SCOTS THESAURUS

D1388216

Edited by
ISEABAIL MACLEOD
with
PAULINE CAIRNS
CAROLINE MACAFEE
RUTH MARTIN

© The Scottish National Dictionary Association Ltd 1990

Polygon at Edinburgh

An imprint of Edinburgh University Press Ltd
22 George Square, Edinburgh

First published 1990 by Aberdeen University Press;
published 1992 by W & R Chambers Ltd
This edition published 1999 by Polygon at Edinburgh

Printed and bound in Finland by WSOY

A CIP Record for this book is available from the British
Library

ISBN 1 902930 03 7 (paperback)

CONTENTS

LIST OF SUB-CATEGORIES

List of sub-categories

INTRODUCTION

"I let fung at his lug an' geed it a gweed doosht." Expressive certainly, and verging on the onomatopoeic. The words *fung* and *doosht*, both in the *Thesaurus*, are here used in a phrase from my own Aberdeenshire dialect. They exemplify the wealth of emotive words and expressions, amongst much else, that readers will find in this great treasure trove of vivid Scots, set out according to themes for easy reference. In fact the *Thesaurus* is a thematically-arranged analysis of almost the whole content, the entire word-hoard, of Lowland Scots, using *The Concise Scots Dictionary* (1985) as the immediate reservoir. Its primary purpose is to provide an enduring service to scholarship and learning at all levels, from the professor finishing off a book, who can use the entries in one of the categories of the *Thesaurus* as a checklist to ensure that he has not missed an important concept, to the casual browser who is simply carried away by the range of riches in these pages and absorbs something of the country's culture as he reads.

The *Thesaurus* takes into account Lowland Scots from its twelfth-century beginnings to the present day. This means that each theme can be viewed in historical depth, a process made easier by the dagger (†) preceding obsolete words. For example, words relating to cattle give many pointers to the past. A sick cow could be †*elf-shot* from a belief that the ailment was caused by the fairies, and there were plenty of other troubles like the lameness †*croittoch*, the disease characterised by continual bellowing †*lowland-ill*, the lung disease †*lungsocht* and one affecting urine and making it red, †*muir*; these are obsolete, but there are plenty of later terms in current use like a form of anthrax called *black spauld*, a glanders-like disease *clyres*, a lameness *crochles*, constipation or diarrhoea called the *dry darn* and *soft darn* respectively, a disease causing the hide to cling to the bone *hide bind*, a wheezy cough *hoose*, an eye-disease *the howk*, and much else. It was obviously a chancy business to rear cattle without some troubles on the way, but that aside, any student of veterinary medicine could have a field day here, pinpointing the diseases of the past as well as of the present, and that not only for cattle but also for sheep, horses and all the other kinds of domesticated creatures we meet in these fascinating pages.

There is another dimension as an aid to study. The entries are localised. We are told that *crochles* is a North East name, like the *dry* and *soft darn* mentioned above, and we can ask ourselves why certain names appear only in certain places. They may once have been more widespread. But there is always a chance that a localised name may give a clue to special local conditions that give rise to a particular disease, and set the researcher on the track of some scientific discovery.

In this context, we have to be aware that the *Thesaurus* entries are the merest digests of heaped up mountains of background information. So the next step is to seek out the repositories where the detail has been already published or is in process of publication. These are the volumes that lie behind *The Concise Scots Dictionary*: the multi-volume *Scottish National Dictionary* (1931–1976) and the *Dictionary of the Older Scottish Tongue* (1931–   ). From these, where words are of course arranged alphabetically and not thematically as in the *Thesaurus*, a fuller pattern can be worked out for change over time and for patterns of regional distributions of terms and the phenomena to which they refer; furthermore, since these Dictionaries incorporate references to books that exemplify the uses of the words, we can readily go from the words to their original sources in the libraries. The *Thesaurus* entries represent the distilled outcome of decades of basic research. Behind every one lies a mass of data, readily available in the Dictionaries mentioned. Few countries are as fortunate in having such a series of step-by-step doorways into the heart of a national culture.

Word lists relating to different specific subjects are indeed to be found, for limited geographical areas, in Gaelic as well as in Scots, but nothing as nationally comprehensive as the *Thesaurus* has appeared before, in Britain or in any other country.

It is comprehensive in another way also. The categories not only give words relating to inanimate objects, the material aspects of culture with which man surrounds himself in his daily life in his striving for the basic essentials of existence like food, shelter, warmth and clothing, but also cover the animate world. We begin with undomesticated birds and animals, with a welter of bird names many of which—like *bullie* the bullfinch, *chaffie* the chaffinch, *maggie* the magpie—have an affectionate ring about them, perhaps a by-product of the deeply-ingrained habit, common to dialectal speech in Scotland and in other countries of Europe, of combining abbreviated forms of the name with diminutives at the end. There is here a whole orchestration of bird-calls and animal noises, mellifluous and raucous, that someone might well set to music sometime, taking into consideration the section on bird behaviour—perhaps the *mairriage* a large gathering of birds, especially rooks and crows—that marks man's close observation of the phenomena of the natural world.

Water Life is another interesting category in the same group. Wherever a creature has been of special importance in the community economies of earlier days—as a matter of necessity rather than as an extension of the divinely anthropocentric plan that in theological teaching once saw all things living as subservient to man's needs and purposes—observant eyes have looked at every detail, and names have been given to all the noted phenomena. A fish full of spawn is *baggit* and one newly-spawned is a *black fish*. If caught high and dry on the shore fish would soon *scag*, become rotten, and what can be worse than the smell of putrescent fish? All stages of growth were known. The coal-fish, once an essential item of subsistence, fished from the rocks of the shore and dried to be eaten as a kind of substitute for bread in hungry seasons, fully reflects its hunger food function in the range of its names: *baddock, bagget, block(an), bluchan, coam,* †*colmie,* †*colmouth, cuddie, cuddin, cuithe, queeth, gerrock, get, graylord, peuchtie, pituchtie, podlie,* †*podler, prinkle, saithe,* †*sey,* †*seeth, stenlock, stan(e)lock*—and this is not to mention the range of Gaelic names that could be added. When economic necessity passes, perhaps as a result of rising living standards, the spread of shops and travelling vans, and more recently of refrigerators and freezers, such intensity of terminology begins to fade. The *Thesaurus* has a strong conservation function in keeping such terms before our minds, though there will always be survivals of old ways in contexts such as fishing trips for pleasure and certain kinds of food retained as prestige items or for fun. It is not so long ago that Aberdeen fathers would bring a bag of *dilse* (an edible seaweed) back from the shore and roast it, wrapped around the poker, on the bars of the coal-fired grate, for the gastronomic delectation of themselves and of their children—who may have enjoyed the game without being over-delighted with the taste.

Plants other than seaweeds and other water plants have a section to themselves, covering wild and domesticated types. Plants and Land taken together (as well as Birds, Animals and Water Life) give a great deal of insight into every aspect of the environment of Scotland, natural and man-made. The *Adam-an-Eves* and *aippleringie,* the *cairt-wheels, creepin eevie* and *dusty millers* bring back the nostalgic scents and blossoms of our old-fashioned gardens. The memory of childhood games is evoked by *cocks and hens* and *curl-doddies,* and I was caught up sharply by the ancient instinct of the hunter-gatherer when I read the word *arnit,* pignut, which as a boy I howked from the field and road edges with a broken knife, to nibble the roots as a triumphant feast.

Beyond such details there are the broad environmental questions, including that of the weather. Man's manipulation of his environment is long-lasting, ubiquitous and constantly changing. The eighteenth-century agricultural improvements first began to systematise the farmed landscape into the patterns we know. Lochs and marshes were drained, fields were enclosed with dyke or hedge, and after the 1830s underground tile drainage gave us the smooth-surfaced fields we now take for granted. The language of such improvement is to be found in the *Thesaurus,* and so also is the language of untamed places, the †*trammel* and the *rone,* both meaning brushwood, the *scrogs* or stunted trees and shrubs, the *etnach* or the juniper, of which there must once have been much more about the countryside. Trees and shrubs played an intimate role in the daily life of the people, providing fuel, building material, implements, furniture and tableware. Estates controlled the extent of tenant use of this resource in former days; now a different viewpoint prevails, for trees are being planted in the wild places, on peat bogs with their own long-established flora and fauna (themselves often overlying traces of human activity in the prehistoric past), and the question is no longer one of conserving the forest or woodland environment but of conserving that of the areas on which commercial interests want to plant trees. The *Thesaurus* may well prove to conserve the names of wild plants, grasses, sedges, mosses, lichens, fungus, ferns, bushes and shrubs, along with notices of the broad localities where they were found. It may be that the names remain even if the species has vanished.

To an even greater extent, perhaps, the *Thesaurus* will conserve for present readers and posterity the details of the changing shape of the human landscape and of obsolete farming techniques. Some of these, like *bruntland*, mossy or peaty ground formerly burnt regularly to fertilise it, have become immortalised in place-names on the map, as have numerous natural features—*brae, cleugh, drum, glack, heuch, kip* etc—of which farmers had to take notice. With the aid of the Land terms in the *Thesaurus*, it is possible to look, as through a magic window, at the well-used landscapes of human activity that lie all around, and see the bones of their history shining through—and this is true also in relation to interpretation of the meanings of legions of farm names, particularly but not exclusively those of the last two and a half centuries.

There is a story about a farmer who always got up at the crack of dawn. He would go to the door, look out and call back the state of the weather to his goodwife still in bed. On the morning after a heavy intake of drams he staggered up as usual but went athwart the room to the kitchen-press door, which he opened: "Maggie, a mochy mornin an' an aafu smell o' cheese!" His weather report was based on a false premise, but not so—or usually not—for the many indicators of weather lore that our forefathers looked for. A *broch* around the moon betided bad weather: "A broch near is a storm far". In fact there was almost a fixation with such halos, which were variously also called *cock's eye, fauld, gow*. Large white snowy clouds on the horizon were *Banff bailies*, a term that surely enshrines the ironic sense of humour that is so widespread. And when the weather was cold and chill, what better could a shivering housewife do than sit close to the warm peat fire, legs spread to get the benefit from the heat? The folk of Angus and Perth called this *meffin*; in the North East, it was "a gweed upthrowe heat". In many ways, such humour and actions are equally part of the human response to the environment.

Man and his interactions with the natural world are strongly in evidence in these sections; and just as in earlier centuries when there was a universal belief that the animal world was a mirror image of human society and political forms of organisation, so also is the *Thesaurus* full of terms for such correspondences. The massive section on Character, Emotions and Social Behaviour, neatly broken down for us in pre-digested analysis, is a bottomless well of information on human attitudes to the environment and to each other. It is like a map of man's mind, in which fragmentary pieces of the lore of the past jostle with perceptions of the present. The outcasts of communities are *bruits, cowts* (colts), †*knappers* (ones who bite with teeth, imitating animals, to drive off cats etc), *tikes*; stupid people can be †*anes* (asses), *gowks* (cuckoos), *hoolets* (owls), *mowdieworts* (moles), *neep heids* (turnip heads), *nowt* or *stirk(ie)s* (cattle) or *yowes* (sheep), and they might have memories like a *hen*. There are local or regional attitudes as represented by derogatory terms for highlanders—†*Glunimie*, †*gluntoch*, †*gluntow*, *Hieland* itself, often prefacing the word *pride*, and *teuchter*, a word beloved of radio comics. There is evidence, in the list of "high class" words denoting social status, of the humorous, sarcastic and sometimes downright cruel tendency that Scots have to level differences, reduce to the lowest common denominator any attempt to climb the social ladder. It is an old habit, as earlier words like †*boldin*, †*boldinit* (affected by or swelled up with pride) and †*dane* (haughty) show, ably continued in the derisory *cockapentie* (snob), *crouse* (conceited), *dink* or *dorty* (haughty), *goich* (a haughty carriage of the head), and many, many more, the stuff that good flytings are made of, and all guaranteed to give the speaker a sense of satisfaction in taking someone *doon a hack*. To this may be allied the terms of gratuitous abuse which again make often unjust analogies with the world of nature: *brock* (badger), *cattle, foumart* (ferret), *golach* (black beetle), *kail-runt*, †*mangrel* (mongrel), *partan* (crab), *whalp* (whelp), *yella yite* (yellowhammer). To some extent we see here aspects, more or less subtle, of social control; levelling or abuse may be the very safety valve that keeps the ultimate peace and preserves the social status quo. At any rate, criticism rather than praise is a kenmark of the Scots language, and avoidance of any expression of strong emotions, especially those of love. Taken over all, there is here the stuff for a dozen dissertations on the psychology of the Scots—and in fact the section is greatly extended by the three others that touch on the Life Cycle and Family, on Physical States, and on Religion, Superstition, Education, Festivals. We do indeed get here a uniquely intimate glimpse of the individual in his setting.

Such critical, kailyard sniping is equally reflected in Law. This large section is not only a most convenient hand-list for budding and experienced lawyers, but also gives much insight into the litigious character of the Scots, who will always seek a †*backspang*, legal flaw or loophole, to avoid excessive *cesses*, rates and taxes, in earlier times as much as for the community charge of the present day. People seem to like long and often latinate words, like the *damnum fatale*, loss due to inevitable accident, that might sometimes afflict their *fungibles*, perishable goods that could be estimated by weight, number or measure. Things could run on a bit, sometimes, each stage in a court process having its legal specific. A *defender's* second answer to a *pursuer* was a †*duply*. The pursuer's answer to this was the †*triply*, and so the game continued through the †*quadruply*, †*quintuply*, †*sextuply* and onwards. The minutiae of the processes of law are hard enough to follow at the best of times. Perhaps this section, with all the intimate detail it presents, will help the investigator's mental clarification.

Against the background of the environment and of mental outlook are to be seen the whole range of activities here documented in such useful detail. We go offshore for a time with the Sea and Ships, we turn to Law to resolve differences or Law turns to us to exert discipline, perhaps after indulgence in War, Fighting, Violence. We see the infrastructure of Trades that takes us now and then into urban and semi-industrial contexts, and learn the terminology that goes into our Buildings and Architecture. But the core of this *Thesaurus* is its reflection of rural Scotland, including its villages and small towns, and it is right that this should be so for the country has been predominantly rural until astonishingly recent times.

Essentially, we are seeing a picture of a non-industrialised countryside, whose occupants knew their environment, their stock of domesticated animals and the ills that could befall them. They knew wild creatures that impinged on their lives as good to eat, or as pests, or simply as starlings that built nests in their chimneys. Somehow—and this is one of the great philosophical matters of outstanding interest in man's development—they gave everything names, thereby encapsulating their knowledge in tangible form and implicitly imposing a degree of order on their surroundings. The thematic structure of the *Thesaurus* allows us to begin the analysis of such patterns.

Of these, Farming gives a major example. It takes us into every nook and cranny of the days of horse and earlier ox draught. The shaping of the face of the land through enclosure and drainage; the seasonal round of ploughing, manuring, sowing, harvesting and grain processing (including the click mills with horizontally turning wheels and the bigger mills with vertically set water wheels); the *cairts* and *coups* and *wains* that transported crops and goods; the range of farm buildings; the peat and turf that fuelled the fires, roofed and walled the houses, bedded the animals in the *byres* and at last completed its energy cycle by returning as fertiliser to the fields; the uses of the farm land and the technicalities of its limitations, such as the *ae-fur-land* that could only be ploughed in one direction because of its steepness; the relationship between tenants and landlords; the constitution of the work force on a farm from farmer to *orra-loon* and *deem* living in the farm-house or in *berrick*, *bothy*, *chaumer* or *hinds' raw* and wearing their *booyangs*, *nickie tams* or *waltams* (leather straps round the trouser legs "to keep the *styoo* (dust) oot o yer een", as a North East wit once put it); the uses of the livestock (this to be taken along with the section on Domestic Animals) and the pointers to the close relationships between the people and their animals, in particular the cows in the byres with their familiar names, often based on terms descriptive of their appearance, and the oxen and horses in the plough and cart, these marking female (all aspects of dairying) and male domains respectively; all these and more are spread before us as clear evidence of the links between farmers and their stock, roughly affectionate as they often were but strictly not sentimental, for the need for food and drink and clothing had to override sentiment and the slaughter of a pig became a moment for rejoicing.

The provision of food was indeed the main aim of all farming activity. The entries under Food and Drink give us a great deal of insight into the eating habits of earlier days. There is an impression that dainty eating was not a primary consideration, if what we see here is any guide: *baible* drink carelessly, *belly* eat voraciously, *blibberin* slobbering soup, *brosie* bloated with too much food, *gilravage* and *gropsie* eat immoderately, and such examples are complemented by derisive terms like *nice-gabbit* fussy about food, *pickie* a poor eater. You ate heartily in the old days and *stapped* or *steched* your stomach full, otherwise there was something wrong with you.

Mealtimes are of considerable interest. In medieval Europe there was a two-meal system later replaced by three meals a day, which translate in Scotland into 'breakfast', 'dinner' and 'supper' or 'tea' (the main meal being dinner at about mid-day, not in the evening according to the 'gentry' habit). There were also in-between snacks, the *by-bit*, †*dorder-meat, efternuin, forenuin,* †*fower-hours* etc, the range of names suggesting that these were by no means rare. Food of a special nature also marked life's occasions and high moments. Harvest's end, the high point of the farming year, had its celebratory supper, *clyack*; a funeral feast was the †*dirgie* and there was a *server* to hand round refreshments, the *service*, at funeral or wedding; a *foy* celebrated a marriage or special occasion; a feast to mark a bride's departure from her old home was the *furthgoing*, matched by the †*in fare* when she came to her new one; and we get an occasional glimpse of obsolete status-related aspects of food, like †*latter-meat*, leftovers from the master's table later served to servants. There is much social history to be teased out from such hints, some of which may even point to questions historians have neither asked nor investigated.

I have given some samples, the merest tip of a great iceberg, of the multifarious range of uses to which a *Thesaurus* like this can be put, and of the continual sparks of fresh interest from individual words and the broader themes to which they belong, as the *fleerish* of the mind strikes the flint of the entries, and sees new and never hitherto thought of relationships. In essence, the *Thesaurus* is a national culture in a nutshell. In particular, it encourages investigation not only into the individual themes, which is useful enough in itself, but also into the linkages between the various elements of that culture. It presents a picture of a world already becoming lost. The last few decades have instituted change at a pace rarely before known in human history. That being so, it is all the more important to have this phenomenal key to the interpretation of the mental, natural and work environment in a world out of which continuing inspiration should come. We do not need to throw away our past in order to be creatures of the present.

Alexander Fenton

HOW TO USE THE SCOTS THESAURUS

The Scots Thesaurus is designed to display the vocabulary of the *Concise Scots Dictionary* in a new way. The main part of the book is divided into groups (see pp iii–vii) covering a wide variety of subjects, including the natural world, human life and society, as well as emotions and character. This arrangement reveals the richness of the Scots language and will help the user to increase knowledge of it and to find words in particular subject areas.

The extensive index (see p 477) will help the user to make the best use of this complex body of material. *The Scots Thesaurus* concentrates on words and their meanings and therefore for etymology and pronunciation the CSD should be consulted.

Headwords

In a book of this kind it is not possible to find space for the large numbers of different spellings found in Scots; for these the reader should consult the *CSD* or the *Scottish National Dictionary*. Most entries here have been limited to one main Scots spelling and, where the word is regularly used in Standard Scottish English, the English spelling.

Grammar

Grammatical information has been kept to a minimum but part-of-speech labels have been inserted when more than one part of speech is included in an entry.

Definitions

These on the whole follow CSD with appropriate adjustments. Cross-references (**X** *see* **Y**) have been kept to a minimum. Bold type within a definition indicates either a straightforward cross-reference to another word in the same category: **sheriff**....... *see* ~ **depute** and ~ **principal** *or* that the word will be found in a Scots rather than an English dictionary; some will be found in the same category, some in another category of *The Scots Thesaurus*; all will be found in *CSD*. Some well-known Scots words, such as clan, scone, whisky have however been given in ordinary type.

Time and place

Obsolete words (ie those for which we have no evidence in the twentieth century) are marked with a †. All the SNDA's dictionaries are based on vast amounts of research but no record of a language is ever complete; the Association continues to fill in as many of the gaps as its resources permit. In particular we are aware that the SND's main research was carried out several decades ago and much needs to be done to bring the picture up to date. If you come across any words or meanings marked obsolete which you know to be still used in some part of the country, please let the Scottish National Dictionary Association know (at the address on p xx).

Where words are used only in a limited area or areas, this is shown by giving the areas according to the list below and map 1 on p xvii.

The more specific labels are based on the pre-1975 counties (map 2), and the boundaries can be compared with their modern equivalents in map 3.

List of dialect areas:

AREA	COUNTY	ABBREVIATION
	Shetland	Sh
	Orkney	Ork
Northern		N
	Caithness	Cai
	Sutherland	Suth
	Ross and Cromarty	Ross
	Inverness	Inv
	Nairn	Nai
	Moray	Mry
North-East	Banff	Bnf
	Aberdeen	Abd

How to use the Scots Thesaurus

	Kincardine	
	Kcdn	
east Angus	Ags	
Central		C
East Central		EC
north East Central		nEC
	west Angus	Ags
	Perth	Per
	Stirling	Stlg
	Fife	Fif
	Kinross	Kinr
	Clackmannan	Clcm
south East Central		sEC
	West Lothian	wLoth
	Edinburgh	Edb
	Midlothian	midLoth
	East Lothian	eLoth
	Berwick	Bwk
	Peebles	Pbls
West Central		WC
	Dunbarton	Dnbtn
	Argyll	Arg
	Bute	Bute
	Renfrew	Renfr
	Glasgow	Gsw
	Lanark	Lnk
	north Ayr	Ayr
South-West		SW
	south Ayr	Ayr
	Wigtown	Wgt
	Kirkcudbright	Kcb
	Galloway	Gall
	West Dumfries	Dmf
Southern		
	Roxburgh	Rox
	Selkirk	Slk
	east and mid Dumfries	Dmf
Ulster		Uls
Highl		
Hebrides		see below

Abbreviations are given in the Thesaurus in the order of this list (roughly north to south), eg *Bnf Abd Ags Fif*. A dash is used to show continuity. *Bnf-Fif* means that the word is found in *Bnf, Abd, Kcdn, Ags, Per, Stlg* and *Fif*.

local Bnf-Fif means that it is found throughout this area but only sporadically.

local NE means that it is found sporadically throughout NE.

local without qualification means that it is found sporadically throughout the whole country.

E is also used occasionally to cover *Sh, Ork, N* and *EC*.

now NE means that the usage is now confined to the North-East, although it was formerly more widespread.

chf SW means that the usage is found chiefly, but not exclusively, in the South-West.

Gen (general) indicates that the word is used throughout the whole Scots speaking area, here used only in such cases as *Gen except Sh Ork*, used throughout except in Shetland and Orkney.

Highl and *Hebrides* label words, chiefly of Gaelic origin, used in the Gaelic-speaking or recently Gaelic-speaking areas (parts of *Cai, Suth, Ross, Inv, Per, Dunbt* and *Arg*) as well as the Western Isles; these areas speak Standard English in various varieties influenced by Gaelic much more than by Scots.

For further information on dialect areas and the use of the abbreviations, see CSD pp xxx–xxxvi.

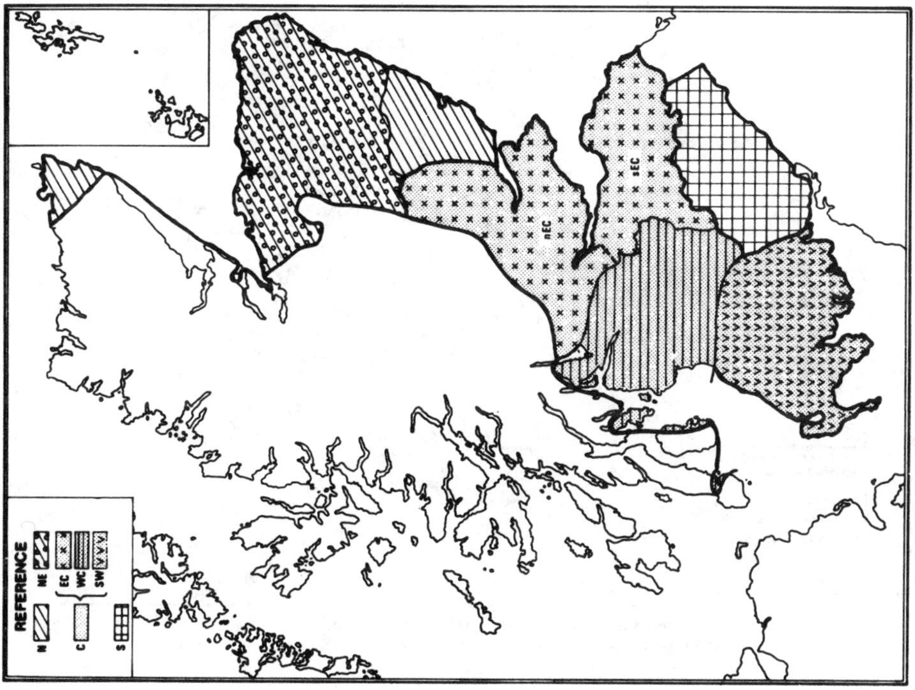

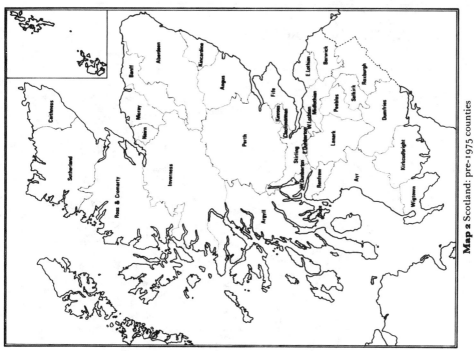

Map 2 Scotland: pre-1975 counties

Map 1 Scotland: the main dialect divisions of Scots

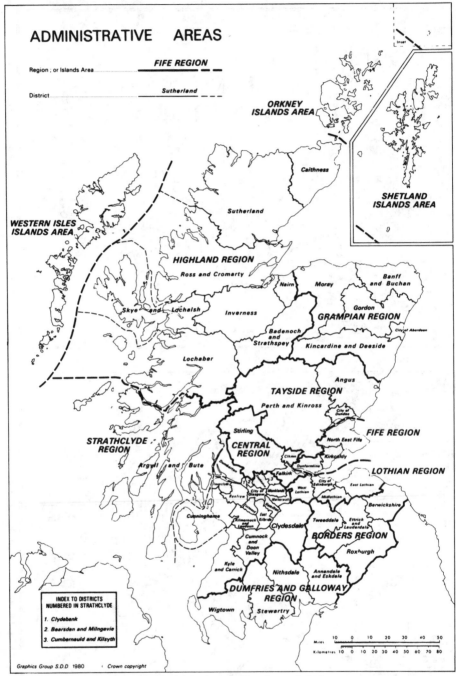

Map 3 Scotland: post-1975 regions and districts
(reproduced by permission of Graphics Group Scottish Development Department)

Index

The Index provides a detailed signposting in English into the intricacies of Scots vocabulary. Numbers indicate the section or sections in which the concept is treated. Common English synonyms are given cross-references, eg **bite** *of food, see* **mouthful**. When the English word has (near) equivalents in Scots, these are given as well as the category number, separated by semi-colons. Where there is more than one Scots word from the same Thesaurus entry, however, the order in that entry is followed rather than a strict alphabetical arrangement; words from the same entry are separated by commas.

Obsolete words are marked with a † but for information on the geographical areas in which they are (or were) used, the text should be consulted. Indications (in italic type) are given where necessary of the part of speech and of the area of meaning of the equivalent, eg **call** *v, animal* treesh.

As many Scots words do not have a direct equivalent in English, it has not been possible to include direct index entries for all words in the main sections. There are however general entries, eg **sewing** 13.1.7, which should lead to the desired word.

Bear in mind when using this section that the Scots words are not, in many cases, exact synonyms of the Standard English words or of each other. If you do not already know the Scots word, its precise meaning(s) can be found in the classified arrangement, along with information about its known geographical distribution (and other restrictions in usage).

List of abbreviations

See also pp xv, xvi.

abbrev	abbreviation
adj	adjective
adv	adverb
appar	apparently
arch	archaic
archeol	archeological
cf	compare
chf	chiefly
colloq	colloquial
comb(s)	combination(s)
derog	derogatory
dial	dialect(al)
eg	for example
Eng	English
erron	erroneous(ly)
esp	especially
etc	et cetera
exclam	exclamation
fem	feminine
fig	figurative(ly)
freq	frequently
gen	general
hist	historical
ie	that is
interj	interjection
joc	jocular(ly)
lit	literal(ly)
Mod	modern
n	noun
obs	obsolete
occas	occasional(ly)
orig	originally
perh	perhaps
phr(s)	phrase(s)
pl	plural
prob	probably
pt	past tense
ptp	past participle
Sc	Scots
sing	singular
specif	specifically
St	standard
univ	university
usu	usually
v	verb

ACKNOWLEDGEMENTS

The editors would like to thank the many people who have contributed to this book in numerous different ways. In particular we would like to express our gratitude to the following:

Professor A J Aitken and Mairi Robinson, who have been editorial consultants to the project from the beginning.

Dr Alexander Fenton for much helpful advice in addition to the Introduction on pp viii–xiv.

Keith Williamson for expert advice on computer systems as well as a great deal of practical help unstintingly given.

Professor Robert Black for his invaluable help on legal terminology.

Elizabeth Glass, whose very efficient keyboarding has once more greatly aided progress.

Sheila Hendry for meticulous help with the proofreading.

Henry Noltie of the Royal Botanic Gardens, Edinburgh, for advice on the plants section.

Over and above the help we have received recently, we are always mindful of the debt we owe to our predecessors in Scottish lexicography, especially to David Murison, the second and main editor of the *Scottish National Dictionary*. Without their years of tireless effort the compilation of the present volume would not have been possible.

We would like to thank Colin MacLean and other members of the staff of AUP for all their help and encouragement, and Ruari McLean for his expert help with the design.

Funding of dictionaries is always a problem and we would like to express our gratitude to the many people and organisations who have recently helped us to continue, in particular the Scottish Arts Council, The Binks Trust, The James Wood Trust and the TSB Foundation Scotland. But above all we would like to thank our Secretary John Gordon and members of the SNDA Council, especially its Chairman, Sir Kenneth Alexander, and Ann Aikman Smith, Chairman of the Fund-raising Committee. Our underfunded work in recent years would have been impossible without the help of a loyal band of volunteers; we would like to thank them all and in particular Betty Philip, Sheila Davies and Henry Pirie.

THE SCOTTISH NATIONAL DICTIONARY ASSOCIATION

The Association was founded in 1929 for the purpose of recording and encouraging the Scots language. In 1976 it fulfilled its first major task when the last of the ten volumes of the *Scottish National Dictionary* was published. The following decade was spent in the preparation of the *Concise Scots Dictionary*, which enjoyed resounding success when it was published in 1985. The policy of bringing the SNDA's researches to a wider public was continued in 1988 with the publication of the *Pocket Scots Dictionary*. This new dictionary continues the programme of publication and research.

With no reliable source of funding, the Association has a constant struggle to keep this programme going and relies to a large extent on contributions from the public, both in money and in practical help of various kinds. If you would like to help, please write to: The Scottish National Dictionary Association, 27 George Square, Edinburgh EH8 9LD.

1. BIRDS, WILD ANIMALS, INVERTEBRATES

1.1 BIRDS

1.1.1 GENERAL

†**aiten** a partridge.

†**awp** a bullfinch.

bird, burd 1 a bird. **2** a young bird, nestling.

blackie the blackbird.

blethering Tam the whitethroat *WC, SW*.

blue bonnet the bluetit.

briskie, brichtie *now Kcb* the chaffinch.

bullie the bullfinch *now Fif.*

†**buntlin** the corn bunting.

bushock *Stlg,* †**bushsparrow** the hedge-sparrow.

capercailzie the wood-grouse.

cattle birds and beasts *in gen now Abd.*

chaffie a chaffinch *!ocal.*

chitty wran the common wren *now Arg.*

†**churr muffit** the whitethroat.

chye the chaffinch *NE.*

†**coal hood** any of several species of black-headed birds.

corbie 1 the raven. **2** *occas* the carrion crow or hooded crow. **3** the rook *local.*

craw the crow, in Scotland *usu* applied to the rook.

†**croupie** the raven *chf Fif.*

craik the corncrake *now Abd Fif.*

cran, crane the swift *local C-S.*

croodlin doo a wood-pigeon *now Bnf Abd.*

croupie the common street pigeon *Fif Edb.*

cushat, cushie(-doo) *Gen except Sh Ork* the ring-dove, wood-pigeon.

cutty wran the wren *chf SW.*

deil, deevil, devil: ~**'s bird** the magpie *now Abd.*

doo a dove, pigeon.

feesant, fasiane, ephesian a pheasant.

feltieflier *now midLoth,* **feltifer** *now Fif,* **feltifare** *now Kcb* **1** *also* **feltie** *now midLoth Dmf* the fieldfare. **2** the missel-thrush.

fern owl the nightjar.

†**fewlume** some kind of bird.

fieldy the hedge-sparrow.

gaiblick an unfledged bird *S.*

get an unfledged nestling *Gall Rox.*

goggie *child's word* an unfledged bird, a nestling *Ags SW.*

gorb *now Ags Kcb Uls,* ~**el** *now NE Per Pbls,* ~**lin** *now NE Ags,* **gordlin** *Abd,* **gorlin** *now Ags Per*

SW, ~**et** an unfledged bird. ~**ellit** *of an egg* containing a developing chick *NE Per Pbls.*

gowd, goold, gold, golden crest(ie) the goldcrest *now midLoth.* **gowdie, goldie** *now nEC Lnk,* **gooldie** *now local Arg-S,* ~ **spink** *now Per Pbls* the goldfinch.

gowk *now local NE-Uls,* ~**oo** the cuckoo.

greenie, green lintie the greenfinch.

grund blackie a blackbird that nests on the ground *now midLoth.*

heather, hedder, hather: ~ **blackie** the ring ouzel.

hedge: ~**ie,** ~ **spurdie,** ~ **spurgie** a hedge-sparrow *now NE Per.*

hempie the hedge-sparrow *S.*

Hieland pyot the missel thrush *NE.*

huid, hood: ~**ie craw, heidie craw** *NE* **1** *also* ~**ie,** ~**it craw,** † ~**ock** the hooded crow. **2** *also* ~**ie,** ~**it craw** the carrion crow.

jakie the jackdaw *EC Lnk SW.*

jay pyot a jay *now Kcb.*

kae the jackdaw.

Katie wren, kittie wren *now Loth Dmf Rox* the wren.

laverock, larick *now Mry Ags,* †**lairick** the skylark.

lintie, brown ~ *now Cai SW,* **gray** ~ *now local* the linnet *Gen except Sh; see also* **rose lintie.**

lintwhite the linnet.

maggie the magpie *local Abd-S.*

mairtin martin, the housemartin *now Abd.*

†**mak(e)** a mate.

mason's ghost the robin redbreast *chf S.*

mavie mavis, the song-thrush.

†**merl,** *chf verse* the blackbird, *freq* ~ **and mavis.**

mune, moon the goldcrest *Rox.*

nightingale, nichtingale the nightingale. **Scotch** ~ the woodlark; the sedgewarbler *now C.*

†**osill** the ouzel, blackbird, merle; *perh also* the ring-ouzel.

ox ee 1 the great tit *now Fif midLoth.* **2** the bluetit *now nEC Rox.*

†**paco(k)** a peacock.

pai(r)trick a partridge *Gen except Sh Ork.*

†**papejay** the parrot.

papingo a parrot *latterly arch, hist, literary or as a heraldic device.*

1

†**parokett** a parrot.

paysie a peahen *NE*.

†**phesand** a pheasant.

pliver's page the dunlin *now Cai*.

pout a young game-bird *now Cai Mry Bnf Kcb*.

†**pown** a peacock.

pud *now Ags Per*, **puddie** *now Rox* name for a pigeon. **pud(die)-doo = pud**; a tame pigeon.

pyot the magpie *now Per Fif*.

†**quailȝe 1** the quail. **2** ? the corncrake

reid, red: ~ **Rab** the robin redbreast *now wLoth Slk*.

rooketty doo a tame pigeon *local C*.

rose lintie 1 the male of the linnet (which has bright red plumage during the breeding season) *now Ork Cai*. **2** the lesser redpoll.

†**rosignell** the nightingale.

sandy swallow the sand-martin.

seed lady the pied wagtail *now Ayr*.

shilfa *now Cai C, S*, **shilly** *now Fif*, †**shoulfall** the chaffinch.

skite the yellowhammer *chf NE*.

skittery feltie the fieldfare *local Stlg-SW*.

snaw, snow: ~ **flake** the snow bunting.

sparra, sparry the sparrow.

†**specht** the green woodpecker.

spink the chaffinch *now Rox*.

spur *chf in combs* a sparrow. ~**die 1 = spur** *now NE Ags Loth*. **2** the hedge-sparrow *Loth Bwk*.

spurg, sprug *joc or child's word, now Cai Fif sEC*, **sp(e)ug** *joc or child's word, Gen except Sh Ork*, **spurgie** *NE* the sparrow.

stirlin a starling.

storm cock the missel-thrush *local N-S*.

strag a stray pigeon *C, S*.

stuckie, stushie the starling *EC, WC*.

swalla, swallow 1 the swallow. **2** the martin *N-WC, S*.

†**tarmagan** the ptarmigan.

thoumie the wren *Mry Abd*.

throstle the song-thrush *now literary*. †~**-cock, thissell-cok** the male song-thrush; the missel-thrush.

tree-speeler the tree-creeper *now local Loth-Dmf*.

†**valentyne** birds, fowls collectively.

waggie *Fif-S*, **waggitie** *Ags Per* the pied wagtail.

†**wallydrag, warridrag** *Bnf Abd*, **wallydraigle** *local C* the smallest, weakest or youngest bird in the nest.

weet-my-fit the landrail or corncrake (from its cry).

weirdie the smallest or least thriving of a brood of birds *nEC*.

wheelie-oe the willow warbler *Ayr*.

whin: ~**-chacker(t)** the whinchat *local Cai-Wgt*. ~**-lintie 1 = whin-chacker(t)** *now Ags Rox*. **2** the linnet *now NE, SW*. **whin-sparrow** the hedge-sparrow *local Kcdn-Wgt*.

†**whishie, whusky,** ~**-wheybeard** the white-throat.

willie: ~**-muff** *or* **-muftie** the willow-warbler. ~ **wagtail** the pied wagtail *Gen except Sh Ork*.

wran(nie) the wren *now local Sh-SW*.

wuid, wood: ~**-lark** the tree-pipit. ~**-pecker 1** the tree-creeper. **2** the woodpecker.

wunda-swalla the house-martin *now Fif Loth*.

yella, yellow, yallock *now Mry*, ~ **lintie** the yellowhammer *Abd Ags Ayr*.

yite, yowt the yellowhammer, *freq* **yella** ~ *Gen except Sh Ork*, **yaldie yite** *NE*.

yoldrin, yorlin *now local N-Uls*, **yarlin** the yellowhammer, *freq* **yella**~. **yaldie** *NE*, †**yeldrick = yoldrin**.

younker *now local Cai-Lnk*, **younk** *now Per* a young bird, a nestling *now local Cai-Lnk*.

1.1.2 MOOR, MARSH AND FRESHWATER BIRDS

†**aithehen = gray hen**.

†**atteal** a species of wild duck.

bell-kite, bel-poot the bald coot.

black cock the (male of the) black grouse.

bleater, blitter, bluiter 1 the bittern *now Kcb*. **2** the cock snipe.

bog-bleater the bittern.

†**brissel-cock, birsel fowl** a kind of (?game-)bird.

bull-o-the-bog the bittern.

burnbecker the dipper *SW*.

chack the stonechat; the whinchat; the ring-ouzel *Bnf Abd Lnk*.

†**clocharet** the wheatear; the stonechat.

coal and candle-light, col-cannel-week the long-tailed duck.

craig: (lang-)~**ed heron** the heron *NE*.

cran, crane 1 the crane. **2** the heron.

earn-bleater, yern-blit(t)er the common snipe *NE*.

esscock the dipper *NE*.

fiddler the sandpiper.

gor-cock *chf literary* the moor-cock or male of the red grouse.

gray: ~**back** the hooded crow *now Cai Ags Per*. ~ **cheeper** the meadow pipit *now Per Pbls*. ~ **hen** the female black grouse. ~ **plover** the golden plover in its summer plumage *now Ayr*.

groose a grouse.

heather, hedder, hather: ~-**bleat(er),** ~-**bluitter** the common snipe. ~-**cock** the black or the red grouse *now local Cai-Kinr.* ~ **lintie 1** the twite or mountain linnet. **2** the common linnet *now Abd Per Slk.* **heather peeper 1** the meadow pipit *Bnf.* **2** the sandpiper *now Per.*

hill lintie the twite.

†**horse-cock** the dunlin; a kind of snipe.

Jenny heron the heron *SW.*

joctibeet the wheatear *Cai.*

lang, long: ~ **Sandy** the heron *NE.*

Mey, May: ~ **bird** the whimbrel *now Uls.*

mire: ~ **drum** the bittern. ~ **duck** the wild duck, the mallard. ~ **snipe** the common snipe *now Ork Cai Wgt.*

moss: ~ **bluiter** the common snipe *Kcb S.* ~ **cheeper** the meadow pipit *C, S, Uls.* ~ **duck** the mallard *NE Renfr.*

muir, moor: ~**cheeper** the meadow pipit *now Per WC.* ~**cock** the male red grouse. ~ **duck** the wild duck, the mallard *now Bnf Kcb.* ~ **fowl** the red grouse. ~**hen** the (female of the) red grouse. ~ **pout** a young red grouse.

nettl(i)e-creeper the whitethroat *Clcm.*

peesweep, peewee(t), peesie *now Ags Per NE* the lapwing.

†**perdrix** a partridge

pickerel the dunlin; any small wading bird.

pliver the plover. ~**'s page** the dunlin (from its habit of flying with the plover) *now Cai.*

quink (goose) the brent goose or the greylag goose *now Ork.*

†**ridlaik** a species of wild goose.

ring fowl(ie) the reed-bunting *now Abd.*

rock lintie the twite; the rock pipit *now Cai.*

†**rout** a species of wild goose.

sand dorbie the sandpiper *Mry Abd.*

sand laverock, sand lairick = sandy laver-ock; *more loosely* the sandpiper *now Abd.*

saw neb the goosander; the red-breasted merganser.

sea lark the dunlin *now Per.*

seed bird the wagtail *now Slk.*

†**shot whaip** a kind of curlew.

stane, stone: ~ **chack** , ~ **chacker** , ~ **chack-art 1** the stonechat *now local Ags-S.* **2** the wheatear *now Sh NE.* ~ **chipper** the wheatear *Lnk SW.*

stankie (hen) *now Per-S.* **stank hen** *now Ags* the water hen.

teuchit *now NE, nEC,* **teewheet** *now Pbls SW,* **teewhip** *Ork* the lapwing, peewit.

Tibbie Thiefie the sandpiper *now Ags.*

titlin the meadow pipit *now Ork Cai.*

walloch the lapwing *now Mry.*

wallop(ie) *Inv NE,* **wallopieweet** *Ork Inv Abd* the lapwing.

water, watter *now local,* **waitter** *now sEC, S:* ~**y** the pied wagtail *Bnf Abd Ags.* ~**y wagtail = watery;** the yellow wagtail. **water blackbird** *now Bwk,* **water bobbie** *now Kcdn Ags Per,* **water cock(ie)** *now Mry,* **water craw** *now nEC Edb Lnk,* **water meggie** *now midLoth Lnk,* **water pyot** *now Per Ayr* the dipper.

whaup the curlew.

whitterick the curlew *local Fif-Rox.*

yella, yellow: ~-**neb lintie** the twite *now Wgt.* ~ **plover** the golden plover *now Mry Ags Fif.* ~ **wagtail** the grey wagtail *now Per.*

1.1.3 SEABIRDS, COAST BIRDS

†**Ailsa cock** the puffin.

Alan the Arctic skua *Sh Ork.* **Allan-hawk** name given to several sea birds, *eg* **1** †the Arctic skua; **2** the great northern diver.

†**assilag** the stormy petrel.

burrow duck the sheldrake.

†**claik** the barnacle-goose.

coot, queet the guillemot *NE.*

cutty the black guillemot.

dirten allen the skua *now Cai.*

†**dovekie** the black guillemot.

earn, yirn the white-tailed or sea eagle *now Ork.*

fulmar a bird of the petrel species, *orig* breeding in St Kilda but now more widespread.

gant the gannet *now Abd Fif.*

goo, gow a gull *N.*

gray willie the herring gull *N.*

huid, hude, hood: ~**ie craw** *Sh,* **heidie craw** *Sh,* ~**it craw** *Ork* the black-headed gull.

Jenny gray the black guillemot in its first or winter plumage *chf Cai.*

lavie the guillemot; the razorbill *Hebrides.*

loch, louch: ~ **maw,** ~ **maa** the common gull *now Sh Cai Wgt.*

loom, leam *NE* the red-throated diver; the great northern diver *now Ork Abd.*

mallduck the fulmar *chf Sh Ork.*

mallimoke, mallie the fulmar *chf Sh Ork.*

marrot the common guillemot; the razorbill *now Abd Fif.*

maw: sea ~ the mew, seagull, *esp* the common gull.

Mochrum elder the cormorant *SW*.

mussel-picker the oystercatcher.

norie the puffin *Sh*.

patie the puffin *WC*.

pellile the redshank *NE*.

pewlie (Willie) a seagull, *specif* the herring-gull, from its wailing cry *NE*.

pickmaw, pickie-maw the black-headed gull *S*.

pictarnie, piccatarrie 1 the common or Arctic tern *now Sh Ork Fif*. **2** the black-headed gull.

pirr the common tern **~-maw, perma** the black-headed gull *SW*.

plee the seagull; the young of the gull before it changes its first plumage *now Sh Fif*.

pleengie a seagull, *specif* the young herring gull *now Kcdn*.

pleep a sea-bird with a thin, high-pitched cry, *specif* the oystercatcher; the redshank *now Mry Per*.

quink (goose) the brent goose or the greylag goose *now Ork*.

reid, red: red-legged crow the chough. **~ neb** the oystercatcher *Bnf Abd*. **~-nebbit pussy** the puffin *Mry Bnf*.

rock lintie the twite; the rock pipit *now Cai*.

†**rood-goose** *Sh Ork Ross*, **rutt** the brent goose.

sand laverock, sand lairick = sandy laverock; *more loosely* the sandpiper *now Abd*.

sand: ~y laverock, ~y lairick the ringed plover *now Cai Abd*.

saw neb the goosander; the red-breasted merganser.

scarf *now Sh-Uls*, **scart** *now local Ags-SW*, **scrath** *chf NE* the cormorant; the shag.

scout one of various seabirds, *eg* the razorbill, the guillemot

sea pyot the oystercatcher *now Abd Ags Gall*.

sea: †**~ coulter** the puffin. **~ doo** the black guillemot *now Arg*. **~ goo** a seagull *Abd*. **~ hen** the common guillemot *now Cai*. **~ lintie** the rock pipit *now Ayr*. **sea-maw** a seagull *Gen except Sh Ork*. †**~ plover** the *Squatarola helvetica*. **~ pyot** the oyster-catcher *local NE-Gall*.

†**skeeling (goose), skelldrake** the sheldrake.

skirly wheeter the oystercatcher *Bnf Abd*.

stock annet the sheldrake *now Ags Fif SW*.

Tammie: **~ cheekie** *Abd Kcdn Ags*, **~ norrie** the puffin.

tarrock, tirrick *Sh* **1** the tern *now Sh*. **2** the (*esp* young) kittiwake *now Fif*.

teistie, †**toist,** the black guillemot *now Sh Ork Cai*.

ware goose the brent goose.

willie goo the herring gull *now Kcdn*.

1.1.4 BIRDS OF PREY

†**aigle** the eagle.

†**bizzard, bussard** a buzzard.

earn, yirn an eagle; *latterly specif* the golden eagle *now Sh Cai*.

gled 1 the kite. **2** applied to other birds of prey, *chf* the buzzard *now Inv Ags*.

†**grape** a gripe, a vulture.

†**gustard** a bustard.

hoolet the owl.

hornie (h)oolet, hornie owl the long-eared owl.

keelie (hawk) the kestrel *local EC-S*.

†**merlȝeo(u)n, marlȝeoun** the merlin, the falcon.

†**mitten** a bird of prey; the male hen-harrier.

ool *now Sh NE Ags*, **oolet** *NE, WC* the owl.

puttock the buzzard *S*.

†**rammasche** *of birds, esp hawks* wild, untamed.

reid, red: † **~ hawk 1** the merlin. **2** the kestrel.

†**reif: fowl of ~** a bird of prey.

†**soir** *falconry* applied to a young bird of prey still with red plummage.

†**stanchel, stenchel** the kestrel.

white hoolet the barn owl *local Stlg-Ayr*.

willie-whip-the-wind the kestrel *Ags*.

1.1.5 BIRD BEHAVIOUR, DESCRIPTION

big build nests.

†**brall** soar, fly.

caif *of wild birds* tame *Rox*.

claut *now Lnk*, **clow** a claw.

cleck hatch.

cleuk *n*, *also* †**clew** a claw *now Ags Fif wLoth*. *v* claw, scratch *Abd*.

clock brood, sit on, hatch (eggs).

†**cocked** *of eggs* fertile.

craw, crow: ~ court a parliament of rooks *now Fif*. **~'s weddin** *etc* a large assembly of crows *local*. **~ widdie** a rookery *local*.

dab peck *now local Bnf-Kcb*.

dorb *n* a peck *now Bnf*. *v* peck, grub *Bnf*.

doup the bottom of an eggshell *now Cai Bnf Abd Fif*.

†**drekters** ? a drake's penis.

est a nest *S*.

flee fly.

flocht a flight or flock of birds. **~er** *of a bird's wings* flutter, flap *now local Sh-Fif*.

forhoo *now NE midLoth Pbls*, **forhooie** *chf NE*, **forvoo** forsake, abandon (a nest).

fung *v* fly up or along at high speed and with a

buzzing noise, whizz. *n, also* **funk** a whizzing noise, *eg* of a bird's wings.

gab, gob, gub, gebbie *Ags Per Fif* a bird's beak.

gebbie the crop of a bird *now local nEC*.

lang, long: lang-craiget *of a bird* long-necked *now NE Wgt.* **~-nebbit** having a long **neb** etc.

mairriage, marriage a large gathering of birds, *esp* rooks *NE Ags wLoth.*

neb *n* the beak. *v, of birds* bill. **nebbit** *usu in comb* having a beak of a specified kind: '*red-nebbit*'.

paek peck *Sh.*

pervoo abandon (the nest) *Abd.*

†pickle peck (up) repeatedly and delicately.

reest *n, v* roost *NE.*

scout diarrhoea, *esp* of birds *now local Cai-Slk.*

†scove *of a bird* fly smoothly, glide

†shed *of birds* cleave (the air).

sitten of an egg on which a bird has been sitting with a developed chick inside, near to hatching *local.*

†strik, strike *of a bird of prey* dart **at** and seize.

swatter flutter or splash in water (like ducks or geese) *now Kcb.*

tove rise into the air, soar *now Bwk.*

weeng a wing.

†welter flutter.

†whidder, whither *chf literary of a bird* dart, flutter.

†yeld *of birds* without a mate.

1.1.6 FEATHERS AND PLUMAGE

†creist a crest.

doon, †doons down, soft plumage.

feather, fedder *now Sh Ork N n* a feather. *v, of a bird* get its feathers *now NE midLoth Bwk.* **†fetherame, feddrame** a coat of feathers, plumage.

huid, hood: **~it** having head colouring etc suggestive of a hood.

marl: **~ie, mirlie** mottled or variegated in pattern *now N-Uls.*

mout *v* moult *now C, S. n, freq* the **~** the process or period of moulting *C, S Uls.* **†** **~it** moulted.

†ostage-fedder an ostrich-feather.

pen a plume, feather; the quill or barrel of a feather *now local.*

pouk a moulting condition *now Per Stlg WC.* **~in** the moult *C.* **~it** plucked *now C, S.* **in the ~** moulting *C.*

puddock hair the down or fluff growing on very young birds.

pyot applied to birds with pied plumage *eg* (**water**) **~** the dipper, **sea ~** the oyster catcher.

tap a tuft of feathers etc; a bird's crest. **~pin** a tuft or crest of feathers on a bird's head *now Wgt.* **~pit** crested, tufted.

1.1.7 BIRD CALLS

†bay the singing of birds.

bick, *chf* (**~**) **~ birr** imitation of the call of the grouse *chf Abd.*

buckartie-boo coo as a pigeon *Bnf Abd.*

cheetle, chittle chirp, warble.

chilp *n* a chirp *Bnf Abd. v* chirp, squeak *Bnf Abd.*

chirawk squawk *Abd Kcdn.*

chirk, chark chirrup.

chirl chirp, warble, murmur.

chirm *n* a bird's call, chirp. *v* warble, murmur.

†chirple twitter *N.*

chitter twitter *local Bnf-Kcb.*

claik *n* a shrill, raucous bird-cry *now chf NE. v* cry *chf NE.*

clatter chatter, call.

craik *v* utter a harsh cry, croak *now local. n* the harsh cry of a bird, *esp* the corncrake *now local.*

craw a crowing sound made by birds, *esp* the rook *Bnf Abd.*

crock croak *local Ork-Stlg.*

croo *now Ags,* **croodle** *now local Bnf-Fif,* **†crood** *of doves etc* coo.

croup *of birds, esp* crows croak, caw *now Bnf Abd Fif.*

†crout croak.

curdoo coo (as a pigeon) *now Fif.*

curroo *of a male pigeon* coo *chf Ags.*

†gale *of the cuckoo* call.

hoo *of an owl* hoot *now Ags.*

kae *n* the call of the jackdaw *now Per. v, of a jackdaw* caw *Bnf Per.*

keck **†***n* the sharp cackling sound made by a jackdaw. *v* make this sound, cackle *now NE.*

keckle *v, of hens, jackdaws etc* cackle. *n* a cackle.

peek *n* the cry of a small bird, a shrill, piping noise, a cheep *NE Ags Uls. v* cheep *Sh NE Uls.*

pew **†***n* the cry of a bird, *esp* the kite. *v* cry, peep.

pleep utter a shrill, high-pitched cry, peep *Sh Cai Per.*

queak make a weak, squeaking noise, cheep *now Bnf Abd.*

rair, roar *of animals or birds not thought of as roaring* call loudly.

rooketty imitating the first notes in the call of a

pigeon. ~**-coo** n the call of a pigeon *Gen except Sh Ork. v* coo.

roup, rolp cry, shout, roar; croak *now NE*.

screel scream, screech.

shatter chatter, chirp.

†shout n a loud noise made *eg* by a bird. v, *of birds* give a loud cry.

skirl v, *of birds* scream, screech. n the loud cry, wail, or whistle of a bird.

skraich, skraik *of birds* screech, utter a high-pitched cry *Gen except Sh Ork*.

skrauch v utter a shrill cry, scream, shriek, shout *now N, S*. n a shriek, screech, a shrill or harsh discordant sound *local*.

spink *of a bird* utter the note 'spink' *now Bnf*.

squaik v, *esp of birds or trapped animals* squeal, squeak, screech, squawk *now local*. n, *esp of a trapped bird or animal* a loud scream or screech *now local*.

†thevis nek the call of the lapwing.

tweeter twitter *now Sh Ags*.

tweetle whistle, warble, sing.

twit chirp, twitter *now Ork Ags*.

weeack chirp *NE*.

whaup whistle shrilly like a curlew *Bwk Dnbtn SW, S*.

wheeber whistle *Bnf Abd Per*.

wheek squeak, whine.

wheep v make a shrill noise, squeak *now NE*. n a sharp cry or whistle *now N-Per*. ~**le** v whistle shrilly or with a long drawn-out note *now Ags Per WC*. n the shrill call or whistle of a bird, *esp* the curlew *now local Ork-Ayr*.

wheetle(-wheetle) *of birds* twitter, chirp *now EC, WC*.

whitter twitter, warble, chirp *now Wgt*.

†wrable, wrible warble.

yabb chatter *now Ork Abd Ags*.

yammer utter repeated cries, chatter *now Per*.

yap v cry shrilly, scream; chirp plaintively *now Sh Cai*. n the call of a bird in distress *Wgt*.

yirm *of a bird* chirp, cry, sing.

yirp *of a very young bird* chirp.

yitter chatter *local Stlg-Rox*.

1.2. WILD ANIMALS

1.2.1 GENERAL, MISCELLANEOUS

Descriptions of wild animals and their behaviour are contained in 2.9 with descriptions of domestic animals.

backie, bawkie, *also* ~ **bird** the bat.

baste 1 a beast. **2** a creature of any sort, a bird, fish, insect etc, a (body- and head-)louse etc. ~**ie** familiar and affectionate form of **beast.**

baudrons a hare *local*.

†baver a beaver.

bawd a hare.

bawtie a hare; a rabbit *Rox*.

†bestial wild animals in general.

bird, burd the young, offspring of an animal.

brawn a boar *SW, S*.

brock the badger.

brod, †brude, brodmell a brood.

†bysyn, bysning a monster.

cattle birds and beasts *in gen now Abd*.

cleckin, clackin a brood, litter.

†con a squirrel.

†cuning, kinnen a rabbit, cony.

†cutty the hare.

†dae, da the doe, the female of the fallow deer.

donie *chf verse* a hare.

†famh *folklore* a small animal somewhat like a mole.

†feitho a polecat.

†fellow deir a fallow deer.

†fiber a beaver.

foumart, thoumart, †fulmart, whumart *Ags Per* the polecat; *latterly chf* the ferret or weasel *now local Abd-S*.

†fowne a fawn.

†fuddie a hare *chf Bnf Abd*.

†fun3eis the fur of the beech-marten.

hedger a hedgehog *now Bnf Ags*.

†hert a hart, stag.

hurcheon *now C,* **erchin** *Abd Fif* a hedgehog.

kittlin, kitling the young of small animals.

land mouse the field vole *local Fif-Wgt*.

lang lugs a hare *Cai Ayr Rox*.

†Laurence, Lowrence name given to the fox.

lavellan the water-shrew *Cai*.

leprone, †laproun a young rabbit.

†lerioun some animal.

†Lowrie *chf literary* name for the fox.

†lucerve a lynx, a lynx skin, lynx fur.

†mak(e) a mate.

mappie, map-map pet names for a rabbit.

maukin a hare *now NE nEC Kcb*.

†mertrick, martrik the pine-marten.

†minnie a mother, dam *C, S*.

moup, moppie, mup-mup *Ayr S familiar or child's word* a rabbit *local N-S*.

mouse, moose a mouse. ~ **weasel** a small female weasel *N Kcb*.

mowdiewort, modewarp, moudie *C* the mole *Gen except Sh Ork*.

†**must-cat** *appar* a musk-deer or a civet cat.

†**nape** an ape

onbeast, †**unbeast** a monster, a wild beast; a frightening bird or animal.

oof, wowf *now Abd* a wolf.

pug(ie) a monkey *now C*.

puss(y) a hare *now Uls*.

rae, †**ra** the roe (deer).

ratton, rotton a rat *Gen except Sh Ork*.

rushyroo the shrew *now Per*.

screw the shrew *now local Ags-SW*.

shear, share: ~ **mouse** the shrew *local Cai-Ayr*.

shirrow the shrew.

†**skurel** a squirrel.

stoat weasel the common stoat or ermine *now local NE-S*.

strae, straw: ~ **mouse** the shrew *now Mry Abd Fif Kcb*.

strow the shrew *Kcb*.

teeger a tiger.

thraw-mouse the shrew *NE*.

tod the fox. ~**-lowrie** the fox *now literary*.

†**urse** a bear.

water dog, †**water mouse** the water-rat or water-vole *now Bnf*.

wheasel *now EC, WC, S,* †**waizel, quhasill** a weasel.

white hare the Alpine, Scottish mountain or blue hare, *esp* in its white winter coat *now N Ags Per*.

whitrat, futrat *N,* **whitterick** *C, S* an animal of the genus *Mustela, chf* the weasel or stoat *local*.

will cat, wullcat a wild cat.

witch used of various animals associated with witches.

1.2.2 REPTILES

dirdy-lochrag, dirdy-wachlag a lizard *Cai*.

ether, edder an adder.

heather, hather: ~ **ask** the common lizard *Bnf Abd Kinr*.

†**lesart** a lizard.

man-keeper the common lizard *SW, S Uls*.

nether *now Cai,* **neddyr** an adder.

†**serpens** a serpent.

†**shell, shall:** ~ **paddock** a tortoise.

slae the slow- or blindworm *Arg Gall Rox*.

†**strik(e)** *of a snake etc* wound with its fangs.

tortie a tortoise.

veeper a viper.

†**venenous** poisonous, venomous.

†**ven(n)ome** venom. ~**(o)us, venamus(e)** venomous; of or like venom.

1.2.3 CALLS, NOISES

brain *v* roar, bellow *now Abd*.

buller *v* a roar, bellow *now Abd Ags. n* roar, bellow like a bull *now Bnf Abd Ags Fif*.

bullie *n, v* bellow, howl *NE*.

croon, crune *v* bellow, roar *now Kcb.* †*n* a bellow.

draunt drawl, whine, drone.

fumper *n, v* whimper *N*.

girn *v* snarl.

grool growl *Mry Abd*.

grumph a grunt.

grunch *v* growl, grunt *now Ork. n* a grumble, grunt, growl *now Rox*.

guff snort, snuffle *now Sh Ork*.

gurl *v* growl *local midLoth-S. n* a growl, a snarl *now local midLoth-Rox*.

gurr, gurry-worry growl, snarl *now local*.

habber, hubber *v* snarl *N. n* a snarl, growl *NE*.

hurr purr *chf Sh Ork Cai*.

mouse, moose: ~ **cheep** the squeak of a mouse.

peek the cry of a small animal, a shrill, piping noise, an insignificant sound *NE Ags Uls*.

queak make a weak, squeaking noise, cheep *now Bnf Abd*.

rair, roar *of animals or birds not thought of as roaring* call loudly.

roup cry, shout, roar; croak *now NE wLoth Ayr*.

rowt *of animals* roar, cry *now Ags Per Ayr*.

snore *of animals* snort *now Kcb*.

snork snort, snore, snuffle *WC-S*.

snot snuffle, snort, breathe heavily through the nose *now Ags*.

squaik, squaich *v, esp of trapped animals* squeal, squeak, screech, squawk *now local. n, esp of a trapped animal* a loud scream or screech *now local*.

weeack *v* chirp, whine, speak or sing in a thin squeaky voice, utter a shrill high-pitched sound *NE. n* a squeak, high-pitched utterance of a person or animal *now Abd*.

wheek squeak, whine.

wheep *v* make a shrill noise, squeak, emit a high-pitched buzz etc *now NE. n* a sharp cry or whistle *now N-Per.* ~**le** whine, whimper *now Ags*.

†**whryne** *v* whine, squeak. *n* whining, a querulous cry.

wow *n* a howl, deep-throated call or cry, bark *local Sh-Loth. v* howl, bark, bay *Sh NE*.

yabb *of animals* chatter, bark etc excitedly *now Ork Abd Ags.*

yammer *v* 1 howl; whimper. 2 *of a bird or animal* utter repeated cries, chatter *now Per. n* wailing, whining, a cry, whimper.

yap cry shrilly, scream; whimper *now Sh Cai.*

yatter *of an animal* yelp.

†yaw mew, caterwaul; squeal.

yirm *of an animal* whine, wail *now S.*

yowl *v, of dogs or other animals* bark, howl, yell. *n* a howl, whine, mournful cry of a dog or other animal.

yowt *v* cry, roar, shout, howl, hoot *now Per Stlg Rox. n* a shout, roar, yell, cry *now Per Stlg Rox.*

1.3 INVERTEBRATES: INSECTS, WORMS, SNAILS, SLUGS

attercap a spider *now local Sh-wLoth.*

beast, baste, *also* ~**ie** a creature of any sort, a bird, fish, insect etc, a (body- and head-)louse etc.

bizz buzz *now Abd.*

blob the bag of a honey bee.

bog a bug *now Loth Lnk.*

boo a louse *now Cai.*

brammel (worm), bramlin a striped worm found in old dunghills and leaf-heaps, used as bait for freshwater fish, *esp* trout.

buckie a snail shell *now wLoth.*

bum *v* make a humming or buzzing noise. *n* a humming or buzzing sound. ~**mer** an insect that makes a humming noise, *esp* a bumblebee or bluebottle. ~**mie** a bumblebee *now Abd Ags Lnk.* ~**bee** a bumblebee. ~**-bummin(g)** a continuous humming sound *now Bnf Abd Fif.* ~**-clock** a humming beetle *now Kcb.*

†bumbard a bumblebee.

bummle *v, of a bee* hum *local Bnf-Ayr. n* a wild bee *now Abd Lnk Kcb.*

butterie a butterfly *Bnf Ags.*

byke *n* a bees', wasps' or ants' nest; a beehive. *v of bees* swarm *now Bnf Abd Ags.*

canny: ~**ca** the woodworm *Fif.* ~ **nanny** a species of yellow stingless bumblebee *C, S.*

cart the crab-louse; the skin-disease it causes *Abd.* **kartie** the crab-louse *now Sh.*

cast *of bees* swarm.

cattle lice etc *now Abd Lnk.*

chackie mill the death-watch beetle *now Abd.*

chirker the house-cricket *chf Dmf.*

cleg, gleg *local E,* **gled** *now Slk* a gadfly, horsefly.

clipshear an earwig *now local EC, WC, S.*

clock a beetle. ~**er** a clock, *esp* a large one; a cockroach *local.* ~ **bee** a flying beetle *now Abd.* ~ **leddy** the ladybird *now Kcb.*

coachbell *chf Lnk,* **scodgebell** *chf Bwk Rox,* **switchbell** *Lnk Rox* the earwig.

cob-worm the larva of the cockchafer *Fif.*

†connoch worm the caterpillar larva of the hawk-moth *local.*

cricket a grasshopper *now Rox.*

deid, dead: ~ **watch** the deathwatch beetle; its ticking sound.

deil's darning needle the dragonfly.

dirt bee *Bnf Ags,* **dirt flee** *now Abd Ags* the common dung beetle.

droner a bumblebee *Bnf Ags.*

dusty miller a kind of bumblebee which deposits a light dust on the hand when seized *local Abd-Rox.*

eariewig an earwig *chf WC Uls.*

eemock, immick an emmet, an ant *now local NE-S.*

elf-mill the death-watch beetle *N.*

emmerteen an ant. *NE.*

ether, edder, adder: fleeing ~ *S,* **†~bell** the dragonfly.

fag a sheep-tick *now Ayr.*

†flae 1 a fly. 2 a flea.

flech a flea *local Sh-Fif.*

flee a fly.

foggie the wild or moss bee *now Ross NE Fif.* **foggie bee** *local NE-S,* **foggie bummer** *now Bnf Abd,* **foggie toddler** *NE Ags Fif* the wild or carder bee.

forker, *sEC, S,* **forkie** *Ork-S,* **forkietail** *local Sh-S* the earwig.

gairy bee the black and yellow striped wild bee *now Rox.*

gavelock, gellock *SW* an earwig or other similar insect *now Ork Cai SW.*

golach, goulock an insect: 1 the carnivorous ground beetle *NE, EC Ayr;* 2 the earwig *now local Cai-Uls.* **forky** ~ *Bnf Abd,* **hornie** or **horned** ~ *now local Bnf-Kcb* the earwig.

gowk, goke: ~**('s)-spit(tle(s))** cuckoo-spit *now local NE-S.*

grannie a hairy caterpillar, the larva of the tiger-moth *now local SW.*

gray horse a louse *now Ags Fif.*

green-kail-worm the caterpillar of the cabbage butterfly *now local Cai-S.*

hair: ~**y grannie** a large hairy caterpillar. ~**y oobit** *Fif Bwk S,* ~**y worm** *Abd Ags Fif* the woolly-bear caterpillar, the larva of the tiger-moth.

heather, hather: ∼-**bill** the dragonfly.

jeck: jecky forty-feet *Cai*, **jeck wi the monie feet** *Arg Kcb* a centipede.

Jenny: ∼-**hun(d)er-feet** *now Cai Per Fif,* ∼-**hun-(d)er-legs** *local,* ∼-**mony-feet** *now Ags midLoth* the centipede. ∼-**lang-legs** *now Cai Abd C, S,* ∼ **Meggie** *midLoth Lnk,* ∼-**nettle(s)** *now Ork midLoth SW,* ∼ **speeder** *Kcb Rox,* ∼ **spinner** *Cai Bnf SW, S* the cranefly, daddy-long-legs.

Jerusalem traveller a louse *Ork Abd-Per.*

kail worm a caterpillar *now local Ork-Ayr.*

ked *now local Sh-Dmf,* **keb** *local Ork-Kcb* the sheeptick.

king: ∼ **alison** *Kcdn,* ∼(**'s**) **doctor ellison** *chf NE,* ∼ **coll-awa** *Kcdn* the ladybird.

lady, leddy: ∼ **lander(s)** *or* **launners** the ladybird *local Ags-Rox.*

loose a louse.

maithe, maid *n* a maggot; the egg or grub of the bluebottle etc *now Sh-Ags. v* become infested with maggots *NE.* **maidie** *Sh,* †**mathie, meithie** maggoty, infested with maggots.

mauk, mauch a maggot *Gen except NE.* ∼**ie** maggoty *now Fif.* ∼**ie fly** *S,* ∼ **flee** *C, S* a bluebottle.

Meg: ∼**gie(-lickie)-spinnie** a spider *N.* ∼(**gie**) (**o** *or* **wi the**) **mony feet** the centipede.

midden flee a dung-fly *now Per Rox.*

midgeck *Abd,* **mudgeick** *Sh Ork,* **midgie, mudge** a midge.

moch *n* a moth *now Sh-nEC. v* be infested with moths *Abd.* ∼**ie** full of moths, moth-eaten *Sh-N.* ∼-**eaten** moth-eaten; infested with woodworm *chf NE.*

moud the clothes moth *Bwk S.*

mouse, moose: ∼ **wab,** ∼ **web,** ∼ **wob** a spider's web, cobweb.

muck flee a bluebottle; a dung-fly *local.*

neet a nit, the egg of the louse, *now chf* the headlouse.

nettercap, netterie = **attercap** *Kcdn nEC.*

nicht, night: ∼ **clock** a night-flying beetle *now Sh Kcb Uls.*

oobit, wobat, woubit: *freq* **hairy** ∼ *Fif Bwk S* a hairy caterpillar, *esp* the woolly-bear caterpillar, the larva of the tiger-moth.

pish: ∼-**minnie** *SW, S,* **pismire** *WC, SW, S Uls,* ∼-**mither** *now Gall,* ∼**mool** the ant.

poulie a louse *C.*

prod the sting of an insect *now SW.*

reid, red, rid: ∼-**arsie** a bee with red markings behind *now NE Ags.* ∼**coat** a ladybird *chf Rox.*

scur the mayfly immediately after its larva stage, *freq* used as angler's bait *chf Ayr.*

shairny flee a dung-fly *local Sh-Kcb.*

sheep taid a sheep-tick *WC-Rox.*

skep(pie) bee the hive- or honey-bee *Abd Kcdn nEC.*

slammachs gossamer, spiders' webs *Bnf Abd.*

slater the woodlouse.

snail a slug.

snake a slug, *esp* the large grey or black garden slug.

sodger *n, also* **red** ∼ *Abd Fif Kcb* a ladybird *now local Inv-Dmf.* **sunny** ∼ the red wild bee *Stlg Fif WC.*

souk-the-bluid a kind of red beetle *now Stlg Rox.*

speeder, spider webster *now Per Ayr* a spider. **speeder jenny** *now SW, S,* **speederlegs** *Sh Ork Rox* the cranefly, daddy-long-legs.

spinner 1 *also* **spinnin jenny** *local N-S,* **spin(nin) maggie** *local NE-S* the cranefly, daddy-long-legs *now local.* **2** a garden spider *now Abd.*

stang *v* sting *Gen except Sh Ork. n* a sting (of an insect etc).

stinging ether the dragonfly *local Stlg-Lnk.*

stripey a red-and-yellow striped worm used as angling bait, a bramble-worm *now Dnbtn Kcb.*

swairm (a) swarm.

taid a sheep-tick *WC, SW Rox.*

Tammie-nid-nod the chrysalis of the butterfly *Lnk Rox.*

†**tap, top:** ∼ **swarm** the first swarm of bees from a hive.

torie, story *Sh Ork Cai* the grub of the cranefly or daddy-long-legs, which attacks the roots of grain crops *chf NE.*

tove swarm or stream out *Bwk Rox.*

†**towl, toll** *of a (queen) bee* emit an intermittent series of single clear notes as a swarming signal.

traveller *joc* a head-louse *Ork NE Dmf.*

wab, wob a web.

wabster a spider *nEC, WC.*

wall-wesher a water-spider *SW, S.*

warback the warble- or gadfly, any of the flies of the family *Oestridae* which breed under the skin of cattle etc *now Cai Per.*

wasp, wap(s) a wasp. ∼ **bike** a wasps' nest *now local NE-WC.*

†**wax cayme** a honeycomb.

weaver, wyver *NE* a spider *local NE-Wgt.*

wirm a worm.

witch *used of various insects associated with witches:* **1** a moth *now Kcdn Ags;* **2** a tortoise-shell butterfly *Bwk S.*

yirdie (bee) a miner bee *Pbls WC.*

yirm, yerm *of an insect* chirp, cry, sing.

2. DOMESTIC ANIMALS

Diseases will be found either under the headings for specific animals or in 2.8.1. Animals calls and noises are in 2.9 and also, where relevant, in the section for specific animals.

2.1 CATTLE

Aberdeen Angus, †Aberdeen and Angus name of a breed of black hornless beef-cattle, *orig* from Abd and Ags.

aff, off *of the ages of horses and cattle* less than one year past the number of years specified: '*he's three aff*'.

†Angus name of a breed of cattle.

Ayrshire (one of) a breed of *chf* dairy cattle with reddish-brown and white colouring and turned-up horns.

back-calver a cow which calves towards the end of the year.

beast, baste, *pl freq* **beas** a cow, any bovine animal *local*.

†beef an ox or cow intended for slaughter.

belloch, belly now *Mry*, **bully** now *Ags, of cattle* bellow.

black spauld a cattle disease which affects the quarters, a form of anthrax.

blin, blind *of a cow's teat* having no opening *now Bnf Arg*.

blue grey *of cattle* applied to a crossbreed of a Galloway cow and a shorthorn bull.

brandie name for a brindled cow *now Abd*.

brocky name for a cow with a **brockit** face *now Bnf Abd*.

bull, bill a bull. **bull-seg(g)** a bull which has been castrated when fully grown *now Abd*.

ca a calf *now Abd*.

cauf, caff a calf.

caur calves *chf NE Ags*.

clyres a disease in cattle similar to glanders in horses.

†colpindach, coupnay, cuddoch *chf SW*, **cowda** *chf SW, S* a young cow or ox.

†connoch a cattle disease, murrain.

coo a cow.

cords an intestinal inflammation in calves *now Lnk*.

cowit *of cattle* polled.

crochles *NE*, **cro** *Cai* a disease of cattle causing lameness.

†croittoch lameness in cattle *SW*.

crommie, crummie a cow with crooked horns, *freq* used as name for a pet cow *now local Bnf-Fif*.

cud *n* the sound of cattle chewing the cud *Mry Wgt*. *v* chew the cud *SW*.

darn: dry, soft *etc* ~ constipation, diarrhoea etc in cattle *now Bnf Abd*.

deep-ribbit *of a cow* large-chested *now Sh Kcb*.

doddie *n* a hornless bull or cow *now Bnf Abd Fif*. *adj, of cattle* hornless *now Bnf*.

dry-haired *of cattle which have been exposed to the weather* not sleek-coated, having a rough dry coat *now Bnf Abd*.

eean a one-year-old horse or cow *NE*.

eisen *of a cow* desire the male *now Bwk*.

†elf-shot a sickness (*usu* of cattle) thought to be caused by fairies.

etterlin a two-year old cow or heifer in calf.

fardel the third stomach of a ruminant, *chf* ~ **bound** a disease of cattle in which the contents of this stomach become impacted.

farrow, ferrow, forrow *of a cow* not in calf; having missed a pregnancy, *locally* either still giving milk or not.

feeder a bovine animal being fattened for market *local NE-SW*.

†fit, fute: at hir ~ *of a calf or stirk* still going with the cow.

Fleckie name for a spotted cow *now Ork Abd Arg*.

follow, fallow: ~**er** the young of an animal, *chf* a cow or hen, *esp* one still dependent on its mother.

†gairy name for a striped cow.

Galloway a breed of hornless cattle, *usu* black. **belted** ~ a breed of **Galloway** cattle with a broad white band round a black body.

gear livestock, cattle.

†geld barren, not giving milk.

green *of a cow* recently calved *now midLoth Rox*.

†guids, goods, guddis livestock, cattle.

†hagg *of cattle* butt with the head, fight.

†hair(e)d, hairt *of cattle* having a mixture of white and red or white and black hair, roan.

hap *of cattle in harness,* turn towards the right.

†hasty, heastie a cattle disease, murrain *chf Cai.*

hawkie a cow with a white face; any cow; pet name for a favourite cow *now chf literary.*

hawkit *chf of cattle, also other animals* spotted or streaked with white; white-faced *now Abd.*

†ha-year auld, hi(gh) year auld *of cattle* a year and a half old.

heat, hate: run wi the ∼ *of cattle* run about in hot weather when tormented by flies. *Cai Abd Kcb.*

heifer a young cow, the precise meaning varying considerably as to whether or not the animal has calved, or how often she has calved.

hide bind a disease of cattle which causes the hide to cling to the bone *now Ork midLoth.*

Hieland, Highland of various breeds of animal native to the Highlands, *eg* the long-horned, shaggy-haired cattle.

hoose a disease in cattle which produces a dry wheezy cough.

hove *v* 1 cause to swell, distend. 2 become swollen or distended, swell, expand. *n* the swelling of cattle *now midLoth Bwk Lnk.* **hoved, hoven,** *chf of grazing animals* blown up with having eaten too much fresh green fodder. **hovie** swollen, distended. **hoving** the state of being swollen.

howk, *chf* **the** ∼ a disease (primarily a stomach disorder) affecting the eyes of cattle *chf Abd.*

hummel, hommill, hammill, humble *of farm animals, chf and orig only of cattle* naturally hornless; also polled. ∼(e)d *of cattle* deprived of horns *now Cai Ags WC.*

†hutheron a young heifer.

Jock a bull *Gall.*

kip, kippit *of a cow's horn* turned or tilted up. ∼**pie,** † ∼**-headed** having upturned horns *local.*

knap bane *in cattle* the knee- or knuckle-joint.

knee ill(s) a disease affecting *esp* the knee-joints of cattle *now Ags Ayr.*

knule a small loose horn *SW, S.*

kyloe, kylie one of a breed of small Highland cattle *local Cai-S.*

lie out *especially of cattle* lie in the open air all night, remain unhoused.

†lowand-ill, lowing ill a disease of cattle characterized by prolonged or continuous lowing or bellowing.

lowse, loose *of a cow* swell with milk in the udder *SW.*

†lungsocht lung disease, esp in cattle

lure the udder of a cow or other animal *now local Ork-Edb.*

milk cow a milch cow.

moniefauld, monieplies the third stomach of a ruminant *now Ags.*

moylie, mowlin a hornless or polled cow or bullock *Gall.*

†muckle, meikle, mickle: ∼ **wame** the stomach of a cow or bullock (as contrasted with the smaller one of a sheep).

†muir, moor: ∼**ill** red-water, a disease of cattle.

mull the lip of a cow *chf Sh Ork.*

mulloch a cow without horns *WC, SW.*

new: ∼ **calf(f)it,** ∼ **cal(d),** ∼ **ca'd** *SW of cows* newly calved.

†norlan(d) a Highland bull, cow or steer.

nowt 1 cattle. 2 an ox, steer *now NE.* ∼ **beast** a bovine animal *now NE.*

oussen oxen.

owse ox.

†painch, paunch puncture the large stomach of (an animal, *esp* a ruminant) to allow accumulated gases to escape, probe.

†pece a head (**of** cattle etc).

pine a disease of cows due to mineral deficiency.

plat: cow-∼ a cow-pat *now Rox.*

pock, poke the udder of a milch animal *now Kcb.*

pork *of a cow etc* prod with the horns, gore *now SW Rox.*

porr prod, poke, thrust at; *of a cow etc* prod with the horns, gore *now SW.*

puslicks the (dried) droppings of a cow *now Abd.*

quey, queyock, †qhoy a heifer.

reed the fourth stomach of a ruminant.

roddikin the fourth stomach of a ruminant *now local sEC, S.*

rowt *v of cattle* bellow, roar *now local Sh-SW.* *n* the bellowing or lowing of cattle; the act of bellowing *now local Sh-Gall.*

†royet, royd a troublesome animal, *esp* a roaming or noisy cow.

runt an ox or cow for fattening and slaughter, a store animal, *freq* a Highland cow or ox; an old cow (past breeding and fattened for slaughter) *now local Cai-SW.*

rush *v, esp of sheep or cattle* suffer from dysentry *now Cai Rox.* *n* dysentry, *esp* in sheep or cattle.

scoul horned *of a cow* having downward-pointing horns *now Ayr.*

scur a rudimentary, loosely-attached horn in polled or hornless cattle *now SW.*

†segg an animal, *esp* a bull, which has been castrated when fully grown.

shag an ox castrated incompletely or when fully grown *now Cai.*

shairn dung, excrement, *esp* of cattle. ∼**y** of cow-dung; smeared with dung.

†**shamlo(c)h** a **farrow** cow.

skibo a Highland bovine animal *chf Ags.*

slink an aborted, premature, or newly-born unfed calf or other animal *now C.*

slip: be ~**pit** *of a cow* have the pelvic ligaments relaxed before calving *local Bnf-SW.*

snug *of cattle* strike, push, try to prod with the horns *now Sh.*

startle rush about wildly, stampede, *esp* of cattle when stung by flies *now SW, S.*

stirk, stirkie a young bullock or (*less freq*) heifer after weaning, kept for slaughter at the age of two or three, *freq in comb denoting sex, eg* **bull(ock)** ~, **heifer** ~.

stot a young castrated ox, a bullock, *usu* in its second year or more. ~ **stirk** a bullock in its second year *now Cai.*

†**strummel** disparaging term for a **stirk**.

stryth the work-animals on a farm, plough-horses and -oxen *Cai.*

suckler *of farm animals* a suckling; a cow giving suck *now C, S.*

summer weed bovine mastitis *local Abd-SW.*

†**taggie** *of a cow* having a white-tipped tail.

†**tail-ill** a supposed disease of the tail in cattle.

tidy *of a cow* giving milk; in calf, pregnant.

tig *of cattle* run up and down, dash about when tormented by flies *now Per Kinr.*

timmer, timber: ~-**tongue** the disease actinomycosis which causes swelling and hardening of the tongue in cattle *N Per WC.*

ting stuff (itself) to the point of acute discomfort *Renfr Ayr.* ~**ed** swollen, ready to burst through eating fresh green fodder, *esp* clover *now Ayr.*

†**towmondall** a yearling cow, steer.

ure the udder, *esp* of a cow or ewe *Dmf Rox.*

veal, vale *now Ork* a calf, *esp* one killed for food or reared for this purpose *now Ork.*

veshel, vessel, weshell the udder (of a cow etc) *Cai Per WC, SW,*

warback the warble- or gadfly, any of the flies of the family *Oestridae* which breed under the skin of cattle etc *now Cai Per.*

West Highland a hardy breed of beef cattle.

†**wuid-ill** a disease of cattle.

yeld, eild *adj of cows etc* not yielding milk because of age or being in calf. *n* **yeld** a barren cow, ewe etc *now Ork.*

2.2 SHEEP, GOATS

awald, avald *of a sheep: adj* lying on its back and unable to rise. *v* tumble down backwards, fall and lie on its back.

blait *v* bleat.

blare, †blere *v of a sheep or goat* bleat.

blea *v* bleat, as a sheep or kid *S.*

braxy, †breakshugh a *usu* fatal intestinal disease of sheep.

brockle a cross-bred sheep, from a Leicester ram and a blackface ewe *now SW.*

caddie (lamb) *Sh Ork,* †**keddie** *Abd* a pet lamb.

cairie a breed of sheep *Cai.* **kairy** *adj, of the fleece* streaked, striped *Cai.*

chaser a ram with imperfectly-developed genitals *now Cai Kcb.*

†**chepe** a sheep.

Cheviot a breed of sheep.

†**cling** diarrhoea in sheep *S.*

coupy a sheep that has turned over on its back and is unable to get up *SW, S.*

crock an old ewe *now Bnf.*

dinmont, †dilmont, dinmound a wether between the first and second shearing, *ie* between one and a half and two and a half years old, *now esp* of the Cheviot breed.

doddie a hornless sheep *S.*

eenie *of a ewe* give birth to (a lamb) *Cai.*

fleesh a fleece *now local Sh-EC.*

gimmer a year-old ewe; a ewe between its first and second shearing.

grass ill a disease of young lambs, a kind of **braxy**.

goniel 1 braxy mutton. **2** a sheep found dead *Dmf Rox.*

gray face a crossbred sheep, black-face crossed with Leicester.

gripping a paralytic disease of sheep.

†**hairst, harvest:** ~ **hog** a lamb smeared at the end of harvest, when it is reckoned to become a sheep.

†**hauselock, haslo(c)k** the wool on a sheep's neck, *freq* regarded as the finest part of the fleece.

†**heid, head:** ~ **mark** *of sheep* an individual characteristic of appearance which distinguishes one from another, as opposed to any artificial means of differentiation.

hog(g) *n* a young sheep from the time it is weaned until it is shorn of its first fleece, a yearling. *v* make a **hogg** of (a lamb), keep a (lamb) on winter pasture during its first year. **ewe** ~ a young female sheep. **tup** ~ a young ram. **wedder** ~ a young castrated male sheep.

†**hograll** ? the skin of a **hogg** *n.*

ingy *of a ewe* give birth to (a lamb) *Cai.*

keb *v, of a ewe* **1** give birth prematurely or to a dead lamb *SW, S.* **2** lose a lamb by early death *chf S. n* **1** *also* ~ **yowe** a ewe that has given birth

to a dead lamb or failed to rear a live one *chf S.*
2 a stillborn or premature lamb *SW, S.*

lamb: lammie-meh pet name for a lamb *local N-S.* **~ bed** the uterus of a ewe *Ork Cai SW.*

†**Lammermuir lion** *joc* a sheep.

†**lang, long: ~ sheep** a Cheviot sheep.

†**Linton** designating a variety of black-faced hill-sheep bred in the Tweed region.

lowpin ill a disease of sheep, symptomized by leaping.

mae *v, of sheep etc* bleat. *n* the sound of bleating, the cry of a sheep or lamb.

maillie a ewe; pet name for a favourite ewe *Kcb.*

maukit, maucht *esp of sheep* infested with maggots *Cai C, S.*

†**meat scheip** *etc* a sheep etc intended to be slaughtered for food, not grown for wool.

mid a lamb of middle quality or growth.

†**milk ewe** a ewe in milk.

milled *of a ewe* mated to a ram of a different breed

morkin a sheep that has died a natural death *Ayr Dmf Slk.*

†**mug** a breed of very woolly sheep with wool even covering the face, imported from England to improve the quality of wool in the Scottish breeds

oo, oull, woo wool.

†**outcum(mit)** *of a sheep* †? that is in lamb.

palie, pallie *adj of young animals, esp lambs* under-sized, not thriving. *n* an undersized, ailing lamb.

park: ~-lamb, ~-sheep a lamb or sheep reared in a field as opposed to moorland pasture *now Cai.*

pet an animal which has been domesticated and treated with affection, *freq* a hand-reared lamb or sheep.

pinding a bowel disorder affecting lambs fed on over-rich milk *now S.*

pine a disease of sheep due to mineral deficiency. **pining** a disease of sheep, **vanquish.**

pluck sheep-rot *NE.*

pock, poke a pouch-like swelling under the jaw of a sheep caused by sheep-rot; the disease itself *now local Sh-Pbls.* †**pocked** *of sheep* having a swelling under the jaw, infected with sheep-rot

puslicks the (dried) droppings of a cow or sheep *now Abd.*

rise the layer of new wool next to the skin of a sheep at shearing time which represents the growth of the new coat *C, S.*

row, roll *of sheep* roll over on the back *EC, WC.*

ruch, rough *of sheep* unshorn, unclipped *Bwk SW, S.*

rush *v, esp of sheep or cattle* suffer from dysentry *now Cai Rox.* *n* dysentry, *esp* in sheep or cattle.

scrapie a sheep disease causing constant itch.

sheep, sheepie, †**schip** a sheep. **sheepie-mae** a sheep, so-called from its bleat *local.* **~ eik** the natural grease in a sheep's wool *Bwk Wgt S.* † **~ head** a sheep's head. **~'s purls, ~ troddles** *Lnk Kcb S* sheep-dung. **sheep shank** the leg of a sheep *now Stlg SW.*

†**shell, shall** *Sh Ork N, of sheep or their wool* become caked with driven snow.

Shetland sheep a breed of small sheep native to Shetland, now much interbred.

†**shoreling** the skin of a recently-shorn sheep; such a sheep.

†**short** *of black-face sheep* relatively short in the body (compared with the **Cheviot** etc).

shot an inferior animal, *esp* a sheep, left over *eg* after a buyer's selection.

sick: ~ (lamb) *Bnf Abd,* **~ie** *NE* a pet lamb brought up on the bottle.

†**side ill** a kind of paralytic disease of sheep.

slack *of a ewe* past breeding age, about to be sold for meat.

sloch, sluch the pelt or coat (taken skin and wool together) from a dead sheep *Per Arg SW.*

†**snuff** a disease in sheep.

soukit gimmer a ewe that has lambed *SW.*

strik, strike *v, of maggots* infest (a sheep's wool) *SW.* *n* the infestation of sheep by maggots *Gen except Sh Ork.*

sturdy 1 a brain disease in sheep, causing giddiness, staggering and ultimately collapse. **2** a sheep affected with **sturdy** *now Kcb.* **sturdied** *of a sheep* affected with **sturdy.**

swingle *of sheep* walk with a swinging jerky motion due to disease of the spine *Cai.*

thorter ill a kind of paralysis of sheep causing distortion of the neck etc.

†**thrunter** a three-year-old sheep, *esp* a ewe *S.*

tops the best sheep or lambs in a flock *Gen except Sh Ork.*

towmond, †**tholmont** a sheep or wether in its second year *Rox.*

tremmlin a virus disease of sheep, causing paralysis, tremor and spasms *now Per WC, SW.*

trintlet a small ball or pellet of sheep's dung *now Per Stlg WC.*

trottle, troddles, trottlicks small round pellets of excrement, *esp* of sheep *local NE-S.*

tuip, tup *n* a ram. *v, of a ram* copulate; sire. **tup-yeld** *of a ewe* barren, infertile *now C, S.* †**tup-hog** a male sheep till its first shearing. **~-lamb** a male lamb.

13

twinter *now Pbls Ayr Slk*, **quinter** *SW, S* a two-year old farm animal, *esp* a thrice-shorn ewe.

udderlocks *n* locks of wool growing beside a ewe's udder *now Cai C, S*. *v* pluck the wool from a ewe's udder to facilitate suckling *now WC*.

†unwollit lacking wool, shorn *Abd*.

ure the udder, *esp* of a cow or ewe *Dmf Rox*.

vanquish, vinkish *now Dmf* a disease in sheep caused by cobalt deficiency *now SW*.

water, watter *now local*, **waitter** *now sEC, S* dropsy; a disease of sheep.

wedder, †wather a wether *now local NE-S*. **†wedder bouk** the carcass of a wether. **wedder lamb** a castrated male lamb.

white-faced *of a sheep* applied to a breed with a white face *now Cai*.

†yean *of a ewe* give birth to (a lamb).

yowe, ewe a ewe. **~ hog** a female **hog**. **~ lammie** a little ewe lamb.

2.3 PIGS

breem *now Fif*, **brim** *now Kcb esp of a sow* be in heat.

chattie a pig, boar *Bnf Abd*.

doorie a pig; the smallest pig of a litter *Arg SW Uls*.

dorneedy *chf of pigs* the runt of a litter *now NE*.

gaut a pig, *chf* a boar or hog *now Sh Ork local N*.

gilt a young sow, *esp* before her first farrowing.

grice a pig, *esp* a young pig, a sucking pig *local Sh Dmf*.

grumph(ie) name for a pig *local Abd-Wgt*.

gruntie *joc* a pig *local Sh-Ayr*.

gruntle 1 the snout of a pig *now Rox*. **2** a grunt *now Rox*.

guff, gouff a grunting, snuffling sound of a pig *now Sh*. **~ie** name for a pig *now Slk*.

gussie *local Arg-S*, **goosy** a pig, *esp* a young pig or sow *now local Ags-S*.

harky, hirki(e) *Sh, sea-taboo or pet-name* a pig *now Sh*.

howk *chf of pigs* root, burrow in the earth.

†jadden the stomach of a sow *Fif*.

†misell, mesell *of swine* infected, tainted.

pock-shakings the smallest pig in a litter.

rag the poorest pig in a litter *SW, S*.

Sandie (Campbell) *joc, freq taboo* a pig *now local Cai-Lnk*.

shott a young pig after weaning *now C, S*.

soo, sow 1 a sow. **2 †**a pig of either sex.

swine a pig, pigs. **† ~ pork** a pig.

titlin(g) the smallest and weakest in a brood, *esp* in a litter of pigs *Kcdn Ags Uls*.

weirdie the smallest or least thriving of a brood of animals, *esp* pigs or birds *nEC*.

†wort *n* the snout of a pig. *v of swine* root or dig **up** (ground).

2.4 HORSES, DONKEYS

aff, off *of the ages of horses* less than one year past the number of years specified: '*he's three aff*'.

a(i)ver, †averill *sometimes disparaging* a workhorse, carthorse; an old or worthless horse.

†am(b)land *chf of a horse* ambling.

†ane, awn an ass.

†asine an ass.

†baggit *of a stallion* testicled.

bassie, bawsey (pet name for) an old horse.

batts the bots, *esp* in horses.

†bekis ? corner teeth (of a horse).

brattle a loud clatter, a rattle, *eg* of horses' hooves.

bung *slang* an old worn-out horse *now Stlg*.

caber an old useless horse *Cai Bnf*.

†cappel a horse, *esp* a cart- or work-horse.

cleek: ~s leg cramps in horses *now Bnf*. **~it** *of horses* having string-halt *NE*.

clip a colt *chf NE*.

†counter the part of a horse's breast immediately under the neck.

cowt a colt. **~ foal** a young horse when suckling *SW, S*.

cruik, crook lame, *esp* of a horse *now Cai*.

cuddy 1 *also* **~ ass** *local Bnf-Arg* a donkey *Gen except Sh Ork*. **2** a horse *local*.

cuit the fetlock *Ayr*.

†cursour 1 *also* **~ hors** a courser, a charger. **2** a stallion *latterly proverb*.

eean a one-year-old horse or cow *NE*.

†eel-backit *of a horse* having a dark stripe along its back.

†fiercie farcy, the disease of horses.

fit, foot *of a horse* kick *now Dmf*.

fliskie *of a horse* apt to kick *now NE*.

frog a young male horse from one to three years old *Bnf Abd*.

funk *esp of a restive horse* kick, throw up the legs *now NE Ags Fif*.

garron 1 a small sturdy type of horse, used *esp* for rough hill work. **2** an old, worn-out horse.

†gillet a mare

gloom *of a horse* show signs of ill-temper or viciousness *now Arg*.

glyde an old worn-out horse.

†goggles, hors goggles blinkers.

gry *gipsy* a horse *local Per-Rox.*

hap *of horses in harness,* turn towards the right.

†harrower a young horse or *chf* mare, unbroken to the plough but used for harrowing *Per.*

hide bind a disease of horses which causes the hide to cling to the bone *now Ork midLoth.*

Hieland, Highland: ~ **pony,** ~ **sheltie** *now local* one of a breed of ponies originating in the Highlands.

†hobyn a small horse.

horse: ~**-beast** a horse *Gen except Sh Ork.* † ~ **fete** the feet of horses; a horse. † ~**-heid** a horse-head, the head of a horse.

†howe backit *of a horse* saddle-backed.

hup *of a horse in harness* go to the right *Gen except NE.*

jaud term of abuse for a horse; a worthless, worn-out nag *now NE Ags Rox.*

†jonet a jennet.

kame, comb *of a horse* rear *Ork Cai.*

†keir *of horses* dun, dark brown or grey. ~ **black** dark-coloured.

kittle *of a horse* become restive *now NE Ags Per.*

lang lugs *joc* a donkey *now Ags Kcb Rox.*

†lyart *chf of a horse* dappled.

mear, mare *freq proverb,* ~**ie** a mare, a female horse.

†mortercheyn a disease of horses, glanders.

naig 1 †*also* **naigie** a nag, a small horse or pony. **2** a horse *in gen.*

nicher *v, of a horse* snicker, neigh. *n* a whinny, neigh.

orra: ~ **beast** *NE,* ~ **horse** a horse kept for odd jobs.

paster, †pasture the pastern.

pownie a pony, *specif* a riding horse.

pret, †prat *of a horse* be disobedient, jib.

pyot, piet a piebald horse *Mry Abd midLoth.*

reest *v of horses* stop and refuse to move, jib, balk *now NE sEC-S.* *n, esp of horses* the act of stopping and refusing to move, *freq* **tak the** ~ jib *now Stlg.* ~**er** a jibbing horse. ~**ie** *of a horse* inclined to jib *local EC-S.*

†runsy a horse.

set *v, of a horse* jib, become restive, refuse to obey the rider or driver *NE Kcb.* †*adj, esp of a horse's tail* stiffened or cocked up. ~**ter** a jibbing horse *Bnf Abd Per.*

sheltie, shalt *Ork Abd,* **†shaltie** a Shetland pony, one of a breed of very small horses, *orig* native to Sheltand; also applied to any pony, *usu* a **garron.**

†side-tailed *of a horse etc* having a long tail.

skeich, skey *now Ags of horses* inclined to shy, restive, frisky, spirited *Stlg WC Wgt.*

skules an inflammatory disease of the gums and palate of a horse *now N.*

smool a snarl by a horse when threatening to bite *SW.*

†sneer *esp of a horse* a snort, noisy breathing (in or out) through the nose.

snippit *of a horse* with a white patch on the face *now Abd.*

†soir, sorre, sorrit *of a horse* of a sorrel colour.

spanker a spirited fast horse *now N Per Kcb.*

spavie spavin *now local Ork-Kcb.* ~**d** affected with spavin.

staig, stag 1 a young horse of either sex, of one to three years old, not broken to work *now Sh-Cai EC, WC Wgt.* **2** a stallion *now Ork-nEC Arg SW.* **3** a young castrated horse, a gelding *local.*

†stalwart strong, sturdy.

stane, stone: stoned *of a horse* not castrated, entire *now Sh Ork Rox.* ~ **horse** *etc* an uncastrated horse.

†steid, sted a steed, horse. ~ **horse** *or* **meir** a stud-horse *or* **-mare.**

†strummel disparaging term for a horse.

stryth the work-animals on a farm, plough-horses and -oxen *Cai.*

†stud a brood-mare.

†stug-tailed *of a horse* with a docked tail.

†sulliart *of a horse* bright, clear-coloured.

tag a skinny, worn-out horse *Bnf Abd.*

teenge colic, *usu* in horses *now Ags Per.*

†towmondall a yearling cow or steer.

†vees vives, hard swellings on the glands of a horse.

witherlock the tuft of a horse's main above its withers *now Cai.*

yaud *n* an old mare or horse, *esp* a worn-out horse *now S.* †*adj of a horse* worn-out.

yunk *of a horse* rear and plunge, buck *Fif Loth.*

2.5 DOGS

baigle a beagle.

†bawtie a dog.

†berk bark.

bick a bitch.

bouch *n* a bark (of a dog) *now Kcb. v* bark.

bouff, bowfer a dog *now Abd.*

Cairn (terrier) a particular type of small **West Highland** terrier, now a separate breed.

collie a sheepdog, *usu* black (and white).

dug, dowg *now local Cai-nEC* a dog.

gansh snatch (at), snap, snarl.

grew a greyhound, *now freq* the **~s** greyhound racing *now WC-Uls*. **~ hound** a greyhound *now Ags Wgt Uls*. †**~ whelp** a greyhound puppy.

guff, gouff a low bark of a dog *now Sh*.

gurlie growling, snarling *now NE*.

gurr *v* growl, snarl *now local*. *n, also* **~ry wurry** *now Ags* a growl, snarl. **~y** *now local SW*, **~y-wurry** *local C* a dogfight.

heather, hedder, hather: **~-claw** a dog's dewclaw, which is apt to catch in heather and is therefore *freq* cut off *now local Cai-Dmf*.

hund, hound *n* 1 a dog *in gen*. 2 a hound, a hunting dog. *v, of a male dog* run about from place to place after females *Abd Lnk*.

†**jolly** *of bitches* on heat.

†**jowler** a heavy-jawed hunting dog.

†**lether, ledder** *of a hound* tear the skin of (a quarry).

†**lying dog** a setter.

†**mangrel** a mongrel.

map *of a bitch* be in heat.

†**mastis** a mastiff, the large watch-dog.

messan 1 †*also* **~ dog**, **~ tyke** a small pet dog, a lapdog 2 *contemptuous* a cur, mongrel *chf C*.

narr snarl *now Bnf Abd*.

nurr the growl or snarl of an angry dog *now Sh Cai*.

nyaff *of a small dog* yelp, yap.

pan tie a pan or kettle to (*eg* a dog's tail), *esp* to make it go home *now Ork Ags*.

penny dog a dog that follows constantly at his master's heels.

pepper and mustard (breed, terrier *etc*) applied to a dog of the **Border** breed now called Dandie Dinmont.

†**ratch** a gundog or hound which hunts by scent.

rin, run *of a dog* move sheep at a brisk pace, range out in herding sheep *SW, S*.

scuddle scurry, roam about aimlessly, often with the intention of keeping out of sight *now Cai*.

scunge prowl or slink about (in search of something), scrounge *local Sh-SW*.

sleuth, †**slow:** **~-hound, slughan** a breed of bloodhound formerly used, *esp* in the Borders for hunting or tracking game or fugitives.

snack *n* a bite, snap, *esp* of a dog. *v* snap with the teeth, bite *now EC-S*.

snoke, snook sniff, smell, scent out (as a dog), snuff, poke with the nose *nEC, WC, SW*.

†**streaker** a kind of hunting dog.

strone *v, freq of dogs* urinate *Ags Edb Rox*. *n* the discharge of urine *now Edb Rox*.

tarrie, terrie, *also* **~ dog** a terrier *now Stlg Ayr*.

tike *usu contemptuous* a dog, a cur.

†**warset, wersslete** a hunting dog, a hound.

weirer a dog which is skilful in herding animals *now Dmf*.

West Highland (terrier), westie a small white rough-haired breed of terrier.

whinge *of a dog, v* whine, whimper *now NE-WC, S*. *n* a whine, whimper *now local Ags-Ayr*.

whink *of dogs v* bark in a sharp, suppressed way, yelp as when chasing game *now Slk*. *n* a sharp, suppressed bark or yelp from a dog *now Slk*.

wirr *of a dog etc v* growl, snarl *NE Ags Per*. *n* the growl of a dog *NE Ags*.

wow *n* a howl, deep-throated call or cry, bark *local Sh-Loth*. *v* howl, bark, bay *Sh NE*.

wowff *n* a low-pitched bark. *v, of a dog* bark in a suppressed way.

yaff, yauff bark, yelp *local EC-Rox*.

yalp yelp *now Ork*.

yamph †*v* bark, yap, yelp. *n* a dog's bark.

yap a yelping dog *N-WC*.

yatter *of an animal* yelp.

yirn *v, of a dog* whine; whimper *now Wgt*. *n* a whine *now Wgt*.

yirr *v, of a dog* snarl, growl *now Sh*. *n* the snarl or growl of a dog *now Sh*.

youch *of a dog* bark *Kcb Uls*.

youp a howling, wailing, as of a dog *Ork NE*.

yowf *of a dog* bark *Sh, N-S*.

yowl *v, of dogs or other animals* bark, howl, yell. *n* a howl, whine, mournful cry of a dog or other animal.

2.6 CATS

baudrons affectionate name for a cat.

cheet, cheetie-pussie a cat.

curmur purr.

fuff *v, of a cat etc* spit, hiss *local NE-Rox*. *v* a hiss or spit of a cat etc *now local NE-Kcb*.

gib, ~bie, ~cat 1 (name for) a cat. 2 *specif* a tom-cat, *esp* a castrated male *local Ork-Dmf*.

kittle *of cats* kitten.

kittlin a kitten.

loll howl like a cat, caterwaul *S*.

maw *v* mew. *n* a miaow *chf SW, S*.

†**mewt** *of a cat* mew.

miauve miaow *NE*.

Muscovy cat a tortoiseshell cat *SW*.

nurr purr *chf S*.

pussy-baudrons affectionate name for a cat *now Abd*.

thrum purr *now Abd Kcdn*. **sing** *etc* **(gray)** ~s purr *Abd-Ags WC*. **three** *etc* **threeds and** *or* **in a** ~ description of a cat's purr *now Ork*.

waw *v* mew piteously, caterwaul, wail *now Ork NE*. *n* the sound made by a cat in distress *now NE*.

†**wraw** mew like a cat.

†**yaw** mew, caterwaul; squeal.

2.7 DOMESTIC FOWL

bantim, bantin(g) a bantam.

bubbly jock a turkey cock.

bunt(ie) a hen without a rump.

buntin a bantam *Bnf Abd wLoth*.

caibie a hen's crop or gizzard *Cai Abd*.

caak *of a hen etc* cackle *Cai*.

caikle cackle *NE, EC*.

chuck, chuckie, chookie *C* a chick, a chicken *local Bnf-Fif*.

chucken a chicken *chf NE*.

clatchin a clutch (of chickens etc, eggs) *Ayr Uls*.

clock brood, sit on, hatch (eggs) ~**er,** ~**ing hen** a broody hen. **clockin** the desire to brood.

cock: ~**ed** *of eggs* fertile. ~**'s eggs** the small yolkless eggs laid by a hen about to stop laying *now Bnf Abd Fif*.

cockieleerie (law) a cock *local*.

cockmaleerie name for the cock *now Bnf Lnk*.

craw *n* a crow, the crowing of a cock *Bnf Abd*. *v* crow.

deuk, juck *now local C* a duck.

†**dumpy** one of a breed of short-legged fowl.

earock a young hen (*usu* in its first year), a pullet just beginning to lay *now Abd WC*.

egg-bed the ovary of a fowl.

faizart a hermaphrodite fowl *now Sh*.

follow, fallow: ~**er** the young of an animal, *chf* a cow or hen, *esp* one still dependent on its mother.

fuff *of a hen etc* puff (feathers) **out** *or* **up** *Sh Ork Abd*.

gaisling a gosling *now local*.

ganner, gain(d)er a gander *now local*.

gizzern the gizzard of a fowl.

goggie *child's word* an egg *Arg Lnk*.

golaich a breed of short-legged hen *now Per*.

guse, geese *Sh-NE* a goose.

habber, hubber *v* make a gobbling noise *N*. *n* the gobble of a turkey *NE*.

habble jock a turkey cock *Ags*.

hard: ~ **birdit** *of an egg* almost ready to hatch *Ags Rox*. ~**-sat,** ~**-sutten** *now local Ags-S* of eggs almost ready to hatch after long incubation.

harigal(d)s *also fig* the viscera of an animal, entrails of a fowl, the pluck.

hen a hen *freq corresponding to Eng* chicken as *eg* ~**-broth,** ~**-hertit.** ~ **pen** the droppings of fowls *now NE, C*.

howtowdie a large (young) chicken for the pot, a young hen which has not begun to lay.

keck *n* the sharp cackling sound made by a hen *now Wgt*. *v* make this sound, cackle, cluck *now NE*.

keckle *of hens* cackle.

lachter, lauchter 1 the total number of eggs laid by a fowl in a season; a single clutch on which she broods *now local NE Uls*. 2 a hatch or brood of chickens *local*.

lay: ~ **bag** *Ork-Per*, ~ **p(y)ock** *chf Sh Abd* the ovary of a fowl. ~ **awa** *of a fowl* lay eggs away from the usual nest.

leerie-la *n* 1 †the call of the cock. 2 the cock. *v* crow *Ags Fif*.

midden: ~ **cock** a barnyard cock *now Kcb Uls*. ~ **fool** a barnyard fowl.

mock the very small egg sometimes laid by a hen and regarded as an omen of misfortune *now wLoth Rox*.

mout *v* moult *now C, S*. *n*, *freq* **the** ~ the process or period of moulting *C, S Uls*, †~**it** moulted.

†**muffed** *of a domestic fowl* having a crest or tuft of feathers at the head, or round the neck or legs.

oon egg a wind egg, an egg laid without a shell *now Per*.

outlay *of a hen* lay away from the regular nest.

pluck a moulting state in fowls *Ork Cai Mry Kcb*.

pouk 1 a moulting condition in birds *now Per Stlg WC*. 2 the short unfledged feathers of a fowl, when they begin to grow after moulting *now Kcb*. ~**in** the moult *C*. ~**it** plucked *now C, S*. **in the** ~ moulting *C*.

poullie a young hen, *esp* one for the table, a chicken, pullet *now Uls*.

poutrie poultry.

†**pown, pon(e)y** the turkey, *esp* the female turkey. **pownie cock** the male turkey, a turkey cock.

pullie a turkey *now Bnf Uls*.

quackie a duck *now Abd Stlg Slk*.

quaick quack, as a duck *now Bnf Abd*.

queeple peep, quack in a squeaking high-pitched tone like a duckling *now Bnf Per*.

roup a catarrhal disease of the mouth or throat in poultry.

scroban the crop of a fowl *Cai-Inv Per Arg Bute*.

shot-cock a young cockerel, to be preserved for breeding *NE*.

sitten *of an egg on which a bird has been sitting* with a developed chick inside, near to hatching *local.*

snotter the red membraneous part of a turkey-cock's beak *now Cai Per Fif.*

snubbert the red membraneous part of a turkey-cock's beak *NE.*

spur scrape or scratch around, as a fowl in search of food *Rox.*

steg a gander *now Rox.*

tappie, tappack pet name for a hen with a tufted crest *now Sh Ork.* **tappint, tappit** *of a fowl* crested, tufted. **tappit hen** a tufted hen.

tickie *child's word* a hen or chicken *NE Ags.*

traik *freq of young poultry* wander, stray, become lost.

tuckie (hen) *child's word* a hen or chicken *now local NE-midLoth.*

weirdie the smallest or least thriving of a brood of animals, *esp* pigs or birds *nEC.*

†wheetle(-wheetie) a young bird, *esp* a duckling or chicken.

yap the plaintive chirping of chickens *Wgt.*

2.8 DESCRIPTION

See also sections for specific animals above. Note that poultry are included here.

2.8.1 GENERAL

angleberry, ingleberry *Loth SW* a fleshy growth on horses, cattle or sheep.

aten out o ply *of an animal* that will not fatten however well-fed. *SW.*

back-gaein not thriving.

†bairntime offspring.

basoned, †bawsant, bassie, bawsie *of an animal, orig a horse* having a white mark or streak on the face.

†bauld bold, fierce.

†beld, bell, baul *adj of horses or cattle* having a white spot or mark on the forehead. *n, only* **bell** a white mark on a horse's face.

bestial domestic animals, livestock.

†birsie bristly; hairy. **birsit** bristly.

†birthful, birthy, berthy prolific, fertile.

blastie *contemptuous* a bad-tempered, unmanageable animal *now Bnf Gsw.*

†bool-horned with curved or twisted horns.

bowdened swollen from overeating *now Bnf.*

brandit, brandered, brannet of a reddish-

brown colour with darker stripes or markings, brindled *now Abd Ags.*

brockit, brocked, brucket having black and white stripes or spots; *esp of a cow or sheep* having a white streak down the face. **brock(ie)-faced** *of an animal* having a **brockit** face *now Cai.*

brudy, breedy *now Bnf Fif Kcb,* **†broody** prolific; able or apt to breed.

†brutal of or like an animal, *usu* ~ **beste.**

†cabbrach lean, scraggy.

†cat-luggit crop-eared.

cootie *of fowls* having feathered legs *SW.*

cricklet the smallest of a litter, the weakest of a brood *WC.*

croot, crit a small or puny creature; the youngest of a brood *chf S.*

cruban a disease of the legs and feet of animals *Cai Arg.*

cruik, crook lame, *esp* of a horse *now Cai.*

†crum(m)et having crooked horns.

†dantit broken in, tamed.

dobbie having spikes, prickly *now Bnf.*

doddit *of cattle or sheep* hornless.

dorneedy *chf of pigs* the runt of a litter *now NE.*

dorty difficult to rear *now Bnf Abd.*

doxy lazy, slow *Bnf Abd Ags.*

dwine pine, waste away, fail in health. **dwiny** sickly, pining *now Fif.*

dyke-lowper an animal which leaps the dyke surrounding its pasture *now Bnf Abd Fif.*

†elf-shot a sickness (*usu* of cattle) thought to be caused by fairies.

fabric an ungainly or ugly animal *local Sh-Fif.*

feeding (sheep etc) being fattened for market.

fence-fed *of animals* fed with titbits brought to the side of the fence; pampered *Abd Ags.*

†fere healthy, sturdy, *chf* **hale and** ~.

fiarter term of abuse for an insignificant or undersized animal *Cai.*

flechy covered or infested with fleas *local Sh-Fif.*

fozie fat, flabby, out of condition *local NE-Gall.*

frame an emaciated animal *local Sh-Kcb.*

fresh *of animals* thriving, fattening *now midLoth SW.*

fuddie *of animals* short-tailed.

funker an animal that kicks.

gawsie *of animals* handsome, in good condition.

growthie well-grown, thriving *now local Ork-Kcb.*

grulsh a fat, squat animal *now Uls.*

†guids, goods, guddis livestock, cattle.

haik an animal given to roaming about, *freq* on the scrounge *local Bnf-S.*

half, hauf: ~-**waxed** *of rabbits etc* half-grown *Dmf Rox.*

18

hawkit, *chf of cattle, also other animals* spotted or streaked with white; white-faced *now Abd.*

heich, high tall.

†hide *pejorative* a female domestic animal.

hove *v* 1 cause to swell, distend. 2 become swollen or distended, swell, expand. *n* the swelling of cattle *now midLoth Bwk Lnk.* **hoved, hoven,** *chf of grazing animals* blown up with having eaten too much fresh green fodder. **hovie** swollen, distended. **hoving** the state of being swollen.

hule a mischievous, perverse or objectionable animal *now Kcb Dmf.*

hummel, hommill, hammill, humble *adj* 1 *of farm animals, chf and orig only of cattle* naturally hornless; *also* polled. 2 *of deer* naturally hornless. *n* an animal that has no horns or has been polled *local Cai-Ags.*

hypal an uncouth, broken-down animal *local.*

ill: ~ **daer** an animal that does not thrive. ~ **willie** bad-tempered *now Rox.*

jabart an animal in a weak or debilitated condition *now Cai.*

jaud term of abuse for a wilful, perverse animal.

karriewhitchit term of endearment for a young animal *Abd Ags.*

keen spirited, lively, eager *local N-SW.*

keeper a store animal, one kept for fattening *NE.*

ket carrion, tainted flesh, *esp* that of a sheep *Bwk S.*

kittlin the young of small animals.

laichy braid a short stocky animal *Bnf Abd.*

lameter a lame or crippled animal.

lang, long: ~-**nebbit** having a long snout etc.

lave-luggit having drooping, pendulous ears *now S.*

lift: a-~**ing** *now Sh Ork Cai,* **at the** *or* **in** ~**in** *especially of animals* in a very debilitated state (from the practice of raising a farm animal to its feet, *eg* after winter starvation).

limb: devil's ~, ~ **o the deil** *etc* a wicked or mischievous animal.

lingel-tailed having a long lank tail *now Fif Dmf.*

marlie, mirlie mottled or variegated in pattern *now N-Uls.*

mean in poor condition; thin *now Ags Uls.*

†meat, mait produce, animal or cereal, while still alive or growing.

mend fatten, (cause to) grow plump *now Kcb Uls.*

midden a gluttonous animal *NE Ags.*

midge a small insignificant animal.

mout, moult moult *now C, S.* †~**it** moulted.

nirl, nurl: ~**ie** dwarfish, stunted *now Sh Ork.*

†open, apen ready to bear young; bearing young; not sterilized.

outerlin(g) the weakling of a brood.

outgane *of an animal's age* past, fully *now Sh.*

outlier, outler *now verse* a farm animal which remains outside during the winter *now local.*

outlying not housed in winter *chf SW.*

paik a worthless animal, *esp* female.

palie, pallie *of young animals* undersized, not thriving.

peerie, peedie *Sh Ork Cai Fif:* ~-**weerie** a thin creature *now Sh Per.*

pet *n* an animal which has been domesticated and treated with affection, *freq* a hand-reared lamb or sheep.

pewl be in a weak state, pine.

pin a small, neat animal *Bnf Abd.*

piner an animal suffering from **pine**; an animal that is not thriving.

pipe-shankit having long thin legs *C, S.*

plaister a fawning animal *now WC.*

plowt a clumsy blundering animal *now Mry Fif.*

pluck a moulting state in fowls or animals *Ork Cai Mry Kcb.*

pluffy having a 'well-padded' appearance, plump, 'puffy', fleshy.

†portrature the external appearance of an animal.

pretty, pratty well-grown, sturdy, well-bred, in good condition *Sh NE.*

prod *contemptuous* a lazy animal.

pud, pod a small, neat animal *now Uls.*

pudget, pudgie *now Sh Abd,* **pudgle** *now Bnf Abd Slk* a small, plump, thickset animal.

punchie *n, also* **punchik(ie)** a short, stout animal *now NE. adj* thickset and short *now NE.*

quick swarming, infested *Sh Ork Uls.*

raff *of animals etc* thriving, flourishing *now Abd.*

rag a lean, scraggy animal *local Sh-Dmf.*

raik a roving animal.

†rammasche *of animals* wild, untamed.

rammish, ramsh mad; uncontrolled.

rammock a large worthless animal *now Bnf*

†ravissant *esp of wolves* ravening.

ribe an emaciated animal *now Gall.*

rickle an emaciated, broken-down animal, *freq* a ~ **o banes.**

rickling the smallest, weakest animal in a litter *Per SW.*

rig[1] a (*freq* white) strip running along the back of an animal *now Sh.*

rig[2] the smallest animal or weakling of a litter *now local Sh-SW.*

riglen 1 an undersized or weak animal or person *now Fif SW.* 2 the smallest animal in a litter *now Ags Per SW.*

riglin a male animal with one testicle undescended *now Ork EC, SW-S.*

rimpin a miserable or annoying animal *SW, S.*

ring: ~**it** *of animals* having a ring of white hair round the eye *now Sh.* ~**gle ee** *of an animal* an eye with a ring of white hair round it. ~**gle-eed,** ~**lit-eed** having a ~**le eye.**

rousie restless, easily excited *S.*

†**royet** a troublesome animal, *esp* a roaming or noisy cow.

rullion a coarse, ungainly, rough-looking animal.

†**trump** contemptuous term for an animal.

rung contemptuous term for: a large, ugly animal; a thin, scraggy animal *now Mry Abd Bwk.*

runk an emaciated, worn-out animal *chf Sh-N.*

runt an undersized or dwarfish animal *local.* ~**it** stunted in growth *Ayr Kcb.*

scaddin a lean, emaciated animal *now Abd.*

scar, skair *esp of animals* timid, shy, wild, apt to run away *now Ork.*

schamlich a weak, puny or slovenly animal *NE.*

scout diarrhoea, *esp* of animals *now local Cai-Slk.*

scrae a stunted, shrivelled or under-developed animal *now NE.*

scrat a puny or stunted animal *now NE Ags.*

scrog, scrag a lean scraggy animal or person *now Cai.*

scrunt a poorly-developed unthriving animal *now NE, C.* ~**it** shrivelled, shrunken, stunted in growth *now local Bnf-SW.* ~**y** stunted, shrivelled, stumpy, wizened *now SW, S Uls.*

set *of animals* stop growing, have the growth checked *now local Ork-WC.*

shaird, shard a puny or deformed animal *now Bnf.*

shairp, sharp: ~**-nibbit** having a pointed nose *Bnf Abd.*

shargar the weakest of a brood or litter *NE.*

shauchle a weakly, stunted, or deformed animal *now Ags Per.*

sheemach *contemptuous* a puny animal *N.*

†**shuit** *of animals* produce horns.

skeer, skeerie *now local of animals, esp horses* nervous, fearful, restive, agitated.

skiddle contemptuous term for a small animal.

skinnymalink(ie) a thin, skinny animal.

sklyte, sklyter *chf NE* a big, clumsy slovenly animal *Abd.*

sleekit smooth, having a glossy skin *now local Cai-SW.*

slink an aborted, premature, or newly-born unfed calf or other animal *now C.*

slounge an animal always on the look-out for food, a scrounger, glutton *Loth Wgt Rox.*

sma(ll) *of animals* slim, slender, slightly-built *now Sh NE Per.*

smatche(r)t a small insignificant animal *now Sh Ork N.*

smout a small animal *Gen except Sh Ork.*

sneck an indentation in an animal's horn as a sign of age *now local Sh-Per.*

†**snores** an animal disease causing snuffling, the snivels.

sodger a wounded or injured animal *local Abd-Dmf.*

†**sonsie** *of animals* tractable, manageable.

soo: ~**-luggit** *of animals* having long, loose-hanging ears *now Per.* ~**-mouthed** *of animals* having a projecting upper jaw *NE, C.*

souk: ~**ie** a suckling *Per Ags Rox.* ~**ing** sucking. ~**it** fatigued, exhausted.

spankie friskie, nimble, spirited.

spean, spane: new ~**ed** newly weaned, just weaned *now Sh Ork N Kcb.* ~**ing brash** an illness affecting young animals on being weaned *now Kcb.*

spittin a small bad-tempered animal *Bnf Abd.*

†**stalwart** *of animals, chf horses* strong, sturdy.

stark physically strong, sturdy, vigorous *now Ork Cai.*

stench *now NE, EC,* **staunch** strong, dependable; in good health *now NE.*

stieve *of animals or their limbs* firm, strong, sturdy *now local Per-Dmf.*

stilp a tall animal with long legs *now NE.*

stookit having short upright horns.

stug, stog a stocky coarsely-built animal.

stump a short stocky animal *now Sh Cai Inv.*

suckler *of farm animals* a suckling, a cow giving suck *now C, S.*

swack *of animals or their limbs* active, lithe, supple *now local Sh-Fif.*

swank *of animals* lithe, agile, strong *now nEC Lnk Slk.*

tarloch a small, weak or worthless animal *now Bnf Abd.*

†**tate** untamed.

taut *n* a tangled, matted tuft or lock of wool, hair etc *now local Sh-SW.* *v* mat, tangle; make matted or tangled. ~**ie** *now C, S,* ~**it** *now local Sh-SW, of hair, wool etc* matted, entangled, shaggy, unkempt; *of animals* having a rough, shaggy head or coat.

tidy in good condition, shapely, plump *now Ork.*

†**traikit** *of animals* having died of exhaustion or disease.

tramshach a big, ungainly animal *Bnf.*

troke, truck worthless specimens *N Bwk Lnk.*

trollop a long, gangling, ungainly animal *local Ork-WC.*

twa year'l *Sh Ork,* **twa year al(d)** *Ayr* two-year-old.

twinter *now Pbls Ayr Slk,* **quinter** *SW, S* a two-year old farm animal, *esp* a thrice-shorn ewe.

vision a puny, emaciated animal *now Sh Ork Stlg Dmf.*

wallie big and strong, thriving, sturdy, plump *now Sh Ork.*

wallop a gangling loose-limbed animal *now Ags.*

wallydrag, warridrag *Bnf Abd,* **wallydraigle** *local C* an undersized animal *now Bnf Abd.*

warback the warble- or gadfly, any of the flies of the family *Oestridae* which breed under the skin of cattle *now Cai Per.*

†**warlock** a savage or monstrous creature.

waster an animal of no further use, due to decrepitude, disease etc *local.*

wearifu troublesome, annoying.

wechtie *of animals* physically heavy and solidly corpulent *now NE.*

weed *of farm animals* a feverish ailment thought to have been caused by a chill; *specif of female animals* mastitis *Gen except Sh.*

†**wicht** strong, vigorous.

wicked, wickit *of animals or their actions* bad-tempered, ill-natured, viciously angry.

willyart *of animals* wild; undisciplined, wayward; unmanageable *now Wgt.*

winter: ~**er** a farm animal kept for fattening over winter *Gen except S.* ~**ing** an animal which is kept over the winter *now Cai Mry.* **weel-** *or* **ill-wintert** *of an animal* well- or ill-fed, (un)healthy *local Ork-Wgt.*

wirl, wrow a puny malformed animal, a stunted or deformed creature, *now Fif.*

†**wirling** a puny or stunted animal.

wisgan *term of abuse* a stunted, useless creature *Bnf Ags.*

wuid, wood, wode *of animals* rabid, mad.

year, 'ear: ~**aul(d)** a yearling.

†**yurlin** a puny stunted creature.

2.8.2 PARTS OF THE BODY

Includes carcasses.

†**beuch** a shoulder or limb.

birse 1 bristles, (a) bristle. **2** a sheaf of bristles.

bun, bunt *Rox* the tail of a hare or rabbit.

cantle the crown of the head *now Abd.*

carcage a carcass *now local Bnf-Fif.*

choller the wattles of a cock *SW, S.*

claut a claw *now Lnk.*

cleuk, †**clew** a claw *now Ags Fif wLoth.*

cloot one of the divisions in the hoof of cloven-footed animals; the whole hoof.

closhach the carcass of a fowl *NE.*

clow a claw.

cluif a hoof, *orig* cloven.

corpus the live body of an animal *now Abd Fif.*

crog a paw *now Cai.*

curpin the behind or rump.

draucht the entrails of an animal *now Mry Ags Kcb.*

faiple a loose drooping underlip *now Fif Dmf.*

flaucht a lock or tuft of hair or wool.

fud the tail of an animal, *chf* a hare or rabbit *local NE-Rox.*

gralloch a deer's entrails.

grunyie the snout.

†**haggis** the stomach.

hainch, hinch, ~**le** *nEC* the haunch.

harigal(d)s the viscera of an animal.

hinders the hindquarters of an animal *now Sh.*

hoch, houch, haugh the hough, hock, the hind-leg joint of an animal.

huif *now Ags Kcb,* **hiv** *now Cai NE* a hoof.

huil *now chf EC, S,* **hull** the skin of an animal.

hurdies the hips, haunches *Gen except Sh Ork.*

inmeat, inmate the viscera of an animal, *esp* the edible parts *now Rox.*

king's hood *or* **head** the second of the four stomachs of a ruminant *now Sh Edb Rox.*

leather, ledder *now Sh Ork NE* the skin, hide.

luif, loof the paw, foot or hoof of an animal *now Wgt.*

lunyie-bane the haunch-bone of an animal.

lure the udder of a cow or other animal *now local Ork-Edb.*

mull the mouth or muzzle of an animal *chf Sh Ork.*

neir a kidney *now Sh-N.*

nick one of the notches or growth-rings on an animal's horns.

oxter the part of an animal that corresponds to the armpit of a person, the underside of its shoulder.

painch, paunch *n* ~**es** the entrails of an animal, *esp* as food. †*v* puncture the large stomach of an animal, *esp* a ruminant, to allow accumulated gases to escape.

†**pap** one of the teats of an animal.

†**pikant** a prickle.

pike 1 a pointed tip or end (of a horn etc) *now Ork NE, EC, S.* **2** a spine or quill of an animal *now Ork.*

pock, poke the udder of a milch animal *now Kcb.*

pow, poll the head, the crown of the head, the scalp, the skull.

prog a spine, prickle *now Per Ayr.*

puddin(g)s entrails, viscera, guts.

puddock, paddock, poddock, paddy: ~('s) **hair** the down or fluff growing on very young creatures.

quern the stomach of a fowl, the gizzard *now NE.*

rig, riggin *now local Ork-Stlg* the back or backbone of an animal *now Sh Cai.*

rumple the rump, tail, haunches (of an animal) *now Sh.*

runt the tail of an animal; the rump, the upper part of the tail *SW.*

shuttle, shittle: ~ **gab** a misshapen mouth, with one jaw protruding beyond the other, *esp* of an animal.

sloch, sluch *n* a slough, an outer skin. *v* slough.

snoot a snout.

spag, spaig *Cai* a paw, hand, foot, *esp* a big clumsy hand or foot *now Cai.*

spaul(d), †**spule 1** the shoulder; the shoulder-bone. **2** †one of the four quarters of an animal, an animal's leg.

†**spinnelled** *chf of diseased teats of animals* spindle-shaped.

spyog a paw *now Cai.*

tait a small tuft or bundle of hair, wool etc *now local Sh-Kcb.*

tap a tuft of hair, wool etc; a forelock.

tartle a tuft of hair or wool at an animal's tail which has become matted with excrement or mud *now Stlg WC Gall.*

thairm an animal bowel, gut, intestine *now local Sh-WC.*

tit a nipple or teat.

torr-bane the prominence on the pelvic bone of a horse, cow or sheep *now SW.*

trollie-bags the intestines or entrails of animals.

ure the udder, *esp* of a cow or ewe *Dmf Rox.*

ush the entrails of a slaughtered animal.

veshel, vessel, weshell the udder (of a cow etc) *Cai Per WC, SW.*

wab, wob, web the omentum of animals *Sh Cai Wgt.*

wan(d) an animal's penis *now Kcb.*

2.8.3 BEHAVIOUR, REPRODUCTION

Includes animal homes; eating and drinking; excretion; reproduction.

baggit very pregnant.

bicker *of living creatures* move quickly and noisily, rush.

binner run, gallop *Abd.*

bourie a rabbit's burrow; an animal's lair.

box *of animals* attack with the horns, butt *now Cai Bnf Abd.*

breem *now Fif,* **brim** *now Kcb esp of a sow* be in heat.

buck push, butt; batter.

cast *of animals* give birth to, *latterly esp* prematurely *now local.*

cave toss (*chf* the head, horns) *now Bnf Bwk Wgt.* †**cavie** rear, prance *NE.*

chack bite *now Lnk Kcb.*

chittle nibble, gnaw *SW.*

clap a rabbit burrow or hare's form *local SW, S.*

†**clappard** a rabbit burrow or hole.

clean(in) the afterbirth of an animal, *esp* a cow *N, S.*

cleck the act of hatching or giving birth *now Bnf.*

cleuk claw, scratch *Abd.*

†**clow** claw.

collieshangie, killieshangie a dogfight *now Bnf.*

cood the cud.

†**cunin(g)ar** a rabbit-warren *in place-names.*

dunch *v* butt *now Fif Kcb.* *n* a butt from an animal *now Kcb.*

ferry farrow, produce young *now local Sh-midLoth.*

flap the lair of a hare or other animal *Bnf Ags Ayr.*

follow, fallow: ~**er** the young of an animal, *chf* a cow or hen, *esp* one still dependent on its mother.

foster *chf of a mother suckling her offspring* feed, nourish *local Sh-Abd.*

fud: cock its *etc* ~ *of an animal* cock its etc tail.

funk *esp of a restive horse* kick, throw up the legs *now NE Ags Fif.*

gae, go *of animals* graze *NE.*

†**gash** gnash, bare (the teeth), snap *NE.*

glamse snap at *now Ork.*

†**gnip** nip, bite.

gnyauve gnaw *N.*

gove start (with fright), toss the head.

hap and *or* **wynd** *of harnessed animals* turn to the right and/or left.

†**hird** a herd, a flock.

†**hoit** *v* move awkwardly or clumsily, *esp* of a well-fed animal trying to move quickly, waddle. *n* a slow hobbling gait.

hose swallow voraciously *now Bnf Abd*.

kindle *of small animals, esp rabbits* produce young *now Dmf*.

kittle *of small animals* produce young. **be in** ~ *of certain small animals* be (on the point of) giving birth *NE, Kcb*.

†**knaw** gnaw.

kned breathe with effort, pant *Cai*.

†**knip** bite or crop grass.

laip *v* lap (liquid) *now local Sh-midLoth*. *n* the act of lapping *now Ags midLoth*.

lizour, †**lezu** graze.

†**loge, luge** an animal's lair.

†**minnie** *of a young animal* run back to its mother.

miss *of a breeding animal* fail to conceive.

moudie(wort) hill(ock) a molehill *now Dmf*.

moup, *also* ~ **on** *or* **at** repeatedly twitch the lips; nibble, munch *now Edb Ayr Kcb*.

nip nibble; graze *now Abd Per*.

open *of female animals* ready to bear young; bearing young; not sterilized.

pawt *of a horse etc* paw (the ground) *now Sh Abd Ayr*.

pick *v, of a female (farm-)animal* abort (her young), give birth to prematurely, *freq* **pick calf** *NE-S*. *n* an aborted or stillborn animal *WC, S, Uls*.

pike *of pasturing animals* eat in a delicate leisurely way, nibble, pick (at food).

pluck a mouthful of grass etc taken by an animal as food *now Sh NE Wgt*.

pork a thrust, prod, poke *now SW*.

purl *n* ~**s, pirlacks** *Ork Cai,* ~**ack** *Per* the small balls of dung excreted by sheep, rabbits etc. *v* defecate *now Sh*.

rag *of grazing animals* spread out in a line, straggle.

riding season *or* **time** the breeding season of animals *now Ork*.

rug *of grazing animals* a bite of grass, a feed *now Bnf Kcb*.

ruit root, dig up with the snout.

rump eat down to the roots *now Kcb*.

scart 1 scratch, scrape with the claws etc. 2 scrape or scratch (the ground) in search of food.

scob hollow, gnaw out with the teeth.

scrat scratch, claw; make a scratching noise *now NE-WC*.

scuddle *of animals, esp dogs* scurry, roam about aimlessly, often with the intention of keeping out of sight *now Cai*.

shuit, shoot: ~ **out** *of animals* produce (horns etc).

slaik, slaich *esp of a pet animal v* lick (dishes) or consume (food) on the sly. *n* a lick with the tongue, a slobbering lick.

slock, sloke appease the thirst of (an animal).

slocken quench the thirst of (an animal).

smurl eat little and slowly without appetite (*esp* if ill), nibble half-heartedly or furtively.

snack *n* a bite, snap, *esp* of a dog. *v* snap with the teeth, bite *now EC-S*.

snash snap, bite *now Ork*.

sotter a considerable number, *esp* of small creatures, a swarm *Rox*.

spean, spane 1 wean (a suckling animal). 2 be (in the process of being) weaned *now Ags Per*. ~**ing time** weaning time *now Cai*.

sten(d) *of animals* rear, start, be restive.

stick *of a horned animal* gore, stab or butt with its horns *now local*.

stot *of an animal* bound, go by leaps *now Bnf Ags*.

suckler *of farm animals* a suckling; a cow giving suck *now C, S*.

†**tod('s) hole** a fox's hole or den.

toddle walk with short, rocking, uncertain or unsteady steps.

tuird *now Ork,* **taird** *now C* a turd.

†**vert** turn up, root up (the ground).

wammle roll about, wriggle writhe *now local Sh-SW*.

whalp *n, v* whelp.

whid *freq of a hare n* a rapid, noiseless movement, a gambol, spurt. *v* move quickly and noiselessly, *esp* in a jerky or zigzag way; whisk, scamper, run.

winch kick, prance.

yeld, eild *of animals* barren, not bearing young because of age or accident *now local Sh-C*.

2.9 CALLS, NOISES

See note at 2 above.

belloch, belly *now Mry,* **bully** *now Ags of cattle* bellow.

†**berk** bark.

bick (bick) birr imitation of the call of the grouse *chf Abd*.

blait bleat.

blea bleat, as a lamb or kid *S*.

bouch *n* a bark (of a dog) *now Kcb*. *v* bark.

bouff *esp of a large dog* bark.

caak *of a hen etc* cackle *Cai*.

caikle cackle *NE, EC*.

clock the clucking sound made by a broody hen *now local Cai-Kcb*.

cockieleerie (law) the crowing of a cock *local.*

craw *n* a crow, the crowing of a cock. *Bnf Abd. v* crow.

curmur purr.

drizzen *chf of cows* make a low plaintive sound *now Abd.*

fuff *v of a cat etc* spit, hiss *local NE-Rox. v* a hiss or spit of a cat etc *now local NE-Kcb.*

loll howl like a cat, caterwaul *S.*

queeple peep, quack in a squeaking high-pitched tone like a duckling *now Bnf Per.*

†quhyn whine.

snag snarl (at) *now Kcdn.* **~ger** snarl, growl *Bnf Abd.*

waw *v* mew piteously, caterwaul, wail *now Ork NE. n* the sound made by a cat in distress *now NE.*

whinge *of a dog v* whine, whimper *now NE-WC, S. n* a whine, whimper *now local Ags-Ayr.*

whink *of dogs v* bark in a sharp, suppressed way, yelp as when chasing game *now Slk. n* a sharp, suppressed bark or yelp from a dog *now Slk.*

wirr *of a dog etc v* growl, snarl *NE Ags Per. n* the growl of a dog *NE Ags.*

wow *n* a howl, deep-throated call or cry, bark *local Sh-Loth. v* howl, bark, bay *Sh NE.*

wowff *n* a low-pitched bark. *v, of a dog* bark in a suppressed way.

†wraw mew like a cat.

yabb *of animals* chatter, bark etc excitedly *now Ork Abd Ags.*

yaff, yauff bark, yelp *local EC-Rox.*

yalp yelp *now Ork.*

yamph †*v* bark, yap, yelp. *n* a dog's bark.

yap the plaintive chirping of chickens *Wgt.*

yatter *of an animal* yelp.

†yaw mew, caterwaul; squeal.

yirn *v of a dog* whine; whimper *now Wgt. n* a whine *now Wgt.*

yirr *v, of a dog* snarl, growl *now Sh. n* the snarl or growl of a dog *now Sh.*

youch *of a dog* bark *Kcb Uls.*

youp a howling, wailing, as of a dog *Ork NE.*

yowf *of a dog* bark *Sh, N-S.*

yowl *v, of dogs or other animals* bark, howl, yell. *n* a howl, whine, mournful cry of a dog or other animal.

3. WATER LIFE

3.1 FISH

3.1.1 GENERAL, MISCELLANEOUS

baggit *adj* big with young; full of spawn. *n, also* **bag(g)ot** a fish full of spawn.

black fish a recently-spawned fish, *chf* salmon *now Fif.*

chollers the gills of a fish *SW, S.*

fush fish.

ginnle the gills of a fish *WC.*

gip the jaw of a fish *now Abd Fif.*

glut slime on fish *now Sh Bwk.*

gut pock the stomach of a fish *now Cai.*

haul(d) *v* hide, lurk under stones *chf S. n* the overhanging bank of a stream, or a stone, under which a fish lurks.

melt, melg *NE* the milt of a male fish.

pock, poke the stomach of a fish *Cai Wgt.*

rag a lean, scraggy fish *local Sh-Dmf.*

rawn, rown, †roan the roe of a fish *now E Kcb.*

redd, †trid *n* fish-spawn, *freq* **fish-~** *now Per Wgt Rox. v, of fish* spawn *now Per Wgt.*

scag *†v, of fish* become rotten by exposure to sun or air. *n* a putrid fish.

†shed, shade *of fish* cleave (the water).

shot(ten) *of fish* spawned *now EC.*

sile, sill the newly-hatched young of fish, *esp* of herring *local Sh-WC.*

†skail 1 a scale (on fish etc). 2 *only in uninflected pl after numerals etc* kinds or varieties (of fish): 'dyuers skaile of fish'.

soom the swimming- or air-bladder of a fish.

soun(d) the swimming-bladder of a fish *now local Sh-Fif.*

3.1.2 SEA FISH

baddock the (young of the) coal-fish *now NE Bwk.*

bagget the coal-fish *NE.*

beggarman a fish, *usu* a flounder *Mry.*

bergell a species of wrasse *Sh Ork Mry.*

birdie a young halibut *Mry Abd.*

blacksmith the halibut *Mry Abd.*

blin ee the dogfish.

block a cod *Bnf.* **~an, bluchan** the young coal-fish *chf SW.* **~ie** a small cod *now Cai.*

bonnet fleuk the brill *now Fif.*

braze any of several species of fish, *eg* the (sea) bream *now Arg.*

bressie the bib or pout *now Fif.*

brigdie the basking shark *Sh Ork N.*

cabelew a young cod *local Sh-Per.*

†cairban the basking shark.

cameral, gamrel a haddock after spawning *NE.*

chat a small haddock *now Bnf.*

coam *Bnf,* **†colmie, colmouth** the mature coal-fish.

cock paddle the lumpfish *now Bnf.*

croon: ~er *local,* **~ick** *chf Bnf,* **~yil** *chf Mry,* **†crunan** the gurnard.

cuddie, cuddin a young coal-fish *now N Fif Arg.*

cuithe *Ork,* **queeth** *NE* the young coal-fish.

cumper the fatherlasher *Ork NE.*

darg a young whiting *NE.* **~ie** the (fry of the) coal-fish.

dinnen skate a kind of skate *local E.*

droud a codfish, *chf* one of poor quality *now Arg.*

fish, fush white fish, as opposed to herring *Cai Ags Fif.*

fitin *NE,* **†whitin** the whiting *now NE.*

fleuk the flounder. **†sole ~** the sole.

flunner the flounder *now N.*

full *adj, of herrings* full of milt or roe, sexually mature *Sh Ork N, EC. n* herring full of milt or roe *E.*

garvie the sprat *now local Inv-Edb.*

gerrock the coal-fish in its first year *NE.*

get a coal-fish in its second stage *now Abd Fif.*

gildee a whiting pout *WC.*

goukmey the grey gurnard.

gowdie, goldie one of various fishes, *eg* the dragonet, the gurnard, the sea scorpion *now Ork NE nEC.*

gray: ~back the flounder *Mry Fif.* **~ fish** the coal-fish, *esp* in its second or third year *now Sh.* **~ lord** the fully-grown coal-fish. *S.* **~ skate** the skate *now Fif.*

great fish white fish as distinct from herring.

†green-bane the garfish, garpike or needlefish.

†guffer the eel-pout.

gundie, gunnie, gunplucker *now Ags* the father-lasher *now NE Ags*.

gutpock herring herring which feed *chf* on small crustaceans *now Arg*.

haddie, haddo, hathock, hoddock *NE* a haddock.

haivel the conger-eel.

halflin(g) a half-mature herring *Fif Loth*.

hardheid the sea scorpion or fatherlasher *now Ayr*.

harrowster a spawned haddock *NE*.

herrin, †har(r)ing a herring. ~ **hake** the hake *now Inv Fif WC*. ~**sile** young herring *now local NE-Kcb*.

hush padle the lumpfish *now Kcdn*.

jabart a lean cod etc, a fish out of season *now Cai*.

jackie downie the bib or pout *chf Arg*.

Jerusalem haddie the opah or kingfish *Ross Abd Ags Fif*.

keelin, killing a cod, *esp* a fully-grown or large one. †~ **sound** the swimming bladder of the cod, used for glue.

Kessock herring a small variety of herring caught in the Inner Moray Firth *Ross Inv Mry*.

keth(r)ie the angler-fish *now Abd Bwk*.

king of the herrings the Arctic chimaera *Sh NE*.

†limp the lump(fish).

Loch Fyne applied to herring caught there.

lythe the pollack *now local*.

†macfische ? mackerel.

†maiden skate a young specimen of the thornback ray, skate, or similar members of the ray species.

marmaid(en)'s purse the egg-case of a ray *now Sh Ork Uls*.

matfull a sexually mature herring.

mattie a young maiden herring with the roe not fully developed *Sh NE Ags*.

muldoan the basking shark *Abd Arg*.

†neck hering ? a variety of herring, ? the shad.

needlach a young eel *Inv*.

†nine-eyed-eel the lamprey.

oof, wolf the angler-fish *NE*.

paidle the lumpfish or lump-sucker *Sh Cai Kcdn Fif*. ~ **cock** the male lump-fish *now Kcdn Ags*.

pelcher the grey mullet *Cai*.

Peter: ~**'s thoom** *Sh-N, WC*, (St) ~**'s mark** *Cai NE, WC* one of the black marks behind the gills of a haddock popularly thought to be the fingerprint of St Peter when he caught the fish for the tribute money (Matthew xvii 27).

peuchtie, pituchtie a young saithe or coal-fish *Arg Ayr*.

pickie the young of the saithe; any small fry of fish *now Ayr*.

piltock the saithe in its early stages, *usu* in the second year *now Sh Ork*.

†pintle fish the sand-eel.

plash, plashack, plashack-fluke the plaice *chf N*.

poach the armed bullhead or pogge *now Ags*.

podlie, †podler the young of the coal-fish at the second stage of its development; the pollack, the **lythe** *NE Ags Fif*.

pout(ie) a small haddock.

prinkle a young coal-fish *NE*.

pullach a species of cod *now Bnf*.

ramper (eel) the sea or river lamprey; any large eel.

rawn, rown, †roan the turbot, *freq* ~ **fleuk** *now Abd*.

redware cod(ling) a young inshore cod *now Sh-EC*.

rock: ~ **cod(fish)** *or* **codling** a kind of cod which lives amongst rocks. ~-**halibut** the coal-fish *NE Ags*. ~-**herring** the allis or twaite shad *now Bnf*. ~ **sole** the Dover sole *now NE*. ~ **turbot** the flesh of the catfish or wolf-fish *NE Ags Bwk*.

rodd(en) fluke the turbot.

ruchie *NE*, **rochie** *NE*, **roughback(-fleuk)** *now Bnf* the long rough dab.

runker 1 the lumpfish *now Cai*. 2 one of several species of wrasse *NE*.

saithe, †sey, seeth the full-grown coal-fish in its third or (*local*) fourth year.

sand: san(d)al, san(d)le *local Cai-Fif*, ~**lin** *now Bnf* the sand-eel. ~ **dab** the dab *local Bnf- Kcb*. ~ **fleuk** the smear-dab *now Bnf Fif*.

sautie the dab *now Bnf*.

scattan a herring *now NE Bute Ayr*.

scule a school, shoal (of fish).

sea: ~ **cat** the wolf-fish. ~ **dog** the dogfish. ~ **soo**, *pl sometimes* ~ **swine** the small-mouthed wrasse *now Kcdn*.

sheer dog *etc* the tope or Portugal shark.

siller: ~-**fish** the bib or pout *now Abd*. †~ **fluke** the brill; the megrim *NE Kcdn*.

skate: †~ **bread** a kind of very small fish. ~ **purse** the ovarium of a skate *local*. †~ **rumple** the part of the backbone of a skate above the root of the tail.

skeet the pollack *N*.

slink an emaciated or spent fish, *esp* a cod or salmon, a kelt *now Ayr*.

sma(ll) fish fish such as haddock, herring etc, caught inshore with **small lines** *now Sh Ags Kcb*.

snap a small cod or haddock *local Ork-Ross*.

soo, sow the ballan wrasse *now Bnf Kcdn*.

soosler a thin fish, *esp* a cod, in poor condition *Cai*.

spent, spyntie *NE adj, of a fish, esp a herring* spawned, in poor condition after spawning. *n* a **spent** fish.

†spirling, sparling, sperling a sprat.

splash *now Abd*, **splashack** *local N* the plaice.

stake, stakie a young ling *Abd*.

†stane, stone: ~ **fish** the gunnel.

stenlock, stan(e)lock the coal-fish, *esp* in its fully-grown or **saithe** stage *now Arg Ayr*.

†sture a sturgeon.

sweltin a cod in poor condition *Sh Kcdn*.

thornie (back) the thornback ray *now Sh*.

tobacco fleuk the lemon sole *NE*.

turbot the halibut.

tusk (fish) a ling-like fish of the cod family, found *chf* in northern Scottish waters *now Sh Ork Cai*.

warry codlin *Sh NE,* **†warcodling** a young inshore cod.

whitie the whiting *now Dnbtn Ayr*.

wide-gab the angler-fish

witch *used of various creatures associated with witches, eg* the pole flounder or dab.

parr a young salmon with dark stripes on its side, at the stage before it becomes a **smolt**.

raggie a diseased salmon *Bwk S*.

rawner, row(a)ner an unspawned salmon *now Per Slk*.

redd, †rid the rut in a riverbed made by salmon for spawning in.

reid, red, rid: ~ **fish 1** a male salmon at spawning time when it turns reddish *now WC, SW*. **2** *used where the name 'salmon' is taboo* salmon.

saumon, salmon, †salmond a salmon. ~ **rawn** salmon roe *now Kcb*.

slink an emaciated or spent fish, *esp* a cod or salmon, a **kelt** *now Ayr*.

smowt, smolt, smout, smelt a young salmon (or sea trout) between the **parr** and **grilse** stages.

spirling, sparling, sperling the smelt *now Per Ayr*.

†whitin an immature sea trout.

whitling an immature sea trout at the stage of development equivalent to the **grilse** of the salmon *now EC Ayr Rox*.

yellow fin the young of the sea-trout *now Abd Dmf*.

3.1.3 SALMON AND SEA TROUT

bill a kind of sea trout *Dmf*.

black fish a recently-spawned fish, *chf* salmon *now Fif*.

†candavaig a variety of salmon *Abd*.

doobrack the smelt or sparling *Bnf Abd*.

finnock a young sea-trout or salmon *now N (except Cai) nEC Arg*.

fish, fush the salmon *local*.

grawl a **grilse** *SW*.

gray: ~**back** a salmon or salmon trout in the autumn run *SW-S*. ~ **scool** an inferior variety of salmon *S*.

grilse, gilse *now Bwk* a young salmon on its first return to fresh water.

herling, hirling an immature sea-trout *SW*.

kelt a salmon or sea-trout on its way back to the sea after spawning. † ~**ed** spawned *S*.

kip, kype the projecting cartilage on the lower jaw of the male salmon at spawning time *chf S*.

Lammasman a young salmon trout which begins its journey up-river from the sea for the first time about the beginning of August.

†lax a salmon *chf NE*.

ligger a newly-spawned salmon, a foul fish *chf SW*.

3.1.4 FRESHWATER FISH

baggie (mennen) a kind of large minnow *local WC-Rox*.

bandie a minnow; a stickleback *now Bnf*.

banstickle a stickleback.

beard, baird: ~**ie 1** the three-spined stickleback. **2** *chf* ~**ie lotchie** the loach.

beeran a small trout *Suth Inv*.

bessie, ~ **bairdie ,** ~ **lotchie** the loach *Rox*.

braze any of several species of fish, *eg* the roach *now wLoth WC*.

doctor a large minnow; the red-breasted minnow *now Fif Edb Ayr*.

eel: ~**at** an eel-like fish, *Myxine glutinosa, N*. **nine-eed** ~ the lesser lamprey.

†gellytroch the char *Kinr*.

guttie the minnow *now Stlg*.

Katie beardie the loach *Ags Fif midLoth*.

lamper eel a lamprey.

loch trout a trout which feeds in a **loch**, *usu* larger than a river-trout.

Lochleven trout a variety of trout peculiar to Lochleven.

minnon, mennen(t) *chf S* a minnow; any small freshwater fish *Gen except Sh Ork*.

peen-heid the young fry of the minnow or stickleback *EC, S.*

podlie a red-breasted minnow *now Loth Rox.*

powan, †pollack a species of freshwater fish, found in Scotland only in Loch Lomond and Loch Eck *WC.*

preenheid the fry of the minnow *C, S.*

ramper (eel) the sea or river lamprey; any large eel.

reid, red, rid: ~ **gibbie** the stickleback *Ags.*

skelly the chub *S.*

sodger the red-breasted minnow *now Abd Lnk Ayr.*

spriklybag the stickleback *Ayr Uls.*

streamer the male minnow near spawning time *now Lnk Ayr.*

troot a trout.

vendace a species of char found in Britain only at Lochmaben, *Dmf.*

3.2 SEA CREATURES

†ballane baleen, whalebone.

bucker a species of whale; a porpoise *now Arg.*

buckie the whelk, edible or otherwise; its shell; sometimes applied to other molluscs.

burr a sea-urchin *now Mry Bnf.*

clabbydhu a large variety of mussel *WC.*

claik the barnacle *Sh Ork Abd.*

clam(shell) a scallop (shell).

cross-fit the starfish *now Abd.*

croy a tiny crustacean on which herring feed *Arg.*

cruban a crab *chf Arg Uls.*

†curale coral.

daichie, daikie a bivalve smooth-shelled mollusc *Fif.*

dunter the common porpoise; the dolphin *now Ork.*

finner a whale of the genus *Balaenoptera, chf Sh.*

groatie buckie a species of cowrie shell *Sh Ork Cai Abd.*

hairy hu(r)tcheon a sea-urchin *now Fir.*

hose-fish, hosack *Abd* the cuttlefish.

†huddoun a species of whale.

John o Gro(a)t's buckie the cowrie shell.

†keavie a species of crab *chf Fif.*

lapster, labster a lobster.

lempit, lempeck *Fif Bwk,* **†lampit** a limpet.

loch-liver *now Abd,* **loch-lubbertie** *now Abd,* **lubbertie** *Kcdn Ags* a jellyfish.

†meer-swine a dolphin; a porpoise.

mettick a soft crab *Abd.*

motherie a small delicately-coloured shell used for making necklaces *Suth Bnf Ags.*

pallawa a small edible crab, *freq* used for bait *Fif.*

†pan-door (oyster) a large succulent type of oyster found in the Forth, *esp* round Prestonpans.

pap the sea anemone *now Kcdn Fif.*

partan the common edible crab. ~('s) **ta(e)** the claw of a crab.

peeler *now NE Ags,* **piller** *local Cai-Fif,* **pillan** *local Ork-Fif* a small crab which has just cast or is about to cast its shell and is therefore suitable for bait.

pellock 1 the porpoise; ? *orig also* the dolphin. **2** †the flesh of the porpoise.

poo the common edible crab *Loth Bwk.*

puffie (dunter) the porpoise *now NE.*

rair, roar: ~**ing buckie** a kind of whelk shell which when held to the ear makes a roaring sound thought to sound like the sea *now Ags Fif.*

rigger worm a kind of marine worm used as bait *local EC.*

rock (partan) the common edible crab *now NE, WC.*

rothick a young edible crab *local N.*

saftie, softie, saftick *NE* an edible crab which has lost its shell, *freq* used for bait *NE Ags Fif.*

sand: ~ **jumper** *now Mry Ayr,* ~ **lowper** *now Ags Per Fif,* ~**y lowper** *Fif midLoth* the sand-flea.

scalder a jellyfish, medusa *Cai NE, SW.*

scaup, scalp the shellfish found on rocks between high and low tide *now Cai.*

scaw a barnacle, a mass of barnacles *now Cai.*

sclushach a crab during the shell-less stage after it has cast its old shell *Bnf Abd.*

scoskie the starfish *N.*

scowder, scouther a jellyfish (because of its burning sting) *now Arg.*

sea: ~ **flech** a sand-flea *Sh Kcdn Ags.* † ~ **fyke** a powder made from the crushed dried egg-capsules of the whelk *Buccinum undatum,* which causes skin irritation. ~ **pa(a)ps** sea anemones *Mry Fif Bwk.*

selch *now NE,* **selkie** *Sh Ork Cai NE,* **†selk, selchy** the seal.

shall a shell *Sh Ork N.*

silver willie the pyramid shell *now local Ork-eLoth.*

skate bubble a jellyfish.

spoonge a sponge.

spout *now Sh Ork Cai Wgt,* **spoutfish** the razor-fish or -clam.

switherel a jellyfish, medusa (from its stinging properties) *now Fif.*

tonie the jellyfish, medusa *Mry.*

whaal *now Sh Abd Fif,* **whaul** a whale. **whaal-bubble** a jellyfish. **†whale schote** spermaceti.

wulk, wilk *now Ork Cai*, **wylk** *Sh* 1 the whelk, the
buckie. 2 the periwinkle mollusc and shell.

3.3 WATER CREATURES

ask, esk a newt, eft.
crud frogspawn *Bnf Fif.*
†gangrel(l) a toad.
gell(ie) a leech.
gener, puddock's ~ frogspawn *Fif.*
horse: † **~ gelly** a horse leech. **~ mussel** a large
 freshwater mussel *now Sh Cai Kcdn.*
kail ladle a tadpole *Per Fif Dmf.*
ladle a tadpole *chf N.*
lavellan the water-shrew *Cai.*
†loch leech the leech.
man-keeper the newt or water-lizard *chf SW Uls.*
powheid, powrit *Fif*, **pallet** *Cai*, **pollywag** *Per
 Fif Ayr*, **†powat** a tadpole
puddock, paddock, poddock, paddy a frog; a
 toad. **~('s) crud(d)les** *local NE-Kcb*, **~ redd**
 now Wgt S, **~ rude** *now Cai* frogspawn. **paddy
 ladle** *now S*, **~('s) pony** a tadpole *Per.*
redd, †rid frogspawn, *freq* **paddock ~** *now Per
 Wgt Rox.*
rodd frogspawn *now Cai.* † **~ing** spawning.
screw, †scrow a freshwater shrimp etc.
skater *C*, **skeeter** *Cai* a water beetle.
taid a toad *Gen except Sh Ork.* **~ie** a little toad.
wall-wesher a water-spider *SW, S.*
washer-wife a water-spider *Mry Abd Ags Lnk.*
water, watter *now local:* **~ baillie** one of the
 water-bug family, *esp* the water-spider *Mry Abd.*
 ~ clearer one of the small insects that skim
 over the surface of water and in so doing are said
 to clean it *local Ags-Lnk.* **~ dog,** † **~ mouse** the
 water-rat or water-vole *now Bnf.*
†yird, yirth: **~ taid** a toad.

3.4 SEA PLANTS

badderlocks *now Ags*, **dabberlacks** *Mry Bnf* a
 kind of edible seaweed.
bellware, beliwar a coarse seaweed *now Abd.*
†black-tang a kind of seaweed, *Fucus vesiculosus.*
blibbans strips of something soft and slimy, *esp*
 seaweed *now Kcdn Gall.*

brook a deep layer of seaweed cast ashore by
 stormy weather, *freq* **~ o ware** *Sh Ork N.*
buss, bush a mass of seaweed growing on sunken
 rocks and exposed at low tide, a ledge of rock
 covered with seaweed *now Bnf Abd.*
currack: tangle *Bnf.*
dilse dulse *now local Cai-Ags.*
green gaw green slimy seaweed or green algae *now
 Abd.*
hen('s) ware an edible seaweed *now Kcdn.*
keys: badderlocks *local Ork-N.*
†pepper dilse a pungent edible seaweed, jagged
 fucus
reid, red, rid: ~ ware the seaweed *Laminaria
 digitata*, from its red colour *now Sh-N Fif.*
roups the stems of seaweed, *specif* of the oar-weed
 Bnf Abd.
sea: ~ ware, † **~ wrack** seaweed, *esp* the coarse
 kind washed up by the tide and used as manure
 now Sh Ork NE.
slake, sloke one of various species of edible fresh-
 and salt-water algae *now Sh Ork Cai.* **†slawkie**
 covered with such weed, slimy.
slattyvarrie the edible seaweed *Laminaria digitata*,
 chf Arg.
tang general name for large, coarse seaweed growing above low-water mark, *esp* the genus *Fucus*,
 chf Sh Ork. **~le** 1 *also* sea **~le** = **tang.** 2 the
 long stalk and fronds of this. **†yellow ~** the
 knotted **tang**, a kind of bladderwrack.
ware, waar a kind of seaweed, *chf* for use as
 manure *now Sh Ork EC, WC.* **wary** covered with,
 living among or generally pertaining to seaweed
 now Sh Abd.
wrack, wreck, wreak 1 fresh- or salt-water weed,
 river or marine algae *now Abd Fif Loth.* 2 seaweed
 and miscellaneous flotsam washed up by the sea
 Gen except Sh Ork.

3.5 WATER PLANTS

glit the slimy vegetation found in ponds *now Arg
 Gall Uls.*
†loch reed the common reed-grass.
†quick moss moss which trembles or in which a
 person can sink.
slake, sloke one of various species of edible fresh-
 and salt-water algae *now Sh Ork Cai.* **†slawkie**
 covered with such weed, slimy.
wrack, wreck, wreak fresh- or salt-water weed,
 river or marine algae *now Abd Fif Loth.*

4. PLANTS

For sea and water plants, see 3.

4.1 GENERAL, MISCELLANEOUS

abraird sprouted *latterly chf arch or verse.*

blate *of crops* backward in growth *now Bnf Ags.*

bleck smut, mildew on plants *now Bnf Ags Bwk.*

bleed **weel** *etc, of grain etc* give a good yield.

bleeze: in a ~ *of a crop* suddenly ripe *now Ags.*

blicht *literary* blight.

†bound a bundle (*esp* of flax).

bow a boll, the seed-pod of flax.

breard, breer sprout above the ground, germinate.

†bunewand, bunwand a hollow plant stem, *eg* of the broad-leaved dock plant or hogweed.

buss a clump of some low-growing plant, *eg* heather, rushes, fern, grass, *now local Cai-Kcb.*

canker *of plants* become infected with blight *Bnf Abd Kcb.*

†cashie luxuriant, succulent *chf Dmf.*

†chip *of buds or seeds* break open; germinate.

chun a sprout *chf SW.*

cocks and hens name for the buds, stems or seeds of various plants, and of games played with *eg* the stems of the ribwort plantain, the leaf-buds of the sycamore, the flowers of the bird's foot trefoil *chf S.*

come *of seeds, plants* germinate, grow rapidly *local Bnf-Loth.*

cow a tufted stem of heather etc.

crop, crap the top of a tree or plant.

deil, deevil, devil: ~'s milk the white milky sap of many plants *Gall.*

dirty *of crops* weed-infested.

dorty delicate, difficult to rear *now Bnf Abd.*

dow fade away, wither. **~it**, **~ed** faded, withered *now Sh Abd.*

†dwine cause to pine or wither.

fair-gyaun *of crops* fairish *Bnf Abd.*

†foilzie a leaf of a plant or tree.

fowd withered vegetation *N.*

fushionless without sap or pith, dried, withered *now local Sh-Arg.*

gae back deteriorate, run down, fall off *Ork C-S.*

gizzen dry up, wither, shrivel *now local Sh-Ags.*

go(r)skie rank, luxuriant *now NE Ags.*

growth 1 growing plants, vegetation; yield, crop. **2** rank vegetation, weeds. **growthie** *of vegetation* growing fast, luxuriant, of abundant growth; weedy *now local Ork-Arg.* **grown-up** overgrown, choked (**with** *usu* vegetation) *local.*

grushie *of vegetation* abundant, lush.

haud *of seeds etc* strike, root *now Abd.*

huil a hull, the husk, pod, skin, shell of a fruit or nut etc.

imp, *now Rox,* **hempe** *Fife* a young shoot or cutting.

jag a prickle, a thorn; something causing a sting, *eg* on a nettle. **~gie** *of nettles* stinging *C.*

job a prick; a prickle *Sh NE nEC.* **jobbie** prickly *Sh NE nEC.*

†kempit the pith of hemp or of a wild carrot, parsnip etc, dried and used as a candle.

ketty *of turf* matted, lumpy.

knee *of the stalks of plants* bend so as to form a knee-shaped angle.

lay flatten (crops) by wind or rain.

lith one of the natural divisions or segments of an orange, onion etc *N, C Slk Uls.*

†lucken *of plants which form a bud or head* grow compact or firm.

†luggie *of crops* growing to leaf and stem, rank and luxuriant with poorly developed fruits *chf N.*

†mauten *of grain or seeds* germinate, sprout; become malt.

†misgie, misgive *of crops* give a poor yield, fail to grow.

misgrown stunted, deformed *now Sh.*

miss *of crops* fail to germinate or grow.

moch *of corn, meal etc* become tainted, fusty or rotten *NE.*

nirl, nurl shrink, shrivel, stunt in growth *local Sh-Lnk.* **~ie** dwarfish, stunted *now Sh Ork.*

pease strae the stalks and foliage of the pea plant used as cheap fodder or bedding for animals *now Kcb.*

pen the stalk of a plant or vegetable, a stalk of straw.

†**pikant** a prickle, thorn.

pike a thorn or prickle on a plant *now Ork.*

pirk a sharp point, thorn, prickle *now Cai.*

porr, purr a thorn, prickle, barb *Cai.*

pricky having sharp points or spines, prickly *NE, SW.*

prod a thorn, prickle *SW.*

prog a thorn, spine, prickle *now Per Ayr.*

proud *of growing crops* (over-)luxuriant *now Sh Mry.*

quern a granule, small seed etc *now Mry Abd.*

raff rank growth *now Bnf.* ~ie thriving, flourishing *now Abd.*

ramp *of plants* climb, ramble *Bnf Uls.*

rapple grow rapidly, shoot up.

reuch, rough *of the growth of grass or crops* strong, luxuriant, dense *local Sh-Kcb.* ~ **blade** the mature leaf of a plant as opposed to the seed leaf *local Ork-Wgt.*

†**ripe** ripen.

roset resin, rosin.

ruit a root.

runkle gnarl, twist, distort, curl *now local C.*

rush a luxuriant growth of vegetation *Sh Ork Ags.*

scam a withering or scorching of plants by frost etc *N Per.*

scrab a shrivelled or stunted tree or plant *now Bnf.*

scrocken *now chf Sh NE,* **skurken** *now chf Sh NE,* **scrockle** shrink or shrivel up with heat or drought.

scruif the layer of vegetation on the surface of the ground *now Sh Cai Abd.*

scrunt a poorly-developed unthriving plant *now NE, C.* ~it shrivelled, shrunken, stunted in growth *now local Bnf-SW.* ~y stunted, shrivelled, stumpy, wizened *now SW, S Uls.*

set stop growing, have the growth checked *now local Ork-WC.*

shank the stem or stalk of a tree, plant, or fruit.

shirp wither, shrivel.

shuit, shoot go to seed. **shot** having run to seed.

sit stop growing or developing, be stunted *now NE-Per Gall.*

skrink, skrunk(le) shrink, shrivel up *now Loth Rox.* **skrinkie** thin, shrivelled *now Rox.*

sloom 1 †(cause to) become soft or flaccid; (cause to) wilt and decay. 2 (cause to) grow or sprout unnaturally *Uls.*

†**smergh** pith.

smuir, smoor bury, cover over thickly, envelop in a dense covering of vegetation.

†**sop** sap.

spire 1 †dry out; become parched. 2 wither, cause to fade, dry up *sEC Rox.*

spirl a small slender shoot *Fif Loth Slk.* ~ie slender, thin, spindly *now Loth S.*

†**spring** the growth of vegetation, *specif* in spring.

sproot sprout.

stickit stunted, checked in growth *now Cai Per.*

stint shrivel, droop *now Ork.*

stock send out shoots, sprout *now N.*

strachle straggle, grow in a loose untidy way *now local Loth-Dmf.*

string *of seedlings, esp turnips* sprout in a line along the drills *Bnf Abd.*

strunty short, stumpy, stunted, shrunken, of poor growth *now Lnk.*

stumpit short, stunted *now local Sh-Dmf.*

tak a state of growth, the sprouting of a crop *local N-Rox.*

tanner(s) the fibres, small or fibrous roots of a tree or other plant.

taupin a main branch of a root; a subsidiary root; a tap-root *now NE Per.*

taw a fibre or filament of a plant or tree, a fibrous root *now Sh.*

unfierdy overgrown *now Sh.*

†**unleifit** without leaves.

†**unthriven, unthriving** unhealthy.

†**vane** a sap-vessel in a plant.

†**verdour, vardour** verdure.

†**virgult** a branch.

wag *of a leaf, plant etc* wave to and fro, shake in the wind.

wallow wither, fade, waste away *now local Cai-Lnk.*

wanthriven, †wanthrifty stunted, in a state of decline, weakly *now Sh.*

†**warroch** a stunted, feeble, ill-grown plant.

wirl a puny malformed plant *now Fif.*

4.2 FLOWERING PLANTS

Adam-an-Eves the tubers of an orchid *local.*

aippleringie, overeengie *NE* southernwood.

alacampine elecampane.

alshinders, alishunners Alexanders; ground elder.

arnit, earnit an edible plant root, pignut.

bad-money the gentian; the spignel (used medicinally in the Highlands).

balderry, bulldairy any of several types of wild orchid, *esp* the heath spotted orchid (sometimes thought to have aphrodisiac powers).

†**banwart** bonewort, the daisy.

bin(d)wood ivy; honeysuckle; convolvulus.

bishop('s) weed ground elder, *Aegopodium podagraria*.

blaw *v* blossom *now Abd*.

blawort, blaver *NE, S* one of several blue plants: 1 the harebell; 2 the cornflower; 3 †the germander speedwell.

blue: ~**bell** 1 the **harebell**. 2 the English bluebell. ~ **bonnets** name of several flowers, *specif:* 1 the cornflower; 2 the devilsbit scabious, sheepsbit.

bluidy fingers the foxglove.

blume bloom.

bob, bab a bunch of flowers *now Abd*.

bog: ~**-hyacinth** a kind of wild orchid *now Abd*. ~**-th(r)issle** the marsh thistle *now Abd*.

bowlocks the common ragwort. *Gall*.

bread-and-cheese the inside of a thistle head *now local Cai-Ags*.

buckie-faulie the primrose *Cai*.

bulls-bags the early purple orchid *now Ags*.

†bunewand, bunwand a hollow plant stem, *eg* of the broad-leaved dock or hogweed.

bunnel the hogweed *Lnk*.

bunweed, benweed (a stalk of) common ragwort.

burr-thistle the spear thistle.

butter blob the globe-flower *now Abd Lnk Kcb*.

cairt wheel a large variety of (ox-eye) daisy *now Abd Lnk*.

camovine camomile *now NE Ags*.

carline, carling: ~ **heather = bell-heather.** *Ags*.

†carmele the bitter vetch.

†carse(s) various cresses, *esp* watercress.

cat: † ~**cluke** the bird's-foot trefoil. ~**'s een** the germander speedwell *now Lnk Kcb*. ~ **heather** various species of heather, varying according to district *Abd Ags*.

cheese the receptacle of the thistle *local Abd-Lnk*.

chickenweed, chickenwort chickweed.

claver, †clever clover.

†clow (gillie flower) the clove pink.

†columby the columbine.

coo: ~**-cakes** the hogweed *now Fif*. ~**-cracker** the bladder campion *C, S*.

craw, crow: ~ **pea(s)** the meadow vetchling *now Bnf*. ~**-tae(s)** 1 the meadow or creeping buttercup *local*. 2 the bird's-foot trefoil *local*. 3 the English bluebell, wild hyacinth *now Kcb*.

creepin eevie convolvulus *NE*.

crochle girs self-heal, said to cause **crochles** (a disease of cattle) *Bnf*.

curl-doddy name for various plants with a rounded flower-head including: 1 the devilsbit scabious *now Bwk;* 2 the field scabious *now Rox;* 3 *also* **carl-doddie** *Bnf Abd Ags Fif Lnk* the ribwort

and greater plantain *now Fif;* 4 various species of clover *chf Ork*.

dainty-lion, †dent-de-lyon the dandelion.

†daseyne *only verse* the daisy.

day-nettle 1 either of two types of hemp-nettle *now Sh Bnf*. 2 various species of dead-nettle *local*.

deid, dead: ~ **man's bellows** bugle *now Ayr.* ~ **man's bells** the foxglove *now Abd*.

deil, devil: ~ **in a bush** the herb Paris *now Abd*.

docken various species of dock, the broad-leaved or curled dock.

†Dodgill Reepan a species of marsh orchid, the roots of which were used in a love potion.

dog: ~ **daisy** the ox-eye daisy *SW.* ~**('s) flourish** one of various umbelliferous plants *local C-S.* ~**heather** heather, **ling** (*Calluna vulgaris*) *Abd Ags*.

doo-docken coltsfoot *Cai*.

dusty miller auricula, a species of primula, so called because of the white powdery appearance of the flowers and leaves.

ellwand: the King's E~ the foxglove *S*.

featherfooly feverfew *now Abd Ags*.

feenich the knot grass, *esp* its flowerhead and seed *Bnf Abd*.

fitch various species of vetch.

†flour dammas auricula.

flour, flooer, flower 1 a flower. 2 a bunch of flowers, a bouquet: '*Here's a wee flower tae ye*.'

flourish *v* blossom, be in flower *now local NE-S. n* blossom, *esp* on fruit or hawthorn trees *Gen except Sh Ork*. †**flurist** flowery.

foos houseleek(s) *now Bnf Abd*.

fox: ~**-fit** creeping buttercup *now midLoth Bwk.* † ~ **trie leaves** foxglove (leaves).

frog's mou(th) the monkey flower *Fif Pbls SW*.

gall bog myrtle *now local Bnf-Gall*.

gaun the butterbur *WC, SW*.

†geraflour the gillyflower.

glen the daffodil *Ayr*.

goldilocks the goldilocks buttercup *now Slk*.

gollan name for various wild flowers, *eg* the daisy, the corn marigold *now Ork Cai*.

gourlins the edible roots or tubers of the pignut *now Kcb*.

gowan 1 *also* **ewe** ~ *now Ags Pbls*, **May** ~ *now Ags* the daisy. 2 *also* (**large**) **white** ~ *local Bnf-Per* the ox-eye daisy *local*. ~**(e)d,** ~**y** covered with daisies, daisied. **horse** ~ applied to various wild flowers, *esp* 1 ox-eye daisy *now local Inv-Rox;* 2 the dandelion. **lapper** ~**, lucken** ~ the globe-flower *now Rox.* **yellow** ~ any of various wild flowers such as the buttercup, marigold etc.

gowk: ~**'s hose** a bell-shaped flower, *esp* the wild hyacinth or the Canterbury bell. ~**'s meat**

the wood sorrel. ~'s-thimles the **harebell** *NE*.

grannie's mutch(es) 1 the columbine *NE-WC*. 2 the snapdragon *Ags Per WC*.

†**grip grass** cleavers.

grund, ground: ~ **avy,** ~ **davy** ground-ivy *now Ork*.

grundiswallow groundsel *now NE Ags*.

guil, guld the corn marigold *now NE Gall*.

guse grass cleavers *now Ork Ayr Rox*.

hard heid(s) name for various plants: 1 †sneeze-wort; 2 common knapweed; the head of this plant *now Kcb*; 3 ribwort plantain *Fife Kcb Dumf*.

harebell *Campanula rotundifolia*, the **bluebell** of Scotland.

healin(g) blade, -leaf the greater plantain *now Cai*.

heather, hather heather. ~ **bell** the flower of the heather ~-**birn(s)** the stalks and roots of burnt heather *now local nEC-Dmf*. ~ **cow** a tuft or twig of heather *now local Sh-Abd*. **bell** ~ a kind of heath with bell-shaped flowerlets, *Erica cinerea; loosely, also* cross-leaved heath, *Erica tetralix*.

hech-how name for various species of umbellifer, *eg* hemlock, the hemlock water dropwort *chf Arg SW*.

hen taes creeping buttercup *local*.

hert of the yearth self-heal *Rox*.

hinniesickle honeysuckle *now Ags Ayr*.

horneck the pignut.

horse: ~('s) **knop** *or* **knot** the common knapweed *now Dmf*. ~-**peas(e)** the common vetch *now Cai*.

humility *Saxifraga sarmentosa* grown as a pot plant *Abd Ags wLoth*.

humlock the hemlock or any of the umbelliferous plants such as the hogweed *now Ags Bwk Rox*.

Jacob's ladder deadly nightshade *now Lnk Uls*.

Jenny, Jinny: ~'s **blue een** the heath speedwell *Abd Fif Lnk*. ~ **nettle(s)** the common nettle *Edb Lnk S*.

jobbie nettle the common nettle *NE-Per*.

†**jonet flour** name for a flower, *orig* any of various yellow flowers.

†**kemps** stalks of the ribwort or greater plantain.

kex the hogweed *now Sh Ork*.

kirrie dumplin the flower cluster of the *Primula denticulata Ags Per*.

knapparts the bitter vetch *N*.

knotty meal the pignut *Inv-Mry*.

†**lad's love** southernwood.

lady, leddy: ~'s **beds** lady's bedstraw *local Ork-Per*. ~'s *or* **ladies' fingers** the cowslip *Fif Loth*. ~ **nit** the greater plantain *Rox*. ~'s **purse** shepherd's purse *now Cai Wgt Uls*. ~'s **thimbles**

1 the **harebell** (the **bluebell** of Scotland) *now Uls*. 2 the foxglove. ~ **o the meadow** meadow-sweet *Cai SW*.

lamb: lammie sourocks sheep's sorrel *Rox*. ~s **ears** *Fif SW Rox*, ~'s **lugs** *NE Ags Loth* the hoary plantain. ~'s **lugs** the plant *Stachys lanata*. ~s **tongue** corn mint *now Cai Wgt*.

lily the narcissus, *esp* the common daffodil and pheasant's eye varieties, *freq* distinguished as **yellow** *or* **white** ~.

lilyoak, laylock *now NE Fif Slk* the lilac.

little guid, little gweedie *NE* the sun-spurge.

†**loukit** *of flower-buds* closed, compact.

lous(e)y arnut the pignut *now Mry nEC Ayr*.

†**lucken** *of flowers* having a compact head as in a bud.

†**luffage** lovage.

maid in the mist navelwort *SW, S*.

mappie('s)-mou(s) name for various plants, *esp* of the figwort family, which have blossoms in the shape of a rabbit's mouth, as the snapdragon, calceolaria *now NE-nEC*.

†**mariguld** the marigold.

†**mascorn** silverweed; its edible root.

†**mather** madder; (dye from) the root of the plant.

maws various species of common mallow *now Sh*.

medick, methick the dandelion *Bnf*.

melgs fat-hen *Nai Mry*.

Mey: ~**sie, maisie** *Ags*, ~ **spink** *now Ags Per* the primrose.

micken the spignel *N, nEC*.

midden weed fat-hen; knot grass.

milky thrissle the (milk) thistle *local Abd-S*.

minnonette mignonette *Abd Ags Wgt*.

moup, -moppie, mup-mup, mop-mop the snapdragon *Ayr S*.

mouse: ~ **pea,** ~ **pease** various species of vetch *now Sh-Cai SW*.

†**muckle wort** deadly nightshade.

muggart (kail), muggins *Abd Uls* the mugwort.

old man southernwood *Fif Edb Slk*.

orpie, wurpie *S* orpine.

†**papple** popple, the corn-cockle.

†**pasper** rock samphire *Gall*.

pee-the-bed *N Ags Edb*, **pish-the-bed** *local* the dandelion.

pinkie the primrose *now NE Ags Ayr*.

pleuchman's love southernwood *Kcdn nEC*.

†**plumrose** the primrose.

plyven the flower of the white or red clover.

porr, purr a thistle *Cai*.

puddock, paddock, paddy: ~ **pipes** the butterbur *Loth S.* ~'s **spindle** a spotted orchid, *perh* the heath spotted orchid *now Ags Ayr.*

puir man's clover self-heal *Bnf Ags Per.*

puppie the poppy *now WC-S.*

†**purpie** the name of some plant, *perh* purslane.

pushion berry the bittersweet *now Lnk.*

queen of (the) meadow meadowsweet *Gen except Sh Ork.*

rabbit: ~'s **sugar** *child's word* the seeds of the common sorrel *Mry Bnf.* ~ **thissle** the smooth sow-thistle *midLoth S.*

ragweed the common ragwort *now local NE-Uls.*

ramps the ramsons.

†**rantie-tantie** a reddish-leaved plant found in cornfields, formerly eaten as a vegetable, *prob* the common sorrel.

rat('s) tail the greater plantain; its seed-head *Gen except Sh Ork.*

reid, red, rid: ~-**shank** name for various weeds with red stems or seed spikes, *esp* the common sorrel, the broad-leaved dock *now C-S.*

ripple-grass the ribwort plantain; the greater plantain.

Robbie-rin-the-hedge *local NE-S,* **Robin-rin-the-hedge** *now Kcb,* **Robin-roond-the-hedge** *now Wgt Rox* cleavers.

rosidandrum rhododendron *local Bnf-Uls.*

†**rosine** a rose.

runch: ~**ick** *now Ork,* ~**ie** *chf Sh, now Ork* the wild radish, found as a weed in cornfields *now local.*

scab one of the umbelliferae, *eg* hemlock *S.*

Scots, Scotch: ~ **thistle** one of the thistle family adopted as the national badge of Scotland (the exact species is disputed though it is most probably the spear thistle).

sea daisy the thrift *now Ork.*

seg the yellow iris. ~**gan** the wild iris *now Arg Bute Ayr.*

sheepie mae a flower of the white clover *local Cai-Arg.*

†**shepherd's club** the great mullein.

shilagie the coltsfoot, *esp* its leaves used by juvenile smokers as a substitute for tobacco *now local Ags-Lnk.*

sit: ~ **fast** a plant, *eg* the buttercup, with roots clinging tenaciously to the soil. ~-**sicker** name for various species of buttercup *now NE.*

sitherwood southernwood.

†**skeldock, scaldrick** the charlock.

skelloch(s), skellie(s) the charlock *now local Cai-Lnk.*

smear dock(en) Good King Henry, a kind of goosefoot used in folk-medicine in ointment for itch.

sodger(s), soldier(s) the stems and flower-heads of the plantain, *esp* the ribwort plantain *now local.*

son-afore-the-father name of various plants whose flowers appear before their leaves: **1** mezereon *Rox;* **2** †the butterbur; **3** †the coltsfoot; **4**†the cudweed; **5** the flowering currant *now Kcdn.*

†**soucye** the marigold.

souk, suck: ~**ie 1** clover *in gen, now Kcdn Ags Fif.* **2** the red clover *now Sh.* ~**ie mae,** ~**y mammy** a clover flowerhead *now Stlg Fif.* ~**ie soo** the flower of the clover *now midLoth.* ~**ie sourocks** wood-sorrel *N nEC Ayr.*

sour: ~**ock** name for various kinds of sorrel. ~ **dock(en)** *Bwk Kcb S,* ~ **leek** *now Kcb Rox* the common sorrel.

†**spanist** *of a flower* expanded, open.

speariment spearmint *EC WC, S.*

speengie rose the peony.

spink one of several species of flower, *eg* the cuckoo flower, primrose or maiden pink *local NE-EC.*

†**spycarie** spikenard.

stick: ~**ers** *now Fif Wgt Rox,* ~**y-Willie** *Gen except Sh Ork* cleavers.

stink: ~**ing Elshender** *now Per Stlg Fif,* ~**in Willie** *now local NE-SW* the common ragwort. ~**in Tam(my)** name for various strong-smelling plants, *esp* the tansy, rayless mayweed *now Bwk S.*

†**strae, straw:** ~ **wald** dyer's rocket.

sucklers the flowerheads of clover *now Stlg midLoth.*

suddrenwood southernwood *now N SW.*

swine('s) th(r)issle the smooth sowthistle *now Rox.*

tansy the common ragwort *now local N-S.*

teer the tare, a wild vetch *NE Ags, sEC.*

threefold the bog-bean *now Sh.*

thummles, thimbles name for various plants, *eg* **1** the foxglove *now Ags Bwk;* **2** †the harebell *N;* **3** the corn bluebottle *now Abd.*

thunner-an-lichtenin the lungwort or other plant with white-spotted leaves *local Bnf-Ayr.*

tirlie-tod the greater plantain *Abd Kcdn.*

tod('s) tail(s) the foxglove *Rox.*

†**triffle** trefoil, the name of various plants.

tushilago 1 coltsfoot. **2** the butterbur *local.*

†**unblomit** *verse* without blossom.

valairie common valerian *Arg Uls.*

†**verbene** verbena.

waid woad.

†**wald** dyer's rocket.

wall raik weeds which grow round a spring *Abd.*

wall, well: ~ **grass** *now Abd,* ~ **girse kail** *now*

Abd, † ~ **kerse** watercress *now Abd.* ~**ink** brooklime *now Dmf.*

wallan(t) *of flowers* withered, faded, drooping *Bnf Abd.*

†**wallie** the daisy *SW, S.*

water purpie brooklime.

waverin leaf *now Sh Ork,* **warba (blade)** *now Cai,* †**wayburn leaf** the greater plantain.

weebie(s) the common ragwort *nEC.*

†**tweedock** a small weed.

what o'clock is it? a popular name for the dandelion from the children's practice of using the seeded head of the flower as a clock *local Ork-Lnk.*

white sookie(s) white clover *now local Ags-Lnk.*

wild fire name of various wild flowers, *eg* spearwort, marsh marigold *now Ags.*

†**wild kail** the wild radish; the charlock *SW.*

wild rhubarb the butterbur *Per-S.*

William and Mary the lungwort *Bnf-Ags.*

willie-rin-the-hedge cleavers *now Bnf Lnk.*

witches' paps the foxglove *Arg Ayr.* **witch(es')-thimbles** the foxglove, *esp* its flowers *Cai Mry C, S.*

wood hyacinth the English bluebell, wild hyacinth, *Scilla non scripta, Gen except Sh Ork.*

wormit wormwood.

wrack, wreck field weeds.

yarr corn-spurrey *N, C.*

yerb a herb *now Ags Dmf.*

4.3 GRASSES AND SEDGES

ae-pointed-gairss name for various species of sedge *local.*

bennel any long reedy grass.

beust withered grass from the previous year *SW.*

blaw grass a hill-grass, a species of bent or purple moor grass *now Ayr Gall.*

†**blue grass** any of various sedges.

bob, bab a small luxuriant patch of grass *Bnf Kcb.*

bog-cotton cotton grass.

†**bruckles** the star sedge *NE.*

bull-grass the soft-brome *now Abd.*

cannach, canna (down) cotton grass, *esp* the harestail cotton grass *now Abd Ags Fif Arg.*

cat('s) tail(s) hairstail cotton grass *now Abd.*

deer('s) hair deergrass.

†**dornell** darnel.

elbow(it) grass marsh foxtail *now Uls.*

flee, fly: ~**in bent** purple moor grass

†**fushloch** the grass that grows in stubble *WC, SW.*

gairdener's ga(i)rtens *or* **garters** the ribbon grass.

garten a leaf of ribbon grass *Per Rox.*

girse 1 *also* **gress** *now local* grass. **2** a stalk or blade of grass *now Abd.* **girsie** grassy.

†**guse grass** verious species of brome.

Hielandman's garters ribbon grass *now Sh Abd.*

†**hose-grass** Yorkshire fog.

kemps the crested dogstail *Cai Ross.*

†**ket** common couch *chf S.*

knot grass name for various grasses with knotty stems etc, *esp* false oat-grass *chf Ork N, C.*

†**lachter** a tuft of grass.

lady, leddy: ~**'s** *or* **ladies' gairtens** *or* **garters** the ribbon grass *local.*

ling the harestail cotton grass; the deergrass *C, S.*

†**loch reed** the common reed.

lonnachs common couch *now Kcdn Ags.*

†**month grass** the sheathed harestail cotton grass *Ags.*

moss *now Cai wLoth,* **mosscrop** *now Ork N, C* cotton grass, *esp* the harestail.

nature grass grass which grows wild and luxuriantly *now NE.*

pile a blade (of grass etc).

pluff grass, pyuff girse Yorkshire fog; creeping soft grass *NE.*

†**pry** one of various species of sedge common in southern Scotland and used for sheep-feeding *S.*

†**pull ling, purlaing** the harestail cotton grass *sEC, S.*

quicken(s) common couch *now EC, SW.*

rammock common couch; its roots *chf Abd.*

rash *n, also* ~**er** *Bwk Rox,* ~**ie** various species of rush. ~ **bush, thrush bush** a clump of rushes. *now NE, SW.*

risp (grass) a species of common sedge or common reed.

ronnachs common couch *now Kcdn.*

†**roseegar** darnel *chf SW.*

†**seg** sedge.

shaker(s) *now Loth Kcb Rox,* **shakie tremlie(s)** *now NE Ags,* **shak-and-trumble** *NE Ags,* **siller shakers** *now Loth Rox* the quaking grass.

†**sleepies** a species of brome, *perh* the rye brome.

sprat a coarse rush growing on marshy ground and sometimes used in rope-making and stack-thatching. † ~**ty** rush-like, rushy.

sprot a rush *both in gen and specif of particular species, now NE Ags Per.* ~**ty** of or like rushes *now Abd.*

star name for various kinds of grass, rush or sedge,

usu growing in moorish or boggy ground, *freq* ~ **grass** *etc.*

string girse common couch *local Bnf-Stlg.*

stuil-bent the heath-rush.

swine('s) arnit the false oat-grass, *esp* its tuberous roots *now Abd.*

tailor, teylor *NE-S:* ~'s **gartens** ribbon grass *local Abd-Rox.*

tait a tuft of grass *now local Sh-SW.*

tathe coarse rank grass which grows on ground where the dung of cattle or sheep has been left for manure *now Lnk.*

tummock, †tammock a tuft or tussock of grass *now Wgt.*

windle strae 1 a tall, thin, withered stalk of grass *now local N-S.* **2** *specif* applied to various kinds of natural grass with long thin stalks, *eg* the crested dogstail grass, Yorkshire fog etc *local N-S.*

wrack, wreck (the roots of) the common couch etc *NE-S.*

4.4 MOSSES, LICHENS, FUNGI AND FERNS

blin: ~ **man's buff** *now Kcb,* † ~ **men's baw** the a species of puffball.

brachan, brechan bracken.

†corkir, corklit *SW* a red lichen used in dyeing.

crottle, crotal dye-producing lichen *local.*

duff (mould) a soft spongy substance, *chf* moss etc *now Sh.*

†ernfern a kind of fern, *esp* polypody (found on high rocks).

fern bracken.

flow moss the spongy moss which grows on mossy, boggy ground.

fog *n* moss, lichen. *v* become moss-grown *now NE Ags.*

fox fit the stagshorn or fir clubmoss *S.*

†hazel raw a type of lichen.

lady, leddy: ~ **bracken** *now Rox,* ~ **fern** *now Dmf Uls* the lady fern.

†nut-gall the oak-gall, *chf* used as a dye-stuff.

puddock, paddock, paddy; ~ **pipes** name for various species of horsetail, *esp* the marsh horsetail *now local NE-Kcb.* ~ **stool** a toadstool or mushroom; any fungus, *usu* stalked.

rannoch fern; bracken *now Per.*

†shot star(s) jelly-like algae found in pastures after rain (thought to be *eg* the remains of a shooting star).

stane stone: ~ **raw** the lichen *Parmelia saxatilis* used for dyeing *now SW.*

tod('s) tail(s) the stagshorn clubmoss *now N.*

white peat a kind of sphagnum moss found under the surface layer of vegetation *now Per.*

4.5 BUSHES AND SHRUBS

†taiten juniper *Abd.*

brammle, bramble the blackberry bush.

breer a briar.

broom, brume broom. ~(s) bushes, a stretch or expanse of broom. ~ **cow** a branch of broom *local.*

buckie breer a wild-rose bush *Dmf Uls.*

buckie-faulie the fruit or flower of the briar *Cai.*

†bullister a wild plum bush.

†buschbome boxwood.

buss a bush. **bussy** *now Bnf Ags,* **bouzy** bushy.

carline, carling: ~ **spurs** petty whin *N.*

etnach the juniper, the juniper berry *now NE.*

jenepere juniper *now Abd.*

lary, †laurean the laurel (spurge laurel or bay laurel).

†melmot juniper *Nai Mry.*

privy hedge privet.

†rammel brushwood, undergrowth.

rone a thicket of brushwood, thorns etc.

†saving a kind of juniper which produces an abortifacient drug, *freq* ~ **tree.**

scrog a stunted or crooked bush or tree; ~s brushwood or undergrowth *now local N-Uls.*

sinnie senna *now Sh Ork Bnf.*

†sylvan ? a forest tree, shrub etc.

†veyton the wayfaring-tree, guelder rose.

†virgult a bush, a shrub.

whin, whun the common gorse. ~s a clump or area of gorse. ~-**bush** a gorse bush *N-S.* **whin-cow** a tuft or branch of gorse *now Per.*

4.6 TREES

Most fruit trees are in 4.7 below.

aik oak *now almost obs or verse.*

aller, arn, †alrone an alder (tree).

belt(in) a clump or line of trees.

†beuch a bough, a branch of a tree.

birk birch. ~s **1** †birch twigs, *esp* as used for decoration. **2** a small wood consisting mainly of birches. ~**en** *adj* birchen. *n* a birch tree.

bonnet fir the Scots pine *Ags.*

bought(y) a branch, twig; a fork of a tree.

bourtree, bountree the elder tree.

brainch a branch.

breeks a forked stick such as is used for a catapult; a fork in a tree *Ags nEC*.

†**brone** a twig.

†**bullister** a wild plum tree.

burr a fir cone *now Bnf*.

caber a long slender tree-trunk.

cheese: ∼**-an-breid, bread-an-**∼ the first green shoots on *esp* hawthorn hedges *now Fif Kcb*.

cloff a cleft, of branches in a tree *chf S*.

cow a twig or branch.

dosinnit *of wood* rotten *now Ags Fif*.

eller the elder *S*.

esh ash(-tree or -wood) *now local WC-Uls*.

esp the aspen tree.

fir: ∼ **tap** *now Fif*, ∼ **yowe** *now NE Ags* a fir cone.

glack the fork of a tree *now Abd Kcdn*.

grain a branch, of a tree *now Per*.

green wood growing trees or branches, living wood *now Cai Kcb*.

gurlie *of trees* gnarled.

haw-bush *now Per Kinr*, **haw-tree** *now local NE-Dmf* the hawthorn tree.

hissel hazel.

hoburn sauch the laburnum *now Bnf*.

hollin holly, a holly-tree *now Bnf*.

†**ibone** ebony.

knablick a knot or root of fir *Bnf*.

knag a knot or spur projecting from a tree *now NE Per Fif*.

†**knapparts** the acorn.

knar a knot in wood.

lady, leddy: ∼**'s meat** the young leaves and buds of the hawthorn *now Cai Kcb*.

larick the larch tree (introduced into Scotland in the late 17th or early 18th century); its wood.

mulberry the whitebeam *Abd Kcdn nEC*.

†**muskane** rotten, decayed.

navis-bore a knot-hole in wood *Bnf Abd*.

†**osare** osier, a species of willow.

palm (tree) one of the various native trees or shrubs, *eg* the goat willow or hazel, used by Roman Catholics or Episcopalians to represent the palm on Palm Sunday; a sprig or branch of one of these trees *now local NE-Uls*.

pea-tree, pease cod tree the laburnum *now S*.

peerie a fir cone *S*.

†**pinule** a young pine tree.

pipe a large ripe acorn with its stalk *Bwk S*.

plane (tree) the sycamore.

plantin(g) 1 †young trees, seedlings. **2** a small wood or grove of trees, a plantation.

preenack a pine-needle *NE*.

pump: ∼**ed** *of a tree* affected by **pumping** or heart-rot, having a hollow stem or trunk *NE-Kcb*. †∼**ing** a disease affecting trees, a form of heart-rot.

quak: ∼**in a(i)sh** *now Abd Kcb*, ∼**in trei** *S*, †∼**in asp** the aspen.

†**rammel 1** small or crooked branches; the rough timber of such. **2** brushwood, undergrowth.

reid, red, rid: ∼ **wood** the wood at the heart of trees.

rice 1 twigs or small branches, brushwood *now Per Ayr*. **2** a branch, a twig.

rodden the berry of the **rowan**; *occas* the tree itself *now N*. ∼ **tree** the **rowan-tree** *now N, local C*.

rone a thicket of brushwood, thorns etc; a patch of dense stunted woodland.

rowan, †**trone,** *also* ∼**-tree,** ∼ **buss** the rowan.

roy a variety of trunk rot in conifers, *esp* the larch *now Mry Bnf*. ∼**ed** affected with **roy** *now Mry Bnf*.

runt an old or decayed tree stump *now local*.

sap spail the sap-wood of a tree *now local Bnf-Per*.

sauch, *n, also* ∼ **willie** *local* various species of willow, including the goat willow. ∼**en** of or pertaining to willow *now local Bnf-wLoth*. ∼ **buss** a willow tree, *prob specif* a low-growing variety *now NE Kcb*. ∼ **tree** a willow tree *now Ags*. ∼ **wan(d)** a twig or branch of willow.

scob a twig or cane of willow or hazel *now SW*.

Scotch mahogany the wood of the alder, which turns red when exposed to light and weather *now WC, Kcb*.

scrog 1 a stunted or crooked bush or tree; ∼**s** brushwood or undergrowth *now local N-Uls*. **2** a gnarled or crooked stump etc of a tree *now Ork NE Ags*. **scroggie** *of a tree* stunted or crooked *now N, EC, SW*.

scrunt a stump of a tree *now NE, C*.

shaw a small, *esp* natural wood, a thicket *now chf literary and in place-names*.

sheepie the cone of the Scots pine *Bnf Abd*.

†**sipling** a sapling, young tree.

sprush spruce.

spyog a bare stumpy branch *Inv Mry Bnf*.

stole *n* a tree stump; a new shoot rising from a group of such stumps after cutting *now Kcb*. †*v*, *of a tree stump* throw up new shoots.

†**stone** *n* a tree stump or trunk left after felling; a cluster of new shoots etc growing on a (cut) tree root. *v, of plants, trees* throw out new growth after pruning etc.

strip, †**stripe** a long narrow belt of trees *NE-S*.

stug, stog a stump of a tree or bush.

†**sylvan** ? a forest tree, shrub etc.

tanner(s) the fibres, small or fibrous roots of a tree or other plant.

tap a fir cone *now Mry Stlg Rox.*

taw a fibre or filament of a plant or tree, a fibrous root *now Sh.*

†**thorter knot** a knot in wood where a branch has grown out of the tree.

†**tree crop** a treetop.

tremmlin tree the aspen *local Mry-Wgt.*

wan(d) 1 a slender pliant stick, *esp* one cut from a young tree. **2** a young shoot of willow used in making baskets *now local NE-WC.*

†**warrock** a knot in wood.

†**wattle** a pliant rod, twig or wand.

whistle, whustle *local:* ~-**wood** any tree with a slippery bark so that twigs can be used to make a whistle *now Dmf.*

widdie 1 a twig or wand of willow or other tough but flexible wood. **2** withy, willow.

willie the willow.

wooding a planting of trees; the trees themselves; a copse or wood.

†**wuid rise** *verse* a small branch.

yowie a fir cone *NE Ags.*

4.7 FRUIT

†**abrico** an apricot.

aipple, apple an apple. †~ **garnet** a pomegranate. †~ **orange** an orange.

†**auchan** a variety of pear.

averin the cloudberry *chf NE.*

black: ~**berry** the blackcurrant *now Abd.* †~ **byde** the berry of the bramble.

blaeberry, blairdie *chf child's word, Bnf Abd,* **blivert** *Abd* the bilberry.

†**blob, honey blob** the gooseberry.

brammle, bramble the blackberry; its bush.

brawlins the berries of the cowberry.

buckie a hip, the fruit of the wild rose *now Abd Arg.* **buckie-faulie** the fruit or flower of the briar *Cai.*

†**bullister** a wild plum (tree or bush).

†**cheston** a chestnut.

chirry a cherry *now Bnf.*

choop *SW, S,* **jupe** *Dmf Rox* the hip of the wild rose.

crack nut a hazelnut.

crane the cranberry *chf S.*

craw, crow: ~(**s**) **aipple** the crab apple. ~**berry** 1 *also* † ~**crooks** the crowberry. 2 *also* ~**crooks** *now Ags* the cranberry.

croupert the crowberry *NE.*

curran, curn *chf Rox* a currant.

†**curson** a fruiting spur.

deaf nut a nut without a kernel.

dog('s) hip the fruit of the dog-rose, the rosehip *now local Abd-S.*

dosinnit rotten *now Ags Fif.*

drop, drap: ~ **ripe** *of fruit* ready to drop with ripeness.

etnach the juniper berry *now NE.*

feg a fig *now Bnf Abd.*

flourish blossom on fruit trees *Gen except Sh Ork.*

†**fruct** a fruit. ~**less** fruitless.

gean the wild cherry, its fruit.

gnashick the bearberry *Mry Bnf.*

†**golden knap, gowdnap** an early variety of pear.

green: ~-**berry** the green gooseberry *now Abd Dmf.* † ~-**gaskin** a variety of gooseberry.

grosell, grosart, groser, groset a gooseberry.

†**gule tree** the barberry.

hagberry, hawkberry the bird cherry.

hap the hip, the fruit of the wild rose *now Kcdn Ags Per.*

haw-stone the seed in a hawthorn berry *now Dmf Uls.*

heather berry the crowberry *now Cai Abd.*

hen(nie(s)) a(i)pple the fruit of the whitebeam or possibly the rowan *now Inv.*

hillberry the crowberry *now Cai.*

hindberry, himberry *now Lnk* the wild raspberry.

hinnie, honey: ~-**blob** a big yellow variety of gooseberry. ~ **pear** a sweet pear *now Edb Gsw SW Rox.*

hippans hips, the fruit of the wild rose *NE.*

kirnel a kernel *now Kcb.*

knot(berry) the cloudberry.

knowperts the crowberry *NE.*

lady('s) *or* **ladies' gartens** *or* **garter(s)** the blackberry *S.*

leamer a ripe nut separating easily from its husk *SW, S.*

leemon a lemon.

†**longueville** a variety of pear.

maumie ripe, mellow.

†**moss mingin** the cranberry.

muck, muckack the fruit of the dog-rose, a rosehip *Cai Ross Inv.*

nit a nut.

noop the cloudberry *N-S.*

oranger, †**orenʒe** an orange.

†**oslin** a variety of early apple *NE.*

paip the stone or kernel of a fruit, a pip *now Dmf Slk.*

peer a pear.

ploom, plum a plum. ~ **damas** a damson plum, damson; a dried plum or prune *now Slk.*

†**pome** an apple.

†**traser** the redcurrant.

rasp the fruit or plant of the raspberry.

rewbard *local N-S,* **roobrub** *now Cai Arg* rhubarb.

rizzar, russle the redcurrant *now local EC Ayr.* †**black** ~ the blackcurrant. **white** ~ the white currant *now Fif.*

rodden the berry of the **rowan**; *occas* the tree itself *now N.*

†**roebuck berry** the fruit of the stone bramble.

rowan, †**rone,** *also* ~ **berry** the fruit of the mountain ash.

†**russer berré** the redcurrant.

scrab the crab apple *now Fif Loth Dnbt Ayr.*

scrog the crab apple (tree) *now sEC, S.*

siven the wild raspberry.

slae the sloe *Gen except Sh Ork.*

sloch, slough the outer skin or husk of certain fruits *now local Cai-Ayr.*

St John's nut a double hazelnut.

stoned *of fruit* having a stone or stones.

strap, strop a cluster of berries, *esp* currants *now S.*

thummles, thimbles raspberries *Mry Abd.*

†**worry-carle** a large coarse winter pear *Rox.*

yap *child's word* an apple *Edb.*

4.8 VEGETABLES

baggie the swede *SE, S.*

†**bane** a bean.

black victual, †**black crap** peas and/or beans *now Stlg.*

blade, blad a leaf of cabbage, turnip, tobacco etc.

blume, bloom: ~**s** potato tops *now Ags.*

bow-kail cabbage *now Bnf Abd Lnk.*

bowstock a cabbage with a properly-developed heart *now Bnf Abd.*

brock small potatoes *now Abd Kcb.*

bullock-yellow a kind of swede *Bnf Abd.*

cabbage: ~ **kail** a cabbage *NE Ags.* ~ **runt,** ~ **stock** a cabbage stalk, a **castock** *chf NE Fif Kcb.*

castock a stalk of **kail** or cabbage *now local Bnf-Kcb.*

chun *n* a sprout, *chf* of a potato *chf SW. v, of potatoes* sprout *SW.*

cob a pea-pod.

cod a pod or husk (of peas, beans) *now Cai Abd Lnk.*

†**crummock** skirret.

curlie kail, curlie green(s) *now local Bnf-Edb Rox,* **curlie(s)** *now Bnf Abd Fif* curly colewort.

†**finkle** fennel.

fozie *of overgrown or rotten vegetables* soft, spongy. **foziness** sponginess *local Sh-Pbls.*

greens green vegetables, *esp* kail.

†**hasterns** early-ripening peas.

†**hasting(s)** an early-flowering variety of pea.

het, hot 1 †*of peas* quickly growing, early maturing. **2** *of root crops* fermenting, decayed through being stored too damp or in a diseased condition *local N-S.*

ingan an onion.

kail, green ~ cole, brassica, *esp* the curly variety; cabbage. ~ **blade** a leaf of kail *now local Sh-Dmf.* ~ **root** the stump left after the head of the kail has been cut *local N-S.* ~ **runt,** ~ **stock** the stalk of the kail plant, a **castock** *now local Sh-SW.* **Kilmaurs** ~ a strong hardy variety, *chf* used for feeding cattle *now WC.* †**lang** ~, **red** ~ great or Scotch kail, a less curly, purplish variety.

knot *of turnips* suffer from finger-and-toe disease *local NE-Loth.*

†**lang craig** an onion which runs to stem *chf Ags.*

†**latuce** a lettuce.

†**loukit kaill** cabbage.

lucken *of cabbages etc* having a firm heart.

neep, turneep *now Ork,* **turmit** *local EC-S,* **turnip, tumshie** *joc or colloq, C, S* a turnip; *in Scotland, chf* a swede.

†**pasneip** a parsnip.

peacod *now Ags,* **pea-huil** *Fif Loth S,* **pea-shaup** *now Fif WC* a pea-pod.

pitawtie the potato.

ploom, plum the fruit of the potato-plant.

raan a disease of turnips *NE Kcb.* ~**ed** affected with **raan** *NE Kcb.*

raw, row *of root crops* come up in rows *now Kcb.*

redcoll the horse-radish.

reefort a radish.

†**reid, red, rid:** ~ **neb** a variety of potato with red markings at one end.

†**ribe** a tall thin (cabbage) plant.

rorie a particularly large turnip *Bnf Abd.*

†**rose (end)** the crown end of a potato tuber.

runk a cabbage-stalk, *esp* when hard and withered *Cai Mry.*

runt the hardened, withered stem of a cabbage or **kail** plant, a **castock.**

scallion a spring onion *C Uls.*

shaup the seed husk of a leguminous plant; a pea-pod *now C.*

shaws the stalks and leaves of potatoes, **turnips** etc.

stock, †stouk the hard stalk or stem of a plant, *esp* of a cabbage etc; the whole plant *now Sh.*

string *of seedlings, esp turnips* sprout in a line along the drills *Bnf Abd.*

swab a pea- or bean-pod *Dmf Rox.*

swade a swede.

swap the shell or pod of peas or beans before they begin to swell; the peas or beans themselves *now Loth.*

sybow, syboe, sybie the spring onion; *orig* a different kind of onion *Gen except Sh Ork.* † ~ **tail** the green shoots of the young onion.

tails onion leaves *now Loth S.*

tattie a potato. ~-**bloom** the flower or complete foliage of the potato *now Cai.* ~-**ploom** the seed-box of the potato plant *now local NE-Kcb.* ~-**shaw(s)** the stalk and leaves of the potato plant.

taupin a tap-root of a turnip *now NE Per.*

victual, vittal leguminous crops; a crop before or after harvesting *now local Kcdn-Loth.*

whaup the seed-pod of a leguminous vegetable, *esp* one before the peas etc have begun to develop or after they have been shelled *now Abd Loth.*

†yam a coarse variety of potato.

4.9 GRAIN CROPS

aicher *Ork Cai,* icker *SW* an ear of corn.

ait(s) oat(s). ~-**seed** the seed of the oat.

ann awn, beard of barley etc *local.*

awny *of grain* bearded.

barley, †barleke barley. **barley-pickle** a grain of barley.

bere, bear bear, barley, *latterly* four- or six-row barley, hardier and coarser than ordinary two-row barley.

bigg a variety of barley.

†blanded *or* blendit bear bere mixed with barley *Fif.*

bob, bab a small luxuriant patch of corn etc *Bnf Kcb.*

†brashloch a mixed crop of rye with oats or barley *SW.*

breard, breer the first shoots of grain etc.

brockit, brucket *of oats* black and white growing together.

buzzle *of grain crops* rustle (indicating ripeness) *Bnf Abd.*

chester: ~ **barley** *or* **bere** a variety of barley *now Ags.*

corn 1 oats. 2 a single grain *now Kcb.* ~**s** crops of grain.

crop, crap a head of corn.

†dour seed late-ripening oats.

en(d)-pickle the grain of corn at the top of the stalk.

†feldeland aitis oats growing on land consisting of a field or fields.

fen(d)less *of corn, straw* short, thin, without substance *NE.*

feuach a very sparse crop of grain *NE.*

†finnie *proverb, of corn etc* full of substance.

fit, fute, foot: upon the ~ *of grain* standing, unthreshed.

girsie *of cereal crops* interspersed with grass.

†gray: ~ **corn** a kind of light grain. ~ **oats** an inferior kind of oats.

grits oat kernels, grain.

†hasterns early-ripening oats.

haver oats, the oat.

het, hot 1 †*of oats* quickly growing, early maturing. 2 *of grain* fermenting, decayed through being stored too damp or in a diseased condition *local N-S.*

hose the sheath enclosing an ear of corn *now midLoth.*

mashlum, †masloch mixed grains or grains and pulses grown and ground together *now local NE-Kcb.*

†mauten *of grain or seeds* germinate, sprout; become malt.

meal('s) corn grain in general *chf Sh-NE.*

†mete cereal while still growing.

oxter pickle the small grain *freq* attached to the full one within the husk in oats *NE.*

pickle, puckle a grain of oats, barley or wheat.

†pildagerst the groats from the naked oat or barley.

pile a grain (of corn etc); a husk *now Dnbtn Kcb.*

†rag *of oats* reach the stage of growth where the grain begins to appear *SW.*

rap(s) rape *now SW.*

redland oats a crop of oats sown after a cleaning crop, *eg* turnips *WC, SW.*

reuch, rough: ~ **bear** = bere.

rissom a single head or ear of oats.

Sandie oat a variety of oat *NE.*

segging a disease of oat-plants *now Kcdn Loth.*

shak, shake the shaking of grain from an ear of corn in wind etc *now Sh Ork N.*

shiak(s) a kind of grey-striped black oats.

shuit, shoot come into ear. **shot blade** the leaf enclosing the corn-stalk and ear *now local*.

†**sloomy** *of corn etc* not well filled out, stunted.

small oats, †**small corn** a kind of oat sown on the poorest soil.

strag a thin, straggly crop, as of corn *now Lnk*.

stuff corn, grain, a crop *now local Ork-SW*.

†**suggeroun** a kind of oats.

tap pickle the highest ear on a stalk of oats, *usu* considered to be of the best quality *now Sh*.

tiller *of corn etc* produce side-shoots from the root or base of the stem *now local Ags-Wgt*.

†**uncorn** poor quality oats.

victual, vittal corn, grain; a crop before or after harvesting *now local Kcdn-Loth*.

†**ware barley, ware bear** *Abd* barley manured with seaweed.

white wheat *NE*.

white victual cereal or grain crops as opposed to green crops *Per Stlg Ayr*.

yawins, yavins *N* awns, the beard or bristle of barley or oats.

4.10 STRAW

bottle, battle, buttle a bundle (of straw) *now Kcb Uls*.

brock the rakings of straw from a harvested field *now Bnf Abd Ags*.

cat a handful of straw laid on the ground without being put into a sheaf *S*.

cavings *now Bnf*, **cuffins** *Bnf Abd* broken straw *now Bnf*.

fen(d)less *of corn, straw* short, thin, without substance *NE*.

†**fushloch** waste fragments of straw, grass etc *WC, SW*.

haver-straw straw from oats.

kemple, kimpill 1 a horse-load of straw or the equivalent quantity. **2** a bundle or load of hay or straw made up in a certain way *Cai*.

pease strae the stalks and foliage of the pea plant used as cheap fodder or bedding for animals.

strab any odd or loose straw *Bnf Abd*.

strae a straw.

4.11 HAY

beust withered grass from the previous year *SW*

bog-hay hay gathered from uncultivated or marshy ground.

bottle, battle, buttle a bundle (of hay) *now Kcb Uls*.

feuach a very sparse crop of grass.

†**fog** grass left in the field in winter.

foggage the second crop of grass after hay.

fowd long coarse grass not eaten down in summer *N*.

go(r)sk coarse, rank grass produced by cattle droppings in a pasture *now Abd Ags*.

hey, hay 1 hay. **2** the hay harvest. ~-**bog** a piece of marshy ground whose grass was formerly used for winter fodder *now Cai Kcb*. ~-**fog** the second growth of grass in a hayfield *now Ags midLoth Rox*.

kemple, kimpill a bundle of hay or straw made up in a certain way *Cai*.

mawin girse meadow hay *Sh Ags*.

mossing a crop of cotton grass *N*.

pine shrink by drying in the open air *now Sh*.

piskie *of grass* dry, withered, shrivelled *SW*.

†**pry** one of various species of sedge common in southern Scotland and used for sheep-feeding *S*.

5 ENVIRONMENT

5.1 LAND

5.1.1 GENERAL, MISCELLANEOUS

back: the ~ of beyond a remote, inaccessible place.

bensell a place exposed to storm *now Per Fif.*

bield a place giving refuge or shelter.

boun(d), boons *NE* a district or stretch of land within certain boundaries *now Bnf Ayr.*

cosie *of places* sheltered, providing comfort and protection.

countra, kintra country.

country-side a rural district or tract of country.

douth gloomy, dreary, dark *S.*

dreich, dree *of scenery etc* dreary, bleak.

†erd-dyn an earthquake.

erse the hinterland, interior *local Ork-Abd.*

fit, fute, foot *freq with local term preceding* the lower end *chf* of a piece of ground: *'baillie Hopes land foot'.*

fusslebare *of land* poor, hilly, exposed *Abd.*

gowstie vast, dreary, desolate; eerie.

grund ground.

iver *freq in place-names* upper, higher, *esp* the higher of two places of the same name.

lan(d) 1 land. **2** ~**s** the fields, the countryside.

†~ gate(s) landwards, in the direction of the country.

larach a site *in gen*, a place, situation.

lea, ley barren, wild.

lee-laik sheltered *SW.*

nether *in place-names* the lower-situated of two places, roads, etc of the same name.

owerhing overhang.

†planet an area of ground.

rig an extent of land, long rather than broad.

†roums domains, territories.

roun(d): the ~ the surrounding country, neighbourhood *Sh Ork local EC.*

scaup, scalp a piece of infertile, stony ground *now Sh NE.* **†scappy** bare and exposed.

†schoir steep; rugged.

scriffin a thin crust or covering; the face of the earth.

†scug, scog: ~y shady; sheltering.

†shaddow half the portion of a piece of land facing north.

shed, shede *now Sh Ork NE* a strip of land, a distinct or separate piece of ground *now chf in place-names.*

sit a sinking or settling down of the surface of the ground or of anything built on it *now NE.*

skelp a long strip or expanse, *esp* of ground, an indefinite area *local.*

smuith, smooth a smooth or level place *Ross Mry Kcdn.*

straik a (*usu* long, narrow) tract of land *now Mry.*

†stripe a narrow tract or strip of country.

track a tract (of land).

†transmeridiane the region beyond the meridian in the Atlantic which separates the New from the Old World.

tryst a conspicuous object chosen as a rendezvous, *eg* for huntsmen etc, *freq in place-names.*

†under, unner *local:* ~**foot** underground.

†upaland in the country as opposed to the town.

upthrou 1 in the upper part of the country, in or from the uplands, in the Highlands, inland from the sea *local Sh-NE.* **2** inland, rural *chf Abd.*

vizzy a view, prospect.

wa(ll) heid(s) the horizon, skyline *chf SW.*

warld, wardle, warle *now NE* the world.

wast, west: ~ land †*n* the west (*freq* Highlands) of Scotland. *adj* coming from or situated in the west of Scotland, western *now Stlg Fif Ayr.*

†wasty desolate, uninhabited.

weather glim a place much exposed to the elements *now Bnf.*

will *of a place* out of the way, desolate *now Abd.*

wilsome *freq in ballads, of a path etc* leading through wild or featureless country, confusing; *of a place* desolate, wild, dreary *now Sh Ork.*

wynd, †twyne a long, awkwardly-shaped or steep piece of land, *orig* ploughed in only one direction by the plough turning left after each furrow.

5.1.2 LAND FEATURES

†ana a river island *Rox.*

†ban(d) a range (of hills); a ridge (of a hill).

bealach *esp mountaineering*, **balloch** *esp in place-names* a narrow mountain pass.

bellibucht a hollow in a hill, running across the slope *SW.*

ben, binn *latterly only place-names* a mountain, hill, **ben** *usu* being applied to the higher Scottish mountains.

bent 1 †~(**s**) a stretch of open ground (covered with bent); a moor. **2** ~**s** a sandy hillock covered with bent.

bink, bench a bank *now Arg.*

boorachie, †boorach, boorock a mound, small hill.

†bord a ridge or rim of a hill.

bore a hole, crevice, *freq* a shelter or hiding-place.

boss 1 a rounded prominence. **2** a round mass; a tussock etc *now Abd Ayr.*

brae 1 a bank or stretch of ground rising fairly steeply; a hillside. **2** the brow of a hill. **3** an upland, mountainous district, *freq* ~**s** in the name of the district: '*the Braes o Balquhidder*'. ~**head** the top of a **brae**. ~-**set** situated on a slope; steep.

brak a hollow in a hill.

brent steep, precipitous.

broo the brow of a hill.

cantle a corner, projection, ledge *now Abd.*

cleugh 1 a gorge, ravine. **2** †a cliff, crag.

clift[1] a cliff *now Arg.*

clift[2] a cleft, fissure; a cave.

clint a cliff, crag, precipice *latterly chf SW, S.*

clivvie a cleft *Bnf Abd.*

Corbett *mountaineering* name for a Scottish mountain of between 2500 and 3000 feet (761-914 metres approx).

corrie a hollow on the side of a mountain or between mountains.

cove a cave, cavern *now Cai Ags.*

craig, crag 1 a crag, rock, cliff. **2** a projecting spur of rock. ~-**and-tail** a formation consisting of a hill with a steep rock-face at one end sloping towards the other in a mass of drift or moraine, caused by the obstruction and splitting of a glacier by hard rock.

†cutter a crack or crevice in a stratum of rock.

dass, dess a ledge on a hillside, cliff etc.

den a narrow valley, *esp* one with trees *Gen except Sh Ork.*

dog hillock a small mound or hillock covered with long grass *now Cai Abd.*

Donald *mountaineering* name for a hill in the Scottish **Lowlands** of 2000 feet (610 m) or over.

doonfa a downward slope *local.*

drum 1 a long narrow ridge or knoll *now Per.* **2** ~**s** an area of ridged land intersected by marshy hollows *Gall.* ~**lin** a long narrow ridge or knoll, *esp* a long whaleback mound of glacial deposit, often occurring in groups in low-lying areas.

†eyllane an island.

fell a (*usu* steep, rocky) hill; a tract of hill-moor.

forest *law* a large area of ground, not necessarily still wooded, *orig* reserved for deer-hunting and belonging to the Crown. **†the F** ~ Ettrick Forest in Slk.

gill a ravine, gully *now local.*

glack a hollow between hills, a defile, ravine *now local N-Arg.*

glen a valley or hollow, *chf* one traversed by a stream or river, and *freq* narrow and steep-sided; a mountain valley as opposed to a **strath**.

gowl a narrow pass or cleft between hills, *esp* **Windy G** ~ on Arthur's Seat in Edinburgh.

grain a branch, arm, offshoot of a valley *now only in place-names.*

gullet a gully, ravine *now local Ags-Dmf.*

hag a hillock of firmer ground in a bog.

hard a piece of firm ground, as opposed to a bog *now midLoth Kcb.*

hause 1 a neck of land *now Ork.* **2** a defile, the head of a pass *Kcb, S in place-names.*

heich a hill, height, an eminence, upland; rising ground *now local Abd-S.* **heich(s)** *or* **heicht(s)** *now local* ~(**s**) **and howes** hill(s) and dale(s).

heicht, hicht a high place, a hilltop etc.

heid 1 the highest part of a valley, parish etc. **2** the summit of a hill.

heuch 1 a precipice, crag or cliff, a steep bank, *esp* one overhanging a river or sea. **2** a **glen** or ravine with steep, overhanging sides *Gen except Sh Ork.* **† ~ heid** the top of a cliff or precipice.

hiddle(s) sheltered spots *now Ags.*

hieland high land, high ground.

hill, hull 1 a hill, a (low) mountain. **2** an (artificial) mound. **hillan** a mound, heap, hillock, *esp* a molehill *now Edb.* ~**er** a little hill, a heap, a small mound *Cai.* † ~**fit(s)** the ground at the foot of a hill; foothills. ~**head,** ~**heid** the summit of a hill *now Sh NE Ayr, freq as a farm name.* ~-**run** *esp of wild moorland* hilly, upland *Cai Inv NE.*

hip a projecting piece of land; a curving projection on the lower slopes of a hillside *now Kcb.*

hirst a barren, unproductive piece of ground, *usu* a hillock, knoll, or ridge.

holl a hole.

hope 1 a small enclosed upland valley, a hollow among the hills *now S.* **2** a hill *now Rox.*

howe 1 †a hole. **2** a depression, a hollow or low-lying piece of ground *now N, EC, S.* **3** *chf in place-names* a stretch of country of basin formation, a wide plain bounded by hills, a vale.

humple, humplock a small heap or mound, a hillock *now local Stlg-Rox.*

inby low-lying *midLoth Kcb Dmf S.*

inch 1 a small island. **2** *in place-names* a piece of rising ground in the middle of a plain.

†inland the inlying or central area of a country.

innerlie inlying, not exposed; in the interior of a district *S.*

kame a long narrow steep-sided ridge, the crest of a hill or ridge *also freq in place-names.*

kip a jutting or projecting point on a hill; a peak *now midLoth, freq in S place-names.* **† ~pit** *of a hill?* having a **kip** or **kips**? **~pie** a hill *local.*

kirn *freq in place-names* a natural feature resembling a churn in shape.

knap a hillock or knoll *local Ork-Fif.*

knock a hillock *now only verse.*

know knoll. **~ head** a hilltop *now local N-Kcb.*

laggin(s) the edge, rim of a hill *now Rox.*

†laich, law a stretch of low-lying ground *freq in place-names.*

law a rounded, *usu* conical hill, *freq* isolated or conspicuous.

lawland(s), lowland(s) 1 †the low-lying area, low-lying lands. **2 L~** any part of Scotland east and south of the Highland line (*sometimes* excluding the Borders).

linn a deep and narrow gorge *SW, S.*

lirk a fold or hollow in a hill, a recess, crevice, ravine *now local Sh-Kcb.*

lum a long funnel-like passage worn by natural forces through a cliff; a rock chimney *now NE.*

month, mounth, mount a stretch of hilly or high ground; a mountain, hill, moor *latterly only in place-names.*

mote a mound or hillock; an embankment *now Sh Uls.*

†mounté a mountain, hill-top.

mou(th) a threshold or entrance to an enclosed place or tract of country *now local C.*

mowdie(wort) hill(ock) a molehill *now Dmf.*

muir, moor moor. **~ish, † ~y** consisting of or abounding in moorland. **~land** moorland.

mull *chf in place-names* a promontory, headland.

Munro name for any Scottish peak of 3000 feet (914.4 metres) or more. **~-bagger, ~-bagging** a person who aims or the act or process of aiming to climb every **Munro.**

munt 1 mount. **2** hilly land, high land, moorland.

muntain a mountain.

nabb, knab *Sh Ork* a hillock, summit *chf Sh.*

neb a projecting tip or point of a piece of land or rock *local.*

ness a headland *chf Sh Ork.*

neuk, nook 1 a projecting point of land, *esp* into the sea. **2** an outlying or remote place. **the East N~** the eastern corner of Fife.

nick *chf in place-names* a narrow gap in a range of hills *chf SW, S.*

pad *chf in place-names* a route over a natural obstacle, a pass through hills etc *C.*

peat-hill *now Sh Ork,* **peat moss** a peat-bog or -moor, the place where peats are dug.

pen a pointed conical hill *chf S, chf in place-names as* **X** ~: '*Ettrick Pen*'.

peth, path a cleft etc running up and down the slope of a steep hill. **†the peths, the paths** name for several ravines crossing the coastal route from Scotland to England near Cockburnspath.

plain, plenn †a small or limited stretch of level ground.

pot, pat a pit or hole in the ground whether natural or man-made.

reuch, rough rough ground. **the rough bounds** name for a mountainous region in the West Highlands from Loch Sunart (Arg) to Loch Hourn (Inv).

rift a cleft, fissure in a rock etc *now local Sh-Per.*

rig a ridge of high ground, a long narrow hill, a hill-crest *now local.* **~gin** the top of a stretch of high ground; a high ridge of land, *esp* running along the side of a plain *now in place-names.*

rive a split, crack, fissure *now Sh.*

scaup, scalp a small bare hill or piece of rock *now Sh NE.*

scaur *freq in place-names* a sheer rock, precipice; a steep, eroded hill *now NE-S.*

s(c)lidder, sclither a narrow steep hollow or track down a hillside, *esp* when stony, a **scree** *now S.*

score a crevice, cleft, gully in a cliff face *now chf in place-names.*

scree a mass of small loose stones on a steep hillside.

shank a downward spur or slope of a hill *now Ags S.*

†shear, share: where wind and water *or* **weather ~s** on a watershed or high ridge.

shin a ridge or steep hill-face, a projecting part of a piece of high ground *now NE wLoth.*

†short *of a hill* low.

†shot heuch a landslip.

sidelin(s) a sloping piece of ground, a hillside *now C Rox.*

†sky the outline of a hill as seen against the sky, the skyline *Abd.*

slack 1 *freq in place-names* a hollow, *esp* between

hills, a saddle in a hill-ridge, a pass *now local.* **2**
†a pit, hole.

slap, slop a pass or shallow valley between hills
now EC, WC, freq in place-names.

slock, sloch, slug *Abd-Ags* a hollow between hills,
a pass *now Cai Inv Mry, freq in place-names.*

slot a pit, hole in the ground, *specif* that on the
shores of Carlingwark Loch at Castle Douglas
Kcb.

snab a steep short slope, a projection of rock *now
midLoth WC Rox.*

sneck a dip in the ground, a saddle between hills
local Sh-Ags.

snib a short steep hill or ascent *Per Stlg Ayr.*

†snout a projecting point of land etc.

†snuke a promontory.

soo('s) back a ridge or natural hump.

spout a narrow enclosed pathway; a gully in a
cliff-face *freq in place-names.*

steel *chf place-name* a steep bank, *esp* a spur on a
hill ridge *S.*

stey *of a hill etc* (very) steep; difficult to climb.

strait *of mountains etc* steep *now local Sh-Per.*

strath a river valley, *esp* when broad and flat.

†summité the summit, top of a mountain.

swallie an abyss.

swire a hollow or declivity between hills; a hollow
or level place near the top of a hill *now Pbls Lnk
S, freq in place-names, chf Pbls S.*

syke a marshy hollow, *esp* one with a stream, a
cleft in the ground *now Dmf Rox.*

tail a long narrow piece of land jutting out from a
larger piece.

tappietourie a **cairn** on a hilltop.

tappin the peaked top of a hill; a **cairn** on a hilltop
now Ayr.

tarbe(r)t an isthmus or neck of land between two
navigable stretches of water, *specif* one over
which a boat could be drawn *freq in place-names.*

†toman a little hill, mound, *freq* one formed by
the moraine of a glacier, in folklore associated
with a fairy dwelling.

†trow the valley or basin of certain rivers in south-
west Scotland: *'the trow of Clyde'.*

tulloch a mound, hillock; *freq* a fairy mound *Cai
Per.*

tummock, †tammock a small hillock; a molehill
now Wgt.

type a low conical hill *Dmf, freq in place-names.*

†upwith rising ground.

vailey a valley *now Sh Loth Slk.*

†wald a wold, a hill, a piece of open country.

water heid the source of a river, the upper end of
a valley *now local Ags-S.*

†weem *also in place-names* a cave, a natural cavity
in the ground, in a rock etc.

†westerne a desert, wilderness.

wham *freq in place-names* a dale or valley, a broad
hollow among hills through which a stream runs
now Sh.

Whangie: the ~ a split rock through which a
path runs in the Kilpatrick Hills, *Dnbt.*

wick a cleft in the face of a hill, *specif* the **Wicks
o Baiglie** on the edge of the Ochil Hills on the
old Kinross to Perth road.

yett a natural pass between hills, *chf in place-names:*
'Yetts of Muckart'.

5.1.3 LAND: SURFACE FEATURES

bent 1 †~(s) a stretch of open ground (covered
with bent). **2** ~s a sandy hillock covered with
bent. †~y covered with bent.

†blout barren, bare.

breerie *adj* briery. †*n* a place covered with briers.

bruntland rough mossy ground, *formerly* burnt
periodically *now Sh.* **birny** consisting of, covered
with or like **birns** (burnt heather stems).

chingly gravelly, pebbly *Ork Bnf Abd.*

cleed cover thickly.

den a narrow valley, *esp* one with trees *Gen except
Sh Ork.*

dog hillock a small mound or hillock covered with
long grass *now Cai Abd.*

dour *of land* hard, barren *local Cai-Rox.*

†firth *verse* wooded country.

forest law a large area of ground, not necessarily
still wooded, *orig* reserved for deer-hunting and
belonging to the Crown. **†the F** ~ Ettrick Forest
in Slk.

†gowan(e)d covered with daisies, daisied.

green *adj* covered with grass, grassy *now Sh Ork
Cai. n* grassy ground; a grassy place.

†grow be covered with growth (**of** vegetation).

†hair grey(ish).

hazelly covered with or abounding in hazels *now
midLoth Kcb.*

heather, hather: ~y heather-covered.

leens pieces of grassy land in a moor or by a river,
freq pastures of natural grass *Cai.*

munt a low tree-covered hill *Fif Ayr.*

†nakit &c, naked *of land* bare, barren

plain, plenn free from hills, water etc; unwooded,
open *now Sh.*

rashie overgrown with rushes.

reesk 1 a piece of moor or marshy ground covered

with natural grass *now Abd Kcdn, freq in place-names Cai local WC-Kcb*. **2** a growth of natural coarse grasses or rushes on rough, waste or marshy ground *now Bnf Abd*. ~**ie** *of ground* having a **reesk** *Abd*.

sauchie abounding in willows.

scabbert a bare, stony piece of land *NE*.

scabbit *of land* bare, infertile *now local Sh-Per*.

scarp a bare barren piece of ground *now Sh*.

scaup, scalp a small bare hill or piece of rock *now Sh NE*. **†scappy** bare and exposed.

scroggie full of **scrogs**, covered with undergrowth *now N, EC, SW*.

seggy abounding in **segs**, sedgy.

sink a hollow, low-lying area where water collects to form a boggy place *now Sh and in place-names*.

spratty *now Ayr Dmf*, **sprotty** *now Abd* producing or abounding in rushes.

stoddert an area of green grass on a hill or heath surrounding a spring of water *NE*.

swaird a sward. **†sward-erd** grassland.

†wald a wold, a piece of open country.

whinnie composed of or overgrown with furze.

white *of hill-land* covered with coarse bent or natural grass instead of heather, bracken or scrub *local Ags-SW*.

5.1.4 LAND: USE

For agricultural use, see also 7.

biel(d) a place giving refuge or shelter.

bore a hole, crevice, *freq* a shelter or hiding-place.

bruntland rough mossy ground, *formerly* burnt periodically *now Sh*.

bunker a small sandpit, *now esp* on a golf-course.

†burgh rudis cultivated land belonging to a burgh.

coal hill ground occupied at a pit-head for colliery purposes *chf Stlg*.

†cummersum *of places* difficult to pass through, full of obstructions.

†deambulatour a place to walk in; a walk.

†difficil difficult to travel or pass over.

green **1** a town or village green. **2** the grassy ground forming part of the grounds of a house or other buildings *freq* **kirk, castle, back, drying** *etc* ~.

grun(d), ground farm-land, a farm, an estate *now local*.

†theather, hather heather-clad hills as a place of concealment.

hey-bog a piece of marshy ground whose grass was formerly used for winter fodder *now Cai Kcb*.

hiddle(s) hiding place(s), sheltered spot(s) *now Ags*.

†hirst a ford.

†house stead the land on which a house is to be built, the site of a house.

meedow, meaddie *EC* marshy grassland where the natural coarse grasses are often cut for hay.

muir, moor rough, uncultivated heathery land considered as part of an estate a tract of unenclosed uncultivated ground held by a proprietor or *chf* a community, the common; *latterly freq* the market green *Gen except Sh Ork, freq in place-names*.

†mute-hill *appar* a hill on which assemblies were held, but sometimes *perh* simply a mound.

neuk, nook an outlying or remote place.

outlan(d) outlying land, rough ground on the edge of arable marginal land.

outlie an outlying piece of ground *NE*.

outset a patch of reclaimed and newly-cultivated (or *orig* newly-inhabited) land, *freq* taken in from moorland *now Sh*.

pad *chf in place-names* a route over a natural obstacle, a pass through hills etc *C*.

†pans *freq in place-names* a group of salt pans or the site occupied by them; a salt works of this kind.

peat: ~**-hill** *now Sh Ork*, ~ **moss** a peat-bog or -moor, the place where peats are dug. † ~ **ʒaird** a place where peats are dug.

peth, path a steep track or road leading down into a ravine and up the other side.

†rink, renk the piece of ground marked out for a contest, combat, race etc.

†saut, salt: ~ **stack** a mound of earth from which salt was manufactured.

s(c)lidder, sclither a narrow steep hollow or track down a hillside, *esp* when stony, a **scree** *now S*.

shed a place where roads branch, a parting of ways *now C*.

sheel, shill: ~**ing hill** a piece of rising ground where grain was winnowed by the wind *now in place-names*.

slock, sloch, slug *Abd-Ags* a hollow between hills, a pass *now Cai Inv Mry, freq in place-names*. **the Slug (Road)** the road through the pass between Banchory and Stonehaven *Kcdn*.

stey *of a road etc* (very) steep; difficult to climb.

swire a hollow or declivity between hills, *freq* one with a road; a hollow or level place near the top of a hill *now Pbls Lnk S, freq in place-names chf Pbls S*.

watch knowe a hill high enough to serve as a look-out station *S, freq in place-names*.

†water fall a slope of the ground sufficient to enable the fall or drainage of water.

wilsome *freq ballad, of a path etc* leading through wild or featureless country, confusing *now Sh Ork*.

water, watter *now local, also* ~ **gate** *S* a river valley, the area and its inhabitants bordering a river *now S*. **†water brae** a slope beside a river. **water lip** the brink of a stream *Ayr*. ~ **side** the side or brink of water, the bank of a river etc.

5.1.5 RIVERBANKS

brae the (steep or sloping) bank of a river or lake or shore of the sea.

broo the overhanging bank of a river *now Lnk*.

carse (*chf* an extensive stretch of) low alluvial land along the banks of a river.

claddach the gravelly bed or edge of a river *Mry SW*.

croy a mound or quay to protect a riverbank *chf Per*.

dippin a place by a river with steps leading down, where pails, clothes etc are dipped.

dry field land above the flood level, *esp* in the Forth and Tay valleys.

hag a ledge of turf overhanging a stream *SW, S*.

haud, hald, hold the overhanging bank of a stream, or a stone, beneath which a fish lurks.

haugh, haugh land, †haugh(ing) ground a piece of level ground, *usu* alluvial, on the banks of a river, river-meadow land.

howm, †holm, ho(l)min(g) (ground) a stretch of low-lying land beside a river *now C, S*.

inch a stretch of low-lying land near a river or other water, sometimes cut off at high tide *now chf in place-names*.

inks low-lying land on the banks of a river estuary *SW*.

lane a marshy meadow *SW*.

leens pieces of grassy land by a river, meadows, *freq* pastures of natural grass *Cai*.

links *esp of the Forth* loops of a winding stream or river, the land enclosed by such.

lochside the side of a loch; the district round a loch.

lowp a place where a river may be or is traditionally thought to have been crossed by leaping.

merse, †mersk flat alluvial land by a river or estuary, *specif* that bordering the Solway *SW*.

mote an embankment *now Sh Uls*.

rin, run the course of a river or stream with the lands bordering it, a river valley *now NE Slk*.

skelvy *of a river bank etc* shelving *now Sh*.

†stank brae the edge of a **stank** (ditch).

5.1.6 MARSH

bobbin-quaw, babanquaw a quaking bog, quagmire.

drums an area of ridged land intersected by marshy hollows *Gall*.

flow a wet peat bog, a morass *now Cai SW, S*. ~ **moss** mossy, boggy ground.

flush a piece of boggy ground, *esp* one where water lies on the surface *now Arg Rox*.

fluther a boggy piece of ground, a marsh.

gullion a quagmire, marsh *Loth Gall*.

hag a hollow of marshy ground in a moor, *eg* where channels have been made or peats cut.

hobble: hobblie *of the ground* quaking under the feet *Bnf Rox*. ~ **bog** *NE*, ~ **quo** *S* a quagmire.

laggery muddy, miry *chf Ags*.

latch, †leche a mire, patch of bog.

†mersk(s) marshland, a marsh *NE*.

mire a peat-bog *Sh*.

misk a damp, boggy, low-lying stretch of grassland *WC*.

moss boggy ground, moorland. ~**y** boggy, peaty. ~ **flow** a wet peat bog, a swamp *C*. ~ **hags**, ~ **holes** dangerous boggy moorland. ~ **pot** a water-filled pit in a peat bog *NE*.

†nesh soft ground, a bog *NE*.

plowter a wet, muddy spot, a bog, mire.

powk a hole or hollow in the ground, *usu* waterlogged or marshy *now Mry Per*.

quak: ~**in-bog** *now Bnf-Wgt*, ~**(k)in moss** *now Cai*, ~**(k)in qua** *Kcb* a quagmire.

quaw a bog, quagmire, marsh *chf Gall*.

†quick moss moss which trembles or in which a person can sink.

shog, shug, shoog: ~ **bog, shoggie bog** *now Lnk Dmf* a soft watery bog, a quagmire.

sink a hollow, low-lying area where water collects to form a boggy place *now Sh and in place-names*.

slack a low-lying, boggy depression in the ground *S*.

slag a marshy place, morass *now Rox*.

†sleugh a slough, a marsh, quagmire *SW*.

slogg a marsh, bog *now Rox*.

sluch a slough, a mire *now Sh NE*.

slump a marsh, boggy place, morass *now Rox.* ~**y** marshy, muddy.

†**slush** a wet marshy place, a puddle, quagmire.

sowp a bog.

spoutie *of soil* full of springs, marshy, undrained *now NE nEC.*

†**strother** a marsh.

swail a wet hollow, a boggy place *now Bnf.*

syke a marshy hollow, *esp* one with a stream, a cleft in the ground *now Dmf Rox.* †**sykie** full of sluggish rivulets, soft, boggy, though dry in summer.

†**waggle, waigle** a marsh, bog *N.*

wall, well: ~ **e(y)e** a place in a bog from which a spring rises.

water hole a hole or pit in which water collects *now Sh N Per.*

wauchie swampy, boggy.

wham a hollow piece of ground in a field etc, a depression, *esp* a marshy one *now Sh.*

5.1.7 MUD

champ a stretch of muddy trodden ground *S.*

clabber, glabber mud, clay, mire *now local Fif-Uls.*

clart, clort mud, mire.

clatchy muddy, sticky *now Bnf.*

droukit stour mud *now Ags.*

dub(s) mud *N.* **dubbie** muddy *now Bnf Abd.*

glaur *n* soft, sticky mud; ooze, slime. *v* make muddy, dirty, soil; make slimy or slippery *now Bwk.* ~**ie** muddy, dirty *local EC-Uls.* ~**sel** completely covered with mud *S.*

gluthery muddy; slimy *now Per Fif.*

goor mud, dirt; muddy, stagnant water *local Sh-Kcdn.* **gorroch** a trampled muddy spot *now Kcb Dmf.* **goory** muddy, slimy *now Kcdn.*

grummel *n* mud, sediment *now Cai Ayr Uls. v* make muddy or turbid. **g(r)umlie** muddy, turbid, full of dregs or gravel *now local Sh-Dmf.*

gullion a pool of mud *Uls.*

gutter: ~**s** mud, mire, muddy puddles *now Sh-C.* **gutterie** muddy, miry, messy *local.*

jaupy splashy, muddy.

lagger mire, mud *chf N.* ~**it** made wet or muddy; besmeared, bespattered. ~**y** muddy, miry *chf Ags.*

lair 1 mud, mire *Ags midLoth Kcb.* **2** a mire *now Abd.* ~**y** miry, muddy *Abd Ags Rox.*

†**plash** a sticky, miry place.

platchie wet, muddy *now Rox.*

plowter, pleuter, ploiter a wet, muddy spot, a bog, mire.

poach a wet, muddy area of ground *now Abd.*

pot hole 1 a small depression in a field which is difficult to drain. **2** a puddle-hole.

powk a hole or hollow in the ground, *usu* water-logged or marshy *now Mry Per.*

†**sea sleech** mud formed by a tidal river or estuary.

slabber mud; muddy, trampled soil *now Abd Kcdn.* ~**y** *of roads* waterlogged, muddy *WC.*

slaiger, slagger 1 bedaub with mud etc *local Cai-S.* **2** walk messily in mud etc *now Pbls WC.*

slaistery wet and dirty, muddy, slimy.

slatch a wet and muddy place *S.*

sleek, slike *now Fif,* **sleech** an alluvial deposit of mud or sludge left behind by the sea or a river, silt *now Ags Fif Kcb.*

sludder something wet and slimy, mud, filth.

slumpy marshy, muddy.

slunk a wet and muddy hollow, a soft, deep, wet rut in a road, a ditch *now Wgt.* ~**y** *of roads* muddy, rutted, full of wet holes *Uls.*

spark *n* a splash or spot of mud etc *now NE. v* spatter with liquid or mud; spot with mud etc *now Sh Ork NE.*

slutch sludge.

5.1.8 ROCKS, SOIL

Includes turf, but see also 7.15.

blaes, †**blae** a bluish-grey hardened clay, soft slate or shale. ~**-beds** layers of **blaes** *now Fif.* **blaes and balls: blaes** with ironstone nodules embedded *now Fif.* **cashy blaes** soft coaly **blaes** *now Fif.*

boolder a boulder.

breese crushed rock, *esp* sandstone or limestone *Ayr.*

brie-stone sandstone *now Loth Lnk.*

cairn a pyramid of loose stones.

†**cam (stane)** limestone.

cauk, †**calk** *n* chalk, lime.

caul(d), cold *of land* stiff, clayey.

chad gravel *now NE.*

channel, channer shingle, gravel *local Abd-Lnk.*

chingle *chf Bnf Abd,* **jingle** *now Gall Uls* shingle. **chingly** gravelly, pebbly *Ork Bnf Abd.*

chuck, chuckie (stane) a pebble.

cley clay.

clinkers broken pieces of rock *now Cai Kcb.*

†**clinty** stony, rocky.

coom peat-dust, fine turf mould *SW, S.*

†**craig, crag** rock as a material. ~ **stane** a detached rock; a large stone.

Crawfordjohn a dark granite, used to make curling stones.

creep *of rocks etc* move slowly, gradually.

†**delf** what is removed by digging; a sod.

divot 1 a turf, sod; a piece of turf thinner than a **fail. 2** †turf; turf in thin pieces.

dowie stane name for one of the large granite stones deposited in the ice-age *Dmf.*

dyke a vein of igneous rock in a vertical fissure in the earth's strata; now in general use as a geological term.

ebb *of the ground, esp in ploughing or mining* shallow, lacking in depth, scant.

elf-cup a small stone 'perforated by friction at a waterfall' *now Rox.*

erd earth.

faik(s) *mining and quarrying* layers of shaly sandstone or limestone.

fail a piece of turf, a sod *now chf N.*

fa(ll) *of limestone or clay* diminish in bulk, crumble, fall to pieces *now Sh Arg.*

flag a piece of turf cut or pared from the surface, a sod.

frush *of soil* crumbly, loose *now local Ork-Dmf.*

glidders small stones, **scree** *chf Rox.*

graivel gravel *now Ags.*

gray stane a grey volcanic rock, *usu* a boulder or monolith used as a landmark or boundary stone *now in place-names.*

grool gritty material, gravel, dusty refuse, coaldust *SW.*

grummel rubbish, *chf* of loose earth and stones, rubble; mud, sediment *now Cai Ayr Uls.*

grush grit, fine gravel *now Pbls Dmf.*

†**hair** *of ground, rocks or stones* grey(ish). ~**stane** a large, grey, moss-covered stone, *specif* a conspicuously-fixed stone or stones used as a boundary mark *now Abd.*

haithen a lump of gneiss etc, a glacial boulder *NE.*

haw clay a kind of clay, formerly used for whitening doorsteps etc, *usu* a tough, clammy, pale-blue clay *now S.*

hirst †a bank of sand or shingle in a harbour, river etc; a ford. **hi(r)stie, hirs(al)ly** dry and stony, barren *now Per Fif midLoth.*

horse heid a large, unbroken lump of earth, a clod *now Abd Ags.*

†**hove** *of light loose soil* rise, puff up.

kingle, kennel a kind of very hard sandstone *now Fif.*

knab(lick) a boulder *NE.*

knibloch a small rounded stone, a hard clod of earth.

†**lame** *verse* loam, earth.

lan(d) stane a loose stone in the soil turned up in digging or ploughing *now Ork SW.*

lapper *of soil* dry out in a caked or lumpy state *Bnf Abd.*

leck a flat stone or slab *NE Kcb, freq in Abd place-names.* †~ **(stane)** a kind of igneous rock which breaks into flat slabs *EC.*

leckerstane a conspicuous stone or stone-heap, *traditionally* associated with burials *chf NE-nEC, now in place-names.*

lime stane limestone.

liver rock a kind of sandstone.

†**maber** marble.

†**marble** marl, a kind of soil *Abd.* **marblie** *of soil* marly *Abd.*

mealie friable *local.*

Moray coast a hard subsoil such as is found along the coast of the Moray Firth *Ross Mry.*

moss ground soil, turf or peat from a bog.

mowrie gravel mingled with sand, shingle *Mry.*

muild, mool, mou(l)d mould, earth etc. ~**s** soil broken up in the process of cultivation, loose soil, lumps of earth. ~**ie 1** crumbled, finely broken up *now Ork Sh.* **2** earthy, deep in the soil *local Sh-SW.*

muir, moor: ~**s** peaty soil; a layer of peat *now Sh Ork.* ~**band** a hard subsoil of sand and clay with embedded stone, impervious to water *now Fif Rox.* ~**stone** the stone from outcrop rock on moorland, *freq* granite *now Bnf.*

neb a projecting tip or point of a piece of rock *local.*

†**outliers** stones found loose above ground, not quarried.

pan †*n* a hard stratum lying below the soil which is impervious to moisture. *v* form into a **pan**, become impervious to rain.

peasie whin a type of stone, *usu* granite, with a marled granular surface *chf Bnf Abd Kcdn.*

peat, pate peat. ~**y** of or like peat; peat-stained.

peeble a pebble *now NE Slk.*

†**ploud** a green sod, a thick piece of turf.

post a thick layer or seam of (particularly hard) stone, *usu* sandstone or limestone *now Fif.* ~**stone** a very hard, fine-grained sandstone *Fif.*

†**puddock-stane** a toadstone.

†**ratchell** a hard stony crust under the soil, a gravelly **till.**

reuch, rough: ~ **stane** a natural boulder *local Per-Gall.*

49

ring *of frosty ground* make a ringing sound under impact or friction *local NE-S.*

rocklie pebbly *local EC, SW.*

rotten *of rock* crumbling.

rummlie *of soil* rough and stony; *hence* loose and crumbly *NE Ayr Wgt.*

†**rum(s)** an inferior bituminous shale; a bend or dislocation in a stratum.

†**sad** *of soil* become dense or solid. ~**dit**, ~**den** *of earth etc* beaten hard, hard-packed *now local Kcdn-Lnk.*

†**sade** (a) turf, (a) sod.

sannie sandy.

scailie slate.

†**scarnach** heaps of loose stones on hillsides, **scree**, detritus.

scaup, scalp a thin shallow soil. †**scappy** *of soil* thin and shallow.

s(c)late slate. ~ **band** a kind of schist *now Fif Lnk.* **sclate stane** *freq in proverbs and similes concerning money* a piece of slate or slate-like stone.

sclenters loose stones, **scree**, a stony hillside.

scraw a thin turf or sod.

scree a mass of loose stones on a steep hillside.

scriddan rocks and gravel brought down by a mountain stream or torrent.

scurdie a kind of whinstone or basalt, *specif* that intrusive into old red sandstone *now Ags.*

shairp, sharp *of soil* containing sand and grit, gravelly, open and loose.

sile soil.

sitfast *n* a stone deeply and firmly embedded in the earth *now Cai Wgt.* †*adj, of a stone* earth-fast.

slabber muddy, trampled soil *now Abd Kcdn.*

soad a sod.

†**soilzie** soil; land.

sole the sub-soil; the under-surface of land.

spoutie *of soil* full of springs, marshy, undrained *now NE nEC.* † ~**iness** a soggy condition (of soil).

stane stone.

stanners shingle *also in place-names.* †**stan(n)ery** stony, gravelly.

swirlie knobby, with an uneven grain *now Sh Cai Abd.*

†**sykie** full of sluggish rivulets, soft, boggy, though dry in summer.

†**table stone** a flat stone.

till a stiff, *usu* impervious, clay, found in glacial deposits and forming a poor sub-soil; now adopted in Eng as a geological term. † ~**ie** composed of **till**. † ~**ie clay** cold, stiff, unproductive soil.

tirr the layer of turf, soil etc removed from the rock of a quarry *local N-Rox.*

travel, traivel: ~**led** *of soil, stones etc* deposited (by natural or human agency) at some distance from the original site; now also Eng geological term.

trouble, tribble *now NE nEC Slk* a break or intrusion in strata; a fault *now C.*

upthrow an upward dislocation of a stratum or seam *now Fif Loth Ayr.*

ure 1 ore. 2 clay containing iron, barren ferruginous soil, red gravelly earth *now Sh.*

†**water sand** freshwater sand as opposed to sand at the sea.

whin 1 also **whinstone** now in StEng as a geological term, †**whin rock** one of several hard crystalline igneous rocks, *eg* basalt, flint or diorite. 2 also **whinstone**, †**whin rock** a piece of **whin**, a boulder, slab or stone *local C.* ~ **boul** a hard nodule of **whin** embedded in sandstone *Ags.* ~ **dust: whinstone** dust or small rubble *EC-Wgt.* **whin-float** an intrusion or surface overflow of igneous rock.

yird, yirth 1 earth. 2 a heap of large boulders forming a den or small cave *Gall.* ~ **fast** *adj* fixed in the ground, earth-fast *now NE Rox.* *n* a stone firmly embedded in the earth *now Mry Bnf.*

†**yolk, yowk** a hard nodule in a softer rock etc.

5.1.9 MINERALS, GEMS

†**beriall** beryl, the precious stone; fine crystal.

†**capper** copper.

†**capprois** copperas, green iron-sulphate crystals.

†**cathead** an inferior kind of ironstone *chf Lnk.*

†**corneill** a cornelian.

cow-lady-stane a variety of quartz *S.*

diamond, †**diamant** diamond.

doggar a kind of coarse ironstone *usu* found in globular concretions; one of these concretions *now Edb.*

†**gum** a clump of ore.

iron, airn: ~ **eer** ferric oxide, rust, *esp* when found as a deposit in soil or water *N.*

jeet jet.

†**jesp** jasper.

jowel a jewel.

lammer, lamber amber.

leid lead.

lunkart a large mass or nodule of one mineral in the layers of another.

†**mercure** mercury.

metal 1 †metallic ore. **2** the geological strata in which minerals occur *now Fif*.

†**sardiane** sardine, a precious stone.

†**sardonice** sardonyx.

saut salt.

s(c)late diamond popular name for iron-pyrite crystals *now Bwk WC*.

Scots pebble, pebble, †**peeble,** a semi-precious stone, *usu* agate or rock-crystal, found in large numbers in streams and rocks, *freq* set in silver, making a distinctively Scottish type of jewellery.

sheep: ~ie's silver *N,* **~ siller** *now WC* white mica, *esp* in small scales.

shells underground quicklime *now local Bnf-Ayr*.

siller silver.

†**spark, sperk** a small diamond, ruby etc.

†**succine** amber.

uilie, eelie oil.

†**ulie peter** rock oil, petroleum.

†**utterfine** *of metals* superfine.

wad black lead, graphite; *hence* a mine of black lead *now Kcb Dmf*.

5.2 WEATHER, LIGHT, COLOUR

5.2.1 GENERAL WEATHER STATES

For temperature in general see 5.2.6.

aheat in(to) a hot or warm condition.

airish cool, chilly.

bask *of weather* dry, withering.

birsle 1 scorch. 2 broil; toast; warm thoroughly. **birsling** scorching.

bladdy unsettled *now Cai Abd*.

blue, bew *NE, WC* a very cold or frosty day *now Abd*.

brak, break cause a change in (the weather) *now Cai*.

brattle a spell of bad weather *now Bnf*.

braw fine, pleasant.

bruckle unsettled *now Bnf Abd*.

caller *adj, of air* cool, fresh, refreshing. *v* freshen, cool *chf NE.* **as ~ as a kail-blade** very cool and fresh *now NE*.

canker gusty, threatening, stormy *now Bnf Abd*.

cast up *of the weather, sky* clear up *now Ags*.

cauld, cold: ~rif(e) cold, causing cold. **~ gab** a period of stormy weather at the beginning of May *Abd Fif.* **the cauld kalends** *(Mry Abd) or* **calendars** *(NE Ags)* the cold spell which often occurs at the beginnings of the spring months, *esp* March or May.

chilpy chilly *Bnf Abd*.

claggy, cleggy *Sh Uls* producing heavy sticky soil.

clam sticky, damp, clammy *now Bnf Rox*.

coo('s) quake a short spell of bad weather in May *now Abd Fif*.

coorse, coarse foul, stormy.

cuil cool.

daak a lull in wet or windy weather *Cai Bnf*.

deid, dead: in the ~ thraw between hot and cold *now Abd Ags*.

dour bleak, gloomy *now Fif Kcb*.

draw to rain be likely to rain.

dreich dreary, bleak.

drouth, droucht drought, prolonged or extreme dry weather; drying breezy weather. **drouthy** dry.

drumlie cloudy, gloomy.

dry: ~achty *of the weather* inclined to be dry *Bnf Abd.* **~ time** a spell of dry weather *Bnf Abd*.

enterin(g) suitable for work, *esp* **~ morning**.

fair clear **(up)**, become fine.

fell severe, inclement *now Abd Fif Bwk*.

flench, flinch be unreliable, give a deceitful promise of improvement, *chf* **a flinchin Friday** *now Bnf*.

flichter: ~some *now Bnf,* **~y** *now Ags* changeable, full of whims.

forcie warm and dry, favourable for crops *NE*.

fordersome, furthersome fine, favourable for work *now Uls*.

fresh *adj* not frosty, open, thawing. *n* (the setting in of) a thaw, a period of open weather *local*.

fuilteach(s) *in contexts describing weather* a period at least partly in February, of varying date and duration *now Abd*.

glorgie sultry, close *Ayr*.

†**goesomer** a spell of mild weather in late autumn, an Indian summer.

gowany, gowan-gabbit (deceptively) bright or fine.

growthie warm and moist, promoting growth.

harden (up) clear up, become settled after rain.

heavy-heartit lowering, threatening rain *now Kinr*.

immis, eemis uncertain, gloomy, likely to rain etc *chf NE*.

keep up stay fine.

lambing-storm a period of severe weather, *usu* about lambing-time in March *N*.

Lammas: ~ flude(s), †**~ spate** a flood caused by a period of heavy rain about **Lammas**.

leesome fine, balmy, mild and bright *NE*.

lithesome gentle.

lock *of weather, snow, mist etc* make (a place) impassable or impenetrable *now Ags*.

loury *of the sky* dull, overcast, threatening rain *now local*.

lown *adj* calm, still *now local Fif-Uls*. *n* calm, unclouded weather.

lowse, loose *of the weather* unsettled *Sh-Cai Gall*.

lunk *local*, **lunkie** *of weather* close, sultry.

mak threaten rain etc *Kcdn Kcb*. ~ **for** *Ork Abd Ags*, ~ **up for** show signs of, 'look like' (snow etc).

†**malagrugrous** grim, forbidding; gloomy, melancholy.

maumie soft, mild.

†**mese** pacify, make calm (the elements, weather etc).

moch a warm moist atmosphere, close misty weather *Abd Ags Gall*. ~**ie, muchtie** *NE* humid; misty and oppressive, muggy *NE-SW*.

mougre hang gloomily, cast a shadow *Arg*.

muith *adj, also* ~**y** oppressively close and humid *now Ork Edb Ayr*. ~**ness** an oppressively hot and moist atmosphere.

oam a warm stuffy atmosphere *Sh NE*.

oorie dull and chilly, raw. **oorlich** damp, raw, bleak *N*.

owercast overcast.

owergaff become overcast after a clear morning *S*.

pet (day) a day of sunshine in the middle of a spell of bad weather *local C-S*.

rack up *of weather* clear *now local Per-Rox*.

rees(t)le, reeshle a spell of bad weather, *esp* windy weather at harvest-time *Cai*.

roukie muggy *now local Cai-S*.

saft, soft mild, not frosty.

shill *adj* chill.

sicker harsh, rigorous *now Ork*.

smochy *of the air* close, sultry, stifling *now Fif*.

†**smolt, smout** fine, fair, calm.

smore a thick, close, stifling atmosphere full of snow, fine rain, dust etc.

smuchter, smucht *Bnf Abd* a thick stuffy atmosphere *NE*.

smuchty smoky, fuggy; misty, close *Bnf Abd*.

snell biting, bitter, severe.

†**snippin** nipping, biting cold.

sour cold and wet, inclement *now local NE-Lnk*.

starrach cold, bleak, disagreeable *Cai*.

stervation bitter cold.

stife a suffocating atmosphere *now S*. **stifin** stifling *now Lnk Ayr*,

†**stith** hard, severe.

sweltry oppressively hot, sweltering, sultry *Sh Ork NE, C*.

swither *v* be very hot, swelter *now Sh Kcdn*. *n* a swelter, a great heat *now Sh*.

teuchit('s) storm a period of bleak wintry weather in March (when the **teuchits** arrive and begin to nest), the date varying in different districts and seasons *NE, nEC*.

thin *of wind, weather* cold, bitter, piercing *Gen except Sh Ork*.

†**thirling** *of weather* piercing cold, bitter *N*.

thrawn *of the weather* disagreeable, inclement *now NE*.

tooterie *of weather* changeable, and so preventing steady outdoor work *NE*.

track a spell of weather *local Sh-WC*.

upslaag *Sh*, **upslay** *Abd Kcdn*, **upsilly** *Abd Kcdn* a change in weather, *esp* from hard frost to milder conditions, *eg* rain and a south wind.

†**variabil** *of weather, seasons etc* changeable.

veecious, vicious *of weather* severe, inclement.

wear to *of weather* turn to, show signs of changing to *now NE*.

weather, wather, wedder 1 weather. **2** *specif* weather suitable for a particular purpose, favourable or seasonable weather *now NE*. ~ **gaw** a bright calm spell between two periods of bad weather thought to forewarn of snow *now NE*.

wersh *Gen except Sh Ork*, †**warsh** *of weather* raw, cold and damp.

yowe, ewe: ~**(s) trummle** a cold spell in early summer, about the time of sheep-shearing *now nEC, S*.

5.2.2 WIND, STORM

Includes squalls of wind and rain; choppy seas.

attery stormy, bitter.

bensell violence (of a storm).

†**bewave** toss about; blow or sweep away.

blashy rainy, wet, gusty.

blaud *v, of storms* buffet, beat *now Ags*. *n* a blast of wind *now Ags*.

blaw *v* blow. *n* a blow, a blast, gust *now Abd*.

bleester, †**blaster** *v, of wind* blow in gusts *Bnf Arg*. *n* a blast of wind *now Bnf Arg*. **blastie** gusty, boisterous *now Bnf Abd*.

blinter, blenter a boisterous gusty wind.

blirt a gust of wind with rain *now Bnf.*

blouster *now Bnf*, **bloster** *now Ayr Kcb* a violent wind with squalls.

blout a sudden burst *now Ayr*. ~**er** a blast of wind *now Abd.*

blowder a sudden gust of wind *NE.*

bluffert a squall (of wind and rain) *NE Ags Ayr.*

bowder a heavy squall, a storm of wind and rain *now Abd Kcb.*

brak the breaking up of a storm *now Abd Ags Fif.*

brash a sudden gust of wind *now local Bnf-wLoth.* ~**y** stormy, wet and windy *now Stlg.*

brattle a sudden blast of wind and rain *now Bnf.*

†**bub** a blast, sudden squall.

buff *of a storm* beat down, flatten (grain) *NE.*

canker gusty, threatening, stormy *now Bnf Abd.*

†**contrary** *of the wind* be contrary.

dad blow in gusts, drive *now local Sh-Bwk.*

daidle *v* buffet *Abd.*

ding, *freq* ~ **on**, **down** descend with great force *now Bnf-Fif.*

doister a stormy wind blowing in from the sea *now Bnf Abd Ayr.*

driffle a gale, a strong wind *now Bnf Abd.*

easter *n* the east wind *chf NE. v* shift towards the east *Sh NE.*

feeding storm *etc* a storm etc which adds more snow to that already lying *now local NE-Gall.*

flaff *v* blow in gusts *now Sh Ags Fif. n* a gust or puff (of wind).

†**flag** a blast or gust.

flan *n* **1** †a blast, storm. **2** a gust of wind, *chf* one blowing smoke down a chimney, a back-draught *now Sh Ork N.* **3** a sudden squall of wind blowing from high land over the sea *Sh Fif Arg. v* blow in sudden gusts *Sh Ork N Fif.* **flannie** squally *Sh Fif Ags.*

flaw a gust or squall of wind, *chf* one bringing rain.

fleg dispel, drive away (stormy weather etc) *now NE Ags.*

flocht a sudden gust of wind *now Abd.*

forester: the muckle ~ the wind *Mry Bnf.*

fuff *v* puff, blow gently. *n* a puff, a gentle gust (of wind), a whiff *now local Sh-Kcb.*

gab: the ~ **o May** stormy weather at the beginning of May *N Kcb.*

gandiegow a squall, heavy shower *Sh Ags Bwk.*

gell *n* a gale. †*adj, of the wind* brisk, keen.

†**gird** *chf literary* a gust, blast.

gliff, glaff, glouf a whiff, puff, breath of air; a gust, blast of hot or cold air *now local Abd-S.*

gouster: ~**ous** dark and stormy *now Dmf.* ~**y** wet and windy, blustery *now Sh Gall Dmf.*

gowk('s) storm a brief storm, a spring storm coinciding with the arrival of the cuckoo *now local NE-S.*

gowl †*v* howl, gust noisily. *n* a howling gust of wind. *now Sh.* ~**ie** windy *Rox.*

gowst a gust.

gowstie wild, stormy; eerie.

†**grashloch** stormy, boisterous, blustering.

gray a light wind, gentle breeze *now Fif midLoth.*

grumlie unsettled, blustery *now NE.*

guff a puff, current of air *now local.*

gurl *v* roar, howl *now midLoth Bwk Ayr. adj* cold, stormy, wild. *n* a gale, a squall. ~**ie** stormy, threatening, bitter *now local.*

haar a cold easterly wind *chf E.* ~**y** cold, piercing *Sh midLoth.*

hard dry *now NE Kcb.*

hash a strong wind, *esp* one accompanied by rain *now Sh Fif Kinr.* ~**ie** wet and/or windy, stormy *now Fif midLoth Kcb.*

hearken blow gently.

hill-clap a rumbling noise in the upper air over hills, said to be caused by an air current *chf Sh.*

hoo howl.

howder a blast of wind, a blustering wind *NE.*

hurl a violent rush forwards or downwards *now local Sh-midLoth.*

hushle *n* a strong, drying, gusty wind *Sh Ork Wgt. v* blow in gusts, blow through (sheaves etc) *Sh-Cai Uls.*

ill stormy *now local.*

jabble *v, of the sea* become choppy *local. n* a choppy area of water or of the sea.

jachelt tossed, buffeted by the wind *now Ayr.*

jaup the splashing of the sea, a breaker, the surf, a choppy sea *Sh Ork SW Uls.*

kav *Sh*, **kaif** *NE of a stormy sea* foam in breaking, throw up a spray *Sh NE.*

†**kene** cruel, violent, terrible.

kittle (up) freshen, blow more strongly and gustily *now NE.*

lambing-storm a period of severe weather, *usu* about lambing-time in March *N.*

lay flatten (crops) by wind or rain.

lough *of the wind* die down *now Ags.*

lowden *esp of the wind* diminish in intensity.

lown *adj, of the wind* lowered, calm *now Loth S. adv, of wind* quietly, gently, moderately. *v* **1** give shelter from the wind, screen. **2** *of the wind, stormy weather etc* moderate, calm, die down *now Fif Loth Kcb.*

†**mask** *of a storm etc* threaten, brew up.

nizzin a buffeting by the weather *NE.*

oam a gust of hot air *Sh NE.*

outerly blowing offshore *now Sh.*

owerset overwhelmed, beaten down (by hostile natural forces, *eg* a storm).

peuch a light blast of air, a puff of wind or breath *now Sh Abd.*

pew *n* a puff or breath of wind etc *SW. v* puff out, rise through the air *now Kcb.*

piner (wind), sea piner a strong north or northeast wind that dies away by degrees *NE.*

†pipe make a low moaning sound; blow gently and softly.

pirl *v* swirl, eddy, ripple *now NE, Uls. n* an eddy or swirl, a ripple, gentle breeze *now NE Rox.*

pirr a sudden sharp breeze; a gentle breath of wind.

quall abate, calm down *now Abd.*

quate, quiet windless, still, calm.

†queat sheltered from the wind.

rack *n* 1 †a rush (of wind). 2 driving mist or fog *now local Mry midLoth. †v, of clouds* fly before the wind, clear away. **~ing** *of clouds* flying before the wind; *of wind* driving *now Per Slk.*

raff a short sharp shower, accompanied by gusts of wind *now Abd.*

ragglish uncertain, gusty with rain *NE.*

rees(t)le, reeshle *v, of wind etc* whistle *now local. n* a spell of bad weather, *esp* windy weather at harvest-time *Cai.*

reevin high, gusty.

reeze †blow strongly. **reezie** windy, blowy; gusty *EC.*

rive blow violently, *chf* **riving wind, a riving storm** *now Sh N.*

roil a storm, a heavy sea *Arg.* **ralliach** choppy, stormy *Arg.*

rout *of the sea, winds, thunder etc* roar, rumble, make a loud noise.

rowsty windy, blustery *Ags Fif.*

†rowt roar loudly.

royet, †troyd wild, stormy, variable *NE.*

rumballiach tempestuous, stormy. *S.*

sab, sob the noise made by a gust of wind or by the rise and fall of the sea.

sair, sore severe, stormy.

saur, savour a slight wind, gentle breeze *Arg Ayr.*

scour a shower of rain, *esp* intermittent with gusts of wind *now local Cai-Ayr.* **~y** blustery with rain, wet and squally *now local NE-Dmf.*

scow, scrow *now NE Ags Per* a sudden, heavy, squally shower of rain.

scudder *n* a driving shower of rain or snow *Bnf Abd. v, of wind etc* sweep along in rainy gusts *now Bnf Abd.* **scuddrie** with cold driving showers *now Bnf Abd.*

†shake-wind a strong blustery wind which shakes off ripe ears of corn.

†sit down *of the wind* become calm, moderate.

skail a strong, scattering or driving storm-wind. **~wind** a scattering wind, hurricane.

skelp a blast of wind, squall, downpour of rain.

skiff a slight gust of wind *now local.*

skirl *v, of the wind* blow with a shrill noise, whistle. *n* the high-pitched sound of a strong wind; the wind itself, gusty weather.

sklent *of wind or rain* a slanting motion.

sma(ll) a period of calm at sea, a lull.

smelt, smilt a calm patch on the sea.

snell *of winds, adj* biting, severe. *adv* keenly, piercingly, with a nip.

†sniffler a strong gusty wind.

snifter *v, of wind* blow in strong gusts *now Sh. n* a strong blast, gust, flurry (of wind, sleet etc) *now local Sh-Loth.*

snirly a gusty biting wind *Sh SW.*

snore make a rushing, whirring, droning sound *now local Sh-Kcb.*

soo breathe, murmur, sigh *now Sh.*

souch, sough, seuch *n* the sound of the wind, *esp* when long-drawn-out. *v, of wind* make a rushing, moaning, murmuring sound.

sowff murmur softly; *of a breeze* puff gently.

spindrift, spunedrift *Sh NE* 1 spray whipped up by gusts of wind and driven across the tops of waves. 2 snow blown up from the ground in swirls by gusts of wind, driving snow *chf NE.*

spleiter a wind-driven shower of rain, snow etc *now Bnf Abd.*

†stalwart *of a storm* violent.

stark violent, rough *now Ork.*

†stench *of storm* come to an end.

storm: † **~y** associated with or indicating storms. **~-stayed** *or* **-stead** held up on a journey by bad weather.

stour a storm, wild weather; a blizzard *now Sh Ork.*

sweevil a gust of wind, a short, sharp gale *now Sh Ork.*

swey, swee a veering of wind.

swirl, sworl a whirling movement of water etc, an eddy, whirlpool.

swither *v* rush, swirl, move with haste and flurry *now Sh. n* a rushing movement, swirl, flurry *now Sh.*

swoof make a rustling, swishing sound, as the wind etc *now Sh.*

tak, take: **~ up** *of wind* rise, begin to blow *Sh SW.*

tattery very windy *Lnk S.*

tear, teir *now NE of wind* blow hard, sweep along in violent gusts, rage *now local Sh-Lnk.*

teuch, tough *of weather* rough, wet and windy *now Sh Cai.*

thin *of wind, weather* cold, bitter, piercing *Gen except Sh Ork.*

thow, thaw: thow wind a wind bringing a thaw *now Cai Per WC, SW.* **dry ~** a thaw after a high wind *local Sh-Wgt.* **weet ~** a thaw unaccompanied by wind or rain *NE, C.*

thud, tud *Sh Ork v, also* †**thudder** *of wind* come in noisy blasts, bluster *now Sh. n* a (noisy) blast of wind, a sudden squall, gust *now Sh Ork.* †**thuddert** a tempest.

†**tift, tiff** a sudden breeze, gust of wind.

tirl a breeze *now NE.*

touk *of the wind* blow in gusts.

tousie *of wind* blustery, boisterous *now Stlg Ayr.*

†**ventulacioun** a motion of the air, a current of air.

waff, wauff *v, of wind etc* blow, waft *chf C. n* a puff, blast (of air etc) *now Sh-C.*

†**wair** ? wild, stormy.

wap, whap a puff or gust of wind *now Sh Abd.*

wast, west *of the wind* veer or back to the west *now Ork Stlg Loth.* **~land** *of the wind* westerly, blowing from the west *now Stlg Fif Ayr.*

weather, wather, wedder †wet stormy weather, rain or snow with blustery winds, rain. **w(e)atherfu** stormy, wet and windy.

wheefle whiffle, blow lightly, shift about *now Lnk Ayr.*

wheeple *of the wind* whistle shrilly *now Ags Per WC.*

whid *n* a squall, (sudden) gust of wind *now Sh Ork. v, of or like wind* sweep in gusts *now Sh Ork.*

whidder *now Sh,* **whither, whudder** *v, of the wind* bluster, blow fiercely in gusts *now Sh. n* a sudden or loud gust of wind; a whirlwind *now Sh.*

whiff, whuff, wheef 1 whiff. 2 drive or carry by blowing.

whip, whup a swirl, gust. **eddy fup** a wind whipping round a corner *NE.*

wind, win, wun *now WC* wind. **~y** windy. **wincasten** blown down by the wind *Sh NE, WC.*

†**wuid, wood, wud(d)** *of wind etc* furious, raging.

5.2.3 RAIN, MIST, SNOW, FROST

Includes rainstorms, but see also 5.2.2.

Banff bailies large white snowy clouds rising along the horizon, regarded as a sign of bad weather *NE.*

barber a freezing coastal mist in calm frosty weather *now Bnf Kcdn.*

bauch *of ice* affected by thaw; not slippery.

bicker *of rain* pelt, patter *now Abd.*

black weet rain *now Ork.*

blash *n* a heavy or drenching shower of rain etc. *v, esp of rain, sleet, snow* batter (against a person or thing) *now Bnf.* **~y** rainy, wet, gusty.

blatter *v, freq of rain, hail etc* rattle, beat with violence. *n* a storm of rain, hail etc *now local Bnf-Ayr.*

blaud *v* buffet, beat *now Ags. n* a downpour of rain *now Ags.*

bleeter rain *now Abd.* **bleatery** cold, raw, showery *Abd.*

blin(d) *of mist etc* dense *now Bnf Abd.* **blin drift** drifting snow.

blout a sudden burst *now Ayr.*

bobantilter an icicle *Cai.*

bore, chf blue ~ *now Bnf Abd,* **borie** *now Abd* an opening in the clouds showing blue sky.

brak, break 1 a fall of snow or rain; a layer or deposit of snow *S.* 2 the breaking up of a storm, frost, ice etc *now Abd Ags Fif.*

brash a sudden burst of rain *now local Bnf-wLoth.*

broo liquid or moisture of any kind, *esp* **snow ~** *now Ags Lnk.*

bullet stane a hailstone *now Bnf.*

cairry, carry the motion of the clouds. **cairries, carries** the clouds in motion.

cast up *of storm-clouds* gather *now Bnf Abd Fif.*

cat's hair cirrus or cirrostratus cloud *Bnf Abd.*

clag a lump or mass of snow etc *now local NE-C.*

clash *n* a downpour. *v, of rain* fall with a crash or splash.

close weather a heavy snowfall *now Abd.*

clud, cloud cloud. †**clud of nicht** darkness of night. †**under ~ of nicht** under cover of darkness.

come a thaw; moisture in the air *Lnk-S.*

cranreuch hoar-frost.

dad blow in gusts, drive *now local Sh-Bwk.*

dag *n* 1 a thin drizzling rain. 2 a heavy shower (of rain) *now Cai Bnf Abd.* †*v* rain gently, drizzle. **daggy** drizzling, moist, misty *now Abd.*

dash: a ~ of rain etc a sudden fall of rain *now Bnf Abd Lnk.*

dawk, †daugh †drizzle. **~ie** drizzly *now Fif.*

†**defund** pour down.

deval *freq of rain or snow* stop, ease *now Gen except Sh Ork.*

dew, deow *NE n* dew. *v* rain gently, drizzle *now Bnf Abd.*

ding, *freq* **~ on, down** descend with great force, fall heavily and continuously *now Bnf-Fif.*

55

dish (on) rain heavily, pour with rain *now Abd*.

†dissle a slight shower, a drizzle.

dooncome a heavy fall of snow or rain *local Bnf-Kcb*.

drabble *of rain* drizzle *Abd Ags*. **drabbly, drab-blichy** showery, drizzly *Bnf Abd*.

drackie damp, wet, misty *chf W*.

drap, drop stop (raining) *Bnf Abd Fif*. **dropping** showery *now local Cai-Fif*. ~**py** showery, drizzly *Bnf Abd*.

dreep a steady fall of light rain *Abd Fif*. ~**in droucht** a showery day during a spell of dry weather *Abd Ags*.

dribble *v* drizzle *local*. *n* a drizzle *now Bnf Abd Fif*.

driffle *v* drizzle, rain or snow lightly *now Gall Rox*. *n* a slight shower of rain or snow *now Dmf*.

drift falling snow driven by the wind. ~**y** snowy.

drow *n* a cold, wet mist, a drizzle *now Bwk Rox*. *v* drizzle *now Bwk Rox*. ~**ie** misty, drizzling, damp. **Liddisdale** ~ a wetting drizzle *Rox*.

drumlie cloudy, gloomy.

dry drift powdery snow *now Abd Ags Fif*.

eident *of rain* continuous, persistent *latterly NE*.

evendoon *esp of very heavy and continuous rain* straight, perpendicular.

feechie rainy, puddly *Kcdn Ags Per*.

feuchter a slight fall of snow.

flag *n* a large snowflake *N*. *v, of snow* fall in large flakes *Bnf Abd*.

flaucht *n* a flake, *chf* of snow *now Sh*. *v* fall in flakes, *chf* ~**in** a flake, fleck *now Ags Per*.

fleg: get a ~ *of snow* diminish appreciably *now Ork NE Ags*.

flicht a flake, a small speck of snow *now Bwk*. **flichan** a flake of snow *now local EC, SW*.

flichter a small particle or flake of snow *now Cai Fif*.

flim a haze, a mist rising from the ground.

freest frost *Abd*.

fresh *n* (the setting in of) a thaw *local*. *v* thaw *now NE Ags*.

frost ice *now local Sh-Fif*. **it is** ~ it is freezing, there is frost.

frozened frozen *Ork Ags Stlg Ayr*.

gait hair *now Rox Kcb*, **goat('s) hair** *Gen except Sh Ork* cirrus cloud.

garb a thin coating (of frost) *SW*.

glaister a thin covering of snow or ice *now SW*.

glotten thaw partially.

glushie *of snow* soft, slushy *now Fif*.

goor slush in running water *now Sh Bnf Abd*.

gray cover with a thin sprinkling of snow *Kcb Dmf*.

greetie inclined to rain, showery *now Mry Ags*.

grime, grim sprinkle, fleck, cover thinly, *esp* with snow, *freq* a griming of snow *now SW, Rox*.

grue the melting snow and ice found on rivers in early spring *now NE Ags S*.

gull a thin cold mist accompanied by a chilly breeze *NE*.

gum a mist, haze *now Cai NE Ags*.

haar a cold mist or fog, *esp* an east-coast sea fog *Gen except Gall*. ~**y** misty, foggy *now Sh Fif Rox*.

haar(-frost) hoar-frost *Cai S*.

hail watter *n* a downpour. *adv* torrentially.

hair 1 hoar **2** †frosty, cold.

hale run down, pour *now Sh midLoth*.

hardy frosty *now midLoth Wgt Kcb*.

ice: ~**-lowsing** a thaw *now Wgt*. ~**-tangle** *NE Ags Fif*, **eeshogel** *Per Bwk Dmf*, † ~**-schok(k)il**, ~**shoggle** an icicle.

jeel *n* extreme coldness, chill, frostiness. *v* freeze, congeal *N-SW*.

Lammas: ~ **flude(s)**, † ~ **spate** a flood caused by a period of heavy rain about **Lammas**.

lapper, lopper melting, slushy snow *SW, S*.

†lash a heavy fall of rain.

lauchin rain an (unexpectedly long) shower of rain from a clear sky *Ags Uls*.

glaur slippery ice; slipperiness.

lay flatten (crops) by wind or rain. ~ **on** *of rain or snow* fall heavily *now local*.

leap *of frost or snow* thaw.

leash *of rain* fall in torrents *Sh Ags*.

leck *of rain* fall in intermittent showers *now Ork Stlg Uls*.

lock *of weather, snow, mist etc* make (a place) impassable or impenetrable *now Ags*.

loom the indistinct appearance of something seen through a haze or at a great distance; a haze or fog *local*.

lowp *of frost* thaw, break *N*.

lowse, loose *of frost etc* thaw *now Sh*.

lying storm a fall of snow which lies long on the ground before melting *now NE Lnk*.

mak, make produce rain etc *Sh Cai*.

mizzle vanish, melt away *now Ags*.

mug *n* drizzling rain, *freq* with mist or fog *now Abd Ags*. *v, also* **muggle** drizzle, *esp* in misty weather *now Abd*. **muggy** drizzling, wet and misty *now Sh NE-Uls*.

nip-nebs Jack Frost.

oam a heat haze *Sh NE*.

onding *n, also* **oncome** *now local Ags-Uls*, **ondag** *NE*, **onfa** *local* a heavy fall of rain or snow. *v* rain or snow heavily.

†oother a light morning mist or haze; a heat haze *S*.

outpour a heavy fall of rain etc, a downpour *NE Ork.*

†owerblaw overblow, *esp* cover (with snow).

packman a type of cloud formation *local.*

pani rain *Rox, orig gipsy.*

peel rushich a heavy shower, downpour; a torrent *NE.*

pelsh a drenching shower of rain, a downpour *NE.*

pewl fall thinly, intermittently or in small amounts *Rox.*

pike: ding on, rain *etc* **auld wives** *or* **puir men an ~ staves (and the ~ ends neathmost)** pour with rain, rain cats and dogs *now NE Ags.*

pile a snowflake *WC.*

pirl *v* swirl, eddy *now NE, Uls. n* **1** an eddy or swirl *now NE Rox.* **2** a snowflake *local C, S.*

pish-oot a heavy downpour of rain, a **thunder-plump** *NE Kcb.*

planet a heavy localized shower of rain.

plash *n* a sudden sharp downpour of rain, a heavy shower. *v* fall in torrents, lash, pelt down *now local Sh-Lnk.* ~**y** rainy, showery.

plowt *v* pelt down *now Sh Abd Ags. n* heavy shower or cascade, a downpour of rain **thunder-plump** *now Sh NE nEC.*

plowtery wet, showery, rainy, puddly.

plump *v* fall heavily, pour, fall in sheets. *n, also* † ~ **shower** a heavy downpour of rain, a deluge, *freq* following thunder.

†plunge a heavy fall of water, a downpour of rain.

plype a sudden heavy shower of rain *now NE Ags.*

pour a heavy shower of rain, a downpour.

purse mou a boat-shaped cloud said to presage high wind *now Ags Per.*

rack *n* driving mist or fog *now local Mry midLoth.* †*v, of clouds* fly before the wind, clear away. ~**ing** *of clouds* flying before the wind; *of wind* driving *now Per Slk.*

rag, raggle *Abd* a wet mist, drizzle *Sh Ork Abd.*

†rair, roar *of cracking ice etc* make a resounding, cracking noise.

rap fall rapidly in a shower or in drops *now Sh Ork.*

rash *v, of rain* pour, come down in torrents *now Ork Cai. n* a sudden downpour of rain or hail.

rattlestane *children's rhyme* a hailstone *local NE-Kcb.*

reek mist, *esp* a morning mist rising from the ground *now Sh Abd.* ~**ie** misty, damp.

rime **1** hoar-frost. **2** a frosty haze or mist *now Sh Ork Ags.* **rimie** frosty.

rind hoar-frost *now Bwk Dmf.*

ringin(g) frost a hard, prolonged frost *local.*

rive *of cloud* break up, disperse *now Sh Fif Wgt.*

rone a strip or patch of ice on the ground; *specif* a children's slide *latterly NE.*

rouk mist, fog *now local.* ~**ie** misty, damp, drizzly *now local Cai-S.*

roup a dense mist *SW, S.*

saft, soft *adj* **1** in a state of thaw. **2** wet, rainy, damp. *n* a thaw; rain, moisture *local Ags-Ayr.* ~**en** thaw *now NE.*

sapple soak with rain *now local Stlg-Kcb.*

scam *v* **1** *of frost* scorch, blight (plants) *now N Per.* **2** cover with a film of moisture, a haze etc. *n* **1** a withering or scorching of plants by frost etc *N Per.* **2** a film of vapour, a haze etc.

s(c)lidder, sclither ice, an icy surface *NE Ags.*

scour a shower of rain, *esp* intermittent with gusts of wind *now local Cai-Ayr.* ~**y** blustery with rain, wet and squally *now local NE-Dmf.*

scowder, scouther *v* **1** *of frost or rain* wither, blight (foliage etc) *now local Per-Slk.* **2** rain or snow slightly *now Ork. n* a slight shower (of rain) *now local Ork-Ayr.* ~**y** beginning or threatening to rain or snow *now Lnk.*

scuff a slight passing shower of rain *now NE Loth SW.*

scullgab a cloud-formation thought to resemble a **scull** (shallow basket), indicating wind direction *Bnf Abd.*

scum a thin coating of ice *Cai Kcb.*

sea haar a sea fog *E.*

seepin *of rain* soaking *now NE.*

†shakers dewdrops.

†shell *of sheep or their wool* become caked with driven snow.

shockle, †scheckle, shuchle an icicle.

†shore threaten (rain or snow).

†shot a sheet (of ice).

shour a shower (of rain etc).

shud a large piece of loose ice etc in a river *chf S.*

simmer, summer: ~ **cowt(s)** a heat haze, the shimmering of the air on a hot day.

†skail *of rain etc* pour down.

skarrach a flying shower of rain; a light fall of snow *now Ags Fif.*

skelp *v* spatter, pelt *local Sh-Kcb. n* a blast of wind, squall, downpour of rain.

skiff *v* rain or snow very slightly. *n* a slight or flying shower of rain or snow, a light drizzle, a fleeting patch of wet mist. ~**in** a slight fall of snow. ~**le** a slight shower of rain *local NE-Rox.*

skift †*v, of rain or snow* fall lightly. *n, also* ~**er** *local Sh-Loth* a light shower of rain or snow. ~**in** a light fall or sprinkling of snow *local, NE-Lnk Rox.*

57

skimmer *Sh NE*, **shimmer** *local Per-Lnk* a light sprinkling, *esp* of snow or rain. ~**ing** a light sprinkling (of snow) *Sh NE Per*.

skippie *of roads etc* slippery, icy *Abd Per*.

skirl *now NE Ags Per*, **skirlie** a flurry (of snow or hail).

skirp *v* rain slightly, spit *chf NE*. *n* a slight shower or spot of rain *chf NE*.

skirvin a thin covering of snow etc *S*.

skite a short sharp shower of rain *now local Bnf-Wgt*.

sklent *of wind or rain* a slanting motion.

slipper a slippery state or condition; that which causes slipperiness, ice etc *now Bnf Abd*. **slippy** slippery.

slumpy *of ice* soft, unsafe.

smirr, smurr *n* a fine rain, drizzle, *freq* ~ **o rain,** *occas* sleet or snow *Gen except Sh Ork*. *v, of rain or snow* fall gently and softly in fine clouds, drizzle.

smizzle rain lightly and thinly, drizzle *SW Rox*.

smoch thick fog *Ags Fif Rox*.

smore *v* **1** cover thickly with snow etc. **2** *of snow etc* fall or come out in a dense stifling cloud; *of atmosphere* be thick with snow etc. *n* a thick, close, stifling atmosphere full of snow, fine rain, dust etc.

smuchter *v, of rain, snow etc* fall in a fine mist, drizzle down persistently *Bnf Abd*. *n* a thin light mist or rain *Mry-Kcdn*.

smuik, smook fine thick snow or rain *Ork Cai Bnf*.

smuir, smoor *v* bury, envelop in a dense covering of snow etc. *n* a thick atmosphere, a dense enveloping cloud of smoke, snow, rain, mist *now local Ork-Kcb*.

snaw, snow snow. ~ **bree** *now NE Dmf*, ~ **broo** *now Kcdn-S* melted snow or ice, *freq* that carried down in rivers, slush. ~ **wreath** a snowdrift *Gen except Sh Ork*.

snifter *v, of vapour etc* escape in clouds *now Sh*. *n* a strong blast, gust, flurry (of wind, sleet etc) *now local Sh-Loth*.

†**sop** a cloud (*of* mist).

sowp rain, wet weather.

spark, sperk *S n* a drop of water, a raindrop *now NE Ags*. *v* rain slightly; spit with rain *now Sh Ork NE*.

spate *n* **1** †heavy downpouring (of rain). **2** a torrential fall or heavy downpour (of rain). *v* rain heavily *now local*.

spindrift, spunedrift *Sh NE* snow blown up from the ground in swirls by gusts of wind, driving snow *chf NE*.

spitter *n* **1** a slight shower of rain or snow *now N*,

C. 2 ~**s** small drops of wind-driven rain or snow *now NE Ags Dmf*. *v, of rain or snow* fall in small drops or flakes, drizzle *now local N-C*.

spleiter a wind-driven shower of rain, snow etc *now Bnf Abd*.

spleuterie wet, rainy *NE Per Fif*.

stob an incomplete rainbow showing only the lower ends of the bow, believed to forewarn of a storm at sea *local E*.

storm *n* fallen snow, *esp* when lying on the ground in some quantity for a long time; a period of wintry weather with alternating frost and snow *now N Per*. †*v* block, cover (up) with snow or frost.

†**stove** a mist or vapour rising from the ground.

straik fill (a road etc) with snow up to its fences etc *now Cai*.

sump a sudden heavy fall of rain, a deluge *Gall S*.

sup a quantity, amount (of rain) *now local NE-Ayr*.

swirl, sworl a whirling movement of water etc, an eddy, whirlpool.

swither *v* rush, swirl, move with haste and flurry *now Sh*. *n* a rushing movement, swirl, flurry *now Sh*.

tak, take: ~ **the air** *or* **lift** *of frost* rise, disperse *now Sh Ork Cai*.

tangle an icicle *now local NE-Fif*.

teem *v, also* **tume** *local of rain* pour, come down in torrents *Gen except Sh Ork*. *n* a very heavy, long-lasting downpour of rain *now C, S*.

†**thicht** *of rain* heavy.

thickness a dense fog or sea-mist *local*.

thow, thaw thaw. **thow wind** a wind bringing a thaw *now Cai Per WC, SW*. **dirty** ~ a thaw brought on by rain *Sh NE Per Ayr*. **dry** ~ a thaw after a high wind *local Sh-Wgt*. **weet** ~ a thaw unaccompanied by wind or rain *NE, C*.

thunder-plump a sudden heavy thunder-shower.

tirl a flurry of snow etc *now NE*.

trashy *of weather* wet, dirty.

tuith, tooth a fragment of rainbow seen near the horizon, regarded as a sign of bad weather *NE*.

upbrak the beginning (of a thaw).

upcastin(g) a gathering of clouds, a cloud formation *now Sh NE*.

upple *chf of rain or snow, freq with* **deval** stop falling, clear *chf N*.

upslaag *Sh*, **upslay** *Abd Kcdn*, **upsilly** *Abd Kcdn* a change in weather, *esp* from hard frost to milder conditions, *eg* rain and a south wind.

ure **1** a damp mist; fine rain, drizzle. **2** an atmospheric haze, *esp* when radiated by sunbeams *now Loth*.

†**wa(c)k** *adj* moist, damp. *n, also* ~**nes** moisture.

waff, wauff a puff, flurry (of snow etc) *now Sh Abd.*

†**walk** a cloud, clouds.

watergaw an imperfect or fragmentary rainbow *now Sh nEC Gall.*

weather, wather, wedder †wet stormy weather, rain or snow with blustery winds, rain. **w(e)atherfu** stormy, wet and windy.

weet, wat *now C, S* rain, drizzle, dew. **weetie** wet, damp, rainy *now Sh NE, EC.*

wersh *Gen except Sh Ork,* †**warsh** *of weather* raw, cold and damp.

white shower a shower of snow *Sh NE.*

wreath, wride *n* a bank or drift of snow, *prob orig* an accumulation of swirls of snow *Gen except Sh Ork. v, of snow* accumulate into drifts; cover or bury *now SW.*

yird, yirth: ~ **drift** drifting snow *now NE.*

yowdendrift, †**ewin-drift** *chf literary* snow driven by the wind.

5.2.4 THUNDER AND LIGHTNING

brattle a peal of thunder.

dinnle *of thunder* peal, roll, drone.

fire-flaucht 1 lightning; flashes of lightning without the sound of thunder *local Sh-Per.* **2** a flash of lightning, a thunderbolt *now Fif.*

†**flaff** a flash (of lightning).

†**flag** a flash (of lightning).

flaucht a flash of lightning *now Sh NE.*

hurl thunder *now Sh Ork Ags.*

rout *of the sea, winds, thunder etc* roar, rumble, make a loud noise.

†**thud** a loud sound (*eg* of thunder).

thunner thunder. **thunder-plump** a sudden heavy thunder-shower.

wild, will, wull: ~**fire** summer lightning, lightning without thunder *now Ork-Per.*

yird, yirth: ~ **din** thunder *now NE.*

5.2.5 WEATHER SIGNS AND FORECASTING

Banff bailies large white snowy clouds rising along the horizon, regarded as a sign of bad weather *NE.*

broch, bruch a halo around the moon, indicating bad weather.

cock's eye a halo round the moon, thought to be a sign of stormy weather *Cai Bnf.*

dog afore his maister the swell of the sea that often precedes a storm *now Bnf.*

fauld a halo round the moon, a warning of stormy weather *now Ayr.*

glaizie *of sunshine* bright but watery, indicating more rain *Arg, Wgt.*

gow a halo around the sun or moon supposed to be a sign of storms *now midLoth.*

lee-gaw a sign of bad weather in the leeward part of the sky *N.*

marcury, mercury a barometer *NE.*

Meg's hole a rift in the sky to the south-west, foretelling clearer weather *now Lnk Ayr.*

midden: be (on her back) in the ~ *of the moon* be surrounded by a lunar bow, foretelling a storm *NE.*

mune: ~ **bow** *now local,* ~ **broch** a halo round the moon, believed to be a sign of an approaching storm. **the auld** ~ **in the airm(s) of the new** *etc* the disc of the full moon faintly illuminated in the crescent moon, believed to be a sign of an approaching storm.

†**phan** a vane, a weathercock.

prognostic *Abd,* †**prognostication** an almanac.

purse mou a boat-shaped cloud said to presage high wind *now Ags Per.*

rosie an effect of light indicating a change in the weather or bad weather *Mry.*

skeel, skill scan expertly, investigate, determine, when looking for weather signs *Bnf Abd.*

stefe, *chf* **stiffie** a broad vertical bar of light across the moon or sun, a sign of bad weather *local N.*

stob an incomplete rainbow showing only the lower ends of the bow, believed to forewarn of a storm at sea *local E.*

†**thane** a vane, a weathercock.

tuith, tooth a fragment of rainbow seen near the horizon, regarded as a sign of bad weather *NE.*

weather gaw 1 a weather gall, an atmospheric appearance regarded as a portent of bad weather *now local Sh-Uls.* **2** a bright calm spell between two periods of bad weather thought to forewarn of snow *now NE.*

5.2.6 TEMPERATURE

For hot and cold weather see 5.2.1 and for boiling liquids see 10.3.

aheat in(to) a hot or warm condition.

air: take the ~ **off** take the chill off.

beek *v* warm (oneself); bask. *n* an act of warming (oneself etc).

birsle 1 scorch. **2** broil; toast; warm thoroughly. **birsling** scorching.

cauld cold. ~**rif(e)** cold, susceptible to cold.

chitter, chitter-chatter *now Abd* chatter, shiver (with cold etc) *now local Abd-Kcb*.

†**chiver** shiver.

cosh snug, comfortable, cosy.

cosie *of persons* warm and comfortable, well wrapped-up.

creep thegither shrink, huddle up with cold.

daver make numb, chill *now Bnf Abd*.

feem *n* a state of sudden heat, a sweat *NE. v* be in a state of great heat or perspiration *NE*.

gell tingle, smart, ache with cold *now Sh Cai*.

glaise a warm at a fire.

grue, gruse *now local Loth-S* shiver from cold *now C, S*.

heat, hate heat *n* the act of heating, a heating, the state of feeling hot, *latterly chf* **get** *or* **gie a** ~. *v* make (oneself or another) warm, *freq corresponding to Mod Eng* warm. **come a-heat** become hot *now midLoth Bwk S*.

hocker crouch over or near a fire for warmth *chf Cai S*.

het, hot 1 hot. **2** warm, comfortable *now Ayr*.

jeel *n* **1** extreme coldness, chill, frostiness. **2** a chill, a chilling sensation *Abd Kcdn Ags. v* freeze, be benumbed with cold *N-SW*. ~**-cauld** cold as ice, stone-cold *NE*.

lew *adj, also* ~ **warm** lukewarm, tepid. *n* a warming, a slight rise in temperature *local Sh-SW. v* become warm *Sh Uls*.

†**lunkit** tepid, lukewarm.

meffin the act of warming oneself at the fire by sitting in front of it with the legs apart *Ags Per*.

†**mese** cool down (something hot).

†**mortfundyit** *adj* deadly cold.

muith(y) oppressed or exhausted by heat.

nip 1 cause to tingle or smart with cold. **2** ache, tingle with cold.

nirl 1 shrink, shrivel, pinch with cold *local Sh-Lnk*. **2** shrivel up in oneself, cringe with cold *now Sh*. ~**ie** *of cold* pinching, nipping *now Sh Fif*.

nither 1 pinch or stunt with cold *now Rox*. **2** shrink or huddle as with cold, shiver *now Loth Lnk S*.

oor †crouch, shiver with cold; huddle. ~**it** cold, shivery, hunched up with cold *now local Sh-Dmf*.

oorie, *now local Sh-Arg,* **oorlich** miserable looking from cold.

†**ovie** giving warmth and comfort.

†**papple** stream with perspiration, be too hot.

peenge look cold and miserable *now Kcdn Ags*. **peeng(e)in** pinched and cold-looking.

perish destroy, kill, bring about the destruction of (a person), *freq* ~**ed with cold**.

plot *v* become very hot, 'boil'; *of persons and animals* 'stew', swelter. *n* an overheated state, a 'sweat', swelter *Sh-Fif*. **plot(tin) het** scalding hot *now Abd Fif Dmf*.

roastit uncomfortably hot *local Sh-Kcb*.

scomfish, scunfis suffocate, stifle, choke, overpower with heat etc *now local*.

smuir, smoor be choked, suffocated, die from lack of air, *esp* by being buried in a snowdrift.

sterve, starve 1 *chf* ~ **o** *or* **wi cauld** be much affected by cold, feel chilled. **2** affect with extreme cold, freeze.

swither *v* be very hot, swelter *now Sh Kcdn*. *n* a swelter, a great heat *now Sh*.

tosie comfortable, cosy, snug.

wall, well: ~**in heat,** *also* **waldin-, welland-** the degree of heat necessary for welding metals *local*.

5.2.7 NATURAL LIGHT, DARKNESS

†**aisle** glow.

†**astrolog** an astronomer, an astrologer.

beek *of the sun* shine brightly.

between the (two) lichts twilight.

†**bicker** *of light, fire etc* gleam, flicker, sparkle.

†**bisom** a comet or its tail.

blear shine dimly *now Abd*.

blink, blent *now Loth,* †**blenk** *v* **1** blink. **2** *chf* **blent (up)** *of light, the sun etc* gleam, shine *now Lnk. n* **1** a blink. **2** *of (a source of) light, esp the sun* a brief or bright gleam; a (short) period of shining, *now esp* of sunshine between clouds. **blinker** a heavenly body. **blinter** glimmer, flicker *now Abd*.

bore, *chf* **blue** ~ *now Bnf Abd,* **borie** *Abd* an opening in the clouds showing blue sky.

bricht bright.

†**brin, brim** a flash, gleam *N*.

broch, bruch a halo around the sun or *esp* the moon, the latter indicating bad weather.

cairry, carry the sky *now Bnf Abd*.

cannle, candle a corpse candle *NE*.

chitter *only verse* flicker, flutter.

clair *adj,* †*v* clear.

cock's eye a halo round the moon, thought to be a sign of stormy weather *Cai Bnf*.

corp candle a will-o'-the-wisp *WC, SW*.

cowslem the evening star *S*.

craw, crow: sit like ~**s in the mist** sit in the dark *local Bnf-Fif.*

creek (o day) break of day, dawn *now Bnf Ags.*

creep: ~ **in** *of daylight hours* shorten. ~ **out** *of hours of darkness* lengthen *now Bnf Abd Fif.*

daaken dawn *Cai.*

daizzle dazzle *now local Bnf Abd Fif.*

Dancers: the (Merry *or* **Pretty)** ~ the northern lights, aurora borealis *chf Sh Ork N.*

darkening twilight.

daw *v* dawn *now local Abd-Kcb.* *n* dawn. †~**ing** dawn, dawning.

day: ~**-daw** dawn *now Abd Fif.* ~**-licht,** †~**is licht** daylight. ~**-set** sunset; nightfall *now Cai.*

dayligaun twilight.

death candle a will-o'-the-wisp, thought to foretell death *now Bnf Abd Fif.*

†**defund** pour down, shed; diffuse.

derk dark *chf S.*

†**dern, darn** dark, dreary, desolate.

†**dirk** *adj* dark. *n* darkness (of night). ~**nes** darkness.

dit darken, dim. ~ **(up)** obstruct, block (the light etc).

†**dook (doon)** *of the day or the sun* draw to a close, go down.

†**doon:** ~**-falling,** ~**-ganging,** ~**-going,** ~**-passing** the setting (of the sun).

†**doup** *of the day* draw to a close; *of darkness* fall. ~ **o day** *or* **een** *verse* the close of day.

douth *of places* gloomy, dreary, dark *S.*

easin(s) the edge of the sky, the horizon *NE.*

†**elf-candle** a spark or flash of light, thought to be of supernatural origin.

ellwand: the King's E ~**, Our** *or* **the Lady's E** ~ *now Ork* the group of stars known as the Belt of Orion.

fair daylight broad daylight *now Abd Ags Wgt.*

fa(ll) *of night* come on.

faucon a mock sun, a parhelion *now Ross.*

fauld a halo round the moon *now Ayr.*

ferrick a mock sun, parhelion.

fire-flaucht a shooting star *WC, SW.*

flaucht a burst of flame *now Sh NE.*

flichter *v* flicker *now Fif Pbls SW.* *n* a flicker, a glimmer (of light) *now Fif.*

flick a glimmering, a streak of light etc *now midLoth.*

†**fuirday** broad daylight.

†**ganging to** the setting (of the sun).

glaik a flash or gleam of reflected light.

glaim, gleam *v* gleam. *n* a flame *now Ags.*

glaise a touch of fire, a burn.

glaizie 1 glittering, shiny *now local Kcdn-Bwk.* **2** *of*

sunshine bright but watery, indicating more rain *Arg, Wgt.*

glancy shiny, shining, bright *now Abd.*

gleed 1 a spark, glimmer of fire or light *now Bwk Slk.* **2** a glowing fire *now Slk.*

gleesh a large bright fire or flame *Bnf Abd.*

gleet *v* gleam, shine, glitter *now Rox.* *n* glistening, glitter; a shine *Rox.*

†**glevin** to glow.

gliff, glaff, glouf a flash, glint.

glim a gleam, glimmer *now Sh Cai Uls.*

glint *v* **1** *also* **glent** gleam, glint, shine, sparkle. **2** cause (a light) to shine, flash **on** *now Ork Abd Ags.* *n, also* **glent** a gleam, flash of light, a faint or momentary glitter. **glintin** dawn, daybreak.

glisk a gleam, sparkle, flash *now WC.*

†**glist** shone, glistened; shining.

glister *v* glisten, glitter *now local.* *n* glitter, brilliance *now local.*

gloam *v* become dusk, grow dark *now NE Ayr.* *n* twilight, a faint light *now Abd.*

gloamin 1 *also* ~ **fa,** ~ **hour** *now Ags, midLoth* ~ **tide** *now Abd,* †~ **grey** evening twilight, dusk. **2** morning twilight, dawn *now Wgt Uls.* †~ **shot** a twilight interval before the lighting of lights.

gloss *of a fire* a bright glow *now Slk.* ~**y** *of a fire* glowing, clear *now Fif.*

glowe glow.

†**glower** *literary, of the heavenly bodies* gleam, shine brightly.

†**glowme** *v* gloom *Rox.*

gloze blaze, shine brightly *now Ags Per.*

gow a halo around the sun or moon supposed to be a sign of storms *now midLoth.*

gray *n* dawn, twilight, *esp* **the** ~ **o the morning** *or* **evening.** *v* dawn *Sh Ork NE.* ~ **dark** dusk *now local C, S.* ~ **(day)licht** dawn *now Sh Cai Abd.*

greking, greek daybreak.

†**horn** the constellation Ursa Minor.

howe-dumb-dead the depth, the darkest point (of winter, night etc) *literary.*

†**lamp** one of the heavenly bodies.

leam *n, chf verse,* light, radiance; a gleam of light *now chf NE.* *v, chf verse* shine, glitter, flash.

licht, light *adj* light, bright. *n* **1** light. **2** *freq* ~**ie** the will-o'-the-wisp (regarded as an omen of death) *chf NE.* *v* light, lighten. *adv* brightly ~**en,** **lich(e)n** lighten. **between (the)** ~**s** twilight *NE Fif.*

lift the sky, the heavens.

†**Lochiel's lantern** the moon.

low *n* **1** a flame. **2** a glow, a radiance as of fire etc.

v gleam, glow, flare. **in a ~ on fire**, alight, glowing.

†**Lucine** the moon.

†**luminar** a luminary.

†**MacFarlane's bouet** the moon.

†**Michaelmas moon** the harvest moon.

midden: be (on her back) in the ~ *of the moon* be surrounded by a lunar bow, foretelling a storm *NE*.

mirk †*adj* dull, murky, lowering. *n* darkness, night, twilight. *v* darken, make or grow dark. **mirken 1** †darken, obscure. **2** grow dark *now Sh*. **~enin** late twilight *now Sh*. **~ing** dusk, nightfall. **~ness** darkness, gloom. **~some** dark, gloomy *now Sh*. **~y** dark, sombre *Gen except NE*. **~ nicht** the dead of night *now Ags Ayr*.

morn: (the) ~ i'e morning daybreak, first light *Gall*.

mornin blink the first glimmer of daylight *now Sh*.

mune the moon. **~ bow** *now local*, **~ broch** a halo round the moon. **the auld ~ in the airm(s) o the new** *etc* the disc of the full moon faintly illuminated within the crescent moon, believed to be a sign of an approaching storm.

nicht night. †**be** *or* **on ~er tale** by night. †**under ~** under cover of night.

†**occasioun** the setting (of the sun).

†**occident** situated in the western part of the sky.

pass doun *or* **to** *of the sun or moon* set, go down.

peek a tiny bead or point of light, a little tongue or jet of flame, *freq* **a ~ o light**.

pen(d) the sky.

†**penny-full** *of the moon* round like a penny, full.

Peter's plough the constellation Ursa Major, the Plough.

pick black pitch-dark, as black as night.

pink(ie) a speck of light.

pit-mirk pitch-dark(ness), dark as a pit.

pleuch the constellation *Ursa Major*, the Plough.

prinkle twinkle, glitter, sparkle.

quarter moon the crescent moon *local*.

rosie an effect of light indicating a change in the weather or bad weather *Mry*.

†**sable** blackness, darkness.

scad a faint appearance of colour or light *now Per Lnk*.

scance *v* gleam, glitter, shine. *n* a gleam, a brief, quick appearance, a tinge *now local Ags-Ayr*.

scarrow 1 a faint light or reflection of light *SW*. **2** a shadow, shade *chf SW*.

†**scheirly** brightly, clearly.

†**scintill** sparkle.

scug, scog 1 †shadow. **2** the shade (of a rock etc) *now local Sh-Fif*.

seeven, seven: the ~ Sisters the Pleiades *now local Cai-Dmf*.

†**share** bright.

shedda *now Sh*, **scaddow** *S*, **shaddie** *Loth Bwk* (a) shadow.

sheen †*adj, also* **schane** bright. *v* shine, gleam, glisten *now Sh NE-WC*.

†**shire, schirly** brightly, clearly.

shuit, shoot emit (flames, rays etc) swiftly and forcibly. †**shot star** a shooting star, meteor.

simmer, summer: ~ blink a momentary gleam or spell of sunshine *now Sh Per*.

skime *v* glance, shine with reflected light, gleam. *n* a gleam of light, flash *now Sh*.

skimmer *of light or a bright object* twinkle, gleam.

skinkle *now chf verse* glitter, gleam, sparkle *now Per Stlg WC*.

skire *adj, of flames, light etc* clear; bright. *v* shine brightly, glitter *now Ork NE*. **skyrin, skyrie** bright *now Ork NE*.

sklent *of light etc* shine in a slanting direction *now Sh*.

skliff, skluif a segment of the moon *Per wLoth WC, SW*.

skreek, skreich, scraich: o day first light, the crack of dawn *local Ork-S*.

sky daylight, the light of the sun, *esp* at dawn or sunset. †**~ break(ing)** daybreak. **~ set(ting)** nightfall.

†**slop** ? a break in the clouds.

†**snip** white bright, dazzling.

spottie the will-o'-the-wisp, *esp* **like ~** at once, with great speed *now Abd*.

spraich of day break of day *now Fif Lnk Ayr*.

†**spring** rise up in the sky.

spunk, *n, also* **~ie** a spark (of fire), quick flicker of light, glimmer *now N nEC, SW*. *v* emit sparks (in all directions) *now Sh Per*. **~ie** the will-o'-the-wisp.

starn, stern, *also* **~ie** *now NE* a star *now Sh-N, Lnk Dmf*. **~ie** starry, covered with stars *now Ork*. †**sternit** starred, starry. **~licht** starlight *now Abd*. †**~ schot** a shooting star.

stefe, *chf* **stiffie** a broad vertical bar of light across the moon or sun, a sign of bad weather *local N*.

†**stellate** *verse* studded with stars.

ster a star *now Rox*.

stime *now chf literary* a glimmer or glimpse of light *now Sh N Stlg*.

straik a stripe of colour, ray of light etc *now local NE-Dmf*.

streamers the Aurora Borealis *now Per Kcb*.

streek o day *etc* daybreak, the first light of day *local Sh-Per.*

†**streke** *of a heavenly body* emit (light).

strip a stripe, a long thin line of colour, light etc *now Abd.*

†**subumbrage** overshadow.

sun, sin (the) sun. ~ **blink** a gleam of sunshine. ~ **broch** a halo round the sun *now E.* ~**down** sunset. †**between** *etc* **the** ~ **and the sky** between dawn and sunrise.

†**tae, to:** ~**-fall (o the day** *or* **nicht)** evening, dusk.

tak, take burn brightly; gleam, glow like fire *Cai.*

†**tender** *of colour or light* delicate; soft

†**terne** *adj* gloomy. *n* gloom.

†**umbrakle** shade, shadow.

†**umbrate** shady.

†**upsun: with (the)** ~ at dawn, at sunrise.

†**ursis** the Great and Little Bear constellations.

†**Vatland streit** Watling Street, the Milky Way.

wa(ll) heids the horizon, skyline *chf SW.*

wade, wad *local, of the moon or sun* move through cloud or mist *now local.*

†**wan** *of the moon* not fully formed.

water burn a name for the phosphorescence seen on the sea *now Mry Kcdn.*

weather glim twilight; a band of clear sky above the horizon often visible at this time.

†**Willie and the wisp** the will-o'-the-wisp.

†**yet** shed (light).

5.2.8 ARTIFICIAL LIGHT

†**bannock, bonnock** a flat cake of tallow or wax.

bleeze *n* 1 a blaze. 2 (1) †a blazing brand, a torch *in gen.* (2) *specif* as used when spearing fish *now Abd Ayr.* 3 a beacon fire, a bonfire *now Ags. v* light up (water) to attract fish *now Ayr.*

blink, blent *now Loth,* †**blenk** *v* 1 blink. 2 *chf* **blent (up)** gleam, shine *now Lnk.* 3 give a spark to or of; light (a lamp) *now Sh. n* 1 a blink. 2 *of (a source of) light* a brief or bright gleam. 3 a momentary use of borrowed light *now Sh Bnf:* 'gie me the blink o a candle'. **blinter** glimmer, flicker *now Abd.*

bouet a (hand) lantern.

cannle, candle 1 a candle. 2 candles; tallow, wax *now Abd.* ~ **doup** a candle-end. **candle fir** split fir-wood used instead of candles *chf NE.* †~ **scheris** candle snuffers.

carle, kerl a tall candlestick *SW.*

†**chan(d)ler, chandelare** a candlestick, chandelier.

cleave cannles make candles of fir roots *NE.*

cruisie, cruise an open, boat-shaped lamp with a rush wick; a candleholder.

†**cut-throat** a dark lantern.

dolly an old-fashioned oil-lamp, a **cruisie** *Bnf Abd.*

doozie a light, a flame (of a candle, lamp etc) *now Ayr.*

doup the end of a used candle.

drieshach the glowing embers of a peat fire *now Abd.*

eelie dollie an oil lamp *NE.*

fir candle = **candle fir** *now Bnf.*

†**gasoliery** a gas chandelier.

†**imp** a small candle or taper.

†**kempit** the pith of hemp or of a wild carrot, parsnip etc, dried and used as a candle.

leerie a lamp *now EC Dmf.*

licht, light that part of a candle which provides light, candle-wax or candle-tallow. *Gall.*

mort hede a turnip lantern representing a skull *NE.*

neepy candle *NE,* **neep lantern** *Sh-nEC* a turnip-lantern, *esp* as at **Halloween.**

†**pan** ? the bowl containing the fuel and wick of a lamp; ? a lamp.

peat-lowe a peat fire, the glow from such a fire.

peek a tiny bead or point of light, a little tongue or jet of flame, *freq* **a** ~ **o light.**

peep a peek, *freq* of a gas-jet. **put the gas at** *or* **in a** ~ reduce the pressure of a gas jet to the lowest point at which it will remain alight. *Gen except Sh Ork.*

†**puir man, peer page** *NE* kind of candlestick used for holding up **candle fir** etc.

†**quinkill** *of a light* go out.

rash *N,* **rasher** *Bwk Rox,* ~**ie** a peeled rush used for a lamp wick.

†**reekie Peter** a **cruisie** *NE.*

reevin blazing *NE.*

rittocks the refuse of melted tallow *chf SW.*

ruffie a torch or light, a fir-brand, a wick of rag smeared with tallow; *specif* a torch used when fishing for salmon at night.

†**shell** the bowl or pan which holds the oil in a **cruisie** *NE.*

skimmer *of light or a bright object* twinkle, gleam.

smore *v* extinguish (a fire, light etc), put out, obliterate *now NE Ags.*

snot *now Bnf,* **snotter** *now NE Kcb* the snuff or burnt wick of a candle.

spail, spell *now Abd* a wooden spill or taper used for lighting etc *now local Ork-Lnk.*

spark, sperk *S* set alight; light (a match, fire etc) *now nEC, WC, SW*.

†**stander** a candlestick.

†**swey, swee** a (street-)lamp bracket.

tally lamp a miner's lamp *Fif Ayr*

tattie-boodie a turnip lantern used at Halloween *nEC*.

tauch, tallow, tallon, tally tallow, **tauch** being sometimes used for the substance in its natural state and **tallow** when it has been melted down.

uilie cruisie an oil lamp.

waster something on the wick of a candle causing it to gutter *now Ags wLoth*.

week a wick (of a candle etc).

whiff, whuff, wheef blow out (a candle etc).

winkie a lamp, light, *esp* an unsteady or flickering one *NE-WC*.

†**yet** shed (light).

†**Yule candle** a large long-burning Christmas candle.

5.2.9 COLOURS

Includes natural markings; stains; patterns.

barken encrust, plaster over, blacken.

bawsant, basoned, †**bassie** *of an animal, orig a horse* having a white mark or streak on the face.

†**begary** variegate with streaks of colour. **begareit** ornamented with stripes or trimmings of another material or colour.

†**beld** *of horses and cattle* having a white spot or mark on the forehead. **bell** a white mark on a horse's face.

bew blue *NE, WC*.

black †*of persons, their complexion, hair etc, freq attached to a personal name* dark: 'blak Archibald of Douglas'. †**blekin** blacken. **~-a-viced, ~-a-vised** dark-complexioned. †**~ broun** dark brown. †**~-gray** (a) dark grey (colour or cloth).

blae 1 blue; bluish; dark bluish grey, livid. **2** livid or bluish from a blow. **3** †*of a blow* making a livid mark or bruise. **4** livid or bluish from cold, bloodlessness etc **5** †*of skin* black, *chf* **bla man.** **~ness** lividness.

blaiken become pale. **~t** made pale or pallid *now Abd*.

†**blechit, blacht** pale, livid.

bleck make black, blacken (*latterly esp* the face with soot etc).

†**bloncat** grey, greyish blue; a cloth of this colour.

bluachie bluish *now Bnf Abd*.

†**boday** a scarlet dye.

brandit of a reddish-brown colour with darker stripes or markings, brindled *now Abd Ags*.

bricht bright.

brockit, brocked *of an animal, esp a cow or sheep* having a white streak down its face. **brock(ie)-faced** *of an animal* having a **brockit** face *now Cai*.

brookit made black or dirty, streaked or smeared with dirt, soot, *now Bnf Abd Ags*.

broon, brown 1 brown. **2** a brown horse *local Abd-wLoth*.

†**browden** stained (with blood).

†**canous** hoary; grey-haired.

casten *of colours* faded *local N-WC*.

chackit checked, tartan *now Bnf Abd Fif*.

changing †*of fabric* showing different colours in different aspects or lights. **chyngin ba** a sweet that changes colour as it is sucked *Mry Ags*.

†**columbie** *of cloth* dove-coloured.

coom dirty, blacken, stain.

cramasie †*adj, chf of materials, esp satin, velvet* crimson. *n* crimson cloth *latterly literary*.

†**crimpson** crimson.

cruik, crook: as black as a *or* **the ~** very black, dirty *now local Bnf Fif*.

cudbear a purple dyestuff, prepared from lichens.

†**cullour** colour. **~ du roy, colour de roy** a purple or tawny dress material.

†**curale** coral, the substance and the colour; coral-coloured cloth.

dark-avised having dark hair and eyes *now Ork Bnf Arg*.

†**deroy (culourit)** purple; tawny.

din 1 dun. **2** *of persons* dark-complexioned, sallow *Gen except Sh Ork*. **~ness** sallowness, darkness *now Cai Bnf*.

†**distene** stain, discolour.

earl o Hell: as black as the ~'s waistcoat pitch black.

†**failzeit** faded in colour.

fair-avised fair-complexioned *now Bnf Fif SW*.

faughie *N*, †**faugh** pale; pale brown, yellowish.

†**faw** variegated.

†**feilamort** the colour of a dead leaf.

flicht a flake, a small speck of soot, dust etc *now Bwk*. **flichan** a small speck of something *now local EC, SW*.

flichter a small particle or flake of soot etc *now Cai Fif*.

gair a dirty streak or stain on clothes *Fif Dnbt*. **~it** striped.

†**galзeard** *of dress etc* gay, bright, gaudy.

gilt 1 gild. **2** become yellow *now Bwk*. †**~in** gilded, gilt, golden.

glog *chf literary* black, dark.

gowden golden.

greenichtie *Bnf Abd,* **greenichy** *Mry Ags* greenish.

grim grey, roan, mottled black and white *now local Abd-Ayr.*

†**gule** yellow.

gyre gaudy *Abd.*

†**hasard** *adj* grey, grey-haired. *n* a grey-haired man.

haw of a pale, wan colouring, tinged with blue or green *now Abd.*

ill coloured having a bad or unhealthy colour.

kairy *of a sheep's fleece* streaked, striped *Cai.*

keel ruddle, red-ochre, *esp* as used for marking sheep *now local.*

†**keir** *of horses* dun, dark brown or grey. ~ **black** dark-coloured.

†**lauchtane** dull-coloured, grey; livid.

lit *v* dye, colour, tinge. *n* a dye, tint, dyestuff *now Sh Cai.*

lyart 1 *of the hair* streaked with white, grizzled, silvery. 2 †*chf of a horse* dappled. 3 variegated, multi-coloured, streaked with two colours, *esp* red and white.

†**milk and watter** bluish-white.

mirk dark, black, gloomy, obscure.

mix *of greying hair* become mixed in colour *local Ork-Kcb.* †**mixt cloth** cloth woven with more than one colour of yarn, marled.

†**oren3e** the colour orange.

†**paintit** *of glass* coloured, stained. ~ **werk** stained glass.

parson gray a dark shade of grey, clerical grey.

†**pasvelour** ? purple.

†**plumb lede** the colour of unworked or untreated lead.

pot black *WC Uls,* **as black as the pot** very black.

†**pullicate** a coloured, *freq* checked gingham-type cotton produced in Scotland.

†**punic** purple.

†**pure** 'pured' fur, fur trimmed so as to show only one colour.

purpie *n* the colour purple *now Mry.* †*adj* of a purple colour, gaudy

†**purpoir** purple (cloth).

pyot *n* a piebald horse. *adj* resembling a magpie in colouring, piebald, multi-coloured, variegated.

†**railya** striped, decorated to give a striped effect.

rand a stripe or section of a different colour or texture *now Kcb.* ~**it** striped or streaked with different colours *now Rox.*

reekie blackened by smoke.

reid, red, rid *adj* red. *v* redden, make or become red.

riach *freq of black and white wool mixed in cloth* greyish-white, drab, brindled *Sh Ork N.*

roant of a roan or variegated colour *Abd SW.*

roarie *of colours* bright, showy; *now chf* glaring, garish, loud *Gen except NE.*

†**roising** rosy.

†**rude** red.

†**sable** blackness, darkness.

scad a faint appearance of colour or light *now Per Lnk.*

†**schip hewit** of the colour of a sheep's fleece.

siller silver.

skire be gaudy *now Ork NE.* **skyrin, skyrie** bright; gaudy in colour, garish *now Ork NE.*

smuik, smook discolour by smoke *now SW, S.*

†**soir, sorit** *of a horse* of a sorrel colour.

spat a spot.

splatch a splodge, blot of colour etc.

spraing *n* a (*usu* glittering or brightly-coloured) stripe, streak or ray of colour. *v* variegate, diversify with stripes or streaks. †**spraingled** striped, streaked.

spreckle, sprackle a speckle, spot, freckle. **spreckled** speckled, mottled, flecked, variegated.

spruttle †a small spot, speckle. ~**d, sprittled** speckled, spotted *now Rox.*

†**sten3ie** *v* stain.

straik *n* a stripe of colour, ray of light etc *now local NE-Dmf.* *v* streak, mark with streaks of a different colour *now Ork Abd Ags Ayr.*

strip a stripe, a long thin line of colour, light etc *now Abd.* ~**pit** marked or ornamented with stripes etc, variegated, ribbed.

†**sulliart** *of a horse* bright, clear-coloured.

†**tannie** tawny.

tash a stain, smudge *now NE nEC Dnbt.*

teenge a tinge.

†**tender** *of colour or light* delicate; soft

thraw, throw discolour, (cause to) fade *now Lnk.*

†**vane** a slender stripe of a different colour or material on a garment.

†**vardour** verdure.

†**varyand** varied in colour, variegated.

†**vermeloun, vermeling** vermilion. **vermillion** painted with vermilion, rouged.

vieve, vive *of colours* bright, clear, vivid, distinct.

†**wald** the yellow dye obtained from weld, the plant.

†**wanhew** *v* stain.

†**wayre** varied or variegated in colour.

white, fite *NE adj, n* white. **fiteichtie** rather white, whitish *NE*. ~**ly** pale, whitish, delicate-looking.

yella, yallow, yella *Sh NE, WC, S* yellow. **yallochie, yallochtie** *Abd* yellowish, slightly yellow *Abd Ags*.

6. WATER, SEA, SHIPS

6.1 WATER, SEA

6.1.1 WATER, LIQUIDS

For boiling liquids and other aspects associated largely with cooking, see 10.3.

addle foul putrid liquid.

†bedovin immersed.

†belch a deep pool, an abyss.

bell *n* a bubble. †*v* bubble up.

†beswakkit soaked, drenched.

bibble bubble *chf NE*.

bicker *of water in gen* move quickly and noisily *now Abd*.

bizz *of liquids* hiss, fizz.

blash *n* 1 a splash of liquid etc. 2 a semi-liquid or soft slimy mass, a dirty mess *now Bnf*. *v* pour down with a splashing noise *now Abd Ags*.

blob, blab *now Mry* a drop of moisture, a bubble.

blybe a large quantity of liquid *Bnf Abd*.

bree liquid or moisture of any kind *now local Cai-Lnk*.

broo liquid or moisture of any kind *now Ags Lnk*.

†brush (cause to) rush or gush.

buck pour or gush out; make a gurgling noise *now Bnf Abd*.

buller *n* a bubble; a whirlpool; a bubbling or boiling up of water *now in place-name:* **the Bullers of Buchan**. *v, of water* boil or bubble up; rush noisily; make a loud gurgling sound *now Abd Ags*.

bummel boil up, bubble; tumble.

burn water drawn for domestic etc use, *latterly esp* from a well or fountain *now Abd wLoth Arg*.

†bush *v* rush or gush **out**. *interj* expressing a gushing sound.

caller cool, fresh, refreshing.

chirt squirt, spurt.

chork squelch.

clashing soaking, dripping *WC*.

clatch, clotch *n* a splashing sound. *v* move with a splashing or squelching sound.

clunk *n* a hollow, gurgling sound made by liquid in motion *now local NE-WC*. *v* make a hollow

gurgling sound as of liquid being poured *now NE*.

coble a pond, a watering place *NE*.

†defund pour down, shed.

deid drap a drop of water dripping on the floor, thought to foretell death.

†din *chf of running water* a slight noise.

†distell distill.

dook *v* bathe. *n* 1 a bathe. 2 a drenching, a soaking *now Bnf Abd*. 3 liquid into which something is dipped.

draigelt soaked through, drenched *now Ork Ags Per*.

draik, drawk *now S* drench, soak *now Bwk Slk*.

drap, drop the dripping of water or the line down which it drops from the eaves of a house *now Bnf-Ags Kcb*.

dreep 1 drip. 2 a wet, dripping condition, *eg* with sweat *now Bnf Abd Fif*. ~**le** *now Abd*, **dripple** *Sh Ags* drip, trickle.

drib a drop, a small quantity of liquid or semi-liquid *now Bnf Abd Fif*.

dribble, dribblach *Bnf Abd* a slight trickle; a drop *local*.

droogled drenched, soaked *now Bnf Abd*.

drouk: droukit drenched, soaked; steeped. **droukin** *adj* dripping with moisture *now Stlg*. *n* a drenching, soaking *now Ags Fif*. **drookle** drench, soak *Sh Bnf Fif*.

drumle *v* make or be muddy or disturbed *now Rox*. *n* mud raised when water is disturbed *S*.

drumlie *of streams or water* troubled, clouded, muddy,

dub 1 a pool, *esp* of muddy or stagnant water; a pond. 2 *also* **dib** a small pool, *esp* of rain water, a puddle. ~**-water** dirty water *now Fif*.

dunk, dank *adj* dank, damp, moist. *n* moisture, a mouldy dampness. *v* dank, make damp or wet. ~**y** damp, moist, wettish.

faem 1 foam. 2 gush *chf Ork*.

fang: lose *etc* **the** ~ lose the power of retaining water *now Abd Stlg midLoth*.

fleet 1 float, rise to the surface of a liquid *now Sh*. 2 flow. ~ **water** water which overflows ground *now C*.

flodder flood, overflow.

†flotter overflow, wet.

flude flood.

flush a pool of water *now Arg Rox.* † ~**an** a large shallow puddle.

freith *chf verse v* **1** foam, froth *now Kcb.* **2** work (a liquid) up into a froth, make a lather in. **3** swill (clothes) quickly through soapsuds *Kcb Dmf. n chf verse* froth, foam, lather *now Kcb.*

fro *n* froth, foam *now local Mry-Slk. v* froth, foam; bubble *local Abd-Slk.*

gang a load, the quantity that can be carried at one time, *esp* of water *now local Cai-Ayr.*

glaur *n* **1** ooze, slime. **2** slippery ice; slipperiness. *v* make slimy or slippery *now Bwk.*

gluthery slimy *now Per Fif.*

goor muddy, stagnant water *local Sh-Kcdn.*

gorge, gurge, grudge 1 choke (**up** a channel) with mud, snow etc *now Sh.* **2** *only* **gurge** *esp of water* swell, surge *now Rox.*

gourd *of water* become pent up *now Bnf Rox.*

grummel, gummle make muddy or turbid. **grumlie, gumlie** muddy, turbid, full of dregs or gravel *now local Sh-Dmf.*

gurl *v* gurgle *now midLoth Rox. n* a gurgling sound *now midLoth Rox.* ~**ie** gurgling *now midLoth.*

hause a narrow stretch of water *now Ork.*

heftit full of liquid to bursting point *now Kinr midLoth.*

hert-dry thoroughly dry *NE Ags.*

hole a shallow pool, a puddle *local Sh-Kcb.*

hurl make a deep rumbling hollow sound, as of rushing water *Sh Cai Uls.*

hush *n* a rushing, gushing sound as of swiftly moving water *now Sh Ork. v, of water* rush forth, gush out *now Sh Uls.*

jabble *v, of a liquid* splash *local. n* **1** a liquid and its sediment stirred up together. **2** a choppy area of water.

japple stamp with the feet in water, splash *Sh Cai Ags.*

jaup *v* **1** dash, splash, spill *now NE Uls.* **2** cause (water) to splash *now Bnf.* **3** splash, bespatter with water, mud etc *now NE, C Uls. n* a splash (of water, mud etc) *now C-Uls. adv* splash!, with a splash *now Fif.* ~**in fu** brimming over *now midLoth SW.* ~**y** splashy, muddy.

jaw *v* **1** pour abruptly, splash, dash, spill *now local NE-Uls.* **2** dash, splash, surge. *n* a rush, spurt, outpouring, splash of liquid; liquid splashed or thrown *now NE Ags Lnk.*

jibble *v, also* ~ **oot, owre, up** spill (a liquid) by agitating its container *now local N-Uls. n* a splash, the splashing or lapping of a liquid *NE Ayr.*

jilp, jilt *v* **1** cause (liquid) to spurt or splash, spill *now NE midLoth Lnk.* **2** *of a liquid* splash about or over *now Sh NE Ags. n* a small quantity of liquid (splashed or spilt), a splash, spurt of liquid *now NE Ags midLoth.*

jirble *v* **1** splash, slop (liquid). **2** pour out unsteadily in small quantities *now local Abd-Rox. n* a small quantity of liquid poured out, a drop *now Lnk S.*

jirg *v* **1** make a squelching or splashing sound, gurgle *now local NE-Gall.* **2** work (something in a liquid) so as to cause a squelching sound *now Abd. n* a squelching sound *NE.*

jow *n* the surge or swell of water or waves *now Kcdn Ags. v* spill (a liquid) from a container by making it move from side to side *midLoth Lnk.*

†jug(g)is swill, dregs, foul or waste liquid.

juitle *v* spill, splash, overflow *now Gall. n* a dash or small quantity of liquid *now Ayr.*

jummlie turbid, muddy *now local.*

junt a large quantity of liquid *Kcb.*

kep catch (a liquid) in a receptacle.

†lake a stagnant pond, a pool.

lapper *of water* freeze *now Abd Ags.*

lappie a small pool of water, puddle *Ags Per.*

†lash a great splash of water.

leck *now local,* **lake** *n, v* leak.

lee lye.

lint: ~**-hole** *now Bnf Fif SW,* ~**-pot** *now Fif* a pond in which flax is steeped.

lip *n* the edge or brink of a stream, pool etc. *v* be full to the brim or overflowing, brim **over** *freq* ~**pin (fou).** ~**-f(o)u** quite full, brimming over *now Sh NE Ags.*

lipper *v* **1** *of water* ripple, be ruffled *now Ork Cai NE.* **2** be full almost to overflowing, be brimming over *local Sh-Pbls. n* a ripple *now Sh-Ags.*

loch, louch a small pool or puddle.

logger, locher drench, soak *Ross Fif Lnk Dmf.*

loit *v* throw down something wet and soggy in a mass on the ground. *n* **1** a small quantity of liquid. **2** a mass of something filthy or disgusting, liquid or semi-liquid *now Kcdn.*

lowp *of water* cascade, roll.

†march a natural frontier or limit (of a stretch of water).

moggan: wet (the sma end o') one's ~**s** be over the ankles in water *Mry Abd.*

moister moisture.

muck: wet as ~ soaking wet *now Sh Kcb.*

oam, yoam steam, vapour; condensation *now Sh Ork NE.*

†ourstrenkle sprinkle, besprinkle.

†overflete flow over, overflow.

†overslide glide over (water).

owergae overflow *now Sh Ork Wgt*.

ower-rin flow over (a surface).

paidle, paddle the act of wading or paddling in water etc *now Cai Bnf Ayr*.

pani water *S*.

papple flow, bubble up *now Abd Loth*.

peat: ~y *freq of water* peat-stained. ~ **bree** the water which drains from peat soil, peaty water *now NE*.

†**peer(ie)** pour in trickles or small drops, trickle.

pink *of small drops of moisture* drip, fall with a sharp, tinkling sound, plop *now Ork Abd*.

pirl *v* swirl, eddy, ripple *now NE, S Uls*. *n* an eddy or swirl, a ripple *now NE Rox*.

pirr *of liquid* ripple; flow, stream *now Sh Uls*.

pish *of water* gush, rush, splash out *now NE Kcb*.

plapper splash about in water *now Mry*.

plash *n* **1** a splash, the noise made by something falling into water *now Sh NE Ags*. **2** a large quantity of something liquid. **3** †a shallow pool. *v* **1** splash (a person, thing etc) with a liquid, wet, drench *now Sh*. **2** walk on water-logged ground, squelch along through mud *local Sh-Kcb*. **3** *freq* ~ **at** work in a messy, slovenly way, mess about in liquids *now Sh*. *adv* splash!, with a splash *now Sh NE Ags*. ~**in** squelching or splashing with moisture, soaking wet. †~**y** causing splashes; water-logged, soaking wet.

platch *n* a splashing, a step or stamping movement in water or mud; a splash of mud etc *Sh midLoth Lnk S. adv* with a splash *Sh S. v* **1** splash, cover with mud *now Sh Bnf*. **2** walk through mud or mire *Sh Fif S*. ~**ie** wet, muddy *now Rox*. ~**in** soaking, sopping *S*.

platter **1** †dabble with the hands in a liquid, work in a messy, slovenly way. **2** splash noisily and clumsily through mud or water *now Sh*.

plinkin tinkling, pattering.

plish-plash †*n* a splashing noise or motion, a splash. †*v, of a liquid* splash, dash, cascade. *adv* with a splashing noise *Sh NE Ags*.

plodge walk on muddy or water-logged ground, squelch along in a heavy slow way *now midLoth S*.

plowp plop *Abd Kcdn Ayr S*.

plowt *v* **1** plunge or thrust (something) **into** a liquid), submerge quickly **in** *now WC*. **2** fall heavily, *freq* into a liquid *now NE Per Wgt*. **3** walk through water or over wet ground, squelch along; dabble in water or mud *now Sh Abd Ags*. **4** *of liquids* fall with a splash *now Sh Abd Ags*. *n* a noisy fall or plunge, *esp* into water etc; a splash, plop *now Sh-Ags Wgt*.

plowter, pleuter *v* dabble with the hands or feet, *usu* in a liquid, splash aimlessly in mud or water, wade messily through wet ground. *n* **1** the act of working or walking in wetness or mud, a splashing about. **2** a splash, dashing of liquid *now Sh Ags*.

plump *of a (semi-)liquid* make a loud bubbling or plopping noise, *eg* when boiling *now Uls*.

†**plunge** penetrate by diving or plunging, plunge into.

plunk **1** fall with a dull heavy sound into water etc, plop. **2** drop (an object) into water, plop.

plype *n* (the noise of) a sudden dash of water; (the noise of) a fall into water *now NE Ags. v* **1** drop suddenly into a liquid, plunge or splash in(to) mud or water *NE Ags*. **2** walk on wet or muddy ground, squelch along *NE Ags. adv* suddenly, with a splash, plop! *Bnf Abd*.

poach a wet, muddy area of ground, a puddle *now Abd*.

pour, also ~**ie** *now Ags Per,* ~**in** *now Sh Ags Uls* a small quantity of a liquid, a drop.

pow, †poll a pool of water, *chf* a shallow or marshy one, a watery or marshy place *now Sh Cai Abd*.

powk a hole or hollow in the ground, *usu* water-logged or marshy *now Mry Per*.

powter paddle or poke about in a liquid, make a noise in a liquid *now Ags Wgt*.

†**puddle** wet with mud or dirty water.

puil pool, a body of water.

ream ower overflow, run over *Sh N, C Slk*.

reek *of hot liquid, damp hay, corn etc* emit vapour or steam *now local Sh-Kcb*.

rin, run *v* **1** be covered with water, mud etc, be awash; leak, stop being watertight *local Sh-Per*. **2** hold (the hands etc) under running water, swill. *n* a flow of water. **rin-water** a natural flow of water, *esp* one which will drive a millwheel without a dam *Abd*. ~ **out** *of a vessel* leak.

†**rowt, rout** *of water etc* roar loudly.

sail be covered over with liquid, be swimming or awash *now Kcdn Ags Fif*.

saip, soap: ~**(y) graith** *now local Ags-Rox,* ~**(ie) sapples** *now C,* †~**y suds** soapsuds, soapy lather. † ~ **bells** soap bubbles.

sap soak, steep, saturate.

sappie wet, soppy, sodden *now NE, C*.

sapple *v* soak, saturate with water etc *now local Stlg-Kcb. n* ~**s** soapsuds, lather for washing *now local C*.

†**scaud, scald** a quantity of scalding liquid.

scout *v* cause (water etc) to spout or spurt out, squirt; *of liquid* spurt or squirt out. *n* a sudden gush or flow of water from a spout etc *now NE, C*.

scruif, scruff the surface of water or the sea *now NE*.

seek percolate, soak, ooze *local Kcdn-SW*.

seep *v, also* **sip** drip, ooze, trickle, leak. *n, also* ~**age** leakage, dripping, oozing. ~**it** soaked, wet through.

shalla shallow.

share pour off (top liquid), separate (a liquid) from its dregs *now SW*.

shaul(d), †**schald** shallow, not deep *now local Sh-Kcb*.

†**ship, scheip:** ~ **fontane** a device for making salt water fresh.

†**shire** *of liquid etc* clear, unclouded.

sink a hollow, low-lying area where water collects to form a boggy place *now Sh and in place-names*.

skail *of a container or its contents* spill out or over, overflow or leak out.

skelp *of liquids* (cause to) splash or dash, spatter, pelt *local Sh-Kcb*.

skiddle, skittle *v* splash (a liquid), squirt (water) about, spill, dabble, potter or splash **about** *Mry C. n* **1** a thin watery liquid *WC*. **2** a mess, muddle, confusion, *esp* with spilling of liquid *nEC Loth WC*.

skink pour (a small amount of liquid) from one container to another; mix (liquids) thus. † ~**in** easily poured, thinly diluted.

skirp *v* **1** sprinkle (water etc), splash in small drops or squirts *chf NE*. **2** *of water, mud etc* splash, fly up in small drops *chf NE*. *n* a small drop, splash, or spurt of liquid *chf NE*.

skit a squirt of water, a jet.

skite *v* cause a spray or splash of liquid, squirt, splash *now Sh-Ags SW*. *n* **1** the act of shooting out or squirting liquid *now N*. **2** a small amount of water *now local Bnf-Wgt*.

sklyte, skloit, sklyter *chf NE n* a soft, wet, half-liquid mass *NE Ags*. *v* pour or throw liquid in a careless noisy way, slop, splash *NE Ags*.

skoosh *v* (cause to) gush in spurts or splashes, squirt. *n* a splash, spurt, jet (of liquid) *N, C*. *adv* with a splash *NE, C*.

slabber wet with a messy semi-liquid substance *now C, S*. ~**y** *of roads* waterlogged, muddy *WC*.

slaiger, slagger *v* **1** besmear with something soft and wet, bedaub with mud etc *local Cai-S*. **2** smear or daub (a soft wet substance) (**on**) *now Cai*. *n* a wet, soggy, or slimy mess *EC, WC, S*.

slaik, slaich something soft, wet or messy which has been smeared on *now Ags Per*.

slair, slairie smear, cover (with something soft, wet, messy) *now local Ags-Dmf*.

slairg, slairk *v* **1** smear, bespatter (with something wet and dirty) *now SW Rox*. **2** smear **on** *or* **in**. *n* a quantity of something messy or semi-liquid, a dollop, smear *now Fif Rox*.

slaister, slyster *v* **1** work messily or splash the hands about in a liquid *Gen except NE*. **2** wade in mud or water *now Sh Cai*. *n* a state of wetness and dirt, a splashy mess, dirty water, slops *Gen except NE*. ~**y** wet and dirty, muddy, slimy.

slam slime, something slimy or oozy *Abd*.

slash *n* a violent dash or clash, *esp* of something wet, a splash *now Sh Bnf Ags*. *v* throw (liquid) with a splash; strike with something wet *now Sh Ork Ags SW*. *adv* with a clash or splash, with violence *now Sh Ags*.

slatch 1 work in something messy, potter or dabble in mud etc *now Rox*. **2** walk or splash through mud, wade about messily *now Rox*.

slaurie *v* daub or splash with mud etc; dirty (one's clothes) *now Stlg WC Kcb*. *n* a smear, smudge, daub of something soft and sticky *now Stlg SW*.

slitter, sluiter *v* **1** work or walk messily in water etc, splash about untidily *now C*. **2** besmear with something wet or messy, make messy or stained *now C Rox*. *n* (messy) semi-liquid matter *now C*. ~**y** wet and messy, sloppy *C, S*.

slock, sloke moisten, soak, drench *Bnf Abd Ags*.

slocken moisten, drench, soak *now Per*.

sloosh *n* a dash of water, a splashing. *v* splash with water, throw water about in large splashes, flush.

slorach a wet, disgusting mess (**of** something) *now NE*.

slouster, sluister *v* dabble in water or mud, work untidily or messily *now Ags Fif Uls*. †*n* something wet or messy.

sludder something wet and slimy, mud, filth.

slunge, slounge *v* **1** wade through water or mud in a clumsy, splashing way. **2** souse with water *Inv C, S*. *n* a plunging motion, a headlong fall, a splash made by a heavy object *now nEC Dnbt*.

slutter, sclutter, skleuter *v* make a splashing sound; plunge, flounder in mud *Bnf Ags*. *n* **1** a mess, a mass of dirty (semi-)liquid *now Sh Ork EC, WC*. **2** a splash, slop. ~**y** messy, soft and wet, sloppy and sticky.

sma(ll) fine, composed of small particles or droplets.

†**sock** soak.

soggit soaked *NE*.

soom, swim an extremely wet state, a flood, *freq* **in a** ~ *local Sh-Ags*. †**be swimming full of** abound with (fish).

soosh swill, splash, wash over *NE*.

sorp be soaked or drenched *S*.

soss *n* a wet state, a sopping condition, a dirty wet mess *now local Sh-Fif.* *v* **1** mix (*esp* liquids) in a messy, incongruous way *now Sh Ags.* **2** make wet and dirty, make a mess of *now Sh NE Ags.*

sotter *v* **1** come bubbling **out**. **2** saturate, soak, wallow *Bwk SW.* *n* a state of wetness *NE.*

souch, sough, seuch *n* the rushing, roaring or murmuring of water *now local Sh-Kcb.* *v, of water* ripple, gurgle, make a slapping sound *now local Sh-Per.*

souk, suck flow in a certain direction, as if drawn by suction *now Ork Ags Per.*

sowff *of water etc* murmur softly.

sowp *v* soak, drench, saturate, steep *now local Bnf-Dmf.* *n* **1** a state of wetness. **2** water for washing, lather *now Lnk SW.*

spairge, sparge, sperge *v* **1** bespatter, besprinkle. **2** scatter, sprinkle, dash (water, mud etc) (**about**) *now Abd.* †*n* a splash, sprinkling, splodge of water, mud etc.

spalter walk awkwardly, stumble; splash through water, flounder *now Wgt.*

spark, sperk *now S n* **1** a drop of water, a raindrop *now NE Ags.* **2** a splash or spot of mud etc *now NE.* *v* **1** spatter with liquid or mud; spot with mud etc *now Sh Ork NE.* **2** throw out a fine spray; sputter, spit forth *now local Sh-SW.*

spate, †speat *n* **1** a flood, a sudden rise of water. **2** †flooding, swollen condition (of water etc). *v* flood, swell.

spicket, spigot, spriggit an outdoor tap, *freq* one supplying water for a locality *local.*

spire **1** †dry out; become parched. **2** wither, cause to fade, dry up *sEC Rox.*

splairge *v* sprinkle, splash (a liquid etc) *now nEC, WC, SW.* *n* a splash, sprinkling, splodge of water, mud etc *now Loth WC-S.*

splatch *n* a splodge, blot, *esp* of something semi-liquid or sticky, a patch of colour, dirt etc. *v* daub, splash *local.*

splatter *v* **1** scatter, splash, sprinkle about, spatter. **2** bespatter, bedaub, splash with liquid, mud etc. **3** splash noisily; walk or run with a clattering or rattling noise *local.* *n* a splash of liquid, mud etc *now Sh Cai.*

spleiter *n* a splash, patch of spilt liquid, blot *now NE Ags.* *v* spill, spatter messily over an area *NE Ags.*

splerrie bespatter, splash with liquid, dirt etc *now wLoth.*

spleut the noise caused by a sudden spluttering gush; the liquid shed or spilled in this way *now Abd.* **~er** burst or gush out with a spluttering noise *Bnf.*

splitter *n* (the noise of) a splashing or splattering of liquid *now Ork C.* *v* splutter, make a spluttering noise; make a mess by splashing liquid about *now Ork C.*

sploit spout, squirt; splash *now Sh.*

splurt a spurt, splutter *now Ags Per.*

spout **1** a forceful discharge of liquid from the mouth of a pipe etc. **2** a small quantity of liquid *local EC-SW.*

spue *of liquid etc* spew, flow, pour (**out** *etc*, in a copious stream.

†spurge spout or gush **out** in a stream.

squatter flutter in water like a duck, flap about in mud or water, splash along *now WC Kcb.*

squirk squirt out suddenly *now Stlg Fif Lnk.*

stank a pond, a pool; a small semi-stagnant sheet of water, *esp* one overgrown with vegetation, a swampy place *Gen except Sh, freq in place-names.*

steepit wet through, sodden.

stench, stanch **1** stanch, check the flow of. **2** †cease flowing.

stoun(d) a stupefying din, a resounding noise (*esp* of water) *now Ags.*

stour *n* **1** a (cloud of) fine spray *now Sh.* **2** a pouring out of liquid, a steady outflow, a gush *now NE.* *v* **1** *of spray etc* swirl, rise in a cloud *now Sh Ork Rox.* **2** (cause to) gush out in a strong stream *now Sh NE.*

stove †*n* a mist or vapour rising from the ground. *v* steam, emit vapour *now Stlg WC.*

straik a (*usu* long, narrow) tract of water *now Mry.*

strick *adj, of running water* rapid, swift-flowing.

strin(d) *n* a very small stream; a trickle of water; the run from spilt liquid. *v* spray, trickle *NE.*

strinkle, †strenkell *v* **1** †besprinkle (**with**). **2** scatter, strew, sprinkle (something) **in, over, on** *now Sh N Rox.* *n, also* **strinkling** *now Abd* a sprinkling; a small amount, *esp* of something liquid or granular *now Abd Stlg Wgt.*

strintle *v* sprinkle, scatter, strew; squirt, spurt; trickle, straggle *now Cai.* *n* a small stream or trickle of liquid; a spurt, squirt *Cai.*

strone *v, of water etc* spout, spurt, gush. *n* a gush or spurt of liquid *now Stlg Bute Kcb.*

†stroube make turbid or cloudy.

stroup the faucet, spout or outlet of a spring or well, a water-tap *now N Per.*

strule a stream or steady trickle of liquid.

sup a quantity, amount (of other liquids, *esp* rain) *now local NE-Ayr.*

swage *of floods etc* subside, settle down, shrink from a swollen state *now Sh Ork N.*

swash *v* dash or splash (liquid) about or over *now Sh Ork.* *n* a splash or plunge in water; a dash of water, the wash of waves against something *now Sh Ork.*

swaw *n* a wave, a ripple. *v* form waves, ripple; undulate.

sweel, swill *v* 1 swill. 2 wash away *local Sh-Kcb.* 3 dash or throw (water) about, cause (a liquid) to swirl round, swallow in copious draughts *local Sh-Kcb. n* 1 a swill. 2 a rinsing, washing or swilling.

swelch, swelt a whirlpool.

swirl, sworl, swurl *n* a whirling movement of water, smoke etc, an eddy, whirlpool. *v* (cause to) move round and round, whirl, eddy.

swither, swodder *now chf NE v* rush, swirl *now Sh. n* a rushing movement, swirl *now Sh.*

switter *of water* plash, ripple.

synd, syne, *v, now freq* ~ **out** 1 rinse (a container etc), swill, wash out *now Cai C-S.* 2 wash (the face, clothes etc), give a quick swill to (an object) by drawing it through water *now Cai C-S.* 3 swill (something) away or out with water etc *now C-S.* ~**ins** rinsings, slops, swill.

sype *v* 1 = *seep now local.* 2 *of a container* drip, leak *now Sh Ork NE, S.* 3 cause to drip or ooze; draw liquid from, drain; drip-dry (clothes) *now Sh Ork Cai Dmf. n* 1 an oozing, leakage *now local Sh-Fif.* 2 a small trickle of water, a small spring. 3 a drip *local Sh-Ags.* 4 a small quantity of liquid, that which drips from an emptied bottle *now Sh Ork.* **sypin, sypit** soaked *now Sh Abd.* **sypins** oozings, leakage; the last drops from a container *now Ork NE Fif.*

tak, take: ~ **someone (up) to** *or* **over** *of water* come up as far on a person as, reach **up to** (a certain height) on a person.

tap, top the surface of water.

teem 1 *also* **tume** empty (a container etc), *now esp* of liquid *now C, S.* 2 *also* **tume** pour, empty out (the contents) from a container *now nEC, S.* 3 *of water* flow or gush copiously *Gen except Sh Ork.*

†**toddle** *of running water* glide, purl, ripple.

totter *now Ags,* †**tottle** *of running water* ripple, purl.

treetle, trytle *now Abd* trickle, fall in drops or in a thin stream *Sh Ork NE.*

†**trigle** trickle.

trinkle *v* trickle *now local NE-WC. n* a trickle *local Ork-WC.*

trinnle, †**trindle, truntle** 1 *of water etc* flow, trickle *now Abd.* 2 cause to roll, flow, trickle *now Stlg Fif Ayr.*

under, un(n)er: ~**water** water below the surface of the ground *now Sh Ork NE.*

†**wa(c)k** *adj* moist, damp. *n, also* ~**nes** moisture.

†**waggle, waigle** a marsh, bog, pool *N.*

wa(ll) drap rainwater dripping from the eaves *Cai Fif wLoth.*

wall, well *n* 1 a natural spring of water which forms a pool or stream *Gen except Sh Ork.* 2 *freq in place-names* a mineral spring reputed to have medicinal qualities. 3 a well. *v* 1 †boil (**up**). 2 well up as a spring of water *now NE.* **wallie** a small well *Mry Abd Ags.* ~ **e(y)e** 1 a place in a bog from which a spring rises. 2 a spring, a well *local N-S.* † ~**heid** a spring which feeds a boggy piece of ground. †**well strand** a streamlet from a spring.

wammle, wamble with a writhing or undulating motion *NE.*

water, watter water. ~**ed** 1 watered. 2 soaked or steeped in water. **water break** a sudden rush of water, a flood. †**waterfall** a slope of the ground sufficient to enable the fall or drainage of water. † ~ **fast** watertight. † ~ **glass** a glass container for water. ~**hole** a hole or pit in which water collects, a well or pool *now Sh N Per.* †**water stand** a water barrel, *esp* one standing on end. †**water stank** a pond, a pool of water.

waver *of water, waves* surge.

†**weel**[1] well, boil, swell up, overflow.

weel[2] a deep pool; an eddy, a whirlpool *freq in place-names.*

weet, wat *now C, S adj, n, v* wet.

weeze ooze, drip, exude.

†**welter** roll down in a stream, flow.

wesh *n, v* wash.

whidder *now Sh,* **whither, whudder** a blowing, spurt of water etc *now Sh.*

†**whummle, whumble, whammle** *of water* overwhelm, drown.

†**wuid, wode, wud(d)** *of wind, water etc* furious, raging.

yat *Sh,* †**yet** 1 pour. 2 pour forth, cause to flow in a flood *latterly Sh.*

yim *n* a thin film or coating on a surface, a scum, a layer of dust, condensed vapour etc *Bnf Abd. v* cover or become covered with a **yim** *Bnf Abd.*

6.1.2 RIVERS, LOCHS

Riversides and -banks are in 5.1.5.

†**boldin, bowdin** swell (up); *esp* rise in flood.

†**brim** a brook, stream.

burn a brook, stream.

caochan, keechan a stream, rivulet *N.*

come doon *of a river* be in flood *now Fif.*

doach name for a rocky stretch of the river Dee at Tongland; a salmon-trap or weir at this point *Kcb*.

doon in flood.

drumlie *of streams or water* troubled, clouded, muddy.

ess a waterfall *NE, chf in place-names*.

fa(ll) subside, *esp* after a flood *now Wgt*.

fluther a slight rise or turbidity in a river.

forkin the point where a river divides into two or more streams *now Abd Ags*.

fuird a ford.

†**gang** the course or channel of a stream.

garth a shallow part of a river or stretch of shingle used as a ford *NE*.

goor *n* slush in running water *now Sh Bnf Abd. v, of streams in thaw* become choked with snow and ice *now Abd*.

grain a branch, arm, offshoot of a stream, river *in place-names*.

great *of a river etc* in flood, high *now Ork*.

grow †*v* rise. *n, of a river etc* a sudden rise, a flood *Mry*.

grue the melting snow and ice found on rivers in early spring *now NE Ags S*.

heavy *of a river* swollen, above its normal height *now local Cai-S*.

hurl-come-gush a noisy rush of water, a mountain torrent in spate.

infa(ll) the inflow of a river, *latterly* of a tributary joining a main river *now NE*.

jouk a bend, meander, twist (of a river) *now Kcb*.

†**lake** *verse* the flowing water of a river or stream.

Lammas: ~ **flude(s)**, †~ **spate** a flood caused by a period of heavy rain about **Lammas**.

lane a slow-moving, winding stream or its bed *SW, also in Gall place-names*.

†**latch** a small stream, *esp* one flowing through boggy ground.

leader a tributary of a stream *now Cai Uls*.

links *esp of the Forth* loops of a winding stream or river, the land enclosed by such.

linn a waterfall, cataract.

lip the edge or brink of a stream, pool etc.

loch, louch a lake, pond (applied to all natural lakes in Scotland, except the Lake of Menteith, Per). ~ **fit** the lower end of a **loch**. ~ **head** the upper end of a **loch**.

loop any natural bend or configuration like a loop, *eg* the winding of a river in its valley.

lowp a place where a river may be or is traditionally thought to have been crossed by leaping; a shelf in a river-bed over which water cascades, or over which fish may leap up-river.

†**pass: burn-** *etc* ~**ing** the act of crossing a burn etc; a crossing-place; the right to cross. ~ **our** pass over, cross a stretch of water.

plumb a deep pool in a river, a drop *now Ayr Rox*.

pot *n, also* ~**tie** a (deep) hole in a river, a pool.

pouch a deep hole in the bed of a river *Fif WC*.

pow, †poll a slow-moving, ditch-like stream flowing through carse land, *esp* bordering the Tay, Forth and Solway *now Per*.

proud *of a river* running high, swollen *now Mry*.

quick water the current (of a river), running water *Gall Slk*.

rack 1 a stretch or reach of a river *now Ags*. **2** a ford in a river, a ridge of gravel or a shallow place *now Kcb Dmf*.

ream *of a turbulent stream,* form a froth or foam.

redd the rut in a riverbed made by salmon for spawning in.

†**ride: not to** ~ *of a river etc* not be fordable by a rider, not allow a rider to cross.

rin, run 1 a stream, rivulet, water channel. **2** the course of a river or stream, *freq* with the lands bordering it, a river valley *now NE Slk*.

scriddan a mountain stream, torrent; rocks and gravel brought down by such.

†**sea, sey:** ~ **sleech** mud formed by a tidal river or estuary.

shaul(d), †schald a shallow part in the sea or a river, a shoal *now local Sh-Ayr*.

sleek, sleech an alluvial deposit of mud or sludge left behind by the sea or a river, silt *now Ags Fif Kcb*.

sma(ll) *of a river etc* low, not in **spate** *NE-S*.

spout a waterfall, cataract *freq in place-names, now local*.

stank a ditch, an open water-course, *freq* a natural stream which has been straightened to serve as a boundary or as part of a drainage system *local*.

step a stepping-stone in a river *now Per Kcb, also in place-names*.

†**stith** *of a stream* strong-flowing.

strand, straun a little stream, rivulet *now Lnk SW*.

strath a river valley, *esp* when broad and flat *in place-names*.

strick *adj, of running water* rapid, swift-flowing. *n* the most rapid part (of a river), the centre of the current.

stripe a small stream, a rivulet *now Sh Ork NE*.

swage *of floods etc* subside, settle down, shrink from a swollen state *now Sh Ork N*.

syke 1 a small stream or water-course, *esp* one in a hollow or on flat, boggy ground, and often dry in summer *now Bwk Lnk S*. **2** a marshy hollow, *esp* one with a stream, a cleft in the ground *now*

Dmf Rox. **sykie** *of ground* full of sluggish rivulets, soft, boggy, though dry in summer.

troch, trough 1 the channel or bed of a river, *esp* a rough part. **2** †the valley or basin of certain rivers in south-west Scotland: '*the trow of Clyde*'.

†**trottin** *of a stream etc* babbling.

up *of a river* in flood *N-Per WC.*

†**wadeable** fordable, that can be crossed on foot.

wample *of a stream* meander, flow gently.

water, watter: waterfit the mouth of a river *now in place-names.* ~**heid** the source of a river, the upper end of a valley *now local Ags-S.* ~ **lip** the brink of a stream *Ayr.* †**watermark** a boundary mark indicating the line of separation between the waters of rivers owned by different proprietors. ~ **mouth** the mouth of a river *now NE Ags Loth.* **water neb** = ~ **mouth**, *specif* the confluence of the Cart and the Clyde. **water run** a runnel of water, a surface drain or gutter for carrying off water, a streamlet. †~ **side** the side or brink of water, the bank of a river etc. †**watter strype** a strip of water, a stream. **water water** river water *S.* ~ **wrack** weeds, leaves, sticks etc carried down by a river *now local Abd-S.*

wham *freq in place-names* a dale or valley, a broad hollow among hills through which a stream runs *now Sh.*

wimple *n, of a stream* a twist, turn, winding or meandering; a twisting movement, a ripple *now local Sh-Loth. v, of a river etc, freq also signifying the sound* meander, twist, turn, ripple *now local Sh-WC.*

wingle *of a stream etc* meander *now Sh Cai.*

6.1.3 ARTIFICIAL WATERWAYS

Mill dams etc are in 7.8.2.

†**bome** a beam, bar; a boom to close a river etc.

brander an iron grating over the entrance to a drain.

†**carry** a weir.

caul a weir or dam *chf SW, S.*

cloose a sluice.

coble 1 †a drainage cistern, cesspool. **2** a pond, watering place *NE.*

†**conduck, conduct** a conduit, a channel for water.

croy a mound or quay to protect a riverbank *chf Per.*

cundy a covered drain, the entrance to a drain *Gen except Sh Ork.*

dam: ~**-dike** the retaining wall of a dam *now SW.* ~**head** a weir *Cai.*

doach name for a rocky stretch of the river Dee at Tongland; a salmon-trap or weir at this point *Kcb.*

†**draucht** the process of drawing off water from a stream etc; a water channel or ditch.

†**draw-dyk** a ditch for drawing off water.

dreep a channel or groove, *esp* one cut for drainage *local C.*

dub a pond.

dutch a ditch *NE.*

ee, eye an opening through which water passes *now Sh Ork.*

flake a weir or lattice fence across a river.

fleet dyke a wall built to prevent flooding *now Ayr.*

†**fontall** coming from a fountain.

funtain a fountain *now Abd.*

gaither dam a dam which collects water from drainage and rainfall only *NE.*

gang water the water supplied by the normal flow of a stream to a mill etc, without a dam *NE.*

gaw, gall a drainage furrow or channel *now Fif.*

gote a ditch, drain, watercourse.

guse dub a goose pond *local, freq in place-names.*

heck 1 a grating placed in or across a stream etc *now local.* **2** †one of the bars of such a framework; *also (chf)* one of the open spaces or interstices between the bars.

†**inhalding** damming (of water).

intak, intake the place where water is diverted from a river, dam etc by a channel.

†**kell,** *chf* ~ **head** a spring, fountain.

kennel a channel, street gutter *now Ayr.*

kep gushes dam the water in a street gutter with the feet *Rox.*

†**land:** ~ **stale**, ~ **stool** the foundation on land of the pier of a bridge or weir.

†**lay in** enclose or retain (*freq* a mill-dam) by means of an embankment.

lonker *now Bute SW,* **lonket** *now Bute SW,* **lunkie** *sEC, SW,* **lunkie-hole** *SW* a hole in a wall, made with a lintel stone, to allow a stream to flow under.

moss pot a water-filled pit in a peat bog *NE.*

pant-well (the mouth of) a public well, fountain etc *Bwk S.*

†**passage 1** an unimpeded flow (of water etc). **2** a water-course, gutter, conduit.

peat-hole an old peat-working on a moor, *freq* one filled with rainwater *now Uls.*

pot hole 1 a small depression in a field which is difficult to drain. **2** a puddle-hole.

pound an enclosed stretch of water, a pond, pool, reservoir *now local C, S*.

pow, †poll a puddle, a pot-hole in the street *Sh Ross*.

puddle a street gutter *NE*.

†restagn dam up (water), cause (water) to cease to flow.

rin, run a small water-channel, a ditch, runnel *now Ork Fif SW*.

†sea, sey: ~ **car** an embankment against the sea, a sea-wall.

sheep drain an open or surface drain in pasture land *Gen except Sh Ork*.

sheuch, sough, shough 1 a trench in the ground, *esp* for drainage, a ditch, open drain. **2** a street gutter *nEC Loth WC*.

slap, slop a gap to let water into or out of a dam, drain, ditch etc.

sloosh a sluice.

slunk, †slonk a wet and muddy hollow, a soft, deep, wet rut in a road, a ditch *now Wgt*.

spout, *also* ~ **well** a natural spring of water streaming from the ground or from a cleft in a rock; *latterly also* an outside tap or standpipe *now local Abd-Rox*.

†spult a spout.

stank *n* **1** a pond, a pool *now Sh*. **2** a ditch, an open water-course, *freq* a natural stream which has been straightened to serve as a boundary or as part of a drainage system *local*. **3** a street gutter *EC, WC*. **4** a grating in a gutter *WC*. *v* make a ditch in; surround with a moat.

strand, straun an artificial water-channel, a (street-)gutter *now local N-Renfr*.

stripe a street gutter.

sweirie well a well which is dependable only after rain *now Cai*.

syver, syre 1 a ditch, drain, water-channel, *specif* a (covered-in) stone-lined field-drain *now Ork N Wgt*. **2** a street gutter *C-S*. **3** the opening of the drain-trap in a street gutter, *freq* including the grating which covers it *Gen except Sh Ork*.

tippit *of a pipe, sink etc* choked to overflowing *Bnf Abd*.

trink a trench, channel, ditch, gutter *now NE Ags Fif*.

†trinsch a trench.

troch, trough *usu* ~**s**, *latterly* **trows** a channel or wooden conduit for water, *esp* that leading to a millwheel *now local Ork-Wgt*.

wa gang an outflow of water, *specif* from a millwheel, the tail-race *now Sh*.

wall, well 1 a well. **2** a drinking fountain *now local*. **3** a water stand-pump *local N-WC*.

water, watter: ~**ings** a trough, pool in a stream etc where farm animals go to drink *now Ork Abd*. ~ **dyke** a flood wall or embankment. ~**-fur** *n* a drainage furrow to carry off surface water *now Ork Stlg Loth*. *v* provide (land) with drainage furrows. **†** ~ **gang** a water course, channel, *esp* an artificial one.**water run** a runnel of water, a surface drain or gutter for carrying off water, a streamlet. **†** ~ **stank** a pond, pool of water.

way-flude, †way lead a water channel *now Bnf Abd*.

†wise lead, conduct (water) in a channel.

6.1.4 SEA(S)

†bewave toss about; blow or sweep away.

brack *adj* briny. *n* brine.

ca(ll) the motion of the waves *Sh N*.

chap, shap a swell, choppiness (of the sea) *now Sh Ags*.

dog afore his maister the swell of the sea that often precedes a storm *now Bnf*.

drag, draig the motion of the tide *now Sh Cai Fif*.

dub 1 *also* **†dib** *joc* the ocean *now Ags Fif*. **2** a sea pool (*esp* one only visible at low tide) *now Fif Bwk*.

†east: the ~**er seas** the Baltic.

†fill flow landward.

fire burn, †fire sea phosphorescence *now Fif Kcb*.

firth, †frith a wide inlet of the sea; an estuary.

gote a narrow rocky inlet of the sea, a creek; a navigable channel *now local*.

gowstie wild, stormy.

†grow rise *NE*.

grumlie sullen, surly, grumbling *now local*.

grun(d), ground the bottom of the sea *now local Sh-Bwk*. ~ **ebb** the ebb-tide at its lowest, low water *local Sh-Abd*.

gullet 1 a narrow, deep channel or rocky inlet *now Gall*. **2** †a narrow channel made or used for catching fish.

hettle name given by fishermen to the rough stony sea-bottom some distance from the shore, beyond the area covered with seaweed *now Cai*.

hole a small bay *now N, EC Arg, freq in place-names*.

hope a small bay or haven *now only in place-names*.

jabble *v* become choppy *local*. *n* a choppy area of the sea.

†jasch the dash of a wave.

jaup the splashing of the sea, a breaker, the surf, a choppy sea *now Sh Ork SW Uls*.

jaw a wave, breaker *now NE Ags.*

jow the surge or swell of water or waves *now Kcdn Ags.*

kav *Sh,* **kaif** *NE of a stormy sea* foam in breaking, throw up a spray.

lake a pool left at ebb-tide, used as a fish trap *Dmf.*

Lammas stream a high and strong tide occurring about **Lammas** *chf N.*

land: ~ **birst,** ~ **brist** the breaking of waves on the shore.

l(e)aky tide a tide in the upper part of the Firth of Forth which seems to lose water temporarily before the full tide, and to gain it before the ebb tide *EC.*

lift a rising swell in the sea *local.*

lipper a broken or choppy sea *now Sh-Ags.*

loch, louch a sea loch.

Mey, May: ~ **flood** a high tide occurring in May *chf Ork.*

†**nairra seis** straits, narrows.

outby outwards; away from the shore, out at sea etc.

outgaun, outgoing *of the tide* ebbing *Sh Ags SW.*

†**pass: the** ~ **(of Calies)** the Straits of Dover.

plumb a deep pool on the seabed *now Ayr Rox.*

pot hole a pool in the rocks on the seashore.

pow, †**poll 1** a creek or inlet (? at the mouth of a slow-moving stream) serving as a wharf for small vessels *now SW.* **2** a sea pool in the rocks *now Sh Cai Abd.*

proud running high, swollen *now Mry.*

roil a storm, a heavy sea *Arg.* **ralliach** choppy, stormy *Arg.*

†**roum se** the open sea.

rug a strong undercurrent in the sea, a strong tide *now Sh-Per.*

rummlin kirn a deep narrow gully on the shore where the tide makes a loud rumbling noise *Kcb.*

sab, sob the noise made by a gust of wind or by the rise and fall of the sea; a full sea, as on the east coast in May.

sang, song the noise of the sea breaking on the shore *local Sh-Kcdn.*

saut, salt: ~ **bree** salt water, water in which salt has been mixed or boiled *Sh NE.*

†**scaud, scald:** ~**ing** *of the sea* boiling, seething.

scruif, scruff the surface of water or the sea *now NE.*

sea, sey the sea. ~ **gust** salt spume driven by wind onto the land *now Sh Ork.* ~ **haar** a sea fog *E.* ~ **loch** an arm of the sea, *esp* fiord-shaped. †~ **sleech** mud formed by a tidal river or estuary.

†**sharp, sherp** make (the sea) rough.

shaul(d), †**schald** a shallow part in the sea or a river, a shoal *now local Sh-Ayr.*

shouder, shoulder, shouther the swelling part of a wave rising to the crest *local Bnf-Gall.*

sleek, sleech an alluvial deposit of mud or sludge left behind by the sea or a river, silt *now Ags Fif Kcb.*

slock, sloch a creek or gully in the sea, a long deep inlet between rocks, often revealed at low tide *Abd-Ags Gall.*

sma(ll) *adj, of the sea, a lake etc* smooth, calm, undisturbed *Cai NE,* C. *n* a period of calm at sea, a lull.

smelt, smilt a calm patch on the sea.

smuith, smooth a smooth or level place, *specif* the sandy sea-bottom *Ross Mry Kcdn.*

sound a sound, a narrow channel.

spindrift, speendrift *NE,* **spunedrift** *Sh NE* spray whipped up by gusts of wind and driven across the tops of waves.

still *of the tide* the pause between ebb and flow *Sh Wgt.*

†**strand, straun** the sea.

swaw *n* a wave, a ripple. *v* form waves, ripple; undulate.

sweel, swill *of water, waves* roll, flow with a swirling motion *local Sh-Kcb.*

swelchie a whirlpool in the sea *Ork Cai.*

tap, top: (in) ~ **flood** *of water* in full flood, at its highest point *now Sh.* **the** ~ **o the water** high water, full tide *Sh N, EC.*

throughlet a narrow passage or channel, *esp* at sea *Renfr Ayr.*

tide the sea, ocean.

†**traduct** a passage, channel.

trink a narrow coastal inlet *now Sh-Ags Fif.*

troch, trough a channel among sea rocks, *esp* a rough one.

water burn a name for the phosphorescence seen on the sea *now Mry Kcdn.*

waver *of water, waves* surge.

waw, wall †a wave (of the sea). **wally** *verse, of the sea* tempestuous, wave-tossed, swelling.

†**wede** *of waves* rage, be furious.

yawn a long sea-inlet or gully *freq in place-names on Kcdn coast.*

6.1.5 SEASHORE

Cliffs are in 5.1.2.

†**bed** a bank in the sea.

brae the (steep or sloping) bank of a river or lake or shore of the sea.

brig a reef, a long low ridge of sea-rocks *now in ECoast place-names.*

chingle *chf Bnf Abd,* **jingle** *now Gall Uls* shingle. **chingly** gravelly, pebbly *Ork Bnf Abd.*

†**cost side** a coast.

ebb the foreshore, sections of which might be assigned to individual fishermen *now local Sh-Abd.*

†**foreland** the foreshore or beach.

grund, ground: ~ **ebb** the lowest part of the foreshore *Sh Cai Abd.*

inch a stretch of low-lying land near a river or other water, sometimes cut off at high tide *now chf in place-names.*

leck a flat rock in the sea *NE Kcb, freq in Abd place-names.*

†**line** a bar or sandbank in a river or harbour.

links a stretch of undulating open sandy ground, *usu* covered with turf, bent-grass or gorse, normally near the seashore *chf E Coast.*

machair 1 a stretch of low-lying land adjacent to the sand of the seashore *chf Hebrides.* **2 the Machairs** the land bordering the Solway Firth or Luce Bay *Gall.*

mowrie 1 gravel mixed with shingle, shingle *Mry.* **2** a gravelly sea beach *Bnf.*

rock, roke: ~**lie** pebbly *local EC, SW.* ~**y-on a** pile of stones built by boys to try to stem the incoming tide *Abd Kdn.*

row, roll the high-water mark on a beach; a roll of seaweed along this line *Ross Mry.*

†**saut, salt:** ~ **fail** seaside turf. ~ **water** the seaside, *esp* as a place for holidaying or recuperation.

scawt *of rocks* covered with barnacles etc *now Cai.*

sea, sey: †~ **craig** a rock by or in the sea. ~ **green** land partially reclaimed from the sea, but still overflowed by spring tides. †**se skar** a sea-cliff. ~ **toun** a seaport town or village *freq in place-names.*

shore head the ground on the upper or land side of a quay or harbour *Fif.*

skellie a ridge of rock running out to sea, *usu* covered at high tide, a **skerrie**, reef *now Abd Ags Fif, freq in place-names.*

skerrie an isolated rock or islet in the sea, *freq* one covered at high tide *chf Sh Ork.*

smuith, smooth a smooth or level place, *specif the sandy sea-bottom Ross Mry Kcdn.*

†**soukand sand** a quicksand.

stack a tall column of rock rising out of the sea, separated from the cliffs by weathering *Sh-Bnf.*

strand a beach or shore of the sea; a sand-bank etc exposed at low water *now Ork Cai.*

tide the foreshore, the land between high and low water marks *now Ags Fif.*

6.2 SHIPS, SHIPPING

6.2.1 SHIPS, BOATS, SAILING

For fishing boats, see 6.3.3.

air an oar.

†**aspyne** a ship's boat.

astarn astern.

†**babord** larboard, port.

bairge a barge.

†**be-eft** after, behind.

†**Bertonar** a ship of Brittany.

beuch the bow of a ship etc *now NE.*

†**bilgit** large-hulled.

†**birlin(g)** a large rowing boat or galley used in the West Highlands.

†**blind** a spritsail.

boat, bait a boat. **boatic, bottick** a boat-hook *now Sh Bnf.*

†**bolm** a boat-pole.

†**bonnet** an additional piece laced to a sail.

bouk *of a rope* increase on a capstan as its coils are wound round *now NE-nEC.*

bowse swing out (*eg* a boat) *now Bnf Abd Ags.*

bowsplit a bowsprit *Bnf Ayr.*

†**boyart** a small one-masted vessel.

buccar a fast-sailing boat used in smuggling.

bugdalin 1 †the inside planking of a ship. **2** anything used to line the hold of a ship before putting the cargo in *now Sh Cai.*

†**bush** a bus, a kind of cargo- or fishing-boat.

†**cabar** = **gabbart.**

†**cabil, capill** a cable. ~ **stok** a capstan. ~ **tow** a cable-rope. ~ ӡ**arne** yarn for making cables.

†**cahute** a ship's cabin; a separate room or space.

caibin a cabin *NE Ags.*

†**cap** sail, keep a course; ? drift.

cast make fast (a rope) by means of a hitch *N Kcb.*

†**challop** a shallop, a kind of large boat.

chatters *Bnf Abd eLoth,* **chathers** *local Mry-Fif* iron staples in a rudder-post into which the rudder is fixed.

cleek anchor a small anchor *Cai Kcb.*

coble 1 a short flat-bottomed rowing-boat, used *esp* in salmon-fishing or lake- or river-fishing. **2** a ferry-boat *now Bnf.*

†**collum** a ship.

†**cordell** a rope, *esp* as part of a ship's tackle.

†cowbrig the orlop-deck of a vessel; material for such a deck.

cowd(le) float slowly, rock gently on waves *chf WC.*

†coy a cabin-bed, berth, bunk.

†crear a small trading vessel.

†cross part of a sail; a cross-sail.

†currach a coracle.

†disrig unrig (a ship etc).

eft *adv* aft. *adj* belonging to the after part; back, rear. **†~ castell, ~ schip** the poop or stern of a vessel.

efter(h)in port side *ECoast.*

faik coil (a rope or line) *now Sh Fif.*

†fall-brig a boarding-bridge on the side of a ship.

†fang a rope for steadying the gaff of a sail.

faran, forin the starboard side of a boat *chf NE.*

fit spar *Sh NE, C,* **feetspur** *now Cai Ross* a bar of wood across the floor of a boat for pressing the feet against when rowing.

†flory boat a boat carrying passengers to and from steamers which cannot get alongside the pier *Fif.*

forethaft the seat next to the bow in a rowing boat *now Sh Bnf Fif.*

gabbart a lighter, barge *chf WC.*

gaillie a galley.

graith the rigging or tackle of a ship *now local NE-Gall.*

†gubernakil a helm, rudder.

hank 1 fore or aft ~(s) the places on each side of a boat where the side-boards come together at stem or stern, the quarters *now Sh.* **2** the stem or *chf* stern compartment of a boat.

†thede tow a head rope on the rigging of a ship.

†helmstok a tiller.

hoise raise, lift up, heave up, hoist (a sail) *now nEC Arg Kcb.*

horn the stem-post (or stern-post *Sh*) of a boat, the prow *now Sh.*

howd *v, of a vessel afloat* pitch or toss about, bob up and down *now Kcdn. n, esp of the motion of a ship* a lurching rocking movement from side to side. **howder** *v* move with a rocking, jolting or bumping motion *now NE. n, of a boat on a rough sea* a rocking, jolting, sideways motion *Bnf Abd.*

howe 1 the hull of a ship. **2** a boat with neither sails nor mast up *NE-Fif.*

howld the hold (of a ship) *now local Sh-Fif.*

jow *of a boat* rock, toss *now Ags.*

keel draucht an iron or wooden covering on the outside of a boat's keel to protect it when the boat is being drawn *now Cai.*

kent *n* a punt-pole. **†v** propel a boat by using a **kent** *S.*

lave bale, remove (water) with a bucket or scoop.

lay: ~ about turn a boat round *Sh Ayr.* **† ~ anker** drop anchor.

†lichter a lighter, a loading boat.

†loft the deck of a ship.

lowrie: ~ hook, ~ tow a hook or rope by which something may be dragged *Sh Ags.*

†lowse *of a ship* free from its moorings.

†lufe 1 a luff, a contrivance for altering a ship's course. **2 ?** the rope which carried forward the clew of a sail to windward.

lum the funnel of a steamship.

†lusty *of a ship* fair, gallant.

†lymphad a West Highland (or Irish) galley.

†mawmar the discharge pipe of a ship's pump.

†mers a round-top, top-castle.

†midschip the middle part of a vessel.

mitch the crutch or rest in which the top of a mast lies when lowered *Cai Fif.*

most a mast *now Bnf Abd.*

†nicht glas(s) *appar* a sand-glass used on a ship to time the night watches.

†nok the tip or extremity of a yard-arm.

†ourloft, ourlop, overlope *orig* the platform or raised gangway(s) joining the raised half-decks at the ends of ships; the deck of a ship; one of the decks, where a ship has more than one.

paidle paddle.

†palm the blade of an oar.

†peges-nos ? the projecting part of the prow, **?** the figurehead of a ship.

†pegy-mast ? a small mast of some kind; **?** a top-mast or **?** a small mast or yard for a pennant on a ship.

pike the pin on the sternpost of a boat *Kcdn.*

†pinnage a pinnace, a small light ship.

puffer a small steamboat used to carry cargo around the west coast of Scotland and the Hebrides.

†pulpit the poop of a ship, from which directions were given.

rae, †ra a sailyard *now Sh.* **~band** the rope attaching the sail to the yard *now Sh Cai.*

rimwale a board round the gunwale of a boat *Sh Fif.*

rither *now Fif Kcb,* **†ruthie** a rudder.

†trone the pipe of a boat's pump.

room the compartment or space between the thwarts of a boat *chf Sh.*

row *of a boat* move along in the water easily or smoothly *now Sh Abd Ags.* **~th** rowing; a stroke of the oar(s).

†**saddle** a block of wood fastened to a spar to take the bearing of another spar attached to it.

†**saule** *n, v* sail. **sailage** ? the speed of a ship under sail.

scaff a light boat, skiff.

†**scharpentyn** a serpentine, a kind of (ship's) cannon.

scow a flat-bottomed boat, *eg* a lighter, barge *now local Cai-Kcb*.

scullrow a notch in the stern of a boat used as a kind of rowlock when the boat is propelled by a single oar *now WC*.

†**se, sey:** ~ **cowbell** a sea-going **coble**.

†**seek up for** bear up for, sail towards.

†**shak, shake:** ~ **out** unfurl and let out (a sail etc) with a shake.

†**ship burd** ? a washboard in a ship.

ship, †**sheip** a ship. † ~ **rae** a sail-yard.

shue *rowing* back water, row (a boat) backwards *now Sh Ork Cai*.

†**smyte** a rope attached to one of the lower corners of a sail.

sneckler a short circle of rope attached to the stern of a **coble** for taking a rolling hitch on standing gear etc *Cai NE*.

†**sneir** *v* sail.

snuve, snoove move smoothly or easily, at a steady, even pace, glide.

spoucher a (*usu* long-handled) wooden ladle or scoop, *esp* for baling a boat or lifting fish from a net.

†**stam** the stem or prow of a ship.

starn the stern (of a boat etc). ~ **stuil** the short seat furthest aft in a small boat, on which the steersman sits *Bnf Kcdn Fif*.

steerer a rudder *now Sh (fisherman's taboo)*.

stent, stint extend, stretch out (a sail, etc) in its proper position, make taut.

†**steven** the prow *or* stern of a boat.

sting, steng *n* a pole used to push off a boat or in punting. †*v* punt.

taik *n, v* tack *now N Fif*.

tak, take: ~**in** *of a boat* let in (water), leak *now Sh N Per*.

tap, top: ~**pin** lift a halyard to set the peak of a mainsail *now Sh.* † ~ **royal** a top-gallant royal (sail).

†**taunt** hoist (a sail).

thaft *now Ork-EC*, **taft** *Sh* a rower's bench, thwart.

thowl *Gen except Sh Ork*, **thow (pin)** *now N-EC* a thole, a pin to hold an oar.

tillie a tiller (of a boat) *now Fif*.

†**track-boat** a boat which is towed.

trochs, troughs a kind of flat-bottomed river barge in two sections with a space through which salmon could be speared *Dmf Rox*.

†**upsail** a hoisted sail.

veshel, weshell a vessel.

wan(d) a pole or stout stick, *esp* a punting pole.

†**weirman** a man-of-war, warship.

†**welter** *of a ship* roll to and fro (on the waves).

wherry a kind of sailing barge with one sail, and a mast stepped forward *now Loth Ayr*.

†**wrang** a rib of a ship.

yatt a yacht *WC*.

†**ʒong frow** ? a dead-eye.

6.2.2 SHIPBUILDING, REPAIR, MAINTENANCE

†**bait wricht** a boat-builder.

brime *Bnf Ags,* **brim** *Cai Ross Mry* fill (a boat) with salt water to swell and close the timbers after it has been lying ashore.

†**calfat** make watertight, caulk. ~**ar** a ship-caulker. ~**ing** caulking.

clink *v* rivet. *n* a rivet *Bnf Abd.* †**clenkett** rivetted.

colf fill in, stop up *chf NE.* † ~**ing, calfin** *n* material for caulking or stopping. †*v* caulk, stop up.

fit eitch a ship's carpenter's long-handled adze held in place by the foot *now Sh Ork Cai Abd*.

geyze become leaky, warp *now midLoth*.

growth the deposit found on the bottom of a boat *now Sh Fif Ayr*.

hauder-on a rivetter's assistant in a shipyard *Loth WC*.

†**lek** *of a ship* leaky, having leaks.

lench launch *now Ork N*.

†**loft** furnish (a boat) with a deck.

mundy a kind of heavy hammer weighing about 20-28 lbs (9-13 kilos) used *esp* by shipwrights *Edb WC*.

†**outred** *v* fit out, equip (a ship). *n* fitting out (a ship) with equipment and provisions for a voyage.

†**outreik, outreche, outrig** *v* make (a ship etc) ready for a voyage or service. *n* 1 equipping a ship for a voyage. 2 the act of outfitting a ship; an outfit (of tackle and stores).

peltie a shipyard hammer *NE*.

pick *n* pitch. †*v* pitch, daub or smear with pitch.

plying hammer a heavy double-faced hammer, used *esp* in shipyards *now WC*.

†**pullan** a kind of sail-cloth.

ruive, roove *esp boat-building* a burr, a metal

washer on which the point of a nail or bolt can be clinched; a rivet *now local Sh-Kcb*.

save draw (a boat) up on the shore for the winter *now Cai*.

seam, sem *Sh* a nail used to fix together the planks of a clinker-built boat riveted by a **ruive**, *freq* **seam and ruive** *now Sh*.

†shute launch (a ship).

†slip a device for drawing ships out of the water for repair.

stuit, stoot, †stut a prop, support (*eg* for a beached boat) *now Kcdn Ags*.

tingle patch a leak in the clinkers of a boat *local Mry-midLoth*.

†tuffing caulking material; oakum.

†wrakling *esp shipbuilding* a large nail.

6.2.3 SHIPPING, NAVIGATION

†aboord aboard.

†awner a shipowner.

†birth the burden or carrying capacity (of a ship).

boat, bait *n* a ferry *now Bnf Abd*. *†v* put into or carry in a boat; go into a boat, embark. **†baitschele** a boatshed, *esp* for a ferryboat.

bow, †buy a buoy *now Mry Bnf*. ~ **rope, †boy rape, burop** a buoy rope *now Mry*.

†brig a gangway for a boat.

†brokin *of a ship* stranded or wrecked.

†buird: on ~ *of a ship* alongside.

†cairt, cart a chart.

card, caird a chart, map.

†dok: ~ **maill,** ~ **silver** dock dues, the charges made for the use of a dock.

ebb 1 *latterly of the contents of a vessel* shallow, lacking in depth, scant *now local Bnf-Rox*. **2** *†of a boat* ground or be grounded at low tide.

enter, inter *now NE Ags* record (a vessel or cargo) in an official register.

fraucht *n* **1** the hire of a boat; the fare or freight charge for transport by water *now Cai Arg*. **2** *†a* ship's cargo. *†v* **1** transport by water. **2** load with cargo. **3** hire (a boat).

free port a port open to all merchants for loading and unloading their vessels.

†fure carry, convey, *chf* by sea. **furing** transporting by sea; the cargo of a vessel; the amount of cargo allowed to a mariner for his own business use.

†gat a navigable channel.

god's-send a wreck or other profitable flotsam etc *Sh Ork SW*.

†gold(en)-penny a shipping due.

graith cargo.

grapple drag (water) for a corpse *now local NE-Uls*.

†grun(d), ground: ~ **leif** leave given to vessels, *esp* in port, to make use of ground in port, to make use of ground on shore; the duty payable for this.

hale *v* haul, drag, pull (up) *now Sh NE*. *†interj* exclam used when hauling.

†half-hyre half of a seaman's pay for a voyage.

†harboury a harbour, shelter for ships.

†havin(ing) a haven. **havin silver** a harbour due.

herbour a harbour.

hine a haven, a (natural) harbour *now Ags Fif, also in place-names*.

hive *only in place-names* a haven, harbour, *chf* Stonehaven *NE*.

†hola haul!

hope, howp *now Abd* a small bay or haven *now only in place-names*.

hythe a harbour, a landing place, an inlet among rocks *Mry Bnf*.

†incuming the coming of vessels into port.

innerlie *of a ship* near the shore *chf Sh*.

†jerkin a jollification, *orig* on a ship's leaving port.

†keyheid the westernmost or most inland part of the quay of Aberdeen.

†laid, load: ~**ening 1** the loading of a ship. **2** a ship's cargo. **laidin 1** loading a ship. **2** a ship's cargo. **laidner** a shipper.

†land: get *or* **take** ~ strike or reach land.

†lastage 1 a port-duty, ? levied on the cargo of a ship. **2** the cargo of a ship measured in lasts (a measure of quantity).

†lay to (the) se to put (ships) to sea.

liver 1 *†*discharge (a ship's cargo), deliver on shore. **2** *†of the ship* unload. **3** unload (a ship) *now N Hebrides*.

†locht a boat-load (of a commodity).

†los, lose 1 *of a vessel* discharge cargo, be unloaded; discharge (its cargo). **2** *of persons* unload (a ship); unload (cargo) from a vessel.

†lyage the lying of goods at a port until collected by the consignee; a charge made for this. **lie day** one of a certain number of days allowed for the loading and unloading of a ship.

meith a sea-mark: **1** *†*a marker in the water; **2** a landmark used by sailors to steer by.

†misguiding steering (of a boat) incompetently.

†navyne navy, a fleet.

†nepe *of a ship* be stranded at neap tide.

†owerbuird overboard.

pall, pawl a pole, a stout post, a beam, *esp* a mooring post for ships *now N Ayr Kcb*.

parch, perch 1 †a perch, a pole set up in a seaway to guide navigation. **2** piles of stones used for this purpose in the Firth of Clyde.

perish wreck (a ship etc) *local Sh-SW*.

†**pike up** sail along, sail close to (the coast).

†**pillage** the share of the contents of a prize-ship due by law to the ordinary members of the ship's company which made the capture.

pow, †poll a creek or inlet serving as a wharf for small vessels.

†**prime gilt** a sum of money paid to the master and crew of a ship for the loading and care of the cargo.

putt a jetty or stone buttress projecting from a river bank, used to alter the current, protect the bank etc *S*.

raid, †reid a roadstead for ships.

†**rowage** rowing dues or charges.

†**sand** run (a ship) ashore on sand.

†**sea, sey: ~ box** a mariner's friendly society, so-called from the box in which the funds were kept. **~ breve** a document allowing reprisals at sea. **be ~ burd** by sea. **~ wrack** property cast up by the sea.

set †*v* sight or make (land). *n* **1** †a berth (in a harbour). **2** *law, chf* action of **~ (and sale)** an action in which a part-owner of a ship can request to buy out or be bought out by his partners or to have the ship sold. **~ ower** ferry across (a river etc) *now Sh*. **tak a ~ o land** take one's bearings *Mry Ags Loth*.

ship, †scheip: † **~ broken** shipwrecked; ruined by shipwreck. † **~ rede** a roadstead. **~ wrack** a shipwreck *now Sh*.

shore *with a place-name or* **the ~** a quay, landing-place, harbour *now N Fif*. † **~ due, ~ mail, ~ silver** a harbour-due. **~ head** the ground on the upper or land side of a quay or harbour *Fif*. † **~ levy** a duty on ships entering a harbour. † **~ master** a harbour-master. **~ porter** *specif, in Aberdeen* a member of an incorporated society of porters, **the Society of S~ Porters,** *orig* called **piners**, no longer only working at the harbour, but also carrying out house removals etc.

shyve throw a rope (*eg* from boat to pier) *NE*.

†**siege, saige** a place on which a ship lies.

sitting doun *of a ship* a going aground.

†**sound** a sounding-line or -lead.

spreath driftwood, wreckage from ships *now Abd Ags*.

spulyie jetsam, anything cast ashore *now Ork*.

†**stell, stile** load (a ship) evenly, trim the cargo in (a ship).

stem keep a certain course.

†**streem: (up)on the ~** *of a ship* lying off the shore of a river.

†**stulage** ? ballast.

swing rope a hawser for making fast a boat *now N Ags Fif*.

†**tether** tie up, moor (a vessel).

vaige *now Sh*, **veage** *now Edb*, †**vod(ge)** *n, v* voyage.

†**waith: wrack and ~** flotsam and jetsam *chf Sh Ork*.

†**warp, werp** run (a ship) aground, *esp* on a sandbank.

†**water, watter: ~ met** a larger measure used for goods sold on board ship.

wrack, wreck, wreak 1 a wreck, a shipwreck etc. **2** seaweed and miscellaneous flotsam washed up by the sea *Gen except Sh Ork*. †**wrack** *or* **wreck goods** *law* goods driven ashore from a wreck. **wrack ship** a wrecked ship *now Sh*. **wrack wid** driftwood *now Ork*.

6.2.4 SAILORS

†**almeral** an admiral.

†**awner** a shipowner.

†**bo(i)t(is)man** a boatman.

†**chaptane** a captain.

†**childer** the common sailors or hands on a ship.

†**contermaister** the mate of a ship.

†**ferryar, ferrio(u)r** a ferryman.

†**frauchtar, ~isman** a person who loads a ship.

hank-(oar)sman a rower seated in the stern of an open boat immediately in front of the helmsman *Mry Bnf*.

keiler a person who coils ropes in the bottom of a boat *now Cai*.

†**key-maister** an officer in charge of the quays in the harbour of a seaport.

killick a leading seaman in the Navy, the anchor badge on his sleeve being likened to a pickaxe *WC*.

†**kippage** the crew of a ship.

lodesman a guide; a pilot; a steersman *now Sh*.

mannie a skipper *NE*.

†**marinall** a sailor, seaman.

†**piner, pioner** a labourer or porter; *specif,* in Aberdeen applied to a member of a society of porters instituted in 1498 and still existing as the **Society of Shore Porters.** † **~ie** *Per,* **~schip** *chf Per* the office or duties of a **piner**.

tarry breeks *etc* nickname for a sailor.

6.3 FISHING

6.3.1 SEA FISHING

†assize herring a royalty of herring due to the king from boats engaged in the herring fishing.

ave a small net used *chf* in herring-fishing.

bauk a rope, *esp* the head rope in fishing lines and nets *now Cai*.

beet replace hooks on (a fishing line) *now Kcdn*.

body a great number of fish *now Bnf Fif*.

†bounty a bonus paid to fishermen for the season's fishing in addition to the price for the fish caught *Cai Mry Abd*.

buird the net closest to the side of the boat *N*.

burth the distance between fishing boats when setting lines *now Ags Cai*.

bush-rope the rope to which the nets of a **drift** are attached *now local Cai-Ags*.

clev the lines protect the **tippin** and hooks before treating a deep-sea fishing line with a preservative after use *N*.

†couper a buyer of herring.

†cran *measure of fresh, uncleaned herrings* one barrel, *latterly* fixed at 37.5 gallons (170.48 litres).

creel a fish-trap, lobster-pot *now local Cai-Arg*.

croy a tiny crustacean on which herring feed *Arg*.

daffins the cords used to fasten drift-nets to the rope from which they are hung *Ork Cai Mry*.

dale each share in a herring-fishermen's profit-sharing scheme. **~sman** a sharer or partner in a ship, fishing boat etc.

dandie *chf herring fishing* keep moving a line up and down in the water *Sh Bnf*. **~s** *now Bnf Abd*, **~ hanlin** *now Bnf* a type of fishing line. **~ line** a line used as above *Sh NE*.

†depin, dipin a section of a fishing net, one fathom in depth.

diacle a small dial or compass, *latterly (Sh Ork)* in a fishing boat.

dorro, darra a trailing cord with hooked lines attached, used in catching cod, mackerel etc *now Bnf*.

draucht net a net drawn to catch fish.

drave 1 the annual herring fishing *now Fif Bwk*. **2** a shoal of fish; a catch.

dreg dredge (shellfish etc).

†drift a set of fishing-nets suspended from a cable and allowed to drift with the tide.

durth stamp down (herrings) in a barrel *now Bnf*.

ebb the foreshore, sections of which might be assigned to individual fishermen *now local Sh-Abd*.

eel ark an eel trap.

farlan a long box into which herrings are emptied for gutting *Sh N Fif Bwk*.

fish, fush fish. **~er 1** a fisherman. **2** a member of a fishing community *local N*. **~er toun** a fishing village *now Abd*. **† ~ boit** a fishing boat. **~-cadger** a fish hawker.

fleet a set of nets or lines carried by a single boat.

fourtie a quarter of the regulation barrel, a firkin, *chf* of herring *NE*.

fresh pack (herring) in ice ungutted, for consumption as fresh *local*. **fresher** a herring-buyer who packs fish as above *local*.

frock 1 a sailor's or fisherman's knitted jersey *Ork Abd*. **2** a short oilskin coat or cape *Sh Cai Fif*.

gauge, gage *net-making* a template to regulate the mesh-size *Sh Cai Kcb*.

gavel, gale *NE* one of the side ropes of a herring-net *Ork NE Fif*.

goshens a good catch of fish.

graith the attachment, consisting of the **snuid** and **tippin** by which the hook is suspended from the line *now NE*.

ground bauk the weighted rope at the bottom edge of a fishing net *now Sh Ork*.

guttag a fish-gutting knife *Cai Ayr*.

gutter a woman employed in gutting fish.

†hake a hook.

†hale a haul (*esp* of fish), the hauling in of nets.

half †a bag-shaped net set or held to retain fish as the tide ebbs *Gall Dmf*. **†halver** a person who fishes with such a net *Dmf*. **go haavin** fish with such a net; go salmon fishing, *esp* on the Solway *now Kcb Dmf*. **halve-net, half-net** = **half** *Gall Dmf*.

handlin a handline *now Sh N*.

hard fish *etc* dried or salt fish *now local Sh-EC*.

heck, haik a triangular spiked frame on which fish are dried *now local Sh-Fif*. **Auld Haik(e)s** name for a fishing ground off the coast of Fife.

heid, head: **~-bauk 1** the float-rope with corks attached, from which the older type of herring-net was suspended in the water *Sh NE*. **2** the vertical edge of a fishing-net *now Sh*. **~ tow** a headrope in a herring-net *Bnf Abd*.

herrie, harry take all the fish or shellfish from (a stretch of water etc). **† ~-watter(-net)** a kind of fishing net.

†herrin drave the annual herring-fishing.

hettle name given by fisherman to the rough stony

sea-bottom some distance from the shore, beyond the area covered with seaweed *now Cai.*

hing, hang: ~ **net** a vertical stake net *now Suth Bwk Kcb.*

hose *of fish* swallow (the bait) *now Bnf Abd.*

huidin *now Sh Ork,* **hiddin** *chf NE* a knot used to join two parts of a fishing line.

hullie a receptacle for storing live crabs and lobsters, *orig* holes in the rocks below the high-water mark, *now* baskets or boxes anchored in the harbour *eLoth Bwk.*

imp a cord of twisted horsehair forming part of a fishing line, to which the hook is attached *Sh-Cai Fif Bwk.*

innerlie *of a ship or of fishing grounds* near the shore *chf Sh.*

iron man a hand-winch used on boats to haul in the nets *Sh Ork E.*

†**jadgear** a gauger, *esp* one who verified that the fish barrels were standard size. **jadgerie** the action or office of gauging.

jig *n* an instrument for catching fish, a sinker or wire frame with fish hooks attached *local. v* catch fish with a **jig.**

†**kaner, kenner** the person appointed overseer of certain fishings and *appar* responsible for paying the **kane** (a rent payment in kind).

kip tie up (hides, fish) in bundles *now Sh.*

klondyke: klondyker, klondyking an exporter or the exporting to the Continent of fresh fish, (*orig* herring, *now chf* mackerel), *orig* by fast ship, *now* direct to factory ships for processing on board.

Lammas drave the summer herring fishing on the Fife coast *now Kcdn Fif.*

†**land:** ~ **rope,** ~ **raip** a rope passing from the end of a drag-net to the shore.

†**Lang Forties** the Forties, a North Sea fishing-ground 75 miles (120 km) off the Abd coast, and only 40 fathoms deep.

lapster, labster, lapster: ~ **creel** a lobster trap. ~ **kist** a box floated in water in which lobsters are kept alive until sent to market *Ork Cai Ags.*

leid, lead: ~ **stane** a lead-sinker for a handline *now Sh Hebrides Ayr.*

lift the amount of fish, *especially* herring that can be lifted aboard by hand in the net, about half a basketful *Abd WC.*

lodge a fisherman's **bothy** *now Sh.*

†**lowp** a basket for catching fish.

lowpin an levin newly caught *chf nEC.*

lucken *adj, of a fish, esp a haddock or whiting* gutted, but not split right down to the tail *now NE. n* a half-split haddock for drying or smoking.

lug the corner of a herring net *now NE Ags.* ~**stane** one of the series of stones attached to the lower corner of a herring-net to make it hang vertically in the water *N.*

maise a measure, *chf* of fish, *esp* herring, = five hundred, *later usu* the long hundred of 120 *chf SW.*

mannie a skipper *NE.*

mash the mesh (of a net) *Ross Ags WC.*

mask *n* the mesh of a net *now Sh-Ags. v* catch in a net; be trapped in a net *now Sh-Cai.*

mast †*n* a net. *v* net (herring) *now Ags Uls.*

mell: cast the ~ assign the stations in **halve-net** fishing *SW.*

†**mete-fisch** freshly-caught fish, as opposed to barrelled or salted fish *chf N.*

mettick a soft crab *Abd.*

mud fish *etc* codfish preserved by being salted wet in bulk in the hold of a fishing vessel *Sh-N.*

murlin a round narrow-mouthed basket used *chf* by fishermen *now Abd.*

noozle one of a row of cords attaching the mesh-work to the headrope of a fishing net *Cai Fif Bwk.*

osel one of the short cords by which a herring-net is attached to the head-rope *local Sh-Arg.*

paidle the pocket or trap in a fishing-net, *esp* in the small stake-net used for catching flounders etc *SW.* ~**-net** a fishing-net containing a **paidle** *now Kcb.*

pallawa a small edible crab, *freq* used for bait *Fif.*

pallet the glass or metal float on a fishing net *NE Fif Bwk.*

peel: † ~(**ed**) *of fish* untreated (as by drying) and bulk packed. ~**er** *now NE Ags,* **piller** *Ork-EC* a small crab which has just cast or is about to cast its shell and is therefore suitable for bait *now NE Ags.* †**in** ~ *of fish* not packed.

pine *of fish* shrink by drying in the open air *now Sh.*

pin-the-widdie a small haddock, unsplit, which is hung in the smoke of the chimney to cure.

piper an unsplit, half-dried haddock *NE.*

pock, poke: ~**net** *n* a kind of fishing net varying between localities *now Sh Ork Cai SW. v* fish or catch (fish) with a ~**-net,** *now Sh Ork SW.*

†**pound** a pond, *esp* a fish-pond.

pow net the first net shot after the buoy from a herring-boat *now Fif.*

preen a fishing hook *Sh.*

†**raise net** a fixed fishing net which rises and falls with the level of the tide *Dmf.*

range agitate (water) to drive fish from a hiding place *S.*

redd *now NE, WC,* **rid** disentangle, unravel, sort out (fishing lines or nets) *now NE, WC.*

reest *v* **1** cure (fish etc) by drying or smoking *now local Sh-Wgt*. **2** *of fish etc* be cured (as above) *now Sh*. *n* a wood or rope framework on which fish, meat etc is smoked *now Sh*.

rigger worm a kind of marine worm used as bait *local EC*.

ring-net a herring net suspended between two boats which gradually sail closer to one another with a circular sweep until the net closes and traps the fish. ~**ting** fishing with a **ring-net**.

rip[1] a round wicker (or straw) basket used for carrying fish, fishing lines etc *Kcdn Ags Fif*. ~**pie** a kind of circular net used in crab-fishing or salmon-poaching *Bnf Abd*.

rip[2] fish with a **ripper** *Sh-nEC*. ~**per** a heavy metal bar fitted with hooks and attached to a fishing line *Sh-nEC*.

rizzered dried, parched; *specif of haddock* sun-dried *now local EC*.

rouse, roose sprinkle (fish) with salt to cure them *now Sh-N Fif*.

rug a tug on a fishing line when a fish has been hooked, a bite *Sh-C*.

saftie, softie, saftick *NE* an edible crab which has lost its shell, *freq* used for bait *NE Ags Fif*.

saw, sow throw out (a fishing-line) from a boat, shoot (a line) *NE*.

†scantack a hooked and baited line fixed along a shore or in a stream, *freq* used by night poachers *Mry*.

scaup, scalp a bank for shellfish in the sea.

scran *n* odd fish, *eg* mackerel among herring, claimed by the crew of a boat *NE*. *v* take (the odd fish found in a catch) as a perquisite *Bnf Fif*.

screenge, scringe fish the sea bottom inshore with a small net *now nEC local WC*. **screenger** a person who fishes with a **screenge net** *now Fif*. ~ **net** a small seine net used as above *now Arg Ayr*.

scull, scoo *local Ork-Bnf* a shallow scoop-shaped basket for holding fish or baited lines *now NE*.

scum catch with a small round net on a long pole (any herring fallen back into the sea as the nets are hauled aboard) *N*. ~**mer** a young crew member who **scums**. ~**(ming) net** a scoop-net for catching salmon in rivers or herring dropped from nets.

set: ~ **a scull** arrange baited fish-lines in a **scull** or basket *Bnf Abd Kcdn*. ~ **up** join together (the parts of a fishing line) *local Sh-Ayr*.

shakins herring which have to be shaken out of the net and are thus damaged, inferior herring *Sh N*.

sheel, shill cut (a mussel) from its shell *now local Sh-Bwk*. ~**blade** a knife for scooping out mussels for bait *NE Fif*.

shot †*n* the **shooting** of a fishing-net etc. *v* cast (lines or nets) *NE*.

sink a (stone or lead) weight attached to the lower corners of a herring-net to make it sink *local N*.

skair *n* a thumb-knot join in a fishing line between the **tippin** and the **snuid** *Mry Abd*. *v* join (the **tippin**) to the **snuid** (of a fishing line) with a thumb-knot *Mry Abd*.

skunk the sole or messenger rope of a herring drift net *WC*.

sky shade (a patch of water) so as to see the bottom *now NE Ags*.

slop *now NE nEC*, **slope** a kind of loose-fitting jacket or tunic, formerly worn by fishermen.

sma(ll): small fish fish such as haddock, herring etc, caught inshore with **small lines** *now Sh Ags Kcb*. ~ **lines** the lines used by inshore fishermen to catch **small fish** *now Sh N, EC*.

smeek smoke (fish etc), *eg* in order to preserve.

smokie, Arbroath smokie an unsplit smoked haddock.

snuid, snood *n* the hemp part of a sea-line to which the hook is attached; the twisted loop of horsehair by which the hook is sometimes attached to this, the **tippin** *now N-WC*. *v* tie (the short hair line) to the hook *now EC*.

sole *now Sh Wgt*, **sole raip** *now local Sh-Ayr* the bottom rope of a fishing net.

spalder, †spald split, lay open or flat (*esp* a fish).

speet, spit *n* a pointed stick or skewer on which fish are hung up to dry *local Sh-Bwk*. *v* hang (fish) **up** by the heads or gills on a **spit** to dry *local Sh-Bwk*.

spel(d) split, cut, slice open (*esp* fish to dry) *now Sh Cai*. ~**ing** *now Sh N*, **speldrin** *now Fif Bwk* a split and dried (or smoked) fish, *esp* a haddock or whiting.

spile hang **up** (fishing lines) on a pole to be cleaned *NE*. **spilin tree**, ~ **tree** a pole on which fishing lines are hung to be cleaned or baited *chf NE*.

splash fish with a **splash net** *now WC Kcb*. ~ **net** a net suspended in the water, into which fish are driven by a splashing in the water *now Arg Kcb*. ~ **netting** a method of fishing using a **splash net** *now Arg Kcb*.

spleeter a person who splits fish and removes the backbone *Sh Cai Kcdn*.

spoucher a (*usu* long-handled) wooden ladle or scoop, *esp* for baling a boat or lifting fish from a net.

spring bauk the main top-rope of a herring-net *now Mry.*

sprool *n* a short length of wire etc pushed through the sinker of a hand-line, with a hook attached at either end *local E. v* fish offshore with a **sprool** *Bnf Ags Fif.*

sprud a knife for prising limpets from a rock *Abd Kcdn.*

stick *in sorting fishing-lines* turn each hook back into the horse-hair of the **snuid** to prevent its entangling the line *Ags.*

stour, †stower a stake, post (for a fishing net etc).

stoy a cork float used to mark the position of sunken fishing-lines or crab-traps *now Mry Bnf Abd.*

strik, strike *of fish* become enmeshed in a net *now Sh E Kcb.*

string a section or proportional length of a fishing-line *now E.*

sucken a small drag or grapnel, *esp* one used by fishermen in searching for lost lines *now Abd.*

surcoat a fisherman's jersey *now Kcdn.*

†sweep a cord or piece of rope by which the stone-sinkers of a herring-net were attached *Mry Bnf.*

swing rope *herring-fishing* the line of nets to the stern of the boat etc *now N Ags Fif.*

tae a section of deep-sea line, with a specified number of hooks attached (*usu* 100 or 120) *now Fif.*

tail net the herring-net first to be **shot** and therefore the farthest from the boat *now Sh Cai.*

tak, take what has been taken, a catch or haul of fish *now local N-WC.*

tame *freq* **tamet** a handline with one or two hooks *Bnf Abd Ags.*

teeset the first of a fleet of lines to be **shot** from a boat; the man whose turn it is to **shoot** the first line and to whom its catch is assigned *NE.*

tenter a bar of wood fitted with hooks on which fish are hung to dry *NE Ags Fif.*

tide leave (fishing lines) for sufficient time to let fish take the bait *now Sh Ayr.* **tidin** the period during which the lines are left down (as above) *NE Ayr.* ~**-line** the last section of a fishing line to be **shot** *Abd Kcdn Ags.*

tip: ~**pet** a length of twisted horsehair to which the hook is attached on a line *now Kcdn Ags.* ~**pin** the horsehair or (*now more freq*) nylon cord used to attach the hook to the **snuid** *now N Ags Fif.*

tome, toum *now Cai,* **tomb** *Sh* a cord of twisted horsehair used as a fishing-line; the cord to which the hook is attached in floating lines; the **snuid** joining the hook to the hemp in a handline *now Sh Ork Cai Ags.*

torn bellie herring which has been split or broken by careless handling *now Sh N Fif.*

trail-en(d) the first of a fleet of herring nets to be **shot** and hence the furthest from the boat *Sh NE.*

†traith a herring-fishing ground.

†tramalt a trammel, a fishing net.

trawl *n* a seine-net. *v* fish with a seine-net, encircling a shoal of herring.

†tug quhiting a whiting caught by a handline.

tusk (fish) a ling-like fish of the cod family, found *chf* in northern Scottish waters; *usu* dried, it was one of the chief exports of Shetland *now Sh Ork Cai.*

†waith the action or practice of hunting or fishing (*chf* unlawfully). ~**ing** fishing; a catch of fish.

want, wint *Bnf Abd Kcdn* a defective or damaged part of a net or line *now Kcdn Bwk.*

washer a person who scrubs and cleans fish after gutting, in preparation for curing *Sh NE.*

weave, wive *NE* make or construct the mesh work of (a herring net) *NE Ags.*

†white herring herring cured by salting only.

winkie the lighted buoy marking the end of a line of herring nets *NE-WC.*

witter the barb of a fish-hook, gaff etc *now Sh Ork N.*

6.3.2 FRESHWATER FISHING

As well as angling this section includes commercial salmon fishing and also poaching.

bangie a man (*occas* a policemen) specially appointed to watch the Solway and Annan for salmon poachers.

†bin(d) a standard measure for the barrels in which certain commodities, *eg* salmon, were packed, *freq* with name of the authorizing town *etc, eg* **the ~ of Banff, Burdeaux ~.**

bleeze *n* a blazing brand, a torch as used when spearing fish *now Abd Ayr. v* light up (water) to attract fish *now Ayr.*

bob, †bobber any fly on a cast other than a tail-fly.

bothy a rough hut used as temporary accommodation *eg* by salmon fishers.

†brae a salmon trap consisting of an artificial gravel-and-stone bank across a river *Mry.*

brammel (worm) a striped worm found in old

dunghills and leaf-heaps, used as bait for fresh-water fish, *esp* trout.

burn light up (water) when fishing at night to attract and spear fish *now Bnf Abd Lnk*.

busk, buss dress (hooks or a fly) for fly-fishing.

cairn net a small net for catching fish lying behind stone-piles in a river *S*.

cast line the thin casting-line attached to the reel-line of a fishing-rod *now Fif*.

cleek, click a salmon gaff.

clep, clip a gaff.

corfhouse a salmon-curing shed.

†**coup** a basket for catching salmon.

cruive, crive, †crue, croy a fish-trap in the form of an enclosure or row of stakes (*orig* of wicker, *latterly chf* of wood) across a river or estuary. ~ **dyke** a rubble dyke extending across a river to hold **cruives** *local*.

†**dammin(g) and lavin(g)** a method of removing water, used in poaching.

doach name for a rocky stretch of the river Dee at Tongland; a salmon-trap or weir at this point *Kcb*.

†**feeth** a salmon net fixed on stakes and stretched into the bed of a river *NE*.

†**fell** cast (a net) from a boat into a river.

fishing wand a fishing rod *now local Sh-Dmf*.

gaud a fishing-rod *now Pbls*.

geg a poacher's hook for catching fish *S*.

ginnle catch (a fish) by the gills *chf WC*.

goory, goories fish refuse, *freq* salmon *now Abd*.

goshens a good catch (of fish).

grain a prong (of a salmon spear etc) *now local*.

grappling a method of catching salmon by means of a special arrangement of hooks *now Ags Ayr Kcb*.

guddle catch (fish) with the hands by groping under the stones or banks of a stream.

†**gullet** a narrow channel in a river made or used for catching fish.

gump, gumph search, grope for, *esp* **guddle** fish *now midLoth Bwk S*.

†**hake** a hook.

half †a bag-shaped net set or held to retain fish as the tide ebbs *Gall Dmf*. †**thalver** a person who fishes with such a net *Dmf*. **go haavin** fish with such a net; go salmon fishing, *esp* on the Solway *now Kcb Dmf*. **halve-net, half-net = half** *Gall Dmf*.

†**Hamburgh barrel** a kind of large barrel, *chf* as a measure of salmon.

hare('s) lug an angling fly, the body of which is dubbed with fur from the hare's ear.

harl, haurle troll for fish with a fly or minnow for bait *now Per*.

†**heckle** a hackle-fly.

heckum-peckum a type of artificial fly used for trout-fishing *local*.

hose *of fish* swallow (the bait) *now Bnf Abd*.

†**hose-net** a small stocking-shaped net fixed to a pole, used for fishing in small streams.

†**inscales**, the gratings or racks placed at the lower end of a wicker salmon-trap.

intae, into: be ~ hook (a fish, *chf* a salmon).

Jock Scott an artificial fly, named after its inventor.

†**keith** a bar across a river to prevent salmon from mounting further *Per*.

†**kist** a kind of fish-trap, *appar* = **cruive** *Inv*.

†**law** a mound of earth and shingle on a river-bank to which salmon nets are drawn *NE*.

†**lax: ~fisher** a salmon fisherman *chf NE*. **~ net** salmon-net.

leader an extension in a salmon-net to lead the fish into the main trap *N Bwk SW*.

leister *n* a pronged spear used (*now* illegally) for salmon fishing. *v* spear (fish) with a **leister**.

lodge a fisherman's **bothy**.

†**lowp** a basket for catching fish.

lugstane one of the series of stones attached to the lower corner of a salmon weir to make it hang vertically in the water *N*.

mell: cast the ~ assign the stations in **halve-net** fishing *SW*.

†**nieve: guddle** (fish) *SW*.

otter 1 the barb of a fishing-hook or **leister** *now S*. **2** a piece of fishing-tackle used by poachers of salmon or trout.

paparap a device consisting of three hooks lashed together and fastened to a weighted string, used in poaching to draw a line out of a river *Mry*.

pirn the reel of a fishing rod *now local NE-Kcb*. **~ in** *or* **out** reel a fishing line in or out.

ply *applied to fishing rivers* condition, state, fettle, *chf* **in (good** *etc)* *or* **oot o' ~**.

†**pound** a pond, *esp* a fish-pond.

powt net a stocking-shaped net fastened to poles, used to force out or to catch fish resting under projecting river-banks.

preen a fishing hook *Sh*.

proud *of fish* slow to take the bait, difficult to catch *now SW*

†**raik, reck** a stretch of river used for salmon-fishing.

range agitate (water) to drive fish from a hiding place *S*.

rip a round wicker (or straw) basket used for carrying fish, fishing lines etc *Kcdn Ags Fif.* ~**pie** a kind of circular net used in crab-fishing or salmon-poaching *Bnf Abd.*

ruffie a torch used when fishing for salmon at night.

rug a tug on a fishing line when a fish has been hooked, a bite *Sh-C.*

saumon, salmon, †salmond: ~ **cruive** a trap in a river to catch salmon *local.* ~ **lowp** a salmon leap.

†scantack a hooked and baited line fixed along a shore or in a stream, *freq* used by night poachers *Mry.*

scum(ming) net a scoop-net for catching salmon in rivers or herring dropped from nets.

scur the mayfly immediately after its larva stage, *freq* used as angler's bait *chf Ayr.*

shiel a temporary or roughly-made hut or shed, *freq* one used by (salmon) fishermen etc. ~ **house** a fisherman's hut.

†sicht, sight a place on a riverbank from which salmon can be watched.

skair one of the segments of a fishing rod *now Sh Cai Per.*

sky shade (a patch of water) so as to see the bottom *now NE Ags.*

slap, slop an opening left temporarily in a salmon weir to allow the fish to swim up-river to spawn. **†Saturday('s)** ~ the period from Saturday night till Monday morning, fixed by law for the free passage of fish up-river.

snigger *v* catch (salmon) illegally by dragging a cluster of weighted hooks along the river bed; fish (a pool) by this method *Gen except Sh Ork.* *n* the grappling implement used in **sniggering** *Cai NE.*

speeder, spider a trout-fly dressed without wings.

stake net a salmon-fishing net fixed on stakes in tidal waters.

†stell, stile, staill a place in a river over which nets are drawn to catch salmon. ~ **fishing** *etc* a fishery with a **stell.** ~ **net** a net stretched out into or across a river.

stem a dam of stones in a stream, used as a fish trap etc *local Cai-Lnk.*

†stent net a fishing net stretched on stakes across a river.

stripey a red-and-yellow striped worm used as angling bait, a bramble-worm *now Dnbt Kcb.*

sun spear (a salmon) while dazzling it with reflected sunlight in the water.

tae, toe a prong of a salmon spear etc.

tak, take: be on the ~ *of fish* rise readily to the bait.

tame, *freq* **tamet** the line on a fishing rod *Bnf Abd Ags.*

tid: in (the) ~ *of a river* in the proper condition for angling; *of a fish* ready to take the bait.

toot-net a salmon-net hung between the shore and a boat (in the Tay estuary), and hauled as soon as a watcher in the boat saw a fish strike the net *Ags-Fif.*

†trail-fly the last fly on a trout-fishing line.

†trout, troot catch trout.

†tug-net a salmon net pulled behind a boat at the mouth of a river, *esp* the Spey.

†waith the action or practice of hunting or fishing (*chf* unlawfully). ~**ing** fishing; a catch of fish.

wan(d), whaun a fishing rod *now Sh-Per.*

wap, whap cast (a fishing line); fish (a river) *now Dnbtn.*

waster a fishing spear with several prongs. † ~**ing** the action of taking a fish with a **waster.**

water, watter *now local* ~ **baillie** a water-bailiff employed to prevent poaching in rivers *now N.* † ~ **keeping** the guarding of a stretch of water against poachers. † ~ **mail** a rent charged for fishing a stretch of water. **†water serjant** one of the constables or officers of the court of the **water** bailie in Glasgow.

†wawsper, wauch spear a (salmon-)fishing spear.

witter the barb of a fish-hook, gaff etc *now Sh Ork N.*

yair, †zair a fish-trap across a river or bay in the form of an enclosure or barrier of stone, wood, or *formerly* wicker, and often also with a net *now Gall.*

6.3.3 FISHING BOATS

baldie a kind of fishing boat *now Bnf.*

bauk a seat in a boat, *esp* a fishing boat.

bum a kind of Dutch fishing boat *now Bnf Abd.*

†bush a bus, a kind of cargo or fishing boat.

coble a short flat-bottomed rowing-boat, used *esp* in salmon-fishing or loch- or river-fishing.

†couper-boit, coping boat a herring-buyer's boat.

den the forecastle of a herring boat *local.*

drave boat a herring boat.

Fifie a type of herring-fishing boat, *prob* first built and used on the Fife coast *E Coast.*

liner a line-fishing boat.

nabbie a type of herring-fishing boat *chf WC, SW.*

ring-netter a boat used in **ring-netting.**

saumon, salmon, †salmond: ~ **coble** a flat-bottomed boat used in salmon-fishing *now local*.

scaith a kind of light fishing boat *Bnf*.

scratcher a trawler which fishes as close as possible to the three-mile limit *NE*.

skiff *NE, C,* **skift** a type of small fishing boat with oars and lugsail.

stock boat a boat used to transport cured herring and equipment between outlying fishing stations and the depots *now Sh Bnf Abd*.

trochs, troughs a kind of flat-bottomed river barge in two sections with a space through which salmon could be speared *Dmf Rox*.

yole a kind of small, undecked, two-masted fishing boat *now Sh-N*.

†zulu, Zulu name for a type of fishing boat common *esp* in the Moray and Clyde Firths *c* 1880-1905, some of which were later fitted with engines.

7. FARMING

7.1 GENERAL, MISCELLANEOUS

†**beggar's bed** a bed made up for beggars, *usu* in the barn.

boutgate the doing of a round of work.

cast dig, cut (peats etc).

delf 1 a place dug out, *latterly esp* in turf; a hole or pit *now Cai.* **2** †what is removed by digging; a sod.

dell delve, dig *Sh-Abd.*

enterin(g) *of weather* suitable for work, *esp* **enterin(g) morning.**

Falkirk Tryst the cattle market held near Falkirk, the largest of its kind in Scotland.

ferm *v* farm.

fiar(s) the price(s) of grain for the year, used to determine ministers' **stipends**, *latterly* fixed in spring by the local **sheriff** in the **Fiars Court**. **strike (the)** ∼**s** fix these amounts.

†**fill** fill in with earth.

grave dig *now Sh.*

herrie, harry exhaust the fertility of (land), as by removing the topsoil *Sh Ork Dmf.*

Highland, Hielan(d): ∼ **Show, Royal** ∼ **(Show), the** ∼ a large agricultural show held annually by *The Royal Highland and Agricultural Society*, *orig* in different centres year by year, but since 1960 at a permanent site at Ingliston, midLoth.

hole dig, excavate; dig up (*now esp* potatoes (*NE Ags*) or turf (*Uls*)).

how †uproot (broom or whins). **come tae the hyow** be ready for hoeing *Cai NE.*

howk, hoke dig (ground), dig into, make (a trench etc) by digging, dig out, uproot.

labour, lawbour *n, also* ∼**ing** *now Sh* agricultural work, tillage *now local Sh-Loth.* *v* till, cultivate *now local.*

†**laidner time** the season when the **laidner mart** was killed and cured for winter provisions.

lonnachs couch grass, *esp* when indicating heaps of the weed gathered for burning *now Kcdn Ags.*

manner *now Sh WC Kcb,* **mainer** *now Rox v* occupy; till. †*n* the utilizing or cultivation (of land).

marrow *of small farmers co-operating in certain tasks* enter into partnership, combine.

†**mislabour** impoverish (land) by overcropping and bad husbandry *Abd Ags.*

muddle grub about in soil etc with the fingers, *esp* work (potatoes) away from the root by hand leaving the stem undisturbed *now Sh Ayr.*

muirburn the controlled burning of moorland to clear the way for new growth, *freq* make muirburn.

neibour, neighbour: ∼ **wi** co-operate with (one's neighbours), *esp* in agricultural jobs *local NE-Uls.*

outby *adv* out of doors, outside, out in the fields *now Loth.* *adj* away from the steading *now Uls.*

owergae overrun, infest, cover over (**with** weeds, dirt etc) *now Sh Ork Wgt.*

padd(er)ed trampled, well-trodden *now Sh Abd.*

plowter, pleuter, ploiter make a mess of, spoil (*esp* a piece of land by bad cultivation) *now Sh Abd.*

†**police** improve or develop (land) by cultivation and planting.

pot, pat *n* a pit or hole in the ground whether natural or man-made. †*v* dig pits in, fill with pits. **pot hole** a small depression in a field which is difficult to drain.

powk dig or excavate in a careless, clumsy way *Bnf Ags.*

rip strip off turf before digging *now Sh.*

rive wrench or force **out**, dig **up** *now local Sh-Kcb.* ∼ **(out)** cultivate (moorland) *now Cai Abd Ags.*

running stock a system of stock-management whereby all stock is sold at regular intervals, and breeding stock is bought in when required *WC, SW.*

scaup pare off the top soil etc from (a piece of ground); denude (soil) *chf Sh.*

†**scourge** exhaust the fertility of (land).

scruif loosen topsoil or skim off weeds etc from *now Sh Bnf Abd.*

scutch *n* a slash, a cutting of twigs, thistles etc, the trimming of a hedge *now SW.* *v* cut or shear with a hook or knife, slash, trim (a hedge) *now Loth WC, SW.*

skin pare the surface layer of soil etc off (land) *N, EC, Ayr.*

†**slay** destroy (vegetation).

sneck cut sharply, cut into or **off**, prune, notch *now local Sh-Ayr.*

sned *v* cut **off** the tops (and roots) of (**turnips**, thistles etc) *Gen except Sh Ork. n* a cut, cutting; a slash, slight wound; a lopping or pruning.

snod prune, cut, trim, smooth, make level *now local NE-SW.*

sour *esp of water on lime* macerate, soften, slake *now local.*

stocking the livestock and gear needed to run a farm.

straik level off (grain etc) in a measure. *now local Sh-SW.*

stug, stog *n* a jagged or uneven cut, anything left rough by careless cutting. †*v* cut with a rough edge.

teel till (land) *now Sh.*

tid *n* a suitable condition of the soil for cultivation *now C.* †*v* cultivate at the right season.

traissle tread or trample down (growing crops or grass) *now Rox.*

tramp tread, press down, crush by treading or stamping *now local Sh-Per.*

tryst a market, *esp* for the sale of livestock, a fair (though not one fixed by charter or statute) *now Bnf Ags Per.*

warranty *with regard to the sale of livestock* a guarantee, assurance *local Ork-Dmf.*

Wednesday each of five winter (cattle) markets held on a Wednesday, *now only* **Big W**~ the main market of the winter held at **Martinmas** *now midLoth.*

white cow remains of heather, **whin** and broom bleached by sun and rain after the annual burning *now Ags.*

yird, yirth press or cause to sink into the ground *now Sh Ork.*

7.2 FARM BUILDINGS

For pens, sties, etc., see 7.3. For mills, see 7.8.2. See also 13 for houses, barns, kilns, etc., viewed as buildings. Terms for farms often refer to the land as well as to the farm buildings (see 7.4).

†**bern** a barn.

bile house a building with a boiler for animal food *local Abd-Fif.*

boose, bease a stall for a horse or cow *now Arg.* **buisin stane** the stone partition between **booses** *now Arg.*

†**bow-hous(e)** a cattle-shed, cowhouse.

byre a cowshed.

cassie the cobbled part of a **byre** or stable *Bnf Abd.*

cot: ~**tar house** 1 a tied cottage. 2 *also* ~ **house** a cottage; a farmworker's cottage. ~**-toun** *now Ags Fif,* ~**tar town** *Ags* a hamlet *esp* of farm cottages.

doocot a dovecote.

ferm, farm: ~**stead** *now Fif,* † ~ **onstead** farm buildings, homestead. ~ **steading** the farm buildings with or without the farmhouse. ~ **toun** the homestead of a farm.

foresta a manger, a feeding trough in a **byre** *NE Ags.*

gang doon the house go to the parlour of a farmhouse, where it is down a step *SW Uls.*

†**girnel, garnel, grinnale** a granary, storehouse.

grainery a granary *now local Bnf-Kcb.*

granzie *gipsy* a barn.

gruip the gutter in a **byre** *Gen except Sh.*

ha(ll) *n, also* ~ **house** *now Sh* a farmhouse as opposed to the farm cottage *now local.* † ~ **board** a dining-table, *latterly* in a farmhouse.

hallan(d) a partition in a **byre** or stable, or between the living-room and the **byre**. ~ **stane** a stone forming a dividing wall between cattle-stalls in a **byre** *Cai.*

hangrell a tree-branch used for holding bridles etc in a stable *S.*

hemmel a shed and an open court communicating with it, used for housing cattle *now Rox.*

hen: ~**-bauk** the tie-beam on the roof of a country cottage (so called because hens roosted there). ~**-laft** a hen-roost; the roof-joists of a house and the space above them.

hinds' raw a row of cottages occupied by farmworkers *midLoth Bwk Rox.*

hire house a farm **bothy** *chf NE.*

howf a rough shelter or refuge *now Ags Stlg Renfr.*

†**husband town** a homestead occupied by a husbandman or *usu* husbandmen; a farm-steading with its cluster of peasants' houses, a settlement of husbandmen.

†**inset** a living room in a farm house *chf WC.*

kill, kiln: ~ **barn** a barn attached to or containing a kiln. *now Ork.*

mains the outbuildings of a farm.

mart a building used for agricultural auctions.

mill toon the buildings comprising a mill; *freq* the adjacent farm or hamlet.

onset a dwelling-site, a **steading** with the dwelling-house and outhouses built on it, a small cluster of houses *orig chf Ork S, now chf SW Uls.*

†**poind fold, poind fauld** an enclosure or build-

ing in which forfeit animals etc were kept, a pound.

raveltree, †realtree *SW-S,* **ravel** the horizontal beam in a **byre** fixed to the tops of the stakes for the tethers.

†runtree a continuous horizontal beam or bar which holds vertical posts firm in a **byre**-stall etc.

†saidle, saddle the part of a stall on which an animal stands *Fif.*

sattle, settle a ledge or raised platform in a **byre** where the cattle stand *now Ags.*

†sit house a dwelling-house on a farm.

sole tree a horizontal beam of wood, *usu* on the ground, which supports the posts forming the manger on the floor of a **byre** *now Sh Per.*

square: the ~ farm buildings, a farm steading, *esp* when forming the four sides of a square *local.*

sta a stall.

stance a stall etc for an animal in a stable *Cai.*

steadin(g), steid *now SW,* **stead** *now SW* the buildings on a farm, sometimes but not always including the farmhouse; the site of the buildings on a farm.

†teind barn a tithe barn.

taft, toft *n, also* † ~**ing** a toft, a homestead and its land etc *now Ags Stlg Fif, freq in Sh Ork place-names.*

toun, town: ~ **end** a row of cottages on a farm *NE Uls.*

travise, treviss 1 the wooden partition between two stalls in a stable or cowshed *now local.* **2** †*also* **triffice** a stall or loose-box in a stable.

walk a passageway in a cowshed *now Sh Ork Cai.*

7.3 ENCLOSURES AND DRAINAGE

†back dyke a back wall.

†barrace a barrier.

†barrere a barrier.

cairn a pyramid of loose stones, as a boundary-marker or other landmark.

cast *v* dig, clear out (a ditch etc) *now Cai-Abd.* †*n* a ditch, cutting; excavation.

cattle: ~ **bucht** *Abd Fif,* ~ **court** *Bnf-Ags,* ~ **reed** *NE nEC* a cattle yard.

cauf ward an enclosure for calves *now Bnf Abd.*

†clap dyke a turf or earth wall.

consumption dyke a wall built to use up the stones cleared from a field *now Abd.*

court a (covered) enclosure for cattle *local.*

craw an enclosure for animals, *esp* a pigsty *now Cai Fif.*

crue, croy, cray *C* an animal pen or fold; *now chf* a pigsty.

cruive 1 a pen, fold *chf NE, EC.* **2** a pigsty.

deval, devolve the amount of downward slope required by a ditch *now Sh Abd.*

dry(-stane) dyke a stone wall built without mortar. ~**r** a person who builds dry-stone dykes.

dyke, dick *now Cai n* **1** a dyke, a ditch; a wall, mound; a boundary wall of stones, turf etc. **2** a hedge *chf SW.* *v* **1** surround with a dyke. **2** †enclose, shut out etc with a dyke. **3** build or repair dykes. ~**-back** the back of a wall.

†face dyke a wall consisting of stones on one side and earth and turf on the other.

fail-dyke a field wall built or covered with sods *Gen except Sh Ork Gall.*

fauld, fold a fold, a pen. † ~**-dyke** a wall enclosing a fold. † ~**in** a cattle- or sheep fold.

fey clean out, scour (a ditch, drain) *Abd Per.*

flake, †fleck a hurdle or framework of crossed slats, *usu* portable and used as a fence, gate etc *Gen except Sh Ork.* ~**s** a temporary pen for sheep or cattle made of such a framework *NE, SW.*

fleet dyke a wall built to prevent flooding *now Ayr.*

†Galloway dyke a **whinstone** wall, the lower part of dry-stone construction topped by a thin course of projecting flat stones, and the upper part a tapering construction of round stones, the whole *usu* being about five feet high.

gaw a drainage furrow or channel *now Fif.* ~**-furrow** a furrow at an **end-rig** used for drainage.

gruip a field drainage ditch *now Ork Abd.*

hain enclose (grassland or a wood) by a hedge or fence; keep unused, preserve from grazing or cutting. † ~**ing** the enclosing of ground by a hedge or fence; the hedge, fence or wall.

heck 1 a grating placed in or across a stream etc. **2** †one of the bars of such a framework; *also* one of the open spaces or interstices between the bars.

hedge root the bottom of a hedge *now Per S.*

heid, head: †the (flat) top or upper surface of a wall. ~**-dyke** the outer wall of a field or holding; a wall separating arable from uncultivated land, the boundary wall *now Uls.*

hill dyke the wall dividing the common moor from the lower arable land *now Sh Ork Dmf.*

†horse wa(i)rd an enclosure for horses.

hutch an embankment built up to check erosion caused by running water *Rox.*

lair a place where animals lie down, a fold or enclosure *now Sh*.

lay 1 plant or make (a hedge) *sEC Kcb*. **2** enclose or retain by means of an embankment. **laid drain** a field drain formed by a row of stones laid on each side and a third course of flat stones laid above these *now Sh Cai Gall Uls*.

let a slip-gate on hurdle used to stop up a gap in a hedge or wall *SW*.

lift the point at which a dry-stone wall begins to rise above the grass at its base *Gall*.

liggat a self-closing gate, *freq* one shutting off pasture from arable land *SW*.

lonker *now Bute SW*, **lonket** *now Bute SW*, **lunkie** *sEC-SW*, **lunkie-hole** *SW* a hole in a wall, made with a lintel stone, to allow sheep to pass through or a stream to flow under.

midden dyke a wall round a dunghill.

outca a small enclosed pasturage for cattle *SW*.

pailin *n*, also **pale** a paling. *v, freq* **pailin aff, up** enclose with a fence or paling. **pailing-stab** a paling post *local Sh-Kcb*.

park, perk enclose (forest etc) (**with** a wall or ditch), form (land) into fields etc *now Sh*. †**~-dyke** a field wall.

parrock, parroch a small enclosure or pen.

†**peel** stake up, support or protect by means of stakes.

pig: ~-crue *now Ags Per*, **~-hoose** a pigsty.

pikit weir barbed wire *NE Ags*.

piling a paling, fence *SW, S*. **~ lett** a slat of wood in a fence *SW, S*.

†**pit** *n* one of a series of holes dug to mark a land-boundary. *v* define (a land-boundary) by means of a series of holes.

†**poind fold** an enclosure or building in which forfeit animals etc were kept in a pound.

privy privet, *chf* **~ hedge** *etc now NE, C*.

puidge 1 a small enclosure, pen or sty. **2** a small enclosure used for fattening cattle *S*.

pumphal a *usu* square enclosure for livestock *now NE*.

pund a pound, an enclosure for animals.

rance the crossbar of a fence.

redd clear out (a ditch, channel etc), remove rubbish or silt from *now NE-C*.

ree, reeve *now NE Per*, **reed** *C* an enclosure or pen for animals, *specif*: **1** a stone-built yard, wholly or partly covered, in which cattle are wintered *now EC, WC*; **2** a pigsty, *usu* a building and an outdoor run *local NE-SW*.

reuch, rough: ~-stane dyke a dry-stone wall *now Ayr Gall*.

rice: stake and ~, also **stab and ~** a method of construction by which twigs are horizontally woven between vertical stakes; a fence constructed thus.

rickle *n* a dry-stone wall; a layer of small stones placed on top of larger stones as a coping to such a wall *local Ork-C*. *v* build without mortar; *freq* **~ up** build (a dry-stone wall) *now Fif*.

rit, rut *v* mark with a shallow trench or furrow as a guide in draining etc *now Sh-Cai Gall*. *n* the shallow preliminary cut or furrow made in draining etc *now Cai*. **~tin(g)-spade** a double-handled spade for making the first cuts in draining *now Cai WC-S*.

ruit, root the bottom of a hedge *now Ags Per Kcb*.

†**runtree** a continuous horizontal beam or bar which holds vertical post firm in a fence.

scarcement the edge of a ditch cut to form a ledge on which bushes etc may be planted.

scutch a slash, a cutting of twigs, thistles etc, the trimming of a hedge *now SW*.

scuttle, scutter hole a sewage pit, drain.

†**sea car** an embankment against the sea, a sea-wall.

sheep drain an open or surface drain in pasture land *Gen except Sh Ork*.

sheuch *n* a trench in the ground, *esp* for drainage, a ditch, open drain. *v* dig, trench, make a ditch (in).

single the one-stone-thick upper part of a dry-stone wall *SW*.

skathie a rough shelter, *esp* a fence or wall used as a windbreak in front of a door *chf NE*.

slap, slop a gap or opening in a wall, hedge etc.

snap †the top layer or coping of stones on a **Galloway dyke** set on their edges so as to taper upwards. **~(-topped)-dyke** a wall built thus *now Kcb*.

sneck a portion of a dry-stone wall built of large stones extending through the whole width of the wall *now Rox*.

soo, sow: ~('s) cruive, ~('s) crave a pigsty *now Ork C, S*.

spadin(g) a trench of one spade-depth *now local*.

spaik, spoke a stake or pale in a wooden fence etc *now Inv Lnk*.

spar a bar or rail of a wooden fence or gate *now NE*.

speeach an oak stake *now Per*.

stane, stone: ~ dyke a *usu* dry-stone wall. **~ dyker** a person who builds dry-stone walls.

stank *n* a ditch, *freq* a natural stream which has been straightened to serve as a boundary or as part of a drainage system *local*. †*v* make a ditch in.

steid, stead a site, foundation, base of a wall *now Sh-Cai.*

stem a dam of stones in a stream, used to form a watering-place for cattle *local Cai-Lnk.*

stent, stint: ~**ing post** a strainer in a wire fence *now local C, S.*

stob *n* a stake, post. *v* fence with stakes, mark or bound with posts *now local WC-S.* ~ **fence** a wire fence fixed on wooden posts.

†stodfald an enclosure for brood-mares.

stower a stake, post (in a fence etc) *now Dmf.*

stuckin a stake *now nEC, S.*

†sunk, sonk a bank or wall, *esp* of earth or turf *Bnf Abd.*

swear dyke a wall of turf *Mry Bnf.*

swine crue *or* **cruive** a pigsty *now nEC.*

syver a ditch, drain, water-channel, *specif* a (covered-in) stone-lined field drain *now Ork N Wgt.*

†taft dyke a (turf) wall round a toft; a turf wall *in gen, SW.*

tappin *now Ayr,* **toppin** *now Ayr,* **tappietourie** a cairn on a hilltop.

†tire a tier, row of stones or turf on a wall.

touk an embankment or jetty built to prevent soil erosion *now Wgt.*

track a trench *N sEC, WC, SW.*

trink a trench, channel, ditch, gutter *now NE Ags Fif.*

wa(ll) wall. ~ **heid** the top of a wall. ~ **stade** the foundation of a wall *now Sh.*

†ward, waird: ~ **dyke** a wall enclosing grazing land.

water: ~ **dyke** a flood wall or embankment. ~-**fur** *n* a drainage furrow to carry off surface water *now Ork Stlg Loth.* †*v* provide (land) with drainage furrows. ~ **gate, water yett** *local C, S* a fence or grating suspended over a stream to prevent animals from straying or floating rubbish from entering a **mill-lade** *now Inv C.*

whin, whun: ~ **dyke** a fence consisting of furze bushes *now Cai nEC Loth.*

yaird, yard: ~ **dyke** a garden wall *now Ork N, C.*

7.4 FARMS AND TENANCIES

See also 7.8.3 below for **thirlage** to particular mills etc.

†bondelesoure, bonelesew ? pasturage connected with bond- or boon-service.

†bone-plewis ploughs used in unpaid tenant service.

bowin(g) a lease of stock and grazing rights on land *now local WC-SW.*

†brew-tak a tack of **brewland.**

†cottery a cottar's holding.

croft, craft *now chf NE, also* **crofting** a croft; *specif* a smallholding *now chf Highl.* ~**ing** the practice of croft-holding.

dale, deal a share, portion or piece of land *now Abd.*

†devoid and red vacate (lands etc).

displenish 1 strip (*now chf* a farm) of furnishings or stock, sell off contents of *now local.* **2** ~**ing sale** *Sh Bnf Abd Ags* a sale of the stock, implements etc on a farm *Gen except NE.*

ferm, farm, †firme 1 a farm, *orig* the condition of (land) being let at a fixed rent etc, *latterly* land leased etc for cultivation etc. **2** †~(**s**) a fixed yearly amount, *freq* paid in kind, as rent for land. **3** †*also* ~ **victual** grain paid as rent. † ~ **bear, corn** *or* meal barley, grain or meal paid as rent.

†free a piece of common land allotted by certain communities to their members.

grund, ground farm-land, a farm, an estate *now local.*

†half: ~-**foot** *Highl,* ~ **manor** *Gall* a system of land use whereby the landlord supplied (*usu* half of) the seed, the tenant grew and harvested the crop, of which the same share was delivered to the landlord as rent. ~-**landis** the half-portion of a landed estate.

†ham(e)lott a holding, ? amounting to a quarter of a forester-stead *Ettrick Forest.*

haud, hald, hold: ~**in(g)** a small farm held on lease.

†hire gang hire, lease of farm animals, utensils or land, *chf* **in** ~.

†horse gang the fourth part of a **plough gate**, the land occupied by one of four persons sharing a plough worked by their four horses.

ingaun, ingoing *n* entry to a new tenancy *local Ork-Gall. adj* entering, taking possession, *esp* ~ **tenant** *etc* the person entering the tenancy of a property on the departure of the previous occupier.

inve(n)tars the stock, crops etc listed in the inventory of a farm and taken over by a new tenant *now local Bnf-midLoth.*

kane a payment in kind, a portion of the produce of a tenancy payable rent, *latterly chf* poultry; such payments collectively.

†labour, lawbour: ~**ing** a farm or holding, arable ground.

land('s)-setting the letting of land and farms to tenants.

led farm a smaller or outlying farm managed through an employee *local Fif-S*.

†**leet peats** peats delivered in **leets** as part of a farm tenant's rent *NE*.

†**loanin(g)** the right of passage for animals by means of a **loan**.

†**lot** a piece of land allotted to a particular tenant.

mail: ~**ing 1** †the action of letting or renting. **2** a tenant farm *now local Bnf-Kcb*. **3** the rent paid for such. † ~ **mart** an ox paid as part of rent.

mains 1 the home farm of an estate, cultivated by or for the proprietor. **2** as part of the farm name: **(the)** ~ **of A** *now N*, **(the) A** ~ *Gen except N*. †**in** ~**ing** *of land* farmed by the proprietor himself as opposed to being leased to tenants.

†**manse** the principal residence of an estate with its attached outbuildings and land.

mean *esp of farm-land and facilities shared by several tenants* possessed jointly or in common, joint-.

mearing a strip of uncultivated land, a **bauk**, marking a boundary *N*.

muckle, meikle applied to the larger of two farms, estates etc of the same name.

nineteen a lease of a farm for nineteen years *now local Ork-Loth*.

†**nolt(is) price** payment due for cattle *SW*.

†**officer corn** grain paid by tenants towards the emoluments of the officer of a **baron-court**.

out-farm an outlying farm, *chf* one worked by a manager or subtenant *now local NE-Lnk*.

outgang an outgoing, departure, *eg* the end of a season etc, one's removal (from a tenancy).

outgaun *of a tenant* outgoing, removing, leaving.

†**outriving** unauthorized cultivating (of land not one's own) and so adding to one's own land; breaking into another's land thus.

†**outware** *appar* services due by tenants on land other than the lord's demesne lands.

†**owerloup** the right of (? occasional) grazing of one's animals in land next to one's own *Kcb*.

†**owersoum** an animal or number of animals in excess of what constitutes a **soum**; the keeping of such animals in excess of the allotted **soum**; a fine or payment for this.

paffle a small piece of land, a **croft**, an allotment.

pair: an ae *etc* ~ **(horse) place** *etc* a farm with one etc team of horses *now NE*.

†**pairt** a portion of land, part of an estate held by a smaller landowner, one of a number of pieces of land into which an estate might be divided for separate disposition.

park, perk to park, enclose (forest etc) (**with** a wall or ditch), form (land) into fields etc *now Sh*.

†**partising** a formal division (of land, goods etc) into shares or portions.

pasturage the right of pasturing animals on another's land.

†**peatery** a **peat moss** belonging to a landed estate; the right to cut peats from this. **peting** the action of getting peat; the right to cut, or the service of cutting peat.

pendicle 1 †a piece of land etc regarded as subsidiary to a main estate. **2** a small piece of ground forming part of a larger holding or farm and *freq* let to a sub-tenant *now C, S*.

place, placie a holding of land, an estate, farm or **croft**.

†**plan** a plot of ground, an allotted **rig** on the **runrig** system; a **croft**.

†**poindage** the right of impounding trespassing cattle; the fine payable for their release.

pot, pat 1 dig holes (in the ground) to indicate a land boundary. **2** place (a boundary-stone) in a pit or hole. **3** mark off the limits of (a piece of land) by pits.

prap, prop an object or objects set up as a boundary marker, *eg* a heap of stones, a pole etc.

†**rig-about** the **runrig** system of land tenure.

rigs *chf literary* the arable land belonging to one farm or proprietor.

room an estate; a piece of land rented from a landowner, a farm, a **tack**, arable holding. †**roum free** not incurring the payment levied on corn for occupying space in a mill while awaiting grinding.

run, rin: rendal, rig and rendale *latterly Sh Ork Cai*, † ~ **dale** a landholding system similar to **runrig** but involving larger portions of (*chf* **outfield**) land. **runrig,** †**rinrig** *n* a system of joint landholding by which each tenant had several detached **rigs** allocated by lot each year, so that each would have a share in turn of the more fertile land; such a portion of land *now only Hebrides. adj, adv* held under this system of tenure, divided by this system.

set a letting or leasing of a farm, house etc, a lease (*esp* thought of from the lessor's point of view) *now Bnf Abd Wgt*.

†**shear(ing) darg** a day's work at reaping or shearing (as a feudal service to a landlord).

†**sheep steid** a sheep farm.

†**skair** a plot of land, *esp* one of the many parcelled out of common lands *Dmf*.

†**snaw mail** a payment made to owners of lowland pasture for grazing hill sheep.

soum *n* **1** *also* † ~**'s grass** the unit of pasturage which will support a certain fixed number of livestock. **2** the number of livestock (*usu* a cow or a proportionate number of sheep) which can be supported by a **soum** *now Sh Highl Per*. *v* determine the number of **soums** which can be supported by (a common pasture) in order to allocate a share among the tenants *now Sh Highl*.

†**spreath, spreach** cattle, *specif* a herd (of cattle) stolen and driven off in a raid, *esp* by Highlanders to the Lowlands.

†**start and owerlowp** the trespassing of farm-animals on a neighbour's land, in which a certain limited latitude was permissible.

†**steelbow** a form of land-tenancy whereby a landlord provided the tenant with stock, grain, implements etc under contract that the equivalent should be returned at the end of the lease; the stock belonging to the landlord under this arrangement.

stent the proportion of pasture in a common allocated to each tenant; the number of animals allowed on each pasturage.

†**stock** *n* that proportion of a crop etc left over after the amount (or its value) apportioned to **teinds** has been taken away. ~ **and teind** *law* the gross produce of a farm etc, without deduction of the **teind**.

store: ~ **farm** a farm, *usu* in the hills, on which sheep are reared and grazed *now SW, S*. † ~ **room** a sheep farm.

†**strenth silver** *appar* money received by a tenant of a **steelbow** farm from his landlord on entering.

tack 1 a lease, tenancy, the leasehold tenure of a farm, *now rare*. **2** *also* ~**ie** *N* the farm or piece of land held on a lease *now local Sh-Wgt*.

taft, toft *also* † ~**ing** a toft, a homestead and its land etc *now Ags Stlg Fif, freq in Sh Ork place-names*. † ~**ing** the tenancy of a **taft**.

†**teind:** ~ **corn**, ~ **fish** *etc* corn, fish etc paid as **teind** or sometimes cash paid in lieu. ~ **sheaf, drawn** ~ every tenth sheaf, paid as **teind**. **third and** ~ a method of renting land whereby the landlord took a tenth of the crop as **teind** and a third of the remainder as rent *chf S*.

toun, town 1 an area of arable land on an estate, occupied by a number of farmers as co-tenants *now local*. **2** a farm with its buildings and the immediately surrounding area *Gen except Sh Ork*. **3** a cluster of houses belonging to the tenants of a **toun**, a village. ~**ship** an area of arable land occupied by a community of **crofters** *esp Highl*. ~**land** the land of a **toun** *now Sh*.

twa-horse ferm *or* place a farm needing only two horses to work it *now local Ork-Per*. **twa-pair** *of a farm* worked by two pairs of horses *Ork Cai NE*.

upper *freq in farm-names, eg* **Upperton**, freq applied to the higher section of a divided estate.

uver *freq in place-names* upper, higher, *eg* the upper or higher of two farms of the same name.

wa, way: ~**-ganging** the departure of a farmer from his tenancy, *freq* ~**-going sale** *N, EC Wgt*, † ~**-gaun crop**.

†**water, watter:** ~ **kyle** meadow land possessed by tenants of an estate in annual rotation.

7.5 FARMERS

7.5.1 FARMERS: TENANTS AND OWNERS

Words for independent tenant-farmers and farmers working their own land. Includes small-holders and crofters.

†**bonnet laird** a small landowner who farmed his own land.

bouman a tenant with a **bow**.

bower a tenant who hires cattle and grazing rights on land *now Lnk Ayr Kcb*.

†**clearances** a series of mass removals of their tenants by Highland landlords *chf* in order to introduce sheep-runs or, on the more fertile land, to enlarge and improve the farms.

coo, cow: ~**-feeder** a dairy farmer *chf Ags*.

cotman *chf SW*, **cottar**, †**cottrall** a tenant occupying a cottage with or formerly without land attached to it.

crofter a person who occupies a smallholding.

dame a (farmer's) wife *now Bnf Abd Fif*.

Eastie familiar contraction of a farm name containing **east** or **easter** applied to the tenant or owner *now NE*.

fermer a farmer.

†**fermorar** a farmer.

†**girse, gress, grass:** ~**man** a landless tenant with only rights of pasture *latterly Abd*.

guid, good: ~**man** the owner or tenant of a small estate or farm, ranking below a **laird**.

hen-wife a woman who deals in poultry.

†**in** with a farm name, indicating a short-lease tenant (as opposed to an owner or principal tenant): '*John Picken in Kirkford*'.

ingaun, ingoing entering, taking possession, *esp* ~ **tenant** *etc* the person entering the tenancy of a property on the departure of the previous occupier.

†**mailer** a tenant (farmer), a **cottar**.

mains name for the farmer of a **mains** according to the Sc idiom of calling a farmer by the name of his farm *Abd*.

missie the eldest unmarried daughter of a farmer *NE, EC Uls*.

†**moss laird** *joc* a tenant given an area of rough moorland rent-free or at reduced rent in return for making it arable *Per Stlg*.

of, o with a farm name, indicating the owner or principal tenant: '*Tam o Shanter*'.

†**on-takis-man** a person who does not hold a **tack** of part of the common *Inverurie*.

†**paffler** a person who farms a **paffle**, a small tenant-farmer.

†**particate man** the owner or a tenant of a **particate** of land *Rox*.

pendicler the tenant of a **pendicle**, a smallholder.

pleuch, ploo, plough †the persons working a plough; the tenants of a **ploughgate**. **haud one's** *or* **the** ~ drive a plough, be a working farmer.

†**store farmer** *or* **master** one who runs a **store farm**.

†**teinder and thirder** a tenant holding a lease under the **third and teind** system.

Wastie familiar contraction of a farm name containing **wast** or **waster**, applied to the tenant or owner *NE*.

7.5.2 FARMERS: GRIEVES

†**catch kow** ? a cattle-pounder.

commissioner a **factor**, steward *now Bnf Abd*.

†**girnel-man** the man in charge of a **girnel**.

†**granitar** an official, *esp* of a religious house, in charge of a granary.

grieve *n* the overseer or head-workman on a farm; a farm-bailiff. *v* oversee.

grund officer the manager of an estate *now Ork-Kcb*.

moss grieve the estate official in charge of the rights of peat-cutting in a **moss** *NE*.

†**peatman** an estate servant in charge of the peat supply.

pick: hae a ~**ie (o) say** have a certain amount of authority or responsibility, be in a position of influence, *specif* of a farm servant etc who has had promotion. ~**ie-say (hat)** the narrow-brimmed

tweed hat, worn as a badge of authority by a foreman or gaffer on a farm *NE*.

†**poind(l)er** an estate officer authorized to impound straying or trespassing animals.

†**pruif man** the person appointed to assess the quality and content of (a given quantity of) grain.

pundler a person whose main duty was *orig* the impounding of livestock, *later* looking after tree plantations *now Mry Bnf*.

tap, top: ~**sman** the chief man in charge of a drove of cattle, the head drover.

†**warander** a warrener, a person in charge of a rabbit-warren.

7.5.3 FARMERS: FARMWORKERS

bailie, cow baillie the person in charge of the cows on a farm *now Bnf Abd Ags Lnk*.

benefit payment in kind as part of a farmworker's wages, *freq* ~ **man** a farmworker who receives such *SW*.

berrick a hut or sleeping quarters for farmworkers etc *local*.

boll payment in food to a farmworker.

†**bondage, bonnage, binage** *Abd* service due from a farmworker to a farmer. **bondager** a person who performs **bondage** service, *chf* a female field-worker supplied by a farm-tenant in accordance with the conditions of his tenancy.

booyangs = **nickie tams**.

bothy *n* 1 a rough hut used as temporary accommodation *eg* by shepherds. 2 permanent living quarters for workmen, *esp* a separate building on a farm used to house unmarried male farmworkers. *v* live in a **bothy** *now local*. ~ **wife** *or* **woman** the woman who takes charge of the **bothy** *now Bnf*.

bouman the man who had charge of the cattle on a farm.

byre: ~**man** a cattleman *now Bnf Kcb*. ~~**woman** a woman who looks after cows *now Bnf Kcb*.

carle *now Bnf Abd Lnk*, **carlie** *humorous, sympathetic or depreciatory, now local Bnf-Fif* a man of the common people, a peasant or labourer.

carsackie an overall, pinafore; a labourer's smock *local NE-S*.

cattler, cattlie a cattleman on a farm *NE*.

chackie a striped cotton bag used by farm servants for carrying their clothes *NE*.

chaumer a sleeping place for farm workers *chf NE*.

clay, cley: ~ **davie** an agricultural labourer *now Abd.*

clean: make a ~ **house** *or* **toun o 1** *of servants, farmworkers* leave. **2** *of the master etc* dismiss (the servants etc), all at one time *chf NE.*

corn kister a type of song sung at farmworkers' gatherings *Bnf Abd Fif.*

cottar, †cottrall *n* a married farmworker who has a cottage as part of his contract. *v* live as a **cottar** in a **cot-house** *NE.* **†cottar('s) beer** barley grown as part of a **cottar**'s remuneration. **cottar-folk** those who live in farm cottages.

countra, kintra: ~ **Jock** *disparaging* a farmworker *Abd Fif.*

darg work by the day.

deem a kitchenmaid on a farm *now Bnf Abd.*

dey a dairymaid *now Cai.*

dock nail a ploughman *Abd Kcdn.*

†dorder-meat a snack given to farmworkers between dinner and supper.

drove drive (cattle or sheep), be a drover.

†fe master a herdsman.

fee *n* **1** *also* ~**s** a servant's wages, *esp* those paid half-yearly or for specific services. **2** an engagement as a servant. *v* **1** engage, hire as a servant. **2** accept an engagement as a servant. ~**in(g) fair** *midLoth Bwk Ayr*, ~**in(g) market** a fair or market, *usu* held at **Whitsunday** and **Martinmas** where farmers engaged servants for the coming **term**.

ferm fowk the workers on a farm *NE Fif SW.*

flit: ~**ting Friday** the **Whitsunday** removal day. **F**~ **Friday** the **Whitsunday** or (*chf*) **Martinmas** removal day for farmworkers *Ags.*

gaud(s)man, goad(s)man a person who drives oxen or horses with a goad.

halflin(g) a half-grown boy, an adolescent youth engaged in farm work.

han(d)sel a piece of bread or other light snack given to farmworkers before beginning work *chf SW Uls.*

hash the workers on a large farm *chf NE.*

hen-wife a woman who has charge of poultry.

herd, hird a person who tends or watches over sheep or cattle, *esp* in order to confine them to a particular pasture in unfenced areas. **†** ~**ing** the post of herdsman. **†common** ~ a **herd** employed by the community.

hind 1 †a farm servant. **2** a ploughman *now local midLoth-Rox.* **3** a married skilled farmworker who occupies a farm-cottage, and has certain perquisites in addition to wages, a **cottar** *chf S.* ~**ing** the work of or a situation as a **hind** *midLoth Bwk Rox.*

hire: ~**r 1** a farm servant. **2** one engaged by the day, or for a short period *chf Cai.* **hiring (fair), hiring market** *etc* a fair or market held for the purpose of engaging farmworkers *now Bwk Rox.* ~ **house** a farm **bothy** *chf NE.* **†** ~**man** a hired servant, *chf* a farmworker. **†** ~**-woman** a female servant.

horseman a man who tends horses, *specif* a farm servant who looks after and works a pair of horses, on larger farms ranked according to seniority as **first, second** *etc* ~ .

howker a person who digs.

Jenny, Jinny: ~ **muck** a female farmworker *Cai NE.*

Jock *sometimes with* **Jenny**, *also* ~**ie, Jack** *now NE,* ~ **hack** *NE,* ~ **muck** *now Cai* a rustic or countryman, a farmworker *now NE, EC Rox.* ~ **hack** *NE,* ~ **muck** *now Cai* a ploughman.

Johndal *contemptuous* a young ploughman *Cai.*

joskin a country bumpkin, a yokel, farmworker *now local NE-Dmf.*

kitchie take one's meals in the farm-kitchen as opposed to living in a **bothy** or **cot-house**, live in *NE.*

†labour, lawbour: ~**er (of the ground)** a cultivator, a landworker.

†land labourer a person who works on the land as a casual labourer.

†little man a junior or adolescent male farm servant.

†livery meal a certain quantity of meal given to farm servants in lieu of board.

loun a young farmworker, a **halflin(g)** *N nEC.*

man: menfolk, †man *or* **men servand(i)s: the** male workers on a farm.

†mel(d)er the meal ground from the corn which formed part of a farm servant's wages.

moggan 1 a protective covering for the legs, of sacking or straw ropes, worn for farm work *N.* **2** a woollen stocking; a stocking foot worn indoors over the stocking or out of doors over the shoe in wet or frosty weather.

Muckle Friday the Friday on which the half-yearly **hiring market** was held; the hiring market itself *Abd Ags.*

nickie-tams a pair of straps or pieces of string, used by farmworkers to secure the trousers immediately below the knees, to keep the legs above the knee clean or to relieve the weight of mud at the ankles.

orra doing casual or unskilled work. ~**ster** an extra hand, casual labourer. ~ **billie** *NE,* ~ **laddie,** ~ **lassie,** ~ **loon** *NE,* ~**man** a person who does odd jobs on a farm.

out (working) out of doors or in the fields, *of farm-*

workers (chf female), eg ~**work(er)**, ~**-girl**, † ~**servant**.

outby worker a field labourer *now Loth*.

peat-caster a person who cuts **peats** and lays them out to dry.

pirler an odd-job man on a farm; a cattleman *now Ags*.

pleuch, ploo, plough †the persons working a plough. **pleuchie** a ploughman *now Ags Per Fif*.

quarterman a farmworker who does miscellaneous jobs and errands *Loth*.

Rascal Fair a **hiring market** for the engagement of men who had failed to get employment at the regular market *Abd*.

†**scallag** a farm labourer *Highl*.

seek *of a farmer* invite (a servant) to remain for the next half-year.

sheep money a yearly payment to a farm servant in lieu of permission to pasture a few of his own sheep on the farm *Bwk*.

†**shiel** live in a summer-pasture hut, herd (cattle) at a **shieling**.

slop *now NE nEC*, **slope** a kind of loose-fitting jacket or tunic, formerly worn by field-workers.

†**spade silver** payment for work with a spade.

speak, spick *NE* ~**ing time** the time of year at which employers, *esp* farmers, renew or terminate workers' contracts. ~ **to** *of a farmer etc* engage (a worker) for a further term.

tasker a worker paid for specified tasks; a pieceworker.

thirl engage as a servant *now Bwk*.

toun, town: ~**die**, ~**-keeper** the person left in charge of a farm when the rest of the household are away *NE*. † ~ **herd** the public herdsman who looked after the cows on the common pasture *NE*. **a clean** ~ a farm from which all the hired servants have left at one term. **keep (the)** ~ act as ~**die** *NE*.

†**walcome** a celebration for the coming of new ploughmen to a farm.

waltams, wull-tams = **nickie-tams** *NE, nEC*.

wisp put warmed straw into (boots, shoes etc) as an insole in cold weather *now Stlg Dmf*.

yanks = **nickie-tams** *Ags Kcdn*.

yorks = **nickie-tams** *local C*.

7.6 FARMLAND

ae coo's meat enough land to grow food for one cow *Sh-Fif*.

ae-fur-land land which can only be ploughed in one direction because of its steepness.

back: ~**land** the back of a piece of ground. ~**side** the space, yard or fields adjoining a building.

†**baittle** *of grass, pasturage* rich, fattening for cattle *latterly S*.

†**bernyard** a barnyard.

biggit *of land* occupied, inhabited; cultivated; built on.

birn a pasture on dry heathy land. **bruntland** rough, mossy ground, *formerly* burnt periodically *now Sh*.

†**birthful, birthy, berthy** prolific, fertile.

bit a small piece of ground *now Lnk S*.

brak, break ground broken up for cultivation; a division of land under the old system of rotation of crops *now local Bnf-Kcb*.

†**brew:** ~**land, Browster land** land connected with the brewing on an estate. ~ **croft** a croft ranking as ~**land**. ~**seat** a piece of **brewland**.

†**brume park** a park or enclosure grown with broom.

ca a cart road, a **loaning** *chf Cai*.

†**cairt gate** a cart road, a road suitable for carts.

cassie 1 *also* **causey** the paved or hard-beaten area in front of or around a farmhouse *NE Lnk Uls*. **2** the cobbled part of a **byre** or stable *Bnf Abd*.

cattle: ~ **creep** a low arch or gangway for cattle under or over a railway *local*. ~ **raik** a road along which cattle are driven to fairs *Ags*.

clean: ~**(t) lan** land after a root crop has been grown on it.

clod free (land) from clods or stones *now Arg*.

close a farmyard. ~ **coort** the square yard round which a farm **steading** is built *NE*.

†**clout** a patch of land.

†**commonité** a common pasture.

coo, cow: ~ **gang** pasturage for a cow *S*. ~**(i)s** *or* †**kyis gress, girs** enough pasturage for a cow *now Kcb Rox*.

corn yaird a stackyard.

†**cotland, cottar land** land attached to a cottage.

cundy, condie a hole in a wall for the passage of sheep etc.

†**cunyie** *appar* a corner piece of ground.

dale, deal a share, portion or piece of land *now Abd*.

deaf *of soil* poor, unproductive, barren.

dirty *of land* weed-infested.

†**drove road** a road or track used for driving cattle to markets.

dyke-side the ground alongside a dyke.

†**eebrek** land ploughed the third year after being left fallow.

fauch †*adj* fallow, not sown, untilled. *n* a fallow field.

†**fauld, fold 1** an enclosed piece of ground used for cultivation; a small field. **2** ~(**s**) the part of the **outfield** which was manured by folding cattle on it. **lime** ~ a place for storing lime.

feedle a field *NE.*

†**felde land** land consisting of a field or fields.

felt worn-out arable pasture consisting *chf* of fine bent-grass *now Per.*

fey the **infield** *Gall.*

†**foggage** winter grazing.

forced grun banked-up ground, ground made up in levelling *now local WC Kcb Uls.*

furr: one ~ **ley** grassland after its first ploughing-up *now WC.*

†**fyle** let (land) become overgrown with weeds.

gang a range or stretch of pasturage, a pasture *now local Abd-S.*

garth an enclosure, yard, garden *now only as place-name esp of farms.*

†**girsing** pasturage, grazing land *now Ork Cai.*

glebe the soil, land; cultivated land, a plot, a field *now Sh Rox.*

†**gracious** *of soil* fertile.

green the grassy ground forming part of the grounds of a house or other building.

guid, good: the ~ **man's craft** a plot of land left uncultivated to propitiate the Devil.

gushet (**neuk**) a triangular piece of **land,** *esp* between adjacent properties; an odd corner of land; a nook *now local Sh-WC.*

haggard a stackyard *chf SW Uls.*

haining a piece of ground enclosed by a hedge or fence *freq in place-names.*

†**heid, head:** ~ **room** the higher or outer part of a **croft**; that side of a **croft** lying on the boundary of the **burghlands** of the estate; the marginal or boundary lands *still in farm names.* ~**3ard** the (farther or outer) end of a yard.

hemp-rig a ridge of land on which hemp was sown *Gall, now only in farm names.*

hen: hen('s) croft part of a cornfield frequented and damaged by fowls *now Bnf Abd.* ~**'s gerse** as much grass or land as would produce food for a hen.

hey, hay: ~**-bog** a piece of marshy ground whose grass was formerly used for winter fodder *now Cai Kcb.*

hill, hull *now NE, WC* **1** a common moor where rough grazing rights are shared by the community *now local.* **2** any piece of rough grazing on a farm *Gen except Sh Ork.*

ill bit a poor, infertile piece of ground *local sEC-S.*

inby in that portion of farmland in the immediate vicinity of the farm-buildings *Ross midLoth Bwk S.*

†**infield** the field or land lying nearest to the farm or homestead; *specif* one of the two main divisions of an arable farm before the practice of crop rotation, consisting of the best land nearest the farm buildings, kept continuously under crop and well manured.

†**ingres** inlying pasture.

†**inland infield** land on a farm or estate.

inlat an entrance, avenue *NE-Fif.*

†**inset, inseat** the **infield** or a part of it.

intak, intake a piece of land reclaimed and enclosed on a farm *now Sh-Ags, Ayr.*

intoun the land adjacent to the farmhouse, *orig* continuously cultivated *chf Abd.*

kill, kiln: ~ **stead** *now Sh,* † ~ **croft** the piece of ground occupied by or attached to a kiln.

†**labour, lawbour:** ~**ing** a farm or holding, arable ground.

lan(d) 1 † ~**s** the fields, the countryside. **2** the fields as opposed to the buildings of a farm *N-SW.* ~ **stane** a loose stone in the soil turned up in digging or ploughing *now Ork SW.*

lea, ley *adj* **1** lea, fallow, unploughed. **2** barren, wild. *n* **1** lea, ground left untilled; ground once tilled but now in pasture, *orig* part of the **out-field**; second-year or older pasture following hay. **2** *chf verse and freq in place-names* a tract of open grassland; an open uncultivated area. ~ **arnut** *joc* a stone lying loose on the soil, and of a size easily thrown *Abd.* ~ **break** fallow ground or old pasture due to be ploughed up in rotation *local N-SW.* ~**field** *N, EC, SW,* ~ **park** *N Gall* a field of established grass. ~ **girse,** ~ **grass,** ~ **ground** established pastureland, grassland not recently ploughed *local.* † ~ **land** land left unploughed. †**lie** ~ lie fallow. ~ **hay** hay grown on old pasture *now SW.* ~ **oats,** ~ **corn,** ~ **crap** oats grown on ploughed up grassland *local.*

leens pieces of grassy land in a moor or by a river, meadows, *freq* pastures of natural grass *Cai.*

lippie's bound the amount of ground to be covered by a **lippie** of seed, *orig* of flax (as one of the perquisites of a farm-servant), *later* of potatoes etc *chf Fif.*

lizour, †**lesu** a pasturage, grazing, meadow.

loan 1 *also* ~**in(g)** *now NE C,* †**loune** a grassy (cattle-)track through arable land, *freq* leading to (common) grazing and also used as pasture, a milking place, a common green *now in place-names*. **2** the part of farm ground or a roadway which leads to or adjoins the house *now NE Per*. ~ **head**, †**heid of the** ~ the higher or outer end of a **loan** *Gen except Sh Ork*. †**commoun** ~ public or communally owned **loan**.

†**manse** a measure or piece of land.

mearing a strip of uncultivated land, *usu* marking a boundary *N*.

meedow, meadow: 1 (a) meadow. **2** marshy grassland where the natural coarse grasses are often cut for hay.

midden, midding: ~-**stead** the site of a **midden** *now local Sh-SW*.

†**mill stead** the ground and buildings comprising a mill.

moss a peat bog; a stretch of moorland allocated to tenants for cutting fuel. † ~ **room** the portion of a **peat moss** assigned to a tenant for his own use *WC, SW*.

muir, moor rough, uncultivated heathery land considered as part of an estate.

neep: ~ **grun(d)** ground prepared for turnips *Sh Ork NE*. ~ **land** ground from which a crop of turnips has been taken *now Sh Ork*. ~ **re(e)t** land from which a turnip crop has been taken, and still so called under the subsequent corn-crop *NE*.

†**oddland** land additional to, or not forming part of some main body of land.

onset a dwelling-site, a **steading** with the dwelling-house and outhouses built on it *orig chf Ork S, now chf SW Uls*.

onstead a steading *chf S*.

outby *of a farm or farmland* away from the **steading** *now Uls*.

outca a small enclosed pasturage for cattle *SW*.

outfield 1 †*in the early agricultural system before enclosures and crop-rotation* the more outlying and less fertile parts of a farm. **2** a poorer outlying patch of ground (previously uncultivated) *only Sh*.

outgang an open pasture for cattle *chf SW*.

outlan(d) 1 †land held in addition to but lying outside the principal holding or estate. **2** outlying land, rough ground on the edge of arable marginal land.

outraik an extensive grazing area *Rox*.

outrun an area of outlying grazing land on an arable farm *Sh-N, WC, SW*.

outset 1 †a smaller piece of land outlying or detached from, but dependent on, a main estate or holding. **2** a patch of reclaimed and newly-cultivated (or *orig* newly-inhabited) land, *freq* taken in from moorland etc *now Sh*.

†**outsteid** a settlement or farm at or near the edge of an estate *chf SE*.

†**out-toun** an outlying field on a farm, the **outfield** *chf NE*.

paffle a small piece of land, a **croft**, an allotment.

park, perk an area of enclosed farm ground, a field.

paster a pasture. †**pasturall** pasture land; grazing.

peat: ~ **lair**, ~-**larach** the area of moor on which newly cut **peats** are laid out to dry *Sh N, SW*. ~ **moss** a peat-bog or -moor, the place where peats are dug.

†**peck** a plot of land, *prob* one requiring a **peck** of oat seed to sow it *Per*.

†**pilmuir** *appar* a piece of common land enclosed by a fence and cultivated as arable ground.

pleuch land land suitable for ploughing, arable land *now Bnf*.

point, pint the tapering part of a field which is not completely rectangular *NE, wLoth Kcb*.

policies the enclosed grounds of a large house, the park of an estate.

port a piece of open ground near a town gate used as the site of a **hiring market** *esp* for farmworkers.

†**quaird** a division of the **infield** land on a farm, used for crop rotation.

†**rag fauch** *or* **fallow** a system of fallowing land by ploughing in the old crop of hay or grass in summer and ploughing once or twice again with manure, before preparing for autumn sowing of wheat.

raik a cattle- or sheep-walk, a pasture *now nEC*.

redland *etc* land cleared of its crop, bare after cropping or ploughing *now Abd C*.

rest, rist *now chf NE of arable land* lie fallow or in grass *Sh-EC*. **ristit** having lain fallow *Sh-EC*.

reuch, rough land in an unimproved, virgin condition *Sh N Ayr*.

rig 1 *early farming* each separate strip of ploughed land, raised in the middle and sloping gradually to a furrow on either side, and *usu* bounded by patches of uncultivated grazing; *now* one of the divisions of a field ploughed in a single operation. **2** *also* **corn** ~ such a piece of land when planted with a crop or being harvested *now Ork NE Ags*. **3** that part of a town left free for cultivation. † ~ **and baulk** arable strips of land separated by uncultivated strips onto which stones and rubbish from the cultivated strips were cleared.

rind the edge, *eg* of a strip of cultivated land.

rodding a narrow track or path trodden out by sheep.

roundel, rounall a circular patch of grass worn smooth by cattle *now wLoth Lnk.*

saw, sow: ~ **doun, out** *etc* sow grass as a rotation crop with corn.

†**shiel (toun)** a summer pasture with a shepherd's hut or huts. **shieling** a high or remote summer pasture, *usu* with a shepherd's hut or huts.

shift each successive crop in a system of crop-rotation; the land or field on which this is grown *Gen except Sh Ork.*

shot a piece of ground, *esp* one cropped rotationally *now only in place-names.*

†**skair** a plot of land, *esp* one of the many parcelled out of common lands *Dmf.*

sole the sward or surface vegetation of a pasture *local N-Gall.*

spread-field the ground where cut peat is spread for drying.

springing grazing from the first grass of the year, spring pasture *SW.*

stack: ~ **hill** the ground or mound on which a peat-stack is built. † ~ **yaird** a rick-yard.

†**stance** an overnight stopping-place for a drove of cattle.

stibble, stubble: ~ **land** the stubble of the first crop of corn after grass. ~ **rig** a ridge of stubble left after harvest.

straik a sheep-walk *now Mry.*

tail a long narrow piece of land jutting out from a **croft** *etc.*

tak, take take over (a crop) for the grazing of livestock *NE Per.*

tathe *n* 1 †the dung of cattle or sheep left for manure on their grazing land. 2 coarse rank grass which grows on ground thus manured *now Lnk.* *v* 1 *also* **ted** *of animals* drop dung on land so as to manure it. 2 †manure (land) by turning cattle or sheep onto it. † ~ **-fold** a piece of enclosed ground on which cattle and sheep are confined to manure it with their dung.

tattie: ~ **grund** potato ground. ~ **park** a field of potatoes *N-Per.*

tear in reclaim (waste or rough ground) *now N.*

†**teel land, teel ryge** tilled land.

torie-eaten infested wth crane-fly grubs *chf NE.*

toun, town: ~ **-loan** an open space round a farmstead or hamlet *now NE.*

under, unner *local* planted, sown or stocked with; used for growing or rearing.

†**unland** non-arable land.

†**waingate** a cart-track.

walk a pasture for cattle *now Ags Lnk.*

†**ward, waird** an enclosed piece of land, *chf* for pasture *now in place-names.*

†**water, watter:** ~ **kyle** meadow land possessed by tenants of an estate in annual rotation.

†**wedder gang** a pasture or right of pasturage for wethers.

wersh *of land* of poor quality, exhausted, lacking fertility.†**wersh crap** the third and last crop taken from the **outfield** before the fallow period.

white *freq in place-names: of arable land* fallow, unploughed *now Cai.*

winter: ~**in(g)** a winter pasture, winter keep for animals *Gen except Sh Ork.* ~ **town** the arable part of a farm as opposed to the summer pasture *now Ayr.*

yaird a yard.

7.7 CROPS

7.7.1 CROPS: PLOUGHING

ae-fur-land land which can only be ploughed in one direction because of its steepness.

awrige the sharp angle of the ridge made by ploughing *Gall.*

back-rape the rope which goes over a horse's back.

bauk *n* 1 a balk, an unploughed ridge. 2 a ridge still apparent in a field after the **bauks** were tilled. *v* leave small strips of (land) inadvertently unploughed. †**balk and burrel** = **rig and fur.**

bout the extent of ground covered as a plough etc moves across a field (and sometimes the distance back again) *now local.*

boutgate the doing of a round of work, *eg* two furrows, outwards and back.

bowed rig a strip of land on a hillside ploughed in winding curves to prevent water from draining off directly and carrying top soil with it *WC.*

brak, break: brak-fur *v* plough (land) lightly *Bnf.* *n* a kind of light ploughing *now Abd.* ~ **in** prepare (a field) for seed by harrowing *now Fif.*

brake a heavy harrow for soil *now Bnf Abd Ags.*

†**burrel** a ridge in the **balk and burrel** method, *freq* ~ **rig** *etc.*

butt a ridge or strip of ploughed land; *later* an irregularly shaped ridge; a small piece of ground cut off in some way from adjacent land *now Abd Ags.*

ca(ll) drive (a plough).

cam the tilt or angle given to a furrow as it falls over from the ploughshare, adjusted by the setting of the coulter, *chf* **gie a fur mair** *or* **less** ~ *NE Fif.*

cas-chrom a crook-handled spade. *Hebrides Highl.*

cleathin *NE*, **cleeding** *Fif* the mouldboard of a plough.

cleave, *also* ~ **down** *or* ~ **oot** *Abd* 'split' (a ridge) *Abd midLoth.*

cooter, culter a coulter.

coup: ~ **facken** shallow autumn ploughing to let the frost into the ground *NE*. ~ **fauch** plough up (the green strip between furrows after **brak-furring**) *NE.*

croon, crown the opening furrow in ploughing *Cai SW.*

cross harrow (a field) across the ploughing *Bnf Abd Arg.*

cut: ~**s** the clevis of a plough *SW*. † ~**widdie** the crossbeam attaching a plough or harrow to the traces. † ~**widdies** the links connecting the mechanism of the implement to the crossbeam.

dock nail the nail used to fix a handle on a plough etc *Abd.*

drag a large heavy harrow.

draucht, draft *now Bnf Kcb Rox* line off (land) with the plough by means of straight furrows *Cai Bnf Ags.*

†**ear** plough.

ebb shallow, lacking in depth, scant, *of the ground in ploughing.*

en(d): ~ **lang** harrow a field along the furrows. ~**-rig** the land at the end of the furrow on which the plough is turned.

fauch *n* the breaking up of fallow land by light ploughing, harrowing or both *chf Abd*. *v* plough or harrow (fallow ground) *now local Sh-Bwk.*

feather, fedder *now Sh Ork N* the projecting wing on the side of the sock of a plough.

feenish *v* cut the final furrow in a **rig**. *n* the final furrow which separates one **rig** from another.

feer make the first guiding furrow on (the land). ~**in 1** the act of making the first furrow. **2** the first furrow made *now Renfr.* ~**in pole** one of the poles set up as a guide in drawing the first furrow.

fit, fute, foot: ~**ick** the chain and hook connecting the muzzle of the plough with the **fit-tree** *Arg SW Uls*. ~ **tree** the wooden spar to which the traces are attached in ploughing etc.

fleed an **end-rig** *NE.*

flot an area of land of varying breadth, ploughed at one turn *Cai.*

furr *n* **1** a furrow made by the plough; the strip of earth turned over in the process. **2** the deep furrow or trench separating one **rig** from another *now Sh*. **3** a deep furrow or rut cut by

the plough to act as a drain for surface water *now Sh Ork Arg*. **4** the act of furrowing, a ploughing *now Ork NE*. *v* **1** plough, mark or make furrows in *now NE Dmf*. **2** make drills in or for *Sh-nEC, SW*. ~**-ahin** *WC*, ~**-beast** *NE Ags WC Dmf*, ~**-horse** *local* the horse in a team immediately in front of the plough on the right-hand side.

furrow the earth turned over in a furrow by the plough.

gaither plough so as to throw the soil into a ridge.

gaw a drainage furrow or channel *now Fif*. ~ **fur(row)** a furrow at an **end-rig** used for drainage.

girn a gaping furrow *now Fif Arg.*

†**glut** a wooden wedge used for adjusting a plough.

gore a deep furrow.

graith = **pleuch graith** *now Stlg-Dmf.*

grubber an iron harrow, *usu* with cultivator tines, *esp* for weeding in drills; a scarifier.

gushet the triangular patch left in ploughing an irregularly-shaped field *local Sh-WC.*

hair *of ploughed ground* dry up *NE.*

hand, haun *n* the horse that walks on the left-hand side of a plough-team, *ie* on the unploughed land *now local Ags-Wgt*. *v* advise or assist a competitor at a ploughing match, *chf* ~**er** adviser, helper *Arg Gall Uls.*

hap in cover up (dung, potatoes etc) in drills with the plough *NE.*

harrow, harra a harrow. † ~ **bill** one of the crossbars or spars of a harrow.

hause, †**thals:** ~**-furr** *etc* the second furrow in ploughing *now Gall.*

heid, head the part of the old **Scots plough** corresponding to the modern sole *now Arg Kcb*. ~ **rig** the ridge of land at the end of a field on which horse and plough etc are turned during ploughing, often including a strip at either side of a field ploughed along with the **rigs** in one continuous journey.

high-cutter a type of plough used in ploughing competitions *local Cai-Arg.*

hilt a plough-handle *Cai Abd Kcb-Rox.*

hin(t) *WC, Dmf Uls*, **hintin(g)** *now local Stlg-Rox* the furrow left between two **rigs**, the **mould furrow**.

horse-tree the swingletree of a plough or harrow *now midLoth Kcb.*

hurkle a single horse-grubber or horse-hoe used for cleaning **turnips** *now Pbls Lnk.*

†**Jockie an his owsen** notches cut on a cowherd's stick, representing the method of yoking an ox-plough team *Abd.*

knee a bend in a part of a plough, as in the plough-beam (*Sh*) or coulter-stem (*Fif Loth*).

lan(d) 1 the soil which has still to be turned over by the ploughshare; the width of the cut made by the plough in the soil. **2** an S-hook attaching the yoke to the muzzle of a plough, by which the **land** can be adjusted *N Fif*. ~**ing** the journey of a plough from one side of a field to another and back again, a **bout** *local EC-S*. ~**er** *local NE-Dmf*, ~ **beast** *local NE-SW*, ~ **horse** *now Arg Ayr Dmf in a plough-team* the left-hand horse, which walks on the unturned earth. ~**('s)-end 1** †the (top) end of a **rig**. **2** the end of a furrow, where the plough turns *chf SW S*. ~ **plate** the side-plate on the left-hand side of a plough *local Fif-Uls*. ~ **side** the left-hand side of the plough *now local N-SW*. **gie (a ploo) mair** *or* **less** ~, **pit on** *or* **tak aff** ~ *Fif SW* adjust the width of the cut to be made by the plough.

lay *v* **1** re-steel (a plough-iron etc) *Gen except Sh Ork*. **2** †lay aside, put (a plough) out of action. *n* the re-steeling of the cutting edge of an implement *Gen except Sh Ork*. ~ **over** turn over (a furrow) in ploughing *Sh-NE Wgt*.

lea, ley: ~ **fur**, ~ **furrow** a ploughing of old grassland *local NE-SW*. ~ **rig** *now only verse* a **rig** or strip of grass left untilled in a ploughed field, a broad **bauk**.

lowse, loose unyoke (a horse from a plough etc or vice versa); unyoke a draught animal, stop ploughing etc.

lug part of the muzzle of a plough *local Cai-Wgt*.

†maister-tree the main swingletree immediately attached to the plough *chf Sh Ork*.

mids *NE*, **mid rig** *local NE-Uls* the dividing furrow between two ridges.

†mowdie(wort) brod the mouldboard of a plough.

muild, mool, mou(l)d: ~ **bred** a mouldboard. ~ **fur(row)** the last furrow of a **rig** ploughed on soil from which the sod has already been turned over *local Ork-Per*.

mumbler an implement for breaking clods, a kind of heavy harrow *now Fif wLoth Rox*.

muzzle, mizzle the bridle of a plough *now C Uls*.

pack lay (the furrows) close together *local Sh-Wgt*.

paidle, paddle a long-handled tool for clearing the coulter of a plough in the furrow *local*.

pair a team of two horses for ploughing and other farm jobs. **an ae** *etc* ~ **(horse) place** *etc* a farm with one etc team of horses *now NE*.

pattle a small spade-like tool, used for clearing the mouldboard of a plough. † ~**ing** scraping clean with, or as with, a **pattle**.

pleuch, ploo, plough *n* **1** a plough. **2** a team of plough-horses or oxen. *v* to plough. † ~ **feast** a ritual entertainment given at the first ploughing of the new season. ~ **graith** the movable fittings and attachments of a plough *now local NE-Dmf*. † ~ **guids** the oxen used for ploughing, a plough-team. ~ **irons** the metal parts of a plough, *esp* the coulter and share. ~ **land** land suitable for ploughing, arable land. ~ **rynes** the reins used for a plough-team *now Kcb*. ~ **slings** *now NE-Per*, ~ **soam** *now Kcb* the hooks connecting the swingletrees to the plough. ~ **soam** the rope or chain by which horses or oxen are yoked to the plough, the traces *now Kcb*. ~ **sock** a ploughshare. ~ **stilts** the shafts or handles of a plough. ~ **theats** the plough-traces *now NE*. **gie a ploo gurr** cut a furrow deeper than usual and at a slant *Bnf Abd*.

point, pint the tapering part of a field which is not completely rectangular; the furrows shortened because of this *NE wLoth Kcb*.

prap, prop an object set up as a guide to mark the course and end of the first furrow of the **rig** *Ork NE*.

rack ban *or* **chain** the chain connecting the bridle of a plough with the swingletree *NE Kcb*.

redd[1] clear (land) by ploughing etc.

†redd[2] the curvature of a ploughshare which helps keep it clear of obstructions.

reest, wrest *now local C n* the mouldboard of a plough *now Abd C*. *v* tilt a plough to the right (*ie* to the mouldboard side) *local EC-WC*.

rib †*n* the ridge left unploughed as below. *v* plough every alternate furrow, turning the soil over onto the adjacent unploughed strip *local N-S*.

ride *of a harrow* override another being drawn alongside it and become interlocked with it *now Kcb*.

rig *n, early farming* each separate strip of ploughed land, raised in the middle and sloping gradually to a furrow on either side, and *usu* bounded by patches of uncultivated grazing; *now* one of the divisions of a field ploughed in a single operation. *v* plough (land) in **rigs** *now local C-S*. † ~**-end** the **end-rig**, the land at the end of the furrow on which the plough is turned. ~**-fit** the foot or lower end of a **rig**. ~**-heid** the crown or high part of the **rig** *now Sh*. ~ **and fur**, ~ **and furrow** *of the pattern on a ploughed field*, ribbed; corrugated.

rin, run: ~ **neeps** *or* **neep dreels** hoe between drills of **turnips** with a horse-hoe *NE midLoth*. ~ **o the rig** the direction or angle at which a field has been ploughed *local Per-S*.

†**ristle** a kind of small plough with a sickle-shaped coulter for cutting a narrow deep rut through strong roots *chf Hebrides Highl.*

rit, rut *v* mark with a shallow trench or furrow as a guide in ploughing *now Sh-Cai Gall. n* the shallow preliminary cut or furrow made in ploughing *now Cai.* **rutter** a marker on a drill plough, which cuts the line of the next drill *now Arg Kcb.*

rive out break up (untilled ground) with the plough *now Cai Abd Ags.*

Robbie Burns an older kind of plough with wooden stilts and beam and an iron body, without a coulter *NE-C.*

s the draught-hook of a plough etc *now local Ork-Loth.*

scart a furrow or mark on the ground *local Sh-Kcb.*

†**Scots plough** a kind of swing- or wheel-less plough.

scrape the shallow first furrow made in commencing a **rig** *WC Kcb.*

scrat the shallow first furrow made in commencing a **rig** *Ork NE.* ~ **aff** mark out with shallow furrows the **rigs** to be ploughed in (a field) *Ork NE Ags.*

seed fur the furrow into which grain is to be sown and harrowed *now N.*

shackle, sheckle 1 the link-fitting which connects the plough-beam with the swingletree *now Cai Kcb.* **2** the clamp which holds the shaft of a plough coulter to the beam *local Cai-Kcb.*

†**shae, shoe** the plate or iron strip on the underside of an old wooden plough etc.

sheth a connecting bar or strut in a plough.

sheuch *n* a furrow made by a plough. *v* make a furrow (in) *now local Per-Wgt.*

shim *n* a horse-hoe, a kind of small plough for weeding, earthing up etc *NE. v* use a horse-hoe, weed etc with a **shim** *NE.*

side casting the act of ploughing along the side of a slope *Per Arg Gall.*

single-horse-tree a swingletree of a plough to which the traces of a single horse are attached *now Per Kcb.*

skail plough **out** (a ridge) so that the furrows fall outward on either side of the **hintin** *now N, C.*

†**slee-band** an iron ring round the beam of a plough to strengthen it where the coulter was attached.

slip a metal ring attaching the swingletrees of a plough to the trace-chains *now Cai.*

soam, †**soum** a chain or rope attaching a draught-ox or -horse to a plough etc *now local Kcdn-Kcb.*

sock a ploughshare. ~ **spade** a spade for removing

stones which might obstruct the **sock** *Fif Loth WC.* † ~ **and scythe** ploughing and mowing.

sole clout the iron shoe covering the sole of a plough *now Kcb.*

soo, sow: ~**s lug** one of the mouldboards of a drill- or double-breasted plough *NE Ags Fif.*

sout a sudden leap, bounce, jolt or bump (as when a plough strikes against a stone) *SW.*

†**speed the ploo** a well-wishing phrase at a **pleuch feast.**

steer[1] plough, *specif* replough in spring (land already ploughed in the autumn) *local.* † ~**ing** ploughing.

steer[2] guide (a plough).

stiel the handle of a plough etc *now Rox.*

stilt one of the handles of a plough.

stoup the **stilt** or handle of a plough *now NE.*

straik *n* the motion or marks of a harrow; the ground covered by one journey of a harrow *now local Sh-Gall. v* harrow (a piece of ground) *now N Ags Per.*

streek put (a plough etc) into action; start work, get going *now Bnf Abd.* †**streiking (time)** ploughing time.

strip a single journey or turn of harrows over a ploughed field *N Loth Kcb.*

†**swaird-cut** chop up the turf of (old pasture), *chf* as ~**ter** a machine which does this.

swing tree a swingletree of a plough etc *now Ork Bnf.*

swiveltree the swingletree of a plough *now Ork Per.*

tear the angle of adjustment between the coulter and the point of the ploughshare, which regulates the cut in the furrow *local Cai-Rox.*

theat 1 ~**s** the traces (attaching a horse to a plough etc) *now N nEC.* **2** a tow, pull by a trace-horse *Ags Per.* ~**er** a trace-horse of a plough *nEC Lnk.*

thorter plough or harrow at right angles to what one has done before *now Abd.*

†**thrapple plough** a kind of single-stilted wooden plough used *esp* in Cai.

threap 1 the angle between the points of the coulter and of the share *Ags Per.* **2** a swingletree *SW.*

†**throck, frock** the third, fourth, or fifth pair of oxen in a twelve-oxen plough team *NE.*

tid the proper or favourable season for ploughing, harrowing etc *now C.*

tie-back a short rope etc tied between two horses of a plough team to prevent their heads moving to the side.

treadwiddie, †**trodwiddie** the draught-chain

(*orig* a twisted withy), with hook and swivel connecting a plough or harrow to the swingletrees.

twa, two: ~**-horse tree** the swingletree of a two-horse plough *now Ork.*

tweel the angle at which the coulter is set in the beam, which determines the lie of the furrow *now Stlg Fif.*

wynd, †twyne: ~**in(s) 1** a long, awkwardly-shaped or steep piece of land, *orig* ploughed in only one direction by the plough turning left after each furrow. **2** a group of **rigs** in a field which is divided into an upper and lower **wyndin** for convenience of ploughing *NE Loth.*

yird, yirth the depth of a furrow; the angle at which the plough-sock is set to achieve this.

yoke *n* **1** the harness of a plough etc; *specif* the main swingletree of a plough *now Cai Abd.* **2** *also* **yokin** the period during which a team of horses or oxen is in harness at one stretch, *usu* half a day's work. †*v* attach (a plough). †**a-** ~, **in(to) the** ~ in(to) harness *NE.*

7.7.2 CROPS: MANURE

addle foul, putrid liquid from dung.

cleek a muck-rake.

coop a small heap of manure.

†coup a closed cart for carrying manure.

fire fangit scorched, spoilt by excessive fermentation *now Ork.*

green *of manure* fresh, unrotted *now Cai Kcb Rox.* ~ **brees** green, stagnant water, *esp* that oozing from a dunghill *now Bnf Abd.*

guid, good: ~**ing** manure.

gullion a pool of semi-liquid manure and decayed vegetable matter *Uls.*

hack *n, also* ~ **muck, muck** ~ a pronged tool used for forking etc *Gen except Sh Ork. v* use a **hack** to drag dung from a cart *midLoth Arg.*

hap in cover up (dung) in drills with the plough *NE.*

harl a rake or scraper used for scraping up dung.

hen-pen the droppings of fowls, used as manure *now NE, C.*

hut, †hot 1 a basket or pannier used for carrying manure. **2** a small heap of manure distributed over a field in preparation for spreading *now local midLoth-S.*

†hutch a small heap or pile of dung.

†kellach a large conical wicker basket or pannier, *usu* with a lid at the lower end, for carrying dung to the fields *N.*

mak, make *v of dung* mature *local Cai-Loth.*

manner, mainner *v* manure; spread manure on (land etc). *n* manure, dung.

midden, midding *n* a dunghill, compost heap, refuse heap. †*v* to heap into a dunghill. ~ **bree** the effluent from a midden *NE.* † ~ **dub** the pool of seepage from a dunghill *chf SW.* ~ **dyke** a wall round a dunghill. ~ **feals** turfs laid on a dunghill to aid the maturing process *now Ork.* ~ **heid,** ~ **tap** *now Ags* the top of a midden. ~ **hole** the hollowed-out foundation of a dunghill *local Cai-SW.* ~**-stead** the site of a midden *now local Sh-SW.*

muck *n* dung, farmyard manure. *v* **1** to clean dung out of (a **byre** or stable). **2** spread with dung, fertilize. † ~ **creel** a pannier or hamper used for taking dung to the fields. † ~ **fail** turf mixed with dung to form a manure or compost *chf Abd.* ~ **midden** a dunghill.

neep muck manure for putting on turnip ground *Sh NE.*

†pare and burn burn the top layer of turf cut from a field before ploughing, for use as manure.

pluck a two-pronged, mattock-type implement used for forking dung etc *NE.*

sea ware, †sea wrack the coarse seaweed washed up by the tide and used as manure *now Sh Ork NE.*

shairn: ~ **bree** the ooze from farmyard manure *Abd.* ~ **midden** a dunghill *Abd.*

skail spread (manure) over the surface of the ground *now Cai Per WC, SW.*

spark in sprinkle, scatter (dung) *now Ork.*

spart scatter (dung) *now Sh Cai.*

stale urine, *esp* that kept for manuring etc.

strang, †strang-wesche urine which has been allowed to stand for some time, used in making manure *now Sh Ork N.* **strang hole, strong hole** a seepage pit in a **midden** *Sh Abd.* **strang pig, strong pig** a large jar etc for holding **strang** *now Ork Abd.*

tathe *n* **1** †the dung of cattle or sheep left for manure on their grazing land. **2** coarse rank grass which grows on ground thus manured *now Lnk. v* **1** *also* **ted** *of animals* drop dung on land so as to manure it. **2** †manure (land) by turning cattle or sheep onto it. † ~**-fold** a piece of enclosed ground on which cattle and sheep are confined to manure it with their dung.

ware *n* a kind of seaweed used as manure *now Sh Ork EC, WC. v* manure with seaweed. † ~ **bear** *Abd,* ~ **barley** barley manured with seaweed.

†willow earth compost made of rotten willow branches.

yird, yirth: ~**ie tam** a mound of earth and weeds, a compost heap *NE*.

7.7.3 CROPS: SOWING

†**ait-seed** the sowing of oats, the season for sowing oats. **ait-seed time, aitsen tyme** the time for sowing oats.

awald *of a crop of grain, esp oats* grown for the second year on the same land: **1** †of the **infield** or **2** of the **outfield**.

†**bere, bear:** ~**-root (crop)** the first crop after **bere**. ~**-sawing** the sowing of barley; seed barley. ~**-seed 1** the seed of the barley; barley for sowing. **2** the (time for) sowing of barley or **bere**.

†**birth** produce of the soil; a crop.

black: ~ **victual** *now Stlg*, † ~ **crap** a crop of peas and/or beans.

blain a bare patch in a field of crops.

†**blander** disperse scantily or over-thinly.

bleeze: in a ~ *of a crop* ready to be thinned *now Ags*.

Bobbin John a kind of hand-sower for turnip seed *now Abd*.

buzzle *of grain crops* rustle (indicating ripeness) *Bnf Abd*.

cast sow (seed) *now local NE-WC*.

caul(d), cold: ~ **seed** late oats or peas.

crap a crop.

cuff remove a layer of soil with a rake from (a piece of ground) before sowing, replacing it afterwards.

doon *of seed* sown *Cai Bnf Abd Fif*.

†**ferd: the** ~ **corne** used in estimates of the value of grain for sowing.

fiddle a hand-machine for sowing grain, worked by turning a flanged wheel with a bow and thong *local NE-SW*.

furr draw soil around (plants) so as to form an edge, earth **up** *Sh-nEC, SW*.

girsie *of cereal crops* interspersed with grass.

gowk aits oats sown after the arrival of the cuckoo *now Abd Rox*.

happer a basket or container, *esp* that from which the sower sows his seed *now Ork NE Ags*. †**happergaw** *n* a gap in growing corn caused by unequal sowing. *v* sow grain unequally (when using a **happer**) so that the resulting crop is patchy.

heuch earth up (plants) in drills, trench *Abd mid-Loth*.

hot-furr a newly-turned strip of earth, used *esp* for sowing early peas *now Abd Fif*.

in under crop, ploughed and sown *now Cai Kcb*.

inpit, input sow (crops) *SW*. †**input** which has been put in, sown, etc.

†**intaking** the breaking in and cropping of previously fallow ground *Abd*.

lazy-bed a method of planting (*usu* potatoes) on beds over undug strips of soil, using manure and sods from adjacent trenches *now chf Hebrides Highl*.

lea, ley: ~ **hay** hay grown on old pasture *now SW*. ~ **oats**, ~ **corn**, ~ **crap** oats grown on ploughed up grassland *local*.

mak prepare (ground) for sowing *now Ork NE, Per*.

†**mete** cereal, while still growing.

miss fail to germinate or grow.

muild, mool, mou(l)d: ~**ie** earthy, deep in the soil *local Sh-SW*.

neep sow (land) with **turnips** *Bnf Abd Loth*. ~**s** the time of year when **turnips** are hoed *Sh NE Per*. ~ **grun(d)** ground prepared for **turnips** *Sh Ork NE*. ~ **land** ground from which a crop of **turnips** has been taken *now Sh Ork*. ~ **machine** a horse-drawn machine for sowing **turnips** *NE Per*. ~ **re(e)t** land from which a **turnip** crop has been taken, and still so called under the subsequent corn-crop *NE*. ~ **seed 1** = **turnip** seed. **2** the time for sowing **turnips** *NE*. ~ **shawin** = **turnip** sowing *NE*.

†**peel** stake up, support or protect by means of stakes.

pit down set plants *esp* potatoes in the ground *Cai Uls*.

profit natural produce, *eg* grain *now Sh Kcb*.

pruif *n* the act of estimating the quality and yield of a grain-crop by examining a random sample; the sample itself *now Uls*. *v* assess the quality and content of (a given quantity of grain) by examining a random sample *now Ork NE Wgt*. ~ **barley, corn** *etc* the barley, corn etc selected as a sample for **pruif** *now Abd Per*.

raw, row *of root crops* plant, come up in rows *now Kcb*.

ruit *v* root.

ruskie a basket for holding seed-corn.

saw, sow sow. ~**in happer** *Ork Abd Ayr*, ~**in sheet** *local* a canvas sheet from which seed was broadcast one-handed. ~**in time** seed-time *NE*. ~ **doun, out** *etc* sow (land) for a grass-crop.

seed †**seed-time**, *freq* **bear** *etc* ~. ~**-like** *of soil* ready for sowing *Cai Bnf*.

set a (portion of a) potato used for planting. ~ **aff** plant out *local Sh-Per*. **setting** a young plant;

the quantity of potatoes planted as seed. ~ **up** earth up (a plant).

sheet a sheet of canvas folded into a pouch to hold corn-seed when sowing one-handed *now Cai*. † ~ **shaking** remains of meal etc shaken from a **sheet** *Abd*.

sheuch *n* a temporary trench or furrow for plants. *v* lay (a plant etc) in the ground; *specif* put (seedlings etc) in a temporary trench for later transplantation or storage.

sinder, sunder single, hoe out (overcrowded seedlings) *NE*.

single thin out (seedlings, *esp* **turnips**).

slap, slop thin out (seedlings etc) *NE*.

spark in sprinkle, scatter (seed etc) *now Ork*.

stitch a furrow or drill *eg* of **turnips** *SW*.

7.7.4 CROPS: HARVEST WORK

acre harvest grain crops at a stated rate per acre *NE*.

back end the end of harvest, late autumn.

bag raip the thick double straw rope round the eaves of a thatched stack *N*.

ban(d) a rope, straw-twist etc used to bind sheaves etc *now Abd*. ~**ster** the member of a party of harvesters who binds the sheaves.

bandwin the band of three to eight reapers who work together and are served by one **bandster**.

†**beet** a sheaf or bundle of flax.

big stack (hay, corn *etc*).

boon a band of reapers, shearers etc *now Uls*.

boss the wooden frame on which a cornstack is built *now Abd Ags Lnk*. **bossin** *now Arg*, **boskill** *now Abd* a ventilation hole in a cornstack.

bottle, battle, buttle a sheaf *now Kcb Uls*.

bout: lying in the ~ *of corn or hay* lying in rows after being cut *Bnf Abd Ags*.

†**braid, broad: in** ~ **band** *of corn* lying unbound on the harvest field.

brath weave (straw ropes) round a stack.

bridle rope (a stack) *now Bnf*.

ca(ll) bring home (**turnips** etc) from the fields.

car, †**ker** a sledge for transporting hay *SW*.

cat a handful of reaped grain laid on the ground without being put into a sheaf *S*.

clod pile up (**turnips**) *Gall*.

cloo a ball of straw rope used in thatching stacks.

clype *rick-building* the person who passes hay or sheaves from the forker to the builder *SW*.

cole *n* a haycock. *v* put up (hay) in cocks. †**collar** a maker of haycocks.

coop a small heap of hay etc.

†**curn** a single grain of corn, *freq* as indicating a proportion of a crop etc.

cutter a reaper, harvester *now Bnf Abd*.

†**darg** the amount (of meadow) which can be mowed in a day.

dass 1 a layer in a pile of hay *now Bwk Kcb*. 2 a cut of hay, etc.

easin(s), esing the part of a haystack corresponding to the eaves of a building. ~ **gang** a course of sheaves projecting a little at the **easin** to keep the rain out *local*.

edder, ether *n* a straw rope used in thatching a haystack *chf Abd*. *v also* **aider rope** (a stack) in order to secure the thatch *Bnf Abd*. ~**in(s)** a straw rope used on stacks, loads etc, a cross-rope *chf NE*.

enter, inter *now NE Ags, also* † ~ **in** *or* to *of harvesting* engage in (a task), begin work *now local Abd-Uls*.

fause, false: ~ **hoose** a conical structure of wooden props built inside a cornstack to facilitate drying *local*.

feather smooth the top and sides of (a rick) *Per Ayr Uls*.

fit, fute, foot: upon the ~ *of grain* standing, unthreshed.

forewin *hand-reaping* the first strip to be cut, done by the most experienced worker; the worker who leads or sets the pace in any farming task *now Arg*.

found, foon a ring of stones and brushwood on which a haystack is built *NE*.

frandie a small rick of hay or corn-sheaves made by a man standing on the ground *Per Fif*.

gait *n* a single sheaf of grain tied near the top and set up to dry. *v* set up (sheaves) thus.

gaither, gather bring together enough corn to form a sheaf *now Abd*. ~**er** a person who **gaithers**.

gang a layer, *esp* of corn-sheaves in a cart or stack *now local Sh-Ayr*.

gaud a wooden slat *approx* nine feet long used to direct the corn to the scythe or binder *NE*.

girse heuk, grass nail *now local Cai-SW* the hooked metal cross-stay between shaft and blade of a scythe *Ork Abd Ags*.

Glesca Jock coir rope used in binding haystacks *Mry Abd*.

gumping the part of a crop left standing between two reapers, *usu* cut the ~**ing** *Gall*.

gushet the triangular patch left in reaping an irregularly-shaped field *local Sh-WC*.

hairst, harst, harvest *n* 1 harvest. 2 *only* **hairst**

or **harst** a harvest job, *esp* **tak a** ~ engage oneself as a harvest labourer *now N Kcb*. *v* **1** harvest. **2** work in the harvest field, gather in the crops. **hairster** a harvester. ~ **fee** the wages paid to a harvest worker *now Abd*. ~ **folk** workers engaged for the harvest *now local Sh-Dmf*. ~ **rig** *now chf literary* a ridge of corn ready for harvesting; the ridge between two furrows in a harvest field; the harvest field itself *now local Sh-Stlg*. **(in the) heid o** ~ (at the) height of the harvest *Abd*.

heckle the network of straw ropes which covers the apex of a cornrick *Bnf Abd*.

heid put the finishing touches to (a rick or stack) and secure its top. ~**ing sheaf** the last sheaf placed on the top of a **stook** (in wet districts) or rick *now local Abd-Uls*. ~**sheaf** the last sheaf of grain placed on top of a **stook** (*now* Arg) or rick.

hert, hairt, heart *n* the central core of sheaves in a cornrick. *v* build up the inner sheaves of a cartload or stack of corn. ~**in(g)** the building up of the inner sheaves; these sheaves themselves.

†**theuk, hook** a reaper.

hey, hay the hay harvest. ~**-bogie** a low haytruck dragged behind a tractor *local midLoth-Rox*. ~**-folk** haymakers *now midLoth Kcb*. ~**-fow** a hay-fork *now Bnf Kcb Dmf*. ~**-neuk** a corner of a **byre** or stable in which hay is stored for immediate consumption *now Sh Dmf Rox*. ~**sned** a scythe or its shaft *local midLoth-Rox*.

hippit, hip-grippit *Cai Abd Kcb, esp of workers in the harvest field* having a feeling of stiffness or overstrain in the lower back, hips, or thighs.

hole dig up (*now esp* potatoes) *NE Ags*.

hooick a small rick of corn or hay *now NE Ags*. **heuicking** the preserving of corn in **hooicks** during a rainy harvest *NE Ags*.

huid, hood *n, also* **hoodin(g)** *now Uls*, †**hood sheaf** one of a pair of sheaves of corn placed on the top of a **stook** or cornstack as a protection against the weather *now Rox*. *v* top (a **stook** of corn) with two protective sheaves. ~**ie** a sunbonnet worn by field-workers *now Ork Ags*.

hut *n* a small stack of corn or hay etc built to protect the crop temporarily from the weather, before its removal to the stackyard *now Ags-Uls*. *v* put up (sheaves of grain) in small stacks in the field as a protective measure against weather or birds *now Ags-Uls*.

hutch *n* a small rick or temporary stack of corn *now Lnk Kcb Dmf*. *v* set (sheaves of corn) in small temporary ricks to dry *Lnk Kcb Dmf*.

ill-hertit *of a cornrick* not packed tightly enough in the centre *Ork Cai NE Wgt*.

in bring (the harvest) in from the fields.

ingaither gather in, harvest (crops).

intak(ing) the act of taking in the harvest.

kame rake (loose hay or straw from a stack to trim it) *local*.

keep: ~ **a stack** trim a hay or cornstack while it is being built *now Kcb Dmf*. ~ **up one's rig** maintain the same rate of corn cutting as the others in the harvest field *now Loth Wgt*.

kicker a tedder, a machine for spreading out newmown hay *Bnf Fif WC, SW*.

kill, kiln the wooden tripod round which a stack of hay or corn is built for ventilation *local NE-Dmf*.

kipper pile or stack **up** carelessly *now Abd*.

lachter the amount of corn grasped and cut in one stroke; a handful of hay *now Cai*.

lap (cock) a small truss of hay *Cai Uls*.

larach, †larach stack the foundation of a hay or cornstack.

lead carry (harvested grain or hay) home or **in** from the field.

lew a warming, a slight rise in temperature, of the interior of stacks *local Sh-SW*.

lib grope in the soil and remove (growing potatoes) without disturbing the tops *now Per Fif Kcb*.

lift 1 take up or out of the ground (*eg* a crop of corn, potatoes). **2** gather (scythed corn into a sheaf for binding) *now local*.

logie the outer opening of a ventilation funnel in a cornstack.

maw mow, cut (hay etc) with a scythe. ~**er** *now Gall*, † ~**ster** *Gall* a mower.

mou *n* **1** a large heap of grain, hay etc *Gen except Sh Ork*. **2** a large vertical section of a houseshaped hay or cornstack *Bnf Ags Kcb*. †*v* pile up (unthreshed grain or hay) in a barn.

†**new corn** harvest-time *S*.

owergaun rapes ropes which go vertically over the thatch on a cornstack *now Loth Kcb*.

pike *n* a round, conical-topped hayrick for drying hay before stacking *now SW, S Uls*. *v* build (hay) into a **pike** *chf S*. ~**r** a person who builds hay into **pikes** *S*.

†**point, pint** the leading member of a team of reapers, the man at the front left-hand-side of the team.

pou, pull pluck (fruit, flowers etc) from the plants or trees on which they grow, gather or collect produce of any kind.

pouk pull out the loose hay at the foot of (a stack) to let air in *local Per-SW*.

prod a wooden pin or skewer used as a thatchingpin *now Per*.

puddock (barrow) a flat, wooden, sledge-like or triangular platform etc, shaped rather like a frog, used for transporting heavy loads of hay etc.

pyot a farm-hand who stands on a cornstack and passes the sheaves from the forker to the builder *NE*.

quile *local Ags-Kcb*, **kyle** *C, S*, **coil** *n* the small heap into which hay is gathered after being cut *now WC Kcb*. *v* rake (hay) into such heaps *now WC Gall*.

raep reap *now Sh Ork Bnf nEC*.

raip *n* **1** the ropes securing thatch on a cornrick *Gen except Sh Ork* **2** a straw band for a sheaf of corn *now NE Loth Rox*. *v* **1** rope. **2** secure the thatch of (a cornrick) with a network of (straw) ropes *local*.

rake rake together stalks of corn left behind on a harvested field. **~r** a person who follows the reapers with a rake to glean.

rascal knot a kind of knot tied on the straw bands of corn sheaves *now Abd Rox*.

raw *of corn-sheaves* damp, not fully dried out *now Sh*.

redd clear (land) by reaping etc. **~ roads** *or* **the bout** scythe corn round the edges of a field to allow space for a reaping machine *NE*.

reek *of damp hay, corn etc* emit vapour or steam *now local Sh-Kcb*.

ree-ruck a small rick of corn set up to aid drying *S*.

rickle *n* a small temporary stack of grain or seed-hay *WC, SW*. *v* build (grain) into small temporary ricks *WC, SW*.

rig: 1 †the team of reapers, *usu* three, assigned to each **rig**. **2** the top, the highest part of, a cornstack, a ridge of corn etc *now local*.

†**ring-gang** the topmost circle of sheaves in the vertical wall of a stack, made to project as eaves.

rip a handful of stalks of unthreshed grain or hay *now local Ork-Bwk*.

road a scythe-cut path round a grain field to clear the way for a reaping machine.

Rob Sorby *joc* name for various sharp-edged tools, *eg* a scythe, a sickle *NE Kcdn Per*.

ruck *n* **1** a hay or cornstack of a standard shape and size *now NE-S*. **2** a small temporary haystack in the field to allow the hay to dry *local Cai-S*. *v* pile up, stack up, build (hay, corn etc) into a stack *now local*. **~ foun(d)** a circular foundation of stones etc on which a stack is built *NE nEC, SW*. **~ heid** the tapering top of a stack *NE nEC, SW*. **~ tow** the rope used to bind the thatch on a stack *NE Per*.

†**sad** *of a haystack etc* become **sad**, shrink in bulk, subside *now Ags Fif*.

scob a twig or cane of willow or hazel bent over to fasten down thatch *now SW*.

scroo *n* a stack of corn, hay etc, *Sh Ork N*. *v* build (corn etc) into stacks *now Sh Ork*.

scythe *v* cut with a scythe, mow. *n* a scytheman *NE*. **~-sned** the curved wooden handle or shaft of a scythe *now NE Per*. **~-straik** a scythe sharpener *now NE Kcb*.

set a team to build cornstacks; the number of **rigs** reaped at one time by a band of reapers *local sEC-Uls*.

shaif, shave *now Ags* a sheaf.

shak, shake the shaking of grain from an ear of corn, *esp* in wind etc; the loss of grain so caused *now Sh Ork N*.

†**shake-wind** a strong blustery wind which shakes off ripe ears of corn.

shank the lower part or sides of a cornstack *N, local C*.

shear, share *v* **1** shear. **2** reap (corn), cut (crops) with a sickle *now local Sh-Per*. *n* the act of cutting (*esp* corn) *now Sh*. *n* the cut end of a sheaf of corn *Mry Abd*. **~er** a corn-reaper, sickleman *now Sh*. **~er's bannock, scone** *etc* a large bread roll etc eaten on the harvest field *local Ags-Bwk*. **~ing** shearing; reaping; harvest.

shig a small temporary hay or cornstack *now Wgt*.

simmen(s) ropes made of straw, heather, rushes etc, used with stone weights to hold down thatch on stacks *now Sh Ork Cai Ross*.

single *now local Bwk-Rox*, **singlin** *local Fif-Rox* a handful or small bundle of gleaned corn.

slip raip a straw binding for a sheaf which, because of a defective knot, slips open *NE Per Lnk*.

smiler *joc* a kind of large wide-toothed wooden hand-rake for stubble *N*.

sned the shaft of a scythe, to which the blade is attached.

†**sock and scythe** ploughing and mowing.

soo, sow, *also* **~ stack** *now Fif Kcb* a large oblong stack of hay or straw *Gen except Sh Ork*.

sookan a one-ply rope of straw etc, used *chf* for binding straw, thatching ricks etc *Ork Dnbt Bute*.

sprat a coarse reedy rush or grass growing on marshy ground and sometimes used in stack-thatching.

†**stack yaird** a rick-yard.

stale the foundation, made of a layer of stones, brushwood etc, on which a corn or haystack is built *now local Per-Rox*.

stamp cole *Dmf*, **stankle** *Ork Cai Inv SW* a small temporary hayrick.

stapple a bundle of straw or rushes tied like a sheaf and used for thatching cornstacks *now Stlg-SW*.

stathel, staddle 1 the foundation of a stack of grain, built of stone, wood etc, to protect from vermin and damp *now local Cai-SW*. **2** the main part of a cornstack; a stack in the process of building or dismantling *now local N*. **stethlin** the foundations of a stack, the materials used for this *now Per*.

steid, stead a site, foundation, base of a corn or haystack *Sh-Cai*.

stibble, stubble stubble. †**stibbler** a harvest-worker who gathers up odd straws, a gleaner. †~ **rig** the leader in a team of reapers.

stob dress or trim (a stack of grain) with a hay-fork *now Ork Bnf Abd*.

stook *n* a shock of cut sheaves, *usu* ten or twelve set up to dry in a field; a bundle (of straw). *v* **1** set up (sheaves etc) in **stooks**. **2** *of corn* go into **stooks** *now Sh Bnf Ags*. ~**er** the worker who sets up the cut sheaves in **stooks**.

strab a stalk of corn that has been missed or merely broken by the scythe or reaper; any odd or loose straw *Bnf Abd*.

straik *n* a tool for sharpening scythes etc *now NE Fif SW*. *v* sharpen (a scythe etc) with a **straik** *now local NE-SW*.

strap the band of corn-stalks used to tie up a sheaf at harvest *SW*.

striddler a farmhand who stands on a cornstack and passes sheaves from the cart to the stack-builder *Bwk Rox*.

†**strip** pull up (a **turnip** crop) in strips, pull up every alternate drill or set of drills.

stug, stog: *n* ~**s** unevenly cut stubble. †*v* cut with a rough edge, *esp* in harvesting grain with a sickle; cut (the stubble) unevenly.

swap throw (a straw rope) up and over a hay or cornstack to hold down the thatch; rope (a stack) thus, **edder** *NE*.

†**swarth** a swath, the cut made by one sweep of a scythe.

sway a swathe, the row of cuts of grass made by a scythe *nEC, WC, S*.

tait a small bundle or wisp of hay or corn *now local Sh-SW*.

tak, take: ~ **about** secure (a crop), harvest successfully *now Sh NE*.

tap(s), top(s) a framework fitted round a cart to facilitate the transport of large loads of hay etc *now Per Fif*.

tattie: ~**-creel** a basket for gathering potatoes. ~

deevil a machine for digging potatoes *NE Ags Fif*. ~ **grubber** a kind of harrow for digging up potatoes *now NE Per*. ~ **holidays** an autumn school holiday to allow children to help with the potato harvest. ~ **holin** *Bnf Abd Ags*, ~ **howkin** *Gen except Sh Ork*, ~**-liftin** the potato harvest. ~ **howker** a person who works at the potato harvest, *esp* a temporary worker from Ireland *Gen except Sh Ork*. ~**-swinger** a foreman, overseer, *esp* of farm-workers at the potato harvest *now Lnk*. ~ **weather** weather favourable for the potato harvest *local Sh-Per*.

taupiner, tapner a curved knife with a hooked tip for **lifting** and topping and tailing turnips *NE Ags*.

thack thatch. ~**-pin** a wooden peg used to fasten down thatch *now Ags Per*. ~**-raip** a straw rope used to secure thatch on a stack. ~ **and raip** the thatch of a stack etc and the ropes tying it down.

theek *v* roof, cover (a hay or cornstack) **with** (thatch). *n* thatch *now WC, SW*.

threave *n* a measure of cut grain, straw, reeds or other thatching material, consisting of two **stooks**, *usu* with twelve sheaves each but varying locally and according to grain type. †*v* act as a **threaver**. **threaver** a reaper paid by the **threave**.

tip a handful of stalks of straw, used *eg* in thatching; a plait, tuft or handful of straw etc *now Bnf Abd*. †~**ple** *n* a bundle of hay tied near the top so that it tapers to a point. *v* tie hay thus.

tramp: ~**-cock**, ~**-cole** *now local Sh-WC*, †~**-rick** a cock of hay compressed by **tramping**.

tummlin Tam a horse-drawn hay-gatherer which turns right over when depositing its load *Ork-S*.

turn, tirn turn (cut hay etc) to dry; dismantle and rebuild (a small stack etc) for drying.

turse *v* truss, pack up, make into a bale etc *now Cai Bnf*. *n* a truss, a bundle, bale of straw, thatch etc *now Ork Cai Arg*.

undrawn *of straw* not arranged in uniform length for thatching *Sh Ork Bnf*.

uplift dig up, harvest (potatoes and other root crops) *now local*.

†**upseed-time** harvest.

uptak, uptake the lifting or gathering of a crop, *esp* a root-crop *Sh NE*.

victual, vittal a crop before or after harvesting *now local Kcdn-Loth*.

wap, wop a bundle of hay or straw.

warp interlace the cross or horizontal ropes in the thatching of a cornstack *Per Fif Loth*.

whittle, whuttle 1 a harvest-hook, sickle, scythe *now Lnk Ayr*. **2** a whetstone for sharpening scythes *now Sh WC*.

win[1] *v* gather in (crops etc), harvest *now local Sh-WC*. *n* the quantity of standing corn cut by a team of reapers while moving in one direction, *usu* one or two **rigs** taken together *now Cai*.

win[2] *of cut corn, hay etc* dry and make or become ready for storage by exposure to air and sun.

win(d)le †*n* a bundle of straw. *v* make up (straw or hay) into bundles. **windlin(g)** a bundle of straw, *usu* as much as a man can carry in the crook of his arm *now Sh Ork N*.

win(d)-raw a row or line into which mown hay is raked *now WC*.

winter the last load of grain to be brought to the stackyard in harvest *now NE*. **get, hae, mak, tak** *etc* ~ have reached the end of the harvest, have brought the crops in.

yaave one of the spokes or paddles on the vane of a corn-reaper or -binder *NE*.

of corn to be cut *S*. ~ **supper** the celebration held when the corn is cut *now Fif Dmf Uls*. **win the** ~ gain the honour of cutting the last sheaf; *of a band of reapers* be the first to finish.

lachter the last sheaf cut in harvest.

maiden 1 *also* ~ **clyack** *NE* the last handful of corn cut in the harvest-field, *freq* shaped into the figure of a girl. **2** †the harvest-home feast and celebrations.

meal an ale the traditional dish (also containing whisky) at harvest-home celebrations; the celebration itself *NE-Per*.

stookie Sunday the Sunday at the height of harvest when all the corn has been cut and stands in **stooks** *now Ork-EC Wgt*.

winter 1 the last load of grain to be brought to the stackyard in harvest *now NE*. **2** †the feast held to celebrate the end of harvest. **3** †the person who removed the last of the grain from the field to the stackyard.

7.7.5 CROPS: HARVEST CELEBRATIONS

bagening rough horseplay at harvest time.

cailleach 1 the last sheaf of corn cut at harvest *local*. **2** the festival of harvest-home *Abd Uls*.

carline, carling the last sheaf of corn; the corn dolly made with it *now Abd*.

clyack 1 the last sheaf of corn of the harvest dressed as a girl or decorated with ribbons, *chf* **tak, hae** ~ *NE*. **2** the end of harvest *NE*. **3** the harvest-home supper *NE*.

grannie the last sheaf cut at harvest-time *Uls*.

hairst, harst, harvest: ~ **plait** a loop of twisted straw worn in a buttonhole, or as a decoration by the horse at harvest time *now Arg Kcb Uls*. ~ **play,** † ~ **vacance** school holidays taken during the harvest *now Cai*.

hare the last sheaf or handful of grain cut in the harvest-field *SW Uls*.

kemp *n* a contest to finish first in the harvest field *now Sh Ork Rox*. *v* compete in a piece of work in the harvest field.

kirn 1 a celebration marking the end of the harvest, a harvest-home *C, S*. **2** the last sheaf or handful of corn of the harvest, *freq* plaited and ornamented etc for display *now Dmf*. ~ **baby,** ~ **dollie** *now Fif* the decorated female effigy made from the last sheaf or handful of corn to be cut, a corn dolly. ~ **cut** the last handful

7.7.6 CROPS: PROCESSING

For milling, see 7.8 below. For the control of vermin, see 7.10 below

ark, †arch a large chest for storing grain etc.

barnman a thresher.

berry thresh (corn) *chf SW, S*.

†bleckit wheat mildewed wheat.

buff thresh (grain) without untying the sheaf.

byke a beehive-shaped straw-covered corn store *Cai*.

caff hoose the compartment connected with a corn-threshing machine which receives the chaff as it leaves the fanners of the winnower *N Fif Kcb*.

cair prepare (threshed corn) for winnowing by separating out the broken pieces of straw etc *N*.

cast 1 †take **in**, store, stack (grain etc). **2** turn over, dismantle (a stack of grain) for airing or threshing *now Ags Bwk*.

cave the corn separate the grain from broken straw etc *now Bnf*. **cavings** broken straw *now Bnf*.

†chaff heat (wheat) by damp.

chap the threshing-floor *NE*.

choffer, †chaffer a portable grate or stove used in a corn-kiln.

chun remove the sprouts from (potatoes) *chf SW*.

corn kist a storage-bin for corn.

cuff winnow for the first time *Bnf Abd.*

dicht sift or winnow (grain) *now local Bnf-Rox.*

dow become musty *chf* ~**it,** ~**ed** not fresh *now Sh Abd.*

drum the cylindrical part of a threshing machine.

dryster the person in charge of the drying of grain in a kiln *now Cai Abd.*

fanner(s) a winnowing machine, grain-sifter.

flail soople the part of a flail which beats out the grain *Sh Ork Abd.*

†flingin tree the part of a flail which strikes the grain.

frail 1 a container with a circular wooden frame and a sheepskin bottom, used for winnowing corn, a **wecht** *midLoth Dmf Rox.* **2** a flail.

girnel, garnel *now chf Ayr n* a storage chest for meal etc. †*v* store (food etc), hold in storage.

gloy thresh (corn) partially or hastily.

†graddan *n* a coarse oatmeal made from parched grain ground by hand. *v* parch (grain) in the ear.

harp the lower fine-meshed sieve in a winnowing machine, that separates weed seeds from grain *Ork Mry Abd.*

hash grain dried in a kiln and then chopped *local Cai-Kcb.*

het, hot *of grain or root crops* fermenting, decayed through being stored too damp or in a diseased condition *local N-S.*

hey, hay: ~**-neuk** a corner of a **byre** or stable in which hay is stored for immediate consumption *now Sh Dmf Rox.*

horse gang the circular track trodden by the horses in driving a threshing mill; the driving apparatus itself.

house store *now Abd.*

huidin the leather hinge or wooden connection joining the two parts of a flail.

hummel, humble remove the awns from (barley etc).

kill, kiln †dry (grain) in a kiln. ~ **beddin** the packed straw on the drying floor of a kiln, over which the grain was spread *now Sh.* ~**man** the man in charge of a corn-kiln.

killogie, kiln-logie applied to various parts of a corn- or malt-kiln: **1** the lower part, under the drying chamber; the kiln itself; **2** *also* **†logie** the fire or fireplace *now Sh;* **3** *also* **†logie** the covered space in front of the fireplace.

knock beat or pound grain *chf* barley. ~**ing mell** a mallet for pounding barley. ~**ing-stane** *now Sh-Cai,* ~**ing trough** a hollowed-out stone in which to pound barley. † ~**it barley,** ~**it bear** barley ground in a **knocking-stane**.

leet a section of an oblong stack of grain or beans *now Loth WC.*

licht, light the light parts of corn seed separated out by winnowing and sifting *now Ross Loth WC.*

logie †a **killogie**, applied to various parts of a corn- or malt-kiln.

†lot an allowance of corn paid to the thresher as part of his fee. ~**man** a corn-thresher.

lowse, loose, *also* ~ **for** *or* tae a mill *Abd* cut or undo the band of a sheaf of corn before feeding it into a threshing mill. **lowser** the person who opens up the sheaves and feeds them to the mill. **lowsin loft** the loft onto which sheaves are thrown for threshing *local N-S.*

mak doon reduce into smaller fragments, grind *now Abd Per Wgt.*

†man milne a handmill.

†mauten *of stored grain* germinate, sprout.

meal: ~ **ark** *now C, Uls,* ~ **kist** a chest for storing oatmeal. ~ **bowie** a barrel for storing oatmeal *NE.* ~ **pock** a bag for holding oatmeal *now Sh-Ags Gall.*

mill, †miln a threshing mill. ~ **coorse** the circular path trodden by the horses driving a threshing mill *Ork Bnf Abd.* ~ **gang** *Cai EC, S,* ~**-rink** *local Bnf-Dmf* the five- or six-sided building which formerly housed the driving apparatus of a horse-driven threshing mill. ~ **lavers** the beams to which the horses driving a threshing mill were harnessed *Ork NE.*

†mortar stane a hollowed stone in which barley was pounded to remove the husks.

mou 1 a large heap of grain, hay etc; a pile of unthreshed grain stored in a barn *Gen except Sh Ork.* **2** the division in a barn where unthreshed grain is heaped *now Per.*

†rag *n* a partial winnowing of corn. *v* winnow partially.

riddling heids the refuse of corn left after riddling *Cai SW.*

ruskie a basket for holding meal.

†Saltoun barley fanner-dressed pot barley.

scree a riddle or sieve, *esp* box-shaped, for sifting grain *local Per-Ayr.*

†scutch strike off (the ears of corn) from the stalk with a stick.

shaif laft a barn loft where sheaves are stacked before being put through the threshing mill *Ork N Kcb.*

shaker(s) the moving racks in a threshing mill *now local Ork-Kcb.*

shaw cut off the **shaws** of (turnips) *Gen except Sh.*

sheel, shill *v* shell (peas, grain, flax seeds etc),

take out of the husk or pod *now local Sh-Lnk. n* the act of husking corn *NE*. ~**ing hill** a piece of rising ground where grain was winnowed by the wind *now in place-names*. ~**ock(s)** the small or light grains of corn blown away during winnowing; the chaff and broken straw riddled off in threshing *now NE*.

†**shelling** husked oats, etc; chaff.

†**slap, slop:** ~ **riddle** a wide-meshed riddle for separating grain from broken straw.

sned cut **off** the tops (and roots) of (**turnips** etc) *Gen except Sh Ork*.

soople, supple the swipple, the part of a flail which beats the grain.

sprout rub or break off the sprouts of (potatoes) *Sh Ork N*.

steam, stame: ~ **mill** a (travelling) threshing mill driven by a steam-engine.

strae: ~ **en** the end of a barn where the straw is built up *now Ork N Loth*. ~ **house** a straw-shed or -barn *now Ork Abd Kcb*.

†**strik, strike** beat (flax) before heckling; tie (it) in bundles; beat (threshed barley) to remove the awns.

struie sweep threshed straw to the side with one movement of the flail *Cai*.

swingletree the free arm or beater of a flail *now Sh Ork*.

†**switch** thresh (grain); beat, scutch (flax).

taisle stir up, turn over (hay) *now Ags Kcb*.

tak, take: ~ **in** dismantle (a cornstack) and carry the sheaves to be threshed.

tasker a pieceworker, *esp* a thresher of corn.

tattie: ~-**bing** *now Sh Ayr*, ~ **pit** *Gen except Sh* a clamp of potatoes.

thane moist, damp, of meal from oats which have not been properly kiln-dried.

thrash, thresh thresh. ~**ing machine,** ~**ing mill** a power-driven machine for threshing.

trimmlin strae(s) unthreshed straw *Bnf Abd*.

tummlin shakker a revolving straw-shaker in a threshing mill *NE*.

†**victual, vittal:** ~-**house** a granary, *esp* the grain-store of an estate.

wase, wease, wassock *now Abd* a circular band of straw used to protect the hands, *eg* when knocking the husks from the ears of barley.

wecht, †**winding wecht** a wooden hoop, about two or three feet in diameter, with skin or canvas stretched over it, *orig* used for winnowing corn *now Sh N Kcb*.

win(d) winnow *now Ork*.

windass a fan for winnowing grain.

winnowster 1 †a person engaged in winnowing.

2 a machine for winnowing corn; the fanning apparatus on a threshing machine *now NE*.

yaave one of the spokes or paddles on the fanner of a winnowing machine *NE*.

7.8 MILLS

7.8.1 GENERAL, MISCELLANEOUS

cannas a canvas sheet for catching grain etc *NE*.

†**capes** grain retaining some part of the chaff or husk.

dicht sift (meal) *now local Bnf-Rox*.

dust particles of meal and husk produced in grinding corn *now Bnf Abd*. ~**y** name for a miller *now Lnk*. ~**y melder** the last milling of a season's crop.

girst grist *now Uls*.

†**graddan** a coarse oatmeal made from parched grain ground by hand.

gray meal the refuse and sweepings of a meal-mill.

†**grindable, grundable** *of grain* suitable for or intended for grinding.

grits oat kernels, grain.

kill, kiln: ~ **cast** the quantity of oats taken to the mill at one time to be ground into meal for household use, *usu* enough to produce four **bolls** *now Wgt*.

†**knaveship** the office of under-miller or miller's assistant; the perquisites of this.

†**lade man, load man** a miller's assistant who collected and delivered corn and meal.

meal *of grain* to yield or turn into meal.

mel(d)er, maillyer *NE* **1** the quantity of one person's corn taken to the mill to be ground at one time *now NE*. **2** the occasion of such a grinding *now Bnf*. **3** †the meal ground from the corn which formed part of a farm-servant's wages. ~**ing** the meal produced in a **melder**.

mill, †**miln: millart,** †**milnar** a miller. †**millart('s) word** a secret password, supposedly current among millers, conferring supernatural powers *NE*. † ~ **knave** an undermiller. ~ **pick** a small tool for roughening the surface of a millwheel *now Ork*. † ~-**ring** the meal remaining in the space between the millstones and the surrounding kerb. ~ **seeds** husks of corn with meal adhering to them *now Ork Kcb*.

†**molendinar** pertaining to a mill or miller.

ongang the starting up or setting in motion of machinery, *esp* of a mill *NE*.

out-dichtings refuse of threshed grain, the sweepings from the mill.

pick(ie)man, †pikeman a man who dresses millstones with a **mill pick** now *Sh*.

pluffings the refuse of corn, husks, chaff *S*.

pron the residue of oat husks and oatmeal remaining from the milling process, bran, **seeds** *local N*.

ring the mill provide the first grain for a mill to grind after the millstones have been picked.

set bring (a mill) to a stop by turning off the water from the wheel now *Bnf Ags Slk*. ~ **on** set in motion, start off (a mill etc).

shag the refuse of oats, barley etc now *Kcdn Ags Per*.

sheel, shill: ~**ing(s)** the grain removed from the husk by milling; *occas* the husks thus removed, the bran now *local Sh-Wgt*. ~**ing seeds** the husks removed from the grain in the first process of milling.

†stickle a small stick laid across the joists of a mill kiln to support the straw etc on which the grain was dried.

thirds the residue of grain left after milling or brewing, third quality flour now *NE-S*.

†thole fire and water *of grain* be dried and ground at a mill.

7.8.2 MILLS: BUILDINGS

ark the curved structure which carries the water off from a breast-shot millwheel; the waterway under a millwheel.

awe, ave *NE* a float-board on an undershot waterwheel. **start-an-**~ **(wheel), startin** ~ an undershot wheel *N*.

back: ~**-fa** the outlet of a **mill lade**. † ~**-water** excess water in a **mill lade**.

†bouthous a building in which flour is bolted.

bowster, bolster a piece of timber used to prevent chafing, or a bearing, *orig chf, later only* for a wheelshaft in a watermill now *Bnf*.

clack the clapper of a mill now *Ags*.

clap a clapper of a mill.

ee, eye the hole in the centre of a millstone now *Sh Abd*.

†foreschete some part of a mill.

†gainshot a cover over the inlet to a millwheel.

gang: ~**ing graith** the moving parts of a mill. ~ **water** the water supplied by the normal flow of a stream to a mill etc, without a dam *NE*.

graith accessory equipment now *Stlg-Dmf*.

happer a hopper.

harp that part of the meal mill which separates the dust from the husks.

hem the outer part of a millstone.

hirst the frame of a pair of millstones, the part of the mill where the stones revolve in their framework.

†hupe the circular wooden frame enclosing millstones to prevent meal from being scattered.

†inlay build (the **inlair**). **inlair** a lade; a small dam leading into it.

intak the place where water is diverted from a river, dam etc by a channel, to supply a mill now *local Cai-Kcb*.

lade, lead now *local Ork-Kcb* a channel bringing water to a mill; a mill-race, *freq* **mill** ~.

lair lay (a millstone) in position *Abd Ags*.

lewder a wooden lever, *esp* one for lifting millstones now *NE*.

†lyar the nether millstone.

mill, †miln a mill. **miller's lift** an upward thrust with the handle of a crowbar, as in setting a millstone now *Cai Fif Ayr*. ~ **caul** a mill-dam. ~ **clap** the clapper of a mill. † ~ **cloose** the sluice of a mill. † ~ **damheid** the embankment forming a mill-dam. † ~**ee** mill-eye, the opening through which meal comes from the millstones. † ~ **graith** the equipment of a mill. ~ **lade, ~-lead** a channel bringing water to a mill; a mill-race. † ~**-ring** the space between the millstones and the surrounding kerb. † ~ **stead** the ground and buildings comprising a mill. ~ **toon** the buildings comprising a mill; *freq* the adjacent farm or hamlet † ~**trow** the wooden conduit carrying water to a millwheel. † ~ **wand** a spar pushed through the central hole of a millstone to trundle it along.

rimmer a hoop or band, one used to protect the runner-stone of a mill.

rin-water a natural flow of water, *esp* one which will drive a millwheel without a dam *Abd*.

shae, shoe the shute carrying grain from the hopper to the millstone now *local Sh-Ayr*.

sheel, shill: ~**ing stane** a millstone, *specif* one to remove the husks in the first process now *Loth*.

†standing graith the fixed or stationary parts of a mill.

†stuiling the framework supporting a mill.

tail-dam now *sEC*, **tail-lead** now *Bnf* the tail-race of a mill.

†trinnle a lantern- or cogwheel in the gearing machinery of a mill. ~**-board** one of the two parallel plates on a **trinnle**.

trows a channel or wooden conduit for water leading to a millwheel *now local Ork-Wgt.* **trowmill** a watermill *now in place-names in S.*

understane the nether or lower millstone.

wa, way: ~**-gang** an outflow of water from a millwheel, the tail-race *now Sh.*

water: ~ **gate,** ~ **yett** *local C, S* a fence or grating suspended over a stream to prevent animals from straying or floating rubbish from entering a **mill lade** *now Inv C.* † ~ **lead** a mill **lade.**

way-flude, †**way-lead** the outflow of water from a millwheel, the tail-race; a water channel *now Bnf Abd.*

win-mull a windmill.

7.8.3 MILLS: MULTURES AND SUCKENS

This section covers the **thirling** or binding of tenants on an estate to use a certain mill, within whose **sucken** they were.

†**astrict(it) multures: multures** to which a mill is entitled from the tenants of certain lands.

†**bannock** a quantity of meal sufficient to make a **bannock,** due to the servant of a mill from each of those using it.

black bitch a bag for fraudulently catching meal from the mill spout *now Kcb.*

†**bunsucken** *of a farm* **thirled** to a certain mill *Bnf Abd.*

†**grana crescentia** used to describe a **thirlage** which applied to all the corn grown on that particular piece of land.

†**insucken (multure)** the **multure** payable by persons within the **sucken** of a mill.

†**invecta et illata** grain brought from outside the **sucken** to be ground at the **superior's** mill.

†**knaveship** a small quantity of corn or meal in addition to the **multure** levied on each lot of corn ground at a mill as payment for the miller's servants.

†**lick:** *esp* a ~ **of goodwill** a small measure of meal given to the under-miller as a gratuity in addition to the **multure.**

†**lock** a small quantity of meal exacted as one of the **sequels** of a mill, *freq* ~ **and gowpen.**

mill, †**miln:** † ~ **bitch** a bag into which the miller secretly diverted some of a customer's meal. † ~ **dozen** every thirteenth peck of grain milled, payable to the mill-owner. † ~ **ee** the profits of the mill *NE.* † ~ **gault** a young pig or castrated boar paid to the miller by estate tenants. † ~ **services** tasks connected with a mill performed

by estate tenants as part of their rent. † ~ **swine** a pig given as a due to the miller.

†**multure, mouter** *n* a duty consisting of a proportion of the grain or meal payable to the proprietor or tenant of a mill on corn ground there; the right to this duty. *v* pay a **multure** on grain; charge **multure** against (a person); levy **multure** on (grain) (at a particular rate). ~**er** an official with the duty or right of collection **multure.** ~**aith** an oath as to the amount and kind of grain which one has had ground other than at the mill to which one is **astricted.** ~ **free** exempt from payment of **multure**; without having to pay **multure**; without exacting payment of **multure.** ~ **malt, meal** *etc* meal, malt etc paid or payable as **multure.**

†**out(in)toun** coming from outside the boundaries of a town; *freq of dues* payable by those from outside the **sucken** of a mill. ~**is multure** a **multure** payable on corn brought in from outside the **sucken** of a mill, an **outsucken (multure).**

†**outmil(n)** a mill outside the town; a mill other than those to which the townspeople were **astricted** *Edb.*

†**outsucken (multure): multure** payable on corn brought in from outside the **sucken** of a mill. **outsuckiner** a person from outside a **sucken.**

†**ring:** *also* ~**-bear,** ~**-corn,** ~**-malt** the meal which falls into the space between a millstone and its casing, regarded as the miller's perquisite.

†**room free** not incurring the payment levied on corn for occupying space in a mill when awaiting grinding.

†**sequels** the small quantities of meal, or money in lieu, given by the tenants **thirled** to the mill to the miller's assistants for their services.

†**sucken** *n* **1** an obligation on tenants or on an estate to use a certain mill; the payment due in kind, service or money for the use of the mill. **2** the lands of an estate on which there was a **sucken**; all the tenants of such land. *adj* bound to a certain mill. ~**er** a tenant of a **sucken.**

†**thirl, thrill** *v* bind (lands or tenants) to have grain ground at a particular mill. *n* the obligation of being bound in **thirlage** to a certain mill etc; the lands subject to **thirlage**, the **sucken** of a mill; the body of tenants **thirled** to a particular mill. *adj* bound in **thirlage to.** ~**age** the obligation on the tenants of an estate to grind their corn at a particular mill and to pay a **multure** or duty, *usu* in kind; the **multure** or payment thus made; the land or body of ten-

ants **thirled** to a certain mill. ~ **multure** the **multure** paid by tenants bound by **thirlage**; the right to exact this **multure**.

†**unthirl** land outside the **sucken** of a particular mill; the dues paid to a mill for the grinding of corn grown on land not **astricted** to it *Rox.* ~**ed** not bound by **thirlage** to a particular mill *Rox.*

†**water corn** the grain paid by tenant-farmers for the upkeep of the dams and races of the estate mill.

7.9 LIVESTOCK

7.9.1 GENERAL, MISCELLANEOUS

Farm animals are dealt with in 2; handling of sheep in 7.13, of poultry in 7.9.3. Includes (the preparation of) fodder, harness and tethers. For calls to animals, see 7.9.4. For milking, see next.

baikie 1 an iron or wooden peg to which a tether was fastened *Bnf Abd.* **2** the stake to which a cow etc was tied in the stall.

bin(d) tether. **binnen,** ~**le** *now NE Ags* a tether, *eg* for cattle.

birn *v*, †*also* **brin** brand by burning. *n* a brand of ownership on an animal, *usu* **skin and birn.** †**brent** burned, branded. †**bir** *or* **bur irne** a branding iron.

blinners blinkers *Bnf Abd Lnk.*

bottle, battle, buttle bundle up (hay or straw) for fodder *now Ags Lnk.*

†**bow**[1] a stock or herd of cattle, *esp* of cows.

bow[2] an ox-bow *now Bnf.*

branks a kind of bridle or halter, *orig* with wooden side-pieces.

brecham a collar for a draught-horse or ox.

buist mark (cattle) with their owner's mark *now Kcb.*

cattle beas(ts) livestock *local Bnf-Lnk.*

cauf's lick a cow-lick *local Cai-Kcb.*

chock roap a flexible appliance for clearing an obstruction in an animal's throat *N.*

chowk band the jaw-strap of a bridle *chf NE.*

clawin post a rubbing post for cattle *chf NE.*

cliver a tether for a cow.

cog feed (*chf* calves) from a **cog** *Bnf Abd.*

coo, cow: ~'**s drink** hot treacle given to sick cows *Ags Fif.*

corn feed a horse with oats or grain. *NE Ags.*

cover, kiver *now Abd Loth Bwk* the maximum livestock a farm will carry.

cowit *of cattle* polled.

cowt halter a halter made of rope or straw *local NE-C.*

crub a crib (for cattle-fodder) *Sh Abd.*

cruive shut up in a pen or stall *Bnf Abd.*

†**cuni(n)gar** a rabbit-warren.

dandy a dandy brush *now Cai Kcb.*

†**dantoun** break in, tame.

dirry: haud on the ~ whip up (horses) *Bnf Abd.*

drauchtit *of a horse* harnessed for work *Abd.*

drave a drove *now Abd.*

dress neuter (a cat).

†**drift** a drove, flock, herd.

droving driving (of cattle).

dyke-louper an animal which leaps the dyke surrounding its pasture *now Bnf Abd Fif.*

eat cause or allow (grass etc) to be eaten by grazing animals, *freq* ~ **grass** *etc* with one's horses *etc now local Sh-Kcb.* ~**en corn** *n* oats eaten by trespassing animals. ~**ing** the eating of grass, growing grain etc, by grazing animals.

eel-stab, eel-stob a V-shaped incision in the ear of an animal as a mark of ownership *now Arg Kcb.* † ~**bed** marked in this way.

†**fe** cattle or sheep.

†**feed** pasture (animals).

ferm, farm: ~ **stockin** farm animals, *esp* cattle and sheep.

ferrier a vet, veterinary surgeon *NE midLoth.*

†**flake, fleck** a kind of rack used for feeding hay to animals.

flit move (tethered animals) to fresh grazing *now Sh Abd Fif.*

fold *n* a herd of (*usu*) twelve Highland cows used for breeding *now Arg. v, also* **fauld** fold, enclose (animals).

fosset a rush mat laid on a horse to prevent chafing by a **currach** (a wickerwork pannier).

fother *n* fodder, food for cattle and horses *local Ork-Uls. v* fodder, feed (cattle and horses) with hay, straw etc *local NE-Uls.*

gaud, †**gad** (**wand**) a goad.

girse, grass, gress pasture (animals). †**girsing** the act or fact of pasturing (animals).

graith *n, also* **horse** ~ the trappings, harness etc for a horse *now C, S. v* prepare, make ready (a horse for riding or work) *now local Per-Uls.* ~**ing** equipment, accoutrements, trappings; harness.

guide treat, use, handle, care for (animals).

haims the two curved pieces of wood or metal forming or covering the collar of a draught horse.

hapshackle, habshackle, hamshackle *v* hobble (a horse etc), tie up (an animal) in such a way as to prevent it from straying *now local Ags-Dmf*. *n* a hobble for tethering a horse etc.

harnish, herness *now Lnk* harness.

†harrower a young horse or *chf* mare, unbroken to the plough but used for harrowing *Per*.

hash slice, cut up, chop (*eg* **turnips** for fodder). **~er** an implement for slicing turnips *now local Sh-Fif*.

haud, hald, hold 1 †keep, maintain (animals). **2** preserve (cattle etc) for stock *now midLoth Bwk*. **~in(g)** the stock of a farm *now Rox*.

heck a rack for fodder in a stable etc, or on a portable frame for use in the open.

heft *v* **1** accustom (cattle) to a new pasture by constant herding to prevent them from straying. **2** *of animals* become accustomed to a new pasture *now Dmf S*. †*n* a pasture which cattle have become familiar with and continue to frequent *Kcb*. **~it** accustomed to a new pasture *now Arg SW, S*.

hemmel a square rack on posts in a cattle court to hold fodder *Rox*.

herd, hird tend, watch over (cattle), *esp* to prevent them from straying onto crops. **~ing 1** †the tending and confining to their own grazing of cattle. **2** a grazing allotted to a particular herd *now Cai S*.

†herdwill capable of keeping cattle in or out *Rox*.

hey-neuk a corner of a **byre** or stable in which hay is stored for immediate consumption *now Sh Dmf Rox*.

†hird a herd, a flock.

hoch band *n* a strap or cord by which the hough-sinew of an animal is constricted to curb its movement. *v* hobble (an animal) with a **hoch band** *now Sh*.

house take, put or drive (animals) into a house; shelter.

kail gullie a blade fixed at right angles to the end of an upright handle, used for cutting and chopping **kail** stems *now Ork local N*.

keeper a store animal, one kept for fattening *NE*.

kenmark a distinguishing mark, a mark of ownership on an animal, a brand *Sh N, Fif*.

kep *v* intercept; stop, head off *now local*. *n* the heading off or intercepting of animals *NE, Lnk*.

kinch fasten a noose round the tongue, lips or muzzle of (a horse) *local NE-Ayr*.

knapdarloch a knot of hardened dirt and dung or matted hair hanging from the coat or tail of an animal *chf NE*.

knewel 1 the wooden pin on the end of a rope or halter *NE Ags Per*. **2** the tag put through the ring

on the rope or chain for tethering cattle in a stall *Abd Fif*.

†laidner mart *chf SW*, **laidner mart cow** *Gall* a fattened ox or cow killed and salted for winter provisions.

lair *n* a place where animals lie down, a fold or enclosure *now Sh, freq in place-names*. †*v* drive (animals) to their resting-place.

†lang helter *or* **halter** the permitting of animals such as cattle to range at will once the crops were harvested.

langle, †langald, langett *n* a hobble, tether (of rope) to prevent an animal from straying *now N Gall Uls*. *v* hobble (an animal) *now Ork N Gall Uls*.

leet the select or prize-winning animals at an agricultural show *SW*.

lib castrate (farm animals).

lift drive (animals) to market *NE-S*.

lingel, †linget *latterly Ags n* a rope for hobbling an animal. *v* hobble (a horse etc) *NE*.

lippie a (wooden, box-shaped) measure of 1/4 of a **Scots peck** for measuring corn for a horse's feed *now N*.

†lizour, lesu *v* pasture.

†loan drive (cattle) along a **loan**.

lowse, loose unbind (an animal) from a stall etc.

†lyam a rope, a tether.

mart 1 an ox or cow fattened for slaughter *now Sh Cai Bnf*. **2** any other animal (*esp* a sheep) or bird which is to be salted and dried for winter meat.

†mask a mash of malt or draff as a feed for a horse etc.

†Mey: ~ kow, ~ wedder an animal paid for in May *Gall*.

mink a cow's tether; a horse's halter *local Bnf-Fif*.

miss *of a breeding animal* fail to conceive.

mou(th): ~-bag, ~ poke *Gen except Sh Ork NE* a horse's nosebag. **~ cord** the rope linking the inner bit rings of a pair of horses to keep them together *WC*.

neep feed (cattle) with **turnips** *Sh-EC*. **~-cutter** an implement for slicing **turnips** *Ork nEC, WC*.

neir: ~ leather, ear leather the back or belly-band of a horse's harness *now Renfr*. **~ strap** a strap in a horse's harness.

nip of hunger the pinch of hunger, the effect of hunger on farm stock *Bwk Rox*.

orra doing casual or unskilled work. **~ horse, ~ beast** *NE* a horse kept for odd jobs.

†ort(s) food for horses etc.

†outhound set a dog to attack or chase (animals or persons).

outlier a farm animal which remains outside during the winter *now local.*

†outsicht plenishing animals kept out of doors.

outwinter keep (cattle) out of doors throughout the winter.

owersee, oversee tend, look after (animals) *now Sh Ork Bnf.*

†oweryear, left or kept over from the previous year.

oxin bow, oussen bow an ox-bow, a curved wooden collar for a draught ox.

pair a team of two horses for ploughing and other farm jobs.

park, pairk rear (animals) in a field or enclosure instead of on free range *now Sh.*

pease strae the stalks and foliage of the pea plant used as cheap fodder or bedding for animals *now Kcb.*

pet make a pet of.

pick *of a female (farm-)animal* abort (her young), give birth to prematurely, *freq* **pick calf** an aborted or stillborn animal *NE-S.*

†piece a head (**of** cattle etc).

piggin a container, *usu* of wood, tub-shaped and with one stave extending to form a handle, used as a feeding dish *now Uls.*

pirkle(s) the spiked nose-band used to prevent a calf sucking *Cai Bnf Bute.*

pirn a twitch for quietening a horse *Bwk S.*

†plenish stock (land) with livestock.

†pluck steal (livestock) **from** (a person).

plump-hasher a heavy implement for slicing **turnips** etc *Bnf Abd.*

poind, pin(d) *v* impound (stray animals etc) as surety for compensation for damage committed by them *now Cai Loth S.* *n* an animal which has been **poinded.**

poll cut the hair of (an animal, head).

†possess with cause (land) to be occupied by (cattle) *Slk.*

prick *of grazing cattle* stampede in an attempt to escape from the stings of insects *NE.*

prob *n* a sharp-pointed instrument for piercing the stomach of swollen cattle to release accumulated gas *Ork NE. v* release gas from the stomach of (cattle) by piercing *Bnf Abd.*

pumphal shut up in a **pumphal** *NE.*

redd clean out and renew the bedding of (a housed animal) *now NE.*

rubbing stock a post in a field for cattle to rub themselves against *now Ork Per.*

rump cut, clip or crop very short *local Bnf-S.*

†rush corn inferior oats fed unthreshed to livestock.

†St Faith's cattle *or* **drove** cattle collected, *chf* from Galloway, into one large herd and drive to St Faith's Market near Norwich.

†schallow a drove, flock.

second, secont: ~ **pair** the pair of horses worked by the second or assistant horseman on a farm *N, SW.*

sell, seal the rope, iron loop or chain by which cattle are bound by the neck to their stalls, *specif* the part of the chain round the animal's neck.

set on put (an unweaned animal) to suck *Bwk Lnk S.*

sicht, sight inspect (a newborn animal) for its sex *local Sh-Edb.*

sinker a weight attached to the rope of a horse's stall-collar to keep it forward in its stall *now N, C.*

soo, sow: ~**'s troch** a pig's trough *local Sh-Per.*

sort 1 *euphemistic* castrate *Sh NE.* **2** feed and litter (*esp* a horse) *now N, C.*

†sow-libber a sow-gelder.

spave spay, neuter (a female animal) *now Kcb.*

sprack a chip of wood, splinter; waste scraps of wood etc, wood or straw litter *Ork Arg.*

stalk raip, stack rope a rope passed through a ring on a stable manger, weighted at one end and tied to the horse's stall halter at the other *now Fif Lnk Dmf.*

stem a dam of stones in a stream, used to form a watering-place for cattle *local Cai-Lnk.*

stoo, stow a cut on the ear (*esp* of a sheep) as a mark of ownership.

strae, straw supply with straw, *eg* for animal fodder or bedding.

Sunday strae an extra amount of straw threshed to tide the animals over the weekend and so avoid threshing on Sunday *Sh-N.*

supper, †sipper *n* the last meal of the day given to an animal. *v* ~ (**up**) give (an animal) its last meal of the day.

sweel, swivel tether (animals) together with a swivel on the rope to allow them limited freedom of movement *now Sh.*

swine: ~ **meat** pigswill *Ork NE, C.* ~ **pot** a pot in which pigs' food is boiled *now Ork Abd Kcb.*

tailer(t) a hand turnip-cutter *Ork N.*

tak, take: ~ **in** house (farm stock), bring under cover *Sh N Per.*

tap, top cut the tip of the ear of (an animal) as an ownership mark *now Sh Kcb.*

tedder tether *now Sh Ork N.*

ten-hours ten o'clock; a small feed given in the middle of the morning to a horse at work.

tent tend, take charge of, look after (animals) *now Wgt.*

thrammel the rope or chain by which cattle are tied in their stalls, *specif* the part linking the post etc to the **sell** *chf NE*.

touting horn a cow's horn sounded by a cowherd driving his animals.

†**towin** tame by beating.

track train or break in (a young animal) *NE*.

traik misfortune, loss, *specif* that caused by disease in farm animals.

†**trannet** some piece of horse harness.

travel, traivel drive (cattle etc) from place to place along a road *now NE Loth Dmf*.

tress a trace, a draught rope etc. **tracer 1** a trace horse. **2** the man in charge of a trace horse.

troch a trough. **~-stane** a stone trough *local Stlg-WC*.

tween heid the part of the reins joining the heads of two horses in a team *local Stlg-Wgt*.

†**unbawndonit** *of animals* loose, not fastened or under control.

veet a vet, veterinary surgeon *Cai Abd*.

waff *of animals* strayed, wandering ownerless.

†**waith** *of an animal* strayed, roaming loose.

water, watter *now local* **~ing(s)** a trough, pool in a stream etc where farm animals go to drink *now Ork Abd*. **watering stone** a stone horse-trough.

wauk, wake guard, watch over (livestock etc), *esp* during the night *now Inv C*.

†**wauken** watch (over), keep an eye on.

†**weasie** an ox-collar.

weir drive (animals) gradually in a desired direction, shepherd *Gen except Sh Ork*.

†**whin, whun** **~-mill** a kind of mill for crushing furze as fodder.

widdie a twig or wand of willow or other tough but flexible wood; several such intertwined to form a rope used for halters and harness.

wile get ot bring by a wile (an animal to or from a place) *now local Sh-Per*.

winter: ~er a farm animal kept for fattening over winter *Gen except S*. **~in(g)** winter keep for animals *Gen except Sh Ork*. **~ing money** money paid for the winter keep of animals *now Per*.

wirk, work look after, herd (animals) *now Ags Per midLoth*.

Yule strae the supply of straw needed on a farm over Christmas and the New Year *NE*.

7.9.2 LIVESTOCK: DAIRYING

For dairy products, see 10. For dairymaids, see 7.5.3.

bally (cog) a milk pail *Bnf*.

beest *now Cai*, **~in** *now Abd*, **beesenin** *now Kcb*, **~y** the first milk of a cow after calving.

bourach a rope etc tied round the hindlegs of a kicking cow during milking.

boyne, bine a broad shallow container in which to skim milk.

brak, break *of milk* curdle, coagulate, either by its becoming sour or in the process of churning *now Sh NE Kcb*. **broken, brokken** *of milk* curdled, *esp* of cream in the churn *now local Cai-Kcb*.

brash *freq in churning* a short turn of work.

butter: ~-brods *Bnf Abd Lnk*, **~-clappers** *now Lnk Kcb* a pair of wooden boards for working butter. **~-kit** a container for butter *local Bnf-Lnk*.

cheese: ~ bandages wrappings for cheese while it is being cured *now Kcb*. **~ bauk** a board or rafter on which cheeses mature *now Abd Lnk*. **~ cloots** wrappings for cheese while it is in the cheese-press *now Abd Lnk Kcb*. **~ stane** a stone worked with a screw for pressing cheese *now Abd*.

clappers, = **butter clappers** (a pair of wooden boards for working butter) *local Cai-Kcb*.

draw milk (a cow) *now Bnf Abd*.

drib extract the last drops of milk from (a cow) *now Bnf Abd*.

efter, after obtain the very last drops of milk from (a cow) by milking it twice *EC Arg*. **~in(g)s** the last drops of milk taken while milking *now midLoth*.

farrow *of a cow* not in calf; having missed a pregnancy, *locally* either still giving milk or not.

†**fauld, fold** the penning of cattle for milking; the milking.

flagon a small metal can used for carrying milk *Abd Ags Per midLoth*.

†**forebroads** the first milk from a cow after calving *Ayr*.

frame a square or hoop of wood hung from the shoulders on which to carry pails *local Ork-Abd*.

gaither, gather *of butter* form, collect in the churn.

glaiks a lever or shaft attached to the churn-staff to facilitate churning *chf Uls*.

hair (the) butter free butter from impurities, *eg* hairs, by passing a knife through it in all directions *now Ork*.

heck a wooden rack (suspended from the roof) for drying cheeses.

heft hold back (milk) in a cow's udder so that it becomes hard and distended; leave (a cow) unmilked *now local EC-S.* ~**it 1** *of an udder* hard and dry, through not being milked *now NE Gall S.* **2** *of milk* accumulated in the udder *now local Abd-S.* **3** *of a cow* having a large quantity of milk in the udder *now nEC, WC Rox.*

jib milk (a cow) to the last drop *now Lnk SW.* ~**bings** the strippings from a cow's udder *now local Lnk-S.*

jummle *v* churn.

†**kaisart** a cheese-vat.

kane a quantity of cheese, *latterly appar* fixed at about 3 tons (3.048 tonnes) *WC, SW.*

kirn *v* churn. *n* a churn; a churnful. ~**ing** one complete act of churning; the quantity of milk required for this *(local)*; the quantity of butter so produced *(local NE-S).* ~**ing day** the day on which churning was done *now local Sh-Ags, Kcb.* ~**ing rung** the plunger of a churn *WC, Dmf.* ~ **staff** *now Sh Ork Abd,* ~ **stick** *now Bnf* (the handle of) the plunger of an upright churn. **the** ~'**s brok(ken)** the milk is beginning to form into butter *local Sh-Ayr.* **milk** ~ a churn for milk *now Sh Ork.*

kye-time milking-time *NE Uls.*

lapper *v, also* **lopper** clot, curdle, *freq* ~**ed.** *n* milk soured and thickened in preparation for butter-making *Gen except Sh Ork Cai.* ~**ing tub** a container used for curdling milk *Abd Loth Dmf.*

lat, let: ~ **doun** *of a cow* yield (milk).

leglin a **lade-gallon**, *latterly chf* with a projecting stave as a hand, used as a milk pail.

lug a wooden container with one or two handles formed from projecting staves, used *esp* as as milking-pail *now local Ags-Gall.*

meal, male a single milking of a cow or cows.

†**meltith** a single milking; the quantity of milk from such.

milk *of a cow or ewe* yield milk (well, badly etc) *local.* ~**ness 1** †an animal's yield of milk. **2** the quantity of milk obtained; its products. ~**bowie** a wooden milk bucket *now NE Ags Per.* ~**-boyne** a broad, shallow wooden vessel for holding milk *C.* ~ **cellar** a small room used as a dairy *Ork Abd.* ~ **house** a dairy. ~**-sye, milsie,** † ~**-syth** a milk-strainer.

pale *n* a small shovel or scoop, used for taking samples of food, *esp* cheese *now Lnk Gall. v* pierce (cheese etc) with a **pale**, remove a sample with a **pale** *now Kcb.*

piggin a container, *usu* of wood, tub-shaped and with one stave extended to form a handle, used as a milk-pail etc *now Uls.*

pilk milk (a cow etc) down to the last drops, **strip** of milk *now Wgt.*

plowt kirn a churn operated by a plunger *now Ork.*

plump: ~**er** the plunger of a **plunge churn** *NE.* ~ **kirn** a **plunge churn** *NE.*

†**plunge churn, plunge kirn** a churn worked by moving a plunger up and down.

ream 1 *of milk* form cream. **2** skim the cream off (milk) *NE-S.* ~**er,** † ~**ing dish** a shallow dish for skimming cream off milk. **raemikle** a round wooden tub for holding milk etc; a pail *now Sh*

rimmer a hoop or band used to shape a cheese.

set leave (milk) standing for the cream to rise.

sile *v* pass (milk) through a sieve, strain, filter *now Bwk WC-S. n* a sieve, strainer, filter, *esp* for milk *Bwk WC-S.*

stan(d), staun: ~**ing kirn** a churn worked by pushing a plunger up and down *local Cai-Kcb.*

stane, stone *freq proverb* press (a cheese) by putting a large box of stones on top of the cheese vat *now Abd Ayr.*

strin(d) the jet of milk from a cow's teat *Bnf Abd.*

strip *v, also* **strib** *now local* squeeze the last drops of milk from (a cow) with the fingers, *now esp* after a mechanical milker. ~**pin(g)s** the last milk drawn off at a milking.

strone the stream of milk from a cow's teat *now Stlg Bute Kcb.*

sye *v* pass (liquid) through a sieve, drain, filter *now local. n, also* **syer** *now Sh-Per* a strainer or sieve for liquids, *esp* for milk *now NE, WC.* **sey clout** a piece of gauze etc, *usu* stretched across a round wooden frame, used for straining liquid *now Sh-N.* ~ **dish** *now NE, nEC,* ~ **milk** *now NE* a milk-strainer.

sythe *v* strain (*esp* milk) through a sieve, filter *now Per. n* a (milk-)strainer, filter *now Per.*

tidy *of a cow* giving milk; in calf, pregnant.

†**tulchan** a calfskin, *usu* that of her own dead calf, stuffed with straw or wrapped round another calf and put beside a cow to induce her to give milk freely.

yirn, earn *of milk* form curds with rennet and heat *now Sh-N.*

7.9.3 LIVESTOCK: POULTRY

bauk, †**balk** a hen roost.

cavie a hencoop *now Ags-Lnk.*

corn feed poultry with oats or grain *NE Ags.*

crib a hencoop *local Cai-Fif.*

cruive a hencoop *Bnf Abd.*

daigh a mixture of meal and hot water for chicken food.

deuk, duck: ∼('s) **dub** a duck pond *now Fif Kcb Dmf.*

gusedub a goose pond *local, freq in place-names.*

hen: ∼**-bauk**, ∼**-cavie** *WC, SW,* ∼ **crae** a hencoop. ∼('s) **croft**, ∼('s) **craft** part of a corn-field frequented and damaged by fowls. ∼'s **gerse** as much grass or land as would produce food for a hen. ∼**-laft** a hen roost; the roof-joists of a house and the space above them. ∼**-ree** a hen run. ∼**-wife** a woman who has charge of, or deals in poultry.

leaven a mixture of oatmeal and water made up as a dough as food for young poultry *Sh N Fif.*

ree, reeve *now NE* a chicken run *NE, SW.*

spaik, spoke the perch of a bird's cage, a roosting bar *now Inv Lnk S,*

7.9.4 CALLS TO ANIMALS

boose, bease: ∼ **up** command to a cow to take its place in a stall etc.

ca(ll) urge on (by calling), drive (animals).

chat a call to a pig *NE.*

chatty-puss *now Bnf Abd Fif,* **cheet(ie-pussy)** a call to a cat.

chay a call to cows to calm them *Uls.*

chew a reprimand to a dog.

chick *n* a clicking noise, *esp* one made to encourage horses etc *local Bnf-Kcb. v* click in this way *now Abd Fif.*

come ather *call to a horse* turn to the left *NE.*

cooch make or command (a dog) to lie down *Abd.*

coo-heel *command, esp to a dog* come away *Ags.*

cop, *freq* ∼ ∼ a call to a horse to approach *local.*

†far yaud a call to a sheep-dog to drive sheep at a distance *S.*

gussie, gus-gus a call to pigs *local Ags-S.*

hap †*interj, n* a call to an animal in harness, *esp* to horses in ploughing, to turn to the right. *v, of horses or cattle in harness* turn towards the right; *sometimes of the driver* command to turn to the right. ∼ **and** *or* **wynd** *of harnessed animals* turn to the right and/or left; *of a ploughman* make the animals do so *now Wgt.*

haud, hald: ∼(**a**)**back** *command to animals* turn left or away *now Abd.* ∼ **aff** (**ye**) *command to animals* turn to the right *now local N-Gsw.* ∼ **up** *command to animals* stand still *local.*

heck a call to a horse to turn left *now Ags Clcm.*

hi *interj* a call to a horse, with various meanings in different areas, but *chf* a command to turn left, *freq* ∼ **here, hey up** etc, *now local. v* direct (a horse) to the left by using this call *now Cai Ags Rox.*

hirr a call to a dog to attack or pursue *now Sh Cai.*

hish *v* 1 make a hissing sound in order to drive (an animal) away or to scare (birds). 2 incite (*eg* a dog) to attack. *interj* a sharp hissing call to drive off animals or to incite a dog to attack. ∼ (**tae**) **cat** a call to frighten away a cat or to incite a dog to chase it.

hisk a call to drive off an animal or to alert or incite a dog to pursue.

hoo a cry used to frighten birds or cattle *NE.*

houxie a call to a cow *Cai.*

hove a call to a cow to come to be milked, or housed for the night *Bwk Rox.*

how a call to incite (horses etc) to action.

hup *interj, n* a call to an animal in harness 1 to turn to the right or off-side *Gen except N;* 2 to increase speed *now Ork NE Uls. v* 1 *of a horse in harness* go to the right *Gen except NE.* 2 *of the driver* call to a horse: (**a**) to go to the right *Gen except NE;* (**b**) to go forward at a quicker pace *NE.* ∼ **aff** go to the right! *now Cai Lnk SW.* ∼ **back** come back, bearing right *now Cai midLoth WC, Dmf.* **wo** ∼ slow down and bear right *Cai Edb WC Rox.*

hurlie a call to a cow to come to be milked *SW.*

hurly hawkie a call to cows at milking time *Gall.*

hush *n, interj* a cry to frighten off birds etc *now Sh Cai NE Uls. v* scare or drive away (birds etc) by making this noise *now Sh Ork midLoth.*

hyte a call to a horse.

isk(y), iskis coaxing call to a dog *now Abd Fif.*

keerie a call to a lamb or sheep *now Per Fif.*

lag, laggie a call to a goose to be fed *SW.*

mappie, map-map call to a rabbit.

pease *Ross Inv C, S,* **peasie** *Per Kcb* a call to food to a tame pigeon.

pet a call to a sheep or lamb *now Cai Ags Kcb.*

piss a call to a cat or kitten *local.* **pistack** a cry to chase off a cat or dog *now Cai.*

potch(ie) potch(ie) a call to a pig *Ross Inv Nai.*

pree: ∼**ay** *NE,* ∼**a** *now Ayr,* **pee-ay** *now Ross Wgt,* ∼ **leddy,** ∼**-may,** ∼ **pree** call-name for a cow or calf, *chf* used to call cows in for milking.

proo 1 a command to a horse to stop *now S.* 2 *also* **pruitchie(-leddy),** ∼**-leddy** *now Lnk Ayr,* **proochie** a call to a cow or calf.

sick, sickie *NE* a call to a lamb or calf to come to be fed from its bottle *NE Ags.*

stan(d), staun *in calls to a horse* stop!, stand quiet! *N, nEC, WC, S.* ∼ **ower** command to a horse move to the other side of the stall *Abd Per.*

sucky, souk (souk) *now local Ork-SW* a call to an animal, *esp* to a calf.

tchick a sound made to urge on a horse *now local Ork-Kcb*.

tick(ie), tick tick a call to chickens to come for food *Ork-Per*.

toch call to a calf to come to food *Cai Suth*.

treesh *v* call an animal *Bnf Abd. interj* a call to cattle, *esp* calves, to come *NE Ags Per*.

troo a call to cows or calves.

troosh a command to an animal, *esp* a dog, to get out of the way *Arg*.

troush a call to cattle *now Bnf Kcdn*.

trwoo a call to cows or calves *Abd Fif*.

tuck, tewk a call to hens to come for food *now N Per Ayr*.

twee a call to calves at feeding time *now Mry*.

vane call to a horse in harness to turn to the left *now C*.

way a call to a sheepdog to make a detour or move away from the sheep.

weesh a call to a horse in harness to turn right *local Sh-Per*.

wha-hup a call to a horse to move off *EC, S*.

wheep make a sharp shrill noise with pursed lips, whistle, to call a dog *local NE-S*.

wheet(ie) a call to ducks, *now Stlg Lnk S*.

wo: ~**-back** a call to a horse to stop or go backwards *Ork-Per*. ~**-hie** a call to a horse to turn left *now Cai Per*. ~**-hup** a call to a horse to turn right *now Cai Per*.

wynd, †wyne †*v* (command (draught-animals) to) turn to the left. *interj* a call to a yoked animal to turn to the left *now SW*. †**wynder, wyner** the leading ox on the right-hand side, which took the first steps to the left on the command to **wynd**.

yain a call to a horse in harness to turn left *Stlg Lnk Ayr*.

†yite: ~ **hub**, ~ **hup**, ~**wo** calls to a horse in harness.

7.10 VERMIN

bockie *Sh-N*, **bogle** a scarecrow.

boodie, *chf* **tattie** ~ a scarecrow *Bnf Abd*.

craw, crow: ~ **bogle** *now Abd Lnk Fif*, ~ **nancy** *now Lnk S* a scarecrow.

fa(ll) a falling mouse- or rat-trap *now local*.

herd, hird: ~ **craws** prevent rooks from interfering with crops *Abd Ags Kinr*.

†lime wand a stick smeared with bird-lime for trapping birds.

moudie *now C, S*, **moudieman** *now wLoth SW, S* a mole-catcher.

molie (*chf* name for) a mole-catcher *N, EC Lnk*.

†pease bogle a scarecrow.

†pitawtie bogle a scarecrow.

†ratton fa a rat-trap.

scaur-craw a scarecrow.

snarl *v* snare *local*.

†snib catch in a trap.

sparrow, sparra: ~ **drift** *or* **hail** *or* **shot** shot for shooting small birds *now local NE-Rox*.

stamp a (rat-*etc*) trap, *esp* one which grips the victim by the foot, a gin-trap *now Per Fif*.

†swar a snare.

tattie: ~**-bogie** *now NE*, ~**-bogle** *Gen except Sh Ork NE*, ~**-boodie** *NE*, ~ **doolie** *now Kcdn Per* a scarecrow, *esp* one in a potato field.

†tod-hunter a person employed to exterminate foxes.

7.11 CARTS

†back widdie the band over a cart saddle, supporting the shafts.

back-rape the rope which goes over a horse's back.

barra, borra a (hand-*etc*) barrow. ~**-steel, barrow-tram** a barrow-shaft.

breist, breast the front or projecting part of a cart *now Cai Bnf*.

britchin, breechin a breeching, a strap round the hindquarters of a shaft horse to let it push backwards.

caddie nail *or* **bolt** a bolt or iron pin used in fixing the body of a cart to its axle *now Ags Per*.

cairt cart. ~**er** a carter. ~**le** *chf NE Ags*, ~ **draught** *now Abd Fif* a cartload. ~ **door** the tail-board of a cart *local NE-S*. ~ **girden** a rope used to secure a load *NE*. ~ **raik** the time taken to dispose of a cart-load *now Bnf Kcb*.

ca(ll) drive (a vehicle, load etc).

cannon: ~ **nail** *S*, ~ **pin** *Abd Ayr* the nail or pin which attaches the cart to its axle.

car, †ker a sledge, latterly for transporting peats or hay *SW*. †**kerfull** a cartload. † ~ **saddle** a saddle designed to take the shafts of a cart.

carron-nail the nail fixing a cart to its axle *Abd Rox*.

clood cart in small loads *Bnf Abd*.

close cairt a farm cart with fixed shafts *now Fif*.

†**coup** a closed cart for carrying manure or earth.
coup-cairt a tipping cart.

dooble cairt a cart pulled by two horses, one in the shafts and one in the traces *now Bnf Abd*.

draucht, draft *now Bnf Kcb Rox* two or more cart-loads brought at one time *now Bnf Abd*.

draw cart (a load) *now Kcb*.

dwang a bar of wood used by carters for tightening ropes etc *now Abd Kcdn*.

forebreist the front (seat) of a cart *Ork NE*.

garron nail a large nail or spike, *esp* as used in fixing the body of a cart to its axle *now local Sh-Fif*.

heck a framework of wooden bars attached to the sides of a cart to enable it to take a high load *eg* of hay *now Abd Kcdn*.

hey-bogie a low hay-truck dragged behind a tractor *local midLoth-Rox*.

hin-door the removable back-board of a box-cart *Gen except Sh Ork*.

†**howe-barrow** a barrow with sides.

hurl †a wheelbarrow. ~**ie**, ~**ie-barrow** *now Cai midLoth*, ~**barrow** a wheelbarrow; a handcart. † ~**-cart** a common cart.

laid tree the centre rail of a frame laid on a hay-cart to enable it to take a heavier load *chf S*.

lang cairt a two-wheeled cart with a long body and sparred sides, used *esp* for carrying grain *local N-Uls*.

lead convey in a cart.

lin-nail, lin-pin *now Ork Rox* a linchpin.

peat-barra a flat barrow with a high end and no sides used for carrying peats.

puddock *n, also* ~ **barrow** *now Ross Abd* a flat, wooden, *usu* triangular platform etc, shaped rather like a frog, used for transporting heavy loads of hay etc. *v* move (stones etc) by means of a **puddock** *NE*.

rackpin *now local Per-Lnk*, **rack stick** a stick used to tighten a rope or chain, *eg* on a loaded cart.

rigbody *EC Arg*, **rigwiddie** *now NE-C* a band (*orig* one made of withes) passing over the back of a carthorse and supporting the cart-shafts.

†**rung cart** an early type of cart made of spars and having solid wooden wheels.

saidle, saddle: ~ **crub** the steel groove in the saddle of a cart-horse in which the back-chain works *now NE*.

shear(s) a piece of metal in which the axle-ends of a wheel or roller turn; the beam of a farm cart between which the shafts are placed *now Per Kcb*.

shelvin(s), shellwing(s) *now Sh-Cai*, **shelmont(s)** *now local Per-S*, **shellband(s)** *now Ayr*

part of the sides of a cart, *now usu* movable boards to allow the carrying of higher or bulkier loads.

sheth a crossbar, *esp* a spar in the frame or sides of a cart etc *now Per Bwk*.

shod the metal tyre of a cartwheel *local*.

shouder, shoulder, shouther: ~ **cleek** the hook on a cart-shaft to which the shoulder-chain is attached *now Loth Dnbt*.

slider the movable metal loop sliding on a rod on a cart-shaft, to which the back-chain is hooked *Ork-EC*.

sling the swivels, hooks and chains of the draught-harness of a cart *now local Abd-Wgt*.

slot a cross-piece or bar in a harrow or cart *now Cai Kcb*.

spar, spare *now Rox* a linchpin *now WC Wgt Rox*.

stang a shaft or draught-pole of a cart.

start one of the uprights of a box-cart onto which the side-boards are nailed *now Abd Per Gall*.

steeker the back-board of a farm cart *Per Fif*.

stiel the handle of a barrow *now Rox*.

stoup the butt-end of the under-rail of a farm cart, on which it rests when tilted *now NE*.

tap(s), top(s) a framework fitted round a cart to facilitate the transport of large loads of hay etc *now Per Fif*.

theat 1 ~**s** the traces (attaching a horse to a vehicle etc) *now N nEC*. **2** a tow, pull by a trace-horse *Ags Per*. ~**er** a trace horse of a cart *nEC Lnk*.

tram a shaft of a barrow, cart etc. ~ **girth** a loose girth attached to the shafts of a cart to prevent a load from tipping back *now Ork*. ~ **horse** a horse harnessed between the shafts of a cart (as opposed to a trace horse) *now Ork*.

tress a trace, a draught rope etc. **tracer 1** a trace horse. **2** the man in charge of a trace horse.

trinnle a wheelbarrow wheel *now Stlg Ayr*.

†**tumbler, tumbling cart** a kind of light box-cart with fixed (solid) wheels.

wain a waggon, a large open two- or four-wheeled cart *now Fif*. † ~ **weight** ? a waggon-load

whiplicker *Fif*, **whipman** *now Pbls* a carter.

wing a detachable board which can be added to the side of a cart to increase its capacity *now Cai Fif*.

yoke *n* **1** the harness of a cart etc *now Cai Abd*. **2** a horse and cart attached in full harness *now Ags Per*. **3** *also* **yokin** the period during which a team of horses or oxen is in harness at one stretch, *usu* half a day's work. †*v* attach (a cart). †**a-~**, **in(to) the** ~ in(to) harness *NE*.

7.12 MISCELLANEOUS IMPLEMENTS

†**backet** a shallow wooden receptacle for lime, salt etc.

blin(d) sieve a basket or tray for carrying grain etc *now Ork.*

byre-claut a **claut** (a scraper) for cleaning out a **byre** *now Ags Kcb.*

caib the iron or cutting part of a spade etc *Suth Ross.*

cannas a canvas sheet for catching grain etc *NE.*

clart clear or scrape with a muck-rake *local.*

claut *n* a hoe; an implement for scraping dung, dirt etc *now Ags wLoth Kcb. v* scrape, clean by scraping, rake *now local NE-C.*

clep, clip a wooden instrument for pulling thistles out of standing corn *now Arg.*

cog *n* a wooden container made of staves, a pail or bowl. †*v* empty into a **cog.**

corn harp an instrument for separating grain and weed seeds *NE.*

den a groove, *eg* for the blade in a scythe handle *now Abd.*

dock nail the nail used to fix a handle on a scythe, etc *Abd.*

faik a strand of rope *now Cai Abd.*

fork a forkful *now Sh Ork Abd Per.*

fow *n* a pitchfork *now NE Gall. v* lift or toss straw, hay etc with a fork *Bnf Abd Kcb Dmf.*

frame a square or hoop of wood hung from the shoulders on which to carry pails *local Ork-Abd.*

furr a turn-over with a spade *now Ork NE.*

†**fute spade** an ordinary digging spade.

†**ganging:** ~ **graith** moving parts. ~ **geir** the working parts of a machine or implement.

gird a hoop-shaped frame hung from the shoulders for carrying two pails *now Bwk.*

glaiks an instrument for twisting ropes from straw etc *SW Uls.*

grain a prong (of a fork, etc) *now local.* † ~**it** pronged.

graip *n* an iron-pronged fork. *v* fork up *local NE-Uls.*

graith 1 materials or equipment (for a particular purpose, job or trade); tools, implements, machinery *now local NE-Gall.* **2** accessory equipment, *esp* of a mechanism *now Stlg-Dmf.* ~**ing** equipment, accoutrements, trappings.

guddle a pointed iron bar for making holes for fence-posts *Kcdn Ags Per.*

hack *n, also* ~ **muck, muck** ~ a pronged tool for breaking up or raking soil etc *Gen except Sh Ork.* ~**(ing) stock** a chopping block.

hag: ~**-block,** ~**-clog,** ~**-stock** a chopping block *latterly SW Uls.*

†**hake** a hook.

hap a covering, *esp* one which protects against the weather *now Loth.*

happer a basket or container, *esp* that in which the sower carries his seed *now Ork NE Ags.*

harl a rake or scraper used for scraping up dung, soft mud, cinders etc *now local.*

harp *n* **1** a sieve or riddle *now Cai-Ags Kcb.* **2** a sparred shovel used *eg* for **lifting** potatoes etc *now Kinr Fif.* †*v* riddle, sift.

heft *n* a haft, a handle of an implement. *v* haft, fit with a handle; fix firmly **in** something. ~**it** handled, fitted with a handle.

hose the socket for the handle on any metal implement, *eg* a fork or rake *now Sh-Cai Fif.* **hozle, hoozle** the socket into which the handle of a pick, fork etc is fitted *now Edb Slk Rox.*

how hoe.

hut, †**hot** a basket or pannier, *esp* one used for carrying manure or earth etc *Gall.*

kent a long staff or pole used for leaping ditches etc.

lat, let: ~ **out** make (straw ropes) by paying out the straw through the fingers while another twists with the **thrawcruik** *NE.*

lay *v* form (a rope etc) by twisting strands together. *n* the re-steeling of the cutting edge of an implement *Gen except Sh Ork.*

lug 1 a projecting flange or spike on an iron instrument, *eg* a a spade *now NE.* **2** one of the hand grips at the top of a full sack.

maun, †**mand** a basket made of wicker or wooden slats.

mid couple a loop of cowhide or eelskin connecting the hand-staff of a flail to the beater *now Uls.*

mou(th) the blade (of a shovel or spade) *Sh-nEC, SW.*

neep: ~**-cleek** a hooked implement for pulling up **turnips** *NE-Loth Kcb.* ~ **hack** a two-pronged iron implement for pulling **turnips** out of frozen ground *now WC.*

orraman any mechanical contrivance used by a man working single-handed *NE.*

†**outsicht plenishing** goods kept for use out of doors.

ower *of ropes etc* going across or over *Bnf Stlg Wgt.*

packet a pannier, a load-saddle *NE.*

paidle *n* a long-handled tool for weeding, scraping earth etc from a hard surface; a hoe *local. v* scrape (floors etc) clean; use a hoe, clean or clear by means of a hoe *now eLoth.*

pattle a small spade-like tool, used *esp* for clearing the mould-board of a plough. †~**ing** scraping clean with, or as with, a **pattle**.

pluck *v* take (**turnips**) out of the ground with a **pluck** *NE*. *n* a two-pronged, mattock-type implement used for taking **turnips** from hard ground, forking dung etc *NE*.

powl *n* a pole, a long, thin, round shaft of wood. *v* pole, furnish with poles.

prang a prong *now Mry Abd Per*.

†**prick measure, prick mett** an iron rod used as a measure for grain.

raip a straw or hay rope.

raip: trail the ~ bring bad luck by twisting a straw rope and pulling it round anticlockwise *NE*.

ree *n* a medium-sized sieve or riddle for cleaning grain, peas, beans etc *now Stlg midLoth*. *v* clean (grain, grass-seed, peas, beans etc) by sieving in a **ree** *now midLoth*.

rip a round wicker (or straw) basket used for carrying eggs *Kcdn Ags Fif*.

†**row, roll** a rounded stick or roller for levelling grain in a measure.

sae a wooden tub, carried by two persons on a pole or rope, used for transporting water *now Sh Ork Cai*.

†**sauch** a rope of twisted willow withes.

scartle a scraper, hoe or rake.

scull, scoo *local Ork-Bnf* a shallow, scoop-shaped basket for carrying potatoes, grain etc *now local NE-Kcb*.

scutch *v* skim or graze the surface of one object with another, flick, **scuff**, sweep, hoe etc, *esp* rather perfunctorily *Cai Bnf*. *n* the act of **scutching**, a grazing or scuffling movement or sound, a swift light motion over a surface, *eg* in sweeping *now Cai*.

scythe: ~**sned** the curved wooden handle or shaft of a scythe *now NE Per*. ~**straik** a scythe sharpener *now NE Kcb*.

search *n* a sieve, strainer, riddle *now NE Ags*. *v* put through a sieve, sift, strain *now NE Ags*.

†**shakefork** a pitchfork.

shimee a straw rope *Suth-Inv*.

shod an iron tip etc on a (*usu* wooden) object to prevent wear *local*.†**shod shovel** a wooden shovel with a metal rim.

shuil, shuffle, shovel *n* a shovel. *v* shovel, work or clean out with a shovel; dig (a hole etc) with a shovel.

skep a wickerwork or straw basket, *esp* one for carrying grain, meal, or potatoes.

slogie-riddle a wide-meshed riddle for separating vegetables *S*.

spadin(g) a spade's depth (or breadth) of earth *now local*.

spail, speal: ~ **basket** a two-handled (potato-) basket made of thin strips of wood.

splicer an instrument for twisting straw ropes, a **thrawcruik** *Fif WC Rox*.

strae, straw: straw crook *now Cai Per Loth*, **strae heuk** *local Sh-Bute* a rope-twister, **thrawcruik.strae raip** a rope of twisted straw.

straik *n* a tool for sharpening scythes etc *now NE Fif SW*. *v* sharpen (a scythe etc) with a **straik** *now local NE-SW*.

swill, sweel a large shallow basket for carrying potatoes etc *Bwk Rox*.

tae, toe a prong of a fork, rake etc.

tang the prong of a digging- or pitchfork *now Sh Cai C*.

tattie-poke a sack for holding potatoes *now NE-Per*.

thoum, thumb: ~-**raip** a hay or straw rope made by twisting the strands under the tip of the thumb *local Bnf-Gall*.

thraw, throw twist (straw, withies etc) together to make (a rope) using an appropriate implement *now Sh N-Per*. ~ **clet** *Renfr Ayr Dmf*, ~**cruik** *now Sh-WC, Rox*, ~**huik** *now NE Arg*, ~-**rape** *local Bnf-SW* 1 an implement for twisting straw etc into rope. 2 a twisted straw rope *local Per-Kcb*.

tramp 1 an iron plate on the sole of a boot or shoe in digging *N, WC Rox*. 2 a horizontal strip of iron on the top of a spade blade for the foot to press on *now local Ork-Ayr*. ~-**pick** a pick or crowbar with an iron bracket for the foot to press on *now N Ayr*.

truan *now local*, **truel** *Ork N Per* a trowel.

turn, tirn twist or spin (a rope) from straw.

tweezlick an instrument used to twist straw or rush ropes, a simplified **thrawcruik** *NE*.

†**tynd** a tine, a prong, spike.

wase, wease, wassock *now Abd* a circular band of straw used to protect the hands, *eg* when knocking the husks from the ears of barley.

wecht, **†winding wecht** a wooden hoop, about two to three feet in diameter, with skin or canvas stretched over it, *orig* used for winnowing corn, *now usu* for carrying grain or potatoes *now Sh N Kcb*. †**wechtfu** the amount contained in a **wecht**.

weedock, **†weidheuk** a weed-hook, an implement for cutting weeds.

†**weeding iron** a tool for removing weeds.

whankie a sickle-blade mounted on a long handle, for cutting down thistles, inaccessible twigs etc *Loth Bwk S*.

whin, whun: ~**-howe** a mattock for uprooting furze bushes *now Gall*.

whip, whup a rope of twisted straw *EC, S*.

wyle, wylie an instrument for twisting ropes from straw, a **thrawcruik** *now sEC, SW, S*.

7.13 SHEEP-FARMING

For calls to dogs see 7.9.4.

†**airie, arrie** a **shieling**.

bat a drove (of sheep) *Bwk S*.

birn *v*, †*also* **brin** brand by burning. *n* a brand of ownership on an animal, *usu* **skin and birn.** †**brent** burned, branded. †**birn** *or* **burn irne** a branding iron.

boucht *n* a sheepfold; *specif* a small inner fold for milking ewes. †*v* enclose (*esp* ewes for milking) in a fold.

brat a cloth put on a **tup-hog** to prevent mating *now Loth*.

breek a cloth put on a ewe to prevent mating *now Bnf*.

buist *n* **1** an identification mark branded or painted on sheep. **2** an iron stamp for marking sheep *SW*. *v* mark (sheep) with their owners mark *now Kcb*. ~**er 1** a person who marks sheep thus *now Cai*. **2** *also* ~**in(g) iron** the instrument used for marking sheep *SW*.

cled score *of sheep* twenty-one in number *SW*.

crummock, †**crummie** a stick with a crooked head, a shepherd's crook *local*.

cundy, condie a hole in a wall for the passage of sheep etc.

cut a group of sheep divided from the rest *now Bnf*.

draucht withdrawn from the flock as being unfit for further breeding *now Bnf Kcb Rox*.

†**drift** a drove, flock, herd.

drove drive (sheep), be a drover. † ~ **road** a road or track used for driving sheep to markets.

dyke-louper an animal which leaps the dyke surrounding its pasture *now Bnf Abd Fif*.

eat cause or allow (grass etc) to be eaten by grazing animals, *freq* ~ **grass** *etc now local Sh-Kcb*: 'he eats the herbage with his sheep'.

eel-stab, eel-stob a V-shaped incision in the ear of an animal as a mark of ownership *now Arg Kcb*. † ~**bed** marked in this way.

eenach the natural grease in sheep's wool *Abd*.

eik the natural grease in sheep's wool *now Rox*.

fank *n* a sheepfold. *v* drive into a sheepfold.

fauld, fold: ~**in** a sheepfold.

†**fe** cattle or sheep. ~ **master** a herdsman.

†**feed** pasture (animals).

fell the skin of a sheep, as distinguished from the wool *S*.

ferm, farm: ~ **stockin** farm animals, *esp* cattle and sheep.

flake, †**fleck** pen (sheep) by means of **flakes** (portable hurdles) *now Bwk Rox*.

†**fute fell** the skin of a lamb dead soon after birth.

gangs sheep-shears *Cai*.

girse, grass, gress pasture (animals). †**girsing** the act or fact of pasturing animals.

gripper the person who catches and holds a sheep to be sheared *now SW*.

guide treat, use, handle, care for (animals).

†**hairst hog** a lamb smeared at the end of harvest, when it is reckoned to become a sheep.

handling, haunling a rounding up and penning of sheep for some special purpose, *eg* dipping or shearing *now Pbls SW, S*.

hanging burn a sheep mark branded on the lower part of the cheek or chin *now Bwk Rox*.

haud, hald, hold *v* round up, pen (sheep) *now Rox*. *n* the action of a sheepdog in holding up sheep at a particular spot *Arg Rox*. ~**in(g)** the stock of a farm, *esp* sheep *now Rox*.

hause lock, haslo(c)k the wool on a sheep's neck, *freq* regarded as the finest part of the fleece.

heft *v* accustom (sheep) to a new pasture by constant herding to prevent them from straying. *n* **1** a pasture which sheep have become familiar with and continue to frequent. **2** the attachment of sheep to a particular pasture *now Arg SW Rox*. **3** the number of sheep that graze on a **heft** *Arg SW*. ~**it** accustomed to a new pasture *now Arg SW, S*.

herd, hird *n* **1** a person who tends or watches over sheep, *esp* in order to confine them to a particular pasture in unfenced areas. **2** a shepherd *now WC Gall S*. *v* tend, watch over (sheep), *esp* to prevent them from straying onto crops. ~**ing** the tending and confining to their own grazing of sheep; a grazing allotted to a particular flock.

hill: gather the ~ gather together flocks pastured on a hillside *local*.

hip locks the coarse wool which grows on the hips of sheep *now Ork Cai SW*.

†**hird** a flock.

hirsel *n* **1** a flock of sheep, looked after by one shepherd or on one small farm *now NE, S*. **2** an area of pasturage to be grazed by a flock of sheep under the care of one shepherd *now C, S. v* arrange in **hirsels** *now Rox.*

hogg *n, also* **hogget** a young sheep from the time that it is weaned until it is shorn of its first fleece; a yearling. *v* †make a **hogg** of (a lamb), keep (a lamb) on winter pasture during its first year. **hogging** a pasture reserved for one-year-old sheep *now Per Gall Rox.* ~**-fence** a pasture saved for the **hoggs**' winter keep *now Rox.*

keb *v, of a ewe* 1 give birth prematurely or to a dead lamb *SW, S.* 2 lose a lamb by early death *chf S. n 1 also* ~ **yowe** *now Fif* a ewe that has given birth to a dead lamb or failed to rear a live one *chf S.* 2 a stillborn or premature lamb *SW, S.* ~ **hoose** 1 a small shed or shelter where a ewe that has lost her lamb is confined while being made to adopt another *S.* 2 a shelter for young lambs in the lambing season *SW, S.*

keel *n* 1 ruddle, red-ochre, *esp* as used for marking sheep. 2 the owner's mark made with ruddle on sheep. *v* mark (sheep) with ruddle. ~**ie** marked with **keel** *Gall.* † ~**man** a dealer in **keel** *SW.*

keep wide keep some distance from the flock so as not to disturb the sheep *local.*

keers a thin gruel given to feeble sheep in the spring *S.*

kenmark a distinguishing mark, a mark of ownership on an animal, a brand *Sh N Fif.*

ket a matted fleece of wool *now Clcm Loth.*

lambing-stick a shepherd's crook used for catching ewes by the neck at lambing-time *WC-S.*

lap a sheepmark made by slitting the ear so as to make a flap *chf Ork.*

lay smear (a sheep's fleece) with butter, tar etc as a protection against wet etc. †**laid wool** wool from sheep which have been so smeared.

lie aff *of a sheepdog* keep at a distance from the sheep *local Sh-SW.*

lift *v* 1 drive (animals) to market *NE-S.* 2 *of a sheepdog* round up (sheep) and move them forward *now Ork Fif Kcb. n* the rounding-up of sheep by a sheep-dog before penning them *local Ork-SW.*

†**lizour, lesu** *v* pasture.

lug-mark *n* an earmark, *esp* on a sheep. *v* mark the ear of.

maud a checked **plaid** or wrap worn by shepherds *chf S.*

†**mete scheip** a sheep intended to be slaughtered for food, not grown for wool.

†**Mey:** ~ **skin** the skin of a lamb which has ? died or ? been slaughtered in May. ~ **wedder** an animal payed for in May *Gall.*

milk *of a ewe* yield milk (well, badly etc) *local.*

ming mix (tar etc) for sheep-shearing *S.*

†**minnie** *of a shepherd* put (a lamb) to its mother.

mort (lambskin) the skin of a sheep or lamb that has died a natural death *S.* **morkin** a sheep that has died a natural death *Ayr Dmf Slk.* †**mortuall** some kind of skin, *perh* that of a young sheep.

†**mutton, moutoun** the carcasses of sheep. ~ **bouk** the carcass of a sheep.

nibbie a shepherd's crook.

nip a sheepmark, a notch cut in the ear *local NE-S.*

outrun the way in which a dog runs out and round sheep in order to gather them for penning *Ork SW, S.*

oversee tend, look after (animals) *now Sh Ork Bnf.*

pack a number of sheep owned by a shepherd which are allowed to pasture along with his master's sheep as one of his perquisites *now Cai Ags Lnk S.*

parrock, parroch *n* a pen in which a sheep is familiarized with a strange or neglected lamb *now SW, S. v* confine (animals etc) in a **parrock** enclose, herd together (*specif* a ewe with a lamb it is intended she should foster).

plaid-neuk a fold or flap in a **plaid** used as a pocket, *esp* by shepherds for carrying young lambs *now eLoth WC, S.*

plot pluck wool from (a sheep).

†**plump** a flock.

pop a small round sheepmark made by dabbing on the marking substance with a stick *Dmf Slk Rox.*

†**pour** smear (sheep) with an oily compound as a protection against insects and wet.

race a passage along a wall where sheep are graded or separated *local Bnf-midLoth.*

raik a sheep-walk, a pasture *now nEC.*

raw, row bring (late-lambing ewes) in single file to a field beside the shepherd's house to keep them under observation.

ree, reeve *now NE Per,* **reed** *C* a permanent stone sheepfold, used during stormy weather, shearing etc *now SW.*

reuch, rough *of sheep* unshorn, undipped *Bwk SW, S.*

rin, run *of a dog* move sheep at a brisk pace, range out in herding sheep *SW, S.*

rit, rut *v* slit (a sheep) in the ear as an earmark *now Sh Slk. n* a sheepmark in the form of a slit in the ear (or nostril) *Sh Ork SW.*

rodding a narrow track or path trodden out by sheep.

roun(d) *local SW, S,* **roundel, rounall** *local Cai-Lnk* a circular sheepfold.

rump cut, clip or crop very short *local Bnf-S*.

†**schallow** a drove, flock.

set on put (an unweaned animal) to suck, *esp* a strange lamb to a ewe that has lost her own *Bwk Lnk S*.

†**shear, share** a shorn animal.

shears (sheep-)clippers.

shed, shede *now Sh Ork NE v* **1** separate, divide (lambs from ewes) *Gen except Sh Ork*. **2** part or comb (a sheep's fleece etc) to one side or the other. *n* **1** the act of sorting out sheep, *freq* as a test in sheepdog trials *Gen except Sh Ork*. **2** the parting of the wool on a sheep's back. **shedder** an instrument for parting, a pen for sorting sheep *Gen except Sh Ork*. **shedding** the act of separating sheep.

sheep: ~ **bucht** a sheep pen, *esp* at a market or for milking-ewes *Gen except Sh Ork*. ~ **fank,** ~ **ree** *now Wgt*, ~ **stell** *now Cai Bwk S* a (dry-stone) enclosure where sheep are gathered for shelter, dipping, shearing etc. ~ **fauld** a sheep-fold *now Cai*. ~ **gang** a sheep pasture, *esp* of hill-grazing *now Loth S*. ~ **net** a net on stakes to confine sheep on a **turnip** field. ~ **raik** a path or strip of ground trodden by grazing sheep. ~ **rodding** a sheep-track. †~ **steid** a sheep farm.

shepherd, †**schipird** a shepherd. ~'s **stirk** a calf reared by a shepherd as one of his perquisites *WC Dmf*.

†**shiel** *n* **1** a temporary or roughly-made hut or shed used by shepherds (and their animals), a **shieling**. **2** *also* ~ **toun** a summer pasture with a shepherd's hut or huts. *v* live in a summer-pasture hut, herd (sheep and cattle) at a **shiel**. ~**ing 1** a high or remote summer pasture, *usu* with a shepherd's hut or huts. **2** a roughly-made hut, *esp* one for shepherds and dairymaids on a **shieling**. ~ **house** a shepherd's hut.

sicht, sight inspect (a newborn animal) for its sex *local Sh-Edb*.

sick, sick lamb, sickie *NE* a pet lamb brought up on the bottle *Bnf Abd*.

slit name for a kind of sheepmark consisting of a cut in the ear *now Kcb*.

sloch, slough remove the wool from a dead sheep by skinning rather than clipping or shearing *SW*.

smear *v, also* **smairg** *now WC Wgt Rox* treat (a sheep's fleece) with a tar-and-grease compound to protect it from damp and parasites. ~**ing house** *etc* the shed in which sheep were so treated.

smot *v* mark (sheep) with tar or other colouring as a sign of ownership *now Bwk*. *n* a mark of ownership on a sheep; sheep or a sheep thus marked *now Bwk*.

smuir, smoor smear (a sheep with tar) *now Cai*.

†**snaw mail** a payment made to owners of lowland pasture for grazing hill sheep.

stell *v* put (sheep) in a **stell**. *n* **1** an open, *usu* circular, enclosure of dry-stone walling, used as a shelter for sheep on a hillside *now WC-S*. **2** a clump or plantation of trees used as a shelter for sheep.

store: ~ **farm** a farm, *usu* in the hills, on which sheep are reared and grazed *now SW, S*. †~ **room** a sheep farm.

straik a sheep-walk *now Mry*.

tap, top *v* cut the tip of the ear of (an animal) as an ownership mark *now Sh Kcb*. *adj* of the best grade. **tops** the best sheep or lambs in a flock *Gen except Sh Ork*.

tar: †~**ry oo** *etc* wool from a sheep which has been smeared with tar. ~ **buist** a box containing tar for smearing and marking sheep *local Cai-S*.

tent tend, take charge of, look after (animals) *now Wgt*.

traik misfortune, loss, *specif* that caused by disease in farm animals.

twin take a lamb from a weak ewe and give it to a strong one to suckle with her own *C, S*.

wauk, wake guard, watch over (livestock etc), *esp* during the night *now Inv C*.

†**wauken** watch (over), keep an eye on.

wauking o the fauld the all-night watch at a sheepfold at weaning time to prevent the lambs returning to their mothers.

†**wedder gang** a pasture or right of pasturage for wethers.

weir 1 *of a sheepdog* stand in front of (a group of sheep) to prevent them breaking loose *now S*. **2** drive (animals) gradually in a desired direction, shepherd *Gen except Sh Ork*.

wide: gae *or* **keep** ~ *of a sheepdog* go ahead but well away from the sheep *now Cai Per Ayr*.

wirk, work look after, herd (animals) *now Ags Per midLoth*.

wise, wice *of a shepherd or his dog* direct, lead (sheep).

†**wollbutter** butter used to salve sheep's wool.

yowe, ewe: ~ **bucht** a pen for ewes at milking- or weaning-time *now Per*.

7.14 FORESTRY

For trees, see 4.6.

back the outermost boards from a sawn tree *now Bnf Ags*.

bang (chain) a chain for fastening a load of heavy logs *now Ags*.

beet plant (trees) to replace others.

buss a thicket; a clump or stand of trees; a wood.

†**currour** a watcher or ranger of a forest.

†**cuthill** *perh* a grove, small wood.

†**cutter** a person who cuts (*esp* wood) without permission.

†**firth** *verse, chf in alliterative phrases* a wood.

†**fosterschip, fostery** forestership, the office of forester.

†**frostar** a forester *NE*.

†**grave** *literary* a grove.

hag *v* **1** hack, cut, chop wood *now C, S*. **2** cut down trees, prepare timber. *n* **1** †a portion of a wood marked for felling. **2** brushwood; felled wood used for fuel *now NE*.

hain enclose (a wood) by a hedge or fence; keep unused, preserve from cutting.

hose remove the bark from the base of (a tree) before felling.

†**land** an open space in a wood, a clearing.

lay in hack a tree around the trunk before felling, *eg* to prevent it splitting upwards *local Abd-Dmf*.

†**park, perk** enclose (forest etc) (**with**) a wall or ditch.

plantin(g) **1** a small wood or grove of trees, a plantation. **2** young trees, seedlings.

†**plenish** stock (land) with trees etc.

†**plump** a clump of trees.

pundler a person whose main duty was *orig* the impounding of livestock, *later* looking after tree plantations *now Mry Bnf*.

shaw a small wood, a thicket *now chf literary and in place-names*.

skelf a wedge of wood driven into the cut in a tree being felled (to ease the motion of the saw) *WC*.

sned chop, lop off (a branch); prune (a tree) *Gen except Sh Ork*. †**~dings** prunings, branches etc removed.

speeach an oak stake; an oak branch without the bark; a small stick *now Per*.

speeler a spiked iron attached to the foot for climbing trees.

sprack a chip of wood, splinter; waste scraps of wood, tree branches etc, wood or straw litter *Ork Arg*.

stell a clump or plantation of trees used as a shelter for sheep.

stole a tree-stump; a new shoot rising from a group of such stumps after cutting *now Kcb*.

strip, †**stripe** a long narrow belt of trees *NE-S*.

switch trim (a tree, hedge etc).

†**tod stripe** a strip of woodland in which foxes have their holes.

turse *v* make into a bundle etc *now Cai Bnf*. *n* a bundle of sticks etc *now Ork Cai Arg*.

†**virideer** an officer of royal forests.

†**ward, waird** a part or division of a forest.

wuid, wood wood. **wooding** a planting of trees; the trees themselves; a copse or wood. † **~ forester** a forester, a person in charge of the woods on an estate. **~ man** a woodman.

7.15 PEAT

bank the place in a **peat moss** where peats are cut.

bink, bench a **peat bank** *now Arg*.

breist, breast a perpendicular cut in peat.

car, †**ker** a sledge for transporting peats *SW*.

cast dig, cut (peats etc).

†**cleit** a small dry-stone structure used for drying peat on St Kilda.

clod *n* a peat *N*. *v* pile up (peats) *Gall*.

coom peat-dust, fine turf mould *SW Uls*.

creel *n* **1** a deep basket for carrying peats on the back, or one of a pair to be carried by a horse or donkey. **2** a basketful **of** (*chf* peats). *v* put into a **creel** *chf S*.

dass a layer in a pile of peats *etc*.

divot *n* **1** a turf, sod; a piece of turf thinner than a **fail**. **2** †turf, peat; turf in thin pieces. *v* cut **divots**.

duff (mould) a soft spongy substance, *chf* peat *now Sh*. **dufftin** a soft, crumbly, inferior peat *Abd*.

fail, feal a piece of turf, a sod *now chf N*.

fill load (peats etc) *Sh Abd*.

fit, fute, foot *v* set (peats) up on end to dry *now local Ags-Uls*. *n* a peat cut with an ordinary spade from the bottom of a **peat-bank** when the upper layers have been removed *NE*.

flae strip (ground) of turf before cutting peat.

flag a piece of turf cut or pared from the surface, a sod.

flauchter pare (turf) from the ground. † **~ fail** a piece of turf cut with **flauchter spade**. **~ spade, flauchter** *SW* a two-handed spade with a broad heart-shaped blade used for cutting turf.

flaw remove turf from (a **peat bank**) before cutting peat *chf Sh.*

foggy peat a rough, spongy peat *now Cai NE Uls.*

fum a wet or spongy peat or turf *now Dmf.*

hag a hollow of marshy ground in a moor, *eg* where channels have been made or peats cut.

hatch a **peat bank**, a row of peats spread out to dry *now Abd.*

hill 1 a piece of rough moorland where peats are cut, a **peat moss** *now local Sh-Abd.* **2** a **peat-stack** *now Cai Abd.*

hole dig up (*now esp* turf) *Uls.*

iron an iron tool used for cutting peats; the amount of peat which can be cut with this tool in one day *Hebrides.*

ket a spongy kind of peat of tough matted fibres *SW.*

lair[1] a patch of ground on which cut peats are laid to dry *NE.*

†lair[2] the floor of a **peat bank**, a trench from which peats have been cut.

lead transport (peat) home from the **moss** *now local.*

leet a stack of peats of a specific size, varying locally and from time to time, *chf NE.*

moss *n* a peat bog; a stretch of moorland allocated to tenants for cutting fuel. *v* to work at cutting peats *etc* in a peat bog. **~er** a person who cuts and dries peats *NE Rox.* **~ aik, ~ oak** bog oak *SW.* **~ bank** a **peat-bank** *N, Per.* **~ hag** *now C,* **~ hole** *Gen except Sh Ork* = **peat hag.** **†~leave** the right or permission to cut peats etc in a **moss.** **†~ mail** rent paid for the right of cutting peat etc in a **moss.** **~ road** a track to a **peat moss** *now Abd.* **†~ room** the portion of a **peat moss** assigned to a tenant for his own use *WC, SW.*

†mou a pile or stack of peats *WC, S.*

mou(th) *of a peat stack* the end from which one begins to draw away the peats for fuel *Abd.*

peat a piece of the semi-carbonized decayed vegetable matter found under the surface of boggy moorland, *usu* cut into brick-shaped pieces, dried and burned as fuel. **the ~s** the work of digging and preparing peat for fuel. **†~ery** a **~ moss** belonging to a landed estate; the right to cut peats from this. **†peting** the action of getting peat; the right to cut, or the service of cutting peat. **~-bank** the bank or vertical face from which peats are cut. **~-barra** a flat barrow with a high end and no sides used for carrying peats. **~ bing** a heap of peats, *usu* the winter's supply, stacked against the gable of the house *Sh Bnf WC.* **~ bree** the water which drains from peat

soil, peaty water *now NE.* **~-caster** a person who cuts peats and lays them out to dry. **~-castin** the act of doing this. **~-clod** a single peat, *esp* one which is still earthy and friable *Sh N Wgt Uls.* **~-coom** *Cai SW, S,* **~ muild, ~ mould** peat dust, the crumbly remains of peat. **~ cassie** *now Sh Ork Uls,* **~-creel** *NE, C Highl Uls* a large straw or rush basket for carrying peats on the back. **†~-gate** the track, road or right-of-way leading to a **peat moss** *chf Abd.* **~ hag** a hole or pit left in an old peat-working. **~-hole** an old peat-working on a moor, *freq* one filled with rainwater *now Uls.* **~ lair, ~-larach** the area of moor on which newly cut peats are laid out to dry *Sh N, SW.* **†~-leading** the carting of cut and dried peats from the **~ moss.** **†~man** an estate servant in charge of the peat supply; an itinerant peat-merchant. **~ moss, ~ hill** *now Sh Ork* a peat-bog or -moor, the place where peats are dug. **†~-pot** a hole from which peats have been dug. **~ rickle** a small heap of three or four peats set up on end to dry *now Abd.* **~ spad(e)** a specially-shaped spade used for peat-cutting. **~-stack** a large pile of dried peats erected out-of-doors as a fuel-store. **†~ ȝaird** a place where peats are dug. **fit the ~s** set peats on end to dry.

pot, pat *n* a pit from which peats have been dug *now Wgt Slk.* **†v** dig holes (in the ground) to extract peat.

reuch, rough: ~-head a turf or peat, *esp* one with the surface grass still attached.

rickle *n* a small heap of peats or turfs, stacked loosely for drying *now local N-Ayr.* *v* stack (peats) loosely for drying *now local N-SW.*

rind the edge, *eg* of a **peat-bank.**

†rit irne a turf-cutter.

ruck a stack or heap, *orig* of fuel, *later also specif* of peats *now Bnf Abd.*

ruit, root a dried tree root used as firewood, *esp* one dug up from a bog *now NE Ags WC.*

†sade (a) turf, (a) sod.

†saut, salt: ~ fail seaside turf.

scaddin a thin flaky turf, the top paring of peat from a bog; a peat turf used for thatching.

scraw a thin turf or sod.

scrocken *now chf Sh NE,* **skurken** *now chf Sh NE,* **scrochle** dry out peats.

scull, scoo *local Ork-Bnf* a shallow, scoop-shaped basket for carrying peats *now local NE-Kcb.*

set stack (peats) in **rickles** to dry *NE.*

shiel *n* a kind of long-bladed peat-cutter *Cai.* *v* cut the top turf of a **peat-bank** with a **shiel** *Cai Ross Inv.*

shirrel, †scherald, scherard, scheratt a (piece of) turf, *esp* from the surface of a peat bog.

skail spread (peat) over the surface of the ground *now Cai Per WC, SW.*

skemmel a **peat bank**, the **hag** left in a **moss** from which peats have been cut.

spade's casting one of various measurements in peat-cutting. **†spadar(r)ack** the number of peats that can be cut with a spade by one man in one day.

spread-field the ground where cut peat is spread for drying.

stack a peat-stack *Sh Cai NE.* ~ **hill** the ground or mound on which a **stack** is built. ~ **mou** that end of a peat-stack from which the peats are drawn for use *Bnf Abd.*

steid, stead *n* a site, foundation, base of a **peat-stack** *Sh-Cai.* *v* lay a foundation (for), make the base (of) (*eg* a **peat-stack**) *Sh Ork.*

taw a conifer preserved in peat *now Sh.*

theek *v* roof, cover (a peat-stack) **with** (thatch). *n* thatch *now WC, SW.*

tirr *now N Bwk Rox,* **tirl** take the top layer off (a piece of ground), remove surface turf or soil from (ground), so as to allow digging for peat. **tirrin** the layer removed before digging *now Ork N.* **tirrin pick, spade** *etc* one used for **tirring**.

turn, tirn turn (peats etc) to dry; dismantle and rebuild (a small stack etc) for drying. ~**-fittin** building piles of peats thus *now Wgt S.*

turr, turf *n, also* **truff** *now Ross Bnf* a surface peat or turf cut as fuel *now local N-Rox.* *v* remove surface turf from *now Cai Mry Bnf.* **turvin** the cutting of turf; sods, surface peats *chf Sh.* † ~ **stack** a peat-stack.

tusk *n* the projecting wing on the blade of a **peat spade** *now Bnf.* *v* cut (peat) from above the bank *N.*

uncassen not cut *Sh NE.*

win *of cut peats etc* dry and make or become ready for storage by exposure to air and sun.

win(d)-raw a row or line in which small piles of cut peats are set to dry *now WC.*

7.16 HORTICULTURE AND MARKET GARDENING

bauk a (garden) path *now Fif.*

blade, blad strip the leaves from (a plant).

†bour a bower.

†curson a fruiting spur.

delve, †delf delve; dig over a garden.

dimple *v* dibble *now Bnf Abd.*

fog house a small garden summer-house built or lined with mossy turf *now Abd.*

front the front garden *local NE-Ayr.*

gairden a garden. **gairdner** a gardener.

garth an enclosure, yard, garden *now only as place-name esp of farms.*

†heidȝard the (farther or outer) end of a garden.

†imp engraft.

Irishman's cutting a cutting taken from a plant, with a portion of the root attached *local Cai-WC.*

kail yaird a cabbage garden, a kitchen-garden.

knot *now Cai Gall,* **flower knot** *now Fif SW* a flowerbed, a formal garden.

†mail: ~-garden(er) a market garden(er). ~ **man** a market gardener.

†peel stake up, support or protect by means of stakes.

†planner a landscape gardener.

pou, pull pluck (fruit, flowers etc) from the plants or trees on which they grow, gather or collect produce of any kind.

raep reap *now Sh Ork Bnf nEC.*

†rider a standard fruit tree used to fill space on a high wall until smaller permanent trees grew high enough.

ripe strip (berries from a bush) *Sh Abd.*

roup, roop prune (a hedge etc) very severely *Per Fif.*

rouse sprinkle with water; water with a watering-can *NE Ags.* ~**r** a watering-can *local NE-WC.*

rump cut, clip or crop very short *local Bnf-S.*

scutch *n* a slash, a cutting of twigs, thistles etc, the trimming of a hedge *now SW.* *v* cut or shear with a hook or knife, slash, trim (a hedge) *now Loth WC, SW.*

sneck cut sharply, cut into or **off,** prune, notch *now local Sh-Ayr.*

sned chop, lop off (a branch); prune (a tree) *Gen except Sh Ork.* ~**der** a pruner. **†sneddings** prunings, branches etc removed. † ~**ding knife etc** a pruning knife etc.

snod prune, cut, trim, smooth, make level *now local NE-SW.*

stob *n* a stake, post. *v* prop up (*eg* plants) with stakes *now local WC-S.*

†stock a stem on which a graft is inserted.

switch trim (a tree, hedge etc).

taft, toft, *freq* plant ~ a small patch of enclosed ground for rearing cabbages etc *Cai.*

tirless, †treilȝeis a trellis on which climbing plants are trained.

truan *now local,* **truel** *Ork N Per* a trowel.

whittle, whuttle a hedge-bill *now Lnk Ayr*.

yaird, yard a garden, *now esp* a cottage- or kitchen-garden. ~ **dyke** a garden wall *now Ork N, C*. ~ **fit** *now Loth Wgt*, † ~ **end** the foot of a garden.

7.17 BEEKEEPING

†**bee skep** a beehive.

bink, bench a hive (of bees etc).

eik an additional ring of plaited straw or wood used to enlarge a beehive *now local Bnf-Kcb*.

nedder †*n* an extension placed below a beehive to give extra room for breeding. *v* place a **nedder** below a hive.

pit down suffocate (bees) with sulphur in order to get at the honey.

port an opening in a beehive for the passage of the bees *Bnf Uls*.

ruskie a straw beehive *NE, EC, S*.

skep *n* a beehive. *v* put (a swarm of bees) into a hive.

smeek *n, also* ~**er** *now Per Fif Kcb* a contrivance for smoking out bees *Bwk-S*. *v, freq* ~ **out** drive out (bees) with smoke fumes *now C, S*.

smuik, smook smoke out (bees) *now SW, S*.

†**stale** the original hive in a colony of bees, from which swarms have come off; a stock of bees.

†**tap, top:** ~ **swarm** the first swarm of bees from a hive.

8. LIFE CYCLE, FAMILY

8.1 GENERAL

ages: be ~ with be of the same age as (someone else).

billy a fellow, lad.

bird *orig only in verse, latterly chf familiar or disparaging* a lady, woman.

body, buddy a person, a human being: **1** *chf* **a ~**, *in gen;* **2 a ~** *referring to the speaker himself or to another* someone, one, a person: *'could you no leave a body in peace?'* **3** *freq* indicating contempt or sympathy: *'a cantie body'; 'a tailor body'.*

boy a man of any age; also used as a term of address. *Hebrides Highl.*

callan(d) an associate; a youth, fellow.

carle *now Bnf-Lnk,* **carlie** *humorous, sympathetic or depreciatory, now local Bnf-Fif* a man, fellow.

carline, carling *freq derog* a *(usu* old) woman *now Bnf Abd Fif.*

chappie *affectionate, familiar* a chap, a fellow.

†childer fellows, people.

†dam a lady, dame.

†ded(e)like mortal, liable to death. **(al) ~s** mortals.

deem a dame.

een a woman *now Sh Ags: 'a braa een'.*

eild †*n* the age of a person. **(be) eil(d)ins, yealin(g)s** (be) contemporaries, person born in the same year.

face: the ~ of clay any man alive *now Bnf Abd.*

fallow, follow *now Sh Cai Abd Uls* a fellow.

†famell females; a female.

fit, fute, foot: (up)on ~ alive *midLoth Bwk.*

fore: to the ~ alive.

fouter a chap, fellow.

fowk, folk 1 folk; people, persons, mankind. **2** individual persons: *'here's twae folks come frae Glasgow'.* **3** human beings as opposed to animals or supernatural beings *now Abd Kcb.*

fremd *now local,* **fremmit,** *now chf* **the ~** strangers, the world at large *now local.*

gadgie a man, fellow *chf S, now child's word, Edb.*

†gersone a fellow.

he a man, a male person *now Abd.*

heidiepeer of equal age or stature.

hizzie, hussy *joc or (slightly) disparaging* a woman, *esp* a frivolous woman.

Jenny, Jinny, *freq with* **Jock** generic term for a woman *now Abd Fif.*

Jock, Jack generic term for a man, the common man *now NE, EC, Rox.* **Jock Tamson's bairns** the human race, common humanity, *chf* **we're a' ~ Tamson's bairns.**

kittie *Sh NE* familiar or contemptuous term for a woman or girl, *specif* a giddy, skittish young woman.

knap a chap *now NE.*

knipe a chap *now Bnf.*

lass, lassie, lassock, lassickie *familiar or joc* a woman.

leddy a lady.

†lede *chf alliterative verse* a person; a man. **all (levand) leidis** *or* **leid** all (living) people, everyone.

leeve live. **leevin** a person, anyone *now local Ork-Gall.*

leuk, look: ~ up be alive: *'had John been looking up to-day'.*

life: in ~ *now Sh midLoth,* **†on ~** alive.

loun a fellow, chap, lad *now N Fif wLoth Wgt.*

†maistres a mistress.

man: ~ body a man as opposed to a woman *local.* **menfolk** men.

manishee a woman *orig gipsy but now also Rox.*

muild, mou(l)d, mool: abune the ~ alive, in this world *Sh Ork NE.*

native the district of one's birth *now NE Ags Dmf.* **† ~ born** born in a country or place.

nick: a ~ in *or* **on one's horn** a year of one's life. **~s** age or experience.

out *esp of one's age* fully, quite: *now NE: 'I'm fifty oot'.* **~leeve** outlive.

parson a person.

past having reached a specified age on one's last birthday: *'Wee Bob's nine past'.*

†quick living, alive.

†schalk a man.

†seck, sect sex, gender.

shither people *Cai.*

skirt a woman.

teenie-bash familiar, *freq* derog form of reference for a woman *EC*.

tike *playfully* a fellow, chap *now N*.

time: this side of ~ in this world, while life lasts *now Sh NE Ayr*.

tuip, tup familiar or disparaging term for a man *now Cai*.

†**vieve** alive.

wicht *freq with contempt or pity* a human being, person.

wife, wifie, wifock, wifockie *chf N* a woman *in gen, now chf disparaging and only* a middle-aged or older woman.

wizzen, wazzin *now Sh Ork Cai* the breath, life itself *now local Sh-Abd*.

woman, wumman, *also* ~**-body** a woman. **women-folk** women. †**on** ~**-wayis** after the manner of a woman or women.

†**wye 1** a man, a person *in gen*. **2** a woman, a lady.

8.2 OLD AGE

†**auld birkie** *colloq* old boy.

†**bever hair** a trembling old man.

bodach *freq contemptuous* an old man *now Cai*.

brae: go *etc* **down the** ~ *of an old person* fail physically.

brolach an old person *now Bnf*.

cailleach an old woman *chf Highl N, WC Uls*.

callan(d) affectionate or familiar term for an older man *now Abd Ags*.

carline *freq derog* a (*usu* old) woman *now Bnf Abd Fif*.

claw: not ~ **an auld man's heid** fail to live to a ripe old age *local*.

creep thegither shrink, huddle up with age.

daver be in one's dotage *now Bnf*.

deem an elderly woman *now Abd*.

doitered witless, confused from old age *now Fif*.

dottered *adj, also* †**dotit** stupid, enfeebled in mind, *chf* from old age. **dotterel** a dotard *now Stlg*. **dottle** †*adj* in a state of dotage, witless. *v* be in or fall into a state of dotage, become crazy *Cai Bnf Abd Ags*.

eild *n* old age. †*v* grow old. ~**it** aged.

elder, eldren old.

get, git: ~ **up in years** grow old.

†**glyde** an old, useless or disagreeable person.

grannie mutch(ie) nickname for an old woman *NE-WC*.

has-been someone past his or her best.

heuk, hook contemptuous term for an old woman *NE*.

†**hogeart** ? a tired-out old man.

horn: lang in the ~ *C*, **auld in the** ~ advanced in years and experience.

kail-runt contemptuous term *esp* for an old woman *Ags Fif Gall*.

long-teethed aged *Abd Ags*.

mutch an old woman *Fif SW*.

old foggie an old decrepit person.

†**rigwiddie** *esp of an old woman* wizened, gnarled, tough and rugged-looking, mis-shapen.

ripe advanced in years.

†**ruddoch** term of contempt for a (bad-tempered) old person.

superannuate senile *now Fif*.

tike-auld very old *now NE*.

turn, tirn: ~ **ower in** *or* **tae years** grow old, age *NE Ags Fif*.

up, up in life, up in years advanced in years, elderly.

veeand in one's dotage *S*.

veed in one's dotage, senile *S*.

warlock *term of abuse* an old, ugly or misanthropic man.

wear: ~ **doun (the brae)** grow old *now Ork Abd*. ~ **on** *now Ork Ags*, ~ **ower** *Sh Abd* be advancing in age, grow older.

8.3 MATURITY

auld, old: ~ **young** middle-aged, mature *now Sh*.

better: (on the) ~ **side (of)** older or younger than *Bnf Abd*.

clockin hen 1 a woman past the age of childbearing *now Loth Kcb*. **2** a woman during the time of bearing and rearing a family *now Bnf Stlg*.

cummer, kimmer a married woman, a wife.

†**Dumbarton youth** a person (*usu* a woman) over thirty-five years old.

†**eild** mature or legal age, full age.

green young, youthful, full of vitality *now local Abd-Uls*. †**keep the banes** ~ preserve good health and youthfulness.

man: ~**-big,** ~**-grown,** ~**-length** *local C,* ~**-muckle** *now Arg SW, S* grown to manhood, adult. ~ **body** an adult man *local*. ~**heid** manhood *now Bnf*. ~**nie,** ~**nikie** *disparaging when used of an adult* a little man *now local*.

†**mid** of medium age. ~**-age(d)** middle age(d).

muckle, mickle, meikle full-grown, adult *now*

Sh Ork NE Kcb. **man** *or* **woman** ~ grown-up now *Clcm Kcb Rox.*

†ripe fully developed mentally or physically.

up, up in life, up in years *of a child growing up* adult, advanced in years.

weel-hained well preserved, in good shape.

wife, wifie, wifock, wifockie *chf N now chf disparaging* a middle-aged or older woman.

woman, wumman: ~**-grown** *now Sh Per,* ~**-length** *Sh Ags Loth,* ~**-muckle** *now Cai Stlg Lnk* grown to womanhood, adult.

youthie young, youthful, looking younger than one is *now Ork.*

8.4 YOUTH, ADOLESCENCE

†bairn a youth, young person. **barnage** youth.

big yins older children *local.*

blinker a lively attractive girl.

†callan a girl *Gall.*

callan(d) an associate; a youth, fellow.

†callet disparaging term for a girl.

chiel(d) 1 *also* **childe** *literary* a lad, (young) man, fellow. 2 a young woman *now Fif.*

come tae grow up *chf Bnf Abd.*

cowt an adolescent boy or girl *now Bnf.*

cummer, kimmer a girl, lass *now Bnf.*

daft days a time of frivolity and fun; *hence* one's youth *now Bnf Abd Edb.*

dame, *also* **damie** *now Ags* a young (unmarried) woman *now Bnf Abd Ags.*

damishell a damsel *now Abd.*

deem a young woman; an unmarried woman *now Ross Bnf Abd.*

dosh term of endearment for a girl *now Sh Abd.*

eild: within ~ under age.

†foichal a girl from sixteen to twenty years of age.

gillie 1 a lad, youth. 2 a flighty girl.

gilly-gawkie a silly young person, *esp* a girl *chf SW-S.*

gilpie 1 †a lively, mischievous youth. 2 a lively young girl, a tomboy.

gilpin a well-grown young person *chf N, SW.*

hairy *somewhat derog* a young woman: 'a wee hairy' *chf Abd Gsw.*

halflin(g), †halflang, halflong *n* a half-grown boy, an adolescent youth. *adj, also* **halflins** half-grown, young.

hallock a thoughtless giddy young woman or girl or *occas* young man *now NE Rox.*

†haspan a young lad, a stripling *S.*

hempie *joc* a mischievous or unruly young person, *now esp* a girl *now local.*

†hensure ? a swaggering young fellow.

†hind a youth, a stripling.

ill guided badly brought up *now Dmf.*

jilt contemptuous term for a girl or young woman.

†kell a caul, a woman's ornamental hairnet or cap; when worn alone, the distinctive head-dress of a young unmarried woman *latterly ballad.*

kelp 1 *chf* ~**ie** a mischievous young person *S.* 2 a big raw-boned youth *NE Ags.*

kittie familiar or contemptuous term for a woman or girl, *specif* a giddy, skittish young woman *Sh NE.*

knap a sturdy lad *now NE.*

knipe a lad *now Bnf.*

lad, lawd *now C, n, also* **laddie** *Gen except Sh Ork,* **lathie** *now Ags* a youth. ~ **o pairts** a promising boy, a talented youth.

lass, lassie, lassock, lassickie 1 a girl. 2 an unmarried woman, a maiden.

look ower the nest *of a young person* begin to act independently *SW, S.*

loun a boy or youth as opposed to a **lassie** or **quine** *N Fif.*

maukin an awkward, half-grown girl.

†mayock ? a little maiden.

Meg a rather unsophisticated girl, *esp* a rough country girl.

†peronall a young woman.

poutie a term of affection for a young person, *freq* a young girl.

†puber a youth, a person between the age of puberty and maturity.

quine, †quean a young (*chf* unmarried) woman, a girl *now NE Ags.*

scargivenet a skinny adolescent.

shanker a young active person *Mry Abd.*

skeer, skeerie *now local, of a girl* flighty, skittish.

†skilt a flighty, giddy young person, a gadabout.

snuid, snood a ribbon etc bound round the brow and tied at the back under the hair, worn *esp* by young unmarried women.

†spink an attractive young person.

spunkie a spirited, lively young person *now NE, C.*

†stibblart a young lad, a (half-grown) youth *Abd.*

strip *n, chf* ~ **of a laddie** *etc* a young fellow, a youth *now Ork Lnk.*

taid, toad term of endearment for a young woman *now NE Ags.*

taupie a giddy, scatterbrained, untidy, awkward or careless young woman *Gen except Sh Ork.*

teenie-bash familiar, *freq derog* form of reference for a girl *EC*.

trimmie a pert, impudent girl, a hussy.

upcomin(g) one's upbringing, development from childhood to adulthood *now Sh*.

wear up grow, advance in age *now Sh NE*.

winch a wench *now local N-S*.

†winklot a wench.

young, †ying young.

younker a youngster, a young lad or girl, a youth *now N, EC Ayr*.

youthheid, youdith *chf literary* 1 youth, the state or time of youth *now literary*. 2 †young people.

youthie young, youthful *now Ork*.

8.5 CHILDHOOD, INFANCY

For 'daughter' and 'son', see 8.11.

ancient, auncient *of children* precocious; having the ways or intelligence of an adult.

†attingent being near or close in age or relationship.

auld-farrant, auld-farran, auld-fashioned, old-fashioned having the ways or shrewdness of older persons; precocious.

babby a baby.

bairn a child or infant. **†barnage** childhood. ∼**heid** childhood, infancy. ∼**ie** a little child.

bed put (children) to bed.

bilch, belge contemptuous term for a child.

bird 1 a term of endearment, *esp* to children. 2 *orig only in verse, latterly chf familiar or disparaging* a girl.

blastie a bad-tempered, unmanageable child *now Bnf Gsw*.

blaud spoil (a child).

boyackie a little boy *Cai Abd*.

breek: ∼**um(s)** affectionate term for a little boy *now Bnf*. †∼**umstoich** a small stout child in breeches.

†brod, brude, brood a young child, the youngest of a family.

bubble weep in a snivelling, blubbering way.

†callan a girl *Gall*.

chappie a little boy.

chiel(d) a child *now local*.

chile *now chf Abd*, **chillie** *Abd* a child. **childer** children.

claik cry incessantly and impatiently *chf NE*.

clip a pert or mischievous child, *chf* a girl *now local NE-SW*. ∼**pie** a pert, sharp-tongued girl *now Ags*.

cockie-bendie *affectionate* a small boy *local*. **cocky-breeky, cock-a-breeky** a small boy, *esp* one who has just been put into trousers *chf Bnf Abd*.

cowlie a boy *Edb*.

crowl a (*freq* tiny) child.

cutty 1 a short, dumpy girl *now Ags*. 2 affectionate name for a child. 3 a mischievous or disobedient girl.

diddle dandle (a child).

dirt contemptuous (*now chf* offensive) term for a troublesome child *now local Bnf-Kcb*.

doo familiar term of endearment for a child.

eeshan *freq derog or playful* a small child *local Cai-Abd*.

faggot term of abuse for a child implying exasperating behaviour.

flairdie a wheedling child *SW*.

fortifee, fortify pet, pamper, spoil (a child) *NE*.

get, git, gyte a child *now local N-S*. ∼**ling** *also abusive* a young child, an infant.

girnie-gib a fretful, bad-tempered child *now Bwk Uls*.

glaikit *of a child* over-fond, clinging *now Fif*.

gorb an infant, young child *now Dmf*.

gorlin a very young person, an urchin *now Kcb*.

gowds pet name for a child *Cai*.

grannie('s) bairn a grandchild, *esp* reared by its grandmother and spoilt *now Abd Ags Rox*.

guddle play messily *now Abd Dmf*.

guide treat, use, handle, care for (persons (*esp*) children). †∼**r** a person put in charge of the guidance and upbringing of a child or young person.

hippin a baby's nappie.

hurb *joc, of a child* a rascal *NE*.

karriewhitchit a term of endearment for a child *Abd Ags*.

kempie a lively child *now Bnf*.

†knave bairn, knave child a male child.

knee hicht a small child, one no higher than the knee *Sh Ork Dmf*.

knip a little, mischievous boy or girl *N*.

lad, lawd *now C, n, also* **laddie** *Gen except Sh Ork*, **lathie** *now Ags* a male child. **laddie wean** a boy.

lambie, my wee lamb affectionate term of address to a child.

lane, lone *of a child learning to walk* unaided.

lass, lassie, lassock, lassickie, lassie wean a girl. **lasslike** girlish, like a girl.

limmer *of a mischievous child* a rascal, rogue *now local*.

linkie a lightfooted girl *S*.

lintie a sprightly, merry girl *now Loth Rox Uls*.

little: littlin, ~ ane, ~ one, ~ body *Ags Fif Uls* a child, an infant *now N nEC.*

loun 1 boy as opposed to a **lassie** or **quine** *N Fif.* **2** *of a boy* a young scamp, a mischievous rogue *now Ags midLoth.*

lovie *child's word* a hug *local NE-Kcb.*

†**maiden barne** a female child.

mammie-keekie a spoilt indulged child *Lnk Dmf S.*

man: **~ bairn** a male child *now C.* **~nie, ~nikie** *affectionate* a small boy.

minnie's bairn a mother's pet *now Ags.*

mither: **~'s bairn** a spoilt, indulged child. **~'s pet** the youngest child of a family.

†**nacket** a boy, youngster.

newser *of a child* a good talker *Sh N.*

nickit: as auld farrant as a ~ bake *(wLoth Kcb)* or **bap** *(Bnf) of a child* old-fashioned, quaint.

paidling toddling, waddling.

palaver, palaiver waste time, trifle, make a great deal of a small task, *freq* of a child, delaying bedtime *now Sh Per WC.*

peat a term of endearment for a child *now Abd.*

peenge a fretful child *Fif S.*

penurious, perneurious *freq of a child* bad-tempered, whining *NE.*

peppint petted, spoilt, pampered *Mry Bnf.*

pet, †**carlingis pet** a petted or spoilt child.

pin, peen a small child *Bnf Abd.*

†**podlie** term of affection for a child.

posy term of endearment for a child *now WC Kcb.*

poutie a term of affection for a child.

pud a term of endearment for a child *Fif wLoth Lnk.*

†**puddock: be in the ~ hair** be very young, be an infant.

quine, †**quean** a female child, a girl up to the end of her schooldays *now NE Ags.*

reuch, rough: ~ie a wild rough boy *N.*

†**rocker** a nurse or attendant whose duty it was to rock a child in its cradle.

royet, †**troyd** wild, unruly, mischievous *now local Sh-Fif.*

rummle, rumble a rough reckless boy *WC, SW.*

scroosh *freq disparaging* a large number of children, a worthless lot.

skellum *playfully to a boy* a scamp, rogue, scoundrel.

†**skelpie (limmer)** a naughty, mischievous girl.

smatche(r)t a pert or mischievous child, a little rogue *now Sh Ork N.*

smool a small child *Gen except Sh Ork.*

smytrie *contemptuous* a collection of children *now Bnf Abd.*

sonsie *of young children* chubby, sturdy.

souk, suck: ~ie *contemptuous* a petted or over-indulged child *now local Cai-SW.* **~-the-pappie** *contemptuous* a fairly old but babyish child, a 'big baby' *local Cai-Kcb.*

sprout a child *now local Bnf-S.*

sprug a bright but undersized boy *Cai Fif Lnk.*

spug, speug a child *now Per.*

steering active, restless, lively.

stirk: be (putten) in the ~(ie)'s sta *etc, of a child* be supplanted in its parents' attention by the birth of a new baby *local N-S.*

stourie *of a young child* active, restless *now Ags Fif WC.*

strange, strynge shy, self-conscious.

strip, *chf* **~ of a laddie** *etc* a young fellow, a youth *now Ork Lnk.*

swarrach a crowd, swarm (of young children in a family) *NE.*

taid, toad term of endearment for a child *now NE Ags.*

tak, take: ~ aff *now Sh Ags,* **tak o** *now Ork Cai* take after, resemble.

teedy cross, fractious; bad-tempered *now Wgt.*

tent tend, take charge of, look after (children) *now Wgt.*

tike *playfully* a mischievous child *now N.*

toddle *v, of a young child* walk with short, rocking, uncertain or unsteady steps. †*n* a toddler, toddling child.

tot(t)ie a small child, toddler.

totum a small child, a little tot *now local N-Lnk.*

tout(er) cry, sob.

trooshter *contemptuous* troublesome children *now Ross.*

trout(ie) term of endearment to a child *local Bnf-Dmf.*

truaghan *joc* a small child *now Cai.*

twa year'l *Sh Ork,* **twa year al(d)** *Ayr* a two-year-old.

upbring training, education, maintenance during childhood *Sh NE Fif Dnbt.* **~ing** rearing, nurture, early training.

upfeshin upbringing, the rearing and training of young people *chf NE.*

warld, world: weel *or* **wise and ~-like** *or* **~(-like) and wise-like** *of a new-born baby* normal physically and mentally *now local.*

warrior, *freq* **a great ~** *joc* or affectionate term for a lively, spirited child.

waw caterwaul, wail *now Ork NE.*

wean a child, *esp* a young one *now C.*

wee: † **~ ane** a young child, a little one. **~ thing**

a small child. ~ **Macwhachle** *joc* a toddling infant *WC*. ~ **yins** younger children *local*.

wench, winch a little girl *now local N-S*.

whick(er) whimper intermittently in a subdued way.

whinge, wheenge whine, whimper, fret whiningly *now NE-WC, S*.

whink a child's sharp cry, a whimper *now Slk*.

†**whippie** term of a abuse for a girl, a hussy.

wick a naughty child *now Abd EC Ayr*.

wife, wifie, wifock, wifockie *chf N* a little girl.

wirl, wurl *applied to a mischievous child* a young scamp, a wicked creature *Fif Slk*.

†**woman bairn** a female child, a girl.

wran term of endearment to a child.

year aul(d) year-old.

yip *of a child* a cheeky, pert person, an imp *chf Rox*.

younker a youngster, a young lad or girl *now N, EC Ayr*.

8.6 PREGNANCY, BIRTH, CHRISTENING

Includes midwives. For physical aspects, see also 9.16; for christening services, see 14.1.9.

bairn make pregnant.

†**biggen** be pregnant.

blithemeat 1 a thanksgiving feast after the birth of a child *now Lnk*. **2** food given to people in a house at the time of a birth *now Lnk*.

bouk(in) pregnant.

ca(ll): ~ **someone for** name someone after *now local*.

canny: ~ **moment** the moment of childbirth. ~ **wife** a midwife *now Abd Fif*.

coat: hae one's ~ **kilted, gae** ~**s kilted** be pregnant *local C*.

come hame be born *now Bnf Ags*.

coup the creels *of a woman* have an illegitimate child *now Fif*.

cry call, give a name to *chf WC*. **be cried** be in labour *now Bnf Abd Fif*. ~**ing** labour; a confinement *now NE*. ~**ing cheese** a cheese specially made at a birth *NE*.

†**cude** a chrisom-cloth.

cummer, kimmer 1 a godmother (*orig* in relation to the parents and other godparents). **2** a midwife. †~ **fealls** an entertainment at the birth of a child

†**deliver** delivered (of a child).

†**depairt** *of a woman* give birth.

doon, down: ~**-lyin** confinement, lying-in, *chf* **at the** ~**-lyin** about to be confined.

†**dreaming bread** wedding or christening cake, so-called because the recipients slept with a piece under their pillow.

fa(ll): ~ take to one's bed through childbirth *NE*. **fa wi bairn** *or* **child** become pregnant.

first fit the first person (or animal) met on a journey, *esp* by a wedding or christening party on the way to church *now Cai Abd Stlg*.

foster *chf of a mother suckling her offspring* feed, nourish *local Sh-Abd*.

get, git, gyte 1 †begetting, birth. **2** offspring, progeny *now local N-S*.

†**green**[1] *of a woman* recently delivered.

green[2] *of a pregnant woman* have a craving (**for** particular foods) *now Mry Kcb*.

†**groaning malt** ale brewed to celebrate a birth.

half, hauf: ~ **gone** about the middle period of pregnancy *now local*.

hame, home *of birth* into the world, *freq of the mother or midwife* **bring** *etc* ~, *of the child* **come** ~ *now local Abd-S*. ~**coming** the festivities that take place on the occasion of a birth.

haud, hald, hold: ~ **up** present (a child) for baptism *now Abd*.

heavy, heavy-footed, heavy o the fit pregnant; in an advanced state of pregnancy.

hole: in the ~ on the point of childbirth *now Abd Fif*.

hoo: hallie ~, **seely** ~ the caul sometimes on the head of a new-born child, regarded as a good omen.

howdie *n, also* ~ **wife** *now local Cai-Lnk* a midwife. ~**ing 1** a confinement *now Lnk Kcb*. **2** midwifery *now Edb*.

hun(d)er: get a ~ **pound** enjoy a birth in the family *local Abd-midLoth*.

inlying *n* a lying-in, confinement *now local*. *adj* confined, in childbed *now local*.

kirk: be ~**it** be churched, of the first church attendance after a birth. ~**in** such a ceremonial attendance at church. ~**in feast** a celebration held after the **kirkin**.

kirsten to christen. ~**ing** christening. **christening bit** *or* **piece** = **baby's piece** *chf Edb*.

kittle *contemptuously, of a woman* give birth.

†**laggin-gird: cast a** ~ bear an illegitimate child.

lichter delivered of a child.

†**maiden cummer** a young woman who acted as attendant to the mother at a christening.

†**mam 1** a wet-nurse. **2** a midwife.

†**medwyfe** a midwife.

†**merry meat** a meal to celebrate the birth of a child.

†**milk wife** a wet nurse.

miscairry 1 to miscarry. **2** be pregnant when unmarried *now Sh.*

muckle, mickle, meikle: ~ **boukit** pregnant *now local Sh-wLoth.*

name: ~ **dochter,** ~ **son** a girl or boy who has been called after someone *now Sh Ork.* ~ **faither,** ~ **mother** the man or woman after whom someone is named. **get the** ~ have a child named after one. **gie (a bairn) its** *or* **a** ~ christen (a child).

nourice a child's nurse, *esp* a wet-nurse or foster-mother *latterly chf literary and ballad.* † ~ **fee** the wages given to a wet-nurse *NE.* † ~**s(c)hip** the occupation or post of **nourice.**

original, oreeginal 1 origin, birth, descent *now Abd.* **2** birthplace *now Abd.*

pairt wi bairn *or* **child** give birth to a premature or stillborn baby; suffer a miscarriage *now Sh NE Uls.*

†**pap-bairn** a child at the breast, a suckling.

road: on the ~ pregnant *NE-S.*

†**saving** a kind of juniper which produces an abortifacient drug, *freq* ~ **tree.**

shae, shoe: cast a ~ have an illegitimate child *now Ayr.*

shour, shower a pang or paroxysm of pain at childbirth.

shout *of a woman* be in labour, give birth *now Kcb.* ~**ing** childbirth; a merrymaking to celebrate it.

slip an abortion, miscarriage *local Cai-Dnbt.*

strae: in the ~ in childbed.

threeplet one of three born together, a triplet *N-S.*

trout: there's a ~**(ie) in the well** said of a woman expecting a child, *esp* if illegitimate *now Abd.*

†**upsetting** a woman's first receiving of visitors after giving birth.

weet the bairn's heid toast the health of a new-born baby.

8.7 DEATH, BURIAL

Covers death in general and any manner of death not dealt with elsewhere (such as violent death in 12.13. For religious services, see 14.1.9.

†**ablach** a mangled carcass.

aff, off: ~**gaun, offgoing** death.

†**aisle** an enclosed and covered burial place, adjoining a church, though not a part of it.

awa, away, *also* ~ **wi't** dead.

banshee a female spirit, *freq* connected with a family, whose wail was thought to forecast death or disaster.

beddal, beadle a gravedigger.

beerie bury.

†**bell-penny** money set aside to pay for one's funeral.

†**beris** *n* a burying place; a burial. *v* bury.

†**bing** a funeral pile.

blacks mourning clothes *chf NE.*

bouk the body of a person (living or dead).

buird a board for laying out a corpse; a bier *now Bnf Abd.*

burial, bural, beerial *NE* a burial: **1** †a burying place. **2** an interment; a funeral; *latterly esp* the occasion accompanying the interment. † ~ **silver** money for a funeral. † ~ **yard** burial ground. **burial letter** an intimation of or invitation to a funeral *now Cai Kcb.*

†**caip: a** ~ **of leid** a lead coffin.

cairn a pyramid of loose stones as a memorial, marking a grave.

†**carcage** a corpse.

challenge a summons by death *Bnf Abd.*

clap bury (a person) *now Sh.*

†**clinkum** a bellman, town-crier, also functioning as gravedigger.

corbie: be a gone ~ be a goner, be done for.

cord one of the ropes (held by close relatives and friends of the deceased) by which a coffin is lowered into the grave.

coronach a funeral lament or outcry; a dirge.

corp 1 a corpse. **2 the** ~ deceased *local Bnf-Lnk.*

coup the creels die.

†**cow** a cow given as a payment to the clergy on the death and burial of a householder.

†**craip** a band of crape on an article of dress.

†**croce-present** a gift due to the clergy from the goods of a householder on his death and burial.

crock *slang* die, croak *local Ork-Stlg.*

deen: be ~ **wi it** be dying *Bnf-Stlg.*

daith death.

†**deces** *v* decease.

dee die.

deid, dead *adj* dead. *n* **1** death. **2** the cause of (someone's) death. †**deadal** *esp of funeral garments* connected with death. ~**ly** deadly. ~ **box** *now Cai Fif Renfr,* ~-**kist,** † ~ **chist** a coffin. ~-**claes** a shroud *now Abd Ags Fif.* ~-**deal** the board on which a corpse is laid *now Fif.* ~-**house**

1 a mortuary *now Abd Fif*. 2 †a grave. †**tak (the) dede** die.

delf a grave *now Cai*.

†**dirgie, dregy** 1 a dirge. 2 a funeral feast, *esp* of drink.

†**dool, dule** *n, also* ~ **habit,** ~ **weeds** mourning clothes. *v* lament, mourn. ~ **string** a piece of black crepe worn round the hat as a sign of mourning.

†**drint** drowned.

droon drown.

eard bury. †**erd-** *or* **erthe-silver** payment for burial-ground.

en(d) die. † ~**day** the last day of one's life.

†**enel-sheet** a winding sheet, shroud.

far, faur: ~ **throu** very ill, at death's door.

†**ferter** a bier.

†**fey** leading to death; fatal. ~ **token** a sign of approaching death.

†**fir fecket** a coffin.

flit die.

funeral, fooneral *S* a funeral. ~ **cairn** a cairn to mark resting places for the bearers on the way to the graveyard *Highl*.

gae, go: †**gaun gear** applied to persons in declining health, *esp* those about to die *NE, SW*. ~ **awa** die *Ork NE, S*.

get, git: ~ **awa(y)** die *local Bnf-S*.

Giant's Grave popular name for the ruins of a neolithic chambered tomb *local*.

graff, graife a grave.

graft a grave *chf sEC, S*.

grapple drag (water) for a corpse *local NE-Uls*.

grave bury (a corpse), inter.

grun(d), ground (the) ground reserved for the burial of a person or family *Gen except Sh Ork*.

†**gumphion, gunfioun** a funeral banner.

hame, home: ~**-gaun** death; the burial of the dead *local*. **gae, gang** ~ die.

han(d), haun(d): ~**spaik** a spoke or bar of wood used in carrying a coffin. **put** ~ **to, in** *etc* **anesel** commit suicide *now Sh midLoth*.

harrows: die in the ~ die while still working, die in harness *now Cai Abd Per*.

has-been someone no longer existing.

hinderend, hinneren(d) the end of life, death.

†**thirsel aff (the stage)** die peacefully, slip away.

†**howdie (wife)** a woman who lays out the dead.

howf 1 †*also* **holf** a burial ground in the centre of Dundee, *orig* the courtyard of the Greyfriars Monastery. 2 a burial ground, *latterly freq* a private burial ground *now Kcdn Ayr*.

hurl the death rattle *local Ork-NE*.

†**thyne** from this world, from this life.

†**ingrave** bury.

†**inlaik** *n* death. *v* die.

Jenkin's hen: die the death of ~, **die like** ~ die an old maid.

kirk: be ~**it** be churched, of the first church attendance after a funeral. ~**in** such a ceremonial attendance at church. ~**in feast** a celebration held after the **kirkin.** † ~ **hole** the grave(yard) *Lnk Ayr*. † ~ **stile** a stile or narrow entrance to a churchyard, where the bier was received into the churchyard at funerals. ~ **yaird** churchyard.

kist *n* a coffin *Gen except S*. *v* put or enclose in a coffin. ~**in(g)** the laying of a corpse in its coffin on the night before the funeral with accompanying ceremonies and entertainment.

lair *n* a burial place or grave, *specif* a burial space reserved for a person or family in a graveyard or church. *v* bury (a person) *now Ags Fif*. † ~ **silver** the price charged for a **lair** *latterly NE*. ~ **stane** a gravestone *chf NE*.

†**lang, long** *of gravestones* tall.

†**law** a grave-mound.

lay doun lay in the grave, bury *chf NE*.

leckerstane a conspicuous stone or stone-heap, *traditionally* associated with burials *chf NE-nEC, now in place-names*.

leuk, look: ~ **on** wait for the end of (a dying person), be at the deathbed of *now Bwk*. ~ **up** be alive: '*had John been looking up to-day*'.

†**life: out of** ~ lifeless.

lift *v* carry (a corpse) out for burial; start a funeral procession *Gen except Sh Ork*. *n* an act of lifting or assisting to lift in carrying a corpse for a funeral.

†**lig** lie in the grave, be buried.

linens a shroud *now Cai Ags*.

†**losenge, lozen:** ~ **armes** funeral hatchments.

†**louk** close (the eyes of a dead person).

lump: a *or* **the** ~ **of someone's death** the chief cause of or an important factor in someone's death *now Sh Kcb*.

lyke, leek *Sh-Ross* 1 a corpse, an unburied body *now Sh*. 2 *also* ~ **wake,** †**latewake** a vigil kept over a corpse until burial, a wake; *also* the (*freq* large and riotous) gathering on such occasions *chf N*. †**funerall** *or* **dedelie lykis** funeral rites.

mae: be at ane ~ **wi't** be at the point of death *S*.

mauk: as dead as a ~ absolutely lifeless.

†**memore** the fact or state of being remembered (*esp* after one's death), *chf in* ~.

†**mening** a peal of bells rung to commemorate a departed soul.

mort †a dead body. † ~ **bell** the bell rung at

funerals. †~ **chest,** ~ **kist** a coffin. ~ **cloth** a pall covering a coffin on its way to the grave, *latterly chf* hire out by the **kirk session** *now local Sh-Kcb.* †~ **cloths, mortcloth money** the fee received from the hire of **mortcloth.** †~ **hede** a human skull, a death's head. †~ **safe** an iron grid placed over a grave or over the coffin to deter body-snatchers. †~ **stand** a set of ecclesiastical vestments or altar-cloths for funeral services.

muild, mou(l)d, mool the grave. ~**(s) 1** the earth of the grave. **2** †*freq with reference to witchcraft* earth as the remains of a buried corpse. †**muldemeyt** *appar* food sacrificed over a grave.

murn mourn. ~**ings** the black garments worn to show grief. ~**ing letter** a black-edged letter of invitation to a funeral *local Sh-Kcb.* †~**ing string** a black sash or black streamer for a hat etc, worn as a sign of mourning.

†**nicht walk** a wake held at night.

†**obeit (silver)** *after the Reformation* an endowment, or the revenue from it, *orig* intended for the provision of an annual memorial service.

outleeve to outlive.

pail 1 †a cloth for draping a coffin or a corpse, a pall. **2** a hearse.

†**pain: dey in(to) the** ~ die in the attempt.

†**passioun(is) of dede, patient(s) o deed** *or* **death** the death throes, the last agonies.

perish destroy, kill, bring about the destruction of (a person), *latterly freq* ~**ed with cold.**

†**pig** a cinerary urn.

pit, put: ~ **awa** *local N-Uls,* ~ **by** *SW Uls,* ~ **down** *now Cai Abd Uls* bury. ~ **oneself awa** commit suicide.

†**poll penny** a charitable offering made at a funeral etc, as it were on behalf of the deceased.

prap, prop an object set up as a memorial, to mark a grave.

†**prevene** *of death* overtake prematurely.

†**priest: be someone's** ~ cause someone's death, 'be the death of'.

†**relicts** the remains of a dead person.

respeck, respect: show ~ attend the funeral of a friend.

resting stane a stone on the road to a churchyard where the coffin was laid while the bearers rested.

ring in be at death's door *now NE Ags Per.*

ruckle *v, of the breathing of a dying person* make a rattling, gurgling or roaring sound. *n* the death rattle *now Rox.*

server a person who hands round refreshments at a funeral *now SW.*

service the serving of refreshments at a funeral *now nEC Lnk.*

shrood a shroud.

†**shuit, shoot:** ~ **out one's fit** *etc* give a convulsive kick, as in a death agony.

†**shusy** a corpse (*prob orig* female) used for anatomical dissection and demonstration, *esp* one stolen from a grave.

sitting (up) the act of watching over a corpse before burial *now Kcb.*

slip: ~ **away** die quietly. ~ **the grip** *now Abd Ags,* ~ **the timmers** *Bnf Abd* die.

smuir, smoor 1 be choked, suffocated, die from lack of air, *esp* by being buried in a snowdrift. **2** drown in a river or bog.

souch awa breathe one's last *now local Sh-Ayr.*

†**sow** a shroud, winding-sheet.

spaik, spoke one of the bars of wood on which a coffin is carried to the graveside *now Per Kcb Rox.*

†**stang** the sting of death.

†**stap, stop:** ~ **someone's breath** *of death* stifle someone, end someone's life.

†**stent, stint** erect (a tomb).

†**stith** stiff, rigid as in death.

†**stour** a death struggle.

strae, straw: ~ **death** natural death (in one's bed), *freq* **a fair** ~ **death** *now Sh Stlg SW.*

straik lay out (a corpse) *now Ork Ags.*

straucht, straight lay out (a corpse) by straightening the limbs *now NE.* ~**en** straighten the limbs of, lay out (a corpse) *now local NE-SW.* ~**in brod** a streekin buird *now NE Kcb.*

streek lay out (a corpse) *now local Sh-Wgt.* ~**in buird** the board on which a corpse is laid out for burial *now NE.*

†**streetch** lay out (a corpse). ~**ing board** a streekin buird.

†**supercloth** a cloth placed over a corpse.

switter struggle like a drowning person, splash or flounder about.

table stone, tombstone table a horizontal gravestone.

tak, take: ~ **about** prepare (a corpse) for burial *Ork Ross NE.* ~ **one's death** get one's death, die *Sh Abd Ags.*

tear: wi the ~ **in one's ee** in mourning or grief *now Per WC Kcb.*

thratch *v* twist the body about, writhe in the death agony. *n* a jerk, twist of the body in the death agony.

throu(gh) at or near one's end, done for *Sh-C.*

†**throwand** suffering the throes of death.

thruch, trouch, *also* ~ **stane** *now SW Rox* a flat

gravestone, *strictly* one resting on the ground, but also applied to one resting on four feet.

torfle pine away; perish, be lost *S*.

tow a coffin cord *NE*.

towl toll (a bell etc).

†**tramort** a putrefying carcass; a corpse.

†**truff** the turf over a grave; the grave itself.

tyne perish, die *now Sh Bnf Ags*.

†**tyre** inter. ~**ment** interment.

umquhile former, late; *esp law* deceased *now literary or arch*.

under, unner *local*: ~**board** *of a corpse* laid out awaiting burial *now Uls*.

wait be on the point of death *now Cai*.

†**warn** invite to a funeral.

wauk, wake *v* stay up all night with, watch over (a corpse). *n* a vigil over a corpse.

wear awa pass away, die.

wede awa(y) *literary* carry off, remove by death.

weed a shroud.

†**whilom** deceased.

whirken, whurken choke, suffocate *S*.

†**whummle, whammle** *of water* overwhelm, drown.

wi: dee ~ die of.

win awa die, pass away, *esp* after great suffering *Gen except Sh Ork*.

†**win(d)** wrap (a corpse) in a shroud.

wuid, wood: ~**en breeks** *now Per Ayr*, ~**en jeckit** *now Ags Ayr*, ~**en overcoat** *WC* a coffin.

yaird, yard, yird a churchyard *now Ork NE, C*.

yird, yirth †the grave. ~**it** buried. †~ **meel** grave-mould, the dust of the churchyard *Abd*. †**yerd-silver** payment for burial ground.

8.8 COURTSHIP, MARRIAGE

For legal aspects, see 11.12; for religious services, see 14.1.9. Courtship is dealt with here, sex in 8.9, though the dividing line is not clear-cut.

†**allekay** the best man, the bridegroom's attendant *Ags*.

†**amouris** love, lovemaking; love affairs.

auld: ~ **maid's bairn** or **wean** *chf proverb* a hypothetical well-behaved child which a spinster has in mind when criticizing the children of others. ~ **marriet man** a married man from the day after his marriage *local*.

bacheleer a bachelor.

band the marriage bond.

†**bandis** banns of marriage.

†**bedding** the ceremony of putting a bride to bed.

begotted, bigottit infatuated.

begunk cheat, deceive, jilt.

†**belovit, belufit** beloved.

best maid a bridesmaid, *freq* the chief bridesmaid.

bid invite (to a wedding etc).

bidie-in, bide-in a person who lives with another of the opposite sex without marriage *Abd*.

billy a lover.

bode, bod an invitation to a wedding *now Sh*.

bowl-money money thrown to children at a wedding *now Kcb*.

boy a bachelor of any age still living with his parents.

†**breek brother** a rival in love.

bride: ~**(s)cake** wedding cake, *orig* a homemade one which was broken over the head of the bride. †~**'s pie** a pie made by the bride's friends and distributed among the company at a wedding.

†**brithal** bridal.

broose a race at a country wedding from the church or the bride's home to the bridegroom's home, *freq* **ride, rin** or **win the** ~.

browden be fond (of) *now Bnf Abd Fif*. ~ **on** enamoured, extremely fond of *now Bnf*.

buckle join or be joined in marriage. ~**-(the)-beggar(s)** a person who performs irregular marriage ceremonies.

buik, book, beuk record the names of (a betrothed couple) in the register of the **session clerk** before marriage *Bnf Abd Ags*.

built: be ~ **up on** be wrapped up in, devoted to (someone) *NE, C*.

bun(d) shafe someone engaged to be married *Abd*.

bundling a form of courtship in which the partners lie in bed together with their clothes on *Sh Hebrides*.

cantrag a festivity to celebrate a forthcoming marriage *Cai*.

chap a lover *N Fif Kcb*.

cheek up till make amorous approaches to *local Cai-Kcb*.

cheep(er) a light kiss *local C*.

cleek, click 1 ensnare, 'hook' (a man) *Bnf Fif*. 2 find oneself a sweetheart *midLoth*.

clockin the desire to marry.

come aifter court, seek in marriage *NE*.

cottar a married farmworker who has a cottage as part of his contract.

court, coort court, *latterly freq* ~ **wi**.

creeling any of various customs to which a newly-married man may be subject, *freq* involving carrying a **creel** *local C*.

creep-at-even someone out late courting *Bnf Abd*.

cruik, crook: tak up wi the ~it stick accept an inferior suitor *now Ags*.

cry: be cried have one's marriage banns proclaimed *Gen except Sh Cai*. **cries** the proclamation of banns, *chf* **gie** *or* **pit in the cries** *now Cai-Fif Kcb*.

†cuittle, cuttle *v* cuddle, caress *SW*.

daft (aboot, for, on) extremely fond of, crazy about.

dame a (farmer's) wife, housewife *now Bnf Abd Fif*.

daut 1 a caress. **2** *also* **~ie** *now local Bnf-Lnk* a darling *now Cai*.

dintit: be ~ be pierced with Cupid's arrow *SW Uls*.

†divortioun a divorce.

doo familiar term of endearment for a sweetheart.

†dote *n* a dowry. *v* provide (a woman) with a dowry.

†dowariar, drowiar a dowager.

†doxie *verse* a sweetheart.

†dreaming bread wedding cake, so-called because the recipients slept with a piece under their pillow.

ee, eye regard, liking, craving: *'you wi a lang ee till another lad.'*

†drowry love, a love-token.

†drurie a dowry *latterly only ballad*.

†enbrace *v* embrace.

†even (someone) to (someone) talk of (someone) as a possible marriage match for (someone).

fain 1 loving, affectionate, amorous. **2** fond **of** *now Sh Ork*. **~ness** liking, love *now Sh*.

fa(ll) on start courting (with) *now Bnf*.

feet-washin(g) the ceremony of washing the feet of a bridegroom or bride, performed by friends on the eve of the wedding *local NE-SW*.

first fit, first foot the first person (or animal) met by a wedding party on the way to church *now Cai Abd Stlg*.

fling jilt *now NE Fif*. **get** *or* **gie someone the ~** be jilted or jilt someone *now NE midLoth Bwk*.

†flird ? talk idly, flirt.

floan *chf of a woman towards men* show affection, *esp* in a sloppy way *Abd*.

fond foolishly keen, infatuated, doting.

forgaither come together in marriage, get married *Abd*.

foy a party to celebrate a marriage etc *local*.

free single, unmarried *now local NE-midLoth*.

furth, forth: ~going the feast given at a bride's departure from her parents' home, a wedding entertainment.

fyke: haud *or* **hae a ~** flirt, have an affair.

gae go: ~ thegither 1 †get married. **2** *of lovers* court. **~ wi** keep company with, court (a lover).

gallant to flirt. **† ~ish** *of women* flirtatious, ostentatious.

gang together get married *Sh Abd*.

garten: get (gie *or* **wear) the green ~** of an older sister or brother when a younger sibling marries first *local Abd-Fif*.

gawk to flirt *now Ags*.

geck 1 turn the head in a coquettish way *now Abd Ags*. **2** †sport, dally.

get, git marry, get for a spouse.

glaik trifle or flirt (with). **† ~it** flirtatious.

†govan, govie flighty, coquettish.

gowds pet name for a married woman *Cai*.

†gree a degree of relationship. **within ~ (defendand)** within the forbidden degrees.

Gretna Green the village in Dmf noted for the marriages of runaway couples, which were celebrated by the blacksmith over his anvil.

guid, good: ~man 1 the head of a household *now local*. **2** a husband. **~wife 1** *freq as a polite term of address* the mistress of a house, a wife or woman in this capacity. **2** a wife *now local*.

gunk *n, freq* **do a ~ (on someone), gie (someone) the ~** disappoint; jilt *now local Pbls-Uls*. *v* disappoint, humiliate; jilt *now Uls*.

gyte made or crazy with longing or desire, love-sick, eager *now local Ork-midLoth*.

half, hauf: ~-marrow a marriage partner *now Ags*. **† ~-merk** a half **merk**, the coin, as the fee or symbol for a clandestine marriage, *freq* **~-merk marriage, ~-merk church**.

hame, home: ~coming the festivities that take place on the arrival of a bride at her new home. **~-fare** the journey of a bride to her new home; the festivities on that occasion *now Sh Ork*.

†han(d), haun(d): ~fast 1 betroth (two persons, *or* one **with** another) by joining of hands. **2** become engaged to marry, *esp* agree to a probationary period of cohabitation with (someone) before marriage. **~fasting** betrothal; trial marriage.

haud hald, hold: ~ up to court, make up to *now Abd Ayr*.

†hause, hals embrace, take in one's arms.

he used by a wife of her husband.

†heary expression of endearment, *esp* used by married couples to each other.

hert-likin affection, love *now Sh Abd*.

hind a married skilled farmworker who occupies a farm-cottage, and has certain perquisites in addition to wages, a **cottar** *chf S*.

hing, hang: be hung have the notice of one's

intention to marry displayed on a registrar's notice board, instead of having the banns read in church *now EC, S*. ~ **in** pay court assiduously, persist in courting someone *chf Abd*. **hing-tee** a mistress, girlfriend *N*.

†**hizzie, hussy 1** a housewife. **2** the mistress of a household.

†**howtowdie** an unmarried woman.

†**infare** the feast given by the bridegroom to celebrate the coming of his bride to her new home. **infar cake** a piece of oatcake or shortbread broken over the head of a bride as she enters her new home.

irregular marriage a marriage contracted without a religious ceremony or formal civil procedure.

jillet a flighty girl, a flirt.

jink *v* flirt *now Cai Kcb Rox*.

jo 1 *term of endearment* sweetheart, darling, dear, *chf* **my ~**. **2** *now chf verse* a sweetheart, lover, *usu* male.

†**kid** *v* flirt.

†**kipple** marry.

kirk: be ~**it** be churched, of the first church attendance after a marriage. ~**in** such a ceremonial attendance at church. ~**in feast** a celebration held after the **kirkin**.

†**kirr** amorous.

†**knit** join in marriage.

lad, lawd *now C*, **laddie** *Gen except Sh Ork*, **lathie** *now Ags* **1** a bachelor *now Cai*. **2** a male sweetheart.

lane, lone: his *etc* ~, **him** *etc* ~ *chf Sh NE* without a mate or companion, on his etc own, solitary.

lass, lassie, lassock, lassickie a sweetheart. **lad and** ~ a pair of sweethearts.

†**lawin** a contribution towards the refreshments at a wedding.

leal faithful, constant in love *now chf verse*. † ~ **love** one's true love, sweetheart.

†**lent: be** ~ *of the affections* have lighted **apon**.

like love, have a strong affection for (a person of the opposite sex).

lock *v* embrace *Sh Ags*.

logan *n* coins scattered for children to scramble for *Abd*. *v* scatter (coins) as at a wedding *Abd*.

†**lucky** a wife, a married woman.

luve, love, loo *v, only verse* love. *n* love. **lovie** a sweetheart, lover *local NE-Kcb*. ~ **blenk,** ~**-blink** a loving or amorous glance. †**lufe-drowry** a love-token. †**luverent** the state or condition of loving or of being loved, love, affection, friendship.

maiden an unmarried woman, a spinster *now NE*.

mairriage, marriage marriage. ~ **braws** wedding clothes *NE-WC*. † ~ **gere,** ~ **gude** a marriage portion or dowry *N*. ~ **lintel** *Fif Kcb*, ~ **stone** *Bnf Fif* the lintel stone of a door bearing the initials and date of marriage (*usu* of the 17th or 18th centuries) of a couple who have set up house there.

mairry marry. ~ **on,** †**upon, with** marry to.

†**maison** a household, family.

†**maistres** a mistress.

mak it up plan to get married.

†**make** *n* a spouse, mate *chf verse*. *v* mate; match.

man a husband.

march: gang ower the ~ *usu of a couple from England coming to be married according to the speedier and less formal procedure of Scots law* elope *Rox*.

marrow *n* a marriage-partner, spouse *now chf literary*. *v*, *also* ~ **wi** marry. ~**less** unmarried *now Ags*. **ill-~ed** of marriage partners ill-matched *Sh NE*.

†**matermony** matrimony.

†**matronize** *v* chaperon.

†**menyie** a family, household.

mercat the marriage market, *chf* **make (one's)** ~ find a husband or wife, become engaged to be married.

mink an entanglement, snare; matrimony *Abd Ags*.

mird have dealings or association **with** sport, dally **with** *chf NE*.

mismarrow mismatch, join together although incompatible. ~**ed** mismatched, ill-assorted *Sh Bnf Lnk*.

mistress 1 designation of one's own or another person's wife. **2 the** ~ the wife of a person of standing in the community, such as a farmer, minister or shopkeeper.

†**mix (one's) moggans** marry *Abd Fif*.

†**morwyngift, mornin gift** a settlement or endowment of money or property made by the husband to the wife on the morning after the marriage.

mot(ie) *derog* **the** old woman, the wife *Bnf Abd*.

moup consort or live **with** *SW*.

munting a bride's trousseau *now wLoth Kcb Slk*.

†**mutch** a close-fitting cap worn by married women.

name: be ~**ed to** be named as the sweetheart of. **gie in** *or* **up the** ~**s** supply the names for the proclamation of marriage banns.

neck *v* embrace.

neibour, neighbour a husband or wife, a bedfellow, partner.

oo woo.

†**orra** *of women* unattached (in marriage).

our ane my wife, my husband *now C Uls*.

oxter (at) embrace, cuddle *NE-WC*.

†**pairt** leave one's spouse after being authorized to do so. **be ~it** be separated formally from one's spouse.

†**pairty** a person proposed or intended as a marriage partner; a lover; a spouse.

†**paraphernal(s)** the personal effects of a married woman, which remained her own property after her marriage.

pawkie roguish, coquettish.

†**pawn(d), pawn(d)s** a sum of money deposited with the **kirk session** by a couple as a guarantee of their intention to marry within forty days and of their chaste conduct in the interval. **lay a ~, lay doon the ~s** make official notification of one's intention to marry, arrange for the proclamation of banns.

peel one's wands begin married life *S*.

pey-wedding, †**penny bridal, penny wedding** a wedding at which a guest contributed a small sum of money, or *occas* food and drink, towards the cost of the entertainment, the surplus of which was given to the couple as a gift *now Loth Kcb*.

†**plenish(ing), plenishment** furniture, household equipment brought by a bride to her new home.

posy term of endearment for a woman, sweetheart *now WC Kcb*.

pour out *exclam* the shout raised at a wedding by children, for coins to be scattered in the street for them to scramble for *now Loth*. *n* the scattering of coins at a wedding *now C, S*.

poutie term of affection for a sweetheart.

pree (someone's) lips *or* **mou** kiss.

†**preivin** a kiss.

proclaim *in regard to banns of marriage* read, publish; read the banns of, announce the impending marriage of. **proclamation** the publication of banns.

providing the household articles, linen etc laid aside by a young woman for her bottom drawer.

†**pursue** follow (a person) persistently with one's attentions; beg (someone) for favours; pay suit to as a lover.

quine, †**quean** a female sweetheart, a lass *now NE*.

†**relict** a widow.

rooketty-coo *of lovers* bill and coo.

rug a good match, a catch, *freq* **no great ~** no great shakes *now Ork*.

rush flirt with, court (a girl) *local Cai-SW*.

sappie *of a kiss* soft, long-drawn out *now Ork Abd*.

scatter *v, at a wedding* throw handfuls of coins or sweets in the street for children to scramble for *C, S*. *n* the scattering of money etc thus *now C, S*.

†**scorn** a snub, brusque rejection of a would-be lover. **~ (someone) wi** tease (*esp* a girl) about (a lover).

Scotch gravat a hug, cuddle *NE, C Slk*.

scour-oot the scattering of coins at a wedding for children to scramble for *Ags Fif*.

seek, sik seek in marriage, ask for the hand of (a woman), propose to.

†**sen(d)** a messenger sent ahead of a bridegroom at a wedding to summon the bride.

service the serving of refreshments at a wedding *now nEC Lnk*.

†**session: be ~ed** *of a betrothed couple* be called before the **kirk session** to record their intention to marry and to lay down their **pawns**.

setting down an equipping or providing for marriage *now Ags*.

shae, shoe applied to a lover or spouse, *chf* **auld shune** an old sweetheart, discarded lover *now local Sh-SW*.

shamit reel *N,* †**shame reel** the first dance at a wedding (danced by the bride and best man, the bridegroom and bridesmaid). †**shame spring** the tune played for this *NE*.

she used by a husband of his wife.

†**siller bridal** a **penny wedding**.

sitting doun a settlement in marriage *Cai C*. **sit-down** a home, settlement gained by marriage *now Ags Per*.

slaik, slaich *v* kiss, caress, fondle over-sloppily *now Ags*. *n* a slobbering kiss *now local EC-S*.

slaver, slever canoodle *local Stlg-Dmf*.

slouster kiss in a sloppy way *Uls*.

smack kiss, *esp* in a loud hearty way.

smirk[1] have a roguish or flirtatious smile.

smirk[2] a kiss *NE*.

smit: get the ~ fall in love.

smuirich *v* exchange kisses, canoodle, cuddle *now NE Ag Per*. *n* a kiss, caress, hug, cuddle *now Sh NE Ags Per*.

soss *now Abd,* **soss up** *or* **about** cuddle.

†**sow** a bride's outfit of clothes, a trousseau.

sowther, solder unite in matrimony; make (a marriage) *now Bnf Ags*.

speak, spick *NE:* **~ to** ask in marriage.

speir, *v, also* **speir for** *now local NE-Wgt* ask in marriage, make a proposal of marriage to, ask for the hand of *Gen except Sh Ork*. **~ing** a proposal of marriage. **~ someone's price** *joc* make a proposal of marriage to someone *now local NE-WC*.

splunt *SW, S*, **sprunt** *chf Rox* go wooing or courting.

†**spousing** marriage-; betrothal-.

†**stan(d), staun** *of a wedding* take place, be celebrated.

stick up to *of a lover* pay court to *Abd*.

stockin(g): throw the ~ throw the stocking of the bride or bridegroom among the guests at a wedding as a way of predicting who will marry next.

strive *v* scatter coins or sweeties at a wedding for children to scramble for *Dmf Rox*. *n* a scattering of coins etc, at a wedding, for children to scramble for *now Inv S*.

†**suit** seek **in marriage**, woo.

†**taigle wi** *etc* hang around, follow about (*esp* a woman).

tairt a girl-friend.

tak, take *freq of a woman* marry, take in marriage.

tether *chf sarcastic* marry, unite in marriage *now N*.

tied: be ~ be married.

tig 1 dally, have playful or amorous dealings **with** *now Sh NE*. **2** touch, twitch, pull playfully, teasingly or amorously *now Sh*. **~-tow** romp, flirt *now Gall*.

†**tirl** a pecking kiss.

tocher *n* a marriage portion, *esp* a bride's dowry *now chf literary*. †*v* endow with a **tocher**, dower. **weel** *etc* **~ed** well etc provided with a **tocher**, well etc endowed, settled. **~less** having no **tocher**. †~ **band** a marriage settlement. †~ **gude** property given as a **tocher**.

touse *v* pull or knock about, handle (*esp* a woman) roughly *now local Sh-WC*. *n* a rough romp with a person of the opposite sex *now Sh NE*. **tousle**, †**tussle** *of lovers* pull one another about playfully, fondle one another.

traik after *or* **upon** follow, pursue in courtship.

treesh run **after**, court *now Bnf Abd*.

tryst betroth, engage to be married *now C*.

†**twine** join, unite in marriage.

upo(n) (be married *etc*) to, with.

†**vacand** a person who is free to take a mate.

†**valentin(e) 1** a Valentine. **2** a custom observed on St Valentine's eve of drawing by lot the name of one's sweetheart for the following year.

wad wed, marry. **~din** a wedding. **~din braws** wedding clothes. **~din fowk** the wedding party.

wall, well unite (people), join.

wanter an unmarried man or woman, a widow(er) *now Ork*.

†**welcome-hame** a celebration in a bride's new house.

†**whistle-binkie** a person who attended a **penny** wedding without paying and had no right to share in the entertainment; a mere spectator (who sometimes whistled for his own amusement).

wi: marry ~ marry, be married to.

widow, weedow 1 a widow, a wife bereaved of her husband: 'widow-woman'. **2** a widower, a husband bereaved of his wife. †**widowity** widowhood.

wife, wifie, wifock, wifockie *chf N* a wife, a married woman.

winch court, keep company with someone of the opposite sex, *orig* of a man with a girl: '*are ye winchin?*'

woman, wumman a wife.

†**wooster** *literary* a wooer.

yoke unite in marriage, *now local Ork-Ayr*. **ill-yokit** ill-matched in marriage *now NE*.

young: ~ **folk** a newly-married couple, irrespective of age *now local Ork-Ayr*. ~ **man 1** the best man at a wedding *Ork NE*. **2** an unmarried man *now Ork*.

8.9 SEX, VIRGINITY

†**abuise, abuse** behave in a licentious way.

†**actual** sexual.

†**bed with** bed, go to bed with (another).

†**bismere** a disreputable woman.

†**black-foot** a lovers' go-between.

†**blink** ogle.

†**blue threid** an indecent or smutty touch (in a story) *now local Sh-Ayr*.

bordel house *now Abd*, †**bordel** a brothel. †**bordeler** a keeper or frequenter of brothels.

†**bugrist** a person who practises buggery.

causey paiker a street-walker.

†**chalmer glew** sexual activity.

cookie a prostitute, tart *Fif WC*.

†**cowclink** a prostitute.

culyie, cullie fondle.

curdoo make love *now Fif*.

†**daffin** licentious behaviour; smutty language.

daftness wantonness.

†**dale** have sexual intercourse *chf* **have** ~ **with**.

dance the reel o Bogie *etc euphemistic* have sexual intercourse.

debosh debauch *now Bnf Abd Fif*.

†**dirrydan, dirrye dantoun** sexual intercourse.

Dodgill Reepan a species of marsh orchid, the roots of which were used in a love potion.

†**dunty** a mistress.

dyke-lowper a person of immoral habits *S*.
†**enflambe** inflame, fire with desire or passion.
ficher wi handle (a woman) indelicately, grope, 'touch up' *local Sh-Ags*.
fin(d) *v* feel with the fingers, grope indecently *local Bnf-Arg*. *n* indecent handling of a woman *local NE-SW*.
†**fornicatrix** a woman guilty of fornication.
†**fornie** *colloq* fornication.
foutie obscene, indecent.
fyke: haud *or* **hae a** ~ flirt, have an affair.
†**glaiks** sensual desire, wantonness.
graip, growp probe; handle, touch indecently *now Rox*.
groff *of language etc* smutty, obscene.
gyte mad or crazy with longing or desire, lovesick, eager *now local Ork-midLoth*.
hairy a woman of loose morals, a prostitute *chf Abd Gsw*.
hash ribald talk, nonsense *now Sh*.
high-kiltit immodest, indecent.
hing-tee a mistress, girlfriend *N*.
hizzie, hussy a woman of bad character.
hochmagandy fornication.
hure a whore.
†**inhonesté** disgraceful conduct, indecency.
†**insolence** licentiousness.
Jenkin's hen: die the death of ~, **die like** ~ die an old maid.
†**jinker** a pleasure-seeker; a libertine, a wanton.
†**jobbing** illicit sexual intercourse.
†**kirr** *adj* wanton.
kittie, †**kittie unsell** a woman of doubtful character, a whore *Sh NE*.
kittle *v* stimulate, please; make excited *now local NE-S*. *n* a pleasurable excitement, stimulus.
†**ladry** base conduct or talk, ribaldry.
†**lamen** a lover. ~**ry, lemmanry** illicit or profane love.
†**larbar** *adj* exhausted, impotent. *n* an exhausted or impotent man.
†**leal** *ballad, of a woman* chaste, pure.
†**lichour** a lecher. **lichory** lechery.
†**lie wrang** *of a woman* lose one's chastity.
lift (a) leg commit fornication *now Ork Abd*.
†**lig** have sexual intercourse **with** *etc*.
limmer a loose or disreputable woman; a man's mistress; a whore.
loun a sexually immoral person: **1** a lewd rascal; **2** *of a woman* a whore. † ~**rie** sexual wickedness, fornication. **play the** ~ behave as a whoremonger or strumpet; commit fornication.
lowp: ~**hunt** a gadding about (esp in search of amorous adventures) *N*. † ~ **on** copulate with.

lurdan *term of reproach, now literary, of a woman* a whore; a slut.
luve, love, loo: ~ **blenk,** ~**-blink** a loving or amorous glance. †**luverent** lust.
†**luxure** lasciviousness, lechery.
maiden 1 an old maid *now NE*. **2** †*of a man, chf Malcolm IV* a virgin.
†**mell** have sexual intercourse (**with**).
misfortune a breach of chastity resulting in the birth of an illegitimate child.
mistak a breach of chastity by a woman *local*.
mistryst seduce *now Kcdn Slk*.
†**mix (one's) moggans** have sexual intercourse (**with**) *Abd Fif*.
mow *of males* copulate, have sexual intercourse (**with**).
†**pamphelet** a woman of easy virtue.
pawn(d), paun(d)s a sum of money deposited with the **kirk session** by a couple as a guarantee of their intention to marry within forty days and of their chaste conduct in the interval.
†**peronall** a wanton woman, harlot.
†**pillie-wantoun** an amorous, lecherous or randy person.
preen-tae an illicit sexual partner, a mistress *now WC*.
†**purchase** *v* procure. *n* concubinage.
†**quean, quine** a mistress, concubine. **querry** associating with prostitutes.
†**racer** nickname for a loose woman.
radge *adj* sexually excited *Gen except Sh Ork*. *n* a loose-living woman *local Abd S*.
randie *adj, of language* coarse, uncouth; obscene *now local Ags-S*. *n* a loose or dissolute woman.
reebald ribald.
reuch, rough lewd, foul-mouthed, indecent *local NE-Kcb*. ~**living** *of a man* living in an immoral way *now Sh NE Per*.
†**riot** wanton, licentious.
scauld, scald (cause to) burn with desire. ~**ing** *of desire* burning, fervent.
sculduddery 1 *literary or joc* fornication, unchastity. **2** obscenity, indecency, *esp* in language.
†**sedouse (with)** seduce.
shairp, sharp: ~ **set** keen, eager for sex *now Ayr*.
†**shed someone's shanks** set someone's legs apart.
†**shute at** *etc* **the shell** *of a man* have sexual intercourse.
sicht, sight scrutinize (a person) indecently *local Sh-Edb*.
skate bree the water in which skate has been

boiled, skate soup, said to have aphrodisiac and other properties *now Wgt.*

†**slicht, slight** of loose moral character.

smicker smile or laugh in a leering way; smile seductively.

snuid, snood a ribbon etc bound round the brow and tied at the back under the hair, worn *esp* by young unmarried women; a symbol of virginity.

strag a loose woman *now Dnbt Lnk Dmf.*

tail a prostitute *C.* † ~-**toddle** sexual intercourse.

tig touch, twitch, pull playfully, teasingly or amorously *now Sh.*

tousle, †tussle *of lovers* pull one another about playfully, fondle one another.

trallop, treelip *NE* a trollop.

troke truck, dealings, association (implying improper familiarity).

undecent indecent.

unricht improper *now Fif SW.*

†**wife** a kept mistress, concubine.

†**woman lowpar** a whoremonger.

wrang, wrong: fa ~ (**to** *or* **till**) *of a woman* lose her virginity, be seduced (by) *SW.*

†**yaud** a whore.

yeukie sexually excited *NE Per Ayr.*

8.10 LEGITIMACY, ILLEGITIMACY

For legal aspects, see 11.12.

†**bastardry** bastardy.

†**bygottin** illegitimate.

†**bystart** a bastard.

come-o-will an illegitimate child *now Abd.*

coup the creels *of a woman* have an illegitimate child *now Fif.*

ill: ~-**cleckit,** ~-**come** *N,* ~-**gotten** *Sh Ags Kcb* illegitimate.

†**laggin: cast a** ~-**gird** bear an illegitimate child.

†**liberal** legitimate *chf Ayr.*

luve, love, loo: ~-**bairn** a love-child *Ork WC.*

merry-begotten conceived out of wedlock, illegitimate.

misfortune a breach of chastity resulting in the birth of an illegitimate child.

shae, shoe: cast a ~ have an illegitimate child *now Ayr.*

trout: there's a ~(**ie**) **in the well** said of a woman expecting a child, *esp* if illegitimate *now Abd.*

wrang, wrong: on the ~ **side o the blanket** out of wedlock.

8.11 FAMILY RELATIONSHIPS

ae only (son etc).

agnate a relative on the father's side.

†**allye** kinship.

†**antecestor** an ancestor.

†**attingent** being near or close in age or relationship.

aul(d), old *indicating family relationships:* great-: '*auld uncle*'; grand-: '*auld mither*'; oldest *now local:* '*auld brither*', '*auld son*'.

auntie *familiar* an aunt.

bairn *expressing relationship* someone's child; offspring of any age. † ~-**time,** ~**teme** a brood of children; offspring.

big sma faimily a large family of young children.

billy a brother.

bird †the young, offspring, *usu derog as* **Deil's bird.** ~-**alane** an only child, the only child left in a family.

blude, blood: ~-**friend** a blood relation *now Sh.* †**of blude** related by blood.

bobbie a grandfather.

brither, †broder a brother. † ~-**barn** a brother's child. ~-**dochter** a niece on one's brother's side. ~-**son** a nephew on one's brother's side.

brod, brude, †brodmal *NE* a brood.

†**cadent** a cadet, a younger son.

chief the head of a clan, **kindred,** or feudal community.

chieftain, †chiftane a chieftain, *specif* a clan chief.

clan a local or family group, *esp* in the Highlands or Borders, bearing a common name (from a supposed joint ancestor) and united under a **chief.** †**clannit** belonging to a clan. ~**sman** a man belonging to a clan.

cognate a relative on the mother's side.

†**conjunct** *latterly law* connected by blood.

consanguinean *law* descended from the same father but not the same mother.

coort kin wi claim relationship with *now Bnf Abd.*

†**dade** dad, father.

dadie daddy.

†**dame** a mother.

dey 1 *child's word* father *now Fif Bwk.* **2** a grandfather, *usu* as respectful term of address for an old man *now Bnf Fif Bwk.*

deyd(ie) a grandfather; a grandmother *NE.*

dochter a daughter. † ~(**is**) **son,** ~ ~ grandson or grand-daughter by one's daughter.

doo's cleckin *or* **sitting** a family of two, *usu* a boy and a girl *local Bnf-Rox.*

drap, drop: no a ~ **of his** *etc or* **no a drap's**

blude ((a-)**kin**) not a blood relation *now local Bnf-Fif.*

†**eem 1** an uncle. **2** *also* **ame** applied to any near male relative.

etion *freq contemptuous* stock, kindred, breed *chf NE.*

†**even** in a direct line of descent.

faimily a family.

faither, faider *Sh NE n* a father. *v* **1** father. **2** show who one's father is by resemblance etc *now Ork N Kcb.* †~ **broder,** ~**sister** a paternal uncle or aunt. †~ **broder son** a paternal cousin. †**father side** the paternal side of a family.

†**famyle 1** a family. **2** a **kindred** or lineage.

far, faur: far aff, ~ **oot** distant in relationship *now Sh NE midLoth.* ~ **awa** *of relationship* remote, distant.

forebearers, forefolk *local Cai-Gall,* †**fore-elders** ancestors, forefathers.

†**foregranddame** a great- or great-great-grand-mother.

†**foregrandfather** a great-grandfather.

†**foregrantsire** a great- or great-great-grand-father.

foster 1 †a foster-child. **2** an adopted child *now Cai.*

fowk, folk the members of one's family, community etc, one's relatives.

fremd *now local,* **fremmit** unrelated *local Sh-Dmf.*

friend a relative, a kinsman. †~**schip** kinship; kindred. **be** ~**s to** *or* **with** be related to *now NE.*

†**fundlin** a foundling.

†**gang** a family or clan.

†**genetrice** a female parent.

get, git, gyte offspring, progeny *now local N-S.*

†**grain** a branch, arm, offshoot of a family.

gran(d), graun(d): †**grandame, grannam 1** a grandmother. **2** a great-grandmother. ~**bairn** *now Sh,* ~**-wean** a grandchild. ~**childer** grand-children *now Uls.* ~**da** *now local,* ~**daddy,** ~**dey** *now Fif,* ~**faither,** ~**fader** a grandfather. ~**-dochter** a grand-daughter. ~**minnie** *now Sh,* ~**mither** *now local Sh-Kcb* a grandmother. ~**sher,** †~**schir 1** a grandsire, a grandfather. **2** a great-grandfather.

†**gree** a step in the familial line of descent.

guid, good -in-law, *as* ~ **brither,** ~ **dochter,** ~ **father,** ~ **mither,** ~ **sister,** ~ **son.** †~ **dame** a or (*chf*) one's grandmother. ~**sire, gut-cher,** †~**schir** a grandfather.

half, hauf: ~**-cousin** the child of one's parent's cousin, a second cousin.

†**thede of kin** the chief of a family or clan.

†**hereditare** hereditary.

ieroe a great-grandchild.

ilk family, race.

kin *n* **1** a kinsman, relation. **2** ancestral stock, familial origin, extraction, *freq* **of** (**royal, gentle,** etc) ~. **3** †the race or stock descended from a particular ancestor. *adj* related, akin. †**kindred, kinrede, kinrent** a or one's family, clan etc, *specif* applied to the extended family groups in the kin-based society of Celtic Scotland. †~**less** without noble or influential relatives. †**be of** ~ be related **to. redd oot** *or* **up** ~ trace one's lineage *local Sh-Dmf.* **not store the** ~ fail to keep up the stock *NE.*

†**kind:** ~**ly** related, of one's kindred. ~**ness** kinship, relationship by birth. **of** ~ by birth or descent.

kith a person's acquaintances, neighbours and kinsfolk.

kizzen a cousin. †**cusines, cousinace** a female cousin.

lad, lawd *now C,* **laddie** *Gen except Sh Ork,* **lathie** *now Ags,* **lad(die) bairn** a male child, a son.

†**lang** belong, as a member of a family or dependent.

lass, lassie, lassock, lassickie, lass(ie) bairn *now local,* **lass(ie) wean** a daughter.

loun a male child, a son, baby boy *N.*

lucky a grandmother *now NE.* ~ **da(d)ie,** ~ **daid** a grandfather *now NE Ags.* ~ **minnie** a grandmother.

†**macalive, makhelve** a portion or endowment in cattle for a child put to fosterage *Highl.*

†**maich, mauch** a male connection by marriage, as a son-in-law, brother-in-law, cousin, uncle or nephew by marriage.

maiden 1 †a daughter. **2** an unmarried heiress; *latterly* the eldest or only daughter of a landowner or farmer *now NE.*

†**maison** a household, family.

mam(mie) *child's word* mother.

manse: a son *or* **daughter of the** ~ a son or daughter of a Presbyterian minister.

†**menyie 1** a family, household. **2** a tribe, race.

minnie affectionate name for a mother.

missie the eldest unmarried daughter of a farmer *NE, EC Uls.*

mither, mother a mother. †~ **brother,** ~ **sister** a maternal uncle or aunt. ~ **side** the maternal line of descent.

†**name** those bearing a particular name, *esp* a family or clan.

†**nation** breed, race, tribe.

†**native** by kinship: '*native moder*'.

†**near** closely related by blood or kinship. ~**nes** closeness of kinship.

†**nece** a nephew.

†**nepote 1** a grandson. **2** a nephew.

nevoy, neffie 1 a nephew. **2** a grandson; a great-grandson. **3** †*literary* a descendant. **4** †a granddaughter; a niece.

nourice a child's nurse, *esp* a wet-nurse or foster-mother *latterly chf literary and ballad.* † ~ **father** a foster-father.

oe, oy 1 a grandchild *now N Arg.* **2** a nephew. **3** †a niece.

†oncle an uncle.

orphant an orphan.

our anes my family *now Uls.*

out-relation a distant relative *now Abd.*

†patruell a paternal first cousin.

paw pa, dad *C.*

pawpie *child's word* grandfather *Fif Bwk Kcb.*

pawrent a parent.

pock shakings the last child of a large family *local.*

†progenytrys an ancestress.

†pronepot, pronevoy a great-grandson.

quine, †quean a daughter *NE Ags.*

Scotch cousin a distant relative *now NE, C.*

†second in blood *etc, law* a person related in the second degree of consanguinity.

shakins: the ~ o the poke the last-born of a family.

shither kinsfolk *Cai.*

sib *adj* related by blood **to**, of the same **kindred** or lineage as. *n* **1** a relative. **2 kindred**, relatives, *freq* ~ **and fremd** *now Sh.* ~**nes(s)** kinship, relationship, affinity. † ~**rent** kinship.

sin a son *now N.*

sister: ~ bairn the child of a parent's sister, a cousin *now Sh Cai.* † ~ **douchtar** a niece, the daughter of one's sister. ~**('s) son** a nephew, the son of one's sister *now Sh Ork.*

sma(ll) faimily a family of young children *now local.*

stap- step-. **stappy** step-father. **step-bairn** *n* a step-child. †*v* treat as a step-child.

staps and stairs: like *etc* ~ *of a family of children* born in quick succession *Sh Ags.*

strind descent, lineage; the inherited qualities which come from this *now Sh.*

†surname a family, **clan.**

swap *n, also* **swype** *NE Per* the cast of someone's features, *esp* as it resembles his relatives, a facial trait or characteristic in a family *now Sh NE Per.* *v* resemble in (*esp* facial) appearance, show a family likeness to *now Ork Wgt.*

tae, to 1 *also* **till** *now Sh N* with (a specified person) as the father: '*she had a child to her cousin*'. **2** *expressing family relationship*: '*son to the Sheriff*'.

tak, take: ~ wi *of paternity* acknowledge, admit one's connection with; own *now NE Ags.*

†tender nearly related, akin, *freq* ~ **of blood.**

the before a surname: **1** †to indicate the chief or leading member of a family: '*Robert the Bruce*'; '*the Chisholm*'; **2** to denote the chief of a Highland clan: '*the Mackintosh*'.

third, thrid: ~**(s) of kin** related in the third degree of consanguinity *now Sh.*

tittie familiar term for a sister.

weel come of good lineage, of honourable parentage *now Abd Dmf.*

wha (i)s aucht ? who is the parent of? *now Ags Per.*

†wowar a guardian, patron.

young *in titles* prefixed to the name of a Highland **chief** or his estate to indicate his eldest son and heir. ~**er** used after a person's name to distinguish him from an older person of the same name, *freq* title for the heir-apparent of a person with a territorial designation as part of his surname or with the style of a Scottish **chief**, *esp* **A, younger of B**, *or (and now officially preferred)* **A of B (the) younger**: '*Malcolm MacGregor of Mac-Gregor, younger*'. † ~ **man** the eldest son and heir.

8.12 SEX ROLES

breeks: wear the ~ *of a wife* wear the trousers.

brolach a weak effete person *now Bnf.*

cockie-bendie a small, bumptious or rather effeminate man *local.*

faizart a puny effeminate man, a weakling *now Sh.*

gilpie a tomboy.

he *of a woman* having masculine manners.

hen-wife a man who concerns himself about matters usually left to women *now Per Kinr Slk.*

†hizzie, hussy a man who interferes with or undertakes women's duties.

hoolet henpeck *Per Rox.*

Jenny, Jinny a man who occupied himself with what are regarded as female concerns; an effeminate man *C, S, Uls.* ~ **Wullock** an effeminate man *EC, WC.*

Jessie, Jessie Ann *Abd,* **Jessie Fisher** *Kcdn Ags Per* an effeminate man or boy.

†John Thomson's man a hen-pecked husband.

lass(ie) boy an effeminate boy *local.*

†minȝart effeminate.

sapsy effeminate *Per Stlg WC.*

souk, suck: ~**-the-pappie** *contemptuous* a 'big baby'; an effeminate man *local Cai-Kcb.*

sweetie-wife *of an effeminate man* a garrulous, gossipy person *local Cai-S.*

wife, wifie, wifock, wiffockie *also* **wife-carl** a man who occupies himself with women's affairs.

9. PHYSICAL STATES

9.1 PHYSICAL TYPES

9.1.1 GENERAL

ablach an insignificant or contemptible person through lack of size.

able physically fit, strong.

†affere manner of bearing, appearance, deportment.

bang agile and powerful.

bauchle a clumsy person.

better-faured better-featured, better-looking.

bilf a sturdy, growing young man *Bnf Abd Ags.* ~**ert** a bigger than usual thing or person *now Bnf.*

black †*of persons, their complexion, hair etc, freq attached to a personal name* dark: '*blak Archibald of Douglas*'. ~**-a-viced, ~-a-vised** dark-complexioned.

bleared debauched-looking.

blind fair *freq of albinos* extremely fair *local.*

bodach a small and insignificant person *now Bnf.*

bodsy a little, dapper, or neat person *chf Abd.*

body, buddy a puny or little person *now Bnf Fif.*

†boldin physically swollen or distended.

boolie-backit round-shouldered *now Bnf Fif wLoth.*

boukit bulky, swollen.

bowsome *chf of a woman* buxom, handsome.

braw *of persons* handsome, of fine physique.

breek: ~**um(s)** a small person; affectionate term for a little boy *now Bnf.*

†brent upright, *freq* **browis** ~.

†bricht a beautiful woman.

brolach an old, weak or effete person *now Bnf.*

buird strong, of sturdy build.

†buntlin short and thick.

caber a big coarse clumsy man *chf NE.*

carle, kerl male; *hence* strong, large.

†cast aspect, demeanour; appearance.

chump *esp of boys or children* a thickset person *Bnf.*

clart a big, dirty, untidy person *local.*

clever handsome, well-made *now Cai.*

clype a big, uncouth, awkward or ugly person *now NE.*

coast bodily girth or frame *S.*

craishan a withered shrunken person *Cai.*

crine 1 shrink, shrivel *Gen except Sh Ork.* 2 cause to grow smaller, shrink, shrivel *now Abd Stlg.*

croot, crit a puny child *C-S.*

cruppen doun shrunk or bent with age *now Fif.*

culsh a big, disagreeable person *Bnf Abd.*

cut: ~**ty** short, stumpy. **a** ~ **of a man** a sturdy, middle-sized man *Cai Bnf.*

cuttag a sturdy, middle-sized woman *Cai.*

daberlack(s) *chf disparaging* a tall uncomely person *Bnf.*

dall a doll, a pretty, silly woman *now Bnf Abd Lnk.*

dance-in-my-loof a very small person *now Ags.*

dark-avised having dark hair and eyes *now Ork Bnf Arg.*

dawlie (a person who is) physically or mentally slow.

decrippit decrepit.

dorbie delicate, weak *Bnf Abd.*

dot, dottle *Bnf Abd* a person of small stature *Bnf Abd Edb.*

dowless feeble, lacking in strength or energy *now Stlg.*

draffie out of condition, unable to walk or run easily *now Cai Ags.*

drod a short, thickset person *now Rox.*

drochle a puny insignificant person *now local Cai-Fif.*

drochlin puny, dwarfish *now Bnf Abd.*

durk a large clumsily-built person *local Sh-Abd.* ~**y** thickset, squat *now Ags.*

durkin a short thickset person *Bnf.*

dwaffle limp, soft; weak, feeble *chf NE.*

dwaible †a weak, helpless person. **dwaibly** shaky, wobbly, weak *now local Abd-Ayr.*

dwamfle flexible, loose, sagging *Bnf.*

eemock a tiny person *Abd Ags.*

eeshan *freq derog or playful* a small child; a small and puny person of any age *local Cai-Abd.*

†fair-farrand handsome.

ferdy strong, active *now Sh.*

faizart a puny effeminate man, a weakling *now Sh.*

†farrant comely.

farrach strength, energy *NE.*

†favour appearance, looks.

feat *of persons or their dress* neat, trim *now Mry eLoth Gall.*

feegur the figure *local Fif-S*.

fell energetic and capable, sturdy *now sEC-S*.

fettle strength, vigour, condition.

fill up increase in bulk or girth *Abd Ags Arg SW*.

flail a tall, gawky person *Cai NE*.

†**fleshlyk** fleshly.

flozent *of the body* swollen, puffed out *Bnf Abd*.

frow(die) a big buxom woman *chf NE*.

garron a strong, thickset man or sturdy boy *NE*.

gash *chf literary* pale, ghastly in appearance, grim, dismal.

gate farrin presentable, comely *NE*.

gawsie plump, fresh complexioned, handsome, imposing.

gear: guid ~ (gangs in) sma buik applied to a small but capable person *local Abd-Rox*.

gentie neat, dainty, graceful *now Abd Fif*.

gillieperous a rough ungainly person *Mry Abd*.

gizzen dry, parched, shrivelled *now Sh Rox*.

gleg quick, keen in perception, *freq* ~ **of** *or* **in sight, hearing, eye** etc.

glipe a clumsy person *now Uls*.

goust(e)rous hearty, vigorous.

gowk: (the) ~ and (the) titlin(g) two inseparable and/or incongruous companions, *esp* a tall and a short person seen together *now Per Fif*.

gowp-the-lift nickname for a person who carries his head high.

green young, youthful, full of vitality *now local Abd Uls*.

gudge a short, strong, thickset person *now Cai Bnf Abd*. **gudgie** short and thickset, squat *now Ags Per Lnk*.

gunch a short, thickset person *chf Cai*.

gurr a strong, thickset, ungainly person.

hand, haun: ~**less** awkward, clumsy, incompetent, slow.

heich, high tall.

heid-mark *orig of sheep etc, later of persons* an individual characteristic of appearance which distinguishes one from another as opposed to any artificial means of differentiation. †**know** *etc* **by** ~ recognise by face or appearance.

heidiepeer of equal stature or age.

heifer *usu of a woman* a big awkward clumsy person *NE Fif midLoth*.

hochle, hachel a person who is ungainly or slovenly in gait, dress or appearance *now Pbls Arg*.

howe-backit round-shouldered; hollow-backed *C, S*.

hugger: ~**t**, ~**ing** round-shouldered *now Mry*.

hurb a puny creature *NE*.

ill: ~ **farrant** ugly, unpleasant in appearance *nEC Rox*. ~ **setten** clumsy *now Ork*. ~**-shaken**

(thegither) ungainly, shambling *NE*. ~**-shaken up** awkward, loutish *Sh Ork NE*.

Jenny Wullock a hermaphrodite, a sexually-deformed male; an effeminate man *EC, WC*.

jimp *now Ork N, C*, **jimpie** *now Abd Lnk* slender, small, graceful, neat, dainty.

junt a squat, clumsy person *Abd Bnf*.

keessar a large uncomely person, *usu* female *NE*.

kelp a big raw-boned youth *NE Ags*.

kibble sturdy, well-built, active, agile *NE*.

kind †the physical nature or constitution of a person. ~ **to** resemble, take after *S*.

knapdarloch contemptuous term for an under-sized person *NE*.

knap a sturdy lad *now NE*. **(k)nappy** stout, sturdy, strong.

knot a sturdy thickset person *now Sh*.

laich: ~**y braid** a short stocky person or animal *Bnf Abd*. ~**-set** squat, stocky *now Ayr Kcb*.

len(g)th a person's stature or height *local*. **breadth an** ~ *Fif midLoth SW*, **one's lang** ~ *Cai NE, EC* one's full length, prone.

†**likely, likly** strong and brave-looking.

little-boukit small in body or bulk, shrunken *now N nEC Dmf*.

loorach an ungainly or untidy person, a trollop *Inv NE Per*.

lour-shouthered round-shouldered, stooping *S*.

lourdie heavy; sluggish, slow.

lout *adj, of the shoulders* bent, stooping, round, *chf* ~**-shouthered**. *n* a stoop *now Sh*. ~**it** bent with age etc; round-shouldered *N Loth*.

loutch *v* stoop, slouch *local Abd-Wgt*. *n* a slouching gait, a stoop *Abd Kcdn mLoth*.

lug a clumsy fellow *now Gsw*.

†**luttard** ? bowed, bent.

makdom a person's form, shape or build.

mannie, mannikee a little man.

†**mass** an amply-proportioned, motherly-looking woman.

maucht physical strength, mightiness.

maukin a feeble person, a weakling *Abd Uls*.

mend fatten, (cause to) grow plump *now Kcb Uls*.

middlin of medium size or stature.

mitten a small squat person or child *Bnf Abd Ags*.

†**mowdiewort** a small dark child with a lot of hair.

muckle, meikle, mickle: ~ **boukit** physically big and broad, burly.

nacket a small, neat person.

nat a small-sized person *now Sh Abd*.

niffnaff a small, insignificant person.

nowt a big unwieldy person *now local Sh-nEC Rox*.

nyaff a puny, insignificant person.

ouf a puny insignificant creature.

outrig outward appearance *now Sh Ags.*

paewae drooping, spiritless *now Sh NE Fif.*

palie, pallie *adj* **1** thin, having a pallid, sickly appearance, listless *now local Fif-S.* **2** stunted in growth, underdeveloped, delicate *now Ayr S. n* a lethargic, sluggish person; a feeble weakling.

pallion a big, gangling, raw-boned person, an ungainly person.

pecht contemptuous term for a small undersized person *now Sh Bnf Abd.*

peesweep, peesie-weesie sharp-featured, gaunt; ailing.

†**petty** *with a proper name, forming a nickname* small in size or stature: 'Pette Johnne'.

pilpert a badly-fed, cold-looking child *NE.*

pin, peen *now EC, S* a small, neat person or animal, a small child *Bnf Abd.*

†**polist** *of persons or their appearance* bright, beautiful; ? adorned, embellished.

†**portrature** the external appearance.

†**pouster** posture.

pretty *of women* well-built, buxom *NE.*

punchie thickset and short *now NE.*

†**quick and quidder** alive and full of vigour.

†**rank** stout, strong.

rapple grow rapidly, shoot up.

†**rax** grow, develop.

†**rigwiddie** *esp of an old woman* wizened, gnarled, tough and rugged-looking, mis-shapen.

riglen, an undersized or weak person *now Fif SW.*

row-shoudert round-shouldered *NE Ags.*

rudas *n, chf* **auld** ~ a coarse or masculine-looking woman *now Bnf. adj, of a woman* ugly, cantankerous, witch-like.

runchie (a) coarsely-built, raw-boned (person).

runt a short, thickset person *Ayr Kcb.*

†**ruskie** (a) strong, vigorous, *usu* rough-mannered (person).

†**sairie** puny.

saur lacking in wit, spirit, energy *NE.*

scart a puny, shrunken person *now Per Dmf.*

schamlich a weak, puny, or slovenly person *NE.*

sclaff: ~**er** a big clumsy flat-footed person *now NE Ags Per.* ~**ert** a clumsy flat-footed person *Bnf Abd.*

scrunt a person shrunken or withered by age, illness etc, a thin scraggy person *now NE, C.* ~**it** shrivelled, shrunken, stunted in growth *now local Bnf-SW.* ~**y** stunted, shrivelled, stumpy, wizened *now SW, S Uls.*

set build, physique, kind *now local Sh-SW.*

setterel small and thickset.

†**shabble** a little, insignificant person or thing.

shaird a puny or deformed person *now Bnf.*

sharg a stunted starved-looking person; a short bow-legged man. ~**ar** a puny, weakly person *now NE Ags.*

shauchle a weakly, stunted, or deformed person *now Ags Per.* **shauchlin** *now N-S,* **shachled** *now C,* **shauchlie** *now NE, C* unsteady or weak on one's feet, shuffling.

short-set small and stockily-built *local Sh-WC.*

singit stunted, shrivelled, puny *now Per.*

sklyte *Abd,* **sklyter** *chf NE* a big, clumsy, slovenly person.

skraich a puny, shrill-voiced person *now Abd.*

skrink *v* shrink, shrivel up *now Loth Rox. n* a shrivelled, unpleasant, or contemptible person, *esp* a woman *now Rox.*

sleug an ugly or ungainly person.

†**sloch, slough** a lumpish or soft person.

smally undersized, small and slight, weakly *now C, S.* ~**-bouk(it)** (of) little bulk, small, compact.

†**smashing** well-built, strapping, vigorous.

smatchet a small insignificant person, *esp* a pert or mischievous child, a little rogue *now Sh Ork N.*

smite a small insignificant person, a weak or puny creature *NE Ags.*

smout a small insignificant person, a small child *Gen except Sh Ork.*

snauchle an insignificant, puny or feeble person, a dwarf *chf SW.*

sober small, slightly-built *NE.*

sonsie **1** *freq as a general term of approbation, of the appearance, looks, face, now local Sh-Kcb.* **2** *esp of women* comely, attractive; *freq of the figure* buxom, plump; *of young children* chubby, sturdy.

sookin teuchit *NE,* **sookin turkey** *etc now Sh-N, SW* a feeble or foolish person.

sowd *Bnf Abd Ags,* **sowdie** *esp of a woman, now Abd Ags* a large ungainly person.

†**spink** an attractive young person.

sprauchle a stunted feeble creature, a weakling *SW.*

sprug, sproug a bright but undersized boy *Cai Fif Lnk.*

spug, speug a child, a small person etc *now Per.*

spurdie a small lively person *NE.*

stalwart *of person or their limbs* strongly built, sturdy.

stammeral, stam(m)rel (an) awkward, clumsy, stupid (person).

stark physically strong, sturdy, vigorous *now Ork Cai.*

†**state** a person's proper form, shape or nature.

stieve *of persons or their limbs* firm, strong, sturdy *now local Per-Dmf.*

stirk(ie) a sturdy young man *now N Stlg Ayr*.

stirrah a (sturdy) young lad.

stodgel, stodger a slow, lumbering, rather stupid person *now NE*.

stoit, styte a stupid, ungainly, blundering person *now Abd*.

stout, stoot stout. ~**rife** strongly built, powerful *Wgt Dmf Rox*.

stowfie sturdily built, stocky, stout, stolid *now Bnf Abd*.

stram a big clumsy blundering man *Bnf Abd*.

strang strong.

strenth, strength strength. †~**ily**, ~**ly** strongly. †~**y** *of persons* strong, powerful; *of a person's body etc* physically strong.

stug, stog a stocky coarsely-built person, one whose movements are stiff and awkward.

stump a short stocky person; a stiff, slow-moving or sluggish person *now Sh Cai Inv*.

stump: ~**er** a short, stocky or dumpy person; a plump sturdy young child *now Cai Ags*. ~**it** stocky, dumpy *now local Sh-Dmf*.

swank, swankie lithe, agile, strong; *esp of a young man* smart, well set-up *now nEC Lnk Slk*. ~**ie**, †~**in** a smart, active, strapping young man *now local nEC-Wgt*.

taistrel a gawky, slovenly, unmethodical person *Gall Rox*.

tak, take: ~ **aff** *now Sh Ags*, ~ **o** *now Ork Cai* take after, resemble. ~ **on** affect physically *local NE-wLoth*.

tangle *n* a tall, lanky person *now Sh N*. †*adj* long and limp, lank and loose-jointed.

tanker-backit round-shouldered and hollow-backed *EC, WC, S*.

targer nickname for a big, active, hustling person *now Dmf*.

teetotum a very small, insignificant person *local N-Dmf*.

thick thickset, muscular, burly *local Ork-Wgt*.

thump a sturdy child *now Per*.

ticht, tight neat in build, well-made, shapely.

†**toddle** a small neat person.

trig trim, neat in figure, dress or manner.

trollop, trallop a long, gangling, ungainly person *local Ork-WC*.

turn *of physical or mental development* become, grow *now local Sh-WC*: 'ye're turnin a big boy'.

twa, two: ~**faul(d)** *freq of persons bent with age etc* bent double *now local Sh-Ayr*.

tweest a small, undersized person *now Abd*.

twitter a very slender, small or feeble person.

undocht a feeble, weak or ineffective person *now Cai*.

unfreely heavy, weighty, unwieldy *now Bnf*.

†**unhalesome** ugly, repulsive.

wa(ll) drap a puny or insignificant person *Cai*.

waff *local EC-S*, **waffish, waff like** feeble in body or mind. ~**-looking** feeble or sickly in appearance *Bwk Lnk S*.

waffle *n* a feeble, silly person *now Loth S*. *adj* inert, limp, feeble, sluggish *now local Cai-Fif*. ~**d** limp from weakness or exhaustion *now Loth*. **waffly** = **waffled**; feeble *local Sh-Fif*.

wallie big and strong, thriving, sturdy, plump *now Sh Ork*.

wallop a gangling, loose-limbed person *now Ags*.

wallydrag *now Bnf Abd*, **wallydraigle** *local C* an undersized person.

wamfle limp, weak *now Bnf Abd*.

wandocht *n* 1 a feeble, weak person. 2 †lack of strength, feebleness. *adj* feeble, puny, inert *latterly literary*.

wanthriven, †wanthrifty stunted, in a state of decline, weakly *now Sh*.

wark, wirk, work affect physically or mentally, *esp* for the worse.

warld, world: ~**like** normal in appearance, like everyone else. **weel** *or* **wise and** ~**-like** *or* ~**(-like) and wise-like** *chf of a new-born baby* normal physically and mentally *now local*. **like the** ~ like everyone else, normal.

waster a person of no further use, due to decrepitude, disease etc *local*.

water, watter: ~**y-nebbit** pale and sickly; starved looking; having a drip at the end of one's nose *Bnf Abd Ags*.

waur-faured more ill-favoured, uglier *now Ork NE Ags*.

†**weary** sickly, puny, weak.

wee-boukit of small size, physically small *now midLoth*.

weel: ~**-faured** well-favoured, good-looking. †~**-lookit** good-looking, handsome. ~ **at anesel** in good physical condition, plump, stout.

wersh sickly, feeble in appearance.

whitely pale, whitish, delicate-looking.

†**twicht** strong, vigorous; active, agile.

weelins: hae the ~ **o** have control or full use of (one's body, limbs etc) *Abd*.

windlestrae *n, contemptuous* a person who is weak in health or character *now NE Ags WC*. *adj* easily blown about; weak, thin, delicate.

winsome attractive in appearance, manner or nature, charming.

wisgan *term of abuse* a stunted, useless, feckless person *Bnf Ags*.

wizen *of any kind of tissue etc* (cause to) shrivel, shrink, wither.

wurf a puny, ill-grown person, *esp* a child.

yite a small person *local Per-Wgt*.

†**yurlin** a puny stunted creature.

9.1.2 FAT AND THIN PEOPLE

†**batie** round, plump.

†**bausy** large, fat, coarse.

beffan a stupid, often fat and flabby, person *chf Bnf*.

belch *freq contemptuous* a stout, *usu* short person *now Kcb*. ~**y** short, plump and thriving *now Dmf*.

bulfie *of persons* fat *Bnf Abd Ayr*.

birk a stout, well-built boy or lad *Bnf Abd*.

burs(t)en fat, corpulent *now Bnf*.

blichan a lean, worn-out, worthless person *SW*.

bowsie, boozy big, fat, corpulent, puffed up *now Bnf Abd Kcb*.

brachton a large, weighty, clumsy man *SW*.

†**breekumstoich** a small stout child in breeches.

brosie stout; soft, inactive *now Bnf wLoth*. **brosie-headit** very stupid, fat and inactive *Bnf Ags*.

buirdly burly.

bumfy *of a person* lumpy in shape *now Abd Edb*.

bunch a small stout girl or young woman *now Lnk*.

bunt a short plump person *now local Abd-Lnk*. ~**in** plump, short and stout.

†**cabbrach** lean, scraggy.

†**chuffie** fat(-faced), portly.

clatch a fat clumsy woman.

clinkit thin, emaciated *now Kcb*.

cloit a dull, heavy person, a stupid and inactive person *now Abd Ags Kcb*.

clump a heavy, inactive person *now NE*.

cutty a short dumpy girl *now Ags*.

deaf nuts: not fed on *or* **wi** ~ plump, well-fed, well developed.

docketie short, round and jolly *Rox*.

drochle a short dumpy person, a puny insignificant person *now local Cai-Fif*.

†**ellwan(d), elvan** long and thin.

erse: aa ~ **an pooches** describing the back view of a stout dumpy man *Abd*.

flodge a fat, slovenly person, *esp* a woman *now Bnf Dmf*.

fluffy puffy, chubby *Abd midLoth Gall*.

fodge a fat, clumsy person *sEC, S*.

fodgel plump, buxom *now Abd*.

fozie fat, flabby, out of condition *local NE-Gall*. **foziness** flabbiness.

frow(die) a big buxom woman *chf NE*.

fuddie short, thick, stumpy.

fum a big, fat, dirty woman *Ayr*.

gaishon a thin, emaciated person, a 'skeleton' *chf SW S*.

gangyls: a gutts an ~ nothing but stomach and legs, fit for nothing but eating and walking *Bnf*.

gavel *NE*, **gable: like the** ~ (**end**) **of a hoose** very big and stout *Abd Kcb*.

gent a tall thin or lanky person *Sh SW, S*.

gilpin a big, stout or well-grown young person *chf N, SW*.

gluntie tall, lean, haggard *Bwk Rox*.

gowstie fat and flabby *now Abd*.

great, gret, grit big, stout *now Sh Abd*.

grulsh a fat, squat person *now Uls*. † ~**ie** sturdy, fat, clumsy-looking.

†**gulsh** a fat, thickset person.

gurk a stout, heavily-built person *Cai NE*.

gurthie corpulent.

gussie a fat person *now Ags*.

guttie *adj* thick; gross; corpulent, pot-bellied *now local Kcdn-Dmf*. *n* a corpulent, pot-bellied person *now Dmf Rox*.

harl: a ~ **o bones** a very thin person *Per Fif Slk Uls*.

hillock a fat sluggish person *Sh N Dmf*.

hotch a big fat ungainly woman *now midLoth WC, S*.

house, hoose: ~-**en(d)** a stout or heavily built woman *Gen except Sh Ork*. ~-**side** a big clumsy person *now Ags midLoth Gsw*.

hush a fat, ungainly, dirty person *now Abd Kcdn*.

ill-thriven badly-nourished, lean, scraggy.

knar a burly stockily-built person *NE*.

lang, long: ~ **drink (o water)** a tall lanky person.

lank a lean creature *now Uls*.

†**leengyie, lignie** fine, thin, slender.

lingel a tall lanky person *N*.

lingit thin, lank, lean *EC, S*.

lipper-fat bulging with fat, gross *chf S*.

†**lotch** a fat lazy person *Ayr Lnk*.

mardle 1 *usu of women* heavy, clumsy, corpulent *NE Renfr*. 2 *derog* a fat, clumsy, idle woman *Sh NE*.

†**mass** an amply-proportioned, motherly-looking woman

meat: like one's ~ plump, well-nourished in appearance.

mend fatten, (cause to) grow plump *now Kcb Uls*.

nairra, narrow: ~-**boukit** thin, lean *Abd Ags Per*.

nakit, naked thin, lean, emaciated *Ags Per Loth*.

pellock, pallo *Ork* a short fat person *now Ork Bnf*.

picket scraggy, shrunken.

pictarnie a thin wretched-looking person, a scarecrow.

pilsh a gross thickset man *NE*.

pilpert a badly-fed, cold-looking child *NE*.

pine emaciated, reduced to skin and bone.

pluffy having a well-padded appearance, plump, puffy, fleshy.

pud, pod a small, neat, *esp* plump person *now Uls*.

pudget, pudgie *now Sh Abd*, **pudgle** *now Bnf Abd Slk* a small, plump, thickset person.

pult a short stout person *now Ork Per Uls*.

punchie, punchik(ie) a short, stout person *now NE*.

rake a very thin person.

rantle tree a thin, stick-like person.

renchel a thin, spindly person *now Slk*.

ribe a long-legged, thin person *now Gall*.

rickle an emaciated, broken-down person, *freq* **a ~ o banes**.

row a plump person, a fat, untidy, lazy woman *SW*. **as ready to ~ as rin** said of a very fat person *Ork Bnf Abd*.

rummle, rumble derog term for a large clumsy person, a 'lump' *WC, SW*.

runk an emaciated, worn-out person *chf Sh-N*.

sappie plump, sleek, fleshy *now Abd Gall*.

scaddin a lean, emaciated person *now Abd*.

scargivenet a skinny adolescent.

scaulin pyock a loose fold of skin under the jaws of a fat person *Bnf Abd*.

selch a fat clumsy person *now Bnf*.

†shangie thin, scraggy, gaunt.

shaupie lank, not plump *now Lnk Ayr*.

shilpie thin, puny, pinched-looking.

shilpit thin, puny, shrunken, starved- or drawn-looking *Gen except Sh Ork*.

shirpit thin, shrunken, with sharp, drawn features *EC, WC*.

skelf a small thin insignificant person *WC Rox*.

skinnymalink(ie) a thin, skinny person.

skleff *of persons* thin; flat-chested *chf S*.

skrank thin, slender, skinny

skrankie thin, scraggy, meagre, shrivelled *now local Sh-Lnk*.

skrinkie thin, wrinkled, shrivelled *now Rox*.

slab a thin person with a broad frame *NE Ags*.

slamp slim, lithe, supple *local Ross-Per*.

slink thin, scraggy, lank. **slunken** lank- or emaciated-looking, sunken *Sh Lnk Dmf Rox*.

slung a tall lanky stupid person *NE*.

sma(ll) slim, slender, slightly-built *now Sh NE Per*.

†snosh chubby and contented.

soadie a big stout woman, a slut *now Stlg*.

†spirie tall, slender, spindly.

spirl a tall thin person *Bnf Abd Slk*. **~ie** *adj* slender, thin, spindly *now Loth S*. *n* a slender person *now Fif Loth S*.

stilch a young fat clumsy man *now Kcb*.

stilpert a tall lanky person or animal with long legs *now NE*.

stab a stout thickset man *now Sh Uls*.

stoussie †*adj* stout and stocky, sturdy, chubby. *n* a plump sturdy little child.

stramlach a tall, lanky, gangling person *Bnf Abd*.

streek: ~er a very tall thin person *now NE*.

strypal a tall, slender, rather handsome person *Cai Bnf*.

sture big, stout, burly, substantial *now Sh*.

sugg a fat, easy-going person *now Ork NE*.

sunk a hefty corpulent person, with a sack-like figure *now Kcdn Ags*.

swabble a tall thin person *now Rox*.

swamp *esp of a formerly plump person* thin, lean.

tanterwallop a tall thin man *Ags Per*.

tripal a tall, thin, ungainly person *now Abd*.

trollie-bags a fat, unshapely person *local N-Lnk*.

tulchan a large or fat person *Bnf Abd Ags*.

tume, toom *of a person or his limbs etc* thin, lean, lank *now local Sh-Stlg*.

wechtie physically heavy and solidly corpulent *now NE*.

whaup, *chf* **lang (teem) ~** a tall scrawny person *Abd Stlg Wgt*.

wheeber a lean, tall, ungainly person *Bnf Abd*.

whitrat a thin, small, hatchet-faced person of an active, ferrety disposition *local Sh-Dmf*.

windlestrae *n, contemptuous* a thin or lanky person; a person who is weak in health or character *now NE Ags WC*. *adj* easily blown about; weak, thin, delicate.

9.1.3 PHYSICAL DEFORMITIES

blastie *contemptuous* a shrivelled dwarf *now Bnf Gsw*.

boo bend, curve; become bent or crooked. **~backit** humpbacked *local Cai-Kcb*.

boolie-backit humpbacked *now Bnf Fif wLoth*.

†bowbackit humpbacked.

bowlt crooked, distorted *now Fif wLoth*.

bowsie crooked.

brockit disfigured.

camshachled distorted, bent, twisted, disordered *now local Abd-Edb*.

†camsheugh crooked, distorted, deformed.

crile a dwarf, a dwarfish or deformed creature.

croot, crit a short misshapen person *C-S*.

crouchie humpbacked *Ayr Pbls*.

crowl term of contempt for a dwarf or very small person *SW*.

†disfigurate disfigured, deformed.

droich a dwarf, a person of stunted growth *now local*.

drochlin puny, dwarfish *now Bnf Abd*.

†dwerch a dwarf.

hulgie- having a hump, hunch(-backed etc) *NE*.

humph, hump a hump, a curvature of the back or spine, a humpback *Gen except Sh Ork*. ~**ed** hunched. ~**ie, humfie** *adj*, also ~**ie-backit** having a hump, humpbacked *Gen except Sh Ork*. †*n* a humpbacked person. **humfy-back** = ~**ie** *Gen except Sh Ork*. ~**-backed** humpbacked *Gen except Sh Ork*.

hunchie a humpback *now Cai Abd midLoth*.

hurkle-backit humpbacked, misshapen *now Dmf*.

knur, nir a decrepit, dwarfish person *chf SW-Uls*.

knurl, knorl, †knurlin a deformed person, a dwarf *chf WC Dmf*.

†mimmerkin a dwarf, a dwarfish creature.

misgrown stunted, deformed *now Sh*.

†myting *abusive, chf flyting* ? a dwarf, a runt.

†rigwiddie *of an old woman* wizened, gnarled, tough and rugged-looking, mis-shapen.

runt an undersized or dwarfish person *local*. ~**it** stunted in growth *Ayr Kcb*.

scart, †scarth a hermaphrodite; a monster *now Rox*.

scrab a shrivelled or stunted person *now Bnf*.

scrae a stunted, shrivelled, or underdeveloped person *now NE*.

scrat a puny or stunted person *now NE Ags*.

shaird a puny or deformed person *now Bnf*.

shargart stunted *now Abd*.

sauchle a weakly, stunted or deformed person *now Ags Per*.

snauchle a dwarf.

strunty short, stumpy, stunted, shrunken, of poor growth *now Lnk*.

sutten on shrunken, dwarfed *now Kcb Rox*.

†unnatural abnormal, monstrous

†warroch a stunted, feeble, ill-grown person.

wirl a puny malformed person, a stunted or deformed creature, a dwarf *now Fif*. ~**ie** puny, stunted, undersized.

†wirling a puny or stunted person, a dwarf.

wrang, wrang *of a person, limb etc* crooked, deformed, out of joint *now Abd*.

†yrle a dwarfish person.

9.2 FACE, HEAD

bap-faced having a face like a **bap**, soft and stupid-looking *local*.

bree the brow, the forehead *now Fif*.

brent *freq of the brow* smooth, unwrinkled.

brinkie-brow *used to children* the forehead *now Bnf Abd Ags*.

broo the brow, the forehead.

brosie-faced having a fat, flaccid face *now Abd*.

†buckie a protuberance on the cheek.

buffie *freq of the face* fat, chubby *now Bnf Abd*.

byke the nose *now Ags*.

cantle (the crown of) the head *now Abd*.

chaft *n* ~**s** 1 jaws. 2 cheeks *now NE Kcb*. **big-**~**ed** big-jawed *now Bnf Abd*. ~ **blade** 1 the jaw-bone. 2 the cheek-bone.

chandler-chafted lantern-jawed *Abd Fif*.

chollers *now Abd Dmf*, **chirles** *now Ork* the jowls, a double chin.

chowks the cheeks, jaws.

chuffie-cheeked *esp of a child* chubby-cheeked.

coontenance a countenance.

cooter ludicrous name for the nose *chf N*.

croon the crown.

†cut-luggit crop-eared.

deafie a deaf person.

dit shut up, close (*chf* the mouth) *now Bnf*.

dull (o hearing) deaf, hard of hearing.

fair: ~**-avised** fair-complexioned *now Bnf Fif SW*.

flytepock a double chin *now Ags*.

foreheid the forehead.

†forestam the forehead.

fraized greatly surprised, having a wild, staring look.

gams the jaws.

†gane an ugly face.

gash †a protruding chin. † ~**-beard** *appar* having a long, protruding chin. ~**-gabbit** having a protruding lower jaw *now Ags Lnk*.

ginnles the cheeks.

gizz the face.

†gowl the jaws.

gruntle *contemptuous, of a person* the nose and mouth, the face or head.

grunyie *contemptuous* the snout of a person.

guffie fat, flabby or fluffy about the cheeks *now Rox*.

haffet *now chf literary*, **†halfhede** the side of the head; the temple, cheek.

harn: ~**s** brains, the brain. ~**pan** the skull *now local Sh-EC*.

heid, head, also ~**ie** the head. † ~**-werk** a headache, a pain in the head.

†hindhead the back of the head.

157

†**holkis** an ailment affecting the face or eyes of a person.

kip a turned-up nose *now Uls.* ~**pit** *of a nose* a nose turned up at the tip *now Rox.*

lang, long: ~**-chafter,** ~**-chaffed** long- or lantern-jawed *now NE-Ags.* **lang lugs** a person with long ears *now Ags Kcb Rox.* **lang-luggit** long-eared *now local NE-S.* ~**-nebbit** having a gnome-like or supernatural appearance *now Ork.*

lap a lobe (of the ear) *now Sh.*

leap *of the face* flush with blushing or with a skin rash *Sh Rox.*

lug 1 the ear as part of the body, the external ear. **2** the ear as the organ of hearing, the inner ear. ~**gie 1** *also used as a nickname* with characteristic ears *now Mry midLoth.* **2** *also* ~**git** having a **lug** *or* **lugs** (of a specified nature) *now Ork.*

mell: ~**-heid** a blunt-shaped head *Rox.* ~**-heidit** hammer-headed *now Rox.*

mouth, mou: wi ~ **and een** (**baith**) in a gaping, staring manner *now Abd.*

nairra, narrow: ~**-nebbit** sharp-nosed *now Uls.*

neb 1 *also* **nib** a person's nose. **2** the whole face. ~**-end** the tip of the nose *local Edb-S.*

neep *joc, implying stupidity* the head *local Sh-EC.*

niz *now joc* the nose. †**nesethrill** a nostril.

nob the nose.

nose thirl a nostril *now Sh N.*

†**now** the head *only proverb.*

open: the ~ **o the heid** the front suture of the skull, the fontanelle *now Sh.*

†**pallet** *chf verse, contemptuous* the head, pate.

pan the skull, the cranium.

†**pash** *joc* the head, 'nut'.

†**pat** the pate, the head.

penny bowls: hae een like ~ have a startled wide-eyed expression, be saucer-eyed *Ork Ags Gall.*

pow, poll the head, the crown of the head, the scalp, the skull.

†**rancie** ruddy-complexioned *Fif.*

red, reid, rid: ~ **face** a blushing face, as a sign of embarrassment or shame, *freq* **give someone** *or* **get a** ~ **face.** ~ **neb** a red nose.

†**rude** complexion.

sair, sore *of the head* aching, painful, throbbing. ~ **heid** a headache.

scaup 1 the scalp. **2** the skull, cranium.

sconeface nickname for a person with a round flat face *now local Ags-WC.*

shairp-nibbit having a pointed nose *Sh Abd.*

sham-gabbit *etc* having the lower jaw protruding beyond the upper, with a projecting lower lip *now C, SW.*

†**shangie-moud** with gaunt cheeks, lantern-jawed.

skrinkie-faced with a wrinkled face (and an unpleasant manner).

snirket *of a face* pinched, wizened, puckered *Sh Rox.*

snotter box the nose.

snout, snoot *contemptuous* **1** the nose. **2** the face, head.

snubbert *joc or contemptuous* the nose *NE.*

swap *n, also* **swype** *NE Per* the cast of someone's features, *esp* as it resembles his relatives, a facial trait or characteristic in a family *now Sh NE Per.* *v* resemble in (*esp* facial) appearance, show a family likeness to *now Ork Wgt.*

tattie *contemptuous* the head *now Sh.*

†**thirl** a nostril.

thrawn *of the mouth, face* wry, twisted with pain, rage etc, surly ~**-faced,** ~**-gabbit,** † ~**-mou'd** having a wry, twisted face or mouth.

top, tap the head *now local Sh-Per.*

tosie *of the cheeks* flushed.

track, tract a feature, trait *now Sh.*

†**visnomy** physiognomy.

†**vult** a face, countenance; *esp* expression of the features, bearing.

whaup-nebbit having a long beaky nose *now Per.*

wulk *joc* the nose, *esp* **pick one's** ~ *Ags Fif Dnbt.*

9.3 MOUTH, TEETH

aisle-tuith a molar tooth; a bicuspid tooth *SW, S.*

buss *n* the mouth, *esp* if pouting; a sulky, bad-tempered expression, *eg* **have a** ~ **on** *now Cai Highl.* *v* pout.

chack 1 snap shut *now Lnk Kcb.* **2** *of the teeth* chatter *now Abd.*

chaft tooth a molar *chf Fif.*

chirk, chark gnash, rub (teeth, gums) **together** *chf NE SW.*

cramsh grit one's teeth *Bnf Abd.*

dummie a dumb person.

faisle a loose drooping underlip *now Fif Dmf.*

†**forder** *of limbs, teeth* front, fore.

gab 1 the mouth. **2** †the palate, taste. **-gabbit** -mouthed.

gams (large) teeth.

gash: ~**le** distort (the mouth etc) *NE.* ~**-gabbit** *now Ags,* ~**-mou'd** *NE Fif* having a sagging, misshapen mouth.

gebbie a person's mouth *now Ags Per Fif.*

†gegger an under-lip, esp when protruding.

girl *of the teeth* be set on edge *S*.

gob the mouth.

gumstick a stick etc used by a teething child *now midLoth Ayr*.

hareshard a hare-lip.

jirg, jirk grate, grind (the teeth) *now Cai midLoth Kcb*.

melt the tongue.

mou the mouth.

muckle-moued having an unusually large mouth *now Sh Ork nEC*.

mull the lip *chf Sh Ork, now Fif*.

muns *cant or gypsy* the mouth, the 'chops' *local*.

neb, nib any projecting tip or point on a person's body *eg* of the tongue.

pou, pull draw or extract (a tooth).

risp grind (the teeth) *now Abd*.

sair teeth toothache *Sh-nEC*.

scash *esp of the mouth* twisted, turned to one side *now Abd Kcdn*.

seam a row of natural or, *more usu*, artificial teeth, *freq* a ~ o teeth *now NE-Per*.

shambling, shammelt *now esp of teeth* twisted, out of alignment *NE*.

shevel †*adj, of the mouth* distorted, twisted. *v* distort (the mouth) *now N Per*. † ~(ing) gabbit *etc* having a wry or twisted mouth.

†skewl screw up, twist (the mouth).

spune-gabbit having a thick, protruding lower lip *local Fif-SW*.

stot a stammer, stutter, speech impediment *now Ork*.

stut stutter, stammer.

tattie-trap *disparaging* the mouth *now Per WC*.

teud a tooth *Fif*.

thrawn *of the mouth, face* wry, twisted with pain, rage etc, surly ~**-faced**, ~**-gabbit**, † ~**-mou'd** having a wry, twisted face or mouth.

tongue-tackit tongue-tied, having a speech impediment, dumb, mute *Gen except Sh Ork*.

†toot-mou'd having protruding lips.

tuith a tooth. † ~y sharp-toothed. **teethache**, † ~work toothache.

wallies a set of false teeth *C*.

†wavel twist (the mouth).

wick a corner of the mouth *local*.

wicker *of the lip or eyelid* twitch, flicker.

†witters the teeth.

worm (i(n) the, thy *etc* **cheek)** toothache *now Ork*.

wummlebore a cleft palate *now nEC*.

yatter *of teeth* rattle, chatter, *eg* from fear *now Ags*.

9.4 HAIR

beld *now Abd*, **bell** *adj* bald. *v* make bald *Bnf Abd*. **bauldy, baldy** bald: '*bauldy-heidit*'.

birr: in a ~ *etc of hair etc* standing up on end, tousled; brushed so as to stand out from the head *now Abd*.

†birsie bristly; hairy.

birstle bristle, the stubble on an unshaved chin *Sh Ork N*.

†canous hoary; grey-haired.

cauf's lick a cow-lick, twist of hair *local Cai-Kcb*.

daberlacks hair in lank, tangled, separate locks *Mry Bnf*.

daik smooth down (the hair etc) *now Abd Ags*.

dossan a forelock *now Cai Ross*.

†felter tangle (hair etc).

flaucht a lock or tuft of hair.

fusker a whisker, a moustache *NE*.

haffets side-locks of hair.

†hasard *adj* grey, grey-haired. *n* a grey-haired man.

hassock a shock of bushy hair *now NE*.

heather, hather: ~y **head** (a person with) a tousled or shaggy head of hair *now NE Rox*.

hudder, huther *chf of hair* shaggy, unkempt, dishevelled *NE*.

Katie beardie name for a woman with a beard or moustache *Cai Abd Ags*.

†lachter a lock of hair.

link a lock of hair, a curl *now Sh*.

lint-tap the bundle of dressed flax put on a distaff for spinning; *chf* describing very fair or grey hair: '*hair like a lint tap*'. ~**-white** *chf verse, of hair* white as flax, flaxen-blond.

†lire *verse* the complexion.

lock: † ~**er** *v* curl. *adj* curly. ~**ering** curling. †**lokkerit** curled, curly.

lyart *of the hair* streaked with white, grizzled, silvery.

matash a moustache *now Ags*.

mix *of greying hair* become mixed in colour *local Ork-Kcb*.

moutache a moustache *NE, nEC*.

†nikkie-now *only proverb* a **nit**-infested head.

nitty now a **nit**-infested head.

penny(s)worths: hang in ~ *of the hair* droop in lank wisps *now Kcb*.

piskie *of hair etc* dry, shrivelled *SW*.

red, reid, rid: ~**-heidit** having red hair and thus popularly believed to be excitable and impetuous *Gen except Sh Ork*.

rush a luxuriant growth of hair *Sh Ork Ags*.

scabbie-heid applied to a person with head lice *local C*.

score a parting in the hair *local C*.

seam the parting of the hair *local Sh-wLoth*.

shed *n* the parting of the hair. *v* part or comb (the hair) to one side or the other.

sheemach a tangled or matted mass of hair etc *NE*.

start *of the hair* stick up in an unkempt way, bristle *Lnk Slk*.

strag thin wispy hair *now Lnk*.

stribbly *of hair* straggly, loose and trailing *NE*.

swirl a tuft or curl of hair, a forelock *now Sh*. ∼**ie** *esp of the hair* having a marked curl or coil, curly, frizzy *now Sh SW*.

tait a small tuft or bundle of hair etc *now local Sh-Kcb*.

tap, top a tuft of hair etc; a forelock. †**tappin, toppin** a crest or topknot of hair, *esp* of an early nineteenth-century men's hairstyle. **tap o tow** a head of flaxen hair *now Kinr wLoth WC*.

taut *n* a tangled, matted tuft or lock of hair etc *now local Sh-SW*. *v* mat, tangle; make matted or tangled. ∼**ie** *now C, S*, ∼**it** *now local Sh-SW* having a rough, shaggy head; *of hair etc* matted, entangled, shaggy, unkempt.

theek, thick any thick covering, of hair etc *now Ags Per*.

tossel a tuft or fringe of hair *Sh NE-Per*.

tousie *chf of the hair* dishevelled; tangled. **touslie** *of the hair* dishevelled, ruffled *C*.

traveller *joc* a head-louse *Ork NE Dmf*.

wase a bushy, unkempt shock of hair, whiskers etc.

9.5 EYES, SIGHT

blear *n, usu* ∼**s** something which obscures the sight; matter in the eye *now Bnf*. ∼**ie** watery-eyed.

bleed-raing become bloodshot *Bnf*.

†**bleezy** *of the eyes* showing signs of intoxication.

blin(d) *adj* blind. *v* close (the eyes) as in sleep *now Bnf Abd*. **blindlins** *now Lnk*, †**blindlin(g)is** blindly; with eyes shut *now Lnk*. **blinner** move the eyelids like a person with defective sight *Cai Bnf*.

blude, blood: ∼ **run** *now Bnf Abd*, ∼**shed** *now local Cai-Ayr* bloodshot.

blue ee a black eye *NE nEC*.

boggle *of the eyes* protrude, bulge with fear or pain *now EC*.

bree †the eyebrow. ∼**rs 1** the eyelashes *now Abd*. **2** the eyebrows *Sh Abd*.

broo a brow, eyebrow.

craw taes crow's feet, wrinkles at the corner of the eye *now Bnf Abd Fif*.

ee, eye, *also* **eenie** the eye. ∼**-bree,** ∼**-broo** an eyebrow. ∼**-brier** an eyelash. ∼**hole,** † ∼ **dolp** an eyesocket. ∼**-wink(er) 1** an eyelash *now Bwk*. **2** an eyelid. ∼ **winkie** *children's rhyme* the eye *local Sh-Ags*.

far awa wi't *of the eyes* dreamy, abstracted *now midLoth Bwk Uls*.

fire a foreign body (*usu* metallic) in the eye *now local Cai-Ayr*.

gledge a squint *now Pbls*.

gley, glee *n* a cast in the eye *local Sh-Edb*. *adj, also* ∼**-eyed** *local Bnf-S* **1** squint-eyed, having a cast or squint in the eye, squinting. **2** one-eyed, blind in one eye *now Per*. **gleytness** the state of having a squint, being squint-eyed *now Sh Abd*.

glimmer *of the eyes* be dazzled; blink *now local Ork-Kcb*. ∼**in** *of the eyes* half-closed, peering *now Bnf Abd*.

gowp-the-lift someone who has a cast in the eye.

greetin ee a watering eye *Sh Abd midLoth Kcb*.

hap, hop *of tears etc* trickle down.

†**holkis** an ailment affecting the face or eyes of a person.

jee, gee: ∼**eed** squint-eyed *now Ags midLoth*.

keeker 1 the eye *local nEC-S*. **2** *also* **blue keeker** a black eye *local Abd-WC*.

†**lucken** *of the brows* knit, close-set, contracted as in a frown.

†**mirkness** blindness.

†**oversile** dim, dull, impair sight.

pearl a cataract (on the eye) *now Uls*.

peerie-wearie strained or short-sighted-looking *now Slk*.

pie peer closely, squint. **pie-eyed** cross-eyed, having a squint *Kcdn WC*.

pink *of the eyes* become small and narrow, be half-shut; *of persons* narrow the eyes, blink, peer.

pinkie *of the eyes* narrowed, peering, winking.

preserves weak spectacles intended to preserve the sight *local Sh-SW*.

rake, rauk rub (the eyes) *now Sh Abd*.

reel *of the eyes* roll or revolve with excitement, greed etc *now NE Ags*.

ring: ∼**it** *of the eye* having a white circle round the iris; *of persons* wall-eyed *now Sh Per Kcb*. ∼**le ee** a wall eye. ∼**le-eed,** ∼**lit-eed** having a ∼**le** eye.

sand blin(d) sand-blind, half-blind; *specif* having the poor sight associated with albinism *now Sh*.

†**sheen** the pupil (of the eye).

shuit, shoot *of tears etc* stream out.

sicht, sight 1 sight. **2** the pupil (of the eye) *local Sh-Lnk*.

skellie *adj, also* ~**-eyed** squinting, squint-eyed *now C (except Ags)*, *S*. *n* a cast in the eye, a squint; a squint or sidelong glance *now Per-S*. *v* squint, be cross-eyed *now local Abd-S*.

skew *v, of the eyes or glance* squint naturally or on purpose. *n* a squint, sidelong glance *now Mry Abd*.

sklent 1 †cast (the eyes) sideways. **2** glance sideways, look askance, squint *now local*.

slabber make a snorting, bubbling sound as in weeping or sleeping *now Dnbt SW*.

spentacles, †**spartickles** spectacles.

†**squink-eyed** squint-eyed.

stane, stone: ~ **blind** completely blind.

star: the ~ **o the ee** the pupil of the eye *local*.

starn: the ~ **o the eye** the pupil of the eye *S*.

†**startle** *of the eyes* start from their sockets.

staul *n, v* squint *now Mry*.

steek close (the eyes).

stell *of the eyes* become fixed in a stare of astonishment, horror etc, stand out *now local Lnk-Rox*.

styan a sty on the eyelid *now Ork Mry Abd*.

†**stymie** a person who does not see well.

†**techyr** a tear.

watshod *of the eyes* wet with tears *now Ayr*.

waul *of the eyes* roll wildly.

wick the corner of the eye.

wicker *of the lip or eyelid* twitch, flicker.

winkers the eyelids, eyelashes.

†**winnel-skewed** suffering from an optical illusion; squint-eyed.

yak *orig and chf gipsy* the eye *Rox*.

9.6 HANDS, ARMS

airm an arm.

†**beuch** a shoulder or limb.

bought the bend of the arm (or leg) *now Abd Fif*.

bran a fleshy part of the body; a rounded muscle of the arm or leg.

car, *adj, also* ~**rie** left (hand side), left-handed. **corrie-fisted** left-handed. **corrie-fister** a left-handed person *WC*. ~**ry-handed** left-handed. ~**-handit,** ~**-pawed** *chf Fif* left-handed.

clauts grasping fingers *now Lnk*.

cleuk a hand *Abd Ags*.

clootie a left-handed person *Abd Uls*.

coorag the index finger *Cai*.

crannie *Bnf-Ags*, ~ **doodlie** *NE*, ~ **wannie** *Abd* the little finger.

crog a big hand *chf Cai*.

curnie(-wurnie) *child's word* the little finger *Fif*.

dirlie-bane the funny bone *now local Bnf-WC*.

elba, elbuck the elbow.

†**fauldit** *of the fists* clenched.

finger neb a fingertip *now Fif Ayr*.

†**forder** *of limbs* front, fore.

gaig *n* a chap in the hands *local Bnf-Dmf*. *v, of the hands* chap *Cai Kcb*.

gardy the arm; *perh specif* the forearm *now Abd*. **gardies** the hands or fists, *esp* when raised to fight.

glack the angle between thumb and forefinger *now Cai*.

gowpen the receptacle so formed by the hands held together in the form of a bowl.

hand, haun *n, also* ~**ie** a hand. ~**less** handless, without hands.

ketach the left hand *Arg Renfr Uls*. ~ **or katy handed** left-handed *Renfr Uls*.

kippie *adj* left-handed *nEC*. *n* **1** a left-handed person *now Per Fif*. **2** the left hand *now Fif*.

knap the point of the elbow *now Sh*.

knockle 1 a knuckle *now NE Per*. **2** the rounded, protuberant part of a bone at a joint, the condyle *Cai SW*.

lirk a fold of the body, a joint; the angle of the elbow or knee when bent *now Slk*.

lith 1 a joint in a finger or toe, a small part of the body, *freq* ~ **and limb** *now Sh N nEC*. **2** †a limb.

†**lucken** *of the hand or foot:* **1** †closed tight, clenched; having the sinews contracted; **2** having webbed fingers or toes.

luif, loof the palm of the hand.

maig, meg a large ungainly hand *chf Sh S*.

†**mell** a clenched fist.

mid-finger the middle finger *now Sh Gall Uls*.

neb, nib any projecting tip or point on a person's body, *eg* of fingers or toes.

nieve, †**nave** a fist.

noup *esp of the elbow* a knob or protuberance *chf Ags S*.

oxter the armpit; the under part of the (upper) arm. **in one's** ~ in one's armpit, in one's arms. **under one's** ~ under one's arm, in one's armpit

pally-handit 1 having a damaged or useless hand *C, S*. **2** left-handed *EC*.

peerie-winkie *nursery rhymes* the little finger or toe *Sh Ork Renfr*.

pinkie the little finger.

pirlie *now Ags*, **pirlie-winkie** *now local NE-Wgt* the little finger.

present a white speck on the fingernail, commonly believed to presage the arrival of a gift *Ork NE C*.

rackle-handed having powerful hands.

ragnail a loose piece of skin or broken nail at the side of a fingernail, a hangnail.

shackle, sheckle, *also* ~ **bane** *now Sh-Per* the wrist *now Fif Ayr*.

shouder, shouther the shoulder. ~ **heid** the socket of the shoulder-bone; the shoulder joint *NE, EC, S*. **~-the-win** (having) a deformity in which one shoulder is higher than the other *local N-Gall*.

sker: **~ry-handit** *now S*, †**~-handed** left-handed.

skibby left-handed *Lnk Ayr*.

southie left-handed *Ayr*.

spag, spaig *Cai* a hand, foot, *esp* a big clumsy hand or foot *now Cai*.

spaul the shoulder; the shoulder-bone. †~ **bane** a shoulder blade

spyog a paw, hand, foot, or leg *now Cai*.

thoum the thumb. **~-hand** the nearest free available hand, *specif* the right hand *NE Ags*.

wallie *of the fist or grip* big, strong.

†**wan bane** the smaller bone of the forearm.

9.7 FEET, LEGS

For bad gaits and walking in general, see 9.17.

†**anklet** the ankle.

†**bane, bone:** **~schaw** sciatica; hip gout.

bap fit a flat foot *NE*.

behouchie *freq to children* the behind, backside *Gen except Sh Ork*.

†**beuch** a limb.

boddam the bottom.

bool a bow-legged person.

bought the bend of the arm (or leg) *now Abd Fif*.

bow: bowdy(-leggit) bandy-legged *now Edb*. **~-houghd** bandy-legged *now Ags Fif*.

bowly-legged bow-legged *WC*.

bowt, bolt: **~foot** a club-foot *now Ags*.

bran a fleshy part of the body; a rounded muscle of the arm or leg, *latterly* the calf.

bumpy the buttocks.

†**bun** the buttocks.

cauf calf (of the leg).

cleavings the crotch *now Abd Ags*.

clift the crotch *now Abd*.

†**cloff** the crotch.

cloot a foot.

cuit the ankle.

†**culum** the buttocks; the anus.

curpin the behind or rump.

†**curple** the buttocks *Ayr*.

deuk-fittit splay-footed *chf SW*.

dock the buttocks *now local Cai-Fif*.

doup the buttocks.

droddum the buttocks *now Bnf Abd Ags*.

drone the buttocks, the backside *now Ags*.

dwaible *chf of the legs* weak, feeble, shaky *now Bnf Abd Fif*.

erse the arse.

fillets the loins or thighs *now Cai Abd*.

fit, foot, fittie a foot. **feetie** feet. **~less** unsteady on the feet, apt to stumble.

forefit the front part of the foot *now Sh Abd Fif*.

forkin the crotch.

fud the buttocks *now Dmf Rox*.

†**gammon** a person's leg or thigh.

girse-gawed *of toes* having cuts or cracks between them.

gowl the crotch, the perineal region *now Cai Bnf Abd*.

grip: hae *or* **tak a guid** ~ **o Scotland** have large feet.

gutter gaw a sore on the foot *now local Ags nEC*.

hainch, hinch, *also* ~**le** *nEC* a haunch.

happer: **~-arsed** **~-hippit** *S* with protuberant buttocks or hips.

happity *freq of a leg* lame *now Ags*.

hen: **~-taed, ~-toed** pigeon-toed.

hinder: **~s** the buttocks. **~lan(d)s, ~lets,** †**~lins** the buttocks. **hinderend** the behind, the backside.

hint-end hindquarters, posterior.

hippit hipped.

hoch, haugh the hollow behind the knee-joint, the back of the thigh; the thigh itself, the upper part of the leg. †**..~ed** having .. thighs, ..-thighed.

hunker-bane the thigh bone *now Cai Per*.

hurdies the buttocks, hips, haunches *Gen except Sh Ork*.

hurkle-bane the hip-bone *local*.

in-kneed knock-kneed *now Ork N Rox*.

intaed, intoed pigeon-toed.

keel *slang* a person's bottom, the backside *now Bwk*.

kep-a-gush a splay-footed person *Rox*.

knap the kneecap *now Kcdn Ags Fif*.

knee-lid the kneecap *now Ags Fif Ayr*.

knockle 1 a knuckle *now NE Per*. **2** the rounded,

protuberant part of a bone at a joint, the condyle *Cai SW*.

knoit a bunion *Kcdn Ayr Uls*.

†knowll-ta a toe swollen at the joints.

knule-kneed ? having swollen or enlarged knee-joints; knock-kneed *chf WC-S*.

lang, long: ∼ **shankit** long-legged *now local NE-S*.

†lendis the loins.

†lid: the ∼ **of the knee** the kneecap, patella.

†limb a leg.

lingel-tailed narrow-hipped *now Fif Dmf*.

lirk a fold of the body, a joint; the angle of the elbow or knee when bent *now Slk*.

lisk the groin, flank *now C*.

lith 1 a joint in a finger or toe, a small part of the body, *freq* ∼ **and limb** *now Sh N nEC*. **2** †a limb.

†lucken *of the hand or foot:* **1** closed tight, clenched; having the sinews contracted; **2** having webbed fingers or toes.

†lunyie the loin.

lyomon, lo(u)man the leg. ∼**s** the lower extremities, *latterly* the feet *chf NE*.

neb, nib any projecting tip or point on a person's body, *eg* of fingers or toes.

nether end the posterior.

†nub, nubbie nickname for a club-footed person *Rox*.

pally-fittit 1 having a damaged or useless foot *C, S*. **2** †splay-footed, flat-footed.

peerie-winkie *nursery rhymes* the little finger or toe *Sh Ork Renfr*.

pin-leg a wooden leg.

pipe-shankit having long, thin legs *C, S*.

pirnie-taed *NE nEC*, **pirn-taed** *Sh NE nEC* pigeon-toed.

plain-soled flat-footed.

reel: ∼**-foot** a club-foot. ∼**-fitted** having a ∼**-foot** *local Sh-Wgt*.

ribe a long-legged thin person *now Gall*.

rumple the buttocks, seat *now Sh*. ∼**-bane** the rump-bone, the coccyx *now local*.

scash *esp of the feet* twisted, turned to one side *now Abd Kcdn*.

scash *NE*, **scashle** *esp of feet or gait* twist, turn to one side.

sclaff: ∼**er** a flat foot *now NE Ags Per*. ∼**ie,** ∼**-fittit** *local N-SW* flat-footed.

sham the leg.

shammie-leggit bandy-legged *Per Stlg Gsw*.

†shammle-shanks *etc* a bandy-legged person.

shankit: ..-∼ having legs of a specified kind: 'sturdy-shankit'.

shuil: ∼**ly** *specif of the feet* like a shovel, flat and

splayed out *now Ayr*. ∼**-fit** a person with flat shuffling feet *now Stlg Ayr*.

skew *of the feet, legs or gait* splay, turn outwards *Bnf Abd*. ∼**-fittit** splay-footed *local NE-Lnk*.

spag, spaig *Cai* a hand, foot, *esp* a big clumsy hand or foot *now Cai*. ∼**ach** flat-footed, with clumsy or misshapen feet *now Cai Inv*.

sparrabaldy having thin legs *Bnf Abd*.

†spauls legs.

splae splay(-foot(ed)) *now Dnbt*.

splashfoot splay foot *now Abd*.

spurtle: ∼ **leg,** ∼ **shank** *now Ayr* a thin leg like a porridge stick. ∼**-leggit** having ∼ **legs** *now NE, C*.

spyog a paw, hand, foot, or leg *now Cai*.

†stane, stone: ∼ **crase,** ∼ **graze** ? a boil or abscess in the foot *SW*.

stumparts (*usu* sturdy) legs *NE*.

tae a toe. **tae('s) length** the length of one's toe *now local Sh-Wgt*.

thee the thigh.

tickie-taed pigeon-toed *Per Fif Loth*.

†tone the buttocks; the anus.

†towdy the buttocks, the posterior.

trampers the feet *now N nEC Ayr*.

trams *esp joc or contemptuous* the legs *now local Sh-SW*.

†tree-leg a wooden leg.

tuckie *of a limb etc* disabled, deformed *NE*.

weaver-kneed 1 knock-kneed *C*. **2** having sensitive or ticklish knees *WC*.

werrock a corn, bunion etc on the foot.

†whorlbane the hip-bone or joint.

9.8 SKIN

bark the skin *now Sh*.

bealin a festering sore, boil, pimple etc.

bile a boil, a suppuration.

†bla *of skin* black, *chf* **bla man**.

†blauds, bladds a disease causing pustules.

blin(d) lump a boil which does not come to a head.

blob, blab a pimple or pustule. ∼**s** a rash *now Ork*.

blush (raise a) blister *Bwk Rox*. ∼**in** a blister; a pustule, as in smallpox *SW Uls*.

†blype a layer of skin as it peels or is rubbed off.

brook a kind of boil, ulcer or sore.

cart the crab-louse; the skin-disease it causes *Abd*.

cattle lice etc *now Abd Lnk*.

cauld ower swarm, be infested (with vermin) *now Bnf Abd Fif.*

cruels scrofula, **the** king's evil *now Bnf Fif Kcb.*

din dark-complexioned, sallow *Gen except Sh Ork.*

dottle the core of a boil *now Abd Fif.*

esscock an inflamed pimple *chf NE.*

ferntickle a freckle. **~ed** freckled.

flech rid (oneself or another) of fleas *N Fif.* **~y** covered or infested with fleas *local Sh-Fif.*

flype *v* 1 tear off (the skin) in strips, peel *local.* 2 *of loose skin etc* curl. *n* the cutting of a strip of skin; a shred or loose piece of skin *Ork Cai Fif.*

galtags inflammation of the skin between the toes *Cai.*

gaw *n* a gall, a sore etc. †*v* gall, make sore, *chf* **gaw(e)d.**

girran a small boil or pustule *now Cai Arg.*

hack *n* a crack or chap in the skin caused by cold or frost. *v, of the skin* crack, chap, roughen.

hail-skinnt having an unblemished skin *local.*

harl peel (off), rub the skin off *now Uls.*

hatter a skin eruption, a rash, *chf* **be in a ~. be in a ~el** be covered with sores *now Bnf.*

hide human skin: 1 *now joc or contemptuous;* 2 †*literary, alliterative with* **hew** *etc.*

hives name for a skin eruption, *esp* red-gum in infants *local Cai-SW.*

horn †a corn on the foot, a piece of hard skin, a callosity. **~ie** horny.

hotterel a mass of festering sores or chaps; one such sore *Abd.*

huil the skin.

humour a skin eruption *Abd Kcdn Rox.*

income a swelling, abscess, festering sore etc *now local Sh-Kcb.*

kell an incrustation of scab or scurf on the head or face *now Ayr.* **~t, ~ed** covered with dirt or scurf *Lnk Ayr.*

kirnel *now Fif-Rox, also* **wax(en)** *or* **waxing kirnels** *local Fif-Rox* a lump under the skin, *esp* in the neck; a swollen gland.

knurl, knorl, *also* **~ick** a lump, protuberance. **~lie** lumpy, knobbly, gnarled *now Cai.*

†**lazarus** a leper.

leather, ledder *Sh Ork NE* the skin.

lipper[1] 1 †a leper. 2 †leprosy. 3 a large festering sore or mass of sores, a scab *now Cai.* †**~ous** leprous. † **~ folk** lepers. † **~ man** a leper.

lirk a crease or fold of the skin, a wrinkle.

luce 1 a skin incrustation, scurf, dandruff, loose dead skin *now Sh.* 2 †seborrhea.

maisle, measle *v* redden the skin of the legs by sitting too near the fire, *chf* **measlet, mizzled** scorched, mottled, blotched *now N.* **mizzle-** *or*

mizlie-shinned with legs blotched, *esp* from sitting too near the fire *local.*

milk-beal(in) a whitlow *SW Uls.*

†**misell** leprous.

moul a chilblain, *esp* a broken one on the heel *now Ayr.* **moulie** affected with chilblains *now Cai.*

mowdiewort *joc* a mole on the skin, a wart *now Renfr Ayr.*

nakit naked.

needle-naked stark-naked *Sh Cai Kcdn.*

nirl, nurl: the ~s a disease characterized by inflamed pustules, a rash *now Ork Per Loth.*

outstriking an eruption of the skin, a rash *now Ags.*

peel skin (one's leg, arm etc), rub or scrape skin off, *usu* by accident.

pick a chap on the skin *Ork Bnf Abd.*

plouk a growth, a swelling; a boil; a pimple. **plookit** covered with pimples, spotty. **plouky** covered with growths, pustules or pimples, spotty.

pock a disease causing eruptions or pustules on the skin, *eg* chicken-pox *now local Sh-SW.* **~(y)arred** pock-marked, having a scarred or pitted skin *now Ayr.*

quick swarming, infested *Sh Ork Uls.*

rankel a festering sore.

rasp a mole; a birthmark, naevus *Per Fif.*

red, reid, rid: ~ nakit stark naked *local Abd-Per.*

†**reef** a skin disease producing scabs.

rimple wrinkle *now Ork Ags.*

runklie wrinkled *now NE nEC, WC, S.*

rush a skin eruption, rash, *specif* of scarlet fever *now local.*

scab †form scabs on. **scabbert** †*n* a person suffering from scab. *adj* scabbed, bare.

scag *of the human face etc* become wrinkled, lose the bloom *Cai.*

scam a spot, crack, injury *now local Sh-Fif.*

scaw, †scall a scaly skin disease *now Ork Ayr.* **scawt** affected with scab, itch, ringworm etc *now NE Ayr.*

score a line, wrinkle on the skin, *esp* of the hand as used in palmistry *now Sh N, WC.*

†**scrubie** scurvy.

scruif, scruff 1 scruff, scurf *now Sh C, S.* 2 a hardened scab, piece of encrusted skin, hair, dirt etc *now Ork C.* 3 †the skin, epidermis.

†**scrumple** a wrinkle, crease.

scuddie *adj* naked, without clothes, or with one garment only *now C, S.* *n, also* **bare ~** *C* the bare skin, a state of nudity *now Abd Kcdn Per WC.*

scur *n, also* **scurl** *now NE Ags Per Rox* a scab or cicatrix which forms over a healing sore or wound *now Abd. v, of a wound or sore* form a scab, crust over in healing *Bnf Abd.*

shilcorn a pimple, a blackhead.

skirl (naked) completely or stark-naked *now local Ags-S.*

sleekit smooth, having glossy skin *now local Cai-SW.*

sotterel: in a ~ affected by a skin disease *Abd.*

spreckle a speckle, spot, freckle.

†strik, strike: ~ out *of the head or face* break out in sores or a rash.

tartan: fireside ~ *local Mry-Ayr,* **Grannie's ~** *local EC-Dmf,* **tink(l)er's ~** *now local N-EC* mottled skin on the legs caused by sitting too close to a fire.

†thack the skin.

walkit *of skin etc* hardened, roughened; calloused *now Sh C.*

weel-skinnt having a healthy clear skin or smooth appearance *now Sh.*

whisky-tacket a pimple on the face ascribed to too much whisky-drinking *now local NE-Lnk.*

whittle, whittle beal(in) *now local Sh-Ayr* a whitlow.

wirlie wrinkled, with wizened features.

wrat a wart *now C, S.*

wrunkle a wrinkle.

9.9 PARTS OF THE BODY

The body itself and parts not covered individually in appropriate sections.

†ablach a mangled carcass *N.*

bag the stomach; the paunch. **† ~gie** the belly, stomach. **~git** corpulent, big-bellied.

bane a bone.

†beef human flesh, the body.

†belch the belly.

blether, bledder the bladder.

blude, blood *n* blood. *v* 1 cause to bleed. 2 bleed; have blood flowing *now Ork.* **bludie** bloody.

boug the stomach, belly *esp* of a child *Cai.*

bouk the body of a person (living or dead).

breist the breast.

brisket the breast *now local Abd-Fif.*

buddie the body.

buffs the lungs *local C.*

†bullerand (in his *etc* **blude)** with blood issuing from the body, bleeding.

cag stomach, belly *now Bnf Edb.*

clap o(f) the hass *or* **throat** the uvula *now Ags Fif.*

cog wame a pot-belly *now Fif.*

corpus the live body *now Abd Fif.*

craig *n, also* **~ie** *now local Bnf-Edb* 1 the neck. 2 *also* **~'s close** *joc* the throat, gullet. **~ed, ~it** -necked, *chf* **lang ~it** *etc.*

creel the stomach. *NE.*

crop, *also* **~pin** *freq joc, now Kcb* the stomach *now Bnf-Fif.*

cuff of the neck the nape or scruff of the neck.

cupplin the bottom of the spine where it joins the sacrum *Bnf Fif.*

cut pock the stomach *NE.*

deep ribbit *of a woman* large-chested *now Sh Kcb.*

dunt a throb or quickened beat of the heart *now Bnf Abd Fif.*

flaff flap, flutter; palpitate. **~er** flutter, flap, palpitate *now NE Ags Fif.*

flichter *of the heart* flutter, quiver, palpitate.

fower quarters the body, the person.

gebbie the stomach.

geck-neck(it) (having) a twisted neck *NE.*

gizzen *chf of the throat* be or become parched *now local Sh-Ags.*

gizze(r)n *joc* the throat *now Ags.*

gley, glee: ~(e)d-necked having a twisted neck *now Cai midLoth.*

†gowl the throat, jaws.

gowp *of the heart or pulse* beat strongly, wildly, palpitate.

grund, ground the pit of the stomach *now Ags.*

†gut: baith ~(s) and ga the whole contents of the stomach; the stomach.

†haggis the stomach.

harigals entrails.

hause 1 the neck *now local Sh-Dmf.* 2 the throat, gullet *now Ork Bnf Ags.* **~bane** the collarbone. **~-pipe** the throat, windpipe *now Ags Ayr.*

hert, hairt, heart 1 the heart. 2 the stomach *now Sh-Cai Abd.* **† ~ pipes** translating Latin *praecordia* the heart, its blood vessels etc.

howe o the neck the nape of the neck *now NE.*

huil the pericardium, the membrane surrounding the heart, *freq* **leap** *etc* **(oot o) the ~** *of the heart* burst.

intimmers *joc* the internal organs *esp* the stomach and bowels *now local Sh-Stlg.*

kettle-bellied pot-bellied *now Cai Wgt.*

†king's hood *or* **head** *joc* the stomach.

kist the chest, the thorax.

knot: the ~ o one's craig *or* **thrapple** the Adam's apple *NE Ags.*

kyte the stomach, belly.

lang craig a long neck *chf Ags.*

lap a lobe (of the liver) *now Sh.*

lapper, lopper *v, esp of blood* clot, curdle, *freq* ~ed. *n* a clot, clotted matter, *esp* blood *now local.*

leader a tendon, sinew *now local.*

lichts, †lighs the lungs.

lingel-backit having a long weak limp back *SW, S.*

link a joint of the body, *esp* one of the vertebrae.

†lire flesh. **bane and** ~, ~ **and bane** flesh and bone.

lith a joint in a finger or toe, a small part of the body, *freq* ~ **and limb** *now Sh N nEC.*

lowp *of the heart, blood etc* throb, race.

mauvie the stomach *Cai.*

melt the milt, the spleen *now local.*

mergh *now Sh,* **mergie, merky** *now Sh Ork* the marrow (of bones).

†middrit the diaphragm, midriff.

muckle, meikle, mickle: ~**-kited** pot-bellied *now NE Fif.*

myave maw, stomach *NE.*

nael, nyvle the navel *chf SW.*

neck the throat, gullet.

neir a kidney *now Sh-N.*

†nobill part a vital bodily organ.

painches, paunches the bowels or intestines *now Ayr Uls.*

pap the uvula, *chf* ~ **o the** *or* **one's hause** *now C, S,* ~ **o the throat** *Cai NE.*

†pechan the stomach as a receptacle for food, the belly.

peenie *child's word* the tummy *C.*

pock *joc* the stomach *Cai Wgt.*

puddin(g): ~**s** entrails, viscera, guts. ~ **market** *child's word* the stomach *Ork Kcdn Ags.*

†punse a pulse.

red, reid, rid: ~ **brae** *local Ags-SW,* ~ **lane** *local,* ~ **road** *local* the gullet.

rig *now Sh Cai,* **riggin** *now local Ork-Stlg* the back or backbone. ~**-back** *now Sh,* ~**-bane** *now Sh midLoth,* ~**gin-bane** *now Ork* the backbone, spine.

†rim the peritoneum.

saw shed (blood).

scroban the gullet or chest *Cai-Inv Per Arg Bute.*

†shed a clot (of blood).

shot a discharge, flow (of blood etc) from the body *now Kcb.*

shuit, shoot *of blood etc* stream out.

sinnon, †sinnie, shinnon a sinew *now Sh NE, C.*

†skelet a skeleton.

slot the hollow depression running down the middle of the breast, *freq* ~ **of his** *etc* **breast.**

†smergh bone-marrow, pith.

†spring gush (**with** blood).

stalk: be ca'ed *or* **loup** *etc* **off the** ~ *of the heart* be stopped by a sudden fright etc *now Fif.*

†stroup, stroop the throat, gullet.

swallie the throat, gullet.

tag a long thin strip or slice of flesh or tissue *now Sh.*

tenon a tendon *now NE.*

thairm, therm a bowel, gut, intestine *now local Sh-WC.*

thrapple the windpipe; *more loosely* the throat, the gullet. ~**-bow** the Adam's apple *chf Mry.*

throttle the throat, gullet, windpipe *Gen except Sh Ork.*

tirr *of one's heart etc* beat, thump *Ags.*

trollie-bags the intestines or entrails.

†trot the throat.

wallop *v, of the heart* throb, beat violently *now Sh-Per. n* a strong beat of the heart or pulse, a throb

wame, wime the belly *now Cai.* ..**-wamed** having a belly of a specified kind, *eg* great, big etc. **wamie** big-bellied *now Ags Fif.*

†whiltie-whaltie: play (a) ~ *of the heart* beat rapidly, palpitate.

†whorlbane a vertebra.

wizzen, weason 1 the gullet *now local Sh-Per.* 2 the windpipe *now local Sh-Abd.* 3 the throat as the source of the voice.

yat gush *now Sh.*

yirnin the stomach *now Kcdn.*

9.10 SENSATIONS

†bang a throbbing pain.

beek *v* warm (oneself); bask. *n* an act of warming (oneself etc).

bide pain *now NE.*

catch a sharp pain, a stitch *local Bnf-Kcb.*

cauld, cold cold. **cauld creep(s)** gooseflesh, the creeps *local Bnf-Lnk.* ~**rif(e)** cold, causing or susceptible to cold.

chitter chatter, shiver (with cold etc) *now local Abd-Kcb.*

†chiver shiver.

claw *n* a scratching, *freq* of the head. *v* scratch gently so as to relieve irritation; scratch (the head) *N.*

commanding *of pain* severe, disabling *local.*

daver make numb, chill *now Bnf Abd.*

day: not hear ~ **nor door** be unable to distinguish sounds.

dead, deid: ~ **bell** a sudden sensation of deafness

and a ringing in the ears thought to foretell death *now Sh.*

deave deafen *now Cai Lnk.*

†**desy** *adj* dizzy. *v* make dizzy.

dingle tingle (with cold or pain) *now Sh Ayr Slk.*

dinnle *v* **1** shake *now local Bnf-Kcb.* **2** *esp of the fingers* tingle with cold or pain; twinge. **3** cause to tremble, vibrate, tingle with pain; shake *now Fif.* *n* a vibrating or tingling sensation, *eg* as caused by a knock on the elbow; such a knock.

dirl *v* **1** pierce or cause to tingle with emotion or pain *now Sh Fif Rox.* **2** cause to vibrate, shake *now local Bnf-Fif.* **3** thrill, quiver or tingle with emotion, pain etc. *n* **1** a knock or blow causing the person or thing struck to **dirl**; a shock, jar. **2** the pain caused by such a blow; a tingling sensation *now local.*

domineer deafen, stupefy with loud noise or too much talk *Bnf Abd.*

dowf *of a part of the body* numb, insensitive *now Sh.*

†**dozen** be or become cold or numb. **~ed** numb, stiff with cold.

draiglet soaked through, drenched *now Ork Ags Per.*

draik, drawk drench, soak *now Bwk Slk.*

dree endure, suffer (pain etc).

dreep *now Bnf Abd Fif,* **dreeple** *Sh Ags* a wet, dripping condition, *eg* with sweat.

†**drint** drenched, drowned.

droogled drenched, soaked *now Bnf Abd.*

drouk a drenching *now Ags Fif.* **droukit** drenched, soaked. **droukin** dripping with moisture *now Stlg.* **drookle** drench, soak *Sh Bnf Fif.*

easement personal comfort etc; relief from physical comfort or inconvenience *now local.*

feem *n* a state of sudden heat, a sweat. *v* be in a state of great heat or perspiration.

fell *of pain etc* severe, acute, grievous *now Abd Fif Bwk.*

fushion bodily sensation, power of feeling *now NE.*

gell, geil *Sh Cai* tingle, smart, ache with pain or cold *now Sh Cai.*

girl *of the teeth* be set on edge *S.*

gowp *v, of sores or pains* throb, ache violently *now local Fif-Wgt.* *n* a throb of pain *now local midLoth-Wgt.*

granich sicken, disgust *NE.*

greeshach shivery, shuddery; chilly *local N.*

grill shiver, shudder *Rox.*

grip, grup: **~s** sharp pains, *esp* in the bowels, gripes *now Sh NE nEC, SW.* † **~pit** seized with pain (as above).

groosie shivery *now midLoth Bwk Slk.*

grue, gruse *now local Loth-S v* shudder, shiver from cold *now C, S. n* a shudder, shiver *now local Cai-S.*

hale *now chf of perspiration* flow copiously, run down, pour *now Sh midLoth.*

heat the act of heating, a heating, the state of feeling hot, *latterly chf* **get** *or* **gie a ~** make (oneself or another) warm. **come a-heat** become hot *now midLoth Bwk Slk.*

heidie apt to make one giddy or dizzy *now midLoth Rox.*

hen: **~('s) flesh,** **~ picks, ~-plooks,** gooseflesh.

hiddie-giddie 1 dizzily. **2** in a confused or giddy state.

hippit, hip-grippit *Cai Abd Kcb, esp of workers in the harvest-field* having a feeling of stiffness or overstrain in the lower back, hips, or thighs.

hotter *v* shudder, shiver with cold *now NE. n* a shiver; a quiver(ing) *now Abd.*

hugger shudder, shiver, hug oneself (to keep warm) *NE.* **~t, ~ing** huddled up or shrunk with cold, pinched-looking *NE-Per.*

hurdie-caikle *or* **keckle** a pain in the back and thighs caused by prolonged stooping.

income a sharp attack of pain, a stitch in the side *now local N-S.*

itchy-coo anything causing a tickling *Ags Fif WC.*

jab *v* prick sharply. *n* a prick, pricking.

job a prick; a prickle *now Sh NE nEC.*

kittle *v, n* tickle. *adj* ticklish *now local.* **kittlie 1** *of things* causing a tickling sensation. **2** *of persons* susceptible to tickling, itchy, ticklish.

licht, light dizzy, light-headed *Loth Renfr.* **~ in the head** = **licht.**

†**lowp** *v* start with pain, surprise, shock. *n* a throb, start.

mirligoes vertigo, dizziness, light-headedness. **in** *or* **on the ~** light-headed, confused.

nip 1 cause to tingle or smart *in gen, specif of cold, of food or its taste.* **2** ache, tingle with cold.

nirl, nurl shrivel up in oneself, cringe with cold *now Sh.*

nither shrink or huddle as with cold, shiver *now Loth Lnk S.*

oor crouch, shiver with cold; huddle. **~it** cold, shivery, hunched up with cold or discomfort *now local Sh-Dmf.*

oorie *of persons* dismal, gloomy, miserable-looking from cold *now local Sh-Arg.* **oorlich** miserable looking from cold.

†**papple** stream with perspiration, be too hot.

perish *latterly freq* **~ed with cold** severely chilled.

†**pined** in pain, tortured, tormented.

pinkle *of hunger pangs* prick, produce a prickling or tingling sensation *now Rox.*

plot, plout an overheated state, a sweat, swelter *Sh-Fif.*

prinkle 1 have the sensation of pins and needles, tingle, thrill, prickle *now Bnf Abd S.* **2** cause to tingle, set pricking; jab with a pin *now Per.*

putt, put pulsate, throb *now S.*

rash produce a stabbing or searing pain, throb.

reel *of the head or senses* be in a whirl, become confused.

reesle *v* shiver, shudder *now Sh. n* an involuntary shiver or shudder.

rug *of pain, hunger, an empty stomach* gnaw, ache, nag *now NE Ags.*

sair, sore 1 sore. **2** causing or involving physical pain or distress: (1) *of pain* severe; (2) *of a task, activity etc* causing physical strain.

sark, serk ~**fu o sair banes** a person stiff or sore from hard labour or from a beating.

scomfish, scunfis disgust, sicken *now Sh NE Ags.*

scunner *v* **1** get a feeling of aversion, disgust or loathing, feel nauseated or surfeited. **2** *freq* ~ **at** feel disgust for, be sickened by. **3** nauseate, surfeit. *n* a feeling of disgust, loathing, nausea or surfeit, *freq* **take a** ~ (**at** *or* **against**) a shudder indicating physical or moral repugnance; a sudden shock.

seepit soaked, wet through.

set disgust, nauseate *now NE Ags.*

shakie tremlie giddy *Kcdn Ags Per.*

shevel make a wry mouth, grimace from vexation, pain, a bitter taste etc *now N Per SW.*

shidder shudder *chf Ags.*

shither shiver, shudder *now Rox.*

shour, shower a pang or paroxysm of pain etc, *specif* of childbirth.

skin: at the ~ (soaked through) to the skin *Sh Abd.*

snoke a smell(ing), sniff *now Stlg WC, SW.*

soo ache; throb, tingle with pain, etc *now Lnk Ayr Dmf.*

sowther, solder, souder mitigate, alleviate (pain etc) *now Ags.*

spurtle grup a sudden gripping pain, a stitch *Ayr.*

stang *v* shoot with pain, throb, ache. *n* a sharp pain, such as that caused by a sting, a pang; the wound caused by a sting or sharp object.

steek a sharp pain, a stitch in the side.

steenge *n* a sharp pain *local Ags-Rox. v* attack with a sharp pain *Bwk Kcb Rox.*

stock *of the body, limbs* become stiff, unwieldy or cramped with cold.

stound[1] *n* a sharp throb of pain; an intermittent ache. *v* (cause to) throb, ache, smart, thrill with pain or emotion.

stound[2] a stunned condition, state of insensibility *now local Bnf-Dmf.*

sweamish squeamish *now Sh Ork Fif.*

†**taibets** physical sensation, feeling; energy, strength.

tak, take: ~ **someone's head** go to someone's head, make someone giddy *now Per.*

thirl vibrate, quiver, pass through with a tingling sensation.

thraw a twisting of the body in pain, a convulsion, spasm *now Dmf.* ~ **one's face, gab** *etc* screw up, twist the face, mouth etc as a sign of pain, exertion.

thrawn *of the mouth, face* wry, twisted with pain, rage etc, surly ~**-faced,** ~**-gabbit,** † ~**-mou'd** having a wry, twisted face or mouth.

tickly ticklish.

torter torture *now Sh N.*

tremmle tremble.

twang a sudden sharp pain, an acute pang *now local Ags-Rox.*

twitter (cause to) quiver or tremble *local Sh-Wgt.*

ug *v* be sickened, nauseated; feel repulsion *now Sh. n* a sensation of nausea or disgust.

wammle, wamble a churning of the stomach, a feeling of sickness *NE Ags Fif.*

†**wark** ache, throb.

†**winch** wince, start back, flinch.

yawk *v* ache *now nEC, WC.*

yerk *v,* throb, ache, tingle *local NE-Dmf. n* a throb of pain; an ache *Abd Ags.*

yeuk *v, of a part of the body* itch, feel ticklish or itchy. *n* itching, the itch; an itchiness. ~**ie** *of a part of the body* itching, itchy.

9.11 BREATHING, RESPIRATORY DISEASES

aynd, end *n* breath *latterly chf Sh.* †*v* breathe (on).

backdraucht the drawing in of the breath, *eg* the gasp in whooping cough.

black-spit a lung disease formerly common among miners *now local.*

blast pant, breathe hard *now Bnf.*

blocher *v* make a gurgling noise in coughing *now Bnf Abd Per Uls. n* a loose, catarrhal cough *now Per Uls.*

boich cough with difficulty *now Abd.*

bouch *v* cough *local Bnf-Rox.*

bouff, *freq* ~ **and host** cough loudly.

braith breath.

broonchadis, broonkaties bronchitis *local Sh-wLoth.*

bucher a fit of uncontrollable coughing; a cough which causes this *Bnf Abd*.

burs(t)en breathless from over-exertion *now Bnf Fif*.

cauld, cold: ~it, ~ed suffering from a cold *now local NE-Lnk*.

chincough = **kink cough**, whooping cough *now Cai Fif Arg*.

chowk choke *SW, S*.

cloch cough *chf Cai*. ~er *n* **1** bronchial mucus. **2** a rough or wheezing cough. *v* cough, expectorate *now Cai*.

clorach clear the throat noisily, hawk *NE*.

close suffer from congestion of the respiratory system *now Abd Ags Fif*. **closing** respiratory congestion; croup.

coch *v* cough *now Cai*. †**coghle** cough weakly; gasp.

cougher cough continuously *now Abd*.

craighle, crechle cough drily or huskily; wheeze *now local Abd-Kcb*.

croichle *v* cough *now Bnf*. *n* a cough *now Bnf*.

croup, crowp speak hoarsely *now Bnf Abd Fif*. ~it croaking, hoarse *now Cai Fif*.

†**crout** croak.

dose: a ~ **of the cold** a cold.

draucht, draft a convulsive gasping or choking *Bnf Abd Fif*.

fesh breathe with difficulty, pant, gasp *now Sh*.

fleem phlegm *now Ags Bwk SW*.

fob, fab pant with heat or exertion, breathe hard *NE*.

fuff puff, blow gently.

glag *now Abd*, **glagger** *Bnf Ags* make a gurgling or choking noise.

gliff, glaff, glouf: a ~ **o (the) cauld** a touch of the cold *local Abd-Edb*.

glisk: a ~ **o cauld** a touch of cold, a slight cold *now Ags nEC Rox*.

glutter a gurgling noise in the throat.

gowp *v (now NE midLoth)*, *n (now Ags midLoth)* gulp.

gowstie breathless from being overweight *now Abd*.

graig make a noise in the throat, *eg* in clearing it *NE*.

graveyaird: ~ **hoast** *etc* = **kirkyaird hoast** *now WC*.

groozle breathe heavily, make a grunting noise *now Kcb Dmf Rox*.

haingles influenza *chf Ags*.

hairse hoarse.

hask give a short dry cough, clear the throat noisily cough up (phlegm) *now local Ags-Uls*. †~y husky, hoarse.

hauch *v* cough, *esp* cough up mucus etc in order to clear the throat *now E, Uls*. *n* **1** a forcible expulsion of breath. **2** a soft loose cough; a clearing of the throat *now local NE-midLoth*.

hech pant, breathe hard or uneasily *now Slk*.

hechle pant, breathe quickly, as after considerable exertion *now local Cai-S*.

hick *n* a hiccup, the act of hiccuping *now Abd Ags*. *v* **1** hiccup *now Abd Ags Fif*. **2** catch the breath and make a hiccuping sound before bursting into tears; sob noisily *chf S*.

hirsel *v* wheeze, breathe noisily. *n* a wheeze or catarrhal sound in the chest.

hoast *n* **1** coughing as an ailment, a cough. **2** a single cough. *v* **1** cough. **2** *chf* ~ **out** *or* **up** cough up *now local Ork-Kcb*.

hooch a sudden expulsion of the breath, a puff.

hurl *v* wheeze because of phlegm in the chest *Sh Ork NE Ags*. *n* **1** the sound of laboured breathing resulting from phlegm in the throat or chest *local Sh-Abd*. **2** the death rattle *local Ork-NE*. ~ie congested with phlegm *Cai Abd Ags*.

husk cough violently *now Ayr Rox*.

intak, intake the act of taking in breath.

keuch *v* cough persistently from a tickling in the throat *now Bwk*. *n* a troublesome, persistent, tickling cough *now Bwk*.

kicher *v* have a short, persistent, tickling cough *local Abd-SW*. *n* a short sharp cough *Abd-Fif Ayr*.

kighle a short, tickling cough.

kink *v* gasp or choke convulsively or spasmodically, *specif* suffer an attack of coughing, *esp* whooping-cough *now local NE-Uls*. *n* a convulsive catching of the breath as in whooping-cough; a fit of coughing *local Abd-Uls*. ~ers *Abd Per Fif*, ~ **cough** *now SW Slk*, ~ **host** *now Sh NE, EC, SW* whooping-cough.

kirkyaird hoast *chf joc* a churchyard cough.

kist(fu) o whistles *joc* a wheezy chest *Cai Ags Per*.

knacks *joc* any complaint characterized by wheezing *chf Rox*.

lift *of the chest* heave, as when there is difficulty in breathing *local C-S*.

load a heavy attack (of cold) *now Sh-N Fif*.

mort cauld *now Sh*, **(one's) morth of cauld** *now Uls* a severe cold, one's death of cold.

neese sneeze *now Sh Ork NE*.

pech *v* **1** breathe hard as from exertion, puff, pant, gasp for breath. **2** move or work so as to pant or gasp with the exertion *NE, WC Kcb*. **3** cough in a subdued asthmatic way *now Ayr*. **4** expel the breath slowly and audibly, sigh, groan. *n* **1** a laboured breath, a pant, gasp; one's breath. **2** an asthmatic wheeze, a breathless cough *NE, C*. ~ie short-winded, asthmatic, wheezy *Gen except*

Sh Ork. ~**in** shortness of breath; the act of panting. ~**(l)t**, ~**(l)ed** out of breath *Abd nEC, S.*

peuch *v, freq* **pyocher, peughle** puff, blow, give a gusty sigh *now Sh Ags.* **peuchle, pyocher** *Sh NE Ags* cough in a choking, asthmatic way, repeatedly clear one's throat and chest of catarrh *now Sh NE Ags. n, also* **peucher** a persistent choking cough *now NE.*

peumonie *joc* pneumonia.

pew a breath, the sound made by exhaling *now Sh.* **not play** ~ stop breathing.

pluff discharge (breath etc) with a small explosion, puff (something) out in a cloud; blow (something) **out** by puffing air on it.

plunk make a plopping or gurgling noise when swallowing etc *now Ags Kcb.*

purfled, purfe(i)t fat and asthmatic, corpulent, plump and wheezing.

rauk †*adj* hoarse, raucous. *v* clear the chest or throat of phlegm, hawk *Ags Fif.*

redd clear (the throat, nose, stomach etc) *N.*

roostie *local Sh-Kcb,* **roostit** *local Sh-WC of the throat or voice* rough, dry; hoarse, raucous.

roup, *freq* **the** ~ hoarseness, huskiness, any inflamed condition of the throat *now local Cai-Fif.* ~**ie** hoarse, rough husky *local N-SW.* ~**it** hoarse, rough, raucous *now local C.*

ruckle *v* make a rattling, gurgling or roaring sound, *specif* of the breathing of a dying person. *n* a rattling or gurgling sound, *specif* the death-rattle *now Rox.*

scomfish, scunfis *v* suffocate, stifle, choke, overpower with heat etc *now local. n* a suffocating atmosphere; a state of suffocation *now Ork.*

†**short ended** short-winded.

sit: ~**ten-doun** *now now Rox,* ~**ting doun** *now Fif, of a cold etc* persistent, chronic.

slorach clear the throat loudly and inelegantly, breathe or speak through catarrh *Bnf Abd Per.*

slork reinhale nasal mucus, sniff or snort *Lnk SW.*

smeek affect or suffocate with smoke or soot *now C, S.* ~**it** stifled or blinded by smoke.

smore 1 smother, suffocate, stifle (*eg* with smoke) *now Sh NE Ags.* 2 be smothered or stifled, choke. **smorin** *of a head-cold* thick, choking, heavy. **be smorin wi the cauld** have a very bad cold.

smuchter *v* be short of breath, breathe with difficulty; *of the voice* be muffled or thick *Abd. n* a thick choking cold, a heavy catarrh *Bnf Abd.*

smudder smother.

smuir, smoor 1 be choked, suffocated, die from lack of air, *esp* by being buried in a snowdrift. 2 cause to suffocate, smother, crush the breath out of.

†**snaffle** snuffle, speak through the nose.

sneer snort, twitch the nose, snuffle, inhale or exhale heavily or noisily *now Ork.*

sneesh, †**snish** sneeze *sEC, WC Rox.*

sneevils a severe cold in the nose, causing difficulty in breathing *now Ork N, C.*

†**sneising** sneezing.

snift puff, snort, blow.

snifter *v* sniff; snivel, snuffle (*eg* with a cold); snort, snore. *n* a (noisy) sniff, from a cold etc, *chf* the ~**s** a (severe) head cold, catarrh, stuffed nose.

snirk *v* snort, wrinkle the nose, snigger *now Dmf. n* a snort, snigger *Sh Dmf Rox.*

snirt *v* snort, breathe sharply and jerkily through the nose. *n* a snort.

snocher *v* snort, breathe heavily and noisily through the nose, snuffle *now NE nEC. n* a snort, snore, the act of breathing heavily through the nose *now NE nEC.* **the** ~**s** a severe nose cold, causing blockage of the nostrils *now NE nEC.*

snoiter breathe loudly through the nose, snore *now Ags.*

snork snort, snore, snuffle *WC-S.*

snotter snuffle, snort, breathe heavily through the nose *now Ags.*

†**snuff** a persistent snuffling.

souch *n* a deep sigh or gasp, heavy breathing, panting *local Sh-Gall. v* breathe heavily, sigh, wheeze, splutter, gurgle *now Sh N Gall.*

sowff †*v* pant, sob, snore, doze. *n* wheezing, heavy breathing.

stech, steigh, stoich gasp, pant, puff etc: **1** from repletion *now Ayr;* **2** from exertion or effort *local Per-S.*

stifle miners' asthma, pneumoconiosis.

†**stoppit** hoarse.

stoury lungs pneumoconiosis; silicosis *Fif Edb wLoth.*

†**stuff** become out of breath.

sture *of the voice* deep and hoarse, harsh, rough *now Lnk Rox.*

†**supire** sigh.

tak, take: ~ **someone's breath** *or* **wind** choke someone *local Sh-Kcb.*

thock pant, breathe heavily with exertion *S.*

through the cold *of speaking* thickly, in a choked manner *now NE Per.*

tuchin a husky cough, hoarseness *Inv Mry.*

waucht a deep breath of air, a full inhalation *now Abd.*

whaisk wheeze, breathe with difficulty, as with a heavy cold, gasp for breath *now Rox.*

whauze, foze *NE,* **wheezle, whazzle** *v* wheeze, breathe with a rasping sound as with asthma or catarrh, pant. *n* **1** a wheeze, hard rough breathing *now SW, NE*. **2 the wheezles** asthma; bronchitis *local Ork-Wgt*.

whirken choke, suffocate *S*.

wind breath, the air breathed.

worry choke (**on** a mouthful of food), suffocate *now local Sh-Per*.

yesk *v* hiccup, belch, vomit. *n* a hiccup, belch.

9.12 SLEEPING, REST, WAKING

For weariness and tiredness, see 9.13.

awauk awake, awaken. † ~**en** awaken.

ba lull, hush (a child) to sleep. **baw baw(s)** *or* **beddie ba(s)** *child's word* bed; the act of going to sleep.

blink a wink of sleep *now local Sh-Kcb*.

boo: not ~ an ee not close one's eyes, fail to sleep *local*.

bow: not ~ an ee not close one's eyes, fail to sleep *now local Bnf-Ayr*.

daak doze for a short time *Cai*.

dot a nap, a short sleep *now Cai*.

dove become drowsy, doze *now Bnf Ags*.

dover *v, freq* ~ **ower** doze off, fall into a light sleep, *n* a doze, a nap. †**doverit** sunk in light sleep.

draw thegither *of the eyes* close in sleep *now Bnf Abd*.

drive swine *or* **pigs** snore loudly *now local Ork-Kcb*.

droosy drowsy.

dwam fall asleep, take a nap *local*.

fa(ll) ower fall asleep.

fauld: ~ one's fit *now Bnf Abd*, ~ **one's hoch** *now Ags Per*, † ~ **one's feet** sit down, rest.

flype fall heavily, flop down for a short rest *NE*.

†**fordoverit** overcome with sleep.

gant, gaunt *v* yawn *Gen except Cai*. *n* a yawn, gape.

gloss doze *now Bnf Abd*.

grouff †*v* snore. *n* a short, disturbed sleep; a snooze.

keep up stay awake *local*.

maffled half asleep, dazed *Dmf*.

misrestit suffering from loss of sleep *Sh Abd SW*.

nid (nid) nodding nodding repeatedly, as when dozing.

†**nop** nap, take a short sleep, *only* ~ **and nod.**

ower off to sleep.

peerie: sleep like *or* **as sound as a** ~ sleep like a top *C, S*.

raise arouse, rouse from sleep *now local Sh-Kcb*.

rap up rouse by knocking *now Cai Kcb*.

rax stretch oneself after sleep etc.

†**trout** *v* snore.

slabber make a snorting, bubbling sound as in weeping or sleeping *now Dnbt SW*.

sleep: ~**ery 1** †sleep-inducing. **2** sleepy, somnolent *now Rox*. ~**ie men, things** *etc* the little specks of matter which form in the eyes during sleep *local*. † ~**ryfe** bringing sleep. **be** ~**it oot** have slept one's fill. ~ **in** oversleep.

†**slide on slummir** *or* **upon a sleip** fall asleep.

sloom *n* a dreamy or sleepy state, a daydream, a light or unsettled sleep *now Kcdn Ags*. †*v* sleep lightly or fitfully, doze.

slug a sleep, a nap, a state of inactivity *WC, SW*.

slumber, †slummer 1 slumber. **2** †a period or occasion for sleep or rest.

snagger snore harshly *Bnf Abd*.

snoiter breathe loudly through the nose, snore; snooze *now Ags*.

snoozle snooze, doze *now Abd Ags*.

snork snort, snore, snuffle *WC-S*.

snotter snooze, doze.

†**sopit** sunk **in** (sleep etc).

souch heavy breathing in sleep; a snooze *now Kcb*.

sowff †*v* pant, sob, snore, doze. *n* a snooze, sleep.

spaik, spoke: drap *or* **fa aff the** ~ collapse with weariness, sleep etc *S*.

wauk, wake *v* **1** wake. **2** be or stay awake, be sleepless or have wakened from sleep. **3** stay up all night with, watch over (a sick person or corpse). *n* wake, abstinence from sleep; *latterly* a vigil over a corpse. ~**rife 1** disinclined or unable to sleep; able to do with little sleep. **2** easily awakened, lightly sleeping *now Ork Abd Ags*. † ~**rifeness** sleeplessness, insomnia. **wide waukin** wide-awake *now Ork*.

wauken, waken 1 waken. **2** arouse (oneself or another) from sleep, wake. **waukened** awake *local Sh-Wgt*.

win asleep get to sleep *local Sh-Per*.

9.13 TIREDNESS, EXHAUSTION

bauch weak, exhausted, seedy.

daviely listlessly, languidly.

defait exhausted, worn out *now Bnf Abd*.

dirt deen extremely tired *Bnf Abd*.

disjaskit exhausted, worn out; weary-looking *local*.

doilt, diled wearied, fatigued *now Abd*.

dowf weary *now local Bnf-Fif.*

dowless feeble, lacking in strength or energy *now Stlg.*

ergh exhausted.

exowst exhaust.

fag fail from weariness.

fail give way under strain, flag, collapse from exhaustion.

fairrie collapse from exhaustion or sudden illness *Abd.*

fauchled tired, worn-out, harassed *now C, S.*

fendless lacking energy *Sh Cai NE, SW.*

†fordone exhausted, worn out *S.*

forfauchlet worn out, exhausted.

forfochtin 1 exhausted with fighting. 2 exhausted with any kind of effort, *freq* **sair ~.**

†forgane exhausted with going.

forjeskit exhausted, worn out *local Sh-Pbls.*

†forjidget extremely tired, exhausted.

fornyawd fatigued, tired, worn out.

forwandert *literary* weary with wandering.

founder 1 collapse, break down with exhaustion etc *Gen except Sh Ork.* 2 **be ~t** be exhausted, worn out, prostrated by fatigue, shock, a cold etc *local NE-S.*

fusionless physically weak, without energy.

haggit weary, exhausted *now Stlg midLoth.*

ha(i)rlt tired-looking *now midLoth Bwk.*

jabb tire out, exhaust, *freq* **~it** *NE.*

jaffled tired, worn out *SW.*

†jamph: be ~it be exhausted or in difficulties.

jaskit jaded, worn out *now Sh Ags.*

jaup exhaust, fatigue (*chf* oneself), *freq* **~it** weary *now Bnf-Ags midLoth.*

kill overcome from weariness *local Sh-SW: 'we're kill'd wi' wark'.*

kned tire out *Ags.*

†larbar *adj* exhausted, impotent. *n* an exhausted or impotent man.

lither lazy, sluggish, lethargic, idle; lax, slack *now Dmf.*

lowsed tired, weary.

mated *Abd,* **mate-out** *S* exhausted, spent.

maukit exhausted, played out *S.*

muith oppressed or exhausted by heat *now Cai.*

oorit tired or ailing-looking.

oxter: wi one's heid under one's ~ with a downcast, drooping look *now Ork Uls.*

pan: knock one's ~ out *or* **in** work very hard, exert oneself to the point of exhaustion.

pech a sigh of weariness, relief, satisfaction etc.

peerie-wearie strained or short-sighted-looking *now Slk.*

pingled overcome with exhaustion.

plet, plait *of the limbs* intertwine as a result of weariness, fold under one *now NE, nEC.*

pouskered exhausted, worn out *Ags WC.*

puggled at a standstill due to exhaustion, done for, at the end of one's resources.

†saughrin lacking in energy, sluggish, soft and flaccid in character or action.

snuil, snool show lack of energy, loaf about shiftlessly, move slowly and lethargically.

socht exhausted *now NE Ags.*

†sopit rendered dull or sluggish.

†sowp, solp weary, tire; become worn out. **~it** exhausted, worn out.

spaik, spoke: drap *or* **fa aff the ~** collapse with weariness, sleep etc *S.*

stane, stone: ~ tired very tired *S.*

stress overwork, fatigue *now local Per-Rox.*

taigled tired, weary, harassed *now local sEC-Rox.*

†taivert exhausted with wandering.

tash fatigue, weary (with hard work) *now local Sh-Kcb.*

taskit fatigued by hard work, exhausted *now local Ork-Wgt.*

tewed exhausted *now Wgt.*

thowless lacking energy or spirit, listless, inactive.

tike-tired dog-tired, worn out.

tire a state of being or becoming tired, fatigue, weariness *now local Sh-Stlg.*

toil exhaust oneself with hard work *now Sh.*

traikit wasted, worn out; fatigued *now WC Wgt.*

trash wear out, exhaust, abuse with overwork and exertion *now Dmf Rox.* **~y** fatiguing *S.*

trauchle: ~d exhausted with overwork, travelling etc, overburdened, harassed. **~some** exhausting, laborious *NE Ags.*

†tuggled fatigued, harassed.

typit worn out by hard work *Bnf Abd.*

useless incapacitated by illness or exhaustion *Sh-N.*

vincust exhausted, tired out *Ags.*

wabbit *Gen except Sh Ork,* **~ out** *chf C* exhausted, feeble.

wauch, wauf unwell, faint, weary.

9.14 EATING, DRINKING

able having an appetite **for.**

appeteet appetite.

†appetized having an appetite, hungry.

bannock hive *joc and derog* a gastric upset caused by overeating.

bind the capacity (of a person etc), *chf* in drinking.

†**bowdened** swollen from overeating *now Bnf.*

brosie 1 bedaubed or fed with **brose** *now local Abd-Lnk.* **2** bloated with too much food or drink *now Bnf wLoth.*

cling shrunken with hunger, hungry *now Bnf-Fif.*

curnawin a gnawing sensation of hunger *now Bnf Abd.*

cut an appetite *Bnf.*

digeest digest. **disgeester** *now Fif,* **disgeestion** *now Bnf Ags* digestion.

drouth thirst. **drouchtit** parched *now Bnf Abd Kcb.* **~y** thirsty, addicted to drinking.

drum-fu as tight as a drum, full (of food) *Abd Ags Fif.*

faimish famish.

fyle the *or* **one's stamach** upset the stomach, make one sick *now NE-WC Rox.*

gled: as gleg as a ~ very hungry.

gulsoch excessive eating; nausea caused by this *now Kcdn.*

†**gut: baith ~(s) and ga** the whole contents of the stomach.

hause: gae doun (into) the wrang ~ *of food etc* go down the wrong way *now local Sh-Dmf.*

heftit 1 swollen with wind, flatulent *now Knr midLoth Dmf.* **2** full to repletion *now Abd midLoth.*

hert, hairt, heart: ~(e)nin strengthening (with food etc) *now Ork NE Ags.* **~ie** *esp of guests at a meal* having a good unrestrained appetite, eager for food *now NE Ags.* **~-hunger** a ravenous desire for food *NE Ags.*

howe hungry, famished, empty (of food) *now Ork.*

hunger starve. **~ed, ~t** starved(-looking). **hungrysome** *now local Cai-Kcb,* **~some** *now Per midLoth* **1** hungry, having a keen appetite. **2** stimulating hunger *now midLoth.*

intak, intake the act of taking in food.

kyte: kytie corpulent, *esp* as the result of good living *now local N-Kcb.* †**~ clung** having the belly shrunk from hunger.

man: be ~ of one's meat have a healthy appetite and digestion *now Ags Ayr.*

nip: ~pit pinched with hunger. **~ of hunger** the pinch of hunger *Bwk Rox.*

oorie dismal, gloomy, miserable-looking from hunger *now local Sh-Arg.* **oorlich** miserable looking from hunger.

pang *v* cram (the stomach) with food, gorge. *adj* crammed with food. **~ f(o)u** *now NE wLoth Uls,* **~'d-fu** stuffed, full to overflowing.

pinkle *of hunger pangs* prick, produce a prickling or tingling sensation *now Rox.*

ram-full crammed full (of food or drink) *Gen except Sh Ork.*

riftin fou full to bursting point.

rug *of pain, hunger, an empty stomach* gnaw, ache, nag *now NE Ags.*

skeichen *adj, also* **skiten** fastidious about food, easily upset or nauseated *NE. n* fastidiousness or fussiness about food; a feeling of disgust for something edible *now Bnf Abd. v* (feel) disgust, (be) repel(led), (be) nauseate(d) *now Bnf Abd.*

slab †slaver, *esp* while eating, eat or drink noisily, slobber. **~ber** *v* slaver, dribble; eat or drink noisily, sloppily *now local N-Dmf. n* a slovenly slack-lipped person, a slobberer *now EC Lnk Gall.*

slerp salivate or slobber, splutter messily, spit *Ork Fif Rox.*

spean put (a person) off food through disgust, fear etc *now NE Per Kcb.*

spuin fou replete, *esp* with drink, to the point of vomiting *now NE Ags Kcb.*

sta, staw *n* a surfeit, a feeling of nausea, disgust or aversion caused by satiety, *freq* **gie, get** *etc* **a ~** *now C, S. v* **1** become cloyed or sated with or nauseated by food etc *local Ags-S.* **2** satiate, sicken or disgust with too much food *C, S.*

stamack: find the bottom *or* **grund(s) o one's ~** feel ravenously hungry *NE Ags Per.* **hae a good** *or* **bad ~** have a hearty *or* poor appetite.

stamagast sicken with a surfeit of food, nauseate *Abd Fif WC.*

stankit sated with food, satisfied *Abd Ags.*

stappit stuffed; replete, gorged *now Sh NE Ags Per.*

stench allay (hunger or thirst); satisfy (a person) with food, satiate *now NE Ags.*

stent, stint distend (the stomach with food).

sterve starve.

swage 1 *of the stomach after a meal etc* subside, settle down, shrink from a swollen state *now Sh Ork N.* **2** relax after a good meal, sit back and let it digest *Ork N.*

ting stuff (oneself etc) to the point of acute discomfort *Renfr Ayr.*

†**tuithy** ravenous.

tume, toom empty of food, fasting, hungry *now local Sh-Per.*

unable for having no appetite for (food).

wamefu *now Ags,* †**wombfull** a bellyful.

wersh *of the stomach or appetite* disinclined towards food; faint from hunger, squeamish *now Abd Kcdn.*

worry choke (**on** a mouthful of food), suffocate *now local Sh-Per.*

wrang, wrong: ~ one's pechan *or* **stamack** make oneself sick with eating too much or the wrong food.

yaup *adj, also* **yamp** *Abd,* **~ish** *now Renfr Lnk* having a keen appetite, hungry. *v* gape with hunger, be hungry.

9.15 EXCRETION, BODY FLUIDS

For blood and blood flow, see 9.8.

atter †corrupt matter, pus. ~**y** purulent, containing or exuding matter.

back-door trots *euphemistic* diarrhoea *local Ork-Ayr.*

beal fester.

bedrite soil with excrement.

befyle soil, defile.

black man a piece of black matter in the nose *C.*

bloit a sudden bowel movement, diarrhoea *SW.*

boakie a piece of hard matter in the nose *now Abd.*

boke, bock *v* belch; retch, vomit. *n* 1 a belch, a retch. 2 nausea *Cai Ags Ayr.* **byochy-byochy** retch, vomit *Ags.* **gie (someone)** *or* **get the (dry)** ~**(s)** (cause to) feel sick, retch or vomit *local C.*

brash bring up liquid into the mouth by belching *now Bnf Kcb.*

broth *v* sweat profusely *now Kcb. n, freq* ~ **o sweat** a heavy sweat *now Stlg.*

bubble mucus from the nose. **bub(b)ly** snotty, dirty with nasal mucus.

buirk *v* belch *now Fif.*

burn urine, *freq* **mak one's** ~ *now wLoth Lnk Kcb.*

cack(ie) *v* void excrement. *n* human excrement.

cadger: bolt *or* **cowp the** ~ vomit *Ags.*

cast vomit (**up**) *now Fif.*

†**caterve** catarrh.

clotterd clotted, congealed, caked *now local NE-C.*

cowk *v* retch; vomit *now Bnf Abd Stlg. n* a retch *NE.*

curmur *v* make a low rumbling or murmuring sound. *n, also* ~**ing** *now Bnf-Fif* flatulence, the rumbling sound associated with it *local NE-Kcb.*

dam the amount of urine discharged at a time (*usu* by children) *now Bnf Abd.*

defluxion a running or discharge, *chf* from the nose or eyes; expectoration, phlegm *now Stlg Fif.*

dirt: ~ **on** defecate on, befoul *now Bnf Abd.* ~**en** dirtied, filthy, soiled with excrement *now Abd Ags.*

driddle urinate in small quantities. †**dridland** suffering from diarrhoea.

drite *v* defecate. *n, chf as term of abuse* dirt, excrement *now Bnf Abd Kcdn Edb.*

†**e(a)se** the act of relieving the bowels, *chf* **do one's** ~.

eik perspiration *S.*

etter *n* corrupt matter, pus. *v* emit purulent matter, fester.

†**fluke** diarrhoea.

foost *v* break wind in a suppressed way *Bnf Abd. n* a suppressed breaking of wind *Bnf Abd.*

fulyie dung, excrement.

fyle defecate *now NE Per Slk.*

ga, gaw gall, bile etc.

geing human excrement *chf C-S.*

glit, glut, glet phlegm, mucus, the thin liquid discharging from a wound etc *now local.*

gob *v* spit *now WC.*

†**goo** *v* retch.

goor mucus, waxy matter, *esp* in the eye *now Sh Ork Cai Ags.*

graith urine *now Sh.*

guff belch *now local.*

gush salivate *now Abd.*

heftit 1 swollen with wind, flatulent *now Knr midLoth Dmf.* 2 full to repletion *now Abd midLoth.*

humour matter or pus from a wound or sore *Gen except WC, SW.*

kich, keech *n* excrement. *v* defecate.

lat, let: ~ **aff** break wind.

loch a discharge of urine *Ork NE Per.*

loit *v* defecate; vomit. *n* a lump of faeces.

meldrop (a drop of) mucus from the nose *latterly Rox.*

†**papple** stream with perspiration, be too hot.

pee *v* urinate, wet with urine. *n* urine; the act of urinating. ~**ins** urine *NE Ags.* ~ **a wallie** *freq in imperative* to coax a child urinate *N.*

pish *n* piss, urine. *v* piss.

press a strong but ineffectual urge to defecate *local Ork-Fif.*

pump *slang or colloq, n* a breaking of wind. *v* break wind.

rair a belch *now Ags Abd.*

rander *of a wound* discharge pus *local.*

reach retch, try to vomit.

reird a noisy breaking of wind *now Abd.*

rift *v* belch. *n* a belch. **hae the** ~ **o** have (food) repeating *Ags Per.* †~ **up** rise on the stomach.

roup *v* vomit *NE.*

rowt, rout break wind *now Fif wLoth.*

rummle-gumption(s) *joc* wind in the stomach, flatulence *now WC Kcb.*

skit *n* diarrhoea *local Sh-Gall. v* defecate *now Sh.*

skite have diarrhoea; soil with excrement.

skitter *n* diarrhoea, liquid excrement. *v* have diarrhoea, void liquid excrement.

slavers, slevers slaver, saliva.

slork reinhale nasal mucus, sniff or snort *Lnk SW*.

sneeshin draps drops of snuff-laden nasal mucus *Bnf Ags*.

snite *v* blow (one's nose), *esp* with the finger and thumb, wipe (mucus) from the nose *now Sh Ork NE*. *n* a blowing or wiping of the nose *now Sh NE*.

snochter nasal mucus, phlegm blown from the nose *Abd WC, SW*.

snotter: ~**s** nasal mucus, *esp* when hanging from the nose. ~**y** slimy, running at the nose *esp* when hanging from the nose, *Gen except Sh Ork*.

spit: ~**s** spittle *Gen except Sh Ork*. ~**tle** a quantity of saliva ejected at one time *now local Ork-WC*.

†**splew** spit out, spew, vomit.

splurt squirt, eject liquid from the mouth in a splash *now local Sh-Per*.

spue a retch, a vomiting motion.

strone *v* urinate *now Ags Edb Rox*. *n* the discharge of urine *now Edb Rox*.

sweet, swat sweat.

teemie *child's word* urinating *C*.

teicher, ticher *esp of a slight wound or sore* exude moisture, ooze *Bwk SW, S*.

thin: the ~ diarrhoea *NE Ags*.

tollie a lump of excrement *Gen except Sh Ork*.

tuird a turd.

wizzy: do a ~ urinate *Edb*.

wursom pus, the discharge from a festering sore *now Sh Ork Cai*.

yesk *v* hiccup, belch, vomit. *n* a hiccup, belch.

yuchle a gob of sputum *wLoth Dnbt Renfr*.

9.16 REPRODUCTION

†**ba-cod** the scrotum.

†**bairn-bed** the womb or a condition affecting it.

biggen swell, grow larger; be pregnant.

bosie the womb.

bubbies breasts.

†**Canongate breeks** venereal disease.

cart the crab-louse; the skin-disease it causes *Abd*.

†**childbedlair** childbed.

cleck bring forth, give birth to. ~**in 1** the act of giving birth *now Bnf*. **2** *derog* a brood, litter of human beings.

coats: hae one's ~ **kilted, gae** ~ **kilted** be pregnant *local C*.

creel the womb *NE*.

cry be in labour. ~**ing** labour; a confinement *now NE*.

cummer a midwife.

†**cuntbitten** poxed.

doddles the male genitals *now Cai*.

egg-bed an ovary.

fud the female pubes.

†**glengore** venereal disease, syphilis. **glengorie** infect with syphilis.

graith the penis.

†**grandgore** venereal disease, syphilis.

†**great** highly pregnant.

†**green**[1] *of a woman* recently delivered.

green[2] *of a pregnant woman* have a craving (**for** particular foods) *now Mry Kcb*.

heavy, *also* ~**-footed,** ~ **o (the) fit** pregnant; in an advanced state of pregnancy.

howdie, howdie wife *now local Cai-Lnk* a midwife. ~**ing 1** a confinement *now Lnk Kcb*. **2** midwifery *now Edb*.

jizzen *now verse*, †**gising** childbed.

†**larbar** *adj* exhausted, impotent. *n* an exhausted or impotent man.

luckie a midwife *now Lnk*.

†**lume 1** the penis. **2** ~**s** the male genitals

†**mam** a midwife.

†**maukin** the female genitals.

†**medwyfe** a midwife.

miscairry miscarry.

muckle, meikle, mickle pregnant *now local Sh-wLoth*.

†**mulls** the labia of the vulva.

pairt, part: ~ **wi bairn** *or* **child** give birth to a premature or stillborn baby; suffer a miscarriage *now Sh NE Uls*.

†**pen** the penis.

pill(ie) the penis *now local*.

pintle the penis.

†**quhillylillie** *familiar* the penis.

riglin a male animal or *occas* a man with one testicle undescended *now Ork EC, SW-S*.

ripples a disease affecting the back and loins, *perh* a venereal disease.

road: on the ~ *of a woman* pregnant *NE-S*.

Robin *child's word* the penis *NE-S*.

†**rubigo** the penis.

see her ain *of a woman* menstruate *Fif*.

shour, shower a pang or paroxysm of pain etc, *specif* of childbirth.

†**sivens** a venereal disease characterized by raspberry-like sores.

slip an abortion, miscarriage *local Cai-Dnbt*.

sookin bairn *etc* a child at the breast, a suckling.

sort *euphemistic* castrate *Sh NE*.

stane, stone a testicle.

taw *child's word* the penis *Stlg Fif WC*.

†**tirly mirlie, tirlie-whirlie** the female genitals.

tit a nipple or teat.

toby *joc* the penis *Abd Ags.*

tossel the penis *local Abd-SW.*

tot *child's word* the penis *N.*

trout: there's a ∼(ie) **in the well** said of a woman expecting a child, *esp* if illegitimate *now Abd.*

†**wallies** the (male) genitals.

wame, wime the womb *now Cai.*

†**wark, werk:** ∼**lume** the penis; ∼**lumes** the male genitals.

weed a high fever, a sudden feverish attack; *specif* puerperal fever *now N Fif Dmf.*

†**weidinonfa** puerperal fever; any fever.

whang the penis *C Slk.*

9.17 ACTIVITY, MOVEMENT

bairge walk with a jerk or spring upwards; strut.

bap walk in a plodding, flat-footed way *now Abd.*

bauchle shamble.

†**braidlingis** flat (on the ground); with the limbs extended.

broostle bustling; hard exertion *chf S.*

ca(ll)-through drive, energy *Bnf Abd Ags Fif.*

cat's lick a hasty superficial wash.

cleuk claw, scratch *Abd.*

†**cleverus** nimble, quick.

†**cliftie** clever, active, nimble.

clinch *v* limp, halt *now NE, SW. n* a limp *chf NE.*

daver stagger (*eg* from a blow) *now Bnf Abd Kcb.*

†**deliverance** activity, agility.

dilp stalk; stump, hobble *now Ags.*

dod move slowly and unsteadily, totter, dodder *now Ayr.*

doddle toddle, walk feebly or slowly *now Bnf Abd.*

doit walk with a stumbling or short step *now Bnf Abd.* ∼**er, ditter** walk or move unsteadily, hang about *now local Bnf-S.*

dotter walk unsteadily, stagger.

dreel energy, forcefulness *now Ags.*

drochle walk slowly and feebly taking small steps *Bnf Abd.*

dump walk with short, heavy steps, stump **about** *now Kcb.*

†**dwaible** totter, walk feebly.

edgie quick, active, mentally and physically *now midLoth Rox.*

†**faik** fold, tuck (a limb) under one; *of limbs* bend, give way under one.

fauchle walk with difficulty due to lack of strength; trudge, plod *now Cai.*

fauld *of the limbs etc* double up, bend under one *now Sh Ags.*

feerie active, nimble.

fend: ∼**fu** energetic *now Ags.* ∼**ie** active, lively, healthy *chf Ayr.*

fersell energetic, active.

fidge *v* fidget; move restlessly from excitement; twitch, itch. *n* a shrug, twitch, jerk *local Sh-EC.*

†**flaucht braid** with the limbs extended like a bird in flight; spreadeagled.

flench flinch *now Sh Bnf Abd.*

fushion physical strength, energy *now NE.*

gae *of a child* at the walking stage *now Sh Ork.*

gangrel(1) a child just able to walk, a toddler *N.*

gleg quick of movement; nimble *local.*

gowdie-lane: gae ∼ *of a child* walk unaided.

hainch, hinch *n* a halt or limp in walking, lameness *now Rox. v also* ∼**le** *Rox* walk jerkily or with a limp *local Abd-Uls.*

hammle walk with a limp, hobble *S.*

hamrel a person who often stumbles in walking, an awkward person *chf Abd.*

hap, hop walk with a limp *now Ags Uls.*

haud, hald, hold: gang *etc* **by (the)** ∼(**s**) *esp of a child or an infirm person* support oneself in walking by holding onto a chair etc *now local.*

haut *v* limp, hop. *n* the act of limping, a hop.

hechle walk or proceed with difficulty, struggle or exert oneself, as climbing a hill etc *now nEC.*

henk walk or move unsteadily, walk with a limp, hop on one leg *now Sh.*

hilch *v* limp, hobble, move with a rolling, lurching gait *local Cai-SW. n* a limp, the act of walking with a limp; an uneven gait *Cai Dmf Uls.*

†**hilt** walk with a limp.

hippity *adv* with a limp, lamely *local. adj* lame, crippled, limping *now Ags Kcb.*

hipple go lame, walk with a limp, hobble *now Bnf.*

hirple *v* walk lamely, limp, hobble; move unevenly. *n* a limp, the act of walking unsteadily or with a limp

hitch hobble, walk with a limp; hop *now midLoth.*

hochle, hauchle *v* walk with a slow awkward hobbling or tottering gait *Gen except Sh Ork. n* an ungainly heaving movement of the body, an awkward shifting of position

hoddle *v* waddle; move with an uneven hobbling gait as an old person; walk with quick short steps *now Ags Edb Dmf. n* a waddling gait, a quick toddling step.

hodge 1 move or walk awkwardly or jerkily, hobble along *now Sh Ork NE.* **2** fidget, twitch, with discomfort *now NE.*

hoit *v* move awkwardly or clumsily, *esp* of a stout

person trying to move quickly, waddle. *n* a slow hobbling gait.

howdle move with a rocking or bumping motion, limp.

humple walk unevenly or haltingly, as in tight shoes, hobble *Rox*.

hurkle walk with the body in a crouching position; stumble along, stagger *now Bnf*.

hyter *v* walk with a lurching, unsteady movement; stumble, trip *NE Ags*. *n* a lurch, a stumble *NE*. *adv* with weak or uncertain stumbling step *Bnf Abd Ags*.

ill gaein clumsy or awkward at walking due to deformity of the feet *Ork Abd Ags*.

jooter saunter, totter *now midLoth*.

jossle shake, totter.

jouk, juke flinch *now local Abd-Ayr*.

kevel hold oneself awkwardly, stumble *now Dmf*.

kim spruce, nimble *Abd*.

kneef physically alert, agile *chf Sh-N*.

†knoit 1 *of the knees* knock. **2** hobble, walk stiffly and jerkily.

†laish relaxed, limp.

†lame *verse* lameness, a crippling injury or infirmity.

lameter a lame or crippled person.

lamp limp, hobble *now local*.

leenge slouch in walking.

leish active, athletic, supple *SW, S*.

licht, light: ~**some** light on one's feet, agile. ~**fit** *now NE Gall*, ~ **set,** † ~**fute** *chf verse* light-footed, nimble.

lift the uneven rising step of a person who has one leg shorter than the other *now Fif WC*.

linking active, agile, brisk *now Fif Ayr*.

lowder walk with a heavy rocking motion as if weary, plod; move clumsily or lazily *now Abd*.

miss a fit trip, stumble.

nimmle nimble.

†olite active, energetic, nimble.

palie, pallie 1 defective, deformed, lame *now C, S*. **2** *of the limbs etc* incapacitated, affected by injury or disease, paralysed *now Per Rox*.

partan-taed having a pigeon-toed gait like a crab *Sh-Ags*.

pauchle: *chf* ~ **alang, awa, on** *etc* move feebly but persistently, shuffle, hobble, struggle along *now Uls Slk*.

†pavie a fantastic movement of the body.

pawt walk in a heavy uncoordinated way *now Cai*.

pergaddus a noisy burst of energy *Abd Ags Fif*.

plet, plait 1 cross or fold (one's legs or arms) *NE-Rox*. **2** walk in an unsteady, pigeon-toed way.

plowd *v, chf* ~**er** walk in a heavy-footed way

(**through** water, mud etc), waddle or plod along *now Bnf*. *n* a heavy ungainly carriage or walk, a waddle *Mry Bnf*.

powl, pale propel oneself with the aid of a crutch *now Kcb*.

powt walk with a heavy exhausted step *Bnf*.

rash active, agile, vigorous *now Rox*.

rax stretch (a cramped limb etc).

redd energy, drive *now Sh Ork*.

reest *of a person or his limbs* come to a (sudden) halt, become rooted to the spot *now Kcb*.

roadit *of a child* able to walk *NE Ags*.

rock stagger or reel in walking *now Sh NE Kcb*.

roddle rock, shake, totter *Lnk*.

scash *NE*, **scashle** *esp of feet or gait* twist, turn to one side; shuffle along with the toes turned out.

sclaff, sclaffer *now NE* walk in a flat-footed or shuffling way *now NE, C*.

sclap walk in a flat-footed or shuffling way *NE*.

sclatch walk or move in an ungainly, slovenly way, shuffle *now Ags Per*.

scush *v, also* ~**le** *now NE* shuffle, walk with a shambling gait *now NE*. *n* a shuffling, scuffling with the feet; the noise of this *now NE*.

shammle shamble, walk awkwardly etc. **schamlich** walk with a shambling gait *NE*.

shauchle *v* walk without lifting the feet, shuffle, walk clumsily *Gen except Sh Ork*. *n* a shuffling, shambling gait *now Abd Kcdn*.

shog, shug, shoog sway, swing, rock from side to side, wobble *NE-Per Ayr*.

skavle walk with a crooked twisting gait, totter, reel *now Ork*.

skleush *v* walk in a clumsy, shuffling, or leg-weary manner *now Cai Bnf Abd*. *n* a trailing, shuffling, heavy-footed gait *now Cai Abd*.

skliff *v* walk with a heavy, shuffling step, drag the feet, scuffle *now NE, C*. *n* a shuffling, trailing way of walking; the noise of this *now local EC-Gall*.

sklute *now Rox*, **skleet** *Cai* set the feet down clumsily in walking, walk in a flat-footed, shuffling or splay-footed way.

slewie walk with a heavy swinging or swaying gait *NE*.

sling *v* walk with a long vigorous stride, swing along *now Rox*. *n* a swinging vigorous gait, a long striding step *now Rox*.

slype walk with a heavy, flat-footed step *Bnf Abd*.

snack, snackie *Bnf Abd* nimble, active, quick.

†snell quick, nimble, active, clever, sharp, smart.

souple *adj* supple. *adv* nimbly, agilely *now Ork NE Per*.

spree spry.

sprush brisk, smart in one's movements, spry.

stacher v stagger, totter *Gen except Sh. n* a stumble, stagger, a false step *NE nEC, SW.* **staucherie** unsteady in gait *NE nEC, SW.*

stammery stumbling, uncertain of one's footing *NE-Fïf, SW.*

stammle stagger, stumble, blunder, hobble *now Rox.*

stavel v walk in a halting uncertain way, stumble, blunder on *now Fif. n* a stumble *Rox.*

staver stagger, stumble about, walk unsteadily *now Fif.*

stechie stiff-jointed, slow-moving due to stiffness, corpulence or indolence, stodgy *local C.*

stilp walk with long stiff steps, stump about, stalk *now Bnf-Ags.* **~ert** walk with long stiff strides, lifting the feet high *local NE.*

†**stilt** walk stiffly, haltingly, lift the legs high in walking.

stodge, studge walk with a long slow step, stump; step uncertainly or unsteadily *now Sh NE Wgt S.*

stoit, styte stagger, stumble from drink etc, walk in a dazed uncertain way *local NE-Uls.* **~er** v walk unsteadily, reel, totter *now local. n* a staggering motion, stumble, reeling about *now local Sh-Wgt.*

stookie: stand *etc* **like a ~** stand in a helpless bemused way as if unable to move.

stot v stagger, walk unsteadily, *eg* from drink, weakness. *n* a sudden erratic movement, a fitful motion; a stumble, stagger *now Sh.* **~ter, stooter** v stagger, totter, stumble *local N-SW. n* the act of **stottering** a stumble, stagger, unsteady gait *local N-S.*

stowff (the sound of) a dull heavy-footed gait *NE.*

strachle, strauchle move or walk laboriously or with difficulty, struggle *now Wgt Dmf.*

stramp go about with a firm or heavy step; stump about, march energetically or purposefully *now local.*

streek 1 stretch (oneself or one's limbs) *now Sh NE, S.* **2** †extend oneself full length, stretch out.

streetch stretch.

stug, stog *of a clumsy, old or infirm person* walk in a heavy-footed way, plod, stump.

stummer stumble, stagger *now Ork.*

stummle stumble.

stump: ~art walk heavily, in a stumping clumsy way *Bnf Abd.* **~er** walk with a clumsy, heavy or hobbling step, stump *Bnf Abd.* † **~le** walk with a stiff hobbling gait, stump.

stunt bound, bounce, walk with a springy step *now WC, SW Rox.*

swack *of persons their limbs* active, lithe, supple *now local Sh-Fif.*

swag sway from side to side, wag to and fro; hang down heavily and lopsidedly.

†**swagger** stagger, sway.

swankin active, agile, athletic.

swaver v totter, sway, move unsteadily or wearily *now Sh Ork NE. n* an inclination to one side, a lurch, stagger *NE.*

swipper adj quick, nimble, active *now NE. n* a lithe, agile person *NE. adv* agilely, nimbly, quickly, abruptly *NE.*

†**tait** lively, active, nimble.

teeter totter or walk with short, tripping or uncertain steps.

through: ~-ca energy, drive *now NE Ags.* **~-gaun** energetic, active *now Fif Lnk Slk.* **~-pit** energy, activity, capacity for or progress at work *now Sh Abd Per Dmf.*

toddle *of a young child, of an old, infirm or drunk person* walk with short, rocking, uncertain or unsteady steps.

toit *now Bnf Abd,* **toiter** *now Abd Ags* walk with short unsteady steps, totter, *esp* from weakness or old age.

tooter v totter, walk with short mincing steps *now Mry Abd. n* a tottery gait, toddle *NE.*

tot toddle; totter *now Lnk Ayr.*

tottle 1 walk unsteadily, toddle, totter *now Ags.* **2** totter and fall, topple over *now Ork Ags.*

trauchle walk slowly and wearily, drag oneself along.

tuckie awkward, clumsy *NE.*

tyauve struggle physically, tumble or toss about *NE.*

unbowsome stiff; unable to bend or stoop *S.*

†**unfeary** inactive, incapable of exertion; weak, infirm, uncertain in one's gait.

†**unhanty** clumsy in figure, movement or action.

waddin, †**waldin** supple, vigorous; young, active.

waffle v stagger, totter *Sh Wgt. adj* supple, pliant *now Cai.*

wammle, wamble stagger, move with a weak, unsteady gait *now local Sh-Lnk.* **wammily** tottery, weak, feeble *now local NE-WC.*

†**wandle** walk wearily or unsteadily.

wannle supple, agile; active *S.*

warsle move in a struggling, laborious way, wriggle, sprawl about, as in an effort to rise or free oneself.

wauchle v walk or make one's way laboriously or with difficulty, walk in a clumsy, ungainly way, stumble with fatigue etc *now Sh-C. n* a staggering ungainly movement, a wobble *now Fif Loth Fif.*

waul supple, nimble, agile *Pbls Dmf.*

wavel rock unsteadily, sway to and fro, stagger *now Sh.*

weelins: hae the ~ o have control or full use of (one's body, limbs etc) *Abd.*

welter reel, stagger, stumble, flounder *now Cai.*

wheeber walk with hurried ungainly steps, scurry *now Abd.*

whippie quick or brisk in movement, nimble, agile *now Fif Wgt.*

whippitie-stourie a light-footed nimble person *now Fif Dnbt.*

whummle go head over heels, fall, tumble or sprawl suddenly; move unsteadily, stumble *now local Sh-SW.*

widdle move slowly and unsteadily, stagger, waddle *now Sh Ork Stlg.*

†**winch** wince, start back, flinch.

wingle walk unsteadily, reel, stagger *now Sh.*

†**wintle** stagger, rock from side to side, roll about. *now Sh.*

yanker a smart agile person.

yare eager, agile.

9.18 GOOD HEALTH

aboot, about on the move, going about (*esp* after an illness): '*Tam's aboot again*'.

abune: get ~ recover from, get over (an illness) *now NE Ags.*

agait on the road, going about, *esp* after illness.

at oneself healthy, flourishing.

bensin bouncing, vigorous *Bnf.*

betak oneself recover *Bnf Abd.*

better completely recovered from an illness. **~ness** recovery *local.* **~-faured** better-featured, better-looking. **~-like** better-looking.

braw well, in good health. **~ and weel** in good health.

ca(ll) through pull through (an illness) *Bnf Ags Fif.*

cantle recover one's health or spirits *Bnf Abd.*

cast aff recover from (an illness) *now Abd Ags Fif.*

cock revive; pick up (after an illness) *now Abd wLoth.*

come: ~ forrit make progress, *esp* in growth *local.* **~ through** recover from an illness.

†**convalesce** become strong, acquire or regain strength.

cower 1 recover, get well *now chf NE.* **2** †restore, revive. **3** get over, recover from (something) *NE.*

fend: ~ie active, lively, healthy *chf Ayr.*

fere healthy, sturdy, *chf* **hale and ~.**

fine in good health.

fit, foot: till one's ~ recovered from illness, up and about. **(up)on ~** well, in good health *Sh Ork NE Ags.*

fleg dispel, drive away (illness etc) *now NE Ags.*

†**freck** able-bodied, vigorous, active.

gaily, gailies *of health* well enough, tolerably well, middling *now local Abd-Dmf.*

gate: be at the ~ again be recovered from an illness *NE Uls.* **haud the** *or* **one's ~** hold one's own (when ill); be in a good state of health *now Abd.*

get through recover from (an illness) *now local.*

green: keep the banes ~ preserve good health and youthfulness.

growthie *of persons* well-grown, thriving *now local Ork-Kcb.*

grushie *of a child* thriving.

hail[1], **whole 1** sound, in a healthy state, wholesome, robust, vigorous. **2** uninjured, undamaged in body or mind. **3** †healthy or fresh in appearance. **get ~ o** recover from. **~ and fere** in full health and vigour; unharmed, undamaged *now literary.*

†**hail**[2] health.

halth health *now Uls.*

hardy in good health *now local Abd-Rox.*

haud, hald, hold continue, keep (in health) *now Ags: 'hoo are ye hauding yoursel?'* **~ forrit** continue to improve (in health) *now midLoth.*

heal: *freq* **guid ~** health, freedom from sickness, physical well-being. †**~ful(l)** healthy, healthgiving.

hech how: (the) auld ~ a return to a former state (of health).

hert, hairt, heart: ~-hale *of the body* organically sound *now local Sh-Dmf.*

horn: as hard as the *or* **a ~** hardy.

keen lively, brisk, with renewed vigour after an illness *local Sh-midLoth.*

keep *v* fare (*as regards health*).

kittle *of health etc* improve *Abd Ags.*

kneef fit, in sound health and spirits *N Per.*

leuk ower the door look outside; *hence* go outside, *esp* be in the open air after an illness *Sh N, C.*

life: lifieness vivacity, vigour *now Sh Ork Fif.* **living and ~like, leevin and ~ thinking** hale and hearty *now Sh.*

liss *v* **1** †relieve (pain or suffering); relieve (a person **of** suffering) *of pain etc.* **2** cease, abate *now Uls.* **lissens, lissance** respite.

livin-like lively, in good health *local Ork-Gall.*

lowpin an levin hale and hearty *chf EC.*

mak, make: ~ **better** improve, get better *now Sh.*

†**mell: keep (the)** ~ **in (the) shaft** keep in a good state of health.

mend 1 restore to health, heal. **2** ~ **of** recover from (an illness). **3** *of a wound, disease etc* get better.

out ower out of bed, up *now Sh-Ags.*

ower weel in very good health *Sh-Cai Uls.*

owercast recover from, throw off (an illness etc); get over.

†**owercome** revive, recover **from** (shock, sickness etc).

poust strength, vigour, power, force *now S.*

poustie 1 †sound physical health. **2** the physical capacity or use of a part of the body.

rambust robust *Bnf S.*

†**refete** recover, recuperate.

†**restore** recover, revive.

†**revert** recover, bring back or return to one's normal state of mind or spirits; recover consciousness *latterly N.*

road: tae the ~ recovered after an illness, able to be about again *NE Ags.*

solvendie strong, in good health, fit.

stout in good health, robust, *freq* with reference to recovery after an illness *now Sh-N Kcb.*

stuffie in good health, sturdy, full of vigour *now nEC-S.*

sturken, storken 1 †become strong; thrive. **2** restore to robustness; recover one's strength *S.*

thole through pull through an illness *Ags wLoth.*

thram thrive *Mry Abd Kcdn.*

tidy in good condition, shapely, plump *now Ork.*

umbersorrow fit, robust; resisting disease or the effects of severe weather *S.*

usual: one's (auld) ~ one's usual state of health, frame of mind; one's old self: *'he's in his usual'.*

weel, well healthy *local.* **weelness** good health.

†**weel-hained** well preserved, in good shape. **weel at anesel** in good physical condition, plump, stout. **well-thriven** well-grown, plump *now Sh.*

win abune get over, overcome, recover from (an illness etc) *now Sh NE Ags.*

yau(l)d active, alert, vigorous, healthy *now Bwk WC-S.*

9.19 BAD HEALTH

For respiratory diseases, see 9.11; for sexually transmitted diseases, see 9.16. Other disorders will be found with different parts of the body in the appropriate sections. Includes fainting.

aff an on *of a (sick) person's health* sometimes better, sometimes worse.

ail an illness.

†**aixies** an attack of ague.

alist: come ~ recover consciousness.

asoond in a faint *now Sh.*

†**attenuat** made thin or weak.

awa, away wasted, reduced in flesh: *'he's awa to skin and bane'.* ~ **frae** past; unable to *Sh N: 'he wis awa fae speakin'.* ~ **wi 't** done for; broken in health.

awald *esp when unconscious* lying on one's back and unable to rise.

back: ~**-gaein** *adj* not thriving. *n, also* ~**-gangin** a relapse *now local N-SW.* ~**-jar** a setback in health or circumstances *now Bnf.* ~**set** something which hinders or causes a relapse *now Bnf.*

bad unwell, in pain, physically ill. ~**ly** ill, ailing.

†**batts** colic etc in human beings.

bed: ~**dit up** confined to bed through illness *NE.* ~**rall** *now Bnf,* ~**al** *now NE,* ~**lar** †*adj* confined to bed, bedridden. *n* a bedridden person, *formerly esp* as an inmate of a hospital or almshouse *now NE Kcdn.* † ~ **evil** an illness confining one to bed. ~**fast** bedridden.

bellythraw colic, bellyache.

bever shaking; a trembling (fever).

blae livid or bluish from cold, bloodlessness etc.

blast a stroke, a sudden attack of illness *now Bnf.* ~**it** paralysed.

†**boldin, bowdin** swell (up).

bowel hive(s) enteritis etc in children *now Stlg Fif.*

branks the mumps *now Fif Loth Lnk.*

brash a short bout of illness; an illness. ~**y** delicate in constitution, subject to illness *now Bnf Stlg Fif.*

brucklie in a weak state of health *now Bnf Abd.*

†**buffed: the best of him** *etc* **is** ~ he etc is in decline, his etc strength is going.

buffets a swelling in the glands of the throat; mumps *now Ags Fif.*

by one's ordinar out of one's usual health *now local.*

care bed a sickbed.

cast back a setback, relapse *now Abd Fif Stlg.*

chockit suffering from quinsy *chf NE.*

†**chokis** quinsy.

clappit having the flesh clinging to the bones; shrunken *now local Bnf-Fif.*

†**clyred** affected with tumours.

compleen, complain be ailing, unwell, *chf* ~**in** unwell, ailing.

corbie: be a gone ~ be a 'goner', be done for.

crazed broken down in health, infirm.

dammisht stunned, stupefied.

daumer stun, confuse *now Bnf.*

daver stun, stupefy, daze *now Bnf Bwk.*

death dwam a death-like faint *now Abd.*

decay a decline (in health), *esp* from tuberculosis.

dishealth ill-health, illness.

distress illness *now Ags Fif.*

doilt, diled dazed, confused, stupid *now Sh Dmf.*

donsie sickly, feeble, delicate *now Arg.*

doon, down: gae ~ **the brae** *or* **hill** *esp of an old person* deteriorate in health.

door: he *etc* **hasn't been** *etc* **over the** ~ he etc hasn't been outside or out of the house.

dorbie delicate, weak *Bnf Abd.*

dortie feeble, delicate, sickly *now Bnf Abd.*

dowie ailing, weak, delicate *now local Bnf-Stlg.*

doze stupefy, stun *now Ork Fif.*

dozened stupefied, dazed, stupid, physically weakened (through age, drink etc) *now local Sh-Lnk.*

drow an attack of illness, a fainting fit *now Abd Ags Fif.*

dwam *n* a swoon, a fainting fit; a sudden attack of illness a stupor. *v* 1 faint, swoon *now Bnf Abd Fif.* 2 ail, decline in health *now Stlg.* ~**ie** *now local Abd-EC,* ~**ish** *now Abd Fif* sickly, faint. **dwamle** *n* a sick or faint turn *now Abd Arg. v* faint, appear faint *now Abd.*

dwine *v* 1 pine, waste away, fail in health. 2 cause to pine or wither. *n* a decline *now local Ork-WC.* **dwiny** sickly, pining *now Fif.*

eemage a ghost of one's former self, a pitiful figure *now local, Sh-Bwk.*

elic passion *orig* appendicitis, *now* colic.

etten and spued unhealthy looking, 'washed out'.

fail: ~**ed,** ~**it** impaired in health, infirm.

fairrie collapse from exhaustion or sudden illness *Abd.*

fa(ll): ~ **awa 1** waste away, decline in health. 2 faint *Sh NE Ags.* ~ **in** *of the body* shrink, shrivel.

far: ~ **awa wi't** feeble; frail, seriously ill *Sh Ork NE Bwk.* ~ **throu** very ill, at death's door.

fash afflict (with a disease).

fauchinless weak, without energy *Mry Bnf.*

faughie pasty-faced, sickly looking *N.*

felled prostrate, *esp* with illness *C-S.* ~ **sick** too ill to move *now Ayr.*

†**felt (gravel)** the disease gravel.

filsh weak, faint.

fit: aff one's *or* **the** ~ *or* **feet** unfit for work *now Cai.*

fivver, fiver a fever, *freq specif* scarlet fever.

fordweblit *literary* very weak, enfeebled.

†**foul** infected with plague.

founder *v* collapse, break down with illness etc *Gen*

except Sh Ork. n **1** a collapse, breakdown in health *local NE-S.* **2** *specif* a severe chill *WC Uls.*

fraik *n* a slight ailment about which too much fuss is made *Ork Ags. v* pretend to be ill, make a fuss about a minor ailment *Ork Ags.*

frame an emaciated person *local Sh-Kcb.*

†**fundy** suffer a chill, become stiff with cold. **fun-dyit** chilled; sensitive to cold.

gae: gaun gear applied to persons in declining health, *esp* those about to die *NE, SW.* ~ **aboot** *of a disease or complaint* be prevalent *local Sh-Ayr.* ~ **awa** faint, swoon *Ags Fif SW.* ~ **back** deteriorate, run down, fall off *Ork C-S.*

gang awa faint, swoon *NE Ags Ayr.*

gate: haud the *or* **one's** ~ hold one's own (when ill) *now Abd.*

glender: ~ **gait,** †~ **gane** on the decline (in health), in a bad way.

gliff, glaff, glouf a slight attack, touch (of an illness) *esp* **a** ~ **o (the) cauld** *local Abd-Edb.*

gowstie, goustly ghastly, wasted, emaciated, pale *latterly Bnf Abd.*

grain be ailing *now Cai Ags Rox.*

graveyaird: ~ **deserter = kirkyaird deserter** *now NE.*

gulsoch jaundice *now Kcdn.*

†**handill** be afflicted (**with** a disease etc).

hard up in poor health, unwell *now sEC, S.*

†**heave** swell, distend.

heels: coup by the ~ prostrate, lay low *now Abd Fif Edb.*

heepocondry *Per Stlg Fif,* †**hypochonderies** hypochondria.

hert, hairt, heart: ~**ie** suffering from a weak heart *local.* ~**-kake** heart-disease *now Sh.* †~**-fever** a febrile condition; an illness causing a feeling of exhaustion. ~ **scad,** ~ **scald** heart-burn. **gar someone's** ~ **rise** make someone sick *Ags Fif Rox.*

hing, hang be in a poor state of health *local NE-SW.* ~**in-like** ill-looking *local Cai-Rox.*

hives inflammation of the bowels in children, causing fever and diarrhoea; *now* any childish ailment without distinctive symptoms *local Cai-SW.*

house, hoose: ~**-fast** *local Sh-Renfr,* ~**-tied** *now Cai Per Renfr* housebound, confined to the house.

hove 1 cause to swell, distend. **2** become swollen or distended, swell, expand. **hovie** distended. **hoving** the state of being swollen.

hushle a person who is unable to work as a result of ill health or incapacity *Renfr Dmf.*

ill illness, disease *now Sh N Ags.* †~ **farandly** in poor condtion. †~ **like** sick looking. **pit (one's**

meat) **in an ~ skin** look thin or half-starved *Gen except Sh Ork*.

income 1 an illness or infirmity with no obvious external cause *N Renfr.* **2** a swelling, abscess, festering sore etc *now local Sh-Kcb*.

indisgestion indigestion.

infeck infect.

it: awa wi't, by wi't, throw wi't ruined in health.

jallisie an illness *Mry Bnf*.

jandies jaundice.

jaw-lock lockjaw *local Ork-Lnk*.

†**jawpish** urethritis.

†**keen** *of pestilence* cruel, violent, terrible.

kind: yon ~ *euphemistic* not quite normal; not up to much, in indifferent health etc *local Sh-Per WC*.

kirkyaird deserter a sickly looking person, one who looks as if he should be in his grave *now NE*.

kirnel *now Fif-Rox, also* **wax(en)** *or* **waxing kirnels** *local Fif-Rox* a lump under the skin, *esp* in the neck; a swollen gland.

kittlie an irritation (of the throat).

knot *of arthritic joints* swell, gnarl *local Sh-SW*. **a ~ in the puddin** a strangulated hernia *Fif Gsw Dmf*.

laid: be ~ aff one's feet *now midLoth Uls*, **be ~ by** *now local*, **be ~ aside** be incapacitated by illness.

†**land: ~ feaver** some kind of illness. **~ ill** a disease, ? epilepsy.

†**lent** *of a fever* slow.

lie be confined to bed by illness. **~ doun** take to one's bed with illness *Gen except S*.

louch in a depressed state of health or spirits *wLoth WC*.

luppen sinnen a ganglion *now Renfr SW*.

maisles measles.

mak, make: ~ naething o it, not ~ much of it, not ~ muckle o't *now Sh NE Ags, of an ill person* fail to show signs of improvement.

mill reek a disease contracted by lead-workers from poisonous fumes *C*.

mirls measles *chf NE Ags*.

misthriven undernourished *Sh Ags Abd*.

molligrups stomach-ache, colic.

nirl, nurl shrink, shrivel, stunt in growth, pinch with cold *local Sh Lnk*.

object a deformed or diseased person.

†**occupe, occupy** *of a disease* take possession of, grip (the victim).

onfa an attack of a disease, *freq* one of unknown origin *chf S*.

onwait of an invalid requiring constant attention *NE*.

ool 1 wreck the health. **2** be dejected, subdued, as from illness *Sh Uls*.

oorie dismal, gloomy, miserable-looking from illness now local Sh-Arg. **oorlich** miserable-looking from illness.

oorit tired or ailing-looking.

owercome a sudden attack of illness.

paewae pallid, sickly *now Sh NE Fif*.

pains: the ~ chronic rheumatism, rheumatic twinges.

pairls, perils: *chf* **the ~** paralysis; a paralytic tremor or weakness *now Slk*. **pairlt** affected with paralysis or a paralytic tremor *now Slk*.

†**palsify** afflict with palsy, paralyse.

†**parlesy** palsy.

patient(s) o deed *or* **death,** †**passioun(is) of dede** the death throes, the last agonies.

peel-and-eat unhealthy-looking, delicate, sickly.

peelie: ~-wally sickly, feeble, pallid, thin and ill-looking. **~-wersh** sickly, delicate *now Rox*.

peenge *v* droop, pine, mope, look cold and miserable *now Kcdn Ags*. *n* a feeble, sickly-looking person *Fif S*. **peengie** sickly-looking, puny, not in good health *now NE Ags Fif*. **peeng(e)in 1** = peengie. **2** ailing, pinched and cold-looking.

peesweep, peesie-weesie sharp-featured, gaunt; ailing.

†**pest** (an outbreak of) any virulent or deadly epidemic disease, *specif* bubonic plague.

†**pestilentious** tending to produce pestilence, noxious to life or health.

†**pestinence** plague, pestilence.

pewl be only half-alive *Ags Per*.

pike *of illness, hunger etc* make (a person) thin and emaciated, reduce to skin and bone *now Ork*. **pikit(-like)** having a gaunt emaciated appearance, thin and unhealthy-looking *now EC*.

pine waste away from disease, become exhausted or emaciated, *now Ork-Per Kcb*. †**pined** in pain, tortured, tormented. **piner** person that is not thriving.

pipsyllis a disease, possibly epilepsy; malingering, feigned illness.

pit, put: sair pit on ill *Cai Per*. **~ up** vomit, bring up.

plottit having a miserable or sickly appearance.

poch slightly unwell, out of sorts *Mry Abd*.

pock a disease causing eruptions or pustules on the skin, *eg* chickenpox *now local Sh-SW*.

†**poplexy** apoplexy, a stroke of apoplexy.

pouk: ~ie dejected-looking, thin and unhealthy-looking *WC Kcb Uls*. **~it** having a miserable, emaciated appearance, scraggy and thin-looking *now C, S.* **in the** ~ not very well, below par.

poustit drained of strength, powerless; not in one's normal state of health or mind, suffering sickness or pain *chf Ork.*

†**purpie fever** some kind of fever causing purplish discolouration of the skin, *prob chf* typhus.

pyauve: pyauvin sickly, ailing; suffering from the heat *now Cai Abd.* **pyauvie** an attack of sickness or faintness, a fit of nausea *now Cai.*

queerways in not quite a normal state, slightly unwell *now Ork Kcb.*

†**rest: the auld** ~ name of a disease.

rheumatise rheumatism.

rheums rheumatic pains *now Bnf Ags Per.*

rimburs(t)in, rimburst *now Ags Per, adj* ruptured. *n, also* †**rimburstenness** a rupture, a hernia.

ring in be near the end of one's powers of endurance; be at death's door *now NE Ags Per.*

ripples a disease affecting the back and loins, *perh* a venereal disease.

road a condition, state *now Abd.*

rush a skin eruption, rash, *specif* of scarlet fever *now local.* ~-**fever** scarlet fever *now wLoth Ayr.*

sair, sore *of an illness* severe. **a** ~ **wame** colic, stomach-ache *now N-nEC.* ~ **awa wi't** far gone, worn out by illness etc *NE-nEC.* ~ **pit on** suffering from an illness *Cai Per.*

†**sairie** in a poor or sorry state.

scrunt a person shrunken or withered by age, illness etc, a thin scraggy person *now NE, C.*

seeck sick. ~ **rife** sickly, slightly ill *now literary.*

shabby unwell, in poor health.

shakers a fit of shaking, from disease or fear *Sh-C.*

shock a (paralytic) stroke, cerebral haemorrhage or thrombosis.

shuit, shoot: shot joint a joint deformed by rheumatism *local.* ~ **out one's fit** *etc* give a convulsive kick, as in a fit or death-agony.

siclike *of health etc* much about the same; so-so, indifferent *local Sh-Dmf.*

silly weak(ly), sickly, delicate.

skiff a slight touch (of an illness) *now Cai Ags WC.*

smit *v, of an infectious or contagious disease or patient* affect by contagion, infect, taint. *n* infection, contagion, *chf* **gie** *or* **get the** ~ infect or be infected by a disease. ~**tal,** ~**tle,** ~**tin,** ~**some** *now Ork* infectious, contagious.

sober in poor or only moderate health, sickly, weak *now NE Ags Per.*

socher pamper oneself, be fussy about one's health.

sound *v* swoon or faint **away** *now Sh Ork Dnbt. n* a swoon, faint; faintness, *freq* **in (a)** ~ *now Sh Ork.* **a** ~ in a faint *now Sh Ork.*

spavie *joc* a rheumatic disease *now local Ork-Kcb.*

†**stane, stone:** ~-**wring** ? colic attributed to the presence of a stone in the kidneys.

†**stith** stiff, rigid as in death.

†**swalm** *adj* swelling. *v* faint, swoon.

swander become giddy or faint; reel about, stagger *Sh Ork Fif.*

swarf *v* 1 faint, swoon *now Sh.* 2 cause to faint; stupefy. *n* a swoon, faint; a stupor *now Sh.*

†**sweiting** sweating sickness.

swelt become faint with weakness or emotion, be physically overcome, swoon.

†**swither, swidder** feel faint or sick.

tak, take: ~ **doun** impair in health or strength, weaken, cause to lose weight *now local Sh-SW.* ~ **ill** *or* **naeweel** become ill *now local.*

†**teesick** 1 phthisic, consumption. 2 a spell of illness, *freq* of an indefinite nature.

tender in delicate health, ailing, weakly *now local Sh-Ags.*

thole amends *freq of health* capable of improvement *now Dmf.*

thratch *v* twist the body about, writhe, *specif* in the death agony. *n* a jerk, twist of the body, *specif* in the death agony.

throu(gh), throch at or near one's end, done for *Sh-C.*

throw throw up, vomit *now N, WC, SW.*

thrown: be *or* **get** ~ **back** suffer a relapse in an illness *now local Per-Rox.*

†**tirl** some disease (*perh* St Vitus dance).

toit an attack of illness, a dizzy turn *now Ork SW.*

torfle decline in health, pine away *S.*

towt a slight or temporary ailment, an indisposition *now Cai Abd C, S.* ~**ie** subject to frequent attacks of slight illness *now nEC, WC Wgt.*

traik *v* be ailing or ill, decline in health; become weak; pine and die. *n* 1 †a plague, pestilence. 2 an illness, *esp* of an epidemic type. ~**ie** sickly, ailing, declining. ~**it** wasted, worn out *now WC Wgt.*

†**tremmlin aixies, tremmlin fever(s)** ague.

trouble, tribble sickness, disease; an ailment: *'he'll diagnose yer tribble'.*

twine a short attack **of** (some ailment) *Bnf Ags.*

†**tympathy** a morbid swelling or tumour.

†**tunable** physically weak, incapacitated.

unco: ~ **like,** ~ **leukin** looking out of sorts, woebegone *now local NE-Ayr.*

†**undercot** suppurate or fester inwardly.

†**unthriven, unthriving** unhealthy.

unweel, unwell not in good health, ill (suggesting a more serious illness than in Eng); sickly, ailing. ~ness bad health, illness now NE.

useless indisposed in health; incapacitated by illness or exhaustion Sh-N.

†visie afflict (a person) with (sickness etc).

vision a puny, emaciated person, one who is wasting away now Sh Ork Stlg Dmf.

waff¹ a slight illness now local.

waff² local EC-S, waffish, waff like feeble in body or mind. ~-looking feeble or sickly in appearance Bwk Lnk S.

waik adj weak. †v weaken.

wainisht shrunken-looking, emaciated.

wait on be on the point of death now Cai.

wallow fade, waste away now local Cai-Lnk.

†wame ill an illness affecting the stomach.

wammle, wamble v 1 †feel nausea, be squeamish. 2 of the stomach or its contents stir uneasily, rumble queasily now Bnf Abd Fif. n a churning of the stomach, a feeling of sickness NE Ags Fif.

water, watter: ~y pox chickenpox Ags Fif. ~y-nebbit pale and sickly Bnf Abd Ags. water brash heartburn.

wauch, wauf unwell, faint, weary.

waumish faint and sick, out of sorts, dizzy Ags Fif.

†wearin(g) a wasting away from disease, a decline.

†weary sickly, puny, weak.

†wede of pestilence rage.

weed 1 a high fever, a sudden feverish attack; specif puerperal fever now N Fif Dmf. 2 an attack of ague, a chill with trembling and chattering teeth.

weel: no or nae (N) ~ unwell, in poor health.

†weidinonfa puerperal fever; any fever.

wersh sickly, feeble in appearance.

whiff of illness etc a slight attack, a touch local.

†worm colic; acidity in the stomach.

wrang, wrong: ~ one's pechan or stamack make oneself sick with eating too much or the wrong food.

yella gum jaundice, esp in the newborn NE Ags Ayr.

9.20 INSANITY, MENTAL HANDICAP

awa wi 't out of one's senses.

bumbazed perplexed, confused, stupefied.

carried delirious, not rational local.

daft crazy, insane; lacking commonsense. ~ie an imbecile; a mentally handicapped person; a fool.

dawlie (a person who is) physically or mentally slow.

deleerit delirious, mad; temporarily out of one's senses now Fif Renfr Ayr.

doit act foolishly, be crazed, enfeebled or confused in mind now Abd. ~ered witless, confused, chf from old age now Fif. ~it, dowtit Fif not of sound mind, foolish, silly. doitrified stupefied, dazed, senseless.

dote: dottered stupid, enfeebled in mind, chf from old age. dotterel a dotard, an imbecile now Stlg. †dotit silly, stupid, chf from old age. dottle †adj in a state of dotage, witless. v be in or fall into a state of dotage, become crazy Cai Bnf Abd Ags.

dozened stupefied, dazed, stupid, physically weakened (through age, drink etc) now local Sh-Lnk.

drumlie muddled, confused now Rox.

eediot an idiot. eediocy idiocy.

founder collapse, break down with drink etc Gen except Sh Ork.

frae: glower, look etc ~ one have a fixed or vacant look, stare stupidly now S.

gane mad, crazy.

gang by oneself go mad now Abd.

gowk(ie) a fool, simpleton, lout.

gyte adj mad, insane; mad with rage, pain etc, freq gang ~. n a madman, fool. gytit half-witted, crazy now Ags.

half, hauf: halfling a half-witted person now Cai. ~ hack(it) now Fif, ~ jeck Arg half-witted.

hazy weak in intellect, mentally unbalanced now EC Arg Slk.

heid: aff at the ~ local, awa in the ~ local Kinr-S off one's head.

horn daft quite mad now Cai Ags.

knot: aff (at) the ~, affen the ~ off one's head, crazed, distraught NE Uls.

†licht demented.

†mangit, mangin confused, crazed.

mixed mentally confused local Sh-Per.

moidert confused, dazed, esp as a result of blows, mental strain etc WC, S Uls.

object an imbecile.

owertaen, overtaken (†with or in) deranged, made helpless now Per.

peerie-heidit in a state of mental confusion now C, S.

raivel speak incoherently, ramble, be delirious now NE nEC Lnk. ~ed confused in mind; rambling, delirious Gen except Sh Ork.

rammish mad, crazy *now Ork.*

red, reid, rid: ~**-wud** stark staring mad, beside oneself with rage, mentally unbalanced *now local N-SW.*

ree over-excited, delirious, crazy *now Ork Fif.*

richt, right: no(t) ~ not in one's right mind, mentally unbalanced; simple-minded.

rizzon, reason: out o one's ~ out of one's mind *now local Sh-Per.*

rove wander in thought or speech, be delirious, rave *now Sh-Cai Ags.*

shilling: want tippence *etc* **o the** ~ be mentally defective, be 'not all there' *local Sh-Kcb.*

silly mentally deficient *now local Sh-Kcb.*

sk(a)ivie, skeevie harebrained, daft, mentally deranged.

†**skire** ? be mad.

slate: want a ~ be feeble-minded, 'have a slate loose'.

sowf a fool, simpleton, stupid, silly person *now Abd.*

sumph a slow-witted person, *usu* a man, an oaf, simpleton *now N-S.*

superannuate mentally deranged, senile; stupefied, dazed *now Fif.*

taiver wander in mind or speech, rave *now Per.* ~**t** bewildered, mentally confused, *esp* through exhaustion or harassment *now Per-Fif.*

tattie *contemptuous* a stupid person, a simpleton *local Ork-WC.*

†**unnatural** simple-minded.

vary 1 †wander in the mind, rave. **2** show the first symptoms of delirium *S.*

veeand in one's dotage *S.*

wandered, waun(n)ert confused, bewildered; mentally disordered *now local Sh-Gsw.*

want: ~**ing** simple, mentally defective. **hae a** ~, ~ **a feather in the wing,** ~ **a bit** be simple, be mentally defective.

will-like having a dazed look *NE.*

wise in one's right mind, sane, rational, *freq* **no** ~ *local Ork-Per.* **no** ~ **eneuch** off one's head, insane *NE.*

†**wit: out o one's** ~ out of one's senses.

wowf touched, mad, violently agitated or excited.

wrang, wrong, *also* ~ **in the heid** *or* **mind** deranged, insane, 'touched' *now NE.*

wuid, wood mad, insane, demented *Gen except Sh Ork.* †~**ness** mad rage, a paroxysm affecting the brain. **aince** ~ **and aye (the) waur** getting madder and madder: daft once, daft always. †**red** ~ stark, raving mad. **rin** ~ go clean off one's head, behave wildly and recklessly.

yonder, yonner: far frae a' ~, **nae (near) a'** ~ half-witted, not all there *NE.*

9.21 SANITY

at oneself in one's right mind *NE, SW Uls.*

gaither, gather recover one's faculties, collect one's wits, pull oneself together, rally *local Abd Uls.*

hiddie kiddie sense, mental stability *Abd.*

judgement reason, senses, wits, sanity, *esp* **lose** *or* **be out of one's** ~.

kneef mentally alert *chf Sh-N.*

solid sane; in full possession of one's mental faculties *now Ags.*

thorow, thorough mentally alert, sane *now Bwk SW, S.*

wise, wice in one's right mind, sane, rational.

wit sanity, reason, one's senses *now Sh-Per.*

9.22 INJURIES

For blows and beatings, see 12.12.

amshach an accident, misfortune; an injury *NE.*

arr a scar, the mark left by a wound. ~**(e)d** marked with scars.

†**back-breed** a fall or throw on the back.

bemang'd hurt, injured.

blae *adj* **1** *formerly freq with* **bludy** livid or bluish from a blow. **2** †*of a blow* making a livid mark or bruise. †*n* a bruise, contusion.

blain a scar from a sore or wound; a weal *now Bnf Abd.*

blatter a heavy fall *now Bnf Kcb.*

†**blaud** an injury.

blue ee a black eye *NE nEC.*

burst *now Bnf Fif,* †**birst** an injury caused by over-exertion.

ca(ll) oot dislocate.

chaff chafe, rub *NE Fif.*

chack, check *v* catch (*eg* fingers in a door), hack, chop *now Fif Edb.* *n* a cut or hack; a bruise, nip *now Fif Lnk Kcb.*

†**clair** harm, injure.

clour a lump, swelling caused by a blow *now local NE-S.*

clunker a lump, a bump *chf Ags.*

coup a fall *Gen except Sh Ork.*

†**debowaill** disembowel.

†**demember** dismember. **demembration** *freq law* dismembering, mutilation.

dinge dent, bruise *Sh Dnbt SW Uls.*

dinnle a vibrating or tingling sensation, *eg* as caused by a knock on the elbow; such a knock.

dirl 1 a knock or blow causing the person or thing struck to **dirl**; a shock, jar. **2** the pain caused by such a blow *now local.*

†**dishort** an injury, a mischief, hurt.

†**dislock** dislocate (a joint).

dob *v* prick *now Sh Ork Bnf. n* a prick *now Bnf.*

docher injury; rough handling, wear and tear.

doup scour a thump on the buttocks caused by falling *Bnf Abd.*

dunt the wound caused by a heavy dull blow *now Cai Bnf Ags.*

†**engreve** do hurt or harm to, injure.

fire inflame (a part of the body) by chafing.

†**fordullit** made dull or stupid.

freet rub, chafe, injure by friction or violence *now Fif.*

†**frusch** become broken, go to pieces.

gaig cut, wound *Bnf.*

†**greve** an injury.

gromish crush, bruise *Cai Abd.*

gruppit sprained *now local Abd-Uls.*

gullie gaw wound, cut, hack, gash *chf N.*

hagger *NE v* cut clumsily, hack. *n* a deep jagged cut.

hail-heidit unhurt *N.*

hoch, haugh hamstring, disable by cutting or striking the tendons of the leg. **cut the ~s** hamstring.

†**injure** physical injury, maltreatment.

jag *v,* also **jog** *now Kcdn C Rox Uls* prick, pierce. *n,* also **jog** *now Kcdn Ags* a prick; a sharp blow.

jeck dislocate (a joint) *Kcb Rox.*

jeelie cause (the nose) to bleed *EC.* **~ neb** *or* **nose** a bloody nose *local EC-Rox.*

keeker, *also* **blue keeker** a black eye *local Abd-WC.*

keel-up a heavy fall on one's back *local Sh-Ags.*

kilhailie a fall *Cai.*

knur, norrie a lump, a weal *Abd Ork.*

†**lame** *verse* lameness, a crippling injury or infirmity.

†**lesed** impaired, injured.

lith disjoint, dislocate *chf NE* †**out of ~** dislocated.

†**Lockerbie lick** *etc* a gash or wound in the face.

†**maggle** cut or hack about, maim, mutilate, mangle. **mag(g)lit** maimed, mutilated or disfigured by cutting; mangled.

†**mainʒie** *n* a crippling or disabling wound or injury, a mutilation. *v* maim, mutilate, disable by a wound or injury.

mairtyr, martyr hurt or wound severely *now Sh.*

malagruize injure, hurt *NE.*

mankit mutilated, maimed *now Abd Edb.*

mar do bodily harm to, maim, injure, kill *orig gipsy but now also Rox.*

massacker severe injury *chf Sh NE.*

mischief a physical injury; bodily harm.

mishanter a physical hurt or injury *now local Sh-Ags.*

†**miss** harm, injury.

mittle do bodily harm to, mutilate *now Ags Per.*

munsie a person who is in a sorry state, who has been knocked about etc *NE.*

†**mutilit** mutilated, maimed.

†**noys** injuries.

prod a prick, stab; the sting of an insect *now SW.* **proddled** poked, jabbed at; pricked as by a thorn *Gall Uls.*

puddin(g) lug an ear which has swollen as the result of a blow, a thick ear *WC.*

rack *v* wrench, dislocate, twist *local. n* a sprain, wrench, dislocation *Gen except Sh Ork.*

rax *v* **1** put (oneself) to great effort, overexert, strain ((a part of) oneself). **2** sprain (a limb). *n* a strain, sprain.

raze gash, cut, tear *now Sh.*

rit *v* scratch *now Sh Cai Edb. n* a scratch *now local Sh-Kcb.*

rive a tear, rip, scratch (in the skin etc) *now local Sh-Lnk.*

scam a spot, crack, injury *now local Sh-Fif.*

scart a scratch with the nails etc.

scaud, scald a sore caused by chafing of the skin *now C, S.*

scaur a scar.

score a scar left by a wound, a weal *now Sh N, WC.*

scrat a scratch, slight wound *now Ork nNE.*

screed a tear, gash, slash; a scratch *now Fif.*

screeve *v* graze (the skin), scratch, scrape *now nEC Lnk S. n* a large scratch *now local Kcdn-Rox.*

scruif, scruff scrape (off) the surface of, graze, skin.

set dislocate (one's neck) *local Sh-SW.*

shammle, shamble twist, strain, dislocate.

skelb a thin flake, slice, or splinter of wood, stone, or metal, now *esp* one lodged in the skin *now NE nEC.*

skelf *now Sh Ork Cai C,* **skelp** *now local Inv-Lnk* a splinter or small chip of wood, *esp* one lodged in the skin *now Sh Ork Cai C.*

skiff a slight touch or graze in passing, an abrasion.

skiver a splinter of wood in the skin *local Ork-WC.*

†**slap** a gash or wound.

sned a slash, slight wound.

sodger a wounded or injured child *local Abd-Dmf.*

†**soo** inflict pain on.

spail, speal, spell a splinter in the skin *Gen except Sh Ork*.

speld wrench oneself or pull one's muscles by falling with the legs apart *now Ork Rox*.

stang sting *Gen except Sh Ork*.

stave *n* a sprain or wrench of a joint. *v* sprain or bruise (a joint) *local Sh-Ayr*.

†**stennis** sprain.

stob 1 a splinter of wood, *esp* one driven into the skin *now NE-Fif*. **2** the wound made thus *NE-Fif*. **3** †a stab wound.

sucky *of a wound or blow* painful, stinging *now Fif Edb*.

target a thin strip of flesh, *esp* from a lacerated wound *now Sh*.

thraw *v* twist (a part of the body), wrench, sprain (a joint etc) *Sh NE nEC*. *n* a wrench of a muscle etc, a sprain *now Sh NE, nEC*.

tramp an injury to the foot by having it trodden on.

trauchled bedraggled, injured, (by dragging, trampling, knocking about etc) *now local NE-SW*.

†**unlamyt** unharmed.

unscaumit not burned or scorched, unscathed *Sh Abd*.

†**wan** a dark-coloured mark produced by a blow, a bruise.

waum a scar, blemish.

wirk, work sprain *now Abd*.

woun, oun *S* wound.

†**wramp** *n* a wrench, twist, sprain. *v* wrench, twist, sprain.

wranch *local Sh-Dnbtn*, **runch** *now Cai WC, SW n* a wrench, a twist. *v, only* **runch** wrench *now Dnbt Kcb*.

wrest, wrist *v* sprain or wrench (a muscle or joint) *now Sh*. *n* a sprain, a wrenching or spraining of the muscles *now Sh*,

yether *n* the mark left by a blow with a cane etc or by tight binding with cord etc, a weal, bruise *SW, S*. †*v* tie very firmly, *esp* so as to leave a pressure mark on what has been bound *SW, S*..

9.23.1 MEDICINE, MEDICAL PROFESSION

†**apothicar** an apothecary.

batter a medicinal plaster *now NE Ags*.

†**bedhous, bede-house** an almshouse, hospital.

†**caddis** surgical lint.

†**chirurgian** *n, also* **chirugenair** a surgeon. ~**rie** surgery.

†**cleister** a clyster, an enema.

†**clenge:** ~**r** a cleanser of infected persons or places, a disinfecter. ~**ing** disinfecting.

†**coulter** a cautery.

cuiter (up) nurse; pamper.

†**dicht** dress (a wound).

droggie *Abd Fif*, **droggist** *now Cai Abd Kcdn* (nickname for) a druggist.

finger steel *now N Bwk*, ~ **stuil** *local Sh-Rox* a finger-stall.

green lady a Health Visitor *Gsw*.

hail heal *Gen except sEC*.

†**hipothecar** an apothecary.

†**hospital(le)** an asylum for lepers.

†**ipotingar** an apothecary.

irons, airns surgical instruments *now midLoth Bwk*.

jag an injection, inoculation.

lance a surgeon's lancet, a scalpel *now local*.

line a prescription.

†**lipper-house** an asylum for lepers.

†**loch leech** the leech.

†**mease** mitigate, allay (pain).

†**medicinary** the art or practice of medicine.

†**mediciner 1** a physician, practitioner of medicine. **2** title of the Professor of Medicine at King's College, Aberdeen.

†**mends** healing, a remedy.

notice tend, see to *now Sh Ork NE*.

oxter staff a crutch *NE*.

†**panse 1** care for (a person) medically or surgically. **2** dress (a wound).

†**pharmacian** a pharmacist, apothecary.

†**phisik** physic. **under (the cure of)** ~ under medical care, receiving medical treatment.

plot, plout foment (a sore) in very hot water.

†**potegar** an apothecary.

poticary *Kcb*, †**pothecar** an apothecary, a druggist.

†**pottingar** an apothecary.

powl, pole a crutch.

receipt a (medical) prescription or preparation *now Ags Ayr Uls*.

sain heal, cure.

scob *n* a slat of wood used as a splint for broken bones etc *now NE Ags*. *v* put (a broken bone) in splints *now NE Ags*.

scour *v* **1** purge or clear out (the bowels, stomach). **2** †flush out with liquid; *joc* drink **off**. *n* a purging of the bowels *now Ork Abd Per*.

†**shear** cut (a person) for the extraction of a stone, *chf* **shorne of the stane**.

†**shusy** a corpse (*prob orig* female) used for anatomical dissection and demonstration, *esp* one stolen from a grave.

skeel, skill skill in the art of healing, *freq* of a non-professional kind *now NE Ags*. ~y having real or supposed skill in the art of healing *now NE Fif*. ~y **wife** *etc* a woman credited with great or supernatural healing powers, *esp* one called to emergencies or confinements.

sneyster cauterize.

sort 1 heal. 2 attend to the wants of (a child or sick person) *now NE*.

spelk, spyolk *n* a surgical splint *now Sh Ork Bwk Rox*. *v* bind (a broken limb) with splints etc *now Sh Ork Cai Bwk*.

stem stop, staunch (bleeding etc).

stench 1 stanch, check the flow of. 2 †cease flowing.

stilt *n* a crutch *now local Stlg-Wgt*. *v* go on stilts or crutches *now local Stlg-Rox*.

stookie stucco, plaster of Paris; *specif* a plaster-cast encasing a broken limb.

stuil a stall (as in finger-stall, head-stall) *now local*.

†**surregerie** surgery.

†**surrigine, surigeoner** surgeon.

thoum, thumb rub or massage (*esp* a sprain) with the thumb *Sh NE Ags*.

wad wadding, cotton wool.

wait on attend to, look after (*esp* a sick or dying person) *now Cai*.

whip a bandage.

†**wip** a bandage.

9.23.2 MEDICINES, MEDICINAL PLANTS

alacompine elecampane, the plant or the extract from it.

bad-money the gentian; the spignel (used medicinally in the Highlands).

†**betteis** ? remedies.

†**buist** a small box for ointment, spices etc.

calamy calomel *now local Bnf-Stlg*.

camovine camomile *now NE Ags*.

cowstick caustic *now Bnf Abd Fif*.

drog a drug *now local Bnf-Kcdn*.

†**electuare** electuary, a medicinal syrup etc.

eyntment ointment.

feesick physic.

†**gait whey** the whey of goat's milk used as a health drink.

graith liquor, medicine.

hailsome 1 wholesome, health-giving. 2 curative, medicinal.

†**hickery-pickery** a purgative of bitter aloes with other ingredients.

Jacob's ladder belladonna *now Lnk Uls*.

†**lib** *n* a (healing) charm. *v* heal, cure (with a charm).

lodomy laudanum *now NE Ags Loth*.

†**muckle wort** deadly nightshade.

need fire fire produced by the friction of dry wood, having reputed prophylactic properties.

peel a pill, a tablet.

†**potegareis** an apothecary's drugs, medicines.

†**pottingary** 1 the art or practice of an apothecary, pharmacy. 2 the drugs or medicines of an apothecary.

pultice a poultice.

pushi(o)n poison. ~**able** poisonous *now Per Dnbt*. **pooshinous** poisonous. ~**t** poisoned.

receipt a (medical) prescription or preparation *now Ags Ayr Uls*.

†**saving** a kind of juniper which yields an abortifacient drug, *freq* ~ **tree**.

saw salve, a healing ointment.

sinnie senna *now Sh Ork Bnf*.

†**smear dock(en)** Good King Henry, a kind of goosefoot used in folk-medicine in ointment for itch.

smeddum a fine powder, *specif* a finely ground meal or malt; a medicinal powder.

†**spycarie** spikenard.

trate a piece of cloth dipped in a mixture of beeswax, lard etc, used as a dressing for sores or boils *Cai Kcdn Fif*.

†**unspoken** *chf folk-medicine, of a curative substance* not spoken over, gathered or handled in silence.

†**unȝement** ointment.

†**virtue, verter** *of a well, spring etc* medicinal *chf SE, S*.

†**vomiter** an emetic.

wall, well *freq in place-names* a mineral spring reputed to have medicinal qualities.

wark, wirk, work purge, act as a laxative on *now local Sh-Per*.

wind: brak the ~ *of a medicine* relieve flatulence *Sh Cai Abd*.

10. FOOD AND DRINK

For names of fruit, see 4.7, of vegetables, see 4.8 of fish, seafood see 3, of farm animals, see 2, of edible seaweed, see 3.4.

10.1 GENERAL, MISCELLANEOUS

air a small quantity, a particle, morsel, taste etc *chf Sh-N*.

auld, old: ~**-tasted** musty *now local Sh-Per*.

barrel 1 a barrel, *esp* as a quantity or measure **of** (some commodity). **2** a dry measure of varying amount *now Bnf Ags*.

†**belechere** good cheer; entertainment.

belly-timber food, provisions.

†**bind** a standard measure for the barrels in which certain commodities were packed, *freq* with name of the authorizing town *etc, eg* **the** ~ **of Banff, Burdeaux** ~ .

†**bit and brat** food and board.

blade a leaf of cabbage, turnip, tobacco etc *now Ork Abd Ags*.

blash *n* a weak mixture of drink, soup etc. *adj, of food or drink* weak *now Abd*.

blear ~**ed** *now Loth Lnk,* † ~**ie** *of liquid food* (too) thin. ~**ie** liquid food, *eg* gruel *now local Cai-Kcb*.

blib a weak watery portion of tea, soup etc *Bnf Abd*.

blithemeat food given to people in a house at the time of a birth *now Lnk*.

blitter a thin watery mess *Abd Edb Ayr*.

†**boll** a dry measure of weight or capacity varying according to commodity and locality, *eg* a ~ **of meal** = 140 lbs (approx 63.5 kg).

brak, break: ~ **on** *or* **o** begin to use (stored food or drink).

brock 1 scraps of bread, meat etc; leftovers *now Fif Arg Kcb*. **2** kitchen refuse used for feeding pigs *local C*.

brose one's living, livelihood *now Bnf Ags*.

bruckie, brocklie friable *now Bnf Ags*.

†**butterman** a dealer in butter.

cairry-out, carry-out food or alcoholic drink bought in a restaurant, pub etc for consumption elsewhere.

caller *of fish, vegetables etc* fresh, just caught or gathered.

capfu a dishful.

†**castellaw** a measure of flour or cheese *Arg*.

cauld kail het again re-heated **broth** or other food.

chiffin a particle, crumb, fragment *Abd*.

chuck food *local C*.

clag a quantity of any kind of soft (sticky) food *local NE, C*. **claggy, cleggy** *Sh Uls* sticky, glutinous.

collie: he never asked *etc* ~ **wull ye lick** *or* **taste?** he never even invited me to have something to eat.

cream (of) the water *or* **well** (draw) the first water from a well on New Year's morning.

†**crote** a particle, crumb. **crottle, crittel** a fragment, crumb *chf SW*. **crotly** fragmentary, crumbly *chf SW*.

cuik a cook. †**maister cuke** the head cook of the royal or other large household.

†**cury** a cooked dish, concoction.

daintess, dentice dainties; luxury food.

†**daintith** a dainty.

divot a thick clumsy piece or slice of bread, meat etc *now local Bnf-Arg*.

dodgel something large of its kind, a lump *now Ork Bnf*.

dog's wages food given as the only wages for service *now Abd*.

dook liquid into which something is dipped.

dorle, darle a small quantity, a piece of something, *esp* of something edible *now Bnf Abd*.

drabble 1 ~ (**s**) spots of dirt, *esp* of liquid food spilt while eating *local Bnf-Arg*. **2** *chf disparaging* a small quantity of liquid food *now Abd Fif*.

dunt a lump, large piece, *esp* of food.

fardel a large slice or piece (*esp* of food) *now Bnf Abd*.

farin food, fare *local NE-EC*.

fau(1)t a want, lack, *freq* of food *now Abd Fif Uls*.

fend fare, sustenance *Abd*. ~**less** without flavour *NE*.

few: a ~ **broth, porridge, soup** *etc* a little **broth** porridge, soup etc *now Stlg WC*.

fineries *chf of food* delicacies *now Sh*.

†**flaur, fleur** flavour, smell.

fleg *of food etc* diminish appreciably *now Ork NE Ags.*

foost *v* become or smell mouldy *now Abd Pbls SW.* *n* a mouldy condition or smell *local NE-Dmf.* **~it, ~y** musty, mouldy.

forpet a **lippie**, now *chf* used for the sale of root vegetables (*eg* = $3\frac{1}{2}$ lb of potatoes) and oatmeal (= $1\frac{3}{4}$ lb) *local Abd-Rox.*

fou, full: ~ man's leavins a very small portion of food left by someone who can eat no more *now local Ork-Per.*

fuid food.

fushion the nourishing or sustaining element in food or drink *now NE Per.* **~less** *of food* lacking in nourishment, tasteless, insipid *local Sh-C.*

gab: fine- *or* **nice-gabbit** fastidious, fussy about food *now Ags Fif.*

gae fae stop, abstain from, lose the taste for *NE Renfr.*

glack a handful, morsel.

goo a strong, persistent, *freq* disagreeable taste *Gen except Sh Ork.* **~ly** tasty, having a distinctive flavour *now Fif Dmf.*

gravy sauce *now Ags.*

grushion an unpleasant or glutinous mess *Bnf.*

guff 1 a (*usu*) unpleasant smell or whiff. **2** a savour, taste, aftertaste *now Rox.*

gussie a segment of an orange *Ags.*

gust *n* taste; a taste; relish. *v* **1** taste (food, drink etc). **2** †take a taste (**of** something). **3** *freq* **~ the gab** *etc* delight the palate, whet the appetite, fill the mouth with tasty food or drink *now Abd Fif.* **~ie** tasty, savoury *now Ayr.*

hair: ~ moul(d) the mould on cheese, bread, jam etc exposed to damp. **~-mouldit** *now Abd Ags Stlg,* **~-moul(e)d** *now Stlg* covered with mould.

hairy-mouldit covered with mould, mouldy *now Sh-nEC Dmf.*

hameower *of food* plain, homely *now Ork Abd Ags.*

hinnie, honey sweet as honey.

hoamed, hoomed musty, mouldy *now Kcdn Ags.*

hogget a measure of liquor, fish, meal etc *now Bute Ayr.*

hummie a pinch (of meal, salt etc), as much as can be taken up between the thumb and four fingers.

humph a 'high' flavour, a taste of a foodstuff going bad.

jibble a small quantity of a liquid or semi-liquid *now NE Dmf.*

jilp a small quantity of liquid or semi-liquid food or drink *now NE Dmf.*

junt a large lump of something, *esp* meat or bread *now NE.*

kail: †~ supper a person who is fond of **broth** *Fife.* **~ wife** a woman who sells vegetables and herbs *now Ags.*

keest tasteless, insipid *S.*

kemple a lump or fragment, *esp* of food *NE.*

kipper a large quantity of food *NE.*

kit a fair amount (of something, *esp* of food) *now Rox.*

kitchen, keiching *n* **1** †*also* **~ meit** an allowance of food from the kitchen, (*eg* of meat) supplied or stored as one's provisions. **2** *also* **kitchie** *Sh N* anything served in addition to a plain food such as bread or potatoes *Gen except N.* **~less** lacking anything that will give taste or savour *now Sh.*

knappie friable; crisp, brittle *now Uls.*

leaf one of the segments of an orange *local Cai-Uls.*

leevin food *now Ags SW.*

lick take a pinch or small quantity of (something, *esp* snuff).

lith one of the natural divisions or segments of an orange, onion etc *N, C Slk Uls.*

†**lithy** *of soup etc* thick, smooth and palatable.

†**loan** provisions for a campaign *chf Highl NE.*

†**lunch** a lump, large slice of food, a chunk.

†**malashes** molasses.

maut: meal and ~ food and drink *now Kcdn Ags.*

†**meal: ~ie bag, ~poke** a beggar's bag for holding alms given in oatmeal. **~('s) corn** food, sustenance *chf Sh-NE.*

meat, mate food *in gen,* for men or animals. **~ rife** having a plentiful food supply *chf S.* **a good** *etc* **~ house** a house where there is always plenty of good food. **hae one's ~ and one's mense baith** said when one's hospitality has been refused, so that one has the credit of hospitality without any expenditure of food *Gen except Sh Ork.*

mess †*n* provisions or supply of food for a person's or household's meals. *v* measure out (a portion for a meal, an ingredient in cooking) *chf NE.*

minschie a crumb, morsel *Bnf Abd Ags.*

mixter mixture.

moch *of corn, meat, meal etc* become tainted, fusty or rotten *NE.*

moost must, mould(er) *now Bnf.*

moul †grow mouldy. **~ie** mouldy *now NE Fif WC.*

moze decay, become musty or mouldy *Sh Ork Cai.* **mozie** decayed, fusty, mouldy *Sh Ork Renfr Ayr.*

muild mealock, moolock, meelackie *now Abd Ags* a crumb, a small fragment. **moolin(g), millen** a crumb, a fragment.

†**neb** sharpness, pungency, *esp* of liquor.

nip *n* pungency, sharpness of flavour. *v*, *of food or its taste* cause to tingle or smart.

oil, eelie oil. † ~ **dolive** olive oil. †**eelie dolly** oil of any kind *Abd*.

†**order** a scheme of the actual or proposed arrangement for a person's or persons' maintenance; regular provision or allowance of board and lodging; one's living standard as determined by this.

†**ordinar** one's regular allowance of (*chf*) food and drink, or pay; a fixed portion or permitted serving.

ort use (food) wastefully. ~**s** leavings, leftovers *now Sh Fif Uls*.

Palie *Heriot's Hospital slang* sweet-tasting, delicious.

pap one of the segments of an orange *NE*.

parritch, porridge food *in gen*, one's sustenance, daily bread.

peck a small quantity of something edible, a scrap of food *local*.

perlaig a disgusting mixture of scraps, *esp* rubbishy food *Bnf Abd*.

pick †a pecking; (a quantity of) food, one's keep. ~**in(g)** a mouthful of food, a frugal meal.

pickant piquant, sharp, keen, biting, tart *now NE*.

piece: ~ **box** the box in which a workman or schoolchild carries a lunchtime snack *local*. ~ **poke** the paper bag etc in which a snack is carried.

†**pigfu** the quantity filling a **pig**, a dishful.

†**pith** the strength-giving quality of food or drink.

plowter a sloppy or sticky mess of food etc *local Sh-SW*.

pock, poke a beggar's bag used for collecting oatmeal etc given in charity.

†**possodie** a poisonous drink.

pot, pat: ~**-tastit** tasting of the pot *now Ork NE*. **pottle** a potful *now Kcdn*.

pottage food *in gen now NE*.

potterlow *freq of food spoilt in cooking* a broken or ruined condition, smithereens, pulp *NE*.

pouther powder.

†**preivin** a taste, a very small quantity.

pronack a crumb, fragment, splinter; a state of mush, a mess, hotchpotch *Cai Per*.

†**proviant** provision, food supply, *esp* for an army.

pudgle a heavy eater *now Bnf Abd Slk*.

†**quart** a gallon, *chf* of wine, ale or oil.

quern a granule, small seed etc *now Mry Abd*. ~**y** *of honey, coarse sugar etc* granular, composed of small grains or particles, coarse to the tongue *now Bnf*.

raik *of food* a spoonful; a helping.

ramp having a strong, coarse flavour or smell *chf SW Uls*.

ramsh *of food* rank, unpleasant, coarse *local Sh-Fif*.

reamy of a creamy consistency.

receipt a recipe *local Cai-Kcb*.

reekit smoke-tainted, acrid.

rodden: as sour as ~**s** very sour or bitter *chf NE Ags Ayr*.

ruch, rough abundant; plentifully supplied, *esp* with good plain fare *now C*: '*a guid ruch house*'. ~ **and round** *of food* plain but substantial.

sappie 1 *of meat* juicy, succulent. 2 *of food* soft, soggy, like **saps** *now local Sh-Per*.

sapsy like **saps**, soft, sloppy *Per Stlg WC*.

saut, salt: as ~ **as lick** very salty *local C*.

scaff food, provisions *now Sh*.

scran *n* 1 food *now local Ork-SW*. 2 scraps or leavings of food, *freq* those acquired by begging *now NE*. 3 any refuse or rubbish which may be picked up by a beggar or scrounger *now Abd Stlg Ayr*. *v* scrounge about for (food etc); scrape together frugally; poke about in or scrounge from dustbins *Abd*. † ~ **bag** *etc* a bag in which a beggar collected scraps of food etc *now Sh Abd WC*.

scrimp use or consume frugally or meanly.

scruifin a thin paring or scraping, *eg* of butter or cheese *Stlg Fif Lnk*.

seg *of sour fruit etc* set (the teeth) on edge.

shall a shell *Sh Ork N*.

sharrow bitter to the taste *now Cai*.

sheave, shave a slice of bread, cheese etc.

shed, sheed a slice, piece divided off *chf Ags*.

shevel, showl *now N Per*, **shile** *SW* make a wry mouth, grimace from a bitter taste etc.

shilp sour, sharp, acid *Cai*.

shilpit sour, bitter; no longer fresh *now Sh Ork Cai*.

shire thin; watery; sparse.

shive a slice (of bread) *now Pbls Bwk S*.

sirple a sip, mouthful, *esp* of liquor.

skelp a large slice or chunk, a slab, *eg* of cheese or butter *now local Ork-Arg*.

skliff a segment, *eg* of an orange *Per wLoth WC, SW*.

slabber something liquid or messy, *esp* food *Abd Per*.

slaiger, slagger a wet, soggy, or slimy mess, a daub, smear of sloppy food etc *EC, WC, S*.

slaister, slyster an unpalatable or nauseating mixture of foods etc *EC, WC, S*.

slaps slops, sloppy food etc.

†**slawkie** smooth, soft and flabby.

slidderie, sclitherie soft, sloppy *now Sh Ags*.

slitter (messy) semi-liquid matter, an unpalatable mixture of food *now C*.

slive a thin slice, a sliver *S*.

sloch, slough the outer skin or husk of certain fruits or vegetables *now local Cai-Ayr*.

smacher a hotchpotch or mixture of food, *esp* sweeties etc *now NE Ags*.

smeerich a thin layer or spread (of butter etc) *Inv NE*.

smell a small quantity, a taste, 'a sensation' (*esp* of drink) *now local Sh-Kcb*.

smervie full of substance or flavour *NE*.

smush fragments, scraps of food etc.

smushlach a mass of tiny crushed fragments, something reduced to pulp or powder, *eg* over-boiled potatoes.

snap a small piece, scrap, *specif* of food *now local Sh-Per*.

snell sharp to the taste or smell, pungent, acrid *now Bnf*.

sorn scrounge food, forage *now Cai Ags*.

soss a mixture of food or drink, a wet, soggy mess of food *now Sh N Per*.

soup *also ironic* a considerable amount, *esp* of spirits *now local Fif-Rox*.

sowce a (messy) mixture of food, *specif* some oatmeal dish such as porridge *now Cai*.

†sowdie a hotchpotch, a heterogeneous mixture.

spicy peppered, peppery.

spleuterie *n* weak watery food *now Bnf Abd*. *adj* weak and watery *now Bnf Abd*.

spune, spoon: ~ **meat** soft or liquid food eaten with a spoon *now local Ork-Dmf*.

stawsome *of food* nauseous, repugnant to the taste or appetite *C, S*.

stieve, steevil *now Ork, of food or drink* strong, thick, full of body.

stuff provisions, a store of food *now Ork Ags*.

†substenance sustenance.

sunkets eatables, provisions, *esp* titbits or delicacies.

†suppins soft, semi-liquid food.

swack soft, moist and easily moulded; *of cheese* not crumbly *now N*.

swash a large amount of drink or food *now Sh Ork*.

tae, to *of food* with, for, to the accompaniment of: 'an egg to his tea'.

tag a long thin strip or slice *now Sh*.

tammie food, provisions.

†test taste.

tewed *of food* tough shrivelled *now S*.

tweest a small amount (of food) *now Abd*.

†unfynit unrefined, unpurified.

unhalesome unwholesome.

†uphalding sustenance.

upstanding *usu of foodstuffs* substance, solidity *NE*.

vivers food, provisions, victuals.

wa, way a lingering taste or flavour; an after-taste *now Sh NE Ags*.

wabble wishy-washy, tasteless drink or liquid food *chf Abd*. **wabblie** wishy-washy, thin *local NE-Wgt*.

wadge *NE-S*, **wedge** a thick slice (of bread, cheese etc) *now Stlg wLoth Lnk*.

walsh, welsh insipid, tasteless; nauseous.

wauch 1 *of a taste or smell* unpleasant, stale, unappetising *now Bnf Abd Ags*. **2** *of food, cooking etc* tasteless, unappetising; not nourishing *now Abd Ags*.

wersh 1 tasteless, insipid, unpalatable; cooked without salt *Gen except Sh Ork*. **2** bitter, harsh in taste, sour *Cai C, S*.

whammle: dish etc o ~ *(now Dmf)* or **whamlin(s)** *(now Lnk Kcb)* joc no food, nothing to eat or drink.

whang, fang a large thick slice of food, *esp* of cheese.

wild, wull strong-tasting, rank *local Sh-nEC*.

10.2 KITCHEN EQUIPMENT

†alcomy a mixed metal (*latterly only* applied to cutlery).

ashet 1 an oval serving plate, *esp* for a joint. **2** a pie-dish *WC*.

back an instrument for toasting; a **girdle** *chf Ags*.

bake: ~ **-board** *now local*, ~ **breid** *now Abd* a baking board. **†** ~ **stule** a stool used in bread making.

†ballance a plate, flat dish.

bally (cog) a milk pail *Bnf*.

bannock, bonnock: †bonnock iron an iron for baking **bannocks**. ~ **stane** a stone placed in the fire, on which **bannocks** were baked.

bassie a wooden basin or bowl for carrying meal to the baking board or in which meal is mixed and kneaded.

bawbrek a kneading trough or board.

†beardie, bairdie a large jar (with the figure of a bearded old man on it).

bicker a beaker, a drinking vessel, *esp* of wood; a (porridge) bowl, *formerly* one made of staves.

bittle, beetle a kitchen implement for bruising barley, mashing potatoes etc.

†boat a barrel, tub.

bool a curved or semi-circular band, forming the handle of a pot, bucket etc.

bow the semi-circular handle of a pail, pot etc *now Bnf Abd Ags*. **bowit** provided with a **bow**.

bowie 1 a broad, shallow dish, bowl or small tub *now Bnf Ags*. **2** a bucket *now Kcb*.

bowl, ~**ie** a bowl; *in Sc used also where Eng prefers* basin: '*pudding bowl*'.

†**braig (knife)** a large knife.

†**brander, brandreth** a gridiron.

†**breidhous** a store room for bread; a pantry.

brook soot on pots, kettles etc *now local Cai- Fif*.

brose: ~**-bicker** *now Bnf Abd*, ~**cap** *now Bnf Ags* a wooden dish for **brose**.

†**brottlet** ? a tablecloth.

buird a table, *freq* one spread for a meal *now Bnf Abd*.

†**buist** a small box for ointment, spices, sweets etc.

butter: ~**-brods** *Bnf Abd Lnk*, ~**-clappers** *now Lnk Kcb* a pair of wooden boards for working butter. ~**-kit** a container for butter *local Bnf-Lnk*.

cap 1 a (wooden) cup or bowl *now local*. **2** a bowl used as a measure for liquor or grain.

caudron a cauldron *now local Bnf-Lnk*.

†**chaffer** a chafing-dish.

chap: ~**per** a beetle for pounding *Bnf Abd Ags*. ~**ping stick** a potato-masher *Sh-Ross*.

clappers = **butter clappers** *local Cai-Kcb*.

†**cleit** a small dry-stone structure used for storing food on St Kilda.

cleps an adjustable iron handle for suspending a pot over the fire.

cog a wooden container made of staves, a pail or bowl.

cood a shallow tub, a wooden dish or basin, *esp* for holding milk *now Abd*.

corcag a small knife *Cai*.

†**counterfute** some kind of plate or dish.

†**coup** a cup.

cran *now local NE-C,* **crane** a means of supporting a pot etc over a fire: **1** an iron frame placed across; **2** a trivet *now Cai;* **3** an iron upright with projecting arm *now Fif Stlg*.

crock an earthenware container for foodstuffs, *eg* milk, salt, butter.

†**crowat** a cruet.

cruet a carafe; a decanter *now Bnf Abd*.

cruik, crook a hook, *esp* a pot-hook. ~ **tree** a beam above the fire from which pot-hooks are hung.

cutty spoon, †**cutty** a short-handled spoon, *usu* of horn.

dale a container (*orig* made of wood), *usu* for milk *now Bwk*.

decanter a table jug *now Abd*.

deep plate a soup plate or similarly-shaped smaller dish.

divide: divider *local Cai-Dmf,* **dividing spoon** *local Bnf-Dmf* a ladle, a serving spoon.

†**dredge box** a flour-dredger.

†**dropping pan** a dripping pan.

†**elcruke** a hook for lifting meat out of a pot.

†**ferekin, firikin** a firkin.

filler a funnel for pouring liquids through.

†**fire vessel** vessels for use on a fire; cooking utensils.

†**flam(m)er flaming spoon** a basting ladle.

flat, flattie *NE* any flat plate etc for placing beneath some other dish etc; a saucer *now Mry midLoth WC*.

†**fraer** a basket (of figs, dates or almonds).

froh stick a whisk made of wood and cow's hair *now Abd*.

†**frything pan** a frying pan.

gab-stick a wooden spoon.

†**gairding, gardenap, gardenat** a protective, *usu* brass mat or plate placed under dishes at table.

gallows a device for suspending a pot over a fire *now Uls*.

gamrel a piece of wood used to separate the legs of a carcass to facilitate butchering *SW, W*.

gebbie a horn spoon *Sh Ork NE*.

girdle an iron plate used for baking, *traditionally* circular with a hooped handle for hanging over a fire.

girnel, garnel, †**girner** a storage chest for meal etc.

goan a wooden bowl or dish *chf SW*.

goblet, goglet an iron pot or pan with a straight handle and *usu* convex sides.

†**gockie** a deep wooden dish *NE*.

grain a prong (of a fork etc) *now local*. † ~**it** pronged.

green-horn a spoon made of a greenish horn.

†**guse pan** a large cooking-pot.

hack(ing) stock a chopping block.

hag: ~**-block,** ~**-clog,** ~**-stock** a chopping block *latterly SW, S*.

hands *Gen except Sh Ork,* **Scotch** ~ *now NE, C Rox* a pair of bats for making butter-pats.

heather: ~ **range** *now Cai Per Kinr,* ~ **reenge** *Abd Ags Kcdn* a bunch of heather stems tied together and used as a pot-scourer.

heck, hake 1 a wooden rack (suspended from the roof) for drying cheeses etc. **2** a plate- or bottle-rack *now local Sh-Pbls*.

henshelstane the stone shelf or slab in front of a baker's oven-door, used to make it easier to slide trays etc into the oven, or to square up loaves before baking.

hinnie, honey: ~**-pig** an earthenware container for drained honey *now Abd*.

jeelie, jelly: ~**-can** *Gen except NE*, ~**-jaur** *local*, ~**-mug** *Ork Renfr Kcb*, ~**-pig** *Abd Ags* a jam-pot. ~ **pan** a (*traditionally*) brass) pan for making jam or jelly.

joug, jug 1 a jug. 2 a mug or drinking vessel.

kail gullie a blade fixed at right angles to the end of an upright handle, used for cutting and chopping kail stems *now Ork local N*.

keiching a kitchen.

kettle, †cattill a large cooking pot. ~ **brod** a wooden pot-lid *Sh N*.

kipper a large bowl *NE*.

knag a small wooden dish with one stave extended to form the handle.

†lade-galloun, lagalloun a wooden bucket used for lading and carrying liquids.

†lai(r)dner a store-room for meat etc.

lappering tub a container used for curdling milk *Abd Loth Dmf*.

†latter meat room a larder for storing food already cooked.

†l(e)aven tub the vessel in which dough is mixed and leavened *chf EC*.

†leck (stane) an oven slab made of a kind of igneous rock which breaks into flat slabs *EC*.

leglin = **lade-gallon**, *latterly chf* with a projecting stave as a handle, used as a milk pail.

link a link in the chain from which the pot-hook hung in the fireplace *now Sh-N Loth*.

luggie a small wooden bowl etc with one or two handles formed from projecting staves, *freq* used for serving milk with porridge *now local N-Rox*.

maun a platter for oatcakes, *usu* made of wooden slats *NE*.

meal, male: ~ **ark** *now C Uls*, ~ **kist** a chest for storing oatmeal. ~ **bowie** a barrel for storing oatmeal *NE*.

†mess a plate, platter, dish.

milk: ~**-bowie** a wooden milk bucket *now NE Ags Per*. ~**-boyne** a broad, shallow wooden vessel for holding milk *C*.

muckle pot the largest cooking pot, a cauldron *now Sh Ork Bnf*.

mug 1 †an earthenware container or jar. 2 *also* **moog** *N* a mug, a drinking vessel.

naipkin, neepyin *local C* a napkin.

nap(pie) a bowl, a drinking vessel.

pale a small shovel or scoop, used for taking samples of food, *esp* cheese *now Lnk Gall*.

parritch, porridge: †parritch cap a wooden

porridge-bowl. ~ **spurtle**, ~ **stick** a stick used for stirring porridge.

†pece a goblet, *usu* of silver.

†pepper curn a pepper-mill.

†pestell, pistoll a pestle.

†petty pan a small metal pan or mould used for pastry.

pig 1 a container, *usu* of earthenware; a pot, jar, pitcher. 2 ~**s** crockery. ~**gery** crockery, dishes *Abd Kcdn*.

piggin a container, *usu* of wood, tub-shaped and with one stave extended to form a handle, used as a milk-pail, feeding dish etc.

pingle(-pan) a small, shallow, metal cooking-pan, *usu* with a long handle, a saucepan *now Uls*.

†plouk, plook a knob, protuberance, *specif* a small knob etc marking a measure on the inside of a container.

pot, pat a pot. ~ **bool**, † ~ **clip** a device for lifting or hanging a pot *now Ork Cai*. **pot fit** one of the legs or feet of a cauldron pot *NE*. **pot lug** the ear or loop by which a pot is suspended *now Sh Ork*. ~ **stick** a stick for stirring porridge etc in cooking, a **spurtle** *now SW Uls*.

†pottinger a bowl for soup, porridge etc, a porringer.

pourie a vessel with a spout for pouring, a jug, *esp* a cream jug; a small oil can with a spout *now C, S*.

prang a prong *now Mry Abd Per*.

†prick a pointed implement, a skewer.

†prop a stopper, bung, wedge.

quaich a shallow bowl-shaped drinking cup, *orig* made of wooden staves hooped with metal, and with two ears or handles, sometimes with silver mountings or made entirely of silver, *now chf* ornamental.

†racks, rax(es) a set of bars to support a roasting spit.

ramhorn (spoon) a spoon made from the horn of a ram *now Kcb*.

ream: ~**er** *now Sh*, ~**ing dish** a shallow dish for skimming cream off milk. **raemikle** a round wooden tub for holding milk etc; a pail *now Sh*. ~ **pig, stoupie** *etc* a jug for holding cream *now NE nEC Kcb*.

reest a wood or rope framework on which fish, meat etc is smoked *now Sh*.

row, roll: ~**er** a rolling pin, *freq* a ribbed or grooved one used in making oatcakes *now NE Kcb*.

†salsar a saucer.

saut, salt: ~ **backet** a salt-box, now *usu* one with a flat back and a curved front made to hang on the wall *now NE nEC*. ~ **dish**, ~ **fat** *now local Sh-Fif*, †~ **foot** a salt cellar. ~ **willie** a salt jar *now Fif*.

scale a shallow drinking bowl; a shallow dish for skimming milk *now Lnk Rox*.

scuit a shallow, wooden, scoop-shaped drinking cup, *freq* ~**ifu** the full contents of this *now Slk*.

scummer a ladle or shallow dish for skimming *now N, EC*.

search a sieve, strainer, riddle *now NE Ags*.

setter a strip of wood supporting the row of end- or side-loaves in a batch in an oven.

†**sextern** a container for liquid.

shankie a small cooking pan with a long handle *now Dmf*.

shell, shall a saucer *Bnf Abd*.

†**siff** a sieve.

sile a sieve, strainer, filter, *esp* for milk *Bwk WC-S*.

skeel a kind of wooden tub for milk or water, *freq* with handles formed by elongated staves *now Ags*.

skellet 1 †a skillet, a saucepan. **2** a tin water-scoop *now Cai Inv Mry*.

†**skiver** a skewer.

skleff *of a dish* shallow, flat *now Loth*.

skoosher a device for sprinkling or spraying, a sprinkler *local Inv-C*.

slap, slop: ~ **bowl** a slop basin.

snipie, snippy a kettle or teapot.

sole a flat plate under a gravy boat, cheese-dish etc *NE*.

sowan bowie, †**sowan boat**, **sowan kit** a wooden barrel or tub used for fermenting **sowans**. †**sowan(s) pot** the pot in which **sowans** was cooked. **sowan sieve** a strainer for **sowans** (after the initial steeping).

speet, spit *n* **1** a (roasting-)spit. **2** a pointed stick or skewer on which fish are hung up to dry *local Sh-Bwk*. **spit rack** a rack for supporting a spit or spits.

†**spice house** a store for keeping spices.

spune a spoon. **spoon creel** a small basket hung on a kitchen wall for holding spoons *now local Ags-Ayr*.

spurtle, spurkle *N, C* **1** a long-handled, flat-bladed implement for turning oatcakes, scones etc *now Ags Per*. **2** a short tapering stick for stirring porridge, soup etc *Gen but rare in Ags*.

stand a tub, barrel or cask set upright to contain water, meal, salted beef etc *now Per*.

stowp 1 a wooden pail or bucket, *esp* a narrow-mouthed one for carrying water from a well *now local NE-Rox*. **2** a jug, *esp* for milk or cream *now NE Ags*.

stroup 1 the spout or mouth of a kettle, jug, pump etc *now Sh-C*. **2** the faucet, spout or outlet of a spring or well, a water-tap *now N Per*.

sweetie bottle a glass jar for holding sweeties.

swey, swee a movable iron bar over a fire, on which pots, kettles etc can be hung. **swee chain** the chain hanging from the **swey** *now Cai Ags*.

swill a large shallow basket for carrying potatoes, etc *Bwk Rox*.

sye *n, also* ~**r** *now Sh-Per* a strainer or sieve for liquids, *esp* for milk *now NE, WC*. **sey clout** a piece of gauze etc, *usu* stretched across a round wooden frame, used for straining liquid *now Sh-N*. ~ **dish** *now NE nEC*, ~ **milk** *now NE* a milk-strainer. ~**-sowans** a strainer for **sowans**.

tass(ie) a cup, goblet etc, *esp* for spirits *now literary*.

tattie: ~**-beetle** a wooden pestle for mashing potatoes *Ork C, S*. ~**-champer**, ~**-chapper** a potato-masher or pestle *now local*. ~**-parer** a potato-peeler.

†**teemse** a fine sieve, *esp* for sifting flour.

theevil *now local N-Dmf*, **theedle** *now local Cai-Fif* a short tapering stick used to stir food as it cooks, a **spurtle**.

tillie-pan a flat iron cooking pan; a saucepan *NE*.

†**timmer, timber** a wooden dish, cup or utensil.

toaster a metal rack or (*formerly*) a stone for drying and toasting oatcakes in front of an open fire *now Abd Ags*.

traicle, treacle: ~ **pig** a treacle jar *N*.

truncher a trencher *now Sh Lnk*.

†**tuip-horn** (a) ram's horn made into a spoon etc.

turning tree a wooden stick for stirring *now Sh*.

une an oven. ~ **pot** *etc* a large shallow pan used as an oven by being set among the glowing embers of a fire *local NE-S*.

†**voidour** a basket etc for clearing dirty dishes, food-fragments etc during or after a meal.

wallie porcelain, glazed earthenware or tiling; a dish made of such *C, S*.

winter an iron or rack which hangs on the bars of a fire-grate to support a kettle or pot; a trivet *now Per*.

wisk a whisk.

10.3 PROCESSES

aboil at or to boiling point.

air: take the ~ **off** take the chill off.

bicker *of boiling water* bubble quickly *now Abd*.

bile, †**builȝe** boil.

†**bishop: the ~'s foot has been in the broth** *etc* the **broth** etc is burnt.

bizz *of liquids* hiss, fizz.

bout bolt, sift (flour etc).

brak, break *of milk* curdle, coagulate, either by its becoming sour or in the process of churning *now Sh NE Kcb*.

brander broil on a gridiron, grill.

†**brewis, browis** broth, stock made from meat and vegetables.

brime brine; pickle *now Bnf Abd Ags*.

broo liquid, *esp* that in which something has been boiled *now Fif Lnk*.

†**brulyie** broil, burn.

†**buff** toast, *eg* on a gridiron (a salt herring which has been steeped in fresh water).

buller *of water* boil or bubble up; rush noisily; make a loud gurgling sound *now Abd Ags*.

bummel boil up, bubble.

caddel stir or mix into a mess *Bnf Kcb*.

cair 1 stir *N*. 2 scrape or rake up *now Abd*.

chack, check hack, chop *now Fif Edb*.

chaff knead or mould (the individual loaves) *now Ayr*.

change, cheenge, chynge *of food* deteriorate, go bad, go off *N*.

chap 1 mash (vegetables). 2 chop *now local Bnf-Lnk*.

†**claut the laggin** scrape or drain a container of food or drink.

cog empty into a **cog**.

cotter scramble (eggs) *Ags Fif*.

crackins the residue from any rendered fat or oil *local*.

creesh *n* fat, grease. *v* grease; oil. **~ie** greasy; fat.

crud: **~le** curdle *now Bnf Kcb Rox*. **~dy** curdled, full of curds.

crummle crumble *now Bnf Abd*.

cuik cook.

daigh dough. **~ie** doughy.

daise become rotten, spoiled by age, damp etc, *chf* **daised** *now Kcb*.

†**dicht** prepare, cook (food, a meal).

draigle mix (flour, meal etc) with water *Bnf Abd*.

drammlicks the small pieces of oatmeal dough which stick to the basin when making oatcakes *now Abd*.

draw *of tea or the teapot* infuse, become infused *local*.

dreep drain, strain (*chf* potatoes after boiling).

†**dropping** dripping (from roasting meat).

een globules of fat in soup etc. **~ie** having the appearance of eyes; *specif of soup or rancid milk* full of **een**.

eik up fill up (a container) *local EC*.

fa(ll) *of fruit in boiling* fall to pieces, diminish in bulk.

fire bake (oatcakes, scones, bread etc) by browning in an oven or over a flame. **fired** *of milk, meat etc* soured by hot weather *now midLoth Kcb*.

†**flam** baste (meat etc).

float grease, scum, *esp* on a boiling pot of soup, jam etc *now Ayr*.

free *of pastry etc* brittle, crumbly.

freith *chf verse, n* foam, froth *now Kcb*. *v* froth, foam, lather *now Kcb*.

fro *n* froth, foam *now local Mry-Slk*. *v* froth, foam; bubble *local Abd-Slk*.

frush *of pastry etc* crisp, short, crumbly *now Ork SW*.

†**frythe** fry.

†**graith** prepare, make ready (food, a meal).

hack, hawk chop up (meat etc).

hair (the) butter free butter from impurities, *eg* hairs, by passing a knife through it in all directions *now Ork*.

harn roast on embers, toast, make crisp before the fire or on a **girdle**, bake or fire *now Sh Ork Kcb Uls*.

hash 1 slash, hack, mangle, as with a sharp instrument. 2 slice, cut up, chop (*eg* bread).

hire season (food), make it more palatable by the addition of rich ingredients *now NE*.

†**hoam, hoan** spoil (food) through damp or steam.

hotter *v, of liquid etc or its container* seethe, bubble, boil steadily *Gen except Sh Ork*. *n* the bubbling noise made by boiling liquor *now NE Fif Dmf*.

huil, hool, hull shell (peas etc), husk.

jeel *of jam, jelly, stock etc* set, congeal.

jeelie jelly, set like jelly.

joice juice *now local Sh-Ags*.

kitchen, kitchie give flavour to, season. **kitchen fee** tallow, dripping, formerly the perquisite of the cook.

lapper, †**lopper** *esp of milk* clot, curdle.

†**laven** leaven.

leam take (a ripe nut) from its husk *SW, S*.

leap *of potatoes being boiled in their skins* burst open *wLoth S*.

leaven a mixture of oatmeal and water made up as a dough for oatcakes or as food for young poultry *Sh N Fif*.

lee side *of a pot* the side boiling less fiercely, the cooler side *now Ork Wgt*.

leep *v* heat partially, parboil *now Sh-N Gall*. *n* a warming; a parboiling *N*. **~it** warmed up; parboiled; scalded.

link: **~ on, aff, up, doun** *etc* place (a pot) on or take (it) off the pot-hook on the **links** (of the pot-hook chain). ~ **up**, ~ **doun** place (the pot-hook) on a higher, or lower, **link**.

lith wring the neck of (a hen) *chf NE*.

lithe, lyde thicken (soup, porridge etc) with oatmeal etc *now Abd Bwk Uls*. **lithin** the flour, meal or milk added to soup, gravy etc *now NE*.

mak, make *of food or drink in the process of cooking* thicken, set, infuse.

meal, male add meal to (soup etc) *chf N*.

†miscook spoil (food) in cooking.

mismak prepare or cook (food) badly *now Ags*.

mouten *adj, of fat* clarified *Mry Bnf*. *v* melt, dissolve; clarify (fat) *chf Mry Bnf*.

nip pinch dough at its edges, make indentations round pastry etc.

oil, eelie oil. **†** ~ **dolive** olive oil. **†eelie dolly** oil of any kind *Abd*.

pale pierce (cheese etc) with a **pale**, remove a sample with a **pale** *now Kcb*.

papple *v, of fat in cooking* sizzle, sputter *local Mry-Wgt*. **†n** a bubble, as in a cooking pot.

Parisian barm flour, malt and water stocked or stored with mature or old barm and used as a medium for the growth of yeast.

particular clean, hygienic, *esp* in cooking *local*.

†patisar a pastry-cook.

peep: put the gas at a ~ reduce the pressure of a gas jet to the lowest point at which it will remain alight.

pilk pick out, shell, peel; top and tail (gooseberries) *now Sh*.

plapper *of a liquid* bubble and plop when boiling *NE*.

play *of a liquid or the vessel containing it* boil, seethe.

plot, plout immerse (the carcass of a fowl, pig, etc) in boiling water to ease plucking or scraping.

plump *of a (semi-)liquid* make a loud, bubbling or plopping noise, *eg* when boiling *now Uls*.

poach reduce (something, *eg* food in a dish) to mush by over-handling, mess about with *Bnf Abd*.

pouk, pook remove the feathers from (a bird), pluck (a fowl) *C, S*.

pour, poor 1 empty (a container) by pouring out its contents. **2** pour the liquid from (boiled food, *esp* potatoes), drain. **~ins 1** the liquid strained of as in **pour 2**. **2** the liquid strained off **sowans** after their fermentation.

pouther, pooder, powder sprinkle (food) with salt or spices in order to preserve it, salt, cure (meat, butter etc).

pree try by tasting.

prinkle *of a boiling pot* bubble, simmer.

pruive, prove, prieve try by tasting, taste *now Sh Ork NE*.

quarter-sponge the first stage of bread-making in which a quarter of the water required has been used.

†quickenin yeast, any fermenting agent.

quinkins dregs or leavings of any kind, scum of a liquid, charred traces of food stuck to the saucepan *now Ags*.

†tramp *of milk etc* become glutinous.

rander, render clarified fat, dripping *now Ork Ags*.

ready cook (food), prepare (a meal) *now Stlg WC, SW*.

ream 1 *of milk* form cream. **2** skim the cream off (milk) *NE-S*. **3** form a froth or foam. **4** be full of a frothy liquid, bubble to the brim *now Mry Bnf Lnk*. ~ **in fou** full of frothy liquid. **~y** frothing.

redd *v* clean (the intestines of a slaughtered animal) of fat *Sh Ork Rox*. *n* fat removed from an animal's intestines, *esp* used for making **puddings** *now Sh Dmf*.

reekit *of food* smoke-cured.

reest 1 cure (fish, ham etc) by drying or smoking *now local Sh-Wgt*. **2** *of fish, ham etc* be cured (as above) *now Sh*.

rin, run 1 *of milk* coagulate, curdle *chf Sh Ork*. **2** put (a batch of loaves etc) in the oven for baking *now Fif*.

rind melt down, render (fat), clarify (butter etc) *now local Sh-Dmf*.

rittocks the refuse of melted lard *chf SW*.

rizzered dried, parched *now local EC*.

roastit *of cheese* toasted.

rouse sprinkle (fish) with salt to cure them *now Sh-N Fif*.

rummle, rumble stir or shake vigorously; mash (potatoes); scramble (eggs) *now Kcb*.

sad 1 *of bread or pastry* not risen, heavy *now Ork NE-S*. **2** *of bread* heavy, not fully baked *local EC-S*.

sair, sore: ~ **done** *of meat* well done, overcooked *now NE*.

same fat, *esp* of pigs, grease, lard *now local*.

sap sop, soak, steep, saturate.

saut, salt: ~ **bree** salt water, water in which salt has been mixed or boiled *Sh NE*.

scaud, scald 1 scald. **2** make (tea) *Kcb S*.

scowder burn, scorch, singe; over-toast (bread etc).

scrammle scramble.

scrumpie baked hard and crisp *now Bnf Abd*.

scum *v* skim, remove scum (from) *Gen except Sh Ork*. *adj* skimmed, *esp* ~ **milk** *Gen except Sh Ork*.

†scuttle serve on a plate, dish up (food); pour

(liquid) from one container to another, spill in so doing.

search put through a sieve, sift, strain *now NE Ags.*

set leave (milk) standing for the cream to rise. **set(t)en on** burnt, frizzled, shrivelled (in cooking) *now Lnk Wgt Rox.*

share pour off (top liquid), separate (a liquid) from its dregs *now SW.*

shaup shell (pea-pods), take (peas) from the husks *now Stlg WC.*

sheave, shave cut into slices *now Sh Abd.*

sheel, shill 1 shell (peas, grain, etc), take out of the husk or pod *now local Sh-Lnk.* 2 cut (a mussel) from its shell *now local Sh-Bwk.*

shire, sheer *now Lnk* pour off (top liquid), separate a liquid from its dregs. **shirins** liquid which rises to the top and is poured off.

shorn *of meat or vegetables* chopped up.

sile pass (a liquid, *esp* milk) through a sieve, strain, filter *now Bwk WC-S.*

sitten on singed in the pan *local Per-Rox.*

skeechan an intoxicating malt liquor produced in the later stages of brewing and formerly used by bakers instead of yeast; sometimes mixed with treacle etc and sold as a kind of beer.

skelf take off (as) in flakes, slice *local Sh-WC.*

skink 1· †pour out (liquor for drinking). 2 pour (a small amount of liquid) from one container to another; mix (liquids) thus. † ~ **in** easily poured, thinly diluted. † ~**le** sprinkle, scatter, spray, or spill in small quantities.

skirl *of something very hot, esp in frying* sizzle, crackle, sputter *now Per.*

skive shave, pare, slice off a thin layer from *local NE-Lnk.*

skiver pierce or stab as with a skewer *now Dnbt.*

slocken make a paste of (meal) *now local.*

smeek smoke (fish, meat etc), *eg* in order to preserve.

smuik cure (meat) by smoking *now SW, S.*

sneyster burn, scorch, roast.

†**sodden** boiled, cooked by boiling.

sodie soda *now Ork Per.*

sooie a lump of dough trimmed off the edges of an oatcake before baking *NE.*

sotter *v* boil, cook slowly, bubble or sputter in cooking *now local Ork-SW.* *n* the noise made by something boiling, frying or bubbling up *now Ags Kcb.*

spalder, †**spald** split, lay open or flat (*esp* a fish).

speet, spit 1 spit. 2 hang (fish) **up** by the heads or gills on a **speet** to dry *local Sh-Bwk.*

speld split, cut, slice open (*esp* fish to dry) *now Sh Cai.*

spilk shell (peas) *NE.*

†**spill** *of food* degenerate, deteriorate, spoil, *freq* **spilt.**

spread spread butter, jam etc on (a slice of bread etc).

sprent a hollow made in a heap of flour to contain liquid before mixing.

spue, spew *of a pudding* burst, split open *Sh Abd.*

stairch, sterch starch.

stap the act of cramming or stuffing *Sh Ork NE Kcb.* **stappin** stuffing, *specif* that used for filling fishes' heads *Abd Ags.*

steep rennet or some other substitute for curdling milk *now Wgt.*

stew a coating or sprinkling of dust or powder *now Abd.*

stove *n* a stew. *v* stew *now local Sh-Bwk.*

swine('s) same lard, pig's fat *now local N-S.*

sye pass (liquid) through a sieve, drain, filter *now local.*

†**syn(dl)ins** rinsings, slops, swill.

sype *v* draw liquid from, drain *now Sh Ork Cai Dmf.* *n* a small quantity of liquid, that which drips from an emptied bottle *now Sh Ork.*

taivers shreds, *freq of meat* **boiled to** ~ *now Sh Ork.*

tappietourie a knob of pastry over the centre hole in a pie *Ayr.*

thairm a gut used as the skin of a sausage etc *now local Sh-WC.*

thickenin(g) an agent which curdles milk, rennet *WC.*

thorter spread butter on bread at right angles to the way one has done it before *now Abd.*

thoum, thumb dab or press (butter on bread etc) with a moistened thumb.

throu(gh) the boil up to boiling point and allowed to boil for a short time *Gen except Sh Ork.*

thunnered, thundered *of liquids, esp milk* tainted, soured, affected by thundery weather *NE nEC Dmf Rox.*

tottle 1 *also* **totter** simmer, boil gently *now Ags.* 2 cause to simmer.

tume, teem *now Per Stlg* drain water from (potatoes).

tyauve knead, work (dough) *now Cai.*

virgus verjuice, sour fruit-juice.

wall, well boil (up).

wat (a cup o) tea make (a cup of) tea *WC.*

weel, well fully cooked, ready to eat. † ~ **baken** well-baked.

whack a cut, incision *now N Per.*

whang cut in chunks or sizeable portions, slice *now EC Rox.*

win dry out, season (cheese etc).

wisk whisk.

wrang, wrong: gae ~ *of food etc* go off, decompose *Sh NE-Per.*

wuss juice, the liquid obtained from boiling or squeezing vegetable substances *now Sh.*

wynted *of food or drink* allowed to spoil, soured, *orig* by exposure to the air *local.*

†**yet** pour.

yirn, earn (cause to) coagulate or curdle; *of milk* form curds with rennet and heat *now Sh-N.* ~ **in 1** rennet *now local Sh-Lnk.* **2** the stomach of an unweaned calf etc used in making rennet *now Sh-Cai.*

†**yowder, euther** steam, smoke, vapour.

10.4 EATING AND DRINKING

able having an appetite **for.**

baible drink carelessly.

beamfill't, beamfoo filled to overflowing; indulged *now Bnf Abd.*

belly eat or drink voraciously *now Bnf.* ~ **gut** *NE,* † ~ **god** *adj, n* gluttonous; a glutton. ~ **rive(r)** a great feast, eating to repletion *Bnf Abd.*

†**bit** *of food* a bite, a mouthful.

blibberin slobbering; making a noise when drinking soup *Abd.*

brosie 1 bedaubed or fed with **brose** *now local Abd-Lnk.* **2** stout, bloated with too much food or drink; soft, inactive.

burst a big feed, *freq* **a hunger or a** ~ a feast or a famine *now local Cai-Arg.*

chat bite, chew *NE.* ~**tle** nibble *now Abd.*

chittle nibble, gnaw *SW.*

chow chaw, chew. **chawl** eat noisily or listlessly *SW.*

corn take food etc.

cow eat up, consume.

craig †drink, swallow. **pit ower one's** ~ swallow *now Bnf Abd Fif.*

cramp munch *N.*

cramsh *Bnf Abd,* **crinch** *now Fif* crunch.

crump crunch, munch *now local NE-C.*

cut an appetite *Bnf.*

cutty sup greedily.

devoor devour *now Bnf Abd Fif.*

dish: get *etc* **a** ~ **o want** get no food at all *N.*

drum-fu as tight as a drum, full (of food) *Abd Ags Fif.*

eat the action of eating *NE.*

flet pour (tea) into one's saucer *now Stlg midLoth.*

forlaithie *n* a surfeit, an excess (**of** something) *now Bnf.* *v* disgust through excess, sicken *Bnf Abd.*

fou, full full of food, well-fed *now local NE-Rox.*

fousome *of food* filling, over-rich *now Sh Abd Ags.*

gamp eat or drink greedily, devour *Rox.*

gaup, gowp *v* devour. *n* a large mouthful, a gulp.

gilravage 1 eat or drink immoderately, indulge in high living. **2** devour *C.*

girsie: get ~ **stibble** enjoy the best of fare *Bnf Abd.*

gizzent sated, surfeited *Abd Slk.*

glock a gulp.

glog *v, chf* ~ **owre** swallow, gulp down *now NE.* *n* a gulp *Abd.*

glunsh gobble, gulp food *Cai Kcb Dmf.*

glut *n* a gulp, draught (of liquid) *now midLoth.* *v* swallow, gulp down *now midLoth.* ~**ter** swallow noisily, disgustingly or voraciously.

gnap a morsel, a bite of food *now Abd.*

gnip(per) a morsel, a bite of food *Bnf.*

gollop *v* gulp. *n* a hasty or greedy gulp *now Arg Ayr.*

gorb eat greedily *Gall Uls.*

gorble eat ravenously, gobble **up** *now Dmf.*

green *of a pregnant woman* have a craving (for particular foods).

gropsie eat gluttonously.

gulch *v* eat rapidly or greedily *now Abd.* *n* a glutton *now Bnf.*

gumsh munch *NE.*

gut: ~**s** eat greedily or gluttonously *local.* ~**sie** greedy, gluttonous. ~**tie** fond of good eating, gluttonous *now Bnf Abd Kcb.*

guzzle a bout of excessive eating and drinking, a debauch.

hanch, hum(p)sh eat greedily and noisily, munch *now Abd Gall Dmf.*

hash munch, chew.

hause, hass: gae doun (into) the wrang ~ go down the wrong way *now local Sh-Dmf.*

heavy: be ~ **on, be a** ~ **neighbour on** consume a great deal of (food or drink) *Gen except Sh Ork.*

heck, hake *n* the ability to eat heartily, appetite *Bwk Dmf.* *v* eat greedily *EC Rox.* ~**er** a glutton, hearty eater *EC, S.*

heid, head: lay one's ~ **till** set about eating (something) *now Abd.*

hose swallow voraciously *now Bnf Abd.*

hum, ham *v* **1** *also* **hummle** chew partially, *esp* chew (food) till soft before transferring it to an infant's mouth *local.* **2** *freq* ~ **amo** or **intae** eat greedily, take large mouthfuls of, crunch *Bnf Abd.* *n* a piece of food chewed as in **hum 1,** and given to a child *now Cai Dmf.*

intak the act of taking in (*eg* food).

kemp compete in eating, eat hurriedly.

knap *v* break or snap with the teeth, munch, eat greedily. *n* a snap, bite; a morsel of food, a bite. ~ **at the wind** (take) a mere bite *Ork NE*.

laib *v* lick up, lap, gobble *now Abd Ags Uls*. *n*, *also* ~**ach** *NE* a mouthful, *esp* of liquid. ~**er** beslobber, bespatter with food *chf S*.

laip *v* lap (liquid) *now local Sh-midLoth*. *n* **1** the act of lapping *now Ags midLoth*. **2** a mouthful or small amount (of liquid) *now Ags midLoth*.

lang: mak a ~ **airm** stretch out and help oneself.

lat, let: ~ **doon** *NE, EC*, ~ **ower** *chf NE* swallow.

lay: ~ **into** *or* **intil** eat greedily. ~ **on** eat heartily *now Ags Loth Uls*. **lay-on** a surfeit *now Ags Loth Uls*. ~ **till** *or* **tae** start to eat *now Sh Uls*.

lerb *v* lap with the tongue, slobber in drinking *Abd*. *n* a lick, a mouthful of a liquid or semi-liquid *Abd*.

lip touch with the lips, taste.

logger, locher slobber (food) *Ross Fif Lnk Dmf*.

lug: lay one's ~ **in(to)** eat or drink heartily of (some food or drink) *now N wLoth Lnk*.

map nibble with twitching of the lips, as a rabbit or sheep *now local Ork-Kcb*.

mattle nibble (like a young animal).

meat, mait eat a meal, receive one's meals *now Sh Abd*.

mimp eat with the mouth nearly closed *Ork Kcb S*.

moup, *also* ~ **on** *or* at nibble, munch *now Edb Ayr Kcb*.

mout fritter **away**, consume gradually *now Sh*.

mouth, mou: ask *etc* **if someone has a** ~ invite someone to eat or drink. **fin one's** ~ convey food to one's mouth *Sh Ork NE, SW*.

nam eat up greedily *chf S*.

nattle nibble, chew awkwardly *Sh Rox*.

nimp, nyim a morsel.

nip *n* pungency, sharpness of flavour. *v*, *of food or its taste* cause to tingle or smart.

nourice nourish.

oam, yoam a warm aroma, *eg* from cooking *Sh Ork NE*.

oof wolf, consume ravenously.

out, oot *of a cup etc, or its contents* emptied, drained, consumed: 'is your cup out?'

†pack stuff (oneself or one's stomach with food).

pang *v* cram (the stomach) with food, gorge *now NE*. *adv* completely filled, full to overflowing; crammed with food. ~ **f(o)u** *now NE wLoth Uls*, ~**'d-fu** stuffed, full to overflowing.

pawl at play with one's food *S*.

†pechan the stomach as a receptacle for food, the belly.

†penfu a (large etc) amount of food or drink.

perish *joc* 'polish off', finish (food or drink) *local Sh-SW*.

pewl, pule †a small morsel (of food), a bite, nibble. ~ **amang, at** *or* **ower one's food** eat listlessly and without appetite, pick at one's food.

pick: ~**ie** a person who picks at his food, a poor eater *now local C-S*. † ~**le** peck (up) repeatedly and delicately; *of persons* eat in a sparing way, nibble.

pike: a ~**-at-one's-meat** a poor or fussy eater *local NE-S*.

pit owre swallow, consume; wash down, make palatable.

pouch eat (something) greedily and with relish, gulp down *Bnf Ags*.

puist cram (the stomach or oneself) with food *chf Rox*.

Rab Ha a glutton, voracious eater *WC, SW*.

ram-full crammed full (of food or drink) *Gen except Sh Ork*.

ramsh munch, crunch, chew vigorously *local Bnf-Loth*.

rax: ~ **doon,** ~ **for,** ~ **till** *etc* at table, reach, stretch out, help oneself to (food).

†repater feed.

retour a second helping of food, round of drinks etc *chf Abd*.

rive *v* **1** ~ (**at**) eat voraciously, tear into (food) *local Sh-Wgt*. **2** *of the stomach* burst from eating and drinking too much *now N Per Lnk*. *n* a bite, a large mouthful; a good feed *now local NE-Kcb*.

†rundge rounge, gnaw, champ; devour greedily.

scaff eat or drink greedily *now Sh*.

scart scrape with a spoon, take the last of food from (a dish).

scoff swallow (food or drink) quickly.

scrump crunch, munch, chew (something hard and crisp) *Bnf Abd Kcdn*.

serve, ser *v* satisfy or content, *esp* with food or drink. *n*, *only* **ser** one's fill, enough, satiety *now NE Ags Rox*. **saired** having one's appetite satisfied, full up *now local*. **ill-saired** not having had enough food at a meal *now NE*. **weel-saired** well satisfied with food or drink *now NE*. **sairin** one's fill (*esp* of food) *now local Sh-Lnk*.

†sey tasting of food or drink.

shairp, sharp: ~ **set** keen, eager, *specif* for food, etc *now Ayr*.

sip eat in spoonfuls or in good mouthfuls *now Bnf Ags*.

sirple *now S,* †**sipple** sip continuously, go on drinking in small quantities, tipple *now S.*

skeichen *adj, also* **skiten** fastidious about food, easily upset or nauseated *NE. n* fastidiousness or fussiness about food; a feeling of disgust for something edible *now Bnf Abd. v* (feel) disgust, (be) repel(led), (be) nauseate(d) *now Bnf Abd.*

slab 1 †slaver, *esp* while eating, eat or drink noisily, slobber. **2** eat **up** noisily, eat **up** greedily *now Kcdn Ags.* ~**ber** *v* **1** wet with saliva, beslobber; stain (one's clothes etc) with saliva or with food when eating *now Cai C, SW.* **2** slaver, dribble; eat or drink noisily, sloppily *now local N-Dmf. n* a greedy or noisy mouthful, a slobber *now Ags.*

slag †mess about with food, gobble up in large spoonfuls. **slaiger, slagger** eat or drink messily *local NE-S.*

slaik, slaich *v* **1** lick, smear with the tongue, beslobber *now local Ags-Wgt.* **2** lick (dishes) or consume (food) on the sly (like a pet animal). *n* a person who eats or drinks excessively *local Per-Rox.*

slairg, slairk sup liquid noisily, slobber at one's food *now Rox.*

slairie slovenly in one's eating habits *Clcm Renfr Lnk.*

slaister, slyster *v* eat or drink messily or greedily. *n* a messy person, *esp* a messy eater *C, S.* ~ **kyte** a messy eater, glutton.

slerp *v* consume noisily or messily *now Edb Kcb Dmf. n* a spoonful of liquid taken with a slobbering sound *now Wgt Rox.*

slitter eat or drink messily *now C.*

sloch *v* swallow (food or drink) in a noisy slobbering way *local Inv-WC. n* a noisy intake of food or drink; a hearty drink, a good swig *now Per.*

slorach *v* eat or drink messily and noisily, slobber, slaver *local NE-Per. n* a noisy gulping down of food *Bnf Kcdn.*

slork *v* make a slobbering noise, *eg* when eating or drinking; suck up (food or drink) noisily *Lnk SW, S. n* a noisy sucking up of food or drink *Lnk SW, S.*

slorp *v* eat or drink noisily and slobberingly *local Kcdn-S. n* a noisy mouthful, a slobber, swig *now Loth Kcb Rox.*

slour a noisy gulp (of food or drink), a mouthful of soft sloppy food *Abd Kcdn.*

slouster swallow noisily and ungracefully, gulp, slobber *now Fif Lnk.*

slubber *v* slobber, swallow sloppy food, eat or drink in a noisy, gulping way *Sh, N, EC, SW. n* a noisy, slobbering way of eating *now Ork N.*

smacher eat in a secretive way, nibble (**at**), munch unobtrusively *now Kcdn.*

smatter awa nibble at (food) *now Ags.*

smurl *of people or animals, esp if ill* eat little and slowly (without appetite), nibble half-heartedly or furtively.

snap gobble (**up**), eat hastily or with relish.

soss eat incongruous, sloppy or messy food; eat in an uncouth, slovenly way.

soup sup.

stap *v* gorge oneself with food *local Sh-Per. n* a surfeit *Sh Ork NE Kcb.*

stech stuff or cram (oneself, one's stomach etc) with food *now nEC Loth.*

stench, stanch *v* allay (hunger or thirst); satisfy (a person) with food, satiate *now NE Ags. n* a satisfying, *esp* of hunger *now NE.*

stent distend (the stomach with food).

stive steeve stuff, pack, cram, *esp* gorge with food *now Per.*

stow fill (the stomach) with food, feed (oneself or another) *now local Sh-Kcb.*

sup *v* take (liquid or soft food) into the mouth, *esp* with a spoon. *n, also* ~**pie** *freq with omission of* **of** etc a mouthful, an amount sufficient to satisfy one for the time being; a drink (of liquor): '*a sup tea*'. ~**pable** fit to be **supped,** palatable *now NE, EC, SW, S.*

swack a big mouthful, a deep draught of liquor *now Edb Rox.*

swage 1 take in and digest (food) *now Sh Cai.* **2** relax after a good meal, sit back and let it digest *Ork N.*

swallie *v* swallow (food etc). *n* an act of swallowing.

synd, syne wash (food) down with drink, swill (something) away or out with water etc *now C-S.*

tak, take: ~ **awa** eat or drink up, eat heartily, toss off (liquor) *now Sh Ork.*

tam a bite, a morsel of food.

taper use (food) sparingly, eke **out** *now Sh Ags.*

taste one's gab, hert *etc* cause a pleasant taste in one's mouth, stimulate the appetite *now local Ork-Rox.*

treat, trait *now Sh nEC* feast, regale (someone (**with** something)).

tume empty of food, fasting, hungry *now local Sh-Per.*

†**wame** fill oneself with food.

worry 1 choke (**on** a mouthful of food), suffocate *now local Sh-Per.* **2** devour, gobble **up** *now Abd Ags.*

wrang, wrong: ~ **one's pechan** *or* **stamack**

make oneself sick with eating too much of the wrong food.

10.5 MEALS

aff-pit a makeshift, *esp* a hasty meal *now Loth S.*

antrum a meal eaten in the afternoon or early evening.

†banket a banquet.

brak, break: brakins the remains of a meal *Abd.* **~fast, ~wast** *now Cai* breakfast.

brod a table spread for a meal *now Bnf Lnk.*

brose a meal of which **brose** was the chief ingredient *now Bnf Ags.* **brosing-time** *mining* a meal-time *now Fif.* **~-time** a meal-time *now NE.*

buird a table, *freq* one spread for a meal *now Bnf Abd.*

by-bit(e) a snack between meals *now Abd Lnk.*

chack a snack.

chat a snack; a morsel *NE.*

cheerie pyke a tasty morsel, a treat *Bnf Abd.*

chit a packed lunch *now Arg Kcb.*

chitterin bit *or* **bite, chattering-bite** *or* **~-piece** *local Abd-Kcb* a snack eaten after bathing.

clyack the harvest-home supper *NE.*

cookie shine a tea party.

cornin time meal-time *now Fif.*

cover the table lay the cloth on the table *now Bnf Abd.*

denner *n* dinner. *v* **1** dine, have dinner *now Bnf Abd.* **2** dine, supply with dinner *now Abd Fif.*

diet a meal, repast *now local Ork-Sllg.* **~-hour** meal-time *now local Cai-Fif,*

dine 1 dinner; dinnertime. **2** *also* common **~s** the communal university dinners in St Andrews University; the place where they are held.

†dirgie, dredgie a funeral feast, *esp* of drink.

†disjune breakfast.

doon-set(ting) a (grand) spread *now Ork Abd.*

†dorder-meat a snack between meals, *chf* one given to farmworkers between dinner and supper.

eat what is eaten, a meal or feast *Bnf Abd.*

†eftermes a second course, dessert.

efternuin a meal taken during the afternoon *now Sh.*

forenuin (bite, bread etc) a mid-morning snack or drink, elevenses *Abd Fif Rox.*

†fower, four: ~ hours a light meal or refreshment taken around 4 pm.

foy a farewell feast; a party to celebrate a marriage, special occasion etc *local.*

furthgoing the feast given at a bride's departure from her parents' home, a wedding entertainment.

hand, haun(d): ~-roun-tea *or* **supper** a tea o supper at which people are served individually and not seated at table. **put in** *or* **oot one's ~** help oneself at table.

handsel a piece of bread or other light snack given to farmworkers before beginning work *chf SW, S.*

†infare the feast given by the bridegroom to celebrate the coming of his bride to her new home.

†intermeis something served between courses at a banquet; an entertainment taking the place of this.

kail a main meal, dinner *now NE nEC Bwk.* **kail-bell** the dinner-bell; a call to dinner *now Ags Per.* **~ time** dinner-time *now local Ags-Lnk.*

kettle a riverside picnic, *esp* on the Tweed, at which newly-caught salmon are cooked and eaten on the spot *now Loth Bwk.*

†latter meat food left over from a meal and served again, *esp* that from the master's table later served to the servants.

lay-on a hearty meal *now Ags Loth Uls.*

lift serve (a dish at table) *N midLoth.*

made diet a cooked meal *Sh NE.*

meal, male: ~ o meat *chf SW, S* a meal.

meltith a meal.

†meridian a social mid-day drink, *esp* among business and professional men.

†merry meat a meal to celebrate the birth of a child.

†mess: at one's ~ at a meal, at (one's) table.

mornin(g): ~ piece *now Sh Ork Uls,* **† ~ drink** a drink or snack taken during the mid-morning break from work.

nacket, nocket a packed lunch, a snack *chf SW, S.*

†noneschankis an afternoon snack; a workmen's afternoon break.

pairt, part divide (food at table) into parts or portions, share *now NE.*

peel-an-eat a potato cooked in its skin; a meal made up of these *now local NE-S.*

†pertinence accompaniments to a main dish.

pick: ~in(g) a mouthful of food, a frugal meal. **~ an dab** a light meal, snack, *specif* of potatoes dipped in salt.

piece a piece of food, a snack; a packed lunch. **~ denner** *NE, EC, S,* **†noon(ing) piece** a lunchtime snack of sandwiches etc. **~ time** a break for a meal or snack during working or school hours. **play ~** a mid-morning snack at school.

schule ~ a child's mid-morning or lunchtime snack at school. **tea** ~ a mid-afternoon snack *Abd Fif.*

pike a bite of food, a light meal *Per.*

pit, put: ~**-by**, ~**-past** *Gen except Sh Ork* a snack, light meal. ~**-owre** a hasty or makeshift meal, a quick snack *now NE.*

pottage one's breakfast *now NE.*

pour, poor: ~ **(the) tea** pour out tea.

rim: ~ **fu** *now Wgt*, ~ **rax(in)** *Abd* a large meal.

say away say grace before a meal *now Ork Bnf Abd.*

Selkirk grace a rhymed grace before meals (wrongly ascribed to Burns).

server a person who hands round refreshments at a funeral *now SW.*

service the serving of refreshments, *specif* at a funeral or wedding *now nEC Lnk.*

set: †~ **by** provide with a makeshift meal. ~ **down** cause to sit down, *esp* at a table for a meal *now local Sh-C.* **set-down** *adj, of a meal* formally served at table *local NE-WC. n* a formal meal, a 'spread'. ~ **in** bring in (a meal), lay (a table for a meal) *now Sh Abd Ags.*

shivering *or* ~**y bite** a snack taken after bathing *now local C.*

shove-by, shove-ower a hastily-prepared or makeshift meal *local.*

shuit, shoot: ~**-aboot** a makeshift meal *Kcdn Ags.*

single *in fish-and-chip-shop usage* not served with chips, by itself *local: 'single fish', 'single pudding'.*

sit: ~ **in (to)**, ~ **to**, ~ **in about** *now NE-Per* draw one's chair in (to a table), take one's seat at a meal.

soup sup, have supper.

†**subcharge, subchet** a second dish or course.

supper, sipper *n* supper. *v* serve or suffice for the supper of *now Cai Abd.* **fish-**~ , **pudding-**~ *etc,* **fish-, (black-** or **white) pudding-**etc-and-**chips,** *esp* as bought from a fish-and-chip shop.

†**surcharge** an additional or second dish or course.

taffie join a social gathering of young people who club together to buy treacle to make toffee.

tatties and point a frugal meal of potatoes only (the non-existent meat etc being symbolically pointed at) *now local Sh-WC.*

tea, tae *chf Sh NE*, **high tea, meat** ~ *WC*, ~ **an till't** *C*, **tousie** ~ *local EC-Rox* a meal eaten in the early evening, *usu* consisting of one cooked course followed by bread, cakes etc and tea. ~**-skiddle**, ~**-skittle** *derog* a tea-party *now Stlg WC.*

thanks: give ~ say grace after (and *later* also before) a meal.

†**tuppeny tightener** *joc* a twopenny portion of fish and chips.

twal, twelve: ~ **hours** a midday snack or drink; a midday meal *now Sh Ork.*

†**unset** not seated at table.

wax cloth a *usu* canvas cloth coated with wax used *esp* for table coverings.

†**win tae** take a seat at table, begin eating.

Yule feast a Christmas dinner *now Sh.*

10.6 BREAD, OATCAKES ETC

ait, oat: ~ **cake** a thin flat crisp biscuit made of oatmeal. †~ **laif** a loaf of oatbread.

anchor-stock a large, long loaf of (*usu*) rye-bread.

auld, old *of bread* stale.

bannock, bonnock, bannie a round flat cake, *usu* of oat-, barley- or pease-meal, baked on a **girdle.**

bap a bread roll, varying locally in shape, size and texture.

batchie a baker; a baker's man.

†**baxter** a baker. **baxtarie, baxtrey** (the craft of) baking.

†**blanter** bread made from oats.

brander bannock a thick oatcake baked on a gridiron.

bran scone a scone made with added bran.

breid, bread 1 bread. **2** a loaf or roll of bread. **3** an oatcake *Cai Bnf Abd.* ~**-berry** small pieces of bread with hot milk poured over *local Abd-Ayr.*

brick a loaf of bread, *freq with an indication of its price or size: 'penny brick'.*

brown scone a scone made with wholemeal flour.

bun in Sc now *usu* less sweet than in StEng.

butter: ~**ie** a bread roll made of a high-fat, cro-issant-like dough *orig NE.* ~ **bannock** a ban-**nock** spread with butter *now Abd Fif Lnk.* ~ **bap** a scone made with butter *now Abd Fif.* ~ **an breid** bread and butter *now local Cai-Kcb.*

cake of bread an oatcake *Bnf.*

†**caper** a piece of bread or oatcake with butter and cheese.

carle: ~**s**, ~ **scones** *Ags* small cakes given to carol-singers.

cat's face a round of six scones *Kcdn nEC.*

clautie-scone a kind of oat bread or scone.

clod a (*usu* wheaten) loaf.

cookie a plain round glazed bun made from a yeast dough. **cream** ~ a **cookie** sliced and filled with whipped cream. **fruit** *etc* ~ a **cookie** with currants etc in.

crumpet, crimpet *Bnf Abd* 1 a crumpet. 2 a large thin **dropped scone**.

cutting loaf bread old enough to be easily cut *local*.

†**derril** a broken piece of bread etc.

drogget scone an oatmeal and potato scone *now Dmf*.

drop(ped) scone a small, round, flat cake, made by allowing thick batter to drop onto a **girdle**, frying pan etc, smaller and thicker than an English pancake and *usu* eaten cold with butter, jam etc, a **pancake**.

fadge 1 a flat round thick loaf or **bannock** formerly of barley meal *now Bwk S*. 2 a kind of **tattie-scone** *Uls*.

fardel a three-cornered cake, *esp* oatcake, *usu* the fourth part of a round *now NE Slg Edb*.

farl a **fardel**, *now also* of scones, rolls. *Gen except N*.

flannen broth milk sops, sweetened with treacle or sugar *Bnf Abd Ags*.

fole a small, soft, thick oatcake *chf Ork*.

foustie *Ags Per*, †**fustian scone** a kind of large thick bread roll, now white and floury but *orig* containing oatmeal, so-called from its coarse texture and *perh* also its colour.

French loaf a loaf made from dough containing a little fat and sugar and shaped so as to give a heart-shaped slice.

garibaldi a kind of bun or scone.

geordie: plain ~ the flat bottom crust of a loaf of bread *Ags Per*.

gnap-at-the-win thin oatcakes, light bread, insubstantial food *NE*.

†**gray breid** bread made of rye or oats.

haben *gipsy* bread *chf Rox*.

half loaf a loaf of **plain bread**, half the size of a standard quartern loaf, *formerly* weighing 2 pounds but successively reduced to 30 and 28 ounces.

hard: ~**ie** a kind of white bread roll with a hard surface *Ags*. ~ **breid** 1 a kind of thin oatcake, *esp* one only baked on one side and then toasted on the other side in front of a fire before eating *now Bnf Abd Uls*. 2 stale bread, *esp* that hardened in the oven, suitable for making into breadcrumbs *local Abd-Loth*.

heel each end of a loaf of bread, *esp* when cut off the loaf.

Hogmanay 1 a New Year's gift, *esp* a gift of oatcakes given to or asked for by children on New Year's Eve. 2 †an oatcake or biscuit baked to give to the children on 31 Dec.

hovie *of bread etc* puffy, well-risen.

Jenny Lind a kind of fancy loaf named after the singer *now local C-S*.

Jew's loaf *or* **roll** a small loaf rounded on top with a brownish glaze *SW*.

Kate: curly ~ the rounded top crust of a loaf of bread *Ags Per*.

laif, loaf 1 a loaf. 2 bread, *esp* wheat-flour bread. **loafie** a kind of currant bun *Kcdn Ags*. ~ **bread** wheat-flour bread (as opposed to oatcakes).

Lon(d)on bun a glazed bun with currants and orange peel, sprinkled with crystallized sugar.

luifie a kind of flat bread roll *Ags*.

†**mainschott** a roll or loaf of the finest wheaten flour.

†**masloch** bread made from mixed meal.

†**mill bannock** a large round oatmeal cake baked at a mill and given to mill-servants or poor people.

muilder crumbled fragments of oatcake *now Sh Uls*.

nacket, nocket a type of small fine loaf.

†**nibbit** an oatcake sandwich.

nickie an oatcake or bun with an indented edge *chf Fif*.

†**toon cake** a thick bun made from oatmeal and yeast, baked in the oven *chf Fif*.

owerday's breid *etc* bread which has been kept for more than one day *now Sh NE Bwk*.

†**paise** the weights and prices of different kinds of bread, periodically laid down by the magistrates of **burghs** etc; the official list or table of this.

pan: ~ **bread** bread baked in a pan or tin. ~ **cake,** ~ **scone** *chf Dmf* = **dropped scone**. ~ **loaf** a loaf with a hard smooth crust, baked in a pan or tin.

pease: peasy-bannock *now Loth*, ~ **bannock** a bannock made of ~-**meal**. † ~-**clod** a roll or loaf made of ~-**meal**. † ~-**scone** a scone made of **peasemeal**.

piece 1 a piece of food, a snack; a packed lunch. 2 a piece of bread etc spread with butter, jam etc; a sandwich: 'a jeelie piece'; 'a piece an treacle'; 'a cheese piece.'

plain: ~ **bread** bread baked as a ~ **loaf**. ~ **loaf** a flat-sided white loaf with a hard black crust on top and a floury brown crust at the bottom, a batch loaf, *formerly* commoner than the **pan loaf**.

potato scone = **tattie scone**.

†**quachet** the name of a kind of loaf of white bread.

quarten loaf a quartern loaf, a four-pound loaf *now S*.

quarter *n*, *also* **corter** the fourth part of a round of oatcakes *now NE*.

ream breid oatcakes made with cream *Abd*.

roun(d)about a circular roll made of coarse flour; a circular oatcake *now Bnf*.

row a roll. **rowie** a flaky bread roll made with a lot of butter *NE Ags.*

rumpie a small crusty loaf or roll *now Per WC.*

saft, soft ~**ie** *local Sh-Fif,* ~ **biscuit** *local Ork-Per* a kind of plain floury bun or roll with a dent in the middle.

sair, sore: ~ **hand** a large thick slice of bread with butter or jam (which looks like a bandaged hand) *C.*

sap a sop. **saps** pieces of bread etc soaked or boiled in milk etc, *freq* as food for children.

†**saut, salt:** ~**ie bannock** an oatmeal **bannock** with a fair amount of salt, baked on Shrove Tuesday.

scaddit scone a scone of barley- or wheat-meal mixed with hot milk or water *Bnf Lnk SW.*

scone 1 a large, *usu* round semi-sweet cake made of wheat flour, baked on a **girdle** etc, or in an oven, and cut into four three-sided pieces; one of these pieces; a similar small round individual-sized cake. **2** an oatcake *now Sh.*

screever a **dropped scone** cooked on a **girdle** *Pbls Lnk Ayr.*

Selkirk bannock *or* **bannie** a kind of rich fruit loaf, made as a speciality by Selkirk bakers.

shearer's bannock, scone *etc* a large bread roll etc eaten on the harvest field *local Ags-Bwk.*

skair scone a kind of oatmeal-and-flour **scone** made with beaten egg and milk.

skinny a bread roll, *esp* a breakfast roll *Dmf Rox.*

slab the first slice cut off a loaf, with one side crusty *local EC Lnk.*

slinger a dish consisting of bread sops boiled in milk *Bnf Abd.*

sma(ll) breid = **tea bread.**

snap and rattle toasted oatcakes crumbled in milk *NE.*

sod a kind of bread, a roll made of coarse flour.

sole the lower crust of a loaf of bread *now Cai-Ayr.* ~ **shaif** the end slice of a loaf, the **heel** *local Cai-Ayr.*

†**souple scones** thin, pliable scones, *usu* of barley-meal.

†**sour cake** a kind of oatcake baked with sour leaven for festivals, *eg* in Rutherglen for St Luke's Fair.

sour poos, sour scone a coarse, sour-flavoured kind of oat bread or scone baked at Christmas-time.

†**souter's clod** a small coarse loaf.

steepies bread sops as food for children, pets etc *NE-Fif.*

sugar piece a slice of bread buttered and sprinkled with sugar *now N Per Kcb.*

sweetie: ~ **bun** *now Sh,* ~ **loaf,** ~ **scone** a bun baked with sweeties or with raisins.

tae, to: ~**bread** an extra loaf etc given free as a discount after the purchase of a certain amount *now Stlg Ayr Rox.*

tammie a loaf of coarse brown bread.

tattie: ~**bannock** *now Sh Ork Cai,* ~**scone** a (flat) scone made of flour, milk and mashed potato.

tea, tae: ~**bread** buns, scones etc, eaten with tea.

†**thirdie** a loaf of coarse or inferior flour, with a large admixture of bran *Kcdn Ags.*

thoum, thumb: ~**piece** a slice of bread etc with butter spread on with the thumb *Ork NE-S.*

†**thraf caik** a cake of unleavened bread.

tod(die) a round cake, scone etc *now S.*

traicle, treacle: ~**scone** a scone made with treacle.

wastel a kind of bread, scone or cake baked with the finest flour; a large scone made of oatmeal and wholemeal flour *now Mry.*

white breid white wheat bread etc as opposed to oat or barley cakes.

wig a kind of small oblong currant bun.

†**Yule:** ~ **bannocks** oatcakes specially baked on Christmas Eve both for one's own family and for children going from door to door. ~ **bread** a richly-seasoned oat-bread baked for Christmas.

10.7 CAKES, PASTRY AND BISCUITS

bake a (*usu* thick or soft) biscuit.

†**birsket, briscat** biscuit, *freq* ~ **breid.**

black bun a very rich spiced fruit cake, baked in a pastry crust and eaten at **Hogmanay.**

bride: ~**scake** wedding cake, *orig* a homemade one which was broken over the head of the bride. † ~**'s pie** a pie made by the bride's friends and distributed among the company at a wedding.

bun 1 in Sc now *usu* less sweet than in StEng. **2** = **black bun.**

butterie a butter biscuit.

cake *specif* cake, fruit loaf etc given to children or callers at New Year *now Fif.*

†**carecake** a kind of small cake eaten on Shrove Tuesday.

chate-the-belly *etc* an insubstantial kind of food, *eg* puff pastry *now Bnf Fif.*

currant bun = **black bun.**

dander a kind of sweet bun or biscuit, a rock-cake *local C.*

†**diet:** ~**cake,** ~**loaf** a kind of sponge cake.

†**dreaming bread** wedding or christening cake, so-called because the recipients slept with a piece under their pillow.

Dundee cake a rich fruit cake with almonds on top.

fardel a three-cornered piece of **shortbread**, the fourth part of a round.

flam name for various kinds of fruit tart or cake.

†**fouat** some kind of cake, *latterly* one similar to a **black bun**.

French cake a kind of small fancy sponge cake, iced and decorated.

gibbery *local N*, **gingebreid** gingerbread.

halie dabbies a kind of shortbread, *esp* that used formerly in place of bread at Communion *chf SW*.

hardie 1 a hard sort of butter biscuit *Abd.* **2** a variety of butter biscuit baked in Cupar and popular as ship's biscuits *Fif.*

heater a wedge-shaped glazed sugared bun *NE.*

heckle(d) biscuit a type of hard biscuit made in Ags with a pinhole surface *Kcdn Ags.*

Pairiser, Pa(i)ris bun a sweet, sugar-topped, sponge-like bun.

pan-jotrals a type of cake made from scraps of other cakes or the scrapings of the baker's board with the addition of fruit *now Mry Bnf Slk.*

parkin, perkin a hard, round, ginger-flavoured biscuit made of oatmeal, flour and treacle, with an almond in the centre.

parlie a crisp, rectangular, ginger biscuit.

†**patisserie** pastries.

penny thing a fancy cake or biscuit, *orig* costing a penny *Ags Loth WC.*

petticoat tails triangular shortbread biscuits cut from a round, with the outer edge scalloped.

Pitcaithly bannock a round flat cake of thick shortbread containing chopped almonds and citron peel.

†**plack pie** a pie costing a **plack.**

porter biscuit a large round flattish bun resembling a roll in texture *C.*

puggy bun a bun consisting of a treacle sponge mixture in a pastry case *Per Fif.*

raggie biscuit a locally-made biscuit with an uneven edge *Per Fif.*

sair, sore: ~ **heid(ie)** a small plain sponge cake with a paper band round the lower part of it *NE-Fif.*

Scotch bun = **black bun.**

shortbread, shortie *local* a kind of biscuit made of a short dough of flour, butter and sugar.

†**singin cake** a sweet biscuit given to children on **Hogmanay** in return for a song etc *Fif.*

snap a ginger snap.

snashters *contemptuous* sweeties, cakes, pastries etc; trashy food *now local Per-WC.*

snysters sweeties, cakes, dainties *now WC.*

St Michael's cake *etc* a kind of cake baked in the Hebrides, *esp* in the Roman Catholic areas, on Michaelmas Eve, the **struan.**

struan a cake made from the various cereals grown on a farm, *usu* oats, barley, and rye, and baked with a special ritual on Michaelmas Eve (29 Sep) *Hebrides.*

†**sugar biscuit** a kind of thin crisp sponge biscuit, baked with sugar on top.

sweet-bread fancy cakes, pastries *now Sh Ork.*

tairt a tart.

tod(die) a round cake, scone etc *now S.*

wastel a kind of bread, scone or cake baked with the finest flour; a large scone made of oatmeal and wholemeal flour *now Mry.*

10.8 GRAINS

See also oats.

†**aigars, aigar-meal** meal from well-dried grain, ground in a hand-mill and *usu* mixed with pease-meal.

bere, bear bear, barley; *specif* four- or six-row barley, hardier and coarser than ordinary two-row barley. † ~**-seed** the seed of the barley; barley for sowing.

flour wheaten flour.

†**graddan** parch (grain) in the ear.

hash grain dried in a kiln and then chopped *local Cai-Kcb.*

mashlum mixed grains or grains and pulses grown and ground together *now local NE-Kcb.*

†**masloch** mixed grain.

meal, male meal *specif* oatmeal as distinct from other kinds, which have defining terms. ~**'s corn** grain in general *chf Sh Ork.*

milk broth a dish made from barley and milk *N.*

†**orgement** barley with its outer husk removed; barley soup or porridge.

†**pairin-meal, -flour** a coarse meal or flour made from the husks of the grain.

pease, pizz pease. **peasie** made of or like ~**meal.** ~**-brose,** ~ **pistils** a dish made of ~**meal** and boiling water stirred to a paste. † ~**kill** a quantity of peas roasted as in (*orig* in) a kiln. ~**-meal** a flour made of ground pease.

pile a grain (of corn etc) *now Dnbtn Kcb.*

pot, pat: ~ **barley** barley from which the outer husk has been removed in milling, used for making **broth** *etc*.

†**Saltoun barley** fanner-dressed pot barley.

†**simmer meill** meal for use until harvest.

smeddum a fine powder, *specif* a finely ground meal or malt.

thirds the residue of grain left after milling or brewing, third quality flour *now NE-S*.

10.9 OATS

ait, oat: ~**s** oats. **aiten** oaten.

Athole brose honey or meal mixed with whisky. *chf Highl*.

†**blanter** food made from oats, *eg* bread, porridge.

blaw *(tinkers')* cant oatmeal *now NE*.

blenshaw a drink made of oatmeal, sugar, milk, water, and nutmeg.

brat the thick(er) surface on a liquid etc, *eg* curdled cream on milk, skin on porridge.

brochan thick or thin gruel (with butter, honey etc); *sometimes (esp Arg Uls)* porridge.

brose a dish of oat- or pease-meal mixed with boiling water or milk, with salt and butter etc added.

brose-meal parched pease-meal for making **brose** *now Bnf*.

buttermilk-an-meal a bowl of buttermilk with oatmeal on top *Bnf Ags*.

cauld steer(ie) oatmeal stirred in cold water (or sour milk), cold **brose** *now N-Per*.

crackins a dish of fried oatmeal *now NE*.

crannachan, cream crowdie a dessert of soft fruit, whipped cream, toasted oatmeal etc.

creeshie mealie oatmeal fried in fat *Ags*.

crowdie, † ~-**mowdie** oatmeal and water mixed and eaten raw.

deochray a kind of **sowans** *chf Cai*.

drammlicks the small pieces of oatmeal dough which stick to the basin when making oatcakes *now Abd*.

drammock a mixture of raw oatmeal and cold water *local Abd-Kcb*.

fat brose: brose made with hot stock or fat instead of boiling water.

foorach buttermilk, whipped cream or whey with oatmeal stirred in *Bnf Abd*.

froh milk a mixture of cream and whey beaten up and sprinkled with oatmeal *NE Ags*.

girsle a fragment of crisp or caked porridge etc.

†**graddan** a coarse oatmeal made from parched grain ground by hand.

grits oat kernels, grain.

gruel 1 gruel; porridge. **2** food made of oatmeal; food *in gen, now Sh Ork*.

grunds, grounds a kind of **sowans**.

haggis the traditional Scottish dish of sheep's offal, oatmeal etc. ~ **bag** the sheep's stomach in which a haggis is cooked.

hasty brose a kind of quickly-made **brose** *NE*.

haver-meal oatmeal *now Dmf*.

hodgel a dumpling, *usu* one made of oatmeal, fat and seasoning *S*.

†**jadden** the stomach of a sow; a **pudding** made therein, a haggis *Fif*.

jaudie 1 the stomach of a pig or sheep, used in making haggis etc *now Fif Kinr*. **2** an oatmeal **pudding** made therein; a haggis *now Fif*.

jerker, *also* **mealie** ~ a white oatmeal **pudding** *Bnf Abd Ags*.

jimmie, *freq* **mealie** ~ a white **pudding**, an oatmeal **pudding** *local NE-Kcb*.

Jock an oatmeal **pudding**, a haggis *Fif*.

kail brose: brose made with the liquid from boiled kail *now N Per Ayr*.

kill, kiln: *joc* ~ **cast** the quantity of oats taken to the mill at one time to be ground into meal, for household use, *usu* enough to produce four **bolls** *now Wgt*.

leaven a mixture of oatmeal and water made up as a dough for oatcakes or as food for young poultry *Sh N Fif*.

lithocks a kind of gruel made from fine oatmeal and *freq* buttermilk *now Stlg wLoth WC*.

meal, male oatmeal as distinct from other kinds, which have defining terms. † ~**ie bag,** ~**ie poke** a beggar's bag for holding alms given in oatmeal. ~-**creeshie, meal-a-crushie** oatmeal fried in fat *WC Wgt Uls*. ~**ie drink** a drink of water into which oatmeal has been sprinkled *Ork Abd Per*. ~**ie dumpling** a round **pudding** of oatmeal and fat with seasoning, boiled or steamed. ~**ie pudding** a sausage-shaped version of this, a white **pudding**. ~ **ark** a chest for storing oatmeal *now C Uls*. ~ **bowie** a barrel for storing oatmeal *NE*. † ~ **kail,** ~ **an kail** *NE* **broth** made with oatmeal and kail. ~ **pock** a bag for holding oatmeal *now Sh-Ags Gall*. ~ **seed** the husk of a grain of oats, used for making sowans *Sh-Fif*. ~ **an ale** the traditional dish (also containing whisky) at harvest-home celebrations; the celebration itself *NE-Per*. ~ **an bree: brose** *now Uls*. † ~ **an thrammel** meal stirred up with water or ale, taken as a snack *NE*.

milk: ~ **brose** oatmeal mixed with boiling milk *local Sh-Dmf.* ~ **porridge** porridge boiled in milk. ~ **and breid** oatcakes crumbled in milk.

muilder crumbled fragments of oatcake *now Sh Uls.*

neep brose: brose made with the liquid in which turnips have been boiled *chf NE Uls.*

nettle brose: brose made with the juice of boiled young nettle-tops *NE.*

pairin-meal, pairin-flour a coarse meal or flour made from the husks of the grain.

†**pap-in** a drink made of light ale and oatmeal with a small quantity of whisky or brandy.

parritch, porridge, poshie *child's word n, formerly freq treated as a pl* porridge, the dish of oatmeal (or rolled oats) boiled in salted water.

pan haggis oatmeal, sometimes mixed with scraps of meat etc, and fried in fat, **skirlie** *Ayr Kcb Rox.*

pot, pat: ~ **brose** a kind of quickly-boiled porridge *NE.*

pottage *formerly freq treated as a pl* oatmeal porridge *now NE.* **milk** ~ porridge made with milk instead of water *now NE.*

pron the residue of oat husks and oatmeal remaining from the milling process, bran, **seeds** *local N.*

†**purry** a savoury dish consisting of oatmeal **brose** with chopped kail stirred into it.

raw sowens *now Sh Ork NE,* **rawsins** *now NE* uncooked **sowans.**

roun(d) meal coarsely-ground oatmeal *now Bnf Abd.*

rummle, rumble: ~(de)**thump** = **skirlie** *now Ags.*

seed, sid *Sh-N Per:* ~**s** particles of (oat-)bran, *freq* used to make **sowans** *now local Sh-Gall.* ~**ie** full of oat husks.

skink a kind of thin, oatmeal-and-water gruel.

skirlie, skirl-in-the-pan *now Cai Ags Per* a dish of oatmeal and onions fried in a pan.

snap and rattle toasted oatcakes crumbled in milk *NE.*

sowans a dish made from oat husks and fine meal steeped in water for about a week; after straining, the liquor was again left to ferment and separate, the solid matter at the bottom being the **sowans,** the liquor **swats,** *usu* eaten like porridge, boiled with water and salt. **sowan seeds** the rough husks of oats used in making **sowans** *now Cai NE.* **sowan-swats** the liquid poured off **sowans** *now Sh Ork Cai.* **drinking** ~ *now NE,* **knotting** ~ *NE* the liquor left after straining **sowans** but before fermenting, *usu* thickened a little by heating.

sowce a (messy) mixture of food, *specif* some oatmeal dish such as porridge *now Cai.*

stourie *now Ork,* **stoorack** *N,* **stoorin** *NE Ags,* ~ **ie drink** *now Ags Per* a kind of liquid fine-oatmeal gruel.

suppin sowans: sowans thick enough to eat with a spoon *Ork NE.*

swats the liquor resulting from the steeping of oatmeal husks in the making of **sowans** *Sh Ork N.*

tam o' tae end a kind of large haggis *SW.*

tartan purry a dish of boiled oatmeal mixed with chopped red cabbage or boiled with cabbage water.

wangrace a kind of thin gruel sweetened with fresh butter and honey etc, and given to invalids.

water broo *now Fif Loth,* **water brose** *now N* oatmeal mixed with boiling water.

whey, fey *N:* **fy brose** *now NE,* **whey brose** *now Ork Abd* **brose** made with whey instead of water. **whey parritch** porridge made thus.

white: † ~ **hause** an oatmeal **pudding** cooked in a sheep's gullet. ~ **meal** oatmeal as distinct from barley meal *now Cai Fif Ayr.* ~ **puddin(g)** a kind of **pudding** or sausage stuffed with oatmeal, suet, salt, pepper and onions.

Yule sowans: sowans specially made for Christmas into which the usual objects of divination of marriage (*eg* a ring, button etc) were stirred before distribution among the company.

10.10 SOUPS

barefit broth *or* **kail: broth** made with a little butter but no meat *NE.*

braxy bree soup made from **braxy** *Bnf Arg.*

bree soup.

†**brewis, browis** stock made from meat and vegetables.

broth *freq treated as pl* in Scotland *usu* a thick soup made from mutton, barley and vegetables, Scotch broth.

cockieleekie, cock-a-leekie chicken and leek soup.

Cullen skink a smoked-fish soup.

†**friar's chicken** a soup made with veal, chicken and beaten eggs.

green kail a non-curly variety of kail; a soup made from this.

hen-broth chicken **broth.**

†**hodge-podge** a thick **broth** made with plenty of vegetables.

jabble a liquid and its sediment stirred up together, *esp* a weak mixture as of tea or soup.

kail, *also* **pan kail: broth** or soup 1 in which cabbage etc is a principal ingredient; made with vegetables with or without the addition of meat, *freq* prefixed by the name of the principal ingredient, *eg* **nettle ~ , pea ~** .

†**lent(r)en kail** soup made with vegetables only, without meat-stock; cabbage boiled in water and then served in milk.

†**meal, male: ~ kail: broth** made with oatmeal and kail.

milk: ~ broth. a dish made with barley and milk *N*. **~ meat: broth** made with skimmed milk *now NE*. **~ soup** soup made with milk.

muslin kail a thin soup made from barley and vegetables without any meat stock.

nettle broth *now Kcb Uls*, †**nettle kail** broth made from nettle-tops.

†**orgement** barley soup or porridge.

partan bree crab soup.

pea, pey: ~ -bree the liquid in which peas have been boiled, pea-soup *Ags Loth WC*.

powsowdie, sheep('s)-heid broth: broth or thick soup made from a sheep's head.

†**raisin kail: broth** with raisins added, a traditional dish at weddings.

scadlips: broth with a small amount of barley (and thus more likely to burn the mouth).

skink a soup, *esp* one made from the **skink** (but *cf* **cullen skink**) *now Sh NE Ags*.

soup tatties potato soup *now NE*.

tattie: ~ -broth *now Ork Ags*, **~ -claw** *now Bwk Rox*, **~ -soup** potato soup.

water kail: broth made without meat.

yaval broth second day's broth *NE*.

10.11 MEAT

For names of animals and poultry see 2.

backsey name for various parts of the loin of beef etc *local*.

beef 1 †an ox or cow intended for slaughter. 2 any butcher's meat.

bisket *now Bnf,* †**birsket** brisket.

black pudding a savoury type of sausage made of oatmeal or flour, suet, seasoning and blood, *usu* of a pig.

†**blaw, blow** inflate, cause (meat) to swell to improve its appearance.

blude, blood: ~y puddin, † **~ puddin** = **black puddin.**

†**bowbreid** *n* a portion of the shoulder of a carcass. *v* 1 remove the **bowbreid** from. 2 **bowbraid** prick or pierce (an animal), *chf* in the flanks before slaughter, to tenderize the meat.

bran brawn (as food). †**brawn** a boar for the table.

braxy the salted flesh of a sheep that has died of **braxy** *local Bnf-Lnk*. **~ ham** the ham of a **braxy** sheep *now Bnf Lnk*.

bree gravy.

breeds the innards of an animal, *usu* as food, *chf* the pancreas, *esp* of a sheep *now Abd*.

bridie, *also* **Forfar bridie** a kind of pie made of a circle of pastry folded over, with a filling of meat, *orig* made in Forfar.

butch butcher, slaughter (an animal) for meat *now Bnf*. **~-hoose** a slaughterhouse *now Abd Fif*.

butcher meat butcher's meat.

caddel beaten eggs, *specif* when scrambled *Sh NE*.

caibie a hen's crop or gizzard *Cai Abd*.

†**cheats** sweetbreads.

chuck *local Bnf-Fif,* **chuckie, chookie** *C* a chick, chicken.

chucken a chicken *chf NE*.

closhach the carcass of a fowl *NE*.

clyre 'a gland in meat'; 'an unsound spot in the internal fat of *eg* cattle' *now Cai Kcb*.

cock's eggs the small yolkless eggs laid by a hen about to stop laying *now Bnf Abd Fif*.

collop a slice of meat.

craig the neck of an animal, *esp* as part of a carcass.

doup the bottom of an eggshell *now Cai Bnf Abd Fif*.

drappit egg an egg poached in gravy made from the liver of a fowl *now Abd*.

draucht the entrails of an animal *now Mry Ags Kcb*.

emmledeug butcher's offal, scraps.

emmlins scraps; entrails, giblets *Abd*.

faa the entrails of a slaughtered animal, used for sausages etc *chf Sh Ork*.

fell slaughter.

flake a side of bacon *midLoth Bwk S*.

†**flay belly flaught** skin (a rabbit etc) by pulling the skin over the head.

flesh butcher's meat *now local Sh-SW*. † **~es** carcasses. **~er** a butcher. **~ing** the trade of a butcher. † **~ crook** a meat hook. † **~ fatt** a beef-barrel. † **~ meat** butcher's meat. † **~ stock** a butcher's block.

foresye a cut of beef from the shoulder, varying

regionally, but roughly corresponding to the Eng forerib and middle rib.

†**furch** the hindquarters of a deer.

gamrel a piece of wood used to separate the legs of a carcass to facilitate butchering *SW, S*.

gigot a leg of mutton or lamb.

girse beef beef from grass-fed cattle.

girsle gristle.

glut slime on decomposing meat *now Sh Bwk*.

goggie an egg *Arg Lnk*.

goniel: braxy mutton *Dmf Rox*.

guga the young of the gannet used as food *Hebrides*.

†**haggersnash** offal, scraps of meat *Ayr*.

haggis the traditional Scottish dish of sheep's offal, oatmeal etc *now chf Sc*. ~ **bag** the sheep's stomach in which a haggis is cooked *now Rox*.

hainch, hinch, ~**le** the haunch.

hangrell a pole knotched at both ends on which' a carcass is hung in a butcher's shop *now Wgt*.

harigals the viscera of an animal, entrails of a fowl, the pluck.

hashie hash, a mixture of chopped meat etc *now Ags midLoth*.

hen *freq corresponding to Eng* chicken as eg ~-**broth,** ~-**hertit.**

heukbone *now local Per-Rox,* **hookbone** the hip bone; a cut of beef from that part of the animal, corresponding to Eng rump.

hoch, hough a hind-leg joint of meat, the shin.

howtowdie a large (young) chicken for the pot, a young hen which has not begun to lay.

†**hutheron** a young heifer; the skin or meat of one. ~ **veal** ? pasture-fed veal as distinct from milk fed veal.

inmeat the viscera of an animal, *esp* the edible parts *now Rox*.

†**jadden** the stomach of a sow; a **pudding** made therein, a haggis *Fif*.

jaudie 1 the stomach of a pig or sheep, used in making haggis etc *now Fif Kinr*. 2 an oatmeal **pudding** made therein; a haggis *now Fif*.

jeel *of stock etc* set, congeal.

jerker, *also* **mealie** ~ a white oatmeal **pudding** *local NE-Kcb*.

jimmie, *freq* **mealie** ~ a white **pudding,** an oatmeal **pudding** *local NE-Kcb*.

jint *n, v* a joint.

Jock an oatmeal pudding; a haggis *Fif*.

keeslip the stomach of an animal used as a source of rennet *chf Slk*.

kirnels animal glands used as food, lamb's fry, lamb's testicles *now Gall*.

knap a shin of beef.

†**lai(r)dner mart** *chf SW,* **lai(r)dner cow** *Gall* a

fattened ox or cow killed and salted for winter provisions.

links a string of sausages or **black puddings**.

lire *in a carcass of beef* the slice of meat near the sternum, the upper portion of brisket *now Cai Edb*.

maiden's hair the coarse sinews in certain cuts of beef when boiled *now local N*.

mart any animal, (*esp* a sheep) or bird which is to be salted or dried for winter meat.

meal, male: ~**ie dumpling** a round **pudding** of oatmeal and fat with seasoning, boiled or steamed. ~**ie pudding** a sausage-shaped version of this, a white **pudding**.

†**mete scheip** *etc* a sheep etc intended to be slaughtered for food, not grown for wool.

mergh *now Sh,* **mergie** *Sh Ork* marrow (of bones).

†**middrits** the heart and skirt of a bullock.

minch, mince mince, minced meat. ~**e(d) collops** minced steak cooked with oatmeal, onion, carrot etc. † ~**ed pie** a pie of finely-chopped meat. *NE*.

moniefauld *now Ags,* **moniplies** the third stomach of a ruminant.

†**mouse (end)** the lump of flesh or tissue at the end of a leg of mutton.

nine holes the cut of beef below the breast *now local Ags-S*.

nowt('s) feet calves' feet, cow-heels as a dish.

oon-egg a wind-egg, an egg laid without a shell *now Per*.

pace egg an Easter egg *now Sh-NRox*.

pan: ~ **haggis** oatmeal, sometimes mixed with scraps of meat etc, and fried in fat, **skirlie** *Ayr Kcb Rox*. ~-**jotral(s)** a dish made from the offal of slaughtered animals *now Mry Bnf Slk*.

plowt *joc* a dish made of meat boiled and jellied in a mould, *esp* **potted heid** *Fif*.

pope's eye a cut of beef from the hip of the animal, corresponding to Eng rump.

potted heid *or* **hoch** a dish made of meat from the head or shin of a cow or pig, boiled, cold, and served in a jelly made from the stock.

poullie a young hen, *esp* one for the table, a chicken, pullet *now Uls*.

puddin(g) a kind of sausage made from the stomach or entrails of a sheep, pig etc stuffed with various mixtures of oatmeal, onions, suet, seasoning, blood etc, and boiled and stored for future use. ~ **bree** the water in which a pudding has been boiled *Ork Abd Per Kcb*.

†**puir, poor:** ~ **man** a dish made from the remains of a shoulder-bone of mutton.

purk pork *Sh NE Ags*.

quern the stomach of a fowl, the gizzard *now NE.*

roast a part of an animal, prepared or intended for roasting.

roddikin tripe *now local sEC, S.*

roun(d)(-steak) a cut of meat, *esp* beef, taken from the hindquarter; *cf* Eng *rump.*

ruch, rough *of a bone* having meat on it *now Per Stlg Ayr.*

rump in Scotland, a cut of beef corresponding to Eng *topside + silverside*, now *usu* called **round-steak**.

runt an ox or cow for fattening and slaughter, a store animal, *freq* a Highland cow or ox; an old cow (past breeding and fattened for slaughter) *now local Cai-SW.*

Sandie (Campbell) *joc, freq taboo* pork or bacon *now local Cai-Lnk.*

sassenger *now rather joc now Ork Cai WC*, **sasser** a sausage.

saster a kind of sausage with a haggis stuffing.

Scots collops thin slices of meat stewed with stock and flavouring.

sey, say a cut of beef from the shoulder to the loin, corresponding to Eng shoulder steak and sirloin.

shank a leg of meat.

sheep('s) heid a sheep's head, eaten as a main course (*also* one used to make **broth**).

shooglie jock brawn in jelly *now Stlg wLoth Lnk.*

shouder, shoulder: ~ lire a cut of beef from the upper foreleg.

shuet suet *now NE local C.*

skemmels a slaughter-house; a meat or fish market.

skink a shin, knuckle, **hough** of beef *now Sh N Per.*

slauchter slaughter.

slingers sausages *Inv-WC.*

†**slot** make one or more slits or scores on (the carcass of a slaughtered animal).

†**sneyster** a piece of grilled meat, a roasted joint; a pork sausage for grilling.

spaul(d) a joint, a shoulder or leg (of mutton, beef etc); the wing or leg of a fowl; a shoulder cut of beef, shoulder steak *now Bnf Abd.* **spale-bone** a cut of beef from the shoulder, blade-bone steak *local.*

†**stock** a butcher's or fishmonger's cutting block or table.

stottin bits scraps of meat used by butchers as make-weights etc *now Ags.*

tailyie a cut or slice of meat for boiling or roasting, *now esp* of pork *now Bwk Rox.*

tam: ~ o' tae end a kind of large haggis; *now* the skin in which a haggis is stuffed *SW.* **trimmlin ~ = potted head** *now Ags Per Lnk.*

tattie pie shepherd's pie *Gen except Sh.*

thocht-bane a wishbone *NE.*

traik the flesh of sheep which have died of exhaustion or disease.

ushaws, †**ushes** the entrails of a slaughtered animals.

veal a calf for slaughter *now Ork.*

wame tripe etc used as food.

†**wedder bouk** the carcass of a wether. **wether gammond** a leg of mutton.

white: † **~ hause** an oatmeal **pudding** cooked in a sheep's gullet. **~ meat** the flesh of poultry or game. **~ puddin** a kind of **pudding** or sausage stuffed with oatmeal, suet, salt, pepper and onions.

womle brees a dish of the same ingredients as haggis but of a liquid consistency *Abd Kcdn.*

yowk a yolk.

Yule mart an ox slaughtered and salted for Christmas and the winter.

10.12 FISH

For names of fish see 3.1.

bervie a kind of split dried haddock.

†**cabbiclaw** a dish of salt cod.

cabelew a young cod; salt cod or pike; a dish of this *local Sh-Per.*

Crail capon a type of dried or smoked haddock *Fif.*

crappit heids stuffed haddocks' heads *now local Bnf-Stlg.*

Cullen skink a smoked-fish soup.

dirken a fir-cone (used in smoking fish) *local Ross-Kcdn.*

Dunbar weather a salted herring.

Finnan: ~ haddock, ~ haddie *etc* a haddock cured with the smoke of green wood, peat or turf.

fresh pack (herring) in ice ungutted, for consumption as fresh *local.*

fry a small number of fish for frying, *chf* when presented as a gift *now local Sh-SW.*

full *adj, of herrings* full of milt or roe, sexually mature *Sh Ork N EC.* *n* a herring full of milt or roe *E.*

Glasgow bailie *Fif Gsw SW*, **Glasgow magistrate** *now Fif Gsw* a salt herring of fine quality; *occas* a red herring.

green *of fish, esp* herring fresh, unsalted *now Sh Dmf.*

hairy tatties a dish made of mashed potatoes and flaked dried salt fish *NE*.

hard fish *etc* dried or salt fish *now local Sh-NE*.

ligger a newly-spawned salmon, a foul fish *chf SW*.

lowpin an levin fresh, newly caught *chf EC*.

lucken a half-split haddock for drying or smoking *NE*.

magistrate a red herring *now Rox*.

†meat-fisch freshly-caught fish, as opposed to barrelled or salted fish *chf N*.

mud fish a codfish preserved by being salted wet in bulk in the hold of a fishing vessel *Sh-N*.

†mussel brose: brose made from mussel-**bree** mixed with oatmeal.

oo: caller ~ fresh oysters *Edb*.

†pandoor (oyster) a large succulent type of oyster found in the Forth, *esp* around Prestonpans.

partan the common edible crab. ~ **pie** a dish of seasoned crab meat cooked and served in the shell. ~ **bree** crab soup.

†peel untreated (as by drying) and bulk packed.

†pellock the flesh of the porpoise.

pine shrink by drying in the open air *now Sh*.

pin-the-widdie a small haddock, unsplit, which is hung in the smoke of the chimney to cure.

piper an unsplit, half-dried haddock *NE*.

rawn the roe of a fish *now E Kcb*.

rizzered *specif of haddock* sun-dried *now local EC*.

saumon, salmon(d): ~ **rawn** salmon roe *now Kcb*.

scag *adj*, †*of fish* become rotten by exposure to sun or air. *n* a putrid fish.

skate: ~ **bree** the water in which skate has been boiled, skate soup, said to have aphrodisiac and other properties *now Wgt*. ~ **purse** the ovarium of a skate *local*. ~ **rumple** the part of the backbone of a skate above the root of the tail.

smokie, Arbroath smokie an unsplit smoked haddock.

spelding *now Sh N*, **speldrin** *now Fif Bwk* a split and dried (or smoked) fish, *esp* a haddock or whiting.

spent *adj*, *of a fish, esp a herring* spawned, in poor condition after spawning. *n, also* **spyntie** *NE* a **spent** fish.

stap: ~**pit haddie** a stuffed haddock *Cai Bnf Abd*. ~**pit heidies** stuffed fish heads *now Cai Bnf Abd*.

†stock a butcher's or fishmonger's cutting block or table.

target a long thin strip of dried skate *now Sh*.

torn bellie herring which has been split or broken by careless handling *now Sh N Fif*.

twa-eyed (beef)steak *joc* a herring or kipper *now Cai Bnf Per*.

white herring herring which is cured by salting only.

yella, yellow: ~ **fish** *now local Ork-Dmf*, ~ **haddie** *or* **haddock** *NE, EC* smoked (*now also* dyed) fish, *esp* haddock.

10.13 DAIRY PRODUCTS

For dairying see 7.9.2.

†beardie, bairdie *of cheese* mouldy, hair-moulded *Loth SW*.

beest *now Cai*, ~**in** *now Abd*, **beesenin** *now Kcb*, ~**y** the first milk of a cow after calving.

blansht *Bnf Abd*, **blenched** *now Bnf* of (skimmed) milk slightly sour.

blased *of milk* slightly soured *now Bnf Ags*.

bledoch, †bladdoch buttermilk.

boyne a broad shallow container in which to skim milk.

brak, break *of milk* curdle, coagulate, either by its becoming sour or in the process of churning *now Sh NE Kcb*. **broken** *of milk* curdled, *esp* of cream in the churn *now local Cai-Kcb*.

brat the thick(er) surface on a liquid etc, *eg* curdled cream on milk, skin on porridge.

buttermilk-an-meal a bowl of buttermilk with oatmeal on top *Bnf Ags*.

buttered made with butter as an ingredient *now Abd*: 'buttered bannocks'.

buttermilk-an-meal a bowl of buttermilk with oatmeal on top *Bnf Ags*.

caufie's cheese a soft cheese or curd made with the milk of a newly-calved cow *Abd Per*.

cauld steer(ie) sour milk or water and oatmeal stirred together *now Abd Ags*.

crap the substance which rises to the top of boiled whey *SW*.

crowdie a kind of soft cheese.

cruds 1 curds. **2** *also* ~ **butter** = **crowdie** *now Bnf Abd*.

crying cheese a cheese specially made at a birth *NE*.

cuppil a measure of butter and cheese sold together *local WC*.

Dunlop cheese a kind of **sweet-milk cheese** *orig* made in west-central Scotland.

†fell *of cheese* strong-tasting, pungent.

fey whey *N*.

fleeting(s) the thick curds formed on the top of boiling whey *Abd*.

float whey a dish made by boiling whey, often with meal and milk, to form a soft floating curd.

foorach buttermilk, whipped cream or whey with oatmeal stirred in *Bnf Abd.*

forebroads the first milk from a cow after calving *Ayr.*

freet milk produce; butter, cheese *Cai.*

froh milk a mixture of cream and whey beaten up and sprinkled with oatmeal *NE Ags.*

†**gait whey** the whey of goat's milk used as a health drink.

glaiks a lever or shaft attached to the churn-staff to facilitate churning *chf Uls.*

goudie Gouda (cheese).

green *of milk* new, fresh *now local Abd-S.*

gurth crushed curd for cheese-making *local WC.*

hangman *Abd,* **hung cheese** *now Bnf Abd* a cheese made by hanging the curds up to dry in a cloth exposed to the sun instead of putting them in a press.

†**hattit kit** a preparation of milk with a top layer of cream, variously flavoured.

heel the rind or last portion of a piece of cheese.

†**kaisart** a cheese-vat.

†**kane** a quantity of cheese, *latterly appar* fixed at about 3 tons (3.048 tonnes) *WC, SW.*

kebbock, †**caboc,** *freq* ~ **of cheese** a cheese, a whole cheese, *latterly esp* home-made. ~ **heel** the hard end-piece of a cheese.

keeslip the stomach of an animal used as a source of rennet *chf Slk.*

kirn *n* 1 a churn; a churnful. 2 *also* ~**ie** *Ags Per Rox* milk in the process of being churned; buttermilk *now Abd Fif. v* churn. ~**ing** one complete act of churning; the quantity of milk required for this *(local);* the quantity of butter so produced *(local NE-S).* ~**ing day** the day on which churning was done *now local Sh-Ags Kcb.* ~**ing rung** the plunger of a churn *WC Dmf.* ~ **milk** buttermilk; curds made from buttermilk *now local.* ~ **staff** *now Sh Ork Abd,* ~ **stick** *now Bnf* (the handle of) the plunger of an upright churn. **the** ~**'s brok(ken)** the milk is beginning to form into butter *local Sh-Ayr.* **milk** ~ a churn for milk *now Sh Ork.* **stannin** ~ an upright churn worked by a plunger *Kcdn Fif Kcb.*

lapper, †**lopper** *v freq* ~**ed** *esp of milk* clot, curdle. *n* 1 a clot, clotted matter, *esp* milk *now local.* 2 *specif* milk soured and thickened in preparation for butter-making *Gen except Sh Ork Cai.* ~ **milk** thick sour milk *local NE-S.*

lithocks a kind of gruel made from fine oatmeal and *freq* buttermilk *now Stlg wLoth WC.*

†**meat-butter** better quality butter, used for food.

milk: ~**ness** the quantity of milk obtained from an animal; its products. ~**-bowie** a wooden milk bucket *now NE Ags Per.* ~ **meat** a dish of milk and meal or bread; **broth** made with skimmed milk *now NE.*

new cheese a dish made from the cream of a newly-calved cow's milk *NE.*

Orkney cheese cheese made in Orkney after the **Dunlop** method (which was introduced into Orkney in the late 18th century).

pell buttermilk, *chf* as **soor** *etc* as ~ *S.*

plowt kirn a churn operated by a plunger *now Ork.*

plump kirn *NE,* †**plunge churn** a churn worked by moving a churn up and down.

plumper the plunger of a plunge churn *NE.*

prent, print a pat of butter *(usu* a quarter- or half-pound) imprinted with a decorative motif using a mould.

ream *n* cream *now Sh NE, C.* ~**y** consisting of or made with cream. ~ **cheese** cheese made with cream *now Bnf.*

short butter butter which is soft and crumbly from being churned too hot *NE Wgt.*

sour: ~ **cogue,** †~ **kit** a sour-cream dish the same as or similar to **hattit kit.** ~ **dook** buttermilk; *latterly also* yoghurt. ~ **milk** buttermilk *now Sh Ayr.*

stibble, stubble: ~ **butter** high-quality butter made from the milk of cows grazed on stubbles *now local N-SW.*

sweet *of milk* fresh, untreated, not skimmed or sour. ~ **butter** fresh, unsalted butter *now Ork NE nEC.* ~**-milk cheese** cheese made from unskimmed milk, *specif* **Dunlop** cheese *now N.*

whig applied to various products resulting from the souring of milk, *specif* whey, buttermilk.

yirn, earn: ~**ed milk** curds; junket *local.*

†**yowe, ewe:** ~ **milk** ewe's milk.

10.14 VEGETABLE DISHES

For names of vegetables, see 4.8.

bowstock a cabbage with a properly-developed heart *now Bnf Abd.*

brock small potatoes *now Abd Kcb.*

†**carlings** peas, variously prepared, *appar* eaten on Passion Sunday.

champ *Uls,* ~**ers** *Edb Lnk Kcb,* ~**ies** *now Bnf Kcb,* ~**it tatties** *local,* **chappit tatties** *now Sh Ork N* mashed potatoes.

chat a small potato *now Bnf Ayr.*

chun a sprout, *chf* of a potato *chf SW.*

clapshot a dish of potatoes and turnips cooked separately and mashed together *Ork Cai.*

curlies greens.

dab melted fat, gravy etc, in which potatoes are dipped. ~**-at-the-stool** potatoes and salt *Abd.*

dip melted fat in which potatoes are dipped *now local Bnf-WC.*

dribbly beards: curly kail boiled in fat stock.

greens green vegetables, *esp* **kail**.

†**hack:** ~**et** *or* ~**um kail** chopped kail or cabbage boiled in water or milk.

hairy tatties a dish made of mashed potatoes and flaked dried salt fish *NE.*

kail: *n, also* **pan** ~ a dish made of **kail**, prepared as a vegetable on its own, boiled and mashed. ~ **blade** a leaf of **kail** *now local Sh-Dmf.* ~ **broo**, ~ **bree** the juice of boiled **kail** *now local Sh-N.* ~ **brose** brose made with the liquid from boiled **kail** *now N Per Ayr.* ~ **kenny,** ~ **kennin** a dish of cabbage and potatoes mashed *N Lnk Kcb.*

neep brose: brose made with the liquid in which turnips have been boiled *chf NE Uls.*

nettle brose: brose made with the juice of boiled young nettle-tops *NE.*

pea, pey: ~ **cod** *now Ags,* ~**-huil** *Fif Loth S,* ~**shaup** *now Fif WC* a pea-pod.

peelock (potato) *SW,* **peel an eat** *now local NE-S* a potato cooked and served in its skin.

peeryorie *street-cry* a potato *Edb.*

pizz pease.

ploom, plum the fruit of the potato-plant *Gen except Sh Ork.*

†**purry** a savoury dish consisting of oatmeal brose with chopped **kail** stirred into it.

rummle, rumble: ~(**de)thump 1** mashed potatoes with milk, butter and seasoning *now Ayr.* **2** mashed potatoes with cabbage (or turnip) *now Ags Stlg Fif.*

skinny tatie a potato boiled in its skin *WC-S.*

sleeshacks a dish of potatoes fried in slices *Ross Inv.*

spilkin(g)s split peas.

stovies, stoved tatties a dish of **stoved** potatoes, onions etc, sometimes with small pieces of meat etc.

stowans lopped leaves etc, *esp* the young leaves of the colewort, used as food *now Sh Abd.*

syboe, sybie: ~ **tail** the green shoots of the young onion.

tails onion leaves *now Loth S.*

tartan purry a dish of boiled oatmeal mixed with chopped red cabbage or boiled with cabbage water.

tattie: ~**-bree,** ~**-broo** *now Ork NE,* ~ **pourins** *local NE-S* water in which potatoes have been boiled *now Ork NE.* ~**-peel(in)** potato peelings *now local Sh-Ayr.* ~**s and dab** *or* **dip** potatoes boiled in their skins and dipped in melted fat, gravy etc *now local Ork-WC.*

whaup the seed-pod of a leguminous vegetable, *esp* one before the peas etc have begun to develop or after they have been shelled *now Abd Loth.*

wuss juice, the liquid obtained from boiling or squeezing vegetable substances *now Sh.*

10.15 DESSERTS

Caledonian cream a dessert of whipped cream, marmalade, brandy etc.

clootie dumpling a **dumpling** wrapped in a cloth and boiled *Gen except Sh Ork.*

Corstorphine cream a preparation of thickened milk and sugar.

crannachan, cream crowdie a dessert of soft fruit, whipped cream, toasted oatmeal etc.

dumpling a kind of rich, boiled or steamed fruit pudding.

Edinburgh fog a dessert of whipped cream, sugar, nuts etc.

jeel(ie) (table) jelly.

mince(d) pie a (fruit etc) mincemeat pie.

puddin pudding.

rowlie-powlie a roly-poly.

Scotch flummery a kind of steamed custard.

trimmlin tam *now EC, WC,* **trimmlin tammie** *EC, WC, Dmf* a table jelly.

10.16 SWEETIES

This section also includes sugar, honey, jams and other sweet preserves, and ice cream.

alicreesh liquorice.

bachelor's buttons = **pan drops** *now local.*

black: ~ **man 1** a kind of toffee; *also* name for other kinds of dark-coloured sweeties *now Fif Loth.* **2** an ice-cream with a plain wafer on one side and a marshmallow-filled wafer with chocolate edges on the other *Fif Edb Gsw.* ~**-strippit ba** a bull's eye *local C.* ~ **sugar** liquorice (juice).

boiling a boiled sweetie.

bool a round sweetie.

candy: candibrod sugarcandy *Abd Ags Fif Rox.*
~ **glue** candy made from treacle *now Ags.* ~
rock candy in blocks or sticks *now Abd Fif.*

†**cannel water** a drink flavoured with cinnamon.

carvey a sweetie containing caraway seed *now Fif
Kcb.* ~ **sweetie** a sugar-coated caraway seed
local NE WC.

†**casnat** cassonade, unrefined cane-sugar, *chf* ~
suggar.

chyngin ba a sweetie that changes colour as it is
sucked *Mry Ags.*

clack a kind of treacle toffee.

claggum treacle toffee *now Bnf Abd.*

conversation (sweetie *or* **lozenge)** a flat sweetie
of varying shape inscribed with a motto *local.*

curlie: ~ **doddy,** ~ **murly** *Ags,* ~ **willie** *Fif* a
kind of sweetie.

curly-andra a sugared coriander or caraway seed
Fif.

doddle a small lump of home-made toffee sold in
little corner-shops *Edb.*

†**dragy muskie** sweeties flavoured with musk.

†**drog** a kind of sweetie, made of spices etc.

Edinburgh rock a stick-shaped sweetie made of
sugar, cream of tartar, water and various
flavourings, *orig* made in Edinburgh.

galshachs sweeties, titbits; trashy (*esp* sweet) food
NE.

†**gib** a kind of sweetie *Edb.*

glass, gless: ~**ie** a home-made sweetie, a kind of
toffee *now Bwk Kcb.*

gob-stopper a large, round, hard sweetie *local.*

grannie's sooker a peppermint sweetie, a **pan
drop** *NE nEC.*

gundy toffee.

Hawick ba a round, brown, mint-flavoured boiled
sweetie made in Hawick.

hinnie honey.

Jeddart snails a kind of toffee from Jedburgh.

lickery, †**licorese** liquorice. ~ **stick** liquorice
root chewed by children as a sweetie *WC.*

lozenger a lozenge, a flavoured sweetie, *orig*
diamond-shaped.

luve-lozenger a **conversation lozenge** *NE Fif
wLoth.*

Macallum vanilla ice-cream flavoured with ras-
berry-juice *C, S.*

mercat mixtures an assortment of small hard
sweeties, commonly sold at markets *Ags Fif.*

pan drop a round peppermint sweetie, a mint
imperial.

pluffy a kind of toffee made fluffy and brittle by
the addition of bicarbonate of soda, puff candy
Ags Slk.

plunkie a kind of homemade sweetie made of
treacle or syrup and flour *NE.*

pokey hat an ice-cream cone *C.*

readin sweetie a **conversation lozenge.**

rock bool a round, hard, candied-sugar sweetie
local sEC-Rox.

rowan jelly a tart-flavoured preserve made of
rowan berries, served with game or meat.

†**scrochat, scorchet** kind of sweetie.

seerup syrup.

slider an ice-cream wafer or sandwich.

slim jim a kind of sweetie consisting of long strips
of coconut or liquorice *WC.*

smag a sweetie, a tasty titbit *Bnf Abd.*

snag a titbit, dainty, *esp* a sweetie *now NE Ags.*

snashters *contemptuous* sweeties, cakes, pastries etc;
trashy food *now local Per-WC.*

snysters sweeties, cakes, dainties *now WC.*

soukers: auld wifie's *etc* ~ mint imperials, **pan
drops** *NE, EC, S.*

sour drap an acid drop *now Sh.* **soor ploom** a
tart-flavoured round green boiled sweetie (*orig*
associated with Galashiels).

spearimint spearmint *Ags Fif WC, S.*

starrie a kind of sweetie *Ags.*

strap black treacle, molasses *local NE-Per.*

strippit ba a round peppermint **boiling** *usu* with
black and white stripes.

succar, shuggar sugar. †**sucker alacreische,**
†**sukker lacrissye** liquorice. **sugarallie**
liquorice, *esp* when made up as a sweetie; a stick
etc of liquorice *Gen except Sh Ork.* **sugar bool,
sugardoddle** *local nEC Lnk* a round boiled sweetie, *freq* striped.

sweetenin a sweetie, a titbit *Ork Bnf Abd.*

sweetie a sweet(meat). ~ **bool(ie)** a round boiled
sweetie *Abd.* ~**-man** a confectioner, sweetie-
seller. ~ **poke** a bag of sweeties *Sh Ork Cai C.* ~
shop a sweetie-shop. ~ **stan(d)** a sweetie-stall
at a fair etc *now Abd Per.* ~ **wife** a female sweetie-
seller.

tablet a kind of sweetie made of butter, sugar etc,
now usu of the consistency of a stiff, friable fudge.

taffie, toffee toffee. ~ **apple** an apple dipped in
slightly candied sugar and held on a stick to be
eaten.

tam trot a kind of toffee *Rox.*

teuch Jean a kind of sticky, chewy boiled sweetie
local Ags-SW.

traicle, treacle treacle; in Scotland, *freq* used of
any of molasses, treacle or syrup. ~ **gundy**
candy or toffee made from treacle *N, C.* **black**
~ molasses *N, WC, Gall.*

†**wax cayme** a honeycomb.

10.17 SPICES AND HERBS

camovine camomile *now NE Ags.*

†**cannel** cinnamon.

carvey caraway *local N-WC.* **carvied** flavoured with caraway *now Abd.*

clow clove *now local Bnf-Fif.*

corrydander coriander *now Abd Lnk.*

dab-at-the-stool pepper and salt *now Stlg Ayr.*

†**ennet seid** dill seed.

etnach the juniper berry *now NE.*

ginge ginger.

jenepere juniper *now Abd.*

†**kimming** cumin.

†**macis** mace.

†**marjolene** marjoram.

mustart mustard.

†**nit, nut:** ~ **mug** a nutmeg.

†**persel** parsley.

†**pudirlumbard** *appar* the name of some kind of spice.

†**ratchell salt** coarse-grained salt.

†**saipheron** saffron.

saut, salt saut. **sma** ~ table salt.

†**sewane** ? a spice.

†**sherville** chervil.

sithe a chive *local Loth-Rox.*

spearimint spearmint *EC, WC, S.*

spice pepper *now Sh Ork N.* **spicy** peppered, peppery.

Sunday salt salt made at the weekend, large-grained from having been left longer to crystallize.

syes chives *now NE Ags.*

†**tarmanick, tarmaluk** turmeric.

yerb a herb *now Ags Dmf.*

10.18 DRINKS

Adam's wine water.

ale, yill *now C, S n* 1 ale. 2 lemonade, or other aerated water. *NE Ags. v* †treat to ale. **aleberry** ale boiled with oatmeal and sugar *NE.* † ~ **cap** , ~ **cop** a wooden ale-cup. †**yill-wife** a woman who sold ale, *usu* of her own brewing.

†**aqua** whisky.

aquavita spirits; *specif* whisky.

Athole brose *etc* honey (or meal) mixed with whisky *chf Highl.*

auld, old: ~ **man's milk** a drink, a kind of egg-flip.

†**auntie** an unmarried woman who kept an inn etc; drink obtained in such an establishment.

barley-bree malt liquor, whisky.

barm 1 mix with yeast *now Sh.* 2 ferment *now Sh Abd wLoth.* ~**y** yeasty; frothy.

†**barrikin** a small cask or barrel.

bead 1 a glass or quantity of spirits: *'he had a good bead in him yesterday'.* 2 (a measure of) the strength of spirits.

bicker a beaker, drinking vessel, *esp* of wood.

birl 1 pour out, serve (wine etc) to (a person). 2 †*also* ~ **at ale** *etc* drink, carouse.

birse-cup a final cup of tea with whisky or other spirit instead of milk *Bnf Abd.*

blade a tea leaf.

blash *usu contemptuous* a large draught (of liquor) *now Bnf Abd Ags.*

†**blaw, blow** a pull (of liquor).

blenshaw a drink made of oatmeal, sugar, milk, water, and nutmeg.

blockin ale a drink taken by the parties to a bargain *NE.*

blubber-totum name for any drink made too thin or weak, *eg* tea, gruel *Abd.*

†**blue** whisky or other spirits.

blybe *n* a large quantity of liquid, *esp* of spirits *Bnf Abd. v* drink heavily *now Abd.*

†**boddoch** a **mutchkin**.

bonailie, †**bonevale** a drink with or toast to a departing friend.

†**bos** a leather bottle for wine etc.

†**bote** a cask, butt (for wine etc).

bothan an unlicensed drinking house or hut, a kind of shebeen *Lewis Gsw.*

bowie a barrel for holding water or ale.

bragwort, †**brogat** a drink made of ale and honey.

brak, break: ~ **a bottle** open a new bottle.

†**branny** brandy.

bree whisky *now local Bnf-Lnk.*

broon, brown porter, ale *now Bnf Abd.* ~ **pig** an earthenware jar for whisky *Abd Ags.* ~ **robin** home-brewed ale *Ags Loth.*

brunt *(Ork NE) or* †**burnt ale** the refuse of a still.

bucket a glass of spirits; a quantity of drink, *freq* **he can take a fair, good** *etc* ~ .

†**budgell** a bottle.

†**caddel** caudle.

cag a keg *now Bnf Fif.*

cairry-out, carry-out food or alcoholic drink bought in a restaurant, pub etc for consumption elsewhere.

cairt: kill the ~ er name for a very strong variety of whisky *local Cai-Stlg*.

ca(ll) aboot circulate, send round (a punch bowl etc).

cap, †cop a bowl used as a measure for liquor or grain.**†cap ale** a kind of beer. **~ out, clean ~ (out)** *chf NE Ags* denoting the emptying of the bowl in drinking. **kiss (a** *or* **the ~(s)** drink out of the same vessel, *usu* as a token of friendship.

†cathel a kind of egg-nog.

cauker a dram of liquor, a bumper *now local N Fif*.

†cauld straik neat whisky, as opposed to toddy.

cave 1 †a wine-cellar. **2** a case for holding bottles of wine or spirits *now Sh*.

†cedar cider.

change one's breath have a drink *local Bnf-Kcb*.

cheepin shoppie a shebeen *Ags Fif*.

†cheerer a glass of spirits; a toddy.

chopin, chap(p)in 1 a Scots half-pint (approx = 0.85 litre) *now Abd Stlg*. **2** †a container of this capacity. **†~ stoup** a drinking vessel holding a **chopin**.

clear: the ~ (stuff) whisky *now Abd Ags*.

cock drink *now Ags*. **~ one's wee finger** drink, tipple.

cog: coup the ~ drink *NE*.

†collep some kind of drinking vessel.

content a drink of hot water, milk and sugar *Bnf Ags Fif Arg*.

coo's drink a hot drink to induce sweating *Ags Fif*.

coup toss off (liquor), quaff *now Bnf Abd Fif*.

cruet a carafe; a decanter *now Bnf Abd*.

cruik, crook: ~ one's elbow drink (alcohol), *esp* rather freely *local*.

cutter a hip-flask holding half a **mutchkin** of whisky *local Cai-Fif*. **rin the ~** carry out liquor from a public house or brewery unobserved *local*.

†cutty stoup a pewter vessel holding ⅛ of a **chopin** *local*.

decanter a table jug.

deochandorus a drink taken when leaving, a stirrup cup.

†deuch a drink; drink, *esp* if intoxicating.

dew whisky *now Bnf Abd*.

†dirgie, dredgie a funeral feast, *esp* of drink.

donal(d) a measure of whisky, about half a gill *local Bnf-WC*.

doo: flee the (blue) ~ send out a messenger surreptitiously for whisky *Bnf Abd*.

dram *n* a small drink of liquor; a drink of any size (*esp* of whisky). *v* drink alcohol, tipple. **be one's ~** pay one's share of the drinks *now Ags Fif*.

drap, drop: a ~pie a drink. **the ~pie** drink.

†dreepin a drink (of liquor etc).

dreg 1 †*chf* **~ wine** inferior wine made from the marc of grapes. **2** *also* **~gle, ~lin** a small quantity, a drop (*chf* of spirits) *now Fif*.

drib 1 a drop, a small quantity of liquid or semiliquid *now Bnf Abd Fif*. **2** † **~s** dregs.

dribble *v* tipple, drink *now Ags*. *n, also* **dribblach** *Bnf Abd* a slight trickle; a drop, *chf* of alcohol *local*.

drink siller a gratuity given to be spent on drink *now Abd Stlg*.

†drumlie *of liquor* full of sediment.

†dry tapster a retailer of ale who did not brew.

ee: a drap(pie) in the ~ just enough drink to make one mildly intoxicated.

eik an additional drink; a little drop more.

†English pint the Imperial pint, one third of a **Scots pint**.

export applied to a superior-quality stonger beer, slightly darker in colour than **heavy**.

feenish a mixture of alcohol and shellac used as an intoxicant by meths-drinkers etc *now Ayr*.

†fell *of drink* potent.

†ferekin, firikin a firkin.

†Ferintosh a kind of whisky formerly distilled at Ferintosh, Ross; whisky *in gen*.

†fit ale a drink of ale to celebrate a mother's rising for the first time after childbirth or the completion of a sale of cattle.

flet pour (tea) into one's saucer *now Stlg midLoth*.

flour the first water drawn from the well in the New Year *local*.

†foy: drink (someone's) ~ drink farewell (to someone).

gantree, gantry *in a bar* a bottle stand.

gardevine 1 a (large) wine or spirits bottle. **2** †a case or chest for holding wine bottles or decanters.

†garnach a wine from the eastern Pyrenees.

†gaskin (wyne) a wine of Gascony.

ginger lemonade or other aerated water *WC*.

Glasgow punch a punch made with rum, cold water, sugar, lemons and limes.

†grace drink a drink taken at the end of a meal after grace has been said.

†graith liquor, medicine.

†graybeard a one- or two-handled jug or pitcher for holding liquor.

†groaning malt ale brewed to celebrate a birth.

half, hauf a half-measure of a specified amount, *esp* of whisky = a half-gill. **a wee hauf** a quarter gill, a small whisky, *orig* less than half an imperial gill, *now usu* one-fifth. **a ~ an a ~** a small whisky with a half pint of beer as chaser.

hard *adj, of intoxicants* strong, undiluted, raw. *n* spirits, *specif* **the** ~ whisky. **the ~ stuff,** ~ **tackle** *now Fif Rox* whisky.

heather ale a drink brewed from heather, hops, barm, syrup, ginger and water *now Ork NE Ags.*

heavy 1 *of a drink, chf of spirits* large, copious. **2** *of beer, freq as noun, corresponding to Eng* bitter.

†**helter-skelter: drink** ~ drink heavily, while also mixing one's drinks.

het, hot: ~ **pint** a drink made from hot spiced ale to which sugar, eggs and spirits may be added, served at christening, wedding or New Year festivities. ~ **waters** spirits, alcohol.

hey-broo a decoction or infusion of hay *now Cai Abd.*

hogget a measure of liquor etc.

hooker a glass of whisky, a dram.

†**Hottopyis** name for a variety of wine, and its standard measure.

howp a mouthful or gulp of liquid, a draught (*esp* of liquor), a dram *NE.*

†**inkie-pinkie** weak beer.

jabble a liquid and its sediment stirred up together, *esp* a weak mixture as of tea or soup.

jaup, jap *chf contemptuous* a small quantity, a drop (of drink, alcohol) *now Bnf Ags.*

jaw a draught, drink *now NE Kcb.*

jilp *esp derog* a thin or insipid drink *now Bnf Abd Kcdn Ags.*

John Barleycorn personification of barley as the grain from which malt liquor is made; ale or whisky.

join, jine the clubbing together of several persons to buy drink; a social gathering or outing *now Bnf.*

joug, jug *n* **1** a jug. **2** a mug or drinking vessel. *v* †tipple, drink.

jute 1 weak or sour ale; bad whisky *now Ork.* **2** any insipid drink, dregs, weak tea etc *now Ork.*

†**keltie:** *chf* **give someone** ~ force a large alcoholic drink on a person who has tried to avoid drinking.

kirsty a whisky jar *now Fif Loth.*

†**kitchen:** *also and chf* **tea** ~ a tea-urn.

knag, knog a keg *now Uls.*

laid as much liquor as one can hold at a sitting *chf S.*

†**land wyne** ? wine grown up-country, not in or near the town (of Bordeaux) *chf Dundee.*

lang, long: ~ **ale** a soft drink *NE.* **Long John** a brand of whisky.

lawin(g) 1 †a session of drinking or entertainment, *esp* in a tavern; a drinking party. **2** a tavern reckoning or one's share of this *now local NE-Ayr.*

leecure *now Sh,* †**licoure** liquor.

leemonade lemonade *now Gall Uls.*

†**lekkage, laikage** wastage of imported wine by leaking from the barrels; an allowance made for this in charging duty.

light applied to a low-gravity beer, the successor of mild.

lippie a glass full to the brim with drink *chf Ayr.*

lug: lay one's ~ **in(to)** eat or drink heartily of (some food or drink) *now N wLoth Lnk.*

Mackay: the real ~ the genuine article, the true original; *specif* a brand of whisky so-named.

madder a square wooden container used as a measure for liquer *SW, S.*

magnum bonum, *also* **magnum** a bottle containing two quarts (2.27 litres) of wine or spirits.

mak, make *of food or drink in the process of cooking* thicken, set, infuse. **mak doon** dilute the strength of (spirits).

mask a brew or infusion, *esp* of tea. ~**ing** an infusion or pot of tea. ~**in pot** a teapot *Ags Ayr.*

maumie *of a liquid* thick and smooth; full-bodied.

maut, malt †ale, liquor. ~ **whisky** whisky distilled from malted barley in a pot-still, as opposed to a blended whisky (made mainly from grain).

meal, male: ~ **ie drink** a drink of water into which oatmeal has been sprinkled *Ork Abd Per.* ~ **an thrammel** oatmeal stirred up with water or ale, taken as a snack *NE.*

mercy, *chf* **the mercies** liquor, *esp* whisky *NE, WC.*

milk add milk to (tea).

miller: droon *etc* **the** ~ add too much water to tea or whisky.

†**moistify** *joc, of topers drinking* moisten, wet.

†**molass, malash** a spirit distilled from molasses; whisky adulterated with this.

moog a mug *N.*

mornin(g) a glass of spirits or a snack taken before breakfast; a mid-morning drink or snack. ~ **piece** *now Sh Ork Wgt,* †~ **drink** a drink or snack taken during the mid-morning break from work.

†**mountain dew** whisky, *esp* if illicitly distilled.

mutchkin a measure of capacity for (*chf*) liquids = $\frac{1}{4}$ pint Scots, *ie* $\frac{3}{4}$ *pint imperial (0.43 litre); a container of this capacity; latterly* sometimes = an imperial pint *esp* of spirits.

nakit *of alcoholic drink* neat *now Fif Wgt.*

nappie *adj, of ale etc* foaming, strong. *n, chf literary* (strong) ale.

nap(pie) a bowl, drinking vessel.

nebfu a beakful; a small quantity *esp* of liquor, a drop *local Sh-Edb.*

neck break the neck of (a bottle etc) *now Kcb.*

pale ale, *formally* **India P~ Ale** a kind of low-gravity beer.

†**pap-in** a drink made of light ale and oatmeal with a small quantity of whisky or brandy added.

†**peaser** a draught of liquor, *esp* whisky.

peat reek Highland whisky, whose characteristic flavour is allegedly from the smoke of the peat fire used in the drying of the malt.

†**pece** a goblet, *usu* of silver.

penny: ~-wabble *Bnf Abd,* †**~ whaup** a thin weak ale formerly sold at a penny a bottle.

†**pichar** the quantity, *esp* of ale held by a pitcher, *appar* accepted as a standard measure.

pig a container, *usu* of earthenware; a pot, jar, pitcher.

†**pinkie** weak beer.

pint stowp a tankard or drinking vessel containing a **Scots pint.**

†**pith: the ~ o maut** whisky.

plash an insipid, tasteless liquid or drink; a large quantity of something liquid.

plottie a hot drink, *specif* mulled wine.

plunk *n* the sound of a cork being drawn from a bottle, a popping sound. *v* make a plopping or gurgling noise as when drawing a cork, swallowing etc *now Ags Kcb.*

prop a stopper, bung, wedge *now Sh.*

†**propine** *n* drink-money. *v* offer or give to drink, present with drink.

pundie 1 a strong type of beer; liquor *in gen now Loth Slk.* **2** a measure of beer given free to brewery workers *Loth Slk.*

†**quart** a gallon, *chf* of wine, ale or oil.

†**ram-(s)tam** the strongest kind of ale, that drawn from the first mash.

raw neat whisky *now Sh Cai.*

ream the froth on top of ale etc *now Bnf.*

red biddy *slang* a mixture of cheap red wine and methylated spirit or other alcohol *now WC, SW.*

†**Rens, Rynche, Rance** *of wine* Rhenish.

retour a second helping of food, round of drinks etc *chf Abd.*

riddle a measure of claret, thirteen bottles arranged round a **magnum.**

†**rin, run** draw (liquor). **~ner** a tapster.

rinse wash **down** (a meal) with liquor *now Bnf Ags.*

roost, rust: ~ie nail a dram of whisky *now EC-Wgt.*

ruch, rough: ~ dram enough liquor to cause drunkenness *N.*

sap a quantity of liquid, *usu* to be consumed with food *now Sh Ork Cai Abd.*

scale a shallow drinking bowl *now Lnk Rox.*

scaud, scald *joc* tea *nEC, WC, SW.*

†**Scherand** name for a kind of wine.

Scotch muffler a drink of liquor, *esp* whisky (regarded as keeping one warm) *Abd nEC Lnk.*

†**scoup aff** *or* **up** drink or toss off (liquor).

†**scour** *v, joc* drink **off**; wet (one's throat etc). *n* a large hearty drink (*esp* of liquor).

screechan, *Sh* †**screich** *slang* whisky.

scuds brisk or foaming ale; beer with a head.

scuit a shallow, wooden, scoop-shaped drinking cup, *freq* **~ifu** the full contents of this *now Slk.*

†**seck** sack.

†**sey, say: ~ drink** a round of drinks paid for by an entrant to a trade when submitting his **sey.**

shilling used until the 1950s in the classification of the strength of beer, from the price per barrel, *eg* **forty-~ ale** (*usu written* **40/-**) a very light beer; *later* re-introduced (without reference to the price) in the 'real-ale' boom of the 1970s.

shilpit *of liquor* insipid, thin *now Sh Ork.*

sirple *now S,* †**sipple** *v* sip continuously, go on drinking in small quantities, tipple *now S.* †*n, only* **sirple** a sip, mouthful, *esp* of liquor.

sitten *of tea* stewed, strong and bitter *N.*

skeechan an intoxicating malt liquor produced in the later stages of brewing and formerly used by bakers instead of yeast; sometimes mixed with treacle etc and sold as a kind of beer.

skiddle a thin watery liquid, *esp contemptuous* weak tea *WC.*

skink drink, liquor, *esp* of a weak, wishy-washy kind.

skirp a drop of liquor, a **dram** *NE.*

skite a small amount of liquor, a **dram** *NE Ags.*

†**skole** *v* drink toasts; drink out. *n* a toast, a health in drinking.

skoosh lemonade or other aerated water *C.*

slock a draught of liquid, a drink *now local Sh-Ayr.* **~in** enough (drink) to slake one's thirst, a drink *Sh Ork NE.*

slocken inaugurate or celebrate with a drink. **~er** a thirst-quencher, a drink *NE-S.*

slushy *of drink etc* weak, insipid *now Sh Ork Cai.*

smell a small quantity, a taste, 'a sensation' (*esp* of drink) *now local Sh-Kcb.*

†**snaker** a small bowl of punch.

snatchack a small quantity of intoxicating liquor, a **dram** *now Ross Inv Mry.*

snipie, snippy a kettle or tea pot.

sorple make a sucking noise when drinking *Dmf Rox.*

soup *also ironic* a considerable amount, *esp* of spirits *now local Fif-Rox.*

†**sowff** a copious drink, a draught.

sowp 1 *also ironic* a larger amount, *esp* of spirits *now local Stlg-WC.* **2** a drink; something to drink.

spairge a drink, a mouthful, a drop of spirits, as much liquid as will moisten one's lips.

†**spark** a nip of spirits.

special *of beer* applied to a later, carbonated version of **heavy**.

speel-the-wa (a nip of) a cheap inferior whisky (from its supposed effects on the drinker) *now Lnk SW Rox.*

spoutrach weak, thin drink *Abd Gall.*

sproosh lemonade or other aerated water *NE.*

†**spunkie** whisky, spirits.

†**standing drink** a drink taken standing; a **deochandorus**.

†**stark** *of liquor* potent.

stowp a flagon, tankard, decanter, mug etc, *freq with its capacity* prefixed, eg **pint** ∼; the measure itself *now nEC Lnk Wgt.*

stroupach, stroupan *Gaelicized* a drink of tea *Cai-Inv.*

stroupie *usu joc* a teapot *now Sh.*

†**strunt** spirits, *esp* whisky toddy.

stuffie: the ∼**ie** whisky *now NE Ags.*

sugarallie water a children's drink made by dissolving a piece of liquorice in water.

swag a quantity of liquid or liquor, a long draught *now Sh Ork.*

†**swap** drink in long quick gulps, toss off.

swash a large amount of drink or food *now Sh Ork.*

swats newly-brewed weak beer; a substitute for this, made of molasses, water and yeast *now Sh Lnk.*

†**swattle** drink greedily or noisily.

sweel, swill *v* **1** wash (the throat) down with liquor; wash (food) down with a drink *local Sh-Kcb.* **2** swallow in copious draughts *local Sh-Kcb.* *n* a hearty drinking *now NE.*

tak, take: ∼ **down** reduce the potency of (spirits), dilute *Sh Per Kcb.* ∼ **out** drink up, drain (a glass) *now Sh.*

tanker a tankard *now EC, S.*

tappit hen a kind of (*usu* pewter) decanter, containing a standard measure, its lid knob resembling a fowl's tuft.

tass(ie) a cup, goblet etc, *esp* for spirits *now literary.*

taste *v* drink liquor in small amounts, have a tipple. *n* a small quantity of alcoholic drink, a **dram. tastin** the drinking of **drams**, a **dram.**

†**taupin** a peg in a drinking vessel; a peg acting as a tappet.

tea, tae *chf Sh NE* tea. ∼**-blade** a tea leaf *nEC.* ∼**-hand,** ∼**-jenny** (*applied to men as well as women*) *N-C* a person who drinks a lot of tea.

†**tersaill** a tierce (of wine) *Abd.*

thrapple: weet one's ∼ have something to drink, quench one's thirst.

throttle: weet one's ∼ slake one's thirst.

†**ticht, tight** *of ale* strong, brisk.

†**tift** drink, toss off (liquor).

†**timothy** a drink, **dram**, a glass (of toddy etc).

tinker's tea tea brewed in a pan rather than in a teapot.

tinnie a small tin mug, *esp* one used by children.

†**tippeny, tuppeny** weak ale or beer sold at twopence a **Scots pint.**

toss a toast, a drink to someone's health; the subject of a toast.

tout *v* **1** drink copiously, tipple *now local NE-Ayr.* **2** drink down, empty (a glass etc) to the last drop. *n, also* ∼(**l**)**ie** *now NE* a draught, swig, *orig* a large single drink, but now rather a small but repeated drink, a tipple *now local Sh-Loth.*

track: ∼ **ie,** ∼ **pot** *NE* a teapot.

traicle, treacle: ∼ **ale** *now local NE-SW,* ∼ **bendy** *now Lnk Slk,* ∼ **peerie** *nEC, S,* ∼ **wheech** *now Bwk* light ale brewed from treacle, water and yeast.

tuith, tooth: ∼**fu(l)** a mouthful, *esp* of liquor.

tume empty (a glass etc) by drinking.

tweest a small amount of drink *now Abd.*

upstanding: be ∼ stand up, rise to one's feet, *specif* ceremonially to drink a toast etc: '*Will you please be upstanding and drink a toast to our guests?*'.

†**usquebae, usquebaugh,** whisky.

†**varnage** a strong sweet white Italian wine.

wall, well 1 a well. **2** a drinking fountain *now local.* **3** a water stand-pump *local N-WC.* **4** a cold-water tap at a sink *local NE-WC.*

water pig a container for water, a pitcher *now ShAgs.*

waucht *v, freq* ∼ **out, ower, up** drink deeply, take large draughts (**of**) drain *now Fif.* *n* a draught of liquid, a swig or gulp of a drink *now NE nEC, WC.*

wee heavy a type of strong beer, *usu* sold in small bottles of $\frac{1}{3}$ pint (approx. 0.2 litre).

weet, wet *n* a drink. *v* celebrate with a drink, drink to the success of (a bargain etc). **weetin** a quantity of liquor, a drinking party *now Stlg Fif Loth.*

wersh *of beer* flat *Gen except Sh Ork.*

†**whauky** whisky.

wheich liquor, booze; whisky *now Per Fif.*

whisky a spirit distilled from malted barley in a

pot still (**malt** ~), or with the addition of unmalted grain spirit (*usu* maize) made in a patent still (**blended** ~). †~-**house** a tavern where whisky could be obtained. ~-**pig** an earthenware jar for holding whisky *now Sh Ork.*

whitter a drink of liquor; liquor *now Stlg.*

willie-waught a hearty swig, *usu* of ale or other liquor.

wine *in urban areas* cheap fortified red wine or sherry *chf Gsw.* ~ **shop** a public-house which serves cheap wine *Gsw.* ~ **slide** a coaster for a wine bottle or decanter which can be slid along a table.

wishy-washy thin watery drink, *eg* weak tea *now Ork Ags Ayr.*

†**wizzen: weet one's** ~ have a drink.

10.19 BREWING AND DISTILLING

acherspyre *v of grain* sprout during malting. *n* the sprouting of grain during malting; a sprout of such grain.

†**ale:** ~-**cunnare,** ~-**tastare** an official inspector of ale offered for sale. ~-**wand** a **wand** indicating ale for sale. **yill-wife** a woman who sold ale, *usu* of her own brewing.

barm 1 mix with yeast *now Sh.* **2** ferment *now Sh Abd wLoth.* ~**y** yeasty, frothy.

†**barrikin** a small cask or barrel.

†**bote** a cask, butt (for wine etc).

bowie a barrel for ale.

brew: †~**ing lume** fermentng vessel. **browst, brewst** a brewing. **brewster, browster** *now Bnf Abd,* a brewer. †**browster house** a brew-house, brewery. **brewsterwife, browster wife** *now Abd Fif* a woman who brews or sells ale; a landlady. †~ **caldron** a brewing vessel. †~ **croft** a croft ranking as **brewland.** †~ **land, Browstar land** land connected with the brewing on an estate. †~ **seat** a piece of **brewland.**

†**bun** a small cask.

cag a keg *now Bnf Fif.*

caochan fermented liquor before it goes through the still.

†**coble** a vat for steeping malt.

cummen, kimming a tub, *esp* as used in brewing.

cummins the rootlets of malt *now Abd.*

†**cun** taste (ale); evaluate by tasting. **cunnar, cunstar** *chf NE* a person appointed to test the quality of ale and fix its price.

†**draff pook** a sack for carrying draff, dregs, the refuse of malt after brewing.

dreg the refuse of malt from the still.

flake (stand) a wooden box containing water through which the worm passes.

foreshot the whisky that comes over first.

geel gyle, wort in the process of fermentation *now Sh Ork.* †~-**house** the place where the wort was set to cool.

†**hammer-stand** a kind of beer barrel.

hat a layer of froth etc forming on the surface of a liquid, *esp* of yeast in brewing *now Sh Ork Bnf.*

hogget a hogshead, a large cask *now Bute Ayr.*

houp hops *now Ork.*

kill, kiln *joc* a whisky still *now Loth.*

†**kinken** a keg, small barrel, *appar* = a firkin or quarter barrel.

†**malashes** molasses.

mask *v* mash (malt); brew (ale etc) *now Ork.* *n* †a single mashing of malt. ~**ing** the action of **masking**; a brewing. ~**in tub** *SW, S,* † ~(**ing**) **fat,** *SW, S* a mashing vat. †~ **rudder,** ~ **ruther** the stick used to stir the steeping malt.

maut, malt 1 malt. **2** †ale, liquor. †~**en** *of grain or seeds* germinate, sprout; become malt. †~-**barn** a building where malt is prepared. †~-**man** a maltster. ~ **silvir** a payment to a maltster for making grain into malt.

newin(g) the working of yeast in the making of ale.

†**play the wort** ? stir or ? boil the wort before adding the yeast.

pot, pat: ~**still** a kind of whisky still in which heat is applied directly to the pot; *orig* one made by adding an attachment to a cauldron-type cooking pot.

pundie 1 a strong type of beer; liquor *in gen, now Loth Slk.* **2** a measure of beer given free to brewery workers *Loth Slk.*

†**quickenin** yeast, any fermenting agent.

†**ram-(s)tam** the strongest kind of ale, that drawn from the first mash.

†**rin, run** distill (whisky).

shouder, shoulder the dome-shaped upper part of the pot of a whisky-still *now NE.*

skeechan an intoxicating malt liquor produced in the later stages of brewing and formerly used by bakers instead of yeast; sometimes mixed with treacle etc and sold as a kind of beer.

†**staff** a stave, a section of a cask etc.

stap a stave of a wooden cask or pail etc *now Rox.*

†**steik** a cask of wine.

stell, still *n* a still, for whisky etc. *v* †distil; discharge (liquid) in small drops. †**sma** ~ *freq implying illicit distillation* a type of small still, supposed to produce mellower whisky.

†**stellage** a local tax on a brewery within a district, *specif* as due to the **burgh** of Wigtown from the county.

†**straik** a level measure (of malt); (the measure of the strength of) the liquor brewed or distilled from this: '*ale o twice the straik of malt*'.

†**tap-tree** a bung inserted in the outlet hole of a (mash-)tub.

†**taupin staff** ? the stave containing the vent-peg in a barrel.

thirds the residue of grain left after milling or distilling *now NE-S.*

†**tree** a wooden, barrel, keg, *esp* for ale.

†**tumill** a funnel used for pouring the wort of ale into casks.

†**voidour** an empty barrel, cask etc.

white: the ~ o the pot the last run of the wash in the (illegal) distillation of whisky *WC.*

wirt, wort wort. † **~ dish, ~ fatt, ~ troch, ~ tube** a vessel for holding wort, a fermentation vat. **~ stane** a stone used in making wort, for keeping the barrel steady *now Ork.*

10.20 TOBACCO

blast *n* a smoke, a puff of a pipe. *v* smoke (tobacco).

blaw, blow *v* smoke (a pipe) *now Lnk Dnbt.* *n* a puff (of a pipe).

bogie (roll) a kind of coarse black tobacco of a medium twist.

cheek-warmer a short-stemmed tobacco pipe.

cut: ~ty (pipe) a short and stumpy (clay) pipe. **~-an-dry** cut-and-dried tobacco *now Bnf Abd.*

dirry the ashes on top of a pipe *now Bnf Abd.*

†**doss** a box or pouch for tobacco or snuff.

dottle 1 the plug of tobacco left at the bottom of a pipe after smoking. **2** a cigarette end *Bnf Fif Ayr.*

doup the stub of a cigarette or cigar.

dowt a cigarette-end *local C.*

draw a puff at a pipe, a smoke.

feech the projecting knob under the bowl of a clay pipe to hold it by when the bowl becomes hot *now Abd.*

feuch *v* puff (at a pipe), smoke *now Bnf Abd.* *n* a draw, a puff (at a pipe) *Bnf Abd Ags.*

fuff cause to emit puffs of smoke, smoke (a pipe).

fuggle an unburnt plug of tobacco in a pipe, the **dottle** *NE.*

†**graddan** home-made snuff.

gun a tobacco pipe, a briar-pipe *now local Abd-Ags.*

lick take a pinch or small quantity of (something, *esp* snuff).

lunt smoke, emit puffs of smoke, smoke (a pipe) *local N-Kcb.*

mill, mull a snuffbox, *orig* incorporating a grinder.

oam, yoam *of a smoker* puff *Abd.*

pen a small spoon or similar object for taking snuff, *orig* one made from a quill *Ork Bnf.*

pipe: ~y-dottle the plug of tobacco and ash in a half-smoked pipe. **~-riper** a pipe-cleaner *Sh-C.* **~-shank, ~ stapple** the stem of a tobacco-pipe.

rackle a small chain on a pipe stem, attaching the lid and a pin for clearing out the pipe *now Abd.*

redd clear (a tobacco pipe) of ashes, poke up or out *Sh NE-C.*

reek *n* the act of smoking a pipe etc, a smoke, a whiff, puff. *v* smoke (a pipe etc) *now Stlg.*

ripe clear (ash etc) out of a pipe; clear (a pipe) of ash *Sh-C.*

row, roll a roll of tobacco *local Sh-Kcb.*

rummle, rumble clear (a narrow passage, *esp* a tobacco pipe) with a rod or wire *now local Bnf-Lnk.*

shilagie the coltsfoot, *esp* its leaves used by juvenile smokers as a substitute for tobacco *now local Ags-Lnk.*

smoke o tobacco as much tobacco as will fill a pipe *local Sh-Kcb.*

sneesh *n* (a pinch of) snuff. *v* take snuff, sniff it up the nostrils *local Abd-S.*

sneeshin, †sneising *chf literary, esp in Highl contexts* (a pinch of) snuff. † **~ box** a snuffbox. **~ horn** a snuffbox shaped from a horn *now Per.* **~ mull** a snuffbox, *orig* one which ground the snuff. † **~ pen** a small spoon or quill for taking snuff.

snuff *n* a pinch of snuff *Gen except Sh Ork.* *v* take snuff. **snuffing** the taking of snuff, *specif* as part of the **Common Riding** ceremony in Hawick *Rox.* **~y hanky** a handkerchief for use after taking snuff *now Per Kcb.* **~ horn** a snuffbox, *specif* one made from a horn tip *now Sh Ags Per.* **~ mill, ~ mull** a snuffbox. † **~ pen** a small spoon or quill for taking snuff.

spaingie, spaingie wan *Bnf Abd* Spanish cane, as a substitute for tobacco etc.

†**spin** roll (tobacco leaf) into a continuous rope or coil, twist (tobacco).

sp(l)euchan a tobacco pouch, *usu* of leather *local Ork-Gall.*

stapple the stem of a (clay) tobacco-pipe *now local.*

strummel the half-smoked tobacco left at the bottom of a pipe, a **dottle**.

tabbie a cigarette stub *now NE nEC.*

taddy a kind of snuff.

thick black a brand of strong tobacco.

tove at smoke, puff (a pipe etc) *now Rox.*

11. LAW

Church law will be found in 14.1.7. Multures, suckens and other legal aspects of milling will be found in 7.8.3.

11.1.1 GENERAL, MISCELLANEOUS

accession complicity, concurrence or assent in some action.

†**actor** an agent, *esp law* one who acts on behalf of another.

adhibit put (one's signature or seal) to a document.

advise reserve for further consideration; review, reconsider.

affix, †**effix** attach (a seal) to a document.

†**agent** act as legal representative (in a cause).

aliment maintenance or support claimed from another; alimony.

allenarly only, solely, exclusively.

†**append, appense** attach (a seal) to a document.

appreciate, appretiate appraise, value. **appreciation** the valuing of **poinded** goods.

†**apprehend** find and seize (goods etc); get or lay hold of as a legal act.

arbiter[1] a person chosen or appointed to decide in a dispute between parties, an arbitrator.

†**arbiter**[2] arbitration.

arbitral, †**arbitrar** of, belonging to, made or pronounced by an **arbiter**[1], *chf* **decreet** or *(latterly)* **decree** ~.

†**assigna(y)** assignee.

assize of articles or payments subject to some regulation, tax etc.

†**assurance** certification; guarantee by act or statement.

atour across; (down) over; out of; above; beyond.

†**atto(u)rnay** the appointment of a legal representative or agent.

augmentation an increase in the amount of a periodical payment, *eg* a minister's **stipend**, rent.

avisandum further consideration.

†**aye and while** until, during the time that.

†**backspang** a legal flaw or loophole.

†**band** a promise, agreement contract; an alliance of mutual interest; **a covenant, league;** a formal or documentary bond or contract entered into by an individual.

†**barrace** an enclosure for judicial combats, tournaments etc.

†**bathe as ane and ane as bathe** jointly and equally.

†**bidden: lawful** *etc* **time** ~ at the time appointed by law.

†**brew talloun** tallow paid as a tax for the privilege of brewing.

†**burgh laws** the code of law governing the burghs, translated in the early fifteenth century from *Leges Quatuor Burgorum.*

by: † ~**ganes** things of the past or done in the past, *esp* past offences or injuries. ~ **and out owre** *now Abd Fif,* † ~ **and atour,** ~ **and besides** *orig freq law etc* in addition to, besides.

†**cachet** a seal or stamp for impressing documents.

†**caduciar** caducary, subject to or by way of.

†**cast** reject or impose as illegal or improper; annul.

†**certiorat(e)** certified.

cess 1 a tax: (1) †the king's or land tax; (2) a local tax *now Abd Ags Fif;* (3) ~**es** rates and taxes *in gen now Bnf.* **2** an exaction of any kind; a tribute *now Bnf.*

†**challenge, challance** a calling to account.

†**clamant** urgent, calling for redress.

†**cled** provided **with** (some material object).

†**cleme** claim.

†**common law** the usual civil law.

†**compositor, componitour** a person who settles disputes etc.

†**compulsitor** compelling performance.

confusion, confusio a mixture of liquids.

conjunct and confident persons persons related by blood and connected by interest, *eg* in a bankruptcy case where recent transfer of property is challengeable.

conjunctly and severally where each of the persons named is singly liable etc for the whole of the obligation etc.

†**contravene** act contrary **to** (a statute etc).

†**contremandment** a counter-order.

†**coram** a quorum.

†**course** usual legal procedure, *usu* **be ~ of com-**

moun law. coursable legal, fulfilling normal legal procedure, *esp* **coursable brevis of one's** *or* **the chapel.**

†**cry down** forbid, suppress, disown by proclamation.

damnum fatale a loss due to an inevitable accident, such as an exceptional flood or storm.

†**daysman** an arbitrator, umpire.

†**deadly: against all** ~ against all persons.

†**debate** a (matter of) dispute as to legal rights etc.

decline reject formally the jurisdiction of.

†**dede** an act of legal import or consequence.

†**defalt, defaut: in his** *etc* ~ through his etc fault, failure, or negligence.

†**defer 1** agree or assent **to** (a legal exception etc). **2** refer (something) **to** (someone's oath).

†**demain** deal with as traitors, thieves etc.

demit resign, give over (an office, possession etc).

†**dependar** a dependant, adherent.

†**desert** given up; annulled; null and void.

desuetude *of old statutes* disuse, *chf* **be, fall in(to)** ~.

deugend litigious *Cai.*

†**dimissioun** the action of giving up or laying down (an office, possession etc), *freq* ~ **and** *etc* **resignation.**

†**doer** a person who acts for another; an agent, **factor.**

†**ease: put to (ane)** ~ bring to a settlement, arrange satisfactorily.

effere, †affere: effeiring, †~and pertaining, appropriate (**to**); corresponding (**to**). (**in form**) **as** ~**s** in the proper way, in due form.

†**efter, after** *in a document or narrative* below: '*as eftir followis*'..

elide annul, quash, exclude.

enorm considerable, severe, *chf* ~ **lesioun** *etc* great detriment.

†**entry, entress:** ~ **silver** money paid on entering into the occupation of land, on being admitted as an apprentice, on bringing goods into port etc.

†**execute** made legally effective.

exemp exempt.

exoner, *chf* ~ **of 1** relieve of an obligation or responsibility; **2** †free oneself by resigning an office etc; **3** †free from blame. ~**ation** the act of being legally disburdened of, or liberated from the performance of a duty or obligation.

expenses costs.

expire †render (a charter etc) void of further effect. **expiry** *of time, contracts etc* termination.

†**extend** apply (a law) specially or more extensively.

†**extent** *n* a levy, contribution or tax imposed by assessment. *v* tax by assessment.

facile easily influenced by others, weak-minded. **facility** being **facile.**

faculty a power given to do something at will.

†**failzie** default (**in**).

fatuous in a state of imbecility and therefore incapable of managing one's own affairs.

†**fore** advantage, profit.

forehand *of payments, now only of rents* made in advance.

foresaid *before or after its noun, now esp law and official* aforesaid, above-mentioned. ~**s** the persons, matters etc previously mentioned.

†**free:** ~**dom** the area over which the immunities of a burgh extended. ~**holder,** ~**haldar** a person who, before the 1832 Reform Act, could elect or be elected a member of Parliament by virtue of holding lands direct of the Crown assessed at or over forty shillings.

†**furious** *of persons* mad, insane, *esp* violently. **furiosity** madness, insanity.

furth of out of, away from, beyond the confines or limits of *now law, literary and NE.*

†**fury** violent insanity.

habile admissible, valid; apt, competent for some purpose.

habit and repute *adj* held or regarded to be (a thief, a married person etc). *n* the state or fact of being so regarded, reputation.

hail, whole: the whole of, **the** full number of: '*the whole Heritors or their agents*'.

hereanent concerning this matter; in regard to what has just been said.

†**heritable jurisdictions** collective term for various ancient rights formerly enjoyed by feudal proprietors of land or by holders of certain offices, entitling them to administer justice in local courts; abolished by the Heritable Jurisdictions (Scotland) Act 1747.

†**thing, hang,** *freq* ~ **to** attach, append (one's seal to a document).

holograph *adj, of a deed or letter* wholly in the handwriting of one person and, in the case of a will, signed by him. *n* a document wholly in the handwriting of one person.

homologate ratify, confirm, approve, render valid, *esp law* ratify (a deed etc which was informal or defective). **homologation** the act of confirming by implication something not previously legally binding.

†**honorary** an honorarium, a fee for professional services, in law considered as a gift made in acknowledgment of services gratuitously rendered.

†idiotry idiocy, the inability to conduct one's own affairs because of mental weakness.

†impediment: mak ~ offer hindrance, opposition or objection. **without, but** *etc* **~** *in precautionary formulae etc* without obstruction, opposition or objection.

†imput impute, lay to the charge of, attribute (a fault, a crime, blame) **to.**

†imput to *or* **upon** impose, levy (a tax etc) on.

in to the amount or extent of: *'fined in forty pounds'.*

indict accuse.

†indors, *also* **indoce** endorse. **~atioun** endorsement.

†indorsate endorsed.

industrial brought about by the industry of man.

†ingiver one who hands in or lodges a document formally for registration etc. **ingiving** giving in a document, submitting it for consideration.

†inhabile unfit, unqualified, inadmissible.

†inhability disqualification, loss of legal rights.

†iniquity lack of equity, partiality.

†injune enjoin.

injure †*n* injustice, wrong, mischief done to a person; an instance of this. *v* do injustice to.

†innovat revised, renewed.

innovation †the alteration of an established form, practice, institution, or legal provision.

†inrin commit (an offence), incur (a loss), fall into (a difficulty etc).

†interchangeably, enterchangeably mutually, reciprocally.

†interpell prohibit, prevent.

interpone 1 †interpose. **2** *of a court* **~ authority to** approve (a private settlement). **† ~ one's authority to** *etc* intervene so as to prevent something.

intimation an official notice given to persons concerned, of something required of them and the penalty in case of default.

†irrevocabill *of a person appointed as an agent etc* authorized irrevocably, whose appointment may not be revoked or rescinded.

irritant to be rendered or rendering null and void.

irritate make void, nullify.

ish, †ush, ischew the termination of a legal term, term of office or service, or any period of time; the expiry (date) of a lease etc.

Jethart, Jedburgh: ~ justice precipitate or arbitrary justice, condemnation without a hearing.

jonick fair play, justice.

†joyse enjoy or have the use of, be in occupation or possession of (lands, office, rights etc).

†judgement judicial authority or the extent or territory of this; jurisdiction.

†jugisment judgement.

†jurant, juror (a person) taking an oath of abjuration in favour of William and Mary, Anne or the House of Hanover. **non-~** (a person) refusing to take such an oath.

†jure jurisprudence.

†justery 1 *appar* one of the districts into which the country was divided for administration of the law by the **justices**; the jurisdiction of a **Justice** within a specified district. **2** = **justiciary** 1, 2. **3** justice, the administration of the law, equity.

justiciary 1 the office or jurisdiction of a **justice** or of the **Justices**. **2** †the judicature as an official body

†ken: be it (made) ~d *formula introducing the principal statement of a legal deed or formal declaration* **make ~d** *in the formula introducing a formal declaration,* make known, declare.

†keyis: use *etc* **the kingis, his hienes** *etc* **~** force entry by virtue of a legal warrant.

†knaw, know make judicial inquiry into, take legal cognizance of. **~lage** judicial or authoritative knowledge; formal investigation to obtain this; legal cognizance, *freq in phrs* **gif a ~lage of** *or* **be ane assise, tak ~lage, pas, put** *or* **tak (something, a person) to the ~lage of ane assise.**

†lang: leave, put *etc* **someone to the ~ sands** subject someone to a lengthy process of litigation.

law, †lauch: ~ful lawful. **~ful day** *etc* a day etc on which it is permissible to transact business. **†law-biding** submitting to the law. **~-paper** a legal document *now Ork Ayr.*

†lawtie integrity in the administration of the law, justice, equity.

†lead administer (the law(s)).

leal 1 †legally valid, just. **2** honest, honourable, law-abiding. **† ~ becumit, ~ come (by), ~ won** lawfully obtained, honestly earned.

†leesome, lefesum morally or legally permissible; right, just.

†leful, leveful, lechfull legally or morally permissible.

†lesed injured in regard to one's interest, property, rights or reputation. **the party ~** the injured party.

†leve: the langar *or* **langest levand** *or* **levar (of thaim)** the survivor.

†lie be, remain, or continue in legal dispute.

†liege poustie the state of being in full possession of one's faculties; soundness in mind and body.

lockfast fastened by a lock, shut and locked, secured under lock and key against interference;

breaking into a ~ place constitutes an aggravation of theft.

locus a place, site, position.

†**majesté: the buke of ~, the Kingis** *or* **Scottis** ~ the early Scottish legal compilation which opens with the words *Regiam Majestatem; loosely* the 'auld laws' as a whole.

†**manrent** homage, vassalary, vassalage. **band, bond** *or* **letter(is) of** ~ the contract between the parties concerned.

†**manuale** *of a signature* written with the hand, autograph, *chf* **subscription ~**.

†**march: day of** ~ a day of truce on which a court of the wardens of the opposing **marches** heard complaints of infringements of the **laws of march. law, statutis** *etc* **of (the) ~(is)** the code of regulations governing Anglo-Scottish relations on the Border.

mediat *of a person* intermediary, intervening; that acts for another.

mid: ~-impediment any event happening between two others which prevents the latter event from becoming effective. †**~man** a mediator. †**~ persoun** a mediator; an intermediary.

mora delay in pressing a claim or obligation which may infer that the action has been abandoned by the **pursuer.**

†**motive: of one's owin (fre, proper)** ~ **will** of one's own free will.

†**mute 1** a formal meeting to discuss and transact official or legal business. **2** litigation.

negative in the negative.

nimious excessive, vexatiously burdensome, *now chf* ~ **and oppressive.**

†**notour 1** (of facts) commonly known or manifest. **2** of facts or circumstances involving no discredit.

now: ~ as then, than as ~ at or for all or any present or future time, for all time.

oblige compel, constrain; consign, commit.

†**oneratioun** a financial burden or charge; a written statement or account of this.

onerous involving payment; granted or created in return for money, services etc received. **onerosity** the fact or condition of being **onerous.**

†**order: as the** ~ **of law will, is usit** *etc* according to the law, in regular legal form. **put** ~ **to, in** *etc* impose order on, exercise authority over, regulate, set to rights, take disciplinary action against.

†**outgiving** giving out, delivering, issuing.

†**outpassing** expiry.

†**outrun** *of time, a due date, contract etc* expire, run out. ~**ing** the expiry of a set period of time etc.

†**out-tane 1** *chf* in bonds of **manrent** excluded, excepted. **2** disclaimed, repudiated.

overture †*n* a proposal or recommendation drawn up for the consideration of a legislative body; a bill etc. *v* submit as a more or less formal proposal to (a legislative or deliberative assembly); propose (a motion) formally; petition.

†**owersicht** failure to take preventive or punitive action; licence, indulgence, toleration, connivance; allowance, special permission (to do something).

oversman, owersman a chief **arbiter**, appointed to have the final decision in the event of a deadlock.

own, awn acknowledge as a relation or acquaintance, give recognition to; deign to be associated with; have to do with; attend to; come into contact with; lay claim to.

patent *of premises, a route, document etc* open to all, generally accessible, public.

†**pertene (un)to** *of a legal issue etc* come under the jurisdiction of.

†**plaintis, plaintuous: be** ~ **(of** *or* **on)** have a grievance (about); express a complaint, *esp* a formal one (about).

†**pley, plie 1** litigate, go to law. **2** sue (a person); take to court. ~**abill** *of a thing in dispute* (that is to be) the subject of litigation. ~**ar** a litigant. **be in** ~ *of a thing in dispute* be the subject of litigation. **but** *or* **without (ony)** ~ without litigation or objection; not liable to plea or counterplea. **enter** *etc* **in** ~ *of a person* engage or be engated in litigation. **move** ~ institute legal proceedings.

†**practicate** legally decided.

principal *adj, of a document* original, not in the form of a copy. *n* the original of a document.

privy seal the seal used to authenticate a royal grant of personal or assignable rights; it was not abolished by the Act of Union but continued subject to regulations made by ensuing Parliaments and is still in existence although no longer a requirement.

†**procure** obtain by formal application, *freq* ~ **a person's seal**.

prorogate defer the termination of (a period of time), extend, prolong (*esp* a lease).

protest make a formal request, demand as a right, stipulate.

proven proved.

†**puir, poor** *followed by a person's name* indicating that he had been given free legal aid because his name was on the **poor's roll**.

†**question** a legal dispute, a litigation.

†**quoniam attachiamenta** name given, from its opening words, to an ancient (now thought to be late fourteenth century) work of Scots Law.

†**ratificatory** confirmatory.

†**ratihabit** express approval of, sanction. ~**ion** approval, approbation, sanction.

†**reable** restore to a former state or position; legitimize.

†**reclaim** make a claim against, sue at law. **reclamation** an appeal at law.

†**re-examinat** re-examined.

†**repute (and halden)** reputed, considered, reckoned.

resile draw back, withdraw (**from** an agreement, undertaking etc).

†**resolve** make or become void, (cause to) lapse.

†**richt, right:** ~**(e)ous** rightful, lawful, legitimate.

†**sanctuar** a sanctuary.

†**scat** a tax or tribute; one of various local taxes.

†**semple, simple** without any strengthening circumstances.

sicker *of laws* harsh, rigorous *now Ork*.

simpliciter simply, unconditionally, without further condition or reservation.

†**sine quo non** an indispensable person.

†**skail** annul (a proclamation).

†**subsidiarie** in a secondary or subsidiary manner, as a second resort.

sundry: all and ~ one and all, all collectively and severally.

†**tanist** *Celtic law* the successor to a Celtic king or chief (of Ireland or Scotland), elected during his predecessor's lifetime from within certain degrees of kinship. ~**ic** of a **tanist**. ~**ry** the system of succession through a **tanist**; the office of a **tanist**.

†**tax roll** a list of its members drawn up by the **Convention of Royal Burghs** with the proportionate liability of each in the total tax payable by the burghs.

†**thirl, thrill 1** reduce to or hold in bondage or servitude. **2** bind or oblige (a person) to give his services or custom to a particular person (*see also* 7.8.3). *n, only* **thrill, threll** a person bound in servitude. *adj* bound in **thirlage** (to). ~**age**, ~**dom** thraldom, bondage. ~**er** a person under **thirlage.**

†**thraill** thrall, servitude.

timeous (sufficiently) early, in good time.

†**touch** ratify (an Act of the Scottish Parliament) by touching it with the sceptre.

†**toust** *n* a rate levied, tax. *v* tax.

umquhile former, late; deceased *now literary or arch*.

†**uncustom** an improper or illegal tax.

†**underly the law** be liable to legal procedures and penalties.

†**unlegittimate** not legitimated.

†**unreason** injustice, impropriety.

†**unreduced** not annulled or repealed.

unricht not right, unjust; dishonest, improper *now Fif SW*.

vacance 1 a vacation, holiday, period of suspension of business etc. **2** †a cessation or suspension (of laws).

†**vacancy** a vacation, holiday.

†**vagabond** *of laws* irregular.

†**valiant** *adj* valid, effective, decisive. *n* value, worth.

†**validat** valid.

verity: of ~ true: '*yet true it is and of verity ..*'

†**vetite** forbidden.

vis major a circumstance, *eg* a natural disaster, which cannot be reasonably expected or prevented, an act of God, a **damnum fatale** which excludes responsibility for loss, damage or the non-performance of a contract.

†**vitiat** rendered null or void; interfered with.

†**vod(e), voud** void.

†**wey, weigh** dispense or administer (justice) impartially.

whereanent concerning which, on account of which.

†**wit: let** ~ let it be known that, take notice that.

wrongous contrary to law, illegal, wrongful.

†**Yule vacance** the Christmas holidays or recess.

11.1.2 QUARTER DAYS

See also 14.4.1

Candlemas 2 Feb, a Scottish quarter day.

Lammas 1 Aug, a Scottish quarter day.

Martinmas the feast of St Martin, 11 Nov; a Scottish quarter day, one of the two legal **term days**, though the date for removals and for the employment of servants was changed in 1886 to 28 Nov.

term one of the four days of the year on which certain payments, *eg* rent or interest, become due, leases begin and end, and (*formerly*) contracts of employment, *esp* on farms, began and ended, **Candlemas, Whitsunday, Lammas, Martinmas**; *latterly* removal **terms** only were fixed as 28 May and 28 Nov. ~**ly 1** occurring or falling due every **term** or at the end of a

term. 2 †in each **term**, once every **term**. ~ **day,** ~ **time** the day or period at which one **term** ends and the next begins.

Whitsunday 15 May, a Scottish quarter day, one of the two legal **term** days, though the date for removals and for the employment of servants was changed in 1886 to 28 May.

11.2 COURTS

11.2.1 COURTS IN GENERAL

†**Admiral(i)ty: (High) Court of** ~ the court in which the **High Admiral** of Scotland exercised extensive jurisdiction (civil and criminal).

†**aire** a circuit court held by itinerant judges or officers.

†**bailie court** a local court held by a **bailie**.

†**baron court** a court held by a baron or his deputy in his **barony**.

†**Bill Chamber** a court separate from, but staffed by judges of, the **Court of Session**.

†**birlaw court** a neighbourhood court for the settlement of local disputes or complaints.

†**bothyn** a **sheriffdom** or **lordship**.

†**bound court** a district court.

†**burgh court** a court held within a burgh.

†**chamberlain:** ~ **aire,** ~ **court** the circuit court held by the **chamberlain**.

chancery an office, *orig* issuing **brieves** directing an inferior judge to try a specified issue with a jury; *latterly* dealing with the **service** of heirs or the recording of **services** etc.

College of Justice collective name for the body of judges (**Lords of Council and Session**) and others composing the supreme civil court.

court-house the building where law-courts are held *now NE*.

district court the lowest criminal court, staffed normally by lay justices of the peace.

†**Exchequer: Court of** ~ a court having jurisdiction in revenue cases (merged since 1856 in the **Court of Session**).

Faculty: the ~ **of Advocates** the members of the Scottish bar.

†**fifteen: the** ~ the **Court of Session** then consisting of fifteen judges, *esp* when acting in a body as a court of appeal.

†**fore-bar** in the old **Court of Session**, the bar at which **advocates** pleaded causes of first instance.

full bench a sitting of the **High Court of Jus-**

ticiary or of the **Inner House** of the **Court of Session** consisting of more than the quorum required for the hearing of criminal appeals generally.

†**green tables** informal name for the **Court of Session**.

†**grete assise** an assize consisting of 25 nobles or gentlemen appointed to try charges against an ordinary assize.

†**head court** *orig* one of the three principal sessions of a **burgh**, **sheriff-** or **baron-court** (which **freeholders** were obliged to attend); *latterly*, a court without judicial function, held once a year at **Michaelmas**, when the **freeholders** of a county met to make up the voters' rolls and, as required, to elect an MP.

Inner House the first and second divisions of judges of the **Court of Session**.

inquiry an inquest, *esp* an investigation into a fatal accident.

†**ish, ush** proceeds or profits (in the form of fines) of a local court of justice.

†**judgement: in** ~ (bring) before a court of law. **in (face of)** ~ during the formal course of proceedings in court, before a court of law, in court. **furth of, out of** *or* **outwith** ~ out of or outside the court. **sit in** ~ sit as a judge or as a duly constituted court of justice.

†**judicialie = in judgement**.

†**justery** a **justice aire** or other **justice court**.

†**justice** †the **Court of Justiciary**. † ~ **aire** the circuit court of the sovereign's **justice** (and) or of the justice of a **regality**. ~ **court, court of** ~ **1** a court presided over by a **justice**. **2 = Court of Justiciary.**

justiciary: †**commission of** ~ a court for trying criminal causes, now absorbed into next. **Court of J** ~ *orig* a court presided over by a **Justiciar**; *now, as* **High Court of J** ~ the supreme criminal court of Scotland (known informally as **the** High Court).

Land Court = Scottish Land Court.

lord: ~s the **Court of Session**. † ~**is auditoris (of Causis and Complaintis)** name for the judicial committees of Parliament for hearing parliamentary causes and complaints.

Lyon Court the Court of Heralds in Scotland.

†**Merk: Ten** ~ **Court** a municipal court dealing with small debts (up to ten **merks**), and with the recovery of servants' wages.

†**Michaelmas (head) court = head court**.

Outer House that part of the **Court of Session** in which cases of first instance are heard.

Parliament: ~ **Hall** the hall of **Parliament**

House which was the meeting place of the Scottish Parliament from 1639 to 1707 and which later became the ante-room to the **Court of Session**; *also* applied to apartments in Edinburgh and Stirling Castles where the medieval Scottish Parliament met. ~ **House** the building in the High Street of Edinburgh where the Scottish Parliament met; *now* the **Court of Session**.

†**Pasch Court** the Easter session of the **head court** of each **burgh**.

†**plain** *of a court* held in the public view and hearing, open.

†**prevene** *of a court or judge* take from (another) the preferable right of jurisdiction, by exercising the first judicial act.

privative *of the jurisdiction of a court* exclusive, not shared or exercised by others.

prorogate extend (the jurisdiction of a judge or court), *usu* by waiving objection to an incompetent jurisdiction.

†**Quarter-sessions** a court of review and appeal held quarterly by the Justices of the Peace on days appointed by statute.

†**regality:** ~ **court, court of** ~ a court held by a **lord of** ~ and presided over by a **bailie** or **stewart** as the **lord's** deputy.

†**seat (of Session)** the **Court of Session**.

session 1 †a court of justice consisting of the **Chancellor** and other persons chosen by the king, which determined causes previously brought before the king and his council. **2 the S~**, *now* **the Court of S~** the supreme civil judicature in Scotland. † ~ **house** the building where the **Court of Session** was held.

sheriff: **S** ~ **Court** the court presided over by the **sheriff**. ~**dom** the area under the jurisdiction of a sheriff, now a group of **regions** or a division of a **region**.

†**side bar** a secondary bar in the **Outer House** of the **Court of Session**.

†**sit down** *of a court* begin its sitting or business, sit.

†**small debt court** a court set up under a JP in 1801 for dealing with debts under £5, and under a **sheriff** in 1837 for debts up to £20.

territory the area over which a judge holds jurisdiction. **territorial** *of a jurisdiction, esp that of a* **sheriff**, limited to a defined area or district.

†**trew: day of** ~ (a day appointed for) a court held by the Wardens of the **Marches** of England and Scotland (on which a truce was held).

†**water court** a court dealing with issues relating to a particular river or canal.

11.2.2 COURTS; ACTIONS

asleep of a civil action where no further step in procedure has been taken within a year and a day after it was first lodged.

†**blude:** ~ **roll** a roll of persons accused of bloodshed. ~**wite,** ~**weck** guiltiness of, or liability to a penalty for bloodshed; an action against a person for bloodshed; a fine for bloodshed; the right of imposing or collecting this.

concourse the simultaneous existence of two actions based on the same grounds.

declarator, action of ~ an action brought by an interested party to have some legal right or status declared, but without claim on any person called as **defender** to do anything.

†**deduce** conduct, prosecute (a process or cause).

†**grounds and warrants** the reasons and documentary evidence on which a **decree** was based and which might be called for in an action of restriction.

insist (in) proceed with (a charge or action at law); continue with (one's case).

†**intend** raise or **pursue** (legal proceedings).

†**intent** the **pursuer's** action in a suit.

†**intented** *of a legal action* raised or instituted.

law-plea a lawsuit, process of litigation *now EC.*

†**mute** 1 an action at law, a plea. 2 litigation.

†**obtene** be successful in, win (an action at law). **optene upon** succeed in getting (costs etc) against (someone).

†**persecution of** (legal) prosecution of: 1 a person or an action at law; 2 a legal claim to (a property etc).

petitory, †**petitor** *chf of an action, freq contrasted with* **possessory** in which the court is asked to order the **defender** to do something, *eg* to pay money, to deliver goods.

plea, †**pley** *n* 1 an action at law, a lawsuit. 2 a plea. *v* 1 †**litigate**, go to law. 2 †**sue** (a person); take to court. 3 contest (a matter), make the subject of litigation. † ~ **abill** *of a thing in dispute* that is (to be) a subject of litigation; *of a dispute* that is being, or may be, argued and decided by a legal process. †**pleyar** a litigant. †**be in** ~ *of a thing in dispute* be the subject of litigation. †**but** *or* **without (ony)** ~ without litigation or objection; not liable to plea or counter-plea. †**enter** *etc* **in** ~ *of a person* engage or be engaged in litigation. †**move** ~ institute legal proceedings.

†**plead** an action at law, litigation; a plea by or on behalf of a litigant; an allegation, a claim.

ploy a legal action; a quarrel, disagreement, breach of the peace.

pursue 1 †prosecute in a court of law, sue. **2** carry on (an action at law), prosecute (a case), claim (damages) in litigation. **3** raise an action in a law court, take part in litigation. **4** †institute a claim **for** by legal action. **†pursuit 1** the action of prosecuting or bringing a suit; an action, suit, prosecution. **2** the prosecution or suing **of** (a person) by another. **3** the prosecution **of** (a legal action or suit) **aganis** or **upoun** (another). **4** the action of seeking to obtain or recover something by legal means.

†reprobator: action of ~ an action to challenge the impartiality or honesty of a witness.

rescissory 1 *of a legal action* purporting to declare a deed or illegal act void. **2** †*specif* of the Act of the Scottish Parliament of 1661 which rescinded all acts since 1633.

sleep *of an action* lapse through passage of time and failure of prosecution.

†souming and rouming a legal action to determine each tenant's **soum**.

spuilzie the taking away or meddling with the **moveable** goods of another without the owner's consent; an action for the restitution of such. **action** *etc* **of** ~ an action for restitution as above.

†suscitate *of an action* promoted.

tender an offer of a sum in settlement made during an action by the **defender** to the **pursuer**.

tenor: proving the ~ an action in which the **pursuer** seeks to set up a lost or destroyed document by proof of its contents.

†tyne lose (a cause) at law.

11.2.3 COURTS: PROCEDURES

abbreviate an abstract, abridgement, *latterly specif* of a **decree** of **adjudication** or, in bankruptcy, of the petition of **sequestration**.

†absents, absence absentees *chf* from a court of justice.

†accusatour an accuser.

†actioun a charge against a person.

adduce bring forward or produce (a person) in proof.

†adjournal, act of ~ a decision of court requiring one person to give satisfaction to another within a specified time.

†adjournay summon for trial.

adminicle a piece of supporting or corroborative evidence.

†adminiculate(d) supported by evidence.

advocate †*ptp* called as an action from a lower to a higher court. *v* appeal from a lower court to a higher one, *now* only in criminal cases; *of the higher court* call (a case) before itself. **†advocation** the calling of an action before a superior court.

†affirm = fence.

†agnosce investigate, establish by proof.

aith an oath.

alter change the judgement of a lower court.

appearance: enter ~ signify one's intention of defending an action in the **Court of Session** or the **Sheriff Court**.

approbate and reprobate assent to part of a deed and object to the rest (a course disallowed by law).

apud acta *of notices etc given in open court* during the proceedings.

†aret accuse.

†argu(e) accuse.

assignation an assignment of a right or rights; the **instrument** by which this is done.

assize a trial by jury; a jury. **†assizer** a juryman.

†attachiament apprehension, seizure.

†atteche attach, accuse, arrest. ~**ment** summons, arrest.

†avay *v* speak or plead at law, present evidence. *n* an argument or plea advanced in court. ~**ment** a legal declaration.

†bill the document used to initiate proceedings in the **Bill Chamber**.

†bodily by a corporal oath. **bodily athe** *or* **faith** a corporal oath.

†bor(r)ow stand surety for, bail (a person). *n* **borch, broch,** *pl* **borrowis** a surety, pledge. ~**gang** the fact of becoming surety; suretyship. **to borch** as a pledge or security. **draw in(to) borch** *or* **borrowgang** put in pledge. **borch, brogh** *or* **burgh of** *or* **and hamehald** a pledge that an animal sold is not stolen.

†box *n* a box in the corridor of **Parliament House**, Edinburgh, containing an **advocate**'s professional papers. *v* **lodge** (papers required in a lawsuit by the **Court of Session**) with the clerk, who put them in the appropriate box for the judge or official concerned. ~**-day** a day in the **Court of Session** vacation appointed for **boxing** papers.

brief, brieve a summons, legal writ.

†burgess oath the oath required of anyone wishing to become a burgess in the major **royal burghs**; there was bitter dispute in the eighteenth century between the **Burgher** and **Antiburgher Seceders** as to whether or not it required the swearer to uphold the Established Church, and thus whether or not it could be sworn with good conscience.

call summon before a court.

†caption *n* arrest.

catechis a catechizing; *latterly also* cross-questioning *now Bnf Abd*.

†cause: in the hour of ∼ at the time appointed for the trial.

caution 1 security; bail. **2** *also* ∼**er** one who stands surety. † ∼**ry**, ∼**arie** suretyship; the obligation entered into by a **cautioner**.

†challenge, challance summon or invite defiantly.

chancellor the foreman of a jury.

†charger an accuser, plaintiff.

†circumduce declare or claim (the term for **leading** a proof) to have elapsed.

†citat cited, summoned.

†clepe and call a legal summons.

cognition authoritative or judicial knowledge or the acquisition of this by inquiry or investigation, cognizance, *freq* **tak** ∼, *latterly specif* a process to ascertain certain facts, *eg* to prove a person insane.

†cognosce make judicial inquiry; take cognizance or jurisdiction (**upon**); declare or assign judicially; adjudicate.

†collitigant an opponent in a lawsuit.

compear appear **before** a court or other authority; present oneself, appear. † ∼**ance** appearance, as a formal act, *freq* **non-, nocht-**.

compensation, compensatio injurarium a plea that a **defender** should not be compelled to pay damages to a **pursuer** on the grounds that the **pursuer** is liable for as great or greater damages to the **defender**.

complainer, †complener a plaintiff, *latterly* a victim of a crime who has reported it to the authorities.

†compulsitour a writ ordering the performance of some act; anything which compels.

conclusion the clause in a **Court of Session summons** which states the precise relief sought.

concourse concurrence *esp* of an authority whose consent is necessary to a legal process, *eg* of the public prosecutor in a private prosecution.

condescendence, †condescendency a specification, statement of particulars, *freq* of legal statements of fact.

conjoin order a joint trial of (two processes involving the same subject and the same parties).

continue 1 adjourn, prorogue, put off (a case etc). **2** †grant (a person) a delay or respite. **con-**

tinuation adjournment, postponement. **†with continuation of days** with provision or allowance for a case etc to be continued or adjourned to a later date.

convene, †convine †summon before a tribunal.

convener 1 a person who assembles along with others, a person who convenes a meeting. **2** the chairman of a committee etc.

cross-speir cross-question *now Bnf Abd Fif*.

†culrach the surety given on removing a case from one court to another; the person acting as surety.

†Cupar justice formal trial after summary punishment.

†dacker search (a house, person) for stolen goods etc (by official warrant) *NE*.

debate the legal argument submitted by the parties on the closed **record**.

declaration the statement made before his committal and in the presence of the **sheriff** by a person whom it is intended to try on indictment.

declinature, †exception ∼ the refusal by a judge to exercise jurisdiction, appropriate in a case in which by reason of relationship to a party or pecuniary or other interest his decision might be thought affected; refusal to accept some office, appointment or benefit, *eg* as a trustee nominated by the truster.

†decourt force out of, dismiss from Court.

defence defence against an accusation, claim etc, or in support of an opinion. ∼**s** the pleading of a **defender** in a civil action. **†mak defens** (attempt to) defend oneself etc.

defender a defendant, *latterly only* in a civil case.

de fideli an oath taken by persons appointed to perform certain public or other duties that they will faithfully carry them out (a breach of which does not amount to perjury).

†delate *v* **1** accuse, denounce. **2 for** *or* **of** *or* **as** (**an offender**), *later esp* to a **kirk session** or **presbytery**. *adj* delated, accused. **delation** (a) denouncement, (an) accusation. **delator** an accuser, informer.

†dependand being still in process or undecided; awaiting settlement.

depone 1 †testify; give evidence on oath. **2** declare on oath. **3** †take, swear (an oath). **†deponar** a person who **depones**.

desert drop, cease to go on with, discontinue (a **summons**, action etc), *latterly chf* ∼ **the diet**.

deteen detain. **†detenar** detainer.

devolution the referring of decisions to an **oversman** *or* arbiters who differ in opinion. **clause of** ∼ a clause devolving some office, obligation, or duty, on a person, *eg* to act as an **arbiter**.

devolve pass a decision over to an **oversman**.

diet 1 †a meeting or session of a court, council or other (*usu* official) body. **2** a day or date fixed for a meeting (*eg* of a court), or for a market. **3** †the list of summonses set down to come before the **Court of Session** from each quarter of the country. †**keep (the, our** *etc*) ~ appear (at a court or meeting) on the day appointed.

dilator †*adj* dilatory, causing delay, *esp* in a legal action. †*n* a delay, *esp* in giving a legal decision; a dilatory plea etc. **dilatory defence,** †**dilator** a defence which is purely technical, not touching the merits of the case.

diligence application of legal means against a person, *esp* for the enforcing of a payment or recovery of a debt; a warrant issued by a court to enforce the attendance of witnesses, or the production of writings.

†**dischairge** forbid, prohibit from doing something.

†**dishabilitate** *v* subject to legal disqualification.

†**dittay 1** *also* **dictay, points of** ~ a statement of the charge(s) against an accused person; an indictment. **2** a body or list of indictments coming before a court for trial. **3** formal accusation, indictment; information forming a basis of indictment. **take (up)** ~ obtain information and proof with a view to prosecution.

document 1 †proof, evidence, testimony. **2** written evidence, a written statement or record of a legal matter.

dominus litis the person really though not nominally behind legal proceedings, liable to pay **expenses**.

donatory a **donator** (*now* only from the Crown).

†**duply** *n* a second answer, *ie* the **defender's** rejoinder to the **pursuer's reply**. *v* answer in a **duply**; allege in a **duply**.

†**ease** a reduction or remission of an amount or service due.

edict †a proclamation made in a public place summoning persons to appear before the courts. ~**al citation** a citation made by **edict**, *now* by sending copies of the summons to the **Keeper of E ~al Citations**. ~**ally** by means of an **edict** or **edictal citation**.

eik *n* an addition or supplement to a document, *latterly esp* an extension of the confirmation of an executor, to cover property not originally included. †*v* make an addition to a document etc.

†**end** settle, come to an agreement.

†**enter, inter 1** appear or present oneself in a court. **2** produce, present (a person) to a court of justice.

†**entry, entress** an appearance or presentation in a court of justice.

†**essonȝe, assonȝe** an excuse, *esp* one offered as a legal defence, a pretext.

evident, †**avedent 1** a document establishing a legal right or title to anything, *freq* **writs and** ~**s**. **2** a piece of evidence, a proof.

†**examinate** examine. **examinator** an examiner, interrogator.

†**excep(t)** make an objection, protest.

exception a plea against a charge etc, a defence; an objection to a judge's charge to the jury in a civil case.

†**excipient** a person who raises an **exception** in law.

execution the writing in which an officer of the law narrates his fulfilment of duty. †**put to** ~ execute, perform.

†**exhibition 1** the presentation (of a person) in court. **2** production or delivery of documents at the instance of a court.

expede complete and issue (a document).

extend make a final copy of (a legal document) for signature.

extract *n* an official certified copy of a judgement of a court or of any other publicly-recorded document. *v* make an official, properly-authenticated copy of (any publicly-recorded document).

†**extrete, extrec(t)** a certified copy of the fines imposed at (*chf*, a **justice aire** or other court; the fines specified in this.

extrinsic *of a fact or circumstance given under oath* not essentially qualifying the matter attested, not inherent to the point immediately at issue.

†**false:** ~**r** a person who challenges a legal judgement. ~**ing** the act of questioning a legal judgement. ~ **a dome, falsifé a dome** deny the justice of a sentence and appeal to a superior court.

†**famous** *esp of witnesses* of good repute, of unexceptionable character *midLoth*.

†**feinȝeit** *of documents* forged, spurious.

fence 1 open the proceedings of (a court or †parliament) by uttering a formula forbidding interruptions. **2** †put under arrest. † ~**ment** the formal opening of a court or of parliament.

†**feriat, feriale:** ~ **time** *etc* a time in which no legal proceedings can be taken.

†**fetters** the restrictions imposed by a deed of entail.

†**follow, fallow: pursue** (a person) at law. ~**er** a **pursuer** or claimant at law. ~**ing a pursuing** at law, the prosecution of a suit or claim. ~ **furth** follow up, prosecute.

†**forspeaker** a person who speaks on behalf of another, an advocate.

free *in calculating time, esp of days between a summons and a trial* clear, non-inclusive.

†**great avizandum** an **avisandum** from a judge in the **Outer House** to the judges in the **Inner House**; a report by the **Lord Ordinary** to the **Inner House** in certain actions.

guid, good: (be)come ~ **for** be surety for *now local.*

habile admissible, valid; apt, competent for some purpose. †**habilitie** the legal competence of a witness.

haver the holder of documents, *specif* those required as evidence in a court.

impreve disprove (a legal document) *chf* as being forged; repudiate; disapprove, condemn.

improbation disproof of a legal deed as invalid or (*chf*) forged; *esp* an action to annul a deed on these grounds. **improbative** liable to **improbation**; not proved to be true.

†**improve** disprove.

†**improvin** *chf of legal deeds etc* disproved.

inclose 1 *also* **enclose** shut a jury in a retiring room for consideration of the verdict. **2** †*of a jury* retire for this purpose.

indictment the form of process by which the accused is brought to trial at the instance of the **Lord Advocate**.

induciae the period of time between a citation to appear in a law court and the date fixed for the hearing.

†**information 1** ~(s) a written argument ordered by a **Lord Ordinary** in the **Court of Session** or by the **Court of Justiciary** when difficult questions of law arose. **2** *in criminal cases* a formal written accusation or statement of the charge.

in litem: oath ~ an oath sworn by the **pursuer** in an action regarding the amount of loss suffered by him.

in retentis *of evidence* taken on oath before a case is heard.

instance the pleading and procedure followed during the hearing of a legal action. †**to** (**someone's**) ~ to the suit or citation (of a **pursuer**). †**with** (**gret**) ~ *in the formula recording the procuring of a seal.*

instruct supply evidence or documentary proof of, prove clearly, vouch for (a fact). † ~**ion** evidence, proof.

interdict *n* a court order prohibiting some action complained of as illegal or wrongful, until the question of right is tried in the proper court, *corresponding to Eng* injunction. *v* **1** restrain (a spendthrift or **facile** person) by law from disposing recklessly of his estate. **2** prohibit or restrain from an action by an **interdict**. ~**ion** the means whereby the actions of a **facile** person are restrained either voluntarily or by a court. ~**or** a person whose consent is necessary before a **facile** person can grant any deed involving his estate. **interim** ~ a provisional **interdict** which can be granted without the participation of the **defender**.

interlocutor *strictly* an order or judgement given in the course of a suit by the **Court of Session** or a **Lord Ordinary** before final judgement is pronounced; any court order. † ~**y,** **interloquutoure** provisional, not finally decisive.

†**interrogators** questions to a witness etc.

intrinsic *of an explanation admitted under oath* not separable from what is sworn and thus qualifying the oath.

irrelevant *of a legal claim or charge* not **relevant**, not sufficient or pertinent in law to warrant the **decree** asked for. **irrelevance** lack of pertinence, impropriety.

†**journall** a register of the **Court of Justiciary**, the **Justice Aire** or another court.

judicatum solvi *of a security* pledged for the payment or satisfaction of a judgement.

juratory caution inadequate security allowed in some civil cases where no better security is available, *similar to Eng* entering into recognisance

†**lat, let:** ~ **to borch** (**borrow**) give up (something) on security, release (a person) on bail.

law, †**lauch** *n* ~**s** the specific points of law cited in support of a plea; the legal basis of one's case. *v* litigate, sue *now Ork Abd Gall.* †**draw onesel** *or* **one's possessions law-borgh** pledge onself etc (not to injure another). **laws burrows,** †**lawborowis, law sovertie 1** legal security required from or given by a person that he will not ijnure another. **2** †*also* **law borch** the person standing as surety as above, *freq* **becum** *etc* **lawborrowis for.**

lead 1 †conduct (legal proceedings); hold (a court); bring (an action); deliver (a judgement): *'quhatsumevir oure saidis counsalouris .. leidis to be done'.* **2** call, produce (evidence, witnesses etc): *'lead proof'.*

†**leal** honest, honourable, law-abiding, *specif* applied to a person required to act (under oath) officially or legally, *esp* in testifying. **bere** ~ (**and suthefast**) **witnes(sing)** give a truthful testimony.

†**ledge** assert, declare, make accusations.

233

†**letters: run one's** ~ await trial; if the prosecutor failed to bring his case within the prescribed period, the prisoner was liberated.

libel *n* a formal statement of the grounds on which a suit or prosecution is brought. *v* **1** specify in an indictment; state as grounds for a suit or prosecution. **2** make a formal charge against. †**libellat** specified in the **libel**; drawn up as a **libel**.

†**liberat(e)** set at liberty, released.

lift *of the police* arrest, apprehend, take into custody. †**instrumentis to (tak,) (ask,)** ~ **and raise** the legal formula in commission of **procuratory**.

litiscontestation the stage at or after which an action in court begins to be contested. †**act of** ~ the judicial act admitting a case to proof.

lodge leave (pleadings etc) in the custody of the clerk of court, *corresponding to Eng* file.

lose be defeated in (lawsuit etc).

†**mane** present formally as a grievance, state as a formal complaint.

†**manswear 1** swear falsely, commit perjury; perjure oneself. **2** refuse or cease to acknowledge, *esp* on oath; disavow, abjure. **3** quit (a place) on oath not to return within the time stated. **manswearing** perjury, bearing false witness. **mansworn** *of persons* forsworn, perjured; *of oaths* sworn falsely, perjured.

†**meet** provide an adequate answer to (contrary allegations etc).

memorial 1 †a statement of facts submitted to the **Lord Ordinary** as a preliminary to a hearing. **2** a document prepared by a solicitor for counsel, giving certain facts and circumstances and indicating the question on which counsel's opinion is sought.

mid couple a piece of evidence linking a claimant with the right claimed.

†**mute** take (a person) to court, litigate.

†**non-entré** the failure to present oneself or another at some appointed place, *chf* in a court of law for trial.

†**oath:** ~ **of calumny** an oath taken at the outset of an action by which both parties swear that the facts pleaded are true. ~ **in supplement** an oath by which a litigant could give evidence in his own favour when impartial legal evidence was incomplete or defective.

†**obliged: be** ~ **in** be pledged or sworn.

obtemper comply with, submit **to** obey (*esp* a court order etc). † ~**ance (of)** complying (with); obedience.

†**oppone** oppose by argument, say or bring evidence to the contrary of, advance as an objection.

†**order of table** the sequence set out in a list of the succession in which causes etc were to be called.

†**ostend** exhibit or present (a document) for scrutiny.

†**ostensioun 1** presentation (of a document etc) for scrutiny. **2** the action of presenting (? by holding up) one's hand in taking of an oath etc.

†**palinode** a formal retraction of a defamatory statement which a **pursuer** could demand of the **defender** as part of the damages in a libel action; an apology.

panel 1 †the place of arraignment in a court, the dock, the bar. **2** a prisoner or (*formerly also*) a group of prisoners at the bar of the court, the accused. †**be** ~**led** be brought to trial, be indicted. †**enter in** *or* **on** ~ present for trial. †**put** *or* **set (up)on (the** *or* **ane)** ~ arraign, try.

†**partial counsel** advice, information etc given improperly to a witness in a case by a judge, juror, witness or other member of the court and constituting a ground for excluding his evidence as biased.

partibus a note written in the margin of a **Court of Session** summons listing the contestants in a case and their counsel and solicitors.

†**pass:** *chf* ~ **(up)on** serve or sit on a jury, inquest etc. ~ **to assise** *or* **probation** *of an accused person or a legal issue* go for trial or adjudication. ~ **(under) the great, privy** *etc* **seal** undergo the process of authentication required for royal grants, deeds etc.

†**perance** appearance, in sight, before a court etc.

perjure *n* perjury. *adj* perjured, perjurious.

petition one of the methods by which proceedings can be brought before the **Court of Session** or the **High Court of Justiciary**. ~ **and complaint** an application to the **Court of Session** for redress of eg complaints of professional misconduct brought against **magistrates** etc; *formerly also* the form for bringing under review by the **Court of Session** the actions of **freeholders** and **magistrates** of **royal burghs** at their **head courts**.

†**piece** a writ establishing a right or title.

plea 1 †state or maintain the claim of a party to a lawsuit, plead as an advocate **for** (a person) *or* **in** (a matter). **2** †put forward a plea; make a formal allegation. **3** †maintain (a plea or cause) by argument. ~ **in bar of trial** *etc* a statement or objection by the counsel for the accused, giving reasons why judgement should not be passed or why criminal proceedings should be dropped. ~ **in law** a short legal proposition at the end of a pleading showing exactly the relief sought and why. **The four ~s of the Crown** criminal cases on murder, robbery, rape and arson, which could only be heard in the **Court of Justiciary**; robbery and arson can now be tried in a **Sheriff Court**.

plead *v, past also* **pled** contend, argue, debate in a court of law; entreat for. †*n* a plea by or on behalf of a litigant; an allegation, a claim. †**pledar 1** a pleader. **2** a litigant.

†**pleen, plenȝe** make a formal complaint. **plenȝe-and** making formal complaint. **(party) ple-inȝeand, plenȝeour** the complainant or **pur-suer**.

†**porteous** an official list of persons to be indicted or otherwise proceeded against. ~ **roll** a list of persons drawn up by the **Justice Clerk** for indictment before the Circuit **Court of Justiciary**.

†**pose** charge (someone) **to declare** something.

†**prattick, practick** a customary usage, a precedent, the usual practice.

precognition the process of **precognoscing**; a statement made by a witness during this investigation.

precognosce carry out an initial investigation of the facts of a case by interrogating the witnesses to find out if there is a case to answer and to make it possible to prepare a relevant charge and defence; examine a witness in preparation for a trial; in criminal cases *orig* carried out by the **sheriff** or **judge ordinary**, *now* done by the **procurator fiscal**.

preliminary defence = **dilatory defence**.

prescribe 1 *of an action, a right etc* become invalid through the passage of time, lapse; *of a debt*, crime etc be immune from prosecution through lapse of time. **2** †make or declare invalid through lapse of time. †**prescriptibility** liability to **prescribe**, the state of being subject to **pre-scription. prescription** the lapse of time after which a right is either established or rendered invalid or a debt etc annulled, if previously unchallenged or unclaimed. **prescriptive** arising from **prescription**, *freq* **prescriptive title** *etc*.

†**prescrive 1** become valid by **prescription**. **2** *of a right or claim* cease to be valid; *of the prescribed period* elapse, run out.

†**presence: (hearing) in** ~ the hearing before an enlarged Court of a case in which the Judges of the **Inner House** have been equally divided.

privileged summons a summons in which the normal period of 27 days between the citation of a person and his appearance in court is shortened.

privy seal the seal used to authenticate a royal grant of personal or assignable rights; it was not abolished by the Act of Union but continued subject to regulations made by ensuing Parliaments and is still in existence although no longer a requirement.

probation the hearing of evidence in court before a judge; evidence, proof and the procedure for demonstrating it. **conjunct** ~ the process of disproving by evidence an opponent's allegations, carried on as part of the process of proving a party's own case. **probative** *chf of a document* having the quality or function of proving or demonstrating, carrying evidence of its own validity and authenticity.

process *n* the legal papers in an action **lodged** in court by both parties. †*v* proceed against in law, sue, bring to trial. ~ **caption** a warrant to imprison a person who has borrowed a **process** and has failed to return it. †**no** ~ a preliminary defence based or sustained on the grounds of a technical error in the procedure which bars trial.

production the exhibiting of a document in court; an article or document produced as evidence, an exhibit. **satisfy** ~ produce a document when challenged to do so in a court of law.

progress a series or progression, *esp* †**charter by** ~. † ~**ive** *of writs or deeds* constituting a series or **progress**.

†**proper improbation** the setting aside or discrediting of a document on the grounds of its falsity or the fact that it has been forged.

propone advance or state in a court of law. ~ **defences** state or move a defence.

†**prosecute** prosecute.

protestation the procedure by which a **defender** in the **Court of Session** compels the **pursuer** either to proceed with his action or to end it.

pruif, proof 1 proof. **2** †a person who gives evidence; a witness. **3** the method by which the disputed facts in a case are judicially determined, including the taking of evidence by a judge or (*formerly*) by a commissioner appointed by the Court, to determine the issues on which trial will take place; *also* (since the introduction of jury trial in 1815) trial before a judge only.

pruive, prieve prove.

†**purged of partial counsel** *of a witness etc* having taken an oath as to the disinterestedness and impartiality of the evidence he is about to give.

pursuer the active party in a civil action, the plaintiff.

†**quadruply** *n* a fourth answer, made by the **defender** in reply to the **triply** of the **pursuer**. *v* answer in a **quadruply**.

qualify *v* 1 establish by evidence, authenticate, testify. 2 †acquire or give legal sanction to by the taking or administration of an oath, *specif* in regard to the Scottish Episcopalians who until 1792 were not permitted to practise their faith until they renounced allegiance to the Jacobite monarchy; swear allegiance to. †**qualified oath** an oath upon **reference** qualified by special limitations restricting it, which must be **intrinsic** to be valid.

†**quality** a proviso, qualification, reservation.

quarter seal one of the seals of the Chancery of Scotland, still available for use but in practice no longer used, *orig* a quarter of the great seal.

†**quintuply** *n* a fifth answer, made by the **pursuer** in reply to the **defender's quadruply**. *v* answer in a **quintuply**.

quoad ultra used in the written pleadings of an action to indicate the point beyond which the **defender** makes no further admission of the **pursuer's** allegations.

†**quote a paper** endorse the title of a paper.

raise draw up (a summons, **letter** etc), bring, institute (an action).

reclaim appeal, *now* from the **Outer House** to the **Inner House** of the **Court of Session**. ∼**ing motion,** † ∼**ing note** *etc* the procedure by which an appeal is made as above.

record the statements and answers of both parties to an action; when adjusted, the **record** is closed and the action proceeds to proof or debate.

†**recounter** *v* oppose (the giving of a pledge). *n* a counter-pledge or security.

†**redargue** refute, disprove (an argument, statement etc).

reduce annul, set aside by legal process. **reducible** *of a deed etc* capable of being set aside by legal process. **reduction** the process of **reducing** a deed etc as above. **reduction-improbation** a **reduction** sought on grounds of forgery. **reduction-reductive** the annulment of an improperly-obtained **reduction**.

refer in a civil action, *chf* ∼ **a matter to an oath** submit a fact at issue to proof by the oath of a **defender**, *esp* in a debt case. ∼**ence** the act of **referring** as above. ∼**rer** a person who **refers** as above.

†**Regulation roll** a roll of the **Court of Session**

listing jury cases or those where no appearance had been made for the **defender**.

relevant *esp of a charge or claim* pertinent, sufficient to justify the appropriate penalty or remedy, if the alleged facts are proved. **relevancy** the state of being **relevant**.

remit the referring of a matter to another authority for opinion, information, execution etc, *specif* the transfer of a case from one court to another; the terms and limits of such a reference.

repel *of a court* reject (a plea or submission); overrule (an objection).

†**replait, resplate** adjourn (a cause); remand (a person).

†**replede** plead again, raise a further plea.

†**repledge** 1 withdraw (a person or cause) from the jurisdiction of another court to that of one's own, under the pledge that justice would continue to be done. 2 take back or take over (something forfeited or impounded) on proper security. ∼**r** a person who **repledges** a criminal. **repledgiation** the act of **repledging**.

†**reply** *n* a counter-answer by the **pursuer** to the answer of the **defender**; *sometimes* this was called the answer and the **reply** was the second rejoinder by the **defender**. *v* answer the plea of a **defender**.

repone restore (a **defender**) to his right to defend his case, *esp* after judgement has been given against him in his absence.

†**reprehend** take (a person) in the act of doing wrong.

†**representation** an appeal against the decision of a judge of the **Court of Session** presented in the form of written pleadings.

†**representing days** the 20 days from the pronouncement of a **Court of Session** judgement during which an appeal against it might be lodged.

†**retourable** *of a document, esp* a **brieve** returnable to the authority issuing it.

ripe search thoroughly, examine (*esp* for stolen property).

†**rogue money** a local tax levied for the expenses of arrest and detention of criminals.

roll a list of cases, applications, motions etc set down for hearing in court.

†**rub** fix (a charge etc) **on** (a person).

†**s(c)lander** charge **with**; accuse **of** (a crime or offence).

†**sea breve** a document allowing reprisals at sea.

seal: pass (by, through *or* **under) the (Great, Privy** *etc* **)** ∼**(s)** *of a document making a gift, granting a warrant etc* be approved and authenticated by being sealed with the appropriate seal with the authority of the Chancery of Scotland or of the **Court of Session**.

sederunt †a meeting of the **Court of Session**. †~ **day** a day appointed for a sitting of the **Court of Session**. **Act of S**~ an ordinance drawn up by the judges of the **Court of Session** to regulate its procedure.

†**septuply** *of the pursuer* make a seventh answer, in reply to the **sextuply** of the **defender**.

†**sextuply** *of the defender* make a sixth reply in answer to the **quintuply** of the **pursuer**.

sheriff *v* act as a **sheriff**. †~ **fee** a fee payable to the **sheriff**. †~('s) **fiars = fiars**. †~('s) **gloves** a perquisite of the **sheriff** levied at a fair.

shewer a person appointed by a court to show a jury premises etc on which litigation is based.

†**signature, signator** a document presented to the **Baron of Exchequer** by a **writer to the signet** as the ground of a royal grant to the person in whose name it was presented.

signet *n* one of the Crown seals of Scotland, *orig* used for private and some official documents of the Sovereign, *latterly* used as the seal of the **Court of Session**. *v* stamp (a document) with a **signet**, *latterly* as the symbol of the authority of the **Court of Session**.

sist 1 stop, stay or halt (a legal process or procedure) by judicial decree, both in civil and ecclesiastical courts. 2 summon or cite to appear in a court case. 3 present oneself before a court, appear for trial or as a litigant.

†**size** a jury.

skill: man *or* **woman of** ~ an expert in a subject, *esp* one called in by a court.

sleep *of an action* lapse through passage of time and failure of prosecution.

†**sopite** settle, adjust, put an end to (a dispute etc).

†**sover** make safe, *esp* by a formal pledge. ~**ty 1** surety. 2 a person who becomes surety.

†**stage** bring (a person) to trial before a court.

stand: †~ (**at**) abide by, obey (a decree). ~ **good for** *Sh-WC,* ~ **in for** now *Sh Abd Ags* stand surety for, guarantee.

state a statement: 1 of facts or figures, *eg* in the pleas of a lawsuit or in financial transactions etc; 2 †*freq* ~ **of a vote** the formulation of a motion as it is to be put to a vote.

strait *of a legal instrument* stringently worded, peremptory.

†**stretch, streetch** a straining or relaxation of the strict import of a law, statement etc; a forced argument or claim.

style the approved form or model for drawing up a legal document. ~ **book** a book containing a collection of **styles**.

†**subscription: sign** *etc* **and** ~ **manual** signature, signed name.

†**subsume** state (in detail). **subsumption (of the libel)** a detailed description of an alleged crime.

†**succumb** fail (in a suit), *usu* for lack of proof.

†**suit** make an application or appeal for; sue for in a court of law. **call the** ~**s** call the names or designations of those bound to attend at a particular court.

†**suithfast** *of an oath or evidence* truthful, reliable.

†**summar** summary, *esp* of proceedings in minor cases in which written pleadings are dispensed with and formalities reduced. ~**ly** in a summary manner, without the formalities of the common law. ~ **roll** a roll of cases which require speedy disposal, going before the **Inner House** of the **Court of Session**.

summary applied to procedures which dispense with the full formalities of the law.

summons *v* take out a **summons** against, *esp* in actions of removal from a tenancy. *n* 1 an official document, *corresponding to the Eng* writ, from the **Court of Session** or *(formerly* in small-debt actions, *now* in **summary** causes) from a **sheriff** informing a person that civil proceedings are being taken against him, detailing the circumstances of the action and the redress sought, and granting warrant to cite him to appear in court. 2 †an order similar to this served on an accused person in criminal cases. 3 *informal* a citation to appear in a criminal court.

†**superinduction** the substitution or imposition of a word or letter in a document in place of another.

supersede postpone, defer, put off.

†**supersedere** a halt or cessation of the process of law, *specif* an agreement among creditors or a **decree** of a court to postpone action against a common debtor.

†**supervenient** *of a right* acquired by the **disponer** subsequently to the act of transmission. **superveniency** the fact or condition of being **supervenient**.

†**surrogate** substitute in respect of a right or claim.

surrogatum something which stands in the place of another, *eg* the price of a thing instead of the thing itself.

suspend 1 *of a court* defer or stay (execution of a sentence etc) until the case has been reviewed. **2** *of a litigant or convicted person* ask for **suspension** as a form of appeal. **~er** a person who **suspends** as in 1. **suspension** (a warrant for) stay of execution of a **decree** or sentence until the matter can be reviewed, used when ordinary appeal is incompetent, *freq* **bill** *etc* **of ~**.

table: lodge a **summons** before a court as a preliminary to its being called.

take, tak †require or accept (a promise etc) in a formal matter from, *freq* **~ someone bound** *etc.* **~ in** arrest, take into custody *local Ork-Kcb.*

†**targe, tairge** treat strictly or severely, *specif* question closely, cross-examine rigorously.

†**tasch** seize, arrest.

†**tenorall** of the tenor or ordinary course or procedure.

test †*n* **1** evidence, witness borne. **2** the oath of declaration prescribed by the Test Act of 1681, aimed at imposing on the extreme **Covenanters** compliance with the Episcopacy in the **Church of Scotland**. **~ing clause** the attestation clause which authenticates a deed by naming the witnesses and date and place of execution.

testifee testify.

†**thief-taker** a person who detects and captures a thief.

thirdsman a third person, *esp* one acting as **arbiter** between two disputants *local NE-S.*

†**thirl, thrill** subject **to** (some condition).

thole an assize *etc* stand trial.

through-pittin a rough handling, a severe rating or cross-examination *now Stlg WC, SW.*

†**tint, taint** prove (a charge).

transference, †transferring the procedure by which an action is transferred to his representative from a person who dies during the process.

†**trew** a suspension of judicial proceedings.

trial 1 in civil cases in Scotland, used only of a trial before a jury. **2** †the testing of a **probationer** before he is admitted to the bench.

†**triply** *n* a third answer, made by the **pursuer** in reply to the **duply** of the **defender**; *occas also* a second rejoinder by the **defender.** *v* make a **triply.**

ultroneous *of a witness* one who gives evidence spontaneously without being formally cited; *of evidence* given voluntarily.

†**unformal** not in proper form, not properly drawn up.

†**unlaw: not worth the King's ~** *of a destitute*

person, esp when challenging his reliability as a witness worthless.

†**unquarrelable** indisputable, unchallenged, incontrovertible.

†**upgiving** a declaration, a statement on oath.

†**uptaking** taking up (of **dittay**).

†**verification** a formal assertion of truth.

†**vidimus** an examination or inspection (*esp* of accounts or documents).

†**visnet** a trial by jury.

†**voche** vouch, assert a claim to.

†**wage, wadge** pledge. **lay in ~** give as security.

†**wairdour** a person in custody, a prisoner.

waken revive (a legal process) in which no action has been taken for a year. **minute** *or* **summons of wakening** the document which **wakens** a case.

†**wan(d)** a staff used as a symbol in various legal transactions. **wand of peace** a baton carried by the king's messenger and used to touch an outlaw to show his restoration to the king's peace; *also* ceremonially broken by the messenger to indicate obstruction in the course of his duty.

†**warrand, warrant** *n* a guarantor; surety, bail. *v* be surety for (someone).

†**water keeping** the guarding of a stretch of water against poachers.

†**will** a clause in a summons expressing a royal command, *chf* the **~ of the summons**.

†**witness: stand in ~** act as a witness. **witnessman** a witness.

writ a formal or legal document or writing, a deed (used *more gen* than in Eng where it is now *usu* restricted to written orders of a court).

11.2.4 COURTS: POWERS

absolvitor *n* a decision by a court in favour of the **defender**. †*adj, following its noun* in favour of the **defender**.

†**act** enact, decree.

adhere confirm or sustain the judgement of a lower court.

†**appell** appeal.

arrest seize (property), apprehend (a person) by legal warrant. **~ee** the person in whose hands the **arrestment** is laid. **~er** a person who arrests, *specif* one who under legal authority arrests **moveable** property belonging to his debtor which is in the hands of a third party. **~ment** the action of arresting, apprehending or seizing by legal authority, the seizing of a debt which is in the hands of a third party.

assoilzie decide in favour of (the **defender**).

brief, brieve 1 an official document; a summons, legal writ. **2** †*latterly chf* **brieve** *specif* a warrant from **chancery** authorizing an inquest or inquiry by a jury, *latterly* in such questions as the appointment of a **tutor** to a **pupil**.

brief: ~ **of division** a brief of **chancery** providing for the dividing of lands between **heirs-portioners**). †~ **of inquest** a **retourable brief** directing the **sheriff** or (in a burgh) **bailies** to try the validity of a claimant's title. †~ **of lining** a non-**retourable brief** out of **chancery**, directed to the **provost** and **bailies** of a burgh for settling the boundaries of holdings by **lining**. †~ **of mortancestry** *or* **mortancestor** a **brief** out of **chancery** directing an inquest into a claim that the raiser is heir to certain property formerly possessed by an ancestor and now wrongfully held by another.

†**caption** arrest; a warrant for an arrest for debt.

†**clenge, clange** clear oneself; declare, prove oneself not guilty; clear by a judicial verdict; find not guilty. ~**ing** clearing from a charge.

†**compell** force (a person) by distraint of property; distrain (goods etc).

†**condampnatioun** condemnation.

†**condampnatour, condempnatour** *adj* condemnatory. *n* a condemnatory sentence or decree.

†**condamp(ne)** condemn.

†**contramand** countermand.

†**contumaxit** declared guilty of contumacy.

†**convict** a conviction, verdict of guilty.

†**court plaint** the feudal privilege of dealing with complaints made to a court of justice.

curator, †curat a person either entitled by law or appointed by the Court or an individual to manage the affairs of a legally incapable person, *eg* a **minor**. †**curatrix** a female **curator**. ~ **bonis** the person appointed to manage the estate either of a **minor** (instead of his legal guardian), or of a person suffering from mental or, less commonly, physical infirmity.

†**curatory, curatry** the office of a **curator**.

dative *adj, after its noun of an executor or* **tutor** appointed by a court. *n* **1** = **decree dative**. **2** †an **executor dative**.

decern, †discern pronounce judicially; decide judicially or formally; decree. **decerniture** a **decree** or sentence of a court.

decree a final judgement. ~ **conform** a judgement by one court to render effective the decree

of another. ~ **dative** the judgement appointing a person executor.

†**decrete** *n* **1** a decision, decree, *esp* of an authority. **2** a judgement, decree of a court or judge. *v* order, decree, *esp* judicially; make, pronounce a decree.

†**defese 1** acquit or discharge from an obligation or penalty. **2** expunge, cancel. **defesance, defaisance** acquittance, discharge.

deliver give a decision or judgement (that ..); decide, settle (an action etc). ~**ance** a formal decision or judgement, *later* a judicial decision; *now* of the orders of the court in **sequestrations** including any order, warrant, judgement, decision.

†**denunce 1** proclaim (as) rebel or traitor. **2** sentence, condemn; proclaim as condemned.

†**denunciation (to** *etc* **the horn)** the act by which a person who has disobeyed a charge was proclaimed a rebel.

†**dischairge** declare oneself to have resigned all claim to something.

†**distrenzie** distrain; subject to constraint; seize (land or goods) by way of enforcing fulfilment of an obligation. ~**abill** liable or subject to distraint.

doom pronounce sentence against, condemn. †**but** *or* **withoutin** ~ **(or law)** without proper (trial and) sentence. †**give (for)** ~ give (as) judgement.

†**enter** place in custody.

†**executor** a person who serves a writ or executes a warrant.

†**fugie warrant** a warrant issued by a **sheriff** to a creditor to apprehend a debtor on sworn information that he intends to leave the country.

†**fugitation** a sentence of outlawry with confiscation of **moveable** property for failing to appear in court on a criminal charge.

†**fugitive: decern and adjudge** *or* **declare** ~ outlaw, pronounce sentence of **fugitation** on.

†**fyle** find guilty, convict, blame. ~ **a bill** find the charge made in a bill justified and the accused guilty.

†**incident diligence** a warrant issued by a lawcourt to enforce the production of evidence in the hands of third persons.

†**laud** a finding in a case of arbitration.

letter 1 ~**s** a **writ** or warrant in missive form, *latterly chf* one issued by the **High Court of Justiciary** or by the **Court of Session** under the **signet**. **2** †a missive from the sovereign by which he intervened by prerogative in the processes of the courts or crown offices, or issued peremptory commands to his officers. †**criminal** ~**s** a form of criminal charge in which the sovereign summoned the accused to answer the charge. ~**s of arrestment** a **writ** to attach property for debt. †~**s of caption** a warrant for the arrest of a person for debt. † ~**s conform,** ~**s conformand** a warrant issued by the supreme court to render effective the judgements of inferior courts. †~**s of cursing** a warrant issued by a decree of the pre-Reformation church courts excommunicating a stubborn offender. † ~**s of fire and sword** a warrant from the Privy Council to enforce court **decrees** of removing and ejection. † ~**s in the first, secund, thrid, ferd form,** ~**s in the four forms,** ~**s of four forms** the warrants (giving up to four successive charges) issued as the first step in a process of **diligence** against a person for debt. ~**s of horning** a warrant in the name of the sovereign charging the persons named to act as ordered, *eg* to pay a debt, under the penalty of being **put to the horn.** ~**s of inhibition** a warrant prohibiting a debtor from burdening or alienating his **heritage** to the prejudice of his creditor. † ~**s of intercommuning** a **writ** issued by the Privy Council prohibiting any communication with the persons named in it. †**letters of lawborrowis** the warrant charging a person to give security that he will not injure another. † ~**s of open doors** a warrant authorizing the forcing open of **lockfast** places containing goods to be **poinded.** † ~**(s) of panis** a missive containing a royal command or summons and specifying the penalties to which the recipient is liable for failure to comply. † ~**s of presentation** the **writ** by which a **presentation** is intimated to the **superior.** † ~ **of procuratory** written authorization for one person to act on behalf of another. † ~**s of slains** a **writ** subscribed by the relative of someone killed in a private feud, acknowledging payment of compensation, abjuring all further claims or revenge, and requesting the sovereign to grant remission. † ~**s of supplement** a warrant from the **Court of Session** enabling an inferior judge to summon a **defender** to appear when he did not live in the jurisdiction.

nobile officium the **Court of Session's** power of equitable jurisdiction in cases where the law itself does not provide a clear remedy.

†**obsolve** absolve.

†**ordinar: ordinar letters, letters** ~ a decree from an ordinary court, including an ecclesiastical court.

†**ourtane: be** ~ be found guilty or be convicted in a court of law (**of** *or* **with** the offence, **for** (as) an offender).

†**pass 1** *of a legal grant, award etc* be issued. **2** issue, give effect to, execute (a grant, warrant etc). † ~ **(ap)on 1** *of an adjudicator etc* proceed to give judgement on. **2** *of a grant, award or decree* be issued or given effect concerning.

†**patent: make** ~ **doors** *of a messenger-at-arms in a* **poinding** *action* force a **lockfast** place with the authority of a warrant.

†**plaint** = **court plaint.**

†**precept** a document instructing or authorizing a certain action, a warrant granted by a judge to give possession of something or to confer a privilege.

†**prevention** a privilege exercised by a superior judge or civil magistrate.

process caption a warrant to imprison a person who has borrowed a **process** and has failed to return it.

†**proper jurisdiction** the authority of a judge when acting in his own person as distinct from the authority delegated by him to a deputy.

proven: not ~ a verdict by the jury in a criminal trial when the whole or a majority find that although there is a suspicion of guilt, the case against the accused has not been proved beyond reasonable doubt; he or she is then unconditionally discharged.

†**quit** free, exonerate, acquit.

rehabilitate restore by **decree** (an attainted or degraded person) to former privileges, rank and possession.

†**relax** release from a legal process or penalty, *esp* from outlawry: '*relax from the horn*'. ~**ation** release from a judicial penalty, *esp* outlawry.

†**remede of** *or* **in law** redress for one's grievances through the appropriate legal channels, *esp* by appeal to a higher court against the decision of a lower one.

†**remission** a formal pardon; a document conveying this.

†**remit** remission, pardon.

†**repone, repose** restore to office or to rights previously held, reinstate. **reposition** the restoration of a person to an office or to rights from which he has been deposed; *esp* the reinstatement of a clergyman.

report *v, of a judge of first instance* remit (a case or part of it) to a body of one's colleagues, *chf* the **Inner House** of the **Court of Session** for decision. *n* the act of **reporting.**

†**retrocess** restore (a right temporarily assigned

to another), reinstate (a person) in a post or office.

†sensement a decision, judgement.

†shaw, show decree, award.

†sickerness safe custody.

sist *v* stop, stay or halt (a legal process or procedure) by judicial decree, both in civil and ecclesiastical courts. *n* a stay or suspension of a proceeding; an order by a judge to stay judgement or execution.

†statute ordain, decree.

†strenȝe distrain.

†sustain *of a court* support the validity of (a claim), uphold authoritatively, approve.

†ticket a certificate; a warrant, licence.

†tint, taint *n* a conviction; *specif* a verdict by a jury. *v* convict.

tolerance a licence or permission given, *freq* by tacit consent, to someone to do or enjoy something to which he cannot establish a formal right.

†trew grant a truce to.

unproven with a verdict of **not proven**.

†Valentin(e) a sealed letter from the Crown to landholders for the apprehension of lawbreakers.

†warding: act *etc* **of** ∼ a warrant for imprisonment for debt issued by magistrates in a **royal burgh**.

†warrand warrant.

†warrandice authorization, authority, warrant; a document conferring such.

11.3 RECORDS

Books of Adjournal the records of the High Court of Justiciary including the **Acts of Adjournal**.

Books of Sederunt the records of the **Court of Session** including the **Acts of Sederunt**.

†imbreve write out in the form of a **brief**; enter in writing.

†journall a register of the **Court of Justiciary**, the **Justice Aire** or another court.

minute 1 a note of the judgements, acts, decrees etc of a court or judge or of the intentions of a party in a suit regarding matters of procedure. **2** *in the* **Register of Sasines** *etc* a summary of the contents of a deed presented for registration, to be recorded in the **minute book**. **3** a memorandum setting out the heads of an agreement. ∼ **book** a systematically kept register of transactions, *esp* those of a notary or court.

†narrate set forth (the relevant facts) in a document. **narration** the act of reporting, *esp* by way of accusation, complaint or slander; a report or accusation, *freq* **fals** *or* **wrang narratioun** false report, misrepresentation. **narrative 1** *†also* **narration** a statement of alleged facts as the basis of a legal action, *freq* **wrang** *etc* **narrative. 2** †that part of a legal document which contains the statement of the alleged facts on which the plea is based. **3** that part of a legal deed which states the relevant essential facts.

†nature the tenor or purport (of a statute, written agreement etc).

note 1 a formal record *esp* in a court register. **2** an appendix to a **decree** in which a judge gives the reasons for his decision.

†outdraucht an extract, abstract or partial copy (of a record or account).

†pratticks, practicks the recorded decisions of the **Court of Session** forming a system of case-law.

protocol book, protocol record, †protocol the book or register in which a notary etc recorded the details of transactions.

†register the record of royal charters etc under the Great Seal; the collection of State and official papers, including parliamentary and judicial records and private deeds, *latterly esp* those concerned with the transfer of **heritable** property, preserved in **R** ∼ **House.**

†responde 1 *chf* ∼ **book,** *also* **buik of** ∼ a book in which records or receipts were kept, *specif*: (1) one in which **non-entry** and **relief** duties due by heirs were entered in **chancery**; (2) one in which decrees and acts were entered by the Clerk of **the Session**, providing a record for the charging of fees. **2** a single entry in **1**.

†sheriff roll the roll on which **sheriff-court** proceedings were recorded.

†transume, transump *v* make an official copy of (a legal document). *n* **transump(t)** a transcript or copy of a document.

†write a written record or document of any transaction, *esp* of a legal or formal nature.

11.4 LAWYERS, LAW OFFICERS

Includes court officials, policemen, executioners.

Accountant of Court an officer of court who supervises the conduct of **judicial factors** etc.

†actorney an attorney.

advocate 1 a professional pleader in a court of justice, a barrister. **2** a solicitor *Abd*. **~-depute** a salaried **advocate** appointed by the **Lord Advocate** to prosecute under his directions.

agent = **law agent**. † **~rie** the office or function of agent.

†**auditour** a judicial hearer **of** (complaints or suits). **A ~ of the Court of Session** *or* **of the Sheriff Court** an auditor who examines the accounts of **expenses** incurred in the respective courts.

bailie 1 †an officer of a **barony** or **regality**. **2** *also* †**bailiff, bailive** a town **magistrate** next in rank to the **provost**, since 1975 used only as a courtesy title by certain local authorities. †**bail(i)ery** the jurisdiction of a **bailie** or the district under him.

bangie a man (*occas* a policeman) specially appointed to watch the Solway and Annan for salmon poachers *Dmf*.

†**baron: ~ bailie** a **baron**'s deputy with both civil and criminal jurisdiction in the **Baron Court**. **B~s of (the) Exchequer** title of the judges of the Scottish Court of Exchequer.

†**basar** an executioner.

†**birlaw-man** one of the group of persons elected or appointed to act as judges or in local disputes.

†**blason** the badge of office displayed by a King's messenger.

bulkie a policeman *now Abd*.

†**burgh clerk** a town clerk.

†**burrio, burreau, burreour** an executioner.

†**captour** a person appointed to catch or detect offenders.

†**chamberlain, chamerlane** one of the chief officers of the royal household, *esp* **~ of Scotland**.

†**chancellor** the highest officer of the Crown and chief legal authority, *freq* **~ of Scotland**.

†**chekker, chakker: ((the) Lordis) auditouris of (the (king's))** **~** those appointed by commission under the **Quarter Seal** to hold the audit and constituting the court of exchequer to hear cases relating to the royal revenues.

Clerk of Session a clerk of court in the **Court of Session**. **Clerk of** *or* (*latterly*) **to the Signet = writer to the Signet**.

†**commissar 1** a commissary, delegate, representative. **2** a civil official taking the place of the former ecclesiastical diocesan commissary, *freq* **C~ of Lanark, Edinburgh** *etc*.

commissary †later name for a **commissar** 2. **~ clerk** the **sheriff clerk** when acting in relation to confirmation of executors.

†**connotar** a notary acting conjointly with another.

constable, †**counstable:** † **~ry, constabulary 1** the district under the jurisdiction of a constable. **2** the rank or office of constable. †**C ~ of Scotland** one of the chief officers of the royal household. **High C~ 1** *also* **Lord High C~ = Constable of Scotland**, the hereditary title, held by the Hays of Errol, being reserved by the Treaty of Union in 1707. **2** a member of a society of special constables created 1611 in Edb, who assume the title **High** in 1805 *now Edb*.

†**coronell** a coroner.

Crown Agent the chief Crown solicitor in criminal matters.

dean the elected leader of the Bar, whether of the **Faculty of Advocates** or of a local Bar of solicitors.

†**dempster, doomster** the officer of a court who pronounced doom or sentence as directed by the clerk or judge.

depute *adj* appointed or acting as deputy: '*advocate depute*'. *n* a deputy. *v* appoint as one's substitute or representative, or to act in some official capacity. †**deputrie** the office of deputy.

†**executor** a person who serves a writ or executes a warrant.

†**extentour** an assessor.

fiscal = **procurator fiscal**.

gaird, guard 1 a guard. **2** †**the ~** = **the town guard**; their headquarters; the lock-up.

†**hangie** *familiar* the hangman.

†**inquest** a body of men appointed to inquire into such matters as cognition of the insane and inheritance.

†**institor** an agent or manager.

†**javelor** a jailer.

jiler a jailer.

justice 1 the presiding judge in the **District Court** (since 1975). **2** *also* **justiciar,** †**Gret J ~** one of the (*orig* three, each with distinct territorial jurisdiction) **officers of state** who, either in person or by deputy, was charged with the holding of **justice aires** and **justice courts**, as presiding judge and in the name of the sovereign; *latterly* the supreme criminal judge but *orig* with jurisdiction also in certain civil matters. **3** *now only in combs* any judge charged with the holding of **justice courts** or **justice aires** in the name of the sovereign; the presiding judge of any particular **diet** of these courts. **4** †the corresponding officer of a **lord of regality**, with jurisdiction equivalent to that of the royal **justices**. **5** †a person with local and separate power of **justiciary** over a particular area. **6** †*in gen, esp literary* a judge. ~ **clerk 1** †an officiating clerk of a **diet** of the **justice court** or **justice aire**. **2 J**~ **Clerk,** *chf* **Lord J**~ **Clerk** the principal clerk of **justiciary,** *orig* the **officer of state** who officiated as clerk of the **justice court** or **justice aire;** *latterly* one of the principal judges and vice-president of the **Court of Justiciary.** †~ **deput** a deputy for the **Justice General** or for a **justice 4. J**~ **General,** *latterly chf* **Lord J**~ **General,** *also* †**J**~ **Principal** the principal **justice 1,** now the president of the **High Court of Justiciary.** †~ **in that part** one who has been granted particular rights of **justiciary,** *usu* over a particular area.

†**justiciar** = **justice,** *now the preferred hist term esp* = **justice 2.**

law: lawer, lawvyer 1 a lawyer *now local.* **2** †a university professor of law. ~ **agent** a solicitor *now in informal usage.* ~ **lord** one of the judges of the **Court of Session** to whom the courtesy title **lord** is given.

†**ledar** a person who administers the law(s).

†**lesson** the public discourse following the examination for admission as an **advocate.**

†**lettern** a lawyer's desk, *chf* **go** *or* **be put to the** ~ pursue legal studies.

†**lockman,** a public executioner, *chf* of a burgh *Ork C.*

lord 1 *as in Eng,* a formal title of certain of those holding high office in the state. **2** †~**(is)** members of Parliament or **General Counsail** or the sovereign's Council, or sections or committees of these, *eg* **the lordis of (the** *etc***) prevy** *or* **secret counsail. 3** †a member of the peerage, with a hereditary right to individual summons to Parliament or to the **General Counsail. 4** †*chf* ~**s of parliament** the lowest rank of the Scots parliamentary peerage, which emerged about 1445. **5** a judge of the **Court of Session** and its antecedents; ~**s** the court itself. **6** †with complements specifying any or all of the **Three Estates. 7** †*in territorial, family and other titles and designations:* the lord or proprietor **of** (a ~**ship**): '*the lord of Doun*'. **8** †*orig* prefixed (*without* **of**) to the family name of certain important barons, and from about 1445 exclusively used as the distinctive style of a **lord of parliament,** prefixed to the family or territorial name: '*(the) lord Gray, lord Halis*'. **9** as a complimentary designation of a ~ **of the session. 10** †**our** ~ *used alone or in apposition* one to whom others owe obedience, a **vassal**'s feudal lord, *chf* **our** ~ **the king. L**~ **Advocate** the principal law officer of

the Crown in Scotland. †~ **chalmerlane** = **chamberlain.** †~ **chancellour** = **chancellor.** †**L**~ **Chief Baron (of exchequer)** the president of the **Court of Exchequer** set up in 1707 and absorbed into the **Court of Session** in 1856. **L**~ **Commissioner of Justiciary** = **L**~ **of Justiciary. L**~ **Justice Clerk** = **Justice Clerk. L**~ **Justice General** = **Justice General. Lord Lyon (King of** *or (not officialy approved)* **at Arms)** the chief officer of arms of Scotland and head of the **Lyon Court. L**~ **Ordinary 1** †one of the regular ~**s of the session. 2** one of the judges (*now* 16 in number) of the **Court of Session** who sit on cases of first instance in the **Outer House. L**~ **President** the president of the **Court of Session** and head of the Scottish judiciary; the same judge now also holds the position of **Lord Justice General.** †**L**~ **Privy Seal** *orig* the (Lord) Keeper of the Privy Seal of Scotland, *latterly* merely a titular office. †**L**~ **Probationer** = **probationer.** †**criminall** ~**s** those ~ **of the session** who became judges of the **Court of Justiciary** by the Act of 1672. †**extraordinar(y)** ~**s of session, supernumerale** *or* **supernumerare** ~**is** those persons nominated by the sovereign to join the fifteen regular ~**s of the session** as additional or supernumerary members of the Court. †**L**~ **of Justiciary** a judge of the **Court of Justiciary.** ~**s of council and session,** ~**s of (the** *etc***) session,** †**the** ~**s of (the** *etc***) counsail,** ~**s of (the** *etc***) sete** the formal collective designation of the judges of the **Court of Session,** the **College of Justice.** †**ordinar** *or* **ordinary** ~ **(of (the) session)** = **L**~ **Ordinary.**

macer an official serving as usher in a court of law etc, who keeps order, acts as messenger etc. †**maserie,** ~**ship** the office of a **macer.**

magistrate title for a **provost** or **bailie** of a burgh as having administrative and judicial powers; also applied to stipendiary magistrates (but not to justices of the peace).

†**mair** an executive officer of the law of the Crown or of a **lord of regality.** ~**('s) corn, land** etc assigned to a **mair** as part of his perquisites. ~**dome** the office or jurisdiction of a **mair.** ~**schip** the office of a **mair.** ~ **of fee** a **mair** holding office, as commonly, by **heritable** right. ~**-of-fee-schip** the office of a ~ **of fee.**

†**man of business** a lawyer.

messenger *n, also* ~ **at** or †**of arms** a messenger of the Scottish Crown; from before 1510 under the authority of the **Lord Lyon** with the main function of executing summonses and letters of **diligence**. † ~y the office of a **messenger**.

†**multurer** an official with the duty or right of collecting **multure**.

†**notar** a notary, a notary public, *freq* ~ **public**, **public** ~ a clerk of court. **office of** ~**ie** the profession of notaryship.

†**odman, oddsman, odpersoun** *in a body of arbitrators* the third, fifth *etc* person, who was accepted as neutral and might give the casting vote. **odmen** arbitrators.

officer an official of any legal, municipal or ecclesiastical court, or similar body whose duty is to keep order at meetings, deliver messages, summonses etc. ~**ship** the position and functions of an officer. † ~ **corn** grain paid by tenants towards the emoluments of the officer of a **baron court**. ~ **of state** one of the important officials of state in Scotland, *eg* the **Lord Lyon, Lord Advocate**.

ordinary, †ordinar *adj* 1 *freq* **judge** ~, **sheriff** ~ *etc* a judge etc with a fixed and regular jurisdiction in all actions of the same general nature. 2 †applied to the regular **lords of session** and to the office of such. 3 †applied to the **lord of session** taking his turn of sitting separately on cases of first instance etc. †*n* 1 = **Lord Ordinary**. 2 = **judge ordinary**. **judge** ~ 1 **judge** ~ **(of the bounds)** a sheriff 3. 2 a **Lord Ordinary**.

oversman 1 a chief **arbiter** appointed to have the final decision in the event of deadlock. 2 †a chief and arbitrating executor; a person appointed by a testament to see that its terms are carried out, and/or to look after the interests of the widow and/or **pupil** or **minor** heirs.

part: in that ~ *of an official or office* by special appointment and with jurisdiction limited either to particular matters or with respect to time or place.

†**peat** an **advocate** reputed to be the protégé of a particular judge.

peg *slang* a policeman *local NE-WC*.

polisman a policemen.

†**Porteous clerk** one of a number of legal officers who investigated the circumstances of crimes to be prosecuted in the circuit courts.

†**prelocutor** a prolocutor, advocate, pleader.

†**president** the head of the **Court of Session**; *see* **Lord President**.

†**probationer** a newly-appointed judge of the **Court of Session** after he has presented his letter of appointment and before he takes the oath.

procurator a solicitor or lawyer practising before the lower courts *now only in formal contexts*. ~ **fiscal** the public prosecutor in a **Sheriff Court**, appointed *formerly* by the **sheriff** or magistrates, now by the **Lord Advocate**, who initiates the prosecution of crimes, and carries out to some extent the duties of an English coroner.

†**prolocutor** a spokesman in court, an **advocate**.

pundler a person whose main duty was *orig* the impounding of livestock, *later* looking after tree plantations *now Mry Bnf*.

†**ratt: the Town R** ~**s** the **town guard**.

red gown the scarlet gown worn by a judge of the **Court of Session** in his capacity as a **Lord of Justiciary** dealing with criminal cases.

register 1 † = **clerk** ~. 2 † = **Lord Clerk R** ~. **Lord Clerk R** ~, †**Clerk of (the** *or* **his)** ~, **clerk** ~, **Lord (Clerk) of R** ~, **Lord R** ~ the official, later **officer of state**, responsible for the framing and custody of the main state registers and records; *latterly* a titular office only (**Lord Clerk R** ~), giving the holder precedence after the **Lord Justice General**; he is also **Keeper of the Signet**. †**Deputy (Clerk) R** ~, **Keeper of the R** ~**s and Records** the official appointed to carry out the duties of the (titular) **Lord Clerk R** ~. **Keeper of the R** ~**s** the official responsible for framing the registers of **sasines**, deeds etc.

reporter the officer responsible for bringing cases before **children's** hearings.

†**scrow: clerk of the** ~ = **Clerk Register**.

†**scur** a sheriff officer or his assistant.

†**searchery** the office of a **searcher**, *esp* a customs-officer.

Senator of the College of Justice official title of a judge of the **Court of Session**.

†**serjeandrie** the office of sergeant in a **sheriffdom** whose duty it was to arrest and incarcerate those accused or suspected of crime under a **sheriff's** warrant.

†**servitor** an apprentice, *esp* to a lawyer, a lawyer's clerk.

†**sessioner** a member of the **Court of Session**.

†**shelly coat** a sheriff officer, bailiff.

sheriff 1 †the (hereditary) chief officer of a shire or county, responsible to the sovereign for peace and order, and having civil and criminal jurisdiction; *see also* ~ **depute** and ~ **principal**. 2 the chief judge of a **sheriffdom**; *see also* ~ **depute** and ~ **principal**. 3 a legal officer who performs judicial duties and certain administrative duties, some of the latter delegated by

the **sheriff principal**; *see also* ~ **substitute.**
~**ship** the office of a sheriff. ~ **clerk** the clerk
of the **sheriff court.** †~ **depute 1** the lawyer
appointed to perform the judicial duties of the
sheriff 1. 2 = **sheriff** 2. ~ **officer,** †~ **mair**
an official or messenger who carries out the warrants of a **sheriff,** enforces **diligence,** serves
writs etc. ~ **principal 1** † = **sheriff** 1.
2 = **sheriff** 2. †~ **substitute** = **sheriff** 3; *orig*
appointed by the **sheriff** 2, *latterly* appointed by
the Crown. ~ **in that part** a person appointed
to substitute for the **sheriff** in certain duties.
signet: Keeper of the S~ the custodian of the
signet, now a titular office, the holder also being
Lord Clerk Register; the actual custodian is
now the **Deputy Keeper of the S**~.
snout *slang* a detective, policeman *local Abd-Wgt.*
solicitor *orig only in informal usage in Scotland; cf*
agent and **writer.** S~ **General (for Scotland),** †**The King's** *or* **His Majesty's S**~ a
senior **advocate** who as a member of the government is the deputy and chief assistant of the
Lord Advocate. S~ **in** *etc* **the Supreme
Court(s) (of Scotland) (S.S.C.)** a member of
an incorporated society of solicitors practising in
Edinburgh.
†**staffman 1** an official carrying a staff of office,
eg a constable *C.* 2 the burgh hangman *Stlg.*
†**stewart, steward 1** an official appointed by the
Crown having jurisdiction over a **stewarty.** 2
the **sheriff** of Orkney and Shetland or of Kirkcudbright. ~**try 1** the territory under the jurisdiction of a **stewart** 2. 2 applied to areas
(Kirkcudbright, Orkney and Shetland) formerly
equal to the above and continuing to be so called
after the abolition of the **stewartry** as an
administrative unit. ~ **court** the court having
jurisdiction within a **stewartry.** ~ **deput(e)**
the judge delegated by the **stewart** 2 to administer justice etc in the **stewartry.**
substitute *in combs, usu following noun* nominated
to act in place of another, as a deputy; *cf* **sheriff.**
substitution a writ or deed appointing a substitute or deputy.
†**sucken** the area of a bailiff's jurisdiction.
†**sugarallie hat** a tall black silk hat, *specif* as *orig*
worn by policemen *C.*
†**thane** a minor noble who acted as an official of
the Crown with certain fiscal, and *later* judicial,
authority over a tract of land; a baron under the
feudal system. **thanage,** ~**dom** the domain or
jurisdiction of a **thane.**
†**usar** a person who enforced or executed a **writ.**
water bailie 1 a water-bailiff employed to prevent

poaching in rivers *now N.* 2 †a magistrate of
Leith and Edinburgh and of Glasgow who had
local jurisdiction over maritime cases in the
Forth and Clyde respectively. †**water bailliery**
the jurisdiction of a **water bailie** 2. †**water
serjant** one of the constables or officers of the
court of the **water bailie** 2, in Glasgow.
writer, *also* ~ **chiel** *etc* a lawyer, notary, solicitor,
attorney. **writer to the Signet (W.S.)** a mem-
ber of a society of solicitors in Edinburgh, *orig*
the clerks by whom **signet writs** were prepared,
latterly having the exclusive privilege of signing
all **signet writs** and drawing up crown **writs,**
charters etc. †**writing** the occupation of a
writer. †**writing buith, writing chamber(s)**
a lawyer's office.

11.5 RIGHTS

Includes servitudes.

assignation an assignment of a right or rights; the
instrument by which this is done.
awe, owe have a claim or right, be entitled (to do
or be something).
†**blude:** ~**wite,** ~**weck** guiltiness of, or liability
to a penalty for bloodshed; an action against a
person for bloodshed; a fine for bloodshed; the
right of imposing or collecting this.
crave, †**creve** *v* ask for as of right; demand or
claim as properly or legally one's due. *n* a request
or petition as above.
delectus personae the right of selection of a particular person to occupy any specific position, *eg*
as a tenant in a lease or as partner in a firm;
important in preventing assignation or del-
egation of a duty by that person.
†**denude** deprive **of** (some possession, right etc);
divest oneself of a right etc.
dominant tenement a piece of land with the
ownership of which goes a **servitude** right over
adjoining land.
eavesdrop the **servitude** by which one has the
right to shed roof-water on an adjoining property.
feal, fail: ~ **and divot** a **servitude** giving the
right to cut turf for building, thatching or fuel.
†**infangthief, infang** the right of the lord of a
manor to try and to punish a thief taken on his
property.
†**inhability** disqualification, loss of legal rights.

†**ish, ush, ischew** right or means of egress, *chf* **(free) ~ and entry.**

†**jure 1** that which substantiates a claim, a ground of right or entitlement. **2** a title, legal right, privilege.

jus tertii the right of a third party (when it is denied that a person has the right he alleges, though it might properly be claimed by another, the third party).

light a **servitude** binding one owner of property not to build or plant on it so as to obstruct the light of his neighbour.

†**moss: ~leave, ~ lefe** the right or permission to cut peats etc in a **moss.** **~ mail** rent paid for the right of cutting **peat** etc in a **moss.** **~ room** the portion of a **peat moss** assigned to a tenant for his own use *WC, SW.*

†**naturality** the rights or position of a native-born subject.

†**outfangtheiff** a franchise granted to the lord of a private jurisdiction, *presum orig* the right to pursue a thief outside one's own jurisdiction and to bring him back for trial; *also* the right to try a thief coming from outside one's jurisdiction.

†**owerloup** the right of (? occasional) grazing of one's animals in land next to one's own *Kcb.*

†**pass: burn-** *etc* **~ing** the act of crossing a burn etc; a crossing-place; the right to cross. **~ fra** give up, renounce, abandon (a right, obligation etc).

pasturage the **servitude** right of pasturing animals on another's land.

†**peat: ~ery** a **~ moss** belonging to a landed estate; the right to cut peats from this. **peting** the action of getting peat; the right to cut, or the service of cutting peat.

personal bar, personal exception, †**personal objection** an impediment to a legal right or action due to a person's own previous statements or behaviour, *corresponding to Eng* estoppel.

†**pit and gallows, pot and gallows** a right of jurisdiction over criminals found within baronial lands.

†**place: have** *or* **give ~** have or give entitlement or a right (to).

praecipuum an indivisible right, *eg* to a peerage, which went to the eldest and not jointly to all **heirs portioners.**

†**precable** that may be asked or demanded as feudal service, impost or tax.

predial servitude *etc* a **servitude** etc connected with land.

prescribe 1 *of an action, a right etc* become invalid through the passage of time, lapse; *of a debt, crime*

etc be immune from prosecution through lapse of time. **2** †make or declare invalid through lapse of time. †**prescriptibility** liability to **prescribe,** the state of being subject to **prescription. prescription** the lapse of time after which a right is either established *or* rendered invalid or a debt etc annulled, if previously unchallenged or unclaimed. **prescriptive** arising from **prescription,** *freq* **prescriptive title** *etc.*

†**prescrive 1** become valid by **prescription. 2** *of a right or claim* cease to be valid; *of the prescribed period* elapse, run out.

regalia rights held by the Crown, comprising **~ majora** which are inalienable, and **~ minora** which may be conveyed to subjects by royal grant.

return: clause of ~ a provision whereby the granter of a right provides that in certain circumstances it may return to himself and his heirs.

servient *of persons or property* subjected to a **servitude,** *freq* **~ tenement.**

servitude an obligation attached to a piece of property limiting the owner's use of it or permitting others to exercise specified rights over it.

†**state** right or title to property.

stillicide = **eavesdrop.**

†**subservient** subject to a **servitude.**

support the **servitude** whereby a building etc rests on the **servient** tenement; *also* the right of an owner of land to have it **upheld** in its natural state, and hence to object to anything prejudicial to this being done by a neighbour.

†**theme** the right of jurisdiction in a suit for the recovery of goods alleged to have been stolen; the process having become obsolete in the twelfth century, *chf* found in fossilized lists of rights etc in charters as **toll and ~,** whence it was misunderstood to mean some kind of duty or impost.

†**ware** the right of gathering seaweed.

†**water: ~ing** the right to take water from one piece of land for use on another. **~ gang** the right of conveying water through a piece of **servient** ground for use on the adjoining **dominant** ground.

11.6 OBLIGATIONS

Servitudes are in 11.5.

†**act: be** *or* **become ~it** have one's name recorded as being under some bond or obligation. **~ one-**

self enter oneself as being under a bond or obligation.

†**astrenȝe** astrain, put under obligation.

astrict bind legally. † ~**ion** a bond, obligation.

†**failzie** failure, non-performance of an obligation; a sum payable in case of failure, penalty. **fail-ȝear, failyier, failer, party failȝear** a person who fails to perform an obligation, a defaulter. **in case of** ~ in the event of failing to comply with a condition or fulfil an obligation.

†**freeth** free or release from a claim or obligation.

innovation the alteration or replacement of a legal obligation.

†**novatioun** the alteration of a legal obligation or status.

obediental *of an obligation* imposed by law as distinct from contract.

†**obligatour** obligatory.

obligement an obligation.

†**pass fra** give up, renounce (a right, obligation etc).

prestation the performance of an obligation or duty.

recompense a non-contractual obligation by which a person is obliged to restore a benefit derived from another's loss.

†**regress** an obligation by a **superior** to readmit a **vassal** to land which he had conveyed in **wadset**, once he was able to redeem it, *freq* **letters of** ~.

relieve release from a legal obligation; *specif* refund the payment of (a **cautioner** or guarantor).

†**surety** a bond or obligation between parties that they will keep the peace and not assault or molest each other.

†**ticket** a bill, a signed obligation.

11.7 REPARATION, COMPENSATION

†**assyth** *n* satisfaction, reparation, compensation. *v* **1** satisfy; compensate (a person); *freq* ~ **of** (the amount at issue): '*fullely assythit of the said fowrty pond*'. **2** pay compensation. ~**ment** compensation for loss or injury by payment; reparation, indemnification.

†**buit** *in compounds* a compensation, payment, reparation, *eg* **kinbutte**.

†**cro** compensation or satisfaction for a killing.

†**enache** amends or satisfaction for a fault or trespass.

†**int(e)res, ent(e)ress** damage, injury, loss; compensation for these.

†**letters of slains** a **writ** subscribed by the rela-tive of someone killed in a private feud, acknowledging payment of compensation, abjuring all further claims or revenge, and requesting the sovereign to grant remission.

†**mending** amends, redress.

mends compensation, reparation; atonement. †**mak a mendis of** make recompense for.

†**plese** satisfy (a person) by payment of compensation **for** (harm done to another).

poind, †pin(d) *v* **1** impound (goods); distrain upon (a person). **2** impound (stray animals etc) as surety for compensation for damage committed by them *now Cai Loth S*. †*n* an article or animals which has been **poinded**, the goods impounded; an act of **poinding** a distraint. ~**able** *of persons, goods etc and property* liable or in a position to be distrained. † ~**age** the right of impounding trespassing cattle; the fine payable for their release. † ~**fold** an enclosure or building in which forfeit animals etc were kept, a pound. † ~ **money** the money realized on distrained goods. ~ **the ground** take the goods on land (*eg* furniture, farm equipment) in enforcement of a real **burden** possessed over the land.

pund †*n* an animals or article taken by distraint. *v* **1** pound, impound straying animals. **2** = †**poind**; fine, levy.

†**refound** make good, repair (an injury etc).

reparation the redress of a civil wrong, *usu* by award of damages.

†**restauration** restoration of stolen goods.

skaith damage etc involving compensation; damages.

solatium damages for injury to feelings or for pain and suffering.

spuilzie the taking away or meddling with the **moveable** goods of another without the owner's consent; an action for the restitution of such. **action** *etc* **of** ~ an action for restitution as above.

†**theftbute** the taking of money from a thief in compensation or as a bribe to prevent prosecution.

†**theme** the right of jurisdiction in a suit for the recovery of goods alleged to have been stolen; the process having become obsolete in the twelfth century, *chf* found in fossilized lists of rights etc in charters as **toll and** ~, whence it was misunderstood to mean some kind of duty or impost.

upmak compensation, reparation *now Sh Ork*. †**upmaking** a compensation.

†**upricht, upright** make reparation to (someone) or for (something), compensate *Abd*.

†**wergelt, wargeld** the sum paid by way of compensation or fine to the victim or his family mainly in cases of homicide, to free the offender from further obligation or punishment.

†**zeld, ʒald** payment for loss or injury, compensation.

11.8 COMMERCIAL LAW

†**borch, brogh, burgh of** *or* **and hamehald** a pledge that an animal sold is not stolen.

†**cofe, coffing** an exchange.

†**colleague** partnership; alliance.

come guid for be surety for; back up *local*.

commodate, commodatum a free loan of an article which must be returned exactly as lent.

†**consign, consing** consign, deposit, (*specif* money) as a pledge or pending judicial action. ~**atioun** the depositing of a sum of money as above.

†**cose, cosse** an exchange (*esp* of lands).

damnum fatale a loss due to an inevitable accident, such as an exceptional flood or storm.

forenail pledge (money) before it is earned, earmark for spending in advance *now NE*.

fungibles consumable goods; perishable goods which may be estimated by weight, number or measure.

guid, good: (be)come ~ **for** be surety for *now local*.

hypothecate give, take or pledge as security, mortgage. **hypothecation** pledging.

impignorate, *ptp* **impignorat,** ~**ed** pawn, pledge, mortgage. **impignoration** pledging; mortgage.

judicatum solvi *of a security* pledged for the payment or satisfaction of a judgement.

juratory caution inadequate security allowed in some civil cases where no better security is available, *similar to Eng* entering into recognisance.

†**lay** reckon up, audit (an account).

†**letters of open doors** a warrant authorizing the forcing open of **lockfast** places containing goods to be **poinded**.

licht, light below the standard or legal weight, underweight.

liquidate, liquid *of debts or other due payments* fixed in advance at a definite sum, specified exactly; *of payments in kind, material damages or services* judicially or authoritatively assessed; having a monetary equivalent ascertained and prescribed by **decree** of court and appointed to be so paid.

†**modify 1** specify the exact amount of (a payment etc), assess at (a precise sum). **2** award (a payment) **to**.

†**moietie** *of a fine, levy etc* a half payment; an instalment of a total payment.

†**patentar** a patentee, a person to whom a patent has been granted.

†**pawn, pand: (lay) in** ~ (put) in pawn, (lay down) as a pledge or security.

peril the hazard of loss of goods bought or borrowed (as falling on the person in possession at the time).

†**plage** a pledge.

†**plicht** a plight, pledge.

portioner a person who shares with another in a joint venture or jointly-owned commercial property.

precarium, †precarious loan a loan given gratuitously and recallable at will.

†**prepositor** a person who employs an agent etc to manage an enterprise, the principal in a business negotiation or undertaking.

prestable able to be carried out, practicable, enforceable; *of money etc* able to be paid out, usable, negotiable, transferable, exigible.

recourse the right of the assignee to claim compensation from the assignor, *esp* in the case of failure to honour a bill of exchange or in the case of eviction.

relocation: tacit ~ the assumed continuation of a lease or contract of employment on unchanged terms if no action is taken at the date of expiry.

repeat †ask back (money or goods); claim; repay, refund, make restitution of. **repetition 1** †the claiming of restitution or repayment. **2** restitution, repayment.

†**rip** a sample of a crop carried to the market cross as a symbol of the right to **poind** it, and as a sample of its quality.

roup *v* **1** sell or let by public auction. **2** sell up, *esp* turn out (a bankrupt) and sell his effects, *freq* ~ **out** *etc*. *n* a sale or let by public auction. ~**ing** a selling or letting by public auction, an auction. **articles of** ~ a formal statement of the conditions of sale at an auction. **put to the** ~ offer for sale or let to the highest bidder *Sh-Per*.

set, *chf* **action of** ~ **(and sale)** an action in which a part-owner of a ship can request to buy out or be bought out by his partners or to have the ship sold.

†**surrogate** substitute in respect of a claim.

surrogatum something which stands in the place of another, *eg* the price of a thing instead of the thing itself.

truster a person who sets up a trust for the administration of property or funds.

†**tyne: able to** ~ **and win** *etc* have the means to risk loss while aiming at profit.

†**wrack goods, wreck goods** goods driven ashore from a wreck.

11.9 AGREEMENTS, CONTRACTS

†**act** enter (an agreement, obligation etc) in a record-book. **be** *or* **become** ~**it, enacted** *or* ~**itate 1** have one's name recorded as being under some bond or obligation. **2** enter oneself as being under a bond or obligation.

†**burdin-taker, burdiner** one who undertakes (*esp* financial) responsibility for another, a guarantor.

†**compositioun, componitour 1** an agreement for the settlement of a dispute etc. **2** a sum paid in settlement of claim, dispute, or obligation; the amount fixed by mutual agreement.

†**compromit** a settlement, agreement.

†**conand** a covenant.

deposit(ation) a contract under which a **moveable** is entrusted by one (the **depositor**) to another (the **depository** or **depositary**) to be kept either for payment or without reward.

gree come to terms, make an agreement, be reconciled *Gen except Sh.*

hinc inde *chf of claims or contracts* reciprocally, on the one side and on the other.

implement *n* the fulfilment or execution of a contractual obligation. *v* complete, execute (a contract or agreement), fulfil (a condition or promise).

irritancy the nullification of a deed resulting from neglect or contravention of the law or of an an agreement. **irritant clause** a clause in an agreement rendering it null and void if any act therein prohibited is performed.

joint adventure a partnership undertaken for a specific and limited purpose.

jus quaesitum tertio a contractual right of one party, arising out of a contract between two others to which the first is not a party.

†**law fere** a lawful partner, a person in partnership with another by legal agreement.

locus poenitentiae the opportunity given to a person to withdraw from an agreement if it is not in the form required by law.

mandate a formal warrant authorizing one person to act on behalf of another (without payment); a commission of attorneyship or proxy. **mandant,** †**mandator** a person who gives a **mandate**. **mandatory, -tary,** †**mandatar** a person to whom a **mandate** is given.

†**marrow** associate, join in partnership; enter into partnership, combine.

minute a memorandum setting out the heads of an agreement.

missive a letter in which a transaction is agreed upon, which may then be succeeded by a more formal legal document, and which may or may not be binding according as whether the contract in view does not or does demand formal writing.

mutuum a contract by which the borrower of goods for consumption, *eg* food, agrees to repay a like quantity of the same goods instead of the actual goods borrowed.

obligant a person who binds himself or is legally bound by a contract, bond or some other obligation.

†**obligatour = lettre** ~. **lettre, lettris** *etc* ~**(is)** a written contract or bond embodying a legally-binding undertaking.

†**oblissing 1** a binding contract, undertaking, oath; the document expressing this. **2** the fact of having pledged or committed one's goods as security. **oblissment** a formal contract or agreement, *freq* to pay a sum of money; an obligation.

†**oblist, obleist, obliged 1** legally or morally bound or pledged; bound by oath, promise or contract (to someone, to do something *or* that something be done *etc*). **2** bound or contracted **to** *etc* another in support, homage, service etc.

†**observar: party** ~ *in penalty clause of contract* the party who kept the terms of a contract, as against the party who failed to do so.

†**paction** *n* an unofficial agreement as distinct from a formal contract. *v* make an agreement or bargain, enter into a compact.

†**pactorial** of the nature of or pertaining to a pact or agreement.

†**privileged deed** a deed which does not require the signatures of witnesses to validate it, *eg* on the grounds of necessity or expediency.

procuratory the authorization of one person to act for another.

purge clear off an **irritancy** by remedying the failure which produced it.

purify fulfil or carry out (a condition), bring an agreement etc into operation by complying with a proviso in it.

rei interventus conduct by one party to an

uncompleted and informal contract with the knowledge and permission of the other party, which makes the contract binding.

relocation: tacit ~ the assumed continuation of a lease or contract of employment on unchanged terms if no action is taken at the date of expiry.

resile draw back, withdraw (**from** an agreement, undertaking etc).

resolutive clause a clause in an agreement whereby it becomes void if some specified event intervenes.

retention the right not to fulfil one's own part of a contract until the other party has fulfilled his, *eg* not to deliver goods until the buyer has paid for them.

rue regret a promise, bargain etc, withdraw from a bargain or contract *now N Per Kcb.*

submission a contract, or the document embodying it, by which parties in a dispute agree to submit the matter to arbitration.

†**submitter** a person who makes a **submission**.

suspensive condition a condition which suspends the coming into force of a contract until the condition is fulfilled.

vis major a circumstance, *eg* a natural disaster, which cannot be reasonably expected or prevented, an act of God, a **damnum fatale** which excludes responsibility for loss, damage or the non-performance of a contract.

11.10 DEBTS, DEBTORS, BANKRUPTCIES

abbey: the A ~ Holyrood Abbey, Edinburgh, the precincts of which were fomerly used as a sanctuary by debtors. †**A** ~ **laird, laird in the A** ~ *joc* a debtor.

abbreviate an abstract, abridgement, *latterly specif* of a **decree** of **adjudication** or, in bankruptcy, of the petition of **sequestration**.

acceptilation the extinction of a debt by an arrangement other than by full payment.

adjudge to assign (property) by **adjudication** to (the creditor).

adjudication the seizure of land or other **heritable** estate in satisfaction of debt.

appraiser a person appointed to value goods which are the subject of a **poinding**.

appreciation, appretiation the valuing of **poinded** goods.

†**apprise** value and sell (a debtor's land) to pay off the debt.

arrest seize (property), apprehend (a person) by legal warrant. ~**ee** the person in whose hands the **arrestment** is laid. ~**er** a person who arrests, *specif* one who under legal authority arrests **moveable** property belonging to his debtor which is in the hands of a third party. ~**ment** the action of arresting, apprehending or seizing by legal authority the seizing of a debt which is in the hands of a third party.

astarn, astern in debt, insolvent *local Sh-Ayr.*

†**bareman** a destitute person; a debtor, bankrupt.

barra: set (doun) the ~ go bankrupt *now NE Kcb.*

brak, break failure, bankruptcy *local Bnf-Fif.* **broken** ruined, bankrupt. ~ **wi a** *or* **the fu han** make a fraudulent bankruptcy.

†**caption** arrest; a warrant for an arrest for debt.

catholic creditor one who holds security for his debt over more than one piece of property belonging to his debtor.

†**cessio bonorum** a process whereby a debtor could escape imprisonment if he surrendered all his means and was innocent of fraud.

charge an injunction issued under warrant of the **signet** to compel *specif* an heir to a debt-encumbered estate or other debtor to act in relation to the **decree** of a court. †**charger** a person who employed a **charge**, *esp* creditor in trying to recover his money.

common †a debt, obligation. ~ **debtor** when A owes money to B which B recovers by taking from C a sum owed by C to A, A is known as the **common debtor**. †**in (someone's)** ~ in debt or under an obligation to someone. †**quit(e)** *or* **repay a** ~ repay a debt or injury.

confusio, confusion a mode of extinguishing a debt, right or claim where either party acquires the title of the other by inheritance or otherwise.

conjunct: ~ **and confident persons** persons related by blood and connected by interest, *eg* in a bankruptcy case where recent transfer of property is challengeable. ~**ly and severally** where each of the persons named is singly liable etc for the whole of the obligation etc.

coup go bankrupt *local.*

†**crack one's credit** become bankrupt; lose one's reputation, trust etc.

crave, †creve press or dun for payment of a debt *now local Cai-Edb.*

deed of accession a deed executed by the creditors of an insolvent, approving and accepting an arrangement by him for settling his affairs.

diligence application of legal means against a person, *esp* for the enforcing of a payment or recovery of a debt.

discuss proceed against one of two possible debtors such as a principal debtor and a **cautioner** before proceeding against the other.

double: ~ **distress** two or more claims on a single fund, an essential of a **multiplepoinding**. † ~ **poinding** = **multiplepoinding**.

†**dyvour** a debtor, a bankrupt. ~**ie** debtorship, bankruptcy.

fitted account, †**futit compt** an account rendered by one party and docqueted as correct by the other without any express discharge; it is presumed that no other amounts are outstanding.

†**fugie warrant** a warrant issued by a **sheriff** to a creditor to apprehend a debtor on sworn information that he intends to leave the country.

†**grace: act of** ~ the act of 1696 providing for the maintenance of an indigent debtor in prison.

heritable: ~ **bond** a personal obligation for a money loan, fortified by a conveyance of **heritage** as security. ~ **security** security for a loan consisting of the right of **heritable** property conveyed by the debtor to the creditor.

hypothec(k) the right of a creditor to hold the effects of a debtor as security for a claim without taking possession of them.

in *of a debtor* ~ **a certain amount (with one's creditor)** in debt (to someone) *NE Ags midLoth Gall.*

†**inbrochting** collecting (*esp* of rents, debts etc).

†**ingettin(g)** getting in, collecting (rents, debts etc).

inhibit place under **inihibition. inhibition 1** a writ prohibiting a debtor from parting with or committing his **heritable** property to the prejudice of a creditor. **2** †an order by which a husband may prevent credit being given to his wife.

†**irresponsall** not answerable, *esp* unable to pay, insolvent.

judicio sisti *of security* involving an undertaking that a debtor will appear in court to answer a claim.

legal (reversion) the period, at different dates seven, five or ten years, during which a debtor may redeem **heritable** property adjudged to his creditors.

letter: ~**s of arrestment** a **writ** to attach property for debt. † ~**s of caption** a warrant for the arrest of a person for debt. † ~**s in the first, secund, thrid, ferd form,** ~**s in the four forms,** ~**s of four forms** the warrants (giving up to four successive charges) issued as the first step in a process of **diligence** against a person for debt. ~**s of horning** a warrant in the name

of the sovereign charging the persons named to act as ordered, *eg* to pay a debt, under the penalty of being **put to the horn.** ~**s of inhibition** a warrant prohibiting a debtor from burdening or alienating his **heritage** to the prejudice of his creditor.

liquidate, liquid *of debts or other due payments* fixed in advance at a definite sum, specified exactly; *of payments in kind, material damages or services* judicially or authoritatively assessed; having a monetary equivalent ascertained and prescribed by **decree** of court and appointed to be so paid.

liquidation judicial valuation or ascertainment of the exact amount of a debt, rent or payment.

lowse, loose 1 †free (lands, **heritable** property) from encumbrance, *eg* of **wadset,** by paying the debt; redeem (**heritage**). **2** withdraw (*eg* an **arrestment**).

†**merk: Ten M**~ **Court** a municipal court dealing with small debts (up to ten **merks**), and with the recovery of servants' wages.

multiplepoinding an action which may be brought by or in the name of the holder of a fund or property, to determine which of several claimants has preferential right thereto or in what proportions the fund or property is to be divided.

notarial protest a **notarial instrument** in which the notary **protests** that a debtor shall be liable on non-payment to the consequences set forth in the instrument.

†**notour 1** openly admitted, *eg* ~ **bankrupt. 2** of crime or other discreditable circumstances, *now* ~ **adultery,** ~ **bankruptcy.**

oath of verity an oath as to the truth of the averment of debt required to be made by a creditor petitioning for or claiming in **sequestration.**

†**oblist, obleist, obliged 1** bound or contracted to another (for a sum of money). **2** under obligation to pay, be owing. **3** commit, engage oneself (**to another**) **in** = for (a sum of money).

†**open account** a debt entered in a book, not constituted by voucher or **decree,** *eg* for goods supplied by shops.

†**outquit** redeem, free (land, **heritage** or annual rent from property) from encumbrance by payment of debt.

†**outred** settle by payment; pay (a sum due), meet or discharge (a debt), pay for (goods or services); redeem (lands etc from pledge etc) by due payment.

paper issue a bill or insert a notice in a newspaper

concerning (a person or thing, *eg* repudiation of a spouse's debts) *now local NE-Kcb.*

†**passive** *of an heir etc* liable for the debts of an estate. ~ **debt** a debt owed to another.

personal diligence, personal execution the procedure of imprisonment for debt.

†**peymaster** a person made responsible for discharging a debt or refunding a loss to another.

†**plack bill** informal term for a bill of **Signet letters**, the summons or warrant presented to a debtor etc in small civil actions.

†**pledge, plage:** ~ **chalmer**, ~ **house** a room or house for confining hostages, sureties or *later* **debtors**.

†**plese** satisfy (a person) by payment **of** or **for** an amount due etc.

poind, †**pin(d)** *v* seize and sell the goods of a debtor. *n* seizure of goods for debt. ~**able** *of persons, goods etc and property* liable or in a position to be distrained. †~**(l)er** a creditor who distrained his debtor's goods.

postpone relegate the claims of (a creditor) by giving others priority of repayment, demote in the **ranking** of creditors.

†**premonition** an official notification or warning, an obligatory period of notice, *freq* **instrument of** ~ a formal notification made by the debtor to the creditor in a **wadset** to appear at an agreed place and receive payment of the debt.

presentation: bond of ~ a written obligation binding the obliger to produce a person freed from custody for debt at a particular time and place, a bail-bond.

†**principal** a person for whom another is surety, the person primarily liable for a debt.

privileged debt a debt owed by the estate of a deceased person, *eg* for funeral expenses, which takes precedence over the debts of ordinary creditors.

raiser the holder of the disputed property in a **multiplepoinding**, called the **nominal raiser** when a claimant initiates proceedings or the **real raiser** when the holder himself initiates.

rank place (a creditor) in his due place on the list of accredited claimants to the realized estate of a bankrupt; *of a creditor* be placed thus. †~**ing and sale** the process whereby a bankrupt estate is sold and the price divided among the creditors.

†**reable, rehabile** *v* restore to a former state or position; legitimize. *adj* legitimate.

rebel a person who disregards or flouts authority; a lawbreaker, disobeyer of summons; a person, *latterly specif* a debtor, declared outside the law

by being **put to the horn.** † ~**lion** disobedience to a legal summons; the consequences of this; *latterly specif of a debtor as above, freq* **civil** ~**lion**.

†**recompense** *v* put forward a counter-claim in a debt action. *n, also* **recompensation** a counter-claim in a debt action.

reest, rest arrest, seize (goods), *chf* for debt, **poind** *now Rox.*

refer in a civil action, *chf* ~ **a matter to an oath** submit a fact at issue to proof by the oath of a **defender**, *esp* in a debt case. ~**ence** the act of **referring** as above. ~**rer** a person who **refers** as above.

relief the right of a person standing security for a debt to reclaim payment from his principal or from his fellow **cautioners** if he has paid more than his share.

relieve release from a legal obligation; *specif* refund the payment of (a **cautioner** or guarantor), *freq* **free and** ~.

requisition a demand by a creditor for repayment of a debt.

†**retire** *of a debtor* seek sanctuary, *specif* in the Abbey of Holyroodhouse in Edinburgh.

ride: riding claim, ~**r, riding interest** a liquid claim on a claimant in a **multiplepoinding** which may be lodged in the **multiplepoinding** itself. **riding claimant,** ~**r** a person who makes such a claim.

roup sell up, *esp* turn out (a bankrupt) and sell his effects, *freq* ~ **out** *etc.*

runk deprive (a person) of all his money, possessions etc, clean out, bankrupt *now local NE-Fif.*

runtit completely deprived of one's possessions, made bankrupt *now NE.*

sequestrate put (the property of a bankrupt) into the hands of a trustee, by appointment of a court, for equitable division among his creditors; make (a person) bankrupt. **sequestration** the act or process of **sequestrating**.

set down go bankrupt *NE Kcb.*

†**small debt court** a court set up under a JP in 1801 for dealing with debts under £5, and under a **sheriff** in 1837 for debts up to £20.

†**supersedere** a halt or cessation of the process of law, *specif* an agreement among creditors or a **decree** of a court to postpone action against a **common** debtor.

vergens ad inopiam in the state preceding bankruptcy, approaching insolvency.

†**warding: act** *etc* **of** ~ a warrant for imprisonment for debt issued by magistrates in a **royal burgh.**

11.11 PROPERTY

†**acquiet** guarantee undisturbed possession of (land), *usu with* **warrand and defend**.

adjudication the seizure of land or other **heritable** estate in satisfaction of debt.

adjudge to assign (property) by **adjudication** to (the creditor).

†**annalzie** transfer to the ownership of another; alienate.

†**annex** *of property* an appurtenance, *freq* ~ **and connex**.

†**annual** an annual payment of rent, quit-rent, duty or interest. **annuellar** one who receives an annual rent.

†**apperand air** an heir apparent.

†**apprise** value and sell (a debtor's land) to pay off the debt.

†**appropir, appropry** assign or make over in possession or property **to** (a person etc); appropriate.

arrest seize (property), apprehend (a person) by legal warrant. ~**ee** the person in whose hands the **arrestment** is laid. ~**er** a person who arrests, *specif* one who under legal authority arrests **moveable** property belonging to his debtor which is in the hands of a third party. ~**ment** the action of arresting, apprehending or seizing by legal authority the seizing of a debt which is in the hands of a third party.

†**assedat** let, leased.

†**assedation** the act of letting or assigning on lease; a lease.

†**aucht** property.

†**author** a person from whom another derives his title, *eg* by sale or gift.

†**average, arrage, harr(i)age** a feudal service of uncertain nature, *chf* ~ **and carriage**.

back: ~ **hand rent** rent payable by agreement later than at the legal term. †~ **ta(c)k** a tack connected with **wadsets**, whereby the actual possession of the **wadset** lands was continued, or returned, to the proprietor or **reverser** on payment of a rent corresponding to the interest of the loan.

bairn's part (**of gear** *etc*) a child's portion of **heritable** property.

base holding *etc* a **subfeu**.

†**beken** admit as possessor.

bequeyst bequest *NE*.

†**bere fra** *etc* dispossess (a person) of land etc; take (something) away from a person.

†**best aucht** the most valuable article or animal owned by a person, claimed by a **superior** on the death of a tenant.

†**black ward** holding in **ward** by a **subvassal** of another **vassal** who also held in **ward** of his **superior**.

blancheferme, blench ferme *n, also* †**blench-duty** a small or nominal quit-rent paid in money or otherwise. *adj, of lands* held in **blancheferme**. *adv* by the payment or on the tenure of **blancheferme**. †**blench-holding** the holding of (land) as above. †**in** ~ = *adv*.

†**boll** a valuation of land according to the quantity of **bolls** it produced.

†**bondelsoure, bonelesew** ? pasturage connected with bond- or boon-service.

†**bone: bonday wark,** ~ **service** work done without payment as part of tenant service. ~**plewis** ploughs used in unpaid tenant service. ~ **silver** money paid in lieu of service.

†**booking: tenure of** ~ a system of land tenure in the burgh of Paisley requiring registration in the burgh register.

bounding specifying the bounds of property, *usu* ~ **charter**.

brief: ~ **of division** a brief of **chancery** providing for the dividing of lands between **heirs-portioners**). †~ **of inquest** a retourable **brief** directing the **sheriff** or (in a burgh) **bailies** to try the validity of a claimant's title. †~ **of lining** a non-**retourable brief** out of **chancery**, directed to the **provost** and **bailies** of a burgh for settling the boundaries of holdings by **lining**. †~ **of mortancestry** *or* **mortancestor** a **brief** out of **chancery** directing an inquest into a claim that the raiser is heir to certain property formerly possessed by an ancestor and now wrongfully held by another.

burden a restriction or encumbrance affecting property.

†**burgage, burrowage, borowage** 1 the form of tenure by which land within a **royal burgh** is held of the king, *usu* **in (fre)** ~. 2 *also* ~ **land** land held in **burgage**.

†**castellward** castle-guard, a payment in commutation of the feudal service of guarding a castle.

†**casualty** an incidental item of income or revenue; *specif* that due from a tenant or **vassal** in certain contingencies.

†**cavel** a division or share of property, *orig* assigned by lot.

†**cedent** a person who assigns property to another.

cess 1 a tax: (1) †the king's or land tax; (2) a local tax *now Abd Ags Fif*; (3) ~**es** rates and taxes *in* *gen now Bnf.* 2 an exaction of any kind; a tribute *now Bnf.*

†**cessioner** a person to whom a cession of property was made.

†**champart** champerty.

†**charter** put in possession (**of** lands) by a charter.

†**chetery** escheat(s).

†**clag** an encumbrance on or claim against property.

†**coble:** ~ **and net** *or* **net and** ~ the symbols used in the transference of the ownership of fishing rights.

collate pool (inheritances) as in next.

collation the pooling of inheritances with a view to their equitable distribution amongst the heirs.

commixtion a mixture of property belonging to different people.

†**commodities** advantages or benefits deriving from the possession or use of property.

communio bonorum the stock of **moveable** property owned jointly by a husband and wife.

confirmation a process whereby executors are judicially recognized or confirmed in their office and receive a title to the property of a deceased person.

conjunct possessed or shared in jointly, *chf* ~ **feftment** *or* **fee.** † ~ **fiar** a person who holds property jointly with another. ~ **and confident persons** persons related by blood and connected by interest, *eg* in a bankruptcy case where recent transfer of property is challengeable.

†**connex** an item of property connected with another, an appurtenance.

†**conquess** acquire (land etc) otherwise than by inheritance.

†**conquest, conques, conquis** acquisition, *esp* of property; property acquired, not inherited.

consolidate, †**consolidat** combine the **superiority** and ownership of (property) in one person. **consolidation** the joining of the **superiority** and ownership of property in one person.

†**cose, cosse** an exchange (*esp* of lands).

†**court plaint** the feudal privilege of dealing with complaints made to a court of justice.

†**courtesy,** *orig* the ~ **of Scotland** a liferent conferred on a widower, of the **heritage** of his deceased wife.

curator, †**curat** a person either entitled by law or appointed by the Court or an individual to manage the affairs of a legally incapable person, *eg* a **minor.** †**curatrix** a female **curator.** ~ **bonis** the person appointed to manage the estate either of a **minor** (instead of his legal guardian),

or of a person suffering from mental or, less commonly, physical infirmity.

†**curatory, curatry** the office of a **curator.**

dale 1 a share, portion or piece of land *now Abd.* **2** †a dealing out, division or distribution, *eg* of land.

dative *adj, after its noun of an executor or* **tutor** appointed by a court. *n* **1 = decree dative. 2** †an **executor dative.**

dead's part (of gear) that part of a person's **moveable** estate which a person can freely dispose of by will.

†**deathbed: (law of)** ~ the law by which an heir could annul deeds made to his disadvantage by a terminally-ill predecessor within 60 days before death, *chf* (**up**)**on the head of** ~.

†**debatable** *of lands, boundaries* subject to dispute.

†**defend** protect (property etc) against encroachment etc; maintain in a legal right.

denude *law, of a trustee* hand over the trust estate on giving up the office of trustee.

dereliction abandonment of something owned.

†**design** assign (something to someone); bestow, grant (*esp* **manses** and **glebes** for the clergy). ~**ation** assigning as above.

destination a direction as to the persons who are to succeed to property, *chf* in a will etc affecting **heritable** property. ~**-over** a **destination** to one person on failure of a precedent gift, usually by will, to another.

†**deviding** formal division (of lands or property).

†**devise** disposition (of property etc); one's will.

†**devoid (and red)** vacate (lands etc).

†**dew service, deservice, do-service** service required from, or rendered by a tenant to a **superior.**

†**disclamation** the renunciation by a tenant or **vassal** of obligation to his **superior.**

†**disheris(h)** disinherit.

dispone 1 make over, convey (land). **2** †dispose or make disposition **of.** ~**r** a person who conveys property. **disponee** the person to whom property is conveyed.

dispositive clause the operative clause of a deed by which property is conveyed.

†**dissasine** dispossession.

division †formal partition (of land etc). **action of** ~ an action by which common property is divided.

†**docquet** a statement appended to an **instrument of sasine** declaring its authenticity.

dominant tenement a piece of land with the ownership of which goes a **servitude** right over adjoining land.

dominium: ~ **directum** the right in land enjoyed by the **superior**. ~ **utile** the substantial right in land enjoyed by the **vassal**, ownership.

†**donator** the receiver of a donation, *esp* in cases of failure of succession, of a forfeiture or ward and marriage. **donatrix** a female donee.

doon, down: ~-**set(ting)** a (good *etc*) settlement, *usu* that obtained on marriage *now Fif Arg Ayr*. ~-**sit(ting)** a settlement, *esp* one obtained by marriage or inheritance.

†**dote** give or grant (lands etc) as an endowment.

duplicand a doubling or doubled amount of feuduty for one year at certain specified intervals or on certain occasions.

†**duty 1** a service due to a feudal **superior**. **2** a payment made to a feudal **superior**; feu duty.

†**dwell** *of things* remain in the possession of a specified person.

eik *n* an addition or supplement to a document, *latterly esp* an extension of the confirmation of an executor, to cover property not originally included.

ejection unlawful and violent expulsion of a person from his **heritage**, ejectment; eviction. **action of** ~ an action either to eject a person or to recover property lost as above.

†**emphiteose** a perpetual feu.

endoo endow *now Ork NE*.

†**enter, inter 1** *freq* ~**in** *or* **to** obtain or assume possession of lands etc. **2** put (a person) formally in possession or occupation of lands, property, or an office.

†**entry, entress** the establishment of an heir as a new **vassal** with his **superior** thereby making his ownership effective.

†**erd, erthe:** ~ **and stane** symbols used in the transference of landed property.

†**erection** *after the Reformation* the creation of a temporal lordship out of a spiritual benefice; the lordship so created.

†**errour, arrour** mistake or wrongful decision of **brief of inquest**. **assise of** ~ an **assize** appointed to **reduce** an erroneous service of **heirship**.

†**escheat, aschaet** *n* **1** property, possession or goods taken from a person by forfeiture or confiscation, *esp* that falling to the Crown thus. **2** the forfeiture of a person's property, **heritable** or **moveable**, on his conviction for certain crimes, and until 1748 on denunciation for nonpayment of debts.

†**es(e)ment, aisment** a material convenience or advantage, *esp* in connection with the occupation of land or buildings, *latterly esp* an opening for entrance, air or light: '*fredomis, commoditeis, & esementis*'.

†**evenar** a person appointed to apportion lands.

excamb exchange (land).

excambion, †**excambium** exchange of land or property.

†**ex capite lecti** = (**up**)**on the head of deathbed** (*see* **deathbed**).

†**executry** the office of an **executor**. **executry** the whole **moveable** property of a deceased person.

†**extent** *n* the valuation or assessment of land; the value as fixed by assessment, *freq* **auld** ~, **new** ~. *v* assess the value of (lands).

factor *n* **1** a person appointed to manage property for its proprietor. **2** †a person appointed by a court to manage forfeited etc property. *v* act as a **factor** 1 for an estate. ~**ship** the office of a **factor** 1. **factory 1** authority granted to a person to act on behalf of another; a deed conferring this. **2** †the office or jurisdiction of **factor**. †**factrix** a female **judicial factor**.

†**failȝand** in the absence or lack **of** (a designated heir etc).

fee: fiar the owner of the fee simple of the property. †~ **and heritage** a feudal holding with **heritable** rights. †**in** ~ **and heritage** in feudal possession with **heritable** rights.

†**fence** an arrest of goods or lands.

ferm, farm, †**firme 1** farm, *orig* the condition of (land) being let at a fixed rent etc, *latterly* land leased etc for cultivation etc. **2** *also* ~**s** a fixed yearly amount, *freq* paid in kind, as rent for land. **3** †grain paid as rent.

feu *n* **1** *orig* a feudal tenure of land where the **vassal** in place of military service, made a return in grain or in money; *latterly* a holding in which a **vassal** has the exclusive possession and use of **heritable** property in return for payment of a **feu duty** to a **superior**. **2** a piece of land held by this tenure. **3** = **feu duty**. *v*, *also* ~ **out** *or* **off** grant **in feu**. ~**ar** a person who holds land **in feu**. ~ **charter** the document granting a new **feu**. ~ **duty**, †~ **mail**, ~ **ferme**, ~ **holding** the fixed annual payment for a **feu**; since 1974 no new contracts may impose a **feu duty** and existing ones may be bought out (and must be on a change of ownership of the **feu**). ~ **ferme** *now only in the formula of a feu charter* = **feu** 1, *freq* **in** ~ **ferme**. †~ **ferm(or)an** the holder of a **feu**. ~ **right(s)** the right(s) established by **feu charter**. **held** ~ *of lands etc* held by this tenure.

(**have** *etc or* **set**) **in** ~ (hold *or* grant) by this tenure.

†**fiall** feudal tenure.

†**foremail** *n* prepaid rent. *v* let (property) for a prepaid rent.

forenail let or sell (property) in advance *now NE*.

†**forest: free** ~**er** person who was granted or claimed the right of **forest**. ~**ry** the district of a forester; a hunting forest; the rights of hunting in such a forest. **free** ~ a forest in which the hunting rights were granted to the proprietor by the Crown under charter.

†**forfaictour** forfeiture.

†**forfault** *v* 1 forfeit. 2 subject (a person) to confiscation of rights or property. *n* forfeit. ~**er**, ~**our**, ~**ure** forfeiture, deprivation of property as a penalty. ~**ry** forfeiture; the property forfeited.

forfeit subject (a person) to forfeiture, confiscate (a person's estates and **heritable** property) as a penalty for treason.

†**franktenement** freehold. ~**ar** a freeholder.

freeholder, †**freehalder** 1 a freeholder, one who possesses a freehold estate. 2 †a person who, before the 1832 Reform Act, could elect or be elected a member of Parliament by virtue of holding lands direct of the Crown assessed at or over forty shillings.

fungibles consumable goods; perishable goods which may be estimated by weight, number or measure.

furth: ~**-coming, action** *etc* **of furth-coming** an action which the **arrester** of property must bring against the **arrestee** in order to make the **arrested** property available. † ~**-putting** eviction from a place.

gear possessions, property, goods, money, *freq* **goods and** ~.

†**goods in communion** = **communio bonorum**.

grassum a sum paid by a tenant or **feuar** at the grant or renewal of a lease or **feu-right**.

†**gratitude** a goodwill payment to a landlord in addition to the rent and **grassum**.

ground: ~ **annual** a perpetual annual rent chargeable on land, the liability for it forming a real **burden** on the land, the relationship between creditor and debtor not being a feudal one. † ~ **richt: heritable** right; right of possession, *chf* of real property.

†**hamelt** claim (an animal) as one's own property.

hau(l)d property held, a holding; a habitation, dwelling place, *latterly freq* **house and** ~ **house**

and home. †**haudin(g), had(d)ing** a small farm or house held on lease.

†**haver** an owner, possessor, occupier.

heir, †**air, ayer** *n* an heir. † *v* **air** be heir to, inherit. **heirship** 1 the state or position of an heir; succession by inheritance. 2 an inheritance *now Bnf*.

†**airschip gudes, gudes of airschip, heirship moveables** the best of certain **moveable** goods belonging to a predecessor, to which the heir in **heritage** was entitled. ~ **portioner** one of several female heirs who succeed to equal portions of a **heritage** failing a male heir; the successor of such a joint heiress. † ~ **of conquest** one who succeeded to lands or **heritable** rights acquired (not succeeded to) by his immediate predecessor. ~**-at-law,** ~ **of line** one who succeeds by law to the **heritable** property of a deceased person. ~ **of provision** one who succeeds in virtue of express provisions, as in a (marriage-)settlement. ~**s what-** *or* **whomsoever** heirs of whatever sort, having a right by proximity of blood to succeed as heirs, as opposed *eg* to those called by **destination**.

†**helter** the possession of an animal or article by one person which is formally challenged by another, *freq* **in** ~; the animal or article itself *Ayr Prestwick*.

†**hereditare** hereditary.

†**herial** 1 *chf* ~ **horse** the best living animal, **best auct** due by feudal custom to the landlord on the death of a tenant; a money payment in lieu. 2 heriot, the right to claim or take such a payment from one's tenants; a particular animal taken or set aside to be given as **herial**.

heritable 1 †capable of being inherited, subject to inheritance; applied to that form of property (houses, lands, and rights pertaining to these) which went by inheritance to the **heir-at-law** as opposed to **moveable** property. 2 pertaining to or connected with houses, lands etc. 3 holding property, office, or privilege by hereditary right. †**heritably** 1 as a **heritable** property, as **heritage**; as held by **heritable** right, by right of inheritance. 2 *in the disposition of property* with **heritable** rights to the disponee.

heritage 1 †property, *esp* landed property, which descended to the **heir-at-law** or the decease of the proprietor, **heritable** estate; such property inherited by a person as rightful heir, sometimes distinguished from **conquest**, *ie* land inherited, not acquired by purchase; an inheritance, birthright. 2 the technical term for property in the form of land and houses. 3 *in reference to a feu* the possession of lands by **heritable** right, *chf* **in** ~.

4 heritable right or title (to lands), *freq* **of** ~ by **heritable** right.

†**heritor 1** the proprietor of **heritable** property. **2** a property-owner, a landowner, a landed proprietor, *specif in parochial law* a proprietor of land or houses formerly liable to payment of public burdens connected with the parish, including administration of the poor, schools, and upkeep of church property. **heretrice, heretrix** a female **heritor**.

†**hesp and staple** symbols employed in giving **sasine**, the symbols of **infeftment** used in **entering** an heir to property held in **burgage** tenure.

†**hosting** military service discharged as a feudal obligation in return for the holding of land.

†**husband:** *n, also* ~**man** a manorial tenant who had, in return for rent and services, a certain holding in land in addition to his homestead. ~**ry 1** the land occupied by the tenant(s) of a manor or estate, as distinct from the demesne lands. **2** the holding of land as a **husband**; the letting of land to such tenants. ~**-land** in SE Scotland, *orig* the land-holding of a **husband**; *later chf* a measure of arable land, varying from district to district but *usu* = two **oxgangs**.

immediat(e) *adj* succeeding directly (as heir). †*adv, of feudal tenure* directly, without intermediary.

†**immixtion** concerning oneself or meddling with property etc, **intromission**.

†**inbrochting** collecting (*esp* of rent, debts etc).

infeft 1 *freq* ~ **in** enfeoffed, invested with legal possession of (**heritable** property). **2** †assign (property) by **infeftment**. **infeftment** the investing of a new owner with a real right in, or legal possession of land or **heritage**, *orig* accomplished by symbolic act, *now* by registration of the deed of transfer; the document which conveys this right. †**infeftment in security** temporary **infeftment** of a creditor in **heritable** property as security against a loan or debt.

†**infeodacione** = **infeftment**.

ingaun, ingoing *n* entry to a new tenancy *local Ork-Gall. adj* entering, taking possession, *esp* ~ **tenant** *etc* the person entering the tenancy of a property on the departure of the previous occupier.

†**ingettin(g)** getting in, collecting (rents, debts etc).

†**inpit, input** grant a lease to, install (a tenant etc).

†**inset,** the **infield** or a part of it.

institute the person first named in a **testament** *or* **destination** of property.

instrument of sasine the deed or document recording the transfer of property.

†**interest** a landed property, an estate.

intromit handle or deal **with** (funds or property, *esp* those of another person living or dead), with or without legal authority. †**intromissatrix** a female **intromitter. intromission 1** the assuming of the possession or management of another's property with or without authority. **2** ~**s** the transactions of an agent or subordinate. **intromitter** a person who **intromits** with another's property. **vitious intromissatrix** a female **vitious intromitter. vitious intromission** unwarrantable interference with the **moveable** estate of a deceased without legal title, whereby liability for all the debts of the deceased may be incurred. **vitious** ~**ter** a person who **intromits** without authority.

invert: inversion the act of **inverting possession.** ~ **possession** exercise proprietary rights over the property of another, *esp* of a tenant using the **subjects** for a purpose not provided for in his lease.

†**inward, inwar** some feudal service, *prob* that due within the lord's demesne.

†**ish, ush** clear (a place) of occupants.

jedge and warrant an order from a **Dean of Guild** specifying repairs or rebuilding (*orig also* new building) of a property.

†**joint feftment** infeftment made to two persons jointly.

judicial factor a person appointed by the **Court of Session** *or* **sheriff court** to administer *eg* the property of a person unable to administer it himself.

jus mariti the right of property vested in the husband on marriage in all his wife's **moveables** except her paraphernalia (*ie* clothes, jewellery and their receptacles).

jus relictae, jus relicti the share of a deceased spouse's **moveable** goods to which the surviving wife (**relictae**) or husband (**relicti**) is entitled: one-third if there are surviving children, one-half if there are none.

†**ken:** ~ **someone to a piece of land** ascertain authoritatively and point out to a person the situation and limits of his or her separate portion of land, thereby formally admitting the person to occupation of the land; recognize a person as legal successor to an inheritance, *latterly chf* ~ **a widow to her terce.** ~ **someone (for, of** *or*

with) **the land** invest with, admit to occupation of, assign the land in this way.

kind †belonging to one by birth or inheritance; lawful, rightful. **~ly 1** †*of a possession, right etc* belonging to one by right of birth or heredity. **2** *of a tenant or tacksman* having a right to the tenancy or **tack** in consequence of its long continued occupation by oneself or one's ancestors, rather than by feudal charter etc, *chf* **~ly tenant** *etc, now only* **King's Kindly Tenants of Lochmaben**. **3** †having the right of a **kindly** occupier **to** (the land etc specified). **4** †*of lands, tacks etc* belonging to a person as the **kindly** occupier, *chf* **~ly rowme, stedding** *etc.* † **~ness 1** the prescriptive right of a **kindly tenant** to his holding or **tack** *orig chf Lnk SW*. **2** *appar* permission to occupy a holding with the friendly consent or goodwill of the landlord. **3** prescriptive or hereditary right or title *in gen*.

†**lady's gown** a gift made by a buyer to the seller's wife on her renouncing her **liferent** in the seller's estate.

land a holding of **burgage land**; a building site; a building erected on this, a **tenement**. **L~ Court = Scottish Land Court**. † **~('s)-setting** the letting of land and farms to tenants. † **~ tack** a **tack** or tenancy of land *Abd*.

†**lang carriage** the feudal duty of carting goods over a relatively long distance.

†**lase** a lease.

†**last: the ~ heir = ultimus haeres**.

†**latter, letter:** **~ mynd, ~ will** a person's intention as to the disposal of his property after his death; a will.

†**lay:** **~ furth, ~ out** put out (furniture) from a house, *especially* in evicting a tenant. **~ in** pay in (rent in kind, pledges).

legal (reversion) the period, at different dates seven, five or ten years, during which a debtor may redeem **heritable** property adjudged to his creditors. **legal rights** the claims which the surviving spouse and/or issue have to share in a deceased's estate, whether or not there is a will.

†**legatar** a person to whom a legacy is left. **legatrix** a female legatee. **universal ~** sole legatee.

legitim that part of a person's **moveable** estate which goes under common law to his or (since 1881) her children (*now* including illegitimate children), one third if there is a surviving spouse, otherwise half; **legitim** only applies after satisfaction of any **prior rights**.

lesion detriment to a person, *esp* a minor, in respect of property or rights.

less a lease, tenancy *NE nEC*.

†**letters of presentation** the **writ** by which a **presentation** is intimated to the **superior**.

liferent 1 a right to receive till death (or some other specified contingency) the revenue of a property, without the right to dispose of the capital, *corresponding to civil law* **usufruct**. **2** †the **liferent** of a **vassal**'s property or of a benefice **escheated** to the **superior** or the patron. † **~ed** possessed in **liferent**. † **~er**, *fem* **~rix** a person who has a **liferent**.

light a **servitude** binding one owner of property not to build or plant on it so as to obstruct the light of his neighbour.

litigious *esp of property* subject to litigation, concerning which legal action is pending (and which therefore cannot be alienated).

location the act of hiring out or renting.

locator a person who lets for hire.

†**Lord of Erection = titular**.

†**love: for ~ (and) favour (and affection)** formula in documents relating to gifts and donations.

†**lows(e) 1** free (lands, **heritable** property) from encumbrance, *eg* of **wadset**, by paying the debt; redeem (**heritage**). **2** revoke (a recognition of or legal interdiction on **heritable** property).

†**lucrative** gratuitous, granted as a free gift, *chf* **~ successor, ~ succession, ~ title** where the heir accepts part of an estate as a gift before the death of the grantor, thereby involving himself in liability for any prior debts.

maister, master 1 †the landlord of a tenant; a feudal **superior**. **2** †a proprietor of lands or of a business. **master of A,** † **~ A,** title for the heir-apparent or heir-presumptive, *orig* to an earldom or **lordship**; *now* for the heir-apparent or heir presumptive to a Scottish peerage which does not possess a subsidiary peerage title which the heir may use as a courtesy title; *also* for a similarly untitled grandson of an earl; *also* for the heir-apparent to a person with a territorial designation as part of his surname; *cf* **younger**. † **~ of the gr(o)und** a landlord.

†**mak, make** make over (land or money to a person). **~ up** complete, establish fully (a title).

†**mar(r)iage** the feudal right of a **superior** *eg* to a payment when an unmarried heir succeeded his **vassal**.

†**mart silver** a money payment as **feu-duty** in lieu of a payment in kind in **marts** (animals kept for winter meat).

mean *esp of farm-land and facilities shared by several tenants* possessed jointly or in common, joint-.

†**in** ~(**is**) in common, as a joint possession or undertaking.

†**mediat**[1] *of an heir* not lineal, collateral.

†**mediat**[2] = **immediat**.

†**meliorate** *chf of a tenant* make improvements on (the buildings, land etc occupied). **melioration(s)** an improvement made by a tenant on the property rented; the allowance made for such improvements on the termination of the lease.

†**mentenant** a person who is under the protection of another as his **vassal** or dependant.

mid: ~-**superior** a person who holds an intermediate position of **superiority** in the occupancy of land between an over-**superior** and a **vassal** or series of **vassals**. ~-**superiority** such a holding.

missive of lease *or* †**tack** a lease drawn up in the form of a **missive**.

†**mobill** *n, pl also* **meubles moveable** property, chattels; possessions, wealth *adj, of goods* **moveable**.

†**molestation 1** the troubling or disturbing of a holder or occupier of lands in his legal possession. **2** *also* **action of** ~ an action taken by a proprietor of land against those who disturb his possession.

mortify †assign or bequeath in perpetuity (lands, property or money) to an ecclesiastical or other body or institution. **mortification** lands, property or money **mortified**; the deed of making such an allocation. †**mortifier** the donor of a **mortification**.

mortis causa *of a deed, bequest* etc taking effect on the death of the grantor.

†**morwyngift, morning gift** a settlement or endowment of money or property made by the husband to the wife on the morning after the marriage.

moveable 1 applied to that form of property which is not **heritable** (personal belongings etc), and which formerly passed to the next of kin instead of to the **heir-at-law**. **2** †*of a tenant* removable, as opposed to **rentalled** tenants, who could not be removed. ~**s: moveable** property.

multiplepoinding an action which may be brought by or in the name of the holder of a fund or property, to determine which of several claimants has preferential right thereto or in what proportions the fund or property is to be divided.

†**native** *of lands* belonging to one by right. ~ **bond, bond** ~ a bondman or bond tenant.

~**man 1** = ~ **bond. 2** *also* ~ **tenant** a **kindly** tenant.

natural possession owner-occupancy of a property.

†**necessaris** necessary rights of access or use (in property).

†**nem: als wele nocht nemmyt** *or* **unnemmyt as nemmyt** *etc* legal formulae used in the specification of possessions, lands etc.

†**nichbourheid** a dispute between neighbours over property rights, boundaries etc; ? the site of such a dispute **Act of** ~ an act for the regulation of such disputes.

nineteen a lease of a farm for nineteen years *now local Ork-Loth.*

†**non-entry** the failure of an heir to a deceased **vassal** to obtain **entry**; the **casualty** payable to the **superior** in the case of such failure.

†**novatioun** the wrongful appropriation to one's own use of land (*esp* common or public) adjacent to one's own; land of this sort.

novodamus the formal renewal of a grant by a feudal **superior** in order to alter or correct a former grant.

nuncupative *usu of a will* oral as opposed to written.

†**on-takis-man** a person who does not hold a **tack** of part of the common *Inverurie.*

†**outgang** an outgoing, departure, *eg* the end of a season etc, one's removal (from a tenancy).

†**outquit** redeem, free (land, **heritage** or annual rent from property) from encumbrance by payment of a debt. **outquitting** redemption from attachment or pawn of **heritage** etc or **moveables**.

†**outriving** unauthorized cultivating (of land not one's own) and so adding to one's own land; breaking into another's land thus.

†**outset** a smaller piece of land outlying or detached from, but dependent on, a main estate or holding.

†**outsetting** the letting out (of land) on lease or feu.

†**overgive** give up, renounce, resign, surrender (property etc).

†**owersoum** an animal or number of animals in excess of what constitutes a **soum**; the keeping of such animals in excess of the allotted **soum**; a fine or payment for this.

†**parcionar** a joint-owner, joint-heir.

part, pairt †a portion of land, part of an estate held by a smaller landowner, one of a number of pieces of land into which an estate might be divided for separate disposition. **(all) part(s)**

(pendicles) and pertinents, †parts and pendicles everything connected with or forming part of lands conveyed (except the regalia) that is not specially reserved from the grant.

passive †of an heir etc liable for the debts of an estate. ~ title the title or right of possession to an inherited estate which carries with it liability for the debts of the granter.

patrimonial referring to property or money, pecuniary.

†peace, pace: ~-warning a notice to a tenant to quit. in (the) ~, in tyme of ~ used in documents, referring to land valuation, perh = by auld extent.

†penny freq as a symbolical payment, chf in property transactions. ~-mail the part of a rent paid in money, rent in cash.

†perceptioune the (? chf wrongful) collection or levy of rents etc.

†permutation an exchange of moveable goods under a contract of consent.

place a holding of land, an estate, farm or croft.

portion: †portionat provide(d) with a portion of an inheritance. ~er 1 the proprietor of a small estate or piece of land once part of a larger estate, orig also a joint heir, chf female, or her successor; a joint tenant; a joint proprietor. 2 †a joint owner, joint proprietor of land.

†portion natural = legitim.

possess be in possession or occupancy of (property etc) as owner or (freq) tenant. † ~ion 1 giving of possession to another; a property given by one to another to possess. 2 a property enjoyed or occupied though not necessarily owned; a tenancy, a piece of ground, small farm etc held under lease. ~ory judgement the legal rule by which an occupant of at least seven years standing cannot be dispossessed by a rival claimant except by a court action of reduction. † ~our(e) possessory.

†precary a grant on request, at the will and during the pleasure of the grantor.

precept: ~ of clare constat a precept of sasine. by which an heir is recognized by the superior. † ~ of sasine the mandate by which the superior authorized his agent to give possession. ~ of warning a written instruction given by a landlord to his agent to notify a tenant to remove from his property within 40 days.

†presentation the granting by the Sovereign to a donatory of heritage acquired by the Crown by escheat.

prior rights the statutory rights of the spouse of a person dying intestate to the deceased's dwelling-house with furnishings and plenishings and a financial provision out of the remaining estate.

†procuratory of resignation, procuratory to resign .. a disposition executed by a vassal in which he resigns his lands to his superior requesting that they be retained by the superior or transferred to another vassal.

progress: †charter by ~ a feu charter which repeated or confirmed a grant of land as distinct from that conveying the original grant. ~ (of title(s) or title-deeds etc) the series of title-deeds, extending over at least ten years, which constitute a person's title to land. †right by ~ a right established under charter by ~.

propel of an heir of entail anticipate (the succession of his heir-apparent) by giving him enjoyment of the entailed property before his succession.

propulsion the act of propelling.

public: ~ burdens taxes etc as they affect land, rates and taxes. † ~ right a heritable right acquired when the purchaser of a property completes his feudal title with the seller's superior, orig a distinct procedure but latterly merely formal in conveyancing practice.

†pureale a perambulation to determine boundaries.

†purpress commit purpresture, encroach on another's land etc.

†purprise make a purpresture or illegal encroachment; enclose or encroach upon.

†purprision encroachment on another's lands, esp on royal or common land, purpresture.

†quot, cote the share (one twentieth) of the moveable estate of a deceased person due to the bishop of his diocese.

radical right the ultimate proprietary right of a truster which survives if the fulfilment of the trust purposes does not exhaust the whole estate.

raiser the holder of the disputed property in a multiplepoinding, called the nominal raiser when a claimant initiates proceedings or the real raiser when the holder himself initiates.

†recognition the resumption of land by a superior, latterly specif when a vassal had alienated half or more of it without the superior's consent.

†recognosce 1 also recognize, raccunys of a feudal superior resume possession of (lands). 2 of lands return to a superior by recognition.

redd, †trede vacate (a property), leave (a house etc) ready for the next occupant, freq void and redd cleared and ready for a new occupant.

reddendo the duty or service to be paid by a

vassal to a **superior** as set out in a **feu charter**; the clause in which this is set out.

†**regress** an obligation by a **superior** to re-admit a **vassal** to land which he had conveyed in **wadset**, once he was able to redeem it, *freq* **letters of** ~.

†**relief** a payment made by an heir of a deceased **vassal** to the **superior** for his recognition as lawful successor.

remove, remuve 1 *of a landlord* compel (a tenant) to quit his holding. 2 *of a tenant* quit a property.

renounce surrender (a lease, inheritance etc). **renunciation** the act of **renouncing**.

rental *n* 1 †*also* ~ **book** a rent-roll, register of tenants. 2 the amount paid or received as rent. 3 †a kind of lease granted on favourable terms by a landlord to a tenant. 4 †an extract from a **rental book** etc confirming such a lease. †*v* 1 enter (a person) in a **rental** 1, or grant (a person) a lease as in **rental** 3 above. 2 record details of (a piece of land, a lease, rent etc) in a **rental** 1; lease (land) on rent. † ~**ler** a person who held land by being entered in a **rental** 1, *latterly* as in **rental** 3 above, a **kindly tenant**.

representation 1 the right to succeed to **heritable** property because one represents a deceased direct heir (*eg* of a grandson succeeding his grandfather). 2 †the right to inherit an estate which carries with it liability for the debts of one's predecessor.

resign *of a vassal* surrender his **feu** to his **superior**. ~**ation** the way in which a **vassal resigned** his **feu**.

resume *of a landlord* repossess (part of a piece of land which has been let) in accordance with the terms of the lease. **resumption** the act of **resuming**.

retour *n* the return or extract of a decision sent to **chancery** by a jury or **inquest**, *esp* one declaring a successor heir to his ancestor; the record of such a return, *esp* one specifying the annual taxable value of the land. *v* make a return to **chancery**, *esp* one declaring a person heir; declare formally as heir; declare the annual taxable value of (the land concerned) on such a return, *freq* ~**ed**. ~**ed duty**, † ~ **duty** the amount of tax payable based on the value recorded in the **retour**.

return: clause of ~ a provision whereby the granter of a right provides that in certain circumstances it may return to himself and his heirs.

reverse: ~**r** a person who borrows money on security of land, a mortgager. **reversion** (the right of) redeeming *esp* mortgaged lands.

†**rig** a strip of ground leased for building in a burgh. ~**-about** the **runrig** system.

†**rin, run:** ~**dale, rendal** a landholding system similar to **runrig** but involving larger portions of (*chf* **outfield**) land. ~**rig** *n, latterly only* **runrig** a system of joint landholding by which each tenant had several detached **rigs** allocated in rotation by lot each year, so that each would have a share in turn of the more fertile land; such a portion of land *latterly only Hebrides. adj, adv* held under this system of tenure, divided by this system.

†**room** an estate; a piece of land rented from a landowner, a farm, a **tack**, arable holding *now in place-names*.

†**ruid, rood** a piece of ground belonging to a burgh rented or **feued** for building and cultivating *now in place-names*.

rural *of a lease etc* relating to land as opposed to buildings (whether in the country or in town).

sasine 1 the act or procedure of giving possession of feudal property, *orig* by symbolic delivery of earth and stones, *now* by registry at the General Register of Sasines in Edinburgh, *freq* **give, take** *etc* ~. 2 †the document which attested **sasine**, the **instrument**. †**sessonar** a lawful possessor (of lands). † ~ **ox** an ox due as a perquisite to a **sheriff** when he gave **infeftment**.

†**scat** a tax or tribute; one of various local taxes.

Scottish Land Court a court set up by statute with a legally-qualified chairman and members with agricultural expertise; its jurisdiction covers the various forms of agricultural tenancy.

search an investigation into the Register of **Sasines** in order to discover the nature of the title, details of the burdens etc, which affect a property offered for sale.

†**sequestrate** 1 divert (the income of an estate etc) into other hands. 2 place (lands or other **heritable** property) under a **factor** or trustee appointed by the **Court of Session** to administer the property and rents from it, *usu* while the ownership is the subject of a legal action. **sequestration** the act or process of **sequestrating**.

†**serve** declare (a person) heir to an estate. ~ **a person heir** declare (a person) heir to an estate through legal process, formerly by an **inquest** and **retour**, *latterly* by petition to the **sheriff**.

†**service** the procedure by which **heritable** property was transmitted to an heir, a **special** ~

referring to particular lands, a **general** ~ having no such restriction.

set †*v* reject, set aside. *n* a letting or leasing of a farm, house etc, a lease (*esp* thought of from the lessor's point of view) *now Bnf Abd Wgt*. †~**ter** a person who lets or gives out on lease, a lessor. †~**ting** the action of letting or leasing (land etc); the right to do this; a lease.

settlement the disposition of one's property by will, a testament.

singular successor a person who acquires **heritable** property by a single title, normally by purchase, as opposed to an heir, whose title is general or **universal**.

sit: ~**ting down** a settlement in marriage *Cai C*. ~ **on** *esp of a tenant at the end of a lease* remain in a place or house; stay on *now Sh NE Per*.

solum soil or ground, *specif* the ground on which a building stands.

†**souming and rouming** a legal action to determine each tenant's **soum**.

†**staff:** ~ **and stik, bastoun, baton** *or* **burdoun** the symbols by which a **vassal** resigned his **feu** into the hands of his **superior**.

standard security the form of **heritable** security which is now the only way of creating a security over land.

†**state** right or title to property. **give** *or* **receive** *etc* ~ **and sasine** *etc* give over or get **heritable** property by a formal act. **in** ~ in possession or seised **of** (land).

†**steelbow** a form of land-tenancy whereby a landlord provided the tenant with stock, grain, implements etc under contract that the equivalent should be returned at the end of the lease; the stock belonging to the landlord under this arrangement.

stillicide = **eavesdrop**.

subaltern *of a land-holder or the land* holding or held of a **superior** who is himself a **vassal**, subinfeudated. †~**ly** by subinfeudation.

subfeu *n* a **feu** granted by a **vassal** to a **sub-vassal**. *v* make a grant of (lands) in **subfeu**, subinfeudate. †~**dation** subinfeudation.

subject a piece of **heritable** property, *eg* a piece of land, a house. †~ **superior** a superior, *freq* when he holds a **superiority** 2.

†**subset** *v* sublet. *n* a sublease.

substitute *n* a beneficiary who will receive property as an inheritance after the death of the first beneficiary. *adj* nominated to replace a predeceasing person in an inheritance. **heir** ~, ~ **heir** an heir of entail.

†**subtack** a sublease or sublet; a house or land so

held. ~**sman** a person who held a subordinate **tack**.

subtenant an undertenant.

†**subvassal, subvassour, subvavassour** an under-**vassal**, a **vassal** of a **vassal**.

†**suit roll** a list of tenants bound to attend at a particular court.

summons take out a **summons** against, *esp* in actions of removal from a tenancy.

†**superintromission: intromission** beyond one's legal rights.

superior a person who has made a grant of land in **feu** to a **vassal** in return for a **feu duty** or (*orig*) for the performance of certain services. ~**ity** 1 *also* †~**ate** the position or right of a **superior**. 2 †a **feu**-title held of the Crown, *orig* of forty-shilling land of old **extent**, *later* of land of £400 **Scots** of valued rent, which conferred the county franchise on its holder before the 1832 Reform Act.

†**surrender** *n* the submission of tithes to the Crown. *v* submit (tithes) to the Crown. ~**er** a person who surrenders tithes to the Crown.

†**symbolic(al) delivery, possession** *etc* the transference of **heritable** property by the delivery of symbols, *eg* earth and stone.

tack a lease, tenancy, *esp* the leasehold tenure of a farm, mill, mining or fishing rights, tax- or toll-collecting etc; the period of tenure *now rare*. †**takkar** a person who grants a **tack**. ~**sman** 1 a person who holds a **tack**; a tenant or lessee *now Mry Bnf Kcdn*. 2 †a chief tenant, *freq* a relative of the landowner, who leased land directly from him and sublet it to lesser tenants. †~**swoman** a female tenant or lessee. †**in** ~ (**and assedation**) on lease, on leasehold terms.

†**tailyie** *n* an entail, the settlement of **heritable** property on a specified line of heirs. *v* determine or prescribe the succession to (an estate), entail.

†**tenandry** land held of or rented from a **superior** by a tenant; rent etc paid by a tenant.

tenement a holding, *specif* land held in tenure and built on. ~**er** the holder of a **tenement** a person who has a **feu** of land in a village *chf Ayr*.

tenendas the clause in a feudal charter which expresses the manner in which lands are to be held of a **superior**.

†**terce** the right of a widow to the life-rent of one third of her husband's **heritable** estate, if no other provision has been made for her, **greater** ~ being applicable when the husband's entire **heritage** was available, **lesser** ~ when the widow of a predecessor still enjoyed **terce** in the lands. **tercer** a widow who has **terce**. ~ **land**

the land of which the rent is assigned to a widow's **terce**.

test 1 †leave by will or testament. **2** make a will, execute a testament.

testament *n* **1** that part of a will in which an executor is appointed, ~ ~**ar(y)** when the testator appoints an **executor nominate** or ~ **dative** when the **sheriff** appoints an **executor dative**. **2** the executor specified in a will. †*v* leave by will, bequeath *Bnf Abd*. ~**ar** testamentary.

†**thirl, thrill** mortgage (land etc). **thirlage** a mortgage.

tinsal *n* forfeiture of a thing or right by failure to perform some stipulated condition. †*v, also* **tensal** subject to loss. ~ **of the feu** forfeiture of a **feu** by failure to pay the **feu duty**.

titles, teetles the title-deeds of land or property.

†**titular (of the teinds** *etc*) a layman to whom, after the Reformation, the Crown transferred the title to church lands, *more specif* to the tithes of church benefices, a **Lord of Erection**.

†**tocher** *n* a marriage portion, *esp* a bride's dowry. *v* endow with a **tocher**, dower. ~ **band** a marriage settlement. ~ **gude** property given as a **tocher**.

†**top annual** *perh* an annual **burden** payable on a building or buildings as distinct from land.

tradition delivery, handing over.

truster a person who sets up a trust for the administration of property or funds.

†**turn** *of property* return **to** (the former owner).

tutor 1 the guardian and administrator of the estate of a **pupil**. **2** †used as a title, with the name of the estate over which the **tutor** had charge: '*the T*~ *of Weem*'. ~**ial** of a **tutor** or his office. †**tutrix, tutrice** a female **tutor**. ~**y** guardianship, protection; the office of a **tutor**. ~ **dative** a **tutor** appointed by a court, *orig* by the Crown. ~ **nominate,** ~ **testamentar, testamentary** ~ a **tutor** appointed *orig* by the father, *now* by either parent of a **pupil** to act in the event of his or her death. ~ **at** *or* **of law,** †~ **legitim** the nearest male relative on the father's side, who becomes **tutor** of a **pupil** in default of one appointed by the parents.

tyne fail to obtain, miss, come short of, forfeit, be deprived of *now NE Ags*.

ultimus haeres last or ultimate heir, a title applied to the Crown when succeeding to the property of someone who has died intestate without any known heir.

†**unanalyt** unalienated.

†**unchargit** not burdened.

†**underset** a subtenant.

†**union** the uniting into one tenantry of lands or **tenements** not lying contiguous, *latterly chf* **charter** *or* **clause of** ~.

universal 1 *of an heir* taking over the total rights, obligations etc of his predecessor, *chf* ~ **successor. 2** †*of an executor* taking custody of all the effects of a deceased.

†**universitas** the whole property, of every kind, of a deceased person.

†**unserved** not returned as heir.

†**unset** *of land, property etc* unlet; not allocated (**to** someone).

†**upgive** give up, deliver up, resign. **upgiving** surrender, abandonment.

uphaud, uphold the support or maintenance of a person, estate etc; the upkeep of property *now Sh-Cai*.

†**upricht, upright** *of an heir* true; undoubted; rightful.

†**uptak, uptake** take possession of, occupy.

urban *of a lease etc* relating to a building, as opposed to land (whether in town or country).

†**usualfruit** usufruct.

†**vacant** a vacant estate.

†**vaik** *of a* **tack** *or tenancy* fall vacant; remain vacant.

†**valent** the value of an estate or piece of land, *chf* ~ **clause** the clause in a **retour** or **special service** in which the **auld** and **new extent** of the lands were specified.

†**valued rent** a valuation of land made in 1667 for the purpose of computing the land-tax and the apportionment for public and parochial expenditure, superseding the **auld** and **new extents**.

vassal a person who holds **heritable** property in **feu** from a **superior**.

†**vest** place, establish (a person) in full or legal possession or occupation of something, *orig only* ~**(it) and sesit (in)**.

†**vicennial prescription** a twenty-year period of **prescription** applied to **retours** (making them unchallengeable) and to holograph bonds (making them unenforceable).

violent profits penal damages due from a tenant when he refuses to vacate premises after termination of his lease etc.

†**wadset** *v* pledge (land or other **heritable** property) in security, mortgage. *n* a mortgage of property, with a conditional right of redemption. ~**ter** the creditor or holder of a **wadset**.

†**ward, waird** *n, also* **simple** ~ the oldest form of feudal land tenure, *ie* by military service, with various rights and obligations, *esp* that of the

superior to uphold and draw the rents of the lands of a deceased **vassal** while the heir was not **infeft** or was a minor, as recompense for the loss of military services during this period. **wardater** the person given by the original **superior** the enjoyment of lands held in **ward** while the heir was a minor. **ward-holding** the tenure of land by **ward**. **ward lands** lands held in **ward**. **ward vassal** a **vassal** who holds his land in **ward**. **hold ward** *of a vassal* hold lands by **ward**; *of lands* be held under **ward**.

warrandice the undertaking by a granter or seller to indemnify a grantee or buyer of *esp* **heritable** property threatened with eviction through defect of title.

†**waverand** *of a person* having a doubtful or uncertain title.

†**with** in ownership of, as owner of; in possession of.

wind and watertight *chf of a house, esp in leases* secure against wind and rain or flood.

†**yeartak** a year's lease *Gsw*.

younger used after a person's name to distinguish him from an older person of the same name, *freq* title for the heir-apparent of a person with a territorial designation as part of his surname or with the style of a Scottish chief, *esp* **A, younger of B,** *or (and now officially preferred)* **A of B (the) younger.**

11.12 FAMILY LAW

adhere *of a husband or wife* remain with and be faithful (to the other). **adherence** the fulfilment of the legal obligation of residing with one's spouse.

agnate a relative on the father's side.

aliment alimony.

†**bairn's part of gear** *etc* a child's portion of property.

†**bastardry** bastardy.

brief, brieve 1 a summons, legal writ. **2** *latterly chf* **brieve** *specif* a warrant from **chancery** authorizing an inquest or inquiry by a jury, *latterly* in such questions as the appointment of a **tutor** to a **pupil**. †**bore breiff** a birth certificate.

†**cled** provided **with** (a husband or wife).

communio bonorum the stock of property owned jointly by a husband and wife.

†**conjunct** connected by blood.

consanguinean descended from the same father but not the same mother.

consistorial *orig* pertaining to or competent before a **consistoré**, *latterly in any court* pertaining to actions between spouses involving status (*eg* for divorce, separation).

†**courtesy,** *orig* **the** ~ **of Scotland** a **liferent** conferred on a widower, of the **heritage** of his deceased wife.

curator, †**curat** a person either entitled by law or appointed by the Court or an individual to manage the affairs of a legally incapable person, *eg* a **minor**. †**curatrix** a female **curator**. ~ **bonis** the person appointed to manage the estate either of a **minor** (instead of his legal guardian), or of a person suffering from mental or, less commonly, physical infirmity.

†**curatory, curatry** the office of a **curator**.

dative *adj, after its noun, of an executor or* **tutor** appointed by a court. *n* **1** = **decree dative**. **2** †an **executor dative**.

†**donator** the receiver of a donation, *esp* in cases of failure of succession, of a forfeiture or ward and marriage. **donatrix** a female donee.

doon, down: ~**-set(ting)** a (good *etc*) settlement, *usu* that obtained on marriage *now Fif Arg Ayr*. ~**-sit(ting)** a settlement, *esp* one obtained by marriage or inheritance.

eild †mature or legal age, full age. **within** ~ under age.

filiate determine the paternity of (a child), *chf* **filiation** the act of or legal action for doing this.

forisfamiliate *adj, of a minor* living independently of his or her parents because of being married, having a separate estate etc. *v* provide separately for (a son or daughter). **forisfamiliation** the separation of a child from his family under such conditions.

†**goods in communion** = **communio bonorum**.

†**gree: within** ~ (**defendand**) within the forbidden degrees.

irregular marriage a marriage contracted without a religious ceremony or formal civil procedure.

†**jus mariti** the right of property vested in the husband on marriage in all his wife's **moveables** except her paraphernalia (*ie* clothes, jewellery and their receptacles).

jus relictae, jus relicti the share of a deceased spouse's **moveable** goods to which the surviving wife (**relictae**) or husband (**relicti**) is entitled: one-third if there are surviving children, one-half if there are none.

†**lady's gown** a gift made by a buyer to the seller's wife on her renouncing her **liferent** in the seller's estate.

legal rights the claims which the surviving spouse and/or issue have to share in a deceased's estate, whether or not there is a will.

legitim that part of a person's **moveable** estate which goes under common law to his or (since 1881) her children (*now* including illegimate children), one third if there is a surviving spouse, otherwise half; **legitim** only applies after satisfaction of any **prior rights**.

†**legitimatioun** legitimacy.

lenocinium the connivance or encouragement by one partner in a marriage of the adultery of the other (constituting a bar to divorce).

†**less:** ~ **age** minority, the condition of being under legal age. **of** ~ **age** minor.

†**liberal** *of offspring* legitimate *chf Ayr*.

†**macalive** a portion or endowment in cattle for a child put to fosterage *Highl*.

†**mar(r)iage** the feudal right of a **superior** *eg* to a payment when an unmarried heir succeeded his **vassal**.

minor (a person) under 21 or (*now*) 18 years of age; *Sc law* a male over 14 or a female over 12 and under 18 or 21; *cf* **pupil**. ~**ity** the state of being a **minor**, *latterly freq* ~**ity and lesion**.

†**morwyngift, morning gift** a settlement or endowment of money or property made by the husband to the wife on the morning after the marriage.

nominate: executor *or* **tutor** ~ an executor or **tutor** named and appointed in the will of the testator or parent.

†**ogthiern** one who ranked with the son or grandson of a **thane**.

†**paraphernal(s)** the personal effects of a married woman, which remained her own property after her marriage.

†**parted: be** ~ be separated formally from one's spouse.

†**partising** a legal separation or divorce.

†**perfit, perfect:** ~ **age** *etc, chf in legal contexts* the age at which a person attained legal competence, *usu* the age of majority, 21 years.

praepositura the right of a wife to incur debts on behalf of her husband for food and household requirements.

prior rights the statutory right of the spouse of a person dying intestate to the deceased's dwelling-house with furnishings and **plenishings** and a financial provision out of the remaining estate.

pro-curator a guardian or **curator** who has not been legally appointed.

pro-tutor a guardian of a **pupil** who has not been legally appointed. **pro-tutrix** a female **pro-tutor**.

pupil a child under the age of **minority**, 12 for girls and 14 for boys. ~**larity** the state of being a **pupil**.

quadriennium utile the four years following on the attainment of majority during which a person may by legal action seek to withdraw from any deed done to his prejudice during his minority.

recrimination *in a divorce action* a counter-charge on grounds of adultery.

representation the right to succeed to **heritable** property because one represents a deceased direct heir (*eg* of a grandson succeeding his grandfather).

†**second in blood** *etc* a person related in the second degree of consanguinity.

†**silence: putting to** ~ the court action to **interdict** another from putting about an unfounded claim to be married to the **pursuer**.

sitting down a settlement in marriage *Cai C*.

†**terce** the right of a widow to the **life-rent** of one third of her husband's **heritable** estate, if no other provision has been made for her, **greater** being applicable when the husband's entire heritage was available, **lesser** when the widow of a predecessor still enjoyed **terce** in the lands. ~**r** a widow who has **terce**. ~ **land** the land of which the rent is assigned to a widow's **terce**.

†**tocher** *n* a marriage portion, *esp* a bride's dowry. *v* endow with a **tocher**, dower. ~ **band** a marriage settlement. ~ **gude** property given as a **tocher**.

tutor 1 the guardian and administrator of the estate of a **pupil**. 2 †used as a title, with the name of the estate over which the **tutor** had charge: '*the T* ~ *of Weem*'. ~**ial** of a **tutor** or his office. †**tutrix, tutrice** a female **tutor**. ~**y** guardianship, protection; the office of a **tutor**. ~ **dative** a **tutor** appointed by a court, *orig* by the Crown. ~ **nominate,** ~ **testamentar, testamentary** ~ a **tutor** appointed *orig* by the father, *now* by either parent of a **pupil** to act in the event of his or her death. ~ **at** *or* **of law,** †~ **legitim** the nearest male relative on the father's side, who becomes **tutor** of a **pupil** in default of one appointed by the parents.

11.13 CRIMES, OFFENCE

†**accessor** accessory **to** (a crime).

†**actioun** a civil or criminal offence.

†**aggrege** increase the gravity of (a misdeed, penalty etc); aggravate.

art and part denoting participation in a crime.

bangstrie violence (to person or property).

†**barrat:** ∼**our** a person who obtained benefices by underhand means. ∼**ry** the crime: **1** by an ecclesiastic, of corrupt purchase of benefices; **2** by a judge, of pronouncing a particular judgement in return for a bribe.

†**birthinsake, burthensack, burdingseck** a theft of only as much food as could be carried on the back.

†**black mail** a payment exacted or made in return for protection from plunder or injury; an illegal exaction.

†**blude:** ∼ **roll** a roll of persons accused of bloodshed. ∼**wite,** ∼**weck** guiltiness of, or liability to a penalty for bloodshed; an action against a person for bloodshed; a fine for bloodshed; the right of imposing or collecting this.

†**broken** *of persons, esp in the Highlands and Borders* outlawed for some crime; having no feudal **superior** or chief; ruined, impoverished, and living irregularly or lawlessly, *usu* ∼ **men.**

†**bud** *n* a bribe; a private reward for services rendered. *v* bribe.

buy buy over, bribe (a person).

cab pilfer, filch *now Abd.*

†**chaud mellé,** *chf* **of** *or* **from (sudden)** ∼ *of a murder* committed in the heat of the moment.

cheatry *n* cheating, deceit, fraud. †*adj* fraudulent, deceitful.

chore steal *local E, S.*

†**cod pease** pilfer pea-pods *SW.*

colleague *v* associate **with** for purposes of crime or mischief, plot, conspire *now Abd.* †*n* collusion.

†**contrafait, compterfit** counterfeit.

†**corp-lifter** a body-snatcher *chf NE.*

†**counterfute** counterfeit.

†**criminabill** capable of being regarded or indicted as a crime; capable of being accused of a crime.

culpable homicide a killing caused by fault which falls short of the evil intention required to constitute murder, *corresponding to Eng* manslaughter.

†**cutter** a person who cuts (*esp* wood) without permission.

†**dede** a criminal act; an act of violence. ∼**-doer** the doer of a deed of violence; a murderer.

defamation *corresponding to Eng* libel *or* slander.

†**defamatoir** defamatory.

†**deficient** a person who fails to comply with a requisition or demand; a defaulter.

deforce *v* **1** †rape, violate (a woman). **2** impede, prevent by force (an officer of the law or body of officials) from the discharge of duty. †*n* = **deforcement.** † ∼**r** the committer of a **deforcement.** ∼**ment,** †**deforciament** the crime of **deforcing.**

delict a wrong, now only a civil, but formerly also a criminal one.

†**depredation** the offence of driving away cattle etc with armed force.

†**deroub** rob.

†**disturs** rob, strip (someone) **of.**

dole the corrupt, malicious, or evil intention which is an essential constituent of a criminal act.

effusion: to the ∼ **of (one's) blood** applied to cases of assault where blood is shed.

†**enorm, 1** *also* **inorme** heinous. **2** *of persons* acting irregularly or without regard for law.

false: ∼**hood,** † ∼**t** the crime of fraud or forgery; an instance of this. † ∼**r** a forger.

†**faltive** *of persons* having committed a fault, guilty of wrongdoing.

†**fang: (be taken) in** *etc* **a** ∼ (be caught) in the act of stealing. **(be taken) with the** ∼ (be caught) in possession of stolen goods.

†**felny** felony.

†**fine** *of a magistrate* compound **with** (an accused person).

fire-raising arson.

force and fear illegal pressure to make a person do something, duress.

†**forethocht** premeditated, thought out beforehand. ∼ **felony** malice aforethought.

†**free:** ∼ **forester** a person who poached on deer forests. ∼ **trade** smuggling.

†**fugitour** a fugitive.

†**gileynour, golenȝour** a cheat, swindler.

†**grip** seize, lay hands on, take possession of (lands or belongings) violently or illegally.

hamesucken (the crime of committing) an assault upon a person in his own house or dwellingplace.

†**hand-hav(e)and** *of a thief* with the stolen article in the hand, red-handed.

†**harl** money or property obtained dishonourably or with difficulty.

†**huird** harbour, entertain (criminals or wrongdoers) *esp* secretly or clandestinely.

†**hurt-majesté** high treason.

†**imbazel** embezzle.

†**improvin** *of persons* convicted of preparing or presenting disproved documents.

†**inbreak** a breaking in, intrusion by force.

†**inrin** commit (an offence).

intak, intake 1 a fraud, deception. **2** a swindler *local Cai-Bwk*.

†**intercommune 1** be in communication (with enemies, rebels, outlaws etc). **2** prohibit from intercourse with others, ban, outlaw. **intercommuned** denounced in **letters of intercommuning** proscribed, outlawed. **intercommuning** the fact or practice of being in communication with rebels or denounced persons.

†**keping: be on one's ~** be a fugitive or in hiding. **go** *or* **run upon one's ~** save oneself by flight or concealment, abscond.

†**le(a)sing** lying, slandering; a lie, a slander. **~-maker** a person who is guilty of **~-making**. **~-making** the spreading of calumny against the Crown likely to cause sedition or disaffection. **mak, make ane ~, mak ~s** lie, tell lies. **mak (a) ~ of** tell lies about, slander.

lift a theft, that which is stolen *local N-SW*.

lockfast fastened by a lock, shut and locked, secured under lock and key against interference; breaking into a **lockfast** place constitutes an aggravation of theft.

†**loun** a lawless or violent scoundrel, a robber.

†**mak, make** commit (a crime, fault or sin).

malverse †*v* betray the trust attaching to an office by acting dishonestly, corruptly, or oppressively. †*n* a breach of trust, a piece of grave misconduct. **malversation** corrupt behaviour in a position of trust.

mobbing and rioting the joining together of a number of people to act in a way which is against peace and good order.

murther murder. **~er** a murderer. †**mak ~ (up)on** murder.

†**mutilation** the (crime of) wounding or disabling of a person in a limb, whether or not it is severed.

†**nicht: ~ waker, ~ walkar** a person who goes about at night, *esp* for nefarious purposes.

†**notour 1** *(of wrongdoers)* known by common knowledge, notorious. **2** of crimes or other discreditable circumstances, *now* **~ adultery, ~ bankruptcy**.

†**nunlaw** = **unlaw**.

obreption the obtaining of a gift, dispensation etc by false statement.

†**outfang** ?theft committed outside the jurisdiction, but *perh* merely formulaic.

†**outhound** incite (to mischief or crime). **~er** instigator.

†**output** issue (false coinage). † **~ar 1** a person who **puts out** others' property (as in **outputting 1**). **2** a person who issues or circulates *eg* coinage unlawfully. **~ting 1** the conveying of stolen goods out of the district etc; *also perh* the exposure of another's property to thieves with whom one is in league. **2** issuing (of false coin).

†**oversile** deceive, delude (a person).

†**ower: take** *etc* **something** *or* **someone ~ another's heid** dispossess someone of land, customers etc unfairly (*eg* by offering better prices).

†**owersoum** an animal or number of animals in excess of what constitutes a **soum**; the keeping of such animals in excess of the allotted **soum**; a fine or payment for this.

pauchle, pochle steal, embezzle, pocket *C, S*.

†**perduellio(u)n** hostility against the state or government, treason.

†**perjure** *n* perjury. *adj* perjured, perjurious.

†**pick** be a petty thief, pilfer. **~ery, pekery** *WC, SW* **1** theft, *esp* petty theft, pilfering; articles pilfered. **2** an act of **pickery**, a petty theft.

picky-fingered light-fingered *now Per*.

pike steal, pilfer; indulge in petty theft *now Abd*. †**piker, pekar** a thief, robber, pilferer. †**pikery** petty theft. †**pikin(g)** *n* the action of stealing, petty theft. *adj* engaged in petty theft, dishonest. † **~-purse** a person who stole purses or their contents.

†**pikkillar** a petty thief or pilferer *Fif*.

pilk pilfer, pocket, indulge in petty theft *now Sh*.

plagium the offence of child-stealing or kidnapping.

†**pleyar** a litigant; a disturber of the peace.

†**plicht** wrongdoing, sin, crime.

ploy a legal action; a quarrel, disagreement, breach of the peace.

†**plu(c)k** steal (livestock) **from** (a person).

pouch put (something) into one's pocket, take (something) either legitimately or dishonestly; *fig* steal, pocket.

†**procure** prevail upon, induce, persuade (a person to do something criminal).

†**purspyk** a thief who picks purses, a pickpocket.

quasi-delict an act of negligence not motivated by criminal intent but making a person liable to an action for damages.

rebel a person who disregards or flouts authority; a lawbreaker, disobeyer of summons; a person, *latterly specif* a debtor, declared outside the law by being **put to the horn**. † **~lion** disobedience to a legal summons; the consequences of this; *latterly specif of a debtor as above, freq* **civil** ~**lion**.

red hand, *also* †**with** ~ (captured) in the act of a crime.

†**reft** robbery.

reive 1 *also* †**rive** despoil, rob; deprive (a person) **of** (something). **2** take away; steal, remove by theft or pillage *now Bnf Ags*.

reset *v, also* †**recept, ressait 1** receive, harbour, give shelter or protection to (*esp* a criminal, enemy, fugitive etc). **2** receive (stolen goods), *usu* with the intention of reselling. *n* **1** †a place of refuge, *later esp* for criminals etc. **2** †a person who receives or shelters criminals. **3** †the receiving or harbouring of criminals. **4** the receiving of stolen goods, *freq* ~ **of theft.** ~**ter** a person who **resets**.

†**reylock** robbery.

†**rin the cutter** evade the revenue cutter when smuggling.

†**riot** unlawful bodily harm or violence to another person, assault and battery.

rook plunder, clean **out**; remove by theft.

†**rug and reive** practise robbery.

†**rummle, rumble** pick (someone's pocket), rob.

rump = **rook** *local Bnf-Slk*.

†**rundge, ronge** clip (coin).

†**scaff:** ~**er** an extortioner. ~**ery** extortion.

†**scandal** an actionable report defaming a person's character, defamation.

scoff steal, plunder.

†**sheepman** ? a sheepstealer, rogue.

†**shusy** a corpse (*prob orig* female) used for anatomical dissection and demonstration, *esp* one stolen from a grave.

†**skaith** damage done by trespass of animals; the act or offence of trespass, **in his, that** *etc* ~ trespassing on him, that place etc.

skin *slang* a robbery, what has been stolen; a petty swindle *C*.

smool *literary* remove stealthily, filch.

sneck snatch, seize, steal *now local Abd-Rox*.

snigger catch (salmon) illegally by dragging a cluster of weighted hooks along the river bed; fish (a pool) by this method *Gen except Sh Ork*.

†**spill** ravish, violate (a woman).

spoach poach *Rox*. ~**er** a poacher *chf Rox*.

spreath, spreach 1 †cattle, *specif* a herd (of cattle) stolen and driven off in a raid, *esp* by Highlanders to the Lowlands. **2** †booty, plunder. **spreacherie 1** †a foray to steal cattle, a cattle raid. **2** booty, plunder, loot; things acquired furtively or on the sly.

spuilzie, spuilyie *v* **1** rob, despoil, plunder (a person or place). **2** deprive (someone) **of** (something) by stealing. **3** take as spoil or plunder, steal; carry off (another's **moveable** possessions) without legal warrant or against his will *now Abd*. **4** plunder, maraud *now Per*. *n* **1** (an instance of) depredation, spoliation, plundering, devastation. **2** *chf* **spuilzie** the taking away or meddling with the **moveable** goods of another without the owner's consent; an action for the restitution of such. **3** †an illegal seizure of another's goods, differing from theft in being done openly with the intention of claiming them as one's own or of returning them after use. **4** booty, spoil, plunder. †~**er** a robber, plunderer.

†**spung** rob (someone **of** something); pick someone's pocket.

†**stalker 1** a person who prowls about for purposes of theft. **2** a person who stalks game illegally, a poacher.

†**start and owerlowp** the trespassing of farm-animals on a neighbour's land, in which a certain limited latitude was permissible.

stellionate 1 a crime for which there is no specific name, applied to a kind of fraud in which the same right is granted to two or more different people. **2** †a real injury against the person.

stouth †theft, robbery. ~**erie** theft; stolen goods; gear, goods and chattels. † ~**reif** theft with violence, forcible theft.

†**strain, stre(i)nзe** extort (money, confessions etc).

†**stupration** violation (of woman).

†**subreption** the act of obtaining gifts of **escheat** etc from the Crown by concealing certain facts.

†**suddenty** a sudden outburst of rage, an act done in hot blood, *freq* **of** *or* **on (a)** ~ without premeditation.

†**swag** a bag or wallet, *esp* one carried by a beggar or thief.

tangs: find something where the Hielandman fand the ~ take something from its rightful place and appropriate it, steal something.

tarry *now local Sh-Kcb*, **tarry-fingered** light-fingered, having a tendency to pilfer.

†**tascal** restore (stolen property, *esp* cattle) after payment of a reward. ~ **money** a reward offered in the Highlands for information about stolen cattle and their thieves.

†**temerarité** reprehensible or culpable heedlessness or negligence.

theft a legal term in Sc; in Eng the legal term was *larceny* until the Theft Act of 1968. † ~**dom** theft; thievery. † ~**bute** the taking of money from a thief in compensation or as a bribe to prevent prosecution.

thief steal *local Cai-SW*.

tirr rob (a fruit-tree) *NE*.

†**traditor** a betrayer, traitor.

†**traffeck, traffic** have illicit or secret dealings, intrigue, conspire (**with**).

traison treason.

†**tratour** a traitor.

†**tresgressor** transgressor.

†**truff** steal, pilfer.

†**unhappin** *of a crime* miserable, wretched.

†**unlaw, unlach** an illegal act.

wa, way: ~**-takin** removal, carrying off, by theft or violence.

†**waith** the action or practice of hunting or fishing (*chf* unlawfully). ~**man** a hunter, *esp* a forest outlaw.

†**way: by ~ of deid** by means of violence.

†**wee pawn** an unlicensed pawnbroker, often one engaged in illicit dealings.

wrang, wrong †violation, transgression or infringement of law. **wrongous 1** contrary to law, illegal, wrongful. **2** unjust, injurious; ill-gotten. **wrongously** improperly, illegally.

11.14 PIRACY

†**cape: caper** a privateer. **cap(er)ing** privateering.

†**peratt** a pirate.

†**pillé 1** rob, plunder (a ship or those sailing in it). **2** steal (goods or possessions), *esp* from a ship.

†**revar** a pirate, sea-robber.

†**scummer** a pirate.

†**se(a) revar** a pirate.

11.15.1 PUNISHMENT: LEGAL

†**absolʒe** absolve.

†**adju(d)ge to** *or* **in** sentence judicially to (a certain fine).

†**admoneis** admonish.

†**aggrege** increase the gravity of (a misdeed, penalty etc); aggravate.

†**amand** a fine.

†**amerciat** *ptp* subjected to or punished by a fine, fined. *v* fine.

†**apayn of** on pain of, under the penalty of.

assoilʒie 1 decide in favour of (the **defender**) in

an action, acquit of a charge. **2** †absolve **one-self**.

†**banis, beneis** banish. ~**ment** banishment.

†**barisdall** (subject to) an instrument of torture invented and used only by MacDonald of Barisdale.

†**birning** branding as a punishment.

†**bludewite, bludeweck** a fine for bloodshed.

†**boyis** leg-irons for the confinement of prisoners.

†**branks** *n* an instrument of public punishment, an iron bridle and gag used to punish breaches of the peace or abusive language. *v* punish with the **branks**.

†**bridle** punish (a person) by the application of a bridle or **branks**.

†**buitis, boots** *n* an instrument of torture. *v* torture with the **buitis**.

†**bull's head** a symbol of condemnation to death, warning of immediate execution.

†**buttock mail, buttock hire** a fine for sexual immorality.

†**cashielaws** an instrument of torture.

†**cave** a cellar, dungeon.

certification a warning of the penalty to be inflicted for non-compliance with an order, *chf* with ~ (**that**) .. introducing the penalty clause.

†**charge** order or commit **to ward** *or* **prison**.

†**chokis, chowkis** the **jougs**.

†**compell** force (a person) by distraint of property; distrain (goods etc).

†**comprise** attach, distrain (property).

†**conding** condign. ~**ly** condignly.

†**dampnis** damages.

†**defese** acquit or discharge from an obligation or penalty. **defesance, defaisance** acquittance, discharge.

†**distrenzie** distrain; subject to constraint; seize (land or goods) by way of enforcing fulfilment of an obligation. ~**abill** liable or subject to distraint.

†**dool tree** a gallows tree.

†**enter, inter** return (**again**) to prison.

†**entry, entress** the return of a prisoner to custody.

†**execute** *ptp* put to death.

†**extrete, extrec(t)** a certified copy of the fines imposed at (*chf*) a **justice aire** or other court; the fines specified in this.

†**failzie** failure, non-performance of an obligation; a sum payable in case of failure, penalty. **under the ~ of** under the penalty of (a certain sum).

†**faut** subject to a penalty.

†**festinance** custody, confinement.

†**fleme** banish, drive into exile; put to flight, drive away, expel.

†**forfaictour** forfeiture.

†**forfault** *v* 1 forfeit. 2 subject (a person) to confiscation of rights or property. *n* forfeit. ~**er**, ~**our**, ~**ure** forfeiture, deprivation of property as a penalty. ~**ry** forfeiture; the property forfeited.

forfeit subject (a person) to forfeiture, confiscate (a person's estates and **heritable** property) as a penalty for treason.

†**free prison** prison without fetters or with the privilege of going out temporarily.

†**freeth** set free, liberate; set or make free **from** or **of**; free or absolve oneself **of**.

†**fugitate**: ~(**d**) declared a fugitive from justice, banished. **fugitation** sentence of outlawry with confiscation of **moveable** property for failing to appear in court on a criminal charge.

†**gade** an iron bar with rings to which prisoners' shackles were attached, *chf* **the lang** ~.

†**gadloup**: **loup** *etc* **the** ~ run the gauntlet.

†**gene** (an instrument of) torture.

†**goif, gove** *n* a pillory. *v* **gove** put in a pillory.

†**gorgets** an iron collar used as a form of pillory.

†**gravat** a hangman's noose, *freq* **hempen** ~.

†**guidman** a manager, *esp* the keeper of a jail.

†**hands**: **in** ~ in captivity, under arrest.

†**hangrell** the gallows.

Heart of Midlothian *orig* name for the old **Tolbooth** of Edinburgh (demolished 1817), *now* the site of this marked by a heart-shaped arrangement of cobbles in the roadway.

heid †behead, decapitate, *freq* ~ **and** *etc* **hang**. **want** *etc* **the** *or* **one's** ~ be beheaded, have one's head cut off.

horn †*n* the trumpet used to proclaim an outlaw, *latterly chf* a debtor, *chf* **at the** ~, **put to the** ~ prolaimed as an outlaw or bankrupt. *v* = **put to the** ~ proclaim as an outlaw or rebel (though still competent, in practice now superseded), *chf* ~**ing**. † ~**er** a person who has been put to the horn.

†**impreson** imprison.

†**inbring** fetch in (persons) as prisoners

incarcerated, †**incarcer(at)** imprisoned.

†**infer**: ~ **the pain(s) of law**, ~ **a punishment** *etc* involve or lead to a certain penalty.

†**inpit, input** put (a person) in prison.

†**irrogat** *adj of a penalty* imposed. *v* impose (a penalty).

†**javell** a jail.

jile a jail. **get the** ~ be sent to prison.

†**jog** put in the **jougs**.

†**jougs** an instrument of public punishment consisting of a hinged iron collar attached by a chain to a wall or post and locked.

†**justify** execute justice upon, convict, condemn; execute (a convicted criminal); put (a criminal etc) to death. ~ **to (the) dede** put (a criminal etc) to death.

†**keep** charge, custody.

†**kelchyn** a fine paid to the kinsmen of a person killed.

†**kinbut(t)e** compensation paid for manslaughter by the slayer to the kindred of the slain, **assythment**.

kittie prison, jail, the village lock-up *S Uls*.

†**law: the** ~(**s**) **of Clan Macduff** a privilege granted to the kin of the Earls of Fife (or to Fife men) of remission of the penalty of slaughter, on payment of compensation by the slayer according to a prescribed rate.

†**letters of fire and sword** a warrant from the Privy Council to enforce court **decrees** of removing and ejection.

†**lock** entrap, imprison.

†**maiden** name for a guillotine used in Edinburgh for beheading criminals; any instrument of the sort.

†**mand** a fee, fine.

†**massymore** the dungeon of a castle.

†**mear** a wooden frame on which wrongdoers were made to 'ride' as a public punishment.

†**merciment** a fine imposed by a court; the condition of being liable to a fine at the 'mercy' or discretion of a court or judge.

†**modify** 1 specify the exact amount of (a fine etc), assess at (a precise sum). 2 determine and decree the nature and extent of (a penalty or punishment).

†**moietie** *of a fine, levy etc* a half payment; an instalment of a total payment.

†**mones** monish, admonish.

†**monest** admonish(ed), charge(d), exhort(ed).

nick *n* prison, the police-station. *v* imprison.

†**nunlaw** = **unlaw**.

†**obsolve** absolve.

†**obtene** take (a person) into custody or into one's hands.

†**ordeen, ordain** sentence (someone) to suffer a certain penalty or punishment.

†**outputting** expulsion, ejection; banishment.

†**owersee** fail to take action against; allow to go uncensured or unpunished; overlook, tolerate.

†**owersoum** an animal or number of animals in excess of what constitutes a **soum**; the keeping

of such animals in excess of the allotted **soum**; a fine or payment for this.

†**owertak** catch up with and punish.

†**parcage** *only in documents concerning Border disputes* the act of enclosing stray cattle or sheep; the fine payable to obtain their release.

†**pass 1** *of a criminal or a crime* go unpunished. **2** *freq of a judicial body* let (someone) off all or part of a penalty, obligation etc; remit (a punishment).

†**peace, pace** an outlaw's pardon; his re-admission to allegiance.

†**pilliewinkis** an instrument of torture for squeezing the fingers.

†**pin** part of a gallows, *perh* the peg over which the rope was slung.

poind, †pin(d) *v* **1** impound (goods); distrain upon (a person). **2** impound (stray animals etc) as surety for compensation for damage committed by them *now Cai Loth S*. †*n* an article or animal which has been **poinded**, the goods impounded; an act of **poinding**, a distraint. **~able** *of persons, goods etc and property* liable or in a position to be distrained. † **~age** the right of impounding trespassing cattle; the fine payable for their release. † **~fold** an enclosure or building in which forfeit animals etc were kept, a pound. † **~ money** the money realized on distrained goods. **~ the ground** take the goods on land (*eg* furniture, farm equipment) in enforcement of a real **burden** possessed over the land.

prison take or keep prisoner, imprison *now Sh Ork*.

pund †*n* an animal or article taken by distraint. *v* **1** pound, impound straying animals. **2** †**poind**; fine, levy. †**pund law** a fine for something impounded.

†**pundlane** the due payable for the release of animals impounded for trespass.

†**rack** stretch (the neck); hang, be hanged.

rax stretch (a person's neck), hang (a person).

†**re-enter** *v* put (a person) **in** (a place of custody) again. *n* the act of **re-entering**.

†**relax** release from a legal process or penalty, *esp* from outlawry: '*relax from the horn*'. **~ation** release from a judicial penalty, *esp* outlawry.

†**remission** a formal pardon; a document conveying this.

†**remit** remission, pardon.

saint, †St Johnston('s) ribbon *etc* the hangman's noose or rope.

†**scaffat** a scaffold.

†**sentence money** *or* **silver** a percentage of the sum decreed, payable as a fee to the **sheriff depute** by the litigants in a case.

sequestrate confiscate. **sequestration** the act or process of **sequestrating**.

†**service** compulsory or forced labour as a penalty for crime, penal servitude.

shangies manacles, handcuffs *now Abd Ags Per*.

†**skaith** penalize, fine.

snitchers handcuffs *now local Mry-SW*.

solatium damages for injury to feelings or for pain and suffering.

†**stang** *n* a rough pole or tree-trunk on which an offender against the laws or local conventions (*eg* a wife-beater, nagger, adulterer) was mounted astride and carried about in public; the punishment itself. *v* cause to **ride the ~**, humiliate (a person) thus. **ride the ~** suffer the punishment as above. **ride the ~ on** deal out this punishment to an effigy of, or someone impersonating (the offender).

†**stark** *of an instrument of torture etc* inflicting severe pain.

†**stent** extend (a person) **on** *etc* (an instrument of torture).

†**stingis-dint, stockisdint** a fine for an assault with a stick.

†**strap** bind and hang (a person); be hanged.

†**streke** stretch (a person) on a rack etc.

†**strenʒe** distrain. **~able** subject to distraint, liable to be distrained.

†**tether** a halter, hangman's noose.

†**thief's hole** a cell or dungeon, *esp* in a **tolbooth** in which thieves and other malefactors were imprisoned.

†**thumbikins** a thumbscrew used to torture **Covenanters** during the 1680s.

†**timmer, timber: ~ meir** a kind of wooden horse used as an instrument of punishment.

†**tinsel, tensal** punish by a fine.

†**tit** pull **up** in a halter; hang.

†**tolbooth** a town prison, jail (*formerly freq* consisting of cells under the town hall).

torter torture *now Sh N*.

tow a gallows rope, hangman's noose.

†**trams** the two upright posts of a gallows.

†**treen mare** a kind of wooden horse used as an instrument of punishment.

†**tron** a pillory, the post of the **tron** (public weighing machine) being used as such, or as a place of public exposure and punishment.

†**tyne** incur (a penalty).

†**unforgiven** without any remission.

†**unhed**, behead (a person).

†**unlaw** *n, also* **unlay** a fine, penalty. *v* **1** fine (*chf* **for** an offence **in** a sum). **2** pay a fine.

violent profits penal damages due from a tenant

when he refuses to vacate premises after the termination of his lease etc.

†**wairdour** a person in custody, a prisoner.

†**ward, waird** n custody, imprisonment; jail *latterly literary*. v keep (a person) in custody, imprison, confine. **warded** detained in **ward**, imprisoned. **warding** imprisonment. **warding place** a jail, prison. ~ **house** a guard-house for prisoners.

†**water hole** a detention cell under the old Guardhouse in the High Street of Edinburgh, so-called because there was always water in it.

widdie the gallows rope. **cheat the** ~ escape hanging.

wrongous imprisonment false imprisonment, imprisonment without the due form of law.

11.15.2 PUNISHMENT: GENERAL

Specific school punishments, especially with the notorious tawse, will be found in 14.3.2. Beatings and thrashings in general will be found in 12.12 (see note there).

†**bauchill** denounce openly; disgrace, discredit (publicly).

berry thrash (*esp* a child) *chf SW, S*.

†**blaw out on** denounce formally or after blowing a horn to attract public attention.

broom: sing the ~ cry out because of punishment inflicted *Bnf Abd*.

†**bussom** a bunch of twigs used as a scourge.

buttock mail a spanking *Abd*.

†**catlill** punish by pressing the finger into the hollow under a child's ear *SW*.

cauker a stroke on the palm of the hand from a strap *now Abd Ags Fif*.

chasteeze chastise *now Ags*.

chastify chastise, castigate.

†**chestee** reprove; chastise.

claw: ~ **someone's hide** *or* **skin** punish, beat *local Bnf-Fif*. **gar (ane)** ~ **whaur it's no yeuky, gar (ane)** ~ **without a youk** give (someone) a drubbing.

clearin a scolding, beating.

coal: bring out o'er *or* **tak ower the** ~**s** haul over the coals.

†**cob** beat or strike, *usu* on the buttocks *S*.

coffee: gie (someone) his ~ scold roundly, chastise.

†**conray, cumray** handle or deal with severely.

cow a birch used for whipping *NE*.

cowdrum: get ~ get a beating or severe scolding *NE*.

crack the lash of a whip *now local Cai-Kcb*.

dichens a reproof, beating, *now Rox*.

dirdum punishment; retribution. **dree the** ~**(s)** bear the punishment, take the consequences *now Fif*.

droddum: dress someone's ~ punish someone, give someone a thrashing.

†**esson3e** v excuse.

excaise excuse.

†**faik** spare, excuse, let (someone) go.

fairins: get *or* **tak one's** ~ be punished, get one's deserts. **gie someone his** ~ punish someone *now local Abd-Rox*.

feather beat, chastise *Bnf Abd*.

flag flog, whip.

†**fleme** banish, drive into exile; put to flight, drive away, expel.

†**forflutten** severely scolded.

free clear (someone of a suspicion), absolve or acquit (someone or something of being or intending something) *Sh NE: 'I widna free 'er to try some queer pliskie on 'im'*.

get (one's) hands on catch (someone) for purposes of punishment.

†**gokstule** a cuck(ing) stool.

hame: pay ~ pay back, retaliate on, punish *now Sh*.

hazel beat or thrash, as with a hazel stick *now Cai Rox*. ~ **oil** *joc* a caning, a sound beating (with a hazel stick) *now Ags Dmf*.

heckle a severe beating, sharp criticism; a person who gives this *now Dmf*. **come** *or* **gae ower** *or* **through the** ~**-pin(s)** be roughly handled; be subjected to strict examination *now Ags*.

heid: get one's ~ **in one's hands** *usu in threats* receive *or* give a severe scolding or punishment.

het, hate, hot: get *or* **gie (some) a** ~ **skin** get or give (someone) a sound thrashing. **get** *or* **gie (someone) it** ~ **(an reekin)** be scolded or beaten severely, scold or beat (someone) severely.

hey-ma-nanny: get (one's) *or* **give** ~ get or give a drubbing, (be) scold(ed) or punish(ed) vigorously *Gen except Sh Ork*.

†**hipsie-dipsie** a thorough thrashing, *chf* **gie (somebody)** ~.

hoch hamstring, disable by cutting or striking the tendons of the hough.

keep: ~ **in aboot** restrain, keep in order, discipline *local*. ~ **in one's hand** restrain oneself, refrain from striking: '*Keep in your han, gudewife; the bairn meant nae ill*'. *now Bnf Fif Loth*.

†**keltie:** *chf* **give someone** ~ give someone a double dose of punishment.

laldie a thrashing, punishment, *chf* **get** ~, **gie someone** ~ *C, S*.

†**myter** a paper hat worn as a punishment, *usu* inscribed with the nature of the offence.

nail beat; scold *chf Rox*.

norter *n* rigorous discipline, chastisement, rough treatment *Abd*. *v* discipline, chastise *now Abd*.

owergang a drubbing, dressing-down *Sh NE Kcb*.

paik *v* beat, strike, thrash, punish *now Kcdn Ags Ayr Uls*. *n* a blow, stroke, thump *now Bnf Ayr*. ~**in** a thrashing, punishment, 'beating-up' *local*. **get one's** *or* **gie someone his** ~**s** get one's or give someone his deserts.

pap, pop beat, thrash. †**pappin** a whipping, drubbing.

peg †whack, beat. **peggin** a beating, drubbing *wLoth S*.

pey, pay *v* beat, chastise. *n* a blow, punishment, chastisement. *n* **peys,** †**pey** punishment, chastisement, a beating, thrashing *now Ork Ags*. ~ **(someone) hame** give (someone) his deserts, repay in full. ~ **someone's skin** *etc* give someone a good beating, thrash someone *now Sh*.

pike scold, beat, chastise.

pin beat, thrash. ~**nin(g)** a beating, scolding *now Wgt Slk*.

plaister, plaster a chastisement, beating; a dressing-down, swearing *now Sh Cai*.

pran bruise, buffet, beat, punish *NE*.

ram punish by bumping the buttocks against a wall or by caning the soles of the feet.

saut, salt punish, take revenge on.

scaud cause grief or pain to, punish *now Ags WC*.

scone slap with the open hand, smack (*esp* a child's bottom) *NE*. **scondies** *child's word* smacks, a spanking *NE*.

scud *v* beat with the open hand or a strap, smack, spank. *n* a blow, smack with the open hand.

skeeg *v* whip, strike, slap, spank *chf NE*. *n* a blow, smack *esp* on the bottom *NE*.

skelp smack with the open hand etc. ~**it leathering** a thrashing, spanking *Per WC*.

†**snib** check, restrain, reprove, punish.

†**snod** punish, defeat.

soosh beat, punish severely.

sort deal with by rebuke or punishment.

spaingie, spaingie wan *Bnf Abd* Spanish cane, or any cane, as used for punishment.

†**stang** *n* a rough pole or tree-trunk on which an offender against the laws or local conventions (*eg* a wife-beater, nagger, adulterer) was mounted astride and carried about in public; the punishment itself. *v* cause to **ride the** ~, humiliate (a person) thus. **ride the** ~ suffer the punishment as above. **ride the** ~ **on** deal out this punishment to an effigy of, or someone impersonating (the offender).

†**ticket** a severe beating or punishment.

†**unchestiable** unchastizable, impossible to chastize.

unction *ironic* punishment *NE*.

†**visie** punish (a sin etc).

†**wan(d)** *n* a rod or stick used for punishment, a switch. *v* beat with a wand or switch.

whacks: get one's ~ be punished, get one's just deserts *local N-Kcb*.

whang a thong for whipping; a whiplash.

whips a whipping, *chf* **get, gie** *or* **hae one's** ~**s** *now EC Rox*.

†**wrake: in** ~ **of** in revenge or punishment for.

12. WAR, FIGHTING, VIOLENCE

For crimes of violence, see 11.13 and for piracy see 11.14. For quarrels and quarrelling, see 15.5.9, for bullying and belligerent behaviour in general, see 15.3.4. Castles and other defensive buildings will be found in 13.3.5.

12.1 ARMY, ARMY LIFE, SERVICES

†**affere, effere** an array or display of armed force.

airmy an army *now NE Ags*.

Argyll: the ~shire Highlanders a Scottish regiment raised in 1794; linked in 1881 with **The Sutherland Highlanders** to form the **~ and Sutherland Highlanders (Princess Louise's)**.

†**bilget, billiet** a document containing a military order.

black: the B~ Watch a Scottish regiment raised from the **Independent Companies** in 1739, so called from their dark green and black tartan.

†**brak, brek** break up, disband (a company).

†**bront** the front rank(s) of an army.

†**Cameron (Highlander) 1** a soldier in **The Queen's Own Cameron Highlanders**. **2 The ~s** informal name for **The Queen's Own Cameron Highlanders**.

Cameronian a soldier in the Cameronian Regiment (Scottish Rifles) raised in 1689 among the **Cameronians** or **Whigs** in the west of Scotland in support of William of Orange; *now* represented only in the Territorial Army; 1786 became 26th Cameronian Regiment; 1881, linked with 90th **Perthshire Light Infantry** to form The Cameronians (Scottish Rifles).

†**chakwache** a patrol.

†**cheriot** a chariot.

†**city guard** = **town guard**.

†**commo(u)n(is)** the foot-soldiers in an army.

†**contramand** countermand.

†**contremandment** a counter-order.

†**cors-gard, crose-gaird** a corps de garde, a small body of soldiers on guard-duty; a guard-room.

†**cursour** a courser, a charger.

†**discover** reconnoitre.

dreel drill.

†**engage: enga(d)ger** one who took part in the **engagement** of 1647-48. **~ment** the undertaking of 1647-48 to send an army to England in support of Charles I.

†**fencible 1** capable of and liable for defensive military service. **2** capable of or actually serving for defence or protection.

†**fifteen: the F~** the Jacobite rising of 1715.

†**follow, fallow: ~ing** a body of retainers, domestic or military.

†**force** a body, troop or company.

†**forebront** the van of an army or a charge.

†**forepartie** a vanguard.

forty: †**the F~-five** the Jacobite rising of 1745. **the F~-twa** the **Black Watch**, *orig* the 42nd Highland Regiment of Foot *local NE-Dmf*.

†**fraction** a proportional payment for horses used for military service; a certain number of persons required to provide and pay a leader of horse.

Glasgow Highlanders a battalion of part-time volunteers, *latterly* the 9th (territorial) Battalion of the **Highland Light Infantry**.

Gordon Highlander *now freq abbreviated to* **Gordon 1** a soldier in **the Gordon Highlanders**. **2 the ~s** the regiment raised by the fourth Duke of Gordon in 1794, or 100th and later **the 92nd Foot (Ninety-Twa)** which became linked in 1881 with the 75th Highlanders.

†**gudget** a camp follower.

†**harboury, herboury** encamp.

†**there** *verse* an army, a host, a company.

Highland, Hieland: ~ Light Infantry a Scottish regiment, raised in 1777 and so called from 1807, mainly recruited in Glasgow and its neighbourhood; *usu* referred to as **the H.L.I.**; in 1881, linked with the 74th Highland regiment; in 1959, merged with the **Royal Scots Fusiliers** to form the **Royal Highland Fusiliers**. **~ regiment** one of the regiments of the British army *orig* raised in and recruited from the Highlands, whose members are entitled to wear Highland dress.

host, †**ost** *n* **1** *also* †**great ~** a host, an armed company. **2** †*also* **~ing** the assemblage or assembling of armed men summoned by the sovereign or regent for military service, *usu* on a specific occasion or for a specific campaign; the

Scottish army; the campaign for which such a force is raised. *v* †serve in an armed force, take part in a campaign etc, raid. † ~ing 1 campaigning, active military service. 2 *only* **osting** ? an army. 3 *only* **hosting** military service discharged as a feudal obligation in return for the holding of land. *adj* as used on active service, field-. †in ~ing on campaign. †in ost as an army.

†**Independent Companies** companies of Highland troops first recruited during Charles II's reign, and again (1725-30) by General Wade to keep order in the Highlands, formed in 1739 into the **Black Watch**.

†**ingadge** enlist.

†**Inglis: the** ~(**is**) the English troops of the Commonwealth.

†**intercommune** be in communication (with enemies, rebels etc).

†**kene** *of war* cruel, violent, terrible.

king: K ~'**s Own Scottish Borderers**, *now familiarly* **the KOSBs**, †**K** ~'**s Own Borderers** the Scottish regiment first raised in 1689 as **Leven's** or **the Edinburgh Regiment.**

†**knot** a closely-massed group of fighting men, a company or troop.

†**leve-gard, love-guard** a lifeguard, a bodyguard of soldiers.

†**leviat** enlisted, recruited.

†**liberate** set at liberty, released.

†**lift, list** raise or levy (troops).

†**ligger** a military camp, *esp* of a besieging force. ~ **lady** a female camp-follower.

list enlist into the army, recruit; enlist (oneself) as a soldier.

†**loan** provisions for a campaign *chf Highl NE*.

†**local** *of troops' quarterings* allocated to a specified district, not temporary or transient. ~**ity** 1 a levy or the allowance provided from it for maintaining troops in quarters, *latterly chf* a requisition of forage for their horses *latterly chf SW*. 2 the district allocated to a particular body of troops to provide its **locality** (as above). ~**lie** *of lands and teinds from which a compulsory or troops' maintenance is to be levied* (distributed) district by district, separately in each district.

†**lo(d)ge** a military camp or camping place.

†**maintenance** the monthly pay due to serving troops (*appar orig* of the Army of the **Covenant**); *chf* the tax first imposed on the Scottish shires and burghs in 1645 to provide this.

mairch march.

†**menyie** a body of troops.

†**merdale** camp-followers.

†**midfield** the centre division of an army.

Ninety Twa the 92nd Regiment of Foot, the **Gordon Highlanders**.

†**ontaking** engaging oneself for a post, enlisting as a soldier.

†**outputting** the finding and equipping of men for military service.

†**outred** fit out (a person or troops) for an expedition etc.

†**outreik, outreche** *v* provide and equip etc (*esp* men for military or naval service). *n* 1 finding and equipping troops or their mounts; fitting out troops etc for military service. 2 a levy of troops; a tax or contribution raised for the finding or equipping of troops.

†**outsetting** support, maintenance with money, provisions, equipment or troops; equipping.

†**outwach(is)** an outlying watch or watchmen; guards etc placed outside the body of an army, a town etc.

†**pallion, palʒoun** 1 a large and stately tent, a pavilion. 2 ~**is** a tented camp; an army's lines.

†**park** lodge (troops) in a camp or fortification.

†**partiment, parsment** a division; a company.

†**passage** a military or naval expedition.

†**Perthshire Light Infantry** a Scottish regiment, raised in 1794 as The 90th Perthshire Volunteers; 1815 became 90th Perthshire Light Infantry; *cf* **Cameronian**.

†**pese, pais** end (a war). **hald** *or* **kepe in** ~ maintain in a state of peace. **in(to)** ~ in freedom from war.

pipe: ~ **band** a band made up of pipers and drummers with a drum-major. ~**s and drums** the formal collective name for the pipers and drummers who make up a pipe band.

†**proviant** provision, food supply, *esp* for an army.

†**punʒe** a handful of men, *usu* soldiers.

Queen: The ~'**s Own Cameron Highlanders** the name from 1881 of the regiment raised in 1793 as the **79th** or **Cameronian Volunteers** by Major Alan Cameron of Erracht, *later* (1806) known as the **79th** or **Cameron Highlanders** and in 1873 granted the title **79th** ~'**s Own Cameron** Highlanders by Queen Victoria. ~'**s Own Highlander** a soldier in the ~'**s Own Highlanders** (**Seaforth and Camerons**). ~'**s Own Highlanders (Seaforth and Camerons)** the regiment formed in 1961 by the amalgamation of the **Seaforth Highlanders** and The ~'**s Own Cameron Highlanders.**

rangle, †rangale, rangald 1 †camp followers. 2 a rabble, (*esp* of soldiers).

†**ratt, rot** a file (of soldiers).

†**recognosce, recognize** reconnoitre.

†**recreu** reinforce (an army).

†**relieve** assist **with** (munitions of war).

Royal: ~ **Company of Archers** the Sovereign's bodyguard in Scotland. ~ **Highland Fusiliers** a regiment formed in 1959 by the amalgamation of the ~ **Scots Fusiliers** and the **Highland Light Infantry.** ~ **Scots** a regiment, *orig* raised 1633 as a regiment in the French service; so called since 1812; from 1920, **The** ~ **Scots (The** ~ **Regiment).** ~ **Scots Dragoon Guards (Carabiniers and Greys)** a regiment formed in 1971 by the amalgamation of the ~ **Scots Greys** and the 3rd Carabiniers (Prince of Wales Dragoon Guards). † ~ **Scots Fusiliers** a regiment, *orig* raised 1678; so called 1881-1959; cf ~ **Highland Fusiliers.** † ~ **Scots Greys** name given officially to the **Scots Greys** in 1877; *cf* **Royal Scots Dragoon Guards**.

Scots of military bodies consisting of Scotsmen, both as mercenaries in foreign service and in the British Army. † ~ **Greys** a Scottish (cavalry) regiment (2nd Dragoons formed from Independent Troops of Dragoons in 1681).

†**Seaforth 1** a soldier in the regiment raised in 1778 by the Earl of Seaforth; a ~ **Highlander. 2** The ~s the ~ **Highlanders.** ~ **Highlander** a soldier in the ~ **Highlanders.** ~ **Highlanders** name given to the regiment formed in 1881 by amalgamation of the **72nd Duke of Albany's Own Highlanders** (raised by the Earl of Seaforth in 1778) and the **78th Highlanders, Ross-shire Buffs** (raised in 1793 by Colonel Francis Humberston MacKenzie), *now* (since 1961) amalgamated with **The Queen's Own Cameron Highlanders** to form the **Queen's Own Highlanders (**~ **and Camerons).**

†**sowd** sold, (soldiers') pay.

†**spear silver** a form of military tax or levy.

†**stale** a body of armed men (posted in a particular place for ambush etc); the main body of an army.

†**stench** *of war* come to an end.

†**stuff** furnish (troops) with support; support, aid (a war).

†**supply** an additional body of troops.

†**Sutherland** *n, also* ~ **Highlander** *etc* a soldier in the ~ **Highlanders.** ~ **Highlanders** a regiment raised *orig* in 1799 as the 93rd Highland regiment; in 1861 it became the 93rd **Sutherland Highlanders;** cf **Argyll and Sutherland Highlanders.**

†**tak, take:** ~ **on** take up (arms). ~ **up** take (land) into occupation.

†**town, toun:** ~ **guard** an armed corps, *chf* of ex-soldiers, enrolled for police duties *Edb*.

†**tranont** shift one's position, *esp* rapidly and stealthily; make a forced march **upon**.

†**trew, trewis, trowis** *n* **1** a truce. **2** a document recording the terms of a truce. *v* grant a truce to.

†**trip** a troop, company (of men).

†**uptaking** the levying (of men).

†**vangaird** a vanguard.

wadge wage.

†**wappenshaw, weaponshaw,** *also* ~**ing** a periodical muster or review of the men under arms in a particular lordship or district.

†**ward, waird 1** an appointed station or post (for a body of soldiers). **2** *law* the oldest form of feudal land tenure, *ie* by military service, with various rights and obligations, *esp* that of the **superior** to uphold and draw the rents of the lands of a deceased **vassal** while the heir was not **infeft** or was a minor, as recompense for the loss of military services during this period. **3** ward. **watching and** ~**ing** one of the duties of a burgess in a **royal burgh,** *namely* taking one's turn to patrol the streets and help suppress disturbances.

weir war. †**pass in werefare** go to war. † ~**lie** martial, warlike. ~**like** warlike. † ~**man** a man-of-war, warship.

12.2 SOLDIERS AND OTHER SERVICES PERSONNEL

†**almeral, ammiral** an admiral.

†**backman** a follower (in war).

†**ban(n)erman** a banner-bearer.

†**caddie** a military cadet.

†**campioun** a champion.

†**cannonar** a cannoneer.

†**capitanry** a captaincy.

†**carmagnole** a soldier in the French Revolutionary army.

†**castellane** one of the garrison of a castle.

†**chaptane** a captain.

†**cornel** a colonel.

†**crownell, crowner** a colonel.

†**discoverour, discurr(i)our** a scout.

†**empriour** a military commander.

†**fencible** a soldier called up for home defence.

foggie a veteran soldier, an army pensioner *local C*.

†**forray, furrow:** ~**our** a forayer; a person sent in advance to secure quarters or supplies.

†**garitour** a watchman on a tower or wall.

†**hagbutar** a soldier armed with a hackbut.

Highlander, Hielander a soldier in one of the Scottish regiments.

Jock (nickname for) a soldier in one of the Scottish regiments.

†**kemp** a champion: **1** one who fights in single combat; a professional fighter; *latterly only ballad and place-names*; **2** one who fights on behalf of another or for a cause.

killick a leading seaman in the Navy, the anchor badge on his sleeve being likened to a pickaxe *WC*.

kiltie a soldier in a Highland regiment.

lieutenand a lieutenant. † ~ **general** the senior military commander after the sovereign.

†**locumtenant** a lieutenant.

†**marischal** *in the army of Scotland* the title of a low-ranking regimental officer of regiments of foot.

offisher, †**officiar** an officer. ~**ship** the position and functions of an officer.

†**ordinar** an officer or other person who had a regular or permanent appointment or engagement; *specif* a (permanently engaged) gunner.

†**outputtar** a person responsible for finding and equipping men for military service.

†**outreiker** a person who found and equipped a man for military service.

†**pikoneir** a soldier armed with a pike.

pipe: ~**r** military title give to certain members of a regimental ~ **band**. ~ **major**, (*informally*) **pipie** the leader of a ~ **band**; *specif* as a military title, the equivalent of the regimental bandmaster in an English regiment.

†**pricker** a light horseman, skirmisher, *esp* a **reiver**; the light pony on which he rode.

†**reform(ie)r** an officer left without a command but retaining his rank and receiving full or half pay.

†**reid, red:** ~ **friar** a templar. ~**-shank** nickname for a Highlander, *esp* a kilted soldier, from his bare legs.

Royal *informal* a soldier in the ~ **Scots**.

†**sairgin, seriand** a sergeant.

†**single** *of members of the armed forces* of the lowest rank.

sodger a soldier.

†**sour-dook (sodger)** nickname for a member of the Lothian militia.

†**suddart** a soldier.

†**town, toun:** ~ **major** the major of the **town guard** *Edb*.

†**wach** a spy, look-out man.

†**wager** a mercenary soldier.

†**waiter** a watchman at the gates of Edinburgh.

†**weirman** a fighting man, warrior, soldier.

†**werriour** a warrior.

†**wye** a fighting man, warrior, soldier.

12.3 FLAGS, BADGES, SYMBOLS

†**banere, benner** a banner.

†**cressen(t)** some sort of decoration (sometimes of satin) on harness or armour.

†**croishtarich, crosstarrie** the **fiery cross**.

†**ensenʒe 1** *also* **ansenʒe, handsenze** a distinguishing emblem or symbol; ~**s** insignia of dignity or office. **2** a flag.

†**fire: fiery cross,** ~ **cors,** ~ **cros** a wooden cross burnt at one end and dipped in blood at the other, carried from place to place by a succession of runners to summon the fighting men of the district to arms.

heckle, hackle a cockade of hackle-feathers dyed in various colours and worn in the bonnets of certain Scottish regiments.

†**medalʒe** a medal.

†**pallion, palʒoun** a flag or banner.

†**pannoun** a pennon.

†**pensil** a (small) pennon or streamer, a standard, a set of colours.

†**pinnet** a small flag or standard, an ensign, streamer.

12.4 UNIFORM, ARMOUR

Shields are in 12.5.

†**abilʒeit** arrayed, dressed; equipped.

†**abuilyiement, bulyament** equipment, arms.

airmour armour *now local Sh-Ags*.

†**banderoll** a bandoleer.

†**barding** horse armour.

†**birny, byrne** a mail-coat; a cuirass or breast-plate.

†**bonnet, bannet** a (metal) helmet.

†**brace** *archery* a guard for the wrist.

†**brigantine** a kind of armour.

†**capricht** ? part of the dress or armour of a horse.

†**dorlach, darloch** a bundle used by Highland soldiers instead of a knapsack.

†**foregere** armour for the front of the body.

Glengarry a kind of flat-sided cap or bonnet (shaped rather like a modern forage cap) pointed at the front and back and *freq* with two ribbons hanging behind, *appar* a development of the **cockit bonnet**, now *usu* worn with Highland dress.

graith equip, array, dress (a person), *esp* in armour.

†**greis** pieces of armour for the shins.

†**haberschoun, aubirchoun** a habergeon, a coat of mail.

†**habilʒementis** apparel, equipment.

habuliment dress, attire, (military) equipment *now Sh.*

†**halcrek** a half-suit of light armour, worn by footmen and horsemen.

†**hogtoune** a sleeveless padded jerkin worn under the hauberk, and occasionally alone as a fencing jacket.

†**hoomet, hewmond** a helmet.

†**hummel bonnet** a plain bonnet without a crest of feathers worn by Highland regiments.

†**journee** a kind of travelling cloak worn over armour.

†**knapscall, knapscap** a metal shell or skullcap, worn defensively, commonly under a bonnet; *latterly sometimes also* shell and bonnet together. ∼ **bonnet** a bonnet for covering a **knapscall**; *latterly* shell and bonnet together.

†**mailʒe** (chain-)mail.

†**pans** a piece of armour to protect the belly or abdomen.

†**pissane** a piece of armour to protect the upper chest and neck.

plaid a rectangular length of twilled woollen cloth, *usu* in tartan, *formerly* worn as an outer garment *esp* in rural areas, *later* also as a shawl by women in towns, and *now* surviving as part of the ceremonial dress of members of the pipe bands of Scottish regiments.

†**plate, pleit:** ∼ **glufe** *or* **slefe, gluve of plate** a glove or sleeve consisting of or reinforced by plate-armour.

†**pullane** a piece of defensive armour covering the knee.

†**reist** a piece of armour which held the butt end of a lance.

†**secret** a coat-of-mail concealed under one's ordinary clothes.

†**sellet** a sallet, a light helmet.

†**sicker** *of armour* dependable, reliable.

strip[1] the stripe of a non-commissioned officer *now Abd.*

†**strip**[2] ? some piece of armour.

†**stuff** the quilted material worn under armour; defensive armour itself.

swurd *now Ork,* **sourd,** †**swerd:** ∼ **belt** a belt from which a sword in its scabbard is suspended.

†**thee pess** a piece of armour for the thigh.

trews close-fitting trousers made of fine, *usu* tartan cloth, with the legs extended to cover the feet (somewhat like modern tights), formerly worn by Highlanders; *later* tartan trousers worn by certain Scottish regiments or short tartan trunks worn under a kilt.

†**tymmer, tymber, tymeral, tymbrall** the crest of a helmet.

†**ulʒeat** a stud for armour.

†**vysar, vesar** a visor.

†**wed** *n* armour.

12.5 WEAPONS

†**abuilyiement, bulyament** equipment, arms.

airra an arrow *now NE Ags.*

aix an axe.

†**amonitioune** ammunition.

†**anarmit** armed.

†**artailʒeit** provided with artillery.

†**artilʒerie, artailʒe** artillery.

†**awblaster** a crossbow.

†**bag(o)net** a bayonet.

bare unsheathed.

†**bastion** a cudgel, truncheon.

†**batoun** *n* a baton. *v* strike with a baton.

†**battard** a kind of small cannon.

†**bauch** *of blows* inflicted with a cudgel etc as opposed to a sharp weapon.

beetyach, bittock a sword, dagger, small knife.

belt fasten on (a sword etc) with a belt.

†**bendit** *of a gun etc* cocked, made ready for firing.

†**bers, bas, barse** the smallest kind of cannon.

blad, bled a blade.

blunderbush a blunderbuss *now Abd.*

†**boden** furnished with arms; equipped for fighting.

bool a cannon-ball.

†**bouk** stop up (the touch-hole of a cannon).

bow, †**boll** a bow. †**bowar,** ∼**maker** a maker of bows. **bowit** provided with a **bow.** † ∼ **butts, merkis** ground for archery practice *now in place-names.* † ∼**-sting** a bowstaff, a stick suitable for making into a bow.

†**brade,** lift, throw, draw **out** *etc* with a quick movement.

†**braig (knife)** a large knife.

†**brandis** brandish (a weapon).

†**brangle** shake, brandish (a weapon).

†**brog(g)it staff** a staff with an iron point, a pike.

†**buge** a kind of (hooked) weapon, *freq* ~ **staff.**

†**bullax** an axe, hatchet *chf N*.

bullet, †**billet** a bullet. † ~ **stane** a round stone, used *eg* as a missile.

†**burdoun** a stout staff, a cudgel.

butts ground for archery practice *now Abd Fif*.

†**byknife** a knife carried beside a dagger.

calms, caums moulds, *esp* bullet-moulds.

†**cartow** a quarter-cannon, throwing a ball of a quarter of a hundredweight (12.7 kilos).

†**chargeour** an appliance for charging a gun.

claymore the Highlanders' large two-edged sword; *also* the basket-hilted single-edged broadsword.

†**cleg** a missile used by rioters against troops or police, *esp* during the Radical movement *C*.

clod pelt with missiles.

colfing, calfing gun-wadding *now NE*.

†**condampne** damage, *esp* with artillery fire.

†**craw, crow:** ~ **tae** a crow's foot, a caltrop (for impeding cavalry etc).

†**culmas** a curved sword; a sabre.

†**culvering 1** a hand-gun. **2** a culverin, a large cannon.

†**cut-throat** a kind of light artillery or firearm.

dab pierce slightly, stab *now local Bnf-Kcb*.

†**delasch** discharge, let fly.

†**dens ax(e)** a long-bladed axe.

dert a dart.

†**ding 1** batter, beat down with shot. **2** pierce with a violent thrust.

†**dog** a kind of cannon.

†**dorlach, darloch** a quiver (for arrows).

†**doup** stab (a person); thrust (a weapon) into.

draps, drops small shot, pellets *now local Bnf-Fif*.

durk, dirk *n* a short dagger worn in the belt by Highlanders. *v* stab with a **durk.**

†**elf-arrow, elf-shot** a flint arrowhead, thought to be used by fairies.

†**enbrace, embrace** put (a shield) on the arm.

ettle aim, direct (a missile).

†**feir: in** ~ **of were** in warlike array.

†**fencible** *of arms etc* capable of serving for defence.

†**fire:** ~ **spere** a spear carrying fire with it. ~**werk 1** fittings for guns. **2** ~**werk(s)** firearms.

†**flane** an arrow.

†**flas** a powder-flask.

†**flegear** a fletcher, an arrowmaker

†**frizzel, frezel** the hammer of a flintlock pistol or gun.

†**frusch** a crashing noise, the crash of breaking weapons.

†**funȝe** fence, make thrusts.

†**ganȝe** an arrow or a bolt for a crossbow.

†**gerit** provided with arms and armour.

gley, glee *v* look with one eye, take aim *now Abd Ags*. *n* aim; the act of aiming *now NE Ags*

†**graith** the accessory apparatus of a gun or cannon; ammunition; the priming materials of a firearm, powder and shot. **small** ~ small shot; the priming materials of a firearm, powder and shot.

†**guddle** stab, hack (a body).

gullie (knife) a large knife.

†**hagbute** a hackbut. ~ **of crok, crochat** a hackbut supported on a mounting by an iron hook attached to the barrel.

hail small shot, pellets *C Uls*.

†**half:** ~ **bend** a half-cocked firearm. ~ **haggis** a smaller size of **hagbute.** ~**lang,** ~**long** *chf of swords* of half the full or usual length; short.

hash slash, hack, mangle, as with a sharp instrument.

†**heck** a metal hook or loop on a scabbard through which the sword-belt passed.

†**hede:** ~**pece** an accessory for a musket. ~**steke** a piece of large artillery, a kind of cannon.

hissel a hazel stick used as a cudgel; a stout stick of any wood.

†**huke** the barb of an arrow.

†**hulster** a holster.

hummel unarmed.

†**inarme** enarm, equip with weapons.

†**javeling, jeffelling** a javelin.

†**Jedburgh, Jethart:** ~ **staff** a weapon similar to a bill or halberd, *orig* from Jedburgh (represented on Jedburgh's coat-of-arms).

jockteleg, jackteleg a clasp-knife *now Sh Ayr*.

†**knife** a knife worn with a sword or **whinger,** *appar* in the same sheath, a **byknife.**

†**lance-staff** a piked staff, a lance or pike.

leash a leash used for whipping *now Sh midloth*.

†**Leith-ax** a kind of halberd.

†**libber-la(y)** a cudgel.

lip a notch in the edge of a knife- or sword-blade *Loth S*.

Lochaber axe *etc* a kind of long-handled battle-axe; *now only* ceremonial arms carried by the attendants of Edinburgh's **Lord Provost.**

†**Lumbard paper** an expensive kind of paper used for cartridges.

†**lunt: with** *or* **of** ~ **werk** *of firearms* having a matchlock.

mark, merk take aim *now Kcdn nEC Ayr*.

†**mass(e), measse** a mace.

†**Meg** applied to a large cannon, *appar* = **Mons Meg**.

†**mik** a wedge for sighting a cannon.

mint brandish (a weapon) *now NE*. † ~ **to make as if to draw** (a weapon etc).

†**misgie** *of a gun* fail to go off, misfire.

Mons †a large 15th-century cannon cast probably at Mons in Flanders and now at Edinburgh Castle. ~ **Meg** the name later given to this cannon.

†**moppat** a mop, *esp* for cleaning gun barrels.

†**mors(e)** prime (a gun). **moshin hole, motion hole** the touch-hole of a gun. **morsing powder** priming powder.

†**moyen, myane** *adj, of a culverin* of the middle size. *n* a medium-sized culverin.

†**nakit** unarmed.

†**nipschot** *of a bowman, of cannon* **schute** *or* **play** ~ *appar* shoot amiss in some way.

†**nit** some accessory part of a gun.

ordinance ordnance.

†**outschute** outshoot.

†**outsetter** some implement used in gunnery.

†**pair of arrows** a set of three arrows.

†**partisan (staff)** a long-handled spear.

†**pasvoland** a passe-volant, a type of small cannon.

†**patrontash** a pouch or case for holding cartridges and other ammunition.

†**patroune** a paper container for the charge of a cannon or pistol; a (paper) cartridge.

†**pellok** a more or less spherical missile shot from a **pellok-bow** gun etc; a ball, bullet or canonball. ~ **bow, pellet** a type of hand-bow or crossbow which shot pellets.

†**pestolat** a pistolet.

†**pestoll** a pistol.

†**phise** ? a device operated by screws, for mounting a cannon or attaching a cannon to its stock.

pick a light stroke or tap, *usu* with a pointed instrument.

†**pik 1** a weapon consisting of a long wooden shaft or pike-staff, with a pointed head of iron or steel; a pike-staff. **2** *literary* applied to earlier staff weapons.

†**pik-moyane** a kind of culverin, a large cannon.

pile a pellet (of shot) *now Dnbtn Kcb*.

pin strike as with a small sharp-pointed missile, hit a sharp quick blow, pelt with stone etc *local Sh-C*.

†**pluffing** firing, shooting.

†**pluke** a club, bludgeon; a stout stick.

†**plummet** the pommel on the hilt of a sword, *freq* weighted with lead.

porr, purr stab.

pot, pat: ~ **pece** a gun with a large bore, a mortar.

†**pouder myll** a mill for making gunpowder; ? the place where this was done.

prime charge, load.

prod a prick, stab *now SW*.

prog *n* a piercing weapon or instrument, a barb, dart, arrow *now Sh Ork Cai*. *v* stab, pierce, prick.

†**punce** a dagger.

putt the recoil from a gun *now Sh-N Kcb*.

†**quavyr (case)** a quiver, a case for arrows.

†**Queen Ann(e)** a long-barrelled, large-bore flintlock musket.

†**rack** *of a gun* go off, fire.

racket a rocket, a firework; a missile.

†**ramforce** ? jam up (cannon).

†**ratch, roch** the barrel of a gun.

rebound a loud explosive noise as of gunshot, a reverberation *now Abd Kcdn Fif*.

†**rever** *archery* rover, a mark selected at random.

rit, rut thrust (a sword etc) through; stab *now Sh*.

rung a stout stick; a cudgel *now N Kcb*.

†**scawbart** a scabbard.

†**scharpentyn** a serpentine, a kind of (ship's) cannon.

set aff cause to explode, let off an explosive charge, shot etc *now Abd Kcb*.

†**seven** seven similar cannon used at the Battle of Flodden.

†**shabble** a curved sword, a sabre, cutlass.

†**shed** cleave (with a weapon).

shiel *now NE*, †**scheld** a shield.

shod fit (an arrow etc) with a metal tip etc.

†**short sword** a short-bladed sword.

shot shoot *now Sh-nEC*. †**shotter** a missile, weapon.

shuit shoot.

skean, sgian a (Highlander's) short-bladed black-hilted sheath-knife or dagger. ~ **dhu, sgian dubh** a **skean**, now commonly worn in the stocking as part of Highland dress. †**skeen occle** a **skean** concealed in the upper part of the sleeve under the armpit.

skirp a small flying fragment of metal, stone etc, a pellet, splinter *NE*.

†**slacky** a kind of sling or catapult.

†**slot staff** some kind of staff used as a weapon.

slung[1] a sling (for hurling stones).

†**slung**[2] a serpentine or culverin.

†**snap gun, snap work** a firelock.

†**souple** a cudgel, a stout stick.

sparrow, sparra: ~ **drift** *or* **hail** *or* **shot** shot for shooting small birds *now local NE-Rox*.

†**sperthe** a battle-axe.

†**sport staff** a quarter-staff.

spurtle, spurkle *literary, disparaging, or joc* a sword.

†**stab** make thrusts with a staff or club.

†**staff:** ~**ing** the action of striking with staves. ~ **sling** a sling, the cords of which are attached to the end of a staff.

†**stair** thrust (a weapon).

stane stone.

†**stark** *of an instrument of torture etc* inflicting severe pain.

†**steik** pierce, stab; transfix.

stick stab, thrust a knife into, finish off. ~**er** a stabber, a slaughterer.

†**sting** a staff etc used as a weapon, the shaft of a pike etc, *freq* **staff and** ~.

†**stob** *n* a stab-wound; a poke, a prod. *v* stab.

†**stock:** ~**er** a workman who makes or fits gun-stocks. ~**ing** the parts forming the stock of a gun. **stokmaker** a maker of gun carriages. **stoke quhele** ? a wheel for a gun-carriage.

†**stock swerd** a thrusting sword.

†**stoke** thrust, drive home (a sword).

†**stoop** plunge (a knife) **in** (a person's body).

†**streke** hold out, launch (a weapon etc).

strik, strike: ~ **off** cut off with a stroke of a sword, axe etc.

stug a prick, stab with some pointed object; such an object, a dart.

†**swack** brandish (a sword).

swap brandish (a weapon), make a swipe with (a sword etc), wave about *now Sh.*

swash *v* bluster with or as with weapons *now Abd Ags.* *n* a clashing against or on.

swurd *now Ork,* **sourd,** †**swerd** a sword. † ~ **slipper** a sword-sharpener.

†**tairge** a targe, a shield.

†**thraw-mou** *appar* name for a cannon **thrawn-mou'd** *of a gun* having a twisted mouth.

†**thud** a loud sound (*eg* of a cannon).

†**titup** the trigger of a crossbow.

tooch the sound of a shot, a bang, puff *Bwk S.*

†**tree** a cudgel, club.

†**tress, trast** a rest for a fire-arm.

tricker the catch or trigger (of a gun) *now N Lnk.*

tume discharge (a gun) *now Abd Ags Stlg.*

†**tynd** a tine, prong, spike.

†**unbend** uncock (a firearm).

†**unermit** unarmed.

†**unsmart** *of a bow* slack.

†**unsonsie** *of a weapon etc* severe, harmful, causing death or injury.

†**ure** the point of a weapon.

vizzy *v* take aim (with a gun etc), aim **at** something) *now Sh.* *n* **1** an aim (with a weapon), *usu*

take a ~ *now Sh.* **2** the sight on the barrel of a gun

†**wad shooting** a challenge shooting match for staked prizes *chf Ags.*

wag brandish (a weapon).

wage, wadge brandish or hurl (a weapon) *NE Ags Fif.*

wald *now Ork,* **weel** *chf Abd* wield.

†**wampish** wave, flourish, brandish.

wapinschaw a rifle-shooting competition organized by volunteers, private rifle clubs etc *now Bnf.*

wappen a weapon.

†**whinger** a short stabbing sword, *usu* hung from the belt.

whisk, wisk a brief rapid sweeping movement (of a weapon etc).

†**windlestrae** *contemptuous* a weapon, dagger etc.

wise aim, propel, shoot (a missile).

†**yetlin(g)** a small cannon.

12.6 MUSIC

gathering a signal on drum or bagpipe to (fighting) men to assemble; a tune used for this purpose; one of the types of **pibroch**.

†**outhorn** a horn blown by officers of the crown to give the alarm, *eg* to summon the lieges in pursuit of a fugitive.

pipe: ~**r** military title given to certain members of a regimental ~ **band.** ~ **band** a band made up of pipers and drummers with a drum-major. ~ **major,** (*informally*) **pipie** the leader of a ~ **band;** *specif* as a military title, the equivalent of the regimental bandmaster in an English regiment. ~**s and drums** the formal collective name for the pipers and drummers who make up a pipe band.

†**touk, tuck** *v of a drum* sound, beat; beat (a drum). *n* the beat or tap of a drum.

12.7 FIGHTING

†**allyat** allied.

†**allye** **1** allies. **2** an ally, associate.

back †put or force back. **with** *etc* **one's** ~ **to** *or* **at the wall** hard-pressed, facing desperate odds.

†**bargain, bergan** *n* contention, conflict, struggle. *v* contend, fight (with).

†**barlafummil** a cry for truce.

†**bataiȝe** a battle.

†**be** have as followers, *esp* in fighting.

bicker *v* fight with arrows, stones, or other weapons; make skirmishing attacks; engage in (street) fights. *n* a fight with missiles; a skirmish; a street- or school-fight.

blue day a day on which some disturbance takes place *now Bnf*.

†**brattle** a fight, struggle.

†**brek lowse** rise in arms.

buck batter; fight.

†**carmusche** skirmish (**with**).

†**chairge, charge** press heavily upon; charge in battle.

†**chaser** a pursuer (in battle).

†**colleg** join as an ally.

collieshangie, killieshangie a dog-fight *now Bnf*.

conduck a safe-conduct *now Abd Fif*.

†**debate** fight for; fight against; stop by force; overcome.

†**dispeace** dissension, enmity, disquiet.

†**ensenȝe, ansenȝe, handsenȝe** a war-cry, a rallying cry or signal.

†**fa, fae** a foe *now verse*.

†**fewter** close in combat.

forfochtin exhausted with fighting.

fraca a fracas.

†**gain-stander** an opponent, enemy.

gang ower overcome, beat *now Ork NE*.

grips: come to ~ close (**with**), engage in a struggle at close quarters (**with**). **be, go, keep** *etc* **in** ~ wrestle, tussle with, struggle with at close quarters.

handshaking a grappling at close quarters; a fight to settle a grudge *Rox*.

hobble *now Kcdn*, **hubble** *Sh C, S* a mêlée.

†**hurkill** come into violent collision.

hurry a disturbance, riot, quarrel, commotion *now local Inv-Uls*.

†**inanimitie** enmity, strife.

†**inimy** enemy.

†**jeopardie, juparty 1** a daring exploit, a feat of arms; a battle, raid etc. **2** martial daring, valour, prowess.

joogle joggle, shake, wrestle **with**.

†**juffle** scuffle.

keep aff o anesel act defensively in fighting; stand up for oneself *N Fif Kcb*.

kelter wriggle, undulate, struggle *now only verse*.

†**kene** *of combat* fierce, violent.

†**licht, light** *of battles or fights* involving small numbers or few casualties.

†**march: day of** ~ a day of truce on which a court of the wardens of the opposing **marches** heard complaints of infringements of the **laws of march**.

†**mell** mingle, come together in combat.

†**mellay** mingle in combat, fight.

†**mellé 1** fighting, *esp* close combat. **2** a battle or engagement, *esp* one involving a close combat between individuals. **3** a closely-packed mass of men fighting.

†**mese** pacify, make calm.

†**meting** the action of engaging (an enemy) in battle; a fight.

†**nichbour** *of enmity or war* internal, domestic.

nieves fisticuffs *now Sh Ork*.

†**offer** offer (oneself) in battle.

†**ost** a confrontation or joining in battle of two opposing armies; two such armies.

†**outer, utter** *of a horse or its rider, in combat?* swerve aside, refuse the encounter.

†**pairt, part:** ~-**tak** support, side with, defend. ~-**taker** a supporter, an ally; an accomplice.

†**pairty, partie 1** take sides, make common cause **with**. **2** support, take the part of.

†**poinȝé** a battle, skirmish.

†**rambarre** beat or force back.

rammy a free-for-all, violent disturbance, scuffle.

†**reconter** encounter.

redd *v*, *also* †**rede** separate (combatants); put an end to (fighting) *now Abd*. † ~**er, ridder** a person who intervenes to stop a fight or quarrel. ~**er's lick** *etc now Bnf*, ~**in straik** *now local Sh-nEC* a blow received by a person trying to stop a fight.

†**reel** *of an army etc* waver, give way.

reid, red bloody, resulting in bloodshed. † ~-**wat** *literary* blood-stained. † ~-**wat shod** *literary* up to the ankles in blood.

rug and rive struggle, tussle.

sair, sore *of a battle, struggle etc* hard, severe, fierce.

†**sarray** in close order or array.

†**sattle, settle** cause (troops) to fall back, yield ground.

sconce a screen or shelter (of stone, wood etc) for concealment, defence etc.

†**scrim** skirmish. **scrimmage** a skirmish.

†**semble** meet in conflict.

†**semblé** a hostile meeting, conflict.

†**senȝe** a battle-cry, rallying cry.

†**set** *of a battle* pitched.

shak a fa try a fall, have a wrestling bout or tussle *chf Bnf Abd*.

shangie a row, disturbance, fight *now local Bnf-Lnk*.

sharrie quarrel, fight *NE*.

†**shield, scheld: with spear and** ~ in battle array; by force of arms.

†Shirramuir: the ~ the Jacobite rising of 1715 which ended in the battle of Sheriffmuir, near Stirling.

†singular combat single combat.

†slap *n* a gap or breach in the ranks (of an army etc). *v* make breaks or breaches in (a body of troops).

slogan, †slug(h)orn a war- or rallying-cry, *usu* the name of a clan chief or clan rendezvous, used by Highlanders and Borderers, *orig* as a signal to arms or as a password.

†soverance assurance; safe-conduct; truce.

†squabblement a wrangle, disturbance of the peace, associated *esp* with the Langholm **Common Riding.**

†stale: in ~ in ambush; in battle array.

†stalwart *of a fight* severe, hard, violent.

stan-tae a set-to, a tussle *Sh N Fif Wgt.*

†stench 1 restrain (**from** violence etc). **2** *of persons* cease from violence.

stour *chf literary* strife, conflict, battle *now local Bnf-Wgt.*

†strik, strike fight (a battle).

taisle a severe brush or tussle *now Kcb.*

tirrivee a disturbance, fight *N, C, S.*

tirr-wirr quarrel, fight noisily. *Ags Per Stlg.*

tissle tussle, struggle *now Ork.*

tousle a struggle, tussle, contest.

†trew, trewis, trowis *n* **1** a truce. **2** a document recording the terms of a truce. *v* grant a truce to.

tulyie *n* a quarrel, brawl, fight *now local Sh-Bwk. v* **1** **†tulʒie** harass. **2** quarrel, contend, fight *now Sh Ork Mry.* **† ~-mulie** a broil, turmoil.

tyarr fight, be prone to quarrel *now Cai.*

†vassalage a brave or chivalrous act; a gallant exploit.

wap, whap a disturbance, brawl, din, quarrel *now NE Per Dmf.*

warsle, wrastle *now Sh,* **†wirstle** *v* **1** wrestle. **2** wrestle with, engage in about with, overcome *now local Sh-WC. n* a wrestling match, a physical tussle *now local Sh-Per.*

widdle a struggle.

†yed *verse* strife, wrangling; struggle.

yoke †join battle **with. yokin** a fight, contest, scuffle *now NE.*

12.8 CHALLENGES

brag, braig *n* a challenge. *†v* challenge, defy.

cooardy lick a blow given as a challenge to fight *now Fif Lnk.*

cooch a blow or tap on the shoulder as a challenge to fight *now local C.*

coorgy a blow or push given as a challenge to fight; a challenge *Loth Lnk.*

fugie a light blow, accompanied by the word, given by one schoolboy to another as a challenge to fight.

scart someone's buttons run one's fingers down another's jacket buttons, as a challenge to fight *now Rox.*

12.9 ATTACK, DEFENCE

†adversare, adversour an adversary.

†assaill assault, attack.

†assailʒe, assalʒe assail. **assailʒeour** an assailant.

†assalt, assaut *n* assault.

†attempat an attempt involving violence or wrong.

†beligger beleaguer.

bicker attack with arrows, stones etc.

blude, blood †an act of bloodshed; an assault causing bleeding. **bludie** bloody. **† ~-drawing** the drawing of blood by assault or wounding.

†brash *n* an attack, assault in battle. *v* break through or down by assault; bash, batter.

†brattle a sharp assault.

†brush *n* a violent impetus, onrush or onset. *v* force or drive violently.

cock raise (a fist) in a threatening manner *Cai-Fif.*

†debate *n* a struggle, a defence *Dmf Uls. v* **1** fight for; defend. **2** fight against; stop by force; overcome.

†defens: mak ~ (attempt to) defend oneself etc.

†ding attack violently.

draw raise (one's hand, foot etc) in attack.

fang acquire, catch, seize, capture.

fend a defence, resistance.

fettle fall upon, 'go for' (a person) *now Bwk.*

†forray, furrow a foray. **rin** *or* **ride a forray** make an attack.

gain-stand withstand, oppose.

gardies the hands or fists, *esp* when raised to fight.

grip seize, lay hands on, take possession of (lands or belongings) violently or illegally.

hain keep from harm, protect, spare.

†handle lay hands on (a person) in a hostile way, seize, capture. **handling** hostile treatment, seizure, capture.

†hot-trod the tracking down and pursuit of Border

marauders by the aggrieved party; the signal for such pursuit.

hund, hound 1 hound. **2** †drive **out** *etc* with dogs or by violence.

†**inbreak** a breaking in, intrusion by force, *fig* violation.

†**incontrare** against, in opposition to; in violation **of**.

†**incuming** an invasion.

†**infa(ll)** a raid.

†**intaking** the taking of a place by assault.

invade 1 attack, assault (a person). **2** †take possession of, usurp, by armed force.

†**ish, ush** sally forth, make a sortie.

†**jeopardie, juparty** a daring exploit, a feat of arms; a raid etc.

keep aff o anesel act devensively in fighting; stand up for oneself *N Fif Kcb*.

†**lap** press round in a hostile way, hem in.

†**ledder, ladder** set a ladder or ladders to (a wall etc), *chf* in attacking a fortified place.

†**lepe** rush or spring in attack.

licht, light: ~ **on**, ~ **to**, ~ **til** set upon, attack.

†**lie** lurk; lie in wait **for** (a person).

†**lig at (the) wait** *or* **await** lie in ambush.

†**ligger** a siege.

lirk lurk *NE*.

lock entrap, imprison.

†**lug: tak someone be (the lap of) the** ~ take someone by the ear, lay hold of someone.

†**maisterfu(l), maistriful** *law, of robbers, beggars or their actions* overbearing, threatening, using force or violence.

mak into *or* **intil** make or force one's way into.

†**mell** a clenched fist.

mint *v* **1** make a threatening movement, feint *now NE*. **2** † ~ **to** make as if to draw (a weapon etc). **3** brandish (a weapon), aim (a blow), threaten (a person) *now NE*. *n* a pretended blow, a feint *now NE*.

†**nakit** exposed to attack.

onding an attack, onset, outburst (*esp* of noise).

†**onfa(ll)** a military attack.

†**onsetter** an assailant.

†**onsetting** attacking, assailing.

†**ourset** the threat of defeat; the condition of being hard pressed or violently attacked; overthrow, subjugation by force.

†**ourta** come at or get at with hostility; seize, arrest, catch.

†**outfall** a sally, sortie.

†**outhalding** holding or keeping out or back; keeping out (by force).

†**outhound 1** incite (to mischief or crime). **2** set a

dog to attack or chase (animals or persons); raid (cattle) with a dog. ~**er** instigator.

ower-rin overrun.

†**pairt-tak** support, side with, defend.

†**pass** make an attack on.

†**press** make a charge or an assault (**on**).

†**prick (ap)on (someone)** attack (someone).

†**pursue, persew** attack, assail, besiege. **persewar** an assailant, a besieger. **pursuit, persuit** an attack, assault; a siege.

†**raible** mob, assault with overwhelming numbers (*specif* an Episcopalian clergyman by a hostile Presbyterian congregation, after the Revolution settlement of 1688-89).

raid a foray or predatory expedition on horseback; *more generally* a sudden or surprise attack.

raise on turn on in anger, attack *local NE-Ayr*.

†**ramforce 1** block up, barricade (a door etc). **2 ranforce** force, break open (a door).

randie behave belligerently.

†**rapt 1** rape. **2** an abducted woman.

†**travis, revis** ravish.

†**rebel** oppose rebelliously.

†**rebet** renew one's attack **on**.

†**rebut(e)** deprive **of** (something) by driving the person off.

†**refutation** military repulse **of** (a person).

†**reir** go backwards, retreat.

†**renew** begin a fresh attack **upon**.

†**riot** unlawful bodily harm or violence to another person, assault and battery.

†**saige** *n* a siege. *v* besiege.

†**sailӡe** make an assult on.

†**scallet 1** *also* **scalade** (e)scalade, the scaling of walls with ladders. **2** a scaling ladder.

scatterment a scattering, dispersal, rout *now Abd*.

sconce a screen or shelter (of stone, wood etc) for concealment, defence, etc.

†**scour** drive (an enemy) **out of**.

†**serve** attack (**with** weapons).

set: † ~ **down** put down, quell. ~ **to** set upon, attack *NE-S*.

skail 1 rout, put to flight *Gen except Sh Ork*. **2** †raise (a siege).

†**slate** incite or set (a dog) on.

†**sorn 1** exact free board and lodging by force or threats, beg importunately, *freq* **thig and** ~. **2** trouble or harass by exacting free board and lodging.

†**sort** sally out; make a sortie.

†**spill** ravish, violate (a woman).

steekit nieve the clenched fist.

†**stren(g)th** *of a position etc* strong against assault.

†**stupration** violation (of a woman).

†**subscrived: be** ~ be engaged in a plot (**against**).

†**supprise** surprise, unexpected attack.

tak, take an act of seizing, a capture, catch.

†**tar and tig** *etc* sport or toy (*esp* with one's victim or prey)

thrapple grip by the throat, throttle.

†**thraw** force by torture or violence.

†**tit** catch forcibly, clutch, seize.

†**tulyie** *v* assault.

†**turn agane** retreat, flee.

†**umbeset** surround, beset.

†**unbrachte** unattacked, unassailed.

†**underset** beset.

†**upcast** throw or force open (a gate).

†**upset** insurrection, revolt.

†**upweir** defend.

†**usurp** practise or inflict (cruelty etc).

violent †treat with violence, use coercion on (a person). **lay** ~ **hands on** *etc* attack, seize with violence.

wa, way: ~-**takin** removal, carrying off by violence.

†**wait** *v* watch with hostile intent, spy upon, lie in wait for. *n* an ambush. **at (the)** ~ on the watch. **lie** ~ lie in wait. **take under** ~ capture or surprise by an ambush.

†**waken** watch (over), keep an eye on.

†**walt** cast or throw **down.**

†**walter** *v* overturn, overthrow. *n* an upset, upheaval, overthrow.

†**wanlas: at the** *or* **a** ~ in an ambush.

†**warn** stop the way of, oppose (someone).

†**warrand, warrant** a protector, defender.

watch 1 be on the look out. **2** †fulfil the duty of a watchman, sentinel or guard. ~ **knowe** a hill high enough to serve as a look-out station *S, freq in place-names.*

wauk guard, watch over (places, livestock etc), *esp* during the night.

weir 1 guard, defend, protect from attack etc stand guard over, keep a watch on, hold (an entrance etc); *now S.* **2** *freq* ~ **aff** keep off, ward off, hold at bay.

wipe strike, beat, attack.

yoke on, yoke to set on (a person), attack.

12.10 PLUNDER BOOTY

†**blackmail** a payment exacted or made in return for protection from plunder or injury; an illegal exaction.

brigane †a brigand. †**brigancy** brigandage; robbery with violence. **brigan(n)er** a brigand, thief, robber *now Bnf.*

†**cape:** ~**r** a privateer. **caping,** ~**ring** privateering.

†**cateran** a Highland marauder; a band of these.

†**creagh** a Highland foray, raid; the booty obtained.

†**depredation** *law* the offence of driving away cattle etc with armed force.

†**depulȝe** despoil.

†**dispoilȝe, dispulȝe** despoil.

†**drago(u)n: rais** ~ commit devastation.

†**extors** subject to extortion or oppression.

fang booty, plunder, stolen goods *now Abd.*

gilravage, gulravage rove about, *esp* to plunder.

grab a thing grabbed, plunder, booty *now Abd midLoth.*

herrie 1 harry, rob, plunder. **2** ruin (persons) by extortion or oppression, impoverish *now NE Dmf.* ~**ment 1** †plundering, devastation. **2** that which causes devastation, ruination *now Bnf.*

†**hership 1** ~**s** armed incursions, *esp* to carry off cattle etc, predatory raids. **2** the act or practice of harrying, plundering or pillaging by an army or armed force, *freq* **mak** ~. **3** harm or hardship inflicted on a person by violence or robbery; destitution, impoverishment caused by harrying or violent treatment. **4** booty, plunder, *esp* cattle.

†**licht, light:** ~ **hors(e)man** a (? mounted) raider or **reiver.**

†**lift** steal (cattle), take by a raid.

†**Locheil's lantern, MacFarlane's bouet** the moon (because the moon's light guided Highland cattle-raiders).

†**maisterfu(l), maistriful** *law, of robbers or their actions* overbearing, threatening, using force or violence.

†**Michaelmas moon** the harvest moon; the booty from Highland and Border raids at this time of year.

†**moss trooper, mosser** a Border cattle-**reiver.**

nip seize, catch; snatch, make off with.

†**onspulȝeit** unspoiled.

†**overharle** despoil.

†**peel, pele** plunder, rob, pillage, cheat.

†**poind, pind** an animal or cattle seized as plunder.

†**pund, pound** a seizure of animals in a raid etc; cattle so taken.

†**rapt** robbery, plunder.

†**reif** plunder, booty, spoil; the act or practice of robbery; plundering.

reive *v, also* **rive** rob, plunder, pillage, *later esp* in the course of a raid *now local NE-S*. †**reiver** a plunderer, robber, *esp* one riding on a raid.

†**ride** ride out on a foray, *esp* in the **Borders**. ~**r** a person who rode as above, a **reiver**. **riding** a raid on horseback.

†**riffle** *v* rifle, plunder. *n* a depredation, sacking.

†**rin, run:** ~**ning** a raid or foray.

†**riot** ravage, harry (a country).

ripe rifle, plunder.

rook plunder, clean **out**.

roup plunder, rob, deprive of everything *local NE-S*.

scoff steal, plunder.

spreath, spreach †*n* 1 booty, plunder. 2 a foray to steal cattle, a cattle **raid**. †*v, only* **spreth** pillage, plunder. †**spreacherie** booty, plunder, loot.

spulyie *v* 1 rob, despoil, plunder (a person or place). 2 take as spoil or plunder, steal *now Abd*. 3 plunder, maraud *now Per*. *n* 1 (an instance of) depredation, spoliation, plundering, devastation. 2 booty, spoil, plunder.

†**waith** spoil, booty.

12.11 VICTORY, DEFEAT

†**abandoun, enbandown** subdue, conquer.

beast overcome, vanquish *now Bnf*.

†**concreour** a conquerer.

†**conques, conquest, conquis** *v* conquer. *n* conquest.

†**debate** stop by force; overcome.

†**debuish** oust, get rid of *WC*.

defeat, †**defait** defeated *now local Bnf-Fif*.

†**deliverance** the act of surrendering (a stronghold, hostage, prisoner etc).

†**ding** defeat, overcome (with blows).

†**discomfish** discomfit, overcome, defeat.

†**escheve** overcome, vanquish.

†**expugnate** taken by storm.

gang ower overcome, beat *now Ork NE*.

†**hause: hald in the** ~ have in one's power, at one's mercy.

lamp defeat *local NE-EC*.

lose be defeated in (a battle etc).

†**obtene** gain possession of by conquest.

occupy, †**occupe** 1 take or hold possession of (territory etc) by conquest or settlement. 2 †gain or have (authority or rule) by conquest or usurpation; usurp the possession of; appropriate to one's use.

†**ourset** overthrow, subjugation by force.

†**outputting** expulsion, ejection; banishment.

†**overharle** 1 oppress, tyrannize over; despoil. 2 overthrow, overwhelm.

†**overquhelme** overwhelm.

owercome overcome.

owergae overpower, overwhelm, oppress *now Sh*.

owergang overcome, oppress, dominate *now Sh*.

†**owerhail** overhale, oppress; overthrow.

owerhan(d), †**overhand** victory *now local*.

ower-pooer overpower *now Sh Cai*.

†**owerthraw, overthrall** overthrow.

pit, put: ~ **down** defeat, beat, overcome *now Sh Uls*.

†**ramvert** overthrow.

redd, †**rede** put an end to (fighting) *now Abd*.

†**shent** defeated (in a fight).

†**snod** punish, defeat.

spit and gie (it) ower *or* **up** give in, admit defeat *now Abd Kcdn Ags*.

†**still stand** an armistice.

†**succumb** bring low, overwhelm.

†**supprise** conquest, defeat.

†**thring down** throw down, overthrow.

†**tobet** beaten.

†**vanquer** a conqueror.

†**victor** victory.

vinkish *now Dmf*, †**vencus, vanquis** vanquish. †**vincust, vencust, vanquest** defeated, overcome, subdued.

†**wandis** retreat, give way.

warsle, wrastle *now Sh*, †**wirstle** wrestle with, engage in a bout with, overcome *now local Sh-Per*.

whang beat, defeat *now Kinr Fif Rox*.

win, won 1 win. 2 beat, defeat, overpower *now N*. **won,** †**winning** won.

†**ȝelde, ȝald** yield.

12.12 BLOWS, BEATINGS

Beatings and thrashings include those meted out as punishment as it has not always been possible to distinguish those from the beatings of bad temper or criminal violence. School punishments with the tawse, however, will be found in 14.3.2. For blows with specific weapons, see 12.5. Includes injury.

Aberdeen sweetie a sharp tap on the head with a flick of the thumb *now Mry Bnf*.

at within reach of (so as to thrash etc); meddling with, hurting: '*Who was at ye?*'.

†**awkwart** with a backward stroke.

†**back-breed** a fall or throw on the back.

baiss baste, beat soundly, *now Bnf*.

baitchel beat *S*.

bang surpass, excel, beat, overcome, thrash.

bash *v* beat, smash (**in** *etc*). *n* a heavy blow, *usu* so as to smash on something.

bate, bet beat.

†**beft 1** struck, beat(en). **2** delivered blows.

belaubir belabour, thrash *now Sh Bnf Ags*.

belt *n* a blow, a hit. *v* beat or thrash (with or without a belt).

bemang'd hurt, injured.

bensell beat or thrash soundly *now Bnf*.

betak deliver (a blow) *now Abd*.

berry thrash (*esp* a child) *chf SW, S*.

†**bevel** a staggering blow.

†**bilf** a blow.

bittle, beetle thrash.

blatter a blow *now Bnf Kcb*.

†**blaud** *v* make a violent thrusting motion; slap, strike. *n* an injury; a blow.

blaw a blow, a stroke.

bleach *v* strike; beat *now Abd*. †*n* a blow, stroke.

blinter, blenter †*n* a strong sharp blow or hit. *v* strike.

bluffert, blaffart a blow, slap *NE Ags*.

brain hurt, *esp* by a blow to the head, wound, beat severely, *freq* as a threat to children *now local Abd-S*.

breenge: let ~ aim a blow.

brizz, birse bruise, crush; *freq* break (bones etc) by crushing.

buck batter. ~**ie** *n* a smart blow, *esp* on the jaw *Abd Ags*. *v* strike or push roughly *Bnf Abd*.

buff *n* a blow, *esp* one making a dull sound *now Bnf Abd Lnk*. *v* strike, beat, buffet *now Bnf Abd Lnk*.

†**bullerand (in his** *etc* **blude)** with blood issuing from the body, bleeding.

bum strike, knock *now Fif wLoth*.

cadge shake up, knock about, jostle *NE*.

ca(ll) a knock, blow *local Abd-Loth*.

carmudgel bash, crush, damage *now Abd*.

chap *n* a knock, blow. *v* knock, strike.

†**clair** harm, injure.

clamihewit a blow, a drubbing.

†**clank** a resounding blow.

clap a heavy blow, stroke.

clash *n* a resounding impact, a blow. *v* strike, slap.

claught a blow *now Ags*.

claw beat, strike *N*. ~ **someone's hide** *or* **skin** punish, beat *local Bnf-Fif*. **gar (ane)** ~ **whaur**

it's no yeuky, gar (ane) ~ **without a youk** give (someone) a drubbing.

clearin a scolding, beating.

cleesh *v* whip, lash with a whip *S*. *n* a lash with a whip; a blow *SW, S*.

clink *n* a blow. *v* strike, slap, beat *now Abd Fif*.

cloot *n* a blow. *v* strike, slap.

clour *n* **1** a blow. **2** a lump, swelling caused by a blow *now local NE-S*. *v* deal a blow to, batter, thump.

cluff a cuff or slap *chf S*.

clype a blow *now Bnf Abd Fif*.

clyte *n* a smart blow *local*. *v* strike *local*.

cob †*v* beat or strike, *usu* on the buttocks *S*. *n, also* †**keb** a blow *WC Gall*.

come: ~**again** a beating *NE*. ~ **a blow** *etc* **out ower** strike *now local NE-C*.

cooardy lick a blow given as a challenge to fight *now Fif Lnk*.

cooch a blow or tap on the shoulder as a challenge to fight *now local C*,

coorgy a blow or push given as a challenge to fight *Loth Lnk*.

coup by the heels prostrate, lay low.

cowdrum: get ~ get one's deserts; get a beating or severe scolding *NE*.

crack strike sharply *NE*.

creesh beat, thrash *now Abd Kcb*.

crunt *n* a heavy blow *Ayr*. *v* strike a blow on (the head).

dab *v* pierce slightly, stab *now local Bnf-Kcb*. *n* a blow, slap *now local N*. ~**ach** a stroke, blow *Bnf Abd*.

dad a heavy blow, thud.

†**dandiefechan** a slap; a stunning blow.

dang strike, knock *now Kcb*.

†**dede** a criminal act; an act of violence. ~**-doer** the doer of a deed of violence.

deg *v* strike (a sharp-pointed object) quickly into something *now Bnf Abd*. *n* a sharp stroke *now Bnf*.

†**deid strake** a death blow.

†**demaim** injure, maim.

†**demember** dismember. **demembration** *freq law* dismembering, mutilation.

†**dere** *v* harm, hurt, injure. *n* hurt, harm, injury.

devel, davel *n* a severe and stunning blow. *v* strike with violence; beat; dash.

dichens a reproof, beating, *chf* **get one's** *or* **gie someone his** ~ *now Rox*.

dicht a blow, smack, swipe *now Abd*.

ding *v* **1** knock, beat or strike (with a heavy blow). **2** strike, force, drive **from, out of, off** (a person, thing etc). **3** beat, cast, throw **down**. **4** drive, force, beat **back, up** etc. n a knock or blow, a smart push local Bnf-Kcb.

dinge dent, bruise Sh Dnbt SW Uls.

dird a hard blow, knock now Bnf Abd.

dirdum a heavy stroke or blow.

doctor do for, finish off, eg in a fight now Sh Lnk: 'he fairly doctored Jock this time'.

doist, dyst a heavy blow now Abd-Kcdn.

doon-set(ting) a laying low (eg from a heavy blow) now Bnf Stlg.

doose v strike, knock, thrash local. n a heavy blow; a butt, push now Sh Ork Bnf Abd.

doosht n a dull, heavy blow, a push; a thud, a beat Sh Cai Bnf Abd. v strike with a dull, heavy blow, thump now Bnf Abd.

draw aim (a blow); raise (one's hand, foot etc) in attack now Bnf Abd Kcb.

drib beat, thrash Bnf Abd.

†**drive** a forceful blow (at a person).

dump v beat, thump, kick now local Ags-Kcb. n a blow, a thump, a thud now Abd.

dunch v punch, thump, bump, nudge. n a blow, a bump, a nudge. ~**ach** a heavy blow, a thud now Abd.

dunner a violent, noisy blow.

dunt n a heavy, dull-sounding blow or stroke, knock. v beat, strike or stamp heavily, thump, bump, knock, so as to produce a dull sound.

dush v push or strike with force, butt now Ork Bnf Abd. n a heavy blow, a violent jolt now Bnf.

†**engreve** do hurt or harm to, injure.

ettle aim, direct (a blow or missile).

fell v injure; thrash. n a knock-down or stunning blow now Wgt Dmf.

feuch a resounding blow NE.

filbow a blow, thump Abd Kcdn.

†**flae** flay, strip.

flag flog, whip.

fleg a severe blow, a kick.

†**flewit** a blow, a stroke, a slap.

†**flichter** bind (the limbs) with cords.

flist: let ~ let fly (a blow), hit out Cai NE.

flocht knock down, knock out now Abd.

fornacket a hard slap, a wallop now Abd.

fortak hit, deal a blow at NE.

founder fell, strike down (a person, animal etc) local NE-S.

freet rub, chafe, injure by friction or violence now Fif.

†**fulyie** trample underfoot, beat down, overcome.

fung, funk v strike with the hands or feet now NE. n a blow from the hand or foot, a cuff, a kick now NE Fif Wgt.

†**gird** strike, deliver a blow, freq **let** ~.

glent a glancing blow, a slap Dmf.

gowf n a blow, slap, buffet. v hit, strike, slap.

†**greve** an injury.

†**guddle** stab, hack (a body).

gullie †cut, knife, slash. ~**gaw** wound, cut, hack, gash chf N.

guzzle take by the throat, throttle now local Bnf-midLoth.

hatter batter, knock about, bruise. now Sh.

hazel beat or thrash, as with a hazel stick now Cai Rox.

†**heezie** a drubbing, rough handling.

hert, heart strike in the region of the heart so as to wind or knock out.

†**hipsie-dipsie** a thorough thrashing, chf **gie (somebody)** ~.

hit a blow, a stroke.

†**hochs: cut the** ~ hamstring.

huizlin(g) a severe drubbing Rox.

jag, jog now Kcdn Ags a prick; a sharp blow, prod.

jass a violent throw, a heavy blow now Abd.

jeelie, jelly cause (the nose) to bleed EC. ~ **nose** a bloody nose local EC-Rox.

jirk a smart blow now Abd Ags.

jirt a sudden or sharp blow, squeeze or push, a jerk now Sh.

†**joss** jostle.

jouk (one's head) duck, dodge a blow etc.

jundie n a push, as with the elbow, a shove, a jolt, a blow now Gall Uls. v push, jog, jostle, elbow now NE Uls.

kame: claw someone's ~ Loth, ~ **someone's hair, head** etc **for** or **til him** give someone a drubbing.

kep parry, ward off (a blow) now local.

kibbling a cudgelling, beating now Wgt Rox.

kilch n an unexpected blow, a push chf Gall. v push, shove, jerk, ram now Dmf Rox.

kill 1 thrash, beat local N-Uls. **2** hurt badly local.

knack v strike or slash sharply now local Sh-Per. n a sharp blow, a crack now Ork NE.

knap, knab v knock, strike sharply, rap now local. n **1** a sharp knock or blow, a rap now local. **2** a snap, bite now Sh Ork.

knidge, †**gnidge** v rub, squeeze, press, esp with the knee now Sh N. n a forceful squeeze, an application of pressure, esp with the knees Sh N.

knoit n a sharp blow now local Cai-Kcb. v knock, beat, strike sharply now Abd.

knool, (k)noll beat, strike, knock.

†**knuitle** strike or squeeze hard with the knuckles; keep striking.

knuse, noozle squeeze, press down, bruise; pummel, drub.

knype knock, strike sharply *NE Uls*.

lab *n* a blow, stroke *chf Bwk S*. *v* beat, strike.

labour beat, thrash *local*.

lamp beat, thrash *local NE-EC*.

lat, let: ~ **drive,** ~ **gird,** ~ **skelp** let fly, strike out. ~ **at** hit out at *now local N-Uls*. ~ **intil** strike violently, let fly at *N*.

lay: ~ **at** strike at, beat *now local Sh-Loth*. ~ **till** or **tae** beat *now local*.

leash *n* a stroke of a lash *now Sh midLoth*. *v* lash, flog *now Sh*.

leather, ledder *NE* a heavy blow *Sh SW*.

leerup a sharp blow or smack, a lash *chf N*.

len(d) deal (a blow).

lewder, louther *n* a heavy blow (from a stout stick) *Abd Per Uls*. *v* hammer; thrash.

†licht, light: ~ **on,** ~ **to,** ~ **til** *of a weapon or a blow* strike (on a particular place).

lick a hard blow. ~**s** a thrashing, chastisement.

lift one's hand (to) hit, strike.

line beat, thrash *now Cai Abd*.

†Lockerbie lick *etc* a gash or wound in the face.

lounder *v* 1 deal heavy blows on. 2 aim or lay on blows, hit out. *n* a heavy blow. ~**ing** a beating.

†lounge belabour, beat.

†maggle cut or hack about, maim, mutilate, mangle.

†mainʒie *n* a crippling or disabling wound or injury, a mutilation. *v* maim, mutilate, disable by a wound or injury.

mairtyr hurt or wound severely *now Sh*.

malagruize injure, hurt, punish with physical violence *NE*.

malvader stun with a blow; punch with the fists.

mar do bodily harm to, maim, injure, kill *orig gipsy but now also Rox*.

massacker, missaucre maul, mutilate, bruise, beat (a person) *now local*.

mell strike as with a heavy hammer, thrash; trounce *now local Per-Kcb*.

melt fell (a person or animal) with a blow near the spleen; thrash *now Fif WC*.

mint aim (a blow) *now NE*.

mischieve injure, give a beating to (a person), treat cruelly *now Sh NE Ags*.

mishandle mangle, maim, knock about *now Sh Uls*.

mishanter hurt, injure *Bnf Abd*.

†mislear hurt, abuse, maltreat.

mittens: claw *(chf Fif Rox)* or **†lay** *(Abd)* **up (someone's)** ~**s** do for; trounce.

mittle do bodily harm to, mutilate *now Ags Per*.

muggin a beating *now wLoth Lnk*.

nail hit, strike down *now local*.

neck break the neck of *now Kcb*.

nevel *n* a sharp blow with the fist, a punch. *v* punch, pummel, batter; squeeze, pinch.

nib a nip; a prod.

nodge *v* nudge, push *now Sh*. *n* a nudge, a jog *now Sh*.

ower-rin run over *now Ork*.

paik *v* beat, strike, thrash, punish *now Kcdn Ags Ayr Uls*. *n* a blow, stroke, thump *now Bnf Ayr*. ~**in** a thrashing, punishment, beating-up *local*.

pap, pop *v* beat, thrash. *n* a tap, rap; a swift blow.

pardoos a thump; a resounding blow, whack; a violent fall *now Sh*.

peelick a blow, buffet *Ags Per*.

peg †whack, beat. **peggin** a beating, drubbing *wLoth S*.

pelt, †palt a hard blow, a buffet *now Ork Ags*.

pergaddus a heavy blow or fall, thump *Abd Ags Fif*

pey, pay *v* beat, chastise. *n* ~**s** a blow, punishment, chastisement *now Ork Ags*. ~**ment** punishment, chastisement, a beating, thrashing *now Bnf Abd*. ~ **someone's skin** *etc* give someone a good beating, thrash someone *now Sh*.

pin beat, thrash now Cai S.

pinkin a beating, thrashing *S*.

†platt a blow, stroke.

plowt a dull blow, punch, thump *Sh Abd*.

plunk strike with a dull thud, hit with a thump *local Sh-SW*.

†poss strike or hit with the knees or feet, knee, kick, trample.

†pouss, push *v* poke or thrust (a stick etc); prod, strike with a sharp thrusting blow, punch. *n* a thrust, prod, blow, stroke, knock, push.

pran bruise, buffet, beat, punish *NE*.

prog *n* a stab, thrust, poke etc, the act of pricking or stabbing *local*. *v* stab, pierce, prick; poke, prod, jab *local*.

punce *n* a light blow with the elbow, foot etc, a nudge, poke, thrust. †*v* buffet.

†quell knock **down**, strike.

†quheiss a blow with something pliant, a lash.

racket a violent stunning blow, a thump, stroke *now Sh*.

ramiegeister a sharp stroke or blow *NE*.

ramscooter trounce, drub, drive off in terror *local N-Kcb*.

rap dash, thump, knock, strike with a sharp thud *now local Sh-Kcb*.

289

rattle a sharp blow, a thump, crash.

rax deal (a person a blow) *now local.*

reak deliver (a blow) *now Sh Kcb.*

†rebegeaster a stroke with a stick.

reemis(s) a heavy stroke, blow or beating *Bnf Abd.*

reesle *v* beat, whack, thrash *now Ags wLoth. n* a heavy blow or stroke *now Sh EC.*

†revel a severe blow.

rhubarb: gie someone ~ give someone a sound thrashing *Abd Gsw Wgt.*

ring *v* give a resounding blow to (*esp* the ear, the head) *now Sh N-C. n, also ~er local* a resounding blow or cuff, *esp* on the ear or head *Sh NE-C.*

rive tear at or maul an opponent in a fight.

rug and rive pull on tug vigorously.

†rout a violent movement, a heavy blow, stroke.

rummle, rumble *v* strike or beat severely; jolt, handle roughly *C, S. n* **1** a resounding blow or whack *now local Sh-Ayr.* **2** a rough knocking or beating *now NE, WC.*

rung *n* a blow with a stick; a thump, whack *local Sh-Stlg. v* beat with a stick, cudgel *now local Sh-N.*

†rusk a blow.

†rymmyll, remel a blow.

sackfu: give someone a ~ o sair banes give someone a beating *now local*

sairin a thorough beating or trouncing *now NE.*

sarkfu: a ~ o sair banes a person stiff or sore from a beating *now local.*

†saw, sow shed (blood).

sclaff *v* strike with the open hand or with something flat, slap *now Abd C. n* a blow with the palm of the hand or with something flat, a falling flat, a thud; the noise of this *NE, C.* **~ert** a blow with the palm of the hand or with something flat *N.*

sclap a heavy blow, hard smack, *esp* with something flat *now NE.*

†scob close or obstruct (the mouth).

scone *n* a slap (with the flat of the hand), smack *local NE-Lnk. v* strike the surface of (something) with a flat object, crush flat with a slap *now local Ork-Ags.*

scour a blow, stroke, box (on the ear) *NE.*

screenge *v* whip, flog *now Bnf Abd. n* a lash of a whip etc, a beating.

†scrim(mage) beat, strike vigorously.

scult strike with the palm of the hand, slap, smack *now Ags.*

†scum strike with the hand across (the cheek), slap (someone's face).

sicker *of a blow* hard and effective, telling *now Sh Ork.*

sing a whizzing blow, wallop *now NE Dmf Rox.* **lat ~** let fly, hit out *NE Ags Dmf.*

skeeg *v* whip, strike, slap, spank *chf NE. n* a blow, smack, *esp* on the bottom *NE.*

skelp *v* **1** strike, hit, *esp* with something flat, *eg* the palm of the hand, slap, smack (*specif* someone's bottom). **2** hit, strike, drive with blows, kicks, etc; beat, hammer. *n* a stroke, blow, *esp* with a flat object, a smack with the open hand, a sword, whip etc.

skite *v* strike, hit (a person) *Cai C. n* a sudden sharp glancing blow *Gen except Sh Ork.*

skivet a sharp hard blow *S.*

skliff *v* strike with a glancing blow, scuff, rub against *local Stlg-Rox. n* a blow with a flat surface, a swipe in passing; the noise of this *now Loth WC Rox.*

slatch a resounding blow, a heavy thud *now Sh Slk.*

sleesh a swipe, cutting stroke; a lash, as with a whip *Ork Bwk Rox.*

slop slap, smack *N.*

slype *n* a hard slap or smack *now NE. v* throw down forcibly with a hard smack *Bnf Abd.*

snap a sharp blow *Sh N.*

snipe *n* a smart blow *now Rox. v* strike smartly *now Rox.*

snite *v* strike, hit, deliver a blow at *now Rox. n* a sharp blow, *esp* on the nose.

soorldab: *freq* **gie someone his ~** put paid to, finish off *local C.*

soosh beat, punish severely.

souch a whizzing blow *now local Sh-wLoth.*

souflet a stroke, a blow with the hand, a smack *local Sh-Kcdn.*

souse *v* strike, cuff, thump *now Cai WC Wgt. n* a heavy blow, *esp* on the head, a thump *now Cai SW. adv* violently, heavily, with a thud *now SW.*

souter get the better of, worst, trounce *now Dmf.*

†sow inflict pain on.

sowff a stroke, blow, smack *Abd-Ags.*

†spang a smart rap, a sharp blow.

splay a stroke, slap *Rox.*

squat strike with the open hand, smack, slap *now Kcdn.*

†stave *n* a forceful blow, a jab. *v* aim blows **at**, hit, belabour.

†steik pierce, stab.

†stint stop (a blow).

†stob a stab-wound.

stoit, styte a buffet, blow *now Dmf Rox.*

stot a sharp (recoiling) blow *Ags Dmf.*

stoun(d) *v* stun, stupefy, make insensible with a blow *local EC, S. n* a stunning blow *now Ags.*

stour: knock (the) ~ out of beat, thrash (someone) *now local*.

straik *n* a stroke, a blow etc. †*v* strike, beat, aim a blow **at**.

†**streke** stretch (a person) on a rack etc.

strik, strike *v* strike. *n* a stroke, blow; a striking.

sub *school slang* kick *WC*.

sucky *of a blow* painful, stinging *now Fif Edb*.

swabble *v* beat, thrash with a belt, cane etc *now Rox*. *n* a thrashing *Bwk*.

swack *n* a sudden heavy blow *now Loth Rox*. †*v* throw forcibly, dash down.

swap *v* strike, hit *now Sh. n* a blow, stroke, slap *now Sh*.

swash *v* dash down, cast against the ground; slash; beat *now Kcb*. *n* (the noise of) a severe blow.

sweech a sweeping blow, a swipe *Ags*.

swinge *v* beat, flog, drive with blows *now Sh. n* a heavy blow, a dash or clash, a forcible impetus *now local wLoth-Dmf*.

†**swither** beat (hard), batter (a person) *Ayr Rox*.

tabour, toober beat, thrash *C, S*.

taisle a buffeting or knocking about *now Kcb*.

tak, take: ~ someone's breath *or* **wind** choke someone *local Sh-Kcb*. **~ one's hand aff (someone's face** *etc*) slap, smack (someone) *now Abd*.

thackin a beating.

thresh thrash.

thrumple the state or condition of being knocked about *NE Ags*.

thud †*v* beat, strike, thump. *n* a buffet, thump, blow with the fist *now Ork Cai*. **~din** a beating *now local Stlg-Rox*.

†**ticket** a severe beating or punishment.

†**till-hew** hew or cut to pieces.

time o day *ironic* a severe manhandling *now Lnk Ayr*.

timmer, timber beat, thrash *now NE Ayr Uls*.

†**tirr** a thumping, shaking *Ags*.

tirraneese, tarraneese treat roughly, bash or batter about *Bnf Abd*.

†**to-perce** pierce entirely.

†**to smyte** struck very hard.

touse pull or knock about, handle (*esp* a woman) roughly *now local Sh-WC*. **tussle** tousle, pull about (roughly); rumple.

touther, towder *v* handle roughly *now Sh Fif. n* a rough handling *now Sh Fif Loth*.

†**tow(i)n** beat; tame by beating.

tuggle *v* pull (about) roughly and jerkily. *n* a pulling about *Sh Cai Abd*.

†**twistle** rough treatment, a shaking, pulling about.

tyauve pull or knock about, treat roughly *NE*.

uncannie *esp of a blow* hard, violent, severe *now NE Ags Per*.

†**unsonsie** *of a blow etc* severe, harmful, causing death or injury.

wap, whap *v* strike, thrash, hit *now Ork. n* a blow, a thump *now Ork NE*.

warm beat, thrash, hit.

†**warp** thrust one's hand **forth**, strike.

†**weel-peyed** thoroughly beaten.

whack, whauk †*v* slash, cut severely with a sharp instrument. *n* a sharp, heavy stroke or blow, a thump, smack.

wham a blow *local*.

whang *n* a stroke, blow; a cut with a whip *now local Sh-SW. v* beat, lash (as) with a whip *now Kinr Fif Rox*.

wheech *v* beat, whack, hit *now local Ags-Ayr. n* a blow delivered with a whizzing sound *now local Kcdn-WC*.

whidder, whither *v* beat, hit. †*n* a blow, smart stroke.

whinner †*v* hit, strike (a person). *n* a resounding blow, a whack, wallop *now Sh Ork*.

whisk, wisk †*v* beat, whip (a person). *n* a blow, swipe.

whistle, fussle *NE n* a wallop, swipe, swingeing blow *now Bnf Abd. v, only* **fussle** beat sharply, cuff *NE*.

whummle, whammle knock down, push or bowl over *now Fif*.

win, won deliver, drive home (a stroke, blow etc) *S*.

wipe strike, beat, attack.

wrang, wring cause physical harm or injury to, hurt *now local Ork-Lnk*.

†**wreik, wryke** injure.

†**yank** a sudden severe blow, *esp* with the hand.

yerk *v* beat, whip, strike; hammer *now local Sh-SW. n* a blow, a hard knock, a slap *now Sh NE Ags*. **~in** a beating, a blow *Bwk Rox*.

yether *n* a severe blow with *eg* a cane or the hand *SW, S*. †*v* beat or lash severely, bruise with a cane *S*.

yird, yirth bring violently to the ground; strike with force *NE*.

yokin a rough handling, a severe dressing down *now NE*.

yowff *n* a sharp blow, a swipe, thump *now Bnf Abd. v* knock, strike, swipe.

12.13 KILLING

†**ding to dede** *etc* kill by blows or strokes.

†**black: mak a ~ cock of** shoot (a person).

†**boucheour** a butcher, a slaughterer, *freq* **bludy ~**.

†**brittin** *only verse* hack or hew to pieces; slaughter.

†**debowaill** disembowel.

†**dede-doer** the doer of a deed of violence; a murderer.

†**deid strake** a death blow.

en(d) kill, despatch.

extirpit extirpated *now Abd*.

fell slaughter, kill.

guzzle throttle *now local Bnf midLoth*.

†**kele** kill.

†**lire: bane and ~, ~ and bane** flesh and bone, *specif* in contexts of burning or utterly destroying.

†**mairtyrdom** slaughter, *esp* **mak (ane) (gret** *etc*) **~** (on *etc* the victims).

mar kill *orig gipsy but now also Rox*.

mittens: claw *(chf Fif Rox)* or †**lay** *(Abd)* **up (someone's) ~** kill, polish off, 'do for'; trounce.

†**murdris, murthrys** *v* murder. **murderissar** a murderer.

murther *n* murder. *v, also* †**mak ~ (up)on** murder. **~er** murderer.

nail hit, strike down, kill *now local*.

†**nick the thread** kill.

†**occisioun 1** slaughter, mass killing. **2** the killing of one person, murder.

†**peris** destroy, kill, bring about the destruction of (a person).

pit, put: ~ down kill, put to death. †**~ off** do away with, kill.

†**posset, possodie** a poisonous drink.

†**priest: be someone's ~** cause someone's death, be the death of *NE*.

pushion poison.

slauchter slaughter.

slay, †**sley** slay. †**~ doune** kill completely.

stick stab, thrust a knife into, finish off. **~er** a stabber, a slaughterer.

†**strap 1** bind and hang (a person). **2** be hanged.

tak, take: ~ someone's breath or **wind** choke someone *local Sh-Kcb*.

thrapple grip by the throat, throttle.

†**thro(a)tcutter** a cut-throat, an assassin.

worry, wirry *now Sh* strangle *now Sh Ork*.

13. TRADES, BUILDING(S), ARCHITECTURE

13.1 TRADES AND OCCUPATIONS

13.1.1 GENERAL, MISCELLANEOUS, INCLUDING TOOLS

aix an axe.

backet a shallow wooden receptacle for lime, salt etc.

†**backsprent** a spring or catch used as a hold or check.

bandit secured or strengthened with (metal) bands.

barra a (hand-*etc*) barrow. **~-steel, barrow-tram** a barrow-shaft.

bass a workman's tool-basket or bag *local*.

bat *n* an iron batten or bar; a staple or loop of iron. *v* fasten or secure with **bats**.

batter *v* paste, fasten (to a wall, together), stiffen as with paste. *n* a paste or glue.

beam steep (a barrel, tub etc) to make it tight.

bed a flat base or foundation; a level structure.

bee a metal ring or ferrule *Dmf Rox*.

besom, bisom a besom; any broom.

bishop an instrument for ramming down stones and earth *now Abd*.

bittle a beetle, a mallet.

block a pulley or sheaf of pulleys.

blondin a cableway between two towers with a skip which can carry *eg* stone in a quarry backwards and forwards or up and down *chf Abd*.

bool a curved or semi-circular band, forming: **1** the handle of a pot, bucket etc; **2** the bow of a key; **3** the ring joining the blades of a pair of shears or the finger and thumb holes in scissors.

bot a bolt

†**bow-saw** a narrow-bladed saw on an arched frame.

bowster, bolster a piece of timber used to prevent chafing, a bearing, *orig chf, later only* for a wheel-shaft in a watermill *now Bnf*.

bowt (a) bolt.

†**braig knife** a large knife.

†**brig** a connecting part of a mechanism or implement.

brods the scales of a weighing-machine.

bullax an axe, hatchet *chf N*.

bursen grease lubricating grease which has become thin through friction *Bnf Abd*.

†**bush, timmer** ~ a warehouse or timber yard, *esp* in Leith.

ca awa drive **in** (nails etc); fix **on** by hammering.

cadden nail *now Abd*, **cathel nail** *Per Fif Ayr*, **caddle** *NE* a large nail or iron pin.

†**cake** a sheet or slab of metal, *esp* lead.

cannel *n* the sloping edge of an axe, chisel or plane after sharpening *now Bnf Ags Kcb*. *v* give the wrong bevel to (the edge of the tool being sharpened) *NE*.

cauk, †calk *n* chalk, lime. *v* mark, treat or wash with chalk.

cheen chain.

cheeve a sheave, a pulley-wheel *N*.

†**chuffel** a shovel.

†**claith of lede** a sheet of lead.

†**claitt** a cleat.

clamp *v* patch; make or mend clumsily *now NE*. *n* a patch *Sh Ork NE*. **~er** a metal plate or patch.

clams a clam, clamp, pincers, vice.

clink *v* clench, rivet. *n* a rivet *Bnf Dmf*. †**clenkett** rivetted.

cloot, clout *n* a patch, a patch of metal etc *now Abd Fif*. *v* repair (pots, pans, footwear etc) with a metal plate.

cod a bearing, *esp* an axle-bearing *local*. **~-needle** a curved needle with the eye in the point for binding besoms *Abd*.

cog *n* a wedge or support *Kcb-Uls*. *v* steady by means of a wedge; wedge, scotch (a wheel) *now Bnf Abd Kcb*.

coll cut; cut obliquely, taper; shape *now Abd Kcb*.

come the angle between a tool and its user *Abd*.

†**coop** make or repair casks.

corcag a small knife *Cai*.

crackin(g)s, cracklings the residue from tallow-melting.

†**crampet** the iron guard at the end of a staff.

cran a crane.

†**craw iron** a crowbar, *esp* with a claw for drawing nails.

creeper a grappling iron, grapnel *now Arg*.

creesh *n* grease. *v* grease; oil; lubricate.

cross-tailit band a tie or connecting piece with a crossed end.

cruik, crook a hook.

†cuiter mend, patch up.

cuttle sharpen, whet.

darg *n* **1** a day's work. **2** the result or product of a day's work *now Edb*. *v* work, toil *now Bnf Abd Fif*.

dook a plug, a bung of a cask, boat etc *Bnf*. ~ **hole** the plug hole of a cask *now Kcb*.

dreel drill.

dwang a tap-wrench *now Gsw Rox*.

†edge lume an edged tool.

ee, eye the hole in the head of a pick or hammer into which the shaft is fitted *WC, SW*.

eik add (**to**) by way of repair; lengthen, patch.

ell-wan(d), elvan a measuring rod, one **ell** long; *latterly* a yardstick.

en(d)-gird *now Sh*, **†en(d)-hooping** the end-hoop of a barrel etc.

enter engage in (a task), begin work *now local Abd-Uls*. **enterin(g)** *of weather* suitable for work, *esp* **enterin(g) morning**.

†exerce carry on (a trade or calling).

†fadmel a weight or quantity of lead.

faik **1** fold the mouth of (a sack etc) outwards and downwards. **2** coil (a rope or line) *now Sh Fif*.

faize make (metal or wood) rough, splintered or jagged *now Bnf Abd*.

fang *n*, *of a pump* the capacity for suction, *chf* **aff the ~** (*local*), **oot o ~** (*Mry midLoth Wgt*) having lost its suction. *v* prime a pump in (a well etc) *local NE-SW*.

feeze a screw; a screwing or twisting motion.

filler a funnel for pouring liquids through *NE Ags*.

fillie a felloe, (part of) the rim of a wheel.

fire edge the sharp edge of a new tool *NE Fif Arg*.

fit, foot, fute: ~ **brod** a footboard, treadle, footrest *now Abd*.

fleg *of a pile of work etc* diminish appreciably *now Ork NE Ags*.

flench *coopering* bevel the stave ends of a barrel *now Abd*.

fluise roughen, blunt (*chf* tools) *chf Kcb*.

†fornace a furnace.

frame a square or hoop of wood hung from the shoulders on which to carry pails *local Ork-Abd*.

furlie a piece of machinery or equipment, *esp* one that revolves or has wheels.

futtle an inefficient or useless instrument or tool *Cai*.

†ganging geir the working parts of a machine or implement.

gavelock a crowbar, lever.

gibble: ~**s** tools, implements, articles *now local Bnf-nEC*. **gibblet** an implement, tool, utensil *now midLoth Dmf*.

gird[1] **1** †encircle, fasten with a band. **2** provide (a barrel) etc with hoops *now local*. ~**ing 1** the act of **girding 2. 2** †material for girths or hoops.

gird[2] a band or hoop for a barrel etc.

†girth *n* = **gird**[2]. *v* provide (a barrel etc) with hoops. ~**ing 1** providing with hoops. **2** material for girths. ~**sting, gersting** a length of wood suitable for using as a barrel-hoop.

Glesca, Glasgow: ~ **screwdriver** a hammer *now Per Fif Lnk*.

graith 1 materials or equipment (for a particular purpose, job or trade); tools, implements, machinery *now local*. **2** accessory equipment, *esp* of a mechanism, *eg* a mill, plough, loom *now Stlg-Dmf*. **†iron** ~ iron equipment or accessories.

guddle a crowbar *now Per Fif*.

gudge †*n* a gudgeon, a pivot. *v* raise or separate by driving in wedges *Bnf Ags*.

†gum a small parcel (of awls).

haimmer a hammer.

†hake a hook.

hand, haun(d): ~ **barrow** a wooden frame with shafts, which can be carried by two people. ~**makin** the making of an article by hand *now Ags*. ~**spaik** a spoke or bar or wood.

handling a task, a job in hand; *specif* a difficult task, a handful.

†hap an implement used to scrape up ooze from the sea-bed to make salt.

haud, hold: ~**-fast** a staple etc used for fixing *now local Per-Dmf*.

†heeze hoisting tackle.

heft *n* a haft, a handle of an implement. *v* haft, fit with a handle. ~**it** handled, fitted with a handle.

heuk a hook.

hooch breathe hard on an object before polishing it.

horse a trestle, support.

hose the socket for the handle on any metal implement, *eg* a fork or rake *now Sh-Cai Fif*. **hozle, hoozle** the socket into which the handle or shaft of a hammer, pick, fork, etc is fitted *now Edb Slk Rox*.

huidin *now Sh Ork*, **hiddin** *chf NE* a point of juncture, a fastening, a hinge.

hurlie, hurl-barrow, hurlie-barrow *now Cai midLoth* a wheelbarrow; a handcart.

ile *Gen except S*, **uilie** *now Sh*, **eelie** *v* oil. *n, also* **†eelie dolly** oil *Abd*. **uilie pig** an oil barrel etc *now Sh*.

†imploy employ.

†inemmell *v* enamel.

†ingill a goldsmith's weight, 1/2 ounce.

ingine an engine, a mechanical contrivance.

ingle a kiln- or furnace-fire *now Ork Cai Kcb.*

†**ingraif** engrave.

†**inhalding** damming (of water).

intimmers the internal structure, the mechanism *Sh Ork NE Wgt.*

jam mend, patch *Sh Ork.*

Jennies callipers, *specif* hermaphrodite callipers with one leg with a short bend and the other with a point.

jockteleg a clasp-knife.

†**journall, journee** one minting or portion of work in coinage, *orig* a day's work; the quantity of coins so produced.

†**keelin sound** the swimming bladder of the cod, used for glue.

kemp compete in a piece of work.

kill, kiln: ~**-crack** a small crack appearing in the glazing of pottery which has cooled at an uneven temperature, *chf* ~**-crackit** covered with such cracks.

†**killick** the 'mouth' of a pickaxe.

kip tie up (hides, fish) in bundles.

kirn bore with a drill or circular chisel *now Fif.*

knee *of a nail or staple* bend so as to form a knee-shaped angle *now Per Fif.* † ~**d** *of a metal bar or band* having an angular bend.

knewel a cross-bar or toggle of wood or metal *local NE-EC.*

†**knit** welded.

labrod a lapboard, a board laid across the knees for working on *now Ork Bnf.*

laggin 1 the projection of the staves beyond the bottom of a barrel etc *now local Sh-Loth.* **2** †the bottom hoop of such a vessel. **3** the angle inside a vessel or dish where sides and bottom meet *now Sh NE.* ~**-gird,** ~**-hoop** = 2 *now Sh.*

lap *v* patch *local Sh-Wgt.*

lated *of iron or steel* softened or reduced in temper by: **1** †heating or **2** through rusting.

†**lay**[1] alloy; an alloy.

lay[2] the re-steeling of the cutting edge of an implement *Gen except Sh Ork.*

lay[3] a turning lathe.

leerie pole the pole used by lamplighters *Abd EC Gsw.*

lether, ledder a ladder.

lewer a lever *chf SW, S.*

†**lingott 1** a block of metal, *usu* silver or gold, which has been cast in a mould, an ingot. **2** an ingot mould.

lug any projecting part of an object, *esp* one by which it may be handled, attached or lifted.

†**Lumbard paper** an expensive kind of paper used for both cartridges and books.

lume an instrument or tool of any kind.

lump a mass of iron in the process of manufacture.

mak, make †the action of manufacturing. ~ **doon** reduce into smaller fragments, grind *now Abd Per Wgt.*

†**manufactor** manufacture; a manufactory.

†**materials 1** equipment, implements, tools for some operation. **2** the matter from which something is made, raw materials.

meenie a fine awl *Cai Ross.*

mell *n* **1** a maul, a heavy hammer; a club. **2** a heavy blow, as given by a large hammer. *v* strike with a heavy hammer *now local Per-Kcb.*

mouse a small lead weight tied to a cord, used by joiners to guide cords into a sash window and by electricians to drop wires.

mouten *of metal etc* molten, melted; moulded, cast.

mouth, mou the blade (of a shovel or spade) *Sh-nEC, SW.*

muild 1 a mould, a pattern etc. **2** *also* **meelie** *NE* a button-mould of bone or metal; a button made of such a mould covered with cloth; *latterly* a flat linen-covered button.

†**muller** a frame or moulding, *chf* of wood. ~**it** furnished with a moulding or ornamental framing, framed.

natch make a notch or incision in *chf Sh Abd.*

neb the point of a pin, knife etc.

†**need-nail** fasten securely, nail up.

†**neve** the hub of a wheel.

†**office** a workshop, factory, shop. ~**-hous** a workshop, an outbuilding.

ongang the starting up or setting in motion of machinery, *esp* a mill *now NE.*

ontak (the taking on of) a task or responsibility; a big job *Sh NE.* ~**ing** (the start of) an undertaking *now Sh.*

orra *of persons or things* spare, unoccupied *now Sh-Per.* ~**man** any mechanical contrivance used by a man working single-handed *NE.*

†**outred** *v* finish off, complete (a piece of work or an artefact). *n* completion (of a piece of work).

owergaeing the act of working over an area etc, *eg* in cleaning, painting *chf NE.*

owerhaul drive (a screw or bolt) too tightly, so that the thread is damaged *latterly N.*

owertak, overtake 1 †deal with, get through (work etc). **2** catch up on (a piece of work or business).

Paddy barrow a barrow without sides, *freq* used for carrying large stones *local Ork-Ayr.*

Paisley: ~ **screw** a screw driven home with a hammer instead of a screwdriver, suggesting laziness *WC.* ~ **screwdriver** a hammer *WC.*

palm the grippers or claws of a pair of tongs *now Ork Uls.*

passer *NE Gsw,* **parson hoop** *NE* a large iron hoop for holding the staves of a barrel in position during construction.

pauchle a bundle, a small load (of goods or merchandise) *now Per Fif eLoth.*

pellet a pelt, a raw skin of a sheep etc before dressing or tanning *now Slk.*

†**pelt** keep hammering or striking (**at** *etc*).

†**pene** hammer metal (**out**) flat and thin.

†**pennok** a measure or quantity of skins.

†**perfit, perfect** complete (a task etc), finish a job.

†**perfurnis** bring to completion, finish, carry out (a task etc).

†**phise 1** ? a type of vice or clamp operated by turning a screw. **2** ? a mechanical device used in warehouses; ? a type of screw-operated hoist.

†**pick** pitch, daub or smear with pitch.

picker *in a sawmill* the man who arranges the sawn timber according to size *now NE Ags.*

†**pike** a pick, pickaxe.

pinch *v* move (a heavy object) by levering it. *n* a pointed iron rod or bar for levering or making post holes, a crowbar. ~**er 1** ~(**s**) a tool for pinching, *eg* tweezers, pliers. **2** *also* ~**ing bar** a crowbar *local.*

pinned tied down (to work), not having a moment's leisure *now Mry Bnf.*

†**pistoll** pestle.

†**plat** a sheet of metal, *freq* ~ **copper, leid** *etc* sheet metal.

plucker a kind of spokeshave, a tool for planing a curved surface, *eg* the outside of a barrel *now Bnf Abd.*

†**pluking** the action of stopping up a barrel with a plug or wedge.

plying hammer a heavy double-faced hammer, used *esp* in shipyards *now WC.*

pourie a small oil can with a spout *now C, S.*

prent print.

prise an instrument used for levering, a lever.

prog a piercing instrument, a barb *now Sh Ork Cai.* ~**ger 1** a pricker, marking point *WC.* **2** a long spike or rod *local EC, WC.*

pry prise, move by leverage *Gen except Sh Ork.*

puil pool, make a hole in.

pulley: ~**shee,** †~ **scheif** the sheave or grooved roller over which a rope runs in a pulley-block.

†**pump-staff** a pump-rod.

†**puncheon irn** an instrument for punching *eg* letters on plate, coinage dies etc.

†**queem** join or fit closely.

rackle, †**reckle** a chain.

rackpin, rackstick a stick used to tighten a rope or chain *now local Per-Lnk.*

rag[1] a whetstone *now Fif Edb Rox.*

rag[2] a rough projection on a surface, *eg* after sawing, filing. ~**gle** make an uneven or ragged cut in, cut jaggedly *now Sh Ayr.*

raip rope. **raperee** a ropery, ropeworks.

rake turn over and smooth out (seaweed) in the last stages of kelp-burning *now Sh Ork.*

†**rand** melt (tallow).

rapple make or mend hurriedly and roughly.

rattle do with great haste, make speedily and not too carefully, *freq* ~ **up.**

†**redschip** tackle, equipment.

ricket a ratchet brace or drill *now Fif WC.*

rimmer a hoop or band.

rind *v* melt down, render (fat, tallow) *now local Sh-Dmf. n* melted tallow *now Ags Stlg.*

ringing bed *etc* a bed of stone or a metal plate on which a red-hot metal rim is placed on a wheel and shrunk to fit it *N-Fif.*

risp *v* **1** file, smooth off with a file; cut or saw roughly. **2** make a grating noise with a **risp**; use (a **risp**). *n* a coarse file or rasp.

rit *v* scratch, score, groove *now Sh Cai Edb. n* a scratch, score, groove *now local Sh-Kcb.*

rittocks the refuse of melted lard or tallow *chf SW.*

Rob Sorby *joc* name for various sharp-edged tools, *eg* a scythe, a sickle, a saw *NE Kcdn Per.*

rub(b)er a hard brush for rubbing or scrubbing, a scrubbing-brush *now Lnk.*

†**ruch, rough** *of hides* undressed, untanned (with hair still on).

†**trug:** ~ **saw** a two-handed or cross-cut saw.

ruive rivet, clinch (a nail or bolt) *now local Sh-Kcb.*

rummle, rumble clear (a narrow passage) with a rod or wire *now local Bnf-Lnk.*

rump cut, clip or crop very short *local Bnf-S.*

rung make or fit with spars or rungs.

†**saip, soap: soapery,** ~**work(s)** a soap factory.

†**saut, salt:** ~ **stack** a mound of earth from which salt was manufactured.

sawin(g)s sawdust *now Abd Lnk.*

scaffie cairt a refuse-collector's cart or lorry *local.*

†**scale** a ladder.

scillop *esp coopering* an auger with a rounded tapering blade *now local.*

scob 1 a twig or cane of willow or hazel, *esp* one bent over to fasten down thatch, make baskets etc *now SW.* **2** †a rod of wood, or *occas* metal, used for various purposes. **3** a slat of wood used for repairing a wooden shaft etc *now NE Ags.*

scree a riddle or sieve, *esp* box-shaped, for sifting grain, sand, coal etc *local Per-Ayr.*

†**scrows** long strips or thin scraps of hides or skins, used for making glue.

†**seal: burning** ∼ an iron for branding casks.

set a whetstone *Fif Loth Rox.* ∼ **stane** a whetstone for razors, chisels etc.

shairp, sherp, sharp *n* the act of sharpening (an implement etc) *now NE Kcb. v* sharpen. ∼**ing stone** a whetstone .

shank fit (a tool etc) with a **shank** or handle *local Ags-SW.*

shave a sheave, a pulley(-wheel).

†**shavelin, chaveling** a tool for smoothing hollow or circular wood *NE.*

shear a pair of shears.

sheer pour off (top liquid), separate a liquid from its dregs *now Lnk.*

shouder pick a pickaxe which is wielded over the shoulder *NE.*

shuil, shuffle, shiel *n* **1** a shovel. **2** an act of shovelling *now NE, C. v* **1** shovel, work or clean out with a shovel. **2** dig (a hole etc) with a shovel.

skive shave, pare, slice off a thin layer from *local NE-Lnk.*

†**slite** make sharp, whet.

slock, slocken *now N, C* slake (lime)

sneck cut sharply, cut into or **off**, prune, notch *now local Sh-Ayr.*

sodger a packing piece or plug, used *eg* to fill a bolt-hole *now Loth Ayr.*

†**souple** soften by soaking, soak.

sour *esp of water on lime* macerate, soften, slake *now local.*

sowther, souder *v* solder.

spaik, spoke one of the rungs of a ladder *now local Per-Rox.*

spar a rung of a ladder *NE, C, S.*

speet a rod for suspending the wicks in the making of tallow candles.

†**spune** a spoon-shaped implement, *eg* for heating, assaying.

stand, staun a complete set or outfit of various kinds of equipment, *eg* ropes, knitting needles *now Sh-EC, SW Rox.*

stave hammer (two pieces of metal) together, make a joint by striking (*esp* lead) when heated.

steep: † ∼ **stone** a hollowed stone trough in which something may be steeped. **in** ∼ in the process of being soaked or macerated *now Abd.*

†**steik** a piece (of work).

stick come to a premature halt in, break down in the middle of (a job etc), botch *now Sh-Per Kcb.* ∼**it, stuck** *of a task etc* left spoilt or incomplete *now Per.*

†**stickle** a small stick.

stow *coopering* a stack or stockpile of barrels stored away ready for use *local NE-SW.*

straik a whetting or paring motion *now Sh Cai.*

strip draw an edged tool across a rough surface in order to trim or sharpen it *Bnf-Ags Kcb.* ∼**pin(g) block** a block or frame with a flat file, over which a saw is drawn to reduce the teeth to a uniform height before sharpening *Bnf-Ags Kcb.*

stuil a bench, counter, trestle *now NE nEC Ayr.*

†**sugary, sugar work** a sugar factory.

swatch match, select; make, copy, or supply according to a pattern.

sweel a swivel.

swey, sway **1** a lever, crowbar *now Sh.* **2** †a derrick or crane for lifting heavy objects; a steelyard.

†**swing** *v* labour, toil.

swink work hard, toil.

s(w)ooper a brush.

swurd a slat of wood or tang of metal on the end of a ladder, used to prevent it from slipping *Per Fif.*

tackle to set to work vigorously on.

tangs *freq treated as sing* tongs: '*a tangs and shovel*'.

tarleathered *of a hide* having had a **tarleather** (a strip from the belly) cut off.

taw *now Ags Pbls,* **tew** knead, draw out, twist (something adhesive, plastic, stringy or fibrous).

teep *n* type, a representation; stamp; letters etc in printing. *v* stamp (a letter, figure etc) on wood or metal with a die *C.*

teethe set teeth in, provide with teeth or spikes *now Sh Cai.*

tenor, tanner: ∼ **saw** a tenon saw.

thairm gut dried and twisted into a string or cord for various purposes, catgut: **1** *in gen, now Sh Per;* **2** *freq* **therm** as a cord for the mechanism of a pendulum clock or watch *now Abd Ags Renfr.*

through-pit production, output.

†**tight** *v* set **with** (jewels).

till airn a crowbar *now Ayr Wgt.*

tip remove the tip of *now Per.*

†**tow** raise or lower by means of a rope.

tramp steep, soak (in).

tramp-pick a pick or crowbar with an iron bracket for the foot to press on *now N Ayr.*

†**traschor** ? a tracer, a tool for marking out designs.

tress a trestle for holding up a board, table etc, *freq* including the bench it supports *now local.*

†**trinnle,** a trindle, a wheel or similar circular object.

tuil a tool; *freq also* applied somewhat *joc* to any implement, piece of equipment etc.

tume *of machinery* idling, not actually processing material *now Per Stlg Loth*.

tune, toon put (an implement) in proper working order, adjust *now Cai*.

turkas a pair of pincers or pliers, *esp* as used by a blacksmith etc *now NE*.

turn a stroke or spell of work; a piece of work, a chore, duty *now Ags*. ~**ing loom** a turning lathe *now Sh*.

†**tynd nale** a spike.

une an oven.

†**uppit, up-put:** ~**tar** a person who raises or erects. ~**(t)ing** the action of erection, building, setting up.

†**upwark** cessation of work *N*.

†**utterfine** *of metals* superfine.

wadge wedge.

†**waffer** some kind of engineering work, ? a fan.

wage wield (an implement) *NE Ags Fif*.

wa(ll) iron a crowbar *NE*.

wall, well weld, join (metals) by means of heat *now local Ork-SW*. ~**in heat**, *also* **waldin-, well-and-** the degree of heat necessary for welding metals *local*.

wallie porcelain, glazed earthenware or tiling *C, S*.

wand *n* a young shoot of willow used in making baskets *now local NE-WC*. †*v* interweave, plait.

wap *v* bind, tie, join, *esp* by splicing; whip with cord *now Ork*. †*n* a tie, a splicing or joining by means of a cord or twine tied round, a turn of string etc round something.

wark *n* work. *v* **wirk** work. ~**lumes** tools, implements, instruments *now Sh*. **wirk one's** *etc* **wark** do (one's) work, perform what one etc is employed to do *now Sh Ork NE*. **wirk wi** employ, use *local Sh-Per*.

†**water** cover (one metal) **with** a film of another metal in a thin solution, wash.

Water of Ayr stone a kind of stone found on the banks of the Ayr used for making whetstones and in polishing *now WC*.

wear get through a task by degrees *Ork N*.

whang cut with a slicing movement, slash, chop, snip.

white, fite *NE* cut with a knife, pare, whittle *now local NE-S*.

whitter diminish by taking away small portions; whittle *now Ork Ags Lnk*.

wickers wickers collectively, wickerwork.

†**widdie** a certain quantity of iron.

wisker a bunch of feathers, short straws etc whipped at one end to form a kind of handbrush *NE*.

†**wrack** examine (goods etc) with a view to rejecting those which are faulty.

wranch a spanner or wrench for tightening bolts etc *now local Sh-SW*.

†**wummle** a drill for boring through soil and rock for coal, water etc.

wup *v* **1** bind together by wrapping string, tape etc round and round a joint, splice, whip *now Sh-nEC*. **2** wind (a cord etc) round an object tightly *now Ork N*. **3** tie, join by tying, lash *now Ork*. *n* a splice, a tying or binding with coils of string etc *now NE*.

yat 1 found, cast (metal). **2** †set or fix (*eg* iron in stone) by means of molten lead.

yerk beat, whip, strike; break by striking; hammer *now local Sh-SW*.

13.1.2 CONDITIONS OF WORK

adae(s) business, occupation; concerns, affairs.

afftak a deduction (of wages).

arles, arle(s) money earnest money.

atween hands in the intervals of regular occupation.

billy a brother, actual or as a fellow member of a craft etc.

blin Saturday the Saturday of the week in which no pay is given to the fortnightly-paid *local nEC-Slk*.

†**blue blanket** the banner of the craftsmen of Edinburgh.

bountith a bounty, gratuity, *latterly usu* a gift stipulated in a contract of employment in addition to money wages, *freq* **fee and** ~.

boutgate the doing of a round of work.

†**box penny** a market duty levied for the benefit of a **box** of a craft or burgh.

boy an apprentice.

brither, brother admit or initiate into a trade, corporation or society *now WC*.

bum a factory siren *local Abd-Lnk*.

†**buntha** a bounty, a gratuity.

by: ~**-hand** *now Abd Fif*, ~**-behan(d)** *NE* finished, over and done with, *esp* of work. ~**-hours** time in addition to ordinary work, overtime *now Bnf*. **bye-job** an additional job on the side *now local Bnf-Stlg*.

†**cap(pie) (and) cog(gie)** *appar* a contribution paid by carpenters to the common fund of their **incorporation** *Gsw*.

†**cardow** work at a trade illegally without being a freeman, *chf* ~**er** one who does this.

†**club** a member of a trade, *esp* shoemaking, who

has not gone through a full or formal apprenticeship.

convener the president of the **Incorporated Trades** in a burgh, the **deacon convenor**. † ~**y** the court presided over by a **convener** (as above).

cork a master tradesman.

†cosnant wages without board. **costanent** working for wages without board *chf Uls*. ~ **work** etc work unpaid either in money or board.

cost payment in kind for rent, dues or wages *chf Ork*.

darg *n* a day's work.

day tale the daily wage of a day labourer *now Bwk*.

deacon 1 the chief official of a craft or trade; the president of one of the **Incorporated Trades** of a town (formerly an *ex officio* member of the Town Council). **2** a master of a craft; an expert *now Fif, Kcb*. ~ **convener** the **deacon** who convenes and presides over meetings of the **Incorporated Trades** of a town.

†eik give an increase, *eg* in payment to (a person etc).

†enter put to work.

†entry silver, entress silver money paid on entering on being admitted as an apprentice etc.

†exerce carry on (a trade or calling).

†freedom full membership of a guild or trade.

grieve oversee.

hand, haun(d): (at the) far *or* **near** ~ *applied to applicants for membership of the incorporated trades, as* **far** ~ a stranger *or* **near** ~ a relative or apprentice of an existing member: '*John Finlay, near-hand (son)*'.

handsel *n* **1** †earnest money, a first instalment of payment. **2** the money received by a trader for his first sale, either the first of the day or the first of a new business, thought to bring good luck. *v* present (someone) with earnest money at the beginning of an employment.

heave: get *or* **gie someone the** ~ (be) sack(ed) or dismiss(ed) from a job.

idleset lack of work, unemployment *now WC Rox*.

incorporated formally constituted as a corporation, *latterly freq* as **Incorporated Trades** the trade association in a burgh.

incorporation an association of tradesmen, *orig* belonging to the same craft, with burgess rights and duties and until 1846 holding the monopoly of their craft in their burgh.

inwark, inwork indoor work *now Ork Ags Per*.

jots small or occasional pieces of work, odd jobs.

leave dismissal, notice to quit. **†get one's** ~ be given one's discharge, be dismissed.

lie: lying time, ~ **time** *EC Lnk* **1** *orig mining* a period of time worked by an employee either at the beginning of a new job for which he is not immediately paid, or between the closing of the books for the week's work and the payment of wages, payment being retained until the person leaves the employment. **2** an accumulation of work postponed, arrears *NE*. ~ **day** a day of **lying time** *local EC-WC*.

lowse †release or dismiss (a workman etc) at the end of a turn of work. ~**d** freed of the day's work *now Loth Slk*. ~**in time** time to stop work, the end of the working day. ~**-fittit** not bound to one place by one's work, engagements etc, free to travel *now local Sh-Kcb*. **†be castin** ~ lose one's job or one's livelihood. **brek, go** *etc* ~ leave one's job; take to vagrancy.

maister, master a master of a craft *now Rox*. † ~ **of craft** an inspector of the quality of work produced by members of a Trade **Incorporation** in a burgh. **†maisterstick** the piece of work produced by a craftsman to prove himself qualified for acceptance as a 'master'.

minute *in a factory* a tea-break *NE Ags*.

†nob a blackleg in a strike; an interloper or unqualified person in a trade.

†noneschankis a workman's afternoon break.

†occupatioun the body of those following a particular trade or occupation, a craft **incorporation**.

†office a workshop, factory or shop.

†omnigaddrum a miscellaneous group of crafts, not **incorporated** separately, and treated for certain purposes as a single unit *Stlg*.

†operatioun practical work of some kind, *esp* as a trade or occupation; craftsman's work; a job of work.

orra 1 *of persons* unemployed *now Sh-Per*. **2** *of a job* casual, odd, unskilled. **3** *of a person* doing casual or unskilled work.

†ouk, week: ~**-day** a day of the week other than market day. ~**(i)s penny,** ~**ly penny** the weekly contribution to the funds of a craft made by its freemen.

pad the road trudge around looking for work.

pauchle a small quantity of something taken by an employee from his employer either furtively or as a perquisite *now local Per-Slk*.

peel one's wands begin an apprenticeship etc *S*.

†pendicle 1 a specialized craft regarded as a subdivision of a general craft. **2** a trade or tradesman not fully incorporated and having limited rights or occupying an ancillary or subordinate position.

299

13. Trades, Building(s), Architecture 13.1.2

†**perfit, perfect** train or instruct (a person) completely in a trade, skill etc.

piece time a break for a meal or snack during working hours.

pit, put: ~ **awa** dismiss from employment, sack *now Sh-Per.* ~ **to** apprentice (someone) to (a trade).

†**prentice, printeis** *n* an apprentice, a learner. *v* apprentice (a youth) to a trade or craft, indenture or bind as an apprentice *now Abd.*

†**profit: put to** ~ put to a remunerative employment.

†**quarter:** ~ **master** an official in an **incorporated** trade who looked after the affairs and probably collected the dues of a quarter or subdivision of the members. ~-**pennies** the sum of money contributed per quarter by each member of an **incorporated** trade etc.

quattin time time to stop work, 'knocking-off' time *now SW.*

road: get the ~ be dismissed, get the sack *Per WC Kcb.*

sap money money given to workers in lieu of a milk or ale allowance.

†**schargant** an officer of a guild.

†**seal of cause** a charter granted by a town council to a body of craftsmen, forming them into an **incorporation**.

seek 1 ask for, request, as wages etc *Sh-C.* **2** require, demand, expect as one's due *now Cai Ags Per.*

sellarie, †**cerrlarie** a salary.

†**service** labouring or unskilled work, *specif* in building a house.

†**servitor** an apprentice, *esp* to a lawyer.

set aff send off or away, dismiss from one's job.

†**sey, say,** ~ **piece** a test-piece, sample, *specif* one submitted as proof of competence for entry to a trade **incorporation**. ~ **drink** a round of drinks paid for by an entrant to a trade when submitting his **sey**.

shift 1 †a way of earning one's living, *chf* **honest** ~. **2** a change of situation, abode or employment *local.*

siller gun a small silver replica of a gun used as a shooting trophy, *esp* that presented to the **Incorporated Trades** of Dumfries by James VI *Dmf Kcb.*

sit down a situation, a job *now Ags Per.*

sitivation, seetiation a situation.

†**speaking drink** a payment by the master of an applicant for entry to a trade **incorporation**.

speel, spail, spell *n* a time of rest or relaxation, a break in work *now local Sh-Wgt.* *v* take a turn at

work for (someone), relieve (someone) at work, substitute for (someone) *now local Sh-Gall.*

†**squaremen** the **Incorporated Trade** which comprised those in a burgh who regulary use a square, *esp* a carpenter or mason.

†**stallenge** the fee paid by a **stallenger. stallenger** a small trader or craftsman who was neither a member of a merchant guild or trade **incorporation** nor a freeman of the burgh who paid a fee for the privilege of trading at fairs or in the burgh market(s).

steg *v* cause a hold-up of work (in a factory, mine etc) *Lnk Ayr.* *n* a hold-up of work in a factory etc *Lnk Ayr.*

stent *n* an allotted task, a portion of work to be covered in a given time *now NE-S.* *v.* apportion (work); allocate an amount of work to (a person); make (a person) work hard.

stick *come to a premature halt in.* ~**it, stuck** halted in their trade or profession, failed, insufficiently qualified.

thrift work, industry, profitable occupation *now Sh Per Fif.*

trade, tread a corporation of master craftsmen in any one trade in a burgh which formerly elected members to the town council. **the T**~**s,** ~**s holiday(s)** the annual summer holiday, *orig* of the craftsmen of a town, *esp* Edb, *later* extended more generally (*orig* one day, *now* two to three weeks). ~**s hall** a meeting house of the **Trades** in a burgh. †~**s hospital** a home for pensioners of the **Trades** of a burgh *specif* Gsw. ~**s house** a deliberative body or council consisting of representatives of the fourteen **Incorporated Trades** of Glasgow, presided over by the **Deacon Convener.** ~**sman** a person who practices a trade, an artisan, craftsman. **to** ~ by profession or occupation: *'a tailor to trade'.*

turn a stroke or spell of work *now Ags.*

†**unfree** not having the rights of a freeman or burgess in a burgh not being a member of a **guild** or **incorporation.** ~**man** an **unfree** person.

†**ungang** a turn or spell of work *Abd.*

uppitting a (servant's) place or situation.

†**upset 1** the act of setting up in business on one's own or of becoming a freeman in a particular trade. **2** the sum paid to a particular **incorporation** when so doing. ~**er** a person who sets up as a master workman, a person who starts in business, a founder.

upstand *of wages* regular, fixed, basic *WC, S.*

†**vacance** a vacancy, an unfilled post; the fact of becoming vacant, the vacation (of a post).

†**vaik** be at leisure, be free **from** (some occupation or business).

wash an apron celebrate the arrival of a new apprentice or an apprentice becoming a journeyman with an initiation ceremony which included the washing of his apron and a drinking party.

wey, way: ~ **o daein** a means of livelihood, a job *now Ork NE-S.*

whip: ~**licker** a carter; *specif in St Andrews* a member of the **Incorporated** Society of Whiplickers or Carters *Fif.* ~**man** a carter; a member of one of the several societies of carters and ploughmen, *now only* in West Linton, where the local society celebrates an annual festival *now Pbls.*

win earn, gain by labour *now local Sh-WC.*

yearn earn (wages etc).

yoke set (a person) to do something, start (a person) to work *now Abd Ags Per.* **yokin 1** the starting of a spell of work, *freq* **yokin time.** **2** a spell of work, a stint, shift *local N-S.*

13.1.3 PEOPLE

†**auntie** an unmarried woman who kept an inn etc.

barrowman a person who helps to carry a handbarrow *now Bnf.*

†**burn:** ~**-ledar,** ~**man** a water-carrier.

caibe a cabinet-maker *local Ags-Ayr.*

†**caird** a tinker, *specif* the craftsman who mends pots etc.

capper 1 †a cupbearer; a keeper of cups. **2** a maker of wooden bowls or other wooden articles *now Abd.*

†**cardower** a travelling tailor or tinker.

carle, carlie *humorous, sympathetic or depreciatory, now local Bnf-Fif* a man of the common people, a peasant or labourer *now Bnf Abd Lnk.*

carsackie an overall, pinafore; a labourer's smock *local NE-S.*

†**challender** a maker of coverlets.

chapper-up a person whose job is to wake people by banging on their doors *chf Dundee Gsw.*

clay davie an agricultural labourer or navvy *now Abd.*

†**collig** colleague.

cork 1 an overseer; a master tradesman; a small employer. **2** name for anyone in authority *local.*

couper a cooper, a maker of casks etc.

†**cultellar** a cutler.

dancie a dancing master *now local Bnf-Lnk.*

darger, darker a casual unskilled labourer *now Bnf Abd Fif.*

†**daysman** an arbitrator, umpire.

dog-dirder a dog-handler, kennel-attendant *Bnf Abd Kcb.*

droggie *Abd Fif,* **droggist** *now Cai Abd Kcdn* (nickname for) a druggist.

dryater the person in charge of the drying of grain in a kiln *now Cai Abd.*

†**fiall** a paid workman.

foresman a foreman, the head workman *local Sh-Dmf.*

fowk employees *Gen except Sh Ork.*

†**furrour, furiour** a furrier.

†**grieve** the overseer or foreman of a gang of workmen, mine, works etc.

†**hair-kaimer** a barber.

himsel name for the head or chief male person in any body or institution, a male boss.

hogger a kind of slipper like a stocking foot, knitted from flax rove and worn by factory-workers *Ags.*

†**horner** a person, *esp* a tinker, who makes articles of horn, *esp* horn spoons or combs.

ingineer an engineer.

†**intrant** newly appointed, just beginning or entering on a profession, function etc.

Jenny muck a working woman *Cai NE.*

jotter an odd-job-man *now midLoth.*

Kilmarnock, *also and orig* ~ **hood** *etc* a knitted woollen conical skull-cap worn by indoor workers such as weavers.

†**lapidar** a jeweller; *latterly* a connoisseur of precious stones.

leerie a lamplighter.

loolie *child's word* a lamplighter *Inv.*

loun *among workmen* a boy who does the odd jobs *N nEC.*

†**maister, master** the manager or supervisor in a business or works.

marrow a colleague, fellow-worker, mate; an associate or partner in business.

†**mealmaker** a person who prepares and deals in meal

†**mec(h)anic(k)** *of a person* that performs manual labour or belongs to the class of artisans.

mill yins factory workers.

†**muckman** a day-labourer whose chief duty was to act as a street cleaner.

†**nacket** a cook's or miller's lad.

†**neibour** a workman's mate.

nettie a woman who goes about the country collecting wool *chf Slk.*

†**office-man** an officer, official.

†**ontaking** engaging oneself for a post.

orra: ~**ster** an extra hand, casual labourer *Bnf Abd.* ~ **billie** *NE,* ~ **laddie,** ~ **lassie,** ~ **loon**

NE, ~**man** a person who does odd jobs, *esp* on a farm.

†**towersman, over(s)man** a craftsman appointed to supervise his fellows and their work.

†**pechler** a pedlar dealing in earthenware, a travelling handyman or tinker.

peltin pyock a shabby garment, a worthless rag, worn as protective clothing for rough work *NE*.

†**peutherer, pewder(er), pewder-makkar** a worker in pewter and also in lead and tin; a pewterer.

picker *in a sawmill* the man who arranges the sawn timber according to size *now NE Ags*.

pig: ~**(g)er** a dealer in earthenware, a maker or seller of crockery *now NE, Ags*. †~ **maker** a potter, a maker of coarse pottery.

pipe-maker a maker of **pipes**, *chf* a specialist in the making of bagpipes.

†**pockman** a porter.

prenter a printer.

ragger a person who collects rags *N*.

†**saip, soap:** ~**man** a soapmaker, soap-boiler.

sauter a salter, a saltmaker; a salt-worker.

scaffie street-sweeper, refuse collector.

scodge, scodgie brat a rough apron worn for dirty work *wLoth S*.

secretar a secretary *now NE Ags*.

†**seer** an overseer; an inspector.

†**servant** a workman's assistant.

shantieglan an itinerant knife-grinder *WC*.

†**shear grinder** a person who grinds **shears**.

shore porter *specif, in Aberdeen* a member of an incorporated society of porters, **the Society of S~ P~s** *orig* called **piners**, no longer only working at the harbour, but also carrying out house removals etc.

†**sinker** a person who engraves designs on dies.

†**suityman** a chimney-sweep.

tailsman a sawmill worker who takes and sorts the timber from the saw *Gen except Sh Ork*.

tasker a worker paid for specified tasks; a pieceworker.

tinkler a tinker, worker in metal; an itinerant tinsmith and pedlar. †**tincklarian** of the tinker sort.

tinnie name for a tinsmith *now local NE-Rox*.

†**tronman** a city chimney-sweep (*orig* with headquarters near the **tron**) *Edb*.

warkman 1 a workman. 2 †a porter.

watchie a watchmaker *now NE Ags*.

wee man an odd-job man *Lnk Dmf*.

wheecher, coal-wheecher a coal-carter, coalman *Loth*.

white: †~**-iron man** a tin-plate worker, a tinsmith. **fite-iron wife** a female tinker *NE*.

†**windass man** a windlass operator.

†**winder** a windlass operator.

wricht a wright, craftsman.

13.1.4 SERVANTS

†**allekay** a footman, lackey.

†**arle** engage for service by payment of a sum of money.

assiepet a scullery-maid.

†**bridle silver** a gratuity given to a servant for leading a horse.

†**chaumer: chalmirleir** a chambermaid. ~ **cheild** a young attendant; a valet.

†**conduce** engage the services of, hire.

†**cude** the butler or storekeeper at George Heriot's Hospital *Edb*.

fee *n* ~**(s)** a servant's wages, *esp* those paid half-yearly or for specific an engagement as a servant. *v* 1 engage, hire as a servant. 2 accept an engagement as a servant.

†**fiall** a paid servant or workman.

fowk servants, employees *Gen except Sh Ork*.

gang oot amang folk work as a charwoman, washerwoman etc in private houses *Ork Abd Ayr*.

†**gillie** a male servant, *esp* an attendant on a Highland chief.

go-between a between-maid.

†**gudget** a servant, a drudge.

hame *of employment* into service, *freq* **enter** etc ~.

hire engage oneself as an employee, take service. †~**man** a hired servant, *chf* a farmworker. †~**woman** a female servant.

hizzie, hussy *joc or (slightly) disparaging* a servant girl.

house place a situation as a domestic servant.

inwark, inwork domestic or indoor work *now Ork Ags Per*.

†**jack fallow lyk** *of a servant* presumptuous, behaving like his master's equal.

†**jakman** an attendant, retainer.

janitor a doorkeeper; a caretaker of a public building, *esp* a school etc. **jannie** *colloq* a (*usu* school-) janitor.

jurr contemptuous term for a servant-girl.

†**knape** a lad, attendant.

†**lad** a serving lad.

lass a maidservant. **servant** ~ a servant girl.

†**leckie** a lackey.

maiden a female attendant, a maidservant *now Ags*.

†**mam(m)ie** a wet-nurse.

†**man** *or* **men servand(i)s** men-servants.

maukin a young house-servant.

nourice a child's nurse, *esp* a wet-nurse or foster-mother *latterly chf literary and ballad.* † ~ **father** a foster-father. † ~ **fee** the wages given to a wet-nurse *chf NE.* † ~**s(c)hip** the occupation or post of **nourice**.

onwait: † ~**er** a person who attends to another; an attendant, assistant, servant. ~**ing** attendance, service.

†**orra** *specif of women* unattached (as a servant) *C.*

†**outliverais** bounty given to servants.

†**pantréman** a man in charge of or employed in a pantry.

pauchle the personal belongings of someone in service and living away from home, *usu* as kept in a trunk etc *now Per Fif eLoth.*

quean a maidservant *now NE.*

recommend A to B as a servant recommend a person as a servant to a master *now Abd Ags:* '*I wadna recommend you to him as a servant*'.

†**retener** a retainer, a servant.

†**rocker** a nurse or attendant whose duty it was to rock a child in its cradle.

scodge, scodgie *Per* a servant who does light, rough or dirty work, *esp* a kitchen-boy or -girl *now local Cai-WC.*

†**scuddler** a scullion, kitchen-boy; *latterly* a maid-of-all-work.

servant: ~ **chiel** a young male servant *now Abd.* ~ **lass** a maidservant.

†**serviable** belonging to the servant class.

serving lass a maidservant.

†**servitrix, servitrice** a female servant.

†**somler** a butler.

†**stuffat** ? a groom, lackey.

teenie *derog* a junior domestic servant *Gen except Sh Ork.*

thirl engage as a servant *now Bwk.*

uppit(t)ing a servant's place or situation.

†**wad:** ~ **man,** ~ **wife** a man or woman who kept a kind of servants' registry *Edb.*

†**wally** a valet, a personal servant.

†**will: what's your** ~ formula used by a servant in answering a summons.

13.1.5 MINING

back *n* a fault in a seam; a main (almost) vertical joint by which strata are intersected. *v, also* ~ **out** throw coal along the face to the **roadhead** to be filled into **tubs** *now Fif.*

†**bearer** a person, *usu* a woman or girl, who carried coal in baskets from the workings to the shaft.

ben *adv* inwards, towards the workings *now Fif.* *n* a miner's right to enter the pit, *freq* **claim one's** ~ *now Fif.*

bing a slag-heap.

black: ~**s** coaly **blaes** *now Fif.* ~**-back** nickname for a miner *Fif Ayr.* ~ **coal** coal which has been slightly burned by igneous rock *now Fif.* ~**-spit** a lung disease formerly common among miners *now local.*

blind coal a kind of anthracite *now Fif.*

blue cap the blue haze over the flame of a safety-lamp when fire damp is present in the air *now Fif.*

bonnet a portion of a seam left as a roof *now Fif Lnk.*

boss *n* the waste or exhausted workings of a mineral *now Fif. v* undercut (a thick seam) *now Fif.*

bottomer the person who loads and unloads the cages at the bottom or intermediate landings in a shaft *now Fif.*

bouff the thud heard when a roof is cracking *now EC.*

bouking segments of wood etc used for increasing the diameter of a drum *now Fif.*

boutgate *in a shallow pit* a secondary access road to the mine, independent of the shaft *nEC Ayr.*

box a **hutch** *now Fif.*

brassy coal coal with veins of iron pyrites *now Fif.*

british a wall, block of mineral etc which supports the roof of a working *now Fif.*

brosing-time a meal-time *now Fif.*

brush remove part of the roof or pavement of a working to heighten the roadway *now Fif Edb Lnk.* ~**ing** the part removed as above *now Fif.*

burnt coal coal which has been altered and carbonized by the intrusion of igneous rock *now Fif.*

burster a blast into a seam without previous cutting or boring *now Fif.*

carsy coal a kind of coal found near Bo'ness *wLoth.*

chap signal by means of a striking apparatus *now Fif.*

cherry-coal a type of shiny, freely-burning coal *now Fif.*

chirls small coal *now Fif-Edb.*

chows small coal, nuts *local Ork-Kcb.*

cleave a division of a seam, *usu* of ironstone *now Fif.*

cleed the wood of the box of a **hutch** etc *now Fif.*

cleek, click a hook attaching the **hutches** to the pulley, *chf* **stop, taigle** etc **the** ~ interrupt the output of coal. † ~**s-man** the man in charge of the **cleek** who unhooked the baskets of coal at the pithead.

†**coal fauld** a coal yard; a recess or cellar for keeping coal.

coal, coll coal. †**colȝear** collier. † ~**bearer** the woman who carried the coal on her back from the workings to the surface. ~ **coom** *local*, ~ **gum** *now Stlg* coal dust. †**coll-ever** a horse for carrying coal. † ~ **heuch** a coal-working or -pit. ~ **hill** ground occupied at a pit-head for colliery purposes *chf Stlg*.

coomy a miner *chf Ayr*.

coup, cowp a sudden break in a stratum of coal *now Fif*.

cover the strata between the workings and the sea-bed *now Fif*.

cowsy a self-acting incline on which one or more full descending **hutches** pull up a corresponding number of empties *local*. ~ **wheel** the drum or pulley on a **cowsy** *now Fif*.

craidle line (a shaft) with stone *now Fif Ayr*.

†**craigleif** leave to dig coal from a **heugh**.

craw: ~**s** *now Fif*, ~ **coal** *local* an inferior coal. ~ **picker** a person who picks stones from coal or shale at the pit-head *Fif Ayr*.

cross-road a moderately-inclined main road *now Fif*.

cuddy a loaded bogie used to counterbalance the **hutch** on a **cuddy-brae** *now Fif*. ~-**brae** an inclined roadway with a **cuddy** on it *now Fif*.

cut coal in **stoup-and-room** working, coal cut on two sides where two **rooms** meet *now Fif*.

†**dale** a certain quantity or measure (of coal) *E*.

†**dalk** one of several types of clay found in coal.

†**dammin(g) and lavin(g)** a method of removing water, used in mining.

dass a cut of coal etc.

daugh soft coaly fireclay, *esp* in a coal seam *now local*. ~**er** a long thin pick for use in a **daugh** band *now Fif*.

dirt material produced other than coal, ore or mineral *now Fif*.

doggar a kind of coarse ironstone *usu* found in globular concretions; one of these concretions *now Edb*.

dook an inclined roadway *now Fif Ayr*.

dross small coal, coal dust.

duffie *of coal* soft, inferior *now Edb*.

dumper 1 a tool for keeping a borehole circular. **2** a tool used in paving roads, a rammer *C*.

dyke a vein of igneous rock in a vertical fissure in the earth's strata; now in general use as a geological term.

ebb of the ground.

edge coals *or* **seams** seams lying at a very steep angle *now Fif*.

ee, eye an opening or entrance into a shaft.

ell coal a type of coal normally found in seams averaging one **ell** in thickness *now Lnk*.

faik(s) layers of shaly sandstone or limestone.

fest, fast: ~ **place** a working place in advance of the others *now Fif*. **fast in the foot** *of a pump* choked *now Fif*.

fire: ~ **coal** coal supplied to workmen connected with a colliery *now Fif*. ~ **stink** the smell of coal burning spontaneously *now Fif*.

float a sheet of intrusive rock lying roughly in the same plane as the surrounding strata *now Ayr*.

†**following** an overlying soft stratum which comes down as the coal is extracted from under it.

foulness an impurity or irregularity in a seam *now Fif*.

free coal coal which breaks or burns easily *local*.

†**gate: gating** a drift or passage in a mine. ~**sman** a person who makes drifts or passages in a coal-mine.

gib a prop.

gig a winding engine *Fif*.

†**goldin myne** a gold mine.

†**gordie** a rope and chain for pulling **hutches**.

goting a drainage gutter cut in the pavement of a mine or working.

†**grieve** the manager or overseer of a mine etc.

†**grool** gritty material, gravel, dusty refuse, coal dust *SW*.

growth the rate of inflow of water in a working.

grund, ground, *also* ~ **coal** the seam next to the floor *now Edb Ayr*. **grund heid** the stratum above the **grund** *Loth Ayr*. **grund-shot, grunsher** one of a series of shots placed along the bottom of a seam where the coal is too hard to undercut *Fif Ayr*.

gum coal dust *C*.

gun *of a charge* go off without splitting the mineral, blow back out of the charge-hole *now Ags*.

hack, hawk a miner's pick-ended hammer *now midLoth*.

hasson a vertical gutter or drainpipe between water rings in a shaft.

herrie cut away coal from pillars left as supports; remove all coal from a working.

heuch a pit, mineshaft *now Ayr*.

†**heuk, hook** the proportion of the proceeds from the sale of coal cut by a group of miners allotted to each one.

hill 1 †the dump of hewn coal at the pithead. **2** the pithead, the surface. ~ **cart** a small low cart. ~ **clerk** the person who weighs the mineral dispatched. †~ **man** a man who worked at the pithead; a colliery official. ~ **woman** a female worker at the pithead.

hose an iron clasp at the end of a rope.

howk hew, mine (coal).

humph name for poor quality coal.

†hurlie a hutch.

hutch the box-like container in which coal is conveyed from the face.

ingaun ee (the entrance to) a drift mine or coal seam at the surface outcrop, *esp* where the seam is not entered vertically.

inside: gae tae the ~ go from the pit-bottom to the coal face *Fif Loth Lnk*.

jeeg *v* jig.

Jock 1 an iron rod attached to the rear of a train of **hutches** as a safety check if a rope breaks *now Fif*. **2** a lump of stone in the coal *Fif Dmf*. ~ **brit** *contemptuous* a miner *now Stlg eLoth*.

justiceman a checkweighman *now Fif Lnk*.

keps = **shuts**.

†kettle a cylindrical or barrel-shaped vessel of wood or iron used to raise and lower materials and men during the sinking of a pit.

†leidin myne a lead mine.

level a water-level, a passage for drainage.

†licht coal splint coal (used for illumination as well as heat).

lid the cover or flap of a valve; a flat piece of wood on the top of a prop *now Fif*.

lie a railway siding, especially in a coal-mine. **lying time,** ~ **time** *EC Lnk orig mining* a period of time worked by an employee either at the beginning of a new job for which he is not immediately paid, or between the closing of the books for the week's work and the payment of wages, payment being retained until the person leaves the employment. ~ **on** work an extra shift, do overtime *Fif Loth*.

lift the first seam of coal removed from a mine; a slice taken off a pillar of coal *now Fif*.

lipe a small intrusion or irregularity in the joints of a coal-seam, the joints being usually glazed *Fif Ayr*. **lipey** *of a coal-seam* intersected by small, irregular, glazed joints *Fif Ayr*.

lodge *n, also* ~**ing** a pithead shed or shelter. ~**ment** a reservoir or water store underground *now Fif*.

maggie an inferior quality ironstone.

main coal the principal or best seam of coal *now Fif wLoth WC*.

†march the limit of a working in a coal-mine.

metal(s) 1 †metallic ore, in the mine or before refinement. **2** the geological strata in which minerals occur.

mine a passageway or tunnel running from the surface to a mine-working or connecting one underground working with another; a drift, level.

mistress a protective covering for a miner working in a wet shaft or for a miner's lamp.

†mote reinforce the stonework of a mining shaft with a mixture of clay and water, making it watertight.

mozey, coal mozey a coal seam of variable thickness *Clcm*.

†muirment stones and rubbish which blocked up the workings in Sheriffhall Colliery.

neck the upper part of a shaft, above the coal *Fif*.

†nip an interruption in a seam of coal.

nose o coal coal left protruding where it has been inadequately stripped.

†odwood *Fawside colliery ?* coal supplied in addition to the amount regularly contracted for.

oncost 1 *also* †~**s, uncosts** additional expenses; overheads. **2** *also* ~**er,** ~ **man** a timeworker.

onsetter the person who loads the hoist at the pit bottom.

owersman, oversman 1 †? the manager (*appar* one superior to the overseer) of a coalmine. **2** an overseer or inspector in a coalmine.

pan a conveyor in a coal or shale-mine *Fif midLoth*. † ~**-wood 1** *also* ~ **coal** small coal or **dross**, *chf* used as the fuel of saltpans. **2** a measure of coal or **dross** used as such.

parrot coal *now Kcdn C Rox,* **†parrot** a highly volatile bituminous coal which ignites easily and burns with a clear bright flame and a crackling sound.

pass water *of a bucket* leak.

pearl a small piece of coal of the next size to **dross**.

peas a grade of very small coal *Loth*.

peerie a surveyor's large brass plumb-bob.

peeweet a miner's singlet, *usu* blue-grey (the colour of a lapwing's wings) *Fif*.

pelt a low-grade type of coal containing a large proportion of stone, shale and slate *now wLoth*.

picker a sharp piece of metal used to trim the wick of a miner's lamp.

pickman a miner, coal hewer.

piercing-shot a blast of explosive in the roof or **brushing** designed to bring down an increasing thickness of stone.

†piling driving in stakes, *chf* to indicate the limits of mineral workings.

pin *n* a miner's distinctive tally used to label the

hutches of coal he has filled. *v* put a **pin** on a **hutch** of coal, *esp* substitute one's own **pin** for that of the rightful owner *C.*

pirn a disc on which flat ropes are wound *now Dmf.*

pit-bottomer an **onsetter** *now Fif Dnbt.*

place the length of coal-face assigned to each miner *now Fif Ayr.*

plane a working room driven at right angles to or facing the plane joints.

platform a junction of two or more lines in a **hutch** railway, *orig* laid on a raised board.

plug blast rock by means of **plug shots.** ~ **shot** a charge in a small hole to break up a stone.

ply a thin layer of hard rock separated by a softer one from another hard layer, a rib.

policeman a movable guard over or round a pit-mouth or at mid-workings, safety gates.

post a thick layer or seam of (particularly hard) stone, *usu* sandstone or limestone.

†**pot, pat** a mine or pit for minerals; a mine shaft.

prick pierce (rock etc) with the point of a pick; cut into a layer of soft fireclay at the bottom of a seam by hand. ~**ing** a thin stratum suitable for holing in.

pugs a stratum of hard coal in a **free coal** seam *now Lnk.*

raggle cut into the coal-face *now Fif midLoth.*

raik a train of loaded **hutches** *local Stlg-Lnk.*

rance a prop to strengthen a wall of coal or the roof of a working; a pillar of coal left for this purpose *now Fif.* †~ **wall** a wall of coal supporting the roof of a working.

rattlehead a suction pipe *now Fif.*

redd *v* clear away waste or debris from *now NE, WC. n* waste material from a coalpit or quarry *now local EC, S.* †~ **bing** a mound of waste at the surface of a mine or quarry *now Fif Loth.* ~ **box** a truck for carrying rubbish to the pit-head *now Fif.* ~**sman** the person who keeps the passages in a pit clear of debris *now Fif.*

ree a yard or enclosure for storing coal and from which it may be sold retail *C.*

reed the line in a coal seam along which the strata split off *now midLoth.*

rib a wall of solid coal or other mineral *now Fif.* ~-**side** a face of solid mineral left projecting beyond the next face *now Fif.*

†**richt** a document substantiating a claim or title.

ride travel up and down the shaft in a cage *now Fif Lnk.* ~ **the shaft** *or* **tow** go down the pit by sliding down the shaft rope *now Fif.*

rimle probe or stir *now Fif.*

road: ~ **coal** coal cut from the face at road-level *Fif Loth.* ~**head** the end of an underground

passage at the working face *now Fif Loth Lnk.* ~**(s)man** a mine official responsible for the making and maintenance of haulage roads *now Fif Loth Lnk.*

rone a wooden water-channel *now Fif.*

room the working space left between supporting pillars of coal *now wLoth Ayr.* ~ **and rance** a kind of **stoup-and-room** working.

†**ruch, rough:** ~ **coal** a kind of inferior coal *now Fif Lnk.*

†**rum(s)** an inferior bituminous shale; a bend or dislocation in a stratum.

sclit slaty or fissile coal, coaly **blaes**, a clayey stratum *now Fif Lnk.*

†**scour** an apparatus for washing gold-bearing soil.

scree *n* 1 a riddle or sieve, *esp* box-shaped, for sifting coal etc *local Per-Ayr.* 2 an arrangement of parallel bars for riddling coal at a pit-head. *v* riddle, sift (coal etc) *now Fif Loth Lnk.*

scutch make a vertical cut in a coal face with a pick *now Fif.*

set aff cause to explode, let off an explosive charge, shot etc *now Abd Kcb.*

shangie a (straw or hemp) washer put round a drill or bolt to prevent leakage *now Abd WC.*

shank *n* the vertical shaft of a mine *now Fif. v* sink (a shaft) *now Fif.*

shear a contrivance for attaching coal **hutches** to the haulage rope *now Fif.*

†**shearing** a preliminary vertical cut.

short coal coal with wide joints in the seam *Fif.*

shuts sliding or hinged boards on which the cage rests at the pithead *now Fif.*

sink a pit-shaft, a coal-pit. ~**(s)man** a person who sinks pit-shafts *now Fif.*

sit a subsidence due to excavation below *now Fif Loth Ayr.*

skew a piece of rock slanting upwards and over-hanging a working place.

skin-for-skin *of props etc* set so close as to be touching *now Fif.*

†**slipe** a curved wooden box on iron runners for taking coal away from the cutting-face.

smiddy: ~ **coal,** ~ **coom** *now Kcb* a small smoke-less type of coal suitable for smiths' work.

sneck: ~**s** points on a **hutch** railway. ~-**shifter** a pointsman *now Fif.*

snibble a bar of wood or iron used as a brake or drag on a waggon etc *now local Fif-Ayr.*

soo, sow: ~**('s) back** a ridge in the roof or pavement of a coal working *now Fif Lnk Ayr.*

spar(ry) coal a kind of coal 'the backs or joints of which are filled with carbonate of lime' *Fif.*

splint *n, also* **splint coal** a hard coarse splintering coal which burns with great heat *C.* ~**y** *of coal* like **splint coal** *now Fif.*

stane, stone: ~ **mine** a road from underground workings which cuts across the strata *Fif Lnk Ayr.*

stap(p)le a short shaft connecting one coal-seam vertically with another *now Fif.*

stell a prop, wooden stay etc used for underpinning a roof *now local Fif-Ayr.*

step a fault or slip in the strata of a mine *Ayr.*

stey coal a coal seam set at a very steep angle *Fif midLoth.*

stifle foul air from an underground fire; miners' asthma (from this or from coal dust), pneumoconiosis *now Fif.*

stinking coal an impure kind of coal which burns with a strong sulphurous smell *now Fif Lnk.*

stoup a pillar of coal left to support the roof of the working. ~**-and-room** pillar-and-stall, a method of working coal by leaving pillars of coal to support the roof.

†**streamer** a person who washes deposits to obtain ore.

†**streek** the horizontal course or direction of a seam of coal; a coal level.

strum the fuse of a shot or explosive charge, a narrow tube of paper etc filled with gunpowder and placed in a blasting borehole *now local Fif-Kcb.*

swipe a crossing-switch or curved plate in a mine railway *now Fif Ayr.*

table a platform or plate on which coals are screened and picked *now Fif wLoth WC.*

taigle the cleek hinder the working of a pit *now Fif.*

tail the end or edge of water in a mine *now Fif Ayr.* ~ **of level** the lower or discharging end of a drainage shaft etc *now Fif Ayr.*

tally lamp a miner's lamp *Fif Ayr.*

taps, tops, tap coal the uppermost division of a seam of coal or mineral *now Fif.*

†**tender** *of coal etc* soft, easily broken or split off *WC.*

thirl cut through (a wall of coal) *now Fif. n, also* † ~**ing** a hole connecting one working with another *now Fif.*

thraw a fault or dislocation in a vein or stratum *now Fif Lnk.*

thrower, througher a passage made by the removal of coal from a seam worked **stoup and room**, a **room** driven between two levels etc for ventilation *now Fif.*

thummle, thimble an iron ring etc round a heart-joint in a pumping apparatus *now Fif.*

till hard laminated shale formed from **till**, a kind of fireclay or **blaes.** † ~**ie** composed of **till**.

tow 1 the winding-rope which hoists or lowers a cage *now Fif Loth WC.* **2** the cage itself *now Fif Loth WC.* **3** the journey up or down in the cage *Fif.*

tree *n* a pit-prop *now Fif Loth WC. v* provide (*eg* the roof of a coal working) with supporting timbers or props.

triping coal from which the larger lumps have been separated; later unscreened coal from the workings; a kind of **drossy** coal *now Fif WC.*

trouble, tribble a break or intrusion in strata; a fault *now C.*

tub a **hutch** for carrying cut coal; a measure of coal (varying in weight) *now Fif.*

tumbler an apparatus for tipping coal **hutches** etc *now Fif.*

tumphy coaly fireclay *now Fif.*

underply a band or division of the upper portion of a thick seam of coal.

upcast 1 a fault in a seam of coal which forces it upwards. **2** *also* ~ **shaft** the shaft by which the ventilating current returns to the surface *now Fif.*

upgae a rise or ascent in the stratum of a coal-seam.

upset a working place driven upwards following the course of the seam *now Fif.*

upthrow an upward dislocation of a stratum or seam *now Fif Loth Ayr.*

vise the line of fracture of a fault in a coal-seam, *usu* marked by a deposit of earth etc.

†**wab, web, wob** the extent of a face of coal, *esp* in thickness.

wad black lead, graphite; *hence* a mine of black lead *now Kcb Dmf.*

wa(ll) coal the middle section of coal in a seam *now Fif.*

want a **nip** *now Fif.*

watered *of a coal-mine* subject to flooding. **water money** extra payment for working in wet conditions.

wee coal a shallow-seam coal.

wheel: ~**er** *Fif Loth,* ~**sman** *Fif* the person who operates the **wheel-brae.** ~**-brae** a **cowsy** *now Fif.* ~ **tree** the wooden post or pivot on which the wheel of a **wheel-brae** turns *C.* ~ **a brae** operate the haulage system on a **wheel-brae** *Fif Loth.*

whirlie a **hutch** *now Lnk.*

wild: † ~ **coal** poor quality coal *WC.* ~**fire** firedamp *now Fif.* ~ **parrot** an inferior kind of soft coal *Fif sEC, WC.*

win †extract (coal etc) by mining or quarrying; sink a pit or shaft to (a coal seam). **~ning** a pit and its fittings and machinery, a seam, a working or extraction of coal *now Fif*. **~ out** widen out a working *now Fif*.

wind draw (coal) to the pithead by means of a winding-engine *now Fif*.

windass a windlass, *latterly specif* one used for taking up water from the shaft of a coal-mine *now Fif*. †**~ cord** a rope on a **windass**. †**~ man** a windlass operator.

†**wuid** an inferior type of small coal.

†**wummle** a drill for boring through soil and rock for coal etc.

yolk, yowk a kind of soft, free, good-burning coal.

13.1.6 TEXTILES, WEAVING, SPINNING

†**backin(g)** providing with a back; material for this. **~s** refuse of wool, tow etc. **~rock** a distaff for spinning **backings** *Fif*.

bank a basket of bobbins of yarn used in making up the warp in a loom; a section of the warping frame in which the bobbins are set up *now Ayr*.

†**bead lam(b)s** part of the mounting of a silk-loom.

†**beet** a sheaf or bundle of flax.

†**birl quheil** a spinning wheel.

boam a wooden framework on which yarn is hung to be shaken and dried *now Fif*.

bore a hole in a series, the space between holes, *eg* on a belt or the yarn beam of a loom *now Abd*. **~ staff** the part of a loom which maintains tension on the warp.

bout a hank or skein of thread or worsted *now Stlg*.

†**braboner** a weaver.

†**breards** the short flax obtained from a second hackling of the first tow.

†**bred** a unit of quantity (of budge, a kind of lambskin).

broach, brutch the spindle on which newly-spun yarn is wound *now Abd*.

caird *n* a card, the instrument for carding wool etc *latterly chf N. v* card (wool etc).

calme(s) heddles *Ags*.

†**chak reel** a reel, *appar* with a check or catch for measuring the thread.

cheese a bobbin without flanges which when full resembles a cheese *Ork Fif Ayr*.

†**clove** break or split (flax) fibres before heckling.

cogster a person involved in the dressing of flax, the scutcher *Rox*.

cork name given by weavers to a manufacturer's agent *local*.

†**crib** a reel for yarn *S*.

crisp fold (cloth) lengthwise after weaving *Ags Uls*.

†**customer wark** orders carried out for a private customer as opposed to factory or speculative work. **~ or customary weaver** a weaver who works for private customers.

cut 1 a length of cloth. **2** a quantity of linen or woollen yarn, *usu* 120 rounds of a 93-inch reel, *ie* 300 ells or 310 yards (283.46 metres).

†**dadgeon wabster** *or* **weaver** a weaver of linen or woollen material for country neighbours *WC*.

†**doup end** a loop or the set of loops of the short **heddle** used in weaving gauze.

dress prepare (a web) for the loom with a starch made from flour etc.

en(d) a warp thread of yarn or silk *now Fif WC Slk*.

evener an instrument for spreading out the yarn on the beam *now Kinr*.

feeze aff, on *etc* twist, screw, cause to revolve (a spinning wheel etc).

felter a defect, a mistake *Fif*.

fill fill (the bobbins) with yarn *now Ags Fif*.

†**fine** sort out (wool) by separating the fine from the coarse parts. **fining quhele** a spinning wheel for making a fine woollen yarn.

fingering 1 a kind of worsted, *orig* spun from combed wool on the small wheel. **2** a kind of woollen cloth.

†**flachtit** *of wool* carded.

flichts the fly of a spinning wheel, which guides the thread to the spool *Sh NE Ags*.

gang a row: **1** †of decoration on a garment; **2** *in knitting, plaiting or weaving, now Sh Ork Cai*.

gaw a gap in cloth where weft threads are missing, *eg* between the end of one piece and the beginning of the next *local Ags-S*.

†**gouffer** decorate (cloth), *perh* with an impressed design.

†**graith** the heddles for a loom.

green *of cloth* unbleached, *esp* of unprocessed linen yarn *now Ags WC Uls*.

grist the size or thickness of yarn *now Abd Ayr S*.

†**grund, ground** the refuse of flax after dressing.

†**thank** a skein of gold or silver wire or thread.

hards the coarse refuse of flax or hemp separated by **heckling**, oakum, tow. †**~ weik, hard weik** candle-wick made from **hards**.

†**harl** the reed or brittle part of the stem of flax separated from the filament.

harnish, harness 1 the mounting of a loom. **2** †an intricate form of weaving common in west

Scotland, *esp* Paisley. ~ **shawl**, †~ **plaid** a **plaid** (*esp* one made in Paisley) or shawl of fine quality or intricate pattern.

hasky *of flax or fibre* rough, coarse.

†**heck** *n* **1** the toothed part on a spinning-wheel for guiding the spun thread onto the bobbin. **2** a part of a warping machine or of a jacquard loom. *v* work a fringe on a small loom.

†**heckle:** ~**ed** *of lint etc* having been combed with a **heckle**, dressed. **heckling house** *etc*, ~ **house** the place where flax etc was dressed.

†**heere** a length of 600 yards (548 metres) of linen yarn, one sixth of a hank. **herrin band** a string dividing cuts or **heeres** of yarn into separate bundles.

hesp a length of yarn, a hank or skein of wool etc of a certain length, the precise amount varying according to district.

†**hiddles** heddles.

holeiepied *of open-work embroidery or broderie anglaise* full of holes *NE*.

ingie in weaving a pattern, hand the requisite threads in a loom to the weaver *local Fif-S*. **ingier** the person who does this *local Fif-S*.

jeanie a (spinning-)jenny *chf Ayr*.

jesp a small gap or opening; a flaw, *esp* in the weave of a fabric, a broken thread *EC Rox*.

†**jink** move jerkily to and fro as when spinning.

†**kaming stok** a support to which carding- or rippling-combs were fixed.

keel the mark made with ruddle by the warper at each end of his warp to ensure that the weaver returns the correct amount of woven yarn.

†**key** an accessory part of a wool-comb.

Kilmarnock, *also and orig* ~ **hood** *etc* a knitted woollen conical skull-cap worn by indoor workers such as weavers.

kinch fasten loops onto (bridles).

knock *v* beat or pound (flax or cloth). †*n* a wooden mallet for beating linen etc, after bleaching. † ~**ing stane** a flat stone on which to beat linen after bleaching.

†**knok (lint)** a bundle (of hemp, flax etc).

†**lap** fold up (newly-woven linen) for storage or dispatch.

†**lash** a looped string fastened so as to raise groups of warp-threads in a loom together. ~**er** a person who fastens **lashes** in a loom *Renfr*.

lay the framed part of a loom, which strikes home each successive weft thread, the batten *now local*.

lease *v* separate or sort out (the yarn for the warp threads) before weaving *chf Rox*. *n* the division of the threads in a warp before it is put on the loom *now WC*.

†**leengyie, lignie** *specif of textiles* fine, thin.

link *freq of spinning* act with speed and energy; work vigorously (**at**) *now Cai Abd Fif*.

lint flax in the process of manufacture for spinning. ~**-beet** a bundle of flax cut and ready for processing *now Renfr Uls*. ~**-dresser** a flax-dresser *now Renfr*. ~**-hole**, ~**-pot** *now Fif* a pond in which flax is steeped *now Bnf Fif SW*. ~**-mill** a flax-factory or its machinery *now local Bnf-SW*, *freq as farm-name*. † ~**-tap** the bundle of dressed flax put on a distaff for spinning. ~**-wheel** a spinning wheel for flax *now only Uls*.

lume a (weaving-)loom.

maiden an upright post of a spinning wheel bearing the yarn-spindle *now Sh Uls*.

mail a metal eye through which the warp thread passes in a loom *local*.

†**mantill** a set of skins of fur containing a specific number. ~**ing** ? making up (furs) into **mantills**.

†**mat** a sack made of matting *N*.

†**misbeet** *of thread or yarn* become crossed or tangled.

muckle, meikle, mickle: ~ **wheel** a spinning wheel consisting of a large hand-turned wheel connected by a band to the spindle.

nabble *chf clothmaking* work with speed and deftness *Ags Per*.

niffler a comb-like appliance between whose teeth the web is spread on the loom, an **evener** *chf Fif*.

†**nok** a small hook; a hook holding the thread in a distaff.

†**nops** wool flock.

oo, woo(l): † ~**ster** a wool-stapler. ~**-card** the spiked board used for teasing wool *now Sh Ork*. ~ **mill** a tweed mill *NE Ayr*. † ~ **wheel** a spinning wheel.

paise one of the weights in the pulley which controls the tension of the warp threads.

Paisley with reference to the thread and textile industries of ~, *esp* the manufacture of shawls of the **Paisley pattern**; the pattern itself or any fabric bearing it. ~ **pattern** an elaborate colourful design based on Hindu and Arabic motifs, used in the **Paisley shawl** (1805-1870) and subsequently copied throughout the world.

pap a paste or dressing, *eg* of flour and water, used to give body to a web.

†**pasmentar** a passement-weaver or -worker.

pass, pace a passage between looms in a weaving shop or machines in a factory; a team of weavers etc *now Renfr Ayr*.

pick throw the shuttle across the loom *local Ags-*

Uls. ~er, ~er stick *etc now Ayr* a mechanism for shooting the shuttle across the loom.

picker the person who cuts off any loose or protruding threads from the web *now Ayr*.

†**pinto** a pin or bolt used as a handgrip for turning the beam in a loom.

†**pippane** a reel onto which a definite length of thread was wound.

pirn 1 a spool for holding the weft yarn in the shuttle, a bobbin. **2** the amount of yarn that can be wound on a **pirn** *now Mry Slk*. **3** †a stripe or band in a piece of cloth, of a different colour or texture from the rest; an irregularity, flaw. † ~ed, ~it woven of threads of different colours or textures, striped, variegated. † ~ie variegated, striped, uneven or irregular in weave. ~-mill a mill where weavers' bobbins are made *Ags Per*. ~ wheel a wheel for winding yarn onto bobbins. † ~-winder a person who loads a weaver's bobbins with yarn. **fill a ~** wind yarn on to a weaver's bobbin *now Ags*.

†**plash:** ~-mill a fulling mill driven by a waterwheel. ~-miller the operator of a fulling mill.

†**plotter** a person who trimmed the nap on woollen cloth.

†**pob tow** the refuse of flax (*later* also of jute) after scutching, any fibrous or dusty waste material; rope or twine teased into fibres *now Bnf*.

porter a section of the reed in a loom containing 20 interstices through which the warp threads are passed.

†**printfield** a cotton-printing works *now in placenames*.

rack a frame for stretching wet cloth in the process of fulling *now Ags Slk*.

raivel, reavel, rael *v* **1** *of thread, yarn etc* get into a tangle or confusion. **2** *of thread or yarn* unwind itself from a reel. *n* a broken or frayed thread, a loose end *now Ags Uls*.

rapery a ropery, ropeworks.

reel wind (yarn etc) on a reel; fill (a spool) with thread.

†**rig** the centre line of a web of cloth along which it is folded, the folded edge.

†**rock** a distaff with the wool or flax attached; the quantity of wool or flax placed on a distaff for spinning.

row, roll †*v* form (cotton or newly-carded wool) into a roll before it is spun. *n* a roll of wool etc drawn out and slightly twisted. ~ing a roll of cotton or wool rolled as above.

†**truch, rough:** ~-spun coarsely-made *now nEC*.

ruind, rind, †**roon** the border or selvage of a web of cloth; a strip of cloth *in gen, now Ork Slk*.

scob *n* a defect in which the shuttle passes on the wrong side of the warp threads *local Ags-Slk*. *v* miss (threads), allow the weft to miss (the warp) *now nEC Slk*.

screener *linen trade* a person who examines cloth for flaws and faults *Per Fif*.

scribble card or tease (wool) mechanically. † ~r a person who cards wool.

scrim a kind of thin coarse linen or canvas, made in narrow widths.

scutcher, †**scutch** the stick used for scutching flax, a swingle; the corresponding part in a machine.

†**seat tree** the weaver's seat in a handloom.

seckie a kind of linen overall worn by foremen in a weaving factory *Ross Lnk Ayr*.

†**seed** weave a pattern of spots, resembling seeds, in (a piece of muslin or linen).

†**shear:** ~er a person who removes the nap of cloth by shearing. ~ shope a place where cloth is manufactured.

shed, shae, shede *now Sh Ork NE* an opening, gap, *esp* between the two sets of threads in a loom *now C*.

shift *jute and linen spinning* change the bobbins on a spinning frame *EC Renfr*.

shorts the refuse of flax tow after carding *Abd Ags*.

shot a single movement of the shuttle carrying the weft across the web *now local Ags-Ayr*.

show the refuse of flax stems broken off in scutching *now Renfr*.

shuttle, shittle *n* a shuttle. *v* weave, drive the shuttle in a loom, be a weaver *now Ags Stlg Ayr*. ~r a weaver; a boy who fills carriages and bobbins in a lace factory *now Ags Stlg Ayr*.

slip a measure of yarn, *usu* in the form of a two-pound hank, consisting of 12 **cuts** *now Rox*.

sma(ll) shot †a strong strengthening thread inserted in **Paisley shawls** at intervals *Renfr*. **sma shot (Satur)day** a Paisley holiday on the first Saturday of July (*orig* a weavers' union holiday) *Renfr*.

snuve twist, twirl, spin, make yarn.

sowans a flour-and-water size applied to warp threads *now Ags*.

spinle, spindle 1 a spindle. **2** †a (varying) measure of yarn.

split a small piece of split reed etc, *later* thin metal, forming one of the divisions through which a warp thread passes in a loom *now nEC, WC, S*.

sprat a coarse reedy rush or grass growing in marshy ground and sometimes used in rope-making.

†**sprunt** the yarn a weaver contrived to keep for himself *Fif*.

spule 1 a spool, a bobbin. **2** the shuttle in which the bobbin is placed *now Sh Ags.*

†**stent, stenter-tree** *cloth-milling* a tenter.

†**stoup: the four ~s o misery** the (four-posted) hand-loom, from the poor living it provided in competition with industrial looms.

†**streek** a strick, a bundle of broken flax for scutching.

†**strik** beat (flax) before heckling; tie (it) in bundles.

sweerie a box or basket for holding bobbins of yarn, constructed so as to make easier the spinning of two- or three-ply thread *now Sh Ork.*

†**swingle: ~ hand, swinglind** a swingle.

†**switch** beat, scutch (flax).

tag (hole) a weaving fault in cloth, producing a hole where there should be pattern *Stlg Fif Ayr.*

†**tail** *damask weaving* the horizontal section of the cords in the harness of a loom.

tait pull or pluck out (fibres etc), tease out *now Sh.*

tap[1] *rope-making* a conical, grooved piece of wood used to keep the strands apart and tensed *now Sh Cai.*

†**tap**[2], **top** the tuft of flax or tow put on a distaff at one time.

tash a rope or strap, *esp* one for tying bundles of flax.

†**teer** *calico printing* coat with colour the pad etc on which the printer presses his block. **~er, ~ boy** the person who **teers**.

temper-pin the wooden screw which controls the tension of the band of a spinning wheel.

tenter a weaver's assistant, *now specif* a loom-tuner *now nEC, WC.*

tew taw, prepare (flax etc).

thairm gut dried and twisted into a cord for the driving-belt of a spinning wheel *now Sh.*

†**thripplin kame** a rippling comb, a ripple (for removing the seeds from flax).

thrum: ~mie covered with or made of **thrums** (waste threads), like **thrums**, frayed *Kcdn Ags.* †**~ keel** the ruddle mark at the end of a web of cloth.

tosslin the forming of the thread-ends of a web into tassels *nEC Ayr.*

tow band a strap or band of woven tow *now Bnf Abd.*

†**tow: ~-card** a toothed instrument for carding flax. **~-rock** a distaff used in spinning hemp.

treadle-hole an open space under the loom for the treadle shafts *now Lnk Ayr.*

tweel *n* twill, a diagonally-ribbed cloth produced by passing the weft threads over one and under two or more warp threads. *v* weave as above. **~ing** cloth, *usu* linen, woven thus.

twiner the person or machine employed to twist spun yarn into a thicker thread *S.*

wab, web, wob: ~ gless a magnifying glass for examining a web of cloth *Fif.* **gie in the ~** assist a weaver to thread his loom by handing him the threads *C.* **have one's ~ oot** have one's piece of cloth completed and off the loom *Ags Ayr.*

wabster, webster a weaver.

waft, woft *n* the woft, weft, the woof or cross-threads of a web of cloth. *v* weft, form a web.

waft clew a hank or ball of yarn *now Abd.*

†**walt: ~ing** a selvage. **~ened** having a selvage.

warp weave; plait. † **~ing ale** *or* **dinner** a drink of ale or some food given to the weaver after setting up a warp of homespun wool. † **~ing fatt** a tub or trough in which the clews of yarn are laid for warping. † **~in staik** one of the set of wooden uprights round which the yarn is wound in warping.

†**water** produce a wavy lustrous finish on (silk etc) by moistening and pressing.

waulk, walk 1 full (cloth), make (cloth) thick and felted by a process of soaking, beating and shrinking. **2** *also* **~in** *of cloth* shrink as a result of being wetted. **~it** *of wool etc* matted, hardened, roughened *now Sh C.* † **~er, walkster** a fuller of cloth. **waulking song** any suitably rhythmic Gaelic song *formerly* sung by a team of women engaged in **waulking** cloth in the Hebrides. **~ mill** a fulling mill *now NE Per WC.*

wheelin(g) a coarse thick type of worsted yarn, *orig* from uncombed wool spun on the **muckle wheel**. **~-band** the driving belt of a spinning wheel, *usu* made of dried animal gut *now Sh Ork Cai.*

†**whip** a thread separate from the basic warp and weft which is introduced into the weave to form a pattern.

whisks a pair of small reels used to facilitate the winding of yarn onto a bobbin.

white: whitie-broon *now Ork Ags Fif,* **fitit-** *Bnf Abd* or **whited-broon** *Abd* applied to linen thread in which the brown colour of the flax has been lightened by washing but not bleaching. **~ room** a room in a textile factory where cloth is inspected and prepared for despatch after finishing *Dnbt Ayr.*

whurl a whorl, the small perforated stone flywheel of a spindle.

†**windle** wind (thread).

windles a device for winding yarn or thread on to bobbins.

yairn now Ork Cai C, S, **yarn** yarn. **yarlins** NE,
~ **winnles** a yarn-reel for winding yarn into
skeins.

†**yaud** of yarn a thread that has not gone properly
round the reel but is left hanging between the
spokes.

yowder the fluff or dust of flax.

13.1.7 SEWING

†**a-jour** needlework of openwork.

Ayrshire needlework fine needlework on muslin
orig chf Ayr.

baiss baste, sew loosely.

†**boikin** a bodkin.

bool the ring joining the finger and thumb holes
in scissors.

†**browd** embroider. ~**en** embroidered.
~(in)**stare, browstar** an embroiderer.

†**brusery** embroidery.

†**brusit** embroidered. **brusoure** an embroiderer.

†**cardower** a travelling tailor.

chizors scissors.

cleed of a tailor make a suit of clothes for.

cloot, clout n a patch now Abd Fif. v patch, mend
(clothes). † ~**er** a patcher.

†**ee, eye** an eyelet.

†**fleeing tailor** a travelling tailor.

flour, flower embroider (flowers or similar
designs).

flourish embroider now Ork Abd Ags.

guse †press or iron with a tailor's goose. **gusing
iron** a tailor's goose now Per.

heel-cap patch, mend or reinforce the heels of
(stockings).

hussy a pocket-case for holding needles, thread
etc now Ork Cai.

†**jag-the-flae** contemptuous name for a tailor.

jam mend, patch Sh Ork.

knotless threid a thread that has no knot and
tends to slip out of the needle.

lay: †**laid wark** couched work. ~ **in** turn up (a
hem) local Ork-Kcb.

†**leill** a single stitch, eg in a sampler.

†**lincum twine** twine or thread made or as made
at Lincoln.

mantie-maker a dressmaker now Sh NE Slk.

†**natch** ? small scissors used by tailors.

neb the point of a pin.

†**nerve** n a band of material used to decorate a
garment. v apply such a band to (a garment).

opensteek a kind of open work stitch now Ork.

owerlay, overlay n the kind of hem in which one

part of the cloth is folded or laid over the other.
v sew (a hem) as above now Sh Ork Ags.

peen a pin.

†**pettie-point** petit point.

pirn a small spool of sewing thread, orig of gold,
silk etc; a reel of or for thread.

preen n a metal pin. v 1 †sew, stitch up. 2 fasten
with a pin. ~**-cod** a pincushion now Ork Cai EC.
~**-heid** a pin-head now Sh NE.

†**prick** fasten or secure with a pin etc. ~**-the-
louse**, ~**louse** contemptuous a tailor.

ranter v 1 sew together, darn, mend now Cai. 2
mend or stitch hastily or roughly. n a rough,
hasty stitching or sewing.

redd disentangle, unravel, sort out (thread, yarn
etc) now NE, WC.

†**seam-biter** joc a tailor.

sey the armhole of a sleeve.

shape v cut (cloth) in a certain pattern or shape,
freq ~ **and sew** now Sh-N. n a dressmaking
pattern, a pattern piece. **shapin(g)s** left over
cuttings or shreds of cloth now Abd.

shear(s) (a pair of) scissors.

shew, †**sue, she** v sew. n the act of sewing; a spell of
needlework. ~**ster** a seamstress, needlewoman
now NE.

spatch n a patch, as on a garment now Rox. v patch,
mend (clothes etc) S.

spat o prins a round pincushion with pins in it.

splay v finish a seam by hemming the upper projecting edge down over the lower one local Sh-
SW. n a hem sewn as above now Abd Ayr.

steek, stick v stitch, sew Gen except Ork. n a stitch.

stockin(g) needle a darning needle Gen except Sh.

surfle gather, ruck a hem; overcast an edge of
cloth; trim with lace bordering.

swatch a pattern or sample of a piece of cloth.

†**taging iron** a tailor's tool for tagging cloth.

†**tailyie** cut (to shape).

tak, take: † ~ **aff** take measurements for (new
clothes). ~ **doun** make (one garment) from
another now Sh Kcb.

tallie iron, talian iron an Italian or goffering
iron now Fif Lnk Rox.

†**tapescher** a tapestry-maker.

†**tent** ? embroider in a frame.

thrapple draw (a hole in cloth) roughly together,
instead of darning Bwk S.

threid thread, freq linen thread.

thummle a thimble.

twilt n, v quilt now local.

walt n the welt (of a garment etc) now local. †v welt.
† ~**ing** an edging, hem. †**waltened** bordered,
edged, having a welt.

†**whip the cat** *chf of a tailor* go from house to house practising one's trade.

white: whitie-broon *now Ork Ags Fif*, **fitit-** *Bnf Abd or* **whited-broon** *Abd* applied to linen thread in which the brown colour of the flax has been lightened by washing but not bleaching. ~ **seam** plain needlework.

†**windle** wind (thread).

13.1.8 KNITTING, CROCHET

cleek, click a crochet-hook.

cuffock a coil in a ball of wool, with the strands wound in one direction *Abd*.

gang a row in knitting *now Sh Ork Cai*.

intak, intake: ~**s** the number of stitches decreased in order to shape a garment, *eg* a sock. ~**ing** the decrease of stitches in knitting socks etc.

lat doun drop (a stitch) *now NE*.

lift pick up (stitches) *now NE*.

loop, loup a stitch. **tak a** ~ take up one's knitting, knit *now Sh N Dmf*.

oncast the first row of stitches; the casting on of this *local Sh-Arg*.

outlatting the increase in the stitches in the heel of a stocking *Sh Abd*.

pearl purl.

rip out *or* **down** undo (a piece of knitting).

shank *n* the leg of a stocking; a stocking, or *later* any garment, in the process of being knitted *now local Bnf-WC*. *v* knit stockings etc *now Abd-Ags*. ~**er** a knitter of stockings *chf Abd*.

sheath a kind of pad on a belt used to hold knitting needles when not in use *now Sh N-WC*.

stand, staun a complete set, *eg* of knitting needles *now Sh-EC, SW Rox*.

swarra a kind of thick, heavy, woollen yarn used for knitting jerseys, scarves and underclothing *now Sh*.

tyne drop (a stitch) *Abd*.

warp knit, cast **on** (stitches).

weave knit (*chf* stockings) *now NE Ags*. **weavin** knitting; a piece of knitted wool *now NE Ags*.

wire a knitting needle. ~**s** a set of knitting needles.

wisker a bunch, *usu* of straw used as a sheath for knitting needles at a woman's waist *NE*.

13.1.9 DYEING, TANNING

aum *n* alum. *v* treat with alum, *esp* to cure (skins).

bark: ~**ened** *of leather* tanned. † ~**er** a tanner. † ~**it** barked, tanned. † ~**hole** a tanner's bark-pit. † ~ **pot** a pot or pit for tanner's bark.

†**blacht, blaugh** bleached.

†**bleachfield** a bleaching works with its adjacent drying-ground.

bleck(in) blacking (for leather).

†**boday** bow-dye, a scarlet dye.

†**brissell** brazil, the wood or the dyestuff obtained from it.

†**Cashub ash(es)** a kind of wood ash used in bleaching.

†**corkir, corklit** *SW* a red lichen used in dyeing.

crottle, crotal dye-producing lichen *local*.

cudbear a purple dyestuff, prepared from lichens.

†**daker, daiker** a set of ten hides.

dyester a dyer *now local Cai-S*.

graith stale urine used in washing and dyeing.

†**leck** a container in which bark for tanning was steeped.

†**leid** a large vat (not necessarily of lead), as used *esp* in dyeing.

lit *v* dye, colour, tinge *now Sh Cai*. *n* a dye, tint, dyestuff *now Sh Cai*. †**litster, littistar** a dyer. † ~**-house** a dye-house.

lucken *of leather* consolidated and thickened by tanning and hammering.

†**mather** madder, (dye from) the root of the plant.

†**nit, nut:** ~**gall** an oak-gall, *chf* used as a dye-stuff.

†**orchard-litt** name of some dye.

†**please madame** a type of dyestuff; the colour obtained by its use, or a stuff of this colour.

†**pot, pat** a tanner's pit for bark or lime.

†**ruch, rough** *of hides* undressed, untanned (with hair still on).

stale urine collected for making bleach etc *now Per*.

stane, stone: ~ **raw** the lichen *Parmelia saxatilis* used for dyeing *now SW*.

strae wald dyer's rocket.

†**tannage** a tannery, leatherworks.

tew taw, prepare (leather).

†**waid** woad.

†**wald** dyer's rocket, the plant; the yellow dye obtained from it.

13.1.10 LAUNDRY

airn iron.

boyne, bine a shallow tub, *latterly esp* a wash-tub *now Bnf Kcb*.

facing iron a smoothing iron with a polished surface.

†**gouffer** goffer.

graith stale urine used in washing.

guffer goffer *Abd Ags.*

†ladinar, lathenar a washerwoman, laundress.

maister, master stale urine, used as a detergent.

stairch starch.

stale urine collected for making bleach *now Per.*

†souple soften by soaking, soak; wash.

steamie a public wash-house *local C, S.*

stiff: ~**en** starch (clothes) *local.* ~**ing** *now N Rox,* ~**ening** *now Stlg WC* starch.

tramp steep, soak (in).

wash, wesh *v* wash. *n* 1 wash. 2 stale urine used as a cleansing agent *now EC Lnk S.* **washer wife** a washer-woman, laundress *local Ork-Ayr.* **washing boyne, wash bine** *now WC* a (portable) wash-tub. **washing house** a wash-house. *now WC.*

13.1.11 SHOEMAKING, COBBLING

birse *n* the bristle fixed on a shoemaker's thread. *v, of shoemakers etc* attach a bristle to a thread. **†birsit** *of thread* supplied with a bristle.

bog *of shoemakers working in a customer's house* work at a daily rate.

cauker, cacker an iron rim fixed on a clog or shoe to minimize wear *Abd SW.*

cloot, clout *n* a patch, a patch of metal etc *now Abd Fif. v* repair (footwear etc) with a metal plate. † ~**er** a patcher, cobbler.

†club a member of a trade, *esp* shoemaking, who has not gone through a full or formal apprenticeship.

†cordiner a shoemaker.

deil *now Abd,* **deil's fit** *now Abd Ayr colloq* a shoemaker's last.

en(d) the (*now* waxed) thread used in sewing leather.

fit, foot, fute: ~ **fang** *NE,* ~ **wang** *Sh* a strap used by cobblers looped round knee and foot and over the work to keep it firmly in position.

†gum a small parcel of awls.

heel: ~**-cap** patch, mend or reinforce the heels of (shoes or stockings) *now Dmf.* ~**-ring** a circular piece of metal fastened to the heel of a boot to reduce wear *Abd Ags Kinr.* ~**-shod** a piece of iron used to protect the heel of a heavy boot or shoe *now local Cai-Dmf.*

†hob(b)ell *v* cobble, mend (shoes) roughly. *n* some part of a shoe, *perh* a patch.

inseam the seam which attaches the welt to the insole and upper of a boot or shoe.

†jimp a strip or sliver, *specif* of leather as used to build up the heel of a shoe.

lingel the waxed thread used by shoemakers. ~**en(d)** the tip of the **lingel** to which the **birse** was attached for threading it through the leather; the piece of **lingel** itself *C S.*

lint linen thread, *esp* that used by shoemakers to make their **lingel** *Sh NE Ayr.*

lug a flap of a shoe.

meenie a fine awl *Cai Ross.*

†mett-stick a stick cut to the exact length of the foot and sent to the shoemaker as a measure for fitting shoes.

outseam awl an awl for sewing shoes from the outside *Sh-Per.*

†petrie-ball *prob* = **peter bowie** *NE Fif.* **peter bowie** a wedge or stick used by shoemakers for rubbing the seams of shoes before sewing.

priest and devil a shoemaker's last *Per Uls.*

rackstrap = **fit fang** *Bnf Abd.*

roset rub with resin. ~**ty-en(d)** a shoemaker's thread *now Kcb.* ~**-en(d)** a resined thread, used for sewing leather *NE-C.*

rubbing stick a stick used by shoemakers to rub leather smooth *now Ork.*

ruind, rind, †roon: ~ **shune** shoes made of strips of selvages of cloth.

shae, shoe hobnail (shoes) *now local Ags-Kcb.*

shod fit (a bootlace etc) with a metal tip etc.

snab, snob a cobbler; a cobbler's boy or apprentice *now nEC Gsw Rox.* ~**bin** shoemaking, cobbling *now Fif Edb.*

souter *n* a shoemaker, cobbler. *v* cobble, make or mend shoes *now NE, SW.* ~**('s) ends** *now Bnf Abd Per,* **sutter's lingles** *now Abd Per* the waxed thread used by cobblers, **lingel-ends**.

tacket a small nail, *latterly esp* a hobnail, used to stud the soles of shoes etc. ~**ed,** ~**y** studded with **tackets,** hobnailed: '*tackety boots*'. ~**y jock** a shoemaker's last *local Stlg-Ayr.*

walt *n* the welt (of a shoe etc) *now local.* †*v* welt.

†wanpa a vamp of a shoe.

whatstick a hone or emery-board with a wooden handle used by cobblers *local Abd-Rox.*

yerk bind tightly, tie firmly together (*eg* shoe-leather in shoemaking) *now local Sh-Kcb.* **yerkin** the side seam in a boot or shoe *now Sh.*

†yickie-yawkie a wooden tool used to polish the soles of shoes *SW.*

13.1.12 BLACKSMITHING

brookie name for a blacksmith *now Abd.*

bruntie a blacksmith *now Ags.* **burn-the-wind** *slang* a blacksmith *now local Abd-Lnk.*

cauk calk (a horse), fix a guard on or sharpen (a horseshoe) to prevent slipping *Abd Fif.* **~er, cacker** a calkin, a horseshoe treated as above.

chap knock, strike with a hammer as in a smithy *local Cai-Kcb.*

†**cruik study** a beaked anvil.

danders the refuse of a smith's fire; clinker.

dog a lever used by blacksmiths in hooping cart-wheels etc *now Abd.*

dwang a large iron lever used by blacksmiths *now Gsw Rox.*

ferrier a farrier *NE midLoth.*

flaw the point of a horseshoe nail.

†**forehaimmer** a sledge-hammer.

gow a blacksmith *now chf literary or as a surname.*

hud the seat by the fire on a blacksmith's hearth.

†**lorimer** a maker of the metal parts of a horse's harness, a maker of small metalwork.

†**owerhip** *of a smith* striking the metal by raising the hammer over the shoulder.

†**pelt** keep hammering or striking (**at** *etc*).

†**pene** hammer metal (**out**) flat and thin.

pike provide with a pike or pikes or with a spike or spikes, *specif* shoe (a horse) with **sharps** to give a grip on icy roads *now Abd.*

plat(ten) flatten down (the point of the nails attaching the shoe to a horse's hoof), clinch (a nail) *now Sh.*

powie a smith's hand-hammer with both striking faces bevelled or rounded off *nEC midLoth.*

shae, shoe: ~in box the box in which a blacksmith keeps his smaller tools *Abd Kcb.* **~in shed** a shed as part of a smithy in which horses are tied up to be shod *Ork Abd Kcb.*

shairp, sherp, sharp *n* a frost-nail on a horse's shoe *now N, C.* *v* provide (a horseshoe) with frost-nails, rough (a horse) *N, C.*

shod, shoad furnish with shoes, put shoes on; shoe (a horse).

†**skivet** a smith's fire-tool.

smiddy a smithy. **~ coal, ~ coom** *now Kcb* a small smokeless type of coal suitable for smiths' work. †**~ craft** smithcraft. **~ sparks** the sparks of iron which fly off a smith's anvil.

stave thicken (iron) by heating and hammering *now Inv WC Kcb.*

studdie, stiddie a stithy, an anvil *now local.*

swedge *n* a tool for making the grooves and nail-holes in a horseshoe. *v* make a groove or hole in (metal), *eg* on a horseshoe *now Bnf.*

turkas a pair of pincers or pliers, *esp* as used by a blacksmith etc *now NE.*

13.1.13 ROADMAKING

blin pack (the large stones forming the bed of a road) with smaller material to give strength and firmness.

bow an arch of a bridge *local.* **~ brig** an arched bridge.

brander *n, also* †**brandreth** a framework of metal or *freq* wood, wooden supports as used in the construction of bridges etc, a trestle. *v* support with a **brander**. **~ing** the material or structure forming a **brander**.

brig 1 a bridge. **2** †a drawbridge. †**~-wark** the work of building or maintaining a bridge.

†**coom, cowm** the wooden frame on which the arch of a bridge is built.

crib *Fif Kcb,* **crib-stane** *now Abd* a kerb.

†**lan(d) stale, lan(d) stool** the foundation on land of the pier of a bridge or weir.

†**ledging** the parapet of a bridge.

metal rock broken up and used in road-making.

†**pament** *n* paving. *v* pave.

parpen the parapet of a bridge.

pen(d) 1 the arch of a bridge. **2** *also* **~ stones** the stonework of an arch.

putt 1 †a buttress of a bridge. **2** a jetty or stone buttress projecting from a river bank, used to alter the current, protect the bank etc *S.* **~ stone** *now Cai,* **peat (stane)** the keystone of an arch.

ravel a bridge parapet.

road-harl a scraper for removing mud from a road *now Stlg.*

†**rummlin** *of a drain etc* filled with loose stones.

spring the rise, slope, height (of an arch) *now WC Kcb.*

†**stag** support with piles *Abd.*

whin, whin-stone *now in StEng as a geol term,* †**whin rock 1** any hard stone used as road stone. **2** a piece of whin-stone, a boulder, slab or stone *local C.*

13.1.14 PLUMBING

aprin a strip of lead folded over the edge of a gutter etc to conduct rain-water into it.

channel a gutter *now Ags.*

cock and pail spigot and faucet *now Ork.*

crampet a roof-gutter bracket, a support *Abd.*

gitter a gutter *C, S.*

jaw-box *C, Uls,* **~ hole,** †**jawer-hole** *Edb Ayr,* **jaw-stane** a sink, drain.

reed *n* a longitudinal defect in a lead pipe *WC*. v, *of a lead pipe* split longitudinally *WC*. ~ie *of a lead pipe* liable to split (as above) *local EC, WC*.

rone, *also* oaccas ~ pipe the horizontal gutter for rainwater running along the eaves of a roof. ~ pipe, *also* occas rone the more or less vertical pipe for draining water from the rone.

spout a horizontal roof gutter, a rone *now local Sh-S*.

stroup the faucet, spout or outlet of a spring or well, a water-tap *now N Per*.

tippit *of a pipe, sink etc* choked to overflowing *Bnf Abd*.

13.1.15 JOINERY

aeger an auger *Sh Abd Fif Ayr*.

†angular a brace-piece or tie in the interior angle of a wooden frame.

back the outermost boards from a sawn tree *now Bnf Ags*.

†bell-heidit *of nails* with a bell-shaped head.

bilget a piece of wood prepared for various purposes, *latterly esp* as a support for shelves.

†blind nale ? a blunt nail.

boral, borell a boring tool.

box †wainscot, cover with boards. ~in wainscotting *now Ayr*.

breist bore an instrument for boring *now Fif*.

†brissell brazil, the wood.

†brod fit with a board or boards, *esp* shutters.

brog a bradawl.

buird, boord board. †burdin made of boards.

bun(d) joined or fitted together, *perh esp* by mortise-and-tenon joints; *also* referring to the covering of a join with beading, *orig freq* bundwark *now Lnk Kcb*.

cadden nail *now Abd*, caddle *NE*, cathel nail *Per Fif Ayr* a large nail or iron pin.

ca drive in (nails etc); fix on by hammering.

caibe a cabinet-maker *local Ags-Ayr*.

†carpoll a pole or spar.

chack, check a groove or notch cut to receive an edge or serving as a check, a rabbet.

cladding cladding boarding; lining with such.

†claitt a cleat.

clift a plank, board.

countercheck a tool for cutting the groove which unites the two sashes of a window *now Abd Kcb*.

covetta a plane for moulding framed work, a quarter-round *local*.

†crampet a cramp-iron.

†craw iron a crowbar, *esp* with a claw for drawing nails.

cuddy a joiner's trestle.

cut a piece of timber cut off a larger piece, beam or tree. † ~ting a piece (of wood) produced by cutting.

dale a deal, plank.

dook *n* a wooden peg etc driven into a wall to hold a nail. *v* insert such wooden pegs etc in (a wall). ~ hole a hole cut in a wall for a dook *NE Ags Kcb*.

†Eastlan burdis boards from the eastern part of the Baltic.

eetch an adze.

faize make (wood) rough, splintered or jagged *now Bnf Abd*.

field sink a margin round (a wooden panel) *local*.

†fit gang a length of plank for workmen to work on.

flaw a kind of nail.

fluir floor. † ~ing (nail) a flooring-nail.

garron nail a large nail or spike *now local Sh-Fif*.

geelum a rabbet-plane.

grannie's tuith *or* teeth a router plane *Abd Ags Per*.

gruip, grip, †grib cut a groove in (a board) for fitting into a corresponding 'tongue'.

gudge *n* a gouge *now Sh Ork NE*. *v* gouge *now Sh Ags*.

hack, hawk a joiner's adze *now midLoth*.

halflin(g), *chf* ~ plane a large-size plane used by carpenters, *now* the largest, *orig* the second in size to the jointer plane.

hard *of joints* pressing closely together at one place and not at another *now midLoth*.

heel the part of an adze into which the handle is fitted *local*.

hirsel an iron pin or auger used when red-hot for boring holes.

jint joint.

joiner, jiner a woodworker, carpenter. joinery a joiner's workshop *Abd Ags Fif*.

kirn bore with a drill or circular chisel *now Fif*.

knappel, †knapholt, knappart, knapwood, knarholt, knapburd clapboard, split oak smaller than wainscot, *chf* used as barrel-staves and as panelling or boarding.

knee *of a nail or staple* bend so as to form a knee-shaped angle *now Per Fif*.

†knit secured by a joint.

laft, loft: ~ing boarding *in gen*.

lay a turning lathe.

mouse a small lead weight tied to a cord, used to guide cords into a sash window. ~ moulding a narrow moulding filling the angle between floor and skirting board or wall.

†nail string the iron rod from which nails are cut.

navis-bore a knot-hole in wood *Bnf Abd*.

†need-nail fasten securely, nail up.

†pannelling (wooden) panels or panel-work.

plant, †plaint attach or lay in a piece of moulding.

plat, platten clinch (a nail) *now Sh*.

plenshin(g) naill, †plencheoun-naill, plen-schell-naill, plensher (nail) a flooring nail.

plucker a kind of spokeshave, a tool for planing a curved surface *now Bnf-Abd*.

powl *n* a pole, a long thin round shaft of wood. *v* pole, furnish with poles.

pownie a carpenter's trestle for supporting planks of wood for sawing etc *N Fif Uls*.

rack a stay, strut *local Mry-midLoth*.

raggle *v* cut a groove in wood to receive a board, *eg* in the steps of a stair. *n*, *also* **raglet, raglin** such a groove.

†trammel the rough timber of small or crooked branches.

rance a prop, wooden post used as a stay or strut, *specif* the stretcher of a table or chair *now Mry Ags Kcb*.

†reid, red: ~ **wood** the wood at the heart of trees.

rind, reen *chf N* a strip or slat of wood, a thin piece cut off the edge of a board, a piece of beading *now Sh-nEC*.

rip the act of sawing wood etc along the grain *now Sh-Per WC*.

ruive clinch (a nail) *now local Sh-Kcb*.

rybat a rabbet.

scillop an auger with a rounded tapering blade *now local*.

scrieve scratch or incise a mark on (wood), *eg* to show the shape in which something is to be made *now Ayr*.

scrunt 1 plane (a board) roughly to remove a thick shaving *local Abd-Lnk*. **2** the act of planing roughly; a thicker rough shaving of wood *now Abd Lnk*.

seam fit one edge of (a plank) to another *now Sh Cai*.

skair *n* **1** a slanting cut or notch in a piece of wood by which it can be joined to another of similar shape *now local Sh-Fif*. **2** a piece of wood so fashioned *now Sh Cai Per*. *v* splice (two pieces of wood etc) *now Sh Ork Cai Per*.

skifting a narrow piece of boarding *EC, WC, S*.

sole tree a horizontal beam of wood, *usu* on the ground, which supports posts *now Sh Per*.

spail a splinter, chip or sliver of wood (broken off by an axe or plane); wood-shaving; a thin strip

or lath or wood. ~**ing** a wood-shaving *now Per*.

spar, spare *now Rox* a spar. **sparred** slatted. **†sparret** a small spar or bar.

sprag a bradnail *now NE nEC, WC*.

square: ~ **man** a workman who regularly uses a square, *esp* a carpenter or mason *now only free-masonry*. ~**wright** a carpenter, *specif* one who makes furniture.

stob 1 *also* ~ **nail** *now Bnf Rox* a short thick nail. **2** a bradawl *now Sh NE Ags*.

stoothe make (a wall etc) with lath and plaster *SW, S*.

†straik a measure of timber.

strap *n* a strip of wood serving as a base to which something else may be nailed. *v* fix strips of wood on (a wall) as a base for lath, skirting etc.

suit, shuit: ~ **stock** *etc* a bevel, adjustable square *now N*.

†tie fasten or fix (with nails).

†timmerman a carpenter.

turning loom a turning lathe *now Sh*.

†tynd nale a large sharp-pointed nail.

variorum a decoration (in furniture etc) *now Sh Ork nEC SW*.

vernish varnish.

warp a strut or struts, a brace or angle-piece.

†warren tre a hard oak.

wash, wesh *v, chf* ~ **down** *or* **off** cut to a slope or bevel *now WC*. *n* a bevelled edge or slope on a board etc *Abd Fif*.

win, wun dry out, season (wood etc).

wricht *n* a woodwright, carpenter. *v* follow the occupation of a wright, work as a carpenter or joiner *NE Ags*. † ~**work** carpentry, joinery.

wuid, wood: ~**laid** floored with wood *Cai Abd Loth*.

wummle an auger, gimlet *now Sh-Per Slk*. ~**-bore** an auger hole *now NE Per Fif*.

13.1.16 MASONRY, BRICKWORK

aislar *n*, *also* † ~ **stane** ashlar, square-hewn stone. ~ **wark** masonry constructed of such stone.

†allouring the material of which the stone pavement placed behind the battlements of a hall is built.

band stane a bondstone *now Sh*.

†barcatt a kind of wooden trestle or support.

barra, barrow: ~**man** a person who helps to carry a hand-barrow; a person who carries building materials on a barrow *now Bnf*.

bat *n* a lead wedge for securing lead flashings in masonry joints. *v* fasten or secure with **bats**.

bed a flat base or foundation.

†**bowal** build or join (a wall) with a recess.

†**brace** a band of stonework, wood etc used to strengthen a structure; *latterly esp* the breast or arch of a chimney.

brander *n*, *also* †**brandreth** a framework of metal or *freq* wood, wooden supports as used in the construction of buildings; a trestle. *v* support with a **brander**. **brandering** the material or structure forming a **brander**.

caip *n* a coping *now Abd*. *v* furnish with a coping. ~ **stane**, †**caip** a coping-stone.

†**calfat** make watertight, caulk.

cat *n*, *chf* ~ **and clay, claut and clay** a handful of straw mixed with soft clay used in building or repairing walls. *v* build or repair with **cat and clay** *S*.

catchie-hammer one of the smallest of a stonemason's hammers *now Bnf Per*.

†**centreis** the timbers used to support an arch in the process of building.

clash repair by throwing wet mortar into joints and crevices.

clatch up build carelessly or clumsily *now Ags Lnk Kcb*.

†**cleidin(g)** a covering or facing applied to a framework etc; the act of making or fixing this.

clour dress or chisel (stone). ~**er** a stone-dressing chisel.

codding stones acting as supports for various constructions.

†**condampne** block, fill up (a door etc).

†**coom, cowm** the wooden frame on which an arch is built.

cowan 1 a builder of **dry-stane dykes**. **2** *disparaging* one not properly apprenticed and trained as a mason.

†**crampet** a cramp-iron.

†**cuistis** pieces of stone used in building an oven.

†**cunyie** a quoin.

deafening sound-proofing (of a building) by pugging.

deval a sloping surface, a slope *now Sh Abd*.

†**develling** a covering of centres or **cooms** used in building arches.

dorbie a stonemason *now Bnf Abd Rox*.

dress cut and smooth (stone), prepare for building.

drove *n* a stonemason's broad-faced chisel *now Cai Bnf Abd*. *v* prepare stone for building using a **drove** *now Abd*.

dry(-stane) dyker a person who builds **dry-stane** dykes.

dyke build or repair **dykes**. **dyker** a builder of **dykes**.

†**fog** *n* moss, lichen used for packing walls. *v* pack (a wall) with moss.

foundin pint a drink given to workmen after laying the foundations of a building as an omen of good luck *now Ork Ags*.

freestane a block of freestone *now local*.

†**fute gang** a plank or planks for workmen to walk on while engaged in building etc.

gaberts scaffolding.

giblet-check a rabbet cut in masonry to allow a door to fit flush with the wall *now Abd Ags*.

gouf underpin or underbuild (a wall or building) to secure its foundations or put in a damp-course *chf Gsw*.

grip: the ~ the 'lump', the system of sub-contracting work to casual labour.

grund, ground: ~**-stane** a foundation stone *now Sh*.

hap a covering, *esp* one which protects against the weather *now local*. ~**per** the last hour of a mason's working day when work is covered up against frost etc *now NE Ags*.

hard *of joints* pressing closely together at one place and not at another *now midLoth*.

harl *v* roughcast with lime and small stones. *n* a mixture of sand and lime used for roughcasting. ~**ing 1** = **harl**. **2** the action of roughcasting.

†**heather an dub** clay mixed with cut heather used instead of mortar *chf Abd*.

horse a trestle, a support, *specif* as used by masons to support scaffolding.

hudd a hod.

inband a header, a stone with its short side in a wall face, a quoin or jamb stone.

ingoing, ingo the reveal of a door- or window-case where the stonework turns inward at right angles to the wall.

intak, intake the offset on a wall, a ledge in a wall where its thickness is reduced *now Fif*.

kilt a tilt, the slope of a stone to allow water to run off, *esp* that on a staircase etc.

lime mortar, cement, *freq* **stone and** ~ masonry.

†**lintel, lentell:** ~ **ale** a drink given to the masons at a building job when the door-lintel was put on.

†**lip** point (a wall).

†**lodge, ludge** a shed or workshop for masons.

†**mason:** ~**er** a mason *Arg Kcb*. ~ **werk 1** *also* ~**ry** mason's work. **2** masonry, stonework.

mear, mare 1 a wooden frame used as a trestle to

support scaffolding *now NE*. **2** †a bricklayer's hod *C*.

†**needle** a spar used as a support in scaffolding. **nedling** the setting of a transverse support.

nidge dress (a building stone) roughly, by picking with a sharp-pointed hammer.

†**togeour** ? an ogee arch, or a moulding which when doubled constituted such an arch; a stone cut for such an arch.

†**tonbaykyn** *of brick etc* not baked in a kiln, not exposed to heat.

out o thraw *of a stone* into alignment, straightened, squared *now Abd Wgt*.

outband a stretcher, a stone with its long side along a wall face, *specif* a quoin or jamb stone. **out and in bond** alternate headers and stretchers in the angles of walls, and of window and door jambs.

†**outstriking (of)** striking out, making an opening (for a door etc).

†**oversailyie** bridge over (a **close** or alley).

parpen a stone which passes through the entire thickness of a wall.

peat (stane), putt stone a gable stone supporting a coping-stone; a coping-stone; the keystone of an arch.

peen: a coping *now Sh Mry Ags*. ~**er** a mason's peen-hammer *now Fif Loth*.

†**pen(d) 1** form into an archway, vault. **2** furnish with arching or vaulting, arch or vault over. ~**stone** a stone shaped for building into an archway.

pin, peen *now EC, S* consolidate masonry with **pins**. ~**s**, ~**ing(s)** *now Sh NE*, † ~ **stones** small stones wedged into the crevices between larger stones in a wall to consolidate it. † ~**ner** a piece or rafter of wood used to fasten or stabilize a structure.

pincher a blunt chisel used for chipping the edge of a squared-off stone.

plinth, †plint 1 a plinth. **2** the uppermost projecting part of a cornice; the eaves course or wallhead course.

point, pint indent a stone face with a pointed tool *NE Per*.

pox spoil (a stone) by bad cutting *now Abd*.

punish reduce (a stone) in size by cutting and dressing *now Cai*.

pup a small size of brick *Stlg Fif WC Rox*.

raggle *v* cut a groove in stone to receive another stone, *eg* in the steps of a stair, the edge of a roof. *n, also* **raglet, raglin** such a groove.

reel a mason's medium-weight hammer with two oblong faces.

†**reprise** an indentation of stone.

rice: stake and ~, **stab and** ~ a method of construction by which twigs are horizontally woven between vertical stakes.

rickle build without mortar; *freq* ~ **up** build (a **dry-stone** wall) *now Fif*.

rin, run: ~ **lime** mortar poured liquid into the crevices of stonework and left to set *chf NE*.

rise: ~**r** *rubble-walling* a stone which reaches to the full height of the course. ~**band** a vertical joint rising through several courses without bonding *Per Dnbt*.

†**ruid, rood** an area of 36 square **ells** or *later* **yards**.

saving stone a stone built over a lintel to distribute the load of the wall above onto the jambs *now Per Ayr*. **safe lintel** a wooden lintel placed for additional support behind the stone lintel of a door or window *Gen except Sh Ork*.

†**saxeane** made of stone.

scrunt rough down (pointing) with a handpick *local Abd-Lnk*.

scutch dress (a stone) roughly with a pick.

†**service** labouring or unskilled work in building a house.

shivers splinters of stone, *esp* as broken off in stonedressing *now EC Lnk*.

siege a wooden or stone bench on which a mason dresses his stones.

skew *n* a stone forming part of the coping of the sloping part of the gable; the coping itself. *v* build a skew on. ~ **corbel**, ~ **putt**, ~ **stone** *now Kcb* the lowest stone in a gable coping.

slap, slop make a gap or break in (a wall etc) or for (a door, window etc).

slump a rough estimate.

sneck close or fill **up** (a crevice in a rubble wall) by packing smaller stones tightly between the large ones, or by filling the interstices with lime *now NE*. ~**s** small stones packed in between the larger ones in a rubble wall *NE*.

†**sparge** roughcast.

squareman a workman who regularly uses a square, *esp* a carpenter or mason *now only freemasonry*.

†**stag** support with piles *Abd*.

stane, stone: ~ **dyker** a person who builds (**drystane**) walls. ~ **and lime** masonry, masoned stone.

steid, stead lay a foundation (for), make the base (of) a building *Sh Ork*.

strik, strike make (a door or window) by knocking a hole through a wall *now Abd*.

319

stug, stog dress (stone) roughly with a pointed chisel *now EC Rox*.

suit, shuit: ~ **stock** *etc* a bevel, adjustable square *now N*.

tabling the stone coping of a wall or gable.

†**teethe** point (a wall etc) with mortar.

throu-band *local*, **thorough-band** a stone etc which goes through the whole thickness of a wall.

truan, trone 1 a trowel *now local*. **2** a tool for smoothing cement or plaster *now Fif Dnbtn*.

tuith tuil a serrated chisel or punch used for the second dressing of stones *Fif Bnf Rox*.

tusks *now local Abd-Loth*, **tusk stones** *now local Abd-Loth*, **tuskin(g) (stones)** *local NE-Edb* projecting end-stones for bonding with an adjoining wall, toothing.

upstart an upright or vertically set jamb- or reveal-stone in a window-case.

wash, wesh *v, chf* ~ **down** *or* **off** cut to a slope or bevel *now WC*. *n* a bevelled edge on a stone etc *Abd Fif*.

whigmaleerie *sometimes derog* a piece of ornamentation in stonework etc.

3.1.17 QUARRYING, BUILDING MATERIALS

blondin a cableway between two towers with a skip which can carry *eg* stone in a quarry backwards and forwards or up and down *chf Abd*.

brie-stone sandstone *now Loth Lnk*.

†**cake** a sheet or slab of metal, *esp* lead.

cauk chalk, lime.

†**claith of lede** a sheet of lead.

faik layers of shaly sandstone or limestone.

fail, feal turf as a material for building *now chf N*.

freestane freestone, a kind of easily worked sandstone *now local*.

gun *of a charge* go off without splitting the stone, blow back out of the charge hole *now Ags*.

heuch a quarry-(face) *now Ayr*.

howk quarry (stone).

†**kevel:** ~ **hammer,** ~ **mell** a large hammer for breaking stones.

kingle, kennel a kind of very hard sandstone *now Fif*.

kinsh a lever used in quarrying stones.

limestane limestone. † ~**s** pieces of limestone.

mash (hammer) a heavy two-faced hammer, used for stone-breaking etc.

pancratch a precipitate of lime forming on the

side of salt pans, formerly used for rendering or **harling** walls.

post a thick layer or seam of (particularly hard) stone, *usu* sandstone or limestone; the working face between main joints in a granite quarry *now Fif*. ~**-stone** a very hard, fine-grained sandstone *Fif*.

quarrel 1 a stone-quarry *now Per SW, also in place-names*. **2** the stone etc taken from a quarry *now N*.

†**quereour** a quarrier, a person who quarries stone.

redd waste material from a quarry etc *now local EC, S*. † ~ **bing** a mound of waste at the surface of a quarry etc *now Fif Loth*.

shoddie a natural building stone, used roughly dressed *local Inv-Ayr*.

stane, stone: ~ **knapper** a person who breaks stones *NE-S*.

swey, sway a lever, crowbar used in a quarry to raise stones *now Sh*.

tirl take the surface off (a piece of ground) for quarrying.

tirr *v* remove surface turf or soil from (ground) so as to allow quarrying for stone etc *now Bwk Rox*. *n* the layer of turf, soil etc removed from the rock of a quarry *local N-Rox*. ~**in pick, spade** *etc* one used for **tirring**.

†**win** extract by quarrying.

13.2 STRUCTURE OF BUILDINGS

13.2.1 MISCELLANEOUS STRUCTURES

backstair backstairs.

bed a level structure.

bole, bowall a small opening in a wall.

boo an arch *Abd*.

bow an arch, an arched gateway *local*.

box-ladder a narrow staircase, like a step-ladder but enclosed with wood behind and walls on both sides *now Stlg wLoth*.

†**buttereis, butterage** a buttress.

cat-steps crowsteps on a gable *Rox*.

close an **entry**, passageway, alley *orig Edb*.

common stair in a **tenement**, the communal staircase giving access to the flats etc.

coom, cowm †an arch or vault. ~**ed** vaulted, arched.

†**corbell sailȝe** a series of corbels.

corbie stanes = **crawsteps** *local*.

craw, crow: ~**steps** step-like projections up the sloping edge of a gable.

†**crownell** a stone or band forming the top of a door, pillar, etc.

cundy 1 a covered drain, the entrance to a drain *Gen except Sh Ork*. **2** a tunnel, passage *Gen except Sh Ork*.

cunyie a quoin.

entry an alley or covered passage, *usu* public, in or between houses.

†**flat** a level part of a structure.

†**forestair** an outside staircase leading to the first floor of a building.

forewa(ll) the front wall of a building.

found(s), foon(s) a foundation.

gavel a gable. ~ **end** a gable-end.

gushet the corner of a building, a corner in a building *now Ags*.

†**half gavill** one side of a gable which is common to two houses; the right to build on such *local WC*.

house, hoose: ~ **en(d)** the end or gable of a house. ~**-side** the side of a house.

jamb a projecting wing or addition to a building *now NE*.

jaw-hole, jaw-box *C Uls,* †**jawer hole** *Edb, Ayr,* **jalling stane 1** a primitive drain; *orig* a hole in the wall of a house for pouring away slops etc *now Fif midLoth Dmf*. **2** the mouth of a cesspool, a sewer *now local Abd-SW*.

kilt the slope of a stone to allow water to run off, *esp* that on a staircase.

†**knock house** the part of a building, *chf* the steeple, in which a public clock was placed.

larach a site or foundation of a building, the remains of an old building *chf NE Per*.

†**naiphouse** a dormer.

†**outjet** a projection, jutting-out part of a building. ~**ting** jutting out.

outshot *n* a projecting part of a wall or building; an extension built onto the side of a building *now local C-Uls*. *adj* projecting, protruding, bulging *now EC*.

†**pannell** a prefabricated section of wooden walling making up part of the external wall, *eg* of a house.

†**parpen (wall)** a thin wall (? *orig* of **parpen** stones) used as a partition; a partition wall of any material.

†**peatch** a piazza, an arcade.

†**pellar** a pillar.

pen(d) *n* **1** an arch, vault, the arch of a gateway etc. **2** † *also* ~ **stones** the stonework of an arch or vault. **3** *also* ~**-close** a vaulted or arched

passageway or **entry** *esp* one leading from the street into the back-court of a block of houses, *orig* running through the building, *later* between houses whether built over or not.

plat *now Ags Per Kcb,* **plettie** *Dundee* a landing on a stair.

pricket a pinnacle or small spire on a building, a pointed finial.

†**putt** a piece of masonry projecting from a wall, a buttress.

†**rag** *of a wall* develop cracks and bulges, come out of alignment *Renfr*.

rail stair a stair with a handrail *now Abd Lnk*.

riggin the top, the highest part of a wall *now local*.

†**rin, run:** ~**-wall** a light partition wall from one side of a house to the other.

roundel *now nEC, SW,* **roun(d)** a round turret.

rummle *Cai Ayr,* **rumble** *Cai Ayr,* †**trummlin** *of a drain* filled with loose stones.

scale stair a straight (as opposed to a spiral) stair.

scarcement, scarsement a horizontal ledge.

scuncheon the open finished end of a wall.

scuttle, scutter: ~ **hole** a hole in the ground, a sewage pit, drain.

shuit, shoot *of walls etc* protrude, bulge; collapse *now Ork*.

spring the rise, slope, height (of an arch) *now WC Kcb*.

stair a flight of steps or stairs leading from one floor of a building to the next, a staircase; a **common stair**. ~**heid** the landing at the top of a flight of stairs or at the top of a **common stair**. **stairfit** the foot of the staircase.

stap a step *now NE Ags Fif Rox*.

steid, stead a site, foundation, base of a building or wall *now Sh-Cai*.

tappietourie a turret, towered structure.

tour, tower *n, also* †**torne** a tower *in gen*. **toorie, ~ock** a little tower; something rising to a point *now Sh Abd*.

trap *now local,* **trap ladder** *now Ork,* **trap stair(s)** *now local N-S* a ladder, a (movable) flight of steps (leading up to a loft etc).

turn: ~**pike, tirnpike,** † ~**grese,** ~**gree,** ~**pek,** ~**pike stair** a spiral stair, a stair revolving round a central axis *now Cai Stlg WC*. † ~**pike foot** the foot of a ~**pike stair**. † ~**pike heid** the head of a ~**pike stair**.

vowt, †**volt** a vault *now Edb*.

†**wacht** a wall of a house.

wa(ll) wall. ~ **heid** the top of a wall. † ~ **rase** a wall-plate. ~ **stade** the foundation of a wall *now Sh*.

†**wattle** interwoven twigs used to form the walls of buildings. **wattlin** twigs etc which have been or can be plaited to form wattle-work.

weeper a small cross-wall between the sleeper-walls in the foundation of a house, constructed so as to direct the ventilation through the foundations and dry out condensation *EC Wgt*.

13.2.2 ROOFS

bellcast a decrease in the pitch of a roof near the eaves.

bottle a rounded piece of timber running along the ridge of a roof, over which a covering of lead or zinc is fixed *now WC*.

camceil, *also rare* **coomceil** a sloping roof *Stlg WC*. **camsiled** having a sloping roof *now WC*.

codding the last course of short slates below the roof ridge.

†**divot** thatch with turf.

easin(s) the eaves of a building.

fail, feal turf as a material for roofing *now chf N*.

†**fog** *n* moss, lichen used as thatching material. *v* thatch (a roof) with moss.

fowd worn-out thatch *N*.

gloy straw, *esp* as used for thatching *now Sh Ork Cai*.

gray slate laminated sandstone, *freq* used in roofing *now Abd Ags*.

heid, head the ridge of a house-roof.

house-heid the roof of a house *now Cai Abd Rox*.

kemple a truss of straw prepared for thatch *Cai*.

†**leid** the lead sheeting covering a roof.

pan *n, also* ~-**tree** one of a number of horizontal timbers fixed to the **couples** of a roof and running at right angles to them, a purlin *now Dmf*. †*v, chf in phrs, eg* ~ **and ruif** build a roof.

peen 1 a peak or apex, a point *now Sh Mry Ags*. **2** one of the sloping ridges at the corner of a hipped roof, where two adjacent sloping surfaces meet *now Abd C*. ~-**roof** a hipped, ridged or pavilion roof *N Loth*.

†**platform, pletform** *n, also* ~ **ruf** a flat roof; *orig also* a partially flat roof serving as a walk on top of a building. *v* provide (a building) with a flat roof or roof-walk.

ragglin(s) the space for the edges of the slates under the coping-stones of a gable.

raip, rope the ropes securing thatch *Gen except Sh Ork*.

riggin *n* the ridge of a roof; the roof itself; the materials of which it is made. *v* roof (a building).

~ **divot** a turf used as a ridge-coping for a thatched roof *chf NE*. ~-**heid** the ridge of a roof *NE nEC, WC, SW*. ~ **stane** a stone used as a ridge stone of a roof *now NE-C*. ~ **tree** the ridge-beam of a roof *now Sh Per*.

†**rin, run:** ~-**joist** a beam running along the side of a roof across the rafters to support the thatch, a purlin. ~-**roof** the roof over the main part of a building.

†**ruid, rood** *slaterwork* an area of 36 square ells or *later* yards.

ruif a roof.

sark cover the rafters of (a roof) with wooden boards, line (a roof) with wood for the slates to be nailed on. ~**ing** roof boarding.

scaddin a peat turf used for thatching.

scant a type or size of slate *Abd Per*.

sclate slate.

scraw a thin turf or sod, *esp* as used for roofing.

shouder, shoulder, shouther point (the inside joints of slating) with mortar.

simmens, simmonds ropes made of straw, heather, rushes etc, used with stone weights to hold down thatch *now Sh Ork Cai Ross*.

skew *n* a stone forming part of the coping of the sloping part of the gable; the coping itself. *v* build a **skew** on. ~ **corbel,** ~ **putt,** ~ **stone** *now Kcb* the lowest stone in a gable coping.

stapple a bundle of straw or rushes tied like a sheaf and used for thatching *now Stlg-SW*.

sting †*n* a stick with a forked iron tip used by thatchers to push straw into the roof. *v* use a **sting** in thatching; thatch with a **sting**.

stob *n* a Y-shaped stick used like a staple in thatching; a two-pronged stick used to push thatching straw into position *now NE*. *v, also* ~ **thack** *now NE* thatch with **stobs** *now Bnf*. †~**ber** a thatcher.

strae-thackit thatched with straw *now Ork NE Ags*.

†**swap thak** wooden slats used in thatching.

syle put up a ceiling over, roof *now Abd*.

†**temple** a (hazel) rod used to hold down thatch.

thack, thatch thatch. †**thack-divot, thack-turf** a roofing turf. ~ **gate** the sloping top of a gable-wall which has no coping and is overlaid by the thatch *now Sh*. **thack-pin** a wooden peg used to fasten down thatch *now Ags Per*. **thack-raip** a straw-rope used to secure thatch. **thack and raip** the thatch of a house etc and the ropes tying it down.

theek, thick *v* 1 †roof (a building) **with** (stone, slate, lead etc). 2 roof, cover (a building) **with**

(thatch). *n* thatch *now WC, SW.* ~**er** a thatcher; a roofer of houses. ~**ing spurtle** a flat-bladed implement, sometimes forked, for pushing thatching straw into position on a roof.

threave a measure of cut straw, reeds or other thatching material, consisting of two **stooks**, *usu* with twelve sheaves each but varying locally.

†**tild** a tile.

tippet a handful of stalks of straw, used in thatching *now Bnf Abd.*

tirr, turr strip or tear off (thatch, roofing etc) *now N Fif.*

undrawn *of straw* not arranged in uniform length for thatching *Sh Ork Bnf.*

wase *now Kcdn*, **wassock** *now Abd* a bundle of straw for thatching.

water barge a stone or wooden ledge on the edge of a roof etc for protection from rain.

wattles the interwoven twigs on which the turf or thatch was laid *now Per.* †**wattlin** twigs etc which have been or can be plaited to form wattle-work.

13.2.3 BEAMS

bauk a balk, a wooden beam; a crossbeam, rafter.

†**bennel** a reed or rush mat used in poorer houses to line the ceiling rafters etc *Bwk Rox.*

bougar, buggar a crossbeam in a roof; a rafter. †~ **stake** the lower part of the **bougar**, that reached to the ground in old houses *S.*

brander fix cross-strips of wood to ceiling joists to support (the ceiling) *now Ayr Kcb.*

bridle a retaining band or beam; a crossbeam supporting the ends of joists.

caber 1 a rafter, beam *now chf NE.* **2** †a side- or subsidiary rafter, one laid across the main beams and supporting the thatch.

camceil a sloping ceiling *Stlg WC.*

†**ciel** a ceiling *SW, S.*

coom, cowm the sloping part of an attic ceiling *local.* ~**ed** *of a ceiling* sloping. †**coomceil, cumsiel,** ~**-syle** furnish with an arched ceiling. **coomceiled** having a sloping ceiling.

couple, kipple *now WC-S* a pair of rafters, forming a V-shaped roof support; one of these, a principal rafter. **coupling 1** †the framing of a roof with **couples.** 2 a rafter *now Per Slk.* ~ **leg** one of a pair of rafters *now Cai Bnf Fif.*

cove ceiling an arched or vaulted ceiling *local.*

crap o the wa the space between the top of a wall and the roof of a building *now Bnf Abd Ags.*

†**cross, cors:** ~**-tailit band** a tie or connecting piece with a crossed end.

dwang a transverse piece of wood inserted between joists or posts to strengthen them.

easin(s) the angular space between the top of the side wall and the roof inside the house *now local N-Arg.*

easwas the top of the walls of a house, on which the rafters rest; the inner angle between the level top of a wall and the sloping edge of an unlined roof, often serving as a shelf *chf Cai.*

garron a wooden beam *now Ork Cai.*

†**hattyr gestis** *appar* maple beams.

hen: ~**-bauk** a tie-beam on the roof of a country cottage (so called because hens roosted there). ~**-laft** a hen-roost; the roof-joists of a house and the space above them.

hinging post one of the wooden posts supporting a roof *now Per.*

†**hoo** a roof rafter.

jeest *n* **1** a joist. **2** †a large timber beam. †*v* joist, furnish with joists. ~**ing** joisting, the timberwork, structure or furnishing of joists.

laft, loft provide (a building) with a loft by flooring joists etc. ~**ing 1** *also* †**loft** a joisted boarded ceiling. **2** furnishing with a loft or joisted ceiling.

lat a lath, *esp* one stretched across roof beams for storage *now Kcb.*

lath, †**laith** (a) lath. † ~**in(g)** (a) lath, *esp* as roof-boarding. †**lauthing** covering with laths. † ~ **brod,** ~ **bord** lath-boarding, laths collectively.

maister wood the principal beams of wood in a tenant's house-roof *Cai.*

owertree a crossbeam, lintel *now Ayr.*

pan, †**pantree** one of a number of horizontal timbers fixed to the **couples** of a roof and running at right angles to them, a purlin *now Dmf.*

rack a stay, strut *local Mry-midLoth.*

raft, raghter a rafter.

†**rantle, rannle:** ~ **tree** a roof-beam, rafter.

rib a horizontal roof-timber joining rafters *now Bnf midLoth.*

roost the open cross-joists of a cottage living room *now Sh.*

ruif, roof the ceiling of a room. ~**-tree** the main beam of a roof.

†**run-joist** a beam running along the side of a roof across the rafters to support the thatch, a purlin.

sile[1] a roof rafter or couple, *usu* one of a pair.

†**sile**[2] cover (an interior roof).

simmer a beam.

sole a sill, a supporting or strengthening beam.

†**spur band** a strut or diagonal stay in a roof.

standart, standard an upright timber, pole, post etc, a support.

stoup a wooden post, pillar, prop *now local Sh-Kcb*.

syle put up a ceiling over, roof *now Abd*.

†**sylour** a ceiling.

†**tree** a wooden rafter, beam, strut etc.

wa(ll) heid the top of a wall; the space between this and the roof-beams, used for storage.

13.2.4 DOORS, GATES

†**back:** ~**sprent** a spring or catch used as a hold or check. ~ **yett** a back gate or door.

band a hinge, fastening for a door etc *now Bnf*.

barge a slat of wood etc to protect doors etc from rain or flood-water.

†**barras ʒet** *or* **gate** *now only as place-name* a gate in or beside a barrier. *Abd*.

boss: ~**-heid** the piece of metal on a door frame into which the bolt of a lock fits *local*. † ~ **lok** a type of lock.

†**bot** a bolt.

bow an arched gateway, *freq* in names of town gateways, *eg* **Netherbow** *local*.

†**catband** an iron strap or bar for securing a door or gate.

chapper a door knocker *Bnf Abd Arg*.

check a door-key *now Stlg*.

cheek the side of a door or gate.

cleek, click a latch, a catch.

close 1 an **entry**, passageway, alley *orig Edb*. **2** the **entry** to a **tenement**, the passageway giving access to the **common stair** *chf WC, SW*. ~ **mou** the entrance to a **close**.

common stair in a **tenement** the communal staircase giving access to the flats etc.

†**condampne** block, fill up (a door etc).

†**conter-tree** a crossbar preventing a door being opened from the inside *NE*.

†**crownell** a stone or band forming the top of a door etc.

†**cruik, crook** a hook on which a door or gate is hung.

door, †**dure** a door. ~**-cheek** a door-post; a door, doorway. ~**-heid** the upper part of a door-case *now Bnf Abd Rox*. ~ **sole** *now Ork Cai*, ~**-stane** *local Sh-Fif*, ~**-thrashel** *NE* the threshold. ~**-stane** a flagstone in front of the threshold of a door *local Sh-Fif*. ~**-staple** an iron hook on the door-post to secure the bar or bolt on the inside of a door *now Bnf Ags*.

entry, †**entress** a place of entry: **1** an alley or covered passage, *usu* public, in or between houses *now Gen except Sh Ork Abd*; **2** the front doorway of a house; an entrance-lobby or porch, *latterly esp* in a block of flats *now local*; **3** the entrance to an avenue leading to a house; the avenue itself *now local NE, EC*.

†**fore entré, fore entres** a front entrance, a vestibule.

foredoor the front door of a building *now NE Fif Ayr*.

†**fore-ʒett** a front gate.

gae, go: ~ **tae** shut, close *Sh Abd SW*.

gate slap an opening, gateway *NE, SW*.

gavel *of a door* stand wide open *NE*.

†**geblet-doir** a door fitting flush with the wall *Abd*.

†**gin** a bolt, lock, latch.

†**hallan(d):** ~ **door** a door into or through the **hallan**. ~ **stane** the threshold, doorstep.

harr the hinge of a door or gate *now Sh*.

†**heck door** a hatch-door, a door divided in two horizontally.

hesp *n* a hasp, a catch or clasp. *v* fasten with a hasp, fix *Gen except Sh Ork*.

†**hirst** a threshold, door-sill.

ingang, ingate, ingaun an entrance, entry *Sh NE Ags*.

†**inlok** ? a lock inserted in a door.

kep a contrivance for checking, stopping or holding doors *now Kcb*.

knee of a staple, bend so as to form a knee-shaped angle *now Per Fif*.

†**knock** a knocker on a door or gate.

lid, led one of the leaves or halves of a double door, *freq* one enclosing a **box bed** *now Ags*.

liggat a self-closing gate *SW*.

lintel, †**lentell 1** a lintel. **2** the threshold of a door *local*.

lock, †**louk** lock. **lokkit** locked (**up**); furnished with a lock or locks. ~**fast** fastened by a lock, shut and locked, secured under lock and key against interference.

main door a door giving sole access to a private house, as opposed to a common entrance to a block of flats.

ma(i)rriage lintel *Fif Kcb*, **ma(i)rriage stone** *Bnf Fif* the lintel stone of a door bearing the initials and date of marriage (*usu* of the 17th or 18th centuries) of a couple who have set up house there.

open on, to *etc, of a door etc* face onto or towards (a place or direction).

outgang *now local Sh-EC*, **outgate** *now Sh* a way out, a means of getting out.

owertree a crossbeam, lintel *now Ayr*.

†**paddok-lok** a portable lock; a padlock.

parpen *of a door* in exact alignment, true, exactly parallel or perpendicular *now NE*.

pass: ~-**key** a key for opening a particular lock. †~-**lock** one of a set of locks which can be opened by the same key.

†**patent** *of a doorway etc* wide, unobstructed, open. **the most** ~ **door** *of a church etc* the main door, that at which public proclamations were made.

pen(d) *n, also* ~ **close** a vaulted *or* arched passageway or **entry**, *esp* one leading from the street into the back-court of a block of houses, *orig* running through the building, *later* between houses whether built over or not. ~ **gate 1** †an arched gate. **2** a gate closing the entrance to a **pend(-close)** *Ags Per*.

†**pin 1** a kind of door-knocker consisting of a vertical, serrated, metal rod fixed to the door and a ring which was drawn up and down it to produce a rattling noise. **2** the latch of a door.

pit to close (a door), sometimes with the implication of not engaging the catch.

port(s) a gateway or entrance, *esp* of a walled town or a castle *now only in place-names*.

†**postrum** a back or side door; a private door; a door or gate other than the main entrance.

pozie a narrow alleyway or passage between buildings, a **close** *now Bnf*.

rack tie the latch of (a door) so that it will not open *now Per*.

rance *n* a bar for securing a door *now Loth*. *v* make fast, close up, *esp* by wedging a bar across an opening, fasten firmly to prevent motion *now Per Loth Stlg*.

†**rest** some part of the ironwork of a gate.

†**risp** a kind of door-knocker, a **pin**.

rochel a porch, vestibule *Bnf*.

safe lintel a wooden lintel placed for additional support behind a stone lintel *Gen except Sh Ork*.

†**schyll** a sill.

scuncheon the inner edge of a door jamb.

†**shiel(d)** a keyhole plate.

shut to close (*esp* a door) properly.

slap, slop a narrow passage or lane between houses *Mry Bnf*.

slip bolt a door-bolt or sash-bolt made to slip into a cylindrical socket, a barrel-bolt.

slot, †**slote** *n* a bar or bolt *now local*. *v* bolt, lock (a door or window), secure with a bolt or bar *now local Cai-SW*.

sneck *n* a latch, catch. *v* **1** latch, fasten (**up**) with a latch etc; make (a catch) fast. **2** lock **up** *or* **in**, catch (something) **in** (a door) *now WC-Slk*. **3** *of a door* close on a latch, shut. **draw** *or* **lift a** ~

open a latch. **aff the** ~ unlatched, with the catch left off. **on the** ~ latched but not locked.

snib *v* fasten with a catch. *n* a catch, small bolt.

sole a sill, a supporting or strengthening beam in a door-case.

spar, spare *now Rox, n* **1** a wooden bolt for securing a door *now WC Wgt Rox*. **2** a bar or rail of a wooden gate *now NE*. †*v* fasten (a door or gate) with a bolt.

stainchel a bar for securing a door or gate *now WC, SW*.

stand to the wa *of a door* be wide open *Sh Ork NE-Per*.

steek *v* **1** close, shut, fasten (something), close the entry to *now local Sh-SW*. **2** shut, make fast. **3** shut, come to. *n* a clasp, a fastening *now Abd Kcdn*.

†**stekin(g)** a lock.

steeple a staple (for securing a bolt etc).

†**stekill** the bar of a door.

†**stent** ? a staple or hole for the end of a bar.

steyband a crossbar of a door; a bar to fasten the two leaves of a double door from the inside *now local Abd-Lnk*.

stoup 1 a wooden gatepost *now local Sh-Kcb*. **2** the pillar of a gateway *now Sh Abd*.

sword the crossbar in a barred gate *now Cai*.

thrashel *now Mry Abd Dnbt*, **threshwart** a threshold.

thraw turn (a key) in a lock, (a knob) on a door etc *now local N-Kcb*.

througang a passage(way), thoroughfare, lane, corridor *now Ork wLoth WC*. **througate** a passage(way), alley, lane *now wLoth WC, SW*. **throughgaun** providing access from one street, house etc to another *now C*.

tirless, †**treilʒeis** *n* **1** a trellis, a lattice, grill, grating. **2** *also* **tirlie** a barred wicket etc; a turnstile *now local*. †*v* trellis, fit with a trellis, lattice, grate.

trance a narrow passage between buildings, an alley, lane *now local Sh-Kcb*. ~ **door** the door of a passage, *esp* an inner door leading from the outside door to the kitchen of a cottage *now NE Ags WC*.

troch, trough, trochie a narrow passage between houses, a **vennel** *now Abd*.

turn, tirn: aff the ~ *of a door* at rest, still *local Abd-Ayr*: '*the door's never off the turn wi' them*'.

†**turnpike yett** a gate or door at the foot of a **turnpike stair**.

upstart an upright or vertically set jamb- or reveal-stone in a door-case.

wallie close a tiled **close**, considered a sign of social superiority *WC*.

vennel a narrow alley or lane between houses *now chf in street names.*

†**warp** *v, of a door* open **wide** *etc.*

whirly-gate *now local Fif-Ayr*, **furlin yett** *Mry Bnf* a turnstile.

wide to the wa *of a door* wide open *now Sh Ork NE.*

yett a gate. † ~ **cheek** the side-post of a gate.

◆

13.2.5 WINDOWS

For bolts etc, see 13.2.4.

astragal a glazing bar in a window.

†**barge** a slat of wood etc to protect windows etc from rain or flood-water.

boss: ~**ing** the woodwork on the recessed part on the inside of a wall below a window. † ~ **window** a bow or bay window.

brod *n* a (window) shutter. †*v* fit with shutters.

†**case** a window frame; a casing. **casit** fitted with a frame. ~ **windo(k)** a casement window.

chess a window-sash, window frame *now Ags Stlg Lnk.*

countercheck a tool for cutting the groove which unites the two sashes of a window *now Abd Kcb.*

glass, gless glass. † ~**in** *adj* made of glass, fitted with glass. *n* glazing. † ~**inwerk** glass, glazing. † ~**(in)wricht** a glazier. † ~ **band** one of the strips of metal or wood for securing the panes of glass in a window.

†**latchet** a window lattice; one of the pieces of wire or metal-work of which it was made.

ledgit the top of the lower sash of a window *NE.*

lintel, †**lentell** a lintel.

†**lokkat, lockart** a metal crossbar in a window.

lozen a pane of glass, *orig* a small diamond-shaped pane in a latticed window *now local N-WC.* ~**ed** *of a window* glazed *Mry Ags.*

†**minʒell** a monial, a mullion in a window.

mouse a small lead weight tied to a cord, used to guide cords into a sash window.

O, †**round** ~ **1** †a circular window. **2** the looped brass fitting for raising a window sash *Per WC.*

open on, to *etc* face onto or towards (a place or direction).

†**paintit** *of glass* coloured, stained. ~ **werk** stained glass.

†**pannell** a rectangular pane of glass in a mullioned window.

parpen *of a window-frame* in exact alignment, true, exactly parallel or perpendicular *now NE.*

peen a pane, a sheet of glass *now NE.*

pottie putty.

safe lintel a wooden lintel placed for additional support behind a stone lintel *Gen except Sh Ork.*

†**schyll** a sill.

scuncheon the inner edge of a window jamb.

†**shot** *n, also* ~ **window** a small opening in the wall of a house, closed by hinged shutters, sometimes with a few panes of glass at the top. ~ **hole** the opening for this.

shuts window shutters.

sole a sill, a supporting or strengthening beam in a window-case.

stainchel *n, also* **staincher** *now local* an iron bar forming part of a grating for a window etc *now SW, S.* †*v* fit (a window) with iron bars.

staincheon a stanchion *now Ork Cai Bnf.*

storm window, stormhead window *now Cai Kcb*, **stormont window** *now Cai Kcb* a projecting window with a small roof and sides, a dormer window.

tirless, †**treilʒeis** *n* a trellis, a lattice, grill, grating. †*v* **1** trellis, fit with a trellis, lattice, grate. **2 terlys** enclose in a trellis or grating.

†**wicket** a small opening or unglazed window in a wall.

window, windie *C*, **wundae** *C, S* a window. †**window-band** the hinge of a window. ~**-bole** an opening in the outer wall of a house, the lower half *freq* being unglazed, with wooden shutters *now Abd Per.* ~**-brod** *or* **-board** a window-shutter *now Abd Per.* ~**-cheek** the side of a window *NE.* ~**-chess** a window-sash *now local Sh-Lnk.* ~**-sneck** a window catch *Sh Ork NE, WC.* ~**-sole** a window-sill.

winnock, windock, †**wink** a window *now NE-WC.* ~**-bole** a **window-bole.** † ~ **brod,** ~ **bred** a **window-brod.** † ~**-bunker** a window-seat. † ~**-neuk** a window-corner. ~**-sole** a **window-sole.**

†**wire, weir** a thin metal glazing- and frame-bar in a church- or similar window.

yolk, yowk an opaque part of window glass.

13.2.6 ROOMS, STOREYS

Words for W.C. are included here although some are in fact outside toilets.

aumry, almery a cupboard, pantry.

backside the back part of a house or building.

†**barge** a kind of shutter similar to a venetian blind, used in drying-sheds.

†**bell-house** a tower etc to hold a bell or set of bells.

ben *adv, also* **there~** in or towards the inner part of a house etc; in or to the best room; inside. *prep* through (a house) towards the inner part; in or to the best room, *freq* ~ **the hoose**. *n* the inner room, the best room. ~**most** furthest in, in the second, inner room.

bole, bowall a recess in a wall, *now* one used as a cupboard.

but *prep* through (a house etc) towards the outer part *now local Bnf-Arg. adv* **1** in or towards the outer part of a house etc; into the kitchen or outer room; out. **2** *rare* into the parlour or best room *now Bnf. adj* **1** outer, outside; of the **but** *now Cai Abd Fif.* **2** of the parlour or best room *Bnf Abd. n* the kitchen or outer room, *chf* of a **but and ben**, *Gen except Edb Arg.* ~ **and ben** at opposite ends (of the same house, passage or landing). ~ **the hoose** **1** the kitchen or outer end of a **but and ben** (two-roomed cottage) *now Cai Bnf Ags.* **2** the best room *NE*.

†**cahute** a separate room or space.

†**cap almery, capburd** a cupboard. **cophous(e)** a store-room for cups or plates.

†**cape house, cap-house** a small erection on top of another building.

†**cave** a cellar, dungeon; a wine-cellar.

†**charter hous** a room for the keeping of charters.

chaumer **1** a chamber. **2** a private room, *orig* a bedroom, *latterly also* the parlour.

cludgie a W.C. *Fif Edb WC*.

crannie a recess in a wall *NE*.

†**deas, dais** a dais. **chamber of** ~ *orig* a private room (at the dais end of a hall); *latterly* a best room.

doon the hoose in the best room *SW Uls*.

dunny a basement *C*. **dunnies** the underground cellars and passages usual in old **tenement** buildings *C*.

en(d) a room, *orig* one room of a two-roomed cottage.

entry an entrance-lobby or porch, *latterly esp* in a block of flats *now local*.

†**fire room** a room with a fireplace.

first: ~ **flat**, ~ **floor** the ground floor of a building *local*.

flat **1** a floor or storey of a house. **2** a set of self-contained apartments, occupied by one family, on one floor of a house of two or more storeys.

†**flet** the inner part of a house.

†**fore entré, fore entres** a front entrance, a vestibule.

†**forechalmer** a front room.

†**forehouse** an outer apartment by which a house is entered.

†**foreshot** a projecting part of a building overhanging the street.

†**forewerk** a front portion of a building.

gaillie a garret, *esp* in a **bothy** *NE Ags*.

†**ha(ll)** the principal room of an ordinary house. ~ **chamer** a small room off a hall.

hallan(d) **1** *also* ~**-wa** an inner wall, partition, or door-screen erected between the door and the fireplace, *usu* of mud or clay mixed with stones, or moulded over a wood and straw framework *now Cai*. **2** a similar partition in a **byre** or stable, or between the living-room and the **byre**. **3** †the inside porch, passage etc formed by such a partition. ~**-end** the area between the wall of the house and the **hallan**.

heich, high **1** occupying the higher situation, raised. **2** situated in the upper part or on the upper floor of a building, **the** *or* **an** upstairs (room etc) *now Arg Ayr*.

house, *also* **hoosie** a separate portion of a building occupied by a single family etc and consisting of one or (*usu*) more rooms, with a separate door opening onto the common passage or stair, a flat. †~**ing** a canopied niche or recess in a wall.

†**ingle-en(d)** the side of a house or room where the fire is.

†**inland** the inner part of a **tenement** *Abd*.

†**inner house** an inner apartment of a building.

innery a **tenement** to which access is gained by a common passage and stair *Rox*.

†**jack** jakes, a privy.

John Gunn a privy, latrine *Bnf Abd*.

laft, loft **1** a loft. **2** *also* **loft-house** *now Uls* the upper storey of a two-storey building *Gen except S*. †~**ing** an upper storey.

laich, law situated in the lower part of a building, *eg* the ground floor or basement. ~ **house** *now Abd Fif Edb*, **laigh room** a room or rooms in the lower part of a building, *eg* a cellar. **laigh shop** a cellar in a shop; a basement shop *now Abd Fif Edb*.

little house a privy, W.C. *now local WC-Uls*.

†**lug** a hidden recess from which one might overhear the conversation in a room.

Michael, mickey *joc* a privy *now C*.

mid house **1** †the central storey(s) of a building. **2** *also* **mid-place** *now Abd* the small middle room of a **but-and-ben** *Bnf Abd*.

†**nestreis** privies, *or perh* a privy.

†**nether** the downstairs or basement (part): '*over kitching .. nedder kitching*'.

offie a privy, dry closet *local Ags-S.*

†**oratory, oratour** a study.

organ loft an organ-gallery, *esp* in a church.

outby in or towards the outer part of a room, away from the fire, nearer the door *now Sh Ork.*

outroom an outer room, *latterly specif* of a room attached to a cottage and under the same roof, but entered from the outside by a separate door *N.*

†**pairple wall** a partition, *freq* of wood or a similar light material.

pass an indoor passage or corridor *now Uls.*

pletform a platform.

press a large cupboard, *usu* one built into a recess in the wall.

rochel a porch, vestibule *Bnf.*

second, secont applied to the storey immediately above the ground floor of a building.

self-contained *orig only of houses, but latterly also of flats* having their accommodation and entrance restricted to the use of one household.

shankie a lavatory *C.*

single en(d) a one-roomed house or flat *Gen except Sh Ork.*

skiff a thin partition or screen *now NE Fif.*

†**spire-wall** a wall or screen between the fire and the door, *freq* fitted with a seat, a **hallan**.

stairfit the foot of the staircase, and the adjacent space or flat.

†**stance** a room, cell.

tenement a large building, *usu* of three or more storeys divided into **flats** for separate householders; the section of such a building served by one stair.

through: ~ **flat** a tenement **flat** with rooms facing both the front and the back *local*. **throu-gang** a passage(way), corridor *now Ork wLoth WC.*

trance a passage within a building, *esp* that connecting the two main rooms of a cottage, a lobby, corridor *now N Ags Lnk.*

tympany, timpan the gable-shaped raised middle part of the front of a house *now Abd.*

up the house into the interior of a house, from the door inwards *now Sh Ork Ags.*

†**uver, over** *in a building* upper; upstairs.

vowt, †**volt** a vault *now Edb.*

watery a W.C. *local Ork-Fif.*

wee house an earth closet, an outside closet *Gen except Sh Ork S.*

yuffie a W.C., *esp* one on a **tenement** stair.

13.2.7 FIREPLACES

auld wife a rotating chimney cowl.

backstane a broad stone or projection of a wall, at the back of a fireplace.

brace 1 †a band of stonework, wood etc used to strengthen the breast or arch of a chimney. **2** a fireplace *now Lnk.* **3** a mantelpiece *now Lnk.* **4** †a chimney made of straw and clay.

brigs the division between flues in a chimney *now local.*

can, *freq* **chimley** ~ a chimney-pot.

cat-hud the large stone used as a back to the fire on the hearth of a cottager's house.

chaffer, choffer a portable grate or stove used as a heater etc.

cheek the side of a fireplace.

chim(b)ley 1 a chimney *now local Cai-Stlg.* **2** a grate, hearth, fireplace *now Abd.* ~ **brace** *now Ayr,* ~ **heid** *local Abd-Fif* a mantelpiece. ~ **cheek** the side of the fireplace or grate *now Abd Fif.* ~ **heid** a chimneytop *local Bnf-Kcb.* ~ **lug** the fireside *now chf NE.* ~ **neuk** the chimney corner *now Cai-Fif.* ~ **rib** *a bar of a grate Abd Ags Fif.*

fire: ~ **end** the fireside, the end of a house or room where the fireplace is *local C.* ~ **stane** a hearthstone *Ork Abd.*

fore-face the front of a fireplace, consisting of an iron framework *Fif.*

grannie a chimney-cowl *now Abd S.*

greesh a stone abutment built against the gable wall inside a cottage, forming the back of the fireplace.

†**hairth** a hearth.

hinging lum a wide wooden chimney, projecting from the wall, which descended from the roof above an open fire.

hud 1 the back of an open fireplace, consisting of a stone or clay block resembling a seat *chf S.* **2** a small shelf or recess at each side of an old-fashioned fireplace, used as a hob for pots etc *Kcb Dmf Rox.* †~ **stane** the stone which forms the **hud** *SW.*

ingle an open hearth, the fireside, a chimney corner *now local Cai-Uls.* ~-**cheek** *now local Cai-Rox,* ~-**neuk** the fireside, chimney corner. ~-**stane** a hearthstone *now Per Kcb Rox.* ~-**en(d)** the side of a house or room where a fire is.

inthrow inwards, towards the fireside *now Sh.*

jamb-stane the upright of a fireplace.

†**kilchan** *Abd,* **coulichin** *Mry* a rack hung in the chimney for drying **fir-candles**.

lintel, †**lentell** a mantelpiece.

lug *chf literary* the chimney corner *now NE nEC Uls.*

lum 1 a chimney, the smoke-vent or flue of a fireplace, a chimney-stack. **2** *specif* (1) †a wood-lined opening in the ridge of the roof, for light and ventilation and the escape of smoke, less primitively having a wooden canopy suspended over the fire to serve as a smoke-vent. (2) the whole structure of a chimney and fireplace with the adjacent recesses, a chimney-piece, chimney corner *now local Sh-Kcb.* ~**mie** a chimney on fire *Ags Edb.* ~**-can** *local Sh-Per,* ~ **pig** *WC, SW* a chimney-pot. ~**-cheek** the chimney corner, fireside *Sh Ags Per Kcb.* ~**-heid,** ~**-tap** *Sh N Per Kcb* the chimney top, the part of the chimney rising above the roof.

outby in or towards the outer part of a room, away from the fire, nearer the door *now Sh Ork.*

peat, pate: ~ **bing** a heap of peats, *usu* the winter's supply, stacked against the gable of the house *Sh Bnf WC.* ~**-house** an outhouse used for storing the winter's supply of peat *now Sh Bnf.* ~**-neuk** a corner or alcove, *usu* in the kitchen, used for storing peats for immediate use *Sh-N Wgt.* ~**-ree** an enclosed recess, either inside or outside, for storing peats *local NE-Kcb.* ~**-stack** a large pile of dried peats erected out-of-doors as a fuel-store.

pig an earthenware chimney-pot *now Ayr.*

pou, pull *of a chimney etc* have a strong draught, draw *local NE-SW.*

rumford †improve the draught of (a chimney) by narrowing the vent. ~**in** a sheet of metal used as a lining or casing for the back of a fireplace *now Ags Per Slk.*

shank a chimney-stack *WC.*

stalk a chimney-stack *NE-S.*

swey, swee a movable iron bar over a fire, on which pots, kettles etc can be hung. **swee chain** the chain hanging from the **swey** *now Cai Ags.*

up *of a chimney* on fire *local Ork-Per.*

vent *n* **1** the flue of a chimney; the duct used to convey smoke out of a room. **2** the opening of a fireplace *now Sh NE.* **3** a chimney-head or -stack *now local.* *v, of a chimney, room etc* discharge or emit smoke, allow smoke to pass through or from it *now local Sh-Lnk.*

whirlie *Kcdn Lnk Rox,* **whirligig(um)** *C, S* a revolving chimney cowl.

win(d)skew a smoke-deflector in a chimney, a chimney cowl *now Ork.*

13.2.8 FITTINGS, FINISHINGS

†**baudkin, bakin** a richly embroidered cloth; a baldachin, canopy.

†**batter** paste, fasten (to a wall, together), stiffen as with paste.

†**brod** a panel painted with a picture on a coat of arms.

†**conform** *of furnishings etc* matching, in keeping with the rest.

coomceil, coomsyle lath and plaster (a ceiling).

†**curliewurlie** an elaboration, an ornamentation.

†**da** a canopy over a throne etc.

dale a shelf *now local Cai-Kcb.*

†**fyall** a finial.

graith †*v* provide with appropriate or necessary additions; ornament, decorate. *n* furnishings, effects *now local NE-Gall.*

†**grate** a grating.

†**kneed** *of a metal bar or band* having an angular bend.

†**knit** secured by a joint, welded.

†**lay** *v* paint.

†**muldry** moulded work, moulding; ornamental masonry on the cornices etc of a building, similar ornamentation in joinery.

†**muller** a frame or moulding, *chf* of wood. ~**it** furnished with a moulding or ornamental framing, framed.

†**over-fret with** *or* **of** decorated, adorned all over with.

†**overgilt** gild over; overlay **with** (gold).

owergaeing the act of working over an area etc, *eg* in painting *chf NE.*

owergang a going over, an application of something to a surface, *eg* a coat of paint *Sh NE Kcb.*

†**owerlay, overlay** paint (timber or metal).

paint, pent 1 paint. **2** the painted woodwork of a room or building, the paintwork. ~**it** painted.

†**pargen** ? cover or daub with plaster, plaster. ~**ar** a plasterer.

†**phan** a vane, a weathercock.

pike a spike (of a railing etc) *now Ork NE, EC, S.* **pikit weir** barbed wire *NE Ags.*

plaister, plaster 1 plaster. **2** †*also* **plaistirman** a plasterer.

†**plet** *of metal bars in gratings, window openings etc* set criss-cross, interwoven.

pricket a pinnacle or small spire on a building, a pointed finial.

rail fit (a stair) with a handrail *now Abd.* ~**ing** a handrail.

ravel *n* a rail, railing; a balustrade. †*v* supply or enclose with a railing. † ~**ing** railing; railings.

†**ruif** a canopy, tester.

scrim fill (a crevice, joint etc) with **scrim** (narrow widths of cloth).

†**shorn** carved.

†**sile** cover (interior walls).

skelf a shelf *now Ork Cai NE Ags.*

skifting (board) skirting-board *EC, WC, S.*

†**sparge** plaster.

†**spargen** parget, plaster.

stoothe cover (a wall etc) with lath and plaster *SW, S.*

†**tabulet** panelled.

†**teer** coat with plaster etc.

†**thane** a vane, weathercock.

torr, tore any ornamental projection *local.*

toupie *Sh,* **toupican** *NE* any high pointed object, a knob on the top of something.

truan, trone a tool for smoothing cement or plaster *now Fif Dnbtn.*

†**tyster** a tester, a canopy.

wallie porcelain, glazed earthenware or tiling; an ornament made of such *C, S.*

†**wash, wesh:** ~**ing board** skirting-board.

whigmaleerie *sometimes derog* a decorative object.

13.3 BUILDINGS

13.3.1 GENERAL, MISCELLANEOUS

†**back and fore** *esp designating a whole property* (in) back and front.

baronial, Scottish baronial applied to an ornate style of architecture characterized by numerous turrets, crow-stepped gables etc, used *esp* for 19th century country-houses and Edinburgh Old Town **tenements.**

†**beild, bould** build.

big build, construct, erect. ~**gin(g) 1** (the act of) building. **2** a building. † ~ **up 1** (re)build, repair. **2** close or block up by building.

boo a bend or curve *Abd.*

†**cast** a ditch, cutting; excavation.

clatch a badly built, clumsy structure, one unfit for use *now Ags Kcb.*

come in collapse *Fif.*

†**demoleis** demolish, pull down.

deval the amount of downward slope required by a ditch *now Sh Abd.*

drap, drip 1 the dripping of water from the eaves of a house *now Bnf-Ags Kcb.* **2** *also* **dreep** *Bnf Abd Ags Fif* the line down which water drips from the eaves *now Bnf-Ags Kcb.*

†**erd, earth: at (the)** ~ completely demolished.

†**esedrop, easing drop** the dripping of water from the eaves of a house; the space liable to receive this.

†**failzeit** in bad condition, dilapidated.

gowstie *of a building* large, bare, cheerless *now Bwk Rox.*

gutsie roomy, commodious *local Abd-Ayr.*

heich 1 occupying the higher situation, raised. **2** situated in the upper part or on the upper floor of a building, **the** *or* **an** upstairs (room etc) *now Arg Ayr.*

house-hicht the height of a house, one or more storeys *now midLoth Renfr.*

jamb an overlarge, rambling house *now NE Kcb.*

jedge, *chf and latterly only* ~ **and warrant** an order from a **Dean of Guild** specifying repairs or rebuilding (*orig also* new building) of a property.

larach a site or foundation of a building, the remains of an old building *chf NE Per.*

†**lay** build.

liner *chf Gsw,* †**lynster** *Elgin Kirkcudbright* a member of a **Dean of Guild** Court which supervised the erection or alteration of buildings in certain burghs. (**decree of) lining** permission to proceed with building after due inspection of the boundaries.

†**lodgeable** habitable.

†**mid** situated midway up a building.

owerfa: at the ~**in** on the point of falling down, very dilapidated *Abd Ags.*

pant(-well) (the mouth of) a public well, fountain etc *Bwk S.*

†**patent** *of premises, a route etc* open to all, generally accessible, public.

†**pavilzeon** a pavilion, a tent.

†**perfurnis** ? to construct.

†**policy** the improvement or development of a town, estate etc by the erection of buildings, plantation or enclosure etc, (provision of) amenity; the buildings etc involved in this.

rack a stay, strut *local Mry-midLoth.*

raible, rabble, rabblach a carelessly erected building etc, something ruinous or dilapidated *now Sh Bnf.*

rance *n* a prop, wooden post used as a stay or strut *now Mry Ags Kcb.* *v* prop up, brace, stay (a building etc) *now Fif midLoth Lnk.*

rebig rebuild *Sh Ork N.*

†**refresh** restore, renovate (a building).

†**rewyne** a ruin.

rickle 1 an old or mean building. **2** an untidy collection or huddle of buildings *now Sh Ork Abd.* **ricklie** badly-constructed, ramshackle, rickety.

rummle, rumble a badly-built piece of masonry, a ruin *Sh NE*.

sevendle strong, firm, securely built.

sit a sinking or settling down of the surface of the ground or of anything built on it *now NE*.

†**slicht** raze to the ground, demolish.

sodger, soldier a packing piece or plug, used *eg* to fill a bolt-hole *now Loth Ayr*.

†**soun(d)** test (a building) for its acoustics.

stent, stint *v, also* †**stend** pitch (a tent). † ~**er** a person who sets up tents.

†**substantious** substantial, solid

superb of noble proportions etc.

†**tect-demolished** having the roof removed.

trink a trench, channel, ditch, gutter *now NE Ags Fif*.

underwater water below the surface of the ground; water that has accumulated in the foundations of a house *now Sh Ork NE*.

†**unsufficient** unsound, insecure.

†**upbeild, upmak** *Abd* build, construct.

upbiggit built up *now Abd*.

†**upbringing, up-putting** the action of building.

wa(ll): ~ **drap** rainwater dripping from the eaves *Cai Fif wLoth*. ~**s** a roofless building, ruins *chf SW*.

†**wark 1** *also* **work** a building. **2** a building operation.

†**waste, wast** *adj* ruined; unoccupied, empty. *n* a ruin. **wasty wanes** a stripped or emptied house.

win(d) and watertight *chf of a house, esp in leases* secure against wind and rain or flood.

†**wrake** a wrecked edifice.

13.3.2 BUILDING PLOTS AND GROUNDS

aurea, aurrie an area, an open space.

back: ~**land** the back of a piece of ground. ~**side** the space, yard or fields adjoining the back part of a house or building.

big †occupy (land), *esp* by building on it; build on (land or ground). ~**git** *of land* occupied, inhabited; built on. **ill** *etc* -**biggit** (badly etc) built, constructed.

close an enclosure, courtyard *now chf Edb*.

†**foreland, foreplace** a piece of land next to the street.

†**houseste(a)d** the land on which a house is to be built, the site of a house.

kill stead, †**kill croft** the piece of ground occupied by or attached to a kiln *now Sh*.

lan(d) a holding of **burgage land**, a building site. † ~ **and tenement, tenement of** ~ a **tenement** in a burgh.

larach a site or foundation of a building, possibly with the remains of an old building *chf NE Per*.

†**mill stead** the ground and buildings comprising a mill.

onset *orig chf Ork S, latterly chf SW Uls,* †**outset** a dwelling-site, a **steading** with the dwelling-house and outhouses built on it.

outland outlying.

†**pailace** an official residence of the Scottish sovereign; the precinct of such a residence.

place an area or building customarily used for a certain (*freq* specified) purpose, *eg* **buriall** ~.

†**rig** a strip of ground leased for building in a burgh.

stance, building stance a building-site for a house etc.

steid, stead a site, foundation, base of a building or wall *now Sh-Cai*. **steadin(g)** a building site; a piece of ground on which a house or row of houses is built; the site of the buildings on a farm.

tenement land held in tenure and built on.

tron the place where the **tron** (public weighing machine) stood and the area round it; the market-place; the town centre *now in place-names in Edb Gsw*.

13.3.3 TYPES OF BUILDING

For farm buildings, see 7.2.

backland the building on the back of a piece of ground; a house built behind another.

big house the principal dwelling house of the **laird** etc on an estate.

biggin(g) a collection or cluster of houses. ~**s** subsidiary buildings on an estate, *now specif (perh also orig)* cottages.

†**black house** *or* **hut** a Hebridean or West Highland house of turf and rough stones with a thatched roof and a central fireplace on an earthen floor.

boorach a small, humble house *now Ags*.

bothy a rough hut used as temporary accommodation *eg* by shepherds, salmon-fishers, mountaineers.

buith a booth.

but and ben a two-roomed cottage.

caibin a cabin *NE Ags*.

†**chekker hous** the house occupied by the exchequer.

†**cleit** a small dry-stone structure used for drying peat and storing food on St Kilda.

†**corshous** a house standing crossways to others.

cot house, cottar house, †**cote house** a cottage.

†**crue, croy** a hovel.

cruive a hovel *now Rox*.

doocot a dovecote.

†**easements** accommodation, buildings, lodgings etc.

fa-tae a lean-to building *local NE-S*.

fire house a house with a fireplace, a dwelling-house as opposed to out-buildings *now Bnf Abd*.

fog house a small garden summer-house built or lined with mossy turf *now Abd*.

†**forebuthe** a front booth or shop.

†**forehouse** a house facing the street.

†**foreland, foreplace, foretenement** a tenement facing the street.

gaillie a **bothy** *NE Ags*.

gushet house a house standing at a corner or forming the angle between two roads.

†**hag-house** a woodshed *chf Edb*.

half house a semi-detached house *NE*.

ha(ll) a hall.

†**hallan(d)** a cottage, house.

†**heid-house** the principal house of an estate, the manor-house; the main building or great house of a manor-house group.

hole i(n) the wa a small house or apartment, *freq* in a recess between two larger buildings, and entered directly from the street, *usu* used as a shop or public house *local Abd-Dmf*.

house, hoose, *also* **hoosie** a house. ~**ing** a dwelling place *now Abd*. ~ **within itself** a **self-contained** house or flat *now Abd*.

howf a rough shelter or refuge *now Ags Stlg Renfr*.

†**hunt hall** a hunting lodge.

laich, law: ~ **house 1** †*also* **laich bigging** a lower building, *freq* one of a group, attached to a main building of several stories. **2** a one-storey building, *freq* of rural cottages *now local Ork-Gall*. † ~ **houses, laich biggings** outbuildings.

lan(d) a building erected on a holding of **burgage land,** a **tenement.** † ~ **and tenement, tenement of** ~ a **tenement** in a burgh.

lodge, ludge 1 a lodge; a porter's lodge. **2** †any shed or cabin, *eg* for storage. **3** †*mining* a pithead shed or shelter. **4** a fisherman's **bothy** *now Sh*. **lodging** a dwelling, a residential building.

lunkart a temporary shelter; a small temporary hunting lodge *now Ags*.

main door flat *or* **house** a ground-floor flat of a block of flats, which has a door to itself direct from the street.

†**maner place** a manor-house.

manse 1 †a large or stately dwelling, a mansion; the principal residence of an estate with its attached outbuildings and land. **2** the dwelling-house provided for the parish minister. **3** †a house reserved for the occupants of particular chairs at Aberdeen University.

mill, †**miln:** ~ **toon** the buildings comprising a mill; *freq* the adjacent farm or hamlet.

office a workshop, factory, shop.† ~**-hous** a workshop, an outbuilding.

onset *orig chf Ork S, latterly chf SW Uls,* †**outset** a dwelling-site, a **steading** with the dwelling-house and outhouses built on it, a small cluster of houses.

†**pack-house** a warehouse, a shed for storing merchandise.

†**pailace 1** a palace. **2** an official residence of the Scottish sovereign.

puidge a hut, a hovel.

raw, row a row of houses, *usu* of a uniform construction with common gables, *freq* applied to miners' or farm-workers' cottages; a street of such houses.

self-contained *of houses* having their accommodation and entrance restricted to the use of one household.

†**shade** a shed, a roofed structure used as a shelter or store.

†**shiel 1** *also* ~**ing** a temporary or roughly-made hut or shed, *freq* one used by (salmon) fishermen or shepherds (and their animals). **2** a small house, hovel. ~ **house** a shepherd's or fisherman's hut.

single end a one-roomed house or flat *Gen except Sh Ork*.

†**sit house** a residence, a dwelling-house, *esp* on a farm.

slate, sclate: ~ **house** a house with a slate roof *now Sh Ags*.

tae, to: ~**-fall** a lean-to porch or outhouse *now local Sh-SW*.

tenement a large building, *usu* of three or more storeys divided into **flats** for separate householders; the section of such a building served by one stair.

thack, thatch: ~ **house** a thatched house.

through house a house whose rooms lead off one another, with no lobby *Fif Ayr Dmf*.

tour, tower 1 *also* †**torne** a tower *in gen*. **2** used in names of **tower houses:** '*Smailholm Tower*'. **toorie,** ~**ock** a little tower *now Sh Abd*. **tower**

house, †tour house a high tower *orig* used both as a residence and for defence (mostly built between the fourteenth and sixteenth centuries), a **peel**.

†trades hall a meeting house of the **trades** in a burgh.

tron the place or building where the **tron** stood and the area round it *now in place-names in Edb Gsw*.

†wark, work a public or imposing building.

white house a house built with stone and lime as opposed to a **black house** *Cai Hebrides Highl*.

within itself *of a house* not shared in its accommodation, **self-contained** *now NE*.

13.3.4 ANCIENT MONUMENTS

†Arthuris hufe, Arthur's Oon an ancient monument near the Roman Wall at Falkirk, demolished 1743, traditionally associated with King Arthur, so called because of it oven-like shape.

barp a chambered cairn *Hebrides*.

broch a late prehistoric structure (dating *chf* from the first century BC and the first two centuries AD), found *chf* in Ork and Sh, the Western Isles and the adjacent Scottish mainland, consisting of a large round tower with hollow stone-built walls; popularly but erroneously supposed to have been built by the Picts; *now in general use as an archaeological term*.

crannog *now archaeol* an ancient lake dwelling.

dun a small stone-walled defensive homestead of the iron age, *freq* situated on an isolated site, found *chf* in western and central Scotland; in general use as an archaeological term.

erd, earth: ~-house a building with earthen walls; *latterly* an Iron-Age underground walled dwelling etc.

Giant's Grave popular name for the ruins of a neolithic chambered tomb *local*.

†Grimes Dyke, Grahame's Dike the Antonine Wall.

†Julius Hoff name for a round building that stood near Carron.

pecht, pict: ~s' house an underground dwelling, a **weem** or earth house, *chf* dating from the first two centuries AD *Sh Ork N*.

rath a circular earthwork, a defensive homestead or settlement *freq in place-names*.

roundabout a circular prehistoric fort *now Ayr Rox*.

†Scots dyke an earthwork (built in the late 16th century) along part of the Scottish-English border.

wag name for the remains of Iron Age houses in Cai.

weem an Iron Age underground storehouse, *chf* in the form of a curved slab-lined passageway *chf Sh Abd Ags*.

13.3.5 CASTLES ETC

†allouring the stone pavement placed behind the battlements of a hall etc.

†bailȝe a bailey, the (upper or lower) court of a castle.

†barmekin, barnekin a battlement, battlemented wall; a wall of defence.

†barras ȝet or gate *(Abd) now only as place-name* a gate in or beside a barrier.

†barrere a barrier.

†barteshing, bartisan a battlement, parapet.

†bastailȝe, bastle a bastille, a fortified tower; a siege-tower.

†bertisse a brattice, breastwork, parapet.

†brig a drawbridge.

†cave a cellar, dungeon.

†forth a fort.

†forteres, fortrace a fortress.

†foussie, fowsie *n* a ditch. *v* provide or surround (a wall, piece of land etc) with a ditch.

†house a stronghold, a castle.

†kirnell 1 a crenel, a notch in a battlement. 2 ~s battlements.

†machcolin(g) machicolations.

†maiden castle name for Edinburgh Castle.

†manteel wall a curtain- or outer wall, a rampart, a screen wall.

†massymore the dungeon of a castle *chf literary*.

†mote a tidal moat which encircled Kircudbright town.

peel a defensive palisade or stockade; the ground enclosed by such; a fortified house or small defensive tower, ? *orig* one built within a palisade (*chf* in the Border counties of both England and Scotland), *latterly hist*, also in place-names as **P~ of X**. † ~-house a fortified dwelling or refuge.

†portculȝeis a portcullis.

†stacket a palisade.

stank *n* a moat. *v* surround with a moat.

tour, tower 1 *also* †torne a tower *in gen*. 2 used in names of *tower houses*: 'Smailholm *Tower*'. **tower house, †tour house** a high tower *orig* used both as a residence and for defence (mostly built between the fourteenth and sixteenth centuries), a **peel**.

†**turnpek** a turnpike, a spiked barrier.

†**wall toun** a walled or fortified town.

†**weir wall** a rampart.

yett *archaeol* a kind of door made of interlacing iron bars.

13.3.6 CHURCH BUILDINGS

†**aisle** an enclosed and covered burial place, adjoining a church, though not a part of it.

†**arch** an ark.

bauks a church gallery *now Loth*.

†**bell house** a tower etc to hold a bell or set of bells.

bottom room, boddom breadth *now Bnf Abd Ags* the amount of space necessary for a person to sit in a church pew.

†**boucht** a square pew in a church.

box-seat a square pew in a church *now Ags Lnk*.

breist, breast the desk board of a pew *Abd Ags*. ~**-seat** the front seat in the gallery of a church *Bnf Abd*. ~ **o the laft** the front of the gallery in a church.

buik, book: ~ **buird** a bookshelf in a pew, pulpit etc *now local NE-Lnk*.

chaipel, chapel 1 a chapel. **2** a Roman Catholic or (*local*) a Scottish Episcopalian church.

†**chancellar** belonging to the chancel of a church.

cock laft the gallery in a church.

cross, corse a cross. ~ **kirk 1** †a transept. **2** a church founded because of a cross.

dask, desk a seat or pew in a church *now local Ork-Lnk*.

deas, dais *n* a desk or pew in a church. †*v* provide with a dais, seats or benches.

†**fit, fute, foot:** ~ **gang** a length of plank flooring to walk on between church pews.

forebreist (o the loft) *now local N-EC*, **front-breist** the front (seat) of the gallery in a church.

†**foredask** a desk or pew in a front position in a church.

†**foreseat** a front seat; *specif* a seat or bench forming the front part of an enclosed pew.

kirk a church. ~ **door** the church door. †~ **house** a house belonging to or adjoining a church. †~ **stile** a stile or narrow entrance to a churchyard. ~ **toun** *chf* the town or village in which the parish church is situated *freq in place-*

names. ~**yaird** a churchyard. †~ **werk** building work on a church.

knock laft a clock loft or gallery in a church *now Fif*.

laft, loft a gallery in a church *Gen except S*.

lamp of Lothian name *orig* for the medieval church of the Franciscan Priory in Haddington, *now* for the tower of the parish church.

lettern, lateron 1 a lectern. **2** the desk of the reader or **precentor** in post-Reformation churches.

Lowrie name given to the great bell of a church, *freq* one dedicated to St Lawrence.

manse the dwelling-house provided for the parish minister.

organ loft an organ-gallery, *esp* in a church.

pass, pace the passage between the pews in a church, an aisle *now NE*.

†**patent: the most** ~ **door** *of a church etc* the main door, that at which public proclamations were made.

pumphal a kind of square church pew, with a seat or bench round the inside, entered by a door or gate and with a small table in the centre *now NE*.

pupit a pulpit.

queir a choir, *chf* a chancel; *latterly* a pre-Reformation cruciform church or its ruin.

range *NE*, †**reenge** *Fif* the seat(s) in a church just below the pulpit, used by the elders etc.

†**room** seating space for one in a church pew.

†**ruid altar** an altar of the Holy Cross.

session house the room in or attached to a church, in which the **kirk session** meets.

soundin box a canopy etc over a pulpit to bounce the speaker's voice out into the congregation *now Sh Ags Per*.

†**tent** a movable pulpit (with steps and canopy) erected in the open air, *esp* at half-yearly Communion services when the congregation was too large for the church.

trance an aisle in a church.

Tron Church *or* **Kirk** name of a church standing near the site of the **tron** *Edb Gsw*.

†**wire, weir** a thin metal glazing- and frame-bar in a church-window.

yaird, yird a churchyard *now Ork NE, C*.

13.3.7 KILNS

chaffer, choffer a portable grate or stove used in a corn-kiln.

ingle a kiln-fire *now Ork Cai Kcb*.

kill, kiln 1 a kiln. 2 †a lime-kiln. ~ **barn** a barn attached to or containing a kiln *now Ork*. ~ **door** the steps up to the entrance to a kiln *now Sh*. ~ **ee** the open space in front of a kiln fireplace *local*. ~ **head** the roof of a kiln, also forming the floor of the drying chamber on which the grain is spread to dry *now Sh*. ~ **plate** one of the perforated metal plates forming the surface of the drying floor in present-day kilns *local Ork-Dmf*. ~ **pot** the heating chamber under a corn-kiln *chf Sh*. ~ **rib** one of the small movable wooden bars laid across the kiln joists to support the bed of straw on the drying floor *now Sh*. ~ **stick(le)** *now Sh*, ~ **tree** *now Sh Ork* one of the beams which support the drying floor.

†**simmer** a beam or joist in the floor of a corn-kiln.

sornie the flue from the fireplace to the underside of the drying platform of a kiln; the fireplace itself *Cai*.

14. RELIGION, SUPERSTITION, EDUCATION, FESTIVALS

14.1 RELIGION

14.1.1 FAITH, BELIEFS

†**bill: burn one's** ~ perform an act of recantation.

†**braid benisoun** *or* **malisoun** full blessing or curse.

†**cauldrife** lacking in religious zeal.

†**devote** devout, pious.

Elfin *eupemistic* Hell.

†**faggot: burn (one's)** ~(**s**) renounce heresy.

far ben in favour with God *now local*.

halie, holy holy. †~ **blude** the blood of Christ or of a saint. †~ **gast(e), halie ghoist** the Holy Ghost. †~ **spreit, ~sprit(e)** the Holy Spirit.

†**heid** a separate item of a statement of religious belief, an article (of faith).

†**hele** spiritual well-being, salvation.

†**there:** ~ **awa(y)** on this earth, in this life. ~ **doun** here below, here in this world.

†**herrie** harrow (hell); lay waste (heaven).

†**thevin impyre** the empyrean, the highest heaven.

hindmaist, hindmost: ~ **day** the Day of Judgement *now local*.

†**huil, hull** the body as the container of the soul.

hyne from this world, from this life.

ill pa(i)rt Hell *now NE*.

†**illustratioun** (spiritual) enlightenment.

judgement-like characteristic of divine displeasure, appearing to threaten divine retribution, awful.

laich, low: ~ **road** the road below the earth along which the dead were supposed to travel.

land: the ~ **of the leal** the land of the faithful, Heaven.

†**lavatoure** the spiritual cleansing of baptism.

†**law wark** theology based on Mosaic law, implying formal morality rather than evangelical religion.

†**legal** *of a preacher or his doctrine* stressing Old Testament law and salvation by works rather than justification by faith.

low a spiritual glow, a state of ardour or excitement, a blaze of feeling.

mairtyr a martyr. ~**dom,** †**martyry** martyrdom.

†**mak, make** commit (a crime, fault or sin).

†**malison** *n* a malediction, curse. *v* curse.

†**matron** as the distinctive designation of a married female saint, *esp* St Anne.

†**medicine** a spiritual remedy.

†**merito(u)r** meritory, *esp* serving to earn reward from God.

†**michts** divine powers or influence.

†**middle-erd** the world, viewed as half-way between heaven and hell.

†**mirkness** spiritual darkness, unenlightenment.

mistak do wrong, transgress *now Ork Ags*.

muckle hell the depths of hell *now Sh*.

†**neck break** one's downfall, or a cause of this; a stumbling block.

†**novatioun** a (*chf* wrongful or undesirable) change or innovation in religious doctrine or polity.

†**novator** one who makes wrongful or undesirable changes in religious matters.

†**obsolve** absolve.

†**oecumenick** ecumenical.

†**outbreaking** a breaking out into sin.

†**outgate** a way out of *esp* a moral or spiritual problem.

†**pine** the pains of Hell *latterly ballad*.

place: the bad ~ *NE*, **the ill** ~ *now Sh* Hell. **the guid** ~ Heaven *now Sh*.

†**pot (of) hell** hell.

†**preveen** *of God's grace* prevent, go before with spiritual guidance.

professor a person who makes open profession of religious faith, an acknowledged adherent of some religious doctrine.

†**pruifs, proofs** scriptural texts used as proof or illustration of the doctrines in the catechisms, *esp* those of the **Shorter Catechism** printed as a schoolbook.

†**rademe** *v* redeem. *n* the act of redeeming.

releegion religion.

†**restauration** the reinstatement of man in divine favour.

ruid the rood, the cross of Christ.

sain *v* **1** *also* **sene** protect from harm by a ritual sign, *esp* by making the sign of the cross, consecrate, bless: *with the hand etc or with an object;* cross oneself, protect oneself from harm by prayer. **2** bless, call down blessings on (*esp* as a sign of gratitude). *n* a blessing, a gesture or invocation of goodwill and good fortune. (**God**) ~ .. (God) bless..!

saul *now local Sh-SW*, **sowl** a soul. ~**ful** enough to fill the soul.

saunt, †sanct a saint.

†saynd the act of sending, a message, gift, God's ordinance; a messenger.

shak, shake shake the faith of (a person).

sin: † ~ **guilt** an act of sinning. ~ **one's soul** incur the guilt of sin (*esp* by telling lies) *local Sh-Kcb*.

speerit, spreit spirit.

†support spiritual help.

Tarnty Trinity *now in place-names*.

†terreall earthly, terrestial, mundane.

†tinsal perdition, damnation.

†tryst *of God, fate etc* appoint, ordain (a person's lot), arrange for; bless **with**; visit **with** (misfortune).

†ubiquiter a ubiquitarian.

†unfaithful not in accordance with faith, irreligious.

†unhovin unbaptized.

†untreuthfull unbelieving, infidel.

voo vow.

†wary *of God, the Church etc* pronounce a formal curse against. **weriour** a person who curses.

14.1.2 RELIGIOUS ATTITUDES

begotted bigoted.

†devote devout, pious.

gospel greedy regularly attending church, fond of church-going *now Stlg Kcb Uls*.

gracie full of spiritual grace, devout, virtuous.

guid, good: ~**ly** godly, pious *now NE Ags*. † ~**lyheid** *verse* godliness, sanctity. **goody-good** goody-goody *now Ags*.

halie holy.

kirk: ~**ie** enthusiastically devoted to church affairs *local*. (**not**) ~ **greedy** (not) zealous in attendance at church *NE-S*. ~ **reekit** bigoted. **ride (on) the rigging o the** ~ be an excessive partisan of one's own church *N Fif SW*.

left abandoned (by God's grace), left to follow one's own foolish or sinful devices.

†lele faithful in religion; Christian.

†lese-majesty treason in relation to God.

lip labour *freq of prayer* empty or useless talk *now Sh*.

†manswear swear falsely or blasphemously by (a god).

nairra, narrow: ~-**nebbit** bigoted, *esp* in religious matters, strict.

†outgate a way out of *esp* a moral or spiritual problem; a solution.

†penalité a troubled state of mind due to an awareness of the weakness of human nature and sin.

†pieté godliness, devoutness, reverence.

†pietuous pious.

regaird, regard: ~**less** heedless of religious practices, irreligious *now Sh Cai*.

releegious religious.

saint, saunt, †sanct play the saint.

†sairie, sorry serious, solemn.

sanctitude holiness, sanctity.

†sappie unctuous, over-full of fervour.

shak, shake shake the faith of (a person).

†sinistrous erroneous, perverse, heretical.

†solem(p)niouslie solemnly. **solem(p)nit, solennit** solemn.

stoup a loyal enthusiastic supporter, a 'pillar' (of a church) *now local Sh-WC*.

Sunday('s) face a solemn, somewhat sanctimonious look.

thirled hidebound by an idea, belief etc.

threap a vehemently held opinion etc, an aggressive assertion of one's beliefs etc *now N nEC*. ~ **down someone's throat** *etc,* (**up**)**on** *etc* **someone** force one's opinion(s) on someone, try to make someone believe ..

unco: the ~ **guid** *chf literary (after Burns)* the self-righteously moral or pious.

†unfaithful not in accordance with faith, irreligious.

warsle, wrestle, wrastle *now Sh* a mental or moral struggle *local Sh-Per*.

14.1.3 GOD

almichty, †almichtine Almighty.

best: the B ~ Providence, God *chf Ork*.

guid, good: (**the**) **G** ~, **the** ~ **man** *child's word* God. **guidness** God, *freq* by ~**ness**.

†la(i)rd Christ.

michty the Almighty *now Sh Kcb*.

†wy(e): the ~ God.

14.1.4 THE DEVIL

auld *in names for the Devil:* '*Auld Nick*', '*The Auld Ane*'.

Bobbie: auld ∼ the Devil *now Abd.*

Carle: the Auld ∼ the Devil *Bnf Abd Ags Fif.*

Chield: the Auld ∼ the Devil *now Abd Fif.*

Cloot: (auld) ∼**(s), auld** ∼**ie** the Devil.

deil, deevil the Devil.

deviltry devilry *now local Bnf-Kcb.*

earl o Hell the Devil *Sh C, S.*

enemy, †**inimy: the** ∼ the Devil.

fient a fiend.

foul: the ∼ **thief** the Devil *now Sh.*

Hornie, *chf* **Auld** ∼ nickname for the Devil.

ill: the ∼ **man** the Devil.

lad: the auld (black) ∼ the Devil *now Loth Uls.*

†**lees: the father of the** ∼ the Devil.

†**little guid** the Devil.

†**Mahoun** name for the Devil.

man: the Auld M∼ *now local Ork-Ags Uls,* **the bad** ∼**, the black** ∼ *local,* **the guid** ∼ *familiar* the Devil.

†**member** an agent or 'limb' of Satan.

†**mishanter: the** ∼**, Auld M**∼ *in imprecations* the Devil.

muckle, meikle, mickle: ∼ **deil** the Devil, Satan *now Sh Loth Gall.*

Nick, Auld ∼**,** ∼**ie-ben,** † ∼**ie** the Devil.

Ruffie cant or slang name for the Devil *now Ayr.*

Sandie, *freq* **auld** ∼ the Devil, Satan.

Sawtan, Sathan Satan, the Devil.

Sim, *chf in dim* **Sim(m)ie** *joc* name for the Devil.

smith: the auld ∼ the Devil *NE.*

sorra, sorrow (the) Devil *now local Sh-Wgt.*

Suitie: Auld ∼ the Devil *local Bnf-Rox.*

tary *freq in imprecations* the Devil *NE.*

teind to hell a tribute or price required of his minions by the Devil.

thief, teef *Sh Ork, freq* **the auld, black** *etc* ∼ the Devil, Satan *now Sh Ork.*

thrummy (caip) the Devil *NE.*

†**waghorn** a character in fable, the greatest of all liars; the Devil himself.

wee man the Devil, *chf* **in the name o the wee man!** *local.*

†**wirricow** the Devil.

14.1.5 ORDERS, SECTS

†**Antiburgher** a member of that section of the **Secession Church** which separated in the early eighteenth century from the rest of the mem-bership over the question of taking the **burgess oath**.

†**Associate** in titles of various sects of the **Secession Church,** *eg* ∼ **Presbytery, General** ∼ **Church**.

†**Bereans** a Protestant sect.

Billy *slang* a Protestant, Orangeman *Gsw.*

blue nose *contemptuous term used by Roman Catholics* a Protestant *Fif WC.*

†**Bourignonism** the emotional and visionary religious doctrines of Antoinette Bourignon, a seventeenth-century French mystic, popular among the Episcopalians and Jacobites of the North East in the early eighteenth century.

†**Buchanite** one of a fanatical religious sect, founded by Mrs Buchan, the wife of a Glasgow dyer *SW.*

†**Burgher** a member of that section of the **Secession Church** which upheld the lawfulness of the **burgess oath**.

†**burgess oath** the oath required of anyone wishing to become a burgess in the major **royal burghs**; there was bitter dispute in the eighteenth century between the **Burgher** and **Antiburgher Seceders** as to whether or not it required the swearer to uphold the Established Church, and thus whether or not it could be sworn with good conscience.

Cameronian 1 †a follower of Richard Cameron, the **Covenanter**; a member of the **Reformed Presbyterian Church**. **2** a soldier in the Cameronian Regiment (Scottish Rifles) raised in 1689 among the **Cameronians** or **Whigs** in the west of Scotland in support of William of Orange; *now* represented only in the Territorial Army.

†**charterour** a Carthusian.

Church of Scotland title of the established reformed church in Scotland, for most of its history presbyterian.

†**Cisteus** Cistercian(s).

†**congregatioun** the body of those forming the Protestant party at and after the Reformation.

†**covenant:** *n* **the C**∼ the National Covenant (1638) *or* the Solemn League and Covenant (1643). *v* be a supporter of either of these, *chf as* **C**∼**er, C**∼**ing. non-**∼**er** one who did not support the **covenant**.

†**Culdee, Kildé** a Culdee, a member of an ascetic religious movement in the Celtic Church.

Dan(nie boy) nickname for a Roman Catholic *WC.*

†**Disruption: the** ∼ the split which took place in the Established Church of Scotland in 1843

when 450 of its 1200 ministers formed themselves into the **Free Church**.

dook baptize as a Baptist *Ags Stlg*.

English Episcopal, Episcopalian

Episcopaulian Episcopalian.

field: † ~ **conventicle** a meeting of **Covenanters** in the open air *Gall*. ~ **preaching** *local*, † ~ **meeting** a religious service held in the open air, a relic of **Covenanting** times, still surviving in special commemorative services.

†**Forty: the** ~ (**Thieves**) a group of ministers in the **Synod** of Glasgow who withdrew their support from the **Disruption** as it became imminent and tried to find a compromise.

free: the F ~ = **Free** or **United Free Church**; a member of these churches. **F** ~ **Church (of Scotland), F** ~ **Kirk** name: 1 †adopted by the body which broke away from the Established Church at the **Disruption**; 2 now applied to the minority which refused to enter the union with the **United Presbyterian Church** in 1900. **F** ~ **Presbyterian, F.P.** *esp wHighl* a member of the body which seceded from the **Free Church of Scotland** in 1892. **wee** ~ *derog* a member of the **Free Kirk** 2.

†**General Associate Synod** that section of the **Secession Church** which refused to take the **burgess oath**, the **Antiburgers**.

†**gentle: the** ~ **persuasion** the Episcopalian denomination, adhered to by many of the upper classes *NE*.

†**Glasite** a member of the religious sect founded by the Rev. John Glas (1693-1773); later known as a **Sandemanian**.

†**gray sisteris** nuns of the third order of St Francis.

†**Green Tables = table**.

†**Haldan(e)ite** a follower of the brothers Robert and James Haldane, leaders of an early nineteenth-century Scottish evangelical movement, now represented partly by the Congregational and partly by the Bapist Church in Scotland.

†**high-flyer** name for a member of the Evangelical Church party, the successors of the **Covenanters**, as opposed to a **Moderate**.

†**hill:** 1 ~ **folk** name given *orig* to the **Covenanters** of *c*.1670-1688 who worshipped secretly in the hills because of persecution, and later to their successors, the **Reformed** Presbyterian Church. 2 one of the ~ **folk**.

†**Howdenite** *appar* a follower of John Halden, an extreme **Covenanter**.

†**keeper** a person who conducts or is present at a conventicle.

†**killing-time(s)** name for the period of the greatest persecution of the **Covenanters** in 1685, later extended to cover the whole period 1679-1688.

kirk 1 †*esp* before the Reformation, applied to the Roman Catholic Church, in Scotland and beyond. 2 after the Reformation, applied to the reformed church in Scotland both when episcopalian and when presbyterian in organization; since the late seventeenth century largely replaced by **church** in most formal contexts, but reappearing in recent years, *usu* as **the Kirk**, in all contexts except the official title **Church of Scotland**. (the) **Auld K** ~ the established Church of Scotland as opposed to other presbyterian denominations, *esp* after the **Disruption**. **K** ~ **of Scotland** title of the established reformed church in Scotland.

†**league:** The Solemn League and Covenant.

left-fitter disparaging name (used by Protestants) for a Roman Catholic *C*.

†**lele** faithful in religion; Christian.

licht, light: auld ~, **new** ~ 1 †the moderate or more latitudinarian element (**new** ~) as opposed to the stricter conservative and evangelical section (**auld** ~) of the Church of Scotland. 2 the two corresponding groups which split both branches of the **Secession Church**, the **Burghers** in 1799 and the **Antiburghers** in 1806, the **New Lichts** from both combining in 1820 to form the **United Secession Church** and the **Auld Lichts** in 1842 to form the **Synod of Original Seceders**.

†**lifters** *in the Secession church* the group which approved of the minister raising the communion elements before consecrating them *Ayr*.

†**lord (of) Sanct John(is)** Preceptor of the Knights Hospitallers of St John.

†**loun-minister** applied by the **Covenanters** to a minister who accepted the episcopalian and royalist regime.

†**Macmillanite** a follower of Rev John Mac-Millan of Balmaghie, Kcb, a **Cameronian**.

†**malignant** used by the **Covenanters** of their adversaries. ~ **kirk, kirk** ~ church malignant (applied to the Roman Church by the early Protestants).

†**Marrow** short for *The Marrow of Modern Divinity* by E Fisher, whose strongly Calvinistic doctrines were condemned by the **General** Assembly in 1720, a prolonged controversy ensuing. ~**-folk,** ~**-men** supporters of these doctrines.

†**martyr** one of those who suffered death in the seventeenth century in the cause of spiritual

independence as set forth in the National **Covenant** or in the Solemn League and **Covenant**. ~('s) **stone** *etc* a stone marking the grave of a **martyr**.

missionar a member of an Independent church.

†moderate *adj* applied to the less rigorously Calvinist party in the **Church of Scotland**. *n* a member of the **Moderate** party in the **Church of Scotland**. **moderation** the principles of the **moderate** party of the Church.

†Morisonian a follower of the Rev James Morison of Kilmarnock, who was suspended from his charge in 1841 for opposition to certain Calvinist doctrines and later founded the Evangelical Union.

†mountain: ~ **men,** ~ **folk** *etc* the persecuted **Covenanters** (1670-88) who took refuge in the mountains, *esp* of Galloway; the **Macmillanites**.

†Negative Confession the King's Confession, or Second Confession of Faith (1580-1).

†non-conform nonconformist (applied to dissenting ministers of the Presbyterian party during the Restoration period).

†Original Seceder a member of the church formed in 1842 by the reuniting of the **Burgher** and **Antiburgher** elements in the **Auld Licht** church, now merged with the **Church of Scotland**.

†out referring to **the Disruption** of 1843: having left the established Church for the **Free Church**.

†outstander a person who opposed the National **Covenant** or its adherents.

paip *derog* a member of the Roman Catholic Church *chf WC*. **papery,** popery *now Ayr Kcb*. **papish, †papisher** *chf derog* a Roman Catholic, a papist. **†papist** papistical, popish.

†Pend Folk a small religious sect, of Baptist principles, taking its name from its meeting-house in a **pend-close** in the High Street of Paisley.

†persecuting time(s) the worst period of the persecution of the **Covenanters**.

piskie *colloq* a member of the Scottish Episcopal Church.

†prioressy a nunnery or convent presided over by a prioress.

Prod(die) *contemptuous, local C Uls*, **prodistan** *Gsw, Uls* a protestant.

†profession a religious system or sect.

†Protesters the name given to those Presbyterians who opposed union with the Royalist party in 1650.

†qualify acquire or give legal sanction to by the taking or administration of an oath, *specif* in

regard to the Scottish Episcopalians who until 1792 were not permitted to practise their faith until they renounced allegiance to the Jacobite monarchy. **qualified chapel** *etc* an Episcopalian Chapel etc whose members had renounced allegiance to the Jacobite monarchy.

†raible mob, assault with overwhelming numbers (*specif* an Episcopalian clergyman by a hostile Presbyterian congregation, after the Revolution settlement of 1688-89).

rector a clergyman in charge of a full congregation of the Scottish Episcopal Church.

Reformed Presbyterian Church the church (or any of its courts) descending from those **Covenanters** who continued to oppose the Revolution Settlement after 1688 and who consider themselves to be the surviving remnant of the true **Covenanted Kirk**; most of them joined with the **Free Church** in 1876 and only a few congregations remain. **Reformer** a member of the **Reformed Presbyterian Church**.

†relief freedom from ecclesiastical oppression, *esp* with reference to the eighteenth-century controversy in the **Church of Scotland** led by Thomas Gillespie, concerning the right of a congregation to elect its own minister; this led to the formation of the **Relief Church**.

†reliever a member of the **Relief Church**.

†religion members of a religious order.

†remnant name (used by themselves) for the extreme **Covenanters** who refused to accept the Revolution Settlement of 1688, *esp* members of the **Societies**, the **Macmillanites**, the **Reformed Presbyterian Church**.

†residuary *chf derog after the* **Disruption**: pertaining to the Established Church of Scotland.

†Resolutioner one of the church party which, in opposition to the **Protesters**, supported the **engagement**.

†Sandemanian a member of a religious body organized from the **Glasites**.

†scoloc *Celtic church, orig* the first-born son of a monastic tenant, given to the church to receive an ecclesiastical education; *later* any monastic tenant.

Scots: † ~ **Confession** the 1560 Confession of Faith of the reformed Scottish Church, the first published document of the Scottish Reformation. **Scottish Episcopal** a member of the Scottish Episcopal Church. **†old ~ Episcopal** an adherent of that branch of the church which had been proscribed for its Jacobitism and whose clergy were not **qualified**.

secede in reference to the **secession**. **Seceder 1** a member of any of the branches of the **Secession Church**. 2 a member of the **Free Presbyterian** Church *Highl Hebrides*. **secession** the departure from the **Church of Scotland** in 1732 by a group of ministers led by Ebenezer and Ralph Erskine; *chf* **Secession Church**, the church formed after this event; the term was first used officially in 1820 in the title **United Secession Church**.

†**Societies, Societies-Men** *etc* name for certain groups of Presbyterians who refused to recognize the 1679 Indulgence and 1688 Revolution Settlement, and who later united under the leadership of the Rev John Macmillan to form what became the **Reformed Presbyterian Church**.

†**Tables** the four boards or committees, consisting of representatives of nobles, ministers, **lairds** and burgesses which framed the National **Covenant**.

†**templary** an estate or benefice belonging to the Knights Templar.

temple-land land belonging to the Knights Templar and as such not subject to **teinds** *now only in place-names*.

†**test** the oath or declaration prescribed by the Test Act of 1681, aimed at imposing on the extreme **Covenanters** compliance with Episcopacy in the **Church of Scotland**.

†**thumbikins** a thumbscrew used to torture **Covenanters** during the 1680s.

†**true blue** (of) a seventeenth century **Covenanter** (from their chosen colour, the blue of the St Andrew flag); *hence* (of) any staunch or devoted Presbyterian; (of) a supporter of the **Whigs** of the seventeenth and eighteenth centuries.

†**tulchan** a substitute, a person appointed nominally to some office, the power and emoluments being diverted to another; *specif* one of the bishops created by Regent Morton in 1572 to enable him and his supporters to appropriate Church revenues.

†**Twa-penny Faith: The** ~ popular name for Archbishop Hamilton's tract *Ane Godlie Exhortatioun* published in 1559.

†**unconform** non-conforming. ~**ist** non-conformist.

United in titles of Presbyterian churches which united or reunited after schisms and separations: †~ **Associate Synod (of the Secession Church)**, ~ **Secession Church** name taken by the **New Licht** parties in the **Burgher** and **Antiburgher** branches of the **Original**

Seceders on their reunion in 1820. ~ **Free (Church** *or* **Kirk), U.F. 1** (1) †the church formed by the union in 1900 of the majority of the members of the **Free Church of Scotland** with the ~ **Presbyterian Church**, the majority of whose members later (1929) joined the Church of Scotland. (2) *also* **Continuing** ~ **Free Church** the minority group of members of the ~ **Free Church** who did not rejoin the Church of Scotland in 1929. **2** *also* **U.F.** a member of 1 (1) or (2). ~ **Presbyterian Church, U.P. 1** the church formed in 1847 by the union of the **United Associate Synod** and the **Relief Church**. **2** *also* **U.P.** a member of that church. †~ **Secession Church** = ~ **Associate Synod**.

†**wark, work** a religious revival; *specif* the evangelical campaign at Cambuslang in 1742.

†**whig** nickname for an adherent of the **National Covenant** of 1638 and hence of Presbyterianism in the seventeenth century, later applied to the **Covenanters** of South-West Scotland who rose in arms in the reigns of Charles II and James II. **whig(g)ing** playing the part of a **whig** adhering to Presbyterian and anti-Jacobite principles.

†**whiggamore** a **Covenanter**, *orig* one who participated in the Whiggamore Raid of 1648, a Presbyterian of the 17th century, a **whig**.

whistle kirk a church with an organ, *freq specif* an Episcopalian Church since they favoured the use of church organs in contrast to the Presbyterians *now literary*.

†**Wiclefit** a Wycliffite, a follower of Wycliffe.

†**wild** nickname for the extreme Evangelical party in the **Church of Scotland**.

†**withdrawer** a person who did not conform to the established church.

†**yellow stick: the religion** *etc* **of the** ~ enforced Presbyterianism on the island of Rhum in the eighteenth and early nineteenth centuries.

14.1.6 CHURCH ADMINISTRATION AND INSTITUTIONS

For church finance and for offences and punishments, see 14.1.7.

†**abbacy** the office or dignity of an abbot; an abbey.

adherent a (*usu* young) person who attends the services but but is not in full communion.

†**archedene, ersedene** an archdeacon.

†**archibischop** an archbishop.

†**archidiacone** an archdeacon.

†**archpriestrie** the office of head priest (at Dunbar).

assembly 1 †a meeting of a congregation or **kirk session. 2** the **General Assembly.**

†**almosar, almessar** an almoner.

beadle, †**beddal, bedrall, pedell** an officer in the service of an ecclesiastical organisation etc; **a kirk officer.**

bishop, †**beschop** a bishop. † ~**rie** a bishopric.

black coat taboo term for a clergyman, minister *ECoast.*

†**bow** a bull, a papal seal or letter.

buik, book record the names of (a betrothed couple) in the register of the **session clerk** before marriage *Bnf Abd Ags.*

ca(ll): be ~**ed to a church** be invited formally by a congregation to be its minister.

†**capellane** a chaplain.

†**chaipel** an ecclesiastical chancellery.

†**channery, chanounrie** a canonry.

†**chapterly** *adj* having or belonging to an ecclesiastical chapter. *adv, also* **cheptourly** as a chapter, in full chapter, *freq* ~ **gadderit.**

†**cheplane** a chaplain. ~**ry, chaplanry** a chaplaincy.

†**cheptour** a chapter.

church officer = kirk officer.

city name for some of the (*esp* larger) burghs which were or had been episcopal seats.

†**class** a **presbytery,** *specif* when meeting for religious exercises and study *Ayr.*

†**collationate** put in possession **of** or appointed **to** (a benefice).

commissioner a member of the **General Assembly** of any of the Scottish Presbyterian Churches.

†**curat** a curate.

deacon, †**diacon 1** a deacon. **2** one of the laymen or -women elected and ordained to manage the temporal affairs, of a congregation. **D** ~**s' Court** a committee which runs a congregation's temporal affairs, consisting of the minister(s), elders and **deacons.**

†**dane** a dean with local designation, as ~ **of Glasgow** *etc.*

†**degraduat** deposed, degraded.

deliverance the findings or decisions of the **General Assembly** or other church court on a report from a committee or special commission.

†**dewar** the hereditary keeper of a relic of a (Celtic) saint, *esp* a bell or staff, *latterly also a personal name.*

†**diet** a church meeting for worship or business *Inv Abd.*

†**diocesie, diocie** a diocese.

†**Book of Discipline** either of two books adopted in 1560 and 1581 respectively, laying down the constitution of the Reformed Church and also dealing with education.

disjoin detach or separate (one church or parish from another).

disjunction the disjoining or dividing up (of parishes).

†**dominie** a clergyman.

†**ebdomadare** a member of a college or chapter taking a weekly turn in performing the services in the church.

elder a person elected and ordained to take part in church government as a member of the ecclesiastical courts, *eg* the **kirk session,** who does not have who does not have the authority to teach, *freq (though now less freq)* called **ruling** ~, in contrast to minister or **teaching** ~; only men up to 1966, thereafter also women. ~**ship 1** the office of **elder. 2** the **kirk session** of a church. **3** †an assembly composed of **ministers** and **elders** of a number of parishes.

†**elect** a bishop elect.

†**enunte** anointed.

exerceese, exercise a **presbytery.**

†**exhortar** a person appointed to give religious exhortation under a minister.

†**expectant** the prospective occupier of a post, *esp church* a candidate for the ministry, a **probabtioner.**

fathers and brethren the members of the **General Assembly** or of the **Synods** *or* **Presbyteries.**

General Assembly *in the Presbyterian Churches* the highest church court as represented by delegate ministers and elders assembled annually, *chf* in Edinburgh, and presided over by a **Moderator.**

†**gorbie: God's** ~ a clergyman.

†**granitar** an official, *esp* of a religious house, in charge of a granary.

halie, holy: † ~ **band** the **kirk session.** ~ **hoose** a church. † ~ **kirk** = Holy Church, the corporate church. †**in (the) face** *etc* **of** ~ **kirk** within the Church. †**in** ~ **kirk** in a church.

Hall: the (Divinity) ~ one of the theological colleges of the **Church of Scotland** or of one of the **Free Churches.**

heich, high: ~ **kirk** the principal church in a town or region, *eg* St Giles in Edinburgh.

helper, helpender *now Abd* a minister's assistant.

herd, hird a spiritual guide, a pastor.

†**hostilary, ostillary** lodging etc provided as a right to a church dignitary; a lodging belonging to a monastic community.

†**immediat** *of ecclesiastical rank* directly, without intermediary.

†**inbuke** enter in a book, record, enrol.

induct *Presbyterian Churches* install (an ordained minister) in a charge. ~**ion** the act of installing an ordained minister in a charge, and *in gen* the ceremonial service which takes place.

†**indult** a special privilege, licence or permission, *esp* one granted by the Pope.

†**intrant** a person who enters the ministry of a church or a new charge.

†**intrude** thrust oneself or another into any benefice or church living to which the intruder is regarded as having no claim, *esp* against the wishes of the congregation. **intrusion** the **presentation** and (forcible) introduction of a minister to a charge against the wishes of the congregation.

†**irregular** a disobedient or disqualified ecclesiastic.

jus devolutum the right of **presenting** a minister to a congregation, which falls to the **presbytery**, if the charge has remained vacant for six months.

kirk 1 church. **2** †the ruling body or **kirk session** of a local church. **3** †the **General Assembly** of the **Church of Scotland**. ~**less** *of a minister* without a church *now local Sh-Loth.* ~ **book** an offical record book of a church *now Ork Kcb.* ~ **door** a chuch door, *specif* the place where various public ceremonies were performed, *orig* baptisms and marriages, *later esp* acts of repentance; also used for the collection of offerings, reading of proclamations etc. ~ **man**, †**man of** ~ an ecclesiastic *now Sh Ork.* † ~ **master 1** *also* **maister of the** ~**-werk** the official appointed by the burgh etc to take charge of the upkeep of the church building. **2** a church treasurer or deacon appointed by the **kirk session**. **3** a paid **kirk officer** appointed by the burgh. **4** an elected officer of a craft or the merchant guild responsible for the upkeep of the fraternity's altar and chaplaincy in the parish church *Edb Gsw.* ~ **officer,** † ~ **bedell** *now usu* anglicized as **church officer**, a paid official with the job of keeping order in the church and parish, attending the **kirk session**, and carrying out its edicts; a **beadle.** ~ **session** *Presbyterian churches* the lowest court, consisting of the ministers and elders of the congregation and exercising its function of church government within a parish.

†**laich kirk** a church which is not the chief church in a town.

lair a burial place or grave, *specif* a burial space reserved for a person or family in a graveyard or church.

lamp of Lothian name *orig* for the medieval church of the Franciscan Priory in Haddington, *now* for the tower of the parish church.

†**lawic** lay, not of the clergy.

†**layit** lay, of the laity.

†**lerit** educated; *hence* belonging to the clergy.

licence, leeshence *n* the permission granted after examination to a divinity student by a **Presbytery** to preach and become a **probationer** available to be called to a ministerial charge, *corresponding to Eng* holy orders. *v* grant a **licence to.**

†**leid, laid** the leaden seal of a papal bull, **under the** ~.

licentiate †*v* = **licence**. *n* a person who has been **licensed**.

†**life: successive .. in thare** ~ *of papal successions* (each) in his own (successive) lifetime or reign, in succession.

lift one's lines withdraw formally from the communicant membership of a certain congregation.

†**lite** a bishop-elect.

lord: L~ **(High Commissioner),** † ~**is commissionaris** the representative(s) of the sovereign, *formerly* (till 1707) in the Scottish Parliament, *also* in the **General Assembly.** † ~**s of the clergy** the Bishops as the ecclesiastical estate in the post-Reformation parliament.

†**lowse** release (a minister) from his charge.

Maister, Master, †**Mes** prefixed to the Christian name and surname, of a clergyman. †**Mes John** *freq joc* name for a (*chf* **Presbyterian**) **minister** or for ministers as a class.

manager a member of a board of management of the temporal affairs of certain Presbyterian churches, *eg* of **quoad sacra** churches and of the former **United Presbyterian Church.**

minister a clergyman, *esp* of the **Church of Scotland. ministry 1** the profession of minister, *esp* of the Church of Scotland. **2** the ministers of the Church, the clergy. **3** †the minister and elders of a congregation as a court of the Church; the **kirk session.** ~**'s man** the manservant of a minister, *freq* also in country parishes performing the duties of **church officer.**

missionar an itinerant evangelical preacher *now NE Ags Uls.*

missionary a lay preacher, *esp* in the **Free** and **F.P. Churches** *now Hebrides Highl*.

moderate preside over, act as chairman of (any of the courts of the Presbyterian Churches). †**moderation** the office of a **moderator**. **moderator** the minister who presides over a Presbyterian church court, *specif* **the Moderator** the minister chosen to preside (*now specif* for one year) over the **General Assembly** of the **Church of Scotland** and to perform certain ceremonial duties. ~ (**in**) **a call** *of a presbytery*, preside over the election and **induction** of a minister to a vacant charge.

†**Non** a person who disagrees with the policy of **intrusion** *chf Abd Ags*.

†**oeconomus, iconomus** the steward or manager of property and finances of a religious house.

officer an official of any ecclesiastical court, or similar body whose duty is to keep order at meetings, deliver messages, summonses etc.

one: 121 informal name for the offices of the Church of Scotland since 1929 situated at 121 George Street, Edinburgh.

†**oratour** a person who offers up prayers for another: **1** applied by the sovereign to members of the clergy; **2** applied by petitioners to themselves as praying for the person addressed (*freq* the sovereign); **3** a person whose duty or employment it is to pray on another's behalf, *chf* a chaplain, a bedesman.

ordeen ordain.

ordain admit (an elder or deacon) to office.

†**order** *Reformed Church* a scheme for territorial reorganization or for the regular and settled provision of ministers' **stipends**.

†**ordinar** a person who invests or ordains (an ecclesiastic).

†**outed** *of a clergyman from his parish* ejected, turned out.

overture a proposal or call for legislation brought before a higher church court by a lower body, *usu* made by a **presbytery** to the **General Assembly**.

paip a pope.

pairish, parish 1 a parish. **2** the inhabitants of a parish. †**parochin** *latterly chf literary* **1** a parish. **2** the inhabitants or members of a parish. †**parochinar, pareeshioner** a parishioner, a member or inhabitant of a parish. †**parochial visitation** a periodical inspection, by the **Presbytery** of the religious affairs of a parish. †**parish school, parochial school** one of the schools set up by the **Church of Scotland** to provide instruction in the rudiments of edu-

cation and in Latin, and to equip promising pupils for University entrance.

†**paper minister** *or* **priest** *derog* a minister or priest who read his sermon; this was looked on as a sign of lack of inspiration or real conviction.

†**parliamentary church** *or* **parish** one of a number of **quoad sacra** churches or their parishes, *esp* in the Highlands and Islands created by Acts of Parliament in 1810 and 1824.

†**parochy** a parish.

†**patent: the most** ~ **door** *of a church etc* the main door, that at which public proclamations were made.

†**pawns** a sum of money deposited with the **kirk session** by a couple as a guarantee of their intention to marry within forty days and of their chaste conduct in the interval.

†**pendicle** an ecclesiastical dependency.

†**person** a parson.

place settle a **probationer** in his first charge; *occas* induct (an ordained minister) to a new charge. ~**d minister** *etc* an ordained or practising clergyman in charge of a parish or congregation.

†**plant** *v* provide (a church etc) **with** a minister; appoint (a minister) to a charge. *n* the action of appointing a minister; the action of supplying a church with an incumbent.

†**plat, plot 1** a scheme of the actual or proposed distribution of churches and arrangements for their supply, within a particular area or over a limited period. **2** the scheme for the reorganization on the Presbyterian system of the post-Reformation church, *esp* in regard to parishes and **stipends**. **3** *also* **Commission of Plat** the body which implemented and administered this scheme, *later (1617)* replaced by the **Commission of Teinds**.

†**pleban** a rural dean *Pbls*.

†**postulat** *n* a person nominated *eg* to a bishopric, although canonically disqualified, while awaiting a papal dispensation of the impediment. *adj* nominated and awaiting papal sanction as above.

preach in conduct a service to welcome (a minister) to a new charge after his **induction**.

†**prebendar** a prebendary.

†**precept** a written authorization issued by an individual or corporate body to make a payment from funds, *freq* in reference to payments made by the **kirk sessions** to the poor.

†**prelot** prelate.

Presbyterian applied to a system in which the church is governed by elders.

presbytery *in the Presbyterian churches* **1** an ecclesiastical court above the **kirk session** and below the **synod** consisting of the minister and one **ruling elder** from each parish or congregation within a designated area. **2** the area represented by and under the jurisdiction of a **presbytery**, one of the units of organization in the **Church of Scotland**. **presbyterial** of or belonging to a **presbytery** or its functions.

†**prescriver** a prescriber, one who appoints or ordains.

†**present** put forward the name of (a **licensed probationer** or minister) to the **presbytery** so that he may be approved for admission to a parish. ~**ation** the action of **presenting**.

†**primacy** the ecclesiastical province or see of a primate.

Primus *Scottish Episcopal Church* the bishop chosen by his colleagues to be the president of their episcopal meetings, but without metropolitan or special authority.

†**privy censures** a meeting of a **kirk session** or **presbytery** at which each member was examined separately and questions were put to his fellow-members about his church duties and his behaviour in his private life.

probabtion: ~**ary** relating to a **probationer**. ~**er** a student minister during the period between his **licensing** and his ordination.

†**proportion** the district assigned to an elder for visiting etc, a **quarter**.

†**provincial** a provincial synod.

provost *Scottish Episcopal Church* the minister of a cathedral church.

†**publican** an excommunicated person.

†**puir's box** a collecting box for poor relief kept by the **kirk session**; the poor fund itself.

purge check or verify (the roll of communicants in a congregation) by removing the names of lapsed members.

quarter one of the areas, *orig* a fourth part, into which burghs and parishes were divided for administrative purposes, *esp* for poor relief and the distribution of elders' duties.

quoad omnia 1 applied to a parish which combined secular as well as ecclesiastical functions. **2** *of a church constitution* in which the **kirk session** is responsible for all matters and which does not allocate secular functions to a congregational board.

quoad sacra applied to a parish which functions for religious purposes only, created by statute because the existing parish became too large for a single minister; the original parish remained the unit for civil administration until such mat-

ters were transferred to other local government bodies.

†**repone** restore (a deposed minister) to his charge.

†**repose** = **repone**. **reposition** the restoration of a person to an office or to rights from which he has been deposed, *esp* the reinstatement of a clergyman.

†**riding commission** *or* **committee** a committee appointed to examine the causes of rejection of a candidate by a **presbytery** or congregation, and to override these if they are found to be insufficient.

ruling elder a person who has been ordained as an elder, *strictly* any elder, *but in practice* one who is not a minister.

sang scule a school attached to a church, for the teaching of (*chf* ecclesiastical) singing and music *local*.

sattle, settle install (a minister) formally in a charge; provide (a vacant parish) with a minister. ~**ment** the placing of a minister in a charge.

†**saul hird** a shepherd of souls.

seat †name for the **kirk session**. ~ **rent** the rent paid for the use of a seat in church.

†**sederunt** a meeting of the **General Assembly** or other court of the Presbyterian Churches.

†**segstar** a sexton.

†**segyrstane** the sacristan in a religious house.

†**senzie** a synod, deliberative meeting of clergy.

session = **kirk session**. ~**al** relating to or administered by the **kirk session**. †~**er** a member of a **kirk session**. ~ **book** the minutebook and register of a **kirk session**. ~ **clerk** the clerk or secretary of a **kirk session**.

†**spiritual** an ecclesiastic or cleric. **spirituality** ecclesiastical property etc received for spiritual services.

†**stallar** a vicar who served in a cathedral. ~**y** the office of a **stallar**.

†**stibbler** a **probationer** in the Presbyterian church not yet in a **settled** charge, who preaches here and there as required.

†**subsynod** a division of a **synod**.

†**superintendence** a body of **superintendents**.

†**superintendent** a minister appointed to supervise the administration of the newly-reformed Church in a particular district.

sustain *of a church court, specif a presbytery* give formal approval to (a call from a congregation to a new minister).

†**sustentation fund** *Free Church of Scotland, in the Presbyterian churches* a fund for the support of the ministry.

synod a court intermediate between the **Pres-**

bytery and the **General Assembly**; in the smaller churches with no **General Assembly** the **synod** is the supreme court. † ~**al** a synodal assembly, a synod.

†**territorial** of a church (*esp* in a large town) serving an area not coterminous with the parish.

†**testificate** a solemn declaration of fact or belief put in writing, a certificate, testimonial, *esp* a character reference, issued by a minister or **kirk session** to a person applying for membership of another church.

†**theologue** a theologian; a theological student.

†**ticket** a Communion **token** *Ags Ayr*.

†**token, taiken 1** a metal badge worn by beggars to indicate a right to beg within a parish. **2** a small piece of stamped metal used as a pass to the Communion service in a Presbyterian (and sometimes in an Episcopal) church (now replaced by a printed card).

translate transfer (a minister) from one charge to another. **translation** the act or procedure of **translating**.

transport 1 = **translate**. **2** remove (a congregation) to a different part of a parish or to a different parish. †**act of ~ability** a formal permission granted by a **presbytery** to one of its ministers to accept a call from another congregation if **presented**. ~**able** enabled to be **transported** in this way. † ~**ation** the act of **transporting**.

trial(s) the examinations of a **probationer** by a **Presbytery** before he is **licenced** as a preacher.

†**vaik** of an ecclesiastical office or position, fall vacant; remain vacant, unfilled.

†**Veto Act** an act passed by the **General Assembly** in 1834, providing that no minister should be **presented** to a parish against the wish of the congregation; the precipitating cause of the **Disruption**.

†**vicar** the church **precentor** who was given the **vicarage teinds** as his salary *Peebles*.

†**vice** applied to the right to **present** a minister to a parish where the patronage was shared by two or more **heritors** who exercised their right in turn.

young communicant a person intending to become a communicant member of a Presbyterian Church, who *usu* attends an instruction class.

14.1.7 CHURCH LAW AND FINANCE

Includes offences against church discipline and their punishment; church courts are in 14.1.6. Includes church finances of property as well as assignment of payment to clergy, benefices etc.

†**annat, ann(a)** the first half-year's (*or orig* year's) income of a benefice legally due to the executors of the deceased previous incumbent.

†**assume** levy, collect as a due (from ecclesiatical property). **assumption** the collecting **of** (the **thirds of benefices**).

augmentation an increase in the amount of a periodical payment, *eg* a minister's **stipend**, rent.

†**barrat: ~our** a person who obtained benefices by underhand means. ~**ry** the crime, by an ecclesiastic, of corrupt purchase of benefices.

Barrier Act an act passed by the **General Assembly** of the Church of Scotland in 1697, which provided that acts involving an important change in church law must be approved by the **presbyteries** as well as by the **General Assembly**.

†**collectorie** that part of the royal revenue derived from the collection of the **thirds of benefices**.

†**commend: in ~** *of a benefice* to be held by a bishop etc (in additon to his own preferment) or by a layman. **commendatare, commendatour** a holder of a benefice **in commend**.

†**commissar 1** a commissary, delegate, representative. **2** a civil official taking the place of the former ecclesiastical diocesan commissary, *freq* C~ **of Lanark, Edinburgh** *etc*.

†**commissariat** the office, jurisdiction or court of a **commissar**; the district included in such jurisdiction.

†**compear** appear **before** a congregation, *esp* for rebuke.

†**consistoré, const(e)rie** a consistory, *specif* a bishop's court or the later **commissar** court. **consistorial** *orig* pertaining to or competent before a **consistoré**.

constitute give legal or official form to (an assembly) *latterly chf church*.

†**coursable** legal, fulfilling normal legal procedure, *esp* **coursable brevis of one's** *or* **the chapel**.

†**creepie** the **stool of repentance**.

†**croce-present** a gift due to the clergy from the goods of a householder on his death and burial.

†**cutty stool** = **creepie**.

†**dale, dele** an ecclesiastical division of land.

†**debar** exclude formally from Communion (those guilty of certain sins).

†**delate** accuse, denounce **for** or **of** (an offence) or **as** (an offender) later esp to a **kirk session** or **presbytery**.

†**denunce** proclaim as condemned by the church.

†**design** bestow, grant (**manses** and **glebes** for the clergy). ~**ation** assigning as above.

†**dulapse** a second offence against church discipline.

edict a legally authoritative public **intimation** from the pulpit. ~**al citation** law and church a citation made by **edict**, now by sending copies of the summons to the **Keeper of E** ~**al Citations**. ~**ally** by means of an **edict** or **edictal citation**.

†**erd-silver** payment for burial-ground.

†**erection** after the Reformation the creation of a temporal lordship out of a spiritual benefice; the lordship so created.

fama a report of scandalous behaviour, chf against a minister or **probationer**.

fama clamosa a widely-circulating rumour of scandalous behaviour usu by a minister or **probationer**.

fauter a wrongdoer, specif one who offends against Church discipline.

†**fiar(s)** the price(s) of grain for the year, used to determine ministers' **stipends**, latterly fixed in spring by the local **sheriff** in the **Fiars Court**. **strike (the)** ~ fix these amounts.

†**forloppin** freq of monks, friars or priests runaway, renegade.

glebe, glibe the portion of land assigned to a parish minister in addition to his **stipend**.

†**gravatour** a letter from the official of an ecclesiastical court censuring a person found guilty of an attempt to defraud or to escape due payment.

†**heritor** in parochial law a proprietor of land or houses formerly liable to payment of public burdens connected with the parish, including administration of the poor, schools, and upkeep of church property. **heretrice, heretrix** a female **heritor**.

instrument n a formal narrative, duly authenticated, of any proceedings of which a person wishes to preserve a record, latterly chf with a view to protesting or appealing against them. †v register a protest against (a person) by means of an **instrument**. † ~**ary witness** one who witnesses the signing of an **instrument**. **ask, take** etc ~**s** request, obtain etc an **instrument**.

†**judicatory** chf church a court of judicature in church or state, a tribunal having judicial authority.

kirk land church land, a **glebe** now local Sh-Ayr.

†**kow** a cow given as a payment to the clergy on the death and burial of a householder.

†**letters of cursing** a warrant issued by a decree of the pre-Reformation church courts excommunicating a stubborn offender.

libel n a charge against a person in an ecclesiastical court. v make a formal charge against.

local †adj, of stipends assigned parish by parish out of the ecclesiastical revenues of each, esp out of the **teinds** of lands within each parish. v assign (a parochial **stipend** or **augmentation**) out of the **teinds** or other ecclesiastical revenues of parish; apportion the liability for payment of the same among the **heritors**. † ~**ity** 1 the authoritative apportioning of liability for payment of **local stipend** or **augmentation** of **stipend** among the **heritors** or other possessors of the **teinds** of lands lying within the parish. 2 the liability thus apportioned for payment of (an increase in) a parish minister's **stipend**. 3 such a **stipend**. †**decree** or **decreet of** ~**ity** the decision of the **Commission of Teinds** confirming the allocation of liability as in **locality** 1. †**locallie** (assigned, paid) as **local stipend** or as appointed by a **decreet of locality**.

†**Lord of Erection** = **titular**.

†**mala fama** a report of bad behaviour, in cases of church discipline.

manse a dwelling house provided for the parish minister.

†**mensal** applied to a church or benefice the revenues of which were appropriated to the bishopric, ? orig for the maintenance of the bishop's table.

†**modify** determine the amount of (a parish minister's) **stipend**. **modifiar** a person who prescribed the amount of a minister's **stipend**. **modification** the assessment of a minister's **stipend**.

†**monitioun** 1 a formal charge or warning by an ecclesiastical authority to a backslider to amend. 2 a formal charge or injunction by an ecclesiastical judge that a certain action be carried out or refrained from, or that the terms of a contract be adhered to.

†**monitour** a monitory, a missive setting out a formal charge or injunction of an ecclesiastical judge; the charge or injunction itself.

†**mortify** assign or bequeath in perpetuity (lands, property or money) to an ecclesiastical or other body or institution.

†**offerand(s)** Church offerings, *esp* as viewed as part of the regular income of a church or benefice.

†**ordinar, ordinary:** ~**is lettres** letters from an ecclesiastical ordinary, *eg* a bishop. **ordinar letters, letters** ~ a decree from an ecclesiastical court.

†**parsonage = parsonage teinds.**

†**Pasch(e) finis** collective term for a certain payment made at Easter in local churches.

†**patrimonial** constituting part of the patrimony of a bishopric.

†**pawns** a sum of money deposited with the **Kirk Session** by a couple as a guarantee of their intention to marry within forty days and of their chaste conduct in the interval.

†**penitent stuil = stool of repentance.**

†**pensionar** the recipient of a pension from an ecclesiastical benefice; a beneficed person.

†**pensionary** an ecclesiastical benefice which pays out a pension.

†**pillar** a pillar in a church or street regarded as a place of public repentance, punishment etc; a raised platform on which wrongdoers were ordered to appear publicly at specified times.

†**pittance silver** the revenue from a bequest or endowment, *orig* given to a religious house to make additional provision of food, wine etc for the religious on special occasions.

procurator an **advocate** appointed as official advisor in legal matters to the **General Assembly.**

proven rental a scheme of a minister's rental proved in a process of **augmentation.**

†**quadrulapse** a fourth offence against church discipline.

†**quart** ? the fourth part of the great tithes.

†**quot, cote** the share (one twentieth) of the **moveable** estate of a deceased person due to the bishop of his diocese.

†**relapse** (a person) having twice offended against church discipline.

†**repent: place of** ~**ance** the area of a church where penitents stood to be rebuked. ~**ance stool, stool of** ~**ance,** ~**ing stool** a seat in a prominent place in a church, *usu* in front of the pulpit, on which offenders, *esp* against chastity, sat to be rebuked.

†**royal bounty** an annual payment made by the Crown to the **Church of Scotland** for the promotion of religion in Highlands and Islands.

†**sack:** ~**en** *of the penitential garment* made of sackcloth. ~**brab,** ~ **goun** a sackcloth garment worn when doing public penance.

†**Sanct Nicholas bischop** a boy bishop elected for a festival of choirboys or schoolboys on or following St Nicholas Day.

†**searcher** a church elder or other official appointed to look out for and report to the **kirk session** any absences from divine service, disorderly behaviour etc.

†**seizer = searcher.**

†**session** summon or take before the **kirk session** for offences against church discipline. **be** ~**ed** *of a betrothed couple* be called before the **kirk session** to record their intention to marry and to lay down their **pawns.** ~ **box** the box or chest containing the church funds, *esp* those to be distributed as charity.

†**sheriff('s) fiars = fiars.**

†**spur silver** money paid to choristers in certain privileged chapels by anyone entering with spurs on.

†**stage** bring (a person) to trial before a court, *esp* a church court. **bring to** *or* **keep on the** ~ bring to *or* prolong a trial before a church court.

stipend, steepend the salary of a Presbyterian minister.

†**stuill = stuil of repentance.**

†**surrender** *n* the submission of tithes to the Crown. *v* submit (tithes) to the Crown. ~**er** a person who surrenders tithes to the Crown.

teind, †**tein** *n, chf* ~**s** an allocation of a tenth of the produce of a parish for the support of religion, after the Reformation expropriated by the Crown and granted to landowners; *now* an amount, in 1925 standardized (on the average **fiar's prices** from 1875-1925), payable by the owner to the **Church of Scotland** and used as part of the parish minister's **stipend.** *v* tithe, take the **teind** of (crops etc); assess for **teind.** †~ **barn** a tithe barn. †~ **corn,** ~ **fish** *etc* corn, fish etc paid as **teind** or sometimes cash paid in lieu. †~ **free** exempt from payment of **teind.** †~ **sheaf, drawn** ~ every tenth sheaf, paid as **teind.** †~ **silver** money paid as **teind** in lieu of goods. **Clerk of T**~**s, T**~ **Clerk** the principal clerk to the **Court of Teinds. Commission(ers) of T**~**s,** †**Court of T**~**s, T**~ **Court** the names (at various dates) of the body administering the **teinds,** since 1707 as part of the **Court of Session. exhausted** ~**s** the **valued teind** already used in its entirety for payment of the minister's **stipend** and thus with no surplus left to provide an increase. **free** ~**, unexhausted** ~ that part of the **teind** not yet allocated to the minister's **stipend. great** ~**s, parsonage** ~**s,** †**personage** ~**s** that part of

the **teind** of a parish formerly due to the parson.
†**small** ~s, **vicarage** ~s: teinds taken from produce other than grain, *orig* paid to the vicar of a parish. **valued** ~ the **teind** assessed by a less variable method than crop-size, *eg* the value of the land, etc.

†**thrids** *or* **thirds** (**of benefices**) a third of the ecclesiastical revenues, collected by the Crown and used in particular to ensure adequate pay for the reformed clergy.

†**titular** (**of the teinds**) a layman to whom, after the Reformation, the Crown transferred the title to church lands, *more specif* to the tithes of church benefices, a **Lord of Erection**.

†**trilapse** *adj, of person* guilty of a **trilapse**; *of the offence* occurring for the third time. *n* a third offence against church discipline, *esp* fornication. **trelapser** a person who is guilty of a **trilapse**.

†**vicar** a layman who claimed the title of the **vicarage teinds** as his salary *Peebles*.

vicarage 1 †a benefice attached to a parsonage. **2** the lesser **teinds** reserved for the actual incumbent of a parish, and exacted only by custom, not by law.

†**victual stipend** that part of a minister's **stipend** formerly paid in grain or the cash equivalent thereof.

†**visie, vesy** punish (a sin etc).

14.1.8 CHURCH PRACTICES, SERVICES IN GENERAL

†**absolʒe** absolve.

†**add** make an **addition** to the **exercise**. ~**er** a person who makes the **addition** to the **exercise**. ~**ition** a discourse made after the **exercise**.

†**administrate** administer (a sacrament or oath).

†**anniversar** a mass said annually on the anniversary of a person's death; payment for this.

†**assoilzie** absolve.

†**bairn, barne** a child at school or in a choir; a schoolboy or chorister.

band a (church) choir.

†**beteach** commit, commend, *esp* **to** (God or the Devil).

†**blasphematioun** blaspheming; blasphemy.

bliss bless.

†**bodily** by a corporal oath. ~ **athe** *or* **faith** a corporal oath.

†**bone** a prayer; the thing prayed for.

borrow ransom, redeem, release (a person's soul).

buik, book 1 the Bible. **2** the reading of the Bible,

family worship *now local*. **tak the B**~(**s**) hold family worship *now local*.

carritch(es) the catechism *now local Abd Kcb*. **mither's** ~ a simplified form of the **Shorter Catechism**.

catecheese catechize.

catechis 1 a or the catechism *now Bnf Abd Stlg*. **2** catechizing *now Bnf Abd*.

cauld, cold: ~ **morality** a sermon lacking fervour.

†**cod** a support or bearing for a bell.

†**commandiment** commandment.

comman(d)s the ten commandments *now local*.

†**common head** an exercise or discourse on a general point.

†**coup** set (a church-bell).

diet *now Abd Arg Kcb*, ~ **of worship** *now local Abd-Kcb* a church service. †~ **of examination** a meeting held in a house by a minister to examine the religious knowledge of the residents of a district.

†**dishaunt** cease to frequent, stay away from (*esp* a church or religious services).

edict a legally authoritative public **intimation** from the pulpit.

Effectual Calling name for and opening phrase in the answer to Question 31 in the **Shorter Catechism**.

engage pray, launch into prayer *NE*.

examin(e) an examination by a Presbyterian clergyman of the theological knowledge of his parishioners, in preparation for Communion. †**examinable persons** those eligible for this.

exerceese, exercise *n* **1** *also* **family** ~ family worship, prayers. **2** †practice or occupation in study or discussion, *esp* of religious themes. **3** †the exposition or discussion of a passage of Scripture, either as part of a church service or by the members of a **presbytery**. **4** †an exegetical sermon or discourse delivered to a **presbytery** by one of its members, or by a divinity student before ordination. *v* perform the **exercise** 3: **1** †in **presbytery**; **2** as part of public or private worship. †**exerciser** the **minister** performing the **exercise** 3. †**make** ~ hold family worship. †**make the** ~ perform the **exercise** 3.

expoond expound, explain (*esp* Scripture).

exposeetion exposition, *chf* of a passage of Scripture.

†**field:** ~ **conventicle** a meeting of **Covenanters** in the open air *Gall*. ~ **preaching** *local*, †~ **meeting** a religious service held in the open air, a relic of **Covenanting** times, still surviving in special commemorative services.

fit, foot, fute: ~ **folk(s)** pedestrians, *esp* those attending church etc on foot *local NE-Kcb*.

gae, go: ~ **in** *of a church* assemble.

gallopin Tam a much-used sermon, *esp* one preached in several places by a candidate for a church.

gathering: ~ **note** a lengthened note sung at the beginning of the first and sometimes certain subsequent lines of a hymn or psalm *chf C*. ~ **psalm** the psalm sung at the beginning of a church service *local*.

grund, ground the text (of a sermon) *now local Sh-Ayr*.

guid, good: ~ **words** (*chf*) children's prayers etc *now local*. **the G** ~ **Book** the Bible.

ha, hall: ~**-bible** a large family bible.

†**haunt, hant** attend (divine service etc).

hear listen to a preacher, attend church. ~**er** one who listens to the preaching of a certain minister, a churchgoer *now local*.

hime a hymn *local Sh-WC*.

hunder(t): the Auld H~, **the Old Hundredth** the long-metre version of the 100th Psalm in the Scottish Psalter (*see* **psalm**); the tune to which this is sung.

hunker (doon) squat; seat oneself in a crouching position or on one's haunches, *freq* derisive in reference to kneeling and genuflexion in non-Presbyterian worship.

ingaun, ingoing the assembling in a building for a church service *now local Cai-S*.

interval the period of time between morning and afternoon church services.

intimation a formal notification or announcement from the pulpit.

†**inunct** anointed.

jow, jowl *chf literary, n* a single peal or stroke of a bell; the ringing or tolling of a bell *now local NE-midLoth*. *v* 1 ring, toll (a bell) *now Kcdn midLoth*. 2 *of a bell* ring, toll *now Kcdn*.

kirk: be ~**ed** be churched, *orig chf* of the first church attendance after a birth or marriage, *latterly* also after a funeral or *eg* on the appointment of a civic or academic body. ~**in(g)** a ceremonial attendance at church as above: 'kirking of the council'. ~**in fest** a celebration held after the ~**in**. ~**in time** the time of church service *Ork NE, SW*. ~**less** not attending or not a member of a church *now Dmf*. ~ **claes** one's Sunday clothes. ~ **folk** churchgoers, frequenters of the church; the congregation. ~ **man** a regular churchgoer *now Sh NE*. ~ **road** a road or path used by parishioners going to the parish church, and constituting a right of way

chf NE. ~ **shune** shoes kept for churchgoing *local Sh-Dmf*. ~ **skail(ing)** the dispersion of a congregation after worship *local*. † ~ **stile** a stile or narrow entrance to a churchyard; *latterly* common as a meeting-place, where announcements were made and the bier was received into the churchyard at funerals.

†**lecture** *n* a reading in church of a passage of Scripture accompanied by a running commentary. *v* deliver such a reading and commentary.

†**legend** a passage of Scripture or of a saint's life read as part of divine service *Abd*.

lettergae the **precentor** in a church *now literary*.

line a line of a metrical **psalm** read or intoned by the **precentor** before being sung by the congregation, *eg* **give out the** ~.

lip labour *freq of prayer* empty or useless talk *now Sh*.

†**mak, make:** ~ **a prayer** say or recite a prayer. ~ (**up**) **a sermon** write a sermon

Men: the ~ name for a group of extremely strict spiritual leaders in a parish *N*. **the** ~'**s day** the Friday preceding the half-yearly Communion service, used by **the** ~ for religious exhortation.

mense: gie a garment kirk *or* **Sunday** ~ wear something for the first time at church on Sunday *Bwk SW, S*.

mind, mine mention in one's prayers, pray for *now Sh Abd Ags*.

†**offerand 1** a religious offering. **2** church offerings, *esp* as viewed as part of the regular income of a church or benefice. **3** ? the offertory, the point in the Mass when offerings were made.

†**oratioun** the act of praying, prayer; a prayer.

ordinar, ordinary (one of) a series of sermons given by a minister on one text. †**ordinary** (**reading**) a regular reading from the Bible as a religious observance within a household. †**collation** ~ regular induction to a benefice.

†**orisioun** a prayer.

†**outlier** an absentee from church.

†**outlying** staying away, absence (from church services etc).

pair o questions the Shorter Catechism *local NE-WC*.

paiter patter, repeat prayers.

†**pale** peal, the ringing of bells.

paper, *freq* **the** ~ the manuscript of a sermon. † ~ **minister** *or* **priest** *derog* a minister or priest who read his sermon; this was looked on as a sign of a lack of inspiration or real conviction.

paraphrase one of a collection of metrical versions of scriptural passages, collected and prepared by a Committee of the **General Assembly** for congregational singing, adopted in 1781 and now printed with the metrical **psalms** at the end of the Scottish Bible.

paumer a palmer, a pilgrim.

pilgrimer a pilgrim.

†**pitter-patter** repeat (words, prayers etc) rapidly and mechanically.

†**popular sermon** the sermon preached to the people of the parish by a **probationer** as part of his **trials** for entry to the ministry.

portion a passage chosen from the Bible for reading, *esp* at family worship *now Abd*.

†**pose** put a question or questions to, interrogate, question.

precent 1 lead the singing in a church, act as **precentor** *now chf Hebrides Highl*. **2** sing (a line of a **psalm** etc) as a lead to a church congregation *Hebrides Highl*. ~**or** an official appointed by the **Kirk Session** to lead the singing by singing the line for the congregation to repeat, *now chf* in the smaller denominations where instrumental music is disapproved *now Hebrides Highl*.

†**preface** *of a minister* deliver a paraphrase of or commentary (on a **psalm** to be sung by the congregation).

psalm in Scotland *esp* referring to the metrical version of the Psalms adopted from French Protestant usage in the sixteenth century, the 1650 version being regularly used in congregational praise in the Presbyterian churches. †**psalmistry** psalms.

pu(l)pit: wag one's pow *etc* **in a** ~ be a minister.

put out the line *of a* **precentor** sing the line of a **psalm** for the congregation to repeat *Hebrides Highl*.

†**pystle** a New Testament epistle.

questions, quastions (the questions in) the **Shorter Catechism** of 1648, so called because it takes the form of a series of questions and answers on Calvinist doctrines. †**question book** a copy of the Catechism.

read *of a preacher* read a sermon, rather than preach extempore. ~**er** a person appointed to read Scriptures etc in the absence of an ordained minister. ~**ing** a reading from the Bible, *esp* in family worship.

†**remembering prayer** the intercessory prayer.

retiring collection an extra collection for some special purpose taken as the congregation leaves.

ring in *of church bells* increase in tempo before stopping or reducing to a single bell as a sign that a service is about to begin *now NE Ags Fif*.

rousing bell a bell rung to let distant worshippers know it is time to get up for church *local EC*.

†**run-line** the singing of a **psalm** by a congregation in two or more continuous lines, instead of the earlier practice of one line at a time after the **precentor** had read or intoned it.

say awa(y) say grace before a meal *now Ork Bnf Abd*.

scripter scripture, *esp* Holy Writ. †**scriptured** warranted by Holy Scripture.

Selkirk grace a rhymed grace before meals (wrongly ascribed to Burns).

†**sermon** *without the article* divine service, an act of church worship.

Shorter Catechism the shorter of two catechisms approved by the **General Assembly** in 1648.

†**shrif, schirryve** shrive.

†**single:** ~ **catechism(s)**, ~ **carritch(er(s))** the **Shorter Catechism**, without the scripture-proofs appended to each question.

sit: † ~**ter** a person who regularly occupies a seat in a church. ~ **below** attend the church of, listen to the preaching of (a certain minister) *now Per Kcb*. ~ **(doun) on one's knees** sink to one's knees, kneel, remain kneeling *now local NE-SW*.

skail 1 dismiss (a congregation). **2** *of a group of persons in a church* break up, disperse, separate.

souch a high-pitched, nasal way of speaking, a whine, *esp* in preaching.

speir questions catechize.

spell swear, blaspheme *Kcdn C Rox*.

Sunday: ~ **blacks** the black suit formerly universally worn by men for attending church on Sunday. ~**('s) claes** one's church-going clothes, one's best clothes. ~ **name** one's formal baptismal name, as opposed to a familiar form of it *C*.

†**superstition** religious observance.

suree, soirée a social gathering, *esp* one organized by a church, Sunday school etc.

tak, take: †**taker-up** a precentor. ~ **up** lead (the praise) in church, act as **precentor**

†**Tantonie bell** a small church bell; a hand-bell.

†**terce** a third part, the third canonical hour.

thanks: give ~ say grace after (and *later* also before) a meal.

†**threap kindness on** *etc* beg kindness, mercy etc from (God etc).

towl toll (a bell etc).

track a tract, a (religious) pamphlet *now N*.

upstanding: be ~ stand up, rise to one's feet, *specif* ceremonially for a prayer etc: '*Will you please be upstanding for the benediction*'.

†**uptak:** ~**er** a **precentor** *latterly NE.* ~**ing** the action of **precenting**.

†**use** a part of a sermon etc devoted to the practical application of a doctrine, a specific precept drawn from a general theological principle.

†**vangel** gospel.

†**vangelist** an evangelist.

walk a ceremonial procession *local*.

warsle, wrestle wrestle in prayer, pray earnestly.

wirship worship.

word, wird: ~**s** prayers. **put up a** ~ say a prayer *local Sh-C.*

worship family prayers.

14.1.9 SPECIAL SERVICES

†**action** the celebration of the sacrament of the Lord's Supper or the Mass. ~ **sermon** the sermon preceding the celebration of the sacrament of Holy Communion.

baby's piece a slice of cake, cheese and a coin offered to the first person to see a baby after its christening.

bapteese baptize.

†**baptime** baptism.

†**cockie-law** the Thursday preceding the spring Communion, kept as a fast day *chf Gsw.*

cry: be cried have one's marriage banns proclaimed *Gen except Sh Cai.* **cries** the proclamation of banns, **pit in the cries** *now Cai-Fif Kcb.*

cummer, kimmer a godmother (*orig* in relation to the parents and other godparents).

dook baptize as a Baptist *Ags Stlg.*

fast day a day in the week preceding the celebration of half-yearly Communion, treated as a holiday with a service of preparation for the **Sacrament** *now chf Highl.*

fence the tables at a communion service, explain the significance of the **sacrament** and indicate those who may properly partake *now Highl.*

fooneral a funeral *S.*

gie, give: ~ **up** hold up a child for baptism *now Abd.*

†**god ba(i)rne gift** a baptismal gift to one's godchild.

guid, good: ~ **breed** bread baked for wedding, baptisms or funerals; the bread used at Communion *now Rox.*

†**halie, holy:** ~ **blud(e) mes** a mass in honour of the **haly blude**.

haud, hald, hold: ~ **up** offer (a child) for baptism *now Abd.*

†**heave** lift (a child) from the font as sponsor; stand sponsor to; baptize.

kirsten, christen christen. ~**ing** christening. **christening bit** *or* **piece = baby's piece** *chf Edb.*

†**knele** kneel, with reference to the question of kneeling to receive Communion.

†**lady messe** a mass celebrated in honour of the Virgin.

†**maiden:** ~ **cummer,** ~ **kimmer** a young woman who acted as attendant to the mother at a christening.

†**matin(e)s 1** *also* **matutines** matins. **2** applied to the Little Office of Our Lady.

†**mening** a peal of bells rung to commemorate a departed soul.

†**mess** (the) mass, Eucharist.

†**mort bell** the bell rung at funerals.

name: gie (a bairn) its *or* a ~ christen (a child). **gie in** *or* **up the** ~**s** supply the names for the **proclamation** of marriage banns.

†**obit** *after the Reformation* an endowment, or the revenue from it, *orig* intended for the provision of an annual memorial service. ~ **silver = obit**; payment for such a service.

occasion the celebration of the Lord's Supper; the periodical Communion Service.

†**pirlicue** *n* the summary formerly delivered by the parish minister at the end of the four-day Communion season, of the sermons preached during that time by visiting ministers. *v* deliver the **pirlicue**.

preaching a sermon, a religious service, *specif* one leading up to and following the communion service.

prepare: †**preparation-day, -Sabbath, -Saturday** *etc* the day(s) preceding the communion service when special services of preparation were conducted. **preparatory service** a service held on a weekday, *usu* the preceding Friday, in preparation for the communion service.

present offer (a child) for baptism.

sacrament 1 the Eucharist. **2 the** periodical Communion service of the Presbyterian Churches. **3 the** ~**s** the period Thursday to the following Monday including the communion and other services *now Hebrides Highl.* ~ **Sunday** *etc* the Sunday *etc* of the communion service.

†**saul, soul:** ~ **mass** a mass for the soul of a dead person.

sealing ordinance(s) the Sacrament of the Lord's Supper and/or baptism *now formal.*

service the serving of the elements at Communion.

table, *freq* the ~**(s)** the Communion table; Communion; a series of dispensings of the **Sacrament** by relays. †**serve (the)** ~**s** *of a clergyman* administer the **Sacrament**; *of the elders* distribute the elements to the **tables**.

thanksgiving (service) the service after the service after Communion, in which special thanks are given to God.

†**ticket** a Communion **token** *Ags Ayr*.

†**token, taiken** a small piece of stamped metal used as a pass to the Communion service in a Presbyterian (and sometimes in an Episcopal) church (now replaced by a printed card).

whistlin *or* **fusslin Sunday** the **fast day** (*usu* a Thursday) before Communion on which whistling was permitted *now Kcdn*.

†**worship, wirship** a funeral ceremony.

14.1.10 CHURCH FESTIVALS

See also 14.4.

†**Alhallow** Allhallowtide. ~**day** All Saints Day. ~ **evin** Halloween. ~**mes, A(ll)hallomes** the feast of All Saints.

†**Ander(s)mess** St Andrew's Day, 30 Nov.

†**Ask-Wedinsday, As Wodinsday** Ash Wednesday.

Bannock Day *or* **Night** Shrove Tuesday.

Beltane a pagan fire festival on 1 or 3 May (and sometimes also on 21 June); identified by the Church as the feast of the Invention of the Cross (3 May).

†**Care Sonday** the fifth Sunday in Lent, Passion Sunday.

Chrissenmas, †**Christinmes** Christmas *now Bnf-Ags*.

fastern's een, fasting even Shrove Tuesday.

†**gude Wednisday** the Wednesday before Easter.

†**thalie:** ~ **day** a holy day.

hallow, hal(l)a-: *chf* **H**~ All Saints. ~**day** *now Ags Ayr*, ~**mas(s)** *now Sh Ags* All Saints' Day. ~**een,** ~ **even** 31 Oct, the eve of All Saints' Day.

†**Laif-So(u)nday** Low Sunday.

†**lentren** Lent.

†**lord: the L**~**'s mornin** *or* **nicht** Sunday morning or night. **the Lordis Saboth** Sunday.

Martin Bullion's day the day of the Feast of the translation of St Martin, 4 July (Old Style), 15 July (New Style), St Swithin's day *now Sh*.

Mary, Marie: † ~ **day** one of the festival days of the Virgin: **first** ~ **day** the Annunciation (25 March) or *(chf)* the Assumption (15 Aug); **latter** ~ **day** *chf or only* the Nativity (8 Sep). ~**mas(s)** = ~ **day.**

†**Michael day** Michaelmas, 29 Sep *Abd*.

†**mid-lentroun** the middle of Lent.

†**offerand** the Presentation of Christ in the Temple, as celebrated at Candlemas.

Pace, Pasche, Pask Easter. ~ **Day** Easter Day. † ~ **evin** Easter eve; the day before Easter. ~ **Saturday, Sunday** *etc* Easter Saturday, Easter Sunday etc *now Sh Cai*.

palm one of the various native trees or shrubs, *esp* the willows, used by Roman Catholics or Episcopalians to represent the palm on Palm Sunday; a sprig or branch of one of these *now local NE-Uls*.

†**Patrickmes** the feast of St Patrick, 17 Mar *chf WC, SW*.

ruid, rood: ~ **Day (in barlan),** ~ **mass** the day of the Invention of the Cross, 3 May. ~ **day (in hairst),** ~ **mass** the day of the Exaltation of the Cross, 14 September. ~ **even** the eve of ~ **day,** *latterly N*.

Skire(s) Thursday Maundy Thursday.

†**Sanct Nicholas bischop** a boy bishop elected for a festival of choirboys or schoolboys on or following St Nicholas Day.

†**Tayne: immunitie of** ~ the sanctuary of St Duthac of Tain.

†**uphali(e)day, uphalimes** the festival of Epiphany as the end of Christmastide.

whistlin *or* **fusslin Sunday** the **fast day** (*usu* a Thursday) before Communion on which whistling was permitted *now Kcdn*.

Whussunday Whitsunday.

Yule, Yeel *N n* Christmas; the day itself; the festive season associated with it, *freq* beginning before Christmas day and (*esp Sh*) continuing until after New Year *now chf literary*. †*v* keep Christmas. ~ **day** Christmas day. ~ **e'en,** ~ **even** Christmas eve. **Auld** ~ Christmas day (Old Style): *orig* 5 Jan; *later* 6 Jan; *now* 7 Jan *Sh NE*.

14.1.11 VESTMENTS ETC

†**antepend** a veil or covering for the front of the altar.

†**arch** an ark.

bands the two short white linen strips hanging from the collar, worn as part of the pulpit or officiating dress of an ordained minister.

†**baudkin, bakin** a richly embroidered cloth; a baldachin, canopy.

brod a (church) offertory or collection plate *now local NE-nEC.*

†**caip** a cope.

†**charbukyll** a fabric used for church vestments or cloths.

†**chelleis** a chalice.

†**cheseb** a chasuble.

corse a cross.

†**cude** a chrisom-cloth.

†**eucharist** the vessel containing the consecrated bread.

†**gaady** one of the larger beads on a rosary; a bead.

†**hostie** the host, consecrated bread.

kirk: † ~ **box** a box in which church funds were kept; a church collection box, *latterly specif* the box containing the fund for the parish poor. ~ **ladle** a small box on the end of a long handle for taking a collection.

ladle a long-handled church collecting box.

lettern, lateron 1 *also* †**lectroun** a lectern. 2 the desk of the reader or **precentor** in post-Reformation churches.

†**linens, linen clathis** penitential garments.

†**matin(e) buke** a book of hours or primer.

†**mort stand** a set of ecclesiastical vestments or altar-cloths for funeral services.

†**neuk: (four) ~it bonet** *or* **cap** a square cap, *esp* as worn by Roman Catholic or Episcopal clergy

†**orphus** an orphrey, an ornamental band or border on an ecclesiastical vestment etc. **orpheist** adorned with an orphrey; bordered **with** (some rich material).

palm one of the various native trees or shrubs, *esp* the willow, used by Roman Catholics or Episcopalians to represent the palm on Palm Sunday; a sprig or branch of one of these trees *now local NE-Uls.*

†**paraling** an ornamental trimming for a vestment.

†**pend(en), pendale** a valance for an altar.

†**pendice** an ornamental strip hanging from a bishop's mitre.

†**pendicle** a hanging cloth such as a valance, *eg* on an altar.

†**piece** one of the containers used for collecting church offerings.

†**porteous** a portable breviary.

quigrich the name given to the pastoral staff of St Fillan.

†**rocket** a bishop's surplice.

†**sacrament house** a tabernacle.

†**sark, serk** a surplice.

†**tent** a movable pulpit (with steps and canopy) erected in the open air, *esp* at half-yearly Communion services when the congregation was too large for the church.

14.1.12 NON CHRISTIAN RELIGIONS

eedol an idol *now Bnf Ags.*

†**Goddis inymyes** *etc, usu* the saracens.

haithen heathen.

Jew, †**Jow** 1 a Jew. 2 term of abuse for an unbeliever, infidel.

†**Mahoun** Mohammed.

†**manswear** swear falsely by (a god).

†**mistrowand** *adj* unbelieving, infidel. *n, also* **mistrowar** an unbelievier, infidel.

†**oratory, oratour** an inner shrine of a temple, as the seat of an oracle.

†**oratour** an oracle.

†**Pace, Pasche, Pask** the Passover. ~ **evin** the day before Passover.

†**vaticinar** a prophet.

†**vaticinatress** a prophetess.

†**weird** a decree (of a god).

14.2 SUPERSTITION

14.2.1 GENERAL, MISCELLANEOUS

For customs bringing good luck, see also 14.4.

ban curse; swear, utter curses.

†**burry man** a public scapegoat, on whom was laid all the bad luck of the fishing and who was then chased out of the village; *later* a man dressed in wool and covered with burrs etc, paraded through a town to bring luck in the fishing season *chf NE.*

canny 1 favourable, lucky, of good omen. **2 not** ~ unnatural, supernatural *now wLoth Sllg:* 'this is no canny'.

cantrip a spell, charm; magic, *chf* **cast ~s.**

chancy *latterly chf* **not** ~ unfortunate, unlucky: 'that's no chancy.'

†**clavie** a torch carried round the fishing boats on New Year's Eve to ensure a successful season *Mry.*

†**Curse of Scotland** the nine of diamonds.

deasil the custom of walking sunwise round a person or thing to bring good fortune.

dint: be ~**ed** be pierced with an elf-arrow *SW Uls.*

eerie affected by fear or dread, *esp* by a fear of the supernatural which gives rise to uneasiness or loneliness *Gen except Sh Ork.* ~**some** uncanny, gloomy *now Abd.*

eldritch weird, ghostly, strange, unearthly *now chf literary.*

elf-candle a spark or flash of light, thought to be of supernatural origin.

†**ether, adder:** ~**stane** a small perforated pre-historic stone or bead, used as an amulet.

ferlie a strange sight, a marvel, a curiosity.

fit, fute, foot: be *or* **have a guid, ill, lucky** *etc* ~ be a person who brings good *or* bad fortune *local Sh-EC.* **first** ~ the first person to enter a house on New Year's morning, considered to bring good (or bad) luck for the year.

foundin pint a drink given to workmen after laying the foundations of a building as an omen of good luck *now Ork Ags.*

freit 1 ~**s** superstitious beliefs, observances or acts *now local N-Rox.* **2** a superstitious saying, an adage *now Bnf.* ~**y** strongly believing in superstition *now Fif.*

gastrous horrifying, unearthly *Abd S.*

glamour(ie), gramarie *literary* magic, enchantment, witchcraft.

guid, good: the ~ **man's craft** *etc* a plot of land left uncultivated to propitiate the Devil.

halie, holy: ~ **man** *euphemistic* the Devil, *chf* in names for ground left untilled as an act of propitiation, *eg* ~ **mans ley,** ~ **man('s) rig**

hallow: ~**een ,** ~ **even,** ~ **eve** *now Uls* 31 Oct, the eve of All Saints' Day, the last day of the year in the old Celtic calendar, associated with witches and the powers of darkness; *see also* 14.4.2.

handsel, *n* **1** a gift intended to bring good luck to something new or to a new beginning, *eg* the New Year, a new house or new clothes. **2** the money received by a trader for his first sale, either the first of the day or the first of a new business, thought to bring good luck *now local Ork-Loth. v* **1** give or offer a **handsel** to (a person) at the beginning of a year or day, or to mark some special occasion. **2** inaugurate with some ceremony or gift etc in order to bring good luck. **3** celebrate the first use of (something) with a **handsel**; use for the first time; be the first to try, test or taste (something).

horse man one of a fraternity of **horsemen** (farm servants who look after and work the horses on the farm) with initiation ceremonies, passwords etc, *usu* regarded as a relic of Devil-worship, *esp*

in comb eg **horseman's word** a secret word by which the initiate gains complete control over his horses *now local Cai-Lnk.*

ill harm, injury, mishchief from supernatural causes. ~ **ee** the evil eye *now Ags Wgt.* ~ **fittit** bringing bad luck *Sh Rox.*

†**inchant** enchant. ~**ment 1** enchantment, the act of enchanting. **2** a method of enchanting, a spell or charm.

†**lammer, lamber:** ~ **bead** an amber bead, *freq* used as a charm or amulet.

†**Lee-penny** a small, red, roughly heart-shaped stone set in a groat of Edward IV of England (1442-83) and possessed by the Lockharts of the Lee near Carluke, Lnk, used as a healing charm; the theme of Scott's *Talisman, Lnk.*

†**lib** *n* a (healing) charm. *v* heal, cure (with a charm).

†**lustrale** *of a sacrifice* purificatory.

†**malison** *n* a malediction, curse. *v* curse.

†**millart('s) word** a secret password, supposedly current among millers, conferring supernatural powers *Bnf Abd.*

†**mirk Mon(an)day** 29 March 1652 (Old Style), on which occurred a total eclipse of the sun, the day being later regarded as one of supernatural darkness.

misfortune: ~**at ,** ~**it** unfortunate, unlucky *NE Gsw Uls.*

misluckit dogged with bad luck, unfortunate *NE.*

mock the very small egg sometimes laid by a hen and regarded as an omen of misfortune *now wLoth Rox.*

mows: nae ~**s** no laughing matter; serious, dangerous, uncanny *now NE Ags.*

†**needfire** fire produced by the friction of dry wood, having reputed magical or prophylactic properties.

†**pissance, puissance** supernatural power.

†**pruif, proof:** ~ **of lead** *or* **shot** a supposed magic protection from bullets.

†**puddock-stane** a toadstone.

†**purse penny** a coin, *usu* of high value, kept in the purse for luck.

skeely having real or supposed skill in the art of healing *now NE Fif.* ~ **wife** *etc* a woman credited with great or supernatural healing powers, *esp* one called to emergencies or confinements.

†**smooring (the fire)** a ritual damping down of the domestic fire at night, once common in Highland Catholic districts.

square man a workman who regularly uses a square, *esp* a carpenter or mason *now only free-masonry.*

threap an old superstition, idea or saying *C, S*.

†**unable, onabill** unlucky.

uncannie *of things* unlucky, inauspicious, tempting Providence *now Sh Cai Abd*.

unchance †misfortune, calamity. **unchancy 1** inauspicious, unlucky; ill-omened, ill-fated. **2** dangerous, threatening, treacherous, not to be meddled with.

†**unhap** bring misfortune.

†**unseely** *of conditions etc* causing or involving misfortune, unhappiness or danger *latterly Abd*.

†**unsell** unlucky, wretched; wicked.

†**unspoken** *chf folk-medicine, of a curative substance* not spoken over, gathered or handled in silence.

†**unweirdit** subject to adverse fate, ill-fated.

wan, whaun a wand.

warlock bewitched, magical, supernatural; malevolent, mischievous.

weird *n* **1** *now chf literary* fate, fortune, destiny; one's own particular fate. **2** †**~s** the Fates, the three goddesses of destiny. **3** someone with supernatural skill and knowledge. †*adj* having the power to control the destiny of men. *v* ordain by fate, destine; assign a specific fate or fortune **to**. **~fu** fateful, fraught with the supernatural. **~ly** magical, eerie, dismal, sinister.

†**widdle** invoke or inflict a curse on.

withershins, widdershins, witherlins *chf Abd*, **widderwise** *Sh*, †**witherwardis** anti-clockwise, in a direction contrary to the apparent course of the sun, *usu* with the implication of bad luck or disaster *now Sh C*.

†**word, wird,** *chf* **mason** *etc* **~** the secret watchword of an initiated craftsman.

Yeel: brak ~'s gird disturb the peace of Christmas by weeping on Christmas day, and so incur bad luck for the following year *NE*.

14.2.2 SUPERNATURAL BEINGS

banshee a female spirit, *freq* connected with a family, whose wail was thought to forecast death or disaster.

bawcan a bogle, ghost *now Arg*.

billy blin a **brownie**, a benevolent spirit.

black: ~ man *in threats to children*, **the** bogyman *local*. †**~ ox** an imaginary black ox said to trample on someone who has suffered a bereavement or other severe calamity.

bockie a hobgoblin *Sh-N*.

†**bodach** a spectre, bugbear.

bogle, boggle an ugly or terrifying ghost or phantom; a bugbear. **bogly** haunted by **bogles** *now Abd*. †**~bo** a hobgoblin, spectre.

bo-man a bogyman *now Bnf*.

boodie a ghost, hobgoblin *now Bnf Abd*.

bowsie(-man) a bogyman, an imaginary monster invoked to frighten children *now Kcb*.

broonie, brownie a *chf* benevolent sprite, supposed to perform household tasks in the night; *latterly also* a more malevolent goblin.

†**bysun** a monster.

cow a hobgoblin; an object of terror.

†**deblat** a little devil, imp.

deil, deevil a devil. **deevilock** a little devil, imp *now Bnf Abd*.

doolie a hobgoblin, a spectre *now Ags*.

draigon a dragon.

eemock, immick a fairy *Abd Ags*.

†**eldritch** belonging to or resembling the elves or similar beings.

elf: ~-arrow, †**~-shot** a flint arrowhead, thought to be used by fairies. **~-ring** a fairy ring *now Uls*. **~-shot** *v* shot by an **~-arrow**; bewitched *now Uls*. †*n* a sickness (*usu* of cattle) thought to be caused by fairies.

Elfin fairyland, the land of the elves.

erd hun a mysterious animal (actually a mole?) supposed to burrow in graveyards *NE*.

†**etin** a giant.

†**fair folk** fairy folk.

†**fairy raid** the ride of the fairies to their celebrations at **Beltane**.

†**famh** *folklore* a small animal somewhat like a mole.

†**fanton** an unreal thing or state, a phantom.

ghaist a ghost *now local Ags-Rox*.

†**golk of Maryland** the cuckoo of (?) fairyland.

grapus the Devil, a hobgoblin *now Ags*.

green lady a spectre, *perh* portending death, from the association in folklore of green with death *now local Ross-Fif*.

†**grephoun** a griffin.

guid, good: the ~ folks, †**~ neebors** the fairies, brownies etc.

gyre carlin(g) a supernatural being, *chf* female, an ogress, witch *now Sh*.

†**habbitrot** = **Whippitie-Stourie**, *specif* a fairy for the spinning *S*.

kelpie a water demon, *usu* in the form of a horse, which is said to haunt rivers and fords, and lure the unwary to their deaths.

lang, long: ~-nebbit having a gnome-like or supernatural appearance *now Ork*.

little folk(s), little foukies *literary* the fairies.

†**marmaid:** ~**en,** ~**yn** a mermaid.

Meg, †**Mag** *chf N* ~**(gie) Mulloch** a familiar spirit traditionally associated with the Grants of Tullochgorum in Strathspey *chf Mry Bnf.*

murmichan a **bogle** or wicked fairy used to frighten children *now Ags.*

onbeast a monster, a wild beast.

†**Redcap** a fairy or goblin said to haunt old buildings.

†**shelly coat** a water-sprite wearing a shell-covered coat.

†**shuit, shoot:** ~ **to** *or* **a deid** kill or harm (*esp* cattle) by magic (*eg* by fairy arrows).

sithean a fairy hill or mound *freq in place-names.*

tak awa *of the fairies* take away (a human child) and substitute one of their own, *chf* **ta'en-awa** a fairy changeling.

†**toman** a little hill, mound, *freq* one formed by the moraine of a glacier, in folklore associated with a fairy dwelling.

tulloch a fairy mound *Cai Per.*

†**waff** an apparition, ghost.

†**wag-at-the-wa** a household goblin *S.*

†**waghorn** a character in fable, the greatest of all liars; the Devil himself.

†**warlock** a savage or monstrous creature.

†**warwolf, warwoof** a werewolf.

water: † ~ **cow** *Celtic folklore* a mythical amphibious beast supposed to live in lakes. ~ **horse,** ~ **kelpie** *chf Celtic folklore* a mythical spirit in the form of a horse which frequents lakes and rivers. † ~ **wraith** *folklore* a water spirit, a goblin which haunted streams and lakes.

Whippitie Stourie name for a kind of household fairy or **brownie.**

wicht, wight a supernatural being; a being with supernatural powers.

wirricow, †**worricow** a hobgoblin, demon *now Lnk SW Rox.*

†**wrath, warth** a wraith.

yird, yirth: ~ **pig** *or* **swine** = **erd hun** *NE.*

14.2.3 WITCHCRAFT

†**beglamour** bewitch.

blink 1 glance at with the evil eye. 2 bewitch. 3 turn (milk etc) sour *now Bnf.*

†**can** supernatural power, witchcraft.

canny: *chf* ~ **man,** ~ **wife,** ~ **woman** a person who deals in the supernatural *now Abd Fif.*

cantrip a spell, charm; magic, *chf* **cast** ~**s.**

carline a witch *now Bnf Abd Fif.*

covine a coven, a group of witches.

†**cummer, kimmer** a witch.

forspoken put under a spell, bewitched, *latterly esp* by excessive praise *now Sh Ork Cai Abd.* **forespoken water** water used to undo a spell.

†**gillatrype(s), jolly-tryp(s)** name of a witches' dance.

glamour(ie), gramarie *literary* magic, enchantment, witchcraft.

hair-tether *chf witchcraft* a tether made of hair *now Cai.*

hattock, huttock ? a little hat, *chf* **horse and hattock** a call, *orig* by witches, to be covered and ride.

†**ill: cast** ~ **on** bewitch, put the evil eye on.

†**luckie** a witch, hag.

†**maiden** designation of an 'office' held by one of the younger witches at a meeting of witches.

†**mark, merk** an insensitive spot supposedly placed on the body of a witch by the Devil as a mark of his possession.

†**muilds** earth as the remains of a buried corpse.

†**saga** a witch.

†**score abune the breath** make a scratch (*freq* the sign of the cross) on the forehead of a suspected witch, *usu* with an iron instrument, as a means of thwarting her power.

†**skaith** harm or injury attributed to witchcraft or the evil eye.

St John's nut a double hazelnut, supposed to be a charm against witchcraft.

taen(-like) bewitched *now Stlg WC.*

teind to hell a tribute or price required of his minions by the Devil.

†**trail the raip** bring bad luck by twisting a straw rope and pulling it round anticlockwise *NE.*

uncannie *of persons* mischievous, malicious, malignant; not safe to meddle with, as being in league with supernatural forces etc *now local Sh-Lnk.*

†**unsonsie** bringing bad luck, ill-omened, associated with evil powers.

warlock *n* 1 a man thought to be in league with the powers of darkness and to have supernatural knowledge and means of bewitching and harming others, the male equivalent of a witch; *occas* used of women. 2 a wizard, magician. *adj* bewitched, magical, supernatural; malevolent, mischievous.

†**weser** a wizard.

wise, wice skilled in magic, possessing powers of witchcraft, *chf* ~ **wife** *or* **woman** a witch, sorceress *now Ork.*

†**witch:** ~ **bird,** ~ **carline** a witch.

14.2.4 FORTUNETELLING

†**augurian** *adj* augural. *n* an augur.

blue clue *see* **wind**.

bod bode, portend. **bodement** foreboding *now Abd*.

burn nits burn nuts at Halloween to foretell the marriages of the younger members of the party.

cast *v* drop (eggs) into water for the purpose of divination *chf NE*. *n* one's lot, fortune, fate *now Abd-Lnk*. ~**ing the glass(es)** a method of fortunetelling using egg-white *now Ork Cai*. ~ **the cup** tap the cup prior to 'reading' the tea-leaves *now Bnf Abd*.

†**cauk and keel** chalk and ruddle, as used by fortunetellers.

death: ~ **candle** a will-o-the-wisp, thought to foretell death *now Bnf Abd Fif*. ~**chap** a knocking, thought to foretell death *now local Cai-Fif*.

deid, dead: ~**-bell** a sudden sensation of deafness and a ringing in the ears, thought to foretell death *now Sh*. ~**-chack** the ticking of the death-watch beetle, thought to foretell death. ~**-drap** a drop of water dripping on the floor, thought to foretell death. ~**-licht(s)** a strange light, thought to foretell death *now Abd*. ~**-rap** an unexplained knocking, thought to foretell death. ~**-spail** = **spail**.

drap, drop: ~ **glasses** drop part of an egg-white into a glass of water in order to foretell the future *now Sh*.

fey fated to die, doomed, *esp* as portended by peculiar, *usu* elated behaviour; *more vaguely* otherwordly. †~**dom** the state of being **fey**, a portent, *chf* of death; doom. †~ **token** a sign of approaching death.

foregang *Sh Cai Bnf*, **forego** an image of a person or some other supernatural sign, *eg* a light, thought to foretell a death; any premonition of misfortune.

for(e)rinner forerunner, precursor, harbinger.

†**foretaiking** a foretoken, an omen.

freit an omen, a presage *now Ross Ags*.

guest an object thought to foretell the arrival of a stranger *now Sh Ork*.

†**hechle** foretell, prophesy.

licht(ie) the will-o'-the-wisp, jack-o'lantern, regarded as an omen of death *chf NE*.

†**pou, pull:** ~ **stalks** pluck stalks of corn or cabbage plants for use in divination, *eg* at **Halloween**.

read interpret (a dream, riddle etc), foretell the future, *freq* ~ (**the) cups, cards** *etc*.

†**riddle: turning (of) the** ~ (**and the shears**)

a method of divination, used *esp* for the discovery of theft.

score a line, wrinkle on the skin, *esp* of the hand as used in palmistry *now Sh N, WC*.

second sight a supposed faculty or power of seeing future or distant things as if they were actually present; the image thus seen; *more gen*, the ability to foretell future events, telepathic powers. ~**ed** having this faculty.

spae *v* 1 prophesy, foretell, predict, tell (fortunes) *now literary*. 2 read (someone's hand) *now Bnf Abd*. 3 utter prophecy, tell the future **about**. †*n* a prediction; an omen. † ~ **craft** the art of predicting the future. † ~**man** a fortuneteller; a diviner, prophet. ~**wife** a female fortuneteller.

spail a shroud-like shape of candle grease on a guttered candle, thought to foretell the death of the person in whose direction it forms *now Mry Ags Per*.

stranger anything thought to foretell the arrival of an unexpected visitor, *eg* a tea-leaf etc floating on the surface of a cup of tea.

†**taghairm** a form of (magical) divination said to have been practised in the Highlands.

†**taisch** a vision seen in **second sight**, *esp* an apparition of a person about to die.

†**takenar** a portent.

warning a premonition, a portent *now Sh Ork Cai Ags*.

†**weird** *n* 1 an omen of a future event. 2 a prophecy, prediction; a mysterious saying. *v* prophesy (someone's fate); warn ominously. ~ **wife** a prophetess, fortuneteller.

wind the *or* **a blue clue** wind a ball of worsted in a kiln at Halloween in order to divine the name of one's future spouse.

†**Yule sowans: sowans** specially made for Christmas into which the usual objects of divination of marriage (*eg* a ring, button etc) were stirred before distribution among the company.

14.3 EDUCATION

14.3.1 GENERAL, MISCELLANEOUS

†**astrolog** an astronomer, an astrologer.

†**Book of Discipline** either of two books adopted in 1560 and 1581 respectively, laying down the constitution of the Reformed Church and also dealing with education.

buik: ~**-lare** learning, education *local NE-C*. **at**

one's ~ reading, studying *now local NE-C*. **far i the** ~ well-read, learned, clever *now Ork*.

†**clark play** a play composed or acted by clerics or scholars.

cless a class.

†**cun** get to know; learn.

dask a desk.

educate, eddicate educated. **eddication** education.

†**entechment** instruction.

†**examinate** *v* examine. *ptp* examined.

examinator an examiner, interrogator.

gremmar grammar *NE*.

†**guttam** *orig school usage* a drop (*orig* of ink).

ken †teach. ~**ning** teaching *now Sh Lnk*.

lair, lear *n* 1 †lore, act of teaching. 2 learning, knowledge, education, lore, doctrine. †*v* learn. †**at** *or* **to (the)** ~ under instruction, at or to school, at study.

lear 1 †teach, instruct. 2 learn, ascertain. †**lerit** educated.

learn, leern *Abd* 1 learn, ascertain. 2 teach, instruct.

†**lesson** the action of reading or study.

misca(ll) mispronounce (a word) in reading *local*.

†**oratory, oratour** a study.

†**pedagoge,** pedagogy.

†**philosophour naturall** a student of natural phenomena.

prentice *n* an apprentice, a learner. *v* apprentice (a youth) to a trade or craft, indenture or bind as an apprentice *now Abd*.

†**quin** study, learn.

†**scientive** well-versed, learned.

tairm a term.

†**techment** teaching, instruction.

upbring training, education, maintenance during childhood *Sh NE Fif Dnbt*.

vacance a vacation, holiday, period of suspension of business etc.

†**vacancy** a vacation, holiday.

14.3.2 SCHOOLS

academy *orig* a public or private secondary school in a burgh, *freq* replacing a grammar school or providing a more modern curriculum, *later* applied to many state secondary schools irrespective of their origins.

Accies nickname for pupils or former pupils of an **academy**, *esp* when organized as a team.

†**bairn** a child at school or in a choir; a schoolboy or chorister.

†**belt: the** ~ the **tawse**.

†**bent silver** money paid by schoolchildren to provide bent grass for the schoolroom floor.

big: ~ **school** informal name for secondary school. ~ **yins** older children *local*.

birl a school's whistle; the sound made by a whistle *C*.

†**bleeze money, bleeze silver, Candlemas bleeze** *SW, S* a gift made by pupils to a schoolmaster at **Candlemas**.

blin swap the exchange of articles by schoolchildren with their eyes shut or with the articles in closed hands.

†**burgh school** a school maintained by a burgh.

†**burnt-nebbit** *of tawse* having had the ends hardened in the fire.

cadger's whips *said by children learning to write* letters such as *r* which have a curve resembling a **cadger's** whip *Ags*.

†**Can(d)lemas king,** *local Abd-WC* title given to the boy who gave the highest money present to the schoolmaster at **Candlemas** *local*.

canker a stroke on the palm of the hand from a strap *now Abd Ags Fif*.

cauld iron used as a solemn pledge by schoolchildren *Abd Ags Kcb*.

†**caum** slate pencil.

censor title of an official in a school, *usu* the person who called the roll or kept the attendance register.

Certificate *secondary education* ~ **of Sixth Year Studies,** *also colloq* **SYS** a state examination at a more advanced level than the **Higher** Grade examinations; the certificate awarded to the successful candidates, introduced 1968. †**(Higher) Leaving** ~ a certificate awarded for proficiency in certain subjects or groups of subjects on the results of examinations conducted annually by the Scottish Education Department from 1888 to 1961 in secondary schools in Scotland at the end of the secondary course, replaced in 1962 by next. **Scottish Certificate of Education, SCE** the various examinations *ie* **Highers**, **O Grades** and ~ **of Sixth Year Studies,** replacing preceding since 1962. **the SCEs** *colloq* these examinations.

†**cooling stone** a stone at or near a school, on which boys who have been whipped were made to sit *Abd Ags*.

copy a copy-book.

count *v* do arithmetic. *n* ~(**s**) arithmetic, sums.

†**cude** the butler or storekeeper at George Heriot's Hospital *Edb.*

dick a schoolmaster *Abd-Ags.*

dobbie, doobie the dunce of a class *now Fif Stlg Edb Kcb.*

†**doctor** an assistant-master in a school. **doctrix** an assistant school-mistress.

dominie, dom *Bnf Abd,* **domsie** *Bnf Abd Stlg* a schoolmaster.

dult the pupil at the bottom of the class *now Gsw.*

dux the best pupil in a school, class or subject.

†**English School** a school where English was taught, as opposed to a grammar school (where Classics was taught).

ephor a prefect at the Edinburgh Academy *Edb.*

†**extranean** a boy from a country district attending Aberdeen Grammar School for a short time to study intensively for the University **bursary competition** *Abd.*

fab a truant *Stlg.*

†**faction,** *Aberdeen Grammar School* a section of a class; the bench at which each section sat.

fits the foot of the class, the dunce *now Ags Uls.* **fittie** the dunce of a class *Ags Rox.*

fugie *n* a truant from school. *v, chf* ~ **the schule** play truant *now NE.*

gae, go: ~ **in** assemble.

gang doon *of a school* close for holidays *Stlg Kcb.*

†**gar:** ~**rer** a senior boy at George Heriot's Hospital who made a younger boy his fag. ~**ring law** the system of fagging etc at George Heriot's Hospital.

George Square informal name for George Watson's Ladies' College, from 1871-1980 situated in George Square, Edinburgh.

get 1 *chf* **gyte** name for a junior pupil at the Royal High School of Edinburgh. 2 *chf* **geit** name for a boy in the first year of the Upper School of the Edinburgh Academy.

gove, govie nickname for a headmaster or school governor.

†**Gray** an arithmetic text book (by James Gray of Peebles (1781-1810)).

gutties gymshoes *WC.*

hairst, harvest: ~ **play** *now Cai,* †~ **vacance** school holidays taken during the harvest.

half: halfie a half-holiday *local.*

hearken someone his lessons *etc* hear someone repeat lessons etc *now local Cai-Gall.*

heid: ~**s,** ~**ie** the top pupil in a class *Rox.* ~**ie** a headmaster.

helper, helpender *now Abd* a minister's or teacher's assistant.

Herioter a pupil of George Heriot's School *(formerly* Hospital) in Edinburgh.

High School name for the principal school in many Scottish burghs; a grammar school; a **senior-secondary school**; a comprehensive school.

Higher *adj, secondary education* at a more advanced or difficult level, of both a State examination and the certificate awarded to successful candidates. *n, colloq* one of these examinations or certificates.

†**Inglis schole** = **English School.**

†**intermediate,** applied to the type of school providing a three year course for 12- to 14-year-old children, which ended with a state examination and the **Intermediate Certificate.**

janitor 1 a caretaker in a school. 2 †an usher or junior master in a school. **jannie** *colloq* a (*usu* school-)janitor.

jick: play the ~ play truant *now Lnk Rox.*

jink dodge (school, a class), play truant *N Fif.*

jotter a school exercise book.

jouk play truant (from) *local NE-Uls.*

†**junior secondary (school)** a state secondary school providing less academic courses than the **senior secondary school**, attended by pupils who were not successful in the **qualifying examination.**

keepie-in a pupil detained after school as a punishment *NE Per Edb.*

kip play truant from school *now nEC midLoth Rox.* **play (the)** ~ play truant *now Stlg Fif Edb.*

†**lair, lear: at** *or* **to (the)** ~ under instruction, at or to school, at study.

leave 1 permission to a pupil to leave the classroom during a school lesson. 2 the playtime interval in school.

†**lector** a pupil learning to read. ~ **schole** an elementary school.

line a note requesting or explaining a child's absence from school etc.

linn a kind of fireclay formerly used as slate pencil *Ayr.*

†**locality** a schoolmaster's stipend.

Lochgelly a leather strap or **tawse** for punishing school children, manufactured in Lochgelly, Fif.

lockerstrae a small pointer, reed or straw used in teaching children to read, or in keeping one's place on a page when reading aloud *NE.*

†**Lower** *adj* at a less advanced level, of both a State examination and the certificate awarded to successful candidates. *n, colloq* one of these examinations or certificates.

luiffie = **palmie** *local Ags-Slk.*

maister, master, †magister a schoolmaster 1 *usu* **the** ~ the only or principal teacher in a small rural community. **2** prefixed to the Christian name and surname *orig, chf* of a Master of Arts, *freq* a schoolmaster.

†matin(e) buke a book of hours or primer.

maxie a gross error in a Latin translation, entailing the highest deduction of marks *chf NE*.

medie an error in Latin translation less serious than a **maxie** with a lesser penalty *Abd*.

†milk an annual entertainment in a school, when the pupils presented a small gift or sum of money to the teacher and were given a treat of curds and cream etc.

minute, meenit an interval or recreation time. *NE Ags*

miss pass over, skip, *eg* in reading *local Ork-Per*.

Ordinary *or (chf)* **O** at a less advanced level, of a state examination, the course leading to it or the certificate awarded to successful candidates. *chf* **O (Grade)** one of these examinations, courses or certificates.

pair o taws(e) a schoolmaster's strap with several thongs *now Sh Ags Kcb*.

palmie, pawmie *n* a stroke with a strap or cane on the palm of the hand as a punishment. *v* administer **palmies** to.

pandie *n* a stroke with a cane etc on the palm of the hand, a beating, *esp* from a schoolmaster. *v* beat on the palm of the hand with a cane etc; punish *local NE-Uls*. **get a** ~ *or* ~**s** be beaten with a cane etc.

†parchment *orig* a parchment certificate issued to a qualified teacher in a state school on which comments on his proficiency were annually recorded by the School Inspectorate and which served as an authorization to teach; *latterly* a certificate given to a qualified teacher on satisfactory completion of a two-year probation period.

†parish school, parochial school one of the schools set up by the **Church of Scotland** to provide instruction in the rudiments of education and Latin, and to equip promising pupils for University entrance.

†Parliamentary school a school in one of the **parliamentary parishes** in the Highlands, supported by State aid.

†pauper a school pupil who received free education in return for various cleaning and supervisory duties *N*.

†penny: ~ **book(ie)** a child's first school primer, *orig* costing a penny; *hence* the first class in a primary school. ~**-buff** a child's first school reading book.

†pense a (spell of) study, a school exercise.

piece: ~ **box** the box in which a schoolchild carries a lunchtime snack *local*. ~ **denner** *NE, EC, S*, **†noon(ing)-piece** a lunchtime snack of sandwiches etc. ~ **poke** the paper bag etc in which a snack is carried *local NE-Kcb*. ~ **time** a break for a meal or snack during working or school hours. **play** ~ a mid-morning snack at school. **schule** ~ a child's mid-morning or lunchtime snack at school.

†plant the action of appointing a schoolmaster; the action of supplying a school with an incumbent.

play: *usu* **the** ~ time off school for recreation; a holiday from school or college. † ~ **day** a holiday or half-holiday from school. ~**-Saturday, -Tuesday** *etc* the Saturday, Tuesday etc of a **play**.

plug dodge (school), play truant *C, S*.

plunk dodge (school), absent oneself from school without leave *C, S*. ~**er** a truant *C, S*.

preliminary examination, *colloq* **prelim** applied unofficially to the class examinations taken before the **Highers** etc to provide an estimate of the candidate's ability *local*.

public school a state-controlled school run by the local education authority, *usu* non-fee-paying and supported by contributions from local and national taxation.

qualify †pass the **qualifying examination** for admission to secondary education. **†qualifying examination,** *colloq* **the quallie** an examination at the end of primary education which decided which type of secondary education pupils should have. **quallie dance** a party for pupils in their last year at primary school *Edb*.

quarter the fourth part of a year, referring to a school term or similar period of instruction. ~**ly** an examination held at the end of a school term.

†Queen Street informal name for The Mary Erskine School for Girls (*earlier* The Edinburgh Ladies' College), from 1871-1967 situated in Queen Street, Edinburgh.

†raith a term at school, three months of full-time education.

rector a headteacher of a secondary school. **R ~ship** the office of **rector**.

†reediemadeasy a first school reading book.

†Sanct Nicholas bischop a boy bishop elected for a festival of choirboys or schoolboys on or following St Nicholas Day.

sang scule a school attached to a church, for the teaching of (*chf* ecclesiastical) singing and music *local*.

scailie 1 (a) slate. **2** a slate pencil. †~ **brod** a slate for writing on.

scholar a school pupil.

schule, school a school. †~**adge**, ~ **wages** school fees. †**school board** an elected body set up in each parish or burgh by the Education Act of 1872 to provide universal elementary education there. ~ **wean** a schoolchild *WC, SW*. **learn the** ~ be a pupil at school *now NE, EC*.

scroll-book a school rough notebook *Edb*.

scud a blow, smack with the open hand, a stroke with the **tawse** or cane.

scult *v* strike on (the palm), cane, **tawse**. *n* a blow with the flat of the hand, a slap, stroke of the cane or **tawse** on the hand.

†**senior secondary (school)** a state secondary school providing more academic courses than the **junior secondary school**, attended by pupils who were successful in the **qualifying** examination.

†**side school** a subsidiary school, *esp* in an outlying part of a parish.

†**siege** a bench or form; a class.

†**sit down** *of a school* begin its sitting, sit.

skail 1 dismiss (a school). **2** *of a group of persons in a school* break up, disperse, separate.

skirt play truant from (school) *now eLoth WC Kcb*.

skulk play truant from (school) *now Ork NE Ags*.

spell 1 spelling, a spelling lesson *now Bwk*. **2** †*also* ~ **book** a spelling book. †**big** *etc* ~(**-book**) a spelling book in capital letters. †**wee** ~(**-book**) a spelling book in lower-case letters.

Standard Grade applied to a certificate, examination or course (replacing the **O Grade** in stages from 1984 on) awarded to all pupils in secondary schools at the end of the fourth year.

stendie a stroke of the **tawse** *chf Fif*.

†**supplementary** *adj* applied to a course between the end of the Primary course and the school-leaving age, for children who were not intending to continue with academic education. *n* the course itself.

†**syllab** divide words into syllables, *esp* in teaching a child to read.

tae one of the thongs at the end of a **tawse** *now Sh Ork N*.

tag *n* the strap used for punishment in schools, the **tawse** *NE Ags*. *v* beat with a **tag** *NE*.

tak, take: ~ **up** *of a school or college* reopen after a holiday.

tards a school punishment strap, a **tawse**.

task a set lesson to be prepared, a piece of school homework *local Sh-Per*.

tattie holidays an autumn school holiday to allow children to help with the potato harvest.

taw *n, chf in pl,* **taws(e)** *sometimes treated as sing and occas with double pl* **tawses** a whip with tails, *specif* a leather punishment strap with thongs, used in schools (only rarely used in recent years and now banned in state schools). *v, also* **tawse** beat, whip with a **tawse**.

the before the names of schools or colleges: '*at the Waid Academy*'.

throosh play truant from (school) *Kcb*.

tick: play the ~ play truant *Fif*.

†**tippeny (book)** a child's elementary reading book, succeeding the **penny book**.

†**trap** correct another pupil's mistake and thus take his place in order of merit in a school class.

troon, trone *n* a truant (from school), *freq* **play the** ~. *v* play truant (from), *freq* ~ **the schule** *local Cai-Dmf*.

version 1 the translation of a passage of English prose into Latin *chf* as a school exercise; the passage so translated *NE Ags Loth*. **2** †*specif* one associated with the **bursary competition** in Aberdeen University.

†**victor** the **dux** of a school.

†**wages** school fees *chf SW*.

Watsonian a pupil or former pupil of George Watson's Boys' or Ladies' Colleges in Edinburgh, which amalgamated 1974-5 to form George Watson's College; a member of the **Watsonian Club**, since 1980 open to former pupils of these schools and of John Watson's School, and to past and present members of staff. †**Women Watsonians** name of the former pupils' club of George Watson's Ladies' College.

wee: ~ **school** the infant department in a school *local*. ~ **yins** younger children at school.

wheechs strokes with the **tawse**, a belting at school *Fif Loth Lnk*. **wheeky-whacky day** a day at school in which the **tawse** is much in use *Fif Loth Lnk*.

whipper-in a school attendance-officer *Gen except Sh Ork*.

write book a (school) writing- or exercise book *now Ork*.

yards, yairds a school playground, *specif* at the High School, Edinburgh and at the Edinburgh Academy.

yite play truant *Ags Per Fif*.

14.3.3 UNIVERSITIES

†**Atholl Crescent** informal name of the Edinburgh College of Domestic Science.

†**bachelor** a third-year student at St Andrews or Glasgow University.

†**beddal, pedell** an officer in the service of a university.

bedellus the chief porter and macebearer in the Universities of St Andrew's, Glasgow and Edinburgh.

bejan(t), †bajan a first-year student at a Scottish university *now only St Andrews*. **bejantine** *St Andrews Univ*, †**bejanella** *Aberdeen Univ* a female first-year student.

†**black stone** a dark-coloured stone, *later* part of a chair, on which students sat during an annual public examination.

bunk the lodgings of a St Andrews student *Fif*. ~**wife** a landlady of a St Andrews student *Fif*.

bursar a holder of a **bursary**. ~**y, †burse** a scholarship or endowment given to a student in a school, university etc. ~**y competition,** *also informal* ~**y comp** a competitive examination for university **bursaries** held by each of the four older Scottish universities (and *latterly* the University of Dundee), *now only* in Aberdeen, Dundee and Glasgow.

Candlemas term the second or spring term in the Universities of St Andrews and Glasgow.

cap confer a degree on (a **graduand**) by touching his or her head with a cap.

censor title of an official in a university, *usu* the person who called the roll or kept the attendance register.

college, *n* 1 *chf* **the** ~ a or the university. 2 a course of lectures. *v* educate at a university *chf C*.

collegianer a student at a college or university.

collie doug *Gsw*, **Buttery Wullie Collie** *Abd* a university student.

come out to be study to be (..), qualify for (a particular profession).

curators, *also* **C**~**s of Patronage** *Edb Univ* the seven persons, appointed by the Town Council (*now* Edinburgh **District Council**) and the University Court, who have the power of appointing to the office of **principal** and to some professorships.

dean: dean of the Faculty, †dean of Faculty *freq* ~ **of Arts** *etc* the head of a faculty in a Scottish university. **D**~ **of Faculty** *Gsw Univ* a general officer of the University; *post-Reformation* an auditor of the accounts, *now* honorary.

diet of examinations a group of university degree examinations at a particular time.

dine: (common) ~**s** *St Andrews University* the communal university dinners; the place where they are held.

Do-School, Dough School familiar name for any of the Colleges of Domestic Science *Abd Edb Gsw*.

Dumf familiar name for the Dunfermline College of Physical Education after it left Dunfermline.

†**foundit** provided for by the foundation of a college etc.

general designating a first-year, non-specialized course *now St Andrews*. **G**~ **Council** the deliberative body in the four older Scottish Universities *now* consisting of the University Court, professors, lecturers of more than one year's standing and graduates, the main functions of which are to elect the Chancellor and four Assessors of the Court and to represent the graduate body.

†**goun, gown:** ~ **class,** ~ **curriculum** *Glasgow Univ* a class qualifying for or the curriculum leading to the Arts degree. ~ **student** *Glasgow Univ* a matriculated student attending a ~ **class** and intending to take the full course for a degree, hence entitled to wear the Arts student's **red gown**.

graduand a person about to graduate.

Hall: the (Divinity) ~ one of the theological colleges of the Church of Scotland or of one of the Free Churches.

hebdomader †*in universities and grammar schools* the member of staff whose turn it was to supervise the conduct of the students. ~**'s room** *Univ of St Andrews* a room *orig* used by the **hebdomadar,** *now* used for meetings of committees etc.

humanity 1 the formal name for the study of the classical languages and literature, *esp* and *now only* Latin. 2 the chair or class of Latin.

†**immatriculat** matriculated.

†**intrant** 1 a person who enters or becomes a member of a college. 2 *St Andrews and Glasgow Universities* the student chosen by each **nation** to represent it in voting for the **rector**.

iron: fresh *or* **new aff the** ~**s** fresh from one's studies.

Kate Kennedy a mythical personage in whose honour a historical pageant is performed annually in spring by the students of St Andrew's Univeristy.

kirk: be ~**ed** be churched, of the first church attendance on the appointment of an academic body.

laureate †*ptp* admitted to a university degree. †*v* confer a university degree on. †*adj* graduate. **laureation** university graduation, *now specif* applied to the complimentary address with which honorary graduates are promoted.

†**lawer** a university professor of law.

†**lectioun** a university lecture.

†**lector** a lecturer in a university.

†**libertine** *in King's College Aberdeen* a student with no **bursary** or scholarship.

†**licentiat** a licentiate, holder of the university degree of 'licence'.

†**luminator** *St Andrews Univ* a member of class who, in return for fees paid by the other students, was responsible for providing fire and light in the lecture-room and for keeping the attendance-roll.

magistrand an undergraduate in the fourth or final year at a Scottish university. † ~ **class** the class in Natural and Moral Philosophy usually taken by students in their final year.

maister, master 1 †a teacher in a university. **2** *only* **Mr A** by a university teacher in formally designating a male student. **3** *also* †**magister** prefixed to the Christian name and surname *orig, chf* of a Master of Arts, *freq* a clergyman or schoolmaster.

manse a house reserved for the occupants of particular chairs at Aberdeen University.

†**manumission** the conferring of a university degree upon a **graduand**.

Martinmas Term the first or autumn term in the Universities of St Andrews and Glasgow.

Meal Monday a Monday holiday in the Universities of St Andrews, Edinburgh and Glasgow.

†**mediciner** title of the Professor of Medicine at King's College, Aberdeen.

†**nation** one of the regional divisions of the student body in the Universities of Glasgow and Aberdeen, and until 1858 St Andrews.

natural philosophy the study of natural phenomena, physics: the formal name of the subject and its chair.

†**oeconomus 1** *also* **iconomus** the steward or manager of property and finances, *esp* of a religious house or a college. **2** *also* **economus** *Abd St Andrews*, **economist** *Abd* the keeper of student lodgings at a university .

ordinary applied in the Faculties of Arts and Science to the general courses in any particular subject, passes in a certain number of which lead either to an **Ordinary Degree** or to the higher classes of an Honours course. **Ordinary**

(**Degree**) an academic degree gained by a number of passes in **ordinary** courses, according to varying regulations.

†**pedagogy, pedagoge** *appar* the *orig* name of the teaching institution of the Faculty of Arts: **1** in St Andrews Univ, with the building housing it; **2** in Glasgow Univ, with its body of teachers; **3** alternative term for the University or College (of St Andrews or Glasgow) viewed as a teaching institution.

†**philosophy** applied to the courses in Ethics, Physics and Metaphysics which constituted the later and greater part of the MA degree; the term was extended to cover the preliminary studies in Latin and Greek and so came to designate the Arts course as a whole.

†**pneumatic(s)** pneumatology, a branch of metaphysics.

†**preliminary examination,** *colloq* **prelim** an examination for entry to a Scottish University set annually by each of the Universities for their own prospective students.

†**primar 1** the **Principal** of a college or university *St Andrews Univ.* **2** a student of the first grade in social rank, the son of a nobleman, who paid higher University fees than the **secondars** and **ternars** and wore a better-quality gown. **~iat** the office of **Principal**.

Principal the academic head of a (university) college; *latterly* also the head of a university (who also acts as Vice-Chancellor).

†**private school** *Edb Univ* a small classroom. **~s** *St Andrews Univ* a seminar or tutorial as opposed to a public lecture.

†**procurator** *Abd, Gsw and St Andrews Univs* a student representative appointed by each **nation** to preside over it (and in Aberdeen to vote on its behalf) in **Rectorial** elections.

professional examination one of a series of examinations, called the **First, Second** *etc* **Professional Examination**, taken by students of medicine and veterinary medicine.

promoter the official, *usu* a senior member of the academic staff, who presents students for their degrees at graduation ceremonies.

†**pro-rector** *St Andrews Univ* the vice-**Rector**.

provisor *Abd Univ* the title of the steward of the Students' Union.

quaestor *St Andrews Univ* the chief financial officer of the University, the University Treasurer.

raisin Monday *St Andrews Univ* a Monday in the winter term when senior students formerly demanded of first-year students a pound of raisins in return for their protection.

rank *St Andrews Univ* a division in the order of merit awarded to students at the end of the class work of the academic year (before the degree examinations).

rector 1 *also informal(ly)* **Lord Rector** a high-ranking official, the office varying in the four older Scottish Universities and throughout the centuries; the **Rector** is now a public figure elected for three years by the students; he or she represents them on the University Court and gives a **rectorial** address at his or her inauguration. **2** † = **regent** 1. **†R~ate** the office of **rector** 1. **~ial** the canvassing and ceremonial connected with the election and inauguration of a **rector** 1. **R~ship** the office of **rector** 1.

red gown the scarlet gown worn by an arts undergraduate of one of the four older universities (no longer worn regularly).

regent *n* **1** †*Sc Univs* a teacher who took a class of students through the full four-year Arts course in language, physics and philosophy. **2** a lecturer etc who acts as adviser and consultant to students assigned to him *St Andrews and Aberdeen Univs*. †*v* act as a **regent** 1. † **~rie** the office or function of a **regent**.

sacrist the chief porter and mace-bearer of King's College and of Marischal College, Aberdeen.

†secondar *St Andrews and Glasgow Univs* a student of social rank just below a nobleman, who had special privileges and paid higher fees.

semi *n, also* ~ **bajan** a second-year university student, *usu* in the Arts faculty *now St Andrews*. † ~ **class** the second-year class as above.

senatus, *in full* **S~ Academicus,** *latterly also (usu less formally)* **Senate** *in the older Sc Univs* the body, consisting of the Principal, Professors and, more recently, a number of Readers and Lecturers, which superintends and regulates the teaching and discipline of the University.

servitor *Edinburgh Univ* a janitor or attendant.

session *Sc Univs* the portion of the year during which teaching is carried on.

†shusy a corpse (*prob orig* female) used for anatomical dissection and demonstration, *esp* one stolen from a grave.

special *of courses in Sc Univs, latterly of a second or sometimes third year class at St Andrews* advanced.

†stent-masters a committee of final-year students at Glasgow University appointed to assess the graduation fee for their fellow-**graduands**.

student, †studient 1 a student. **2** an undergraduate; a pupil of a particular university teacher. **S~s' Representative Council,**

S.R.C. a statutory body elected by the matriculated students of each of the Scottish universities to discuss student affairs etc, and represented on the University Court.

†sub-principal the deputy of the **Principal** of King's College, Aberdeen.

†suppost, supposit a member of St Andrews or Glasgow Universities.

tak, take: ~ **out** enrol in (a class) or for (a subject) at a university. ~ **up** *of a school or college* reopen after a holiday.

†ternar *St Andrews Univ* a student of the third or lowest social rank.

tertian *Sc Univs, n* a third-year Arts student *latterly St Andrews and Aberdeen, now only St Andrews*. †*adj* in the third year of the Arts course, third-year.

the before the names of schools or colleges: '*at the College Hall*'.

†theologue a theological student.

toga *Sc Univs* the scarlet gown worn by undergraduates, *esp* at Aberdeen.

Whitsun Term the third or summer term in the Universities of St Andrews and Glasgow.

14.4 FAIRS, FESTIVALS, SPECIAL OCCASIONS

14.4.1 FAIRS, SAINTS' DAYS, LOCAL FESTIVALS

†abbot: A~ of Na rent, A~ (of) Unreason the leader of the revels in a burgh festival which burlesqued religious institutions etc and was suppressed at the Reformation.

ba(ll) 1 the ~ the annual game of football *formerly* played in some areas on Shrove Tuesday. **2** *chf* **the Ba** a game of **handball** played on certain annual holidays in the **Borders** and in Ork.

Bartle: ~ **day** St Bartholomew's day, 24 Aug. ~ **fair** a fair held on that day, *esp* that at Kincardine O'Neil, Abd.

Beltane 1 a pagan fire festival on **Beltane**, 1 or 3 May (and sometimes also 21 June). **2** an old Scottish quarter day, 1 or 3 May (or possibly other days in May). † ~ **day** the day of the **Beltane** festival or fair.

Can(d)lemas Candlemas, 2 Feb, a Scottish quarter day. ~ **ba** a football match played on 2 Feb *now Bnf Kcb*.

cast the colours perform the flag-waving ceremony at Selkirk **Common Riding** *Slk*.

Common Riding name for the **Riding of the Marches** in certain towns, *eg* Selkirk, Hawick.

cornet *in ceremonies of Riding of the Marches* the chief rider and standard-bearer of the burgh *chf S*.

cry: † ~**it fair** a fair or market proclaimed in advance. ~**ing (of) the burley** the proclamation of the town's charter at the annual **Riding of the Marches** *Slk*.

Curd: ~ **Fair**, ~ **Saturday** a holiday in Kilmarnock around the time of the old **hiring fair** in May *Ayr*.

doonie a member of the **handball** team playing towards the downward goal, the **doonies** *usu* coming from the lower part of the town *Ork Rox*.

†Dudsday applied to various **hiring markets** *Ayr*.

†exerce hold (a fair or market).

fair †a gift bought at a fair. **the F**~ the annual summer holiday, *esp* **the Glasgow F**~, *now* the last two weeks in July; *also* the first Monday of this period, held as a public holiday. ~**in(g)** a present, *freq* food from a fair or at a festive season.

Falkirk Tryst the cattle market held near Falkirk, the largest of its kind in Scotland.

fee: ~**in(g) fair** *midLoth Bwk Ayr*, ~**in(g) market** a fair or market, *usu* held at **Whitsunday** and **Martinmas** where farmers engaged servants for the coming **term**.

flit: **F**~ **Friday** the **Whitsunday** or *(chf)* **Martinmas** removal day for farmworkers *Ags*. † ~**ting Friday** the **Whitsunday** removal day.

Glen Saturday a Saturday (the first or third) in April on which the children of Kilmarnock went to Crawfurdland Castle to pick daffodils *Ayr*.

groset fair an agricultural fair, *esp* the one held in Kilmarnock at the beginning of August *Ayr*.

Guid Nychburris festival the Dumfries festival of the **Riding of the Marches**.

hallow fair a market held on 1 Nov in various places, *esp* Edb.

hand, haun: ~**ba(ll)** a team game played in the Borders in which a small ball is thrown with the hands *S*.

Hawick ba a game played at Shrovetide with a football in the River Teviot.

Highland, Hieland: ~ **Show, Royal** ~ **Show, the** ~ a large agricultural show held annually by The Royal Highland and Agricultural Society, *orig* in different centres year by year, but since 1960 at a permanent site at Ingliston, midLoth.

hiring *now Bwk Rox*, **hiring fair** *or* **market** a fair or market held for the purpose of engaging farmworkers.

Honest: the ~ **Lad, the** ~ **Lass** the leading participants in the annual festival in Musselburgh.

Kelso laddie the leading male participant in the Kelso **Riding of the Marches**.

†Kowanday *prob* St Congan's day (13 Oct) when one of Turriff's two fairs was held *NE*.

lad the young bachelor chosen as the central male participant in various annual local festivals, *eg* the **Riding of the Marches**.

Lammas 1 Aug, a Scottish quarter day. ~ **Fair** a fair held at **Lammas** in various places. ~ **market** = ~ **Fair**, *esp* one held in Kirkwall and St Andrews.

lanimer(s) †the annual ceremony of inspecting the boundaries, **Riding of the Marches. Lanimer Day** *etc*, **†landsmark day** the day etc of celebrations accompanying the annual **Riding of the Marches** in Lanark *Lnk*. **Lanimer Queen** the girl chosen as Queen at the **Lanimer Day** celebrations *Lnk*.

lass the central female participant in various local festivals, *eg* the **Riding of the Marches**.

†latter fair the last of the annual fairs in Stirling.

†Legavrik one of the eight annual fairs of Inverness, held on 1 Feb.

†Lilias-day a July holiday and fair in Kilbarchan, Renfr.

Lord Cornet = **cornet** *Lnk*.

Lowrie name of two fairs held in Rayne (Abd), and Laurencekirk (Kcdn) in mid August.

†Lukismes the festival of St Luke, 18 Oct, a customary date for payment of debts and dues; the date of one of the annual fairs in Rutherglen *chf C*.

Martinmas the feast of St Martin, 11 Nov; a Scottish quarter day.

Mary: ~**mass**, ~**mes**, † ~ **day** one of the festival days of the Virgin. **†first** ~ **day** the Annunciation (25 March) or *(chf)* the Assumption (15 Aug). **†latter** ~ **day** *chf or only* the Nativity (8 Sep). ~**mas Fair** a Fair etc held at **Marymas**.

Michael Fair a fair held in Oct at Aboyne *Abd Ags*.

molly-dolly an Aunt Sally at a fair *Dnbt Ayr*.

†muck bell a silver bell given annually in Dumfries to the winner of the **muckmen's** (ie street cleaners') horse-races.

Muckle: Mucklie the fair held on **M**~ **Friday** *Kcdn Ags Fif*. **M**~ **Friday** the Friday on which the half-yearly **hiring market** was held; the hiring market itself *Abd Ags*.

nicht: the ~ **afore the morn** the eve of an important occasion, *eg* the **Common Ridings** in the Borders or the **Lammas Fair** in Kirkwall.

Northern meeting a social gathering held at Inverness, *orig* with Highland Games etc, *now* a formal ball held in late summer and at Christmas-time.

†**palm fair** an annual two-day fair formerly beginning on the fifth Monday in Lent *SW*.

†**Pasch Fair** a fair held in various districts at Eastertime.

†**Patrickmes 1** the feast of St Patrick, 17 Mar *chf WC, SW*. **2** the date of one of the annual fairs in Dumbarton.

†**peace of the fair** the special protection granted to merchants and traders travelling to or from, or attending, a fair.

†**pensil** the standard carried at the celebration of the **Common Riding** in Hawick.

†**Peter:** ~ **fyir** a bonfire made for **Petermes**. ~**mes** the feast of St Peter and St Paul (29 June); the feast of St Peter and Vincula, **Lammas** (1 Aug).

†**play** a country fair or festival. ~ **day** a day of festivity or one on which a play or pageant was performed; a day of recreation or freedom from task-work.

†**pluck-up fair** a 'grab and buy' sale; a scramble in which everyone tries to get as much as he can for himself.

pursuivant an attendant on the **cornet** at the **Riding of the Marches** ceremony at Dumfries.

Queen of the South the Dumfries schoolgirl chosen as the festival queen at the annual local **Riding of the Marches**.

Rascal Fair a **hiring market** for the engagement of men who had failed to get employment at the regular market *Abd*.

Reiver the chief male participant in the annual festival at Duns *Bwk*. ~**'s Lass** the female partner of the **Reiver** *Bwk*.

ride: Riding of the Marches the traditional ceremony of riding round the boundaries of common land to inspect landmarks, boundary stones etc, *latterly* the focus of an annual local festival in certain, *esp* Border towns. ~ **the marches** perform the ceremony of **Riding of the Marches**. ~**-out** one of a series of rehearsal rides of a section of the boundaries in the weeks before the **Riding of the Marches** *Dmf Rox*.

rowlie-powlie 1 a form of **kyles** or ninepins played at fairs. **2** †a fairground stallholder in charge of this.

ruid, rood: 1 R ~ Day (in barlan), ~mass *now Cai* the day of the Invention of the Cross, 3 May.

2 R ~ day (in hairst), ~mass the day of the Exaltation of the Cross, 14 September. **R ~ even** the eve of **R ~ day** *latterly N*. **R ~ fair** a fair or market held on **R ~ day** *now SW*.

St Michael's cake *etc* a kind of cake, the **struan**, baked in the Hebrides, *esp* in the Roman Catholic areas, on Michaelmas Eve.

†**simmer tre** a flower-bedecked pole erected during summer games.

Skire's Thursday Maundy Thursday; a fair or market held on that day.

sma(ll) shot (Satur)day a Paisley holiday on the first Saturday of July (*orig* a weavers' union holiday) *Renfr*.

snuffing the taking of snuff, *specif* as part of the **Common Riding** ceremony in Hawick *Rox*.

†**squabblement** a wrangle, disturbance of the peace, associated *esp* with the Langholm **Common Riding**.

Standard-Bearer the chief male participant in the Selkirk **Common Riding** who carries the burgh flag round the town's boundaries *Slk*.

struan a cake made from the various cereals grown on a farm *usu* oats, barley, and rye, and baked with a special ritual on Michaelmas Eve (29 Sep) *Hebrides*.

swey, sway: *chf* ~ **boat** a swing-boat at a fair *Kcdn nEC midLoth*.

Tenants-Day a fair day and holiday held on 18 Aug (Old Style) in the town of Beith in Ayrshire *now Ayr*.

teribus (and teriodin) the slogan of the town of Hawick, Rox; a local popular song with these words in its chorus, sung *esp* at the Hawick **Common Riding** *Rox*.

†**the** before the names of feast days or times associated (at some period) with religious observance: '*about the Martinmas*'.

timmer market a fair held in Aberdeen at the end of Aug (*orig chf* for the sale of wood or wooden objects).

Toun Champion the chief male participant in the festival of the **Riding of the Marches** at Musselburgh, with the duty of protecting the **Turf Cutter**.

trades holiday(s), the Trades the annual summer holiday, *orig* of the craftsmen of a town, *esp* Edb, *later* extended more generally (*orig* one day, *now* two to three weeks).

Turf Cutter one of the participants in the **Riding of the Marches** ceremony at Musselburgh, with the duty of marking the **marches** by digging a turf at each.

uppie in **handball** a member of the team playing

towards the upward goal, the **uppies** *usu* coming from the upper part of the town *now Ork S.*

whipman a member of one of the several societies of carters and ploughmen in West Linton, where the local society celebrates an annual festival *now Pbls.*

Whuppity Scoorie a traditional custom among young people in Lanark celebrated on 1 Mar *Lnk.*

Whussenday, Whitsunday Whitsunday, a Scottish quarter day.

14.4.2 MAJOR FESTIVALS

For saints' days, see 14.1.10 and 14.4.1.

April(e): ~ **errand** an errand on which an April fool is sent *Sh-Fif WC.* ~ **gowk** an April fool *now Ags Fif midLoth.*

auld: ~ **lang syne** the song or the tune of this name, *now esp* Burns' song and its tune, played and sung at the close of social gatherings and at midnight on **Hogmanay. A** ~ **Year** (always in contrast with **New-year**) the previous year; the year that is about to end; the last few days of the year. **A** ~ **Year's Day** *or* **Night** = **Hogmanay. A** ~ **New Year's Day** New Year's Day (Old Style) *now Sh Ork.*

Bannock Day *or* **Night** Shrove Tuesday.

†bene: King *or* **Queen of B** ~ the person in whose portion of Twelfth-Night cake the bean was found.

Burns: ~ **Night** 25 January, the anniversary of the birth of the poet Robert Burns. ~ **Supper** an annual celebration of the birthday of Robert Burns, with various traditional features such as the serving of haggis, **neeps** and whisky, the reciting and singing of Burns' poems and songs, the making of various speeches.

cake cake, fruit loaf etc given to children or callers at New Year *now Fif.* **C** ~ **day** = **Hogmanay** *Fif Rox.*

†carlings peas, variously prepared, *appar* eaten on Passion Sunday.

Chrissenmas, †Christinmes Christmas *now Bnf-Ags.*

Christmas a Christmas present, Christmas box: *'there's yer Christmas'.*

cream (of) the water *or* **well** (draw) the first water from a well on New Year's morning *now Abd Ags Fif.*

daft: the ~ **days** the period of festivity at Christmas and New Year.

dook for apples *Halloween game* attempt to get hold of apples floating in a tub etc with one's teeth, by dipping one's head in the water and without using one's hands.

fastern's een, fastingeven Shrove Tuesday.

first fit, first foot *n* the first person to enter a house on New Year's morning, considered to bring good (or bad) luck for the year. *v* be the first to visit (a person) in the New Year; go on a round of such visits. **first fitter, first footer** a person who does this.

flour the first water drawn from the well in the New Year *local.*

Galatian, Galoshan 1 *also* ~**s** a play performed by boy **guisers** at **Hogmanay**; a mumming play or entertainment at this time *C, S.* **2** the name of the hero in such a play, a mummer, harlequin *now Ayr Rox.*

gowk *n* **1** *also* ~**ie** a fool. **2** a joke, trick *esp* an April Fool's Day joke *now midLoth.* *v* fool, deceive, *freq* in connection with April fooling *now local NE-Uls.* ~**'s day** April Fool's Day *now nEC.* ~**'s errand** a fool's errand *now local.*

†gude Wednisday the Wednesday before Easter.

guiser a mummer, masquerader, *now esp* one of a party of children who go in disguise from door to door offering entertainment *esp* at Halloween. **guising** going about as a **guiser.**

hallow: H~**een,** ~ **eve(n) 1** 31 Oct, the eve of All Saints' Day, the last day of the year in the old Celtic calendar, associated with witches and the powers of darkness, and celebrated with bonfires, divination rites etc. **2** a children's festival when they go around as **guisers**, *freq* with turnip lanterns. **†** ~ **fire** a Halloween bonfire.

Han(d)sel Monday the first Monday of the New Year on which the New Year's **handsel** was given, regarded as a holiday *now local Ags-Ayr.*

het pint a drink made from hot spiced ale to which sugar, eggs and spirits may be added, served at christening, wedding or New Year festivities.

Hogmanay 1 31 Dec, the last day of the year, New Year's Eve. **2** a New-Year's gift, *esp* a gift of oatcakes etc given to or asked for by children on New Year's Eve. **3** †the cry uttered in asking for the New Year's gift. **4** *esp* **your** *etc* ~ any form of hospitality, *esp* a drink given to a guest to celebrate the New Year, or a gratuity given to tradesmen and employees on that day. **5** †an **oatcake** or biscuit baked to give the children on

31 Dec. **haud** *etc* ~ celebrate the passing of the old year.

huntegowk *n* **1** the game of April fool, a fool's errand, *esp* on April Fool's Day *Fif sEC, WC Dmf.* **2** April Fool's Day *now Fif Gall Dmf.* **3** an April fool, a person sent on a fool's errand *now Ork C-S. v, also* **hunt the gowk** go on a fool's errand, be made a fool of, *esp* an April Fool *now EC, S.*

Immortal: The ~ **Memory** name for the honorific speech in praise of Robert Burns given at **Burns Suppers.**

Jenny reekie a hollow cabbage stalk packed with tow, used to blow smoke into a house as a Halloween prank *Fif Kinr.*

magowk make an April fool of. ~'s **day** April Fool's day *Gsw SW.*

†**Mey play(s)** the entertainments etc of May Day or early May.

Mod: the ~ the annual Gaelic festival of music and literature, first held at Oban in 1892.

mort hede a turnip lantern representing a skull *NE.*

neep lantern *Sh-nEC,* **neepy candle** *NE* a turnip lantern, *esp* as at Halloween.

New-year, Ne'er 1 the New Year. **2** *also* ~('s) **day** a gift, or a drink or food given in hospitality at the New Year. ~('s) **day** New Year's Day. ~('s) **even** New Year's Eve, **Hogmanay.** †~(**is**) **gift** a New Year gift. ~('s) **mas** New day or tide *now Sh.*

Pace, Pask 1 Easter. **2** †the Passover. ~ **Day** Easter Day. **p**~ **egg** an Easter egg *now Sh-N Rox.* **pace egg day** Easter Monday *Bwk Rox.* †~ **evin** Easter eve; the day before Easter or the Passover. ~ **Saturday, Sunday** *etc* Easter Saturday, Easter Sunday etc *now Sh Cai.* **Pace-yaud** a person who fails to observe the custom of wearing something new for Easter.

†**play day** a day of festivity or one on which a play or pageant was performed; a day of recreation or freedom from task-work.

†**pou, pull:** ~ **stalks** pluck stalks of corn or cabbage plants for use in divination, *eg* at Halloween.

preen-tail day the day following All Fools' Day when paper tails were attached to the backs of unsuspecting persons as a joke *Bwk Rox.*

†**sautie bannock** an oatmeal **bannock** with a fair amount of salt, baked on Shrove Tuesday.

shannack, shanacle a **Halloween** bonfire *Per Fif.*

sing: ~**in cake** a sweet biscuit given to children on **Hogmanay** in return for a song etc *Fif.* † ~**in**

e'en: Hogmanay, when children went from house to house singing songs for cakes etc *Ags Fif.*

skitterie winter the last person to arrive for or leave work on **Hogmanay** *WC.*

sowans nicht Christmas Eve (Old Style) *NE.*

sownack a **Halloween** bonfire; a heavy bog-fir torch used in **Halloween** fires *now Per.*

tailie (day) 2 April, when children fix paper tails with various messages to the backs of unsuspecting victims *local Ork-Rox.*

tannel a bonfire, *esp* one kindled at certain festivals, *eg* at Midsummer Eve or **Halloween.**

tattie-bogle a turnip-lantern used at **Halloween** *nEC.*

†**uphalie(day), uphaliemes** the festival of Epiphany at the end of Christmastide.

†**valentin(e)** a custom observed on St Valentine's eve of drawing by lot the name of one's sweetheart for the following year.

†**wauks, wakes** a small band of musicians, maintained by a town to play in the streets, *usu* a Christmas and New Year.

whistlin *or* **fusslin Sunday** the **fast day** (*usu* a Thursday) before Communion on which whistling was permitted *now Kcdn.*

winter the last person to turn up for work on **Hogmanay** *now WC.*

Yule, (y)eel *N n* **1** Christmas; the day itself; the festive season associated with it, *freq* beginning before Christmas day and (*esp Sh*) continuing until after New Year *now chf literary.* **2** the entertainment provided at Christmas, Christmas cheer *now Sh.* †*v* keep Christmas. † ~ **bannock** a gratuity of oatmeal paid at Christmas by tenants of a **barony** to the **baron court** officer. ~ **bannocks** oatcakes specially baked on Christmas Eve both for one's own family and for children going from door to door. † ~ **bread** a richly-seasoned oat-bread baked for Christmas. † ~ **candle** a large long-burning Christmas candle. ~ **day** Christmas day. ~ **e'en,** ~ **even** Christmas eve. ~ **feast** a Christmas dinner *now Sh.* † ~ **girth** a time of immunity granted at Christmas. †**brak Yeel's gird** disturb the peace of Christmas by weeping on Christmas day, and so incur bad luck for the following year *NE.* ~ **mart** an ox slaughtered and salted for Christmas and the winter. ~ **pins** *now Sh,* † ~ **preens** *NE* pins used as stakes in a Christmas game. ~ **sowans: sowans** specially made for Christmas into which the usual objects of divination of marriage (*eg* a ring, button etc) were stirred before distribution among the company. † ~ **stok** ? a

Yule log. ~ **tide,** ~ **time** *now Sh* the season of **Yule.** †~ **vacance** the Christmas holidays or recess. ~'s **yaud** *latterly chf N,* ~ **shard** *Abd abusive* a person ill-prepared for **Yule**, *eg* one who leaves work unfinished before Christmas or the New Year or who has nothing new to wear for the festivities. **Auld** ~ Christmas Day (Old Style), *orig* 5 Jan, *later* 6 Jan, *now* 7 Jan *now Sh NE.*

14.4.3 MISCELLANEOUS OCCASIONAL CELEBRATIONS

For the celebration of major life events, such as birth and marriage, see relevant sections of 8.

†**bale** a bonfire.

†**banefire** a bonfire.

beverage a fine in the form of money, drink, or a kiss demanded from a person wearing something new, *chf* **gie, get** *etc* **the** ~ **o** (the new garment).

bleeze a bonfire *now Ags.*

deochandorus a stirrup cup.

dump: gie someone his *or* **get one's** ~**s** give or get thumps on the back as a birthday ritual, the number of thumps corresponding to the age reached *now Loth Dnbt.*

first fit, first foot the first person (or animal) met on a journey *now Cai Abd Stlg.*

foundin pint, foonin pint a drink given to work-men after laying the foundations of a building as an omen of good luck *now Ork Ags.*

foy a farewell feast; a party to celebrate a special occasion *local.* †**drink (someone's)** ~ drink farewell (to someone).

hack, hag: strike, put *etc* **a** ~ **in the post** *or* **jamb** celebrate an event *chf WC SW.*

han(d)sel *n* a gift intended to bring good luck to something new or to a new beginning, *eg* the New Year, a new house or new clothes. *v* **1** give or offer a **handsel** to (a person) at the beginning of a year or day, or to mark some special occasion. **2** inaugurate with some ceremony or gift etc in order to bring good luck. **3** celebrate the first use of (something) with a **handsel**; use for the first time; be the first to try, test or taste (something).

heat the house *etc* hold a house-warming party *now midLoth.*

†**infare** an entertainment on entering a new house.

†**lintel ale** a drink given to the masons at a building job when the door-lintel was put on.

†**pleuch, ploo:** ~ **feast** a ritual entertainment given at the first ploughing of the new season.

sain inaugurate with some act or ceremony *now Bnf.*

slocken inaugurate or celebrate with a drink.

tannel a bonfire, *esp* one kindled at certain festivals, *eg* at Midsummer Eve or **Halloween.**

†**warping ale** *or* **dinner** a drink of ale or some food given to the weaver after setting up a warp of homespun wool.

15. CHARACTER, EMOTIONS, SOCIAL BEHAVIOUR

15.1 GENERAL AND NEUTRAL TERMS

aboot a bat equal in ability.

†affere, effere manner of bearing, appearance, deportment. **~s, feirs** manners, ways, actions.

aicht: a (common) five ~(s) an average or ordinary person *local*.

awfu remarkable.

†bere carry oneself; act; behave.

billy, *usu the* **~** a person etc particularly characterized by something.

bin(ner) humour, mood *NE*.

bon humour, mood *now Ags*.

buff: not *etc* **play ~** make no impression.

cast aspect, demeanour; appearance.

conteen bear or conduct oneself. **~ing** behaviour, bearing.

†convoy deportment, bearing.

cuttance: no ~ no encouragement *local Abd-Stlg*.

deid, dead: in the ~ thraw between one state and another *now Abd*.

†demain treat or deal with in a particular way.

†dreaddour hesitate.

eel-drowner *usu ironic* a person who can do the impossible, an exceedingly clever person: *'he's nae eel-drowner'*.

efter-ane alike, uniform, unchangeable, the same *now NE: 'he's aye efter-ane'*.

even, e'en bring to the same level or condition *now Ags*. **† ~lyness** equality. **†evenlikly** equal in character, size, force.

†exerce practise (a virtue, vice etc).

†faculty one's personal character, disposition.

farrant, farand of a certain disposition, *eg* **auld-farrant, fair-farrand**.

fashion, †fassoun: †~t of a specified appearance, manner etc, *eg* **fair, ill ~t**. **~s** manners, behaviour, *chf* **fair** *or* **ill ~s** *now local*.

†father better *or* **war** better or worse than one's father.

faut, fault: hae nae ~ til have no fault to find with *local*.

fin(d) feel, be conscious of.

†ingine mental quality, disposition, temperament; the mind or disposition of a person or persons.

key mood, humour, *chf* **be in a ~** *local Sh-Kcb*.

kilter good spirits, fettle, *chf* **in** *or* **out of ~**.

kippage (good etc) spirits, fettle *Cai Kcb*.

lair, lear habit, custom, *usu* **ill ~** *Cai*.

lay mood, temper *chf Sh Ork*.

like: be ~ anesel act up to one's reputation.

muid mood.

†offcome the way in which one comes out of an affair, or is seen to conduct oneself in it.

†ondreyd not dreaded *Abd*.

owercome *v* overcome.

raploch ordinary, undistinguished *now Ags*.

sakeless guileless, simple; inoffensive, harmless.

scone: a ~ o the day's *etc* **baking** one of the same kind as others, an average or typical person.

ser, sair treat (in a certain way), behave (in a certain way) towards *local Sh-Kcb*.

set *now sometimes ironic* be seemly or suitable for, become, suit: *'It sets us to be dumb a while'*.

sevendle, sevendable thorough, out-and-out, extreme.

shape, †shap *v, chf* **~ to** to turn out, show promise of being etc; adapt oneself to. *n* an attitude, posture; conduct, manner.

†slocken abate, subdue, do away with, suppress.

smuir, smoor deaden; quench.

souch, sough general feeling or opinion, attitude, style *now Ayr*.

speed: come (good, bad *etc*) **~** be (very, not at all etc) successful *now Ork NE, EC*.

spune, spoon: mak a ~ *or* **spoil a horn** either succeed or fail in a big way.

†state a person's proper nature.

strind the inherited qualities which come from descent, lineage *now Sh*.

taik a mood, humour, disposition *Sh Abd*.

tether, tedder scope, the limits (of conduct, resources, endurance etc), 'rope' *now Sh Ork N*.

tholeable bearable, tolerable *Gen except Sh Ork*.

tid a mood, humour *now C, S Uls*.

tift, †tiff humour, fettle, frame of mind *now Ayr Wgt Rox*.

track a feature, trait *now Sh*.

tune mood, humour, temper, *freq* **(in) guid** *or* **ill ~** *local Sh-Wgt*.

†unirkit not irked, not wearied (**of**).

up wi on an equality with, as good as *now Cai Ags*.

usual, uswal: one's (auld) ~ one's usual state of health, frame of mind; one's old self: *'he's in his usual'*.

wame the seat of the passions or thoughts, the heart, the mind.

ware spend, employ, waste (one's time, life, efforts etc).

warld, world, wardle: like the ~ like everyone else, normal.

warmer *of a person, used in admiration or disapproval* an extreme example of his or her kind, 'a right one' *C, S*.

whiff, whuff *of a mood etc* a 'touch' *local*.

15.2 SOCIAL STATUS AND INHERENT QUALITIES

15.2.1 HIGH CLASS

almichty, †almicht *verse* almighty.

†athill noble.

below lower oneself.

better-mais(t) better-class.

big of consequence.

†boldin affected by extreme pride etc.

†boldinit swelled with pride etc.

causey: crown of the ~, casey croon *local Abd-S* a public, conspicuous, creditable, respectable or dominant position, *eg* **keep the crown of the ~**.

cockapentie a snob.

come doun with one's spirit humble oneself *now Abd Lnk*.

crouse conceited, arrogant, proud *now Bnf Abd Ags*.

daddies: be a their ~ excel, be the best, be an extreme example *local Bnf-Rox*.

†dane haughty, reserved, dignified.

†danger disdain.

†deaf: nae ~ **nit(s)** no inconsiderable person.

†dedenʒe *v* disdain.

†digne worthy; of great or exceptional worth or merit.

din-bonnets: nae ~ not to be despised, first-rate *Abd*.

dink haughty.

†disdene disdain.

dorty haughty *now Ork Ags Kcb*.

†exalt exalted.

expensive extravagant *now local Sh-Pbls*.

†Falkland bred well-mannered, as if bred at court.

fallauge lavish, profuse, prodigal with money *Abd*.

far kent known far and wide, famous *local*.

fawmous famous *NE*.

fiddle: look *etc* **like the far (awa) end of a (French)** ~ have a long face, look disdainful *local*.

fill an fesh ben (*NE*) *or* **mair** *(now Abd Ags Kcb)* extravagant living.

†gadge talk haughtily without justification.

genteelity 1 gentility. **2** gentry, people of gentle birth *now Sh WC Uls*.

gentie genteel; courteous, well-bred *now Abd Fif*.

†gentle *adj* gentlemanly, genteel *NE*. *n* a person of gentle birth.

gentlemanny gentlemanly *now Sh NE Ags*.

gentrice 1 †the character or behaviour natural to a person of gentle birth or rank. **2** good birth or breeding, gentility. **3** people of good birth or breeding, gentry.

gentry 1 the character or behaviour natural to a person of gentle birth or rank *now Abd Ags*. **2** good birth, rank of a gentleman *now Ags*.

get well up rise in position, succeed.

glore *n* glory *latterly arch*. †*v* glory, take pride (**in**), boast.

goich a haughty carriage of the head *Arg*.

gree pre-eminence, supremacy, first place, victory in a contest; the palm, the prize, *freq* **win** *or* **bear the** ~ *now literary*.

gret, grit (the) great.

guid, good distinguished in rank or social standing, worthy, respectable *now local*.

hack: a ~ **abeen the common** a cut above ordinary people *Sh NE*. **tak, pit** *or* **haul doon a** ~ take (someone) down a peg *Sh NE*.

†ha(ll) binks are sliddery *proverb* great men are not reliable in their support.

†hautane haughty.

heck: live *etc* **at** ~ **and manger** live extravagantly, 'be in clover' *now Mry nEC, WC*.

heelie(fou) proud, haughty, arrogant.

heich, high, †thie *adj, also* ~**-heidit** *now Sh N nEC* arrogant, proud, condescending. *adv* proudly, haughtily, disdainfully. **carry a** ~ **heid** behave haughtily *E*. **be very** ~ **in the bend** be very condescending *now midLoth Dmf*.

†heicht, also ~**ynes** haughtiness, pride, insolence. ~**y** proud, haughty, arrogant. **at** ~ at the height of dignity, greatness etc.

heid, head: ~**ie** proud, haughty *now Bnf Kcdn Per*. ~ **bummer** a manager, a prominent or important person. ~-**heich** with the head high, proudly, confidently, with dignity *NE midLoth Uls.*

†**therely** stately, splendid.

high-bendit dignified in appearance, haughty, ambitious *now midLoth.*

hing, hang: ~-**the-gither** clannish *Arg Ayr.*

ilka: nae ~ **body** not everybody, no ordinary person *N Per.*

jouk bow deferentially; humble oneself, show deference *now midLoth.* ~ **under** be subservient to *now Abd midLoth.*

kick show off, walk haughtily *N.*

†**kid** renowned.

†**kith** knowledge of how to behave, courtly or refined behaviour, *only in* **cumly in, to** *or* **with** ~.

knab, nabb a person of importance or prestige; a person of moderate wealth, a person with social pretensions, a snob *now local N-S.* †**knabbie** having rank, means or position; genteel, pretentious.

lady: ~**ness** the quality or character of a lady *now Ork Ags Uls.* ~ **body** a ladylike woman *Ork Abd Ags.*

†**lair, lear:** (**well** *etc*)-~**ed** (well-)educated.

laird †**lord it** (**over**). ~**ly** lordly, aristocratic; lavish, extravagant *chf Abd.*

lairge, large lavish *now NE.*

lanerly reserved in manner.

†**laureat(e)** worthy of the laurel crown symbolizing distinction, pre-eminent.

†**lout** humble oneself.

maist chief, most powerful, greatest *now Ayr Rox.*

†**maister-man** a chief or leader, a mighty man.

major-mindit haughty in demeanour, high-minded *now EC, S.*

marked notable, distinguished *local.*

†**mauchty** powerful, mighty *chf N.*

†**memorial** posthumous reputation, fame.

mense do honour to; grace, adorn; honour with one's presence *now SW.* ~**ful** well-mannered, polite *now N, SW,S.*

†**miskennand** disdainful (of others), neglectful.

muckle, mickle of high rank or social standing *now local Sh-Edb.*

namely noted, famed, of good repute.

neb: cock (**up**) **one's** ~ look haughtily.

†**nice** disdainful, haughty. ~**nes** hauteur.

†**nobilitate** distinguished, renowned.

†**nobill** a person of great distinction or renown.

†**ogart** pride, arrogance, presumption.

outward cold in manner, aloof, reserved *Rox.*

†**parage** (noble) lineage.

pauchtie supercilious, haughty, arrogant *now Kcb.*

†**pauchtily** haughtily, arrogantly, superciliously.

†**pensit** proud, conceited, arrogant; puffed with pride.

†**politik** refined, cultured, polished.

potestater: in one's ~ at the height of one's career, influence etc, in a state of full well-being and prosperity, in one's prime *Sh NE.*

†**precede** go before or beyond (another) in quality or degree; surpass.

†**preclare** distinguished, illustrious.

†**prefer** surpass, excel.

pridefu haughty, arrogant, snobbish. †**prydy** characterized by pride, proud.

primp haughty, conceited *now Sh.*

proud †a proud person; a person of high degree. ~**fu** haughty, prideful *now Bnf Ags Kcb.*

puddock term of abuse or contempt for an arrogant person.

†**rank** proud; noble, grand.

†**ray** a king, used as a respectful term for a man.

†**reginal** queenly.

†**rich, ryke** powerful, mighty.

sanshach disdainful, surly *NE.*

saut, salt: nae sma ~ 'no small beer' *Ags Per Fif.*

†**senʒeourabill** of a lord, lordly.

sheep shank: nae ~ a person of some importance *now Stlg SW.*

skeich, skey *now Ags adj, esp of women* shy, coy, disdainful, saucy, haughty *now Lnk Ayr Wgt.* †*adv* shyly, coyly, disdainfully, saucily, spiritedly.

skit *esp of a woman* an arrogant person *now Sh.*

sma(ll): be *etc* **nae** ~ **drink** be a person of some importance.

sneist behave in a contemptuous, arrogant way, be scornful or supercilious.

†**sneith** smooth, polished.

†**snifty** haughty, disdainful *sEC Wgt Rox.*

snottery surly, brusque, snooty *nEC, WC, SW.*

†**solemn** famous, renowned.

spicy proud, testy.

†**statelike** in a stately manner.

stench, stainch, staunch serious, severe-looking, reserved *now NE.*

†**stey, steich** reserved, haughty.

†**stingy** haughty, supercilious.

stinking offensively haughty, snobbish, supercilious *now Sh NE Ags.*

streetch, stretch strut about haughtily *now Kcb.*

†**strenthy** strong, powerful.

strunt strut, walk about in a stately way *now local Ork-Gall.*

†**succudrus** presumptuous, arrogant.

†**succudry** presumption, arrogance.

†**tarrow at** *or* **on** show disdain at.

†**trump: the tongue of the** ∼ the main or most active person in a group; the spokesman.

†**unthrift** lack of thrift, extravagance.

†**upsticken** priggish, snobbish.

wanthrift extravagance, lack of thrift *now Sh.*

wasteful *NE-SW*, **wastrife** *now NE-S*, **wastry** *now Rox* wasteful, extravagant. †*n* **wastry** reckless extravagance, *esp* in living; wastefulness.

weel-come of good lineage, of honourable parentage *now Abd Dmf.*

15.2.2 LOW CLASS

auld, old: ∼**-fashioned, auld-farrant** old-fashioned; quaint. †**auld-gabbit** speaking an ancient tongue; ancient looking. **auld warld** belonging to past time, old, antique; old-fashioned.

Auntie Beenie a rather old-fashioned looking woman *local C.*

†**barbar** *adj* barbarous, barbarian. *n* a barbarian.

bard, baird *freq derog* a poet; a strolling singer or player; a vagabond minstrel, buffoon.

†**bellamy** a rough person.

†**borrel** rough, rude.

†**broken** *of persons, esp in the Highlands and Borders* outlawed for some crime; ruined, impoverished, and living irregularly or lawlessly, *usu* ∼ **men.**

bruit brute.

buirdly rough *now Abd.*

cabbrach a big, disagreeable, uncouth person *Bnf Kcb.*

caddie a ragamuffin, a rough lad or fellow *now Abd Fif Uls.*

caird a vagrant or rough person.

carle, carlie *humorous, sympathetic or depreciatory, now local Bnf-Fif* a man of the common people, a peasant or labourer *now Bnf Abd Lnk.*

cavel, kevel a low, rough fellow.

†**chuff** a churl, a rude, coarse person.

clamjamfry rabble, riff-raff.

†**clucane** ? a yokel.

clype a big, uncouth, awkward or ugly person *now NE.*

clytach talk in a strange language, *esp* chatter *NE.*

†**codroch** *n, also* **codderar** *Abd* an idle low-class person. *adj* **1** low-class. **2** having country manners, rough.

coof a lout, rustic *now Fif.*

coorse 1 coarse. **2** rough, awkward, over-direct in manner(s).

countra, country: countryfeed countryfied *local NE, nEC.* ∼ **Jock** *disparaging* a farmworker *Abd Fif.*

cowt a rough awkward person *now Abd.*

donsie unfortunate, luckless.

doon-come a fall in status, humiliation *local.*

drumshorlin having an uncared-for or miserable appearance.

Englisher *now usu derog* an Englishman *now nEC Rox.*

†**ethnik** a heathen, pagan.

far back backward as regards progress, ignorant *Ross Abd Ags.*

filget an untidy, disreputable-looking person *Bnf Abd.*

filsh a big, disagreeable person, a lout *Bnf Abd.*

†**flear** a fugitive, a person who flees.

fleep a lazy lout, an oaf *Ork Cai NE.*

flunkie *chf contemptuous* a manservant, *esp* in livery, a footman, lackey.

fugie a runaway, a fugitive *now Ags.*

†**fugitour** a fugitive.

geordie a rustic, yokel *local Inv-S.*

gheeho an uncouth, blustering fellow *Arg.*

gillieperous a rough, ungainly person *Mry Abd.*

gilpin a loutish person *chf N, SW.*

†**Glunimie, gluntoch, gluntow** *derog* a Highlander.

†**graith** *contemptuous* people, riff-raff.

groff 1 *of language etc* vulgar, coarse. **2** *of persons* coarse, rough *now local Sh-Abd.*

gustless in bad taste, tasteless *now Fif.*

gutterbluid a lowly-born or ill-bred person, a guttersnipe.

hairy a woman slum-dweller *chf Abd Gsw.*

haithen outlandish, incomprehensible *now Sh Uls.*

hallach *now NE,* **hallockit** *Gen except NE,* **hallirackit** *local Sh-Ags* uncouth, noisy.

hameart unpolished, unsophisticated *now Ags.*

hamit rough and ready, uncouth, untidy *now Fif.*

heap a coarse rough person *local Mry-Kinr.*

heather, hather: ∼**y** rough, dishevelled; mountain-bred. ∼ **an dub** rough, poor, unrefined *NE.*

Hieland, Highland referring to the mental or moral qualities or traits of character supposed to be typical of Highlanders, *freq pejorative* owing to the suspicion and dislike of them once prevalent in the Lowlands: **1** having an exaggerated sense of birth and lineage, *esp* ∼ **pride. 2** uncouth, unskilled, inelegant, rough and ready. **3** not quite truthful or honest, shifty, evasive *now NE.* **4** naive, gullible, unrealistic, impractical, 'green'.

hill-run uncultured, rough, boorish *NE Ags Fif.*

hobby a person who dressed in coarse rustic clothing; a stupid slovenly fellow.

hodden rustic, homely *now Fif.* ~ **gray** a person dressed in a simple rustic fashion.

hugmahush a lout *now Kcdn.*

hummle humble. †**hum(m)il(l)y** humbly.

hummlie 1 †a rustic, *specif* a Highlander. **2** a native of Buchan *Abd.*

hurb an uncouth creature *NE.*

†**hurcheon** an unkempt, uncouth person.

hypal an uncouth, unkempt, broken-down or good-for-nothing person *local.*

†**ignorant(is)** ignorant people.

ill: ~**-faured** ill-mannered, bad-tempered, coarse. ~**-guided** badly brought up *now Dmf.* ~**-shaken-up** untidy, disordered, awkward, loutish *Sh Ork NE.* ~**-towdent** poorly-clad, neglected-looking; unkempt *Bnf Abd.*

incomer in Sc *chf derog* implying an intruder.

†**jakfallow** *lyk of a servant* presumptuous, behaving like his master's equal.

†**Jock:** ~ **the laird's brither** *proverb* a person treated with familiarity or little respect. ~ **upaland, John up(on)land** a rustic.

joskin, geeskin a country bumpkin, yokel, farmworker *now local NE-Dmf.*

keelie a rough male city-dweller, a tough, now *esp* from the Glasgow area.

†**kittok** term for a woman or girl of low rank or character.

†**knapper** one who bites or snaps with the teeth (to drive off cats etc); a boor.

†**ladry** base conduct or talk.

landward, landwart rustic, awkward, uncouth *now EC Ayr.*

†**lawit, lewit** unlearned; unpolished; common.

†**licht, light** be brought low, *chf fig* be degraded or humiliated.

†**lithry** a crowd of rather disreputable characters, a rabble, mob.

loun †a fellow of the lower orders, one of the riff-raff, a rough; a rascally servant, a menial. † ~**rie** baseness. ~**-like** disreputable, shabby, scruffy *latterly Ags.*

†**lour** grovel.

lown humble, unassuming.

lowp-(the-)coonter *contemptuous* a male shop-assistant *local N-Wgt.*

lubbard a lubber, a lout *now Kcb S.*

main mean, common; inferior.

mane: to ~ to be pitied *now local N-S.*

Meg, maggie, meggie a rather unsophisticated girl, *esp* a rough country girl.

menseless unmannerly, objectionable in behaviour.

Michael a person of lowly rank, a rustic.

midden: ~ **mavis** *joc* a female searcher of refuse heaps. ~**-raker** a searcher of refuse heaps *now WC.*

minker a ragamuffin, vagrant *Abd Edb.*

miraculous clumsy, loutish *Cai Abd.*

mislearit ill-bred, unmannerly, rude *now Ork Ags Per.*

†**mislernit** ill-bred, misconducted; *of speech* unmannerly.

†**misnurtourit** ill-bred, unmannerly, boorish.

muirland moorland-bred or -grown, rustic, uncouth.

†**munsie** *disparaging* a Frenchman.

neeger 1 a nigger. **2** a savage, barbarous person.

new-start-up (an) upstart.

†**obeyand** submitting, obedient or subject (**to**).

†**outdwellar** one who lives outside the burgh, a stranger, outsider.

outlan(d) an outsider, stranger, outcast *now local Sh-Fif.*

outrel, outeral a person from a different country, district or family; an alien, stranger, incomer *now local Sh-Lnk.*

†**outwale** an outcast.

†**pet(e)ous, pietuous** piteous, deserving pity.

pilsh a boorish, low character *NE.*

pleuchie a ploughman; a rustic, yokel *now Ags Per Fif.*

†**popular** a commoner; the common people.

†**quent** quaint.

†**rabiator, rubeatour** a lout, boor.

rag: ~**gety,** ~**git** wearing ragged clothes.

ragabash *n* **1** †a ragamuffin. **2** a ragged, motley crew, riff-raff *now Ags.* †*adj* rough, uncouth *chf S.*

ramgunshoch bad-tempered, rude and boorish *now Wgt.*

rammock a big, coarse person *now Bnf.*

ram-stampish rough and ready, unceremonious.

randie 1 *of a woman* loud-voiced, coarse and aggressive *now Bnf Ags midLoth.* **2** *of language* coarse, uncouth *now local Ags-S.*

ranegill a rough character, *esp* a tinker *Abd Kcdn Rox.*

raploch ordinary, undistinguished; crude, uncouth *now Ags.*

raucle, rackle 1 rough, crude, tough, uncouth. **2** *of speech* rough, unpolished.

†**reebaldaill** rabble; low company.

reechnie a rough, uncouth person, *esp* a woman or girl *Bnf Abd*.

reuch, rough *adj* rough. *n* a rough, coarse woman *Abd*. ~**some** rough, crude, uncouth *now Dnbt Kcb*. ~**-spun** *of manners* rough, crude, unpolished *now nEC*. ~ **and right** rough and ready, having somewhat rough manners, blunt *now Sh*.

rinagate a runagate, a fugitive, rascal *local Sh-SW*.

†**roid** unlearned; unrefined; inelegant.

rothos, rothie a rude, coarse person *Abd*.

rudas *n, chf* **auld** ~ a coarse woman *now Bnf*. †*adj, of a man* cantankerous, stubborn, rough-mannered.

rullion a coarse, ungainly, rough-looking person.

rum boorish, coarse in manner or speech *NE Lnk SW*.

†**ruryk** rustic.

†**ruskie** (a) strong, vigorous, *usu* rough-mannered (person).

†**rusticate** countrified, boorish.

sagan *contemptuous* an uncouth person *Abd*.

†**Sandie, Sawny, Saunders, Sannock** a young man, *esp* a countryman, yokel; *chf Eng slang* a Scotsman.

scaff (and raff) riff-raff.

scawt, †**skaid** scruffy, mean.

scourie scruffy, disreputable, broken down (in appearance) *now Stlg Ayr*.

scruff riff-raff *C*.

scuff riff-raff *now local Per-WC*. ~**y** shabby, worn, tarnished, mean-looking *now NE-S*.

†**scurr** a buffoon, jester.

scurryvaig a vagabond; a lout.

†**silly** deserving of pity or sympathy.

sing sma adopt a deferential or submissive tone or attitude.

skybal(d) *n* a ragged, unkempt person, ragamuffin. *adj* tattered, ragged.

†**sober** of low degree; humble.

stirrah, †**stirrow** contemptuous term for a rough unmannerly youth *now Rox*.

strag a vagabond, roaming person *now Dnbt Lnk Dmf*.

sture rough in manner or appearance *now Slk*.

tatterwallop a ragged person, ragamuffin *Ork NE*.

tattie: ~**-bogie** *now NE*, ~**-bogle** *Gen except Sh Ork*, ~**-boodie** *NE*, ~ **doolie** *now Kcdn-Per* a scarecrow, a ragamuffin.

teuch, tough rough, coarse *local Sh-Wgt*.

teuchter *freq* disparaging or contemptuous term for a Highlander, *esp* a Gaelic-speaker, or for anyone from the North; an uncouth, countrified person *now Cai EC, WC*.

tike *contemptuous* a rough person, a clumsy, ill-mannered boor.

tinker, tinkie *NE Ags Per, now usu* **tink** *contemptuous term for a person* a foul-mouthed, vituperative, quarrelsome, vulgar person.

toun, town: ~**ser** *usu disparaging* a town-dweller as opposed to a countryman etc *NE-Per*.

track a poorly- or untidily-dressed person, a sight *NE*.

trag riff-raff *Bnf Abd*.

troke, truck worthless specimens, riff-raff *N Bwk Lnk*.

trooshlach trash, worthless people *Abd Arg Wgt*.

†**trowane** a vagabond.

truaghan a poor, destitute person, a down-and-out *now Cai*.

unco *adj* 1 *also* ~ **like** unknown, unfamiliar, strange *now NE, C*. 2 †rude, uncouth, unseemly. †*n* 1 the world outside one's own circle, strangers. 2 ~**s** strangers, foreigners. † ~ **body** a stranger, outsider, newcomer. ~ **folk** strangers *now NE nEC, SW*.

†**uncouth** 1 unknowing, ignorant. 2 foreign.

unfarrant unrefined, unsophisticated, rude.

unkenning, †**unkennand** unknowing, ignorant *now Sh*. **unkent (by)** unknown, unfamiliar, strange (to).

†**unsell** unlucky, wretched.

†**unskilful** uncouth.

†**unsonsie** luckless, hapless, unfortunate.

†**upland(is)** living out in the country; rustic, rural.

vagabon *n* a vagabond. *adj* vagabond, wandering, nomadic.

†**vagring** vagrant, wandering; nomadic.

vaig a vagrant, vagabond, tramp *now Uls*.

†**vagand** a vagrant. ~**in(g)** roaming, vagrant, straying *now chf literary*.

waff, waif *n* a waif. *adj* 1 †vagrant, homeless. 2 *also* ~**ie** *local Cai-Fif*, ~**ish**, ~ **like**, ~**-looking** *Bwk Lnk S* vagabond-like, good-for-nothing; *freq of appearance* scruffy *now Cai nEC Wgt*. ~**ie** a vagabond *now Fif*.

†**waffinger** a vagabond.

†**wanhap** unfortunate.

†**waverand** wandering, vagrant.

weirdless unfortunate *now local Abd-Loth*.

†**whistle-binkie** a person who attended a **penny wedding** without paying and had no right to share in the entertainment; a mere spectator (who sometimes whistled for his own amusement).

†**wilrone** *chf as a term of abuse* a savage creature.

wratch, a wretch.

yack(ie) *occas contemptuous* an Eskimo *now local Sh-Ags.*

yaup a fool, oaf, yokel *Ags Fif S.*

yeukie mean, shabby, rough, filthy *local Fif-S.*

yochel a yokel *now Ags Per.*

yon kind *euphemistic* used to describe persons in a poor state *Sh N.*

15.2.3 INTELLIGENCE

For the misuse of intelligence, see 15.3.8.

aboot: hae mair ~ one nor have more sense than *NE.*

†astuce astute.

auld: ~-farrant *of persons, their ways, sayings etc* sagacious, prudent, witty, ingenious. **~-mou'd** wise, wily, crafty *chf NE.*

buik, book: far i the ~ well-read, learned, clever *now Ork.*

canny cautious, careful, prudent, astute.

cleek, click: ~ie cunning, astute *now Mry.*

cleverality cleverness *now Fif.*

cowshus cautious *now local Bnf-Fif.*

crafty skilful, ingenious, clever *now local.*

dungeon o learnin a person of great knowledge *local Bnf-Kcb.*

edgie quick, active *now midLoth Rox.*

eel-drowner *usu ironic* a person who can do the impossible, an exceedingly clever person: *'he's nae eel-drowner'.*

far: ~ ben, ~ in deeply versed, having deep or specialized knowledge *now Ork Abd.* **~ north** astute, wide-awake *Abd WC Rox.* **~ seen** far-sighted *now Ags Uls.*

fell clever, shrewd *now local EC-S.*

few show promise or aptitude.

flinty keen, sharp, lively *now Ayr.*

forehand far-seeing, having thought for the future *local.*

†foresichty foresighted, provident.

forethochty cautious, having foresight *now Clcm.*

gash sagacious, shrewd.

gleg *adj, also* **~-witted** *now Sh midLoth WC* keen, smart, alert, quick-witted, *freq* **~in, of** *or* **at the uptak. ~ness** sharpness, keenness, cleverness *now Sh Abd Rox.*

gumption common sense, native wit.

hair: have a ~ on one's head be clever, cautious or wise *now Arg Ayr.*

heid, head: ~ie clever, showing proof of brains. **~ie knite** *or* **knot(ar)** a clever fellow *NE.*

hiddie kiddie wit, sense, mental stability *Abd.*

in alert, attentive *NE Ags midLoth Kcb.*

judgement reason, senses, wits, sanity.

Kilmaurs: sharp *or* **gleg as a ~ whittle** quick-witted *Ayr.*

lang, long: ~ heid shrewdness; a shrewd or sagacious person. **~-heidit** shrewd, sagacious. **lang-luggit** shrewd *local C.* **lang-nebbit** sharp, astute, having an eye to one's own advantage *now local Ags-S.*

mense common sense, intelligence *Gen except Sh Ork.* **~ful** sensible *now N, SW, S.*

†natural ? sagacious, ? *orig and chf* knowing a country as or as if a native. **naturality** a native endowment, *esp* mental; ability, intelligence.

neb: see far afore one's ~ have foresight *now Sh Ork Ags.*

nizwise far-seeing, perceptive *now Abd Kcdn.*

†nobill distinguished for learning.

pawkie 1 *also* **~-witted** wily, crafty; shrewd, astute. **2** having a matter-of-fact, humorously critical outlook on life, characterized by a sly, quiet wit.

pensefu thoughtful, meditative, pensive *now Ags.*

quirky cunning, resourceful, tricky *now Bnf Abd Ags Kcb.*

rumgumption *local Sh-Wgt,* **rummle-gumption** *now N, C* common sense, understanding, shrewdness.

sairious serious.

sanshach wily, shrewd, **pawkie** *now Bnf.*

sicker prudent, cautious, *esp* with money, wary *now local Ork-Per.* **~ly** prudently, cautiously *now NE.*

slee, sly wise.

smairt smart. **~er** *Cai C,* **smartie** a lively and efficient person, one who is quick to understand and act. **~ly** smartly; sharply, keenly.

snack *now Cai Abd,* **snackie** *Abd Dmf* quick in mind, acute, clever, sharp-witted.

†snap quick, eager, smart. *now Sh.*

†snar astute, sharp (in one's dealings); *of a housewife* shrewd, efficient.

†snarp sharp, keen.

†snell quick, nimble, active, clever, sharp, smart.

solid sane; in full possession of one's mental faculties *now Ags.*

†solomonical characteristic of Solomon.

†sonsie sensible, shrewd.

souple, supple ingenious, cunning, astute, devious *now local Sh-Kcb.*

sparkie bright, sharp, quick-witted *now Abd Kcdn Per.*

spune, spoon: have mair than the ~ pits in

(**the heid** *etc*) be more than usually clever *now local NE-Kcb*.

†**suttaille** subtle.

tentie cautious, careful, prudent *now Abd*.

thocht, thought: ~**ie** serious-minded. **thocht-ish** serious, pensive *Rox*.

tholemoody pensive.

thorow, thorough mentally alert, sane *now Bwk SW, S*.

uptak(e) the capacity for understanding, power of comprehension, intelligence, *freq* **gleg** *etc* **in, of** *etc* **the** ~.

†**vertie** cautious, prudent.

†**vesynes** caution, foresight, prudence.

†**wasie** wise, clever, quick-witted *Bnf Ags*.

wise, wice *adj* 1 in one's right mind, sane, rational, *local Ork-Per*. 2 wise, clever, knowing, well-informed *now local Ork-Per*. †*adv* wisely. ~**like** *adj* prudent, sensible, reasonable *now local Sh-Per*. *adv* prudently, sensibly, reasonably *now local Sh-Per*. ~-**spoken** wise, sensible in speech *now local Sh-Per*.

wit, wut 1 wit. 2 intelligence, wisdom, common sense. 3 †a person of great mental ability. †**wit-tandly** wisely, skilfully.

wylie clever, sagacious, wise *now Sh Ags*.

†**yaup** clever, cunning; shrewd.

15.2.4 STUPIDITY

ablach a person insignificant or contemptible through lack of intellect.

amitan *disparaging* a person who plays the fool; a person lacking common sense *Cai Gall*.

†**ane** an ass.

aumeril an awkward stupid fellow.

†**aumry** a clumsy, stupid person.

beffan a stupid, often fat and flabby, person *chf Bnf*.

begoyt foolish, mad.

bladry foolishness, ostentation, harm.

blate dull, stupid, easily deceived *Bnf Ags C*.

blether(an)skate, blether(um)skite a silly foolish person.

blicker (the talk of) a stupid person.

bluff a credulous person *now Abd*.

blumf a dull, stupid person *now Bnf Abd*.

blunk(art) a dull, lifeless person *now Bnf*.

blunt a stupid fellow *now Abd*. † ~**ie** a stupid fellow, *chf* **look like** ~**ie**.

boss destitute (of brains).

†**bowbart** a dull or sluggish person.

brosie-headit very stupid, fat and inactive *Bnf Ags*.

†**bumbard** a stupid person.

bummer a stupid person, a fool *now Ags*.

bumph a stupid person *now Kcb*.

cloit, clyte a dull, heavy person, a stupid and inactive person *now Abd Ags Kcb*.

coof a fool, simpleton.

custril a fool *S*.

daffin foolish behaviour. †**daffery** folly, foolishness.

daft foolish, stupid, lacking intelligence; lacking common sense. ~**ie** an imbecile; a mentally handicapped person; a fool. ~**ness** foolishness.

dauk stupid; sluggish.

†**daupit** stupid, slow-witted.

daver be stupid *now Bnf*.

dobbie a dull, stupid, clumsy person *now Fif Stlg Edb Kcb*.

dochle a dull, stupid person, a fool.

docus a stupid person *local C*.

doilt dazed, confused, stupid *now Sh Dmf*.

doit *v* act foolishly, be crazed, enfeebled or confused in mind *now Abd*. *n* a stupid person, a fool. ~**ered** witless, confused *now Fif*. ~**it** not of sound mind, foolish, silly. **doitrified** stupefied, dazed, senseless *now Bnf Ags Fif*.

donnert dull, stupid.

donsie dull, stupid *S*.

doolie a stupid, dithering, nervous person *local C*.

dottered stupid, enfeebled in mind. **dotterel** a dotard, an imbecile *now Stlg*. †**dotit** silly, stupid. †**dottle** witless.

dovie *adj* stupid *Fif*. *n* a stupid-looking person *now Fif*.

dowf *adj* stupid *now local Bnf-Fif*. *n* a stupid person *now Ork Abd*. ~**art** *adj, verse* stupid. †*n* a dull stupid person. ~**fie** †*adj* dull, slow, stupid. *n* a stupid person, a dolt.

dozie *adj* stupid *local Fif-Rox*. *n* a stupid person *Bwk SW Rox*.

driddle an awkward, helpless person.

dulbert a stupid person, a fool *SW*.

dult a dolt *now Renfr Lnk Kcb*.

ebb *of the mind* shallow, lacking in depth. † ~**ness** shallowness.

eediot an idiot. **eediocy** idiocy. **idiotical** foolish, senseless, stupid *NE, EC*.

flup a stupid, clumsy person. †**floop-like** stupid and awkward.

†**fon** *n* folly, foolishness. *v* be foolish, play the fool.

forget (an instance of) forgetfulness, absent-mindedness. **forgettle** forgetful.

fozie unintelligent, dull, stupid *now midLoth*. **foziness** stupidity.

fuil, fool *n* a fool. *adj* foolish, silly *now Sh-C*. ~**-like** foolish *C*.

fuilitch foolish.

gaibie a stupid person *S*.

gaikit silly *Sh Abd Ags*.

gamaleerie a foolish clumsy person *now Fif*.

ganner wander aimlessly or foolishly about *Abd S*.

gansh a stupid, clumsy or stammering person *Uls*.

gaupie *n, also* **gaup** *chf N, SW* a simpleton, fool, a person who gapes. **gaupit** stupid, silly *Abd Ags Loth Uls*. **gawpus** a fool, a clumsy, stupid lout *now local Ork-Edb*.

gawk *n, also* ~**ie** an awkward, clumsy person, a fool. *v* 1 *also* ~**ie** play the fool, behave foolishly *now Ags*. 2 fool around, wander aimlessly *now Ags Kcb*. 3 stare vacantly *now Ayr Kcb*. ~**it** stupid, clumsy. **gawkus** a fool *Ork Ags*.

geck a fool.

†**gend** foolish, simple.

gillieperous a fool *Mry Abd*.

gilly: † ~**gacus** a fool. ~**-gawpus**, † ~**-gawpy** a stupid person, a gaping fool *now Ags*.

glaik *n* a silly, thoughtless person *now local*. †*v* look foolishly. † ~**ery** foolish behaviour. ~**it** foolish, stupid, of low intelligence.

glipe an uncouth, clumsy, thoughtless or stupid person *now Uls*.

glundie a fool.

goamless stupid *C, S*.

gomach a fool, simpleton *now Uls*.

gomerel *n* a fool, stupid person. †*adj* foolish, stupid.

goniel a fool *now Dmf Rox*.

gove a vacant stare. **govie** an awkward or silly person *now Uls*.

gow a fool *now Wgt*.

gowk *n, also* ~**ie** a fool, simpleton, lout. ~**ie** stupid, loutish *now midLoth*. ~**it** foolish *now NE Ags midLoth*.

greenhorn a raw inexperienced person, a simpleton.

guff a fool, simpleton *now EC, S*. ~**ie** stupid *now Rox*.

†**guk** talk or behave foolishly. ~**(k)it** foolish, silly.

gumph, gamf *now Ags Ayr*, ~**ie** *now Rox*, **gumpus** *now Bnf Abd Ags* a fool *now local N-Uls*.

gype *v* stare foolishly or open-mouthed *NE Ags Per*. *n* a foolish awkward person, a silly ass, a lout *now Sh NE Ags*. **gyperie** nonsense, foolishness *Abd*. **gypit** silly, foolish, witless *Sh N Per*.

gype play the fool *now Sh Ags*.

haiverel *n* a foolishly chattering or garrulous person, a fool, a halfwit. *adj* foolish, stupid, nonsensical.

hallockit, hellicat, †**hallirakus** a fool.

harnless stupid *now local Sh-Kinr*.

†**hawkie** a stupid person.

hawkit foolish, stupid, harum-scarum.

hazy weak in intellect, mentally unbalanced *now EC Arg Slk*.

†**heepie** a melancholy or foolish person.

heid, head: ~**-banger** *slang* an idiot, very stupid person *local C*.

hen: have a memory like a ~ have a bad memory, be very forgetful *local*.

hinkum sneev(l)ie a silly stupid person *Abd*.

hocus a stupid person, a simpleton *now Cai*.

hoolet applied to persons showing real or imagined characteristics of the owl (*eg* stupidity).

howffin a clumsy, shy and rather stupid person *NE*.

hyter a stupid person *now Kcdn*.

kae-witted hare-brained, half-witted *chf Ags*.

kiow-ow act frivolously, caper about, play the fool *N Gall Uls*.

†**lurdan** heavy, dull; clownish, stupid, rascally.

mappit stupid, thick-headed *Abd nEC*.

mell-heid a stupid person, blockhead *Rox*. ~**-it** stupid *now Rox*.

menseless stupid, foolish *now Bnf EC, S*.

moniment an object of ridicule or distaste, a 'sight', a laughing-stock *Sh-Per*.

mowdiewort a slow-witted or slovenly person *Abd Fif Loth*.

muckle, mickle: ~ **to hoi,** ~ **tae hae** a gawky empty-headed fellow *now Ags Rox*.

neep heid a stupid person *local Sh-EC*.

nowt a big unwieldy person, an oaf, a blockhead *now local Sh-nEC Rox*.

oanshach a foolish person, an idiot *Mry Abd Arg*.

object an imbecile.

ouf an imbecile, a stupid fool *now Bnf*.

preen-heidit stupid, of low intelligence *NE nEC*.

prod *contemptuous* a waster, lazy creature, fool.

puddin a stupid or clumsy person.

puppie: mak a ~**-show o anesel** make a fool of oneself, make an exhibition of oneself *now nEC, WC*.

richt, right: not ~ simple-minded.

sakeless without sense, silly *S*.

sappie-headed simple-minded, silly, foolish *Ags Per*.

scatter-wit a scatterbrain *now local Abd-Slk*.

scrimpness scantiness, deficiency in wits.

379

shilling: want tippence *etc* **o the** ~ be mentally defective, be not all there *local Sh-Kcb*.

silly mentally deficient *now local Sh-Kcb*.

skate contemptuous term for a stupid person *local*.

slung a tall lanky stupid person *NE*.

smerghless, smeerless lacking in spirit or energy, sluggish, feckless, stupid *N*.

sneuter a slow, unskilful, stupid person *NE*.

snoddie a stupid person *Rox*.

snot *n, also* ~**ter** *now Cai* a stupid person *now local Inv-Rox*. ~**ter box** a soft, stupid, untidy person.

sn(u)ivie a dull-witted person *now chf Rox*.

sot a fool, simpleton, stupid person.

souk, suck a stupid person *now Rox*. ~**in teuchit** *NE,* ~ **turkey** *etc now Sh-N, SW* a feeble or foolish person.

sowf a fool, simpleton, stupid, silly person *now Abd*.

spune, spoon: have nothing but what the ~ **pits in (the heid** *etc*) be more than usually stupid *now local NE-Kcb*.

stammeral (an) awkward, clumsy, stupid (person).

stirk(ie) a stupid oafish fellow *now N nEC, S*.

stodgel, stodger a slow, lumbering, rather stupid person *now NE*.

stoit a stupid, ungainly, blundering person *now Abd*.

stookie a slow-witted, dull, person *now N, C Rox*.

stot a stupid clumsy person.

stump a stupid person *now Rox*.

stupe a fool, stupid person *now local Inv-wLoth*.

stupit stupid.

stymel a person who does not see or understand quickly *chf Rox*.

sumph *n* a slow-witted person, *usu* a man, an oaf, simpleton *now N-S. v* act like a **sumph** *now NE, C.* ~**ish** *now NE, C,* ~**y** *now NE* stupid, doltish.

taibetless heedless, foolish, silly.

tattie a stupid person, a simpleton *local Ork-WC*.

†**taupie** foolish, awkward, slovenly, foolishly thoughtless. **taupit** foolish.

timmer, timber wooden, dull, stupid, unresponsive.

trosk a slow-witted, slovenly person, *esp* a woman *Cai*.

tume empty-headed, foolish, witless *now Sh*. ~**heidit** silly, foolish.

tumfie a dull, stupid, soft person.

†**unnatural** simple-minded.

unsensible lacking sense or reasoning power.

unwiselike indiscreet, imprudent, foolish *now N*.

uptak(e) the capacity for understanding, power of comprehension, intelligence, *freq* **slow** *etc* **in, of** *etc* **the** ~.

veeand lacking common sense *S*.

waff, waif *adj, also* ~**ish,** ~ **like** feeble in mind *local EC-S*.

want: ~**in** simple, mentally defective. **hae a** ~, ~ **a feather in the wing,** ~ **a bit** be simple, be mentally defective.

†**wanwit** foolishness, lack of wit. **wanwitty** foolish, stupid.

willie goo a lost- or stupid-looking person *Abd Kcdn Ags*.

willyart backward, dull *now Wgt*.

wuid, wud: aince ~ **and aye (the) waur** daft once, daft always.

yaup a fool, oaf, yokel *Ags Fif S*.

yonder, yonner: far frae a' ~, **nae (near) a'** ~ half-witted, not all there *NE*.

†**yowe, ewe** a stupid, weak-willed person *NE*.

15.3 CHARACTER TYPES

15.3.1 MISCELLANEOUS POSITIVE TYPES

a'body's body a general favourite.

beezer *child's word* a person bigger or better than usual.

†**bening** benign.

birkie a smart (*usu* young) fellow.

bore: tak in *or* **up a** ~ turn over a new leaf *Bnf Abd*.

brave splendid, excellent, fine *now Abd Fif*.

braw *adj* **1** fine, splendid. **2** *slightly familiar* worthy.

bummer a person who is very wonderful of his or her kind *now local Bnf-Kcb*.

by: ~**ous** wonderful, extraordinary, exceptional *now Ags*. ~**common,** ~**usual,** ~ **the common,** ~ **the ordinar** out of the ordinary, unusual. ~**ordinar,** ~**ornar** extraordinary, unusual. ~**spel** an extraordinary person; extraordinary, wonderful.

canny gentle, quiet, steady; pleasant.

canty lively, cheerful; pleasant.

dacent decent.

†**digne** worthy.

douce 1 sedate, sober, respectable. **2** sweet, pleasant, lovable *local Bnf-Lnk*.

†**even:** ~**lik(e)** just, equitable. ~**likly** equitable, just.

†**exerce (oneself in)** practise (a virtue).

faisible respectable, decent *now midLoth Slk*.

†**fashiont** well-mannered, respectable.

†**flyting free** blameless.

furth the gait candid(ly), honest(ly), straightforward(ly) *now NE*.

gainin winning, winsome *now Uls*.

gey, gay: ~ **(like)** excellent, splendid.

grow increase, make progress (**in** a quality, property etc).

guid, good distinguished in social standing, worthy, respectable *now local*. †**gud mither tochter** the daughter of a good mother.

hert, hairt, heart: the ~ **o corn** one of the best, a good fellow *Gen except Sh Ork*.

hinnie sweet as honey.

honest of good character and standing, worthy, estimable. **honesty** decency, decorum; a mark of respectability *now Abd Per Renfr*. ~ **like** *of persons, or their dress or appearance* decent, respectable.

†**jellie** upright, honest, worthy, excellent.

jonick, gennick genuine, honest, fair, just *now NE-Per*.

†**lack: but** ~ without fault, blamelessly.

†**lamp** a shining light or example, a paragon. ~ **of licht** a person of extreme excellence.

†**lawtie, lauteth** faithful adherence to high standards of conduct, upright behaviour.

leal honest, honourable, law-abiding.

†**lovabill** *of persons, their actions or attributes* praiseworthy, honourable, satisfactory, acceptable.

luvesome, lusum lovable, admirable.

†**mak faith** possess credence, be valid or trustworthy.

†**makeles** matchless, peerless.

†**meid** the quality of deserving well, merit, worth.

†**memorative** mindful.

†**memore: of gude** ~ of happy or blessed memory.

mend 1 reform, improve (one's character or habits) *now local*. **2** reform oneself.

†**mends** improvement, betterment (in morals).

mense 1 *also* †**mensk** honour, credit *now SW, S*. **2** moderation *now sEC, SW, S*. **3** something which brings credit or honour to one *chf SW, S*.

†**meritis** the condition or fact of deserving well, of being entitled to reward or gratitude. **meritabill** worthy of reward or praise.

namely noted, famed, of good repute.

†**order** decorous personal behaviour, decency, propriety.

†**original justice** innate sense of justice.

past ordinar outstanding, remarkable, exceptional *now Uls*.

†**pleasant** *of a person's appearance* agreeable, pleasing.

pretty fine, good-looking, having an impressive and dignified bearing.

principal excellent, first-rate, outstandingly good *now Sh*.

real honest, forthright, genuine *now Sh Ags Wgt*.

†**rememorant** mindful.

†**round** *of speech* honest, plain.

saint, saunt, †**sanct** a saint.

shaw, show: ~ **well** *etc* have a good etc appearance, make a good etc show.

shouder, shoulder, shouther: never look ower one's ~ never look back, go steadily forward, not fail or relapse *NE-S*.

†**shrive oneself of** renounce.

sin: hae nae ~ **o** bear no blame or reproach for *now Sh*.

sodger-clad but major-mindit *usu complimentary* having a strong sense of pride and self-respect in spite of a humble position *now Abd Ags Stlg*.

solit solid *now Bwk Ayr*.

sonsie *of the appearance, looks, face* bringing good fortune; lucky; good, honest *now local Sh-Kcb*.

stang: the ~ **o the trump** the indispensable or most effective person in a group or activity, the best of the bunch *NE Ags*.

stob-feather beginning to be equipped for life *chf NE*.

straucht, straight: ~**-oot(-the-gate)** frank, candid *now Ork*.

†**suit** sweet.

suithfast soothfast, truthful, reliable.

tak, take: ~ **up** improve in conduct or character, pull oneself together *now Per Rox*.

†**tee'd ball** a person bound to succeed.

thoum, thumb: turn one's ~ make an effort, bestir oneself *Abd Ags SW*.

torn: be ~ **out** be asked out a lot, be popular *NE*.

†**trewthelie** honestly.

trumph a splendid person etc.

†**unsinnand** unsinful.

upstannin upstanding, erect.

†**vertu** virtue.

weel-faured decent, respectable.

winsome attractive in appearance, manner or nature, charming.

wise, wice: ~**like** *adj* respectable, proper, decent *now Cai C*. *adv* respectably, properly, decently *now Cai C*.

worthy, wordy, †**wirdy** worthy.

†**wye** a man of good strong character.

†**wyteless** blameless, innocent.

15.3.2 MISCELLANEOUS NEGATIVE TYPES

For gratuitous abuse (the boundary is unclear) see 15.7.5.

†**aucht** applied to persons, with adjs of blame or (ironic) praise: '*a bad aucht*'.

awa, away: ~ **wi't** done for.

†**awmous, alms** *ironic* one's just deserts.

bauchle an old, useless, worn-out person.

†**bellamy** an unpleasant person.

†**bismere** a disreputable woman.

black gate the road to ruin *now Mry Bnf*.

blear, blare: ~**ed, blerit** debauched-looking.

blichan a lean, worn-out, worthless person *SW*.

bluiter a big clumsy useless person *now Bnf*.

bodach a small and insignificant person *now Bnf*.

brak: ye've pu'd a stick tae ~ yer ain back you will suffer from the consequences of your own actions *Bnf Ags Stlg*.

brave *ironic* splendid, excellent, fine *now Abd Fif*.

by: † ~**-sle(e)ve** a hanger-on, nonentity. ~**spel** *ironic* an extraordinary person; extraordinary, wonderful.

ca(ll): no worth ~in oot o a kail-yard useless *now Cai Ags*.

†**carmagnole** a rascal.

Carnwath(-like) awkward; odd-looking *C*.

ceepher a person of no significance, an impudent or empty-headed person *local Abd-Rox*.

cess a burden (to another) *now Bnf*.

chowed: look like *etc* **a ~ mouse** have a debauched or worn-out appearance *chf S*.

†**clag** a fault, cause for reproach.

clem *chf schoolboy's word* mean, unprincipled *Edb Rox*.

colleague *chf derog* associate, be friendly **with** *now Bnf Abd*.

†**coof** a rogue.

coorse hard, trying; disagreeable *Bnf-Ags*.

†**crack one's credit** lose one's reputation, trust etc.

craw: be shot amo the ~s be involved in trouble through bad associates *local Ork-Per*.

†**cummerwarld** a useless encumbrance.

cush a soft, useless person *chf Rox*.

dae, do: ~**-na-gude** a ne'er-do-well *now Abd Fif*.

daeless helpless, feeble, useless *now Stlg*.

†**defame** ill fame; disgrace, discredit.

defection a defect, flaw; a failure *now Ags*.

dirten mean, contemptible *now Abd*. **dirtrie** worthless people.

douchtless powerless, worthless *now Fif*.

drochle a short dumpy person, a puny insignificant person *now local Cai-Fif*.

dyvour a rogue, a good-for-nothing.

†**eilest** a fault, flaw or defect.

fa(ll): ~ **ower the brim** go to one's doom or destruction *now Abd*.

†**faltive** having committed a fault, guilty of wrong doing.

fang a rascal, disagreeable person *NE*.

faut, fault: ~**er** a wrongdoer.

fen(d)less lacking resource or energy *Sh Cai NE, SW*.

find frost run into difficulties, *chf* of one's own making, suffer unpleasant consequences from one's own actions *now Ork*.

fit: aff one's *or* **the ~** *or* **feet** morally astray *now midLoth Bwk*.

†**flyredome** an object of scorn.

†**forlane** despicable, worthless.

fouter term of abuse, *orig* for a hateful, objectionable person, *now much weaker* an exasperating person *now chf N*.

foutie mean, despicable, underhand *now Mry Abd Wgt*.

fum a useless person *Ayr*.

gang throu it dissipate one's resources, come a cropper, go bankrupt *NE Ags*.

†**gang to (the) gate** go to wrack and ruin, be destroyed *chf WC*.

gey, gay: ~ **(like)** *freq ironic* disreputable, wild.

glender on the decline (in morals etc), in a bad way.

gleyd: gae *or* **gang ~** go astray, *esp* morally *now Ags midLoth*.

†**glittous** filthy, base, vile.

†**glyde** an old, useless or disagreeable person.

gray: (gang) a ~ gate (follow) a disastrous course, (come to) a bad end *now Wgt*.

hallockit, hellicat, †**hallirakus** a good-for-nothing.

hasp: buckled wi ae ~ tarred with the same brush, birds of a feather *now Sh-Cai Kcb*.

hatesum hateful *now Cai*.

heel: come to one's ~-hap(pin) *proverb, of a person who persists in pursuing a wrong course* come to grief *NE*.

hingum-tringum worthless and somewhat disreputable; barely presentable *Bnf*.

horse: be sic mannie, sic horsie *usu contemptuous* be all of one kind, be birds of a feather *NE*.

hule a mischievous, perverse or objectionable person *now Kcb Dmf*.

hurb a good-for-nothing creature *NE*.

†**thutit** reviled, execrated; detested.

hypal an uncouth, unkempt, broken-down or good-for-nothing person *local*.

ill: ~-**farrant** unpleasant in behaviour *nEC Rox*. ~-**gate** a bad habit *Ags Fif midLoth*. ~-**likeit** unpopular. ~-**looked-upon** held in disfavour, unpopular *Sh Ork midLoth*. ~ **for** inclined to (some bad habit etc), having a vicious propensity to *N midLoth SW*. ~ **name** a bad name, a bad reputation *local Sh-WC*.

†**inding** unworthy.

†**jaloused: be** ~ be regarded with suspicion.

jiff(er) a person of doubtful reputation *NE*.

kame: bring *or* **get an ill** ~ **for** *or* **to one's hand** bring mischief upon oneself *now Fif*.

keiler *derog* a useless or insignificant person *now Cai*.

ken o't *freq in threats* know by dire experience, suffer for one's actions *local*.

†**kid** notorious.

†**lack** *n* a fault or failing such as to bring shame or disgrace. *adj, latterly freq ballad* deficient in quality, inferior. **to** ~ to blame; blameworthy, despicable.

lair, lear habit, custom, *usu* **ill** ~ *Cai*.

†**licht: sit in one's own** ~ be an obstruction to oneself.

lirk an unusual trait of character, a kink, a mental twist *now Abd*.

little: ~-**boukit** of little importance, insignificant *NE*. ~ **worth** of worthless character.

†**losel** *chf literary* a scamp, scoundrel, loafer.

loun 1 †a dishonest rascal. **2** a rogue, wretch, scoundrel, worthless person *now local EC Uls*. ~-**like** disreputable, shabby, scruffy *latterly Ags*.

†**lurdan** clownish, stupid, rascally.

†**mailȝe:** *chf* **nocht** *or* **nevir worth a** ~ not worth a halfpenny.

†**mainȝie** a defect, flaw.

†**mal-grace** disfavour, disgrace *chf* **in** ~.

†**maling** act wrongfully, err.

mane: not to ~ not to be pitied *now local N-S*.

†**maugre** odium, the state of being regarded with ill-will.

mend: there's no ane o them to ~ **anither** they're all equally bad *C, S*.

menseless unmannerly, objectionable in behaviour.

†**meschant** *of persons, their character and conduct* spiritless, feeble, worthless. ~**ly** miserably; feebly.

†**mess and mell** to interfere; mix *or* have dealings (**with**).

mird meddle, have dealings or association **with** *chf NE*.

misfare come to grief *now Sh*.

†**misgae** go astray.

†**misordinate** disorderly, immoderate.

†**mistemperance** over-indulgence, excess.

mote a flaw, blemish *now Abd*.

munsie a person deserving contempt and ridicule *now Abd*.

neir-do-gude, neir-do-weel a good-for-nothing.

nestie nasty.

niffnaff a small, insignificant or trifling person *now Sh Bnf Lnk*.

nocht: ~**ie** good-for-nothing, insignificant. ~**less** worthless, of no account *now Sh-S*.

notour *of wrongdoers* known by common knowledge, notorious, openly admitted, *eg* ~ **bankrupt** *now only law*.

nyaff a worthless person, good-for-nothing.

O a cipher, a nonentity.

object someone deserving of pity.

†**off-falling** a decline or lapse in morals.

onhanger a hanger-on *now Uls*.

orishon *contemptuous* an odd-looking or insignificant person *SW*.

orra worthless, shabby, disreputable *NE Ags Per*. **orraster** a disreputable person *Bnf Abd*.

ouf a puny insignificant creature.

outerlin(g) the black sheep of a family, a reprobate.

†**outwale** an unworthy person.

paik *of a woman* a worthless creature.

pallion a rough, ungainly or worthless person *NE*.

peek an unimpressive, insignificant individual *Bnf Abd*.

peelie-wersh insipid, nondescript *now Rox*.

peety, pity: ~**ifu(l)** arousing pity and compassion, pitiable.

pell *contemptuous* a dirty, worthless person, reprobate, tramp *now Sh Ork*.

†**pelt** a person of little value.

†**perverst** perverted.

†**piece** *derog* a (bad etc) untrustworthy etc person.

pingling ineffectual, feeble, lacking character or energy.

pirn: wind (oneself *or* **another) a** ~ *or* **into a bonnie** *etc* ~ create difficulties for oneself or another.

pit: I wadna ~ **it by him** *etc* I wouldn't put it past him etc (to do something discreditable).

pot, pat †of a (reprehensible) quality: '*the pot of ignorance*'. **gin I be pottie ye're pannie** you are as bad as I am, you are in no position to criticize *Bnf Abd*.

potterlow: (gane) tae ~ gone to the devil, to wrack and ruin *NE*.

potterneeshin a state of ruin or chaos, a mess, shambles, *chf* **gae to** ~ get into a state of ruination, go to the dogs *Abd*.

pushion *n* an unpleasant person, a horror *Sh N*. *adj* unpleasant, detestable, foul *now Sh Ork Fif*. ~**able** unpleasant *now Per Dnbt*.

†**qued** *slang*, **quaid**, vile, bad.

radical a wild, unruly person, a rogue, rascal *now Sh Bnf Abd*.

†**tragabash** *n* a good-for-nothing, a ragamuffin. *adj* good-for-nothing *chf S*.

rap a good-for-nothing *now Fif*.

reebald a good-for-nothing, a scoundrel *now Sh Ork*.

†**retrospiciant** a person who turns back; a renegade.

rinagate a runagate, a fugitive, rascal *local Sh-SW*.

†**ruddoch** term of contempt for a (bad-tempered) old person.

†**run deil** an out-and-out rogue.

runk contemptuous term, *esp* for a bad-tempered woman *Mry Abd*.

runt contemptuous term, *esp* for a coarse, gnarled, ill-natured person, *esp* an old woman *now local Sh-Fif*.

Sammy dreep a 'drip', a spiritless, ineffective person *local Bnf-Kcb*.

scabbit mean, worthless.

†**scant-o-grace** a scapegrace, reprobate.

scoon(d)rel a scoundrel.

scourie *adj* scruffy, disreputable, broken down (in appearance) *now Stlg Ayr*. †*n* a scruffy, disreputable-looking person, a rascal.

scoutie worthless in character, scruffy *now Per WC*.

scroosh *freq disparaging* a large number of people, a worthless lot.

scruff a worthless person or persons, riff-raff *C*.

scum a worthless disreputable person *now local Sh-Ayr*.

scunner an objectionable person.

†**scur** a despicable person, rascal, 'scab'.

†**shame is past the shed of his** *etc* **hair** he etc has lost all sense of shame.

†**sham:** ~**ful** shameful. ~**fully** shamefully.

shent *v* put to shame, disgraced, ruined. †*n* disgrace.

†**shirrow, shrew** wicked, bad.

shortcome a deficiency, shortage; a fault in character or conduct *local Sh-SW*.

shurf *contemptuous* an insignificant person *S*.

sin one's soul incur the guilt of sin (*esp* by telling lies) *local Sh-Kcb*.

†**sinistrous** erroneous, perverse, heretical.

skate contemptuous term for an objectionable person *local*.

skellum *contemptuous term for a man* a scamp, rogue, scoundrel.

skit *esp of a woman* a disagreeable person.

skite a nasty or objectionable person *now local Inv-Lnk*.

skrink a shrivelled, unpleasant, or contemptible person, *esp* a woman *now Rox*. ~**ie-faced** with a wrinkled face (and an unpleasant manner).

skybal(d) *n* a rascal, rogue, worthless person. *adj* rascally, disreputable, worthless.

skybe, skipe a mean rogue, a bad-mannered or worthless person *now Rox*.

†**slait** a nasty person.

†**sleeth** a worthless person *NE*.

sleug an unpleasant person.

slink a low despicable character *now C Rox*.

sloosht a disreputable character, a reprobate *Abd*.

slung a disreputable person, a rascal *NE*.

smaik contemptuous term for a person; a rogue, rascal. † ~**ry** mean or contemptible behaviour.

smatchet a small insignificant person.

smool an insignificant person.

smout a small insignificant person *Gen except Sh Ork*.

†**smy** a knave, rascal.

†**snapper** make a slip in conduct, get into trouble.

snauchle an insignificant, puny or feeble person *chf SW*.

snifty an insignificant person *sEC Wgt Rox*.

snite *esp contemptuous or abusive* a worthless person, a small insignificant person *now Sh Bnf Abd*.

snot *now local Ags-Rox*, **snotter** *now Cai* a contemptible, or worthless person.

†**sop of ..** a person in respect of some pervading specified quality: 'sop of sorrow'.

sorra, sorrow a rascal, a pest of a person *now Sh N Per*.

†**speculation** a spectacle, subject for remark or gossip, an object of contempt.

squeeb a mean, scrounging, insignificant person *NE*.

squeef term of abuse for a mean, disreputable, shabby, or worthless person *now WC-S*.

†**stark** arrant, unmitigated: 'sterk thefis'.

step aside commit a fault, go astray.

sticky-fingered having a tendency to steal.

surfeit excessive, immoderate, intemperate.

†**swinger, swounger** a rogue, scoundrel.

tarloch a small, weak or worthless person *now Bnf Abd*.

tash a blot on one's character, slur, stigma *now Sh*.

thief general term of contempt for a person; a rascal, scoundrel. ~**like** *now Sh*, ~(**t**)**ie** *local* disreputable.

too-hoo a spiritless, useless person *local Kcdn-S*.

toosht a nasty unpleasant person *now Bnf Abd*.

torn-doun disreputable, dissipated, broken-down *now Sh.*

†**tresgressor** a transgressor.

troke, truck worthless specimens, riff-raff *N Bwk Lnk.*

trooshlach trash, worthless people *Abd Arg Wgt.*

trucker a rascal, rogue.

trusdar an untrustworthy person, a rascal *N Highl Arg.*

†**tutivillar** a rascal.

ug a person with disgusting manners *NE.*

†**unduchtie** lacking in good qualities; worthless, vile.

†**unlikely, unlikly** unattractive, unacceptable, disagreeable, objectionable.

†**unremembrand** forgetful.

unthochtful unthoughtful.

†**unworth** unworthy, worthless.

vaig 1 a rough-living disreputable person, a rascal, rogue *now Kcdn Ags.* **2** *of a woman* a gadabout, a coarse, disreputable, gossipy person *now Ags.*

vision an insignificant characterless person *now Sh Ork Stlg Dmf.*

wa drap a puny or insignificant person *Cai.*

waff, waif *n* a worthless person *now Cai. adj, also* ~**ie** *local Cai-Fif,* ~**ish,** ~ **like,** ~**-looking** *Bwk Lnk S* vagabond-like, good-for-nothing. ~**er** a good-for-nothing *local Fif-Rox.*

†**waffinger** a good-for-nothing.

wandocht †*n* a silly, sluggish, worthless person. *adj* contemptible, worthless *latterly literary.*

†**wangrace** lack of grace, bad behaviour.

wanwordy unworthy, worthless *now literary.*

wanworth *n* a worthless person, a good-for-nothing *now Sh. adj* unworthy, worthless.

warroch, *chf* **a weary** ~ a good-for-nothing, ne'er-do-well.

warse *adj* worse. *v* **warst** worst.

waster a person of no further use, due to decrepitude, disease etc *local.*

wauch, wauf good-for-nothing, worthless, feeble.

waur *adj* worse. *n* the worse.

weel: ~ **wared on** *etc* **him** *etc* it served him etc right. **the** ~ **warst** the very worst, the worst of the lot *now NE.*

weeshie-washie wishy-washy.

wheeber a person with disagreeable manners *Bnf Abd.*

widdie, wuddie: cheat the ~ a rogue *local.*

wiffer-waffer a nonentity, a useless, ineffectual person *Abd Kcdn.* **wifferty-wafferty** ineffectual, doddering *Kcdn Ags.*

wile warst the very worst *Abd Kcdn.*

wirk for deserve, earn (punishment or retribution) *now local Sh-Per.*

wisgan *term of abuse* a stunted, useless, feckless person *Bnf Ags.*

†**wissel: get the** ~ **of one's groat** *etc* be paid in one's own coin, get one's just deserts.

witter, wutter a sharp, active, restless, impatient, *freq* disagreeable person *now NE Ags.*

worth: gae *etc* **(aa)** ~ go to pot, become spoilt or useless, go to ruin *now NE.*

wunner, wonder contemptuous term for a nasty, unpleasant or insignificant person *now N.*

yeuk: his *etc* **neck is** ~**in** he etc is heading for the gallows.

yon kind *euphemistic* not quite normal; not worth or up to much, in indifferent health etc *local Sh-Per WC.*

15.3.3 WARM, FRIENDLY

back chap a helping hand *now Ags.*

†**back-friend** a supporter; one who does his best for another.

†**bien** handsomely; liberally.

big friendly, intimate *now Mry Abd.*

billy a (close) friend, comrade. **billies,** *freq* **grand** *etc* **billies** on very friendly terms *now Mry.*

†**Bonaccord** concord; friendly agreement.

bowsome obliging; amiable; *chf of a woman* pleasant, agreeable.

cadgy friendly, hospitable.

canny pleasant; good, kind.

canty lively, cheerful; pleasant.

cap: kiss (a *or* **the)** ~**(s)** drink out of the same vessel, *usu* as a token of friendship.

cast a friendly turn; help, assistance *now Abd Ags Fif.*

cheek for chow(l) cheek by jowl, close together, very friendly *now local Cai-Kcb.*

chief intimate, friendly, 'thick'.

chum accompany as a friend.

cleek, click: ~ **in** *or* **up wi(th)** associate, be intimate with *now Abd Lnk.*

clever, cliver good, nice.

come tae become reconciled *local.*

compaingen a companion *Cai Bnf Abd.*

†**companionrie** companionship.

compluther, comploiter mix, associate **with**.

concord agree; come to an agreement.

condescendence, condescendency agreement, acquiescence.

condingly agreeably, lovingly *N.*

considerin considerate *local.*

†**convene** come to an accord, agree.

cosh friendly, intimate *local.*

couthie, †**couth** agreeable, sociable, friendly, sympathetic.

cowshus unassuming, kindly, considerate *now Abd.*

cracky talkative, affable; loquacious *local.*

†**culyie** receive, entertain kindly.

†**curcuddoch** cordial, kindly.

curmud close, near, intimate *S.*

dab: common *or* **plain** ~ a plain, ordinary or unpretentious person *NE Per.*

dainty, denty pleasant, agreeable *now Bnf-Fif.*

discreet civil, polite, well-behaved.

docketie short, round and jolly *Rox.*

doo a kindly loving person *local E.*

douce sweet, pleasant, lovable *local Bnf-Lnk.*

draw agree, get on together *now Fif Lnk Kcb.* ~ **up** become friendly (**with**), get to know *now Ags Fif.*

†**effectionat** affectionate, well disposed; loving.

fain loving, affectionate *now Sh Ork.*

fair: ~**-spoken** frank, friendly *local Bnf-Slk.* ~ **furth the gate** *now Abd,* ~ **oot** *now NE Fif SW* candid(ly), straightforward(ly).

fere companion, comrade *latterly arch or verse.*

fine pleasant-mannered, likeable.

fodgel a plump, good-humoured person *now Uls.*

forgaither associate, keep company **with**.

†**forspeaker** a person who speaks on behalf of another, an advocate.

fraca an intimate, demonstrative friendship, a warm affection *Abd Fif midLoth.*

frequent associate, keep company **with** *local Sh-midLoth.*

friend, freen *n* friend. †*v* befriend. † ~**ship** friends. † ~**full** friendly. † ~**lyk** friendly, in a friendly way.

frugal frank, kindly, hospitable *Sh Cai Abd.*

furth: ~**ie, forthy 1** †frank, friendly, affable. **2** generous, hospitable, liberal *now Fif.* ~ **the gait** candid(ly), honest(ly), straightforward(ly) *now NE.*

gae, go: ~ **in wi** agree with *local Sh-Dmf.*

†**galland** gallant.

†**gal3eard** gallant; lively.

gentie courteous, well-bred *now Abd Fif.*

†**gleefu** kind-hearted, considerate, compassionate.

gracious friendly, on good terms *now Abd Wgt.*

†**gratitude** a service or benefit performed, kindness or favour conferred.

great, gret, grit intimate, friendly.

gree 1 reconcile (persons) *now Ork Abd Ags Rox.* **2** come to terms, make an agreement, be reconciled *Gen except Sh.* **3** be or live in harmony, be friends; be of one mind. ~**able 1** †agreeable. **2** harmonious, living in peace and goodwill *now Abd Ags Wgt.* ~**ance** concord, agreement *now Abd.* ~**ment,** †**griment** agreement, harmony, concord *now local Ork-Arg.*

guid, good ~**willie** generous, hearty, cordial *now local Bnf-Bwk.* †**gude zeill** good intent, kindly disposition.

gun: be great ~**s (wi)** be close friends (with) *Sh N Ags.*

†**habit: be in** *or* **on good** *etc* ~**s** be on good terms.

hame, home: ~**ly 1** homely. **2** friendly, kind(ly), courteous. ~**liness 1** †familiarity, lack of ceremony, intimacy; fellow feeling; *orig also* kindness. **2** homeliness. ~**ower 1** *of speech* homely, simple, in the (Scots) vernacular *now local Ork-Arg.* **2** *of habits and manners* plain, simple, natural, without reserve *now local Ork-Ags.* **3** familiar, intimate *Ags.*

hamelt 1 homely, familiar, plain, simple *now Cai Bnf Ayr.* **2** †*of speech* vernacular; in the native (Scots) tongue.

hamit home-loving, homely, familiar; vernacular.

help: ~**lie** helpful; willing to help. † ~**like** helpful, serviceable.

†**thende** *n* a gentle or courteous person. *adj, also* ~**ly** skilful, pleasant.

†**herbourous** hospitable.

hert, hairt, heart: ~**ie 1** *also* † ~**ily** hearty, cordial. **2** liberal, open-handed *local.* ~**-likin** affection, love *now Sh Abd.* ~**-warm** deeply affectionate, sincerely warm, cordial *now Sh.*

Hieland, Highland warmly hospitable *now local.*

hing, hang: ~ **tae** join in, adhere, attach oneself to some person or cause, fall in with another's plans *Cai NE midLoth.*

hinnie: nothing but *or* **a'** ~ **and jo(e)** all affability, all smiles *now Ags midLoth.*

hodden rustic, homely *now Fif.* ~ **gray** a homely, unaffected individual.

ilka body's body a popular person, a general favourite, *esp* a friendly obliging person *local N-Kcb.*

inner friendly, kindly, sympathetic, affectionate *now S.*

innin an entrance, introduction, friendly reception *local Abd-Dmf.*

†**inwart, inward** on intimate terms, in favour.

jellie pleasant, attractive, agreeable.

†**Jock, jock:** ~**-fellow-like** *of inferiors' relations with their superiors and vice versa* intimate(ly), familiar(ly).

keep in guid wi keep in with, on good terms with *now local Cai-Kcb.*

†**knit up** make firm (friendship etc).

†**kythesome** pleasant, of prepossessing appearance, *always* **blythesome and** ~ *Per WC.*

lairge, large generous *now NE.*

lang syne, auld lang syne, †**long syne** old times, memories of the past, old friendship.

†**largité** liberality.

leal faithful, constant in friendship *now chf verse.*

leesome pleasant, lovable *now Ork Uls.*

leuk, luck, look: ~ **the gate o** *local,* ~ **near (han)** *now Abd* heed, see to, take an interest in.

lithe *now NE,* **lithesome** gentle, genial, kindly.

love-darg a piece of work or a service done gratuitously out of friendliness *NE, EC Ayr.*

†**luferent** the state or condition of loving or of being loved, love, affection, friendship.

†**luke-hertit**? warm-hearted.

luvesome, †**lusum** lovable, admirable. †**luf(e)sumly, lusumly** affectionately, cordially.

†**lusty** gallant, valiant.

†**mawsie** an amply-proportioned, motherly-looking woman.

mense courtesy, hospitality *now sEC, SW, S.* ~**ful** well-mannered, polite *now N, SW, S.*

muild (in) mix well together, fraternize or associate **(with)** *now Ork NE Edb.*

naitral-hertit kindly, affectionate *now Uls.* †**naturality** natural human sympathy.

neibour: ~ **(wi)** associate with, consort with. ~**heid,** ~**hood** friendly relations between neighbours, *freq* **gude** ~**heid, evill** *etc* ~**heid.** ~ **like** neighbourly. † ~**schip (till)** neighbourly relations, amicable behaviour **(to).** †**hald** ~**schip to** act as a neighbour towards. ~**t(r)ie** neighbourliness *NE.*

notice care, attentive help *Sh Abd.*

notion: ~ **o, tae** *etc* a liking or affection for (a person).

oncomin ready to make advances, friendly *local.*

out and in, in and out *of neighbours* paying frequent short calls, used to dropping in *nEC, WC.*

pack on intimate and friendly terms, linked by mutual feeling or understanding, in league *now EC, WC, S.*

†**pack up** bring (a dispute) to an amicable agreement.

†**part: kepe (a) gude** *etc* ~ **to** behave towards (a person) in a good etc way.

†**peace** reconcile.

†**plesour** the wish or inclination to please; courtesy.

†**propiciant** well-disposed.

†**reuch, rough:** ~ **and round** simple, homely.

sanshach pleasant, genial *NE.*

say: ~ **ae wey (wi)** agree, be in harmony (with) *local NE-Ayr.* ~ **thegither** agree, be of one mind; be on good terms *NE nEC.* ~ **wi** agree with, concur with.

seilfu pleasant.

sib bound by ties of affection, familiarity etc, mutually well-disposed *now local NE-Slk.* ~**like,** ~**ly** friendly, like members of the same family.

†**skep in wi** hobnob with.

smirk a pleasant smile, a friendly expression. ~**ie** having a good-natured, amiable, friendly expression.

†**solicit, solist** characterized by solicitude or care.

sonsie *of the appearance, looks, face* friendly, hearty, jolly *now local Sh-Kcb.*

†**sort 1** come together, keep company, live in harmony **(with). 2** come to an agreement.

†**sosh** sociable, frank, open.

sowther, solder confirm, strengthen (a friendship) *now NE.*

†**suave** gracious, kindly.

tosh in a comfortable, friendly way.

troke, truck be on friendly or intimate terms **with.**

welcome welcome.

†**warmly** full of warmth.

†**weel, well:** ~**-farrant** of pleasant behaviour. ~**-hertit** good-hearted, generous, liberal. **weill menyt** kindly disposed. ~**-natured** good-natured, kindly and amiable. **well set** well-disposed.

†**wife** affectionate term for a female friend.

15.3.4 AGGRESSIVE

again in hostility to; to the hurt or disadvantage of.

alagrugous grim, ghastly.

†**apirsmart** sharp, severe.

argle-barglous quarrelsome.

at meddling with, hurting: '*Who was at ye?*'

attercap a spiteful or venomous person *now local Sh Ags.*

attery, 1 †venomous, malignant. **2** bad-tempered, spiteful, quarrelsome *Cai.*

austern austere.

awkward, †**ackwart** awkward, ill-natured, hostile, etc.

†**back** repress, harm.

bad-use ill-treat; misuse; abuse *now Sh NE Ags.*

bang fierce, violent, strong. †~**ie** impetuous; quarrelsome.

†**bard, baird:** ~**ie** quarrelsome.

†**barliehood** violent ill-temper.

†**battalous, batalrus** bellicose.

†**bauchle** treat contemptuously, cause trouble or harm to.

bessie an ill-mannered, boisterous, bad-tempered woman or girl.

blaud harm, injure.

†**brastling** noisy and menacing.

†**brath** fierce, violent, strong.

†**breem** furious, fierce, violent.

camstairy perverse, unruly, quarrelsome.

carnaptious irritable, quarrelsome.

cat-wittit spiteful; savage.

cuttit curt, abrupt, snappish *now Bnf Abd.* †~**ly** abruptly, curtly.

†**danger** disdain; displeasure, enmity.

demain 1 demean. 2 treat with severity, harshness or cruelty; maltreat, injure (*formerly esp* criminals at execution) *now Bnf.*

†**dere** harm, hurt, injure.

†**derfly** boldly, fiercely, roughly, violently.

din-raisin quarrelsome.

†**dispite** despite, malice, outrage, injury. ~**fully** spitefully, cruelly.

door: put someone to the ~ ruin someone *now Bnf Abd.*

dour *adj, of persons or actions* determined, hard, stern, severe. †*adv* severely, relentlessly, obstinately.

†**engreve** do hurt or harm to, injure.

†**envy, invy:** ~**fu** full of malice.

ettersome contentious, disagreeable *Sh-Ags.*

even, e'en lower, demean *now Ags.*

†**fairce** fierce.

fecht pugnacity. ~ **wi one's ain taes** be excessively quarrelsome *Sh Cai Abd.*

†**feid: bere, hald** *or* **have** ~ **at** be at enmity with, be hostile towards.

fell *adj* fierce, of cruel disposition, ruthless. *adv* sternly.

†**felloun** fierce, cruel.

fremmitness strangeness, unfriendliness, unfamiliarity.

gaw gall, bile etc.

†**gram** anger, malice.

groff *of the voice* harsh *Sh Mry Abd.*

grugous grim, ugly, surly.

†**haggersnash** tart *Ayr.*

†**harsk** harsh; severe, offensive, rude.

†**hask** severe, rigorous, rough.

†**haterent** hatred.

†**heelie** despise.

horn: have one's ~ **in somebody's hip** criticize severely, be antagonistic towards *now Ork NE Arg.*

ill *n* badness, malice. *adj* 1 harsh, severe, cruel *Gen except WC.* 2 *in curses* malevolent, unfriendly, hostile *now local.* ~**-faured** ill-mannered, bad-tempered, coarse. ~**-gaishon'd** mischievous, ill-disposed *Fif.* ~**-gien,** ~**-gevin** ill-disposed, malevolent *now Sh Lnk Dmf.* ~**-greein** quarrelsome *N-WC.* ~**-hertit** malevolent *Gen except Sh.* ~**-inten(i)t** ill-disposed, with evil intentions *NE.* ~**-kinded** ill-disposed, cruel *EC.* ~**-muggent** malicious *N.* ~**-nature** bad temper, irritability. ~**-natured** bad-tempered, irritable. ~**-set** harsh, cruel *Stlg Fif.* ~**-will** *n* dislike, enmity, malevolence. *v* wish evil to, hate *now Abd.* ~**-willed** hostile, having a dislike to *now Sh.* ~**-willer** a person who wishes evil on another. **ha(v)e** *or* **tak (an)** ~**-will at** *local Sh-Ags,* †**hae** ~**-will to** take a dislike to. ~**-willie** 1 †malevolent, malignant. 2 unfriendly, hostile.

indiscreet rude, uncivil. ~**ly** impolitely.

†**inimity** enmity.

injure do injustice to; hurt, harm; maltreat.

jimp curtail, restrict unduly, stunt *local.*

laith *n* ill-will, loathing, scorn *now Ork.* *v* loathe, detest.

†**leth** ill-will, hatred.

litigious vindictive, spiteful *NE.*

†**malagrugrous** grim, forbidding.

mane: mak nae ~ **for** *or* **about** show no sympathy towards *now Sh-N Uls.*

mark a finger (up)on harm in any way *Bnf Uls.*

†**mavité** *verse* wickedness, malice, evil intent.

mischieve injure, treat cruelly *now Sh NE Ags.*

misguide treat badly, neglect; bring up badly or cruelly *now local Sh-nEC Uls.* †**misguiding** misrule, mismanagement, ill-treatment.

†**miskennand** disdainful (of others), neglectful.

†**misknawlage** refuse to acknowledge, disown, repudiate, neglect.

mislushious malicious, ill-intentioned.

†**mispersoun** treat (a person) with indignity.

†**misregard** disregard, treat with disrespect, despise, ignore. ~**ful** heedless, neglectful.

nairra strict *now Uls.*

nebbie brusque *now local sEC-S.*

negleck neglect.

nip *of a sarcastic speaker or his words* cause to tingle or smart. ~**pit,** ~**py** curt, bad-tempered.

†**nither** oppress, vex.

†**odious** full of hate or enmity; hostile.

†**pairty** antagonistic, hostile **to.**

†**pautener** cruel, deadly.

pictarnie a bad-tempered person.

†**pine** cause pain and suffering, torment, torture.

play the loun act mischievously or wickedly.

plea strife, discord, enmity *now Mry Ags*.

pooshinous unpleasant, spiteful, malicious *now Rox*.

puddock term of abuse or contempt for a spiteful person.

ramgunshoch bad-tempered, rude and boorish *now Wgt*.

ramsh brusque, testy *Abd*.

randie *adj* 1 rough, belligerent, riotous, aggressive, *freq* ~ **beggar** *now Sh C*. 2 *of a woman* loud-voiced, coarse and aggressive *now Bnf Ags midLoth*. *n* any foul-mouthed, brawling, bad-tempered woman.

raucle, rackle *adj, also* **rackle-handed** hard, stern, grim, unbending.

rebat give a curt, brusque or discouraging reply *NE*.

regaird, regard: ~**less** heedless, uncaring.

†**reithe** fierce, cruel.

†**troid** violent, rough, uncivil.

royet an unruly, troublesome person, *esp* a bad-tempered woman *C*.

†**ruddoch** term of contempt for a bad-tempered old person.

rung contemptuous term for a bad-tempered person *now Mry Abd Bwk*.

runk contemptuous term, *esp* for a bad-tempered woman *Mry Abd*.

sair, sore *adj, also* ~ **on** *etc* harsh in discipline, treatment or judgement (towards). *adv* sorely, severely, harshly, so as to cause pain or suffering.

saut, salt *adj, of speech, manner* harsh, unkind *now Kcb*. *v* treat severely.

scouk, skulk 1 scowl, look balefully or furtively from under the eyebrows *now local Cai-Fif*. 2 draw (the brows) together in a frown *Bnf Abd*.

setterel short-tempered, sarcastic *NE*.

shaird, shard a bad-tempered or malicious person *now Bnf*.

side hard or severe **on** *Abd*.

†**sinistrous** malicious, unfair, prejudiced.

skaith, skaid harm, injure, damage. †**do** ~ do harm or injury.

†**snack** sharp or severe in one's dealings or manner, exacting.

snag snarl (at) *now Kcdn*. ~**ger** snarl, growl *Bnf Abd*.

snar severe, strict, tart.

sneisty uncivil, tart.

snell *adj* severe in manner or speech, tart, sarcastic

now Sh NE Ags. *adv* harshly, unfeelingly, vigorously.

snippit, *local Ork-Loth,* **snippy** *now Fif Loth* quick in speech, tart.

snotty short-tempered, curt, huffy *Gen except Sh Ork*.

†**stalwart, stalworth** *of actions* severe, hard, violent.

stang the capacity to injure in word or deed, a harsh or cutting remark *now Sh Abd*.

stench, stainch, staunch inflexible, uncompromising; austere, rigid *now NE*.

step-bairn: mak a ~ **o** treat unkindly, neglect, spurn.

stere harsh, austere, stern, rigorous.

stieve hard-hearted, relentless, obstinate *now Per*.

†**strait** bring into straits, restrict, stint. ~**en** press hard, put in difficulty.

stret strait, narrow; strict *now NE*.

strick strict.

†**strunt** strife, enmity, hostility.

sture grim, gruff, stern; hard, determined, unyielding *now Slk*.

sturt contentious or violent behaviour, *freq* ~ **and strife**. †~**ful** contentious.

targe treat strictly or severely. **targer** a violent, quarrelsome, domineering person, *esp* a woman *local Cai-Kcb*.

†**tarmegant** a violent, blustering, quarrelsome person.

teedy bad-tempered *now Wgt*.

teeger a person with a fierce quarrelsome nature.

†**tigirnes** ferocity.

†**teenfull** malicious.

†**terne** gloomy, fierce.

†**thieveless** cold, frigid, forbidding (in manner).

thin unfriendly *Abd Ayr*.

ticht, tight strict, severely critical *now Cai*.

tifty, tiffy quarrelsome, touchy *Bwk WC Rox*.

tinkler a tough malicious person.

tirr bad-tempered, quarrelsome.

toy treat (a person) in an offhand, frivolous or dismissive way *now Rox*.

tramp on a person's taes encroach on a person's interests or preserves, take advantage of, offend a person *now Sh N Per*.

†**trensand** trenchant, cutting.

†**trouble, tribble** harm; injure.

tuithy, toothy sharp in manner; critical, acrimonious *now local Fif-Wgt*.

†**tulyie:** ~**r** a quarrelsome person, a brawler. ~**some** quarrelsome, contentious.

turk fierce, truculent, sullen *now NE Ags*.

tyarr be prone to quarrel *now Cai*.

uncannie mischievous, malicious, malignant *now local Sh-Lnk.*

uncouthie unfriendly, fear-inspiring.

unfriend one who is not a friend, an enemy, *freq* **be ~ of** *or* **to**. **~ship** enmity, ill-will *now Sh.* †**unfreindfully** unfriendly.

unmainnerfu rude, discourteous, unmannerly *now Sh Abd.*

†**unmoderly** unkindly.

†**unrude** violent, rough.

†**usurp** practise or inflict (cruelty etc).

veecious vicious.

†**vendicatife** vindictive.

†**wait** treat (a person) **with** (unkindness etc).

warlock, †**warlo(ch)** *n* a mischievous or troublesome man. *adj* malevolent, mischievous.

†**warp** plunge (a person) suddenly or roughly **into** (distress etc).

†**weird** troublesome, mischievous, harmful.

whin, whun: **~stone** hard-hearted, inflexible.

whippert hasty and sharp in manner or behaviour.

wicked, wickit *of persons or their actions* bad-tempered, ill-natured, viciously angry.

worry-carl a snarling, ill-natured person *Bwk S.*

†**wraikful** destructive.

wranglesome quarrelsome, contentious *now Sh Ork Abd.*

†**wroke** active ill-will; spite, malice.

15.3.5 PESSIMISTIC

alagrugous grim, ghastly; sour; woebegone.

awkward, †**ackwart** awkward, ill-natured, hostile, etc.

beal swell with rancour.

†**black-baised** depressed *S.*

blue day a day when one is very depressed *now Abd.*

cadger an ill-tempered person *Bnf Abd.*

calshie crabbed, surly *now NE.*

camsheugh surly, perverse *now Bnf.*

canker *v* fret; become ill-tempered *now Abd Ags. n* ill-temper *local Bnf-WC.* **~(i)t** cross, ill-natured. **~some** *SW*, **cankry** *WC* ill-natured.

capernicious short-tempered, fretful, fault-finding *NE.*

cappit peevish, ill-humoured, crabbed.

cark complain, grumble *now Cai Bnf Dmf.*

catter-wurr an ill-tempered person *Bnf Abd.*

cauld, cold: **~ comfort** inhospitality *now local NE-Kcb.* **~rife** cold in manner; indifferent; lacking in cheerfulness *now NE Ags Fif.* **~-wamed** cold in manner, cold-blooded *now Fif.* **~-water** apathetic, indifferent *now Abd.*

channer, chunner grumble.

chilp cry in distress or querulously *Bnf Abd.*

chirm fret, complain.

compleen, †**complenȝe** complain.

crabbit crabbed.

craik grumble, complain *local.*

crankous fretful, captious.

cronachin grumbling.

croup, growp *now Mry* grumble *NE.*

curmurring a grumbling or complaining *local.*

demuired sad, downcast *Cai S.*

derf unbending, sullenly taciturn.

dirdum bad temper, ill humour *now Lnk.*

disjaskit dejected, downcast, depressed *local.*

disjeckit dejected.

doddy sulky, bad-tempered.

dods the sulks. **tak the ~** take a fit of bad temper, sulk *now Stlg Fif.*

†**donsie** glum, dejected.

doolsome, †**doolful, doly, duly** doleful.

doon: **~-looking** sullen, guilty looking. **~-moued** depressed *now Abd.*

dort: **~y** 1 bad-tempered, sulky *now Ork.* 2 fastidious, difficult to please *SW.* †**Meg D~s** a sulky, bad-tempered woman.

dour sullen, humourless, dull *local Bnf-Kcb.* † **~ly** resolutely, stubbornly, sulkily, sullenly.

douth dispirited, depressed *chf S.*

†**dow** dismal, sad.

dowf *adj* sad, melancholy *now Bnf Abd Fif. n* a gloomy person *now Ork Abd.*

dowie sad, dismal; dull, dispirited.

dowly sad, doleful.

draunt *v* whine. *n* a whine.

drearifu, drearysome sad, dreary *local Bnf-Edb.*

dreich depressed, doleful, dull, boring.

†**drevel** feel feeble and wretched.

drum sad, dejected, sulky.

drummoid dull, dejected *Cai Ross.*

drummure serious, sad-looking, dejected *now Cai.*

drunt(s) a fit of ill-humour.

†**dud:** *contemptuous* a dull, spiritless person.

†**dully** doleful, gloomy, dismal.

eerie †gloomy, dismal, melancholy. **eerily** weirdly; drearily. **~some** uncanny, gloomy *now Abd.*

†**engaigne** resentment.

faiple: hang a *or* **one's ~** look glum or sour.

fang without one's usual spirit or skill.

fashious fractious, peevish.

fiddle face a long face; a sad face *now midLoth Arg Ayr*.

freff cold, distant.

fremd †strange in manner, distant, aloof. †**fremmitly** strangely, in a strange or unfriendly way. **fremmitnes** strangeness, unfriendliness, unfamiliarity.

fryne grumble, whine.

gab-gash petulant or voluble chatter *now Inv*.

girn *v* complain peevishly, whine, grumble. *n* 1 a whine, whimper; whining, grumbling. 2 a grousing, peevish or fault-finding person *local*. ~**ie** *adj* peevish, ill-tempered. *n, also* ~**igo** (**gabbie**) a fretful, bad-tempered person *local*.

glooms a state of depression *now NE*.

glum look sullen *now Ags*.

glump *now Ags*, **glumph** *now local Sh-Dmf v* be glum, sulk, look gloomy. *n* **glumph** a sulky or morose person *now local Sh-Kcb*. ~**y** sulky, sullen, morose *now Ags*.

glumsh *v* be or look sulky or morose; grumble, whine *now local Bnf-Fif*. *n* a sulky, sullen, surly mood, look or reaction. *adj* 1 sulky, sour-looking *now Abd Ags*. 2 melancholy *now Per*.

glunsh *v* look sour, scowl; grumble, snap at, *freq* ~ **and gloom** *now local N-Kcb*. *n* a sour look, scowl *now WC*. ~(**y**) sulky, sour, bad-tempered.

grain complain, grumble *now Cai Ags Rox*.

greet complain; grumble ineffectually.

greet: ~**in face** a person who habitually looks miserable or as if he is about to weep. ~**in Teenie** a cry-baby; a person who is always complaining *Gen except Sh Ork*.

gronach grumble, complain *Bnf Abd*.

grudge, †grutch *v* 1 complain, be grieved, discontented or unwilling *now local Sh-Kcb*. 2 grudge. *n* 1 a grudge. 2 †discontent, dissatisfaction; a grievance, misgiving.

grugous grim, ugly, surly.

grummle *v* grumble. *n* 1 a grumble. 2 a grudge, grievance, quarrel *local Abd-S*. **grummlie** sullen, surly, grumbling *now local*.

grumph *v* grumble. *n* a grumbler, complainer *local Bnf-Slk*. ~**ie** ill-natured, grumpy.

grunch grumble; object, refuse *now Rox*.

†grunyie a grudge *Bnf Abd*.

gum ill-will, rancour.

gurl *now Dmf*, **gurlie** *now local Sh-SW* surly.

haggersnash spiteful *Ayr*.

heavysome dull, gloomy, doleful *Kcb Dmf*.

†theepie a melancholy or foolish person.

heepochondreoch listless, melancholy *Abd Kcdn*.

hert, hairt, heart: ~**less** disheartened, discouraged, dejected.

hing, hang: ~**ing-luggit** dejected, crestfallen, abashed. ~**ing mou'd** dejected, sulky *NE*. ~ **one's** *or* **the lugs** look dejected or abashed. ~ **on a** (**lang**) **face** look glum or doleful *now Sh Ork Ags*.

hoolet go about with a miserable expression; be solitary, unsociable.

howes a mood of depression, *freq* **be in the** ~ be depressed, be in the dumps *now midLoth*.

huid, hood: ~**ie craw**, † ~**ock** *contemptuous* a person with a sinister manner or aspect *Abd Per Rox*.

humch be sulky or bad-tempered *Bnf*.

hum-drum dejected, in low spirits; sullen *now local Cai-Slk*.

hummer murmur, mumble, grumble; mutter to oneself *now Cai midLoth*.

humour a feeling of resentment or ill temper.

ill: ~**-haired** ill-tempered, surly. ~**-set** 1 surly, out of humour *Ork*. 2 ungenerous, churlish. ~**-thrawn** ill-natured, cantankerous *Sh Ork Cai SW*. ~**-willie** grudging, disobliging, mean *now Abd*. ~ **tae dae til** (*local Sh-Per*) *or* **wi** (*N-SW*) difficult to please or humour.

kilter spirits, fettle, *chf* **in** *or* **out of** ~.

lanerly reserved in manner.

lang lip a sulky expression *Bnf Uls*.

langour, langer languor; boredom, low spirits.

langsome bored *now Sh-Ags*.

†leuk, luck, look: ~ **down** be melancholy or downcast.

louch in a depressed state of spirits *wLoth WC*.

†malagrugrous gloomy, melancholy.

†malancoly feel melancholy, sadness or resentment.

mane *n* a voiced complaint, grievance, grouse. †*v* bemoan, complain. **mak a** ~ to complain, grumble.

map mope *Ags*.

maroonjous surly, obstinate *now NE*.

meesery misery *now Sh Ork Per*. **meereable** miserable.

†miseritie misery.

molligrant, mulligrumph complain, grumble *now Abd EC Lnk*.

mou(th): doon o ~ in low spirits, down in the mouth *local*.

mowdiewort a recluse *Abd Fif Loth*.

mump *adj* depressed, sullen *local NE-S*. *v* 1 grumble, complain peevishly *Gen except Sh Ork*. 2 sulk, mope around.

munge grumble.

murmell *v* grumble at; mutter, mumble. †*n* the expression of discontent, grumbling *Sh*.

murn, mourn complain.

narr be discontented or complaining, fret.

natterie peevish, bad-tempered *now local*. **nitteret** ill-natured *chf Sh Ork*.

neetie a disobliging person.

neukit cantankerous *NE*.

nyarb be discontented or complaining *NE*.

on about occupied in talking about, harping on.

oolet a disgruntled, peevish, dismal person *Sh NE Ags*.

oorie dismal, gloomy, miserable-looking from cold, illness etc *now local Sh-Arg*.

orp fret, grumble, complain in a peevish, nagging way *now Ags*. **~it** fretful, discontented, peevish.

outward cold in manner, aloof, reserved *Rox*.

oxter: wi one's heid under one's ~ with a downcast, drooping look.

peefer complain querulously, fret.

peek complain, grumble, whine, whimper *NE Ags*.

peenge whine, complain, whimper. **peeng(e)in, peengie** *NE, C, S* peevish, fractious.

peesie-weesie shrill-voiced, whining, complaining *now Wgt*.

penurious, perneurious bad-tempered, whining *NE*.

perskeet hard to please *now Sh*.

†**pevych** peevish. **pevagely** peevishly.

pewl *v* pule, whine, complain *now local Sh-Per*. *n* a moan, complaint *Abd Per*.

pick-thank *NE*, **pike-thank** *Bnf Abd* ungrateful, unappreciative.

†**plaint** complain about, find fault with.

please: not ~ not be pleased, not show contentment: *'He frettit aye an wadna please' now NE*. **nae hae a ~** be incapable of being pleased, be perpetually dissatisfied *NE Ags*.

†**pleen (of)** complain, grumble, mourn, whine.

poukie dejected-looking, thin and unhealthy-looking *WC Kcb Uls*.

rame (on *or* about) dwell on something, harp on **about** (one's troubles).

rodden: have had ~s tae one's supper be in a sour or surly humour *NE*. **as sour as ~s** very sour or bitter *chf NE Ags Ayr*.

†**troust** rancour.

rudas *n, chf* **auld ~** an ill-natured hag, an old witch *now Bnf*. *adj* 1 *of a woman* ugly, cantankerous, witch-like. 2 †*of a man* cantankerous, stubborn, rough-mannered.

runt contemptuous term, *esp* for a coarse, gnarled, ill-natured person, *esp* an old woman *now local Sh-Fif*.

sagan *contemptuous* a surly person *Abd*.

sanshach disdainful, surly *NE*.

sauchen stubborn and sullen, **dour** *now Bnf Abd*.

scone: who stole your ~? why are you so glum? *C*.

scrae an ill-natured person *now Cai*.

scunner repugnance, distaste, dislike, loss of interest or enthusiasm, *freq* **tak a ~** (at *or* against). **~t, ~ed** bored, fed up.

sick-sair(t) *Ork NE*, **sick sorry, seek-stawed** *local wLoth-Dmf* thoroughly sated or bored, sick to death.

†**sitten-up** set in one's ways.

slotch move or walk in a slouching, hangdog way, drag the feet in walking *now Fif Loth Rox*.

smool look petulant or discontented, scowl, frown.

snottery surly, brusque, snooty *nEC, WC, SW*.

†**sopit** rendered dull or sluggish.

sour: ~ock, †**~och** a sulky, perverse, sour-tempered person *now local NE-WC*. **~ cloot** *now local Abd-Kcb*, **~ ploom** *EC, WC*, **~ face** *C* a person of harsh, gloomy or fault-finding disposition. **~ dook** a sour, mean person *local N-SW*. **~-moued** *now NE Ags Per*, **~-like-mood** *NE*, **~-mood-like** *NE* sulky-looking. **~ plooms** 'sour grapes' *now C*.

spaik *now local Inv-S*, **spoke: no ~** an unsupportive person.

†**standfray** aloof, rebellious.

steek one's lugs *or* **hert** refuse to listen, harden (one's heart).

stench, stainch, staunch serious, severe-looking, reserved *now NE*.

stickin stiff and unsocial in manner, unwilling to join in *now C*.

still reserved, taciturn, unforthcoming *now NE Ags Rox*.

strange, strynge aloof. **stringie** aloof, shy, stiff, affected *now Ags Per*.

strounge gruff, surly, sullen, morose *now N*.

stunkard sulky, surly, perversely or sullenly obstinate *now Lnk Wgt Dmf*.

sumph *n* a surly, sullen, sulky person *now NE-S*. *v* act like a **sumph**, sulk, be sullen *now NE, C*.

tak, take: ~ on mope.

tarrow complain; be perverse *now Sh*.

tedisome peevish and slow in one's actions *Per Fif*.

†**terne** gloomy, fierce.

†**tharf, thraf** cold, stiff in manner, unsocial, reluctant.

†**thocht, thought: ~iness** melancholy.

†**thieveless** cold, frigid, forbidding (in manner).

thrain harp constantly on a theme, beg persistently *Fif*.

thraw act perversely, quarrel, grumble *now NE local C, S*.

thrawn perverse, obstinate; intractable; cross, in a **dour**, sullen mood. **~-headed** perverse, contrary *now Ags Per Rox*.

thrum a (perverse) streak in a person's character; a whim, fit of ill-humour *now Ags*.

tig a fit of sullenness *now NE Ags Per*.

tirran a cantankerous, awkward, or exasperating person *now Cai*.

†Tontine face a grimace, distortion of the face from glumness etc *Gsw*.

torn face (a person with) a bad-tempered, sulky, glum face *now Cai C*.

†trist sad; doleful.

tunie moody, changeable in temperament *S*.

turk fierce, truculent, sullen *now NE Ags*.

uggit fed up *now Sh NE*.

unco like, unco leukin looking out of sorts, woebegone *now local NE-Ayr*.

†ungrate ungrateful.

unhearty listless, dispirited; melancholy *now Sh*.

†upsitting indifference, lethargy.

waebegane woebegone *now Sh Cai*.

warlock, †warlo(ch) *term of abuse* an old, ugly or misanthropic man.

wear out of pass from, leave (a friendship) behind *now Abd*.

weary †*adj* sad, miserable. *v* become bored or listless.

weasel-blawn unpleasant-looking, ill-natured.

weest depressed, doleful *Abd*.

weirdly magical, eerie, dismal, sinister.

wersh spiritless, depressed. †**~ly** insipidly, without cordiality.

wheek complain peevishly *now Ags Per*.

wheeple whine, whimper *now Ags*.

whinge, wheenge a whine, whimper, querulous complaint *now local Ags-Ayr*. **whinger** a person who whines or complains *local Stlg-S*.

witter *now NE Ags*, **wutter** grumble. **~ous** of a **crabbit**, stubborn nature, venomous in temper *NE*.

worm-eaten discontented *now Ork*.

wray wry.

wurn be peevish and querulous, be constantly complaining.

yabb harp on a subject, talk incessantly *now Sh-Ags*.

yaff *contemptuous* a peevish insignificant person.

yammer whine, whimper; grumble, complain; harp on, keep insisting.

yap chatter, nag, speak querulously, harp on.

yarp grumble *now Sh*.

yatter: ~in, ~y fretful, querulous, scolding *now Sh*.

yirm complain, whine, harp on *now S*.

yirn *v* wail, whine, complain *now Wgt. n* a complaint, whine *now Wgt*.

yowl complain, whine.

15.3.6 TOUCHY

†amplefeyst a sulky humour.

birkie huffy *now Per*.

bung: ~y huffy *now Bnf*. **in a** *or* **the ~(s)** in the sulks *now Bnf Abd*. **tak the** *or* **a ~** go into a huff *now Bnf Abd*.

buss *n* a sulky, bad-tempered expression, *eg* **have a ~ on** *now Cai Highl*. *v* pout, sulk.

crouse touchy *local*.

dods the sulks. **tak the ~** take a fit of bad temper, sulk *now Stlg Fif*. **doddy** sulky, bad-tempered.

dort *v* sulk, take offence *now Sh-Cai Fif. n* **~(s)** the sulks, the huff, *freq* **tak the ~**. **~y** bad-tempered, sulky *now Ork*. **†Meg Dorts** a sulky, bad-tempered woman.

dour: tak the ~les take offence, take a huff *now Ayr*. † **~ly** resolutely, stubbornly, sulkily, sullenly.

drap, drop: have a ~ at one's nose have something waiting to be done of which one doesn't want to divulge details, *eg* the paying of a debt *now Bnf Ags*.

drum sad, dejected, sulky.

drumshorlin sulky *Lnk*.

drunt(s) the sulks *now Rox*. **take (the) ~** take the huff.

fling jerk the head or body sideways as a gesture of displeasure, flounce *now local*. **tak the ~s** go into the sulks.

flird flounce.

frump(s) the sulks, a bad mood *now Sh*.

fuff *v* go off in a huff *local Abd-Rox*. *n* a huff *now Bnf local EC*.

fung, funk *v* fly into a temper or rage, sulk. *n* a bad temper, huff, tantrum *now local Sh-Kcb*. † **~ie** apt to take offence, huffy.

gee a fit of sulkiness or temper, a mood, caprice, fancy. **tak the ~** take offence, sulk.

glump *now Ags*, **glumph** *now local Sh-Dmf v* be glum, sulk, look gloomy. *n* **glumph** a sulky or morose person *now local Sh-Kcb*. **~y** sulky, sullen, morose *now Ags*.

glumsh sulky, sour-looking *now Abd Ags*.

glunsh, glunshy *now Dmf* sulky, sour, bad-tempered.

gowlie sulky, scowling *now Sh.*

gumphs the sulks, *freq* **tak the gumps** *Fif.*

heelie *v* be offended, take offence. *n* an affront, a slight; a feeling of pique.

hing, hang: ∼**ing mou'd** dejected, sulky *NE.* ∼ **the pettit lip** sulk, have an injured and offended expression.

humch be sulky or bad-tempered *Bnf.*

humdudgeons sulks.

ill: ∼**-taen** taken amiss, resented *local N-S.* **tak something** ∼ **oot** be upset at, averse from, offended by something *local Ork-Lnk.* **tak** ∼ **(wi)** take badly, find difficulty in.

kittle 1 touchy, easily upset or offended, difficult to deal with *now local NE-Kcb.* **2** sensitive, easily roused or provoked.

lip: let *or* **pit down the** ∼ look dismayed, pout *Sh NE-S.*

mistaen, mistaken *of a remark* taken amiss, misunderstood *Sh-EC Kcb.*

molligrant(s), mulligrumph(s) a state of dissatisfaction, a fit of sulks *now Ork EC.*

mump sulk, mope around.

munge sulk.

nervish nervous, easily agitated *N-S.*

†**offend** be offended: '*the Queen offendeth that I vse the title and arms of England*'.

pernicketie cantankerous, touchy, bad-tempered.

pet (cause to) take offence, anger, upset.

†**pick** *n* pique.

pirrie quick-tempered, touchy, easily annoyed.

rue: tak the ∼ take offence or a dislike *Ayr Dmf Slk.*

snotty short-tempered, curt, huffy *Gen except Sh Ork.*

snuff †a rage, huff. ∼**y** sulky, touchy, huffily displeased *now local.*

†**stingy** peevish, petulant.

stots a fit of the sulks, a whim *now Sh.*

stound a mood, whim, a fit of depression, sullenness etc *Ork N.*

strum *n* a fit of pique or bad humour, a perverse mood, the huff, *freq* **tak the** ∼**(s)** *now Mry Abd Per.* *v* sulk, go into a huff, look surly *Abd Ags Fif.*

strunt *n* a huff, the sulks, *freq* **tak the** ∼**(s)** *now C, S.* *v* **1** sulk, go about in a huff *now local Inv-Rox.* **2** offend, pique, affront. ∼**it** offended, in a huff.

stunk sulk, go into a huff *now Abd Kcdn.* **the** ∼**les** the sulks *Abd Kcdn.*

stunkard sulky, surly, perversely or stubbornly obstinate *now Lnk Wgt Dmf.*

sturdy a fit of sulks, a perverse mood, *freq* **tak the** ∼ *or* **sturdies** *now local Ags-SW.*

sumph *n* a surly, sullen, sulky person *now NE-S.* *v* act like a **sumph**, sulk, be sullen *now NE, C.*

tak, take: ∼ **tae oneself** acknowledge the truth of (an accusation), feel guilt or remorse, be sensitive about *now local.*

taum a sullen, sulky mood.

thin piqued, annoyed *Abd Ayr.*

thraw a fit of ill-humour, the sulks *now NE nEC, WC.*

tift, tiff *n*, *also* ∼**er** a fit of ill-humour, the sulks *now Loth WC.* ∼**y** quarrelsome, touchy *Bwk WC Rox.*

tig take a sudden whim, go off in a huff *now Ags.* **tak a** *or* **the** ∼ get a fit of the sulks *local NE nEC.*

towt a sudden (*usu* bad) mood, huff *now local Ork-Wgt.* ∼**ie** touchy, irritable *now local Abd-SW.*

umrage umbrage *NE Ags.*

15.3.7 WEAKNESS OF CHARACTER

ablach a person insignificant or contemptible through lack of will.

aff, off: ∼ **an on aboot** vacillating, undecided, changeable, unsettled.

bairge strut.

bairn: ∼**lie** *adj* childish; childlike. †*adv* childishly. ∼**liness** childishness.

†**barmy** flighty, foolish.

bee-headed hare-brained, unsettled.

big conceited, swollen headed. ∼**sie** proud, conceited *Ork NE.*

birkie a conceited fellow.

bladry foolishness, ostentation, harm.

blaw, blow *v* **1** †utter arrogantly, *chf* ∼ **(a great) bost.** **2** brag, boast; exaggerate. *n* **1** boasting, a boast. **2** a boaster *now Lnk.*

bleeze boast, brag *now Abd Fif.* ∼ **awa(y)** brag, exaggerate *now Bnf.*

blether brag. ∼**(s)** long-winded (boasting) talk.

blether(an)skate, blether(um)skite a boaster *now Fif.*

blicker (the talk of) a boaster.

bloust *n* a boast; boasting *now Cai Ags.* *v* brag, boast *now Cai Ags.* ∼**er** *n* a boaster, braggart. *v* brag, boast.

braggal boastful, smug *Inv.* **braggie** ostentatious, boastful *Ags.*

†**brandis** act showily, swagger.

brank bear oneself proudly, prance, strut *now Abd Fif.*

brolach a weak or effete person *now Bnf.*

†**bruckle** morally weak; readily yielding to temptation.

buckle: up in the ~ conceited.

bull: as prood as ~ **beef** very proud or conceited *Bnf Abd Ags.*

buller blustering talk, nonsense.

bum brag, boast *local.*

cairried conceited *local.*

caleery †*adj* frivolous; vain *Uls. n* a silly, light-hearted person, a harum-scarum *Uls.*

ca(ll) a nail to the head go to extremes, exaggerate *NE.*

canse speak pertly, saucily, in a self-important way *Dmf.*

capernoited capricious, crazy *now Abd Lnk.*

cat-wittit hare-brained, unbalanced *local Cai-Kcb.*

ceepher a person of no significance, an empty-headed person *local Abd-Rox.*

cockie-bendie a small, bumptious or rather effeminate man.

conceit, concait 1 conceit. **2** a good opinion **of** (oneself † *or* another). **conceity 1** †fanciful, flighty. **2** conceited, vain, proud.

†**corky:** ~-**noddle** a feather-brained person. ~-**heidit** feather-brained.

†**cowhuby** ? a weak or silly person.

crack boast, brag. ~(**s**) loud boasts or brags. ~**er** a boaster, braggart.

†**cramp** strut, swagger.

crankie unsteady, insecure, unreliable.

creest brag; put on airs *SW, S.*

creest a self-important person *local.*

crouse confident, self-satisfied. **craw** ~, †**crack** ~ boast, talk loudly and confidently. **croose i the craw** full of self-confident talk *local Bnf-Lnk.*

cude hare-brained *chf S.*

cush a soft, useless person *chf Rox.*

daeless helpless, feeble, useless *now Stlg.*

daft frivolous, thoughtless.

daighie inactive, lacking in spirit.

dall a doll, a pretty, silly woman *now Bnf Abd Lnk.*

†**dalldrums** foolish fancies.

dandilly *n* a (spoilt) pet. †*adj* petted, pampered.

dandrum a whim; a freak *now Bnf Abd.*

daviely listlessly, languidly.

deltit, diltit petted, spoilt *local NE.*

didderums *Arg,* **dodrums** *local C* half-daft notions, bees in one's bonnet.

dird act or walk conceitedly *Cai.*

dirten conceited, disdainful *now Abd.*

†**donsie** neat, tidy (*freq* with the notion of self-importance).

dowf *local Bnf-Fif,* **dowfart** *verse* dull, spiritless.

†**dud:** *contemptuous* a dull, spiritless person.

dwaffle limp, soft; weak, feeble *chf NE.*

†**dwaible** a weak, helpless person.

dwam: ~**ie** *now local Abd-EC,* ~**ish** *now Abd Fif* dreamy.

facile easily influenced by others, weak-minded. **facility** being **facile.**

fair: be taken to the ~ *of an over-confident person* be taken aback, discomfited *local.*

faizart a puny effeminate man, a weakling *now Sh.*

falderal an idle fancy, a fuss about trifles.

fa(ll): fair ~ **masel(l)** who can compare with me? *N.*

†**fallauge** giddy, thoughtless *Abd.*

†**faut, fault: (it war) na(e)** ~ *contemptuous interj used of pretentious people.*

feckless ineffective, weak, incompetent. ~**ness** weakness, incompetence.

fiddltie-fa a trifling excuse, hesitation *Bnf Adb.*

finger-fed pampered *now Abd.*

fittiefie a quirk, quibble; a whim, fussy action *Abd.*

†**flae-luggit** harum-scarum, hair-brained.

flagarie a whim; a piece of frivolity.

flair *v* boast.

†**flaunter** prevaricate.

flauntie capricious, flighty.

†**flaw** boast, exaggerate, tell lies.

flee, fly: ~-**about** a gadabout; a person of fickle principles *now local Sh-Ags.* **flee-up-(i-the-air)** a frivolous or pretentious person *now NE Ags Fif Dmf.*

flicht: ~**ie** flighty, capricious. ~**rife** unsteady, fickle, changeable.

flichtersome *now Bnf,* **flichtery** *now Ags* changeable, full of whims. **flichter lichtie** a light-headed person unable to settle down to any employment *Bnf.*

flird flutter, move restlessly or frivolously from place to place.

flird a vain, fickle person.

fliskie restless, flighty, skittish *now NE Wgt.*

fliskmahaigo, fliskmahoy *now Slk* a flighty or frivolous woman.

flist *v* boast, brag; exaggerate *Cai Bnf. n* **1** a fib, a boast *now Abd.* **2** a boaster, a fibber *now Cai Abd.*

florie †*adj* vain, showy. *v* swagger, strut about conceitedly *now Cai.*

†**flowin(g)** unstable, changeable, fickle.

flumgummery any foolish or frivolous action *Bnf Abd.*

†**fraik** a freak, whim, an odd notion.

free-living self-indulgent *Sh NE Fif Uls.*

freevolous frivolous.

freit a whimsical notion, a fad. **stand on** ~s make a fuss about trifles, be faddy.

†frivole frivolous, of little account or worth; fickle, unreliable.

fuil foolish, silly *now Sh-C*.

full proud, pompous, conceited *local NE-Kcb*.

fushion, fooshion: ~**less** *of persons etc, and their moral or mental qualities* spiritless, faint-hearted, lacking vigour or ability.

fyke a whim, a fussy fad *now local EC*.

†fyke-fack a whim, a contrary or freakish mood.

gaikit silly *Sh Abd Ags*.

†gallantish *of women* flirtatious, ostentatious.

†gallivaster an idle, boastful person, a gadabout *Abd*.

gamphrell a bumptious, foolish person.

gan(d)y talk in a blustering, boastful or pert way *NE*.

gange brag; exaggerate.

†gingebreid gaudy, extravagant.

glaik a silly, thoughtless person *now local*. ~**it** thoughtless, irresponsible.

†glaister talk boastingly, brag, bawl.

†gloriositie self-importance, boastful bearing.

glorious vainglorious *now Ags*.

glousterin blustering; loud-mouthed.

gouster *v* boast, bluster *now Sh Ork Dmf. n* a wild, violent, blustering or swaggering person *now chf Ork Kcb Dmf*.

gowst boast, bluster.

†grashloch boisterous, blustering.

great, gret, grit boastful, proud, elated.

gumptious bumptious.

haithen an intractable or difficult person *now Sh*.

haiver a piece of nonsense, a foolish whim or notion *now local*.

hallach *adj, also* **hallirackit** *local Sh-Ags* crazy, hare-brained *NE. v* behave in a crazy, wild or irresponsible way *now Ags Stlg*.

harrows: rin aff *or* **awa wi the** ~ let oneself go in a dogmatic, assertive way, talk unrestrainedly, exaggerate.

Hieland, Highland having an exaggerated sense of birth and lineage, *esp* ~ **pride**.

hippertie-skippertie light, frivolous, frisky *now Kcdn*.

hizzie, hussy *joc or (slightly) disparaging* a frivolous woman.

horn: blaw one's ain ~ boast.

howe: heicht(s) and ~**s, †heich(s) and** ~**s** moods, tantrums, quirks of character *now local*.

jirkie changeable *now midLoth*.

kae-witted hare-brained, half-witted *chf Ags*.

kick show off, walk haughtily *N*. **kicky** showy, *esp* in dress, dandified *now Kcdn*.

kiow-ow talk or act frivolously *N Gall Uls*. ~**in** tattling, frivolous *N Wgt*.

kirr self-satisfied *SW*.

kittle inconstant, unreliable, fickle *now local NE-S*.

lasslike girlish, like a girl.

leepit fond of warmth, given to coddling oneself, pampered *chf N*.

licht, light dizzy, light-headed *Loth Renfr*. ~**-farand,** ~**-farrant** *Abd Gall* frivolous, giddy in behaviour. ~**-headed** frivolous; changeful.

like wha but him, her *etc* quite the thing, in a grand or confident manner *now NE*.

madge *contemptuous* a silly woman *now Lnk*.

maggot a whim, fancy, bee in one's bonnet *Gen except Sh Ork*. ~**ive** *chf NE*, ~**y** *now Kcdn-S* capricious, perverse.

maik: as daft *(C) or* **feel** *(NE)* **as a** ~ **watch** completely silly.

massie bumptious, full of self-importance, proud *now nEC, WC, S*.

megrim a whim, preposterous notion *local Per-Uls*.

†meschant *of persons, their character and conduct* spiritless, feeble, worthless. ~**ly** miserably, feebly.

midden: craw on one's ain ~ be boastful in one's own environment. **look** *or* **glower at the moon till one falls in the** ~ be so lost in one's dreams that one loses touch with reality and comes to grief.

misken have mistaken ideas of one's own importance, get above oneself *now NE*.

†misknaw have an exaggerated opinion of oneself.

mollop toss the head disdainfully; give oneself airs *S*. ~**s** airs, antics, capers *Rox*.

moniment a silly person *Sh-Per*.

morn: here the day and awa the ~ said of someone unreliable or changeable.

muckle, mickle self-important *now local Sh-Edb*.

†new fangle (excessively) fond of novelty.

norie a whim, a fancy *chf S*.

notionate full of whims or caprices *now Kcb*.

nyaff a small conceited impudent person.

†ostentive ostentatious.

paewae drooping, spiritless.

palaver, palaiver *now local Ork-Per n* **1** a fussy way of behaving, an ostentatious procedure, a great fuss about nothing. **2** a foolishly ostentatious person, an extremely fussy person *now Cai NE Per*. *v* behave in a silly or ostentatious way, fiddle about. ~**in** *n* an ostentatious fuss, an 'act' *now local Ork-Per. adj* capering, ostentatious *now local Ork-Per.*

†**patient** passive, inactive, inert.

pauchtie supercilious, conceited; self-important *now Kcb.*

pavie adopt an exaggeratedly courtly bearing, strut, parade oneself.

pensie self-important, affected, pompous, priggish, prim. †**pensit** proud, conceited, arrogant; puffed with pride.

peppint petted, spoilt, pampered *Mry Bnf.*

phrase *n* a great or ostentatious talk about something, a palaver *now Abd Ags.* †*v* boast, brag, exaggerate, gush.

pingling ineffectual, feeble, lacking character or energy.

pirrie given to sudden bursts of activity, unpredictable, unreliable.

pitten on affected, conceited, insincere *now N-C.*

plaistery a showy, overdressed person *WC.*

poochle proud, self-assured, self-confident *NE.*

pride †take pride **in**, feel proud **of**, be or become proud. †**prydy** characterized by pride, proud. ~**fu** vain.

primp *adj* haughty, conceited *now Sh. n* a straight-laced and self-consciously correct person, a prig, a show-off *S.*

prink strut, move with a swagger, walk in a jaunty, self-conscious way *Ork Ags.* ~**ie** over-meticulous in dress or appearance, fussy over details, ostentatious, conceited *now Ork Bnf.*

pross put on airs, show off.

puff boast, brag *local Abd-Kcb.*

radge silly, weak-minded.

†**rattle scull** a giddy, thoughtless, empty-headed person.

†**ray** a king, used as an ironical term for a man.

rift *v* exaggerate, brag *now Abd. n* an exaggerated account; a boast *now Abd.*

rinabout a restless person, a gadabout.

ruise †*v* boast (**of**). *n* boasting; a boast. †**mak (a) (toom)** ~ boast (unjustifiably).

saft, soft soft. ~**ie** a softie, a weak(-minded) person.

sakeless lacking drive or energy *S.*

Sammy dreep a 'drip', a spiritless, ineffective person *local Bnf-Kcb.*

sapsy *adj* soft, sloppy; effeminate *Per Stlg WC. n* a soft, weak-willed, characterless person *Fif WC.*

sauchen soft, yielding as willow, lacking in energy or spirit *now Abd.*

saucy vain, conceited *local.*

saul *now local Sh-SW,* **sowl, soul: the (wee)** ~,

my (wee) ~ term of mild disparagement. **not say one's** ~ **is one's own** not be independent of others.

saur, savour: ~**less** lacking in wit, spirit, energy *NE.*

†**scance** talk pompously, exaggerate.

scatter-wit a scatterbrain *now local Abd-Slk.*

scrug tug (one's cap) forward over one's brow so as to give one a jaunty or bold air *now Ags.*

set him *etc* **up!** *ironic or contemptuous, of a person who gives himself airs* what a cheek!, the impudence etc! **set-up** conceited, affected, stuck up *local Inv-Slk.*

shalla shallow.

shanker a gadabout *Mry Abd.*

shaul(d) shallow in character, empty-headed *now Sh.*

†**shaup** an empty-headed, frivolous person, a useless creature.

shusy a silly, empty-headed woman *now Bnf.*

†**side** proudly, boastfully.

†**sirken(t)** fond of one's comforts, coddling oneself.

skavie, skeevie rush about in an idle, silly or ostentatious way *now Bnf.*

skech, skaich go about in a silly, vain, idle way *Bnf Abd.*

skeer, skeerie *now local of a girl* flighty, skittish.

†**skit** a frivolous, vain woman.

sma(ll): think anesel *etc* **nae** ~ **drink** think oneself to be a person of some importance.

smerghless, smeerless lacking in spirit or energy, sluggish, feckless, stupid *N.*

socher pamper oneself, be fussy about one's health.

sodie heid a feather-brain, flibbertigibbet *local.*

splore show off, boast, brag (**about**) *now Lnk.*

sprose *v* **1** boast, make a great show, swagger *chf WC.* **2** †brag about (oneself or another). **3** exaggerate, tell a tall story in order to impress *now Ayr.* †*n* a bragging or boasting, swagger, bravado.

stane pirrie hare-brained, scatty *S.*

streetch, stretch strut about haughtily *now Kcb.*

strunt strut, walk about in a stately way *now local Ork-Gall.*

strush *n* a bustling, swaggering gait *Cai. v* bustle, strut, swagger *Cai.*

†**strutly** ? proudly.

sturdy, sturdied giddy-headed *now Sh Cai.*

swash *v* bluster with or as with weapons; swagger, cut a dash *now Abd Ags. n* **1** affected ostentatious behaviour; a swagger; a strutting, haughty gait. **2** a swaggerer, a vain, ostentatious person. ~**y** ostentatious, dashing *now Abd.*

397

taibetless dull, lethargic, spiritless *now local Abd-Bwk.*

tantrum affected airs, whims *now Sh Ork Ags.*

taupie a giddy, scatter-brained, untidy, awkward or careless person, *esp* a young woman *Gen except Sh Ork.*

thowless *Gen except Sh Ork,* **thewless** *now Loth WC Rox,* **thieveless** *now Abd WC,* **thaveless** *Per Uls* lacking energy or spirit, listless, inactive.

tig *v* take a sudden whim, go off in a huff *now Ags. n* a sudden whim, mood or humour *now NE Ags Per.* **tak a** *or* **the** ∼ take a sudden whim or notion *local NE nEC.*

tip: have a guid ∼ **o onesel** have a good opinion of oneself *local Loth-Rox.*

tirrivee a wild extravagant mood, *freq* **take a** ∼ *C, S.*

too-hoo a spiritless, useless person *local Kcdn-S.*

tout (on) one's ain horn *or* **trumpet** blow one's own trumpet *N-WC, S.*

†tovie boastful, *esp* in drink.

†to-waver waver uncertainly, wander.

towt a sudden (*usu* bad) mood, huff *now local Ork-Wgt.*

traik a gadabout *now WC, S.*

tume *of words etc* vain, hollow, insubstantial *now Sh.*

twa-fangelt indecisive *NE.*

†undocht a feeble, weak or ineffective person *now Cai.*

upset *†n* arrogance, an unwarranted assumption of superiority. *adj* haughty, presumptuously ambitious, giving oneself airs *now local NE Dmf.*

vaig gad about *now local Ork-Ayr.* ∼**er** an idle stroller, a footloose person, a gadabout.

vainity vanity *now Sh Ork.*

vaudie proud, vain, ostentatious, showing off.

vauntie proud, boastful, vain *now chf literary.*

†voke arrogance, vanity, conceit. **vogie** proud, elated, vain.

voust *v* boast, brag *now Sh.* †*n* a boast. †∼**er** a braggart. ∼**y 1** † ? puffed up. **2** boastful(ly), proud(ly).

waffle, wuffle *n* a feeble, silly person *now Loth S. adj* inert, limp, feeble, sluggish *now local Cai-Fif.*

waik weak.

†wamfler ? a dandy, gallant.

†wandocht a silly, sluggish, worthless person.

†wanton insolent in triumph or prosperity.

weanish, weanly childish *local C.*

wersh spiritless, depressed.

wha, who: ∼ **but he** a paragon, the 'cock of the walk' *now NE Ags Loth.*

†wheegee a whim.

wheem a whim *local.*

whether-or-no indecisive, dithering *EC Lnk Dmf.*

whigmaleerie a whim, fanciful notion, fad *now local N-Dmf.*

whittie-whattie *n* frivolous excuses, circumlocutions intended to conceal the truth; indecision. *v* talk frivolously, shilly-shally; make frivolous excuses *now Sh.*

win(d), wund *n* a boast, brag; a boaster, braggart *now Sh. v* exaggerate, boast *Bnf Abd Ags.* ∼**y** proud, conceited; boastful *now Per.* ∼**y wallets** a person who talks in a boastful exaggerated way *now Rox.* **win-mull** a notion, fancy *NE.*

win(d)lestrae a person who is weak in character *now NE Ags WC.*

wisgan *term of abuse* a stunted, usesless, feckless person *Bnf Ags.*

yett: as daft as a ∼ **in a windy day** scatter-brained, flighty, crazy *C.*

†yowe, ewe a stupid, weak-willed person *NE.*

15.3.8 TREACHEROUS

For cunning as an element of intelligence, see 15.2.3; for tale-telling, see 15.5.8.

auld-mou'd wise, wily, crafty *chf NE.*

back: go the ∼**gate** act cunningly or deceitfully *now Abd Per.* ∼**spang** (the taking of) an underhand advantage *now Arg.*

beenge bow (humbly or servilely); cringe, fawn.

begeck *v* deceive, disappoint. *n* a trick, disappointment *chf N.*

begowk befool.

begunk *v* cheat, deceive, jilt; befool. *n* a disappointment; a trick.

berry: no the ∼ not to be trusted *Bnf Abd.*

†betraise betray.

†betrump deceive.

blaf(l)um †*n* a deception; a hoax, illusion. *v* cajole, deceive.

bland flattering, pleasant.

blaw, blow: ∼ **in someone's lug** flatter a person. ∼ **up** flatter, hoax, make (a person) believe what is untrue.

blear, blare blear, *usu* ∼ **someone's ee** deceive someone. **draw the** ∼ **ower someone's eye** deceive someone.

blink deceive, cheat. † ∼**er** a cheat, a spy.

brak, break: ∼**er** a breaker (**of** laws, peace, faith etc).

†brigue intrigue, use underhand means.

†**buss: wag as the ~ wags** *or* **wagged** agree sycophantically with someone.

buttery-lippit *etc* smooth-tongued, flattering *Ags Kcb*.

cat kindness cupboard love *now Bnf Abd Lnk*.

catchy ready to take advantage of another *Abd Stlg Kcb*.

causey saint a person who is well-behaved and pleasant when away from home *now Ags Lnk*.

cheat, chate *chf NE* cheat. **~ry** *n* cheating, deceit, fraud. †*adj* fraudulent, deceitful.

cheek in wi court the favour of *NE*.

chim make up to (a person) *NE*. **~ in wi** agree with fawningly *Bnf Abd*.

claw someone's back flatter someone, ingratiate oneself with someone.

cleek, click an inclination to trickery, a trick *NE*. **~ie** cunning, astute *now Mry*.

collogue be in league, have an understanding **with**, scheme *now Bnf Fif*.

corbie messenger a dilatory or unfaithful messenger *now Bnf Fif*.

†**crank** a snare; a wile *SW-S*.

creep a contemptible fellow, a sneak.

crose talk in a fawning, whining way, flatter *now Bnf*.

cuittle †1 coax, flatter *SW, S*. 2 smile ingratiatingly *S*.

deceiverie deceit.

†**dissimulate** dissembled, pretended; dissembling, deceitful.

draucht: deep-~, far-~, lang-~it, † **~y** designing, crafty.

†**faikin** deceitful.

fair: ~-ca'in smooth-tongued, flattering *now Fif*. **~-faced** superficially polite, deceitful *local N-Uls*. **~-farrand** plausible, specious, flattering, superficially attractive.

†**falset** falsehood.

†**fan** fawn.

fause, †**fals(e)** false, break (an oath etc). **~hood,** †**falshede** falsehood.

feeze fawn, get oneself into another's favour.

feingie make pretence, act deceptively. **~it 1** feigned. 2 †*of things* counterfeit, imitation.

Fifer a native of Fife, *freq* with implication of cunning and unscrupulousness.

filschach a dishonest, greedy person *Bnf Abd*.

flair flatter.

flairdie *v* flatter, cajole *Kcb*. *n* flattery; insincerity *SW*.

†**flat** flatter.

†**fleech** use cajoling or flattering words (**with**). **~er** a flatterer, wheedler.

†**flether** flatter, cajole. **~s** flattery.

fluister, flooster coax, flatter *Uls*.

foonge (on) fawn, as a dog, flatter, show affection in a sloppy way *NE*.

foutie mean, despicable, underhand *now Mry Abd Wgt*.

fraik *n* 1 a flatterer, a wheedler *Ags Fif Dmf*. 2 flattery *Ork Cai Ags Fif*. *v* flatter, make a fuss of, pet, pamper *Ork Ags Fif*.

gileynour a cheat, swindler.

glib sharp in one's dealings, smart, cunning *now Sh Ags*.

†**gluther** flatter.

†**goleinʒeis** deceitful or evasive statements or arguments.

gunk *n, freq* **do a ~ (on someone), gie (someone) the ~** cause (someone) pain or chagrin, disappoint *now local Pbls-Uls*. *v* disappoint, humiliate *now Uls*.

ha(ll) binks are sliddery *proverb* great men are not reliable in their support.

†**hand, haun: play with** *or* **tak silver of baith the ~s** act dishonestly or with duplicity.

haud, hald, hold: ~ in wi(th) keep in with, curry favour with.

hidlin secretive, furtive *now local Ags-Bwk*. **~ wise** secretly, by stealth *now Dmf*. **~s** *adv* secretly, stealthily, in secret *now Ags sEC Rox*. *n* concealment, secrecy *now Dmf*. *adj* secret, clandestine, underhand *now local sEC-Rox*. **in ~s** in secret, clandestinely *now sEC, Arg, Kcb*.

Hieland, Highland not quite truthful or honest, shifty, evasive *now NE*.

hing in curry favour *chf Abd*.

hinkum sneev(l)ie an underhand person, a tell-tale *Abd*.

†**hint,** *chf* **~ aboot, aifter** *or* **roun** go about in a sly or furtive way in order to further one's own interests, slink about; watch quietly *Bnf*.

hintback surreptitious, behind the back *Sh Ork*.

hirtch approach in a sly ingratiating way, sidle *now Kcdn Ags*.

house devil a person who behaves badly at home *freq* contrasted with **causey saint**.

hudge-mudge secrecy; furtive whispering *now Ags*. **hudgemudgan** whispering (*esp* behind someone's back) *now Abd Ags*.

huggery(-muggery) *adj* furtive *Ags Rox*. *adv* furtively *now Dmf*.

hunker-slide evade a duty or a promise, act in a shifty manner, prevaricate. **hunker-slider** a slippery customer. **hunker-sliding** *n* dishonourable or shifty conduct, evasive behaviour. *adj* evasive, dishonourable.

hypocreet a hypocrite.

inbearing officious, ingratiating, obsequious *Bnf Abd Ags*.

†ingine: evil *or* **false** ~ deception, guile.

inhaudin obsequious *Cai-Fif*.

†insinuat insinuate.

intak a swindler *local Cai-Bwk*.

jamph fool, trick.

jank evade, give the slip to; fob **off** *now Ags*.

Jock: play ~ **needle** ~ **preen** play fast and loose, act in a double-dealing or shifty way *NE*.

jouk evade, elude, avoid (someone or something). ~**er** a slippery or evasive character. ~**erie** *now C*, ~**erie-pawk(e)ry** trickery, deceit, roguery. ~**ie** evasive, elusive, sly *now Kcb*. ~**ing** dodging, shiftiness, dissembling.

keek a cunning, sly or malicious person *NE*. ~**er** a person who watches surreptitiously, a peeping Tom *now Kcb*.

kiss-my-luif a fawner, toady, effeminate person.

kithan, *also of women,* **kithag** a tricky person *Cai*.

†lamp in the *or* **intill ane lyme** trap as in birdlime.

lat, let: ~ **on** pretend.

lee like false, lying; fictional *SW, S*.

lick: ~ **lip** fawning, wheedling. ~**-penny** a swindling person *now Ags Loth Wgt*. ~**-ma-** *or* **the dowp** an obsequious (person) *now Ags midLoth*. ~**-spit** a lickspittle *now Cai Fif*.

link: hae *or* **pit a** ~ **in one's tail** be crafty or deceitful *SW, S*.

linkie a deceitful, untrustworthy person *S*.

lippen: no to ~ **tae** untrustworthy *N-S*.

loopie deceitful, shifty, crafty *Fif SW*.

†loun a dishonest rascal. **play the** ~ cheat.

†lounder idle, skulk.

†lour lurk, skulk.

†Lowrie a crafty person, a rascal.

†lug: blaw in the ~ **o** flatter, wheedle, cajole.

mak, make: ~ **in wi** curry favour or ingratiate oneself with *now Sh-Cai*. ~**-on** a pretence, humbug; an imposter *Sh NE*.

malverse †*v* betray the trust attaching to an office by acting dishonestly, corruptly, or oppressively. †*n* a breach of trust, a piece of grave misconduct. **malversation** corrupt behaviour in a position of trust.

†Matchevell Machiavel, an intriguer.

†mislippen defraud, disappoint.

mistryst fail to meet, let down, break faith (**with**) *now Kcdn Slk*.

mowdiewort a sneaking, underhand person *now wLoth Ayr*. **mowdy** loiter or prowl furtively about *Lnk Ayr*.

muild (in) curry favour **with** *now Abd*.

nick cheat, trick.

nip get the better of (in bargaining), cheat *now Gall*.

†nob a blackleg in a strike.

†offcome an excuse, pretext, evasion.

†oversile deceive, delude (a person).

†paintit *of words, speeches etc* highly coloured for show or to deceive; feigned, deceitful, insincere.

pauchle a swindle, a piece of trickery, a fiddle *Per WC*.

pawkery trickery, slyness. **pawkie(-witted)** wily, crafty.

†penny dog a sycophant, toady.

peuther importune in a fussy and ingratiating way, bustle about trying to win favour.

phrase *n* **1** an elaborate flowery speech, gushing and effusive talk, flattery *now NE*. **2** something false and misleading *now NE Ags*. *v, also* **†faizle** flatter, praise in an ingratiating and often insincere way, fawn on *NE*. **phraser** a wheedler, sycophant *Bnf Abd*. **phrasing** fulsome, ingratiating, insincere in speech. **mak a** ~ **wi, haud a** ~ **wi** *now Abd* flatter, butter up.

pike-thank, †pick-thank a person who curries favour by discreditable means, a sycophant, sneak, gossip *now Cai*.

pit, put: pitten on affected, conceited, insincere *now N-C*. ~**into 1** insinuate or suggest to, impose (an idea etc) on *NE Ags*. **2** impress, impose on, fool *now Cai Per*. ~**on** insincerity, pretence, falseness *now Sh Abd Edb*.

plaister *n* **1** a person who thrusts himself on the attention or company of others, a fawning or ingratiating person *now WC*. **2** an excessive flatterer *nEC Dmf Uls*. *v* be over-attentive, fawn, intrude obsequiously *Kcdn nEC Rox*.

platter a plotter, conspirator.

†prattick influence or activate craftily.

†quent cunning.

quirk trick, fox, get the better of, cheat *now NE Ags*. ~**y** cunning, resourceful, tricky *now Bnf Abd Ags Kcb*.

rap a cheat *now Fif*.

ride: no tae ~ **the ford** *or* **water on** *or* **wi** not to be depended on, unreliable, untrustworthy *local NE-S*.

ruise, roose *v* praise, extol, *esp* exaggeratedly, flatter *now Sh-N Kcb*. *n* praise, commendation, flattery. **†mak (a) (toom)** ~ give (empty) praise or flattery.

scodge act slyly, sneak idly about *now Cai*.

sconce cheat, get something by false pretences.

scouk, skulk *n* a skulking, cowardly person, a

sneak *now Cai Inv. v* 1 skulk. 2 shun, avoid (in a skulking manner) *now Ork NE Ags.*

scug a pretence, pretext, hypocritical excuse *now local Sh-Kcdn.*

†**sellable** venal.

†**sile** deceive, beguile, mislead (a person).

skech, skaich obtain (something) in an underhand way by wiles, wheedling or filching.

skite: gie *or* **play someone a** ~ deal unfairly or deceitfully with someone.

slee, sly *adj* sly. *adv* slyly, cunningly, stealthily. †*v* go or come silently or slyly.

sleek *adj, also* ~**ie** *now local Abd-S* smooth, oily, fawning and deceitful; cunning, self-seeking, sly *now local Abd-S. v* 1 walk or move smoothly or furtively, slink, sneak *local Sh-Dmf.* 2 flatter, wheedle, ingratiate oneself with *local EC-S.* ~**it** smooth in manner, plausible; sly, cunning, not to be trusted.

slid, †**slide** *of persons or their actions* smooth, cunning; oily, cajoling *now Lnk Slk.*

slidder †slippery. **slidderie, sclidderie, sclitherie** *of persons or actions* sly, deceitful, unreliable, untrustworthy *now local.*

†**slig, skleg** practise deceit *SW, S.*

slim wily, sly, crafty *now Abd Kcb.*

slink †*v* cheat, deceive, act dishonestly. *n* a smooth crafty person *now C Rox.*

slip-ma-labor a lazy untrustworthy person *now Sh.*

slooch, slouch crouch, cower, skulk furtively *now local Sh-C.*

slounge, slunge *v* behave furtively and stealthily. *n* a skulking, sneaking, sly, trouble-making person *chf SW.*

†**smaikry** roguery, trickery.

smook, smuk 1 slink or sneak (**about**). 2 go about furtively looking for something to pilfer *now local Sh-Ayr.*

smool curry favour, fawn, wheedle *now Ags Per Fif.* ~ **in wi** cajole, suck up to *now Ags.*

smool *v* slink, sneak, go about furtively *now NE. n* a wheedler *NE.*

snaik sneak, skulk about, do something in a mean, furtive or underhand way *now Ags.*

sneck: ~**-draw(er)** a crafty, deceitful person. ~**-drawing** guile(ful), artful(ness). **draw** *or* **lift a** ~ insinuate oneself into something surreptitiously, act craftily or stealthily.

sneevil, snivel 1 speak through the nose, speak with a nasal snuffling tone, whine *now local NE-SW.* 2 cringe, act sycophantically or insincerely.

snoke, snowk hunt, nose one's way, prowl, go about furtively *now local Sh-SW.*

snuil, snool submit tamely, cringe, act meanly, deceitfully or spiritlessly.

snuve slink, sneak *now Rox.* **sn(u)ivie** an abject or cringing person.

soother coax, cajole, flatter *chf Arg Uls.*

souk, suck a sycophant, toady *C, S.* ~ **in** curry favour, ingratiate oneself (**with**).

souple, supple ingenious, cunning, astute, devious *now local Sh-Kcb.*

sowd agree (to), sympathize with (so as to curry favour).

†**stouth** stealth, clandestine transactions.

stow(n)lins in a hidden or secretive way, furtively. †**steil someone doun** ruin by secret means.

†**sugurat** *of words* sweet, honeyed.

†**supprise** ensnare, betray.

swick, sweek *n* a cheating rogue, swindler, deceiver *Sh-WC. v* cheat, swindle, deceive. ~**ery** cheating, swindling *now NE.* † ~**ful** deceitful, treacherous.

thief: ~**like** *now Sh,* ~**(t)ie** *local* stealthy, furtive. † ~**ly** by stealth.

†**thift:** ~**fully,** ~**ly** by stealth. ~**uous, theftuous** furtive, stealthy. **by** ~ stealthily, furtively.

†**time-taker** a time-server.

tod a sly, cunning, untrustworthy person *now local Per-SW.* † ~**ly** foxy, crafty.

†**tove** puff up with praise, flatter.

†**traffeck, traffic** have illicit or secret dealings, intrigue, conspire (**with**). **trafficker** a go-between, negotiator; an intriguer.

traisonable treacherous.

†**trigit** trickery, deceit.

trucker a deceiver, cheat.

†**trufinge** deceit.

†**trump** deceive, cheat. ~**er** a deceiver, cheat. ~**ery** deceit, trickery.

†**truphane** a deceiver, impostor.

turn, tirn: tak the ~ **oot o** trick, fool *now Sh Per.*

twa, two: ~**-faul(d)** deceitful, two-faced *now NE.*

tweedle cheat, deceive *now Mry Abd.*

uncannie dangerous, unreliable, insecure, treacherous, threatening.

under, unner: ~ **thoum** secretly, in an underhand manner.

unhonest dishonest *now local.*

†**unsonsie** unpleasant, treacherous, troublesome, mischievous.

†**up-put** the ability to deceive.

†**wansonsy** *literary* mischievous, unpleasant, treacherous.

†**weasel, wheasel** a sharp, restless, prying, sneaky person.

wheetie underhand, shifty, evasive *NE*.

whilly cheat, trick, *esp* by means of wheedling, cajole.

whillywha 1 a flatterer, a person who deceives by wheedling. **2** flattery, cajolery. †*adj* flattering, glib, deceitful, unreliable.

†**whirliwha** flatter, deceive by flattery, trick.

†**white** flattering, fair-seeming, *usu* implying an intention to deceive. **whiting** flattery.

†**widdle** beguile, lead astray.

wile 1 deceive by a wile, beguile. **2** get or bring by a wile (a person to or from a place, or a thing from a person) *now local Sh-Per*.

†**wimple, wumple** tell a story in an involved deceitful way.

†**wise, wice** contrive, obtain by guile.

wratch, wretch cheat, stint.

†**wrenk, wringe** a cunning action, trick.

†**yaup** clever, cunning; shrewd.

15.3.9 BOLD

†**apert** bold.

bang fierce, violent, strong; agile and powerful.

†**bard, baird:** ~**ach** stout, fearless.

bauld bold.

†**beld** bold.

†**brath** fierce, violent, strong.

campy bold, brave.

crouse bold, courageous, spirited *now Bnf*.

derf bold, daring, hardy. † ~**ly** boldly, fiercely, roughly, violently.

douchty doughty.

†**dourly** resolutely, stubbornly, sulkily, sullenly.

facie bold, ready to face danger *now midLoth*.

†**fear: but** ~ without fear.

fechtie courageous, ready to fight *now local Bnf-Fif*.

†**freck** bold, active, eager, forward.

furthie, forthy forward in disposition, bold *now Abd*.

grip: haud the ~ hold to one's faith or purpose; endure, last *now Ags Wgt*.

gumption pluck, self-confidence *now local*.

hail, whole: ~-**heartit** undaunted, stalwart.

hard: as ~ **as a** *or* **the horn** hardy.

hardy: † ~**ment 1** boldness. **2** deeds of valour. **keep up a** ~ **heart** be stout-hearted *now Ags midLoth Wgt*.

†**jeopardie** martial daring, valour, prowess.

jirg: not ~ not to hesitate, waver or budge.

†**keen** *of persons or their actions etc* brave, fierce, courageous, resolute.

kempie a bold or pugnacious person *now Bnf*.

†**likly** strong and brave-looking.

†**lusty** gallant, valiant.

†**man of main** *verse, latterly only ballad* a mighty man.

mettle spirited, mettlesome *now Abd C, S*.

†**mudie** *chf verse* brave, bold.

†**pauchtie** stout-hearted, spirited, gallant.

†**permanence** steadfastness.

pretty *of men* courageous, gallant, manly *Sh NE Ags Slk*.

saul *now local Sh-SW*, **sowl** spirit, mettle, courage.

†**savage** intrepid, valiant.

stalwart, †stalworth *adj* **1** *of persons or their attributes* resolute, determined. **2** valiant, courageous. †*n* a strong valiant man. † ~**ly** strongly, bravely.

†**stout** a brave, valiant person. ~**fullie** stoutly.

stuffie spirited, plucky, game *local Ags-Wgt*.

sture strong, sturdy, valiant *now Sh*.

†**thrae** *adj* stubborn in a fight, sturdy, bold. *adv* boldly.

†**unabasit** undaunted. ~**ly** boldly.

†**unagaist** not aghast; unafraid.

undantit undaunted.

†**unfrayit** undaunted.

wale wight men *ballad* the best and bravest men.

†**weel-hertit** courageous, valiant.

wicht *adj, only verse* **1** valiant, courageous: (1) *of persons, esp warriors*; (2) †*of actions or attributes*. **2** †strong, vigorous. †*n* a valiant man.

†**wirship** valour.

15.3.10 TIMID

bauch backward, timid, sheepish, foolish.

blate bashful, timid, diffident, modest.

†**bluntie** a sniveller, *chf* **look like** ~.

bog-stalker an idle, bashful man.

britchin: hing in *or* **on the** ~ hang back, hesitate *now Bnf Ags Kcb*.

cooard a coward. ~**iness** cowardliness *local Bnf-Fif*. ~**ly** *now local Abd-Fif*, ~**y** *now Fif Stlg* cowardly.

coocher a coward, poltroon.

coof a coward *now Ags*.

coor, cower: ~**ie** timid, cringing *C, S*.

coordie be cowed, shrink *now Bnf Abd Fif*.

crap: get the ~ **on** get the wind up *Bnf Abd Gsw*.

†**crawdoun** a coward.

creenge cringe *local Bnf-Kcb*.

dow: not ~ be unwilling, not have the strength of mind or courage (to do something), not to dare.

ergh †*v* be timid, feel reluctant, hesitate. *adj* timorous; hesitant, reluctant. ~(**ness**) doubt, fear, timidity. †**archly** timidly.

feardie (gowk) *chf child's word* a coward.

†**flear** a fugitive, a person who flees.

freff shy.

fugie *n* a runaway, a fugitive; a coward *now Ags*. *adj* cowardly *Rox*.

hen withdraw from any undertaking or promise through cowardice, chicken out *sEC, SW, S*. **hennie** timid, cowardly *local Abd-Ayr*. ~-**hertit** chicken-hearted.

laithfu bashful(ly).

like, lik: not ~ expressing hesitation or bashfulness: '*I dinna like*'.

†**lirk** shrink, cower, cringe.

†**lour** cower, crouch.

†**meschantly** miserably; feebly, cowardly.

mim-spoken prim or shy in speech, quiet-spoken.

scar, skair timid, shy, wild, apt to run away *now Ork*.

shan bashful, timid, frightened *now Cai*.

skeich, skey †shyly, coyly, disdainfully, saucily, spiritedly. ~**en, ska(i)ken** timid, easily scared, nervous *Abd*.

snuil, snool a spiritless, cringing, abject or cowardly person *now Sh Ags*.

stookie a shy person *now N, C Rox*.

strange, strynge shy, self-conscious. **stringie** aloof, shy, stiff, affected *now Ags Per*.

teet *v* peep, peer, glance slyly, surreptitiously etc *now Sh-nEC*. *n* a shy peep, a sly, secretive glance *Sh-nEC*.

timmer bashful, afraid *Bwk Renfr Rox*.

timorsome nervous, timid, fearful *now nEC, WC, S*.

tongue-tack(it) tongue-tie(d) *now local Sh-Per*.

†**tremebund** inclined to tremble; timorous, timid.

unco reserved, shy, bashful *now Sh*.

†**waynd** flinch; hesitate.

willyart awkward, shy *now Wgt*.

15.3.11 WILD, ECCENTRIC

For drunkenness, see 15.5.6; for uproar 15.5.5; for sexual debauchery 8.9.

†**abandoun:** ~**ly** impetuously, recklessly. **in** *or* **at** ~ impetuously.

†**abuise** behave in a disorderly or licentious way.

awkward obstinate *chf NE*.

back-jaw impudence, abusive language *Bnf Abd Lnk*.

†**bangie** impetuous.

†**bard, baird:** ~**ie** bold, impudent.

†**barns-breaking** a mischievous action.

belli-hooin riotous(ness) *Fif*.

bin(d): be neither *etc* **to haud nor** ~ be beyond control.

bool-horned perverse, obstinate.

†**born head** straight and impetuously.

bousterous boisterous, fierce; rowdy *now local Cai-Kcb*.

bows: gae owre the ~ *Abd Ags*, **be** *or* **gae through the** ~ *Bnf Abd Ags* go beyond all bounds.

braisant brazen-faced *now Bnf Abd Fif*.

†**brank** behave violently or without restraint.

breengin wilful, pushing, sharp-tongued *now local*.

britchin: sit in the ~(**s**) refuse to move *now local Ork-Kcb*.

buckie a perverse, obstinate person, *freq* **Deil's** ~.

bucksturdie obstinate *Ags*.

†**busteous** boisterous.

†**caleery** full of mischief *Uls*.

camsheugh surly, perverse *now Bnf*.

camstairy perverse, unruly, quarrelsome.

canse speak pertly, saucily, in a self-important way *Dmf*.

†**carl: a stalk of** ~ **hemp** a tough or stubborn element.

ceepher a person of no significance, an impudent person *local Abd-Rox*.

†**chat** impudence, impertinent talk.

cheek up cheek, use insolent language to *now Ags Stlg*.

clack, cleck gossip, chatter, insolence.

clippie pert *now Kcb*.

†**contemptioun** insolent disregard **of** (authority), *freq* **in** (**hie**) ~ **of.** ~ **done to** a display of contempt shown to (an authority).

contermacious perverse, self-willed, obstinate *local Bnf-Fif*.

contermin't contrary, perverse *Abd*.

coorse wicked, bad, naughty *chf NE*.

Cupar: he that will to ~ **maun to** ~ a stubborn person will have his way *local*.

cutlack impertinence, impudence *Abd*.

†**deblat** a little devil, imp.

deil, deevil, devil: deevilock a little devil, imp *now Bnf Abd*. **deviltry** devilry. ~'**s bairn** a mischievous person, a rascal *now Bnf*.

deugend wilful, obstinate *Cai*.

ding doun Tantallon go beyond all bounds in conduct.

dinsome noisy, riotous, brawling.

†**disobeyance** disobedience.

disrespeck disrespect.

†**donsie** badly behaved, ill-tempered *SW*.

dorty saucy *now Ork Ags Kcb*.

dour *adj* 1 obstinate, stubborn, unyielding. 2 slow, sluggish, reluctant (to do something) *now Fif WC*. †*adv* severely, relentlessly, obstinately. † ~**ly** resolutely, stubbornly, sulkily, sullenly.

ersit, essart stubborn, perverse *chf SW*.

facie impudent, cheeky *midLoth Bwk Rox*.

faggot exasperating behaviour.

fey behaving in an irresponsible way *now local NE-Uls*.

fiercelins hurriedly, impetuously, violently.

Fifish eccentric, slightly deranged *now Ags Fif*.

fire: (like) ~ **and tow** rash(ly), impetuous(ly) *now Bnf Ags*.

†**flae-luggit** harum-scarum, hare-brained.

†**fordersome** rash, impetuous.

forritsome forward, impudent, bold *now local midLoth-S*.

frawart contrary, perverse *latterly only literary*.

frush frank, bold, rash.

furthie, forthy impulsive *now Abd*.

fyke 1 ~**(s)** the itch, the fidgets, a fit of restlessness *now Cai midLoth*. 2 restlessness, a state or mood of uneasiness.

gab light entertaining talk, chat, cheek. **set up one's** ~ speak out boldly or impertinently *local Cai-Rox*.

gae, go: ~ **ower** be beyond a person's power or control *local Sh-Fif*.

gall(o)us wild, unmanageable, bold; impish, mischievous, cheeky *local N-S*.

gange talk insolently.

gansel a disagreeable comment, an insolent remark.

gash pert, impudent language.

†**gaud** a trick, deceitful practice, prank.

gey, gay: ~ **(like)** *freq ironic* disreputable, wild.

†**gillravager** a wild or lawless person.

gouster a wild, violent, blustering or swaggering person *now chf Ork Kcb Dmf*.

hallach behave in a crazy, wild or irresponsible way *now Ags Stlg*. **hallockit, hellicat,** †**hallirakus** a noisy restless person, a hoyden.

hallion a slovenly-looking or clumsy person, a rascal, a clown *now Sh Ags Gall Rox*.

hard: ~ **neck** brass neck, impudence, effrontery. ~-**neckit** lacking in modesty, forward *now Arg*. ~-**set** wilful, obstinate *now midLoth*.

†**harrow: have** *or* **get one's leg ower the** ~**s** get out of hand, become unmanageable.

haud, hald, hold: ~ **by** have (little etc) respect for *now NE: 'ye haud light by the law'*. **neither to** ~ **nor (to) bind** ungovernable, beyond control.

hawkit stupid, foolish, harum-scarum.

†**heichtynes** temerity.

heid, head: ~**ie** headstrong, passionate, impetuous, violent *Gen except Sh Ork*.

hempie wild, romping, roguish *now Bwk*.

heronious misguided in behaviour, disregarding or defying established habits and ideas, unconventional, outrageous *Ayr*.

het, hot: (ower) ~ **at** *or* **a-hame** *ironical* applied to someone who appears to have left the comforts of home for no apparent reason *local N-SW*.

hilty skilty harum-scarum, heedless.

ignorant ill-mannered, presumptuous, forward.

ill: ~-**chat** impudence *NE Ags midLoth Lnk*. ~-**contrived,** ~-**contriven** 1 tricky, mischievous, badly-behaved *Sh N*. 2 contradictory, intractable *Sh Cai Mry*. ~-**daein** *n* misdemeanour, bad behaviour *now Sh N midLoth*. *adj* badly behaved, dissolute. ~-**dune** wrong, badly behaved, perverse, mischievous. ~-**deedie,** ~-**deedit** *Cai Ags* mischievous, unruly. ~-**designed** mischievously-minded *Sh NE midLoth*. ~-**gab** insolent, impudent language *local EC*. ~-**gates** dissolute behaviour, mischievousness *Ags*. ~-**gated,** ~-**gettit** badly-behaved, perverse *local EC*. ~-**gaitedness** perverseness *chf NE*. ~-**jaw** coarse, abusive language, insolence *Sh N Kcb*. ~-**mou'd** impudent, insolent *local Sh-EC*. ~-**trickit** prone to play tricks, mischievous *Sh-Ags*. **gae** *or* **run an** *or* **the** ~ **gate** live an immoral life *local Sh-Lnk*.

†**impertinat** impertinent.

impident impudent. **impidence** impudence.

†**incounsolabill** refusing counsel or advice.

†**ingere** push oneself in, obtrude oneself.

†**inhonesté** disgraceful conduct.

†**inordourly** disorderly.

†**insolence** wild behaviour.

jeeger *chf contemptuous* an odd or eccentric person *Sh local E Lnk*.

kill: fire the ~ *now Sh midLoth S*, **set the** ~ **on fire** *or* **a-low** *now Sh* start trouble, raise a commotion.

kiow-ow a trick, ploy, carry-on *now Gall Uls*.

kittle cattle persons who are unmanageable, capricious, difficult.

knapdarloch contemptuous term for an undersized, dirty, cheeky person *NE*.

laidron, la(i)therin *term of abuse* a rascal, loafer.

†**lan(d) lowper** a person who roams about the country idly or to escape the law, a vagabond, adventurer.

lenth, length: gae *etc* **a bonnie** *or* **all one's ~** follow one's inclinations or feelings as far as one can or dares *Gen except Sh Ork.*

limb: devil's ~, ~ o the deil *etc* a mischievous person.

†**ling: in(til) ane ~** *verse* quickly, impetuously.

linkie a roguish person, a wag *S.*

loud-spoken having a loud voice, forward or overbearing in speech.

loun a mischievous rogue *now Ags mLoth.* †**play the ~** act mischievously or wickedly.

lowp: ~-the-dyke undisciplined, wayward. **~ ower** go beyond, transgress.

lowse, loose *of persons, their way of life etc* unrestrained by moral consideration, dissolute, immoral. †**brek ~** break out into or turn to disorder, lawlessness, immorality etc.

maroonjous wild, obstreperous; surly, obstinate *now NE.*

mile: gae one's ~(s) go as far as one dares (in wild conduct).

†**milygant** *derog* ? a rascal.

mirkie merry, cheerful, mischievous *now NE.*

misanswer give a rude answer *Bnf Abd Uls.*

misbehaden out-of-place, improper, impolite. *now Sh Ork NE.*

moniment a rascal *Sh-Per.*

nash(-gab) impudent talk *chf Rox.*

neb: ~bie cheeky *local wLoth-Gall.* **~sie** impudent, pert *now eLoth.*

neeger a hard or reckless person.

orishon a wild person *SW.*

orra strange, uncommon, abnormal *now EC.*

†**outbreking** an outburst; a breaking out into sin or rebellion; a bout of disorderly conduct.

outheidie headstrong, rash *Kcdn Ags.*

†**outrage** excessive boldness; foolhardiness, rashness; presumption.

†**outschute** over-reach oneself, go too far.

†**outstrapalous** obstreperous.

ower, over: ~ly unrestrained, unconventional, unusual *now Sh.*

pauchtie insolent, cheeky *now Kcb.*

pawkie 1 *also* **~ witted** stubborn. **2** roguish.

pet-willed headstrong, self-willed, obstinate *NE.*

pliskie mischievous, full of tricks, wily.

poochle cocky *NE.*

positive determined, adamant, pig-headed, obstinate *N, C.*

prat a trick, prank, practical joke, piece of mischief *now Cai.*

prattick 1 †*also* **prettikin** *Sh Ork* an exploit, feat of daring or physical skill, a caper. **2** †*also* **prettikin** *Sh Ork* an escapade, *esp* a discreditable one, a piece of mischief, trick *now NE.* **3** an artful scheme, trick, dodge *now NE.*

†**pratty** mischievous, naughty, restive. **ill-~** mischievous, naughty.

quean *term of abuse* a bold, impudent woman *now NE.*

queer *adj* rather strange, oddish *Ags Per.* *n* an oddity, a queer person *now Ags Edb.*

queeriosity a curiosity, something strange *NE Per.*

†**querty** full of mischief.

†**rabel** oppose rebelliously.

rackless reckless *now Sh Ork Wgt.*

radical a wild, unruly person, a rogue, rascal *now Sh Bnf Abd.*

ragglish wild, unreliable *NE.*

ramagiechan a big, raw-boned, awkward, impetuous person.

†**rammage, rammasche** violent, wild, unruly.

rammish, ramsh impetuous, uncontrolled *now Ork.*

†**ramp** wild, bold, unrestrained.

rampage riotous living.

ramscallion a rapscallion.

ram-stam, †**ram tam** *adj* headstrong, rash, heedless, unrestrained. *adv* in a headlong, precipitate way, rudely, in confusion. *n* a headstrong, impetuous person or action. *v* rush or blunder about in a headlong, impetuous way *Gen except Sh Ork.*

ramstougar, ramstougerous rough in manner, boisterous, disorderly *now Lnk.*

randie *adj* **1** rough, belligerent, riotous, aggressive, *freq* **~ beggar** *now Sh C.* **2** boisterous, wild, dissipated *now Sh C.* *n* a boisterous, mischievous person *now Abd Kcb.*

†**rank** swift, impetuous, turbulent, given to violence or excess.

rap a rake *now Fif.*

raucle, rackle *adj,* also **rackle-handed** bold, impulsive, rash *now Fif.* †**raklie** rapidly, impetuously.

†**reel: make a ~** behave riotously.

reester a stubborn person.

reevin rash, excitable.

reid, red, rid: ~-heidit having red hair and thus popularly believed to be excitable and impetuous *Gen except Sh Ork.*

reuch, rough: ~-living *of a man* living in a dissolute, debauched or immoral way *now Sh NE Per.*

†**reverie** wantonness, wildness.

rhymeless irresponsible, reckless, ineffective *now Bnf.*

rigwiddie stubborn, obstinate; perverse.

rin, run: rinabout *adj* runabout, roving. *n* a vagabond, rover. ~ **thereout** a vagrant, roving person *now NE Ags.*

rizzon, reason: ~ **or nane** with or without reason on one's side; obstinately *now NE.*

royet *adj* wild, unruly, mischievous *now local Sh-Fif. n* an unruly, troublesome person *C.*

rudas 1 wild, undisciplined, irresponsible *now Mry.* **2** †*of a man* cantankerous, stubborn, rough-mannered.

rummle, rumble: rummlin boisterous, full of mischief. ~**garie** †*adj* wild, unruly, devil-may-care. *n* a wild, reckless, or thoughtless person. ~**skeerie** a wild reckless person *local Per-Ayr.*

sacket *term of abuse* a scamp, rascal, a pert impudent person *Ags.*

scamp go, wander **about** *etc, freq* with an idea of mischief *now Bnf.*

scandaleese scandalize.

score: over the ~ beyond the bounds of reason, moderation etc.

set obstinate, *freq* **ill-set** *now Sh-C.* ~ **up one's gab** *etc* utter impudent remarks etc *local Sh-Kcb.*

shape an odd or droll figure *Wgt Rox.*

sharg an impudent man.

†**skellie** naughty.

skemp a scamp *local N-S.*

smatchet an impudent, worthless person, a rascal *now Sh Ork N.*

snash *v* insult, speak impertinently to, sneer at. *n* abuse, hard words, impudence *Gen except Sh Ork.* ~**gab** petulant, insolent talk *now Loth Rox.*

sneist impertinence. ~**y** cheeky *now Rox.*

speak, spick *NE:* ~ **back** reply impertinently and defiantly, talk back.

splairge run wild, squander one's resources or talents heedlessly *now Kcdn Per.*

†**staffage** stubborn, unmanageable.

†**standfray** aloof, rebellious.

stickin obstinate *now C.*

stockit obstinate, stubborn *Bnf Abd.*

tap, top: ~**-thrawn** headstrong, perverse, obstinate.

tear: *freq* ~ **awa, on** *etc* work strenuously, energetically and with speed (**at**). ~**in** †*n* rowdy behaviour. *adj* rowdy, boisterous *now N, C.*

†**temerare** reckless, rash.

†**temerat** adventurous, headstrong.

theat: kick *etc* **ower the** ~**s** kick over the traces *now NE Ags.* **out of (the)** ~(**s**) disordered; out

of control; going beyond normal bounds *now NE Ags.*

†**thowless** immoral, dissolute.

thrae *adj* obstinate, persistent; perverse. †*adv* obstinately.

thraw a fit of obstinacy *now NE nEC, WC.*

thrawart perverse, contrary *now Sh Ork.*

thrawn perverse, obstinate; intractable. ~**-headed** perverse, contrary *now Ags Per Rox.*

†**thrimlar** a pusher, jostler, hustler.

tongue impudence, abuse, violent language *NE Ags WC, SW.*

torn-doun disreputable, dissipated, broken down *now Sh.*

tousie rough, boisterous, rowdy, violent *now Ayr Rox.*

†**tow: ower the** ~ over the traces, out of control, beyond bounds.

traik a person who is always roving about *now WC, S.*

unco unusual; odd, strange, peculiar. ~**ness** strangeness, peculiarity, eccentricity *now Sh.* ~ **like,** *also* ~ **leukin** having a strange or wild appearance *now local NE-Ayr.*

†**undantit** unbridled, unrestrained; undisciplined, disorderly.

†**unrude** dreadful, outrageous.

†**unruleful** unruly, rebellious.

†**unsonsie** unpleasant, treacherous, troublesome, mischievous.

†**unthochtful** not taking thought, unheeding **of.**

†**unvisitly** imprudently.

warld, world: ~'**s wonder** a person whose conduct is notorious and surprising *now Ork NE nEC.*

waywart wayward.

widderwise contrary, stubborn *Sh.*

widdie, wuddie: ~**fu** *now chf joc* a rogue, scamp.

wile wild.

†**willed, willy** wilful, headstrong.

willsome *arch or literary* wilful.

willyart undisciplined, wayward, wilful, obstinate *now Wgt.*

†**worricow, wirricow** a mischievous person.

yip a cheeky, pert person, an imp *chf Rox.*

15.3.12 VILLAINOUS

For criminals, see 11.13.

bangster a violent or lawless person.

black: ~ **guaird,** ~**yirt** a blackguard.

bleck *sometimes joc* a blackguard, scoundrel.

brak, break: ~**er** a breaker (**of** laws, peace, faith etc).

bruit a brute.

coorse wicked, bad, naughty *chf NE*.

†**crackraip** a gallows-bird.

†**custrin** a wicked person, knave, rogue.

†**dagone** a villain.

†**dede-doer** the doer of a deed of violence.

enorm †acting irregularly or without regard for law. ~**ity** extreme wickedness.

†**fox's birds** an evil brood.

gallows, gall(o)us villainous, rascally *chf WC*. †**gallow-breid** a gallows-bird.

†**glittous** filthy, base, vile.

†**hempie** a rogue, a person deserving to be hanged.

ill *adj* evil, wicked, depraved. *n* badness, malice. ~-**daer** evil-doer. ~-**deedie**, ~-**deedit** *Cai Ags* wicked. ~-**designed** evilly disposed, mischievously-minded *Sh NE midLoth.* ~-**gien**, ~-**gevin** addicted to evil ways *now Sh Lnk Dmf.* ~-**intent(i)t** ill-disposed, with evil intentions *NE.* ~-**kinded** having a wicked disposition *EC.* ~-**like** having the appearance of evil, suspect *Sh.* ~-**minted** evil-intentioned *now Sh Ork.* ~-**set** evilly-disposed *Ork N, SW.* ~-**willer** a person who wishes evil on another.

†**infame** infamous, an infamous person: '*he salbe declarit infame*'.

†**infamité** infamy.

†**ivil** evil.

†**jevel** a ruffian, a rascal.

keelie a rough male city-dweller, a tough, now *esp* from the Glasgow area, *orig* with an implication of criminal tendencies.

kithan, *also of women*, **kithag** a rascal, blackguard *Cai*.

†**koken** a rogue.

limb: devil's ~, ~ **o the deil** *etc* a wicked person.

limmer *freq of Border or Highland robbers* a rascal, villain, scoundrel.

loun †a lawless or violent scoundrel, a robber. † ~**rie** knavery, villainy ~-**lookin** knavish-looking, villainous.

lowse, loose dishonest, lawless. †**brek** ~ break out into or turn to disorder, lawlessness, immorality etc.

†**lurdan 1** a ruffian; an oppressor. **2** *term of reproach, latterly literary* a villain, a rogue, rascal. ~**ry** villainy.

†**maisterfu(l)** *of robbers, beggars or their actions* overbearing, threatening, using force or violence.

†**maling** act wickedly, err.

†**mavité** *verse* wickedness, malice, evil intent.

meschant †*of persons, their character and conduct* wicked, bad. † ~**ly** wickedly; wrongfully. ~**ness** heinous villainy, wickedness.

minker a gallows-bird *Abd Edb*.

rabel *law* a person who disregards or flouts authority.

†**rabiator, rubeatour** a scoundrel, villain; a violent, ruthless person.

†**rack sauch** a gallows-bird.

†**raipfu** a gallows-bird.

randie a (*usu* rude or hectoring) beggar, a ruffian *now Cai EC Wgt*.

†**rank** swift, impetuous, turbulent, given to violence or excess.

†**recryand** a recreant.

†**reid, red, rid:** ~ **etin** a giant, a savage monster.

rochian a ruffian *NE Per*.

†**ruffie** a ruffian.

†**savagiously** savagely.

†**shirrow, shrew** wicked, bad.

snaffle, †**snaffler** term of contempt for a wicked person *now Lnk Dmf*.

†**sture** violent, severe.

sturt violent behaviour, *freq* ~ **and strife**.

†**temptise** incite to evil.

†**unsell** *adj* wicked. *adv* wickedly, vilely. *n* a wicked worthless person, wretch.

†**veillane** a villain.

†**velanous** villainous.

†**velany** villainy.

†**warlo(ch)** a warlock, a wicked person.

†**wick** a wicked person. **wickit** wicked.

widdie, wuddie: ~**fu** a gallows-bird, scoundrel. † ~ **neck** a gallows-bird.

wile, vild *now Sh* vile.

wuid, wud fierce, violent, wild.

15.3.13 EARNEST

†**abide** remain faithful to; adhere to. ~ **at** stand by, adhere to.

aefauld simple, sincere; honest, faithful; single-minded. † ~**ly** sincerely, honestly, faithfully.

†**bayne** *adj* ready, willing. *adv* readily, willingly.

boun prepared, ready, *freq* ~ **to** *or* **to do** (something).

†**camp** exert oneself.

clair prepared, ready *latterly chf Sh*.

conceit interest, lively attention, concern, *chf* **tak a** ~ **in** *now Abd Fif*.

†**constant** steadfast in an attachment, *esp* **to** *or* **in**.

conterm(i)t determined.

†**curious** ready, desirous, eager.

†**doggit** dogged.

dour *of person or actions* determined, hard, stern, severe.

†**eernest** earnest.

endaivour endeavour. **do one's ∼(s)** do one's utmost.

ettle: in ∼ earnest in dead earnest *S*.

even doon honest, frank, sincere.

†**exerce onself in** occupy oneself in (an activity).

fash *v* trouble oneself, take pains. *n* trouble, pains.

†**feal** loyal, faithful.

fechter: a bonnie ∼ an intrepid fighter (for a cause).

fond eager, glad (to do etc) *now local WC-S*.

frank willing, eager, ready *now Ags*.

free ready, willing (to do etc) *local Sh-Kcb*.

furth the gait candid(ly), honest(ly), straightforward(ly) *now NE*.

fyke exert oneself, work laboriously, take trouble or pains (**with**) *now local Cai-Stlg*.

gnappin: (in) ∼ earnest (in) dead earnest *Abd*.

guid, good: ∼willed zealous *now Sh*. **∼willie** willing, ready *now local Bnf-Bwk*.

hail: gang ∼-heidit for *or* **intae** devote one's entire energy to *N*. **gang ∼heid erran** go for one express purpose *Cai*.

hatter: like a ∼ with maximum energy or vigour, with all one's might and main *Gen except Sh*.

haud, hold, hald: ∼ at persist in, keep at (something) *now local*.

heid: in *or* **on the ∼ o(f)** busied or occupied with, deeply involved in *now Sh Abd Uls*.

hert, heart: † **∼fully** *freq verse, also* **∼ly** from the heart, with the whole heart, heartily, sincerely. **∼ily** heartily. † **∼lynes** sincerity, heartiness.

hing, hang: ∼ tae join in, adhere, attach oneself to some person or cause, fall in with another's plans *Cai NE midLoth*.

†**thyrit: as they were ∼** (run etc) willingly, eagerly, speedily.

†**lawtie, lauteth** loyalty, fidelity; faithful adherence to one's word; integrity. **lautéfull** faithful, loyal; honourable.

leal *adj* 1 loyal, faithful to one's allegiance or duties *now chf verse*. 2 *of conduct or counsel* dutiful, trusty. *adv* loyally, honestly, sincerely. **∼ty** loyalty. **∼-heartit** faithful, sincere *local Bnf-Rox*.

minute: in a ∼ readily, without a second thought.

nettle-earnest dead earnest *S Uls*.

olite eager, ready, willing.

†**outmost** (do one's) utmost.

†**pain: set one's ∼, tak ∼(s) upon oneself** expend much effort, exert oneself, take the trouble (to do something).

†**pairty** concerned, personally involved; active **in**.

pech: get over something with a ∼ get something done by dint of great effort *NE Ags Wgt*.

†**peremptor** positive, absolutely certain. **be** *etc* **(up)on** *or* **be put to one's ∼s** be precise and formal in one's attitude, stand firm on one's ground.

pith: a' one's ∼ with all one's energy *now Ork N*.

plowd work perseveringly towards a goal, strive, plod *now NE*.

pludisome dogged, persevering, painstaking *now NE*.

positive determined, adamant, pig-headed, obstinate *N, C*.

†**redd, rad** prepared, willing.

†**reithe** zealous, keen.

†**responsal** answerable, responsible, trustworthy.

sair, sore with vehemence or intensity, with all one's strength or feeling.

†**set** apply oneself (to do something).

shairp, sharp: ∼ set keen, eager *now Ayr*.

sicker reliable, loyal; steady, sure *now NE Bwk Wgt*. **mak ∼** make sure or certain.

†**singly** sincerely, honestly.

sowl: for ∼ and body with great vigour, as if one's life depended on it *now Ork*.

†**spleen: from** *or* **to the ∼** from *or* to the heart.

†**stalworth** a stalwart, a dependable supporter.

†**stand: not ∼** not hesitate, not be reluctant (to do etc *or* about).

stench *now NE, EC*, **stainch** 1 staunch. 2 strong, dependable, firm *now NE*.

stent, stint, *also* **∼ at** *Sh* strive, exert oneself.

stieve *adj* steady, resolute, staunch; loyal, dependable *now Per Stlg*. *adv* firmly, stoutly, stiffly, securely, staunchly.

stoup a loyal enthusiastic supporter, a 'pillar' *now local Sh-WC*.

†**stout** with power, strenuously, strongly. **∼fullie** stoutly.

†**straiten** exert oneself to the utmost.

†**subsist** keep on, persevere.

suithfast soothfast, truthful, reliable.

sussie, sizzie: not ∼ not shrink or hesitate *now Sh*.

tattie: the (clean) ∼ the right person, one who can be trusted or relied on *Gen except Sh Ork*.

†**teuch, tough** vigorously, stoutly; persistently, pertinaciously.

thirled bound by ties of affection, duty etc.

†**thrae** keen, zealous, earnest.

threap: keep (up *etc*) *or* **stand** *etc* **to one's ∼**

keep to one's opinions despite all opposition or contradiction, stick to one's guns.

†**traist 1** firm, strong. **2** also **trist** trusty, trustworthy. **~ful** sure, secure; trustworthy. **~ly** faithfully. **~nes** trustiness. **~y** trusty.

†**uterance: at the ~** to the utmost of (one's power).

wark: like a day's ~ with great vigour, for all one is worth *N nEC, SW*.

weel: † **~-willed** favourable; enthusiastic. **~-willie** kindly disposed, ready, willing. †**weill willing** well-willing; ready or keen (to do something).

†**wicks: hing by the ~ of the mouth** hang on with grim determination for as long as possible.

yare ready, prepared *now literary*.

†**yaup** eager, ready.

†**ȝarne** eager(ly), earnest(ly).

15.3.14 INDEPENDENT

bide await the effect of; tolerate, endure.

bo, boo: not be able to say ~ to your *etc* **blanket** not be able to reproach you etc, not be able to injure your etc reputation.

bruik brook, put up with.

†**but specialitie** without partiality or favour.

canny gentle, quiet, steady.

come tae regain one's composure after a time of mental stress *local*.

†**compone** compose, calm (oneself).

conceit, concait a good opinion **of** (oneself).

†**defend** maintain or vindicate (one's fame etc) against attack etc.

†**degest, digest** composed, settled; mature, grave. **degestlie** maturely, carefully, with full deliberation.

douce sedate, sober, respectable.

even, e'en: impartial. **~ oneself** *in a good sense* think oneself entitled **to**.

fend an effort, attempt, *esp* to maintain oneself, *chf* **make a ~** *now local Ags-Kcb*.

flee laich act prudently and cautiously; be modest and unambitious *local Abd-Dmf*.

†**fleme** put away (anger etc) from oneself; refrain from.

fushion strength of character, power *now NE*.

gaither recover one's faculties, collect one's wits, pull oneself together, rally *local Abd-Uls*.

gate: gang one's ain ~ follow one's own opinions etc. **gie (someone) his (ain) ~** give someone his own way, allow him free rein.

hair: have a ~ on one's head be clever, cautious or wise *now Arg Ayr*.

heeze (up) one's heart lift up one's heart, take courage.

hing, hang: ~ by one's ain head be independent and self-supporting, be self-reliant.

jee, jow *Bnf Ags:* **not ~ one's ginger, not jow one's jundie** *Bnf Ags* not show concern, not bother one's head; not become flustered.

jouk an let the jaw gae by *etc proverb* give way prudently in the face of overwhelming force, submit to the force of circumstance.

keep aff o anesel stand up for oneself *N Fif Kcb*.

lowp: ~ dykes weather troubles successfully, tackle difficulties boldly and effectively. **~ a gutter** *chf NE*, **~ a** or **the stank** *NE* avoid or overcome a difficulty or loss.

man o his mind one who thinks and acts for himself, a self-reliant person *now Ags Ayr*.

mense dignity *now sEC, SW, S*.

†**mesing** pacifying, setting at rest.

†**motive: of one's awin (fre, proper) ~ (will)** of one's own free will.

ower oneself (be able to) do what is necessary for oneself without help; cope with a situation, bestir oneself.

†**owerpit** come through (a trial, danger), get over, recover from, get the better of.

†**owerset** overcome, get the better of (a trouble, difficulty etc).

pairt: keep one's ain ~ look after one's own interests, keep one's end up *now Ork Ags*.

†**peace** moderate (one's anger etc).

pensie responsible, sensible, respectable, self-respecting *now NE*.

pit, put: ~ owre make (a period of time, hardship etc) pass more quickly or easily, get through *now Sh NE*.

pretty fine, good-looking, having an impressive and dignified bearing.

pridefu self-respecting, fastidious.

†**refresh** cool (desire).

†**revert** recover, bring back or return to one's normal state of mind or spirits *latterly N*.

road: hae one's ain ~ follow one's own inclination, go one's own way. **never out of one's ~** always able to turn things to one's own advantage; not easily upset *now Abd*.

†**sad** grave, sedate.

†**saft, soft** calm or restrain oneself.

sattle, settle become composed, settle oneself. **settleder** more settled *now NE*.

shire *of the mind* (allow to) become clear *now Uls*.

sit with put up with, tolerate.

sodger-clad but major-minded *usu complimentary* having a strong sense of pride and self-respect in spite of a humble position *now Abd Ags Stlg.*

†**sponsible** responsible, reliable, respectable.

spring: play oneself a ~, tak a ~ o one's ain fiddle *etc* go one's own way, do what one pleases *now Sh.*

spunk up revive in spirits, cheer up *now Ags Per.*

stey, steich: set *etc* **a stout heart to a ~ brae** face difficulties with resolution.

strang strong.

tak, take: ~ o it resign oneself to something, take the consequences, 'lump it' *NE.* **~ on** take the consequences, make the best of it *now Sh.*

thole *v* **1** endure with patience or fortitude, put up with, tolerate. **2** be able to endure; have capacity for *now local N-WC.* *n* patience, endurance *Gall Uls.*

†**traist** *n* confidence, trust; assurance. *adj* assured, confident. *adv* firmly; confidently. **~ly** securely; confidently.

†**ultroneousness** voluntary action.

†**unaffectionat** unbiased, impartial.

†**undoutandly** unhesitatingly, with confidence.

watch look after oneself, be on one's guard, watch out: '*Watch yersel crossin the road*'. †**~ one with** guard oneself against.

will, wull: at one's ain ~ of one's own free will, as one wishes *Cai C.* †**of ~** spontaneously, of one's own accord.

winter: he *etc* **never died o** *or* **a ~ yet** he etc survived, pulled through all difficulties or hardships *local Ork-Ayr.*

15.4 PERSONAL VALUES AND BEHAVIOUR

For religious values, see 14.1.2.

15.4.1 THRIFT, MISERLINESS, AVARICE

bien well-to-do, well-off.

canny frugal, sparing: '*be canny wi the butter*'.

clem *chf schoolboy's word* mean, unprincipled *Edb Rox.*

collie: he never asked *etc* **~ wull ye lick** *or* **taste?** he never even invited me to have something to eat.

†**dring** a miserly person.

earth-worm a money-grubber *now Bnf Abd.*

fen(d)ie able to look after oneself, managing, thrifty *chf SW.*

filschach a dishonest, greedy person *Bnf Abd.*

fou comfortably well-off, well-provided for.

fouthie having abundance, prosperous.

†**gair 1** greedy, covetous *C, S.* **2** parsimonious, niggardly; thrifty, careful *C, S.*

†**gell** brisk, keen.

glamshach greedy, grasping.

gled a rapacious or greedy person.

grab 1 an advantageous bargain, an advantage of any kind, *freq* with the implication of greed or dishonesty *now Bnf Abd Ags.* **2** a miserly or avaricious person *local.* **~bie** greedy, avaricious *local N-S.*

grip: ~pie close-fisted, avaricious, mean; inclined to sharp practice. †**gripping** grasping, avaricious. **hae a guid ~ o (the) gear 1** be well-off *now Ags WC.* **2** be miserly *nEC Ayr Rox.*

grisk greedy, avaricious.

groats: ken *or* **tell one's (ain) ~ in ither folk's kail** be wily or sharp in recognizing one's own property or handiwork or one's own interests.

grub grasp at (money) *now NE Ags Kcb.*

had: be well ~ be well off *now Ayr Uls.*

hame, home: ~-drauchtit selfish, keen to further the interests of oneself or one's home *NE.*

†**hamesucken** selfish.

hard, hard-handed *now Sh-Ayr* close-fisted, stingy *now local.*

haud, hald, hold: ~ in about save, economize, be miserly.

heather, hather: ~-piker term of contempt for a person living in a miserly way *NE.*

heck: live *etc* **at ~ and manger** live extravagantly, be in clover *now Mry nEC, WC.*

herrie-water-net a very selfish person *Cai.*

†**hivie** in easy circumstances, rather wealthy.

hooky crafty, grasping *now midLoth Rox.*

†**huid, hood: ~ock** an avaricious person. **~pyk** a miser, a mean person.

hungry mean, miserly; greedy.

ill: ~-hertit greedy, mean *chf NE.* **~-set** ungenerous, churlish. **~-willie** grudging, disobliging, mean *now Abd.*

inhaudin frugal, stingy *now Abd.*

jimp 1 scrimp, stint, keep in short supply *now Ork-midLoth.* **2** give short or scant measure to (a person) *or* in (a measure) *local N-S.*

keen avaricious, driving a hard bargain *local.*

keep: ~ in one's hand be stingy *now NE Loth.* **~ your ain fish guts for your ain sea maws** *proverb* charity begins at home *now NE.*

knapper-knytlich mean *Abd.*

lairge, large *of persons* having an abundant supply of, rich in *NE.*

lick-penny a greedy, covetous person *now Ags Loth Wgt.*

long, lang: ~**-nebbit** sharp, astute, having an eye to one's own advantage *now local Ags-S.*

meat-like and claith-like well-fed and -dressed *now Sh Ags.*

meechie mean, stingy *local N-WC.*

meeserable mean, stingy, miserly.

menseless greedy, grasping *now Kcb.*

misert *n, also* †**meeser** a miser. *adj* mean, miserly *now Sh Ags.*

mislearit excessively selfish, greedy *now Abd.*

moulie mean, stingy *C, S.*

nabal *n* a miser. *adj* grasping, churlish *now Abd Kcdn.*

†**nagus** term of abuse for a stingy person.

nairra-begaun miserly *local.*

near: ~**-begaun** *local,* ~ **gaun** *chf Sh-N, S,* ~ **the bit** *WC Kcb,* ~ **the bane** miserly.

†**needy** that acts as if in need, parsimonious.

neetie *n* a mean or disobliging person. *adj* stingy.

niggar a niggard, a miser *now Ags Kcb Uls.*

nip: ~**pit,** ~**py** niggardly. †~**caik** a miser. ~**scart** a niggardly person.

†**particular** (an instance of) self-interest, private advantage.

peeng(e)in mean, grudging.

pegral mean, greedy, miserly.

perneurious penurious *now NE.*

peyzart a miser, skinflint.

picket mean.

pinch spend or give meanly, stint, be excessively economical.

pinner an unscrupulous person, one with an eye on the main chance *Bnf S.*

pithy prosperous, well-to-do.

†**play pluck at the craw** take what one can get by any means to hand.

†**prosper** prosperous, successful.

puir, poor: mak a ~ **mou(th)** plead poverty as an excuse for meanness, claim to be poor when in fact one is quite well-off.

puist in easy circumstances, comfortably off *now Kcb Dmf.*

raffie abundant, generous, well-supplied *NE.*

rake a grasping, hoarding person.

reuch, rough in a comfortable or well-supplied state *Ags Per Kcb.*

richt, right: ken the ~ **side o a shillin** *etc* be knowing with money, be good at getting the best value for money *local Sh-WC.* ~ **eneuch** comfortably off, well provided for *Ork-C.*

rimpin a miserable or annoying person, *eg* a mean old woman *SW, S.*

scart scrape or gather together in a niggardly, acquisitive way *now C, S.*

scrae a miser *now Cai.*

scrimp *adj* parsimonious, ungenerous, sparing. *adv* parsimoniously. ~**it** scanty; restricted; mean.

scrub *v* treat meanly. *n* a mean avaricious person, a hard bargainer. **scrubby** sordid, mean, niggardly *now Bnf Abd Loth.*

scrunt a mean miserly person *local Bnf-S.* ~**y** mean, niggardly *local Bnf-S.*

scuddie stingy, penurious *Bnf Abd.*

scuffy niggardly *NE.*

sellie selfish(ness).

sicker prudent, cautious, *esp* with money, wary *now local Ork-Rox.*

†**silver-seck** avaricious.

skybal(d) not providing enough, scrimp *Bnf Abd.*

slughan, slowan a covetous or greedy person *now Rox.*

sneck a greedy grasping person; nickname for an Aberdonian *local Ork-Fif.*

snippit *now Sh N Slk,* **snippy** *now Fif Loth* niggardly, giving short measure.

solid having a large supply, well-stocked *with Sh Bnf Ags.*

†**spare** sparely, in a spare frugal manner.

stieve shrewd in business, prudent, slightly mean.

trift thrift *Sh Ork.*

througal frugal *Ayr.*

ticht, tight parsimonious, close-fisted.

warld, world: ~**lin** a worldling; a mean, grasping person *now Abd.* ~**ly** 1 worldly. 2 greedy.

†**warner** ? a miser.

weel: ~**-daein** well-to-do, prosperous. ~**-foggit** well-off as the result of thrift *NE Ags.*

†**welthy** happy, prosperous.

wheetie mean, stingy, shabby *NE.*

wratch, wretch †*n* a miser, niggardly person. *v* become mean or niggardly. † ~**edly** in a miserly or niggardly way. † ~**edness** miserliness, niggardliness.

15.4.2 SPENDTHRIFTS, SPONGERS

†**Abbey laird** *joc* a debtor.

†**addebted** indebted.

awa, away: ~ **wi't** done for; ruined.

†**bareman** a destitute person; a debtor, bankrupt.

†**beggartie** beggary.

boss destitute.

broken ruined, bankrupt.

cadge beg, sponge.

†**cake fidler** a parasite.

†**crack one's credit** become bankrupt.

cruik, crook: as peer's *or* **like the links o the**
~ very poor; very thin, meagre *NE*.

cuil, cool: ~**-an-sup** live from hand to mouth *chf
S.*

†**dilp** a thriftless housewife.

doless lazy, improvident *now Stlg Dmf*.

†**dring** a poor person.

drink out o a toom cappie be in want *Bnf Abd*.

eat-meat an idler, parasite *Bnf Abd*.

fallauge lavish, profuse, prodigal with money
Abd.

gadger a sponger *chf NE*.

gang throu it dissipate one's resources, come a
cropper, go bankrupt *NE Ags*.

gie's-a-piece a hanger-on, a parasite *now Ags*.

guid: hae ye ony ~ **on ye?, hae ye ony** ~ **on
your mind?** *said when asking for money, C.*

haik a person given to roaming about, *freq* on the
scrounge *local Bnf-S*.

haveless, haiveless 1 †destitute. **2** shiftless,
incapable, careless, extravagant *N*.

†**herbriles** without shelter, homeless.

ill: ~**-aff** badly off, poor. † ~**-hard** hard up.

†**loch leech** a parasite, a rapacious person.

†**milygant** *derog* ? a scrounger.

misguide waste, squander, mismanage *now Sh NE
Ags*.

†**mister** be in needy circumstances. ~**ful** needy,
necessitous. **have** ~ **1** be in distress, be in straits.
2 be in need. **3** be impoverished, destitute. **in
one's (maist** *etc*) ~ when one is in (most *etc*)
difficulty or need.

†**nace, ness** pitiable, destitute *Abd*.

needfu having need or want of, needy; in straitened circumstances *now local*.

pack: bring *or* **ca one's** ~ **to the pins** *or* **till a
preen** squander one's fortunes, be at the end of
one's resources *now Abd Kcdn Ags*.

perneurious penurious *now NE*.

†**prodigue** a prodigal.

puir, poor poor. †**puiranis** poor ones, poor
people. **mak a** ~ **mou(th)** complain of one's
poverty, exaggerate one's need.

puirtith poverty.

†**quit, quite** destitute, deprived **of.**

scaff going about idly, roaming on the scrounge
local Cai-Ags. † ~**er** a parasite, sponger.

scoff, scouf sponge, scrounge.

scrimp having a scanty supply, in want *now Sh
NE Ags*.

scuddie mean, scruffy, shabby-looking, in want
or straitened circumstances.

scunge *v* prowl or slink about, sponge, scrounge
local Sh-SW. *n* a person who **scunges** now *local
Loth-SW*. **scunger** a prowler, moocher *NE*.

sheuch: in a *or* **the** ~ in a state of squalor or
misery, ruined *now wLoth SW*.

sit on a person's coat-tail(s) depend on or make
use of someone else for one's own convenience or
advantage *now Bnf-Per*.

skech, skaich *v* scrounge; *freq* wander about in
search of (food), scrounge (a meal). *n* **1** the act
of **skeching**, *freq* **on the** ~ now *Abd WC Kcb*. **2**
also **skaicher** now *Mry* a scrounger, sponger *local
Abd-WC*.

skemler, †**scambler** a sponger, parasite.

skybal(d) *n* a poor wretch. *adj* not having enough,
needy *Bnf Abd*.

slounge, slunge *v* hang about in the hope of getting food *Sh Wgt Rox*. *n* a person always on the
look-out for food, a scrounger, glutton *Loth Wgt
Rox*.

sober poor, mean, paltry, miserable *now NE*.

sorn: ~ **(on)** scrounge or sponge (on), abuse
someone's hospitality, act as a parasite *now N
Per*. ~**er,** †**soroner** a person who **sorns** *now N
Per*.

sparple, †**sparfle** squander.

spendrife (a) spendthrift *NE Ags*.

splairge run wild, squander one's resources or
talents heedlessly *now Kcdn Per*.

spoach *v* sponge, scrounge around for favours *now
Bwk*. *n* a sponger, scrounger *now Bwk*.

squatter squander *now Ayr Dmf*.

squeeb a mean, scrounging, insignificant person
NE.

tether, tedder: go the length of one's ~ use up
one's resources, exhaust one's means *now Sh*. **win
to the end o one's** ~ reach the limit of one's
resources *Sh Ork N*.

thrieveless, thraveless thriftless, careless, negligent *Gsw Uls*.

†**unthrift** lack of thrift, extravagance.

†**wandreth, wander** misery, hardship, poverty.

wanthrift 1 extravagance, lack of thrift *now Sh*. **2**
†a thriftless person.

waste: ~**r** *n* an idler, a squanderer, good-for-
nothing. †*adj* idle, wasteful, good-for-nothing.
~**ful** *NE-SW*, **wastrife** *now NE-S*, **wastry** *now
Rox* wasteful, extravagant. †**wastry** reckless
extravagance, *esp* in living; wastefulness.

†**weirdlessness** thriftlessness, mismanagement of
one's life and affairs.

win(d), wund let the ~ **in (amang) it** *or* **intil't**
squander one's money or resources *NE*.

15.4.3 AFFECTATION

For affectation in dress, see also next. For vanity in general, see 15.3.7.

†**cavie** walk affectedly.

conceit, consait a quaint or dainty person *now Ags Lnk.*

curious, kwerious *Bnf Abd of words or sounds* carefully or elaborately expressed or modulated; elegant, artificial.

dainshach fastidious, particular *now Cai.*

dichty water (English) the affected speech of a Scot trying to sound English *now Ags.*

dink prim, precise.

dird act or walk conceitedly *Cai.*

Englified anglicized (in speech or manner).

fa(ll) through make a botch of (an attempt at formal speech beyond one's capabilities) *now Abd.*

fite-iron gentry social upstarts; people who make a pretence of gentility *NE.*

fussy affected in dress or manner, dressy, foppish *Abd Ags Fif Rox.*

gless: talk ~ haunles speak politely, use a refined accent *now Fif Ayr Dmf.*

gnap speak mincingly or affectedly.

gnip talk carpingly or affectedly *Mry Bnf.*

half-hung-tee pretentious, affecting gentility *Abd.*

hank a hesitancy in speech, natural or affected *now S.*

high English the stilted, affected, pedantic or distorted form of English used by Scots trying to imitate 'correct' English *now Per midLoth WC.*

jinipperous finicky, over-particular, stiff *Abd.*

Kelvinside, Morningside: a ~ accent, speak ~ denoting a very affected, over-refined pronunciation of Scottish English.

knap *esp of a Scot aping 'fine' English* speak in an affected or clipped, mincing way *now Sh.*

Lord *or* **Lady Muck** name for a person who puts on airs.

mim *adj* prim, restrained in manner or behaviour, *esp* in a prudish or affected way. *adv* in a mincing, prudish way. *v* move or act in a prim, affected way. **~-moued** affectedly prim or demure in speaking or eating. **~-spoken** prim or shy in speech, quiet-spoken. **as ~ as ɑ Mey puddock** very demure and staid.

mimp speak or act affectedly *NE Kcb Rox.*

†**minȝard** dainty, mincing, effeminate.

mou: get roun the ~ wi an English dishclout become affectedly anglicized in speech *NE nEC.*

†**moy** demure, prim, meek. **mak (sa) ~** behave demurely, affect gentility.

neibour, neighbour: ~ like emulating or aping one's neighbours.

nippit narrow in outlook.

†**ogertfu** dainty, affected, fastidious.

pan loaf an affected, ultra-refined way of speaking adopted to impress others *Gen except Sh Ork.*

pensie self-important, affected, pompous, priggish, prim.

perjink *adj* prim, strait-laced. *adv* primly, fastidiously, in a precise and careful way.

phrase gushing and effusive talk, flattery *now NE.* **phrasie** gushing, fulsome *now Abd.* **phrasing** *adj* fulsome, ingratiating, insincere in speech. *n* flattery, gush.

pitten on affected, conceited, insincere *now N-C.*

prent, print: speak like ~ buik speak in an affected way.

prick-me-dainty *n* an affected, self-conscious person *now Mry. adj* over-refined, mincing *now Bnf Renfr S.*

primp *v* 1 make prim and over-neat, arrange or do up in a stiff, affected way. 2 behave or talk in a mincing or affected style *NE-S. adj* fastidious, straight-laced, prim *now Sh. n* a straight-laced and self-conciously correct person, a prig, a show-off *S.* **~ed** 1 affected, elaborately and formally dressed. 2 *of speech* stiff, formal, over-elaborate, correct.

primsie self-consciously correct, demure, straight-laced, old-maidish *now Sh Ork.*

skew, skeuch *NE* sway affectedly *now Bnf Abd.*

speak pink speak in a very affected over-refined way, in an unsuccessful attempt at Received Pronunciation *Kcdn Ags Fif.*

strange, strynge aloof, shy, stiff, affected *now Ags Per.*

†**streiche** stiff, affected.

strunt strut, walk about in an affected way *now local Ork-Gall.*

swash affected ostentatious behaviour.

tattie-peelin *of speech* affected, prim *local Stlg-Pbls.*

upset haughty, presumptuously ambitious, giving oneself airs *now local NE Dmf.*

†**upsticken** priggish, snobbish.

wallie close a tiled **close**, considered a sign of social superiority *WC.*

yap, yaup *applied esp to English speakers or to Scots who ape them* speak in an affected way *local Abd-S.*

15.4.4 DRESS SENSE

auld, old: ~**-fashioned, auld-farrant** old-fashioned; quaint. **auld warld** belonging to past time, old, antique; old-fashioned.

Auntie Beenie a rather old-fashioned looking woman *local*.

barrie smart in appearance *orig gypsy, now also Rox EC*.

best-lyk of best appearance.

bodsy a little, dapper, or neat person *chf Abd*.

bogle a scarecrow.

brank dress up in finery *now Fif*. †~**ie** finely or showily dressed.

braw splendid in dress; well-, prettily- or gaily-dressed. ~**ly** finely; elegantly.

brisken up smarten *local Fif-Kcb*.

bruik, brook used to wish someone well when wearing something for the first time: '*weel may he brook it*'.

conceit, consait a fancy article, a quaint or dainty person *now Ags Lnk*. **conceity** neat, tidy, dainty.

dashle battered, worn *WC Kcb*.

dashy showy *now Bnf Abd*.

dink *adj, now only of women* neat, trim, finely dressed, dainty *now Abd Fif*. *v, freq* ~ **up, out** dress neatly or sprucely, adorn *now Bnf Abd Bwk Rox*. ~**ie** neat, trim. ~**ly** neatly, sprucely, trimly.

disjaskit dilapidated, neglected, untidy *local*.

dockie neat, tidy *SW*.

†**donsie** neat, tidy (*freq* with the notion of self-importance).

doss *adj* spruce, neat, tidy. *v* dress (**up**), make neat *now Bnf Abd*.

douce neat, tidy, comfortable *now Stlg*.

†**draggly** straggly, untidily dressed.

eemage a spectacle *now local Sh-Bwk*.

faisible neat, tidy *now midLoth Slk*.

fettle neat, trim *now SW*.

flary gaudy, showy *SW*.

flird a vain, dressy person.

fussy affected in dress or manner, dressy, foppish *Abd Ags Fif Rox*.

†**galʒeard** *of dress* spruce, gay, bright, gaudy.

gash well or neatly dressed, respectable, smart.

gate farrin presentable, comely *NE*.

†**gaudy** gay, dashing *local*.

†**gentie** *of dress* tasteful.

gim, †**jimmy** neat, spruce *now Bnf Ags*.

†**gingebreid** gaudy, extravagant.

gled: be as (gin *or* **if) one had fa'en frae the** ~**('s feet)** be in disorder, dishevelled.

haspal an untidy, carelessly-dressed person *SW*.

heap be untidy in one's dress, wear clothes carelessly *Abd*.

hing, hang: ill- ~**-tee** *or* **thegither** dressed without care or taste *local Sh-Kcb*.

hingum-tringum worthless and somewhat disreputable; barely presentable *Bnf*.

hochle, hachel a person who is ungainly or slovenly in dress *now Pbl Arg*.

honest *of dress* decent, respectable.

houster a badly-dressed, untidy person.

hudder, huther throw **on** (clothes) hastily or untidily *now Ags*.

hushle *v* dress in a careless or slovenly way *now Sh*. *n* an untidy, carelessly-dressed person, a slattern *now Sh Cai SW*.

ill: ~**-farrant** unkempt, unpleasant in appearance *nEC Rox*. ~**-faured** shabby, faded *Ork Abd*. ~**-shaken-up** untidy, disordered *Sh Ork NE*.

jeety neat, fastidious *Abd Ags*.

jinipperous spruce, trim *Abd*.

kicky showy, *esp* in dress, dandified *now Kcdn*.

kim spruce *Abd*.

like, lik: ~**(e)r** more apt, more befitting, more appropriate *local*: '*a worset goon's the liker you*'.

mack neat, tidy; seemly.

†**moutit** worn away, bare, shabby.

munsie an odd-looking or ridiculously-dressed person *now Abd*.

nackety neat *now NE Per*.

nate neat; trim, smart.

nine: (up) to the ~**(s)** to perfection.

nuif neat, spruce *Gall*.

Pace-yaud a person who fails to observe the custom of wearing something new for Easter *now Ags*.

pensie respectable, self-respecting, fastidious about one's appearance *now NE*.

perjink trim, neat, smart in appearance.

pit: ill, weel *etc* ~**(ten) on** shabbily, finely *etc* dressed.

†**polist** *of persons or their appearance* bright, beautiful; ? adorned, embellished.

poukit shabby, threadbare *now C, S*.

†**prelucent, preluciand** shining, resplendent.

†**prick and prin oneself** dress oneself up, take excessive pains with one's appearance.

primped affected, elaborately and formally dressed.

prink make smart or pretty, titivate. ~**ie** over-meticulous in dress or appearance, fussy over details, ostentatious, conceited *now Ork Bnf*.

purpose tidy-looking *Sh-nEC Uls*.

rag: ~**gety,** ~**git** wearing ragged clothes.

ramshackle unkempt, untidy, rough *now Ork Bnf Ags*.

†**redimite** adorned, beautiful.

sair, sore: ~ **on** destructive, harmful, giving hard wear or usage to: '*she's sair on her claes*'.

saucy fastidious about dress *now WC-S*.

scash(le) †*v* dress in a slovenly way. *n* an untidy or slovenly person or garment.

scuddle make shabby or shapeless by rough usage *now Abd Ags*.

scuff wear away (clothes) with hard usage, make worn and shabby. ~**y** shabby, worn, tarnished, mean-looking *now NE-S*.

seem look becoming in (a piece of clothing) *S*.

set *v* look becoming in *now local. adj* fit, suitable, becoming *now NE-Per*.

shape an odd or droll figure *Wgt Rox*.

skire be gaudy; wear gaudy, garish clothes *now Ork NE*.

sloggerin slovenly in appearance, dirtily or untidily dressed *local Pbls-Rox*.

snod *adj* neat, trim, spruce, smart. *v* make trim or neat, tidy, put in order *now NE-SW*. ~**(die)-up** a tidying, smartening *now NE, SW*.

snug, snog neat, trim, tidy *now Ork Cai*.

sprush *n* a sprucing or smartening up, a tidying or setting in order *now Sh Ags Per. v, adj* spruce.

suit, shuit look becoming in (a colour, dress etc): '*she suits blue*'.

swank, swankie *now local Cai-wLoth, esp of a young man* smart, well set-up *now nEC Lnk Slk*.

target an oddly- or untidily-dressed person *now Mry Abd*.

tash spoil (clothes) by handling roughly or carelessly *now local Sh-Dmf*.

tattie: ~**-bogie** *now NE*, ~**-bogle** *Gen except Sh Ork*, ~**-boodie** *NE* a ragged, unkempt or grotesquely-dressed person.

Teenie f(r)ae Troon *local WC-S*, **Teenie f(r)ae the neeps** *Ags Fif* an odd-looking, oddly-dressed or over-dressed woman.

ticht, tight neat, smart, tidily or carefully dressed.

ticket a person dressed in a slovenly, dishevelled or odd way, a sight.

tippy fashionable, stylish *local Cai-S*.

tosh *adj* neat, tidy, smart. *adv* neatly. *v* make neat or tidy, smarten **up**. ~**-up** a tidy-up.

toutherie dishevelled, untidy, slovenly *now local Sh-Dmf*.

track a poorly- or untidily-dressed person, a sight *NE*.

trig *adj* trim, neat in dress, well turned out. *v, freq* ~ **up, out** make **trig**, smarten up *now NE*. ~**ly** neatly, smartly.

trum trim.

untowtherly, untodderly slovenly in dress or figure, unkempt, dishevelled *NE*.

vauntie proud-looking, ostentatious, jaunty *now chf literary*.

weel to be seen having a good appearance, very presentable *Sh NE Kcb*.

whirligig(um) a piece of unnecessary finery.

15.4.5 SLOVENLINESS, LAZINESS

For slovenliness in work, see 15.5.16; in dress 15.4.4; in eating habits, see next.

aff, off: ~**-pit** 1 excuse, evasion, reason for delay; a delay, waste of time. 2 one who delays *NE, SW, S*. ~**-pittin,** ~**-putting** *n* postponement, evasion, excuse. *adj* delaying, trifling, dilatory. ~**-set** a delay, an excuse.

back late, behindhand.

baigle a disagreeable dirty person; a sight *now Arg Uls*.

†**batie-bum** a feckless person.

bauchle an untidy person.

†**bausy** large, fat, coarse.

beffan a stupid, often fat and flabby, person *chf Bnf*.

bog-stalker an idle, bashful man.

brochle a lazy, indolent person *now Cai Kcb*.

brookie grimy, dirty *now Bnf Abd*.

brosie coarse, clumsy *now Bnf wLoth*. ~**-headit** very stupid, fat and inactive *Bnf Ags*.

†**bumbard** a lazy person.

by: ~**-pit,** ~**-put** a procrastination *now Bnf Abd*.

capper nickname for a late riser *NE*.

clart, clort *n* a big, dirty, untidy person *local. v* act in a slovenly, dirty way *local*.

clatch a dirty, untidy person, a slut; a fat clumsy woman.

cloiter walk in a slovenly way, *esp* in wet or muddy conditions *chf N*.

coof a useless, incompetent person; a feckless person.

cruik, crook: not to ~ **a finger** not to make the least exertion *now local*.

daeinless unprosperous, feckless *now Fif*.

dauble potter about, waste time *now Bnf Abd*.

daw 1 †a lazy person. 2 a slattern.

†**dilly daw** a slow, slovenly person, a slattern.

†**dilp** a trollop, a slovenly woman; a thriftless housewife.

disjaskit dilapidated, neglected, untidy *local*.

doless lazy, improvident *now Stlg Dmf*.

dollop a slut, an untidy woman *Bnf Abd*.

dour slow, sluggish, reluctant (to do something) *now Fif WC*.

doxy, duxy lazy, slow *Bnf Abd Ags*.

draigle a dirty, untidy person *now local Bnf-Edb*.

†drawlie slow and slovenly.

dreich slow; backward; tardy.

driddle potter, idle, waste time *now Abd Ayr*.

†driffle put off (time).

†drift *n* delay, procrastination. *v* delay (to do *etc*). ~ **time** delay, make delays.

dring *v* loiter, delay. *n* a lazy person. ~**le, †drangle** dawdle *now Ork*.

drochlin lazy *now Bnf Abd*.

drool a lazy person.

†dudderon a slut, a lazy, slovenly person.

easy osy *adj* easy-going, inclined to be lazy. *n* an easy-going or lazy person *now Bwk*.

eedle-doddle *adj* easy-going, lacking initiative, muddle-headed *N*. *n* a person with such a character *N*.

faggot term of abuse for a woman or child implying slatternliness *now Arg Bwk*.

fite the (idle) pin fritter away time *Bnf Abd*.

flag a large, clumsy, slovenly woman.

fleep a lazy lout, an oaf *Ork Cai NE*.

flodge a fat, slovenly person, *esp* a woman *now Bnf Dmf*.

fodge a fat, clumsy person *sEC, S*.

foongil a work-shy person; a slovenly, careless individual *chf Ags*.

foost a dirty person, someone with disagreeable habits *Bnf Abd*.

fozie fat, flabby, out of condition *local NE-Gall*. **foziness** flabbiness.

fum a big, fat, dirty woman *Ayr*.

gamfle idle, dally *chf nEC*.

gawk 1 to idle *now Ags Kcb*. **2** stare idly *now Ayr Kcb*.

gilfa, garfa a fit of idleness *SW*.

glaik look idly.

gloid do something in a slovenly, messy or awkward way *Ags*.

gotherlisch slovenly, confused *chf Abd*.

gowstie breathless from being overweight, fat and flabby *now Abd*.

†groosie dirty, greasy, unsavoury.

grulsh a fat, squat person *now Uls*. † ~**ie** sturdy, fat, clumsy-looking.

guddle *v* do things in a careless, slovenly way, mess about, make a mess *now C, S*. *n* a person who does things in a messy, slovenly way *midLoth Dmf*.

gutter do something in a dirty, slovenly or unskil-

ful way; potter, tinker, fritter away time *local N-S*.

habble a coarse or slovenly person.

haik *v* wander aimlessly, rove; loiter *now local*. *n* a person given to roaming about, *freq* on the scrounge *local Bnf-S*.

haingle *v* loiter, hang about. *n* an idle good-for-nothing. *adj* slovenly, careless; lazy, not inclined to work *NE*. **be in** *or* **hae the** ~**s** be in a lazy mood *N*.

haiver *v* dawdle, potter about; lounge *now Ayr Uls*. *n* a lounger, a lazy person *now Sh*.

hallion a slovenly-looking or clumsy person, a rascal, a clown *now Sh Ags Gall Rox*.

harl a slattern, a dirty, untidy or coarse person *now SW Rox*.

hasky *of persons or actions* rough, coarse, dirty.

haveless shiftless, incapable, careless, extravagant *N*.

hawm lounge; loaf about *Bnf*.

heap a slovenly woman *now local NE-Uls*.

hert, hairt, heart: ~**-lazy** exceptionally lazy, naturally indolent.

hillock a fat sluggish person *Sh N Dmf*.

hinder, hinner waste (time) *Sh NE Ags*.

hing, hang delay, hover indecisively *now Ags Fif Arg*. ~ **the cat** *or* **cleek** lounge about, hold things up *Fif Ags*.

hint-han(d) dilatory, careless, late.

hither an yon(t) untidy; careless *now Mry midLoth*.

hochle, hachel a person who is ungainly or slovenly in gait, dress or appearance *now Pbls Arg*.

horn idle having nothing to do, completely unemployed *now Sh Cai Lnk Ayr*.

hotch a big fat ungainly woman; a slut *now midLoth WC, S*.

hudderon a slovenly person *now Cai Lnk*.

hugmahush a slovenly person, a slattern *now Kcdn*.

hum-drum an apathetic, lazy-minded person.

hush a fat, ungainly, dirty person *now Abd Kcdn*.

hushle *v* work or dress in a careless or slovenly way *now Sh*. *n* an untidy, carelessly-dressed person *now Sh Cai SW*.

hush(l)ochy hurried, careless(ly), slovenly.

huther an untidy worker or person, a sloven *now Lnk Dmf Rox*. **hudderie, hutherie, hudderie-dudderie** slovenly, dirty or untidy in appearance or habits *now local Fif-Dmf*. **hudd(e)rin** *chf of a woman* slovenly, slatternly *now Kcb Uls*.

†hutt a lazy person, a slattern.

idleset *n* idleness, laziness *now local Sh-Kcb*. *adj* idle, disposed to idleness.

idlety, †idilteth idleness *now Ork Abd.*

jack easy easy-going, offhand.

jotter a ne'er-do-well, a trifler, a dawdler *now midLoth.*

knot: ~**less** futile, aimless, ineffective *now Loth Bwk.* **a** ~**less threid** an aimless, useless, futile person.

laidron, la(i)therin *term of abuse* a slattern, drab.

†lan(d) lowper a person who roams about the country idly, a vagabond.

langsome tardy, dilatory *now Sh.*

latch *adj* slow, tardy, lazy *NE. v* delay; lag, procrastinate *now NE.* ~**ie** slow, dilatory *NE.* ~**in** *adj* slow, tardy, lazy *NE.* †*n* tardiness, loitering, *chf* **without laching.**

lazy a fit of laziness *midLoth SW, S.*

lither lazy, sluggish, lethargic, idle; lax, slack *now Dmf.*

loll a pampered, lazy person *Abd.*

loonge, lunge *now local* lounge, slouch, loll.

loorach an ungainly or untidy person, a trollop *Inv NE Per.*

†losel *chf literary* a scamp, scoundrel, loafer.

†losengeour a sluggard, idler.

†lotch a fat lazy person *Ayr Lnk.*

†lounder idle, skulk.

maffle procrastination, bungling *Dmf.*

mardle †*adj, usu of women* heavy, clumsy, corpulent; lazy *NE Renf. n, derog* a fat, clumsy, idle woman *Sh NE.*

mart contemptuous term for a clumsy, inactive person *now NE.*

mautent lazy, weary, lethargic *NE.*

midden a dirty, slovenly person.

mirky dirty *Gen except NE.*

mistimeous irregular, unpunctual, slovenly *Cai NE.*

mole, mollach loiter about, wander idly *NE.*

mowdiewort a slow-witted or slovenly person *Abd Fif Loth.*

Mrs MacClarty name for a dirty slovenly housewife *local Kcdn-SW.*

mump loaf around.

niddle fiddle, toy, potter.

niffnaff trifle, dilly-dally.

oozlie slovenly, untidy, unkempt, dirty *SW.*

owerheid untidy, slovenly, rough and ready, careless *now Sh Ork.*

oxter: wi one's airms in one's ~**s** with one's arms folded (implying idleness).

paidling aimless, feckless.

†peeferin trifling, feckless, ineffectual.

pell *contemptuous* a dirty, worthless person, reprobate, tramp *now Sh Ork.*

pirl, purl move idly or half-heartedly *now Mry Bnf.*

plaister go about in a slovenly slapdash way, mess around *local N-Dmf.*

platch go about in a sloppy way, potter *Sh Per S.*

plowter, pleuter, ploiter act idly or aimlessly, potter or fiddle **about.**

prod *contemptuous* a waster, lazy creature, fool.

rachlie dirty and disorderly.

ropach untidy, dirty, slatternly *Highl Per.*

row, roll a plump person, a fat, untidy, lazy woman *SW.*

scabbie-heid applied to a person with head lice *local C.*

scaff going about idly, roaming in search of amusement *local Cai-Ags.*

scawt, †skaid scabby, scruffy *now NE Ayr.*

schamlich a slovenly person *NE.*

scuddle work in a slatternly way, mess about at domestic work *now NE Per.*

scurryvaig *n* an idle, unkempt, or slatternly person. *v* **1** range or roam about or aimlessly (over). **2** live in idleness and dissipation.

scutter *v* do something in a slovenly or bungling way, make a mess (of), spill or splash about *now Sh-Per. n* **1** the doing of work awkwardly or dirtily, a botch, bungle *Sh Ork N nEC.* **2** a person who works in an ineffective, muddled, or dirty way *N Per.*

set aff dawdle, be dilatory *NE Kcb.*

shaviter a slovenly disreputable-looking character.

skavie, skeevie rush about in an idle, silly or ostentatious way *now Bnf.*

sklyte *Abd,* **sklyter** *chf NE* a big, clumsy, slovenly person.

slab a slovenly slack-lipped person, a slobberer *now EC Lnk Gall.*

slaigerin dirty, slovenly, slatternly *local.*

slaik, slaich, sklaik *NE* a careless or slatternly wash, a hasty clean or wipe *local Ags-SW.*

slaister, slyster, sclyster *nEC* a messy person *C, S.* ~**in** untidy, slovenly.

†slait a dirty, slovenly or nasty person.

slap, slop a careless or dirty person *WC Gall.*

slatch a dirty coarse woman *now Rox.*

†sleeth a slow, lazy person *NE.*

slemmer a lazy, idle person *now Ags.*

slerp a slovenly woman, slut *Per Fif.*

slidder, sclidder, sclither *v* walk or move in a casual or lazy way *now Ags WC. n* a slow-moving or dilatory person, a sluggard *now WC.*

slip-ma-labor a lazy untrustworthy person *now Sh.*

slitter, sluiter 1 a state of untidiness or dirt *now C*. **2** a slovenly, untidy, or messy person *C, S*.

slogger a slovenly, dirty, or untidy person *local Pbls-Rox*. ~**in** slovenly in appearance, dirtily or untidily dressed *local Pbls-Rox*.

sloit *v, also* ~**er** walk in a slow, slouching way, stroll idly or carelessly about *now Fif*. †*n* a lazy, slovenly person.

slooch, slouch an idle, work-shy person *now Sh Ags Per*.

slope shirk one's work, dodge duty, idle *NE Lnk Gall*.

slotch a lazy, slouching person, a layabout, ne'er-do-well *now Loth Rox*.

†**slotter** act in a slovenly way, work messily in a liquid; act slothfully. ~**y** sluggish, slothful.

slounge, slunge *v* idle or loaf about, walk in a slouching, lethargic way *now local*. *n* a lazy, lounging, hangdog person *local*. **slounger** an idler, loafer *now Cai*.

slouter a coarse, slovenly, idle person *now local Cai-Ags*.

slouth, sleuth †*n* sloth; laziness. †*adj* slothful, slow, lethargic. *v* **1** carry out (a task) in a lazy, idle, careless way, treat with indifference or neglect *now Abd Kcdn Ags*. **2** †waste (time) in sloth. † ~**ful** slothful.

†**sluggart** a sluggard. **sluggardry** sluggardy, slothfulness.

slughan, slowan a slow-moving, lazy, soft person *now Ork Cai Rox*.

slunk *contemptuous* a lazy, sneaking person, a shirker *now Cai*.

†**slush** a slovenly, untidy person, a slut.

slute *n* a slovenly, sluggish person *now Ork Cai SW*. *adj*, †*also* **slutt** sluttish, untidy.

slutter, sclutter walk in a slouching, slovenly way *local Ork-Per*. ~**y** slovenly, sluttish *now EC, WC*.

slype, sclype *NE highly contemptuous* a lazy, coarse, dissolute, worthless person, *usu* a man *now NE*.

sniffle be slow in action, loiter *now Bnf Abd*. **snifflin** slow, sluggish, lazy, procrastinating, frivolous *Bnf Abd*.

snuil, snool *n* a lazy, inactive person *now Sh Ags*. *v* show lack of energy, loaf about shiftlessly, move slowly and lethargically.

snuit move about in a lazy, careless or stupefied way, laze about, be listless, be at a loose end *now Abd*.

snuve move carelessly, lazily or abjectly, idle *now Rox*. **sn(u)ivie** a layabout *chf Rox*.

soadie a big stout woman, a slut *now Stlg*.

†**sonyie** *n* delay. *v* hesitate, delay, refuse.

†**sorn** idle, loaf.

soss *n* **1** a state of dirt and disorder, a muddle, confusion *Sh N nEC*. **2** a slattern, slut *now Ags Per*. *v* **1** make a mess, work dirtily *N nEC*. **2** take one's ease, lie or remain idle *now Abd*.

sotter idle, loaf, potter **about** *Bnf Ags Per*.

stane, stone: ~ **tired** lazy, bone idle *S*.

stech any disorder or lack of cleanliness *now Ags*.

stechie stiff-jointed, slow-moving due to stiffness, corpulence or indolence, stodgy *local C*.

strushie, strushlach *adj* untidy, slovenly, disorderly *NE*. *n* an untidy, slovenly person, a slut, slattern *now NE*.

sugg a fat, easy-going person *now Ork NE*.

sunk a hefty corpulent person, with a sack-like figure *now Kcdn Ags*.

†**superexpend** spend (time) wastefully.

sweir *adj, also* ~**t** *now Sh NE, C* lazy, slothful, unwilling to work *now N, EC, SW*. ~**ie** rather lazy *now Sh Ork*. ~**tie** laziness *Sh NE*.

taistrel a gawky, slovenly, unmethodical person *Gall Rox*.

tashy having a tattered, slovenly appearance, unkempt *local NE-S*.

tentless inattentive, heedless, careless *now NE, WC, SW*.

through-the-muir untidy, heedless, devil-may-care *NE*.

throuither, through other untidy, disorganized, slovenly, unruly.

toosht a slattern *now Bnf Abd*.

trail *v* wander about idly. *n, also* **trailach** *Bnf SW* a careless, dirty, slovenly person, *esp* a woman *now NE Ags*.

trallop a trollop.

tram a rough, untidy person *N*.

trap an idle, slovenly person, *esp* a woman *Cai*. ~**ach** slovenly, slatternly *Cai*.

troll an untidy, slovenly person, a slattern *Mry Bnf Rox*.

trooshlach dirty, slovenly *NE*.

trushel a slovenly person *Cai*.

tyne spend unprofitably or in vain, waste (time etc).

unlucky: *esp* **foul** ~ slatternly, slovenly *Abd*.

†**unsonsie** slovenly, untidy.

vaig wander about idly, roam aimlessly *now local Ork-Ayr*. †**vagand** wandering. ~**er** an idle stroller, a footloose person, a gadabout. † ~**in(g)** idle rambling, wandering.

wallydrag, warridrag *Bnf Abd*, **warydraggel** *now Bnf*, †**wallydraggle** a good-for-nothing, a slut *now NE*.

waster *n* an idler, a squanderer, good-for-nothing. †*adj* idle, wasteful, good-for-nothing.

whistle, whustle: ~ **(on) one's thoum** do nothing useful, twiddle one's thumbs, be nonplussed after some snub etc *now local Sh-Per.*

†**yaud** *contemptuous* a woman, *freq* a slovenly or dissolute one.

Yerlston fever a fit of laziness, a lazy mood *Bwk S.*

15.4.6 EATING HABITS

belly gut *NE,* †**belly god** gluttonous; a glutton.

†**bootyer** a glutton.

connach devour.

crop, crap: have a ~ **for all corn** be greedy; have a capacity for absolutely anything.

dainshach fussy about food *now Cai.*

gabbit: fine- *or* **nice-**~ fastidious, fussy about food *now Ags Fif.*

gangyls: a gutts an ~ nothing but stomach and legs, fit for nothing but eating and walking *Bnf.*

geenyoch ravenous, voracious, greedy *chf WC.*

glutter swallow noisily, disgustingly or voraciously.

†**gluttery** gluttony.

gollop a hasty or greedy gulp *now Arg Ayr.*

gorb a glutton *Ags Per SW Uls.*

gropsie eat gluttonously.

growk *esp of a child* look longingly at food etc *now Kcdn Ags Per.*

gut: ~**s** eat greedily or gluttonously *local* ~**ser** a glutton *NE Ags.* ~**sie** greedy, gluttonous. ~**tie** *adj* fond of good eating, gluttonous *now Bnf Abd Kcb. n* a corpulent, pot-bellied person *now Dmf Rox.*

guzzle a bout of excessive eating and drinking, a debauch.

heck eat greedily *EC Rox.* ~**er** a glutton, hearty eater *EC, S.*

hungry greedy.

midden a gluttonous person *NE Ags.* **knacker's** ~ a glutton *C, S.*

mim-moued affectedly prim or demure in eating.

nimm expression of pleasure (by or to a child) at something good to eat, = yum-yum *chf Sh.*

pawl at play with one's food *S.*

penurious, perneurious attentive to detail, scrupulous, fastidious, *esp* about food *NE.*

pickie a person who picks at his food, a poor eater *now local C -S.*

†**puddin fillar** a person who lives to eat, a glutton.

Rab Ha a glutton, voracious eater *WC, SW.*

saucy fastidious about food *now WC-S.*

skeich, skey *adj, also* **skiten** fastidious about food, easily upset or nauseated *NE. n* fastidiousness or fussiness about food *now Bnf Abd.*

slab a greedy or noisy mouthful, a slobber *now Ags.*

slaik, slaich a person who eats or drinks excessively *local Per-Rox.*

slairie slovenly in one's eating habits *Clcm Renfr Lnk.*

slaister, slyster, slyster *nEC* a messy eater *C, S.* ~ **kyte** a messy eater, glutton

slounge, slunge *v* hang about in the hope of getting food *Sh Wgt Rox. n* a person always on the look-out for food, a scrounger, glutton *Loth Wgt Rox.*

troch, trough *contemptuous* a person who eats or drinks to excess *local Cai-Dmf.*

†**tuithy, toothy** sharp-toothed, ravenous.

†**vorax** voracious, ravenous.

15.5 SOCIAL BEHAVIOUR

15.5.1 PERSUASION

For flattery, see 15.3.8.

†**ameise** appease, placate, soothe (a person).

†**amove** move to action, influence.

†**artation** instigation, incitement.

at: be ~ **someone about something** try to get someone's support or consent with regard to something.

beseek beseech.

†**brak** overcome by persuasion.

buiks, books: be i the gudeman's ~ be in favour, in a person's good books *now Bnf Abd Ags.*

come paddy owre get round (a person) *now Ags Lnk.*

cook coax *chf NE.*

cowshin pacify, quieten *chf NE Ags.*

craik ask persistently, clamour *now local Abd-Kcb.*

credit: earn someone's ~ gain someone's approval or esteem *Bnf Abd Ags.*

cuddle (up tae) approach so as to coax or wheedle *Bnf Abd Stlg.*

cuiter coax, wheedle *now Bnf.*

cuittle coax, flatter *SW, S.*

culyie, cullie coax, entice.

dill soothe, quieten down, die away.

enteece entice *Bnf-Ags.*

faize (on) make an impression on *now Arg Kcb Uls*.
flairdie a wheedling person *SW*.
fleech 1 coax, flatter, entreat *now local Bwk-Rox*. **2** use cajoling or flattering words (**with**).
†**flether** flatter, cajole.
fluister coax, flatter *Uls*.
fraikie coaxing, wheedling *now Ork*.
gow, *usu* ~ **ower** wheedle, persuade *NE*.
haister perplex, pester, harass *now Gall*.
†**inbearing** impressive, persuasive.
infit: hae an ~ wi have influence on, be in the good graces of *Bnf Abd*.
†**intrait** entreat.
†**lug: blaw in the ~** flatter, wheedle, cajole.
†**mease** pacify, assuage (a person; some emotion, passion or sorrow).
mend reform, improve (a person, his character or habits) *now local*.
mint, mint at *now NE* insinuate, hint, suggest.
moot *v* **1** hint, insinuate *now Sh Abd Ags*. **2** †argue, plead. *n* a whisper, hint *now Sh Abd*.
moyen persuade, induce (someone) *Abd Ags*.
neuk, nook: hold, keep *or* **put (one) in his ain ~** keep under strict control *Sh NE*.
past: pit ~ put (a person) off something.
perswad persuade.
pest trouble, annoy, plague, pester *local Sh-SW*.
pick on make an impression on, affect *Kcb*.
pouss incite, urge, egg on.
†**prattick: prieve a ~** *or* **one's ~s** practise schemes, use wiles **on** (a person).
prig 1 plead **with** (someone) **for** (something) *now Sh-nEC Kcb*. **2** beseech, entreat, importune.
saft, soft: on *or* **up someone's ~ side** into someone's good graces or favour.
sair, sore: ~ face a pathetic expression assumed to elicit sympathy *local Sh-Per*.
soother 1 soothe, calm. **2** coax, cajole, flatter *chf Ags Uls*.
spean draw (a person) away **from** (a habit, idea etc) *now NE nEC Lnk*.
†**straik wi the hair** soothe, humour.
teal entice, coax, wheedle by flattery.
thirl bind with ties of affection, sense of duty or loyalty, force of habit etc.
thrain harp constantly on a theme, beg persistently *Fif*.
tice, †tyst entice, coax, wheedle.
†**treat** beseech, beg, request.
treesh (wi) entreat, cajole, entice in a kind and flattering way *now Abd*.
tryst invite, encourage, entice. ~ **wi** make a fuss of, coax, wheedle *N*.
†**vieve** (making a) vivid (impression).

wear roun prevail on, get round (someone) *now Sh Ork*.
wheetle, wheegle *now local Stlg-Rox* wheedle.
†**wheeze** flatter, coax, cajole *C*.
whillywha wheedle, coax, cajole (a person for something or a thing from a person).
win, wun: ~ farrer ben be admitted to greater grace or favour *Sh Ork Ags*. **~in wi** find favour with.
wise, wice coax, induce, entice, lead round by advice.

15.5.2 COMPASSION

†**apardon** pardon, forgive (a person); make allowances for, excuse; forgive (a person) for (some offence).
†**bete** relieve, lessen (distress, need etc); amend, correct; relieve (a person) **of**.
biel(d) *n* **1** *chf literary* protection; relief, succour *now Bnf*. **2** †a person acting as a protector, comforter etc. †*v* succour, help; protect.
breet *indicating pity, affection, tolerance etc* a (poor etc) fellow, creature *NE*.
cherity charity.
†**dede** a kind or charitable act, *chf* ~ **of alms, mercy** *etc*.
†**essonʒe** *v* excuse.
excaise *C*, **exkeese** *NE v* excuse.
†**faik** spare, excuse, let (someone) go.
forbear bear with, have patience with *now midLoth*.
hert, hairt, heart: ~-peety deep compassion *Sh Abd*.
lat, let: ~ doun (on) refrain from teasing (a person), stop reproaching a person *now NE*.
†**leefu** kind-hearted, considerate, compassionate.
leuk, luck, look: ~ o(w)er pass over, overlook, forgive *now Sh N*.
licht, light make light, lighten, ease, mitigate *now Ags Wgt*.
†**liss** relieve (pain or suffering); relieve (a person **of** suffering).
mane pity or show sympathy towards (a person or his misfortune) *now Cai Ags Rox*. **mak ~ for** *or* **about** show sympathy towards *now Sh-N Uls*. **to ~** to be pitied *now local N-S*.
†**marcie** mercy.
object someone deserving of pity.
peety, pity pity. ~**ifu(l)** arousing pity and compassion, pitiable.
†**pietuous 1** *also* **pet(e)ous** deserving pity. **2** compassionate.

rue on have pity on, feel compassion for *now Ags Fif*.

†**sairie, sorry** *expressing compassion:* 'poor old ..'

saul *now local Sh-SW*, **sowl: the (wee)** ~, **my (wee)** ~ term of pity.

†**silly** deserving of pity or sympathy.

sin pity, a sense of sympathy *now Sh*.

†**slake** relieve **of** (sorrow etc). **slaken** assuage, mitigate.

sowther, solder mitigate, alleviate (sorrow, pain, anger etc) *now Ags*.

stock *usu sympathetic, chf of men* a chap, bloke, creature *now NE Ags*.

vex: be ~**ed for** be sorry for (a person) *Sh-Cai Ags Per WC*.

wicht *freq with pity* a human being, person.

worm, wirm applied to a person, expressing tenderness, playfulness or commiseration *Sh Ags*.

15.5.3 MOCKERY

For mocking laughter, see 15.6.17.

aff, off: ~ **tak 1** a mocking remark, a jeer. **2** a person who ridicules others, a mimic. ~**taking** *n* mockery. *adj* waggish, jeering.

at: be ~ **someone about something** keep finding fault with, tease someone.

bairge taunt loudly *now Bnf*.

bauchle: mak a ~ **o** make a laughing-stock of.

bob a taunt, scoff *now Sh*.

†**brag** threaten, taunt.

chairge, charge chaff (a person) *SW, S*.

collie-fox tease *Uls*.

†**contempnandly** contemptuously, scornfully.

cry names call (someone) names.

†**defoul** treat with scorn; disparage, despise.

disperson treat with indignity, insult, abuse.

†**dispitefully** scornfully, contemptuously.

doon-tak a humiliation, a taunt.

dunt a dig, insult.

†**flyre** *v* grimace, mock. ~**dome** mockery.

†**geck 1** a gesture of derision, a gibe, trick. **2** a scornful or disdainful manner *chf SW*.

girn grin, sneer *now Sh Ork Ags Gall*.

†**gleek** *v* jeer, gibe.

†**guk** a mocking sound.

gype make a fool of *now Sh Ags*.

heeze a practical joke, banter, a teasing *NE*.

†**hething** scorn, derision, mockery. ~**full** derisive, scornful.

hoot say **hoot** to, pooh-pooh, treat or dismiss with contempt *now EC Dmf Rox*.

jamph *v* mock. *n* mockery, a jeer.

joke make a joke against, tease.

kittle (up) provoke, annoy, tease *Gen except Sh Ork*.

knack *v* make fun of; deride *now Ayr*. *n* a mocking retort; a gibe.

laith ill will, loathing, scorn *now Ork*.

lant mock *NE*.

†**lardon** a gibe, a piece of sarcasm.

lat at make a sarcastic thrust at *now local N-Uls*.

light, licht: † ~**lie** slighting, contemptuous, scornful. ~**liefu** slighting, contemptuous *now NE*. † ~**lifullie** slightingly, contemptuously. †**lat** ~**ly of** regard with scorn, disparage.

†**ludifie** make a fool of, ridicule.

mockrife scornful, mocking.

†**mow** *n* a grimace, *esp* derisive. **mak a** ~ *or* ~**s** pull a face, *esp* in derision.

murgeon mock with exaggerated posturing or grimaces.

†**object, objeck** mention in reproach, disparagement or mockery.

rub a slight jibe, reproof or teasing *local Ork-Kcb*.

scorn jeer, scoff **at** *now Sh*.

†**scorp** mock, scoff.

†**scrip** *v* mock, jeer, scoff (at). *n* a scornful grimace.

†**scuff 1** a gibe. **2** scoff, mockery.

setterel short-tempered, sarcastic *NE*.

†**skirp (at)** mock, treat with contempt.

†**sklent** reflect sarcastically **on**, hint **at** by insinuation.

smool look scornful and unfriendly *SW*.

snag nag, grumble, taunt *now Kcdn*. † ~**gy** sarcastic, snappish.

snash insult, speak impertinently to, sneer at.

snaw, snow: throw *or* **cast** ~ **baws** jeer, make insulting remarks.

sneist *n* a taunt, gibe, air of disdain. *v* behave in a contemptuous, arrogant way, be scornful or supercilious. ~**y** sneering *now Rox*.

snell severe in manner or speech, tart, sarcastic *now Sh NE Ags*.

snite someone's niz taunt someone *now SW*.

†**soosh** taunt, upbraid *Ayr*.

span(g) the nose thumb one's nose *Stlg Fif EC, SW*.

taisle *v* tease, irritate, vex *now Kcb*. *n* a teasing *now Kcb*.

tak, take: ~ **on** have (a person) on, chaff *local NE-Slk*. **take one's water off** make a fool of, take a rise out of *now Per*.

†**tant** taunt.

†**tench** ? a taunt, reproach.

tirraneese, tarraneese tease, irritate *NE Ags.*

towt *n* a teasing remark, taunt *Bwk S. v* tease, annoy, taunt *now Bwk Rox.*

turn, tirn: tak the ~ **out o** trick, fool *now Sh Per.*

upcast *v* taunt, reproach, bring up against someone, allege as a fault *local Sh-WC. n* a taunt, reproach, ground or occasion for criticism *now Sh-N Fif Lnk.*

15.5.4 JOY, MERRY-MAKING

For laughter, see 15.6.17.

†**barns-breaking** an idle frolic.

blithe, blide *now Sh adj* **1** blithe; joyous, cheerful, glad, in good spirits. **2** †*of the face, bearing etc* happy, cheerful. †*v* gladden. *adv* happily, cheerfully, kindly. †**blithfull** joyful, glad. **blithesome** cheerful, merry.

cadgy *adj* cheerful, in good spirits. *adv* cheerfully *Renfr Kcb.*

canty lively, cheerful.

cheerisome cheerful, merry *now Sh Loth WC.*

conveevial convivial.

crouse cheerful, merry.

daffery fun, merriment *now Bnf Fif.* **daffin** fun. **on the daffin** out for fun, on holiday *now Bnf Abd.*

divert an amusing person.

†**fainness** gladness, joy.

†**gay** gaily.

geckin lively, playful *Bnf Dmf.*

†**glaikit** playful, full of pranks.

gled *adj* glad. †*v, chf verse* make glad. † ~**ar** a person who cheers or makes glad.

gleg lively, sprightly, merry *now Sh NE Per.*

†**glew** glee, entertainment, sport, mirth.

gyper fun, joking *NE.*

hail at the heart in good spirits *chf N.*

hert, hairt, heart: ~**ie** fond of fun and good company, jovial, cheerful, merry. ~**some** merry, cheerful, lively *now Sh NE Dmf.* ~**somely** cheerfully, heartily *now Sh.* ~**someness** cheerfulness *now Sh.*

humoursome humorous, witty *now N nEC.*

†**jellie** jolly.

†**jo** joy.

joco jovial, merry, cheerful, pleased with oneself *Gen except Sh Ork.*

jokie jocular, fond of a joke.

†**jolious** jolly, merry, joyful.

kim spirited, frolicsome, lively *chf Abd.*

kiow-ow a trick, ploy, carry-on *now Gall Uls.*

kirr cheerful, lively, brisk *SW.*

knackie witty, pleasant in conversation, facetious.

licht, light: ~**some** carefree, cheerful.

†**liking** *chf early verse* happiness, contentment.

linkie a roguish person, a wag *S.*

madderam boisterous fun, hilarity *chf Sh Ork.*

†**melody** rejoicing, joy.

†**merines, mirrines** merrymaking; fun.

merry-courant a riotous revel *chf SW.*

mirkie *adj* merry, cheerful, mischievous *now NE.* *adv* cheerfully, pleasantly, merrily *NE.*

†**mirrie** merry.

†**muith** cheerful.

pawkie 1 roguish, coquettish; lively, merry. **2** quaint, fantastic, amusing *now Cai*

†**playrife** playful, light-hearted, fond of fun.

†**pleasance, plesandis** the feeling of pleasure, joy, happiness, satisfaction.

pleasant humorous, witty, jocular, merry *now NE, WC, SW.*

prank play pranks, meddle, interfere, act in a lighthearted, careless way *now Bnf Ags.*

prat a trick, prank, practical joke, piece of mischief *now Cai.*

†**queer** amusing, funny, entertaining.

†**querty** full of fun.

raffin roistering, merry, boisterously hearty *now Per.*

randie a romp, frolic.

rant *v* romp, make merry, indulge in boisterous fun *now local Sh-Ags. n* a romp, boisterous or riotous merry-making *now Bnf Abd.* † ~**ie** frolicsome, full of boisterous fun. ~**in** roistering, merry, uproarious *local.* † ~**inlie** merrily, uproariously.

set a joke, piece of fun, frolic *now WC, SW.*

shortsome *of persons, things, situations* lively and entertaining, cheerful, making time pass quickly *now N Per.*

†**sportsum** amusing, diverting, sportive.

tear a lively entertaining person, a comic *local Cai-S.*

vaudie frisky, merry.

vogie merry, light-hearted, happy.

†**wanton** jovial, jolly, waggish, free from care.

†**whilking** lively, playful as a kitten.

15.5.5 UPROAR

adae ado, fuss, commotion.

asteer, astir in a commotion.

ball bustle, disturbance *now Sh Bnf.*

†**beir** an outcry, shouting; noise, din.

belli-hooin riotous(ness) *Fif.*

bizz a state of commotion, bustle *now local NE-S.*

†**brainyell** an uproar.

†**brangle** a state of confusion; a tangle; a disturbance.

brulzie(ment), brulie(ment) broil, a turmoil, commotion, etc.

cabby-labby, kebby-lebby a hubbub *local.*

camstairy an uproar *now Fif.*

ca-through a disturbance *Bnf Abd Ags Fif.*

clamihewit a hubbub.

†**crya** a hue and cry.

†**cummer(s)** troubles, commotions.

din a fuss, disturbance *now local Bnf-Kcb.*

dindee, dundee, dinniedeer a noise, uproar; a fuss, disturbance *now Abd.*

dirdum tumultuous noise, altercation, uproar.

†**distribulance** disturbance.

erumption an outburst, uproar *local EC-S.*

feuch a commotion *now Ags midLoth.*

fizz a bustle, commotion, a state of great excitement.

fray a noise, a fuss, a stir.

fry a state of worry or distraction, a disturbance *now local Sh-Stlg.*

fuffle fuss, violent exertion *S.*

fyke a fuss, bustle, commotion, excitement *now Ags Fif Stlg.*

Jock: the Deil's gane ower ~ Wabster *proverb* things have got out of hand; the fat's in the fire *now Cai Kcdn.*

kill, kiln: the ~'s on fire *or* **in a bleeze** *proverb* denoting a state of tumult or excitement *now Ags Loth.*

kip a state of great excitement *Abd Rox.*

kippage disorder, confusion, fuss, predicament.

mank a fuss *Lnk Rox.*

pirr a sudden burst of activity.

raise a reek make a great fuss, cause a stir *now local Sh-Lnk.*

rammy a free-for-all, violent disturbance, scuffle.

†**reel** a commotion, clamour, stir.

reird, raird a loud uproar or clamour. †**rerdour** clamour, tumult.

ribble-rabble in a state of great confusion *now wLoth Slk.*

ricket a noisy disturbance, racket, row *now Ags.*

rippet *n* a noisy disturbance, uproar *now NE Pbls WC.* †*v* create a row or disturbance, quarrel loudly.

rothos, rothie a tumult, uproar *now Mry.*

†**rowt** a shout, outcry, clamour, fuss.

rumble-tumble (full of) noisy confusion *now Ags.*

rumption a state of noisy, bustling disorder, an uproar.

ruther 1 †an outcry, uproar. **2** turmoil, chaos, ruin *Abd.*

sclammer a clamour *NE.*

†**shout and cry** *or* **hoyes** hue and cry.

sonnet a fuss, to-do *Ags.*

souch, sough an uproar, fuss *local NE-Uls.*

splitter a hubbub *now Ork C.*

splore a state of excitement or commotion, a fuss.

†**spree** a disturbance, fuss.

†**squeal** an outcry, uproar.

steer: † ~**age** movement, commotion. ~**ie** a bustle, commotion, muddle. ~**iefyke** confused bustle, agitation, excitement. ~**ing** *of places etc* full of activity, in a tumult.

stew, steuch a hubbub, uproar *now Sh.*

stour commotion, fuss, disturbance, *freq* **raise** *etc* **a ~**.

strow a commotion, bustle, to-do.

strush, stroosh: ~**in** a disturbance, uproar, fuss *Rox.*

sturt strife, trouble, disquiet, annoyance, *freq* ~ **and strife.** *now Sh.*

swither, swidder *now chf NE* a state of confusion, a tangled or muddled condition *local Sh-Gall.*

tartar a disturbance, noise, row *Cai.*

throuither, through other a confusion, row *now Abd.*

time a fuss, great excitement.

tirrivee a state of excitement or bustle; a disturbance, fight *N, C, S.*

tirr-wirr a commotion, disturbance *now NE nEC.*

too-hoo a fuss; hullaballoo *now Sh Ags Dmf.*

towrow a noisy uproar, rumpus, disturbance *now Sh Bnf Ags.*

trevallie a disturbance, brawl.

tulyie trouble, turmoil *now Sh, chf literary.*

†**unquietatioun** a disturbance *Abd.*

†**vociferation** a clamour, an outcry.

wap a disturbance, brawl, din, quarrel *now NE Per Dmf.*

wark, work trouble, outcry *now Sh-WC Dmf.*

wey-dain, wey o daein a fuss; a disturbance, uproar *chf Ags.*

whillilu an uproar, a commotion.

whush a stir, commotion *now Ork C.*

†**widdle** a bustle, tumult.

yammer a great outcry, clamour, incessant talk *now Ork NE-S.*

15.5.6 DRINK

ball a spree *now Sh Bnf*. **on the ~** constantly drinking *now Ags*.

†barlie, barrel: barliehood violent ill temper, obstinacy resulting from drunkenness. **~ fever** intoxication, drunkenness. **~-sick** drunk.

bash: on the ~ having a drinking bout, on the spree.

batter: on the ~ on the spree.

beamfill't, beamfoo intoxicated *now Abd Bnf*.

bedrucken drunken *now Sh Ags*.

bend the bicker, †bend drink hard. **†bender** a hard drinker.

bite: no be able *etc* **to ~ one's fingers** *or* **thoum** be very drunk *now N-Per*.

blab drink excessively *NE*.

bleared debauched-looking.

bleezed, bleezin (fou) very drunk. **†bleezy** *of the eyes* showing signs of intoxication.

blin fou very drunk.

blink, blenk be drunk, under the influence of drink *now Ayr*.

blybe drink heavily *now Abd*.

bung-fu very drunk *now local Bnf Arg*.

burst a bout of drunkenness *local Bnf-Kcb*.

cap, caup: he's as fou's ~ *or* **staup'll mack him** he is completely drunk *Bnf Abd*. **†play cop out** empty the cup, carouse.

capernoitie *now Abd*, **capernoited** *now Abd Fif* intoxicated, giddy.

chippit tipsy *Bnf Abd*.

cock one's wee finger drink, tipple.

corn: ~ed exhilarated with drink, tiddly *chf Bnf*. **waur to water than (to) ~** addicted to drink.

cruik, crook: ~ one's elbow drink (alcohol), *esp* rather freely *local*.

†daidle and drink wander from place to place drinking; tipple.

dram **†drink** alcohol, tipple. **be one's ~** pay one's share of the drinks *now Ags Fif*.

drouth a drunk, a habitual drinker. **~y** thirsty, addicted to drinking.

†drucken, drunken drunken. **~some** inclined to drink too much.

drunkart, †drunkat a drunkard.

dry-mou'd not drinking, not having a glass of liquor *now Bnf Abd Fif*.

due sober quite sober *now Kcb*.

†ee, eye: a drap(pie) in the ~ just enough drink to make one mildly intoxicated.

fill drunk *or* **fou** make drunk.

flee, fly be violently excited by drink, *chf* **fleein** hilariously drunk *local*.

fou drunk, intoxicated, *now also with qualification, eg* **blin ~, roarin ~** *and in phrases, eg* **~ as a puggie.**

fresh *chf of a habitual drunkard* sober, recovered from a drinking bout *now Sh-Ags*.

fuddle get drunk on, drink the proceeds of; spend (time) drinking.

greetin fou at the tearful stage of drunkenness.

half, hauf: ~cock(ie) half drunk.

heid, head: tak one's ~ go to one's head, intoxicate.

jute, jeet *NE contemptuous* a tippler, boozer, drunkard *now Abd*. **juitle** tipple *now Dmf*.

maut: get *or* **hae in one's ~, haud the ~** be drunk. **the ~ gaes, is** *etc* **abune the meal** he *etc* is drunk.

mingin very drunk *local EC-Ayr*.

miraculous very drunk.

†mistaen with overcome by, under the influence of (drink).

mixed muddled with drink *local Sh-Per*.

moidert, modderit confused, dazed as a result of drink *etc WC, S Uls*.

†molassed drunk, *esp* with **molass** *local*.

mortal *adj* extremely intoxicated, dead drunk. *adv* very, *chf* **~ drunk, ~ fou.**

muck: as drunk as ~ very drunk *now Sh Ags Per*.

†nappie slightly intoxicated, 'merry'.

owertaen, †overtaken (with *or* **in)** deranged, made helpless, overcome (by liquor) *now Per*.

pie-eyed cross-eyed, drunk *Kcdn WC*.

pin: ~ner a heavy drinking bout. **pit in the ~** give up drinking.

piper: as fou as a ~ extremely drunk.

plet, plait stagger as with drink *nEC, S*.

rammle, ramble *v* wander about aimlessly, *esp* under the influence of drink *now local Bnf-Uls*. *n* a noisy drinking bout *local NE-S*. **on the rammle** drinking heavily.

ream *of liquor* rouse confusion (in the mind).

ree tipsy, befuddled with drink *now Ork*.

reezie light-headed from drink, tipsy *now Slk*.

richt, right sober, not drunk, living in a sober, well-behaved way *local Sh-Kcb*.

roarie drunk *now Sh Per Gsw*.

rotten drunk drunk *Sh-SW*.

sand bed a very heavy drinker, a 'soak' *now Rox*.

sappie given to drinking too much.

screed a bout of drinking, a few days **on the bash.**

slaik, slaich a person who drinks excessively *local Per-Rox*.

smeekit drunk *chf WC, SW*.

souple, supple limp, helpless (with drink) *local*.

†spate a bout (of drinking).

spin: on the ~ on a drinking spree *now Ags Dmf*.

splore *n* a party, spree, jollification, *freq* with drinking. *v* frolic, make merry *now local Ags-Per*.

spuin fou replete, *esp* with drink, to the point of vomiting *now NE Ags Kcb*.

†squeal a spree.

stavin staggering with drunkenness, stottin *now Inv*.

steamin (wi drink) very drunk *Ork-C*.

stoit, styte stagger, stumble from drink, walk in a dazed uncertain way *local NE-Uls*.

stot stagger, walk unsteadily from drink. stottin (fou) reeling drunk *local N-SW*.

sussie, sizzie care, trouble, bother, *latterly freq* in dealing with a fractious drunk person *now Sh Fif Kcb*.

†swash fuddled with drink.

†swig: play at ~ indulge in drinking.

tosie slightly intoxicated, tipsy and merry.

total teetotal *now NE Rox*.

tout *v* drink copiously, tipple *now local NE-Ayr*. *n*, *also* ~lie *now NE*, † ~ie a drinker, tippler *now WC*.

†tovie boastful, *esp* in drink.

troch, trough *contemptuous* a person who drinks to excess *local Cai-Dmf*.

turn, tirn: ~ someone's head make someone feel giddy, intoxicate someone *local Sh-Per*. ~ up the wee finger tipple, indulge in drinking *Gen except Sh*.

weel upon't *Abd*, †weel to live tipsy.

whiskied, †whiskified affected by whisky, tipsy.

worse: the ~ of drink the worse for drink, having drunk too much alcohol *local*.

wulk: as fou as a ~ very drunk *local NE-Ayr*.

15.5.7 CHITCHAT

For slander, see next.

auld wife a fussy, gossipy man, an 'old woman'.

†blaf(l)um nonsense, idle talk.

blatter talk volubly, noisily and fast.

†blellum an idle, ignorant, talkative man.

blether talk foolishly, loquaciously or idly. ~(s) talk, nonsense; long-winded (boasting) talk. ~(er) a person who talks foolishly or too much. ~ation, ~ie *now Bnf Abd* foolish talk.

blether(an)skate, blether(um)skite a babbler.

blicker the talk of a boaster or stupid person.

bluiter *n* a senseless talker *now Edb wLoth Kcb*. *v* talk foolishly; blurt out *now Bnf Abd Kcb*.

boo speak loudly, monotonously and to little purpose *now local NE-EC*.

braid, broad, *chf* ~ out unrestrainedly, indiscreetly.

buff silly or irrelevant talk, *freq* ~and styte *local Bnf-Lnk*.

buller blustering talk, nonsense.

bummle speak carelessly *now Lnk*.

chant chatter pertly.

clack, cleck *v* gossip, talk loudly and idly. *n* gossip, chatter, insolence.

claik *v* gossip, chatter *now Bnf-Fif*.

clash *n* 1 chatter, talk, gossip. 2 a gossiping person *now Fif wLoth*. *v* tell tales, gossip, chatter.

clash-ma-claver(s) gossip, idle tales *now Bnf Fif Lnk*.

clatter 1 ~(s) noisy idle chatter, gossip, scandal; rumours. 2 a chatterer, a gossip *NE*. ~er a chatterer.

claver *v*, *also* glaver *now midLoth* talk idly or foolishly; gossip. *n* 1 ~s prating; gossip; nonsense. 2 *also* glaver *midLoth* a foolish idle talker *SW, S*.

click-clack loquacity *NE*.

clish repeat gossip. clish-clash, clishmaclash idle talk, gossip. clishmaclaver *n* idle talk, gossip; endless talk *now Bnf Abd*. *v* gossip, chatter *now NE*.

clitter-clatter *n* noisy animated talk, senseless chatter, meaningless verbiage. *v* talk endlessly, chatter.

clype be talkative, gossip *now Bnf Kcb*. clypach *n* a gossip *Bnf*. *v* gossip *now Abd*. clypie talkative, tattling *now Abd*.

clytach *n* senseless chatter, balderdash *chf NE*. *v* talk in a strange language, *esp* chatter *NE*.

crack *v* talk, converse, gossip. *n* an entertaining talker, a gossip. ~er a talker, gossip *now Bnf Fif Stlg*. ~y talkative, affable; loquacious *local*. ~like a (pen-)gun, pea guns *or* two hand guns talk in a lively way, chatter loudly *now Bnf Abd Fif*.

cronachin gossiping, tattling.

curmuring a murmur of talk *now Abd Fif*.

deave *v* annoy with noise or talk; bore. *n* an interminable talker *now Abd*.

domineer deafen, stupefy with loud noise or too much talk *Bnf Abd*.

en(d)less pertinacious; long-winded.

gab *n* 1 light, entertaining talk, chat, cheek. 2 a talkative person, chatterbox, gossip *local Mry-Ayr*. *v* talk idly or volubly. gabbie garrulous, chatty; fluent *Gen except Sh Ork*. gabbit talkative, gossipy *now Sh Kcb Rox*.

gab-gash petulant or voluble chatter *now Inv*.

gange *v* chatter, gossip.

gash *n* prattle, talk. *adj* talkative, loquacious. *v* talk volubly, gossip, prattle. ∼-**gabbit** loquacious, glib *chf Fif*.

gibble-gabble chatter, tittle-tattle *now local Bnf-S*.

giff-gaff *n* interchange of talk, repartee *now sEC Ayr. v* bandy (words) *now local Inv-Bwk*.

glaiber talk incessantly or idly, babble *now Rox*.

gleg-gabbit *now WC*, **gleg-tongued** *now Sh midLoth Rox* smooth-tongued, glib, voluble.

glib, *also* ∼-**gabbit** *now Abd Per midLoth*, ∼-**mou(e)d** *now Abd Ags*, †∼-**by** voluble, fluent (without the implication of insincerity etc) *local*.

gnib quick in action or speech *Bnf Abd*.

guff babble, talk foolishly *now Rox*.

gun gossip, talk rapidly or animatedly *NE*.

gutter talk nonsense, gabble, gibber *now WC*.

gyper *v* talk nonsense *Abd. n* nonsense *NE*.

gyter *n* **1** nonsense, foolish talk *NE*. **2** a stupid, talkative person, a driveller *NE. v* talk a great deal in a silly way *Abd*.

†**habble** babble.

haiver *v* talk in a foolish or trivial way, speak nonsense. *n* a person who talks nonsense *Gen except Sh Ork*. ∼(**s**) nonsense, foolish talk, gossip, chatter. **haiverel** *n* a foolishly chattering or garrulous person, a fool, a halfwit. *adj* garrulous, speaking foolishly *now Kcb*. **havering** *adj* nonsensical, gossiping, babbling, garrulous. *n* chatter, gossip, nonsense.

harrows: rin aff *or* **awa wi the** ∼ let oneself go in a dogmatic, assertive way, talk unrestrainedly, exaggerate.

hash *v* talk volubly, emptily or illogically *chf S. n* ribald talk, nonsense *now Sh*.

hearing news; a long story.

jangle chatter, talk incessantly *now Uls*.

jaun(d)er *v* talk idly, foolishly or jokingly *now Per Kcb Dmf. n* **1** idle, foolish talk *SW Rox*. **2** a chatterbox *Kcb Dmf Slk*.

jibber silly talk, idle chatter *now local N-nEC Uls*.

kiow-ow talk frivolously *N Gall Uls*. ∼(**s**) silly chatter *N*. ∼**in** tattling, frivolous *N Wgt*.

kyaard-tung't given to loose talk *Bnf Abd*.

laberlethin a rigmarole, rambling discourse.

lagamachie, legammachie a rigmarole, a long-winded discourse *NE*.

laibach *n, also* **laib** *Bnf Abd* a rigmarole, a rambling or incoherent discourse *NE. v* babble, chatter *NE*.

laig *v, also* **lig(-lag)** *now Bnf*, **leg-laig** *now Bnf* chatter, gossip *chf NE. n, also* **lig** (idle) talk, gossip *chf NE*.

lamgabblich a long rambling discourse, a rigmarole *NE*.

lay aff *v* talk volubly and confidently (about). *n* a harangue, rigmarole.

leetany a long rambling story, a rigmarole *Sh NE*.

lingel a rigmarole *N*.

lingie a long rambling story, rigmarole *NE Fif Dmf*.

maunner maunder, babble. †**maundrels** nonsense, idle tales.

mill: gang on like a tume ∼ chatter on without pause *now Ags Per*.

nash-gab garrulous talk *chf Rox*.

natter *v* chatter, *esp* peevishly. *n* **1** grousing, nagging talk; aimless chatter. **2** a chatterer *Sh NE, SW, S*.

newser a person who is fond of chat *Sh N*. **newsie** gossipy, talkative *chf NE*

nyaff talk senselessly or irritatingly, yap *now Sh*.

on about occupied in talking about, harping on.

paiter talk in a persistent monotonous way, chatter on endlessly.

†**pratt** prate.

†**prolixt, prolixit** prolix, lengthy. **prolixitnes** prolixity.

pross gossip.

psalm recount (a story etc) at great length and in monotonous detail, reel **off** endlessly in a monotonous whining voice *NE*.

pyot *n* contemptuous term for a chattering, irresponsible person. *adj, of speech* loud, empty, voluble.

raible, rabble *v* utter (a torrent of words) *now Sh Ayr. n, also* **rabblach** a disorderly outpouring of words or noises, a rigmarole; nonsensical talk *now local*.

raivel, ravel speak incoherently, ramble, be delirious *now NE nEC Lnk*. †**reavel-ravel, revill-raill** a rigmarole.

rame *v* drone on monotonously *now Uls. n* a phrase, remark etc repeated over and over.

rander, render *v* talk idly or nonsensically, ramble, maunder *now Sh Cai Uls. n* **1** a great talker *Rox*. **2** ∼(**s**) senseless, incoherent talk *chf S*.

rane, rone, rennie *Abd Ags*, **ronnie** *Abd Ags n* a constant refrain, a prolonged or repeated utterance. *v* keep on repeating *now Ags Fif*.

rat-rhyme, †**rat rane** a nonsensical rigmarole, a tedious repetition.

rave a person who talks volubly and nonsensically, a windbag *local Stlg-SW*.

raverie, reverie nonsense, foolish talk *now Abd*.

426

raw-gabbed *Sh*, †**raw-mowit** voluble in an ignorant, ill-informed way.

†**reeve** chatter, babble.

rhyme repeat, drone **on** monotonously; talk nonsense *local Bnf-Uls*.

†**roy** talk nonsense.

royet †extravagant, nonsensical. **roiter** talk nonsense, babble, rave *Renfr Ayr*.

rummlieguts *contemptuous* a windbag *Loth Dmf*.

say awa(y) 1 a long rambling discourse, a rigmarole *local NE-S*. **2** a loquacious person *S*.

sclore *v* chat, gossip, **blether** (at length). *n* rubbishy talk, a long rambling story.

sheen: gie a story hose and ~ magnify a story in the telling *Abd Kcb*.

slab *v* talk drivel, babble *Fif WC*. *n* ~**s** senseless or foolish talk, idle chatter *Fif WC, SW*.

slaver, slever talk nonsense, chatter in a silly way, **blether** *local Cai-S*.

sonnet a tale, yarn, a (tall) story, nonsense *now Abd Ags*.

stoit foolish talk, stupid rubbish, nonsense *now Ork Cai NE*.

strowd a piece of nonsense; rubbishy talk *Abd*.

sweetie-wife *freq of a(n effeminate) man* a garrulous, gossipy person *local Cai-S*.

taivers idle, foolish talk *now Stlg Ayr*.

tatter talk idly *now S*.

tedisome tedious, tiresome, boring *now local*.

tittle whisper, chatter *now local Sh-WC*.

toner a person who talks endlessly on the same subject *now Lnk Kcb*.

tongue: tonguie glib, loquacious, fluent *now Sh Cai*. ~**-deaving** tiresomely talkative *now Sh Bnf*. ~**-raik** volubility, flow of language.

touter trivial gossip, tittle-tattle *Bnf Abd*.

tove *v* talk in a friendly, animated way, gossip, chat. *n* a chat, talk, gossip.

trattle talk idly; chatter, prattle, gossip. † ~**s** idle talk or tales; gossip; chatter.

†**trittle-trattles** foolish or idle talk.

troke, truck nonsensical talk, rubbish *Sh N*.

tronie a long story, rambling chat *Ags*.

trosk a silly, talkative person *Cai*.

wallop a wagging (of the tongue) *Sh Abd*.

whitter chatter, prattle; a talkative person.

witter *now NE Ags*, **wutter** mutter **on** about nothing.

yaag *v* gossip, chatter *NE*.

yabb *v* harp on a subject, talk incessantly *now Sh-Ags*. *n* a garrulous person, a chatterbox *now Abd Ags*. **yabble, yabber** *now EC* talk volubly or excitedly, chatter, gossip.

yaff *v* chatter, talk pertly *now Lnk*. *n* a chatterbox, a pert person *now local Loth-S*.

yammer *v* talk volubly or incoherently. *n* a great outcry, clamour, incessant talk *now Ork, NE-S*.

yap, yaup *v* chatter, nag, speak querulously, harp on. *n* **1** incessant talking, *usu* implying nagging. **2** a chatterbox; a windbag.

yatter *v* **1** chatter, ramble on, talk interminably. **2** *of a person speaking incoherently or in a foreign language* gabble. *n* **1** continuous chatter, rambling and persistent talk. **2** an incessant talker; a gossip.

yiff-yaff *n* **1** chatter *now Loth Stlg*. **2** a small, insignificant, chattery person *local Fif-S*.

yitter *v* chatter *local Stlg-Rox*.

†**yove** talk in a rambling way; rambling talk.

15.5.8 NOSINESS, SLANDER

For gossip as idle conversation, see 15.5.7.

at meddling with, hurting: '*Who was at ye?*'

bemean disparage, humiliate.

†**blasphematioun** evil-speaking, calumniation.

blaud defame.

bleck blacken in character etc, defame *now Edb*.

†**brute** *n* a rumour involving praise or blame of a person, good or bad report. *v* accuse or credit (a person) by rumour.

ca(ll): ~ **clashes** *or* **the clash**, ~ (**aboot**) **a story** spread gossip *NE Ags*.

†**calumpné** calumny. **calumpniat** calumniate(d).

causey clash street-talk; gossip *now Abd Fif*.

claik *n* **1** ~(**s**) gossip *Bnf-Fif*. **2** a gossip *Bnf-Fif*. *v* gossip, chatter *now Bnf-Fif*.

clapperdin a gossip *NE*.

clash tell tales, gossip, chatter. ~**er** a tell-tale, gossip *now Bnf wLoth*. ~**y** given to gossip *now Cai Bnf Fif*. ~**-bag,** ~**-pyot** a tell-tale.

clatter *n* **1** ~(**s**) noisy idle chatter, gossip, scandal; rumours. **2** a chatterer, a gossip *NE*. *v* gossip, talk scandal. ~**er** a chatterer; a tale-bearer. ~ **bag(s)** a tale-bearer *now NE*.

clink *of news or gossip* spread *now Fif*.

clish repeat gossip. **clishmaclaver** a talkative busybody *now Bnf Abd*.

cloot: a tongue like to *or* **that wad clip** ~**s** a sharp or voluble tongue.

clype *v, also* ~ **on** tell tales, inform against someone. *n* **1** an idle tale, a lie, gossip *local NE-*

WC. **2** *also* ~**-clash** *now Kcb* a tell-tale. **clypach** *n* a gossip *Bnf. v* gossip *now Abd.*

countra, country: ~ **clash** the gossip of the district *local Bnf-Kcb.*

craik ill-natured gossip; grumbling talk *S.*

cummer, kimmer *v* gossip *S.*

curious, kwerious *Bnf Abd* curious. **keeriosity** curiosity *now NE.*

†**defame** defamation.

†**defoul** disparage, despise.

†**deprise** depreciate, despise.

dern, darn loiter, eavesdrop.

†**detractour, detrakkar a** detractor.

dill *of a rumour etc* die **down**, be forgotten, pass out of mind *Sh Bnf Abd.*

din a report, rumour; a scandal *now Bnf Abd Ayr.*

din-raisin *of a tale-bearer* deliberately causing trouble *Bnf Abd.*

†**disparissing** disparaging.

†**disprese** dispraise, depreciate, undervalue.

dunt a slanderous lie.

ee: say black is (the white of) a person's ~ speak ill of a person.

ferlie, fairly: ~**s** gossip; an object of gossip. **spy** ~**s** interfere in someone else's business, be inquisitive *local Cai-Kcb.*

fyle one's fingers *etc* **wi** have to do with, meddle with (something debasing) *now NE Ags Lnk.*

gae, go: ~ **on** make a fuss, talk at length in a badgering or quarrelsome way *local.*

gansel a disagreeable comment, an insolent remark.

glib-mou(e)d gossipy, smooth-tongued.

gnip talk carpingly or affectedly *Mry Bnf.*

†**hame, home:** ~**liness** bluntness in speech.

hearken *v, also* ~ **tae** eavesdrop, play the eavesdropper *local NE-Ayr.* ~**er** a listener, an eavesdropper.

heid, head: be at ~ **an aix wi** be involved, *esp* in a meddlesome or contentious way, with (a person or affair) *now Bnf.*

ill fashiont rudely inquisitive *Sh NE.*

ill: ~**-scrapit** *of the tongue* slanderous, rude, bitter *now Cai Mry.* ~**-speakin** given to repeating slander, slanderous talk *now Sh midLoth.* ~**-spoken o** slandered *Sh Ags.* ~**-tongue** slander. ~**-tongued** slandering. *N midLoth SW.* ~**-wind** scandal, slander *NE.*

inbearing meddlesome, intruding *Abd nEC.*

intromit have to do **with**, consort, interfere **with** *now Abd Ags Fif.*

†**jangle,** calumniate, defame.

kail: scaud one's lips *or* **tongue in** *or* **wi ither folk's** ~ interfere, meddle *now local Cai-Fif.*

†**lack** disparage.

lang, long: ~**-luggit** long-eared *now local NE-S.* ~**-nebbit** inquisitive, critical *now local.*

†**leasing 1** lying, slandering. **2** a lie, a slander. **mak** ~**, mak ane** ~ *or* ~**s** lie, tell lies, backbite, slander. **mak (a)** ~ **of** tell lies about, slander.

lee on *etc* tell a lie about, slander.

let the cat oot of the pock let the cat out of the bag *local Cai-Kcb.*

licht, light: ~**lie** *v, also* ~**ifie** *now NE Per* make light of, disparage, insult. †*n* the act of disparagement, an insult.

likeness: no to leave a body (in) the ~ **o a dog** call someone everything that is bad, defame someone's character.

mak, make: ~ *or* **meddle** *(now nEC, SW) or* **mell** *(now Sh Kcb)* interfere, meddle.

†**maling** malign.

mell concern or busy oneself improperly or intrusively (*chf* **with** an affair, action; goods, property; a person) *now Sh Kcb Slk.*

†**mess and mell** to interfere; mix *or* have dealings (**with**).

michty disgraceful, scandalous.

middle 1 meddle. **2** have to do or associate **with** *now local Bnf-Kcb.*

mird meddle, have dealings or association **with** *chf NE.*

misca speak ill of, slander, disparage.

†**mislear (oneself to someone)** abuse, vilify *only Linlithgow.*

†**mislikely** depreciate; smirch.

†**misliken** speak ill of, disparage; undervalue.

mudge, midge *local Ork-WC* a rumour *now NE nEC Dnbt.*

murmur calumniate.

nash caustic talk *chf Rox.*

nebbie inquisitive *local sEC-Uls.*

plat *adj* direct, clear, downright, *freq* ~ **and plain**. *adv* in a plain, direct way, straightforwardly, flatly, outright, *freq* ~ **and plain** *now Sh.*

queesitive inquisitive *local Sh-Per.*

raucle, rackle *of speech* blunt to the point of rudeness.

†**rave** a vague rumour, an unlikely story.

raverie, reverie a rumour, a piece of gossip *now Bnf Kcdn.*

redd up *or* **out** speak critically of *local Sh-SW.*

richt, right: ~ **oot** outright, unequivocally.

say a remark, piece of gossip *now local Sh-Ayr.* ~ **(a body) wrang** speak ill of (someone) *local Sh-Ags.*

†**scance** reflect, comment **on** *or* **about.**

sclave *v, also* **sclaver** spread (a story) by gossip, *specif* as a malicious rumour; slander (a person) *NE*. *n* a gossip, scandalmonger *NE*.

†**skail** spread (a rumour etc).

skelp an indirect satirical reference, a hit (**at** someone) *NE wLoth Ayr*.

skiver a prowler, prying person *now Lnk Ayr Dmf*.

sloom a rumour, piece of hearsay or gossip *Bnf Abd*. † ~**in** a secret or stealthy report, a rumour *Bnf Abd*.

smore hush **up** (a rumour etc).

souch, sough gossip, rumour, scandal *now NE-S*.

soun(d) a rumour, report; widespread talk or gossip *local Ork-Kcb*.

speak, spick *NE* 1 gossip, scandalmongering *now local*. 2 a subject of current gossip or rumour, the talk (of a place) *now local Sh-Kcb*.

†**speculation** a spectacle, subject for remark or gossip, an object of contempt.

speir a person who is continually asking questions; a prying inquisitive person *now local Bnf-Slk*. ~**ing** inquisitive, searching.

spin a (made-up) story, gossip, rumour *Bnf Abd*.

splairge slander, besmirch.

spoach *v* pry, rummage, poke about **in** *Bwk Rox*. *n* a person who pokes about, a prying, inquisitive person *now Rox*.

spune, spoon: pit in one's ~ interfere in another's affairs *NE Fif WC*.

tale-pyot a tell-tale *now local Per-S*.

tash a blot on one's character, slur, stigma *now Sh*.

tell: ~**ie-speirie** *Ags Per*, ~ **pie(t)** *now Ork Cai* a tell-tale. ~ **on,** † ~ **upon** inform against, tell tales about.

tittle gossip, tell someone something, *esp* by whispering in their ear *now local Sh-WC*.

tongue-betrusht blunt, outspoken *chf Abd*.

toun, town: ~**'s speak** the talk of the town, the local scandal *local NE-S*.

†**tout(er)** spread (a report), blab, broadcast.

vaig *of a woman* a gadabout, a coarse, disreputable, gossipy person *now Ags*.

whitrat *now Sh Ross C, S*, **whiterick** a thin, small, hatchet-faced person of an active, ferrety disposition *local Sh-Dmf*.

15.5.9 QUARRELS

For quarrelsome characters, see 15.3.4.

airgument an argument *NE Ags*.

argie argue (usu implying contention). **argie-bargie** *n* a quarrel, haggling. *v* dispute, haggle.

argifee, argufy, argue-bargue argue. **argle-bargle** *v, also* †**argle-bargain** dispute. *n* a contention, dispute.

back-come recrimination *Sh Ork Per midLoth*.

†**bargain** *n* contention, conflict, struggle. *v* contend, fight (with). **barganour** a quarreller, wrangler.

bargle wrangle, bandy words *now Abd*.

†**bell the cat** dispute, contend, *esp* with a superior.

blacken someone's door darken someone's door *now Ork Ags*.

breed in disfavour, on bad terms (**with**) *now Ork NE*.

brulzie(ment), brulie(ment) broil, a turmoil, commotion, quarrel etc.

bum dismiss without ceremony *now Loth Lnk*.

cabal *n* a violent dispute *chf Bnf*. *v* quarrel, dispute.

cabby-labby, kebby-lebby *n* a quarrel, altercation, wrangle *local*. † *v* wrangle.

cangle wrangle, dispute.

carble *v, also* **carb** wrangle, quarrel *now Bnf Abd Fif*. *n, also* **carb** *Bnf Abd* wrangling, an argument *now Bnf Abd Fif*.

carfuffle a disagreement, quarrel *Ags Fif SW*.

cast: ~ **at** spurn, condemn. ~ **oot** disagree, quarrel.

catterbatter *n* a quarrel, disagreement *Fif Rox*. *v* wrangle *S*.

cattiewurrie *n* a violent dispute *Bnf*. *v* wrangle violently *Bnf*.

chap someone in aboot, chap in someone's taes take someone down a peg, snub *Bnf Abd*.

chaw a disappointment, snub; a cutting retort *now Bnf Abd Fif*.

clamper *v* quarrel, struggle.

clean: mak a ~ **breast wi** speak one's mind to, have it out with *now Bnf Ags Lnk*.

collieshangie a noisy dispute, uproar.

currieshang a dispute, quarrel *Cai*.

currie-wurrie *n* a violent dispute *now local Bnf-Lnk*. *v* dispute violently *Bnf*.

cut harrows sever relations, stop being on speaking terms *Rox*.

†**dabber** *NE*, **dabble** wrangle.

deil, deevil, devil: ~ **speed the liars** a quarrel, dispute *now Bnf*.

dibber-dabber *v* wrangle, argue *Bnf Abd*. *n* wrangling, argument.

†**dispeace** dissension, enmity, disquiet.

†**disperne** disperse, drive away.

door: gie someone the ~ (**in his face**) show someone the door, slam the door in someone's face *local*.

dunt out settle (a quarrel or misunderstanding) by discussion, thrash out.

eelist a cause of offence, disagreement or ill-feeling; a grievance; a ground for a quarrel.

eggle quarrel *Ork N.*

even, e'en: ~ one's wit to condescend to argue with.

†fair: it was nae mair than *etc* ~ **guid day and** ~ **guid een** *etc* they were barely on speaking terms.

far oot on bad terms, not friendly *local Mry-Fif.*

fa-tae a set-to, quarrel, row *now Sh Ork.*

flyte, *chf* ~ **wi** *now Ork Abd midLoth,* ~ **at** *local,* ~ **(up)on** *local* altercate, wrangle violently with. **flyting** scolding, quarrelling, employing abusive language.

fratch quarrel, argue, disagree *Dmf Rox.*

gae, go: ~ **by the** *or* **someone's door** pass someone's house without calling in, shun. ~ **on** make a fuss, talk at length in a badgering or quarrelsome way *local.*

gash argue bitterly *Ayr.*

giff-gaff bandy (words) *now local Inv-Bwk.*

grummle a grudge, grievance, quarrel *local Abd-S.*

gum a disagreement, dispute.

†habble quarrel, wrangle *chf S.*

haggle-bargain, haggle-baggle, †hargle-bargle wrangle, dispute, haggle *now Ags.*

haud, hald, hold a dispute, a tiff *now midLoth.*

heckle wrangle *now Sh midLoth Uls.*

heelie an affront, a slight.

hither an yon(t) estranged *now Mry midLoth.*

intae: that's ~ **ye** *etc of a cutting remark etc* that's one for ..

intil: be ~ *of a pointed remark* be a hit or thrust at (someone) *local Abd-Kcb.*

jirr *v* quarrel *now Abd.*

†kevel scold, wrangle *S.*

†kilfuddoch a meeting and discussion, a debate, a dispute *Ayr.*

knag: at the ~ **an the widdie** at variance, at loggerheads *NE.*

leuk, luck, look: not ~ **the road someone is on** take no interest in, ignore.

†mell come together in a **flyting.**

†miscontentment mutual bad feeling, discord.

†misken refuse to recognise, spurn, ignore.

†misknaw repudiate, ignore, disavow. ~**lage** refuse to acknowledge, disown, repudiate, neglect.

†misregard disregard, treat with disrespect, despise; ignore.

nip-lug back-biting, squabbling.

†nyte disown, abjure (a person).

outcast a quarrel *now Sh-Ags SW.*

outfa a quarrel *now Sh.*

†particular a private grievance or feud.

pat, pot: out like a ~ **fit** in a state of discord, not on speaking terms *NE.*

pervoo *of persons* stop keeping regular company with (someone), drop (a friend) *Abd.*

pilget *n* a quarrel, disagreement, wrangle *NE.* †*v freq of children* quarrel, wrangle, bicker.

†pingle *v* contend, compete; quarrel, disagree. *n* a disagreement, quarrel.

pit, put: ~ **someone by the door** turn someone away, reject, spurn *Sh Abd Uls.*

plea *n* a quarrel, disagreement, argument; strife, discord, enmity *now Mry Ags. v* quarrel, disagree, argue *now Ags.*

†plead a verbal dispute.

ploy a quarrel, disagreement, breach of the peace.

†provoke a provocation.

raggle wrangle, dispute *now Abd.*

rebat give a curt, brusque or discouraging reply *NE.*

†rebut, rabut repel, reject (something offered).

†rent a breach between persons.

saut, salt snub, treat severely.

scash *v* quarrel, squabble *Abd.* †*n, also* ~**le** a quarrel, dispute, brawl.

†scorn a snub, brusque rejection.

set a carry-on, wrangle, fuss *local Abd-Gall.*

sharrie quarrel, fight *NE.*

shirramuir a noisy row, rumpus *now NE.*

skew *v* fall out, disagree *NE. n* a quarrel, row *Mry Abd.*

sneck a cutting remark, snub *now Cai Ags Per.*

snifter a rebuff, quarrel *now Rox.*

snot snub, reprove *now local Inv-Rox.* ~**ter** a snub, rebuke *now nEC, SW, S.*

split a quarrel, rift.

splore a controversy, quarrel.

†spree a boisterous quarrel, a spirited argument.

†squall a row, disturbance, quarrel.

†staff: keep someone at (the) ~(**'s) end** keep someone at a distance, keep aloof from someone.

†strik, strike a quarrel, dispute.

strive (wi) quarrel, dispute (with) *now Sh NE.*

striven having quarrelled, at loggerheads, out of friendship *NE.*

†strunt strife, enmity, hostility.

sturt †*v* contend, make trouble *now Sh. n* contentious behaviour, *freq* ~ **and strife.**

thraw *v* **1** act perversely, quarrel, grumble *now NE local C.* **2** quarrel, contend (**with**) *now NE, local C, Rox. n* an argument, dispute, quarrel *now NE nEC, WC Rox.*

threap *v* argue, contend, be disputatious; quarrel *now Sh-Per SW*. *n* a dispute, quarrel *now Sh Abd Ags Rox*.

tift, tiff: *also* ~**er** a quarrel, dispute; the act of quarrelling *now local*.

tirr-wirr *n* a noisy quarrel, *now NE nEC*. *v* quarrel, fight noisily *Ags Per Stlg*.

tit-tat an argument, altercation *Cai*.

tuithy, toothy critical, acrimonious *now local Fif-Wgt*.

tulyie *n* **1** a quarrel, brawl, fight; a noisy contest, dispute; a struggle, turmoil *now local Sh-Bwk*. **2** a verbal quarrel, wrangle *now Sh Ork Mry Abd*. **3** †quarrelling, contention. *v* **1** harass; quarrel with. **2** quarrel, contend, fight *now Sh Ork Mry*. **3** quarrel verbally, argue, squabble *now Sh Ork Mry*. † ~-**mulie** a quarrel, broil, turmoil.

turn, tirn: ~ **to the door** put out of one's house, eject, expel *now Sh Cai Abd*.

twa words a discussion, argument, dispute *now Ags Per*.

†**umbeschew, umchew** avoid, shun.

†**unreconsiliat** unreconciled.

widdie: in(to) the ~ **necks** at loggerheads, in a violent altercation *Abd*.

†**twitters: be in** *or* **flee in (someone's)** ~ start a quarrel with, fly at.

worry a dispute, wrangle, argument *now Ags*.

†**yed** *verse* strife, wrangling.

†**yellyhooing** shouting and screaming, yelling *local WC, SW*.

†**yoke** start a dispute or quarrel **with**.

15.5.10 OPPOSITION

again in opposition to; in defiance of.

†**aganis** against.

ail: what ~**s ye** *etc* **at** what objection have you to? what grounds of complaint have you etc against?

†**back** put or force back.

†**brag** challenge, defy.

breed(th): i the ~ **o someone's face** *etc* to someone's face, in the face.

ca(ll) again oppose, contradict *now Ags Per*.

†**cheson** objection, exception, demur, *as* **without** *or* **but** ~.

conter oppose, contradict, thwart. **gae** ~ **to** go against (someone's wishes, expectations).

contrair *adj* contrary. *v* go contrary to, oppose, contradict.

†**contravaill** countervail.

deny refuse (to do something), *now esp* refuse to move etc *now Bnf Abd*.

difer ward off, resist.

†**disassent** refuse to agree **that**..

†**enchesone** objection, dissent.

fend a defence, resistance.

gainstand **1** withstand, oppose. **2** †offer resistance, be opposed **to**.

grunch grumble; object, refuse *now Rox*.

†**habbergaw** make objections.

haud, hald, hold: ~**again** opposition *now Abd*.

†**impung** impugn.

kicker: sit the ~, **stand the** ~**s (o)** resist, refuse to budge (for) or be disturbed (by) *NE*.

maugre act in despite of *NE*.

†**moot** protest, object.

na-say refuse, deny.

neck: (in) spite of one's ~ in defiance of one's efforts, wishes etc.

objeck object.

†**oppung** oppugn.

†**pairty** antagonistic, hostile **to**.

†**plead** contention, opposition.

†**quarrel, querel** dispute (a fact or claim), challenge the truth or validity of, take objection to.

†**rabel** oppose rebelliously.

†**sonyie** hesitate, delay, refuse.

stick up to stand up to, oppose defiantly.

stickle have scruples, raise objections.

stimie obstruct, thwart.

†**tap, top** oppose.

teeth: in spite of someone's ~ despite someone's wishes or efforts, in defiance of someone.

teethe face, stand up to, set one's teeth against *Bnf Abd*.

thorter *v* thwart, oppose. †*adj* obstructing, opposing. †*n* opposition, obstruction.

thraw thwart, oppose, cross *now NE nEC, WC*.

threap assert (something) positively, vehemently or persistently, *esp* against contradiction.

15.5.11 ABUSIVENESS

For angry outbursts, see 15.5.14; for terms of abuse, see 15.3.2 and 15.7.5.

abuise abuse.

back: † ~**hash, baghash** abuse, scold vigorously *Ags Per*. ~**-jaw** impudence, abusive language *Bnf Abd Lnk*.

bad-use *v* abuse *now Sh NE Ags*.

bard, baird a scurrilous person.

bemean disparage, humiliate.

ca(ll): ~ **someone for** abuse as being .., *chf* ~ **someone for everything** heap abuse on someone.

†**clesch** *v* abuse.

disperson treat with indignity, insult, abuse.

†**dispite: speak** ~(**s**) use contemptuous or malicious language.

drub scold, abuse *Abd Ags Fif.*

dunt a dig, insult.

flyting scolding, quarrelling, employing abusive language.

forflutten, †**forflitten** severely scolded, excessively abused.

ill *of conduct, language* bad, profane, malevolent. ~-**gab** use abusive language, abuse (a person) *local C.* ~-**jaw** coarse, abusive language *Sh N Kcb.* ~-**mou** vile language, a disposition to use such language, an abusive tongue *Bnf.* ~-**tongue** *n* an abusive tongue; bad language, abuse. *v* abuse. *Cai Mry Abd.* ~-**tongued** abusive, vituperative *N midLoth SW.* ~-**wind** abusive language *NE.*

injure abuse, insult.

jeedge swear, curse *NE.*

lack offence, injury; insult.

licht, light: ~**lie** *v, also* ~**lifie** *now NE Per* make light of, disparage, insult *now NE nEC Lnk.* †*n* the act of disparagement, an insult. † ~**lines** arrogance, contempt; an insult.

likeness: no to leave a body (in) the ~ **o a dog** call someone everything that is bad, defame someone's character.

misca call (a person) bad names, abuse verbally, denounce.

†**mislear (oneself to)** abuse, vilify *only Linlithgow.*

†**mislernit** *of speech* abusive.

†**mispersoun** abuse verbally.

randie a foul-mouthed, brawling, bad-tempered woman.

†**rebalk, rebaik** abuse, reproach.

scaul(d) 1 a scold, a scolding, abusive woman. 2 scolding, railing, abuse. †**scaldrie** abusive speech.

†**shout** shout at, greet with shouts (of insult).

snash *v* insult, speak impertinently to, sneer at. *n* abuse, hard words, impudence *Gen except Sh Ork.*

tinker, tinkie *NE Ags Per, now usu* **tink** *contemptuous term for a person* a foul-mouthed, vituperative, quarrelsome, vulgar person.

tinkler a coarse, foul-mouthed, abusive person.

tongue impudence, abuse, violent language *NE Ags WC, SW.*

up hill and doun dale *esp of someone pursuing another*

with abuse etc relentlessly, without restraint *Sh-Per.*

voo, vow curse, swear *Ork Abd.*

wallipend despise, abuse *chf NE.*

†**wary** *v* curse.

†**winze** a curse, imprecation.

15.5.12 REVENGE

†**aboot, about: be** ~ **wi** be even with, avenged on.

cauk, calk make (someone) pay dearly *now Bnf Abd.*

chape, cheap: be ~ **o** *or* **on** serve (someone) right: '*ye'e got your fairin, an I maun say I think ye're cheap o't.*'

day: get *or* **see** ~ **aboot wi** get one's own back on.

dirdum retribution.

even, e'en: be ~**s (with)** be even or quits (with) *now local EC.*

†**gar (someone) as gude** pay (someone) back, retaliate.

hairst: hae a day in ~ **wi someone, owe someone a day** *etc* **in** ~ have a score to settle with someone *now Abd Ags.*

†**mends: get a seing** ~ **of** see oneself revenged on.

peety, pity: it's a *or* **the** ~**o** *ironic* it serves (you etc) right *Sh Cai Ags Per.*

penny: get one's (flesh) ~(**s**)**worths (out) o** get one's own back on, revenge oneself on, get the better of *local.*

†**pey (someone) hame** give (someone) his deserts, repay in full.

price: be the ~ **o someone** *of an event or happening* serve someone right, be just what someone deserves.

saut, salt punish, take revenge on.

†**syth, syte: get one's heart's** ~ **of** *or* **on** be revenged on.

up wi even with, quits with *now Sh Ags.*

upsides: be ~ **wi, be** ~ **doun wi** *Cai Abd* be even with, have one's revenge on.

†**vengeable** inclined to take vengeance, cruel, destructive.

†**vindicable** vengeful, vindictive.

†**vindicate** exercise (wrath) in revenge.

win, wun: ~ **tae wi** be even with *Abd.*

†**wrake** suffering, punishment, vengeance. **wrack** wreak, give vent to (feelings of vengeance).

wraikful vengeful. **in wrake of** in revenge or punishment for.

15.5.13 MASTERY

back-water: gar someone's ee(n) stan (in) ~ reduce someone to a state of helplessness.

bang surpass, excel, beat, overcome. **~ster** a bully. **~strie** bullying behaviour.

bleck surpass, beat, excel *now Ags*.

boast †*n* a threatening, a menacing. *v* **1** utter threats, threaten *now Sh-N*. **2** command or drive with threats. **3** †announce with threats.

care: take ~ **o** be a match for *NE Ags*.

counger overawe, intimidate *NE, S*.

coup the creels foil the plans or get the better **of** *NE*.

danger power to harm *now Lnk*.

†**dantar** a subduer, controller.

dare, daur terrify, intimidate *now Abd*.

daunton overcome, subdue; intimidate *now Stlg Lnk*.

ding beat, get the better of *now local E*.

ee: put out a person's ~ obtain an advantage over, supplant *Gen except Sh Ork*.

†**evert** overthrow (a person) in an argument.

gae, go: ~ **ower** get the better of (someone) *local Sh-Fif*.

gree pre-eminence, supremacy, first place, victory in a contest; the palm, the prize, *freq* **win** *or* **bear the** ~ *now literary*.

grip *v* get the better of, outsmart *NE*. *n* grasp, control, mastery, power.

hair: a ~ **in someone's** *or* **the neck** a shortcoming etc which gives another a hold over one; such a hold *now Ags Gsw Ayr*.

hatter treat roughly, bully *now Sh*.

haud, hald: ~ **doun** burden, oppress, afflict, *freq* **hauden doon**.

†**hause: hald in the** ~ have in one's power, at one's mercy.

heft: hae (baith) (the) ~ **an (the) blade (to haud) in one's hand** have complete control (of a situation), have the whip hand *Abd*.

king: be a ~ **tae** surpass, be superior to *now Sh-C Slk*.

mair: maister *or* **mistress and** ~ an autocratic, domineering master or mistress, one with the whip hand *EC Slk*.

†**malverse** *v* betray the trust attaching to an office by acting oppressively.

maugre act in despite of; master, worst *NE*. **mag-**erful** domineering, wilful *chf NE*. †~ **a person's hede, neck** *etc* in spite of a person's opposition or resistance.

maun master, control, domineer *now Sh*.

merciment the discretion, disposal, mercy (of a person *in gen*), *chf* **in someone's** ~ at his mercy.

neb: lead by the ~ lead by the nose.

necessitat necessitate, oblige, compel (a person to do something).

new master, oppress, curb *NE*.

nip get the better of (in bargaining), cheat *now Gall*.

†**nither** oppress, vex.

†**obleege, oblige, oblis** compel, constrain.

ool treat harshly, ill-use, bully; wreck the health or spirits of.

outding beat, exceed, surpass *now NE*.

ower: **~ance** control, mastery *now Rox*. †**may** ~ have power over, have mastery or control of: *'gif ony of thame may our his falow be strenth'*. ~ **somebody's heid** at the expense of someone, in spite of someone, without consulting the wishes or rights of someone *now local Ork-SW*.

owercap be superior to, beat *now Sh*.

owergae surpass, excel *now Sh*.

owergang overcome, oppress, dominate *now Sh*.

†**owerhail** oppress.

†**owerhan** the upper hand; mastery.

owermaister overmaster.

ower-pooer overpower *now Sh Cai*.

†**Paddy: come (the)** ~ **ower** get the upper hand of by a trick, bamboozle.

pall, pawl exceed, surpass, *chf* ~ **aa** beat everything *Sh Ork NE*.

†**pass** surpass, excel.

peep: put someone's gas at *or* **in a** ~ put someone in his place *Gen except Sh Ork*.

peter: come the ~ **ower** act in a domineering way over, dictate to.

pit, put: ~ **at** make demands on, press.

poustie power, strength, force, authority, control.

povereese reduce to a condition of poverty; impoverish, over-exploit *now Ork N, SW*.

raivel, ravel bamboozle, outwit *Sh Ork Mry*.

ringin domineering.

shore *v* threaten, use menaces (to). †*n, also* **shoring** menace, threatening.

sit on a person's coat-tail(s) depend on or make use of someone else for one's own convenience or advantage *now Bnf-Per*.

snuil, snool subdue, keep in subjection, humiliate, reprove, snub *now Ork*.

†**succumb** bring low, overwhelm.

swatch: tak *etc* **the** ~ **o** take the measure of, be a match for *now Bnf.*

threat 1 †press, urge *esp* by threatenings. **2** threaten.

†trouble, tribble oppress.

†tyranfull tyrannical, tyrannous. **tirranitie** tyranny.

†vanquish, vencus excel, surpass.

†vice treat arrogantly or oppressively.

†violent treat with violence, use coercion on, ride roughshod over the wishes of (a person).

whummle, whammle get the better of *now Fif.*

will: get, hae *or* **take one's** ~(**s**) **o** get one's way with, do what one likes with, have at one's disposal or mercy *now local.*

win, wun: ~ **in ahin** get the better of, outsmart *NE.* ~ **tae wi** overtake, make up on *Abd.*

worse get the better of, worst, overcome, outdo *now local Sh-Ayr.*

†yoke burden, oppress.

15.5.14 SCOLDING

†admoneis admonish.

antle (on) keep on repeating a complaint, nag, grumble *Cai Dmf.*

at: be ~ **someone about something** keep finding fault with.

†aweband a check, curb, restraint, deterrent.

†backhash, baghash abuse, scold vigorously *Ags, Per.*

bairge speak loudly and angrily; scold loudly *now Bnf.*

†banter scold, drive away by scolding.

bard, baird a scold, a noisy woman.

†bauchle denounce openly; disgrace, discredit (publicly).

†belgh an outburst.

bilsh speak loudly or angrily.

birkie *n* a sharp-tongued, quick-tempered person, *usu* a woman *Edb. adj* sharp-tongued, tart *now Per.*

blash a torrent of words *now Bnf Ags Lnk.*

blast shout loudly, declaim in violent language *now Bnf.*

†blason proclaim with reproach.

boast scold, reprove *now Sh-N.*

bows: take a person throw the ~ take a person severely to task *Bnf Abd.*

†brag reproach, scold.

braid, broad, *chf* ~ **out** unrestrainedly, indiscreetly.

branks: put the ~ **on** restrain, cut (a person) down to size, checkmate *local Ork-WC.*

breengin wilful, pushing, sharp-tongued *now local.*

cabal find fault *Bnf.*

caird *n* a person who scolds *local N. v* abuse, scold *NE Per.*

cast: ~ **something at someone** reproach someone with something *Abd Ags Fif.* ~ **a clod at** reproach *N.* ~ **up,** *chf* ~ **something up to someone** reproach someone with something; cast something in someone's teeth.

chackart term of affectionate reproof *Bnf Abd.*

challenge reprove, find fault with *local Bnf-Kcb.*

chaw 1 a cutting retort *now local Ags-Kcb.* **2** a jaw, a lecture, reprimand *N.*

check rebuke, reprove.

†cheson find fault with, blame, accuse.

†chestee reprove.

claver a fuss, murmur *now Fif.*

clearin a scolding.

coffee: gie (someone) his ~ scold roundly, chastise.

come-again a scolding, reproof *NE.*

†conray, cumray handle or deal with severely.

counger keep in order, scold *NE, WC.*

†cow upbraid, scold, rebuke (one's equal or superior).

cowdrum: get ~ get one's deserts; get a beating or severe scolding *NE.*

craw in someone's crap irritate, annoy or henpeck someone; give cause for regret *now Ags Fif.*

creed a severe rebuke *local.*

crub curb *now local Bnf-EC.* ~ **in aboot** keep under strict discipline *Bnf Abd.*

cunner scold *WC.*

†daunton bring under control; suppress.

dichens a reproof, *chf* **get one's** *or* **gie someone his** ~ *now Rox.*

dicht scold, reproach *now Abd Lnk.*

din make a loud noise or outcry.

ding 1 drive (mad etc) *now Bnf Abd Slg.* **2** †drive into the mind, din into someone's ears.

dirdum a scolding.

dixie a sharp scolding, *chf* **get one's** *or* **gie someone his** ~(**s**) *now Ork Bnf Abd.*

doon: †~**leuk** a displeased look, disapproval. ~**set(ting)** a scolding *now Bnf.*

dreel *v* scold, rebuke *local. n* a scolding, a dressing-down *local Cai-Ags.*

drib scold *now Bnf.*

driffle *v* scold *now Bnf Abd. n* a scolding *Bnf Abd.*

drub scold, abuse *Abd Ags Fif.*

drum major *n* a domineering woman. *v* boss, order around *now Abd Edb.*

†**enchesone** challenge, accuse, blame.

eruction a violent outburst.

fa(ll) oot (up)on lose one's temper with, speak angrily to *Abd Ags.*

faut, fault find fault with, blame *local N-S.* **hae a** ~ **til** have a fault to find with *local.*

fingers: get it ower the ~ be reprimanded.

fit, foot, fute: get up one's ~ be scolded *now NE Ags Dmf.* **gie (someone) up his** *or* **the** ~ scold, rebuke *now local.*

flee, fly: ~ **intae** severely rebuke, scold *NE midLoth Rox.*

flyte *v, chf* ~ **wi** *now Ork Abd midLoth,* ~ **at** *local,* ~ **(up)on** *local* scold, chide, rail at *local Abd-Rox.* *n* 1 a scolding *now Sh Arg Ayr.* 2 a scolding match *now Sh midLoth Bwk.* **flyter** a scold; a person who engages in **flyting. flyting** scolding, quarrelling, employing abusive language.

forflutten, †**forflitten** severely scolded, excessively abused.

gan on aboot make a fuss about *Fif SW.*

gansel *n* a disagreeable comment, a scolding. *v* scold, upbraid.

get on attack verbally, scold *local.*

goller, gulder a verbal outburst, as of oaths *now Ork Wgt.*

gollie scold *Ayr.*

gouster a violent outburst *Sh Ork Dmf.*

gowl scold angrily *now Fif Ayr.*

haims, hems: hae *or* **pit the** ~ **on (someone)** curb, keep in order *Ross Abd C.*

haud, hald, hold: ~ **again** hold back, check, resist *chf NE Ags.* ~ **at** urge on by exhortation, criticism etc, nag *now Cai NE Ayr.*

heckle *v* speak sharply and reprovingly (to), scold severely, wrangle *now Sh midLoth Uls.* *n* a severe beating, sharp criticism; a person who gives this *now Dmf.*

heid, head: get one's ~ **in one's hands, gie someone his** ~ **in his hands** *usu in threats* receive *or* give a severe scolding.

hey-ma-nanny: get (one's) *or* **give** ~ **(be)** scold(ed) vigorously *now NE.*

horn: have one's ~ **in somebody's hip** criticize severely, be antagonistic towards *now Ork NE Arg.*

hurry a scolding *now Abd Fif.*

intae: be ~ find fault with, scold (a person) *now local.* **that's** ~ **ye** *etc of a cutting remark etc* that's one for ..

intil: be ~ *of a pointed remark* be a hit or thrust at (someone) *local Abd-Kcb.*

†**kail:** ~ **wife** a scold, a coarse brawling woman.
get one's *or* **gie someone his** ~ **through the**

reek *now Sh-Per,* **get** *or* **hae one's** ~ **het** *now NE Per* get or give someone a severe scolding.

kame *NE Lnk,* **comb** *NE Lnk, also* ~ **someone's hair, head** *etc* **for** *or* **til him** *local NE-S* scold.

ken o't *freq in threats* know by dire experience, suffer for one's actions *local.*

†**kevel** scold, wrangle *S.*

kittle chide, reprove *now Abd midLoth.*

lesson something from which one may learn; a rebuke etc aimed at preventing a repetition of the offence.

licht, light: ~ **on, to, til** upbraid *now local.*

lowp up at flare up angrily at, chide sharply *Sh NE Ayr.*

lowse, loose *specif of anger or scolding* let oneself go, explode; break **out on** (someone) *now local Sh-midLoth.*

lug: get one's *or* **gie someone his head in his hands** *or* **lap and his** ~**s to play wi** get or give someone a severe dressing-down *local Ork-Gall.*
get one's ~ **in one's luif** be severely taken to task *now Ags.*

Maggie Robb a scolding shrewish woman.

†**mote** find fault with.

nail scold *chf Rox.*

narg *v* keep grumbling, nag *now Sh-Cai.* *n* nagging *now Sh.*

nat a small-sized, sharp-tempered person *now Sh Abd.*

natter *v* chatter, *esp* peevishly, nag, grouse. *n* 1 grousing, nagging talk. 2 a bad-tempered, nagging person *Sh NE, SW, S.*

nebbie biting, nippy, sharp *now Fif WC Kcb.*

need: hae mair ~ **to do** *censorious* ought rather to do, would be better employed doing.

new master, oppress, curb.

nizzin a sharp reproof.

nurring fault-finding *now Sh Cai.*

†**object, objeck** mention in reproach or disparagement.

onset a scolding.

owergaeing a severe reproof *Sh NE Ags.*

pallion a scold *NE.*

peety, pity: it's a *or* **the** ~ **o** *as a threat* it's a bad lookout for *Sh Cai Ags Per.*

phrase: mak a ~ make song and dance, make an outcry.

pin a scolding *now Wgt Slk.*

pipe: pit oot someone's ~ put someone in his place, thwart someone.

pit, put: ~ **frae** 1 prevent, hinder, stop. 2 put (a person) off (a thing or person), give (a person) a distaste for (a thing) *Abd Uls.*

plaister a dressing-down, swearing *now Sh Cai.*

pouk at annoy, harass; criticize *now Kcb.*

puist criticize.

quarrel, †querel find fault with (a person), reprove, rebuke.

rack stock: tak owre (the) ~ take severely to task *Bnf Abd.*

rag scold, reproach severely *now local Bnf-Uls.*

rage at *or* **on** scold, berate *Gen except Sh Ork.* **raging** a scolding *Gen except Sh Ork.*

rally (on) scold, speak angrily to *local.*

†randie behave belligerently, scold.

rant make a great noisy fuss, complain at length *Cai Kcb Uls.*

rebaghle disparagement, reproach.

†rebalk, rebaik abuse, reproach.

rebook rebuke.

reboun(d) a reprimand, severe rebuke *Abd-Stlg.*

†rebut, rabut *v* revile, rebuke, reproach. *n* a rebuke, reproach.

†redargue blame, reprove.

redd: ~**ing-up** a scolding, rebuke *local Sh-Kcb.* ~ **one's crap** get something off one's chest *now Abd.* ~ **up** *v, also* ~ **out** scold, give a dressing-down to *local Sh-SW. n* a scolding, rebuke *now local NE-SW.*

reek: ~**in lum, a sour** ~ **in the house** a source of annoyance which drives one from the house, *esp* a nagging wife *now local Sh-Fif.* **get (**or **gie someone) it het and** ~**in** be scolded severely, scold someone severely *Sh Per.*

reird *n* a loud outburst of scolding *now Rox.* †*v* scold loudly.

repree *Abd,* **†repreif** *v* reprove. *n* a reproof.

†reproche recall (*eg* a promise) with reproaches.

†ring rant, storm, behave in a domineering way (towards).

rouse on become enraged at *NE nEC wLoth.*

†rummiss, rummish protest loudly, make an uproar.

saut, salt: ~**er** a shrew, termagant *local Abd-Per.* **†lay (something) in** ~ *freq in threats of something unpleasant* lay aside, keep in reserve.

say awa(y) say on, hold forth, speak one's mind *now local Sh-Per.*

scam scold severely *now Bnf Per.*

scance (at) criticize, reproach *now Cai.*

scaud 1 *also* **scald** †*of words, language* burn, scald. **2** cause grief or pain to, punish *now Ags WC.*

scaul(d) *n* **1** scolding, railing, abuse. **2** a scold, a scolding, abusive woman. *v* scold.

†scomfish, scunfis discomfit.

scourge a brawling, domineering woman *now SW.*

†scoutherin reproving (severely), blistering (with rebuke). **scoudrum** chastisement *Bnf Abd.*

scronach make a great outcry or fuss, grouse *now Bnf.*

sederunt, sedarin an unpleasant interview, a scolding, a dressing-down *now Abd Ags Per.*

set awa a row, scolding *local NE-S.*

shairp, sharp sharp. **be** ~ **upon** be hard or severe on.

shake one's crap give vent to grievances *NE.*

†shaw, show inflict (shame etc).

sherrack raise a riot about (a person), incite a mob against (a person) by publicly reviling and denouncing him *now WC.*

shirramuir a dressing-down *now NE.*

shirrow a shrew.

shore scold, upbraid *now Sh.*

sicker securely under control, held firm *now Ags.* †~**ly** sharply, severely.

siege scold severely, storm **at** *NE.*

sloan a sharp retort, a snub, reproof *Rox.*

snag nag, grumble, taunt *now Kcdn.*

†snib *v* check, restrain, reprove, punish. *n* a check, rebuke, rebuff.

snite someone's niz take someone down a peg *now SW.*

†snod put to rights morally, put (someone) in his place, punish, defeat.

snot snub, reprove *now local Inv-Rox.* ~**ter** a snub, rebuke *now nEC, SW, S.*

snuil, snool subdue, keep in subjection, humiliate, reprove, snub *now Ork.*

soorldab: gie someone his ~ put paid to, finish off *local C.*

†soosh taunt, upbraid *Ayr.*

sort deal with by rebuke or punishment, put (a person) in his place, scold.

souse reprove, put (a person) in his place, silence *now Ags Per.*

spunk up become heated, flare up in anger or passion *now Fif Wgt.*

†squabash silence (a person) by demolishing his arguments, pretensions etc, squash.

†stang: ride the ~ **on** hold up to public ridicule.

stap: tak a ~ **oot o someone's bicker** *or* **cog** humble someone.

†stripe a scourge.

tap, top: never off someone's ~ always chiding or criticizing, continually quarrelling with someone. **on someone's** ~ attacking, severely reproving someone.

targe *v* scold severely *now local Stlg-SW. n* a violent, scolding woman, a shrew, virago *local Ork-Uls.*

~**r** a violent, quarrelsome, domineering person, *esp* a woman *local Cai-Kcb*. **targin** a scolding *now Stlg SW*.

tatter scold *now S*.

tear †rage at. ~**er** *of a woman* a shrew, vixen *now Sh Cai Lnk*. ~**in** an angry reproof, a thorough dressing-down *Kcdn nEC Lnk*.

telling a warning, admonition, lesson, *freq* **let that be a** ~ **tae ye, take a** ~.

†tench ? a taunt, reproach.

tether, tedder: put a ~ **to someone's tongue** silence a person, restrain someone from speaking *now Sh Cai*.

thackin a severe scolding.

thank: (aa) one's *or* **the** ~ *used in reproach* the thanks for or recognition of a service, which the speaker feels is inadequate *now local Ork-Kcb*.

threap assert (something) positively, vehemently or persistently, *esp* against contradiction. ~ **at, wi** *etc* nag at, be insistent with *now SW*. ~ **down someone's throat** *etc*, **(up)on** *etc* **someone** force one's opinion(s) on someone, try to make someone believe ..

through: ~-**gaun,** ~-**gaen** a strict and censorious examination of a person's conduct *now local NE-Rox*. ~-**pittin** a severe rating or cross-examination *now Stlg WC, SW*. **gie someone** ~ **the wud, laddie** give someone a severe scolding *SW, S*. **throu-the-muir** a severe dressing down, a violent row *now local NE-Stlg*.

thuddin a severe scolding *now local Stlg-Rox*.

ticht, tight strict, severely critical *now Cai*.

time-o-day *ironic* a severe reproof *now Lnk Ayr*.

tinking an abusive scolding, a slanging *Bnf Abd*.

tirr-wirr *n* a scolding match *now NE nEC*. *v* speak snappishly *Ags Per Stlg*.

tongue scold, revile.

†trensand trenchant, cutting.

turn, tirn a rebuff, set-back, a heading-off *now Cai*.

upcast *v* taunt, reproach, bring up against someone, allege as a fault *local Sh-WC*. *n* a taunt, reproach, ground or occasion for criticism *now Sh-N Fif Lnk*.

upreddin a scolding *now Sh Fif wLoth Dmf*.

wauken, waken lose one's temper with someone, break out **on** someone *now Ork N*. **waukenin** a severe reproof, a dressing-down *local Sh-SW*.

whin, whun: gie *or* **tak (someone) through the** ~**s** give (someone) a dressing-down *local EC-S*.

whudder bluster or rage like the wind *now Abd*.

†wide *of speech* unrestrained, violent.

word, wird: speak a ~ **to** rebuke, admonish, advise *now Sh Cai*.

wyte *v* blame, impute blame or guilt to (a person or thing), accuse a (person) of responsibility for something *now local*. *n* blame, reproach, responsibility for some error or mischief. ~ **someone for, o** *or* **wi** blame someone for (something), accuse someone of (something).

yabble, yabber *now EC* scold, be querulous *chf Loth*.

yaff chide, scold, criticize *now local Loth-S*.

yammer *v* harp on, keep insisting. *n* a great outcry, clamour, incessant talk *now Ork, NE-S*.

yap, yaup *v* chatter, nag, speak querulously, harp on. *n* incessant talking, *usu* implying nagging.

yatter *v* nag, harp on querulously, scold *local*. *n* (continual) scolding, grumbling *now Ork Ags*. ~**in,** ~**y** fretful, querulous, scolding *now Sh*.

yerk nag, find fault *now Sh*.

yeuk: (gar someone) claw *or* **scart where it's no** ~**ie** *or* **†where he** *etc or* **it disna** ~ *freq in threats* (make someone) smart or regret what he *etc* has done.

yirp harp on something, wrangle, make a fuss or complain *local Sh-Lnk*.

yirr make an outcry, keep complaining *now Sh*.

yokin a severe dressing-down *now NE*.

15.5.15 SKILL

airt art, skill.

†attent attentive. **attentfully, attentlie** attentively.

billy, *usu* **the** ~ a person etc particularly suited to, good at or characterized by something.

bonnilie prettily; well, satisfactorily.

breid: he *etc* **disna aet the** ~ **o idleseat** he etc works hard for his living *local Bnf-Lnk*.

†bussie busy.

ca(ll) through work with a will *now local Bnf-Lnk*.

can skill, knowledge, ability *chf N*.

canny *adj* skilful, dexterous. *adv* cautiously, carefully. ~ **ways** *NE Ags*, ~**wise** *now Sh Ags* cautiously, gently.

capstride anticipate; perform a task sooner or better than (another).

cawpable capable *NE Ags Fif*.

claw aff *or* **awa** do (something) with speed or eagerness *NE*.

†cleverus nimble, quick.

†cliftie clever, active, nimble.

come speed make progress, get on quickly.

crafty skilful, ingenious, clever *now local*.

437

dock-nail any person indispensable to the efficiency of a job *now Abd*.

†**doucht** power, strength, ability.

dreel work quickly and smoothly *now Cai*.

effeckwal effectual *now Sh Ags*.

eident assiduous, diligent, busy; conscientious, careful, attentive.

†**exercit** exercised, made expert, experienced.

far seen deeply skilled *now Ags Uls*.

feckfu effective, capable, efficient.

feerich ability, activity *now Bnf Abd*.

†**feit** clever, adroit.

few show promise or aptitude.

fordersome active, not slack *now Abd*.

gate a knack *now local Sh-Dmf*.

†**genie** inherent ability, natural bent *chf Ayr*.

†**giftie** a sense of power, an ability.

gleg adroit *local*. †**~ly** smartly, skilfully, adroitly.

graithly well, properly, successfully; carefully, attentively; readily, promptly.

guid gear (gangs) in sma buik applied to a small but capable person *local Abd-Rox*.

†**habile** having ability, power or competence; fit, competent **for** *or* **to**; able, competent (to do etc). **habilitie** ability.

hae, have: ~ **easy** *etc* **dain** be able to do easily etc *now Sh NE Ags*.

hail, whole: ~**-tear** at full speed *local Abd-Wgt*.

handy dexterous, skilful.

†**hende(ly)** skilful, pleasant.

hing: ~ **in** carry out a task with energy, get on with a job, persevere; hurry *local Sh-Kcb*. ~**er-in** a person who perseveres, a conscientious, hardworking person.

†**hire: as they were hyrit** (run etc) willingly, eagerly, speedily.

†**huilie** moderate, slow, cautious, careful *orig only* ~ **pace** *or* **speid**.

†**idoneus** fit, competent, suitably qualified.

in alert, attentive *NE Ags midLoth Kcb*.

kemper a person who strives or contends, a fighter, one who strives to outdo his fellows, a keen worker.

kepper a person who is good at catching *local*.

kittle cunning, adept, skilful *now Ags*.

knackie adroit, deft, ingenious, skilful.

†**laborous** laborious, industrious.

†**latchin** tardiness, loitering, *chf* **without laching**.

like, lik: ~**ly** capable or competent in manner *local EC-S*.

†**listly** *chf verse* skilfully; cunningly, craftily.

lowse, loose set to with vigour (**on** a task etc).

†**maister of, in(to)** a person who is skilled or adept at (doing) something.

muithlie in a soft, smooth way.

†**nait** quick and effective, deft. ~**ly** skilfully, cleverly.

†**necessar** giving necessary or useful service.

†**nobill** distinguished for ability.

†**painful** painstaking, laborious, assiduous, diligent.

particular clean, hygenic, *esp* in cooking *local*.

penurious, perneurious attentive to detail, scrupulous, fastidious *NE*.

perjink *adj* exact, precise, scrupulously careful, fussy. *adv* primly, fastidiously, in a precise and careful way.

pingling painstaking, meticulous *local*.

pludisome dogged, persevering, painstaking *now NE*.

†**ply** apply (oneself) to (a task), work hard and perseveringly.

point, pint: ~**ed** precise, (over-)attentive to detail, demanding; punctual, exact *Ork, local N, S*. ~**edly** accurately, punctiliously, punctually, immediately *now Ags*.

poustie 1 power, strength, force, authority, control. **2** †ability to do or effect something, capacity, might.

†**practicate** practised, experienced, skilled.

†**prattickit** practised, versed.

profite proficient, skilful, expert *now Bnf*.

†**proper** thoroughly.

purpose *n* efficiency, neatness, tidiness *now Ork Uls*. *adj* well-ordered, tidy, methodical; tidy-looking *Sh-nEC Uls*. ~**-like** neat, tidy, methodical, efficient *Gen except Sh Ork*.

†**quent** *adj* skilful, cunning. *adv* skilfully, cunningly.

†**redd, rad:** *also* ~**-handit** quick and skilful (with one's hands).

ringin forcefully, with ease *Bnf*.

†**schapen** naturally fitted **for**.

†**sicker** *adj* having sure mastery (**of** an art). *adv* accurately, precisely.

skeel: ~**y** skilled, experienced, practised *now NE, C*. **hae** ~ **o** be experienced in, have practice in.

skelp do (a piece of work) vigorously, rattle off *now Kcb*.

slee, sly skilled, clever, expert. †~ **in** *or* **of** skilled at.

slicht 1 sleight, craft, cunning, skill. **2** the trick, method, or knack (of doing something) *now Stlg*. † ~**fully** cunningly.

†**solicit, solist** careful.

swick, sweek the knack or ability to do (something).

tent: ~**ie,** *also* †**tent** watchful; attentive; heedful. †~**ily** attentively, with care, gently. †~**ive** attentive. **tak ~ o** take (good) care of, heed.

thocht, thought: †**thochtful on** careful of. ~**ie** heedful, attentive.

thrang busily, assiduously.

through-pit energy, activity, capacity for or progress at work *now Sh Abd Per Dmf.*

ticht, tight competent, capable, alert, vigorous.

up wi equal to, fit for, capable of *now Cai Ags.*

virtue, †**vertu** industry, diligence. †**vertusly** with great skill or excellence.

warklike industrious *now Sh.*

warslin energetic, hardworking.

weel: ~-**handit** good with one's hands, deft; energetic in small matters. †~ **seen** well-versed, proficient, very knowledgeable **in.** †**weill usit** well practised or exercised.

†**yare** *adv* quickly, promptly; well thoroughly.

15.5.16 BAD WORKMANSHIP

For bad housekeeping etc, see also 15.4.5.

bauchle distort, spoil. **mak a ~ o** make a botch of.

blaud damage, spoil by harsh or careless treatment, harm, injure.

bluiter do work in a bungling way.

blunk spoil, mismanage.

bootch *v* botch, bungle, muddle. *n* a botch, bungle, muddle *Bnf Abd.*

britchin: sit in the ~(**s**) not do one's fair share of work *now local Ork-Kcb.*

broggle botch, bungle.

broke handle carelessly or unskilfully; spoil.

bucker *v* make a mess of, bungle *Bnf Abd. n* a mess, bungling *Bnf Abd.*

bullox spoil, make a mess of.

bummle 1 a person who reads, sings or plays badly *now Bnf.* **2** a bungle, mess *now local Bnf-Kcb.* ~**r** a blundering person, a bungler *now Cai.* **bamling, bummlin** clumsy, careless.

clorach work in a slovenly way *NE.*

connach *n* a botch *NE. v* waste; spoil.

corbie messenger a dilatory or unfaithful messenger *now Bnf Fif.*

cowan an unskilled or uninitiated person.

cuil, cool: ~-**the-loom** a lazy worker *chf S.*

daidler a trifler *now Fif.*

disabuse *v* misuse, damage; spoil *now Abd. n* damage, bad usage *Abd.*

driddle spill, dribble, let fall through carelessness.

durk bungle, ruin (a job etc).

fa(ll) through 1 make a botch of, mismanage *now Abd.* **2** abandon (a task) from negligence or laziness *now Ags.*

fang without one's usual spirit or skill.

fauchle *v* work lazily, listlessly or ineffectually *Cai Bnf Gall. n* a slow inept worker, a bungler *now SW.*

feckless ineffective, weak, incompetent. ~**ness** weakness, incompetence.

ficher a fiddling, inept way of working *Bnf Abd.*

†**forsume** neglect, misuse.

fouter a slacker, a muddling, aimless person. ~**ie** fussy, inept.

†**fruster** ineffective, useless.

fushion, fooshion: ~**less** *of actions, speech, writing etc* without substance, dull, uninspired *now Abd C.*

gae through ither make a mess of things *NE-Fif.*

Glesca screwdriver a hammer *now Per Fif Lnk.*

goor make a mess of, spoil *now Kcb.*

greenhorn a raw inexperienced person, a simpleton.

gutter *n* a stupid, awkward, untidy or messy worker *local Cai-Dmf. v* do something in a dirty, slovenly or unskilful way; potter, tinker, fritter away time *local N-S.*

haimmer, hammer *n* **1** †clumsy, noisy working. **2** a clumsy, noisy person *Bnf Ayr. v* work or walk in a clumsy, noisy way *chf N.*

hairy *esp of work* untidy, rough, slovenly *chf Kcb Dmf.*

haister †rush, scamp (a job). ~**ed** ill-done, scamped.

haiver make a fuss about nothing, make a pretence of being busy *now Ayr Uls.*

hamrel an awkward person *chf Abd.*

handless awkward, clumsy, incompetent, slow.

hash *v* spoil, destroy, deface. *n* work done in a hasty careless way *now local Ork-Kcb.* ~**er** a careless, hustling person; a workman who does fast but rough-and-ready work *local NE-Kcb.* ~**ie** slapdash, careless, slovenly *now local.* ~**ter** *n* work done in a slovenly way, or badly arranged; a person who works thus *chf Uls. v* work in a hurried, slovenly and wasteful way *Renfr Ayr.*

hatter work in a careless, slovenly or haphazard way *now Rox.*

hawm (ower) work in a slovenly way *Bnf.*

heesty hasty.

439

Hieland, Highland uncouth, unskilled, inelegant, rough-and-ready.

hing, hang delay, hover indecisively; shirk *now Ags Fif Arg.* ~ **the cat** *or* **cleek** work slowly or to rule; lounge about, hold things up *Fif Ags.*

hint-han(d) dilatory, careless, late.

†**hudder, huther** act in a confused or hasty way; work clumsily or hastily. **hudd(e)rin** awkward, clumsy.

hushle work in a careless or slovenly way *now Sh.*

huther an untidy worker *now Lnk Dmf Rox.*

ill 1 awkward, inexpert, having difficulty in *local.* **2** bad, unsatisfactory, ineffective *now Sh Ork Abd.* ~**-set** be unsuitable for *now Abd.*

inadvertence negligence, carelessness.

jamph trifle, slack (at) *NE.*

jauk idle, dawdle, slack *now Bnf Kcb.*

jeck neglect (work).

jotter work in a dilatory fashion *now midLoth Bwk.*

jottle appear busy without achieving much *now midLoth.*

jouk shirk *now local Abd-Ags.*

keeger mix up messily, mess about, work in a slovenly or ineffective way *Bnf Abd.*

keeroch stir or poke about messily; work awkwardly *now Abd.* **kweerichin** awkward and unskilful *Abd.*

kipper pile or stack **up** carelessly *now Abd.*

kirning footling, inefficient *NE Ags.*

†**laish** slack, negligent.

†**lang, long:** ~ **o(f)** slow in, dilatory about.

latch be negligent; lag, procrastinate *now NE.* †**lacheand** lagging, negligent.

late tardy in (doing something).

maffling procrastination, bungling *Dmf.*

maggle 1 spoil by over-handling *SW.* **2** †mutilate or botch (a literary work etc). †**magglit** botched.

maig spoil by over-handling *S.*

mak a munsie o reduce to a ridiculous or sorry state, spoil, bungle *NE.*

malagruize dishevel, disarrange, spoil *chf NE.*

mank mutilate; deface; spoil; botch (cloth). ~**it** mutilated, maimed *now Abd Edb.*

massacker spoil (something) by mishandling or rough treatment *local.*

mauchle botch; act or work clumsily, exert oneself to no purpose *now Wgt.*

†**miscook** bungle, mismanage.

†**misfare** impair, bring to ruin; mismanage.

misguggle handle roughly or clumsily; rumple; bungle; hack *now Bnf Fif.*

mislippen neglect, overlook *Gen except Sh Ork.*

†**mismaggle** spoil *N Fif.*

moger *v* work in a slovenly or messy way, botch (a piece of work) *N, WC. n* a muddle, mess, bungle *Cai WC.*

ower, over: ~**ly** *adv* carelessly, superficially, in a casual manner. *adj* superficial, casual, careless *now Abd.*

Paisley screw a screw driven home with a hammer instead of a screwdriver, suggesting laziness *WC.* ~**driver** a hammer *WC.*

palaver, palaiver *now local Ork-Per* waste time, trifle, make a great deal of a small task *now Sh Per WC.*

partle waste (time), work in a half-hearted way, trifle.

pauchle work ineffectually, bungle, potter *Fif Loth Gsw.* **be in a** ~ be in a chaotic, disorganized state, be behind with one's work *Mry Fif Uls.*

†**peeferin** trifling, feckless, ineffectual.

peister work in a lethargic half-hearted way.

†**perfunctorious** perfunctory.

peuchle, pyocher *Sh, NE* fuss about or work ineffectually, make a poor attempt at something *now Sh.*

peuther fuss about doing nothing, fumble, make a great show of working *Ork Ags Uls.*

picher work in an unplanned and disorganized way, muddle along *now NE.* ~**in** fumbling, ineffectual, unmethodical *now NE.*

pingle trifle, dabble or meddle **with**, work in a lazy, ineffectual way *now S.*

pirl, purl work idly or half-heartedly *now Mry Bnf.*

plaister *n* a botched or mismanaged job, a mess, shambles *local Ags-Uls. v* work in a slovenly, slapdash way, mess around *local N-Dmf.*

platch work in a sloppy way, potter *Sh Per S.*

plowster an incompetent, messy worker, a bungler *now Rox.*

plowter, pleuter, ploiter *v* **1** work idly or aimlessly, potter or fiddle **about**. **2** make a mess of, spoil *now Sh Abd. n* **1** a botched job, an exhibition of slovenliness or inefficiency. **2** a messy inefficient worker, a muddler *now C.*

plype, plyper dabble or work messily and carelessly in a liquid or some wet material *NE Ags.*

poach work in an aimless or messy way **at**, mess **about** *now S.*

powk dig or excavate in a careless, clumsy way *Bnf Ags.*

puddle *v* work in a muddling, inefficient way, muddle along, mess about *NE Ags Gall Uls. n* an untidy or disorganized worker, a muddler, bungler *now Ags.*

ramstoorie vigorous but slapdash, rough-and-ready *Kcdn-Stlg.*

†**reckless, rackless** neglect; be negligent or heedless of. ~**ly** through carelessness; accidentally.

rhymeless irresponsible, reckless, ineffective *now Bnf.*

†**roid** roughly or hurriedly made, not well finished.

ruit, root work in a clumsy, ineffective way, *freq* **reet and fyke** *Cai.*

rummlin slapdash.

sair, sore: ~ **hand** a mess, a piece of unskilled workmanship *now Ayr.*

†**sairie, sorry** incompetent.

sclatch *v* work messily; make or use clumsily, untidily or carelessly *now local Abd-Fif. n* a mess, bungle *local Abd-S.*

scuddle work in a slatternly way, mess about at domestic work *now NE Per.*

scutter 1 the doing of work awkwardly or dirtily, a botch, bungle *Sh Ork N nEC.* **2** a person who works in an ineffective, muddled, or dirty way *N Per.*

skiff by *or* **ower** do work carelessly or superficially *Sh N Per.*

sklyte work messily or clumsily *EC.*

slab work carelessly, messily or with something wet or messy *now Kcb.*

slaik, slaich, sklaik *NE* a dirty, messy way of working *local Ags-SW.*

slaister, slyster, sclyster *nEC, v* work messily or splash the hands about in a liquid; work awkwardly, clumsily, or ineffectively *Gen except NE. n* a slovenly, dirty worker, a slut *C, S.*

†**slake, sclaik** weaken or decrease one's efforts.

slatch a messy dirty worker *now Rox.*

slim (ower) treat (work) with insufficient care, scamp (a job) *local Cai-Rox.* **slemmer** a person who scamps his work *now Ags.*

slip-by a carelessly-performed task, shoddy work *local Sh-WC.*

slope shirk one's work, dodge duty, idle *NE Lnk Gall.* ~**r** a shirker *now Abd Loth.*

slouth, sleuth carry out (a task) in a lazy, idle, careless way, treat with indifference or neglect *now Abd Kcdn Ags.*

slunk *contemptuous* a lazy, sneaking person, a shirker *now Cai.*

slutter, sclutter work in a slovenly, dirty way, or in something messy *now Cai, C, S.*

smatter, smather work untidily or unmethodically, (appear to) be busy with trivial jobs.

snaffle, †**snaffler** term of contempt for an ineffective person *now Lnk Dmf.*

snuit work in a làzy, careless or stupefied way, laze about, be listless, be at a loose end *now Abd.*

soss make a mess, work dirtily *N nEC.*

sotter work in a dirty unskilful way *local Sh-Per.*

squeeter a state of confusion, a mix-up, a botched job *NE.*

stick: nae great ~**s at** not adept at, not very good at *now Sh NE Ags.*

stickit, stuck 1 halted in one's trade or profession, failed, insufficiently qualified: '*stickit minister*'. **2** *of a task etc* left spoilt or incomplete *now Per.*

strachle labour ineffectually *now Wgt Dmf.*

tash spoil (*esp* flowers or clothes) by handling roughly or carelessly *now local Sh-Dmf.*

thoum, thumb: aside one's ~ in an ineffectual, inept, or uncertain way *now Bnf.*

thowless *Gen except Sh Ork,* **thewless** *now Loth WC Rox,* **thieveless** *now Abd WC,* **thaveless** *Per Uls* **1** lacking initiative, ineffectual. **2** †**thieveless** *of an action* ineffective; unconvincing.

throuither, through other an unmethodical person who is always in a muddle *Ags Lnk Rox.* ~**ness** muddle-headedness, lack of method *now NE.*

†**thrum** twist, coil or tie loosely, carelessly, or in a makeshift way.

toosht rumple, bundle up carelessly *now Ags.*

tooter *v* work ineffectually, potter ineptly *N. n* **1** ineffectual working; a botch, bungle *NE.* **2** a feckless worker, a botcher *NE.* ~**er** a person who **tooters** *N.*

trauchle, trackle *v* bedraggle, injure, spoil (by dragging, trampling, knocking about etc) *now local NE-SW. n* a careless incompetent person, an inefficient slovenly worker *now local Stlg-Dmf.*

twa-han(d)it work work so badly done that it has to be done again *now local Sh-Fif.*

tyne spend unprofitably or in vain, waste (time, labour etc).

†**uncannie** unskilful, clumsy, careless.

unkent (to) inexperienced (in), unfamiliar (with).

weirdless inept, incapable *now local Abd-Loth.*

yeukie *of work* rough and careless, badly finished *now Fif Ayr.*

15.5.17 SHAMBLES

ball put in disorder *now Sh.*

†**barbulyie** disorder, confuse.

boorach(ie), boorock(ie) a muddle, mess, state of confusion *Cai Mry Highl.*

bootch a botch, bungle, muddle.

bucker a mess, bungling *Bnf Abd.*

bullox a mess.

bummle a bungle, mess *now local Bnf-Kcb.*

burble a tangle; something in disorder, *eg* yarn *Lnk SW.* ~**d** tangled, disordered *Lnk SW.*

carfuffle *n* a disorder, mess. *v* disorder, throw into confusion.

clary a mess *local WC-SW.*

clat a mess, muddle *now wLoth.*

compluther, comploiter a mix-up; confusion.

farkage an untidy heap or bundle *now Ork.* **ferkishin** a large untidy amount *S.*

farrach a mix-up *now Ags.*

guddle a mess, muddle, confusion *now C, S.* **guddled** disordered, in a muddle *now Ags.*

gutter, gitter a muddle, mess *local Cai-Dmf.*

hatter 1 a confused heap *now Kinr WC Rox.* **2** a state of disorder *now midLoth Rox Slk.*

heeliegoleerie topsy-turvy, in a state of confusion *now Ags midLoth.*

heels ower gowdie, heelster gowdie *or* **gowrie** *local NE,* **heelster heid(s)** *now Sh Ork NE Uls,* **heels ower hurdie(s)** *now Abd Rox* topsy-turvy, upside-down. **heelster heid(s), heels ower hurdie(s)** *now Abd Rox* in disorder.

heid, head: ~**s and** *or* **or thraws,** †**head(s) and thrawart(s)** lying in opposite directions; higgledy-piggledy. ~**s and thraws** *of articles arranged in a row* in disorder or confusion, higgledy-piggledly *now midLoth.*

hickertie-pickertie higgledy-piggledy *now midLoth.*

hirdum-dirdum topsy-turvy *Rox.*

hirdy-dirdy in disorder or confusion, topsy-turvy *now Ags Rox.*

hish-hash a muddle, confusion, untidy mess *now Sh midLoth.*

hither an yon(t) muddled *now Mry midLoth.*

hixy-pixy in confusion, topsy-turvy *now Ags Per.*

hodge-podge a hotch-potch.

hudder, huther *n* a confused crowd or heap *now Kcb.* *v* heap together in disorder *now Ags.*

huggery(-muggery) *adj* disorderly, untidy *Ags Rox.* *adv* in a confused or disorderly state *now Dmf.*

jummle jumble, mix up, get mixed up with, confuse.

jurmummle mess or mix up; confuse *now Rox.*

kirn a muddle, jumble, confusion *local Sh-Kcb.*

knacker's midden a mess, a shambles *C, S.*

mankit *of a literary work* mutilated; corrupt *Abd Edb.*

midden a muddle, shambles, mess *local.*

†**ming** mix, blend; mix up, confuse.

ming-mang muddle *C.*

mish-mash mix up, throw together confusedly *Bnf Abd Edb.*

mixtie-maxtie *n* a jumble of objects, a mixture, confusion. *adj* heterogeneous; jumbled; in a state of confusion.

moger a muddle, mess, bungle *Cai WC.*

muck clutter up, mar the appearance of *Sh NE.*

owerheid precipitately; in a commotion, in confusion; untidily.

owerum, ower(h)im, ower(th)em (in) a state of muddle or confusion *Rox.*

Paddy's market any confused scene, an untidy room etc *Ags WC.*

panshit, panshine a state of excitement, panic, muddle *now NE.*

plaister a botched or mismanaged job, a mess, shambles *local Ags-Uls.*

plowster a mess; a muddle, shambles *now Rox.*

poach a disordered state of affairs, a shambles, mess *now Abd.*

pronack a state of mush, a mess, hotch-potch *now Cai Per.*

†**puddle** a state of disorder, a muddle, mess, confusion.

puidge a mess, muddle, a pigsty *S.*

rach-ma-reeshil confused, mixed-up, higgledy-piggledy *now Per Fif.*

†**rag-footed** ill thought out.

raivel, ravel *v* get into a tangle or confusion; muddle, disorder. *n* a muddle, tangle, confusion. ~**ed** tangled, confused, in difficulties. ~**ed hesp, pirn** *etc* a knotty problem, a state of confusion *now local Ork-Lnk.* †**travelment** a confusion, tangle.

†**ramshackle** throw into confusion or disorder.

†**rangle** disorder, commotion.

reel: ~**-rall** *n* a state of confusion, a muddle of objects, sounds etc *NE local C. adj* confused, disorganized, higgledy-piggledy *N-C. adv* in a confused way, higgledy-piggledy *N-C.* **out o (the)** ~ out of step or tune, astray, disarranged *NE.*

rothos, rothie a tangle, muddle *now Mry.*

row-chow mixed-up, tangled *now WC Kcb.*

rummle, rumble something confused or disordered *now Sh.*

sair, sore: ~ **hand** a mess, a piece of unskilled workmanship *now Ayr.*

sclatch a mess, bungle *local Abd-S.*

skiddle a mess, muddle, confusion, *esp* with spilling of liquid *nEC Loth WC.*

skitter anything dirty or disgusting, a mess, rubbish *now local Sh-Per.*

snorl a predicament, scrape, muddle, confusion *now Sh Cai NE.*

soss a state of dirt and disorder, a muddle, confusion *Sh N nEC*.

sotter a mess, muddle, confused mass, chaos *now local Sh-Per*.

squeeter a state of confusion, a mix-up, a botched job *NE*.

taigle *n* a tangle, muddle *now nEC Wgt Rox*. *v* (en)tangle, confuse, muddle *now Cai C, S*.

taisle entangle, mix up, put or get into disorder *now local Loth-SW*.

tap, top: ~ **ower tail** upside down, head-over-heels, topsy-turvy.

tapsalteerie, tapsie-tearie, †tapsie turvie *adv* upside down, topsy-turvy, in(to) utter confusion or disorder. *adj* chaotic, muddled, disorderly. *n* a state of disorder or of being topsy-turvy.

tersie versie topsy-turvy, in a random, disorderly way *S*.

throuither, through other *adj* confused, untidy or badly arranged. *adv* **1** (mingled) indiscriminately one with another. **2** mingled or mixed up; into a state of muddle or confusion, in(to) disorder, higgledy-piggledy. *n* a muddle, mess *now Abd*.

tousie untidy, in a disorderly state *local Sh-SW*.

touther, towder *v* handle roughly, throw into disorder *now Sh Fif*. *n* a throwing into confusion; a state of disorder, a mess *now Sh Fif Loth*.

†towt toss about, upset, put in disorder.

trushel a muddle, confusion *Cai*.

wattle a tangle, mix-up, confused mess *Cai*.

15.5.18 BEING HAMPERED

aff, off: ~**-pit** that which delays *NE, SW, S*.

behss *n* bustle, hurry *now Ags*.

block hinder, impede.

bode offer with insistence, press (something) **on** (someone) *now Bnf*.

boorach(ie), boorock(ie) a fuss *Cai Mry Highl*.

breengin bustling *now local*.

bubbly jock: sair hauden doun by the ~ overwhelmed with too much to do *now Bnf Kcb*.

bucker fuss, move or work aimlessly, awkwardly, yet fussily *Bnf Abd*.

bummle bustle about, work noisily but ineffectively, blunder about *now Lnk*.

connach fuss over.

creest an officious person *local*.

cried: like a ~ **fair** in a state of bustle.

†cummer, cumber *n* a hindrance or encumbrance. *v* hamper, impede. **mak** ~ cause trouble or disturbance. **be quit of someone's** ~ be free of trouble etc caused by the person mentioned.

cummersum troublesome, causing trouble or difficulty.

deester *often contemptuous* a person in a position of authority *now Bnf Abd*.

defeeckwalt difficult *now local Bnf-Kcb*.

deid, dead: in the ~ **thraw** between one state and another; undecided *now Abd*.

dirl a hurry, bustle *Sh Abd*.

disabuse disturbance *Abd*.

discomfit put to inconvenience *now Abd*.

disconvenience inconvenience *now Sh Bnf Abd Ags*.

doot, doubt: ~**sum** doubtful, undecided in opinion.

dossach (wi) fondle, pet, fuss over needlessly *Bnf Abd*.

dreich a *or* **in drawing** *etc* slow to move, slow in deciding *now Abd*.

†drift subject (a person) to delay.

dwang subject to pressure, harass, worry *now Ags*.

ersie hinder *chf Sh Ork*.

farrach a bustle *now Ags*.

fash trouble, annoy, anger, inconvenience.

feery-farry a bustle, a state of confusion.

fickle difficult, tricky *local Ork-Renfr*. **ficklie** puzzling, difficult, tricky *now Fif midLoth*.

fiddltie-fa a fuss; a trifling excuse; hesitation *Bnf Abd*.

find frost run into difficulties, *chf* of one's own making, suffer unpleasant consequences from one's own actions *now Ork*.

finick a fussy, fastidious person *local NE-C*. ~**y** fussy, fiddling.

firris a bother, a predicament *Abd*.

†fissle, fistle a bustle, commotion, fuss.

fittiefie a quirk, quibble *Abd*.

fittininment concern, interference *Abd*.

fizz *n* a bustle, commotion, a state of great excitement. *v* make a fuss, bustle.

flocht 1 a bustle, a flurry, a great hurry. **2** bustle, excitement, stress *Abd*.

flochter fluster. **† ~ous** hurried and confused, fluttering *Mry Abd Ags*.

fluister *v* fluster, hustle, bustle *now Sh Ork Rox Uls*. *n* a fluster, hustle, bustle *now Sh Ork Rox Uls*.

foorich bustle, confusion.

fouterie fussy, inept.

fraca a fuss, a bother.

freits: stand on ~ make a fuss about trifles, be faddy.

†fruster frustrate, bring to nothing, make useless.

fyke *n* a fussy, fastidious person, a person who

makes a fuss over trifles *EC, WC, S. v* bustle about in a trifling way, fiddle, make a fuss about nothing very much *local N-S*. **mak a ~** make a fuss (**about**). **~rie** fuss, fastidiousness over trifles *now Sh WC*. **fykie 1** fussy, fastidious over trifles, finicky. **2** *of a task etc* tricky, troublesome, intricate and difficult to manage *now local*.

fyke-facks, ficks facks a trivial fuss.

fyle one's fingers *etc* **wi** have to do with, meddle with (something debasing) *now NE Ags Lnk*.

gae, go a fuss, bother; a state of anxiety, distress or excitement, *freq* **in a ~** *now Sh-nEC*.

gate: †in someone's ~ hampering, obstructing someone.

guddle hard, dirty or messy work *now Ags midLoth Gsw*.

habble hamper *chf S*.

hae, have: ~ ill *etc* **dain** not be able to do easily etc *now Sh NE Ags*.

hair: a ~ to make a tether a fuss about nothing, a trifle used as an excuse *now Sh Arg*.

haister perplex, pester, harass *now Gall*. **† ~ed** flustered, harassed.

haiver 1 a person in a state of fussy indecision, an idler *now Ayr*. **2 ~(s)** a state of fussy indecision *now Ayr*.

hamperit confined, restrained, hindered, cramped *now Sh Ork Arg Uls*.

hank hesitation, delay *now S*.

hash a rush or excessive pressure of work *now local Ork-Kcb*. **~ter** harass *Renfr Ayr*.

hatter harass, vex *now S*.

hechle a perplexing piece of work *midLoth Rox*.

heid, head: ~ bummer *freq sarcastic* a manager, a prominent or important person.

hing, hang: ~ on delay or hinder (someone) in doing something, keep (someone) waiting *NE Ags*. **~-on** (a source or period of) delay, tedium or weariness; an encumbrance, hindrance *Gen except Sh Ork*.

hobble *v* perplex, bother *Cai Uls*. *n* a difficulty, predicament *now Cai*.

hover pause, wait a little (*orig in deliberation, uncertainty or indecision*). **in (a) ~** in a state of hesitation, uncertainty or indecision *now Sh*.

humdudgeon a fuss.

hurried harassed, hard pressed, hard put to it (to do something) *local Ork-Kcb*.

inbearing officious, ingratiating, obsequious *Bnf Abd Ags*.

†inconvenient a state or cause of difficulty.

jam 1 put in a quandary, cause to be at a loss. **2** inconvenience *now local Abd-Lnk*. **3** occupy one's

time to the exclusion of all else, preoccupy oneself exclusively *Bnf Abd Ags Loth*.

jauchle through do (something) with difficulty *now Fif Renfr*.

kiow-owy fussy, pottering *chf Ags*.

made distressed, upset, *eg* because of overwork *NE*.

maitter: make (a) ~ make a fuss *local Sh-Kcb*.

mak, make: ~ ceremony stand on ceremony, fuss, scruple *now Ags Uls*.

mank a fuss *Lnk Rox*.

meddle, middle interfere with, bother, harm *local*.

misgie (cause to) fail, let (a person) down *now Sh Ayr*.

†mismaggle disarrange, interfere with; spoil *N Fif*.

mismak disturb (oneself), put (oneself) about, trouble (oneself) *now WC, S*.

misred tangled, involved, confused *now Sh Cai Kcb*.

murther, murder harass, torment, distress *now Sh Per Uls*.

neef difficulty, bother *Abd*.

nig nay *v* trifle, fuss.

offeecious officious.

†painful causing or involving hardship or difficulty; troublesome, laborious.

pall puzzle, perplex, thwart *now Sh-Cai Mry*.

pavie a fuss about nothing, a commotion; a great state of excitement *now Ags Fif Bwk*.

pea-splittin petty, fussy, cheese-paring *now Uls*.

peremptor, peremptory excessively careful, fussy *now Sh*.

perjink exact, precise, scrupulously careful, fussy.

perskeet fastidious, precise, over-particular; hard to please *now Sh*.

pest trouble, annoy, plague, pester *local Sh-SW*.

peuther importune in a fussy and ingratiating way, bustle about trying to win favour.

phrasie fussy, fastidious *Bnf Abd*.

picher a useless, ineffective person, a person who is habitually in a flap *Bnf Abd*.

pilliedacus: the heid ~ *usu with critical and sarcastic implication* the person in command, the big cheese *now NE nEC*.

pirkas a finicky, troublesome matter, a bother, predicament *Cai*.

pirn: wind (oneself *or* **another) a ~** *or* **into a bonnie** *etc* **~** create difficulties for oneself or another.

pirr a harassed, over-excited state of mind, a panic, rage *now Sh Ork NE*.

pit, put: ~ **aboot** inconvenience, cause trouble to; distress, upset (oneself or another).

plaister make a fuss or useless bother, be over-attentive *Kcdn nEC Rox*.

plet a predicament, quandary *S*.

point, pint: ~ed precise, (over-)attentive to detail, demanding; punctual, exact *Ork, local N, S*.

pouk at annoy, harass *now Kcb*.

prat meddle or interfere **with**, tamper or fiddle **with**.

†prejudge affect unfavourably, work to the prejudice of, harm, hinder, interfere with.

†primineary *joc* a fix, predicament, scrape.

pursue 1 harass, worry, persecute (a person or group), beg (a person) persistently to do something *now Kcb*. 2 †follow (a person) persistently with one's attentions.

raivel, ravel: ~ed tangled, confused, in difficulties. ~ed hesp, pirn *etc* a knotty problem, a state of confusion *now local Ork-Lnk*.

ramfeezle, ramfoozle exhaust *now local Abd-Fif*.

rammis rush about frantically.

ratton's nest a state of perpetual unrest and bustle.

ride on the riggin o be completely preoccupied (with); be very officious (about) *now local Ork-SW*.

sanshach (over-)precise, irritable *now NE*.

scutter *v* 1 be engaged in troublesome, time-wasting, pointless work, fiddle about aimlessly or confusedly, dawdle *now N Per*. 2 hinder with something unimportant, detain through some needless or annoying cause *NE Ags Per*. *n* a footling, time-consuming and irritating occupation *Sh Ork N nEC*. **scutterie** troublesome; *of a job* time-wasting, muddling, footling *NE*.

skitterie *of a task* fiddly, time-consuming *C*.

snorl a predicament, scrape, muddle, confusion *now Sh Cai NE*.

†sonyie *n* hesitation. *v* hesitate, delay, refuse.

sorra, sorrow: ~fu causing vexation, troublesome *now Sh Cai Per*.

soss nurse over-tenderly, fuss over; pester *now Bnf*.

†stap: stand on ~pin stanes be excessively fussy; dither.

stashie, stushie a (*usu* unnecessary) fuss, bother.

steer *v* 1 be in a bustle; be hard-pressed with work etc; work or go about in a confused, harassed way. 2 disturb, molest, pester *now local Abd-Kcb*. *n* stir, movement, bustle. ~ie a bustle, commotion, muddle. ~iefyke confused bustle, agitation, excitement.

stichle *v* rustle, stir, bustle *now Kcdn*.

stress *v* overwork, fatigue *now local Per-Rox*.

strow a commotion, bustle, to-do.

†supersede defer action, hesitate.

sussie, sizzie care, trouble, bother *now Sh Fif Kcb*.

swander hesitate, dither *Sh Ork Fif*.

swey, swee vacillate.

swither, swidder *now chf NE, v* be uncertain, be perplexed about what to do or choose, doubt, hesitate, dither. *n* 1 a state of indecision or doubt, hesitation, uncertainty. 2 a dithering, undecided person *local*.

tag: be in the ~ be oppressed with hard work *NE*.

taigle hinder, get in the way of, harass *now C*. ~**some** tiring, tedious *local sEC-Rox*. ~ **the cleek** hinder progress *local Fif-Ayr*.

†tainghle harass, weary with hard work.

†tary provoke, harass.

teeter hesitate, hover indecisively *local Sh-Bnf*.

†tere(full), tyrefull difficult, tiring, tedious.

†thortersome obstructive.

thrang, throng *n* pressure (of work or business), (a time of) great activity *now Sh C, S. adj, of times, seasons, activities etc* busy, busily occupied; *of persons* busy, fully occupied. **†thronged** busily occupied, stressed with work. **thrangity** busyness, pressure of work; bustle, stir *now Per Stlg*.

tickly puzzling, difficult *now Abd*.

†tig meddle, have to do **with**.

tirraneese, tarraneese harass with overwork *NE Ags*.

titersome *of a job* fiddling, tediously difficult *NE*.

tooterie *of persons* fussy, pottering; *of things* fiddling, irritatingly trivial or intricate *NE*.

trash wear out, exhaust, abuse with overwork and exertion *now Dmf Rox*. ~**y** fatiguing *S*.

trauchle a state of chronic muddle caused by having too much to do *local NE-Wgt*.

trauchle, trackle *v* exhaust with overwork, travelling etc, overburden, harass. *n* tiring labour, drudgery, fatiguing or dispiriting work. ~**d** hampered, troubled, worried. ~**some** exhausting, laborious *NE Ags*.

†tribul bring tribulation upon; distress, harass, afflict.

tyauve fatigue, wear out *now Abd*.

tyne spend unprofitably or in vain, waste (time, labour etc).

uncannie awkward, not easy to manage *local Sh-Fif*.

†uneis not easily, (only) with difficulty, scarcely.

unfordersome, unfurthersome slow, causing delay or hindrance.

†**unsell** a troublesome person.

use, yuise: ~**less** exceedingly, so much as to be ineffectual, far too *now local: 'the maid has put on useless many coals'.*

wark, work a business, fuss *now Sh-WC Dmf.* **hae, haud** *or* **mak a** ~ **about** *etc* make a great fuss over, make a song-and-dance about *now Sh-Per.*

†**wheegee** a humming and hawing, prevarication.

whether-or-no uncertain, indecisive, dithering *EC Lnk Dmf.*

whirr commotion, rush, hurrying about *now Bnf.*

†**wimple, wumple** complicate.

worry: eat the cow and ~ **on the tail** fail or lack success because of one small thing; be a stickler for trivialities.

5.5.19 INDIFFERENCE, RESTRAINT

aff, off: ~**-loof** offhand.

bird-mouthed unwilling to speak out *now Gsw.*

blaw, blow: ~ **lown** make little or no noise; avoid boasting *now Abd.*

care: not ~ not be reluctant, have no objections *now Bnf Ags.* ~**na by** be indifferent *now Ags.*

†**cheson** objection, exception, demur, *as* **without** *or* **but** ~.

†**cure: not** ~ **1** have no anxiety or scruples in some regard. **2** have no care or concern for. **3** have no regard, heed or consideration for, fail entirely to value. **have no** ~ **of** have no concern for or interest in.

†**evenlyness** equanimity.

flee: let that ~ **stick tae the wa** drop a particular (*usu* embarrassing) subject, say no more about a topic.

gae fae lose the taste for *NE Renfr.*

goam: not ~ not heed or notice *now Pbls Bwk S.*

gowan: not care a ~ not care in the least, not care a fig *now midLoth.*

haud, hald, hold: hae't and ~ **it** hide one's feelings *Abd.*

†**ill: for na(ne)** ~ with no bad intention.

jack easy indifferent, not caring one way or the other; easy-going, offhand.

jee, jow *Bnf Ags:* **not** ~ **one's ginger, not jow one's jundie** *Bnf Ags* not show concern, not bother one's head; not become flustered.

†**keep one's tung** keep a check or guard on one's tongue.

lose taste o lose interest in or liking for *local Ork-Per.*

mane: mak nae ~ **for** *or* **about** show no sympathy towards *now Sh-N Uls.*

myowt: not a ~ not a sound, not a whisper *esp* of complaint or protest *NE.*

objections: have no ~ have no objection.

†**onamovit** unmoved.

pou, pull: like ~**ing teeth** extremely difficult (to get money, a response etc from an unresponsive person).

sid(s): never lat *or* **say** ~ never say a word, never make the least remark (**about**) *NE.*

smore, smuir, smoor suppress, conceal (*eg* feelings).

souch, sough: keep *etc* **a calm** *etc* ~ keep quiet, hold one's tongue; keep calm or still.

steek one's mouth *now local NE-SW,* **steek one's gab** shut one's mouth, keep silent.

sussie, sizzie: not ~ **1** not care, not be anxious or concerned *now Sh.* **2** †not refuse (to do something). **3** †not care for or regard.

tak, take check oneself, stop oneself from doing or saying something which one might later regret *now NE.*

thoum, thumb: no care the crack o a ~ be completely indifferent *now Bnf.* **not fash one's** ~ pay no heed, never worry or concern oneself *now NE-Per.*

tinkler: not to care a ~**'s curse** *etc* not to care etc at all.

unmovit unmoved.

up: neither ~ **nor doun** *esp of feelings etc* unaffected by events, the same as before *Sh-C.*

†**upsitten** indifferent, inactive.

wheesht: haud *or* **keep one's** ~ be quiet, keep silent, hold one's tongue.

whistle, whustle: no to gie a ~ not to give a damn, have nothing but contempt for *now local Sh-Per.*

will, wull: hae nae ~ **o** take no pleasure in, have no liking for *now NE.*

wrang, wrong: not come ~ **(to)** not come amiss (to), not be unwelcome (for), not disconcert *local Sh-Lnk.* **not say a** ~ **word** not use harsh, unjust or improper language *Sh-Per.*

5.5.20 OBEDIENCE

bowsome obedient, willing, obliging.

discreet civil, polite, well-behaved.

fleet easy to deal with, manageable *Bnf Abd.*

leuk, luck, look: ~ **efter** take notice of, respect *Abd.*

†**obedient** an obedient or dutiful person; a person who is subject to authority.

†**obeyand** submitting, obedient **to**.

patientfu long-suffering, very patient, submissive.

rander, render order, restraint, decorousness, conformity *now Kcdn*.

said: be easy ~ **til** be yielding or amenable *Abd Kcdn Ags*.

†**serv(i)ble** willing to serve, obedient.

thole *v* 1 endure with patience or fortitude, put up with, tolerate. 2 be patient, wait patiently *now N Per. n* patience, endurance *Gall Uls*. † ~**mode,** ~**mude** patient, submissive, meek. ~**moody** patient.

15.6 EMOTIONS AND STATES

15.6.1 MISCELLANEOUS SOURCES OF CONTENTMENT

abune in good cheer, in or into better condition.

abune: get ~ recover from, get over (a disappointment) *now NE Ags*.

†**amene** *verse* agreeable, pleasing, pleasant.

at oneself in one's right mind; in a calm state *now NE, SW Uls*.

†**avenand** convenient, agreeable.

†**bening** benign.

†**bete** amend, correct.

better better fortune; advantage.

biel(d) *chf literary* protection; relief, succour; refuge, shelter *now Bnf*.

bien *adj* comfortable(-looking), pleasant, cosy. †*adv* handsomely; liberally; comfortably. ~**ly** pleasantly; comfortably; cosily. † ~**ness** prosperity.

†**bightsom** easy, relaxed.

blink a gleam of comfort etc.

bonny beautifully.

bool: the ~**s row** *etc* **smooth** *etc* things are going well.

brisken up freshen, stimulate *local Fif-Kcb*.

bummin very good, worth boasting about *Bnf Ags*.

canny favourable, lucky, of good omen; comfortable, easy.

cantle up recover one's spirits *Bnf Abd*.

canty comfortable *now Ags*.

codgie comfortable, content *Bnf Abd*.

†**commend** commendation, praise.

†**confortable** comfortable.

content pleased, happy *now Fif Stlg*.

cosh snug, comfortable, cosy.

curmud snug *S*.

din: nae ~**-bonnets** not to be despised, first-rate *Abd*.

†**dow** thrive, prosper.

ease †take one's ease, enjoy ease. ~**dom** comfort, leisure, relief from anxiety etc *now Sh Abd*. ~**ful(l)** giving ease or comfort.

easement personal comfort etc; relief from physical discomfort or inconvenience *now local*.

†**enbalden** embolden.

feel comfortable, cosy *S*.

feerious extraordinarily good, excellent *NE*.

fiddle: find a ~ come upon something rare or precious, get a pleasant surprise *now Abd*.

fouthie having abundance, prosperous.

†**gracious** happy, prosperous.

guidly goodly.

†**hailsome** mentally or morally beneficial; salutary.

happy lucky, fortunate, auspicious *now Cai-WC*.

†**haud, hald:** ~ **wi** be content with, be pleased to accept: '*haud wi less drink neist time*'.

heeze (up) someone's heart lift up someone's heart; give courage to, cheer.

hert, hairt, heart *v, also* ~ **up** embolden, hearten *now Kcb*. ~**some** encouraging, animating; cheering, attractive, pleasant. † ~**-heezing** encouraging, uplifting, heartwarming.

lichtsome cheering, enlivening, pleasant.

lift *v* raise (the spirits), elate. *n* help, relief, encouragement. ~**it (up)** cheered up *local*.

like, lik: ~**(e)r** more apt, more befitting, more appropriate *local*: '*a worset goon's the liker you*'.

liss *of pain etc* cease, abate *now Uls*. ~**ance** respite.

luck 1 fare, prosper **well** *now Sh N*. 2 have good fortune; succeed *now Abd midLoth Bwk Kcb*.

mak, make: ~ **weel** make good, succeed *Ork Fif*.

†**mends** improvement, betterment (in fortune).

odds: make (a person's) ~ **even** equalize or level inequalities, adjust.

†**ourdrive** come through (hardship etc) more or less successfully; live through, pass through.

†**outgate** a way out of *esp* a moral or spiritual problem; a solution.

†**owerpit** come through (a trial, danger), get over, recover from, get the better of.

pithy prosperous, well-to-do.

†**plight-anchor** a support or refuge in a crisis or emergency, a sheet anchor.

†**precordial** very comforting or cheering.

†**proper** excellently, handsomely.

†**prosper** prosperous, successful.

puss: as quiet, calm *etc* **as** ~**ie** in a quiet, tranquil way *now local*.

†**queem, quim** pleasingly, smoothly, calmly, neatly.

†**quemfully** pleasantly, agreeably; graciously.

ranter order, tidiness *Abd*.

reel: in gweed ~ in step, in good order, tidy *NE*.

†**revert** recover, bring back or return to one's normal state of mind or spirits *latterly N*.

sad, sod *chf N, now Abd* remarkable, outstandingly good *chf NE*.

seil happiness, bliss, prosperity, good fortune. ~**fu** happy, lucky. ~**y** blessed, lucky, happy.

sicker *adj* 1 safe, secure, free from danger etc *now local NE-Wgt*. 2 †confident, having a sense of security. 3 having assurance or certainty (**of**) *now Sh Abd*. *adv* securely, firmly, stably *now Abd Ags*. † ~**ly** firmly, fast.

snod comfortable, snug, at ease *now N-SW*.

snog snug.

†**snosh** chubby and contented.

sonsie bringing good fortune *freq as a general term of approbation, now local Sh-Gall*.

†**speedfull** profitable, advantageous, expedient.

spin progress favourably, go well *Bnf Abd Ags*.

†**sprete** inspire **with** (courage).

straucht, straight smooth, set to rights *now Sh N, EC*. ~**-forrit** straightforward, straight ahead.

†**sufficient, sufficiand** satisfactory, good enough.

†**tee'd ball** a state of affairs bound to succeed.

thack and raip describing something tidy, comfortable, well-secured.

†**thrift** prosperity, success, good luck.

thrive *v, also* **trive** *Sh Ork* thrive. *n* prosperity, a thriving state, boom *now SW*.

through bearing a way out of difficulty or hardship *now Sh*.

†**tift, tiff** put in good spirits *N*.

tosie comfortable, cosy, snug.

upheeze lift up, raise *now Lnk*.

†**upset** make good, make up for; get over, recover from (a loss etc).

upsteer, upstir stimulate, encourage. †**upstirring** exciting, stimulating.

waff a slight agreeable experience *now local*.

walcome welcome.

wallie *adj* fine, pleasant, beautiful *now Ork*. †*adv* finely, splendidly.

weel: ~ **come** arriving at an opportune moment, welcome *now NE*. ~**-daein** well-to-do, prosperous. † ~**-faurdly** in a decent, proper or pleasant way. ~**-lookit tae** well-looked-after, blessed by fortune *now NE*. ~**-redd-up** tidy, well in order.

†**weirdly** lucky, prosperous.

†**welthy** happy, prosperous; comfortable.

wise, wice: ~**like** suitable, fitting, appropriate.

15.6.2 MISCELLANEOUS SOURCES OF DISCONTENT

†**abaisitness** discouragement.

adae(s) trouble, difficulty, *eg* **have one's ain** ~.

†**aggrege** increase the gravity of (a misdeed, penalty etc); aggravate.

agley wrong, awry.

amshach an accident, misfortune; an injury *NE*.

†**antercast** a misfortune, a mischance *chf N*.

awa, away: ~ **frae** past; unable to *Sh N*: '*he wis awa fae speakin'*.

awfu awful; lamentable.

back: ~**-cast** an unexpected blow. **at a** ~ at a loss *Bnf Abd*. **go up one's** ~ be beyond one's power *now Abd*.

bad badly.

barm *n* blame *Mry*.

†**bask** unpleasant, distasteful.

bather bother.

begunk a misfortune.

big miss a great loss by death, or by the departure of a friend *local*.

black dark, dismal, unfortunate, shameful.

bladry foolishness, ostentation, harm.

blame fault: '*it's not my blame'*. ~ (**something**) **on** (**a person**) ascribe the blame to (a person) for (something).

†**blaw, blow:** ~ **a cauld coal** suffer failure, engage in a hopeless task.

blinlins, †**blindlingis** blindly; heedlessly; with eyes shut *now Lnk*.

blue do *colloq* a poor performance, a failure, a black outlook.

bock: gie (someone) *or* **get the (dry)** ~(**s**) (cause to) feel sick, retch or vomit *local C*.

bonny *ironic* good, excellent, fine.

bree: *chf* **nae** ~ an unfavourable opinion.

broo, *chf* **no** ~ an unfavourable opinion *now local Abd-Lnk*: '*I've nae broo o him.'*

†**buit, boot: na** ~ no alternative or choice.

†**calumpniat** calumniated.

canny: no(t) ~ unnatural, supernatural *now wLoth Stlg*: '*this is no canny'*.

cast: ~ **at** spurn, condemn.

chancy: not ~ unfortunate, unlucky.

chape, cheap: be ~ **o** *or* **on** get off lightly with (something); serve (someone) right: *'ye've got your fairin, an I maun say I think ye're cheap o't'*.

chaw a disappointment, snub; a cutting retort *now Bnf Abd Fif*.

clatty disagreeable *now wLoth Arg Lnk*.

come: ~ **at** *of a misfortune* befall. ~ **ower** *chf of misfortune* happen to befall (a person).

†**condampnatioun** condemnation.

†**condampnatour** condemnatory.

†**condampne** condemn.

†**contemptioun** 1 contempt. 2 the state of being scorned.

conter a reverse, misfortune *now Ags*. **gae** ~ **to** go against (someone's wishes, expectations).

coorse hard, trying; disagreeable *Bnf-Ags*.

†**crank** a difficulty *SW-S*.

†**cruik, crook**, *also* a ~ **in one's** *or* **the lot** a misfortune, difficulty.

†**cummer, cumber** difficulty. ~**sum** troublesome, causing trouble or difficulty.

curmurring a source of complaint *local*.

dae, do: ~**-nae-better** a poor substitute *now Kcb*.

debosh debauch *now Bnf Abd Fif*.

†**default, defaut: in his** *etc* ~ through his etc fault, failure, or negligence.

†**defoul** disparage, despise.

demain demean.

†**deprise** depreciate, despise.

†**dere** hurt, harm, injury.

dirdum *n* blame.

disconvenient inconvenient *now Sh Bnf Fif*.

†**disemal** dismal.

disherten dishearten *now local Bnf-Fif*.

†**disperne** despise.

displeesure displeasure.

doon: gae ~ **the brae** *or* **hill** go downhill, deteriorate in fortune etc.

dow: not ~ be unable, not have the strength or ability (to do something).

drap, drop a disappointment.

dree one's (ain) *or* **a sore** *etc* **weird** suffer the consequences of something.

dreep a disappointment *Cai Fif*.

dreich dreary, long-lasting, persistent; tiresome, hard to bear; *of time, journeys etc* long, wearisome.

dunt a blow to fortunes, feelings; a shock, disappointment.

eelist a cause of offence, disagreement or ill-feeling; a grievance.

eggs: aff (o) one's ~ mistaken *now Ork NE-S*.

†**exorbitant** grossly or flagrantly excessive or unfair.

fa(ll): ~ **ower the brim** go to one's doom or destruction *now Abd*.

faut, fault harm, injury *Sh Abd*. †**in a** *or* **the** ~ in the wrong, at fault.

flamagaster a stunning shock of surprise or disappointment *NE*.

†**fructles** fruitless.

glender on the decline (in health, morals, etc), in a bad way.

gley(e)d mistaken, misguided *now midLoth*.

hairm harm.

handling an unpleasant experience, an ordeal *now Ork Ags*.

hearing, *chf* **fine** ~ *ironical* unpleasant news *now Sh*.

hechle a struggle, a difficulty *midLoth Rox*.

hert, hairt, heart: ~ **scaud** a source of bitter grief, trouble, disappointment or aversion *now NE Ags Uls*. **gang against one's** ~ be distasteful, disliked *NE Ags SW*. ~**less** cheerless, dismal, discouraging *now Abd WC Dmf*. **gar someone's** ~ **rise** make someone sick *Ags Fif Rox*.

howf: hae nae ~ **o** have no desire to associate with, have no liking for.

hyter in a state of ruin *Bnf Abd Ags*.

ill *freq in curses* unlucky *now local*. ~**-brew** an unfavourable opinion *midLoth Kcb*. ~**-contrived, ~-contriven** awkward *now Sh*. ~ **spoken o** slandered *Sh Ags*. ~ **wared** ill-spent, wasted, out of place *now Sh NE Fif*. **ha(v)e** *or* **tak (an)** ~**-will at** *local Sh-Ags*, †**hae** ~**-will to** take a dislike to. **tak something** ~ **oot** be upset at, averse from, offended by something *local Ork-Lnk*.

†**impreve** repudiate; disapprove, condemn.

imput impute, lay to the charge of, attribute (a fault, a crime, blame) **to**.

†**injure** injustice, wrong, mischief done to a person; an instance of this.

†**inordourly** improperly, irregularly.

†**interest** damaged, harmed.

it: awa wi't, by wi't, throw wi't ruined in health or fortune.

†**kep skaith** suffer or incur harm.

kiss the causey 'come a cropper', meet defeat *now Fif*.

lack offence, injury; insult.

laith *adj* loath. †*v* loathe. ~**fu** reluctant(ly) *now Wgt*.

langsome lengthy, tedious. ~**ness** tedious lengthiness.

†**langorius** distressing, painful.

†**laqueat** *only verse* ensnared.

†**lat, let** think (lightly, less etc) **of** (a person etc).

left abandoned (by God's grace), left to follow

449

one's own foolish or sinful devices. **left to anesel** misguided, astray in one's judgment.

leuk, luck, look: ~ **down on** regard with disfavour, hold in contempt.

†**lief, lee** *only verse, esp ballad* solitary, desolate, eerie: '*a' the lee winter nicht*'.

†**light, licht: set** ~ think little of, despise, undervalue.

loss lose.

luck fare, prosper **ill** *now Sh N*.

†**mank** *adj* deficient, defective. *v* be deficient or wanting, come short.

†**may not** not be agreeable (to do etc).

meet the cat in the morning suffer a setback, have bad luck *Bnf Abd*.

michty disgraceful, scandalous *chf NE Ags*.

mill: throo the ~ an ordeal, a searching examination *NE, SW, Uls*.

†**mirk** unenlightened, deluded.

†**miscairrying** erring, blundering.

mischancy, †mischancit unlucky, unfortunate, ill-fated *now local NE-S*.

mischief misfortune, trouble *now Sh Ork Ags Uls*.

†**misfare** *n* misfortune. *v* impair, bring to ruin.

misfortunate unfortunate, unlucky *now NE Gsw Uls*.

misgie misgive.

†**misknaw** misunderstand, misjudge.

mislear †**misinform**, misguide, lead astray. ~**it** misinformed, mistaken, erroneous *now Cai Per*.

misluckit dogged with bad luck, unfortunate *NE*.

miss 1 a loss, want, cause for regret or mourning. **2** †harm, injury; offence, fault.

mistak: in a ~ *adj* mistaken, labouring under a misapprehension. *adv* in error, by mistake.

mote a drawback *now Abd*.

necessitate compelled, *chf* by circumstance (to do something) *NE*.

neck: (in) spite of one's ~ in defiance of one's efforts, wishes etc. †**strike in the** ~ *of disaster etc* overtake (a person).

†**noy** vexation, harm. ~**s** wrongs, injuries.

oorie *of things* sad and depressing *NE*.

†**owersee 1** fail to take action against; allow to go uncensured or unpunished; overlook, tolerate (a crime, fault, person). **2** neglect to insist upon, forego.

†**owersicht** failure to take preventive or punitive action; licence, indulgence; toleration, connivance.

past a' unspeakable, beyond belief, intolerable *now Sh Cai*.

peltry worthless, unpleasant *now Bnf*.

pick: hae *or* **tak a** ~ **at** have or form a dislike for, bear (someone) a grudge *now N Ags Kcb*.

plaint a complaint, protest, grievance; an expression of distress or grief, *freq* ~ **of** *or* (**up**)**on**.

†**plicht** a plight.

pliskie a plight, predicament, a sorry state *now local Sh-Fif*.

provokshin temptation *now Sh*.

pushion *v* make unpleasant, spoil; cause discomfort to. *v* an unpleasant thing, a horror *Sh N*. *adj* unpleasant, detestable, foul *now Sh Ork Fif*. ~**able** unpleasant *now Per Dnbt*. **pooshinous** unpleasant, detestable, horrible *Sh N*.

raip: a thraw *or* **a whaup in the** ~ a snag, drawback, unforeseen difficulty.

†**refound, refond** cast the blame of (something) **on** (a person or thing).

rue regret a promise, bargain etc, withdraw from a bargain or contract *now N Per Kcb*. ~**fu** rueful. **mak a** ~ *now local EC Wgt*. **tak the** ~ repent, regret; change one's mind about a course of action *NE-S*.

sad, sod *chf N, now Abd* causing sorrow, distressing, lamentable.

sair, sore causing mental distress or grief. ~ **fit,** ~ **leg** *now Ags Per* a time of need or difficulty, an emergency, *chf* **lay something aside** *etc* **for a** ~ **fit.** ~ **hert** a cause for grief, a great disappointment. †**sit** *or* **set someone** ~ distress someone.

†**sakelessly** innocently, without just cause.

scam a hurt to one's feelings, a wound, cause of suffering *Bnf Abd*.

scaud, scald *v* cause grief or pain to. *n* a hurt to the feelings.

scomfish, scunfis: get *or* **tak a** ~ **at** take a strong dislike to, be disgusted at *now Sh NE Ags*.

scunner *v* **1** be bored or repelled by. **2** cause a feeling of repulsion, aversion or loathing in (a person), nauseate. **3** make bored, uninterested or antipathetic, *freq* ~**ed, scunnert** disgusted, bored, 'fed up'. *n* repugnance, distaste, dislike, loss of interest or enthusiasm, *freq* **tak a** ~ (**at** *or* **against**).

serve, ser, sair enough of something unpleasant *now NE*.

set a setback, a disappointment *now NE Ags*.

sheuch: up a *or* **the** ~ in error, mistaken *WC Dmf*.

sick-laith extremely unwilling, very reluctant.

skaith, skaid 1 damage, hurt, injury, harm, *sometimes in phrases with* **scorn. 2** †something which harms. † ~**ful** harmful, injurious. **get, tak** *etc* ~ be hurt, damaged etc *now local Kcdn-Lnk*.

skellie an error, a going astray *chf SW*.

skelp *v*, *of the blows of misfortune* hit. *v* a blow of misfortune.

†**snapper** a slip in conduct, blunder; an unfortunate accident.

†**sneg off at the web('s) end** cut off someone's hopes.

snell *of a blow, fortune etc* hard, severe, harsh *now Abd WC*.

†**snib** a calamity, reverse.

snifter a shock, reverse, rebuff *now Rox*.

spite a disappointment, a cause for annoyance or grief *now Abd Ayr*.

stamagast, stammygaster a great and sudden disappointment, an unpleasant surprise, a shock *NE Ags*.

stap: fa aa ~s, gae (aa) to ~s fall to pieces, go to ruin.

†**steid: be ~it** be placed in a difficult or bad condition or position.

stew, steuch *n* trouble *now Sh*.

†**stink in** *or* **into someone's nese** be offensive to someone.

strive (wi) take a dislike (to) or distaste (for) *now Sh NE*.

†**superflue** *adj* excessive, immoderate. *adv* in excess, excessively.

sweir *adj*, *also* ~**t** *now Sh NE, C* unwilling, reluctant, loath. ~**ie** somewhat reluctant (to do something). ~**-drawn** reluctant, hesitating *S*.

swick, sweek: the ~ o the responsibility for (something bad or unfortunate) *NE*.

†**tae, to** as an accusation against, to the detriment of: '*she never heard anything to him*'.

taiglesome tiring, tedious *local sEC-Rox*.

†**tarisum** slow, lingering; wearisome.

†**tarrow at** *or* **on** feel or show reluctance for, show disdain or hesitation at, spurn, refuse.

tedisome tedious, tiresome, boring *now local*.

†**teen** troublesome, distressing.

†**tere(full), tyrefull** difficult, tedious.

†**theat: hae nae ~ o** not like, not have an inclination for.

thole: †**tholance** sufferance, toleration. ~ **wi** put up with, tolerate.

†**thoum, thumb: aboon one's ~** beyond one's reach, power or ability.

thrae reluctant, unwilling.

thraw a check, reverse, setback *now Bnf Abd*.

thrawart adverse *now Sh Ork*.

†**thriftless** unprofitable, useless.

†**tideous** tedious.

time: a fine ~ of day a pretty pass.

tolter, †**towter** unsteady, unstable; insecure, precarious *now Ork*.

traik misfortune, loss, *specif* that caused by disease in farm animals.

†**trigidy** (a) tragedy.

trouble, tribble trouble. **tribblesome** troublesome. †**trublance** troubling; trouble; disturbance.

tyne 1 lose, suffer the loss, destruction or disappearance of, cease to have or enjoy; mislay *Gen except Sh Ork*. **2** spend unprofitably or in vain, waste (time, labour etc). † **~ of** suffer loss of.

ug *v* dislike *now literary*. *n* a dislike, *freq* **take an ~ at** take a dislike to *NE Ags*.

unable †unlucky. **~ for** unfit for, incapable of; *specif* having no appetite for (food).

unfeel unpleasant, disagreeable, dirty, filthy; rough; uncomfortable *S*.

†**unganand** inappropriate, unbecoming, unsuitable.

unheartsome cheerless, melancholy, dismal.

unhearty in poor condition; rather uncomfortable *now Sh*.

†**unlikely, unlikly** unpromising; poor in quality or condition.

unooorament uncomfortable, unpleasant *now Cai*.

†**unreason** unreasonable action or intention; injustice, impropriety.

unricht not right, unjust; dishonest, improper *now Fif SW*.

†**unseely** *of conditions etc* causing or involving misfortune, unhappiness or danger *latterly Abd*.

†**unthrift** lack of success.

†**untymis** untimely.

†**unweirdit** subject to adverse fate, ill-fated.

†**unwillis** against one's will, unwillingly.

†**vilipensioun** the action or fact of despising.

waesome causing sorrow *Gen except Sh Ork*.

†**waik** weaken.

†**wanfortune** misfortune.

†**wanhap** misfortune.

ware waste (one's time, life, efforts etc).

weary depressing, dispiriting *now NE*.

weird: ~less unfortunate *now local Abd-Loth*. **~ly** magical, eerie, dismal, sinister.

wersh *of life, feelings, activity* dull, humdrum, lacking zest.

whaup i(n) the nest *freq proverb* something, *usu* annoying or unpleasant, likely to make its presence felt, something brewing or afoot.

whin, whun: come through the ~s come through an unpleasant or painful experience *local EC-S*.

whistle, whustle: no to gie a ∼ not to give a damn, have nothing but contempt for *now local Sh-Per*.

whummle, whammle a downfall, reversal of good fortune *now Ags Per Dmf*.

will, wull misguided, erring, wayward.

†**wink** shut one's eyes to (an offence, fault etc).

wrang, wrong wrong. ∼**ous** unjust, injurious; ill-gotten. ∼**ously 1** †wrongously. **2** †incorrectly. **3** improperly, illegally.

15.6.3 MISCELLANEOUS SENSATIONS

admiration wonder; astonishment *now Sh*.

†**agitat** perturb, disturb.

†**astonait** astounded, astonished.

†**astonist** astonished.

awfu awful; shocking.

†**awonder** wonder, marvel; astonish, surprise.

baise †confusion, bewilderment. ∼**d** dismayed, confused, bewildered.

†**bash** be confused.

bees: head in the ∼ confused, light-headed.

bumbazed perplexed, confused, stupefied.

claw *n* a scratching of the head as an indication of mild astonishment. *v* scratch (the head) as an indication of astonishment.

clinker a 'stunner', something astonishing, either good or bad *now Sh Ork N*.

confeesed confused *chf NE, EC*.

conflummix confuse, bewilder; a shock *Bnf Abd*.

confoon confound *Bnf Abd*.

creel: in a ∼ in confusion or perplexity *now local Abd-Kcb*.

dabbled bemused, distraught *Bnf*.

dammisht stunned, stupefied.

daumer stun, confuse *now Bnf*.

denumb confound, perplex, stupefy *now Abd*.

doilt dazed, confused, stupid *now Sh Dmf*.

doitrified stupefied, dazed, senseless *now Bnf Ags Fif*.

donner daze, stun, stupefy.

dottle make confused *Bnf Abd*.

drumlie troubled, disturbed, muddled, confused *now Rox*.

dumbfooner(t) dumbfounder(ed), flabbergast(ed).

dumfoutter(t) bewilder(ed), nonplus(sed) *Bnf Abd*.

ferlie, fairly *n, disparaging* a strange sight, a marvel, a curiosity *now Abd*. *v* **1** wonder, marvel, be surprised (at). **2** cause to wonder, surprise

now Sh. adv strange(ly), wonderful(ly). †**ferlifull** wonderful, marvellous. †**have** ∼ marvel, wonder. **na, gret, sma** *etc* ∼ no, great, small *etc* wonder.

fickle puzzle, perplex *local Inv-S*.

flamagaster a stunning shock of surprise or disappointment *NE*.

†**fordullit** made dull or stupid.

†**forwonderit** amazed, astounded.

fraized greatly surprised, having a wild, staring look.

gliff, glaff, glouf *v* gasp (with surprise) *now Ork*. *n* a momentary or sudden sensation (physical or emotional) *now Bwk S*.

glisk a momentary sensation or reaction *now WC*.

habble perplex, confuse *chf S*.

haister perplex, pester, harass *now Gall*.

jabble confusion, agitation *now Sh Per Slk*.

kittle puzzle, perplex, nonplus *now midLoth Rox*.

†**mang 1** bewilder; stupefy. **2** err; become perplexed.

maze *v* amaze *S. n* a state of amazement, perplexity *local*.

†**mervel** marvel.

†**mervellous** marvellous.

mesmerise surprise, astound, dumbfound.

mineer make a din; stupefy with noise *NE*.

†**mistryst** delude, perplex, dismay.

moidert, modderit confused, dazed, *esp* as a result of blows, drink, mental strain etc *WC, S Uls*.

pall surprise, astonish *Sh Ork Bnf*.

penny: hae een like ∼ **bowls** have a startled wide-eyed expression, be saucer-eyed *Ork Ags Gall*.

pichert at a loss, perplexed, unable to cope *Bnf Abd*.

raivel, ravel confuse, perplex, make incapable of coherent thought *Gen except Sh Ork*.

ramfeezle, ramfoozle muddle, confuse *now local Abd-Fif*.

spaik *now local Inv-S*, **spoke: drap** *or* **fa aff the** ∼ collapse with astonishment *S*.

stamagast, stammygaster *n* a great and sudden disappointment, an unpleasant surprise, a shock *NE Ags*. *v* give a sudden surprise or disappointment to, flabbergast, bewilder *now NE Ags Dmf*.

†**stare** a state of staring amazement, admiration etc.

stell *of the eyes* become fixed in a stare of astonishment, horror etc, stand out *now local Lnk-Rox*.

stound stupefy with noise or astonishment, bewilder.

strange marvel or wonder (**at**) *now Sh.*

superannuate stupefied, dazed.

surpreese surprise *now SW.*

taen(-like) surprised, embarrassed, disconcerted; bewitched *now Stlg WC.*

taigle bamboozle; perplex *now Loth Dmf.*

taisle a bamboozling with questions *now Kcb.*

taiver bewilder with talk or questioning. ~**t** bewildered, mentally confused, *esp* through exhaustion or harassment *now Per-Fif.*

tickle puzzle, perplex *local Sh-SW.*

tint lost; forlorn, bewildered.

†uncredible incredulous.

wander, wanner confuse, perplex, bewilder *now Ags Per.*

wauchled perplexed, bewildered, muddle-headed *now Ags.*

whummle, whammle astonish *now Fif.*

will, wull: *also* † ~ **of rede** bewildered, perplexed, at a loss *now NE.* ~**-like** in a perplexity; *freq of appearance* having a dazed look *NE.*

willyart bewildered. *now Wgt.*

†wimple, wumple bewilder, perplex.

yawkin perplexed.

15.6.4 STRONG EMOTION

aflocht agitated, in a flutter.

†agitat perturbed.

†amove affect with strong emotion, excite; be excited.

beal swell with rage, fill with rancour, pain, remorse etc.

†bensell a state of excitement.

†boldin affected by extreme grief, pride etc.

†boldinit swelled with pride, grief etc.

carfuffle a state of excitement or agitation.

case: in a ~ in a state of excitement *NE.*

dabbled bemused, distraught *Bnf.*

dementit demented, *esp* highly excited.

dinnle, †dindill a thrill (of emotion) *now Bnf Abd Ags.*

dirdum violent excitement *now Lnk.*

dirl 1 pierce or cause to tingle with emotion *now Sh Fif Rox.* **2** thrill, quiver or tingle with emotion.

egg: aff (of) one's ~**s** nervous *local Sh-Kcb.*

†fairy a dazed or excited state of mind.

feem *n* a state of agitation or rage *NE. v* fume *NE.*

feerich a state of agitation, excitement, rage or panic *now Bnf Abd.* ~**in** bustling, fumbling because of excitement *now Abd.*

feuch a state of great excitement or rage *now Ags midLoth.*

fey behaving in an excited way *now local NE-Uls.*

fidder flutter, be in a state of excitement *now Kcb.*

fidge fidget; move restlessly from excitement.

firr a state of agitation or excitement *Bnf Abd.*

firris excitement, rage *Abd.*

fizz a bustle, commotion, a state of great excitement.

†flaunter quiver, tremble with excitement or agitation.

flee, fly be violently excited *local.*

flichter *v, of the heart* flutter, quiver, palpitate. *n* a state of excitement *now Abd.*

flocht *n* a flutter, a state of excitement *now Sh Abd. v* excite, flurry *NE.*

flochter a state of excitement *Abd.*

fluffer excite, agitate.

fry a state of worry or distraction, a disturbance *now local Sh-Stlg.*

fung, funk a state of excitement; a state of enthusiasm, commotion.

gae through the fluir, grund *etc* be overcome with shame, embarrassment, astonishment.

gloan excitement *Abd.*

go a state of anxiety, distress or excitement, *freq* **in a** ~ *now Sh-nEC.*

gowp *of the heart or pulse* beat strongly or wildly, palpitate.

great, gret, grit †*of the heart* full with emotion, *esp* grief. ~**-hearted** having the heart filled with emotion, ready to cry, sorrowful *now NE Ags Fif.*

†hache a pain, pang.

hotter shake with excitement *now NE.*

huil: leap *etc* (**oot o**) **the** ~ *of the heart* burst.

jabble confusion, agitation *now Sh Per Slk.*

kip a state of great excitement *Abd Rox.*

kippage disorder, confusion, fuss, predicament; a state of excitement or anger.

kittle (up) become angry, moved or annoyed *now Abd.*

knot: aff (at) the ~, **affen the** ~ off one's head, crazed, distraught *NE Uls.*

†mad upset, troubled; dismayed; dazed.

made distressed, upset *eg* because of pain, overwork, or worry *NE.*

match a bout or fit of ..: '*a greetin match*'.

†tourquhelme overwhelm.

out o anesel beside oneself (with grief, anxiety etc) *now Ork SW Slk.*

overcome *v* overcome.

owertaen, overtaken (with *or* †**in**) deranged, made helpless, overcome *now Per.*

453

panshit, panshine a state of excitement, panic, muddle *now NE*.

†papple be extremely excited.

patience passion *local*.

pelter a state of great excitement *Sh Abd*.

picher a state of confusion or muddle, an excited or overwrought state of mind *NE Ags*.

pilget a state of distress or excitement, a fluster, panic *now NE*.

pirr a harassed, over-excited state of mind, a panic, rage *now Sh Ork NE*.

pit, put: ~ **aboot** distress, upset (oneself).

raised infuriated, wild, over-excited.

ream *of emotion etc* bubble over, effervesce.

ree *adj* over-excited, delirious, crazy *now Ork Fif. n* a state of great excitement or frenzy. *v* become extremely excited, fly into a rage *now Ork*.

reel 1 *of the eyes* roll or revolve with excitement, greed etc *now NE Ags.* **2** *of the head or senses* be in a whirl, become confused.

reevin rash, excitable.

rouse become agitated, excited or enraged *NE-S*.

rug a twinge or pang of nerves or emotions *local NE-Ayr*.

set up arouse, stir up *now Sh Ork*.

skeer, skeerie *now local* nervous, fearful, restive, agitated.

skirl shriek with excitement.

spate a torrent (of words etc); an outburst of emotion.

speerit, spirit, spreit: ~s the mind as the source of emotion, *esp* as affected by circumstances.

stalk: be ca'ed *or* **loup** *etc* **off the** ~ *of the heart* be stopped by a sudden fright etc *now Fif*.

stang a sharp pain, a pang.

†stend a sudden start, a thrill of excitement, fear etc.

stound a pang of mental pain or emotion, a thrill of pleasure or excitement *now Ork-C*.

stramash a state of great excitement *now Sh Cai*.

sweet, sweat a state of excitement.

swelt become faint with emotion, be physically overcome, swoon.

swither, swidder *now chf NE* a state of nervousness or agitation, a panic, fluster *now local Sh-Ayr*.

tak, take a state of excitement, agitation, *etc now S.* ~ **on** get excited or emotional, be worked up.

thirl *v* **1** pierce or affect with emotion; thrill *now literary.* **2** vibrate, quiver, pass through with a tingling sensation. *†n* a thrill.

†tirl quiver, vibrate, thrill.

tirr *v, of one's heart etc* beat, thump *Ags. †n* a thumping, shaking *Ags*.

twang a sudden sharp pain, an acute pang *now local Ags-Rox*.

†unrockit in a state of excitement, *chf* ~ **ʒe** *etc* **raif**.

up in a state of excitement *now NE Ags*.

†vibrant agitated with emotion.

wall, well fever pitch, the heights of passion.

way: in a (dreedfu *etc*) ~ in a state of great distress, worried and upset **about** *local Sh-Ayr*.

†whiltie-whaltie: *chf* **play (a)** ~ *of the heart* beat rapidly, palpitate.

†whisk *of the heart* flutter, palpitate.

wirk affect physically or mentally, *esp* for the worse. ~ **(up)on** operate on, have an influence on, affect.

wowf touched, mad, violently agitated or excited.

yagiment a state of excitement, a flurry, agitation *Abd*.

yivverin in a state of great excitement, very eager or agitated *Abd*.

15.6.5 ELATION

buckle: up in the ~ elated *now Fif Lnk*.

carried carried away, transported, elated *local*.

fey fated to die, doomed, *esp* as portended by peculiar, *usu* elated behaviour; *more vaguely* otherworldly.

gale 1 *†*a state of spiritual uplift, an afflatus. **2** *also* **gell** a state of excitement from anger, joy etc, *chf* **in a** ~.

heich in high spirits, lively, excitable *local Sh-Ayr*.

heicht *of behaviour, emotion etc* a high pitch *now local NE-Uls*.

keevee: on the ~ on the qui vive, on the alert; in high spirits; worked up.

made up wi pleased, elated with.

midden: either (in) the moon or the ~ (in) one of two extremes of mood or behaviour *C, S*.

out: be ~ **o't** be in an exalted state of mind *NE*.

skeich, skey *now Ags* in high spirits, animated, daft, skittish.

sprack *chf literary* lively, animated, alert *now Cai*.

upheeze exalt, elate *now Lnk*.

upliftit elated, in high spirits, proud.

upmade pleased, elated *S*.

vaudie elated.

vauntie pleased, elated *now chf literary*.

vogie proud, elated, vain.

15.6.6 GO

bensell vigorous action; force.

bensin bouncing, vigorous *Bnf*.

birkie lively, spirited *WC*.

birr enthusiasm, verve.

brainy (high-)spirited, lively *now Fif*.

bum go on vigorously *NE Ags*.

busy bee a very busy person.

cant †brisk, lively, smart. ~**y** lively, cheerful.

ca-through drive, energy *Bnf Abd Ags Fif*.

dingle-dousie an active bustling person.

dreel energy, forcefulness *now Ags*.

edgie quick, active *now midLoth Rox*.

feckfu sturdy, forceful, powerful *now Fif*.

feerich ability, activity *now Bnf Abd*.

feerie active, nimble.

fell *adj* energetic and capable, sturdy *now sEC-S*. *adv* vigorously, energetically.

fen(d): ~**fu** able to fend for oneself, energetic *now Ags*. ~**ie** active, lively, healthy *chf Ayr*.

fersell energetic, active.

fire edge the first wave of enthusiasm *Bnf Abd Kcb*.

flech a restless, active person *NE Ags Per*.

flinty keen, sharp, lively *now Ayr*.

forcie vigorous, active, forceful *now Sh NE Ags*.

fung, funk a state of enthusiasm, commotion.

furthie, forthy forward in disposition, bold; go-ahead, energetic *now Abd*.

fushion mental or spiritual force or energy *now NE*.

†galȝeard gallant; lively.

†gaun brisk, active, busy.

geckin lively, playful *Bnf Dmf*.

gloan energy, go *Abd*.

goust(e)rous hearty, vigorous.

gurr drive, spirit *now Abd*.

gustily with gusto, heartily.

heicht *of behaviour, emotion etc* a high pitch *now local NE-Uls*.

kemp: ~**er** a person who strives or contends, a fighter, one who strives to outdo his fellows, a keen worker. ~**ie** *n* a bold or pugnacious person *now Bnf*. *adj* energetic, vigorous *Rox*.

kilter good spirits, fettle, *chf* **in** *or* **out of** ~ .

kim spirited, frolicsome, lively *chf Abd*.

kirr cheerful, lively, brisk *SW*.

kneef 1 mentally or physically alert, agile *chf Sh-N*. **2** fit, in sound health and spirits *N Per*.

laldie: gie it ~ do something vigorously or exuberantly.

lifie full of life, vivacious, brisk *Sh-Fif S*. ~**ness** vivacity, vigour *now Sh Ork Fif*.

linking active, agile, brisk *now Fif Ayr*.

livin-like lively, in good health *local Ork-Gall*.

†querty vivacious, active, in good spirits.

rash active, agile, vigorous *now Rox*.

redd the power to clear or sweep aside obstacles; energy, drive *now Sh Ork*.

†ruskie (a) strong, vigorous, *usu* rough-mannered (person).

shanker a (young) active person *Mry Abd*.

smeddum spirit, energy, drive, vigorous commonsense and resourcefulness.

smergh pith, energy, vitality *now Cai*.

sparkie lively *now Abd Kcdn Per*.

speerack a lively alert person *Cai Ross Inv*.

speerit, spreit, spirit spirit. ~**y** spirited, vivacious, full of energy.

sprack *chf literary* lively, animated, alert *now Cai*.

sprush brisk, smart in one's movements, spry.

spurdie a small lively person *NE*.

stark vigorously, energetically; fully, completely *now Lnk*.

steer: ~**ie** lively, bustling *N nEC Rox*. ~**ing** active, restless, lively.

stourie active, restless *now Ags Fif WC*.

swank: ~**ie**, *also* † ~**in** a smart, active, strapping young man *now local nEC-Wgt*. ~**in** active, agile, athletic.

swashy strapping *now Abd*.

†tait lively, active, nimble.

targer nickname for a big, active, hustling person *now Dmf*.

thrift, trift *Sh Ork* willingness to work, energy, enthusiasm *now Ork*.

through: ~**-ca** energy, drive *now NE Ags*. ~**gaun, ~-gaen** energetic, active *now Fif Lnk Slk*. ~**-pit** energy, activity, capacity for or progress at work *now Sh Abd Per Dmf*.

timmer, timber: *freq* ~ **up** *etc* act oɪ move briskly or vigorously, go at (something) with verve and energy *NE*.

trig active, nimble, brisk, alert.

†trump: the tongue of the ~ the main or most active person in a group; the spokesman.

vertie energetic, active, up early and at work, early-rising *now Bnf Abd*.

†v\ively in a lively way.

virr vigour, energy, force, impetuosity *now local Ork-Loth*.

warrior, *freq* **a great** ~ joc or affectionate term for a lively, spirited person.

waygate speed, progress; push, drive, energy *now Rox Lnk*.

†yaup active.

15.6.7 ANXIETY, CARE

For depression see 15.3.5.

afflickit afflicted.

anxeeity anxiety *now Ags.*

back: with *etc* **one's ∼ to** *or* **at the wall** hard-pressed, facing desperate odds. **∼set** weary; worry.

†barrat distress, trouble, vexation.

blue day a day when one is very anxious *now Abd.*

burnt: be ∼ suffer *now Abd Fif.*

cark care, anxiety, *chf* **∼ an care** *now Bnf.*

†chargeand burdensome, oppressive.

chowed: look like *etc* **a ∼ mouse** have a worn-out appearance *chf S.*

clamant urgent, calling for redress.

claw: in a ∼ in an excited state of annoyance or anxiety *NE.*

come at affect, distress *Sh NE.*

†cummer, cumber *n* trouble, distress. *v* cumber.

dant, daunt daunt. † **∼it** vanquished, subdued.

defeat, †defait 1 defeated *now local Bnf-Fif.* **2** exhausted, worn out *now Bnf Abd.*

dispert despairing; desperate *now Ags.*

distrackit distracted.

doilt wearied, fatigued *now Abd.*

†dolorous having(is) signs of suffering.

doon, down: ∼ draught *now Ags Stlg,* **∼-draw** *now Ags* a depressing influence, a heavy load, a handicap. **∼-drag** a handicap *Bnf Abd Ags.* **∼-haud** a handicap, something that prevents one rising in the world. **∼hadden** kept in subjection. **∼set(ting)** a laying-low (*eg* from a misfortune) *now Bnf Stlg.*

dree 1 endure, suffer (misfortune etc). **2** †pass, spend (time) miserably, drag out (an existence). **∼ one's (ain)** *or* **a sore** *etc* **weird** endure one's fate, suffer a hard etc fate.

†drevel live miserably.

drow a spasm of anxiety *now Abd Ags Fif.*

drumlie troubled, disturbed, muddled, confused *now Rox.*

ergh exhausted in resources.

†extors subject to extortion or oppression.

fauchled tired, worn out, harassed *now C, S.*

fell *of pain, misfortune etc* severe, acute, grievous *now Abd Fif Bwk.*

finnissin fidgeting, anxious *Per.*

focht(en) harassed, worn out *now NE.*

forfauchlet worn out, exhausted.

forfochten exhausted with any kind of effort, *freq* **sair ∼.**

†freet fret, be vexed.

fry a state of worry or distract, a disturbance *now local Sh Stlg.*

fyke *n* **1** restlessness, a state or mood of uneasiness. **2** trouble, bother, worry. **3 ∼s** petty cares. *v* fret, be anxious or troubled *now midLoth.*

girdle: like a hen on a het ∼ restlessly, anxious(ly), impatient(ly).

go a state of anxiety, distress or excitement, *freq* **in a ∼** *now Sh-nEC.*

†grevand grievous, painful, hurtful.

gumple-faced dejected.

haggit weary, exhausted *now Stlg midLoth.*

haggle *v* struggle on *chf S. n* a struggle, a laborious effort *S.*

hard difficulty, hardship, *chf* **if** *etc* **∼ comes** *or* **goes to ∼** if the worst comes to the worst; when it comes to the crunch. **be, come** *or* **gae through (the hans of) the ∼(s)** experience hardship or misfortune *now local Bnf-Fif.*

harlt worried- or tired-looking *now midLoth Bwk.*

harm(s) sorrow, grief, distress *now Sh.*

haud, hold, hald: ∼ doun burden, oppress, afflict, *freq* **hauden doon.**

heavy handfu(l) a heavy burden, an oppressive responsibility.

hechle a struggle; a difficulty; a perplexing piece of work *midLoth Rox.*

hert, hairt heart: ∼'s care anxiety, deep worry *now Sh Ork.* **∼less** disheartened, discouraged, dejected. **∼-rug** a strain on the emotions *now Sh Ork.* **∼-sair** heartsore. **∼-scalded** vexed, sorely grieved *Uls.* **∼ scaud** a source of bitter grief, trouble, disappointment or aversion *now NE Ags Uls.*

hinderend: the ∼ o a' the last straw *chf NE.*

ho: nae (ither) ∼ but no (other) choice, no hope but *Abd.*

ill pit in difficulties, baffled, hard-pressed *local Sh-WC.*

†jamph *v* struggle. **be ∼it** be exhausted or in difficulties.

jaup: ding, knock *or* **gae to ∼** be wrecked or brought to ruin.

kauch care, worry, bustle, anxious exertion *chf SW.*

(k)noolt crushed, dispirited *Gall Rox.*

kyauve a struggle, exertion, a turmoil *chf N.*

little-boukit deflated in esteem *NE.*

†mad upset, troubled; dismayed; dazed.

made distressed, upset, *eg* because of pain, overwork, or worry *NE.*

mae: be at ane ∼ wi't be at breaking point, be at the end of one's tether *S.*

†malese unease or distress.

†**may not** be unable to endure (to do etc).

†**mister** be in distress, be in straits.

munsie a person who is in a sorry state, who has been knocked about etc *NE*.

†**noy** be troubled.

ool be dejected, subdued, as from illness *Sh Uls*. ~**d**, ~**t** downcast, cowed, nervous, bewildered *now NE*.

oorit tired or ailing-looking, dejected.

out o anesel beside oneself (with grief, anxiety etc) *now Ork SW Slk*.

ower beyond the control or capabilities of, too much for *Sh NE Ags*.

owerset overwhelmed, beaten down (by hostile natural forces, *eg* a storm).

pech: a sair ~ a prolonged and weary effort, an exhausting struggle.

pichert at a loss, perplexed, unable to cope *Bnf Abd*.

pilget a fight, struggle, battle against odds *NE*.

pine suffering inflicted as punishment or torture, the pains of Hell *latterly ballad*. † ~**ed**, **pinit** in pain, tortured, tormented.

pingle *v* struggle at a difficult task, exert oneself at something; work hard with little result, drudge. *n* an effort, struggle, fight against odds; a labour with little result *now Fif*. **pingled** hard put to it, harassed with difficulties, overcome with exhaustion. †**pingling** contention, exertion; labour with little success.

pit, put: ~ **aboot** distress, upset (oneself or another). **hard, ill, sair** *etc* **pit(ten) to** hard-pressed, in difficulties.

puggled at a standstill due to exhaustion or frustration, done for, at the end of one's resources.

rack worry needlessly, be over-anxious *Kcb Rox*.

sair, sore *adj* 1 causing mental distress or grief; pressing hard upon one, hard to bear, oppressive. 2 *of a struggle* hard, severe, *now freq (of life in gen)*: **it's a sair fecht**. ~ **awa wi't** far gone, worn out by illness, hard usage etc *NE-nEC*. **sair made** sorely harassed, oppressed, hard put to it *Sh-Ags*.

saut, salt *of experience etc* painful, severe, bitter *now Kcb*.

†**solicit, solist** anxious.

sorra, sorrow: not have one's ~**(s) to seek** have plenty of trouble on one's hands *Sh N, C*.

stieve *of a struggle* hard, grim.

†**strouble** full of troubles.

†**supprise** injury, outrage, oppression.

sweet, sweat a state of anxiety.

†**sweir** oppressed in mind, sad.

†**syte** sorrow, grief, suffering.

taigled tired, weary, harassed *now local sEC-Rox*.

taivert bewildered, mentally confused, *esp* through exhaustion or harassment *now Per-Fif*.

taskit stressed, harassed *now local Ork-Wgt*.

taw work laboriously, struggle *now Kcdn*.

thocht, thought anxiety, care, trouble; a cause for anxiety, a burden, worry. ~**ie** anxious. † ~**iness** anxiety. ~**it** worried, anxious, troubled *now Loth*.

thole *v* suffer, have to bear (pain, grief etc); be subjected to; be afflicted with.

throucome what one has to come through, an ordeal, hardship *Sh NE*.

ticht-hauden hard-pressed, harassed *SW Rox*.

tint forlorn, bewildered.

tire become or be weary or sick **of**.

†**touch** grieve, vex.

trauchle, trackle *v* drudge, labour on in a harassed way, toil and moil. *n* 1 a struggle, a hard time. 2 a source of trouble or anxiety, a burden, encumbrance *now NE*. ~**d** hampered, troubled, worried.

†**travel** travail.

†**tribul** *n, also* ~**ance**, ~**nes** tribulation, distress, affliction. ~**us** full of tribulation. ~**at** afflicted.

†**trist** sadness, sorrow, affliction.

†**troublesome** troubled in mind.

tuggle a struggle *Sh Cai Abd*. †**tuggled** pulled about; fatigued, harassed.

tyauve, chauve *v* strive, struggle (*freq* with little result), live or work hard, exert oneself *NE*. *n* an act of labouring, exertion, a hard struggle *NE*.

typit worn out by hard work *Bnf Abd*.

†**tuneis** not easily, (only) with difficulty, scarcely.

vex a source of sorrow or annoyance.

wabbit, wabbit out *chf C* exhausted, feeble *Gen except Sh Ork*.

†**wandreth, wander** misery, hardship, poverty.

†**wanease** uneasiness.

wanrest unrest, a state of uneasiness or trouble *now Sh*. ~**fu**, ~**ie** *now Sh* restless, unsettled.

†**wanrufe** disquiet, unrest.

warsle, wrestle, wrastle *now Sh, n* a fight against circumstances or hardship *local Sh-Per*. *v* make one's way through life with much toil and difficulty, scrape along *now local*. **warslin** struggling.

wauchle last out (a period of time) in a weary, listless way; make (one's way) with difficulty *now Ork Ags*.

way: in a (dreedful *etc*) ~ in a state of great distress, worried and upset **about** *local Sh-Ayr*.

†**wecht, weight** oppress (the mind).

†**whip, whup: lick a** *or* **the** ~**shaft** kiss the rod, suffer humiliation or defeat.

†**wilsome, wulsome** lost, wandering; forlorn.

wirry worry.

witter *now NE Ags,* **wutter** struggle, carry on with difficulty, earn one's living precariously *NE.*

†**wrake** suffering, punishment, vengeance.

wratch: ~**edly** wretchedly. ~**edness** wretchedness.

15.6.8 MADNESS

See also 9.28. For fury, see also 15.6.13; for the mentally retarded see 15.2.4.

ajee 1 *of the mind* off the straight. **2** in or into a disturbed or disordered state.

awa, away: ~ **i the heid** deranged, lunatic *now Edb.* ~ **wi't** out of one's senses.

begoyt foolish, mad.

brain: ~**ish** wandering in the mind *Ags Fif.* † ~**wode** mad.

†**brank** behave violently or without restraint.

by oneself, †**by one's mind** out of one's mind, insane, beside oneself.

cairried delirious, not rational *local.*

capernoited capricious, crazy *now Abd Lnk.*

cat-wittit hare-brained, unbalanced *local Cai-Kcb.*

crack(-wittet) crack-brained, crazy *Bnf Abd.*

creel: in a ~ mad *now local Abd-Kcb.*

daft crazy, insane. ~**ish** somewhat deranged *now Abd Fif.*

deleerit delirious, mad; temporarily out of one's senses *now Fif Renfr Ayr.*

dementit demented, *esp* highly excited.

doit act foolishly, be crazed, enfeebled or confused in mind *now Abd.* ~**ered** witless, confused *now Fif.* ~**it** not of sound mind, foolish, silly.

dottle 1 become crazy *Cai Bnf Abd Ags.* **2** make crazy or confused *Bnf Abd.*

Fifish eccentric, slightly deranged *now Ags Fif.*

†**flowin(g)** unstable, changeable, fickle.

forby: be ~ **oneself** be beside oneself, out of one's wits *Sh Ags midLoth.*

frainesy (a) frenzy.

gane mad, crazy.

gang by oneself go mad *now Abd.*

gyte *adj* **1** mad, insane; mad with rage, pain etc, *freq* **gang** ~. **2** mad or crazy with longing or desire *now local Ork-midLoth. n* a madman, fool. **gytit** half-witted, crazy *now Ags.*

hazy weak in intellect, mentally unbalanced *now EC Arg Slk.*

heich out of one's mind, raving in delirium *NE.*

heid, head: aff at the ~ *local,* **awa in the** ~ *local Kinr-S* off one's head.

horn daft quite mad *now Cai Ags.*

hyte mad, highly excited, enraged; excessively or madly keen. **gae** *or* **gang** ~ go mad with rage or passion, fly into a hysterical state *now Cai Kcb.*

judgement reason, senses, wits, sanity, *esp* **lose** *or* **be out of one's** ~.

knot: aff (at) the ~, **affen the** ~ off one's head, crazed, distraught *NE Uls.*

licht, light: ~ **in the head,** †**licht** demented.

madderam madness, folly, frantic rage, tantrums *chf Sh Ork.*

†**mang** go distracted or frantic. **mangit, mangin** confused, crazed.

mixed mentally confused *local Sh-Per.*

nail: aff at the ~ deranged.

out o one's head off one's head, out of one's mind *now local.*

peerie-heidit in a state of mental confusion *now C, S.*

queerways in not quite a normal state *now Ork Kcb.*

radge, radgie mad, violently excited, furious, wild.

raivel, ravel: ~**ed** confused in mind; rambling, delirious *Gen except Sh Ork.*

rame talk nonsense, rave.

†**rammage, rammasche** violent, wild, unruly; frenzied.

rammish, ramsh mad, crazy *now Ork.*

ramp an outburst of temper, a violent mood *NE Ags.*

rapture a paroxysm, fit, *esp* of rage *now local Per-Dmf.*

raverie, reverie raving, furious or deranged speech *now Abd.*

ree *adj* over-excited, delirious, crazy *now Ork Fif. n* a state of great excitement or frenzy. *v* become extremely excited, fly into a rage *now Ork.*

reid, red, rid: ~ **wud** stark staring mad, beside oneself with rage, mentally unbalanced *now local N-SW.*

richt, right: not ~ not in one's right mind, mentally unbalanced; abnormal, **uncanny.**

rizzon *now NE,* **reason: out o one's** ~ out of one's mind *now local Sh-Per.*

rove wander in thought or speech, be delirious, rave *now Sh-Cai Ags.*

†**sk(a)ivie, skeevie** harebrained, daft, mentally deranged.

skeer, skeerie *now local* behaving irrationally, mentally unstable.

†**skire** ? be mad. ~ **mad** absolutely, utterly, altogether mad.

skite off one's head, daft *now Bnf Abd.*

stramash a state of great rage *now Sh Cai.*

superannuate mentally deranged, senile *now Fif.*

taiver wander in mind or speech, rave *now Per.*

†**vary** wander in the mind, rave.

wandert confused, bewildered; mentally disordered *now local Sh-Gsw.*

†**wede** be or become mad. **wedand** raging, raving.

wise, wice: no ~ **(eneuch)** off one's head, insane *NE.*

†**twit: out o one's** ~ out of one's senses.

wowf touched, mad, violently agitated or excited.

wrang, wrong: *also* ~ **in the heid** *or* **mind** deranged, insane, touched *now NE.*

wuid, wud *adj* mad, insane, demented *Gen except Sh Ork. adv* crazily, in a daft or demented way; *freq as intensifier* absolutely, 'clean': '*the bodie's gane wood crazy*'. **in a** ~**en dream** with a sudden frantic motion or effort, like fury. † ~**ness** mad rage, a paroxysm affecting the brain. ~**drim** *now literary* a dazed state, a great mental confusion as in waking from a dream; a brainstorm. **aince** ~ **and aye (the) waur** getting madder and madder. **rin** ~ go clean off one's head, behave wildly and recklessly.

15.6.9 JEALOUSY

alagust suspicion, disgust *NE.*

bodement foreboding *now Abd.*

chaw make jealous *now local Ags-Kcb.* ~**some** causing envious disappointment, galling *now Lnk.*

doot, doubt *n* doubt. *v* fear, be afraid, suspect (that..).

†**dreaddour** fear, dread, apprehension, distrust.

dree *v* suspect *now Ags.*

dreid suspect, fear; be in doubt. **ill** ~ grave suspicion, apprehension *local Cai-Fif.*

een(d)il be or become jealous *now Sh.*

†**eldnyng** jealousy.

envy, †**invy** envy. †**invyar** a person who envies. † ~**fu** full of envy, envious **of** *or* **that.** †**invious** envious.

glint a flash of intuition, a slight suspicion *local Sh-midLoth.*

ill-thochted having nasty or suspicious thoughts, nasty-minded *local Sh-EC.*

jalouse suspect, be suspicious of (a person or thing).

jealous, †**jalous** 1 jealous. 2 †suspicious, apprehensive.

†**jolesy** jealousy.

jubish dubious, suspicious *now Ork Cai C Uls.*

ken o anesel be aware consciously or intuitively, have instinctive knowledge *Sh NE.*

misbelieve disbelieve, doubt.

misdoubt *v* 1 distrust, doubt, disbelieve. 2 presuppose, suspect, be afraid (that) *now Sh SW. n* a doubt, suspicion, fear *now Ags Ayr.*

mislippen distrust, doubt, suspect *local NE-S.*

†**mistrow** disbelieve, doubt (something).

suspeck suspect.

†**ware** be apprehensive for. **wary** beware, be on one's guard.

†**weer(s)** doubt, uncertainty, apprehension. **werefull** doubtful.

5.6.10 LONGING

aiver, yivver eager, ardent.

†**asperans** hope.

awid eager, longing.

be fidgin fain be restlessly or excitedly eager *now local Bnf-Fif.*

begotted infatuated.

†**bentnes** inclination, intentness.

†**bid** offer, desire, seek (to do something).

bode expect, desire, aim at *now Bnf.*

browden *adj, chf* ~ **on** *etc* intent on, insistent for *now Bnf. v* be fond (of), be intent (on) *now Bnf Abd Fif.*

crave desire, hankering after *now Bnf Ags.*

ee regard, liking, craving: '*you wi a lang ee till anither lad*'. **have one's** ~ *or* **een in** covet *local.*

ettle: *v* ~ **for, after** *or* **to do** desire very much, be eager for *chf N. n* an ambition, desire.

fa(ll) in fancy wi take a fancy to *Sh Ork Gsw Lnk.*

far ben *of the eyes* dreamy, abstracted *now midLoth Bwk Uls.*

fond foolishly keen, infatuated, doting.

glagger be avid, long **for** *NE.*

gleg: as ~ **as a gled** as keen or eager as a hawk.

green long or yearn **for** *now local Ork-Fif.*

growk *esp of a child* look longingly at food etc *now Kcdn Ags Per.*

†**thameart** childishly attached to home.

hame-drauchtit homesick; drawn to home *NE.*

hert, hairt, heart: ~-**hunger** a longing for affection *Sh Abd Ags.* **hae one's** ~ **an one's ee in** be extremely interested in, be eager to possess *local NE-Arg.*

hyte excessively or madly keen.

ill: ∼**-ee** a longing, yearning *Abd Ags.* ∼ **aboot** desiring greatly, keen on, fond of *now NE.*

inklin(g) an inclination, a slight desire *now Sh Ork N.*

keen: be ∼ **of** be eager for (something) *or* to (do something), be fond of, have a liking for *local N-S.*

lanely lonely. **lanerly** lonely, alone. **lanesome** lonely, lonesome.

lief: I *etc* **wad as** ∼ *or* ∼**er** I *etc* would rather.

mad for extremely eager for or desirous of.

mang be extremely eager or anxious, long *NE.*

†**mind** have in mind, intend, desire.

†**miscairry** fail to obtain (one's desire) *chf Abd.*

misslie 1 alone, lonely through absence of a usual companion. **2** missed, regretted owing to being absent *SW Uls.*

provokshin provocation, temptation *now Sh.*

rife quick, ready, eager **for** *now Sh Ork.*

sair, sore *of temptations* pressing hard upon one, hard to bear, oppressive.

†**scaud, scald** (cause to) burn with desire. ∼**ing** *of desire* burning, fervent.

seek wish, desire (to) *now local Sh-Kcb.*

snell quickly, keenly, eagerly.

think lang long (**for**) *now Sh-Per.*

†**thrae** eagerness, haste.

†**tire** grow weary of waiting **for**, long **for** or **to**.

waff, waif solitary, lonely.

wait await, remain in expectation of *now N nEC Rox.*

wan hope, expectation *now Sh Ork Cai.*

weary for long for (*esp* something or someone missed for some time).

will, wull will, wish, intent. **willin(g), wullint** *now Kcdn C, S* eager, deliberately intending.

wiss, wush, wish *v* want, desire, wish (for): '*Do you wish any more?*' *n* a wish.

wuid, wud: ∼ **for** *or* **to** eager, desperately keen to *now Stlg.*

yare eager, agile.

†**yaup** eager, ready.

yawkin very eager.

yeuk be keen or eager; have a strong urge (to do something). ∼**ie** excitedly eager, impatiently waiting to do something *now local Sh-Stlg.*

†**yird, yirth:** ∼ **hunger** a strong desire to possess land.

yivvery desirous, anxious.

†**ȝarne** *v* yearn; desire earnestly. *adj, adv* eager(ly), earnest(ly).

15.6.11 LIKING

able having an appetite **for**.

†**admeir** admire.

†**applese** please, gratify, propitiate; content, satisfy.

†**appreve** approve.

apprise value, appreciate.

appruve approve *now Sh.*

†**arbiter** will, pleasure.

†**belufit** beloved.

†**bensell** a strong inclination.

†**bentnes** inclination, intentness.

†**blason** blazon, describe or proclaim with praise.

†**blink** glance kindly, look fondly (at).

blithe happy because **of**, glad **of** *now Ags.*

browden *adj, chf* ∼ **on** *etc* enamoured, extremely fond of *now Bnf. v* be fond (of), be intent (on); pet, pamper *now Bnf Abd Fif.*

built: be ∼ **up on** be wrapped up in, devoted to (someone) *NE, C.*

†**care** have regard for: '*he cairis ȝow nocht*'.

cock indulge, pamper, *chf* ∼ (**someone**) **up with** (**something**) *local Abd-Kcb.*

come up one's back fit in with one's own inclination (to do something).

†**commend** commendation, praise.

†**complese** please, satisfy.

†**conceit, concait** a good opinion **of** (another).

content *adj* pleased, happy. *n* satisfaction.

cuiter (up) pamper.

culyie, cullie cherish.

daft: *chf* ∼ **about, for, on** extremely fond of, crazy about.

†**dair** *adj* dear.

daut *n* a darling *now Cai. v* pet, fondle, make much of *now local Cai-Lnk.* ∼**ie** a pet, darling *now local Bnf-Lnk.*

daylicht: not be able to see ∼ **til** *or* **for someone** be blind to someone's faults *now Bnf Abd.*

delicht delight.

†**delyte:** ∼**able** delectable, delightful. **delytably** delightfully, daintily. ∼(**e**)**sum** delightful. **tak** *etc* **in** ∼ take *etc* delight in.

†**devote** devoted **to**.

dint (of) affection, liking, regard (for) *Abd Ags.*

doddle something attractive.

dossach (wi) fondle, pet, fuss over needlessly *Bnf Abd.*

draw to come to like (someone) gradually *now Bnf Abd Fif.*

ee: a person's ae *or* **tae** ∼ a person's favourite, the apple of someone's eye *now local NE-Kcb.*

eedol an idol *now Bnf Ags.*

†**effectioun** affection.

†**emplese, enplese 1** give pleasure or satisfaction (**to** a person). **2** be pleased; choose. **emplesance, emplesour** pleasure, satisfaction.

†**enjose** enjoy.

†**estimy** *v* esteem.

fain fond **of** *now Sh Ork*. † **~est** most gladly. † **~ness** liking, love *now Sh*.

far ben *or* **in** intimate, friendly, in great favour.

fittit pleased, satisfied *now local NE-Rox*.

floan *chf of a woman towards men* show affection, *esp* in a sloppy way *Abd*.

fond foolishly keen, infatuated, doting.

foonge (on) fawn, as a dog, flatter, show affection in a sloppy way *NE*.

fortifee pet, pamper, spoil (a child etc) *NE*.

fraik *n* affectionate fussing. *v* flatter, make a fuss of, pet, pamper *Ork Ags Fif*.

glack someone's mitten gratify someone *chf NE*.

glorifee glorify.

goo a liking, taste (**o** *or* **for**).

graitifee gratify.

†**thamesucken** greatly attached to one's home.

heeze elevate, exalt, extol.

hert, hairt, heart: †**hertly** dear to the heart, beloved. **~-glad** very glad, delighted *Sh-Cai*. **gae** *or* **gang wi** *or* **tae one's ~** be to one's liking *NE Ags SW*. **taste someone's ~** be agreeable to someone's tastes, be to someone's liking *N*.

idoleeze idolize.

†**joyse** take pleasure, rejoice **in**.

keen: be ~ of be eager for (something) *or* to (do something), be fond of, have a liking for *local N-S*.

kirn, *chf* **~ wi** fuss over, mollycoddle; be constantly and demonstratively affectionate towards, pet *NE*.

kittle *v* stimulate, please; make excited *now local NE-S*. *n* a pleasurable excitement, stimulus.

knichtit highly gratified as by some honour, delighted with oneself *Abd*.

kythe to *or* **wi** take after, accord with; be attracted to *now Kcdn*.

licht, light: canna see the ~ o day to be blind to the faults of (a person) *NE, EC, S*.

lief, †**lee** *chf early verse and latterly ballad* dear, beloved, agreeable.

like, lik like. **it ~s** it pleases, suits, is agreeable to (me etc) *now literary*. †**liking** *chf early verse* happiness, contentment; pleasure, satisfaction.

†**little** used to imply modest depreciation, affection etc: '*this lytle buk*'.

†**lofe, love** *v* praise, honour; value highly. *n* praise; honour, glory. **lovage, loving** the act of praising, praise; honour, credit; fame, glory. **lovit, luvit** beloved, dear.

made up wi pleased, elated with.

mak o fuss over, make much of.

mends: get *or* **hae (a** *or* **the) ~ of** get satisfaction from.

past: not to (be able to) see ~ someone be obsessed with someone's virtues or merits, favour someone to the exclusion of all others.

pet *n, also* †**carlingis ~** a favourite person, a petted or spoiled child. *v, also* **pettle** *now S* make a pet of, treat with special ʾvour, fondle, cuddle.

†**pleasance 1** *also* **plesandis** the feeling of pleasure, joy, happiness, satisfaction. **2 ~(s)** a source of pleasure; a pleasure or delight.

†**please** like, approve of, be pleased or satisfied with.

pleasure please, content, give pleasure to, satisfy *now local NE-SW*.

preen-tae a person attached to another *Fif Edb*.

pridefu pleased.

prize 1 value or esteem highly, think much of. **2** †praise, commend.

proud 1 †highly pleasing. **2** pleased, gratified, glad.

†**rajose** rejoice.

reid, red, rid: gae roon a bodie's hert like a yaird o ~ flannan warm the heart, be very palatable or flattering *Sh-N*.

respeck, respect *n* affectionate esteem. *v* regard affectionately, esteem.

ruise *v* praise, extol, *esp* exaggeratedly, flatter *now Sh-N Kcb*. *n* praise, commendation, flattery.

saft, soft: have a ~ side to have a special liking for, be well-disposed towards.

†**sairie, sorry** *expressing affection:* 'poor old ..'

saitisfee satisfy.

†**sasiabilitie** capability of being satisfied.

saul *now local Sh-SW*, **sowl: the (wee) ~, my (wee) ~** term of familiarity.

ser *v, also* **serve, sair** satiate, sate, glut *now N*. *n* one's fill, enough, satiety *now NE Ags Rox*.

set 1 pleased *now Bnf Abd*. **2** disposed, inclined, determined, *freq* **well-~** *now Sh-C*.

†**shore** offer as a mark of favour.

sicht: a ~ for sair een a welcome or pleasing sight.

skeel: hae ~ o have a liking for or favourable opinion of.

†**slocken** sate, satisfy (desire).

†**sover** trust (**in** something).

stench, stanch a satisfying *now NE*.

suit, shuit 1 suit. **2** be agreeable or convenient

to. **3** please, give pleasure to *chf* ~**ed** pleased, satisfied *Gen except Sh Ork*.

†**syth** *v* **1** satisfy, give satisfaction to. **2** be satisfied. *n, also* ~**ment** satisfaction, compensation.

tak, take: be ~**en on with** take a liking to, be attracted by *Gen except Sh Ork*. **be** ~**en up about** *or* **wi** be charmed by, find agreeable *local Sh-Kcb*. ~ **wi** find agreeable, take kindly to *now local Sh-Dmf*.

†**tender** *adj* dear, beloved.

†**thank:** ~**fully 1** graciously; with satisfaction. **2** so as to please, acceptably, satisfactorily. ~**fulness** gratification, satisfaction.

†**theat: hae** ~ **o** like, have an inclination for.

time: haud a ~ (**wi**) make a fuss (of) *Sh N*.

†**tinkle on** *etc* sing the praises of.

†**traist** trust, have confidence **in**.

vauntie pleased, elated *now chf literary*.

wan liking *now Sh Ork Cai*.

waste spoil, pamper (a child, pet etc) *C*.

weel-peyed well-paid, well-satisfied.

wiss, wush, wish: to a (very) ~ just as one would wish, to one's complete satisfaction.

15.6.12 GRATITUDE

†**addebted** indebted.

bunsucken under an obligation, beholden *NE*.

cun someone (nae *etc***) thanks** feel or express (no *etc*) gratitude to someone.

due: be ~ be indebted, owe.

graititeed gratitude *NE*.

hairst, harvest: hae a day in ~ **wi someone, owe someone a day** *etc* **in** ~ owe someone a favour *now Abd Ags*.

mento: in *or* **out of someone's** ~ under or free from obligation to someone *NE*.

thankrife full of thanks, grateful *Fif Ayr SW*.

15.6.13 ANGER

For blind fury, see also 15.6.8.

†**amove** annoy, anger.

anger *n* **1** a cause of grief or vexation. **2** †a fit or spell of rage. *v* become angry. ~**some** provoking, vexatious.

attery *of looks or appearance* grim, angry, forbidding.

barm come to a head, fume *now Sh Abd wLoth*.

†**barrat** distress, trouble, vexation.

beal swell with rage, fill with rancour etc.

birse anger, temper, *chf* **his** *etc* ~ **is up. birsie** hot-tempered, passionate.

botherer annoyance *now Abd Fif*.

†**brain** mad, enraged, furious.

†**breme** furious, fierce, violent.

broo, brow: lat *or* **put doon a** ~ show displeasure *now local Ork-Ags*.

bucker vexation, annoyance; a nuisance *now Bnf Abd*.

bung: in a *or* **the** ~(**s**) in a temper *now Bnf Abd*.

canker put into a bad temper *now Bnf Abd*. ~(**i**)**t** cross, ill-natured.

cantle up bristle with anger *Bnf Abd*.

capernicious short-tempered, fretful, fault-finding *NE*.

capernoited, capernoitie *now Abd* irritable *now Abd Fif*.

carnaptious irritable, quarrelsome.

cat-wittit short-tempered.

chaw provoke, vex *now local Ags-Kcb*.

clamersum noisily discontented, contentious *now Bnf Abd*.

claw: in a ~ in an excited state of annoyance or anxiety *NE*.

†**commove** move to anger, excite to passion.

corruption temper, anger *now local Bnf-Fif*.

crab 1 †annoy, make angry. **2** become angry *now Kcb*.

crabbit in a bad temper, cross.

craw in someone's crap irritate, annoy or henpeck someone; give cause for regret *now Ags Fif*.

cruik, crook: ~ **one's mou** distort the mouth as a sign of displeasure or ill temper.

curst very cross *now Abd Ags*.

cut temper, (bad) humour *local:* '*he's in bad cut*'.

dance: dancin mad in a towering rage *now local Cai-Kcb*. ~ **one's lane** dance with joy or rage *now Abd*.

†**danger** displeasure, enmity.

deave annoy with noise or talk. **deavance** annoyance, nuisance *now Abd*.

desperation a great rage *now Bnf Abd*.

dirdum bad temper, ill humour *now Lnk*.

dockit *of speech or temper* clipped, short *now Bnf Abd Fif*.

eat: ~ **oneself,** ~ **one's thumb(s)** be extremely annoyed or vexed *now Sh Abd Ags*.

†**engrave** annoy.

†**ennoy** annoyance, vexation, trouble.

†**ern, urn** pain, irritate.

faize annoy, inconvenience, ruffle *now Bnf*.

fash *v* **1** trouble, annoy, anger, inconvenience. **2** vex or bother oneself. **3** ~ **at,** ~ **of** be impatient with, grow weary of. **4** †make trouble. *n* **1** annoyance; bother. **2** a troublesome person *now midLoth WC.* **~erie** trouble, annoyance. **~ious** troublesome, annoying.

feem *n* a state of agitation or rage *NE*. *v* fume *NE*.

feerich a state of agitation, excitement, rage or panic *now Bnf Abd.*

feuch a state of great excitement or rage *now Ags midLoth.*

finnissin fidgeting, anxious *Per.*

firris excitement, rage *Abd.*

fizz *v* be in a great rage. *n* a state of great rage.

flist *v* fly into a rage *now NE. n* a sudden outburst of rage, a fit of temper *NE Ags.* **~y** irascible, irritable *NE Ags.*

†freet fret, be vexed.

fuff *v* fly into a temper. *n* a sudden outburst of temper *now Bnf local EC.*

fuffy short-tempered, impatient.

fung, funk *v* fly into a temper or rage, sulk. *NE. n* a bad temper, tantrum *now local Sh-Kcb.*

fyke †cause pain or bother to, trouble, vex. **fykie** restless, fidgety *now local NE-S.*

gale a state of excitement from anger, joy, *chf* **in a ~.**

gaw gall, vex, irritate.

girdle: like a hen on a het ~ restless(ly), anxious(ly), impatient(ly).

†gram anger, malice.

grunch a grumble, grunt, growl *now Rox.*

gyte mad with rage.

heckle-pins: be (kept) on ~ be (kept) in suspense or on tenterhooks *now N nEC.*

heelie affront, hurt, offend.

het, hot: ~-skinned fiery, irascible *now N nEC.*

hodge fidget, twitch, *usu* with impatience or discomfort *now NE.*

hotchin restless with impatience, extremely eager.

humph: set up one's ~ become angry and antagonistic *EC, WC Slk.*

hyte mad, enraged. **gae** *or* **gang ~** go mad with rage, fly into a hysterical state *now Cai Kcb.*

ill-nature bad temper, irritability. **~d** bad-tempered, irritable.

kailier a person who outstays his welcome *Ross Inv Uls.*

kame against the hair ruffle, irritate *NE Fif.*

†ket irascible, quick-tempered *SW.*

kippage a state of excitement or anger.

kittle: ~ (up) 1 provoke, annoy, tease *Gen except Sh Ork.* **2** become angry, moved or annoyed *now Abd.* **~ in the trot** quick-tempered, irritable *NE.*

knapper-knytlich short-tempered *Abd.*

mad infuriated, beside oneself with rage; angry, annoyed.

madderam madness, folly, frantic rage, tantrums *chf Sh Ork.*

miscomfit displease, offend *Bnf Abd.*

misfit offend, displease *Bnf Abd.*

mismay trouble, bother, upset.

†mismuive trouble, disturb.

†misset displease, annoy, disconcert; be displeasing **to.**

†mistemper disturb, upset.

nat a small-sized, sharp-tempered person *now Sh Abd.*

nettles: on ~ on tenterhooks, impatient, ill-humoured.

†nither oppress, vex.

†noy *v* **1** annoy, vex, irritate. **2** be troubled, *chf* be incensed, angry. *n* vexation, harm.

nurr growl like an angry dog, snarl like a cat *now Sh Cai.*

offen offend.

†onrestles *appar* restless.

†outrage a sense of injury; anger, rage.

owercoup upset.

pawt 1 stamp (the foot) in rage *now Sh Abd Ayr.* **2** stamp around angrily *now Cai.*

pest *n* a troublesome, annoying person. *v* trouble, annoy, plague, pester *local Sh-SW.*

pet cause to take offence, anger, upset.

pirr *n* **1** a fit of temper, sudden rage *Sh Ork NE Bwk S.* **2** a harassed, over-excited state of mind, a panic, rage *now Sh Ork NE. v* tremble with anger, fizz with rage *now Sh.*

pit, put: ~ aboot inconvenience, cause trouble to; distress, upset (oneself or another).

plaister *n* a person who thrusts himself on the attention or company of others, a fawning or ingratiating person *now WC. v* intrude inopportunely *Kcdn nEC Rox.*

pouk at annoy, harass *now Kcb.*

preen: be sittin on ~s be in a very nervous, apprehensive state, be on tenterhooks.

provoke 1 a person or thing which causes annoyance, a nuisance, pest. **2** †a provocation, challenge, invitation, summons. **provokshin** provocation, temptation *now Sh.*

pug: get one's ~gy up *now Fife,* **lose one's ~gy** *C, S* lose one's temper.

radge, radgie mad, violently excited, furious, wild.

†radote mutter disconnectedly.

rag: lose one's *or* **the ~** lose one's temper.

raise *v* infuriate, enrage, drive into a frenzy *now Sh-N, SW, S. n* a state of extreme bad temper, a

frenzy *Ags-Stlg.* **~d** infuriated, wild, over-excited.

rampage *v* rage or rush about furiously. *n* an outburst of rage; violent, disorderly behaviour.

ramsh brusque, testy *Abd.*

rapture a paroxysm, fit, *esp* of rage *now local Per-Dmf.*

ree become extremely excited, fly into a rage *now Ork.*

reeho a state of excited impatience, a stir *Bnf Abd.*

reek show anger or fury, fume *now Ayr.* **~in lum, a sour ~ in the house** a source of annoyance which drives one from the house, *esp* a nagging wife *now local Sh-Fif.*

reid, red, rid †mad, furious. **~ mad** furiously angry, demented *now Sh Cai.*

rimpin a miserable or annoying person, *eg* a mean old woman *SW, S.*

rouse become agitated, excited or enraged *NE-S.*

rumballiach *of temperament* tempestuous, stormy *S.*

scaud, scald vexation.

scunner 1 a nuisance. 2 a troublesome person.

seeck, sick tiresome *Fif Ags.*

seed: a ~ in one's teeth *etc* something which irritates or annoys one.

setterel short-tempered *NE.*

short: ~ in the trot *NE,* **~ in the pile** *SW* on *etc* **~ trot** in a bad temper, curt and uncivil.

sick-tired sick and tired.

skime a glance of the eye, a quick (often sideways) or angry look *now Kcb.*

snag snarl (at) *now Kcdn.* **~ger** snarl *Bnf Abd.* † **~gy** sarcastic, snappish.

snap short-tempered, giving a short or evasive reply, ready to find fault *now Sh.* † **~per(t)** snappish, tart, curt. **~pit** snappish(ly) *now Ork Ags.* **~pous** hasty in temper, testy *now Abd.*

†**snuff** a rage, huff.

sorra, sorrow a rascal, a pest of a person *now Sh N Per.* **~fu** causing vexation, troublesome *now Sh Cai Per.*

spittin a small hot-tempered person *Bnf Abd.*

†**spunk(ie)** a hot-tempered, irascible person.

staw *n* an annoyance, nuisance; a pest, a bore *local Bwk-S.* *v, also* **stall** 1 become bored or fed up *local Ags-S.* 2 tire, weary, bore with monotony or repetition *now chf SE, S.* **stawsome** tiresome, boring.

steering active, restless, lively.

stick in one's crap cause resentment, 'stick in one's gullet' *now Abd Stlg Lnk.*

†**stomachat** indignant, angry.

stourie active, restless *now Ags Fif WC.*

†**straik against the hair** annoy, ruffle someone's feelings.

†**strouble** disturb, trouble.

strunt offend, pique, affront.

sturt trouble, disturb, annoy *now Sh.* **~some** disturbing, troublesome, annoying.

†**suddenty** a sudden outburst of rage, an act done in hot blood, *freq* **of** *or* **on (a) ~** without premeditation.

taisle *v* tease, irritate, vex *now Kcb.* *n* a vexing *now Kcb.*

taiver annoy, irritate.

tak, take a state of rage *etc now S.*

tantersome exasperating, annoying *NE.*

tap, top: ~ o lint *or* **tow** a fiery-tempered, irritable person.

†**tary** *n* vexation, trouble, harm. *v* provoke, harass.

taum a fit of rage, bad temper.

tear †rage (at). **~er** a passionate, irascible person *now Sh Cai Lnk.*

teedy cross, fractious *now Wgt.*

teen †*n* wrath, anger, rage. *v* trouble, annoy, provoke. *adj* vexatious, troublesome, distressing. † **~full** angry.

thin piqued, annoyed *Abd Ayr.*

†**thrae** angry, violent.

thrawn cross, in a **dour**, sullen mood.

tiggie fractious, cross *now Ags Per.*

tirr a passion, a fit of bad temper or rage *now Sh Ork Dmf.*

tirrivee a fit of rage or bad temper, a tantrum *freq* **take a ~** *C, S.*

tit a fit of bad temper or rage *now Bnf Ags Fif.* **~tie** short-tempered, irritable *now Fif.*

†**toit** a fit of bad temper.

†**touch** grieve, vex.

toustie testy, irascible.

tow: lat the ~ gang wi the bucket *proverb* give up, get rid of something impatiently, cut one's losses *NE nEC.*

tramp on a person's taes encroach on a person's interests or preserves, take advantage of, offend a person *now Sh N Per.*

ug annoy, upset, exasperate *now Sh NE.* **~gin** objectionable; annoying, vexatious *now NE.* **~git** upset, annoyed *now Sh NE.*

unresty unrestful, ill at ease *now Cai.*

up in a state of irritation *now NE Ags.*

vex a source of regret, sorrow or annoyance.

vexsome full of vexation *now Lnk.*

†**vibrant** agitated with anger.

weary annoying, troublesome. **wearifu** troublesome, annoying *now NE.*

weest anxious, fidgety *Abd.*

whippert hasty and sharp in manner or behaviour.

wicked, wickit *of persons or their actions* bad-tempered, viciously angry.

wirk trouble, annoy.

wirr *v joc of a person* growl, snarl *NE Ags Per.* †*n* a fit of bad temper.

witter *now NE Ags,* **wutter** be restless with impatience, fret.

†**wrack** wreak, give vent to (feelings of rage).

wraith wroth, angry.

wrang, wrong: rise aff one's ∼ **side** get up in a bad temper *now local Sh-Per.*

wrath, wreth *now Sh n* wrath. †*v* make (a person) angry.

wuid, wud furiously angry, beside oneself with rage *now local NE-Dmf.* † ∼**ness** mad rage, a paroxysm affecting the brain.

yoller speak loudly, excitedly, angrily or incoherently, shout, bawl *now Dmf.*

15.6.14 SHAME

†**answer** requite, compensate (a person).

†**bash** be abashed.

beal swell with remorse etc.

†**cormundum: (cry)** ∼ confess one's fault.

doonleuk a hangdog expression *Bnf Abd.* **doonlookin** sullen, guilty-looking.

†**eat in one's words** eat one's words, retract.

†**eschame** feel shame. **eschamit** ashamed.

forthink 1 think of with regret, regret that, repent of *now NE.* **2** †feel repentance.

gae through the fluir, grund *etc* be overcome with shame or embarrassment.

guilt: tak ∼ **til ane(sel)** feel or show guilt, be conscience-stricken *local.*

haud, hald, hold: ∼ **wi** own up to *now local Ork-Kcb.*

hing, hang: ∼**ing-luggit** dejected, crestfallen, abashed. ∼ **one's** *or* **the lugs** look dejected or abashed.

ill-peyed extremely sorry *Abd.*

odds: make (a person's) ∼ **even** atone for or remit his shortcomings or transgressions.

†**prickle** cause (a person) to feel pain or guilt.

reid, red, rid: ∼ **face** a blushing face, as a sign of embarrassment or shame, *freq* **give someone** *or* **get a** ∼ **face.**

†**remord 1** afflict with remorse or painful feelings. **2** examine (one's conscience etc) in a penitent

spirit. **3** recall to mind with remorse or regret. **4** feel remorse.

†**remord** awaken remorse.

remorse express regret or remorse (about), repent, lament *chf Abd.*

rue †repent of. ∼**fu** rueful. **mak a** ∼ *now local EC Wgt* **tak the** ∼ *NE-S.* repent, regret. †**rew a** *etc* **race** repent of the course one has taken.

sairie sorry.

shame, †**sham** shame. † ∼**ful** shaming, affording shame **to.** † ∼**fully** shamefacedly, modestly. **think (black burning)** ∼ be (be very) ashamed.

shent put to shame, disgraced, ruined.

sick sorry very sorry *now Ork Cai.*

sin 1 a sense of shame *now Sh.* **2** †a fear of doing wrong.

sorra, sorrow sad, sorry *now Cai.*

tak, take: ∼ **tae oneself** acknowledge the truth of (an accusation), feel guilt or remorse, be sensitive about *now local.*

†**tobasyt** ashamed.

whistle, whustle: ∼ **(on) one's thoum** do nothing useful, twiddle one's thumbs, be nonplussed after some snub etc *now local Sh-Per.*

yon kind *euphemistic* persons who are uncomfortably embarrassed *Sh N.*

15.6.15 FEAR, DISGUST

For interjections of disgust, see 15.7.2.

†**abaisitness** alarm.

†**abhor** shrink, draw away, deviate **from;** shrink back from, regard with repugnance. ∼ **with** feel repugnance for.

afeard alarmed, afraid.

†**afere** *v* be afraid; fear, be afraid of (someone). *n* fear.

†**affrayitly** in alarm, in panic.

†**afleyd** dismayed, afraid.

alagast suspicion, disgust *NE.*

alairm alarm *now local Sh-Ags.*

†**awfully** causing awe or dread.

backset *v* disgust *Bnf Abd.*

boke, bock a feeling of disgust or revulsion *Cai Ags Ayr.* **gie (someone)** *or* **get the (dry)** ∼**(s)** (cause to) feel sick, retch or vomit *local C.*

†**bre** terrify, frighten.

cauld creep(s) gooseflesh, the creeps *local Bnf-Lnk.*

conflummix a shock *Bnf Abd.*

†**cryne** *v* fear.

dare, daur *v* 1 †*freq* ∼ **at** be afraid of. 2 terrify, intimidate. *n* (an instilling of) a feeling of awe *Fif Bwk*.

†**dirt fear** extreme terror.

†**doot, doubt:** ∼ **for** *or* **to do** .. fear, be afraid of (something) or of doing (something).

†**dreaddour** *n* 1 ∼ **of** fear or dread of; fear on account of or for. 2 fear, dread, apprehension, distrust. *v* fear, dread.

dree *v* fear *now Ags*.

dreid dread.

eerie affected by fear or dread, *esp* by a fear of the supernatural which gives rise to uneasiness or loneliness; *less freq* apprehensive *in gen, Gen except Sh Ork*. †**eeriness** fear, dread.

†**effray** *n* a state of alarm or fear; fright, terror. *v* alarm, scare, terrify. ∼**it** afraid. ∼**itly** in alarm, in fear.

fear *n* a fright, a scare *now Sh NE Fif Dmf*. *v* 1 frighten, scare. 2 ∼ **(o)** be afraid or fear (for) *now Ags Fif*. ∼**ed, ∼t at, o, for** frightened or afraid of.

feartit afraid *Renfr Gsw Ayr*.

feechie foul, dirty, disgusting.

flamagaster a stunning shock of surprise or disappointment *NE*.

fleg *v* 1 frighten, scare *now local*. 2 take fright, be scared *chf NE*. *n* a fright, a scare *Gen except WC, SW*. **get a** ∼ *or* **one's** ∼**s** be scared *now Ork NE Ags*. **tak** ∼ take fright *now NE*.

fley *v* 1 frighten, scare *now local Ork-Dmf*. 2 *chf* ∼ **awa** put to flight, drive off by frightening *now NE Fif Kcb*. *n* 1 a fright, a scare *local NE-Dmf*. 2 a source of fear; a fearsome looking person. **fleit** frightened, scared. †**fleyitnes** fear, fright, alarm. ∼**ed for** frightened of *now C*. ∼**some** terrifying, terrible *now NE, SW, S*.

flichter startle, frighten *now Ags*.

flocht startle, frighten *NE*.

forlaithie a feeling of revulsion *now Bnf*.

fraized greatly surprised, having a wild, staring look.

fricht *n* fright. *v* frighten, terrify. ∼**it for** afraid of *now C*. ∼**some** fearful, terrifying.

frichten frighten. ∼**ed for** frightened of.

gast *n* a fright, *chf* **(put) in a** ∼. †*adj* frightened.

†**gastrous** horrifying, unearthly *Abd S*.

girl shudder with fear or dread *S*.

gliff, glaff, glouf *v* frighten, startle *local*. *n* a sudden fright, a scare, a shock, *freq* **get a** ∼ *now local Bnf-S*.

glocken start with fright *SW*.

granich sicken, disgust *NE*.

greeshach shivery, shuddery.

grue 1 *also* **gruse** *now local Loth-S* feel horror or terror, shudder, shrink in horror or fear. 2 *of the flesh, heart, blood etc* creep, quake, run cold with horror or fear *now local*. *n, also* **gruse** *now local Loth-S* a shudder, shiver, feeling of horror or repulsion *now local Cai-S*. *adj* shuddering with fear, dread or loathing, afraid *now Cai*. **it gars me, my flesh** *etc* ∼ it makes my etc blood run cold. **tak the** ∼ **(at)** become disgusted or fed up (with) *now local Abd-Rox*. †**gruesome** ugly, repulsive, dismal.

hert, heart: ∼ **scald,** ∼ **scaud** a feeling of disgust or repulsion *now WC Uls*. **gar someone's** ∼ **rise** make someone sick *Ags Fif Rox*.

hotter shudder, shiver with fear *now NE*.

laith: ∼**fu** disgusting(ly) *NE Per Loth*. ∼**ly** *adj, also* †**laidly, lailly** loathsome, hideous. †*adv* foully, horribly. ∼**some** loathsome.

†**mismuive** *v* alarm.

quak quake *now local*.

†**trace** a shock, blow.

rad, †red(e) frightened, afraid, alarmed. † ∼**our** fear, terror.

resile recoil (**from** something), shrink away in distaste or disgust.

†**truefu** terrible, dreadful.

scar *n* a fright, scare *now Ork Kcb*. *v, also* **scare** 1 scare, frighten (away). 2 take fright, run away in fear.

scomfish, scunfis disgust, sicken *now Sh NE Ags*. **get** *or* **tak a** ∼ **at** take a strong dislike to, be disgusted at *now Sh NE Ags*.

scunner *v* 1 get a feeling of aversion, disgust or loathing, feel nauseated. 2 ∼ **(at)** feel disgust for, be sickened by, or repelled by. 3 cause a feeling of repulsion, aversion or loathing in (a person), nauseate. *n* 1 a feeling of disgust, loathing or nausea *freq* **tak a** ∼ **(at** *or* **against)**. 2 a shudder indicating physical or moral repugnance. 3 a thing or action which causes loathing, aversion or disgust. 4 a person who causes disgust or dislike. 5 a sudden shock. ∼**ed, scunnert** disgusted. ∼**ation** an object of dislike or disgust, an offensive sight *local Sh-Kcb*. ∼**fu** *NE-S*, ∼**some** *Gen except Sh Ork* disgusting, nauseating, objectionable.

seeck, sick sickening, nauseating *Fif Ags*.

set *v* disgust, nauseate *now NE Ags*. *n* a feeling of disgust or repulsion *NE Ags*.

shaker a fit of shaking; a state of terror or intimidation *Sh-C*.

shidder *chf Ags*, **shither** *now Rox* shudder.

skeer *v* scare. *n, also* ∼**ie** *now local* nervous, fearful, restive, agitated.

skeich, skey 1 shy, startle *now Ayr.* **2** †**skey** ? startle, come upon suddenly. ~**en** (feel) disgust, (be) repel(led), (be) nauseate(d) *now Bnf Abd.*

skirl *v* **1** scream, cry out with fear. **2** utter with a high-pitched discordant sound, cry shrilly, raise a clamour. *n* a scream or shriek of fear etc.

skitter anything dirty or disgusting, a mess, rubbish *now local Sh-Per.*

spean put (a person) off food through disgust, fear etc *now NE Per Kcb.*

stalk: be ca'ed *or* **loup** *etc* **off the** ~ *of the heart* be stopped by a sudden fright etc *now Fif.*

stamagast, stammygaster a great and sudden disappointment, an unpleasant surprise, a shock *NE Ags.*

†**stand aw of someone** be afraid of someone, stand in awe of someone.

†**stare** a state of staring horror, etc.

start, stert *now local* startle, disturb suddenly.

stell *of the eyes* become fixed in a stare of astonishment, horror etc, stand out *now local Lnk-Rox.*

†**stend** a sudden start, a thrill of excitement, fear etc.

stertle startle.

terrel terrible *now Stlg SW.*

terrifee terrify *now NE.* **terrification** the action of terrifying; a state or condition of terror, alarm or fright *now Sh NE.*

ug *v* **1** find offensive or repellent; feel disgust or horror at *now literary.* **2** †feel dread or apprehension. **3** be sickened, nauseated; feel repulsion *now Sh.* **4** disgust, nauseate *now Sh NE.* *n* **1** a sensation of nausea, *freq* **take an** ~ **at** *NE Ags.* **2** an object of disgust; a person with disgusting manners *NE.* ~**gin** †*n* dread, loathing. *adj* disgusting, loathsome *now NE.* ~**git** disgusted *now Sh NE.* † ~**rines** horror. ~**(g)some** disgusting, repulsive, horrible.

uncouthie unfriendly, fear-inspiring.

†**unhool someone's saul** frighten the life out of someone.

Wattie: look like ~ **to the worm** look disgusted or reluctant, look with loathing.

wirricow, †**worricow** a frightening- or repulsive-looking person *now Lnk SW Rox.*

yatter *of teeth* rattle, chatter from fear *now Ags.*

15.6.16 SORROW, TEARS

anger distress, grief.

begrutten tear-stained, sorrowful.

blirt *v* cry, weep, burst into tears *now Bnf Abd Ags.* *n* an outburst (of weeping) *now Bnf.*

bluther, bludder soil, disfigure (the face, eyes, mouth) with tears *now Ags.*

†**boldin** affected by extreme grief.

†**boldinit** swelled with grief etc.

†**bool** weep with a long-drawn-out mournful sound *S.*

broom: sing the ~ cry out because of punishment inflicted *Bnf Abd.*

bubble weep in a snivelling, blubbering way. **bubbly** tearful, blubbering, snivelling.

bum cry, weep *now Bnf Abd Gsw.*

bummle weep *Bnf Abd.*

byke weep, whine, sob *chf SW.*

caterwouling, caterwailing caterwauling *now Bnf-Ags.*

chilp cry in distress or querulously *Bnf Abd.*

claik cry incessantly and impatiently *chf NE.*

cown weep, lament *now Cai.*

croon *v* utter a lament, mourn; sing in a wailing voice *now N.* *n* a wail.

demuired sad, downcast *Cai S.*

doilt grief-stricken *now Abd.*

dool *now verse n* grief, distress. †*v* lament, mourn. *adj* sad, sorrowful.

doon mouth a sad expression *local Bnf-Stlg.*

†**dow** dismal, sad.

dowie sad, dismal; dull, dispirited. ~**ly** sadly, mournfully.

dowly sad, doleful.

drool utter or sound mournfully *S.*

drum sad, dejected, sulky.

fiddle face a long face; a sad face *now midLoth Arg Ayr.*

fuff sniffle as if about to cry *now midLoth.*

gollie weep noisily *now Abd.*

gowl *v* howl, yell, weep noisily. *n, also* †**gule** a yell, howl, bellow, growl.

grain *v* groan *now local Bnf-Rox.* *n* a groan *now local Ags-Rox.*

†**gram** sorrow, grief.

†**grank** groan.

great, gret, grit †*of the heart* fill with emotion, *esp* grief. ~**-hearted** having the heart filled with emotion, ready to cry, sorrowful *now NE Ags Fif.*

greet *v* **1** weep, cry, lament. **2** weep (tears). *n* **1** †weeping, tears. **2** a sob; a fit of weeping, *freq* **hae** *or* **tak a** *or* **one's** ~. ~**ie** *adj* weepy, given to tears *local Sh-Dmf.* *n* a child's whimper. ~**in(g)** weeping, lamentation **the** ~ **in one's craig** *or* **throat** a sob in one's throat *now Sh Abd.* **get one's** ~ **out** relieve one's feelings by weeping *now local.*

†**grief** grieve.

gruntle make a groaning noise *now Rox.*

harm(s) sorrow, grief, distress *now Sh.*

hert, heart: ~-**sab** a sob from the heart *now Per Ayr.* ~-**sair** pain or grief of heart; a great vexation, constant grief *now local.* ~-**scalded** sorely grieved *Uls.* ~-**sorry** deeply grieved. ~-**stoun(d)** a pain in the heart *Gen except Sh Ork.*

ill aboot, †ill at vexed, sorrowful *Gen except N.*

isk *v* sob *Cai.*

†mad full of or expressing distress or dismay, sorrowful.

mane *n* 1 a moan. 2 any mournful sound *now local Sh-Fif.* *v* 1 mourn, lament (*chf* **for** a person or thing) *now local Cai-Uls.* 2 utter a moaning or mournful sound *now Ags Fif.* **†mening** mourning, lamentation. **†mak mening** lament (**for** a person). **mak (a)** ~ lament, mourn *now local.*

match a bout or fit of ..: '*a greetin match*'.

molligrant, mulligrumph a complaint, lamentation *now Ork EC.*

moolet *v* whimper, whine *Ayr Lnk.*

murn, mourn mourn. ~**ing** mourning. **mak (a)** ~ **for** *or* **ower** lament, bewail over *Abd.*

murther *of a child* murmur, whimper, sob quietly.

out o anesel beside oneself (with grief, anxiety etc) *now Ork SW Slk.*

pech *v* expel the breath slowly and audibly, sigh, groan. *n* a sigh of weariness etc.

peuch, pyocher, peughle puff, blow, give a gusty sigh *now Sh Ags.*

pewl *v* cry in a shrill piercing tone *now local Sh-Per.* *n* a wailing cry, shriek *Abd Per.*

†pipes: tune one's ~ start to cry, wail like the sound of bagpipes being tuned.

†pit sunk **in** (sorrow etc).

plaint a complaint, protest, grievance; an expression of distress or grief, *freq* ~ **of** *or* (**up**)**on**.

†plene *v* lament.

†port-youl a sad outcry, a doleful moan, howl, *freq* **sing** ~ cry, lament.

rair, roar weep, cry, *usu,* but not necessarily, loudly, *freq* **roar and greet**.

†regrate *v* lament, feel or express sorrow at; mourn. *n* (an expression of) grief, sorrow or disappointment.

remorse express regret or remorse (about), repent, lament *chf Abd.*

rive 1 tear (the hair), *esp* in grief or anguish *now Sh NE nEC.* 2 burst with pain or anguish *local Sh-SW.*

sab sob.

†saddit made sad.

sair, sore *adj* 1 involving mental distress or grief; pressing hard upon one, hard to bear, oppressive. 2 *of the heart* aching, grief-stricken, sorrowful.

n a grief, a sorrow. *adj, of weeping* in a distressed manner. ~ **hert** a sad or sorrowful state of mind. **†**~ **herted** sad at heart.

sairie, sorry sorry; distressed, sad, sorrowful.

scronach *v* shriek, yell, cry out *now Bnf Abd Kcdn.* *n* a shrill cry, outcry, loud lamentation *now NE.*

shour, shower: a ~ **in the (dam-)heids** a fit of weeping.

sich sigh.

†sing dool lament, bewail one's luck.

skirl *v* 1 scream, cry out with pain or grief. 2 utter with a high-pitched discordant sound, cry shrilly, raise a clamour. *n* a scream or shriek of pain, anguish etc.

slab make a snorting, bubbling sound as in weeping *now Dnbt SW.*

slorp an greet weep noisily and with gulps of indrawn breath, sob convulsively *now Rox.*

sneeter weep, blubber *now Cai.*

snifter a (noisy) sniff, from grief etc; a snivel, whimper.

snotter snivel, weep noisily, blubber *now WC Kcb.* ~**y** tearful, lugubrious *WC Kcb.*

sorra, sorrow sorrow. ~**fu** sorrowful.

souch, sough a deep sigh or gasp *local Sh-Gall.*

†sout shake or heave convulsively with sobs *N.*

spate a flood of tears.

spraich *v* cry shrilly, scream, shriek *now Abd.* *n* a scream, cry, shriek; the sound of weeping or wailing.

stound a throb of grief.

†suspire *v* utter with a sigh. *n* a sigh.

†syte sorrow, grief, suffering.

tear *n, also* **†techyr** a tear. **†***v* 1 weep. 2 fill with tears. **wi the** ~ **in one's ee** in an emotional or tearful state, in mourning or grief *now Per WC Kcb.*

teen *n* sorrow, grief. **†** ~**full** sorrowful.

†thrain a sad refrain, dirge, lamentation *EC.*

tout(er) *v* cry, sob.

†trinkle shed (tears).

†trist *adj* sad; doleful. *n* sadness, sorrow, affliction.

vexsome sorrowful *now Lnk.*

wae *n* woe. *adj* grieved, wretched, sorrowful. ~**fu** woeful *Gen except Ork.* ~**some** sorrowful *Gen except Ork.*

†walawa, willawins *n* a lamentation. *v* make lamentation; screech, yell.

walloch, wallack *Mry Bnf v* cry, shriek, howl *now Abd.* *n* a scream, howl, wail *now Mry Abd.*

watshod *of the eyes* wet with tears *now Ayr.*

wearifu sad, woeful *now NE.*

†whryne whining, a querulous cry.

†woment *v* lament.

yammer *v* howl, lament, cry out in distress. *n* lamentation, wailing, whining, a cry, whimper *now only Sh*.

†yaw caterwaul; squeal.

†yet shed (tears).

yowl *v* bawl, wail. *n* a yell, wail, shriek.

15.6.17 LAUGHTER

bicker laugh heartily *NE*.

buff laugh aloud.

dance one's lane dance with joy or rage *now Abd*.

flicher giggle, give a silly laugh.

gaff(aw) *n* a guffaw, a hearty laugh. *v* laugh loudly and heartily or coarsely, guffaw.

gaggle laugh, giggle, cackle *Edb eLoth*.

goller, gulder a loud laugh *Ork Wgt Uls*.

goo *of an infant* coo *now NE, EC Rox*.

groozle *of a child* gurgle *now Rox*.

guff *n* a suppressed laugh, a snort *now Cai*. *v* cackle with laughter *now Rox*.

heffer *v* laugh heartily, guffaw *midLoth Bwk*. *n* a loud laugh, guffaw *now midLoth Bwk*. **~er** a person who laughs loudly *midLoth Bwk Slk*.

hinderend: lauch one's ~ die laughing *chf NE*.

hobble shake with mirth *NE*.

hodge shake, quiver, hitch the shoulders, *esp* with laughter *now Adb Kcdn*.

hooch whoop with mirth.

hotter shake with laughter or excitement *now NE*.

hurr a purring, murmuring sound expressing pleasure or contentment *now Sh*.

keckle *v* 1 laugh noisily; giggle. 2 laugh with joy or excitement, express unrestrained delight *now Sh NE Ags*. *n* a cackle, chuckle *now Sh NE Ags*.

keechle *v* giggle, titter *local Sh-Dmf*. *n* a short laugh *now Loth Dmf*.

kicher *v* titter, giggle *now Sh Abd-Ags*. *n* a titter *Abd Ags*.

kill: laugh one's ~, get one's ~ (lauchin) laugh one's head off (**at**) *Abd Ags*.

kink *v* choke with laughter *now Abd SW, S Uls*. *n* a violent and irrepressible fit of laughter *local Abd-Uls*.

murr a murmuring sound as made by a baby.

nicher snigger.

olite cheerful.

pech a sigh of relief, satisfaction etc.

reird a loud outburst of laughter *now Rox*.

rive burst with laughing *now Sh N Lnk*.

shevel, showl *now N Per*, **shile** *SW* a wry smile, grimace *now SW*.

skirl *v* shriek with excitement or laughter. *n* a shriek of laughter etc.

smicker smile or laugh in a sniggering or leering way; smile seductively; smile affectedly.

smirk, †smirkle *v* smile in a pleasant friendly way, have a smiling amiable expression; have a roguish or flirtatious smile. *n* a pleasant smile, a friendly expression.

†smirl a sneer, mocking smile; a snigger, sneering laugh.

†smirtle *v* smile in an arch or knowing way, smirk; laugh coyly, giggle, snigger. *n* a sarcastic smile, a smirk of satisfaction.

smudge *v* laugh in a suppressed way, laugh quietly to oneself, smirk *local*. *n* a quiet half-suppressed laugh, a smirk, simper *local*.

smue smile placidly, blandly or ingratiatingly, smirk; laugh in a suppressed or furtive way *now Ork*.

sneeter giggle, snigger *local Ork-Ayr*.

sneister laugh in a suppressed way, snigger *now Sh*.

snicher *v* snigger, laugh in a suppressed way. *n* a snigger, titter.

snifter a snigger.

snirk *v* snort, wrinkle the nose, snigger *now Dmf*. *n* a snort, snigger *Sh Dmf Rox*.

snirl snigger, laugh in a suppressed way *Rox*.

snirt *v, also* **snirtle** snigger, make a noise through the nose when trying to stifle laughter, sneer. *n, also* **†snirtle** a snigger, suppressed laugh *now local Stlg-Rox*.

snitter laugh in a suppressed way, giggle, snigger *now Ayr S*.

snoke, snowk snort, snigger.

souple, supple limp, helpless (with laughter) *local*.

strae: be able *etc* **to bind** *or* **tie someone wi a ~** used to describe someone who is helpless with laughter *now Kcb*: 'ye might hae bund me wi a strae'.

15.6.18 GRIMACES, GESTURES

†bo make a face.

buss *n* a sulky, bad-tempered expression, *eg* **have a ~ on** *now Cai Highl*. *v* pout; sulk.

claw *n* a scratching, *freq* of the head as an indication of mild astonishment. *v* scratch (the head) as an indication of astonishment or uncertainty.

cruik, crook: ~ one's mou distort the mouth as a sign of displeasure or ill temper.

†doonleuk a displeased look, disapproval.

†**fippill** put out the lower lip.

fling jerk the head or body sideways as a gesture of displeasure, flounce *now local.*

flird flounce.

†**flyre** grimace, mock.

froon frown.

girn *v* 1 snarl, grimace. 2 screw up (the face) or gnash (the teeth) in rage or disapproval. 3 grin, sneer *now Sh Ork Ags Gall. n* a grin, grimace *now Sh Cai.*

gloom a frown, scowl *now Dmf Rox.*

glower a wide-eyed stare, an intent look; a scowl, a fierce look.

glunsh *v* look sour, scowl *now local N-Kcb. n* a sour look, scowl *now WC*

gowl scowl *now WC Rox.* ~**ie** sulky, scowling *now Sh.*

grue make a wry face *now local Cai-Uls.*

hing, hang: ~ **the pettit lip** sulk, have an injured and offended expression.

hirsel shrug (the shoulders).

lip: let *or* **pit down the** ~ look dismayed, pout *Sh NE-S.*

lour-brow a frowning aspect *now Ags eLoth.*

mow †a grimace, *esp* derisive. **mak a mow** *or* **mows** 1 †pull a face, *esp* in derision. 2 make a grimace of disapproval, reluctance *chf Abd.*

mudgins, †**mudgeoune** movements of the features, grimaces.

murgeon *n* a grotesque movement of the body or face; a contortion. *v* grimace, posture.

rive tear (the hair), *esp* in grief or anguish *now Sh NE nEC.*

scouk, skulk a furtive look (from under the brows); a frown *now Bnf Abd Ags.*

scoul *v* scowl *now Abd.*

†**scrip** a scornful grimace.

scunner a shudder indicating physical or moral repugnance.

sham, shan make a wry face, grimace *now Sh.*

†**shammle, shamble** twist (the face), make (a wry mouth).

shevel, showl *now N Per,* **shile** *SW v* become distorted; make a wry mouth, grimace from vexation, pain, a bitter taste etc *now N Per SW. n* a wry smile, grimace *now SW.*

smool *v* 1 look scornful and unfriendly *SW.* 2 look petulant or discontented, scowl, frown. *n* a scowl *SW.*

snirk *v* snort, wrinkle the nose, snigger *now Dmf.*

teeger look fierce; clench the teeth and fists *eLoth Bwk.*

thoum, thumb: crack one's ~**s** snap one's fingers in pleasure or derision *now Sh NE.*

thraw a twisting of the face, a wry expression *now Sh Ork Bnf Abd.* **thraw one's face, gab** *etc* screw up, twist the face, mouth etc as a sign of pain, exertion, displeasure or disdain.

thrawn *of the mouth, face* wry, twisted with rage etc, surly. ~**-faced,** ~**-gabbit,** † ~**-mou'd** having a wry, twisted face or mouth.

†**Tontine face** a grimace, distortion of the face from laughing, glumness etc *Gsw.*

†**wray, wry** twist or distort (the face); make a wry face, grimace.

15.7 INTERJECTIONS

15.7.1 MISCELLANEOUS

For euphemisms for hell, see 15.7.4.

ae expressing surprise or wonder.

behear expressing surprise *now Ags.*

†**bethankit** God be thanked!

bit: nae a ~! expressing surprise *NE.*

bummasal by my soul! *Bnf Abd Ags.*

by my fegs a mild oath *now local Cai-Fif.*

certie: (by) my ~ assuredly, *esp* expressing surprise or emphasis *Gen except Sh Ork.*

confooter confound..! *Bnf Abd.*

criffins *now Bnf Gsw Kcb,* **crivens** *now local Bnf-Lnk* exclamation expressing astonishment.

dag, dog: ~ **it** *now Cai Bnf Abd,* ~ **on it** *now local Bnf-Kcb* confound it!

dang *euphemistic* damn.

daver damn ..! *now Loth Lnk Kcb.*

dazent damned *now Abd.*

dear dear Lord *local.*

deed: upon *or* **by my** ~ upon my word! *Ork Bnf Abd.*

†**Deil swarbit on** the Devil's curse on.

ding *in imprecations* dash! *now Cai Bnf Abd.*

dod *euphemistic* God *Gen except Sh-Ross.*

ech expressing pity, surprise.

ee expressing *eg* dismay or foreboding *Abd.*

eh: ~ **aye,** ~ **man,** ~ **sirs** *usu* expressing affirmation, surprise, dismay *now local NE-C.*

†**fack** indeed!, really!

fa(ll) befall, happen to, *chf in blessings or curses.* **fair, foul, shame** *etc* **fa** *now Gen except WC.*

fegs, guid fegs *now Abd,* †**by (my) fegs, my fegs** *expressing emphatic assertion or surprise* indeed!, goodness!

fient *exclam* the devil..! *freq* ~ **nor,** ~ **that** would to the devil that.. ∼(s) **ma(y) care(s)** devil may care, who cares?

foul: the ∼ **thief** *now chf in imprecations* the devil *now Sh*. †∼ **(be)fa** may evil befall..

go expressing surprise or admiration *local NE-Bwk*.

gonterns *interj* expressing surprise or delight.

gor *now Sh N Ayr*, **my** *or* **by** ∼ *now Rox Uls* expressing surprise or incredulity; a mild oath.

gosh: ∼**en(s)**, ∼ **be here** *Sh Abd*, ∼ **bliss me** *now Bnf Ags*, ∼ **me** *local Ags-Rox*, **gude** ∼ *Ags Rox* gosh.

goth a mild oath *now Cai Kcb*.

govanenty expressing surprise *now Cai*.

govie: ∼ **dick**, ∼ **ding** expressing surprise *now local N-S*.

†**guide us** *interj* expressing surprise or consternation.

gweeshtens, gweeshtie gosh!, goodness! *NE*.

haith, heth a mild oath or exclam of surprise.

harro a cry of distress, alarm, encouragement, rejoicing.

heather *exclam* expressing surprise, wonder, doubt, disgust *S*.

hech expressing sorrow, fatigue, pain, surprise or contempt, *freq* ∼ **me** *or* ∼ **sirs.** *n* such an exclamation *now Ayr*. †*v* make such a sound.

heech expressing exhilaration, uttered by dancers in a reel.

hegs expressing emphatic assertion or surprise *now local*.

help ma bob *interj* expressing astonishment or exasperation *C*.

here expressing surprise.

hooch *interj* expressing excitement or exhilaration, *esp* when uttered by dancers during a reel. *v* cry **hooch**, shout. *n* a shout, a loud cry, *esp* that uttered while dancing a reel etc.

hoot: ∼ **awa** *expressing pity or sympathy, esp in soothing children* oh dear! *NE*. ∼ **aye** indeed, certainly

howp, hope: I ∼ blow me if he *etc* didn't *etc now NE Dmf*: '*I hope he'd forgotten the key*'.

hule devil, deuce, *eg* **what the** ∼, **a** ∼ **of a** *now Rox*.

husta expressing surprise, remonstrance or alarm *NE*.

imphm *interj* with varying intonation indicating attentiveness, decided or reluctant assent, sarcastic agreement, hesitancy etc.

jings: (by) ∼ a mild expletive.

keep: ∼ **me** *or* **us (a)** may God keep me or us (all) *local N-S*.

laird *colloq as mild expletive* Christ! *now local Cai-Kcb*.

Lod Lord! *Cai Ags C, S*.

lorie Lord! *Sh-N*.

losh (me), †**loshins** Lord!

lovan(entie) *exclam or surprise or protest* dear me!, good gracious! *now Lnk Dmf*.

man *vocative, used parenthetically and sometimes with the name of the man (or in ModSc occas the woman)* implying surprise, remonstrance or irony: '*Maun, Will, I'm dumfounert*'; *esp in the unstressed forms* **min, mon** *as an emphatic expletive*: '*Hey, mon!, he called to Rab*'.

megstie, mexty expressing surprise, distress or disapproval, *chf* ∼ **me** *Gen except Sh Ork*.

michty, ∼ **be here,** ∼ **me,** ∼ **on's** *etc* expressing surprise or exasperation.

†**mishanter: the** ∼, **Auld** ∼ *in imprecations* the Devil.

name: i(n) the ∼ **(o a')** in heaven's name *NE, WC*.

never a bit really? *NE Per*.

noo na expressing sympathy or mild remonstrance well then!, now then!, really! *now C, S*.

nyod *interj* God! *NE Fif*.

och, ochanee *orig* expressing sorrow, pain, regret; *now chf* expressing exasperation, weariness etc.

od, odds *as a mild oath* God *Sh NE, EC*. ∼ **sake(s)** *now NE, WC*, ∼ **saffs** *now Sh* a mild oath.

ou expressing surprise or vexation; oh! ∼ **yea** really?, is that so? *NE*.

patience: ma ∼! expressing wonder, disbelief, exasperation etc *local*.

peace *as a substitute for* God *etc in phrs, eg* **I wish to** ∼, **surely to** ∼.

peety, pity: ∼ **me!** *exclam* expressing surprise, disapproval, disgust etc.

†**plagued** confounded, blasted, damned.

praise *euphemistic* God, Lord etc, *eg* ∼ **be blessed**.

preserve: (Guid *etc*) ∼ **us (a)** expressing surprise or dismay.

receive *in imprecations* seize, carry off: '*God receive me*'.

sakes me! dear me! *now Cai Ayr*.

sang expressing surprise etc, *freq* **by my** ∼ *local Sh-SW*.

sauf, safe: (Lord *etc*) ∼ **us** *etc* exclam of surprise, apprehension, protest *now Ork Bnf Ags*.

saul *now local Sh-SW*, **sowl, sal** upon my word.

ser's, sirs, surce *exclam* (God etc) preserve us! *now local N-SW*.

set: Deil *or* **sorra** ∼ **you** etc *as imprecation, Abd*.

sic a like *exclamation indicating surprise and usu disparagement* what a ..! *Gen except Sh*.

sink *in imprecations* blast, ruin *now Sh*.

swith *as exclamation* quick!, off!

tary *freq in imprecations* the Devil *NE*.

†**teth** a mild oath.

the in expressions of admiration etc: '*they tell me you're to be the great surgeon*'.

thram: ill ~ .. woe betide .., curse .. *Cai.*

†**tod** a minced oath *Ags Fif.*

trogs *used as a mild oath or expletive* faith, troth, *freq* **by my** ~.

trowth, troth, (the) God's truth *as interj, freq* **in** ~ indeed!, upon my word!

tweel truly!, indeed! *now local Stlg-Ayr.*

vengeance *in imprecations: 'what the vengeance ..'*

†**vow** expressing pleasure, admiration, surprise.

wae[1] well! *now SW, S.*

wae[2]: †~ **(be) to** a curse upon, may sorrow befall. ~ **worth** a curse upon. ~'**s my craws** dear me! *nEC.*

†**wallie** *interj expressing admiration, chf* **o** *or* **a** ~ goodness!, my!

waly fa woe betide .., devil take .. etc.

weary: ~ **fa,** †~ **on,** ~ **tak** *etc used to express exasperation* damn!, the devil take .. *now Uls.*

wee man the devil, *chf* **in the name of the** ~! *local.*

weel (weel) well!, well well!

wha deil who the devil? *now Sh Ork.*

what 1 †how much!, how great! '*quhat loss quhat honour quhat renoun/Was spokin of him*'. **2** how many!, what a lot of!: '*what a hooses*'.

whatten *exclam* what! *now local Sh-Lnk.*

whow expressing astonishment or surprise *now EC Rox.*

wow expressing admiration, astonishment or surprise.

yea *expressing surprise or disbelief* really, indeed *now NE:* '*Yea, d'ye think sae, Tammas?*'.

yod *as an oath* God *Abd.*

15.7.2 DISGUST

ech expressing disgust.

feech expressing disgust or impatience.

foof expressing disgust *now Sh Abd Stlg.*

gad expressing disgust *Gen except S.*

gid gad, gid gow *interj* expressing disgust *Ork Ags Fif Bwk.*

heather *exclam* expressing surprise, wonder, doubt, disgust *S.*

kich an exclamation of disgust, a warning, *usu* to a child, not to touch something dirty or undesirable.

ouch a sound like a gasp or grunt used as *exclam* of disgust.

peety, pity: ~ **me!** *exclam* expressing disgust etc

peuch expressing disgust etc, pooh! *now Sh Ags Per.*

tew expressing disgust *Ayr.*

15.7.3 IMPATIENCE

ou: ~ **ay** oh yes, yes, indeed, that's so; *sometimes* expressing impatience or dissatisfaction. ~ **yea** really?, is that so? *NE.*

ach, expressing impatience, disappointment, contempt, remonstrance etc.

awa expressing incredulity or surprise: '*awa wi ye!*'

behangt expressing impatience.

†**be-licket,** *chf* **Deil** *etc* ~ devil a bit, absolutely nothing.

bit: nae a ~! expressing incredulity *NE.*

blethers nonsense!, rubbish!

boohoo show contempt (for) by using this sound *now Bnf.*

Clyde: I *etc* **didna** *etc* **come up the** ~ **on a banana boat, skin** *etc* I'm no fool *local.*

come on I don't believe a word of it!

deil, deevil, devil: ~ **a fear(s)** not likely, no fear *now Cai Abd Fif.*

doot, doubt: I *etc* **hae my** ~**s** I etc am doubtful.

else *now Bwk,* **ense** *now Ags midLoth or* ~ **no** *ironic* I don't think!

†**fack** indeed!, really!

feech expressing impatience.

fient: (the) ~ **(a)** devil a, never a, not a blessed.. ~ **all** nothing at all, not a thing *local.*

fine: ~ **day** *local Sh-Ayr,* ~ **ham** *chf slang, Abd Fif Gsw Lnk* 'go on!', nonsense!

foof expressing impatience *now Sh Abd Stlg.*

foul a .. not a .., devil a ..

fuff expressing contempt, fsst!, psst!, bah! *now local NE-Dmf.*

fy na no indeed!, certainly (not)! *NE Ags.*

gae, go: ~ **awa(y)!** expressing impatience, incredulity or derision: '*g'wa wi ye*'.

grannie, ~('**s**) **mutch(es)** *now Abd Fif Arg* as a contemptuous riposte, with a *possessive adj, usu* following the repetition of the relevant word: '*We might have improvised ..*' '*Improvised yer grannie*' *Sh NE-S.*

ham-a-haddie *chf exclam and in expressions of disbelief* a confused or unlikely story or situation: '*fine ham-a-haddie (but ye'll no fry it in my pan!*')' *C, S.*

hech *interj* expressing contempt, *freq* ~ **me** *or* ~ **sirs.** *n* such an exclamation *now Ayr.* †*v* make such a sound.

hish an exhortation to be quiet *local Cai-Kcb.*

hoch aye expression of assent, suggesting impatience or resignation *now Abd*.

hoot *interj, also* ~s expressing dissent, incredulity, impatience, annoyance, remonstrance or dismissal of another's opinion. *v* say **hoot** to, pooh-pooh, treat or dismiss with contempt *now EC Dmf Rox*. ~ **awa**, ~ **fie** *now local NE-SW*, ~(**s**)-**toot**(**s**) nonsense! ~ **na**, ~ **no** a strong negative

kae expressing disapproval, contempt or incredulity, pooh-pooh!

kiss my erse expression of abusive contempt.

luif: the outside of the, my *etc* ~ *in various phrs of defiance or derision, now Wgt*: '*and the outside of the loof to them*'.

man *vocative, used parenthetically and sometimes with the name of the man (or in ModSc occas the woman)* implying surprise, remonstrance or irony: '*Maun, Will, I'm dumfounert*'; *esp in the unstressed forms* **min, mon** *as an emphatic expletive*: '*Hey, mon!, he called to Rab*'.

maybe a possibility, *chf proverb* **a** ~ **is not aye a honey bee**. ~ **aye and** ~ **hooch aye** *ironic expression of disbelief* sure!

michty, ~ **be here,** ~ **me,** ~ **on's** *etc expressing surprise or exasperation*.

nae fears! no fear!

nae frichts no fear *now Fif*.

nor *in imprecations* (**God**) ~, **Deil** ~, **fient** ~, **shame** ~, **sorrow** ~ would that, (God) (grant) that, would to the devil that etc.

peuch expressing impatience, disbelief etc, pooh! *now Sh Ags Per*.

†**prute** expressing scorn or defiance, *freq* ~ **no!**, **prutish!, pruts!**

puddin: ~ **lug** *exclam* expressing impatience *now Abd*. ~**s an' wort!** *exclam* expressing contempt or disbelief *now Kcb*.

sake: for any ~ for Heaven's sake.

see someone far enough expression of annoyance wish that someone were out of the way, had not appeared etc.

shame a ..! not a blessed ..!

†**shoo** *rejecting another's statement etc* pooh!, nonsense!

sic a like *exclamation indicating surprise and usu disparagement* what a ..! *Gen except Sh*.

†**snuff** stuff!, nonsense!

soo's tail te ye *etc* expression of defiance or derision.

sorra, sorrow *in impatient questions, eg* **what** (**the**) ~ (**way**), **where in** (**the**) ~ *now Sh N*. ~ **a** not a *now Sh N*.

sot, sut *esp child's word, used to contradict a negative* on the contrary, far from it: '*It is not.—It is sot*.'

teh expressing impatience or derision *EC Lnk Rox*.

tew expressing contempt, impatience *Ayr*.

tillieloot a cry of reproach, a taunt of Galashiels boys to those of the neighbouring parish of Bowden *S*.

toot(**s**), **tits** *interj, freq reduplicated expressing disapproval or expostulation* nonsense! *v* utter the exclamation **toot** *now local Ork-Per*.

†**tutti-taiti**(**e**) expressing impatience, disbelief, derision.

tyach, tach expressing impatience, contempt or petulance.

wa *expressing disbelief, impatience etc, freq* (**gae**) ~ (**wi ye**) go away *local Sh-Lnk*.

what *after verb indicating disbelief or disparagement* indeed *Ork N, C*: '*I worked it aa out in ten minutes.—Did ye what?*'

wi(**th**) **his** *etc* **tale** according to *him* or so *he* says *local*.

yea *expressing disbelief, vague assent or opposition* really, indeed *now NE*: '*Yea, d'ye think sae, Tammas?*'. *chf* ~ ~ *used derisively expressing contempt, now Abd Ags*.

15.7.4 DISCONTENT

†**aich** expressing surprise, sorrow etc.

†**alace** *interj* alas. *n* an 'alas': '*thai grat with mony saire alace*'.

alake, †**alakanee** alack *now arch or verse*.

anee a cry of lamentation *more freq in combs, eg alakanee*.

awa expressing (contemptuous) dismissal (of a person or concept): '*awa wi ye!*'

back: ~-**come** an expression of regret or disappointment *Sh Ork Per midLoth*. ~ **o my hand** contemptuous term of farewell or dismissal **to**.

†**Banff: go to** ~! get lost!, go to blazes!

bile: (**awa an**) ~ **yer heid!** *very familiar* get lost! *now Abd*.

bizz shame!, tut tut! *now Abd*.

bottle: gang tae Buckie *etc* **an** ~ **skate** get lost!, go to blazes! *now Bnf Abd*.

care's my case woeful is my plight *Abd Ags*.

†**chat: ga** ~ **thee** *etc* expression of contempt.

dicht: he *etc* **may** ~ **his** *etc* **neb and flee up** he may as well 'get lost' *now local Abd-Kcb*. ~ **yer** *etc* **ain door steen** be sure that you etc are beyond reproach before criticizing others *Bnf Abd*.

dool, dule alas! *now Sh*.

fear: ye're nae ~**t** *ironic* you are pretty brazen-faced.

foy tut tut! *now Abd*.

Freuchie: gae tae ~ (and fry mice) go to blazes! *local Ags-Ayr.*

give me *etc* **peace** leave me etc alone, don't disturb me etc.

†**gouch** *only literary,* a gasp; *also as interj* ouch!

†**harmisay** *interj* expressing grief or distress.

hech: ~ hey *now Per,* **~ how** *now Slk,* **how hum ~** *now local NE-midLoth* expressing weariness or regret. **~ wow** expressing distress or regret *now Slk.*

Hecklebirnie *euphemistic, usu in imprecations* Hell *now Bnf Abd.*

Hexham: go to ~ *euphemistic* go to Hell, go to blazes *S.*

hoch expressing weariness, regret or disapproval *now Abd Uls.* **~ aye** expression of assent, suggesting impatience or resignation *now Abd.* **~ hey** expressing weariness or sadness, sometimes accompanying a yawn *now Abd.*

hyne: (a) merry ~ to ye go to the devil and good riddance to you! *Abd.*

ill vage to ye bad luck to you *now Sh.*

†**lackanee** alas!

†**lockanties** expressing surprise or disappointment *Ayr.*

lovan(entie) *exclam of protest* dear me!, good gracious! *now Lnk Dmf.*

luif: the outside of the, my *etc* **~** *in various phrases of defiance or derision, now Wgt:* 'and the outside of the loof to them'.

mane: Deil ~ ye *etc* Devil take you *now local Abd-SW.*

megstie expressing disapproval, *chf* **~ me** *Gen except Sh Ork.*

och, ochanee expressing exasperation, weariness etc. **~ane; o(c)hone** expressing sorrow.

ou expressing surprise or vexation; oh!

out *interj, chf in combs* attracting attention and urgency, expressing indignation etc, *eg* **~ ~,** †**~ harrow.**

parritch, porridge: keep *or* **save one's breath to cool one's ~** save one's breath; hold one's tongue, *usu in imperative* mind your own business! shut up!

play: (away, go *etc* **and) ~ yourself** go to blazes!, go away!

quate wi ye! be quiet!

set: Deil *or* **sorra ~ you** etc *as imprecation, Abd.*

snifter a (noisy) sniff, from disdain.

soo's tail tae ye *etc* expression of defiance or derision.

sorra, sorrow *in phrs of malediction, exasperation etc, eg* **~ fa ye** *etc* **(a) ~ on ye** *etc, now Sh N.*

steep your heid don't be silly! *N, C.*

tchick *interj, n, v* expressing annoyance, tut-tut *now local Ork-Kcb.*

thank: (aa) one's *or* **the ~** *used in displeasure* the thanks for or recognition of a service, which the speaker feels is inadequate *now local Ork-Kcb.*

toot, toots, tits *interj, freq reduplicated, expressing disapproval or expostulation* nonsense! *v* utter the exclam **toot** *now local Ork-Per.*

†**trittle-trattle** *interj* expressing contempt.

†**trolylow** expression of contempt.

uts tut!

wae: ~suck(s), ~'s me *Gen except Sh Ork,* **~'s (my) heart** *now Cai Ags* alas!

†**walawa, willawins** *interj* wellaway!, alas!

wally-dye *expressing sorrow, literary or arch* alas!

†**waly** *expressing sorrow* oh dear!, alas!

whow expressing astonishment or surprise, *usu* with regret or weariness *now EC Rox.*

wow *occas* expressing regret.

yeltie, †**yall** you would, would you; be careful; that's enough, now.

15.7.5 GRATUITOUS ABUSE

belge, bilch contemptuous term for a person, *esp* a child.

besom term of contempt for a person, *esp* a woman.

bitch term of contempt for a woman or a man.

†**bladʒean** term of abuse for a person.

blichan contemptuous term for a person *now Ags.*

block contemptuous term for a person *now Ags.*

bluiter term of abuse or contempt for a person.

boch contemptuous term for a person *Cai.*

bool contemptuous term for a man *now Bnf:* 'auld bool'.

†**bos** contemptuous term for a person, *freq* old **~.**

†**brad** term of abuse for a person, *esp* an old man *SW.*

brock contemptuous term for a person.

†**bystour** contemptuous term for a person.

†**caribald** term of abuse for a person.

carle *derog term for a man now NE Fif Lnk:* 'ilk crabbit auld carle'; †'glutton carl'.

carline *freq derog* a (*usu* old) woman *now Bnf Abd Fif.*

cattle term of contempt for persons *local Abd-Lnk.*

†**chittirlilling** term of abuse.

clamjamfry a company, crowd of people.

cowlie contemptuous term for a man *now Cai.*

cullion term of abuse for a person *now Abd.*

†**culroun** term of abuse for a person.

†**cust** term of abuse or contempt for a person.

cutty contemptuous term for a woman *now Bnf Abd Fif.* ~ **quean** *chf* contemptuous term for a woman *now Bnf Abd.*

dirt contemptuous (now *chf offensive*) term for a person *now local Bnf-Kcb.*

doddie contemptuous term for a person.

†**dogone** contemptuous term for a man.

drite *chf as term of abuse* dirt, excrement *now Bnf Abd Kcdn Edb.*

†**fleggar** term of abuse for a person.

†**flindrikin** term of contempt for a person.

foumart, †**fulmart** a term of abuse *chf NE.*

glaur term of contempt or abuse *now Kinr.*

golach an insect, a derogatory term for a person *now Cai Abd.*

grunyie the snout of a person.

hairy a young woman: '*a wee hairy*' *chf Abd Gsw.*

hash contemptuous term for a person *now local Kcdn-Dmf.*

†**hide** a female domestic animal; a woman; *rare* a man.

jaud a worthless, worn-out nag; a woman.

jaw-hole a foul place.

†**Jew** term of abuse for an unbeliever, infidel.

jilt contemptuous term for a girl or young woman.

Jock brit a miner *now Stlg eLoth.*

Johndal *contemptuous* a young ploughman *Cai.*

†**jurr** contemptuous term for a servant-girl.

†**kae** contemptuous term for a person.

kail runt contemptuous term, *esp* for an old woman *Ags Fif Gall.*

keek contemptuous term for a young woman *Abd.*

†**kensy** term of abuse for a man.

kiteral strong term of abuse for a person.

kittie, Katie familiar or contemptuous term for a woman or girl; a giddy, skittish young woman.

limmer term of abuse or contempt for a woman.

†**luschbald** term of abuse for a person.

†**mangrel** mongrel, term of abuse for a person.

mannie, mannikee *disparaging* a little man *now local.*

menyie *disparaging* a rabble *now NE Edb.*

messan a cur, contemptuous term for a person *now local sEC-SW.*

muck-a- *or* **the-byre** a farmer *now Bnf Per.*

partan a crab, an ugly, bad-tempered or stupid person, *freq* ~**-face(d)** *now Bnf Ags Fif.*

pug(gie) term of disrespect or abuse for a person *now Per.*

quine *NE,* †**quean** *term of abuse* a hussy, slut *now NE.*

ratton, rottan a rat, contemptuous term for a person.

†**reep** familiar, slightly derogatory term for a person *Bnf Abd.*

†**rehator** term of abuse for a person.

†**rook, ruke** term of abuse.

†**trump** contemptuous term for a person.

†**scabbert** contemptuous term for a person.

scaddin contemptuous term for a person *NE.*

scart term of abuse *now Per Dmf.*

scat term of abuse.

scout contemptuous term for a person *now local Abd-Kcb.*

scriever *esp derog* a writer, scribbler.

†**scurliquitor** term of abuse.

†**scutarde** *contemptuous* ? a person who defecates.

skiter term of abuse *Bnf Mry.*

smytrie *contemptuous* a collection of people *now Bnf Abd.*

snipe contemptuous term for a person.

†**spink** term of abuse for a person.

†**stickdirt** term of abuse in **flyting.**

†**strekour** term of abuse for a person.

stirrah, †**stirrow** contemptuous term for a man *now Rox.*

stock *sometimes disparaging* a chap, bloke, creature *now NE Ags.*

†**strummel** term of contempt for a person.

†**stuffat** ? a groom, lackey; ? a vague term of abuse.

†**tichle** *usu contemptuous* a troop, string (of people) *Slk.*

tuil term of contempt for a person *now Ork.*

tulshoch contemptuous term for a person *Abd Kcdn.*

vermin *pejorative* a large crowd *now Cai Bnf Ags.*

whalp a whelp, term of abuse for a person *local.*

whaup term of abuse for a person *local.*

wicht *freq with contempt* a human being, person.

yella yite contemptuous term for a person *local Per-Wgt.*

15.7.6 ENDEARMENTS

For pet names in the family, see 8 11.

bird, burd term of endearment.

bonny in terms of endearment: '*my bonnie bairn*'.

chackart term of endearment *Bnf Abd.*

croodlin doo term of endearment *now Bnf Abd Fif.*

†**crowdie mowdy** ludicrous term of endearment.

cushie-doo term of endearment *local.*

doddie humorous term for a person.

doo familiar term of endearment.

dosh term of endearment for a girl *now Sh Abd.*

galat term of endearment to a girl *NE Arg*.

hinnie, † ~-**blob, hynygukkis** term of endearment.

jo *term of endearment* sweetheart, darling, dear, *chf* **my** ~.

†**luck** *term of endearment* attended by good fortune, good.

†**possodie** term of endearment.

posy term of endearment for a child or woman, sweetheart *now WC Kcb*.

pout(ie) term of affection for a child or young person, *freq* a young girl or sweetheart.

ratton, rottan term of endearment for a person.

rosy-posy term of endearment *now Abd Ags*.

scone: my wee ~ term of endearment, *esp* to a child *local C*.

†**slasy** ludicrous term of endearment.

†**suckler** term of endearment.

sweetie *term of endearment* darling.

taid, toad term of endearment, *esp* for a child or a young woman *now NE Ags*.

†**towdy mowdy** term of endearment.

†**wally gowdy** *term of endearment* lovely jewel.

wran, wren term of endearment.

INDEX

abandon *a nest* forhoo, forhooie, forvoo; pervoo 1.1.5.
abashed hinging-luggit 15.6.14.
abate †slocken 15.1; *of pain* liss 15.6.1.
abbey †abbacy 14.1.6.
ability can; †doucht; feerich; †giftie; †habilitie 15.5.15; *natural* †genie 15.5.15.
aboard †aboord 6.2.3.
abort *of an animal* pick calf etc 2.8.3.
abortion slip 9.16, 8.6; a slip 8.6.
abscess income 9.8.
absent-mindedness forget 15.2.4.
absolve *in specific ways* 11.15.1; †absolȝe; †obsolve 11.15.1.
abstain from gae fae 10.1.
abuse 15.7.4; 15.7.5; *n* abuise; ill-jaw, -tongue *or* -wind; scaul(d); †scaldrie; snash; tongue 15.5.11; *v* abuise; †backhash; bad-use; †clesch; disperson; drub; ill-gab *or* -tongue; injure; misca; †mislear (oneself to (someone)); †mispersoun; †rebalk; wallipend 15.5.11; *v, see* ILL-TREAT.
abusive *ill-tongued* 15.5.11; *specif of speech* †mislernit 15.5.11.
abyss swallie 5.1.2.
accessory *in a crime etc* †accessor 11.13.
accommodation *for farmworkers, specific types* 7.5.3; berrick; bothy; chaumer; hire house 7.5.3.
accurately †sicker 15.5.15.
accusation *legal, specific types* 11.2.3; †delation 11.2.3.
accuse †aret; †argu(e); †atteche; †delate 11.2.3; †cheson; †enchesone; faut; wyte 15.5.14.
accused *n* panel 11.2.3.
accuser †accusatour; †delator 11.2.3.
ache *n, see* PAIN; *v* rug; soo; stang; †wark; yawk; yerk 9.10.
aching *of the heart* sair 15.6.16.
acid *adj, of taste, see* SHARP.
acorn †knapparts 4.6.
acquire *property, in specific ways* 11.11.
acquit *in specific ways* 11.2.4, 11.15.1.
acquittance 11.15.1.
acrid reekit; snell 10.1.
acrimonious *of a person* tuithy 15.5.9.
across atour 11.1.1.
action *legal, specific types* 11.2.2, 11.10; law-plea; †mute; †plea 11.2.2.
active *in a cause etc* †pairty in 15.3.13; *of a child* steering; stourie 8.5; *of animals* swack 2.8.1; *of a*

person feerie; fersell; forcie; kneef; linking; †querty; rash; steering; stourie; swankin; †tait; trig; vertie; †yaup 15.6.6; *of persons* 9.1.1, 9.1.2, 9.17; †cliftie; edgie; feerie; fendie; fersell; kneef; leish; linking; †olite; rash; snack(ie); †snell; swack; swankin; swipper; †tait; throughgaun; waddin; wannle 9.17.
activity 9.17; †deliverance; through-pit 9.17.
Adam's apple knot o one's craig *or* thrapple; thrapple-bow 9.9.
adder ether; nether; veeper 1.2.2.
adjourn *a legal case etc* continue; †replait, resplate 11.2.3.
adjust *an implement* tune 13.1.1.
adjustment *of a plough* 7.7.1.
administer *laws etc, in specific ways* 11.1.1.
admirable luvesome 15.3.1.
admiral †almeral 6.2.4, 12.2.
admire †admeir 15.6.11.
admissible habile 11.1.1, 11.2.3.
admonish †admoneis; †mones 11.15.1; †admoneis; speak a word to (*see* word) 15.5.14.
admonition lesson; telling 15.5.14.
adolescence *see* YOUTH.
adolescent *see* YOUTH.
adoption 8.11.
adult muckle; up, up in life *or* years 8.3; *specif of a man* man-big, -grown, -length *or* -muckle 8.3; *specif of a woman* woman-grown, -length *or* -muckle 8.3.
adulthood 8.3; eild 8.3.
advantage better 15.6.1.
advantageous *see* FAVOURABLE.
adventurer †lan(d) lowper 15.3.11.
adversary †adversare 12.9.
adverse thrawart 15.6.2.
adze 13.1.15; eetch; hack 13.1.15.
affable *see* PLEASANT.
affectation 15.4.3.
affected *of a person, in various ways* 15.4.3; †ogertfu; pitten on; strange; †streiche 15.4.3; *specif in dress* fussy; primped 15.4.3; *specif of speech* tattie-peelin 15.4.3.
affection 15.3.3; hert-likin; †luferent 15.3.3; 15.6.11; dint; †effectioun 15.6.11; *for* dint of 15.6.11.
affectionate *see* LOVING.
affectionately luf(e)sumly 15.3.3.
afflicted afflickit; †tribulat 15.6.7.
aforesaid foresaid 11.1.1.
afraid *in various ways* 15.6.15; afeard; †afleyd; †effrayit; feartit;

rad 15.6.15; *of* feart at, o *or* for; frichtit for 15.6.15.
aft eft 6.2.1.
afterbirth *of an animal* clean(in) 2.8.3.
aftertaste guff; wa 10.1.
against *in opposition to* again; †againis 15.5.10.
age *n, legal aspects* 11.12; *of a person* 8.1-8.5; †eild 8.1; *v, of a person, in various ways* 8.2, 8.3; †eild; get up in years; turn ower in *or* tae years; wear doun (the brae), wear on *or* ower 8.2.
aged *see* OLD.
agent *specific types* 11.1.1; †doer 11.1.1.
aggravate aggrege 15.6.2.
aggressive *see* BELLIGERENT.
agile 9.1.1, 9.17; lichtsome; linking; rash; swanking; wannle; waul; whippie; yare 9.17.
agitated *of a person* aflocht; †agitat; skeer(ie); †vibrant; yivve rin 15.6.4.
agitation 15.6.4; jabble; yagiment 15.6.4.
agree *in various ways* 15.3.3; concord; †convene; draw; say ae wey *or* thegither 15.3.3; *with* gae in wi; say (ae wey) wi 15.3.3.
agreeable †amene; †avenand; bien; hertsome; lichtsome; wallie 15.6.1.
agreeably †queem 15.6.1.
agreement condescendence, condescendency; greeance, greement 15.3.3; *legal, specific types* 11.9; *see* CONTRACT.
aground *running (a ship etc) aground* 6.2.3.
ailing *see* ILL.
aim *a blow* let breenge (*see* breenge); draw; ettle; lounder 12.12; *v, a weapon* ettle; gley; mark; vizzy; wise 12.5; *a blow* ettle 12.12; *n* gley; vizzy 12.5.
airs mollops; tantrum 15.3.7.
aisle *in a church* pass; trance 13.3.6.
akin *see* CLOSE.
alarm *n* †abaisitness; alairm; †fleyitness; terrification 15.6.15; *v, see* SCARE.
alas †alace; alake; †alakanee; dool; †lackanee; och(anee), ochane; wae suck(s), wae's me *or* (my) heart; †walawa, willawins; wally-dye; †waly 15.7.4.
alcohol *see* DRINK.
alder 4.6; aller, arn 4.6.
ale yill (*see* ale) 10.18.

someone it het and reekin (*see* reek); gie someone through the wud laddie (*see* through); gie *or* tak someone through the whins (*see* whin) 15.5.14.

berry *specific types* 4.7.

berth *n, in a harbour* †set 6.2.3; *see also* BUNK.

beryl †beriall 5.1.9.

besiege †beligger; †pursue; †saige 12.9.

beslobber slabber; slaik, slaich 10.4.

besmirch *see* VILIFY.

bespatter *with food* laiber; slabber 10.4.

best clothes kirk claes; Sunday claes 14.1.8.

best man †allekay; young man 8.8.

betray †betraise; †supprise 15.3.8.

betroth *two persons* †han(d)fast 8.8; *someone* tryst 8.8.

betrothal 8.8; †handfasting 8.8.

better-class better-mais(t) 15.2.1.

between-maid go-between 13.1.4.

bevel *n* suit stock 13.1.15, 13.1.16; *v, coopering, in specific ways* 13.1.1.

bewilder conflummix; †mang; ramfeezle; stound; taiver; wander; †wimple 15.6.3.

bewildered baised; dabbled; taivert; will, †will of rede; willyart; yawkin 15.6.3.

bewilderment †baise; jabble 15.6.3.

bewitch *in specific ways* 14.2.3; †beglamour; blink; †cast ill on (*see* ill) 14.2.3.

bewitched *in specific ways* 14.2.3; forspoken; taen-like 14.2.3.

bib *the fish, specific types* 3.1.2; bressie; jackie downie; siller-fish 3.1.2.

Bible *specific types* 14.1.8; the Guid Book 14.1.8.

bicker v, *see* SQUABBLE.

bier buird; †ferter 8.7.

big *of persons* 9.1.1, 9.1.2.

bigoted begotted; kirk reekit; nairra-nebbit 14.1.2.

bilberry blaeberry, blairdie, blivert 4.7.

bile ga(w) 9.15.

bill *v, of birds* neb 1.1.5.

bind *in specific ways* wup 13.1.1; *to a mill* †thirl 7.8.3.

birch birk, birken 4.6.

bird burd (*see* bird) 1.1.1.

birdsong †bay 1.1.7.

birth 8.6; †get 8.6; *giving birth* 9.16; **give birth to** *of animals* cast; cleck 2.8.3; *lamb* eenie; ingy; †yean 2.2.

birthday 14.4.3.

birthmark rasp 9.8.

birthplace original 8.6.

biscuit *specific types*, 10.7.

bishop *specific types* 14.1.6; †beschop (*see* bishop) 14.1.6.

bitch bick 2.5.

bite *v* chack 2.8.3; *n, of food, see*

MOUTHFUL, MORSEL; *v* chat 10.4; *n, on a fishing line* rug 6.3.1, 6.3.2.

bitter *of taste* as sour as roddens (*see* roddens); sharrow; wersh 10.1; *of beer* heavy 10.18; *of a person* as sour as roddens (*see* rodden) 15.3.5; *of the tongue* ill-scrapit 15.5.8.

bittern bleater; bog-bleater; bull-o-the-bog; mire drum 1.1.2.

bittersweet pushion berry 4.2.

black *of hair, eyes etc* 5.2.9; glog; mirk 5.2.9; *very black* as black as a cruik; as black as the Earl o Hell's waistcoat; pot black, as black as the pot 5.2.9.

blackberry *see* BRAMBLE.

blackbird *specific types* 1.1.1; blackie; merl; †osill 1.1.1.

black bun currant bun; †fouat; Scotch bun 10.7.

blackcurrant blackberry; †black rizzar (*see* rizzar) 4.7.

blacken barken; †blekin; bleck; coom 5.2.9.

black eye blue ee; blue keeker (*see* keeker) 9.5, 9.22.

blackguard blackguaird; bleck; kithan 15.3.12; *of a woman* kithag (*see* kithan) 15.3.12.

blackhead shilcorn 9.8.

blacking *for leather* bleck(in) 13.1.9.

blackleg †nob 13.1.2; †nob 15.3.8.

blackness †sable 5.2.9.

black pudding blude puddin (*see* blude) 10.11.

blacksmith 13.1.12; bruntie; burn-the-wind; gow 13.1.12.

bladder blether; bledder 9.9.

blade blad 12.5; *n, of an oar* †palm 6.2.1; *of a shovel etc* mou(th) 13.1.1, 7.12; *of grass* girse; pile 4.3.

blame *n* barm; dirdum 15.6.2; *v, for* blame (something) on (a person) 15.6.2.

blast *n, of wind, see* GUST.

blaze *n* bleeze 5.2.8.

bleached †blacht 13.1.9.

bleaching 13.1.9.

bleak *of weather* dour; dreich; oorlich; starrach 5.2.1.

bleat *v* blait; blare; blea; mae 2.2, 2.9; *n* mae 2.2.

bleed blude 9.9.

bleeding †bullerand 12.12.

blessed seily; weel-lookit tae 15.6.1.

blether *n, of a person* blether(er); blether(an)skate; clash; clatter(er); claver, glaiber; cracker; gab; natter; newser; yitter 15.5.7; *v* claik; clash; claver, glaiber; clishmaclaver; clitter-clatter; crack; gab; gange; gash; glaiber; jangle; jaun(d)er; laibach; laig, lig(-lag); †pratt; pross; †reeve; sclore; slaver; tittle; tove; trattle; yaag; yabb; yitter 15.5.7.

blight blicht 4.1.

blind *in specific ways* 9.5; blin 9.5.

blindly blindlins 9.5.

blindness †mirkness 9.5.

blink *n, v* blent (*see* blink) 5.2.7, 5.2.8; *of the eyes* glimmer 9.5.

blinkers blinners 7.9.1; †(hors) goggles 2.4.

bliss seil 15.6.1.

blister *n* blushin 9.8.

blizzard stour 5.2.2.

bloated brosie 10.4.

blockhead gawkus; glipe; gowk(ie); gype; mell-heid; muckle to hoi; neep heid; nowt; puddin; sn(u)ivie; stammeral; stirk(ie); stookie; stot; stymel; sumph; tattie 15.2.4.

block up *a door etc* †condampne 13.2.4, 13.1.16.

blood blude 9.9.

bloodshed 11.13, 12.1.

bloodshot 9.5; blude run, bludeshed 9.5.

blood-stained †reid-wat 12.7.

bloody bludie 9.9; reid 12.7.

bloody nose jeelie neb *or* nose 9.22.

bloom blume 4.2.

blossom *v* blaw; flourish 4.2; *n* flourish 4.2, 4.7.

blot *on a person's character* tash 15.3.2.

blotched *of the skin, in specific ways* 9.8; measlet 9.8.

blow *n, a hit, specific types* belt; †bilf; blatter; †blaud; blaw; †bleach; bluffert; buff; ca(ll); chap; clamiehewit; clash; claught; cleesh; clink; cloot; clour; clype; cob; dab(ach); dicht; ding; dump; dunch; filbow; †flewit; gowf; hit; jundie; kilch; lab; paik; peelick; peys; †platt; plowt; †push; †rebegeaster; rung; †rusk; †rymmyll; scour; skelp; sleesh; sowff; splay; stoit; straik; strik; swap; thud; wap; wham; whang; †whidder; whisk; yerk 12.12; *of fortune, see* REVERSE; *of wind, in specific ways* 5.2.2; waff 5.2.2.

blow out *a candle etc* week 5.2.8.

blubber bubble; slab; sneeter; snotter 15.6.16.

bludgeon *n, see* CUDGEL.

blue bew; blae 5.2.9.

bluebell *Scottish bluebell* blawort, blaver; bluebell; gowk's thimbles; harebell; lady's thimbles; thummles 4.2; *English bluebell* bluebell; craw-tae(s); gowk's hose; wood hyacinth 4.2.

bluebottle bummer; mauk flee, maukie fly; muck flee 1.3.

bluetit blue bonnet; ox ee 1.1.1.

bluish *specific shades* 5.2.9; blae; bluachie 5.2.9.

blunderbuss blunderbush 12.5.

blunt *adj, of speech* raucle; tongue-betrusht 15.5.8; *v, tools* fluise 13.1.1.

bluntly richt oot 15.5.8.

bluntness †hameliness 15.5.8.

blurt out bluiter 15.5.7.

bluster *n* buller 15.3.7; *v, in various*

breast breist; brisket 9.9.
breastfeeding 8.6.
breast-milk pap-milk 8.6.
breastplate †birny 12.4.
breasts bubbies 9.16.
breastwork †bertisse 13.3.5.
breath *specific types* 9.11, aynd, end; braith; pew; wind 9.11.
breathe *in specific ways* 9.11; †aynd, end 9.11.
breathless *in specific ways* 9.11.
breeding season *of animals* riding season *or* time 2.8.3.
breeze *specific types* 5.2.2; tirl 5.2.2.
breviary *specific types* 14.1.11.
brew *ale etc* mask 10.19; *of a storm* †mask 5.2.2.
brewer brewster 10.19.
brewery †browster house 10.19.
brewing 10.19.
briar breer 4.5.
bribe *v, in specific ways* 11.13; †bud; buy 11.13; *n, specific types* 11.13; †bud 11.13.
bribery 11.13.
brick 13.1.17; *specific types* 13.1.16.
brickwork 13.1.16.
bridesmaid best maid 8.8.
bridge *n* 13.1.13; *specific types* 13.1.13; brig 13.1.13.
bridle *specific types* 7.9.1.
brigand †brigane, brigan(ner) 12.10; *specif Highland* †cateran 12.10.
brigandage †brigancy 12.10.
bright 5.2.7, 5.2.9; bricht; licht; †share; †sheen; skire, skyrie, skyrin; †snip white 5.2.7; *specif of colour* vieve 5.2.9.
brightly licht; †scheirly; †shire, schirly 5.2.7.
brill bonnet fleuk; †siller fluke 3.1.2.
brindled brandit; riach 5.2.9; brandit 2.8.1.
brine brack; saut bree 6.1.4; brime 10.3.
brisk *of a person* †cant; edgie; †gaun; kirr; lifie; linking; sprush; trig 15.6.6.
bristle birstle 9.4.
bristle(s) birse 2.8.2.
bristly †birsie, birsit 2.8.1.
broil †brulyie 10.3.
broken *in health* awa(y) wi't; crazed 9.19.
brome *specific types* 4.3.
bronchitis broonchadis, broonkaties; the wheezles (*see* whauze) 9.11.
brood *n* cleckin 9.16; *of young animals see* LITTER; *of chickens* lachter 2.7; *of children* †bairntime; brod, †brodmal 8.11; *see also* SWARM; *v, of birds* clock 1.1.5.
brood-mare †steid-meir; †stud 2.4.
broody *of a hen* clockin 2.7.
brook *specific types* 6.1.2; †brim; burn; caochan, keechan; rin, run; strand, straun; stripe 6.1.2.

brooklime wallink; water purpie 4.2.
broom *the plant* brume (*see* broom) 4.5.
brose *specific types*, 10.9, 10.12, 10.14; meal an bree (*see* meal) 10.9.
broth *specific types* 10.10; †brewis 10.10.
brothel bordel house, †bordel 8.9.
brother billy; brither 8.11.
brother-in-law guid brither; †maich 8.11.
brow *of a hill* brae; broo 5.1.2; *see* EYEBROW, FOREHEAD.
brown *specific shades* 5.2.9; broon 5.2.9.
bruise *n* †blae; chack; dinge 9.22; *v* gromish 9.22; *in various ways* 12.12; hatter; knuse; massacker; pran 12.12.
brush besom; s(w)ooper 13.1.1.
brushwood *see* UNDERGROWTH, TWIG.
brute bruit 15.2.2; *of a person* bruit; †reid etin 15.3.12.
bubble *v, in specific ways* 6.1.1; bibble; bummel; fro 6.1.1; *n* bell; blob; bibble 6.1.1.
buck *of a horse* yunk 2.4.
bucket *specific types* 10.2.
buffet *v, of a storm, see* BEAT; *of wind* daidle 5.2.2.
buffeted *by the wind* jachelt 5.2.2.
buffoon bard; †scurr 15.2.2.
bug bog 1.3.
bugger *n* †bugrist 8.9.
bugle *the plant* deid man's bellows 4.2.
build †beild; big, †big up; †lay; ?†perfurnis; †upbeild, †upmak 13.3.1.
building biggin(g); *specif action* †upbringing, †up-putting; *specif structure* †wark 13.3.1.
building site *specific types* 13.3.2; lan(d); stance, building stance; steid, steadin(g) 13.3.2.
build on *land* †big 13.3.2.
built on *of land* biggit 13.3.2.
built up upbiggit 13.3.1.
bulge *v, of a wall* †rag; shuit 13.2.1.
bull bill (*see* bull); Jock 2.1.
bullet †billet (*see* bullet); †pellok 12.5.
bullfinch †awp; bullie 1.1.1.
bullock stirk; stot 2.1.
bully *n* bangster 15.5.13; *v* hatter; ool 15.5.13.
bullying *n* 15.5.13.
bumblebee *specific types* 1.3; †bumbard; bummer, bummie, bumbee; droner 1.3.
bump *see* BLOW.
bumptious †grashloch; gumptious; massie; muckle; pauchtie; pensie 15.3.7.
bunch *of flowers, see* BOUQUET.
bundle *of flax, specific types* 13.1.6; †beet; †knok (lint) 13.1.6; *of hay or straw* bottle, battle 4.10, 4.11; wap 7.7.4; *of straw* stook; win(d)le, windlin(g) 7.7.4; *of hay*

or corn tait 7.7.4; *see also* SHEAF, BALE.
bung *n, of a cask* dook 13.1.1; *see also* STOPPER.
bungler bummler; fauchle; gutter; plowster; plowter; puddle; scutter; tooter(er) 15.5.16.
bungling *adj* bamling (*see* bummle); kweerichin (*see* keeroch) 15.5.16; *n* bucker; maffling 15.5.16.
bunion knoit; werrock 9.7.
bunk *on a ship* †coy 6.2.1.
bunting *see* CORNBUNTING, REED-BUNTING, SNOW BUNTING.
buoy bow, †buy 6.2.3.
burden *n, of persons* cess; †cummerwarld 15.3.2.
burdensome †chargeand 15.6.7.
burial 8.7; †beris; bural (*see* burial); hame-gaun; †tyre 8.7.
buried yirdit 8.7.
burly 9.1.2; buirdly 9.1.2.
burn *v, food* †brulyie; scowder; sneyster 10.3.
burning *of desire* †scauding 15.6.10.
Burns Supper 14.4.2.
burrow *n, rabbit's* bourie; clap; †clappard 2.8.3.
burst *n, of rain, specific types* 5.2.3; *v, of the heart* leap (oot o) the huil (*see* huil); be ca'ed *or* loup off the stalk (*see* stalk) 15.6.4; *of a pudding* spue 10.3; *with anguish* rive 15.6.16; *with laughter* rive 15.6.17.
bury *a body* 8.7; beerie; †beris; clap; eard; grave; †ingrave; lair; lay doun; pit awa, by *or* down; †tyre 8.7.
bush 4.5; buss; †virgult 4.5.
bushy bussy; bouzy 4.5.
busily thrang 15.5.15.
bustard †gustard 1.1.4.
bustle *v* bummle; fizz; fluister; steer; stichle 15.5.18; *n, specific types* 15.5.18; behss; flocht; foorich; steer; thrangity; whirr 15.5.18; a dirl; farrach; feery-farry; †fissle; fizz; flocht; fluister; steerie; strow 15.5.18.
bustling breengin 15.5.18.
busy †bussie; eident 15.5.15; *of a business, worker etc* thrang 15.5.18.
butcher flesher 10.11; *slaughterer*, †boucheour 12.13.
butler *specific types* 13.1.4; †somler 13.1.4.
butt *n, see* CASK; *v, of cattle* †hagg 2.1; *with the horns* box; buck; dunch 2.8.3.
butter *specific types* 10.13; freet 10.13.
butterbur gaun; puddock pipes; †son-afore-the-father; tushilago; wild rhubarb 4.2.
buttercup *specific types* 4.2; yellow gowan 4.2.
butterfly *specific types* 1.3; butterie 1.3.
buttermilk bledoch; kirn(ie), kirn

Index

milk; pell; sour dook *or* milk (*see* sour); whig 10.13.

buttocks *specific types* 9.7; behouchie; boddam; bumpy; †bun; curpin; †curple; dock; doup; droddum; drone; fud; hinders, hinderlan(d)s, hinderlets, †hinderlins; hinderend; hint-end; hurdies; keel; nether end; rumple; †tone 9.7.

buttress †buttereis; †putt 13.2.1; *specif of a bridge* †putt 13.1.13.

buxom 9.1.1, 9.1.2.

buzz *v* bizz; bum 1.3; *n* bum 1.3.

buzzard †bizzard; gled; puttock 1.1.4.

cabbage *specific types* 4.8; bow-kail; cabbage kail; †loukit kail 4.8; *dishes* 10.14.

cabbage stalk *specific types* 4.8; cabbage runt, cabbage stalk; castock 4.8.

cabin caibin; †lodge 13.3.3; caibin; 6.2.1; *specif on a ship* †cahute 6.2.1.

cabinet-maker caibe; squarewright 13.1.15; caibe 13.1.3.

cackle *n*, *v* keckle 1.1.7; *v* caak; caikle; keck; keckle 2.7, 2.9; *with laughter* guff; keckle 15.6.17; *n*, *of laughter* keckle 15.6.17.

cadet †cadent 8.11; *military* †caddie 12.2.

cage *n*, *mining* 13.1.5; tow 13.1.5.

cairn tappin, tappietourie 7.3.

cake *n*, *specific types* 10.7.

calamity *see* REVERSE.

calceolaria mappie('s)-mou(s) 4.2.

calf ca; cauf; veal 2.1; *pl* caur 2.1; *of the leg* bran; cauf 9.7.

calk *a horse* cauk 13.1.12.

calkin cauker 13.1.12.

call *of specific birds* 1.1.7; clatter 1.1.7; *v*, *an animal* treesh 7.9.4.

callipers Jennies 13.1.1.

calloused walkit 9.8.

calls *to animals* 7.9.4.

calm *adj* lown 5.2.1; *n* lown 5.2.1; *adj*, *of a person at oneself* 15.6.1; *of wind, sea, in specific ways* 5.2.2; quate, quiet 5.2.2; *v*, *of wind, see* DIE DOWN; *n*, *at sea* 6.1.4; *oneself* †compone; †saft; sattle 15.3.14.

calmly †queem 15.6.1.

caltrop †craw-tae 12.5.

camomile camovine 10.17, 4.2.

campaign *specific military campaigns* 12.1.

camp *military* †ligger; †lo(d)ge; †pallionis 12.1.

camp-follower †gudget; †ligger lady 12.1; *pl* †merdale; †rangle 12.1.

campion *specific types* 4.2.

candid furth the gait; real; straucht-oot(-the-gate) 15.3.1; *see* FRANK.

candidly furth the gait 15.3.1, 15.3.3.

candle *specific types* 5.2.8; *substitutes* 5.2.8; cannle 5.2.8.

candle-end cannle doup 5.2.8.

Candlemas Can(d)lemas 14.4.1.

candle snuffers †cannle scheris 5.2.8.

candlestick *specific types* 5.2.8; †stander 5.2.8.

cannon *specific types and names of particular cannon* 12.5.

cannon-ball bool; †pellok 12.5.

cannoneer †cannonar 12.2.

canoodle *see* DALLY.

canopy *specific types* 13.2.8; †baudkin; †da; †ruif 13.2.8.

cantankerous *see* ILL-NATURED.

cap *see* BONNET.

capable cawpable; feckfu; likely 15.5.15; *of* up wi 15.5.15.

capacity *to do something* †poustie 15.5.15; *for work* through-pit 15.5.15.

capricious aff an on aboot; capernoited; flauntie; flichtie, flichtrife; flichtersome, flichtery; †flowing; †frivole; jirkie; kittle; licht-headed; maggotive, maggoty; notionate 15.3.7.

capstan †cabil stok 6.2.1.

captain †chaptane 6.2.4, 12.2; *see also* SKIPPER.

capture *in various ways* 11.2.4, 12.9; fang; †ourta 12.9; *specif lands or goods* grip; †invade; *specif lands* †occupe (*see* occupy) 12.11; *specif a person* †handle; lay violent hands on (*see* violent) 12.9; *n* tak; *of a place* †intaking 12.9; *see also* PLUNDER.

carafe *see* DECANTER.

caraway carvey 10.17.

carcass carcage 2.8.2; *of a fowl* closhach 2.8.2; *of specific animals* 10.11; *pl* †fleshes 10.11.

card *v*, *wool etc* caird 13.1.6; *specif mechanically* scribble 13.1.6.

care *n*, *see* ANXIETY, WORRY.

carefree lichtsome 15.5.4.

careful eident; †huilie; †solicit 15.5.15.

carefully canny (ways *or* wise); graithly 15.5.15.

careless *in various ways* 15.5.16.

carelessly owerly 15.5.16.

carelessness 15.5.16; inadvertence 15.5.16.

caress *v* †cuittle; slaik 8.8; *n* daut 8.8.

caretaker janitor, jannie 13.1.4; *of a school* janitor, jannie 14.3.2.

cargo *of a ship, specific types* 6.2.3; †fraucht; †fure; graith; †laid, load, laidin 6.2.3.

carouse †play cop out (*see* cap); splore; †play at swig (*see* swig) 15.5 6.

carpenter *see* JOINER, CABINET-MAKER.

carpentry *see* JOINERY.

carrion ket 2.8.1.

carrion crow corbie; huidie (craw), heidie craw, huidit craw 1.1.1.

cart *n*, *specific types* 7.11; cairt;

†hurl-cart 7.11; *refuse-collector's* scaffie cairt 13.3.3; *v*, *in various ways* 7.11; cairt; draw 7.11.

carter cairter; whiplicken, whipman 7.11.

cartload cairtle, cairt draught; †kerfull (*see* car) 7.11.

cartridge †patroune 12.5.

cartridge case †patrontash 12.5.

cart road ca; †cairt gate; †waingate 7.6.

carved †shorn 13.2.8.

cask *n*, *specific types* 10.19; †bote 10.18, 10.19.

cast *adj*, *of metal* mouten 13.1.1; *v*, *metal* yat 13.1.1; *n*, *in the eye, see* SQUINT; *v*, *fishing lines or nets, in specific ways* 6.3.1, 6.3.2; shot 6.3.1.

castle 13.3.5; †house 13.3.5.

cast on *in knitting* warp 13.1.8.

castrate *livestock* lib; sort 7.9.1.

casual *of a job* orra 13.1.2.

cat *specific types, colours, ages* 2.6; baudrons; cheet(ie-pussie); gib(bie), gib-cat; pussy-baudrons 2.6.

catapult *specific types* 12.5.

cataract *in the eye* pearl 9.5.

catarrh †caterve 9.15.

catch *n*, *of a marriage partner* rug 8.8; *of a window* window-sneck 13.2.5; *see also* LATCH; *v*, *fish, in specific ways* 6.3.1; *n*, *of fish, specific types* 6.3.1; drave; tak(e) 6.3.1; †waithing 6.3.1, 6.3.2.

catechism *specific types* 14.1.8.

catechize catecheese; speir questions 14.1.8.

caterpillar *specific types* 1.3; kail worm 1.3.

caterwaul loll; waw; †yaw 2.6, 2.9.

catgut thairm 13.1.1.

Catholic Dan(nie boy); left-fitter; paip, †papisher 14.1.5.

cattle *farming* 7.9.1; *specific breeds, types, colours, ages* 2.1; gear; †guids; nowt 2.1.

cattle diseases 2.1.

cattleman bailie, cow baillie; bouman; byreman; cattler, cattlie; pirler 7.5.3.

cattle market *specific types* 7.1.

cattle raid †spreath 12.10; *pl* †herships 12.10.

cattle raiding †depredation 12.10.

cattle yard cattle bucht, court *or* reed; court; †fauldin; ree, reeve, reed 7.3.

caudel †caddel 10.18.

caul *on a newborn baby* hallie *or* seely hoo (*see* hoo) 8.6.

cauldron caudron; muckle pot 10.2.

caulk †calfat 13.1.16; *v* †calfat; †colfing 6.2.2.

caustic cowstick 9.23.2.

cauterize sneyster 19.23.1.

caution †vesynes 15.2.3.

cautious canny; cowshus;

convolvulus bin(d)wood; creepin eevie 4.2.

coo v buckartie-boo; aroo, croodle, crood; curdoo; curroo; rooketty-coo 1.1.7; *of an infant* goo 15.6.17.

cook n cuik 10.1; v cuik; ready 10.3.

cool caller 6.1.1; *of weather, atmosphere* 5.2.1; airish; caller; cuil 5.2.1.

cooper couper 13.1.3.

coopering 13.1.1.

cope n caip 14.1.11.

coping caip; peen; skew; tabling 13.1.16.

coping-stone caip stane, †caip; peat (stane), putt stone 13.1.16.

copper †capper 5.1.9.

copperas †capprois 5.1.9.

copse plantin(g); shaw; wooding 4.6; *see* CLUMP.

copulate *make love* curdoo; dance the reel o Bogie; †mell; †mix (one's) moggans 8.9; *with* †have dale wie (*see* dale); †lig with; †mell with; †mix (one's) moggans with 8.9; *specif of the man* †lowp on; mow; †shed someone's shanks; †shute at the shell 8.9; *see also* FORNICATE; *of a ram* tuip 2.2.

copy n, *specific types, legal* 11.2.3; *of a legal document* †transump(t) 11.3.

coquettish *see* FLIRTATIOUS.

coracle †currach 6.2.1.

coral †curale 3.2; *the colour* †curale 5.2.9.

cordial †curcuddoch; guid willie; hertie, †hertily, hert-warm; sonsie; †warmly 15.3.3.

cordially †luf(e)sumly 15.3.3.

coriander corrydander 10.17.

cormorant Mochrum elder; scarf, scart, scrath 1.1.3.

corn *on the foot* werrock 9.7.

corn bunting †buntlin 1.1.1.

corn-cockle †papple 4.2.

corncrake craik; weet-my-fit 1.1.1.

corn dolly carline; clyack; kirn baby *or* dollie; maiden (clyack) 7.7.5; *see also* CLYACK.

corner *building* cunyie; gushet 13.2.1.

cornflower *specific types* 4.2; blawort, blaver; blue bonnets 4.2.

corn-kiln 7.7.6.

corn-spurrey yarr 4.2.

cornstack *see* STACK.

coroner †coronell 11.4.

corpse *specific types* 8.7; bouk; †carcage; corp; lyke; †mort; †tramort 8.7.

corpse candle cannle, candle 5.2.7.

corpulent 9.1.2; gurthie 9.1.2.

corridor pass; througang; trance 13.2.6.

corrupt *of a text* mankit 15.5.17.

corruption 11.13.

cosy bien; cosh; curmud; snod; snog; tosie 15.6.1; cosh; tosie 5.2.6.

cottage *specific types* 13.3.3; cot house, cottar house; †hallan(d) 13.3.3; *pl* biggin(g)s 13.3.3.

cottar cotman, cottar, †cottrall; †mailer 7.5.1.

cotton grass *specific types* 4.3; bog-cotton; cannach, canna (down); moss crop 4.3.

cotton wool wad 9.23.1.

couch, common †ket; lonnachs; quicken(s); rammock; ronnachs; string girse; wrack 4.3.

cough v, *in specific ways* 9.11; bouch; cloch; coch; croichle; hoast 9.11; n, *specific types* 9.11; cloch; croichle; hoast 9.11.

coulter cooter 7.7.1.

counterfeit †contrafait; †counterfute 11.13; *adj* †feingit 15.3.8.

countermand †contramand 11.2.4, 12.1.

counter-order †contremandment 12.1.

countervail †contravail 15.5.10.

country *as opposed to the town* 5.1.1.

country side 5.1.1; lan(d)s 5.1.1.

courage saul 15.3.9.

courageous †apert; bauld; †beld; campy; crouse; derf; douchty; †weel-hertit; facie; fechtie; †freck; furthie; †keen; †lusty; †mudie; pretty; †savage; stalwart; sture; †thrae; wicht 15.3.9.

court n, *of law, spwcific types* 11.2.1; *Incorporated Trades* †convenery 13.1.2; *church, specific courts* 14.1.6; v gae thegither; winch 8.8; *someone* coort (wi) (*see* court); gae wi; haud up to 8.8.

courteous gentie; hamely 15.3.3; *see also* POLITE.

courtesy mense; †plesour 15.3.3.

courtship 8.8.

courtyard close 13.3.2; *see also* 7.6.

cousin *specific types* 8.11; kizzen 8.11; *second half-cousin* 8.11.

Covenanter(s) 14.1.5.

cow beast, baste; coo 2.1.

coward cooard; coocher; coof; †crawdoun; feardie (gowk); fugie 15.3.10.

cowardice cooardiness 15.3.10.

cowardly *adj* cooard(l)y; fugie; hennie, hen-hertit 15.3.10; *adv* †meschantly 15.3.10.

cowberry brawlins 4.7.

cowed (k)noolt; oolt 15.6.7.

cow-lick cauf's lick 7.9.1, 9.4.

cow-pat cow-plat 2.1.

cowrie *specific types* 3.2; John o Gro(a)t's buckie 3.2.

cowshed †bow-hous(e); byre 7.2.

cowslip lady's fingers 4.2.

crab *specific types* 3.2; cruban 3.2; *specific types used as bait* 6.3.1.

crab apple craw(s) aipple; scrab; scrog 4.7.

craftsman 13.1; tradesman 13.1.2; wricht 13.1.3.

crafty auld-mou'd; cleekie; deep-, far- *or* lang-drauchtit, †drauchty (*see* draucht); glib; loopie; pawkie(-witted) (*see* pawkery); †quent; quirky; sleek(ie); slid; slim; sneck-drawing; souple; †todly; †yaup 15.3.8.

crag *see* CLIFF.

cram *the stomach, see* GORGE.

cramp-iron †crampet 13.1.15, 13.1.16.

cranberry crane; crawberry, crawcrooks; †moss mingin 4.7.

crane n cran; †swey 13.1.1; *bird* cran 1.1.2.

cranefly *see* DADDY-LONG-LEGS.

crazily wuid 15.6.8.

crazy capernoited; cat-wittit; crack (wittet); daft; doitit; Fifish; gane; gytit; hazy; rammish; ree; †sk(a)ivie; skite 15.6.8; *see* INSANE.

cream n ream 10.13.

creamy reamy 10.11.

credit n, *see* HONOUR.

creep *of the flesh* grue 15.6.15.

cress †carse(s) 4.2; *see also* WATERCRESS.

crest †creist 1.1.6; *of feathers etc* tap; *on a bird's head* tappin 1.1.6; *of a helmet* †tymmer 12.3.

crested tappit 1.1.6.

crevice *see* CLEFT.

crew n, *of a ship* †kippage 6.2.4.

crib n crub 7.9.1.

cricket *specific types* 1.3.

crime 11.13; *specific types* 11.13.

crimson †cramasie; crimpson 5.2.9.

cringe coordie; creenge; †lirk; †lour 15.3.10.

crisp *adj, of food* knappie 10.1.

criticize *in various ways* 15.5.14; cabal; challenge; †cheson; faut; †mote; pouk at; puist; scance (at) 15.5.14; *specif a person* quarrel; yaff 15.5.14.

croak crock; †crout; roup 1.1.7; *of birds* croup 1.1.7; *of persons* †crout 9.11

crochet 13.1.8.

crochet-hook 13.1.8.

crockery pigs, piggery 10.2.

croft craft, crofting (*see* croft); paffle; place, placie; †plan 7.4.

crofter pendicler 7.5.1.

crook *shepherding, specific types* 7.13; crummock, †crummie; nibbie 7.13.

crooked *of a tree* scroggie 4.6; *see* BENT.

crop n, *specific types* 7.7.3; †birth; crap 7.7.3; *of a bird* gebbie 1.1.5; *of a fowl* caibie; scroban 2.7; v, *hair, wool* rump 7.9.1, 7.13.

crossbar *of a door* steyband 13.2.4; *of a window, specific types* 13.2.5; *of a barred gate* sword 13.2.4.

crossbeam *specific types* 13.2.3;

bauk; bougar 13.2.3; *of a plough or harrow* †cutwiddie 7.7.1.

crossbow †awblaster 12.5.

cross *adj* canker(i)t; crabbit; curst; teedy; thrawn; tiggie 15.6.13; *n* corse (*see* cross) 13.3.6.

cross-examination through-pittin 11.2.3.

cross-examine cross-speir; †targe 11.2.3.

crotch cleavings; clift; †cloff; forkin; gowl 9.7.

crow *v, of a cock* craw; †leerie-la 2.7, 2.9; *n* cockieleerie (law); craw; †leerie-la 2.7, 2.9; *specific types* 1.1.1; craw 1.1.1; *see also* CARRION CROW, HOODED CROW.

crowbar *specific types* 13.1.1; †craw iron 13.1.1, 13.1.15; gavelock; guddle; pincher, pinching bar; swey; till airn; wa(ll) iron 13.1.1.

crowberry *specific types* 4.7; crawberry, †crawcrooks; croupert; hillberry; knowperts 4.7.

crowing *of birds* craw 1.1.7.

crown *of the head* cantle; pow 2.8.2, 9.2.

crow's feet craw taes 9.5.

crowsteps cat-steps; corbie stanes; crawsteps 13.2.1.

crude *see* COARSE.

cruel *of a person* †felloun; ill (-kinded *or* -set); †pautener; †reithe 15.3.4.

cruelly †dispitefully 15.3.4.

cruet †crowat 10.2.

crumb *n* air; chiffin; †crote, †crottle, †crittel; minschie; mealock, meelackie, moolin(g) (*see* muild); pronack 10.1.

crumble crummle 10.3.

crumbly bruckie; †crotly (*see* crote); knappie *of pastry, see* SHORT 10.1.

crumpet crimpet (*see* crumpet) 10.6.

crunch *v* cramsh, crinch; crump; hum (amo *or* intae); knap; ramsh; scrump 10.4.

crust *of bread: bottom* plain geordie (*see* geordie); sole 10.6; *top* curly Kate (*see* Kate) 10.6.

crustacean *specific types* 3.2.

crutch oxter staff; powl, pole; stilt 9.23.1.

cry *n, of birds, specific types* 1.1.7; *v, of birds* claik; pew; roup; yirm 1.1.7; *v, in specific ways* 1.2.3; yowt 1.2.3; *of a bird or insect* yirm 1.1.7, 1.3; *n, specific types* 1.2.3; yammer; yowt 1.2.3; *v, in various ways* 15.6.16; *see also* WEEP; *v, of a child, in various ways* 8.5; tout(er) 8.5.

crystal *specific types* 5.1.9.

cuckoo gowk, gowkoo 1.1.1.

cuckooflower spink 4.2.

cuckoo-spit gowk('s)-spit(tle(s)) 1.3.

cud cood 2.8.3.

cuddle *v* †cuittle; oxter (at);

smuirich; soss up *or* about 8.8; *n* Scotch gravat; smuirich 8.8.

cudgel *specific types* 12.5; †bastion; †burdoun; †libber-la(y); †pluke; rung; †souple; †tree 12.5.

cudweed †son-afore-the-father 4.2.

cuff *n, slap* cluff; fung 12.12.

cultivate *see* TILL.

cultivated biggit 7.6.

cultivation *see* TILLAGE.

cultured *of a person* †politik 15.2.1.

cumin †kimming 10.17.

cunning *see* CRAFTY.

cup *n, specific types* 10.2; †coup 10.2.

cupboard *built in, specific types* 13.2.6; aumry; †cap almery, †capburd, cophous(e); press 13.2.6.

curb *n* †aweband 15.5.14; *v, a person* put the branks on (*see* branks); counger; crub; †daunton; hae *or* pit the haims on (*see* haims); haud again; new; †snib: snuil 15.5.14.

curdle *of milk* brak; lapper 7.9.2.

curdled cruddy 10.3; *of milk* broken (*see* brak) 7.9.2, 10.13.

curds *specific types* 10.13; crap; cruds; fleeting(s); yirned milk 10.13.

cure *meat etc, in various ways* 10.3; *fish, in specific ways* 6.3.1.

curiosity 15.5.8; keeriosity (*see* curious) 15.5.8.

curious *see* INQUISITIVE.

curl *n* link 9.4; *v* †locker 9.4.

curlew *specific types* 1.1.2; whaup; whitterick 1.1.2.

curly lockering, †lokkerit; swirlie 9.4.

currant curran, curn 4.7; *flowering currant* son-afore-the-father 4.2; *see also* BLACKCURRANT, REDCURRANT.

curry favour sleek; smool; souk in 15.3.8; *with* hand in wi(th); mak in wi; muild (in) with; smool in wi; souk in with 15.3.8.

curse *n, specific types* 14.1.1; †malison 14.1.1; ban; †malison 14.2.1; †winze 15.5.1; *v* jeedge; voo; †wary 15.5.11.

curt cuttit; nippit, nippy; †snack; snotty; tuithy; whippert 15.3.4.

curtly †cuttitly 15.3.4.

custody †festinance; †keep; †ward 11.15.1.

custom *see* HABIT.

customs *connected with annual events* 14.4.2.

cut *n* whack 10.3; *specific types* 9.22; *of meat, specific types* 10.11; *v* †gullie; †maggle; †whack 12.12; *to pieces* †till-hew 12.12; *v, cloth* shape; †tailyie 13.1.7; *v, in specific ways* 9.22, 13.1.1; *peats, in various ways* 7.15; cast 7.15; *turfs* divot 7.15.

cutler †cultellar 13.1.3.

cut-throat †thro(a)tcutter 12.13.

cutting †a cast 7.3; *plants, specific types* 7.16.

cuttlefish hose-fish, hosack 3.2.

dab *fish, specific types* 3.1.2; sand dab; sautie 3.1.2.

dad †dade; dadie; dey; paw 8.11; *see also* FATHER.

daddy-long-legs Jenny Meggie, Jenny-nettle(s), Jenny speeder, Jenny spinner; speeder jenny, speederlegs; spinner, spinnin Jenny, spin(nin) maggie 1.3.

daffodil glen; lily 4.2.

dagger *specific types* 12.5; beetyach; †punce; †windlestrae 12.5.

dainty *of persons* 9.1.1.

dairy *n* 7.9.2; milk house 7.9.2.

dairymaid dey 7.5.3.

dais †deas 13.2.6.

daisy *specific types* 4.2; †banwart; †daseyne; ewe gowan; gollan; gowan, May gowan; †wallie 4.2.

dally †geck; slaver; smuirich 8.8; *with* mird with; tig with 8.8.

dam *animal mother* †minnie 1.2.1; *n, water, specific types* 6.1.3; *parts thereof* 6.1.3; caul 6.1.3; *v, in specific ways* 6.1.3.

damages *specific types* 11.7; 11.15.1; †dampnis 11.15.1.

dame *see* LADY.

damn *in imprecations* confooter; dang; daver; ding; sink; weary fa, †weary on *or* tak 15.7.1; *it* dag (on) it 15.7.1.

damnation †tinsal 14.1.1.

damned *in imprecations* dazent; †plagued 15.7.1.

damp dunk(y); †wa(c)k 6.1.1; *of corn-sheaves* raw 7.7.4; *of weather* 5.2.3.

damson ploom damas 4.7.

dandelion dainty-lion, †dent-de-lyon; horse gowan (*see* gowan); medick; pee-the-bed, pish-the-bed; what o'clock is it? 4.2.

dandle *a child* diddle 8.5.

dandruff luce 9.8.

dappled †lyart 5.2.9; *see also* BRINDLED.

dark *adj* derk; †dern; †dirk; douth; mirk(some), mirky 5.2.7; *in colour* glog; †keir-black; *of hair, eyes, complexion* 5.2.9; *see also* BLACK; *of persons, in specific ways* 9.1.1.

darken dit; mirk, mirkening, †mirken 5.2.7.

darkness †dirk(nes); mirk; †sable 5.2.7.

darling daut(ie) 8.8, 15.6.11; *see also* ENDEARMENTS.

darn *sewing* ranter 13.1.7.

darnel †dornell; †roseegar 4.3.

dart dert 12.5; *specif a missile* prog; stug 12.5.

daughter *specific types* 8.11; dochter; lass(ie), lassock, lassickie; lass(ie) bairn, lass wean; †maiden; quine 8.11.

daughter-in-law guid dochter 8.11.

Index

gilt †giltin 5.2.9.
ginger ginge 10.17.
gingerbread gibbery, gingebreid 10.7.
girdle *for baking* back; †bannock iron 10.2.
girl *specific types* 8.5; bird; †callan; lass(ie), lassock, lassickie; †maiden barne; quine; wench; wife, wifie, wifock(ie); †woman bairn; younker 8.5; *see also* LASS.
girlfriend †doxie; hing-tee; jo; lass(ie), lassock, lassickie; lovie (*see* luve); quine; tairt 8.8.
girlish lasslike 15.3.7; lasslike 8.5.
give way †reel 12.7.
gizzard caibie; gizzern 2.7; caibie; quern 10.11; quern 2.8.2.
glad gled 15.5.4; *of* blithe of 15.6.11.
gladden †blithe; †gled 15.5.4.
gladness †fainness 15.5.4.
glass *n* gless, †glassinwerk (*see* glass) 13.2.5; *adj* †glassin 13.2.5.
glazed *of a window* lozened 13.2.5.
glazier †glass(in)wricht 13.2.5.
glazing 13.2.5; †glassin(werk) 13.2.5.
gleam *n, specific types* 5.2.7, 5.2.8; †brin; glim; glint; glisk; leam; scance; skime 5.2.7; *v, in specific ways* 5.2.7, 5.2.8; †bicker; blink, blent; glaim; gleet; glint; low; scance; sheen; skime; skimmer; skinkle 5.2.7.
glean rake 7.7.4.
gleaner raker; †stibbler 7.7.4.
glib gash-gabbit; gleg-gabbit *or* -tongued 15.5.7.
glimmer *v* blinter; gleet 5.2.7; *n* flichter; gleed; glim; spunk(ie); stime 5.2.7.
glitter *v* gleet; glister; prinkle; scance; skinkle 5.2.7; *n* gleet; glister 5.2.7.
globe-flower butter blob; lapper *or* lucken gowan (*see* gowan) 4.2.
gloom †glowme; mirkness; †terne 5.2.7.
gloomy dour; dreich; drumlie; †malagrugrous 5.2.1; †dully; †eerie, eeriesome; heavysome; †malagrugrous; †terne 15.3.5; mirksome; †terne 5.2.7.
glorify glorifee 15.6.11.
glory *n* glore 15.2.1; *v* †glore 15.2.1.
glow *n, specific types* 5.2.7, 5.2.8; †aisle; low 5.2.7; *v* †glevin; glowe; low 5.2.7.
glue *n* batter 13.1.1.
glum *see* DOWNCAST.
glutinous claggy 10.1.
glutton belly gut, †belly god; †bootyer; gorb; gutser; hecker; midden, knacker's midden; †puddin fillar; Rab Ha; slaik; slaister kyte; troch 15.4.6; belly gut, †belly god; gulch; hecker; Rab Ha; slaister kyte 10.4.
gluttonous belly gut, †belly god;

geenyoch; gutsie, guttie; hungry; †tuithy; †vorax 15.4.6; belly gut, †belly god; gutsie, guttie 10.4.
gluttony 15.4.6; †gluttery 15.4.6
gnarled *of trees* gurlie 4.6.
gnash †gash 2.8.3; *teeth* chirk 9.3; girn 15.6.18.
gnaw chittle; gnyauve; †knaw 2.8.3; chittle; †rundge 10.4.
goad *n* gaud, †gad wand 7.9.1.
gobble glunsh; gorb; gorble; gulch; guts; hanch; hum(p)sh; heck; laib; lay into; nam; scaff; †slag; slaister; slerp; snap 10.4; *n, v, of a turkey* habber 2.7.
go-between †black-foot 8.9; †trafficker 15.3.8.
goblet †pece; tassi(ie) 10.2, 10.18.
goblin *specific types* 14.2.2.
God the Best; (the) Guid, the guid man, guidness; †the wy(e) 11.1.3; *in exclams* dod; nyod; od(d)s; peace; praise; †tod; yod 15.7.1; *see also* GOSH.
godliness †guidlyheid; †pieté 14.1.2.
godmother cummer 8.6.
goffer †gouffer; guffer 13.1.10.
goldcrest golden crest(ie); mune 1.1.1.
golden †giltin; gowden 5.2.9.
goldfinch gowdie, goldie, gooldie, gowd spink 1.1.1.
good *see* FINE.
good-for-nothing *n* dae-na-gude; fang; hallockit, †hallirakus; hurb; loun; neir-do-good *or* -weel; nyaff; outerlin(g); pallion; †ragabash; rap; reebald; †scant-o-grace; scum; skybe, skipe; †sleeth; sloosht; snot(ter); waff(er); †waffinger; wanworth; warroch 15.3.2; *specif of a woman* paik 15.3.2; *adj* little worth; †meschant; †nocht *or* nevir worth a mailʒe (*see* mailʒe); nochtless; †ragabash; scabbit; scoutie; skybal(d); †unworth; waffie, waffish, waff like *or* -looking; wanwordy; wanworth 15.3.2.
good-looking *of persons* 9.1.1, 9.1.2; weel-faured; †weel-lookit 9.1.1.
goodly guidly 15.6.1.
good-natured *see* KINDLY.
goods *specific types* 11.8.
good turn cast 15.3.3.
goosander saw neb 1.1.2.
goose guse, geese 2.7; *wild, specific types* 1.1.2, 1.1.3.
gooseberry *specific types* 4.7; †blob, honey blob; grosell, grosart 4.7.
gooseflesh cauld creep(s); hen('s) flesh, hen('s) picks, hen-plooks 9.10; cauld creep(s) 15.6.15.
goosefoot *specific types* 4.2; *see also* FAT HEN.
go out *of a light* †quinkill 5.2.8.
gore *v, of a cow* porr 2.1.
gorge *n, see* RAVINE; *v* pang; puist;

stap; stech; stent; stive; stow; †wame 10.4.
gorged pang, pan('d)-fu; ram-full 10.4.
gorse whin 4.5.
gosh 15.7.1; go; gor; goshen(s); goth 15.7.1.
gosling gaisling 2.7.
gospel †vangel 14.1.8.
gossamer slammachs 1.3.
gossip *n, specific types* 15.5.8; causey clash; claik(s); clatter(s); clype; ferlies; souch; speak; spin 15.5.8; *person* claik; clapperdin; clash; clasher; clatter; clypach (*see* clype); sclave 15.5.8; *see also* CHIT-CHAT. *v* claik; clash; clatter; clype; cummer 15.5.8; *see also* BLETHER.
gossipy clashy; glib-mou(e)d 15.5.8; *see also* TALKATIVE.
grace *n, prayer at meals, specific types* 14.1.8; *v* mense 15.2.1.
graft *v, a plant cutting* †imp 7.16.
grain 4.9; *in gen* meal's corn 4.9; *of specific plants* 4.9.
grammar gremmar 14.3.1.
granary †victual-house 7.7.6; †girnel; grainery 7.2.
grand- *indicating family relationship* aul(d) 8.11.
grandchild gran(d)bairn, gran(d)-wean; oe 8.11; *pl* gran(d)childer 8.11.
grand-daughter *specific types* 8.11; †nevoy 8.11.
grandfather bobbie; dey; deyd(ie); gran(d)da, gran(d)daddy, gran(d)-dey, gran(d)faither, gran(d)sher; guidsire; †guidschir; lucky da(d)die, lucky daid; pawpie 8.11.
grandmother deyd(ie); †grandame; gran(d)minnie, gran(d)mither; †guid dame; lucky (minnie) 8.11.
grandson *specific types* 8.11; †nepote; nevoy 8.11.
granite *specific types* 5.1.8.
granular querny 10.1.
granule quern 10.1.
graphite wad 13.1.5, 5.1.9.
grapnel creeper 13.1.1.
grass 4.3; *specific types* 4.3; girse, gress 4.3.
grasshopper cricket 1.3.
grassland 7.6.
grassy girsie 4.3; *of land* 5.1.3, 5.1.4; green 5.1.3.
grate chim(b)ley 13.2.7.
grateful thankrife 15.6.12.
gratification †thankfulness 15.6.11.
gratified knichtit; proud 15.6.11.
gratify †applese; graitifee 15.6.11; *someone* glack someone's mitten 15.6.11.
grating †grate 13.2.8; *farming* 7.3; *on a window* 13.2.5; tirless, †treilʒeis 13.2.5; *over a river etc, specific types* 6.1.3.

Index

gratitude 15.6.12; graititeed
15.6.12.
gratuity bountith; †buntha
13.1.2; *specific types* 13.1.4.
grave *n* †deid-house; delf; graff;
graft; †kirk hole; lair; muild;
†truff; †yird 8.7.
gravedigger *specific types* 8.7;
beddal 8.7.
gravel *specific types* 5.1.8; chad;
channel, channer; graivel; grool
5.1.8.
gravelly chingly 5.1.3, 6.1.5; *of soil*
sha(i)rp 5.1.8.
gravestone *specific types* 8.7; lair
stane 8.7.
graveyard *specific types* 8.7; †burial
yard; howf; †kirk hole 8.7; *see
also* CHURCHYARD.
gravy bree 10.11.
graze *v* screeve; scruif 9.22; *of
animals, in various ways* 2.8.3;
gae, go; †knip; lizour; nip 2.8.3;
n skiff 9.22.
grazing *see* PASTURAGE.
grease *n*, *specific types* 13.1.1; creesh
13.1.1; *v* creesh; ile 13.1.1.
greasy creeshie 10.3.
great gret 15.2.1.
great- *indicating family relationship*
aul(d) 8.11.
greatest maist 15.2.1.
great-grandchild ieroe 8.11.
great-grandfather
†foregrandfather; †foregrantsire;
gran(d)sher 8.11.
great-grandmother
†foregranddame; †grandame 8.11.
great-grandson nevoy;
†pronepot; †pronevoy 8.11.
great-great-grandfather
†foregrantsire 8.11.
great-great-grandmother
†foregranddame 8.11.
great tit ox ee 1.1.1.
greenfinch greenie 1.1.1.
greenish greenichtie, greenichy
5.2.9.
green woodpecker †specht 1.1.1.
grey *specific shades* 5.2.9; †bloncat;
grim; †hasard; †lauchtane
5.2.9.
grey-haired †canous; †hasard
5.2.9, 9.4.
grey mullet pelcher 3.1.2.
griddle *see* GIRDLE.
gridiron †brander, brandreth
10.2.
grief 15.6.16; *specific types* 15.6.16;
anger; dool; †gram; harm(s);
†syte; teen 15.6.16.
grief-stricken doilt 15.6.16; *specif
of the heart* sair 15.6.16.
grievance eelist; plaint 15.6.2.
grieve †grief 15.6.16; †touch
15.6.7.
grieved hert-scalded 15.6.7; *in
various ways* 15.6.16; wae
15.6.16.
grievous fell; †grevand 15.6.7.
griffin †grephoun 14.2.2.
grim *of a person* alagrugous;

grugous; †malagrugrous; raucle;
sture; †thieveless 15.3.4.
grimace *n*, *specific types* 15.6.18;
girn; †mow; shevel, shile; thraw;
Tontine face 15.6.18; *v*, *in various
ways* 15.6.18; †flyre; girn; grue;
mak a mow *or* mows; murgeon;
sham; †shammle; shevel,
showl; thraw one's face, gab *etc*;
†wray 15.6.18.
grind mak doon 7.7.6, 13.1.1; *teeth*
jirg, jirk; risp 9.3.
gristle girsle 10.11.
grizzled lyart 5.2.9.
groan *n* grain; †grank; mane
15.6.16; *v* grain; †grank;
gruntle; mane; pech 15.6.16.
groin lisk 9.7.
groove *n*, *masonry* raggle, raglet,
raglin 13.1.16; *n*, *v* rit 13.1.1.
grope *v*, *indecently* ficher wi; fin(d);
graip 8.9; *see also* FONDLE.
gross *of persons* 9.1.2.
ground grund 5.1.1.
ground elder alshinders;
bishop('s) weed 4.2.
grounds 13.3.2, 7.6.
groundsel grundiswallow 4.2.
grove †cuthill?; †grave; plantin(g)
7.14.
grow *of persons, in specific ways* 9.1.2;
†rax 9.1.1.
growl *v*, *of an animal* grool; grunch;
gurl; gurr(y-worry) 1.2.3; *n*
grunch; gurl; habber 1.2.3; *v*
snag(ger); wirr 2.9; *specif of a dog*
gurr; yirr 2.5; *n*, *specific types* 2.5,
2.9; gurr(y-wurry) 2.5, 2.9; *specif of
a dog* yirr 2.5, 2.9; *v*, *of a person*
grunch; nurr; wirr 15.6.13.
grow up come tae 8.4.
grudge *n* †grutch (*see* grudge);
grummle; †grunyie 15.3.5; *v*
†grutch (*see* grudge) 15.3.5.
grudging *adj* ill-willie 15.3.5.
gruel blearie 10.1; *specific types* 10.9.
grumble *v* cark; channer; chirm;
compleen; craik; croup; fryne;
girn; glumsh; glunsh; grain;
greet; gronach; grudge;
grummle; grumph; grunch;
hummer; †mane, mak a mane;
molligrant; mump; munge;
murmell; murn; orp; peek; peenge;
pewl; †pleen; tarrow; thraw;
witter; yammer; yarp; yirm; yirn;
yowl 15.3.5; *n* grummle; mane;
pewl; yirn 15.3.5.
grumbler greetin Teenie;
grumph; whinger 15.3.5.
grumbling *adj* cronachin;
grumlie; peesie-weesie 15.3.5; *n*
girn; †murmell 15.3.5.
grumpy *see* ILL-NATURED.
grunt *v* grunch 1.2.3; *n* grumph;
grunch 1.2.3; *of a pig* gruntle;
guff 2.3.
guarantor †warrand 11.2.3.
guard *v* gaird 11.4, 12.9; †waken;
wauk; weir 12.9; *n* †cors-gard;
†outwach(is) 12.1.

guardian †wowar 8.11; *legal*
11.12.
guard-room †cors-gard 12.1.
gudgeon †gudge 13.1.1.
guelder rose †veyton 4.5.
guffaw *v* gaff(aw); heffer 15.6.17;
n gaff(aw); heffer 15.6.17.
guilds 13.1.2.
guile †evil *or* false ingine (*see*
ingine); pawkery; sneck-
drawing 15.3.8.
guileless sakeless 15.1.
guillemot *specific types* 1.1.3; coot;
lavie; marrot; scout; sea hen
1.1.3.
guilty *in specific ways* 11.13.
guiser *see* MUMMER.
gull *n*, *bird*, *specific types* 1.1.3; goo;
pewlie (Willie); plee; pleengie; sea
goo; sea-maw 1.1.3.
gullet craig; hause; neck; red brae,
red lane, red road; scroban;
†stroup; swallie; thrapple;
throttle; wizzen, weason 9.9.
gullible blate 15.2.4.
gully *see* RAVINE.
gulp *n* gaup; glock; glog (owre);
glut; gollop; slour 10.4; *v* glog;
glunsh; glut; gollop; hose; pouch;
slouster 10.4.
gun *specific types* 12.5.
gunnel †stane fish 3.1.2.
gunner †ordinar 12.2.
gun-wadding colfing 12.5.
gurgle *v*, *in specific ways* 9.11; gurl
6.1.1; souch 9.11; *of a baby*
groozle 15.6.17; *n*, *gurgling noises*
6.1.1; *of a baby* murr 15.6.17.
gurnard *specific types* 3.1.2; crooner,
croonick, croonyil, †crunan;
gowdie 3.1.2.
gush *n*, *specific types* 6.1.1; stour;
strone 6.1.1; phrase, phrasing
15.4.3; *v*, *in specific ways* 6.1.1;
†brush; pish, faem; strone
6.1.1.
gushing *of talk* phrasie 15.4.3; *of a
person* phrasing 15.4.3.
gust *n*, *of wind, specific types* 5.2.2;
blaud; blaw; bleester; blouder;
flaff; †flag; flan; flaw; †gird; gliff,
glaff; gowst; howder; skelp;
snifter; thud; †tift, tiff; wap,
whap; whid 5.2.2; *v*, *in specific
ways* 5.2.2; bleester; dad; hushle
5.2.2.
gusty *of wind, see* BLUSTERY.
gut *of an animal* thairm 2.8.2.
gutter 13.1.14; channel; gitter
13.1.14.
guttersnipe gutterbluid 15.2.2.
habit lair 15.1.
habitable †lodgeable 13.3.1.
haddock *specific types and ages* 3.1.2;
haddie, haddo, hathock, hoddock
3.1.2; *dried or cured in various ways*
10.12.
haft *n*, *v* heft 13.1.1, 7.12.
haggard *of persons* 9.1.2.
hailstone bullet stane; rattlestane
5.2.3.
hair *specific types, colours* 9.4.

500

Index

Index

Index

loach beardie lotchie; bessie, bessie bairdie, bessie lotchie; Katie beardie 3.1.4.

load *v* prime 12.5; *a ship, in specific ways* 6.2.3.

loaf *v* haiver; hawm; loonge; mump; slounge; snuil; snuit; †sorn; soss; sotter about 15.4.5; *n, specific types* 10.6; laif 10.6.

loan *n, specific types* 11.8.

loathing laith 15.3.4.

loathsome *see* HIDEOUS.

lobby *n* entry; trance 13.2.6.

lobe *of the ear* lap 9.2; *of the liver* lap 9.9.

lobster lapster, labster 3.2.

lobster-pot creel; lapster creel 6.3.1.

lock *n, specific types* 13.2.4; †gin; †louk; †stekin(g) 13.2.4; *of hair, specific types* 9.4; flaucht; †lachter; link; swirl; tossel 9.4; *v* †louk 13.2.4; *up* sneck up 13.2.4; *in* sneck in 13.2.4.

locked lokkit, lockfast 13.2.4.

lockjaw jaw-lock 9.19.

lodge ludge (*see* lodge) 13.3.3; *hunting, specific types* 13.3.3; †hunt hall 13.3.3.

loft *specific types* 13.2.6; laft 13.2.6.

loggerheads *at* at the knag an the widdie (*see* knag); out like a pat fit (*see* pat); striven; in(to) the widdie necks (*see* widdie) 15.5.9.

loin †lunyie; *pl* †lendis 9.7.

loiter dring; haik; haingle; mole, mollach 15.4.5.

lonely lanely, lanerly, lanesome; misslie; waff 15.6.10.

long *v* mang; think lang; †tire; †ʒarne 15.6.10; *for* glagger for; green for; think lang for; †tire for; weary for 15.6.10.

longing *n* 15.6.10; ill-ee 15.6.10; *adj* awid 15.6.10.

long-suffering patientfu 15.5.20.

long-winded en(d)less 15.5.7.

look out 12.9.

loom 13.1.6; lume 13.1.6.

loose-limbed *of persons* 9.1.1.

loot *see* DESPOIL, PLUNDER.

loquacious *see* TALKATIVE.

loquacity click-clack; tongue-raik 15.5.7.

Lord *in exclams* laird; Lod; lorie; losh (me), †loshins 15.7.1.

lordly lairdly; †senʒeourabill 15.2.1.

lorry *refuse collector's* scaffie cairt 13.1.1.

lose loss; tyne 15.6.2.

loss *n, specific types* 11.8, 15.6.2; miss 15.6.2.

loud-mouthed glousterin 15.3.7.

louse *specific types* 1.3; gray horse; Jerusalem traveller; loose; poulie 1.3; *head-louse* traveller 9.4.

lousy *of hair, head* 9.4.

lout *specific types* 15.2.2; †chuff; coof; gillieperous; hugmahush; lubbard; †rabiator; scurryvaig; yaup 15.2.2; *see also* BOOR.

loutish ill-shaken-up; miraculous 15.2.2; *see also* BOORISH.

lovage †luffage 4.2.

love *n* 8.8; †amouris; †drowry; luve 8.8; †lamenry 8.9; *the emotion* fainness; hert-likin; luve, †luverent 8.8; *v* like; luve 8.8; *see* AFFECTION.

lover billy; chap; jo; lad(die); lovie (*see* luve); †pairty 8.8; †lamen 8.9.

love-sick gyte 8.8.

love-token †drowry; †lufe-drowry 8.8.

loving †effectionat; fain; hert-warm; inner; naitral-hertit 15.3.3.

lovingly condingly 15.3.3.

low *of a river etc* sma(ll) 6.1.2.

low-class 15.2.2; †codroch; main 15.2.2; *specif of a person* †sober 15.2.2; *see also* COMMON.

lower *of a place* nether 5.1.1; *v, oneself, see* HUMBLE.

lowing *of cattle* rowt 2.1.

low-lying *of ground* 5.1.2.

Low Sunday †Laif-So(u)nday 14.1.10.

low tide *see* EBB-TIDE.

loyal †feal; †laúteful; leal; sicker 15.3.13.

loyally leal 15.3.13.

loyalty 15.3.13; †lawtie, lauteth; lealty 15.3.13.

lozenge *specific types* 10.16; lozenger 10.16.

lubricate creesh 13.1.1.

lubrication 13.1.1.

lucky sonsie 15.3.1; *bringing luck* canny 14.2.1; *see* AUSPICIOUS, FORTUNATE.

lukewarm *see* TEPID.

lull *in weather* daak 5.2.1, 5.2.2.

lumbering *of persons* 9.1.1.

lump *n, on the skin, specific types* 9.8; *of food* dodgel; dunt; junt; kemple; †lunch; skelp 10.1; *see* SWELLING.

lumpfish *specific types and ages* 3.1.2; cock paddle; hush padle; †limp; paidle; runker 3.1.2.

lump-sucker *see* LUMPFISH.

lumpy *of persons* 9.1.2.

lungs buffs; lichts 9.9.

lungwort thunner-an-lichtenin; William and Mary 4.2.

lust 8.9; *n* †glaiks; †luverent; †luxure 8.9.

luxuriant *of plant growth* 4.1; †cashie; gorskie; growthie; grushie; proud; reuch, rough 4.1.

lying-in *see* CONFINEMENT.

lynx †lucerve 1.2.1.

mace *plant* †macis 10.17; *weapon* †mass(e) 12.5.

machinery graith 7.12, 13.1.1.

mad begoyt; †brainwode; in a creel (*see* creel); deleerit; gane; gyte; hyte; radge, radgie; rammish; wuid 15.6.8; *totally* horn daft; reid wud; †skire mad 15.6.8; rammish 2.8.1; *see also* RABID, INSANE.

madder †mather 4.2, 13.1.9.

madman gyte 15.6.8.

madness 15.6.8; madderam 15.6.8.

maggot maithe, maid; mauk, mauch 1.3.

maggoty †mathie; maukie 1.3.

magic *see* ENCHANTMENT.

magpie deil's bird; maggie; pyot 1.1.1.

maiden dame, damie; damishell; deem; lass(ie), lassock, lassickie; quine 8.4; *see also* LASS.

maid-of-all-work †scuddler 13.1.4.

maidservant lass; maiden; quean; servant lass; serving lass 13.1.4.

mail *see* CHAINMAIL, COAT-OF-MAIL.

maim †maggle; mittle 9.22; *see* MUTILATE.

maimed mankit; †mutilit 9.22.

†mains manse 7.4.

malevolence *see* HOSTILITY.

malevolent *see* HOSTILE, MALICIOUS.

malice †gram; ill; †mavité; †wroke 15.3.4.

malice aforethought †forethocht felony 11.13.

malicious †envyfu; ill-hertit, -muggent *or* †-willie; mislushious; pooshinous; †sinistrous; †teenfull; uncannie; warlock; †weird 15.3.4.

malign †maling 15.5.8.

malignant †attery 15.3.4.

mallard mire duck; moss duck; muir duck 1.1.2.

mallet bittle 13.1.1.

mallow *the plant* maws 4.2.

malt maut 10.19.

malt-kirn 7.7.6.

maltreat *see* ILL-TREAT.

maltster †mautman.

man boy; carle; carlie; gadgie; he; Jock; †lede; man body; †schalk; tuip; †wye 8.1; *pl* menfolk (*see* man) 8.1.

manageable *of animals* †sonsie 2.8.1; *of a person* fleet 15.5.20.

manager †grieve; †maister 13.1.3; *specif of a coalmine* owersman 13.1.5; *of an estate* grund officer 7.5.2.

manger foresta 7.2.

manhood manheid 8.3.

mankind 8.1; fowk; Jock Tamson's bairns; †all (levand) leid(is) (*see* lede) 8.1.

manly pretty 15.3.9.

manners †afferes, feirs; fashions 15.1.

manor-house big house; †heid-house; †maner place; †manse 13.3.3.

mansion †manse 13.3.3.

manslaughter culpable homicide 11.13.

mantelpiece brace; chim(b)ley brace *or* heid; lintel 13.2.7.

manufacture 13.1.1; †manufactor 13.1.1.

manure *n, specific types* 7.7.2; guiding (*see* guid); manner;

muck 7.7.2; *v, in various ways* 7.7.2; manner; muck 7.7.2.
marble †maber 5.1.8.
march mairch 12.1.
mare †gillet; mear(ie) 2.4.
marigold *specific types* 4.2; yellow gowan (*see* gowan); †mariguld; †soucye 4.2.
marjoram †marjolene, 10.17.
mark *n, of ownership on an animal* 7.9.1, 7.13; kenmark 7.9.1, 7.13; *see also* BRAND; *v, livestock* buist 7.9.1, 7.13; *see also* BRAND.
market *agricultural* 7.1, 7.5.3; *see also* FAIR, HIRING FAIR.
market garden 7.16; †mail-garden 7.16.
market-place tron 13.3.2.
marking *specific types* 5.2.9.
marriage 8.8; mairriage 8.8; *legal aspects* 11.11, 11.12; *services* 14.1.9.
marrow *of bones* mergh, mergie; †smergh 9.9; *as food* mergh, mergie 10.11.
marry *join in marriage* buckle; †knit; mairry; sowther; tether; †twine; wall; yoke 8.8; *to mairry on,* †upon *or* with 8.8; *get married, see* WED.
marsh 5.1.6; *specific types* 5.1.6; fluther; †mersk; †nesh; quaw; †sleugh; slogg; slump; sowp; †strother; swail; †waggle 5.1.6.
marshland 5.1.6; †mersk; moss.
marshy 5.1.6; slumpy; wauchie 5.1.6; *of ground* 5.1.4.
martin mairtin; swalla, swallow 1.1.1; *see also* HOUSE-MARTIN, SAND-MARTIN.
martyr mairtyr 14.1.1.
marvel *v* †awonder; ferlie, †have ferlie; †mervel; strange 15.6.3; *n* ferlie; †mervel 15.6.3.
mash *v, malt* mask 10.19; *vegetables* chap; rummle 10.3.
mason *see* STONEMASON.
masonry 13.1.16; †mason werk; stane and lime 13.1.16.
mass *religious service, various types and aspects* 14.1.9; †mess 14.1.9.
massage *in specific ways* 9.23.1.
mast *of a ship. specific types* 6.2.1; most 6.2.1.
master *of a craft* cork; deacon; maister 13.1.2.
masterpiece †maisterstick 13.1.2.
mastery 15.5.13; grip; owerance; †owerhan; poustie 15.5.13.
matching *of furnishings* †conform 13.2.8.
matchless †makeless 15.3.1.
mate *n, of a bird or animal* †mak(e) 1.1.1; 1.2.1; *on a ship* †contermaister 6.2.4; *workman's marrow;* †neibour 13.1.3.
matrimony †matermony; mink 8.8.
matted *of hair, wool etc* tautit 2.8.1; *of wool* waulkit 13.1.6.
mattock *specific types* 7.12.
mature *adj, in years* auld young 8.3;

of a person †degest 15.3.14; *v, of dung* mak 7.7.2.
maturely †degestlie 15.3.14.
maturity *in a person* 15.3.14.
maunder maunner; rander; roiter (*see* royet); slab 15.5.7.
Maundy Thursday Skire's Thursday 14.1.10, 14.4.1.
May Day 14.4.2
maypole †simmer tre 14.4.1.
mayweed *specific types* 4.2.
meadow leens *pl*; lizour; meedow 7.6; *by a river, specific types* 5.1.5; haugh 5.1.5.
meadow pipit gray cheeper; heather peeper; moss cheeper; muir cheeper; titlin 1.1.2.
meadowsweet lady o the meadow; queen of (the) meadow 4.2.
meal *specific types* 10.5; diet; eat; meal o meat; meltith 10.5; *grain, specific types, see* 10.8.
mealie pudding jerker, mealie jerker; jimmy, mealie jimmy; Jock; †white hause, white puddin(g) 10.9, 10.11.
meal-time *specific types* 10.5; brosing-time, brose-time; cornin time; diet-hour 10.5; *mining* brosing-time 13.1.5.
meander *n, v, see* BEND.
measles maisles; mirls 9.19.
measure *n, of liquor* 10.18; *of food, specific types* 10.1; *specific quantities of fish* 6.3.1, 6.3.2.
measurement *of coal* 13.1.5; *of thread, fabric, etc* 13.1.6.
meat *butcher's meat* beef; butcher meat; flesh, †flesh meat 10.11.
mechanism intimmers 13.1.1.
medal †medalȝe 12.3.
meddle *in various ways* 15.5.8; scaud one's lips *or* tongue in *or* wi ither folk's kail (*see* kail); mak *or* meddle *or* mell; mell; †mess and mell; middle; mird 15.5.8.
medicinal hailsome 9.23.2.
medicinal plants 9.23.2.
medicine *art of* †medicinary 9.23.1; *substance* feesick; graith 9.23.2.
meek †tholemode 15.5.20.
meeting *of church courts, specific types* 14.1.6; *of legal bodies* 11.2.3.
megrim †siller fluke 3.1.2.
melancholy *adj, see* SAD; *n* †thochtiness 15.3.5.
melt *in specific ways* 5.2.3; mouten 10.3.
membership *of a guild etc* 13.1.2.
menace *v* cock; mint 12.9.
mend *in various ways* 13.1.1; †cuiter; jam 13.1.1; *specif sewing* 13.1.7; ranter; spatch 13.1.7; *specif shoes, see* COBBLE.
menial *n* †loun 15.2.2; *see also* LACKEY.
menstruate see her ain 9.16.
mentally handicappd *in specific ways* 9.20; gytit; half hackit, half

jeck; no(t) richt (*see* richt); silly; wanting 9.20.
mentally-handicapped person daftie; eediot; gowk(ie); halfling 9.20.
mercenary †wager 12.2.
mercury †mercure 5.1.9.
mercy †marcie 15.5.2.
merit *n* †meid 15.3.1.
mermaid †marmaiden 14.2.2.
merry blithesome; cheerisome; crouse; gleg; hertsome; joco; joly, †jolious; mirkie; †mirrie; pawkie; pleasant; vaudie; vogie 15.5.4.
mess 15.5.17; boorach(ie); bucker; bullox; bummle; carfuffle; clary; clat; guddle; gutter; knacker's midden; midden; moger; plaister; plowster; poach; †puddle; sclatch; skiddle; skitter; sotter; throuither; touther 15.5.17; *of (semi-liquid)* 6.1.1; *of food, specific types* 10.1.
mess about *in specific ways in liquid etc* 6.1.1.
messy *wet and messy states* 6.1.1.
metalwork 13.1.1.
meteor *see* SHOOTING STAR.
meticulous †painful; perjink; pingling; pludisome; pointed 15.5.15.
mettle saul 15.3.9.
mew *v* †yaw 1.2.3; maw; †mewt; miauve; †wraw; †yaw 2.6, 2.9; *n* maw 2.6.
mezereon son-afore-the-father 4.2.
miaow *see* MEW.
mica *specific types* 5.1.9.
Michaelmas 14.1.10.
midden *see* DUNGHILL.
middle age 8.3; †mid-age 8.3.
middle aged auld young; †mid (-aged) 8.3.
middle-sized *of persons* 9.1.1.
midge midgeck, mudgeick, midgie, mudge 1.3.
midriff †middrit 9.9.
midwife canny wife; cummer; howdie(wife); †mam; †medwyfe 8.6; cummer; howdie (wife); luckie; †mam; †medwyfe 9.16.
midwifery howdieing 8.6, 9.16.
mighty †mauchty; potent; †rich 15.2.1.
mignonette minnonette 4.2.
milch cow milk cow 2.1.
mild *of weather* lithesome; maumie; saft, soft 5.2.1.
mildew *on plants* bleck 4.1.
military service † (h)osting 12.1.
milk *v, a cow* draw 7.9.2.
milking 7.9.2; †fauld 7.9.2; meal; †meltith 7.9.2.
milking-time kye-time 7.9.2.
milk pail *specific types* 7.9.2; bally (cog) 7.9.2.
mill 7.8.2; †miln (*see* mill) 7.8.2; *for making gunpowder* †pouder myll 12.5.

mill-dam mill caul 7.8.2.
miller millart, †milnar 7.8.1.
milling 7.8.
mill-race †inlair (*see* inlay); lade; mill lade; †water lead 7.8.2.
millstone 7.8.2; sheeling stane 7.8.2.
millwheel 7.8.2.
milt melt, melg 3.1.1.
mimic *n* aff tak 15.5.3.
mincing †minȝard; prick-me-dainty 15.4.3.
mind *the seat of the thoughts* wame 15.1.
mindful †memorative; †rememorant 15.3.1.
mine *v* howk 13.1.5; *n* †pot 13.1.5; *gold* †goldin mine 13.1.5; *graphite* wad 13.1.5; *lead* †leidin mine 13.1.5; *see also* PIT.
miner coomy; Jock brit; pickman 13.1.5; *see also* COLLIER.
minerals 5.1.9.
mineral waters *see* lemonade.
mineshaft *specific types* 13.1.5; heuch; †pot; shank; sink 13.1.5.
mineworkings 13.1.5; winning 13.1.5.
mining 13.1.5.
minnow *specific types* 3.1.4; bandie; guttie; minnon, mennen(t) 3.1.4.
minor *in legal age* 11.12.
mint specific types 4.2.
mire *see* MUD.
mirth 15.5.4, 15.6.17; †glew 15.5.4.
miscarriage slip 8.6, 9.16.
miscarry miscairry 8.6, 9.16; *specif in pregnancy* pairt wi bairn *or* child 8.6, 9.16.
mischief 15.3.11; deviltry (*see* deil) 15.3.11.
mischievous †caleery; gall(o)us; ill-contrived, -contriven, -dune, -deedie, -deedit *or* -trickit; mirkie; pliskie; †pratty, †ill-pratty; royet; rummlin; †unsonsie 15.3.11; *specif of a child* 8.5; royet 8.5.
mischievousness ill-gates 15.3.11.
miser †dring; grab; heather-piker; †huidpyk; misert, †meeser; nabal; niggar; †nipcaik, nipscart; peyzart; rake; scrae; scrunt; ?†warner; †wratch 15.4.1.
miserable *of a person* meeserable; †weary 15.3.5.
miserliness †wratchedness 15.4.1.
misery meesery; †miseritie 15.3.5.
misfire †misgie 12.5.
misfortune amshach; †antercast; begunk; conter; †cruik (in one's *or* the lot) 15.6.2; *see also* TROUBLE.
misgive misgie 15.6.2.
misguide †mislear 15.6.2.
misguided gley(e)d; left to anesel; †miscairrying; will 15.6.2.
misinformed mislearit 15.6.2.

misjudge †misknaw 15.6.2.
mismanage blunk; fa(ll) through; †misfare 15.5.16.
mismatched *of marriage partners*, *see* ILL-MATCHED.
missed *of a person etc* misslie 15.6.10.
missel-thrush feltiflier, feltifer, feltifare; Hieland pyot; storm cock; †throstle-cock 1.1.1.
missile racket; †shotter 12.5.
mist *specific types* 5.2.3; gum; rouk 5.2.3.
mistaken aff (o) one's eggs (*see* eggs); gley(e)d; mislearit; in a mistak (*see* mistak); up a *or* the sheuch 15.6.2.
mistress *of a house* 8.8; *concubine* †dunty; hing-tee; limmer; preen-tae; †quean; †wife 8.9.
misty daggy; drackie; haary; reekie; roukie 5.2.3.
misuse *v* disabuse; †forsume 15.5.16.
mix *v*, *socially*, *see* ASSOCIATE.
mix-up compluther; farrach; snorl; squeeter; wattle 15.5.17.
moat *specific types* 13.3.5; †foussie; †stank 13.3.5.
mob *n*, *see* RABBLE.
mock *v*, *in various ways* 15.5.3; †flyre; jamph; knack; lant; †scorp; †scrip; †skirp (at) 15.5.3.
mockery 15.5.3; afftaking; †flyredome; †hething; jamph; †scuff 15.5.3.
mocking *adj* mockrife 15.5.3.
mock sun faucon; ferrick 5.2.7.
moderate *v*, *of wind*, *see* DIE DOWN.
moderation mense 15.3.1.
Mohammed †Mahoun 14.1.12.
moisture *specific types* 6.1.1; bree; broo; moister; †wa(c)knes 6.1.1.
molar aisle-tuith; chaft tooth 9.3.
molasses †malashes 10.19; *see* TREACLE.
mole *animal* mowdie(wort), modewarp 1.2.1; *on the skin* mowdiewart; rasp 9.8.
mole-catcher moudie, moudieman; molie 7.10.
molehill moudie(wort) hill(ock) 2.8.3; mowdie(wort) hill(ock); tummock 5.1.2.
mollusc *specific types* 3.2.
molten *of metal* mouten 13.1.1.
money-grubber earth-worm; grab; †huidock; lick-penny; scrub; warldlin 15.4.1.
mongrel †mangrel; messan 2.5.
monkey pug(gie) 1.2.1.
monkey flower frog's mou(th) 4.2.
monster †bysun; onbeast; †warlock 14.2.2; †bysyn; onbeast 1.2.1.
monuments *ancient* 13.3.4.
mood 15; bin(ner); bon; key; lay; muid; taik; tid; tift; tune 15.1; *bad* gee; stots; stound; strum; sturdy; taum; towt 15.3.6.
moody tunie 15.3.5.

moon *specific stages* 5.2.7; †Lochiel's lantern; †Lucine; †MacFarlane's bouet; mune 5.2.7.
moor *n* muir 7.6; *farming* 7.6; *specific types* 5.1.2, 5.1.3, 5.1.4; bent; mo(u)nth; muir 5.1.2; *v*, *a ship etc* †tether 6.2.3.
mope map; mump; tak on 15.3.5.
morose *see* SULLEN.
mortal *of humanity* †ded(e)like 8.1.
mortality 8.1.
mortar lime 13.1.16.
mortgage *v*, *in specific ways* 11.8, 11.11; hypothecate; impignorate 11.8; *n*, *specific types* 11.8, 11.11.
mortuary deid-house 8.7.
moss *specific types* 4.4; duff (mould); fog 4.4.
moth *specific types* 1.3; moch; witch 1.3.
moth-eaten mochie, moch-eaten 1.3.
mother *n* †dame; †genetrice; mither 8.11; *see also* MUM.
mother-in-law guid mither 8.11.
motion *of waves* 6.1.4; *of the tide* drag, draig 6.1.4; *of a ship or boat* 6.2.1.
mottled marlie 1.1.6.
mould *n specific types* 13.1.1; muild 13.1.1; *for baking* †petty pan 10.2; *fungus* foost; hair moul(d) 10.1.
mouldboard *specific types* 7.7.1; cleathin; reest 7.7.1.
moulder moch; moost; †moul; moze 10.1.
moulding †muldry; †muller 13.2.8.
mouldy foostit, foosty; hair-moul(e)d, hairy-mouldit; hoamed; moulie; mozie 10.1; *of cheese* †beardie 10.13.
moult *v* mout 1.1.6, 2.7; *n*, *moulting state* pouk(in) 1.1.6, 2.7; *specif of fowls* 2.7.
moulted †moutit 2.8.1.
moulting *adj* in the pouk 1.1.6, 2.7.
moulting state pluck 2.8.1.
mountain *see* HILL.
mourn †dool; murn 8.7; *in various ways* 15.6.16; †dool; mane; †mak (a) mening; murn; †regrate 15.6.16.
mournfully dowiely 15.6.16.
mourning 8.7; *n* †mening (*see* mane); murning 15.6.16.
mouse moose 1.2.1.
mouse-trap *specific types* 7.10.
moustache fusker; matash; moutach 9.4.
mouth *specific types* 9.3; gab, gaw; gebbie; gob; mou; muns; tattie-trap 9.3; *of an animal* mull 2.8.2; *of a river, specific types* 6.1.2; waterfit, water mouth 6.1.2.
movement *of persons* 9.17.
mow maw; scythe 7.7.4.
mower †mawster; scythe 7.7.4.
muck-rake cleek; hack (muck), muck hack; harl 7.7.2.
mucus *specific types* 9.11, 9.15; glit 9.15.

overcome *v* gang ower; warsle 12.7; owercome 15.1, 15.6.4; *a trouble etc* †owerset 15.3.14; *see also* DEFEAT; *adj, emotionally, in various ways* 15.6.4; owertaen 15.6.4; *see also* DRUNK.

overcooked sair done 10.3.

over-excited dementit; raised; ree; yivverin 15.6.4.

overflow juitle; †overflete; owergae; flodder; †flotter; ream over; †weel 6.1.1; *see also* FLOOD.

overgrown *of plants, in specific ways* 4.1; grown-up; unfierdy 4.1.

overheads *mining* oncost, †oncosts 13.1.5.

over-indulgence †mistemperance 15.3.2.

overlook †owersee; thole wi; †twink 15.6.2; *a crime etc* †owersee 11.15.1.

overpower *see* DEFEAT.

overrun ower-rin 12.9.

oversee †grieve 13.1.3.

overseer cork; †grieve; †seer 13.1.3; *farming* grieve 7.5.2.

oversleep sleep in 9.12.

overthrow †overharle; †owerhail; †ramvert 12.11; *see also* OUST.

overtime by-hours 13.1.2.

overwhelm †ourquhelme 15.6.4.

overwhelmed *of a person, in various ways* 15.6.4.

overwork *v* stress; tirraneese; trash; tyauve 15.5.18.

overworked sair hauden doun by the bubbly jock (*see* bubbly jock); made; †thronged (*see* thrang) 15.5.18.

owl *specific types* 1.1.4; hoolet; ool, oolet 1.1.4.

own *see* POSSESS.

owner †haver 11.11.

own up *to* haud wi 15.6.14.

ox owse 2.1; *pl* oussen 2.1.

ox-bow bow; brecham; oxin *or* oussen bow; †weasie 7.9.1.

ox-collar *see* OX-BOW.

oyster *specific types* 3.2; *as food* 10.12.

oystercatcher mussel-picker; pleep; reid neb; sea pyot; skirly wheeter 1.1.3.

pacify cowshin; †mease; soother 15.5.1.

paddle *v* paidle 6.2.1.

paddock *specific types* 7.3; †horse wa(i)rd 7.3.

padlock †paddok-lok 13.2.4.

pagan *see* HEATHEN.

pail *specific types* 7.12, 10.2.

pain *n, specific types* 9.10; bide 9.10.

painful *of a blow* sucky 12.12; *of experience* saut 15.6.7.

pains fash 15.3.13.

paint *n* pent (*see* paint) 13.2.8; *v* †lay; †owerlay; pent (*see* paint) 13.2.8.

paintwork paint 13.2.8.

palace †pailace 13.3.3.

pale *in colour, in specific ways* 5.2.9; †blechit, blacht 5.2.9.

paling a pailin, pale; piling; spaik 7.3.

palisade †peel; †stacket 13.3.5.

pall *n, specific types* 8.7; †pail; †supercloth 8.7.

palm *of the hand* luif, loof 9.6.

palpitate flaff(er); flichter; gowp 9.9.

pamper *in various ways* 15.6.11; browden; cock (someone up with something); cuiter (up); daut; fraik; pet(tle) 15.6.11; *specif a child or pet* waste 15.6.11.

pampered †dandilly; deltit; finger-fed; leepit; peppint 15.3.7.

pan *specific types* 10.2.

pancake *in the Scots sense* dropped scone; pancake 10.6.

pane *specific types* 13.2.5; lozen; peen 13.2.5.

panel *specific types* 13.2.8; *wooden* 13.1.15.

panelled †tabulet 13.2.8.

pang *emotional* †hache; rug; stang; stound; twang 15.6.4; *of grief* stound 15.6.16.

panic *n* pilget; pirr; swither 15.6.4.

pannier hut; packet 7.12.

pant *v, in specific ways* 9.11; fesh; hech; hechle; pech; †sowff; thock 9.11; *n* pech 9.11; *of animals* kned 2.8.3.

pantry aumry 13.2.6; †breidhous 10.2.

paragon †lamp 15.3.1.

paralysed *in specific ways* 9.19; blastit 9.19.

paralysis pairls, perils 9.19.

parapet †barteshing; †bertisse 13.3.5; *of a bridge* †ledging; parpen; ravel 13.1.13.

parasite *of a person* †cake fidler; eat-meat; gie's-a-piece; †loch leech; †scaffer; skemler 15.4.2.

parboil leep 10.3.

parched drouchtit 9.14.

pardon *n, specific types* 11.2.4; 11.15.1; †remit 11.2.4; 11.15.1.

pare skive 10.3; skive; white 13.1.1; *top soil* scaup; skin 7.1.

parent pawrent 8.11.

paring scruifin 10.1.

parish *specific types* 14.1.6; pairish, †parochin; †parochy 14.1.6.

paroxysm rapture; †wuidness 15.6.8; *of rage* rapture; †wuidness 15.6.13.

parrot †papejay; †papingo; †parokett 1.1.1.

parry *v* kep 12.1.

parsimoniously scrimp 15.4.1.

parsley †persel 10.17.

parsnip †pasneip 4.8.

parson †person 14.1.6.

particle *see* CRUMB.

parting *in the hair* score; seam; shed 9.4.

partition *n, specific types* 13.2.6; †pairple wall 13.2.6; *wall, specific types* 13.2.1; †parpen (wall) 13.2.1.

partner *specific types* 11.9.

partnership *specific types* 11.8; †colleague 11.8.

partridge †aiten; pai(r)trick 1.1.1.

pass *in mountains, specific types* 5.1.2, 5.1.4; bealach; slack; slap, slop; slug; yett 5.1.2.

passageway *in a byre* walk 7.2

passion patience 15.6.4.

Passion Sunday 14.4.2; †Care Sonday 14.1.10.

Passover †Pace, Pask 14.4.2.

paste *n, v* batter 13.1.1.

pastern paster, †pasture 2.4.

pastries †patisserie; snashters; sweet-bread 10.7.

pasturage *specific types* 7.6; †girsing; lizour; †pasturall (*see* paster); sole 7.6.

pasture *specific types* 7.6; gang; lea girse, grass *or* ground; paster; raik 7.6; *v* †feed; girse; †lizour, †lesu 7.9.1, 7.13.

patch *n* clamp; cloot 13.1.1; *specif on a garment* spatch 13.1.7; *specif on a shoe* ?†hob(b)ell 13.1.11; *v, in various ways* 13.1.1; clamp; cloot; †cuiter; jam; lap 13.1.1; *specif sewing* spatch 13.1.7.

path *specific types* 5.1.2, 5.1.4.

patience 15.5.20; thole 15.5.20.

patient *adj* patientfu; †tholemode, tholemoody 15.5.20.

patrol *n* †chakwache 12.1.

pattern *specific types* 5.2.9

pave †pament 13.1.13.

pavement †pament 13.1.13.

pavilion †pavilʒeon 13.3.1; *see* TENT.

paw *n* crog; luif; spag; spyog 2.8.2; *v, the ground* pawt 2.8.3.

pawn *n, v* 11.8.

payment *specific types* 11.1.1, 11.8, 11.11; *in kind* cost 13.1.2.

pea *specific types* 4.8.

peacock †paco(k); †pown 1.1.1.

peahen paysie 1.1.1.

peak *of a hill, specific types* 5.1.2; kip 5.1.2.

peal *n, of bells* jow(l); †pale 14.1.8; *of thunder* brattle 5.2.4; *v, of thunder* dinnle 5.2.4.

pea-pod *see* POD.

pear *specific types* 4.7; peer 4.7.

peas *as a vegetable* 10.14; pizz 10.14.

pease pizz (*see* pease) 10.8.

peat 7.15; *specific types* 7.15; clod; peat-clod; reuch-head 7.15. divot; duff (mould) 7.15.

peat bank bink; hatch; moss bank; peat-bank; skemmel 7.15.

peat-bog mire 5.1.6.

peat bog 7.15; hill; moss; †pete ʒaird (*see* peat) 7.15.

peat-hag hag; moss hag; peat hag *or* -hole, †pete-pot (*see* peat); pot, pat; skemmel 7.15.

peat-stack 7.15; hill; †mou; peat bing; ruck; stack; †turr stack 7.15.

pebble chuck, chuckie (stane); peeble 5.1.8.

plaister; †sparge; †spargen; †teer 13.2.8.

plasterer †pargenar; †plaister, plaistirman 13.2.8.

plaster(-cast) stookie 9.23.1.

plasterwork 13.2.8.

plate *specific types* 10.2; †ballance 10.2.

platform †deas; pletform 13.2.6.

platter *specific types* 10.2.

plausible *of a person* fair-faced *or* -farrand; sleekit; †white 15.3.8.

playful geckin; †glaikit; kim; †playrife; †querty; †whilking 15.5.4.

plea *specific types* 11.2.2, 11.2.3.

plead *in specific ways* 11.2.3, †moot 15.5.1

pleasant *of a person* bowsome; canny; canty; dainty; douce; fine; †furthie; †greeable; †hende(ly); jellie; †blythsome and kythesome (*see* kythesome); leesome; lithe(some); luvesome; sanshach; seilfu; †weel-farrant *or* -natured 15.3.3; *of things, see* AGREEABLE.

please *v, see* SATISFY, GRATIFY.

pleased *in various ways* 15.6.11; content; fittit; pridefu; set; vauntie 15.6.11.

pleasing *of things, see* AGREEABLE.

pleasure *enjoyment* †emplesance, emplesour; †liking; †pleasance 15.6.11.

pledge *n, specific types* 11.2.3, 11.8; †plage; †plicht 11.8; *v, in specific ways* 11.2.3, 11.8.

pliers pincher(s); turkas 13.1.1; *blacksmith's* turkas 13.1.12.

plight †plicht; pliskie 15.6.2.

plimsolls gutties 14.3.2.

plinth †plint 13.1.16.

plod *see* TRUDGE.

plop *v, of liquid* pink; plowp 6.1.1; *n* plowt 6.1.1.

plot v, *in a crime etc* colleague 11.13; *n, see* BUILDING SITE; *of land* dale; †free; †plan; †skair 7.4; *specific types* 7.6; bit; †clout; dale; glebe; paffle; †skair 7.6.

plough *n, specific types* 7.7.1; pleuch 7.7.1; *v, in various ways* 7.7.1; †ear; furr; pleuch 7.7.1.

plough-handle hilt; pleuch stilts *pl*; stiel; stilt; stoup 7.7.1.

ploughing 7.7.1.

ploughman dock nail; hind; Jock hack *or* muck; pleuchie 7.5.3.

ploughshare pleuch sock; sock 7.7.1.

plough-team †pleuch guids 7.7.1.

plover *specific types* 1.1.2; pliver 1.1.2.

pluck *v, a fowl* pouk 10.3; *wool from a sheep* plot 7.13; *n* gumption 15.3.9.

plucky *see* SPIRITED.

plumage †fetherame 1.1.6.

plum *specific types* 4.7; ploom 4.7.

plumbing 13.1.4.

plump *of animals* pluffy; tidy 2.8.1; *of persons* 9.1.1, 9.1.2.

plunder *n, specific types* 12.10; fang; †hership; †rapt; †spreath, spreacherie; spulyie; †waith 12.10; *v, in various ways* 12.10; herrie; †peel; reive; †riffle; ripe; rook; roup; scoff; †spreth (*see* spreath); spulyie 12.10; *specif cattle* †lift 12.10; *see also* DESPOIL; *v, in specific ways* 11.13; scoff; spulyie 11.13; *n, specific types* 11.13; spulyie 11.13.

plunderer †spulyier 11.13.

plundering *see* DEPREDATION.

plunger *of a churn* kirning rung, kirn stick; plumper 7.9.2, 10.13.

pneumoconiosis stoury lungs 9.11.

pneumonia peumonie 9.11.

poach *steal fish, in specific ways* 6.3.2, 11.13; spoach 11.13.

poacher spoacher; †stalker 11.13.

pock-marked pock(y)arred 9.8.

pod huil 4.1; cod; swab; whaup 4.8; *pea-pod* cob; peacod; pea-huil; pea-shaup; shaup 4.8.

pogge poach 3.1.2.

point *n, of a pin, knife etc* 13.1.7, 13.1.16; *of a weapon* †ure 12.5; *v, the inside joints of slating* shouder 13.2.2; *a wall* †lip; †teethe 13.1.16.

pointsman sneck-shifter 13.1.5.

poison pushi(o)n 9.23.2, 12.13.

poisonous pushionable, pooshinous 9.23.2.

pole †carpoll; powl 13.1.15; *specific types* 7.12; powl 7.12.

polecat †feitho; foumart, thoumart 1.2.1.

policeman bulkie; peg; polisman; snout 11.4.

polished *of a person, see* REFINED.

polite discreet; menseful 15.3.3; *see also* COURTEOUS.

pollack lythe; skeet 3.1.2.

polled *chf of cattle* cowit; hummel 2.1; *of cattle* cowit 7.9.1.

polypody †ternfern 4.4.

pomegranate †aipple garnet 4.7.

pommel †plummet 12.5.

pompous full; pensie 15.3.7.

pond *specific types* 6.1.1, 6.1.3, 6.3.1, 6.3.2; coble; dub; pound; stank; †water stank 6.1.3.

pony pownie 2.4.

pooh-pooh hoot 15.7.3.

pool *specific types* 6.1.1; puil; stank; †waggle; waterhole 6.1.1; *specif in a river* 6.1.2; *in the sea* 6.1.4.

poor ill-aff; †misterful; needfu; puir; scrimp; skybal(d); sober 15.4.2.

pope paip 14.1.6.

popple †papple 4.2.

poppy puppie 4.2.

popularity 15.3.1.

porcelain wallie 10.2, 13.1.1; *manufacture* 13.1.1, 13.1.3, 13.3.7.

porch *specific types* 13.2.6; entry; rochel 13.2.6.

pork purk; Sandie (Campbell) 10.11.

porpoise dunter; †meer-swine; pellock; puffie (dunter) 3.2.

porridge *specific types* 10.9; gruel; parritch; pottage 10.9.

porringer bicker; †parritch cap; †pottinger 10.2.

port *n, side of ship* †babord 6.2.1; *harbour (town)*, *specific types* 6.2.3; *adj* efter(h)in 6.2.1.

portcullis †portcul3eis 13.3.5.

portend bod 14.2.4.

portent *see of death, specific types* 8.7; †fey token 8.7; *specific types, esp of death* 14.2.4; †foretaiking; freit; †spae; †takenar; warning; †weird 14.2.4.

porter *specific types* 13.1.3; †pockman; warkman 13.1.3.

portion *see* SHARE.

Portugal shark *see* TOPE.

possess *land, property, in specific ways* 11.11.

possession *of land, in specific ways* 11.11.

post standart; stoup 13.2.3; stob 7.3; *specif in a fence* stower 7.3; *military* †ward 12.1.

postpone supersede 11.2.3.

posture †pouster 9.1.1.

pot *n, specific types* 10.2.

potato 10.14; *specific types* 4.8; pitawtie; tattie 4.8.

potato cake fadge; potato-scone; tattie scone 10.6.

potent *see* STRONG.

potful pottle 10.1.

pot-hole *specific types* 6.1.3.

potter *v* dauble; driddle; †driffle; fite the (idle) pin; gutter; haiver; niddle; plowter; sotter 15.4.5; *n* †pig maker 13.1.3.

poultry poutrie 2.7; *farming* 7.9.3.

pound *for animals* †point fold 7.2; †point fold; pund 7.3.

pour *in specific ways* 6.1.1; †yat 6.1.1; *liquids, in various ways, see* 10.3; *of rain, in specific ways* 5.2.3; dish (on); hale; rash; †skail; teem 5.2.3.

pout *n, the fish, see* BIB; *v* buss; let *or* pit down the lip (*see* lip) 15.3.6, 15.6.18.

poverty puirtith; †wandreth, wander 15.4.2.

powder *n* pouther 10.1.

powder-flask †flas 12.5.

power *in a person* †doucht; poustie 15.5.15; *legal* 11.2.4.

powerful *see* MIGHTY.

poxed †cuntbitten 9.16.

practise *a virtue, vice, etc* †exerce 15.1, 15.3.1.

praise *v, in various ways* 15.6.11; †lofe; †prize 15.6.11; *n* †commend; †lofe, lovage, loving; ruise 15.6.11.

praiseworthy †lovabill 15.3.1.

prance †cavie; winch 2.8.3.

prank †gaud; kiow-ow; prat; prattick 15.3.11.

clatter; din; mudge; raverie; sloom; †sloomin; soun(d); spin 15.5.8.

rump curpin; runt 2.8.2.

rung n, of a ladder spaik; spar 13.1.1.

runrig runrig (see run); †rig-about 7.4.

runt of a litter, see WEAKLING.

rush n, the plant, specific types 4.3; rasher, rashie; sprot 4.3.

rust iron eer 5.1.9.

rustic n, see YOKEL; adj countryfeed (see countra); hodden; landward; muirland; †ruryk; †rusticate; †upland(is) 15.2.2.

ruthless fell 15.3.4.

sack n, the drink †seck 10.18; v †lowse; pit awa; set aff 13.1.2; someone gie someone the heave 13.1.2; see DESPOIL.

sad dowf; drearifu, drearysome; drum; †eerie; glumsh; heepochondreoch; †malagrugrous; unhearty; †weary 15.3.5; adj see DOWNCAST, SORROWFUL.

saddened †saddit 15.6.16.

sadly dowiely 15.6.16.

safe sicker 15.6.1.

safe-conduct conduck; †soverance 12.7.

saffron †saipheron 10.17.

sail n, of a ship, specific types, parts 6.2.1; †saule; v, in specific ways 6.2.1, 6.2.3; †cap; †saule; †sneir 6.2.1.

sailor specific types, ranks 6.2.4; †marinall; tarry breeks 6.2.4.

saint saunt, †sanct (see saint) 15.3.1, 14.1.1.

saints' days 14.1.10, 14.4.1.

saithe see COAL-FISH.

salary sellarie 13.1.2; of clergy 14.1.7.

saliva slavers 9.15.

salivate gush 9.15.

sally n †outfall 12.9.

sally forth †ish; †sort 12.9.

salmon specific types and ages 3.1.3; fish; †lax; reid fish; saumon, †salmond 3.1.3.

salt saut 5.1.9; specific types 10.17; saut 10.17.

salter sauter 13.1.3.

salt fish specific types 6.3.1; hard fish 6.3.1.

salt water see BRINE.

salty as saut as lick 10.1.

salvation †hele 14.1.1.

sample of cloth swatch 13.1.7.

sand freshwater †water sand 5.1.8.

sandbank specific types 6.1.5.

sand-eel †pintle-fish; san(d)al, sandlin 3.1.2.

sand-flea sand jumper, sand(y) lowper; sea-flech 3.2.

sand-martin sandy swallow 1.1.1.

sandpiper fiddler; heather peeper; sand dorbie; sand laverock; Tibbie Thiefie 1.1.2.

sandpit on a golf-course bunker 5.1.4.

sandstone specific types 13.1.17; brie-stone 13.1.17, 5.1.8.

sandwich specific types 10.6; piece 10.6.

sandy sannie 5.1.8.

sane at oneself; solid; thorow; wise 9.21; solid; thorow; wise 15.2.3.

sanity judgement; wit 9.21; judgement 15.2.3.

sap of plants, specific types 4.1; †sop 4.1.

sapling †sipling 4.6.

sap-wood sap spail 4.6.

sarcasm 15.5.3.

sarcastic setterel; †snaggy; snell 15.5.3.

sardonyx †sardonice 5.1.9.

sate ser(ve); †slocken 15.6.11.

sated gizzent 10.4; in specific ways 9.14; with food stankit 9.14.

satiate with food 9.14; sta(w) 9.14.

satiety ser, sairin 10.4, 15.6.11.

satisfaction content; †templesance, emplesour; †liking; †pleasance, plesandis; †sythment; †thankfulness 15.6.11.

satisfactory †sufficient 15.6.1; of persons or their actions †lovabill 15.3.1.

satisfatorily bonnilie 15.5.15.

satisfied fittit; suited 15.6.11.

satisfy †applese; †complese; †emplese, †enplese; pleasure; saitisfee; suit; †syth 15.6.11; with food serve, ser; stench 10.4.

saturate see SOAK.

sauce gravy 10.1.

saucepan specific types 10.2.

saucer flat, flattie; †salsar; shell 10.2.

sausage specific types 10.11; sassenger, sasser; slingers pl 10.11.

savage adj, see FIERCE.

savagely †savagiously 15.3.12.

savour n guff; gust 10.1.

saw 13.1.1; n, specific types 13.1.1; Rob Sorby 13.1.1; v, in various ways 13.1.1.

sawdust sawin(g)s 13.1.1.

sawing 13.1.1.

saxifrage specific types 4.2.

scabbard †scawbart 12.5.

scabbed scabbert 9.8.

scabby scawt 15.4.5.

scab n scur(l) 9.8.

scabious specific types 4.2.

scaffold n †scaffat 11.15.1.

scaffolding 13.1.16; gaberts 13.1.16.

scald scaud 10.3, 15.5.14.

scalded leepit 10.3.

scale v, a wall, military 12.9; n, on fish †skail 3.1.1.

scaling ladder †scallet 12.9.

scallop clam(shell) 3.2.

scalp pow; scaup 9.2; pow 2.8.2.

scalpel lance 9.23.1.

scamp n †losel; skellum; sorra 15.3.2; v †haister; skiff by or ower; slim (ower) 15.5.16.

scandal clatter(s); din; ill-wind; souch 15.5.8.

scandalize scandaleese 15.3.11.

scandalmonger sclave 15.5.8.

scandalmongering speak 15.5.8.

scandalous michty 15.5.8.

scar n arr; blain; scaur; waum 9.22.

scare birds 7.9.4, 7.10; alairm; †effray; fear; fleg; fley; flichter; flocht; gliff; †mismuive; scar; skeer 15.6.15.

scarecrow bockie, bogle; boodie, tattie boodie; craw bogle or nancy; †pease bogle; †pitawtie bogle; scaur-craw; tattie-bogie, -bogle, -boodie or doolie 7.10; of a person bogle; tattie-bogie, -bogle or -boodie 15.4.4.

scarifier grubber 7.7.1.

scarlet fever fiv(v)er; rush-fever 9.19.

scatter at a wedding 8.8; n logan; pour out; scatter; scour-oot; strive 8.8; v logan; scatter; strive 8.8; seed spark in 7.7.3; dung spark in; spart 7.7.2.

scatterbrain scatter-wit 15.3.7.

scatter-brained see FLIGHTY.

scheme v †brigue 15.3.8.

schemer †Matchevell 15.3.8.

schist specific types 5.1.8.

school 14.3.2; specific types 14.3.2; schule 14.3.2.

school attendance officer whipper-in 14.3.2.

schoolbook specific types 14.3.2.

schoolchild specific types 14.3.2; scholar; schule wean 14.3.2.

school examination specific types 14.3.2.

schoolmaster dick; dominie, dom, domsie; maister, master, †magister 14.3.2.

school punishment specific types 14.3.2.

schoolteacher specific types 14.3.2; nicknames for 14.3.2.

sciatica †baneschaw 9.7.

scissors 13.1.7; specific types 13.1.7; chizors; shear(s) 13.1.7.

scold v, in various ways 15.5.14; †banter; boast; †brag; caird; counger; †cow; cunner; dicht; dreel; drib; driffle; drub; flyte (wi, at or (up)on); gansel; gollie; be intae (see intae); †kevel; nail; rally (on); †randie; shore; tatter; tongue; yaff 15.5.14; n caird; flyter; pallion 15.5.14; specif of a woman bard; †kail wife; scaul(d) 15.5.14.

scolding n 15.5.14; clearin; come-again; dirdum; doon-set(ting); driffle; flyte; gansel; hurry; onset; pin; raging; redd up; scaul(d); set awa; targin; upreddin 15.5.14; adj yatterin, yattery 15.5.14.

scone specific types 10.6.

scoop n pale 10.2.

scope of conduct tether 15.1.

scorch birsle 5.2.1, 5.2.6.

scorching birsling 5.2.1, 5.2.6.
scorn 15.5.3; †hething; laith 15.5.3.
scornful †hethingfull; †lichtlie; mockrife 15.5.3.
scornfully †contempnandly; †dispitefully 15.5.3.
scoundrel *see* ROGUE.
scourge *n, of a person* †stripe 15.5.14.
scout †discurr(i)our 12.2.
scowl *n* gloom; glower; glunsh; smool 15.6.18; *v* glunsh; gowl; scoul; smool 15.6.18.
scowling *adj* gowlie 15.6.18.
scraggy *of animals, v* †cabbrach; mean 2.8.1; *of persons* 9.1.2.
scramble *eggs* cotter; rummle 10.3.
scrape cair 10.3; *see* SCRATCH.
scraps *of food* brock; orts; scran; smush 10.1; brakins 10.5.
scratch *v* cleuk; scart; scrat 2.8.3; cleuk 1.1.5; *in specific ways* 9.10; *in specific ways* 9.22; rit 9.22; *n, specific types* 9.22; rit; rive; scrat; screed 9.22.
scream *of animals, v* screel; skirl; skrauch 1.1.7; yap 1.2.3; *n, of animals* 1.2.3; *specific types* 1.2.3; *of persons: v, in fear* skirl 15.6.15; *n, of fear* skirl 15.6.15.
scree glidders; †scarnach; sclenters 5.1.8.
screech screel; skirl; squaik 1.1.7; *of birds* skraich 1.1.7; *n* skrauch 1.1.7; *see* SCREAM.
screw *n* feeze 13.1.1.
scrimp haud in about; jimp; pinch 15.4.1.
scrofula cruels 9.8.
scrotum †ba-cod 9.16.
scrounge scoff; scunge; skech; sorn; spoach 15.4.2.
scrounger *specific types* 15.4.2; gadger; ?†milygant; †scaffer; scunge(r); skech, skaicher; skemler; slounge; sorner; spoach 15.4.2.
scrubbing-brush rub(b)er 13.1.1.
scruffy *see* SHABBY.
scruple *v* stickle 15.5.10.
scrupulous penurious 15.5.15.
scuffle *n* rammy; yokin 12.7; *see also* DISTURBANCE; *v* †juffle 12.7.
scullery-maid assiepet 13.1.4.
scullion scodge, scodgie; †scuddler 13.1.4.
scum float 10.3.
scurf *specific types* 9.8; luce; scruif 9.8.
scurry *of animals* scuddle 2.8.3.
scurvy *n* †scrubie 9.8.
scutch knock; †strik; †switch 13.1.6.
scutcher cogster; lint-dresser 13.1.6.
scutching 13.1.6.
scythe hey-sned; whittle 7.7.4.
sea 6.1.4; sey (*see* sea); †strand, straun; tide 6.1.4.

sea anemone pap; *pl* sea pa(a)ps 3.2.
sea creatures 3.2
sea eagle earn 1.1.3.
sea fish 3.1.2.
sea fog sea haar 6.1.4.
sea gull *see* GULL.
seal selch, selkie; †selk, selchy 3.2; *legal, specific types* 11.1.1, 11.2.3.
seaman *leading* killick 12.2.
seam *mining* 13.1.5; *specific types* 13.1.5.
seaport sea toun 6.1.5.
search *v, legally, in specific ways* 11.2.3.
sea scorpion *see* FATHERLASHER.
seaside †saut water 6.1.5.
season *v, wood* win 13.1.15.
sea trout *specific types and ages* 3.1.3.
sea-urchin burr; hairy hu(r)tcheon 3.2.
seaweed *specific types* 3.4.
seborrhea †luce 9.8.
secrecy 15.3.8; hidlins; hudge-mudge 15.3.8.
secretary secretar 13.1.3.
sect *names of various religious sects* 14.1.5; †profession 14.1.5.
secure sicker 15.6.1.
securely sicker; †sickerly 15.6.1.
security *legal, specific types* 11.2.3, 11.8, 11.10; caution 11.2.3; *of mind* 15.6.1.
sedate canny; douce; †sad 15.3.14.
sedge *specific types* 4.3; †seg 4.3.
sedge warbler Scotch nightingale (*see* nightingale) 1.1.1.
seduce debosh; mistryst; †sedouse (with) 8.9.
seed *n, specific types* 4.9, 4.1. **go to seed** shuit, shoot 4.1.
seed-time sawin time; †seed 7.7.3.
seek *in marriage* come aifter; sik (*see* seek); †suit 8.8.
segment *n, of an orange, onion etc* leaf; lith; skliff 10.1.
seize *property, in specific ways* 11.11; arrest 11.11; *see also* CAPTURE; *the goods of a debtor* poind; reest, rest 11.10.
self-confident poochle 15.3.7.
self-contained *of a house* within itself 13.3.3.
self-heal crochle girs; hert of the yearth; puir man's clover 4.2.
self-importance 15.3.7; †gloriositie 15.3.7.
self-important *see* BUMPTIOUS.
self-indulgent free-living 15.3.7.
selfish hamedrauchtit; †hamesucken; mislearit; sellie 15.4.1.
selfishness sellie 15.4.1.
self-reliance 15.3.14.
self-respect 15.3.14.
self-respecting pensie; pridefu 15.3.14.
self-satisfied crouse; kirr; †?vousty 15.3.7.
selvage ruind; †walting 13.1.6.
senile doitered; dottered, †dotit,

†dottle; superannuate; veeand; veed 8.2.
senility 8.2.
senna sinnie 4.5, 9.23.2.
sensation gliff 15.6.3; *physical* fushion; †taibets 9.10.
sense *see* COMMON SENSE.
sensible menseful; †sonsie; wiselike 15.2.3; *specif in speech* wise-spoken 15.2.3.
sensibly wiselike 15.2.3.
sentence *v, in specific ways* 11.2.4, 11.15.1; *v, see* CONDEMN.
sergeant †sairgin 12.2.
serious *of a person* sairious; thochtie, thouchtish 15.2.3.
sermon *specific types* 14.1.8.
serpent †serpens 1.2.2.
servant *specific types* 13.1.4; †fiall; †gudget; †hireman; †onwaiter; †retener 13.1.4; *pl* fowk; *specif male* †gillie 13.1.4; *pl* †man *or* men servand(i)s 13.1.4; *specif a boy* servant chiel 13.1.4; *specif female* †hire-woman; †servitrix 13.1.4; *specif a girl* hizzie; jurr; lass 13.1.4;
serve *a dish* lift 10.5; *wine* birl 10.18; (*someone*) *right* be chape o *or* on (*see* chape) 15.6.2.
service 13.1.4; onwaiting 13.1.4; *religious specific types* 14.1.8, 14.1.9; diet (of worship) 14.1.8.
setback *see* REVERSE, SNAG; *specific types* 9.19.
set *n, of knitting needles* stand; wires 13.1.8; *v, of jam etc* jeel 10.3; *of food* mak 10.3; *of the sun* pass doun *or* to 5.2.7; *with jewels* †tight with 13.1.1.
settle *a debt etc* †outred 11.10.
settlement *legal, specific types* 11.11, 11.12; *marriage* sitting doun, sit-down; †tocher band 8.8.
severe *of a person* †apirsmart; dour; †harsk; †hask; ill; side; †snack; snar; snell; †stalwart 15.3.4; *of weather, in specific ways* 5.2.1; fell; sicker; snell; sour; †stith; thin; thrawn; veecious 5.2.1; *of wind, a storm, see* VIOLENT.
severely *see* HARSHLY.
sew †preen; shew; steek 13.1.7; *specif hastily* ranter 13.1.7.
sewing 13.1.7.
sex *n, gender* †seck 8.1; *sexual intercourse* 8.9; †chalmer glew; †dale; †dirrydan, †dirrye dantoun; †tail-toddle 8.9; *see also* FORNICATION; *v* sicht 7.9.1, 7.13.
sexual †actual 8.9.
sexuality 8.9.
shabbily-dressed ill-pit(ten) on (*see* pit) 15.4.4.
shabby drumshorlin; ill-towdent; loun-like; scawt; scourie; scuffy; yeukie 15.2.2; *of dress* ill-faured; †moutit; poukit; scuffy 15.4.4.
shad *specific types* 3.1.2.
shade *n* scug; †umbrakle 5.2.7.
shadow †scug; shedda, scaddow, shaddie; †umbrakle 5.2.7.

Index